Probability and Mathematical Statistics (Continued)

PURI, VILAPLANA, and WERTZ • New Persp
  Applied Statistics
RANDLES and WOLFE • Introduction to the
  Statistics
RAO • Linear Statistical Inference and Its Applic
RAO • Real and Stochastic Analysis
RAO and SEDRANSK • W.G. Cochran's Impact
RAO • Asymptotic Theory of Statistical Inference
ROHATGI • An Introduction to Probability Theory and Mathematical Statistics
ROHATGI • Statistical Inference
ROSS • Stochastic Processes
RUBINSTEIN • Simulation and The Monte Carlo Method
SCHEFFE • The Analysis of Variance
SEBER • Linear Regression Analysis
SEBER • Multivariate Observations
SEN • Sequential Nonparametrics: Invariance Principles and Statistical Inference
SERFLING • Approximation Theorems of Mathematical Statistics
SHORACK and WELLNER • Empirical Processes with Applications to Statistics
TJUR • Probability Based on Radon Measures

Applied Probability and Statistics

ABRAHAM and LEDOLTER • Statistical Methods for Forecasting
AGRESTI • Analysis of Ordinal Categorical Data
AICKIN • Linear Statistical Analysis of Discrete Data
ANDERSON, AUQUIER, HAUCK, OAKES, VANDAELE, and WEISBERG • Statistical Methods for Comparative Studies
ARTHANARI and DODGE • Mathematical Programming in Statistics
BAILEY • The Elements of Stochastic Processes with Applications to the Natural Sciences
BAILEY • Mathematics, Statistics and Systems for Health
BARNETT • Interpreting Multivariate Data
BARNETT and LEWIS • Outliers in Statistical Data, *Second Edition*
BARTHOLOMEW • Stochastic Models for Social Processes, *Third Edition*
BARTHOLOMEW and FORBES • Statistical Techniques for Manpower Planning
BECK and ARNOLD • Parameter Estimation in Engineering and Science
BELSLEY, KUH, and WELSCH • Regression Diagnostics: Identifying Influential Data and Sources of Collinearity
BHAT • Elements of Applied Stochastic Processes, *Second Edition*
BLOOMFIELD • Fourier Analysis of Time Series: An Introduction
BOX • R. A. Fisher, The Life of a Scientist
BOX and DRAPER • Empirical Model-Building and Response Surfaces
BOX and DRAPER • Evolutionary Operation: A Statistical Method for Process Improvement
BOX, HUNTER, and HUNTER • Statistics for Experimenters: An Introduction to Design, Data Analysis, and Model Building
BROWN and HOLLANDER • Statistics: A Biomedical Introduction
BUNKE and BUNKE • Statistical Inference in Linear Models, Volume I
CHAMBERS • Computational Methods for Data Analysis
CHATTERJEE and PRICE • Regression Analysis by Example
CHOW • Econometric Analysis by Control Methods
CLARKE and DISNEY • Probability and Random Processes: A First Course with Applications, *Second Edition*
COCHRAN • Sampling Techniques, *Third Edition*
COCHRAN and COX • Experimental Designs, *Second Edition*
CONOVER • Practical Nonparametric Statistics, *Second Edition*
CONOVER and IMAN • Introduction to Modern Business Statistics
CORNELL • Experiments with Mixtures: Designs, Models and The Analysis of Mixture Data

The Theory and Practice of Econometrics

Wiley Series in Probability and Mathematical Statistics

The Theory and Practice of Econometrics

Second Edition

George G. Judge
University of Illinois

W. E. Griffiths
University of New England

R. Carter Hill
University of Georgia

Helmut Lütkepohl
Universität Osnabrück

Tsoung-Chao Lee
University of Connecticut

John Wiley and Sons

New York *Chichester* *Brisbane* *Toronto* *Singapore*

Library of Congress Cataloging in Publication Data:

The Theory and practice of econometrics.

Includes bibliographies and index.
1. Econometrics. I. Judge, George G.
HB139.T48 1985 330'.028 84-7254
ISBN 0-471-89530-X

Printed in the United States of America

10 9 8 7

To

Marge
Jo Ann
Todd and Peter
Hilde and Karlheinz
Nancy

Preface to Second Edition

The topical content of the first *Theory and Practice of Econometrics* and the pace of developments in econometrics over the last four years have made it necessary to rewrite and restructure the first edition completely. We have added chapters concerned with asymptotic distribution theory, Bayesian inference, time series, and simultaneous equation statistical models. The distributed lag chapters have been rewritten within a time series context and the nonlinear estimation and estimation and hypothesis testing involving nonsample information have been extensively rewritten to take account of recent research results. In the other chapters, some results that are mainly of historical interest have been deleted and relevant new research results have been included.

Given the state of computer development and availability, we have deleted the Monte Carlo sample data contained in the first volume. Those who do not have computer facilities to develop Monte Carlo sample data for the various statistical models considered in this edition are referred to the instructor's manual for the book *Introduction to the Theory and Practice of Econometrics*, published by Wiley in 1982.

The research and instructional objectives and uses of the book are the same as those enumerated in the first edition. Chapters 2 through 7 are concerned with the theoretical basis for statistical inference in economics. The remainder of the book is concerned with using these tools to cope with the stochastic, dynamic, and simultaneous characteristics of economic data and determining the statistical consequences of changing (1) the statistical models, (2) the amount and type of information used, and (3) the measure of performance employed. For introductory material relating to the various chapters contained herein, we refer the interested reader to our *Introduction to the Theory and Practice of Econometrics* and the first edition of this book.

The criticisms and suggestions we received from colleagues and students who used the original book and/or read early editions of the new and revised chapters, were very helpful in eliminating some errors and in determining the contents and organization of this volume. We cannot here acknowledge each individual contribution but we do indicate our debt to these readers and to each we offer our sincere thanks.

For a book of this nature a skilled technical typist who has patience and who can type rapidly while emphasizing accuracy and consistency, is a necessity. Dixie Trinkle not only possesses these talents but her interest in the book and willingness to do repeated versions of each chapter, contributed much to its quality and style. Partial support for this work was provided by a National Science Foundation grant.

George G. Judge
William E. Griffiths
R. Carter Hill
Helmut Lütkepohl
Tsoung-Chao Lee

April 1984

Preface to First Edition

This book is concerned with the problems facing those who wish to learn from finite samples of economic data. Over the last half century, econometricians have, in conjunction with theoretical and applied statisticians, developed a varied and sometimes curious set of methods and procedures that serve as a basis for this learning process. In the theory and practice of econometrics, the economic and statistical models, the method of estimation and inference, and the data are all interdependent links in the search and discovery process. Therefore, economists who apply quantitative methods face many choices as they attempt to give empirical content to their theoretical constructs. Many of these alternatives are interrelated, and the choices actually taken condition the inferential reach of the results and their usefulness in a decision context.

As an information base to aid in the choice process, two types of econometrics books appear in the literature. Texts on econometric theory examine an array of alternative statistical models and, under prescribed sets of conditions, evaluate the sampling properties of a number of estimators and test statistics. Alternatively, applied econometric texts specify and statistically analyze a range of economic relationships such as supply, investment, consumption, and production functions and give examples of how the empirical results may be used in practice. Both types of books provide valuable information for the student and the researcher. In many cases, however, traditional books fail to identify a range of alternatives by being either too model- or too case-specific or fail to aid the student or researcher in coping with a particular sequence of questions or choices. Consequently, a basis may not be provided for choosing the statistical specification and estimation procedure that is most appropriate for the problem at hand. Within this context, this book is directed to specifying an up-to-date set of procedures that researchers may use to identify and mitigate the impact of econometric problems arising from the use of passively generated data and incomplete information concerning the appropriate economic and statistical model.

Our objective of improving the efficiency of the learning and quantitative research choice process is addressed in the following way:

1. We identify a sequence of questions, and thus problems, faced in econometric work.
2. We clarify, summarize, and integrate the latest theoretical developments or state of the art relevant for each decision-making problem.
3. We discuss the statistical consequences of alternative specifications and research strategies, and based on these evaluations, make various recommendations or provide a framework for choice.

The book can serve as (1) a text for theoretical and applied courses in econometrics, (2) a handbook for those who are in one way or another searching for quantitative economic knowledge, and (3) a reference book for undergraduate and graduate courses in econometrics and statistics. Although directed toward econometrics, the statistical problems considered have implications for analyzing and learning from data relating to all social science areas.

In developing and discussing a wide range of econometric problem areas, we assume that the reader has an introductory knowledge of calculus, linear algebra, economic theory, and inferential statistics and is familiar with an array of statistical models usually covered in a first basic or survey course in econometrics. The sequence in which the chapters are used is not of great consequence. However, Chapter 2 is designed to present the notation to be used throughout the book and to provide a bridge between the prior econometrics exposure of the reader and the topics covered in this book. An introduction is provided for each part of the book, and in each chapter flowcharts are presented to illustrate the relationship between the various sections and subsections and to assist the reader in identifying the part of the chapter most relevant to the problem at hand. Problems are given at the end of each chapter to help firmly establish the sampling theory and Bayesian approaches to inference.

Many persons have contributed directly or indirectly to this work. Helmut Lütkepohl not only wrote the chapter on models nonlinear in the parameters but also read and commented on every chapter in the book. Stuart Low and Tom Fomby read and made editorial comments on several of the chapters. Richard Esposito made valuable and timely comments concerning format and organization. We are also grateful to Professors Malcolm Dowling, of the University of Colorado; Peter Zadrozny, of New York University; and Albert Link, of Auburn University, for having made many useful comments on portions of the manuscript. Students in a range of classes labored through some of the early drafts and helped us eliminate many errors of omission and commission. Debbie Greene, Hazel Landers, and Marlene Youman, with patience, interest, and skill, typed the chapters through their many, many versions. To these colleagues and to many others we express our warm thanks and appreciation. Writing this book has been a joint and enjoyable effort, and the order of the names on the title page is of limited significance.

Partial support for this work was provided by a National Science Foundation grant.

George G. Judge
William E. Griffiths
R. Carter Hill
Tsoung-Chao Lee

April 1979

Contents

The Theory and Practice of Econometrics

Chapter 1

Introduction

This book is concerned with the problem of measurement in economics, and it is directed toward developing, reviewing, and synthesizing some of the analytical methods that may be employed to analyze and learn from economic data. Over the last half-century, a great many achievements have been realized through a systematic use of economic data in conjunction with economic and statistical models and the sampling theory and Bayesian approaches to inference. These productive efforts have given content to both the theory and practice of econometrics.

Economic theory is concerned with explaining the relationships among economic variables and using that information within a general theory of choice to explain production, allocation, and distribution decisions for a system that must operate within the implications of scarcity. On the other hand, statistical inference is concerned with drawing conclusions from limited data or bits of information, and the existence of this type of scarcity has led to the development of a general theory for dealing with decision problems under conditions of uncertainty. Consequently, both economics and statistical inference are concerned with generating information that may be used to improve decision making or strategy formation.

If the goal is to select the best decision from a set of economic choices, it is usually not enough to know that economic variables are related. In addition, we must also know the direction of the relation and, in many cases, the magnitudes involved. Toward this end, econometrics, using economic theory, mathematical economics, and statistical inference as analytical foundation stones and economic data as the information base, provides a basis for (1) modifying, refining, or possibly refuting conclusions contained in the body of knowledge known as economic theory, and (2) attaching signs, numbers, and reliability statements to the coefficients of variables in economic relationships so that this information can be used as a basis for decision making and choice.

Progress in economics in general and econometrics in particular depends on at least three related activities:

1. Development of tools to facilitate both the formulation and the testing of possible economic generalizations.
2. Collection, or generation and accumulation of observations on economic processes and institutions.
3. Application of the tools and the observations to enlarge the body of established generalizations about economic affairs.

Given a basis for organizing knowledge, and given the usefulness or indeed the necessity of quantitative economic knowledge, the next important question involves how to go about searching for it. If all economists had IQs that were 300 standard deviations above the mean, this question might be of limited importance. However, many of us do not fit into this category, and the question of how to get on the efficient search turnpike is a real one.

1.1 THE SEARCH PROCESS

Much of the knowledge in economics is gained by a process of abstraction. Economic systems, like mathematical systems such as the number system, are invented, not discovered. Therefore, we start with the phenomena the scientist seeks to understand, and we develop a mathematical system or theory that consists of a set of assertions from which consequences are derived by using the rules of logic. The model of reality that results reflects an attempt to reconstruct in a simplified way the mechanism thought to lie behind the phenomena under study by the scientist. Therefore, the model represents the outcome of the process of abstraction, whereby tentative explanations are formulated. These tentative explanations, which are formulated as propositions, provide the hypotheses that may be tested. Consequently, the postulation process by which certain components of the phenomena under study are mapped into a formal deductive system with real-world interpretations tells us nothing about the truth or falsity of the conclusions. It only gives us the possibilities, provided that we have correctly made use of logic. In economics, partial equilibrium, general equilibrium, and aggregative economics are three systems methods that have been developed and used to organize knowledge and that form one basis for drawing economic conclusions.

The use of postulation and logic to obtain knowledge may be viewed, following Thrall, Coombs, and Raiffa, through the flow diagram shown in Figure 1.1.

Other routes that have been proposed and possibly tried as a basis for going from phenomena to conclusions are revelation, magic, mysticism, and intuition. Various claims have been made concerning the role and success of each.

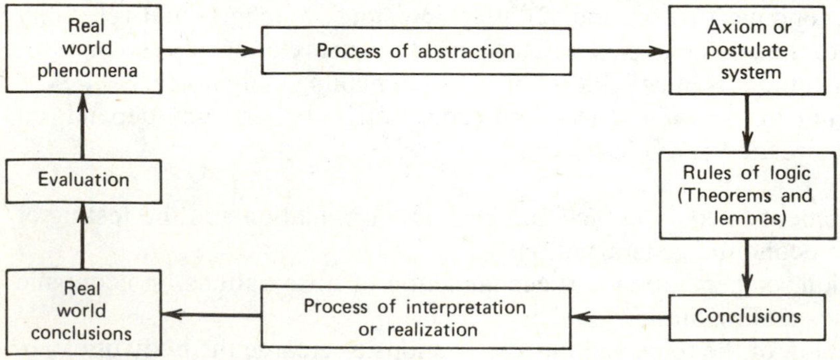

Figure 1.1 The postulation approach.

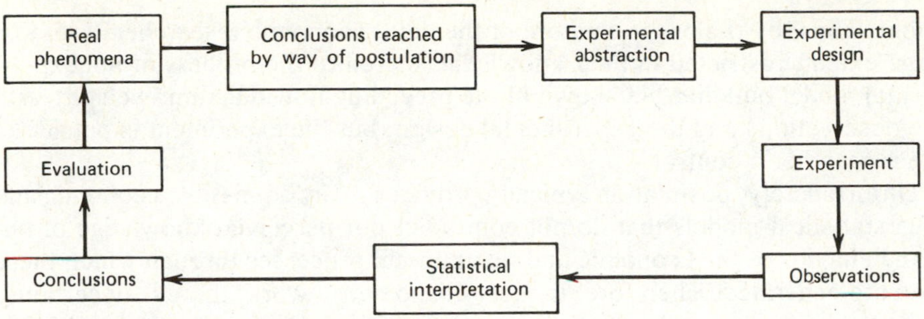

Figure 1.2 The experimental approach.

Since postulation only provides a range of possible conclusions and indicates nothing about the real-world truth content, the urge is strong to find a way to sort out fact from fiction or reduce the number of alternatives. Therefore, as was recognized early, one way to obtain knowledge is to observe the outcome of experiments that yield reproducible knowledge. In this process, a theoretical model is proposed and the uncontrolled elements are handled by the use of probability. In essence the postulation route to knowledge provides the theoretical model that may be used in the experimental search process or in alternatively learning from passively generated data.

The process by which choices between the tentative explanations, reached by postulation, may be made and theoretical parameters converted to useful information for decision purposes may be viewed as shown in Figure 1.2. Thus measurement provides one basis for choosing between the model alternatives and permits us to say, relative to the relationship between economic variables, something about how much, or at least the probability of how much. Disagreement between the statistical conclusions and those reached by postulation provide a basis for reevaluating the economic and experimental models and starting the search process again.

Given these knowledge-search processes, the task of econometrics is to use postulation and experimentation to generate information that may be used to reach conclusions of both a descriptive and prescriptive nature about economic processes and institutions.

1.2 THE NONEXPERIMENTAL MODEL-BUILDING RESTRICTION

Economic theory, through a formal deductive system, provides the basis for experimental abstraction and the experimental design, but society in most cases carries out the experiment, possibly using its own design. Therefore, the economic researcher observes the outcome of society's experiment or performance but has little or no impact on the experimental design and the observations generated. This means that the economist is often asked to estimate the impact of a change in the mechanism that produces the data when there is limited or no possibility of producing the data beforehand in a laboratory experiment. Thus, by the passive nature of the data, economic researchers are, to a large extent, restricted in their knowledge search to the process of nonexperimental model building. As shown in the preceding flow diagram, we start with the observations and the experimental design, but the experiment is outside of the researcher's control.

Unfortunately, postulation typically provides many admissible economic and thus statistical models that do not contradict our perceived knowledge of human behavior or the economic and institutional processes through which these data are generated. Therefore, in most econometric work, there is uncertainty as to the economic and statistical model that is used for estimation and inference purposes and the sampling model that actually was the basis for the data generation.

When econometric models are correctly specified, statistical theory provides well-defined procedures for obtaining point and interval estimates and evaluating the performance of various linear and usually unbiased estimators. However, uncertainties usually exist about the correct underlying economic and statistical models, such as the variables that should appear in the design matrix, the algebraic form of the relation or the type of nonlinearities that should be considered, the dynamic or lag structure between the economic variables, and the stochastic assumptions underlying the statistical model. In many cases, these uncertainties lead to models that are incorrectly specified and thus invalidate the sampling results that are traditionally claimed and generate estimators whose sampling performance is unknown. Consequently, to a large extent, econometrics is concerned with efficient procedures for identifying or mitigating the impacts of model misspecification.

The nonexperimental restriction also means that in addition to being efficient in using the data that are available, one must, in many cases, use nonsample information in order to adequately support the parameter space. Thus, much of econometrics is concerned with how to sort out and make use of this nonsample information in conjunction with the sample observations. In fact, much of the success in handling many of the problems in this book springs from how effectively this prior information is used. Therefore, in econometric work, as one goes from the conceptual model to the observed data and from prior information to the estimated relations, many interrelated questions face the researcher.

1.3 THE OBJECTIVES OF THE BOOK

Given the plethora of admissible economic and statistical models and the nonexperimental or passively generated nature of economic data, the general objective of this book is to provide the student and the researcher with the statistical consequences of a range of models and rules and to present an array of estimating procedures that are appropriate and effective in providing information that may be "useful" for a range of economic decision problems and data sets. Emphasis is directed to understanding the statistical consequences involved in the search for quantitative knowledge and not to mechanics and technicalities.

In particular, the purposes of this book are as follows.

1. To consider a range of traditional and nontraditional estimating and hypothesis testing rules, within both a sampling theory and a Bayesian framework.
2. To question, in some cases, the use of conventional statistical properties in evaluating the performance of estimators and to use a decision theory framework for evaluating estimator performance.
3. To indicate the statistical consequences of traditional and ad hoc rules for hypothesis testing and model selection.
4. To recognize that econometricians may, to a large extent, work with false models and to suggest procedures to cope with this fact of econometric life.
5. To recognize that much information exists other than sample information and to propose and evaluate procedures that combine both sample and this other information.
6. To provide an up-to-date and modern treatment of some of the most important questions and statistical models encountered in attempting to learn from economic data.

1.4 ORGANIZATION OF THE BOOK

In specifying and analyzing an array of statistical models, we have organized the book in six parts. Parts One and Two are concerned with the basic statistical models and the basis for inference, that is, the tools of econometric analysis. Parts Three and Four recognize the dynamic, stochastic, and heterogeneous nature of economic data and consider statistical models consistent with these data generation processes. Part Five is concerned with statistical models that recognize that much economic data are generated by systems of relations that are *dynamic, stochastic,* and *simultaneous*. Part Six recognizes that (1) some economic variables are either nonobservable or measured with error, (2) some economic variables are discrete rather than continuous, (3) some economic parameters are stochastic or variable rather than fixed, (4) not all random variables of interest are normally distributed, (5) not all statistical models used in practice have design matrices with correct column dimension and finally, (6) some design matrices are ill conditioned. Three appendices to the book are concerned with (1) matrix and distribution theorems that are used throughout the book, (2) numerical optimization methods that provide a computational base for a range of nonlinear models considered throughout the book and (3) Kalman filter models that provide a rather general framework for handling a range of economic models.

Given an understanding of the concepts developed in Parts 1 and 2, the sequence in which the other chapters are read is not of great consequence.

1.5 ECONOMETRIC THOUGHT

In order to understand the intellectual basis underlying econometrics, it is useful to see it through the eyes of a variety of practitioners in the field. The list of persons who have contributed to the development of econometric theory and application is rich and long. In this closing section, we include a sampling of articles that will introduce the reader to the literature in the field.

After the casual empiricism of the nineteenth century there was a concerted effort to make systematic and scientific use of statistical data. The statistical study of demand that started with Moore (1914) culminated with Schultz's classic work *The Theory and Measurement of Demand* (1938). Working (1926) in a provocative paper raised the interesting question, "What do statistical demand curves show?" and gave us the concept that we refer to today as the identification problem. Based on the productive efforts of these men along with those of others such as Frisch, Tinbergen, and Tintner, the early 1940s marked the beginning of the era of modern econometrics.

In formulating statistical models consistent with the way we visualize economic data are generated, the following publications stand out: two articles by Haavelmo (1943) and Mann and Wald (1943) and a monograph by Haavelmo entitled, *The Probability Approach to Econometrics* (1944). A monograph edited by Koopmans (1950) summarizes the productive efforts of many during the 1940s. Some who have traced the evolution of econometrics in the 1950s and 1960s include Tintner (1966), Leser (1968), Wold (1969), Klein (1971), and Judge (1975). The 1960s were especially important in developing statistical models that provide systematic ways of combining sample and nonsample information, and in this context Zellner's book, *An Introduction to Bayesian Inference in Econometrics* (1971), stands out in both content and influence. The 1960s was also the beginning of the use of an idea, first introduced by Wald (1950), which emphasized statistical decision theory. We hope this incomplete trek through econometric history will provide the reader with some feeling of the debt we owe our precursors, and will give some insight as to the foundation stones on which the chapters to follow rest. Perhaps at this point in econometric life the great impediment to discovery is not technical incompetence but rather the illusion of knowledge.

1.6 REFERENCES

Haavelmo, T. (1943) "The Statistical Implications of a System of Simultaneous Equations," *Econometrica,* 11, 1–12.

Haavelmo, T. (1944) *The Probability Approach to Economics,* supplement to *Econometrica,* 12, 1–118.

Judge, G. G. (1975) "Estimation and Inference in Economics," *Quantitative Methods in Agricultural Economics,* G. Judge, R. Day, S. Johnson, and G. Rausser, eds., University of Minnesota Press, Minneapolis.

Klein, L. R. (1971) "Whither Econometrics," *Journal of the American Statistical Association,* 66, 415–21.

Koopmans, T. (1950) *Statistical Inference in Dynamic Economic Models,* Wiley, New York.

Leser, C. E. U. (1968) "A Survey of Econometrics," *Journal of the Royal Statistical Society,* Series A, 131, 530–566.

Mann, H. B. and A. Wald (1943) "On the Statistical Treatment of Linear Stochastic Difference Equations," *Econometrica,* 11, 173–220.

Moore, H. L. (1914) *Economic Cycles: Their Law and Cause,* Macmillan, New York (reprinted in 1967 by H. M. Kelly).

Schlutz, H. (1938) *The Theory and Measurement of Demand,* University of Chicago Press, Chicago.

Tintner, G. (1966) "Some Thoughts About the State of Econometrics," *Structure of Economic Science: Essays on Methodology,* S. R. Krupp, ed., Prentice Hall, Englewood Cliffs, N.J.

Wald, A. (1950) *Statistical Decision Functions,* Wiley, New York.

Wold, H. (1969) "Econometrics as Pioneering in Non-Experimental Model Building," *Econometrica,* 37, 369–81.

Working, E. (1926) "What Do Statistical Demand Curves Show?" *Quarterly Journal of Economics,* 41, 212–235.

Zellner, A. (1971) *An Introduction to Bayesian Inference in Econometrics,* Wiley, New York.

PART ONE

SAMPLING THEORY AND BAYESIAN APPROACHES TO INFERENCE

In the following three chapters, we review the sampling theory and Bayesian approaches to inference when the underlying sampling process can be described by a variant of the traditional linear statistical model. Basic concepts and definitions underlying statistical decision theory are presented and the statistical implications of (1) using conventional hypothesis testing (estimation) procedures, (2) combining sample and nonsample information, and (3) the nontraditional family of Stein-rule estimators are explored and their sampling performances evaluated under a squared error loss measure. Finally, the concepts underlying the Bayesian approach to inference are introduced and applied in the linear statistical model case. Some matrix and distribution theorems that are useful in formulating and evaluating the statistical models in Part 1 are presented in Appendix A at the end of the book.

Chapter 2

The Classical Inference Approach for the General Linear Model

Within a classical inference framework, in this chapter we (1) specify linear statistical models that reflect alternative ways of modeling sampling or data generating processes, (2) demonstrate alternative estimation rules and evaluate their sampling properties, and (3) propose alternative test statistics that may be used as a basis for checking the compatibility of the data and general linear hypotheses. Since there are alternative ways of modeling the sampling process underlying the observed economic data, the statistical consequences of incorrectly modeling the sampling process or specifying a statistical model that is inconsistent with the data generation process are considered. Within this context, the major purpose of this chapter is to provide a quick review of some basic results of classical inference as it relates to linear statistical models and to establish a notational basis for the chapters to follow. Those seeking a more detailed development of these traditional estimation and inference procedures are referred to Chapters 6, 7, 10, and 11 in Judge, Hill, Griffiths, Lütkepohl, and Lee (1982) or to books referenced at the end of this chapter. An overview of the chapter is given in Table 2.1. Some matrix and distribution theorems that are used in this chapter and indeed throughout the book are summarized in Appendix A at the end of the book.

2.1 CLASSICAL INFERENCE FOR THE TRADITIONAL LINEAR STATISTICAL MODEL

In many cases we have limited knowledge about the relationships among economic variables. Facing this situation, one way to gain knowledge is to experiment. If we visualize the observed values of economic variables as the outcomes of experiments, then we must have a theoretical framework on which to base the experimental design or to act as a basis for modeling the data generation or the sampling process. Within this context consider the following linear statistical model

$$\mathbf{y} = X\boldsymbol{\beta} + \mathbf{e} \tag{2.1.1}$$

TABLE 2.1 ***SAMPLING THEORY APPROACH TO ESTIMATION AND INFERENCE***

The Linear Statistical Model

$\mathbf{y} = X\boldsymbol{\beta} + \mathbf{e}$; Unknown Parameters $\boldsymbol{\beta}$, σ^2

$\mathbf{e} \sim (\mathbf{0},\sigma^2 I_T)$	$\mathbf{e} \sim (\mathbf{0},\sigma^2 \Psi)$	$\mathbf{e} \sim N(\mathbf{0},\sigma^2 I_T)$	$\mathbf{e} \sim N(\mathbf{0},\sigma^2 \Psi)$
Point Estimation $\boldsymbol{\beta}$		**Point Estimation $\boldsymbol{\beta}$**	
Least squares estimator (Section 2.1.1)	Generalized least squares estimator (Section 2.2)	Maximum likelihood rule (Section 2.1.2)	General maximum likelihood rule (Section 2.2)
Sampling Properties		**Sampling Properties**	
Best linear unbiased (Section 2.1.1a)	Best linear unbiased (Section 2.2)	Best unbiased sufficient (Section 2.1.2a)	Best unbiased sufficient (Section 2.2)
Point Estimator of σ^2		**Interval Estimation**	
(Section 2.1.1b)	(Section 2.2)	(Section 2.1.3a)	(Section 2.2)
Sampling Properties		**Hypothesis Testing**	
Unbiased (Section 2.1.1b)	Unbiased (Section 2.2)	(Section 2.1.3b)	(Section 2.2)

Point Estimator of σ^2 (for $\mathbf{e} \sim N(\mathbf{0},\sigma^2 I_T)$):

Maximum likelihood (Sec. 2.1.2)	Unbiased (Section 2.1.2a)	Minimum mean square (Section 2.1.2a)

Sampling Properties (Section 2.1.2a)

Biased	Best unbiased	Minimum mean square error

Hypothesis Testing and Interval Estimation (Section 2.1.3)

where $\mathbf{y}$ is a $(T \times 1)$ vector of observable values of the random variable y on a sample space defined on the Euclidean line, X is a known $(T \times K)$ nonstochastic design matrix of rank K, $\boldsymbol{\beta}$ is a K-dimensional fixed vector of unknown parameters and $\mathbf{e}$ is a $(T \times 1)$ vector of unobservable random variables with mean vector $E[\mathbf{e}] = \mathbf{0}$ and finite covariance matrix. As a basis for describing a simple data-generating process, let us assume that the elements of the random vector $\mathbf{e}$ are identically and independently distributed. Therefore, the covariance matrix is $E[\mathbf{ee}'] = \sigma^2 I_T$, where the scalar σ^2 is unknown and I_T is a Tth-order identity matrix. We denote this specification for the real random vector $\mathbf{e}$ as $\mathbf{e} \sim (\mathbf{0}, \sigma^2 I_T)$.

The $(T \times K)$ design matrix X is assumed to be composed of K fixed (explanatory) variables. In an experimental context these variables would be considered treatment or control variables and their design would be specified by the researcher. In economics the experiment is usually designed and carried out by society, and the researcher is a passive observer in the data generation process. The assumption that X is a matrix of fixed variables means that for all the possible situations that might take place under repeated sampling, the matrix X would take on the same values. However, the observable vector $\mathbf{y}$ would vary from sample to sample. In reality, usually only one sample vector $\mathbf{y}$ is actually observed. In this situation, if both X and $\mathbf{y}$ are thought of as random variables, then the repetition of X implies that it has a singular distribution. Alternatively, $\mathbf{y}$ may be thought of as a random vector with a distribution that is conditional on the matrix of fixed variables X.

Other than the functional form specified in (2.1.1) it is assumed that only sample information is used and that no other information is either available or introduced about the unknown parameter vector $\boldsymbol{\beta}$ and the unknown scalar σ^2. Furthermore, the design matrix is assumed to be correctly specified, and the outcome vector $\mathbf{y}$ and the treatment variables in the design matrix X are assumed to be observable and measured without error. In the sections to come we will consider more general data generation schemes and thus change the stochastic assumptions that are made relative to the distribution of the real random vector $\mathbf{e}$.

2.1.1 The Least Squares Rule

For the statistical model (2.1.1), the observed values of the random variables $\mathbf{y}$ contain all of the information available about the unknown $\boldsymbol{\beta}$ vector and the unknown scalar σ^2. Consequently, the point estimation problem is one of finding a suitable function of the observed values of the random variables $\mathbf{y}$, given the design matrix X, that will yield, in a repeated sample sense, the "best" estimator of the unknown parameters. If, in estimating the unknown coefficient vector $\boldsymbol{\beta}$, we restrict ourselves to the class of rules that are linear functions of $\mathbf{y}$, we may write the general linear estimator or rule as

$$\mathbf{b}_0 = A\mathbf{y} \tag{2.1.2}$$

where A is some $(K \times T)$ matrix. This means that the estimation problem is reduced to determining a $(K \times T)$ matrix A that "appropriately" summarizes the information contained in $\mathbf{y}$.

Obviously, there are a number of criteria we might insist on in choosing A; if we use the sampling theory approach one way of proceeding is to (1) select a criterion, (2) determine the A matrix, and thus the estimator of $\boldsymbol{\beta}$ that it leads to, and (3) evaluate the sampling performance of the estimator. For example, if we use the criterion of choosing the estimate of the coefficient vector $\boldsymbol{\beta}$ that makes the sum of the squared errors of the disturbance vector **e** a minimum, we would then minimize the quadratic form

$$\ell = \mathbf{e}'\mathbf{e} = (\mathbf{y} - X\boldsymbol{\beta})'(\mathbf{y} - X\boldsymbol{\beta}) = \mathbf{y}'\mathbf{y} - 2\boldsymbol{\beta}'X'\mathbf{y} + \boldsymbol{\beta}'X'X\boldsymbol{\beta} \quad (2.1.3)$$

This criterion results in the optimizing condition

$$\frac{1}{2}\frac{\partial \ell}{\partial \boldsymbol{\beta}} = X'X\mathbf{b} - X'\mathbf{y} = \mathbf{0}$$

which leads to the optimizing vector

$$\mathbf{b} = (X'X)^{-1}X'\mathbf{y} \quad (2.1.4)$$

This linear rule (linear function of **y**) is appropriately known as the least squares estimator and means that one candidate for A is $A = (X'X)^{-1}X'$.

2.1.1a Sampling Properties of the Least Squares Estimator

In conventional sampling theory, properties such as unbiasedness, efficiency, and invariance are proposed as a basis for evaluating and choosing among estimators or decision rules. Thus properties are identified that may be desirable under certain circumstances, and these properties then form the basis for rating or ranking various estimators or rules.

First, let us look at the property of unbiasedness for the linear estimator (2.1.4). Note that since the least squares estimator **b** is a linear function of the random vector **y**, it is also a random vector with mean vector

$$\begin{aligned} E[\mathbf{b}] &= E[(X'X)^{-1}X'\mathbf{y}] = \boldsymbol{\beta} + E[(X'X)^{-1}X'\mathbf{e}] \\ &= \boldsymbol{\beta} + (X'X)^{-1}X'E[\mathbf{e}] = \boldsymbol{\beta} \end{aligned} \quad (2.1.5)$$

where we have used the assumption $E[\mathbf{e}] = \mathbf{0}$ and that X is nonstochastic. We remind the reader that $E[\ ]$ stands for the expectation of the argument. These results imply that the linear decision rule (2.1.4) is on the average correct and is thus unbiased, a property that is sometimes given high priority in evaluating sampling theory estimators.

Given the unbiased property, the next question concerns how the linear unbiased rule (2.1.4) compares with other linear unbiased rules in terms of the precision (variance–covariance) matrix. The covariance matrix for the random vector **b** is

$$\begin{aligned} \Sigma_{\mathbf{b}} &= E[(\mathbf{b} - E[\mathbf{b}])(\mathbf{b} - E[\mathbf{b}])'] = E[(\mathbf{b} - \boldsymbol{\beta})(\mathbf{b} - \boldsymbol{\beta})'] \\ &= E[(X'X)^{-1}X'\mathbf{e}\mathbf{e}'X(X'X)^{-1}] = \sigma^2(X'X)^{-1} \end{aligned} \quad (2.1.6)$$

which follows from the assumptions $E[\mathbf{e}\mathbf{e}'] = \sigma^2 I_T$ and X is nonstochastic.

Given this covariance result, the Gauss–Markov theorem provides proof that out of the *class of linear unbiased rules* for the statistical model (2.1.1) the least squares estimator is best, where best is defined in terms of minimum variance. That is, any arbitrary linear unbiased estimator $\mathbf{b}_0$ will have a covariance matrix

$$E[(\mathbf{b}_0 - \boldsymbol{\beta})(\mathbf{b}_0 - \boldsymbol{\beta})'] = \sigma^2(X'X)^{-1} + \Delta \tag{2.1.7}$$

where Δ is a positive semidefinite matrix. Therefore, for the linear rule (2.1.4), the least squares estimator is equal to or better in terms of sampling precision than all others in its class. This is a beautiful result, which does much to explain the popularity of the least squares rule.

2.1.1b An Estimator of σ^2

Having obtained a point estimator for the unknown coefficient vector $\boldsymbol{\beta}$, we now turn to a basis for estimating σ^2, the variance of the elements of the random vectors $\mathbf{y}$ and $\mathbf{e}$. The quadratic form (2.1.3) that was used in obtaining a least squares estimator of $\boldsymbol{\beta}$ does not contain σ^2, and therefore does not provide a basis for its estimation.

From our stochastic assumptions regarding the error vector $\mathbf{e}$ we know that $E[\mathbf{e}'\mathbf{e}] = T\sigma^2$. Thus it would seem that if we had a sample of observations for the random error vector $\mathbf{y} - X\boldsymbol{\beta} = \mathbf{e}$, we could use this sample as a basis for estimating σ^2. Unfortunately, since $\boldsymbol{\beta}$ is unknown and unobservable the random vector $\mathbf{e}$ is unobservable. If we are to estimate σ^2 on the basis of information that we have, this will involve the observed random $\mathbf{y}$ vector and its least squares counterpart $\hat{\mathbf{y}} = X\mathbf{b}$. Thus the vector of least squares residuals, $\hat{\mathbf{e}} = \mathbf{y} - X\mathbf{b}$ provides a least squares sample analogue of the vector of unobservable errors $\mathbf{e}$. Since

$$\hat{\mathbf{y}} = X\mathbf{b} = X(X'X)^{-1}X'\mathbf{y} \tag{2.1.8}$$

then

$$\hat{\mathbf{e}} = \mathbf{y} - X\mathbf{b} = \mathbf{y} - X(X'X)^{-1}X'\mathbf{y} = (I_T - X(X'X)^{-1}X')\mathbf{y} \tag{2.1.9}$$

and

$$\hat{\mathbf{e}} = (I_T - X(X'X)^{-1}X')(X\boldsymbol{\beta} + \mathbf{e}) = (I_T - X(X'X)^{-1}X')\mathbf{e} = M\mathbf{e} \tag{2.1.10}$$

where $\hat{\mathbf{e}}$ is expressed as a linear function of the unobservable random errors and the matrix M is of dimension $(T \times T)$ and symmetric. The $(T \times T)$ symmetric matrix M has the property

$$\begin{aligned} MM' &= MM = M^2 = M \\ &= [I_T - X(X'X)^{-1}X'][I_T - X(X'X)^{-1}X'] = [I_T - X(X'X)^{-1}X'] \end{aligned}$$

and thus is an idempotent matrix. If we use the quadratic form $\hat{\mathbf{e}}'\hat{\mathbf{e}}$ instead of $\mathbf{e}'\mathbf{e}$ as a basis for estimating the scalar σ^2, then it can be written as

$$\begin{aligned}\hat{\mathbf{e}}'\hat{\mathbf{e}} &= \mathbf{e}'(I_T - X(X'X)^{-1}X')(I_T - X(X'X)^{-1}X')\mathbf{e} \\ &= \mathbf{e}'M'M\mathbf{e} = \mathbf{e}'M\mathbf{e} = \mathbf{e}'(I_T - X(X'X)^{-1}X')\mathbf{e} \end{aligned} \tag{2.1.11}$$

If we investigate on the average what would happen if we made use of (2.1.11), then by using the expectation operator and the concept of a trace of a matrix

$$\begin{aligned}E[\hat{\mathbf{e}}'\hat{\mathbf{e}}] &= E[\mathbf{e}'(I_T - X(X'X)^{-1}X')\mathbf{e}] \\ &= E[\mathbf{e}'M\mathbf{e}] \\ &= E[\text{tr}(\mathbf{e}'M\mathbf{e})] = E[\text{tr}(M\mathbf{e}\mathbf{e}')] \\ &= \text{tr}\{ME[\mathbf{e}\mathbf{e}']\} = \sigma^2\text{tr}[I_T - X(X'X)^{-1}X'] \\ &= \sigma^2[\text{tr}(I_T) - \text{tr}(X(X'X)^{-1}X')] = \sigma^2[\text{tr}(I_T) - \text{tr}(I_K)] \\ &= \sigma^2(T - K) \end{aligned} \tag{2.1.12}$$

Consequently,

$$E\left[\frac{\hat{\mathbf{e}}'\hat{\mathbf{e}}}{T - K}\right] = \left(\frac{1}{T - K}\right)\sigma^2(T - K) = \sigma^2 \tag{2.1.13}$$

Thus if we let $\left[\dfrac{\hat{\mathbf{e}}'\hat{\mathbf{e}}}{T - K}\right] = \hat{\sigma}^2$, then

$$\hat{\sigma}^2 = \frac{(\mathbf{y} - X\mathbf{b})'(\mathbf{y} - X\mathbf{b})}{T - K} = \frac{\mathbf{y}'(I_T - X(X'X)^{-1}X')\mathbf{y}}{T - K} \tag{2.1.14}$$

is a quadratic form in terms of the observable vector $\mathbf{y}$. By (2.1.13), the quadratic estimator $\hat{\sigma}^2$ for the unknown scalar σ^2 is an unbiased estimator. The variance of the random variable $\hat{\sigma}^2$ will be evaluated in the next section.

2.1.2 The Maximum Likelihood Rule

Once a distributional assumption is made about the random vector $\mathbf{e}$, the maximum likelihood principle provides another basis for estimating the unknown parameters $\boldsymbol{\beta}$ and σ^2. Under the maximum likelihood principle the observations $\mathbf{y}$ are the only elements in the sample space $\mathcal{Y}$ that are relevant to problems of decision or inference concerning the unknown parameters. Thus, in making decisions about the unknown parameters after $\mathbf{y}$ is observed, all relevant sample information is contained in the likelihood function. Under the maximum likelihood criterion, the parameter estimates are chosen so as to maximize the probability of generating or obtaining the observed sample. If the assumption is made that the random vector **e** or **y** is multivariate normally distributed and the assumption $E[\mathbf{ee}'] = \sigma^2 I_T$ is retained we may write the likelihood function for the linear statistical model (2.1.1) as,

$$\ell(\boldsymbol{\beta},\sigma^2|\mathbf{y}) = (2\pi\sigma^2)^{-T/2} \exp\left[-\frac{(\mathbf{y} - X\boldsymbol{\beta})'(\mathbf{y} - X\boldsymbol{\beta})}{2\sigma^2}\right] \tag{2.1.15}$$

The corresponding maximum likelihood estimators for $\boldsymbol{\beta}$ and σ^2 that maximize the likelihood function (2.1.15) are

$$\tilde{\boldsymbol{\beta}} = (X'X)^{-1}X'\mathbf{y} = \mathbf{b} \tag{2.1.16}$$

and

$$\tilde{\sigma}^2 = \frac{(\mathbf{y} - X\tilde{\boldsymbol{\beta}})'(\mathbf{y} - X\tilde{\boldsymbol{\beta}})}{T} \tag{2.1.17}$$

2.1.2a Sampling Properties

The maximum likelihood estimator for $\boldsymbol{\beta}$ is the same as the least squares estimator and thus we know it is a best linear unbiased estimator. Also, since $\tilde{\boldsymbol{\beta}}$ is a linear function of the normally distributed random vector **y**, we can say that the random vector $\tilde{\boldsymbol{\beta}}$ is normally distributed with a mean of $\boldsymbol{\beta}$ and a covariance of $\sigma^2(X'X)^{-1}$ [i.e., $\tilde{\boldsymbol{\beta}} \sim N(\boldsymbol{\beta},\sigma^2(X'X)^{-1})$].

The maximum likelihood estimator $\tilde{\sigma}^2$ is a quadratic function of normal random variables and has a mean

$$E[\tilde{\sigma}^2] = \frac{1}{T} E[\mathbf{e}'(I - X(X'X)^{-1}X')\mathbf{e}] = \sigma^2 \frac{(T - K)}{T} \tag{2.1.18}$$

and thus is biased in finite samples. However, the estimator $[T/(T - K)]\tilde{\sigma}^2 = \hat{\sigma}^2$ is as we know an unbiased estimator. Since $\tilde{\sigma}^2[T/(T - K)]$ is a quadratic form in terms of the normal random vector **e** (see Section 7.1.3c in Judge et al., 1982 or Appendix A) the quadratic form

$$\frac{\mathbf{e}'(I - X(X'X)^{-1}X')\mathbf{e}}{\sigma^2} = (T - K)\frac{\hat{\sigma}^2}{\sigma^2} \tag{2.1.19}$$

is distributed as a chi-square random variable with $(T - K)$ degrees of freedom [i.e., $(T - K)\hat{\sigma}^2/\sigma^2 \sim \chi^2_{(T-K)}$]. Also since $\hat{\mathbf{e}}$ and $\tilde{\boldsymbol{\beta}}$ are independently distributed random vectors, it follows that $\tilde{\boldsymbol{\beta}}$ and $\hat{\sigma}^2$ are independently distributed.

We can use these distributional results to determine the mean and variance of $\hat{\sigma}^2$ and $\tilde{\sigma}^2$ as follows

$$E[\hat{\sigma}^2] = \frac{\sigma^2}{T-K} E[\chi^2_{(T-K)}] = \sigma^2 \tag{2.1.20}$$

and

$$E[(\hat{\sigma}^2 - \sigma^2)^2] = \frac{\sigma^4}{(T-K)^2} \operatorname{Var}(\chi^2_{(T-K)}) = 2\sigma^4/(T-K) \tag{2.1.21}$$

Likewise,

$$E[\tilde{\sigma}^2] = \frac{\sigma^2}{T} E[\chi^2_{(T-K)}] = \frac{(T-K)}{T}\sigma^2 \tag{2.1.22a}$$

and

$$E[(\tilde{\sigma}^2 - E[\tilde{\sigma}^2])^2] = \frac{\sigma^4}{T^2} \operatorname{Var}(\chi^2_{(T-K)}) = 2\sigma^4(T-K)/T^2 \tag{2.1.22b}$$

Thus $\tilde{\sigma}^2$ has a bias $-(K/T)\sigma^2$ and a variance which, in finite samples, is smaller than the variance for the unbiased estimator $\hat{\sigma}^2$. If one visualizes a trade-off between bias and precision, interest might focus on a minimum mean squared error (MSE) estimator of σ^2. That is an estimator $\bar{\sigma}^2$ where

$$E[(\bar{\sigma}^2 - \sigma^2)^2] = \text{variance}(\bar{\sigma}^2) + (\text{bias}(\bar{\sigma}^2))^2 \tag{2.1.23a}$$

is a minimum. To investigate this question consider the estimator $\hat{\sigma}^2 (T-K)/(T-a)$ where a is unknown. This estimator has mean $[(T-K)/(T-a)]\sigma^2$, a bias of $[(a-K)/(T-a)]\sigma^2$, variance $(\bar{\sigma}^2) = 2\sigma^4(T-K)/(T-a)^2$ and mean squared error $2\sigma^4(T-K)/(T-a)^2 + \sigma^4(a-K)^2/(T-a)^2$. The choice of a that makes the mean square error a minimum is $(K-2)$ and thus the minimum mean squared estimator is $\bar{\sigma}^2 = \hat{\sigma}^2(T-K)/(T-K+2)$ and has mean

$$E[\bar{\sigma}^2] = \sigma^2(T-K)/(T-K+2) \tag{2.1.23b}$$

with bias $-2\sigma^2/(T-K+2)$ and variance

$$E[(\bar{\sigma}^2 - E[\bar{\sigma}^2])^2] = 2\sigma^4(T-K)/(T-K+2)^2 \tag{2.1.23c}$$

The mean squared error of $\bar{\sigma}^2$ is always less than the variance (MSE) of $\hat{\sigma}^2$. Finally, the optimum divisor of the quadratic form to get an unbiased estimator is $(T-K)$ and in this class of estimators $\hat{\sigma}^2$ is the minimum variance unbiased estimator of σ^2.

2.1.2b Cramér-Rao Inequality

Since we have unbiased estimators for $\boldsymbol{\beta}$ and σ^2 let us use the normality assumption to investigate the lower bound for the sampling variance of estimators that can be chosen from the class of all unbiased estimators. These results will provide a reference point for gauging goodness of performance if we stay in the unbiased class and use finite samples of data. Similar asymptotic results will be considered in Chapter 5.

In developing this lower bound we will use the *Cramér-Rao inequality* and the resulting *information matrix*. The Cramér-Rao inequality makes use of the fact that the square of a covariance is at most equal to the product of the corresponding variances. In stating this result for the normal linear statistical model we will represent the $(K + 1)$ unknown parameters as $\boldsymbol{\gamma} = (\beta_1, \beta_2, \ldots, \beta_K, \sigma^2)'$ and remember that the likelihood function $\ell(\boldsymbol{\gamma}|\mathbf{y},X)$, as a function of the random sample $\mathbf{y}$, is random, and therefore the derivatives of the likelihood function with respect to $\boldsymbol{\gamma}$ are random. If we assume that the likelihood function is twice differentiable the information matrix for $\boldsymbol{\gamma}$ is defined as

$$I(\boldsymbol{\gamma}) = -E\left[\frac{\partial^2 \ln \ell(\boldsymbol{\gamma}|\mathbf{y},X)}{\partial\boldsymbol{\gamma}\, \partial\boldsymbol{\gamma}'}\right] \tag{2.1.24}$$

which is the negative of the expectation of the matrix of second-order derivatives.

The inverse of the information matrix provides a lower bound for the sampling precision for unbiased estimators of $\boldsymbol{\gamma}$. That is, $\Sigma_{\hat{\boldsymbol{\gamma}}} \geq I(\boldsymbol{\gamma})^{-1}$ in the sense that $\Sigma_{\hat{\boldsymbol{\gamma}}} - I(\boldsymbol{\gamma})^{-1}$ is positive semidefinite. For our statistical model the elements of the matrix (2.1.24) are the second order derivatives of the likelihood function (2.1.15) and thus

$$\begin{aligned} I(\boldsymbol{\gamma}) &= -E\begin{bmatrix} -\dfrac{1}{\sigma^2} X'X & -\dfrac{1}{\sigma^4}(X'\mathbf{y} - X'X\boldsymbol{\beta}) \\ -\dfrac{1}{\sigma^4}(X'\mathbf{y} - X'X\boldsymbol{\beta})' & \dfrac{T}{2\sigma^4} - \dfrac{1}{\sigma^6}(\mathbf{y} - X\boldsymbol{\beta})'(\mathbf{y} - X\boldsymbol{\beta}) \end{bmatrix} \\ &= \begin{bmatrix} \dfrac{1}{\sigma^2} X'X & 0 \\ 0 & \dfrac{T}{2\sigma^4} \end{bmatrix} \end{aligned} \tag{2.1.25}$$

and

$$I(\boldsymbol{\gamma})^{-1} = \begin{bmatrix} \sigma^2(X'X)^{-1} & 0 \\ 0 & \dfrac{2\sigma^4}{T} \end{bmatrix} \tag{2.1.26}$$

The covariance for the unbiased estimators $\tilde{\boldsymbol{\beta}}$ and $\hat{\sigma}^2$ is

$$\Sigma_{(\tilde{\boldsymbol{\beta}},\hat{\sigma}^2)} = \begin{bmatrix} \sigma^2(X'X)^{-1} & 0 \\ 0 & \dfrac{2\sigma^4}{T-K} \end{bmatrix} \tag{2.1.27}$$

and this means that the Cramér-Rao lower bound is attained by the covariance of $\tilde{\boldsymbol{\beta}} = \mathbf{b}$ but not for the unbiased estimator $\hat{\sigma}^2$. This gives us a stronger result than the Gauss-Markov theorem because it means that the maximum likelihood estimator of $\boldsymbol{\beta}$ is best in a larger class of estimators that does not include the linearity restriction. Also, although the variance of $\hat{\sigma}^2$ does not attain the lower bound, an unbiased estimator of σ^2 with variance lower than $2\sigma^4/(T-K)$ does not exist.

2.1.3 Interval Estimation and Hypothesis Testing

Since the maximum likelihood estimator $\tilde{\boldsymbol{\beta}} = \mathbf{b}$ is a linear function of the normally distributed vector $\mathbf{y}$ we may work with the following model in developing interval estimates and hypothesis tests:

$$\mathbf{b} = \boldsymbol{\beta} + (X'X)^{-1}X'\mathbf{e} = \boldsymbol{\beta} + \mathbf{v}$$
$$\mathbf{v} \sim N(\mathbf{0},\sigma^2(X'X)^{-1}) \tag{2.1.28}$$

Therefore $(\mathbf{b} - \boldsymbol{\beta}) \sim N(\mathbf{0},\sigma^2(X'X)^{-1})$. Since $(X'X)^{-1}$ is a positive definite symmetric matrix there exists (Appendix A) a square nonsingular P matrix such that $(X'X) = P'P$ or $(P')^{-1}(X'X)P^{-1} = I_K$. Consequently,

$$\mathbf{z} = P(\mathbf{b} - \boldsymbol{\beta}) \sim N(\mathbf{0},\sigma^2 I_K) \tag{2.1.29}$$

and $\mathbf{z}$ is a K-dimensional vector of independent normally distributed random variables with mean zero and variance σ^2. Therefore, the quadratic form

$$\frac{\mathbf{z}'\mathbf{z}}{\sigma^2} = \frac{(\mathbf{b} - \boldsymbol{\beta})'P'P(\mathbf{b} - \boldsymbol{\beta})}{\sigma^2} = \frac{(\mathbf{b} - \boldsymbol{\beta})'(X'X)(\mathbf{b} - \boldsymbol{\beta})}{\sigma^2}$$
$$= \frac{\mathbf{e}'X(X'X)^{-1}X'\mathbf{e}}{\sigma^2} \sim \chi^2_{(K)} \tag{2.1.30}$$

where $X(X'X)^{-1}X'$ is an idempotent matrix of rank K.

Alternatively we have for the model involving general linear combinations of the parameters

$$R\mathbf{b} = R\boldsymbol{\beta} + R(X'X)^{-1}X'\mathbf{e} = R\boldsymbol{\beta} + \mathbf{v}_1$$
$$\mathbf{v}_1 \sim N(\mathbf{0},\sigma^2 R(X'X)^{-1}R') \tag{2.1.31}$$

where R is a $(J \times K)$ matrix of rank $J \leq K$.

As above, $(R\mathbf{b} - R\boldsymbol{\beta}) = R(\mathbf{b} - \boldsymbol{\beta}) \sim N(\mathbf{0},\sigma^2 R(X'X)^{-1}R')$ and there exists a matrix Q such that $[R(X'X)^{-1}R']^{-1} = Q'Q$ and

$$\mathbf{z}_1 = QR(\mathbf{b} - \boldsymbol{\beta}) \sim N(\mathbf{0},\sigma^2 I_K) \tag{2.1.32a}$$

Therefore

$$\begin{aligned}\frac{\mathbf{z}_1'\mathbf{z}_1}{\sigma^2} &= \frac{(\mathbf{b} - \boldsymbol{\beta})'R'Q'QR(\mathbf{b} - \boldsymbol{\beta})}{\sigma^2} \\ &= (\mathbf{b} - \boldsymbol{\beta})'R'[R(X'X)^{-1}R']^{-1}R(\mathbf{b} - \boldsymbol{\beta})/\sigma^2 \\ &= \frac{\mathbf{e}'X(X'X)^{-1}R'[R(X'X)^{-1}R']^{-1}R(X'X)^{-1}X'\mathbf{e}}{\sigma^2} \sim \chi^2_{(J)}\end{aligned} \tag{2.1.32b}$$

and $X(X'X)^{-1}R'[R(X'X)^{-1}R']^{-1}R(X'X)^{-1}X'$ is an idempotent matrix of rank and trace J. We previously noted in Section (2.1.2a) that the random variable

$$(T - K)\hat{\sigma}^2/\sigma^2 \sim \chi^2_{(T-K)} \tag{2.1.33}$$

This result in conjunction with (2.1.32b), and the fact that these two quadratic forms are independent, can be used to construct t and F statistics for interval estimation and hypothesis testing.

2.1.3a Interval Estimation

If R is a $(1 \times K)$ row vector the random variable

$$\frac{R(\mathbf{b} - \boldsymbol{\beta})}{\hat{\sigma}[R(X'X)^{-1}R']^{1/2}} \tag{2.1.34}$$

is distributed as a t random variable with $(T - K)$ degrees of freedom. Therefore at the α level of significance we can write

$$Pr\left\{-t_{[(T-K),\alpha/2]} \leq \frac{R(\mathbf{b} - \boldsymbol{\beta})}{\hat{\sigma}[R(X'X)^{-1}R']^{1/2}} \leq t_{[(T-K),\alpha/2]}\right\} = 1 - \alpha \tag{2.1.35a}$$

and this yields the interval estimator

$$R\mathbf{b} \pm t_{[(T-K),\alpha/2]}\hat{\sigma}[R(X'X)^{-1}R']^{1/2} \tag{2.1.35b}$$

If interest centers on joint confidence intervals then when R is a $(J \times K)$ matrix then

$$\frac{(\mathbf{b} - \boldsymbol{\beta})'R'[R(X'X)^{-1}R']^{-1}R(\mathbf{b} - \boldsymbol{\beta})}{J\hat{\sigma}^2} \sim F_{(J,T-K)} \tag{2.1.36}$$

that is, it is distributed as an F random variable with J and $(T - K)$ degrees of freedom. The joint confidence interval is in the form of an ellipsoid with $R\mathbf{b}$ as its center.

In addition, since

$$\frac{(T - K)\hat{\sigma}^2}{\sigma^2} \tag{2.1.37a}$$

is distributed as a central chi-square random variable with $(T - K)$ degrees of freedom, then

$$P[\chi^2_{(T-K,a_1=\alpha/2)} \leq \chi^2_{(T-K)} \leq \chi^2_{(T-K,a_2=1-\alpha/2)}] = 1 - \alpha \tag{2.1.37b}$$

or

$$P\left[\chi^2_{(T-K,a_1=\alpha/2)} \leq \frac{(T - K)\hat{\sigma}^2}{\sigma^2} \leq \chi^2_{(T-K,a_2=1-\alpha/2)}\right] = 1 - \alpha$$

This implies the inequalities

$$\frac{(T - K)\hat{\sigma}^2}{\chi^2_{(T-K,a_2=1-\alpha/2)}} \leq \sigma^2 \leq \frac{(T - K)\hat{\sigma}^2}{\chi^2_{(T-K,a_1=\alpha/2)}} \tag{2.1.37c}$$

and in a repeated sampling sense the set of upper and lower bounds computed from the samples will contain σ^2, $(1 - \alpha)$ percent of the time.

2.1.3b Hypothesis Testing

After estimating the unknown parameters of the statistical model, the researcher is usually interested in testing one or more linear hypotheses about individual parameters or linear combinations thereof. The interval estimation procedures developed in the previous section and the distribution theorems of Appendix A provide the underlying basis for testing linear hypotheses. In developing a test procedure consider the models

$$\mathbf{y} = X\boldsymbol{\beta} + \mathbf{e}$$

where

$$\mathbf{e} \sim N(\mathbf{0},\sigma^2 I_T) \tag{2.1.38a}$$

and

$$R\mathbf{b} = R\boldsymbol{\beta} + \mathbf{v}_1$$

$$R\boldsymbol{\beta} = \mathbf{r}$$

$$\mathbf{v}_1 \sim N(\mathbf{0},\sigma^2 R(X'X)^{-1}R') \tag{2.1.38b}$$

where R is a $(J \times K)$ hypothesis design matrix and $\mathbf{r}$ is a $(J \times 1)$ known vector. $R\boldsymbol{\beta} = \mathbf{r}$ is the null hypothesis.

If R is a $(1 \times K)$ row vector and the linear hypothesis $R\boldsymbol{\beta} = r$ is correct, the ratio

$$\gamma_1 = \frac{R\mathbf{b} - R\boldsymbol{\beta}}{\hat{\sigma}(R(X'X)^{-1}R')^{1/2}} = \frac{R\mathbf{b} - r}{\hat{\sigma}(R(X'X)^{-1}R')^{1/2}} \tag{2.1.39}$$

is a central t random variable with $(T - K)$ degrees of freedom. The traditional test mechanism for the null hypothesis H_0: $R\boldsymbol{\beta} = r$ against the alternative H_1: $R\boldsymbol{\beta} \neq r$ is to reject the linear hypothesis H_0 if the value of the test statistic γ_1 (2.1.39) is greater than some critical value c that is determined for a given significance level α for the random variable $t_{(T-K)}$.

The test statistic γ_1 and a statistic for the general linear hypothesis $R\boldsymbol{\beta} = \mathbf{r}$ when $J \geq 2$, can be derived using likelihood ratio procedures that test the compatibility of the hypotheses with the sample data. In developing the test [see Section 7.3.1, Judge et al. (1982)], use is made of the ratio of restricted and unrestricted likelihood functions

$$\gamma_J = \frac{\max[\tilde{\ell}(\boldsymbol{\beta},\sigma^2|\mathbf{y},X)]}{\max[\bar{\ell}(\boldsymbol{\beta},\sigma^2|\mathbf{y},X,R\boldsymbol{\beta} = \mathbf{r})]} \tag{2.1.40}$$

where $\tilde{\ell}$ and $\bar{\ell}$ are the maximum values of the likelihood under H_0 and H_1. This ratio leads to the quadratic forms

$$\frac{(\mathbf{b} - \boldsymbol{\beta})'R'[R(X'X)^{-1}R']^{-1}R(\mathbf{b} - \boldsymbol{\beta})}{\sigma^2} = \mathbf{e}'X(X'X)^{-1}R'[R(X'X)^{-1}R']^{-1}R(X'X)^{-1}X'\mathbf{e}/\sigma^2 \tag{2.1.41}$$

where $R(\mathbf{b} - \boldsymbol{\beta}) \sim N(\mathbf{0},\sigma^2 R(X'X)^{-1}R')$ and

$$\frac{(\mathbf{y} - X\mathbf{b})'(\mathbf{y} - X\mathbf{b})}{\sigma^2} = \frac{\mathbf{e}'(I - X(X'X)^{-1}X')\mathbf{e}}{\sigma^2} = (T - K)\frac{\hat{\sigma}^2}{\sigma^2} \tag{2.1.42}$$

which are distributed as χ^2 random variables with J and $(T - K)$ degrees of freedom respectively. When the independent χ^2 random variables are divided by their respective degrees of freedom, the ratio

$$\lambda_J = \frac{(R\mathbf{b} - \mathbf{r})'[R(X'X)^{-1}R']^{-1}(R\mathbf{b} - \mathbf{r})}{J\hat{\sigma}^2} \tag{2.1.43}$$

is distributed as an F random variable with J and $(T - K)$ degrees of freedom, when the hypothesis $R\boldsymbol{\beta} = \mathbf{r}$ is correct. The statistic λ_J is a simple transformation of γ_J, and as in the case of the single hypothesis, the hypothesis $R\boldsymbol{\beta} = \mathbf{r}$ is rejected if the value of the test statistic λ_J is greater than some critical value c, which is determined for a given significance level α for the central F distribution with J and $(T - K)$ degrees of freedom.

In general what we look for in a statistical test is one that has a low probability of a Type 1 error when the null is true, has a low probability of a Type 2 error when the null is false (power large) and is robust to misspecifications of the statistical model.

It is interesting to note that in the context of (2.1.38) we may write the Lagrangian for the restricted likelihood as $\ell(\boldsymbol{\beta},\sigma^2|\mathbf{y},X) + 2(\mathbf{r}' - \boldsymbol{\beta}'R')\boldsymbol{\lambda}$ and this leads to optimum values of the Lagrange multipliers

$$\tilde{\boldsymbol{\lambda}} = (R(X'X)^{-1}R')^{-1}(\mathbf{r} - R\mathbf{b}) \tag{2.1.44}$$

If the restrictions are correct $\tilde{\boldsymbol{\lambda}} \sim N(\mathbf{0},\sigma^2[R(X'X)^{-1}R']^{-1})$ and the quadratic form

$$\tilde{\boldsymbol{\lambda}}'Q'Q\tilde{\boldsymbol{\lambda}} = \tilde{\boldsymbol{\lambda}}'[R(X'X)^{-1}R']^{-1}\tilde{\boldsymbol{\lambda}} = (\mathbf{r} - R\mathbf{b})'[R(X'X)^{-1}R']^{-1}(\mathbf{r} - R\mathbf{b})/\sigma^2 \tag{2.1.45}$$

is distributed as a $\chi^2_{(J)}$.

Hypothesis testing frameworks are considered again in Chapters 3 and 5 and are used in one form or another in most of the chapters to follow. To complete this discussion let us note that for testing H_0: $\sigma^2 = \sigma_0^2$, the ratio $(T - K)\hat{\sigma}^2/\sigma_0^2$, is distributed as a central $\chi^2_{(T-K)}$ when the hypothesis is correct.

2.1.4 The Orthonormal Model

In statistical model (2.1.1) it is assumed that the $(T \times K)$ design matrix X has rank K and thus $X'X$ is a $(K \times K)$ positive definite symmetric matrix. Consequently, using the matrix theorems discussed in Section 7.1.3c in Judge et al., (1982) and Appendix A of this book, there exists a positive definite symmetric matrix $S^{1/2}$, such that $S^{-1/2}X'XS^{-1/2} = I_K$, where $S^{1/2}S^{1/2} = S = X'X = C'\Lambda C$, $\Lambda = CSC'$, and $S^{-1/2} = C'\Lambda^{-1/2}C$. Here C is an orthogonal matrix of order $(K \times K)$ and Λ is a diagonal matrix whose diagonal elements are the characteristic roots of $X'X$. Therefore, we may rewrite the statistical model (2.1.1) in equivalent form as

$$\mathbf{y} = XS^{-1/2}S^{1/2}\boldsymbol{\beta} + \mathbf{e} = Z\boldsymbol{\theta} + \mathbf{e} \tag{2.1.46}$$

where $\boldsymbol{\theta} = S^{1/2}\boldsymbol{\beta}$, $Z = XS^{-1/2}$ and hence $Z'Z = I_K$. The mean and covariance of the random vectors $\mathbf{e}$ and $\mathbf{y}$ remain unchanged. This transformation is known as a canonical reduction, and in this case the specification has been reparameterized from the $\boldsymbol{\beta}$ space to the $\boldsymbol{\theta}$ space.

Note that if we reparameterize the statistical model as in (2.1.46) the least squares estimator of $\boldsymbol{\theta} = S^{1/2}\boldsymbol{\beta}$ is

$$\hat{\boldsymbol{\theta}} = S^{1/2}\mathbf{b} = (S^{-1/2}X'XS^{-1/2})^{-1}S^{-1/2}X'\mathbf{y} = (Z'Z)^{-1}Z'\mathbf{y} = Z'\mathbf{y} \quad (2.1.47)$$

with covariance matrix

$$E[S^{1/2}(\mathbf{b} - \boldsymbol{\beta})(\mathbf{b} - \boldsymbol{\beta})'S^{1/2}] = \sigma^2 S^{1/2}(X'X)^{-1}S^{1/2} = \sigma^2 I_K \quad (2.1.48)$$

It will usually be assumed that $\mathbf{e}$ is normally distributed in which case the elements of the coefficient vector $\hat{\boldsymbol{\theta}}$, will be normal independent and identically distributed random variables. All the sampling properties previously derived in this chapter hold for this reparameterized model. The statistical model (2.1.46) may, since $Z'Z = I_K$, be written as the K mean statistical model

$$Z'\mathbf{y} = \boldsymbol{\theta} + Z'\mathbf{e}$$

or

$$\mathbf{z} = \boldsymbol{\theta} + \boldsymbol{\omega} \quad (2.1.49)$$

where $\mathbf{z}$ has a K variate normal distribution with mean vector $\boldsymbol{\theta}$ and nonsingular covariance matrix, $\sigma^2 I_K$, which we may without loss of generality let be equal to I_K if we wish to assume σ^2 known.

This specification is used from time to time in the chapters ahead, when for expository purposes it is more convenient to work in the $\boldsymbol{\theta}$ rather than the $\boldsymbol{\beta}$ space. In some cases this reparameterization will not cause a loss of generality.

2.2 NONSCALAR IDENTITY ERROR COVARIANCE MATRIX

Up to this point we have made the simplifying assumption that the elements of the random vector $\mathbf{e}$ were independent and identically distributed random variables. Although this assumption may describe a sampling process consistent with much economic data, it is inappropriate for situations involving such problems as heteroscedasticity, autocorrelation, and equation error related sets of regressions. These and other violations of the scalar identity covariance assumption are discussed in detail in Chapters 8, 11, 12, and 13 and Chapters 10, 11, 14, 15, and 16 of Judge et al. (1982). In this chapter we consider the case in which

$$E[\mathbf{ee}'] = \sigma^2\boldsymbol{\Psi} = \boldsymbol{\Phi}$$

where $\boldsymbol{\Psi}$ is a known real positive definite symmetric matrix. Thus we consider the statistical model

$$\mathbf{y} = X\boldsymbol{\beta} + \mathbf{e} \quad (2.2.1)$$

where $\mathbf{y}$ is a $(T \times 1)$ vector of observations, X is a known $(T \times K)$ design matrix, $\boldsymbol{\beta}$ is a $(K \times 1)$ vector of unknown coefficients, and $\mathbf{e}$ is a $(T \times 1)$ real random vector with mean vector $E[\mathbf{e}] = \mathbf{0}$ and covariance matrix $E[\mathbf{ee}'] = \boldsymbol{\Phi} = \sigma^2\boldsymbol{\Psi}$, where $\boldsymbol{\Psi}$ is a $(T \times T)$ known positive definite symmetric matrix and σ^2 is an unknown scalar.

In the statistical model (2.2.1), the covariance matrix $\sigma^2\boldsymbol{\Psi}$ of the disturbance vector $\mathbf{e}$ is assumed known except for an unknown scalar σ^2. The $(T \times T)$ matrix $\boldsymbol{\Psi}$ is a known positive definite symmetric matrix, which means that for *all* $(T \times 1)$ vectors $\boldsymbol{\delta} \neq \mathbf{0}$, $\boldsymbol{\delta}'\boldsymbol{\Psi}\boldsymbol{\delta}$ is positive and thus $\boldsymbol{\delta}'\boldsymbol{\Psi}\boldsymbol{\delta}$ is a positive definite quadratic form in $\boldsymbol{\delta}$. Alternatively, $\boldsymbol{\Psi}$ is positive semidefinite if $\boldsymbol{\delta}'\boldsymbol{\Psi}\boldsymbol{\delta}$ is nonnegative. It should be noted that if $\boldsymbol{\Psi}$ is symmetric positive definite, then $\boldsymbol{\Psi}$ is nonsingular and all of the characteristic roots of $\boldsymbol{\Psi}$ are positive. If $\boldsymbol{\Psi}$ is symmetric positive semidefinite, then all the characteristic roots are nonnegative.

If $\boldsymbol{\Psi}$ is a $(T \times T)$ real symmetric nonsingular matrix, there exists a $(T \times T)$ orthogonal matrix $C = (C')^{-1}$ whose columns are characteristic vectors of $\boldsymbol{\Psi}$ such that $C'\boldsymbol{\Psi}C = \Lambda$, a diagonal matrix with diagonal elements that are the characteristic roots of $\boldsymbol{\Psi}$. If $\boldsymbol{\Psi}$ is positive definite, each diagonal element of Λ is positive. Therefore, if $\boldsymbol{\Psi}$ is a positive definite symmetric matrix, there exists a nonsingular $(T \times T)$ matrix P such that $P\boldsymbol{\Psi}P' = D'C'\boldsymbol{\Psi}(D'C')' = D'C'\boldsymbol{\Psi}CD = D'\Lambda D = I_T$, where D is a diagonal matrix with the reciprocals of the square roots of the characteristic roots on the diagonal. Therefore, if $P' = CD$, then $P\boldsymbol{\Psi}P' = I_T$, $\boldsymbol{\Psi} = P^{-1}(P')^{-1}$ and $\boldsymbol{\Psi}^{-1} = P'P$.

Given these results, the statistical model (2.1.1) may be transformed by using the above P matrix as follows.

$$P\mathbf{y} = PX\boldsymbol{\beta} + P\mathbf{e} \tag{2.2.2}$$

or

$$\mathbf{y}^* = X^*\boldsymbol{\beta} + \mathbf{e}^*$$

where the random vector $P\mathbf{e} = \mathbf{e}^*$ has a mean of $\mathbf{0}$ and a covariance matrix of $\sigma^2P\boldsymbol{\Psi}P' = \sigma^2I_T$. This implies that the elements of the random vector $P\mathbf{e}$ are independently and identically distributed. Whenever $\boldsymbol{\Psi}$ is known, the statistical model can be reduced without loss of generality to the special case of σ^2I_T for analytical purposes. Note that under the P transformation the parameter space is not transformed.

Under the least squares criterion, this leads to the generalized least squares rule

$$\hat{\boldsymbol{\beta}} = (X'P'PX)^{-1}X'P'P\mathbf{y} = (X'\boldsymbol{\Psi}^{-1}X)^{-1}X'\boldsymbol{\Psi}^{-1}\mathbf{y} \tag{2.2.3}$$

where $\boldsymbol{\Psi}$ is a $(T \times T)$ known matrix. Since (2.2.2) is equivalent to (2.1.1) all the results of previous sections hold and $\hat{\boldsymbol{\beta}} \sim (\boldsymbol{\beta},\sigma^2(X'\boldsymbol{\Psi}^{-1}X)^{-1})$ and is, in fact, a best linear unbiased estimator. Similarly

$$\hat{\sigma}_g^2 = (\mathbf{y}^* - X^*\hat{\boldsymbol{\beta}})'(\mathbf{y}^* - X^*\hat{\boldsymbol{\beta}})/(T - K) = (\mathbf{y} - X\hat{\boldsymbol{\beta}})'\boldsymbol{\Psi}^{-1}(\mathbf{y} - X\hat{\boldsymbol{\beta}})/(T - K) \tag{2.2.4}$$

is an unbiased estimator of σ^2.

If we add the assumption that the random sample vector $\mathbf{y}$ or that the random error vector $\mathbf{e}$ is normally distributed the likelihood function may be written as

$$\ell(\boldsymbol{\beta},\sigma^2|\mathbf{y},X) = (2\pi\sigma^2)^{-T/2}|\boldsymbol{\Psi}|^{-1/2} \exp\left[-\frac{(\mathbf{y} - X\boldsymbol{\beta})'\boldsymbol{\Psi}^{-1}(\mathbf{y} - X\boldsymbol{\beta})}{2\sigma^2}\right] \tag{2.2.5}$$

and the maximum likelihood estimators are

$$\tilde{\boldsymbol{\beta}} = (X'\boldsymbol{\Psi}^{-1}X)^{-1}X'\boldsymbol{\Psi}^{-1}\mathbf{y} \tag{2.2.6a}$$

and

$$\tilde{\sigma}_g^2 = (\mathbf{y} - X\tilde{\boldsymbol{\beta}})'\boldsymbol{\Psi}^{-1}(\mathbf{y} - X\tilde{\boldsymbol{\beta}})/T \tag{2.2.6b}$$

which is a biased estimator of σ^2. The maximum likelihood estimator $\tilde{\boldsymbol{\beta}} = \hat{\boldsymbol{\beta}}$ is best unbiased via the Cramér-Rao inequality and the same can be shown for $\hat{\sigma}_g^2$.

Since

$$R\tilde{\boldsymbol{\beta}} = R\boldsymbol{\beta} + \mathbf{v}$$

$$\mathbf{v} \sim N(\mathbf{0},\sigma^2 R(X'\boldsymbol{\Psi}^{-1}X)^{-1}R') \tag{2.2.7}$$

where R is a $(J \times K)$ known matrix, the quadratic form

$$(\tilde{\boldsymbol{\beta}} - \boldsymbol{\beta})'R'[R(X'\boldsymbol{\Psi}^{-1}X)^{-1}R']^{-1}R(\tilde{\boldsymbol{\beta}} - \boldsymbol{\beta})/\sigma^2 \tag{2.2.8}$$

is distributed as a $\chi^2_{(J)}$. Consequently if the hypothesis $R\boldsymbol{\beta} = \mathbf{r}$ is true the test statistic

$$\frac{(R\tilde{\boldsymbol{\beta}} - \mathbf{r})'[R(X'\boldsymbol{\Psi}^{-1}X)^{-1}R']^{-1}(R\tilde{\boldsymbol{\beta}} - \mathbf{r})}{J\hat{\sigma}_g^2} \sim F_{(J,T-K)} \tag{2.2.9}$$

and may be used as a basis for hypothesis testing and interval estimation.

If we incorrectly specify the sampling process and assume $E[\mathbf{ee}'] = \sigma^2 I_T$, when it is in fact $E[\mathbf{ee}'] = \sigma^2\boldsymbol{\Psi} \neq \sigma^2 I_T$, and use the least squares rule $\mathbf{b} = (X'X)^{-1}X'\mathbf{y}$ we face the following consequences.

1. The covariance matrix of the least squares estimator **b** will be $\sigma^2(X'X)^{-1}X'\Psi X(X'X)^{-1}$, not $\Sigma_{\mathbf{b}} = \sigma^2(X'X)^{-1}$.
2. The estimator **b** will be unbiased but will be inefficient relative to the generalized least squares estimator $\hat{\boldsymbol{\beta}}$, that is $\Sigma_{\mathbf{b}} - \Sigma_{\hat{\boldsymbol{\beta}}} = \Delta$ a positive semidefinite matrix.
3. The estimator $\hat{\sigma}^2 = (\mathbf{y} - X\mathbf{b})'(\mathbf{y} - X\mathbf{b})/(T - K)$ will be a biased estimator of σ^2.

Consequently, the usual interval estimation and hypothesis testing procedures are no longer appropriate. See Judge et al. (1982), Chapter 10 for details.

2.2.1 Error Related Sets of Equations

The statistical model in which $\Psi \neq I_T$ can be extended to sets of linear statistical models that are error related. In this context we may, following the original idea of Zellner (1962), write a set of M linear statistical models as

$$\begin{bmatrix} \mathbf{y}_1 \\ \mathbf{y}_2 \\ \vdots \\ \mathbf{y}_M \end{bmatrix} = \begin{bmatrix} X_1 & & & \\ & X_2 & & \\ & & \ddots & \\ & & & X_M \end{bmatrix} \begin{bmatrix} \boldsymbol{\beta}_1 \\ \boldsymbol{\beta}_2 \\ \vdots \\ \boldsymbol{\beta}_M \end{bmatrix} + \begin{bmatrix} \mathbf{e}_1 \\ \mathbf{e}_2 \\ \vdots \\ \mathbf{e}_M \end{bmatrix} \tag{2.2.10}$$

or compactly as

$$\mathbf{y} = X\boldsymbol{\beta} + \mathbf{e} \tag{2.2.11}$$

where $\mathbf{y}$ is a $(MT \times 1)$ vector of observations, X is a block diagonal matrix of M design matrices, each having dimension $(T \times K_m)$, where $m = 1, 2, \ldots M$, and $\boldsymbol{\beta}$ is a $(\Sigma_m K_m \times 1)$ vector of unknown coefficients. The $(TM \times 1)$ random vector **e**, is assumed to have mean vector zero and covariance matrix

$$E[\mathbf{ee}'] = \begin{bmatrix} \sigma_{11}I_T & \sigma_{12}I_T & \cdots & \sigma_{1M}I_T \\ \sigma_{21}I_T & \sigma_{22}I_T & \cdots & \sigma_{2M}I_T \\ \vdots & \vdots & \ddots & \vdots \\ \sigma_{M1}I_T & \sigma_{M2}I_T & \cdots & \sigma_{MM}I_T \end{bmatrix} = \Sigma \otimes I_T = \Phi \tag{2.2.12}$$

where $\otimes$ denotes the Kronecker product and Σ is an $(M \times M)$ known positive definite symmetric matrix. Since the $(MT \times MT)$ positive definite symmetric matrix $\Sigma \otimes I_T$ is known, we may, as in the single-equation linear statistical model, minimize the weighted quadratic form

$$(\mathbf{y} - X\boldsymbol{\beta})'(\Sigma^{-1} \otimes I_T)(\mathbf{y} - X\boldsymbol{\beta}) \tag{2.2.13}$$

The optimizing vector $\hat{\boldsymbol\beta}$ is

$$\hat{\boldsymbol\beta} = (X'(\Sigma^{-1} \otimes I_T)X)^{-1}X'(\Sigma^{-1} \otimes I_T)\mathbf{y} \tag{2.2.14}$$

which is the Aitken or generalized least squares estimator, or for normal errors the maximum likelihood estimator, for the set of linear statistical models. When the design matrices are identical, that is, $X_1 = X_2 = \ldots = X_M$, or when the covariance matrix (2.2.12) is diagonal, the Aitken estimator applied to (2.2.11) or the least squares estimator applied to each equation separately yield identical results.

The sampling characteristics of $\hat{\boldsymbol\beta}$ are identical to those discussed above. Thus $\hat{\boldsymbol\beta} \sim N(\boldsymbol\beta,(X'(\Sigma^{-1} \otimes I)X)^{-1})$ and with known covariance Σ, and true linear hypothesis $R\boldsymbol\beta = \mathbf{r}$, the quadratic form

$$(\mathbf{r} - R\hat{\boldsymbol\beta})'[R(X'(\Sigma^{-1} \otimes I)X)R']^{-1}(\mathbf{r} - R\hat{\boldsymbol\beta}) \sim \chi^2_{(J)} \tag{2.2.15}$$

provides the basis for hypothesis testing and interval estimation.

2.3 GOODNESS OF FIT MEASURES

In applied work a commonly used measure of the adequacy of an estimated linear model is the coefficient of multiple determination, denoted by R^2. This measure has a number of interpretations and, when we are considering the single-equation model $\mathbf{y} = X\boldsymbol\beta + \mathbf{e}$, where X contains a column of ones and $E[\mathbf{ee}'] = \sigma^2 I$, its definition is unambiguous.

However, when $E[\mathbf{ee}'] = \sigma^2\Psi$ with $\Psi \neq I$, or when estimating a set of equations like that discussed above the definition of an R^2, or an appropriate goodness of fit statistic, is not obvious.

For the statistical model (2.1.1) we can write, making use of the least squares estimator $\mathbf{b} = (X'X)^{-1}X'\mathbf{y}$,

$$\mathbf{y} = X\mathbf{b} + \hat{\mathbf{e}} = \hat{\mathbf{y}} + \hat{\mathbf{e}} \tag{2.3.1}$$

Now, if we let $\mathbf{j} = (1, 1, \ldots, 1)'$, $\bar{y} = \Sigma_{t=1}^{T} y_t/T$, *subtract* $\mathbf{j}\bar{y}$ from both sides of (2.3.1) and premultiply each side of the result by its own transpose, we get

$$\begin{aligned}(\mathbf{y} - \mathbf{j}\bar{y})'(\mathbf{y} - \mathbf{j}\bar{y}) &= (\hat{\mathbf{y}} - \mathbf{j}\bar{y})'(\hat{\mathbf{y}} - \mathbf{j}\bar{y}) + \hat{\mathbf{e}}'\hat{\mathbf{e}} + 2(\hat{\mathbf{y}} - \mathbf{j}\bar{y})'\hat{\mathbf{e}} \\ &= (\hat{\mathbf{y}} - \mathbf{j}\bar{y})'(\hat{\mathbf{y}} - \mathbf{j}\bar{y}) + \hat{\mathbf{e}}'\hat{\mathbf{e}} - 2\bar{y}\mathbf{j}'\hat{\mathbf{e}}\end{aligned} \tag{2.3.2}$$

The second line of Equation 2.3.2 uses the result $X'\hat{\mathbf{e}} = X'(\mathbf{y} - X\mathbf{b}) = \mathbf{0}$. If, in addition, X contains a constant term, then $\mathbf{j}'\hat{\mathbf{e}} = 0$ and Equation 2.3.2 becomes

$$(\mathbf{y} - \mathbf{j}\bar{y})'(\mathbf{y} - \mathbf{j}\bar{y}) = (\hat{\mathbf{y}} - \mathbf{j}\bar{y})'(\hat{\mathbf{y}} - \mathbf{j}\bar{y}) + \hat{\mathbf{e}}'\hat{\mathbf{e}} \tag{2.3.3}$$

where $(\mathbf{y} - \mathbf{j}\bar{y})'(\mathbf{y} - \mathbf{j}\bar{y})$ is the total sum of squares or total variation in $\mathbf{y}$, $(\hat{\mathbf{y}} - \mathbf{j}\bar{y})'(\hat{\mathbf{y}} - \mathbf{j}\bar{y})$ is the regression sum of squares or variation in $\mathbf{y}$ explained by the estimated equation, and $\hat{\mathbf{e}}'\hat{\mathbf{e}} = (\mathbf{y} - \hat{\mathbf{y}})'(\mathbf{y} - \hat{\mathbf{y}})$ is the residual sum of squares or variation in $\mathbf{y}$ not explained by the regression. The coefficient of multiple determination is defined as

$$R^2 = 1 - \frac{\hat{\mathbf{e}}'\hat{\mathbf{e}}}{(\mathbf{y} - \mathbf{j}\bar{y})'(\mathbf{y} - \mathbf{j}\bar{y})} \tag{2.3.4}$$

and, because of the decomposition in (2.3.3) it lies between zero and one and may be interpreted as a measure of the proportion of the variation in $\mathbf{y}$ explained by the estimated equation.

Also, R^2 is equal to the square of the correlation coefficient between $\mathbf{y}$ and $\hat{\mathbf{y}}$ and thus can be viewed as a measure of the model's predictive ability over the sample period. In this context

$$R^2 = \frac{((\mathbf{y} - \mathbf{j}\bar{y})'(\hat{\mathbf{y}} - \mathbf{j}\bar{y}))^2}{(\mathbf{y} - \mathbf{j}\bar{y})'(\mathbf{y} - \mathbf{j}\bar{y})(\hat{\mathbf{y}} - \mathbf{j}\bar{y})'(\hat{\mathbf{y}} - \mathbf{j}\bar{y})} \tag{2.3.5}$$

Another useful expression is the relationship between R^2 and the F statistic used to test whether the regression relationship is a "significant one." If $\boldsymbol{\beta}$ is partitioned as $\boldsymbol{\beta}' = (\beta_0, \boldsymbol{\beta}_s')$, β_0 being the intercept, then the F statistic used for testing the set of linear restrictions $\boldsymbol{\beta}_s = \mathbf{0}$ or $R\boldsymbol{\beta} = \mathbf{r}$, where $R = [0, I_{(K-1)}]$ and $\mathbf{r} = \mathbf{0}$, can be written as

$$F = \frac{R^2}{1 - R^2} \cdot \frac{T - K}{K - 1} \tag{2.3.6}$$

The acceptance of the null hypothesis $\boldsymbol{\beta}_s = \mathbf{0}$ implies that there is insufficient evidence to suggest that any of the explanatory variables influences y. Note that the F value is monotonically related to R^2.

Because the addition of new explanatory variables will always increase R^2, an alternative coefficient, the "adjusted R^2" is frequently used as a goodness of fit measure. It is given by

$$\bar{R}^2 = 1 - \frac{\hat{\mathbf{e}}'\hat{\mathbf{e}}/(T - K)}{(\mathbf{y} - \mathbf{j}\bar{y})'(\mathbf{y} - \mathbf{j}\bar{y})/(T - 1)} \tag{2.3.7}$$

which can fall with the addition of an "unimportant" variable.

Most of the above interpretations and expressions for R^2 depended on the result $\mathbf{j}'\hat{\mathbf{e}} = 0$ (the residuals sum to zero) which follows directly from $X'\hat{\mathbf{e}} = \mathbf{0}$ when X contains a constant term. When X does not contain a constant term, there are a number of possible definitions of R^2. The main difficulty arises because the total variation in $\mathbf{y}$ around its mean is now given by (2.3.2) and not by (2.3.3). As a result, if R^2 is defined as $R^2 = 1 - \hat{\mathbf{e}}'\hat{\mathbf{e}}/(\mathbf{y} - \mathbf{j}\bar{y})'(\mathbf{y} - \mathbf{j}\bar{y})$, its range will be from $-\infty$ to 1 and it is difficult to interpret it as the proportion of variation in $\mathbf{y}$ explained by the regression. Also, this definition will not be equal to the square of the correlation between $\mathbf{y}$ and $\hat{\mathbf{y}}$ or related to the F statistic as in (2.3.6). There are two alternatives that seem reasonable. The first is to measure the variation in $\mathbf{y}$ around zero not $\bar{y}$. If it is reasonable to specify an equation without a constant, then it is likely that such a measure of variation is also reasonable. Then

$$\mathbf{y}'\mathbf{y} = \hat{\mathbf{y}}'\hat{\mathbf{y}} + \hat{\mathbf{e}}'\hat{\mathbf{e}} \tag{2.3.8}$$

and R^2 can be defined as

$$R^2 = 1 - \frac{\hat{\mathbf{e}}'\hat{\mathbf{e}}}{\mathbf{y}'\mathbf{y}} \tag{2.3.9}$$

This value will be between zero and one and, for testing the hypothesis $\boldsymbol{\beta} = \mathbf{0}$, it will be related to the F statistic in a similar way to (2.3.6), though the degrees of freedom will be different.

A second alternative is to define R^2 as the squared correlation between $\mathbf{y}$ and $\hat{\mathbf{y}}$, as it appears in the last expression in Equation 2.3.5. Defined in this way, R^2 will be a measure of the predictive ability of the equation over the sample period and it will be between zero and one, but it will not be equal to the definition in (2.3.9).

2.3.1 A Single Equation with Nonscalar Covariance Matrix

In the single-equation model $\mathbf{y} = X\boldsymbol{\beta} + \mathbf{e}$, where $E[\mathbf{e}] = \mathbf{0}$ and $E[\mathbf{ee}'] = \boldsymbol{\Phi} \neq \sigma^2 I$, the potential for misusing R^2 is high, particularly if one reports, without question, the number given by most computer programs. If we define $\hat{\mathbf{e}}$ and $\hat{\mathbf{y}}$ from the equation

$$\mathbf{y} = X\hat{\boldsymbol{\beta}} + \hat{\mathbf{e}} = \hat{\mathbf{y}} + \hat{\mathbf{e}} \tag{2.3.10}$$

where $\hat{\boldsymbol{\beta}} = (X'\boldsymbol{\Phi}^{-1}X)^{-1}X'\boldsymbol{\Phi}^{-1}\mathbf{y}$, the first line in (2.3.2) will still hold with these new definitions and so we have

$$(\mathbf{y} - \mathbf{j}\bar{y})'(\mathbf{y} - \mathbf{j}\bar{y}) = (\hat{\mathbf{y}} - \mathbf{j}\bar{y})'(\hat{\mathbf{y}} - \mathbf{j}\bar{y}) + \hat{\mathbf{e}}'\hat{\mathbf{e}} + 2(\hat{\mathbf{y}} - \mathbf{j}\bar{y})'\hat{\mathbf{e}} \tag{2.3.11}$$

However, in this case the last term will not disappear even if X contains a constant. This is because $X'\hat{\mathbf{e}} = X'\mathbf{y} - X'X\hat{\boldsymbol{\beta}} \neq \mathbf{0}$, the normal equations being, in this case, $X'\boldsymbol{\Phi}^{-1}\mathbf{y} - X'\boldsymbol{\Phi}^{-1}X\hat{\boldsymbol{\beta}} = \mathbf{0}$.

Thus, as was the case for model 2.2.1 when there was no constant term, the measure

$$R^2 = 1 - \frac{\hat{\mathbf{e}}'\hat{\mathbf{e}}}{(\mathbf{y} - \mathbf{j}\bar{y})'(\mathbf{y} - \mathbf{j}\bar{y})} \tag{2.3.12}$$

will have a range from $-\infty$ to 1, and so it will be difficult to interpret it as the *proportion* of variation in $\mathbf{y}$ explained by the regression. It does have one possible advantage over another measure (mentioned below), namely that we are measuring the variation in $\mathbf{y}$ in its original units, not in terms of a transformed $\mathbf{y}$ or a "weighted variation in $\mathbf{y}$."

The above is not the number reported by many computer programs. A large number of programs would apply least squares to the transformed model

$$\mathbf{y}^* = X^*\boldsymbol{\beta} + \mathbf{e}^* \tag{2.3.13}$$

where $\mathbf{y}^* = P\mathbf{y}$, $X^* = PX$, $\mathbf{e}^* = P\mathbf{e}$, and P is such that $P'P = \boldsymbol{\Phi}^{-1}$. Then, if the formula in (2.3.12) is used on the transformed observations, the resulting R^2 definition is

$$\begin{aligned} R^2 &= 1 - \frac{\hat{\mathbf{e}}^{*\prime}\hat{\mathbf{e}}^*}{(\mathbf{y}^* - \mathbf{j}\bar{y}^*)'(\mathbf{y}^* - \mathbf{j}\bar{y}^*)} \\ &= 1 - \frac{\hat{\mathbf{e}}'\boldsymbol{\Phi}^{-1}\hat{\mathbf{e}}}{(P\mathbf{y} - \mathbf{j}\mathbf{j}'P\mathbf{y}/T)'(P\mathbf{y} - \mathbf{j}\mathbf{j}'P\mathbf{y}/T)} \end{aligned} \tag{2.3.14}$$

where $\hat{\mathbf{e}}^* = \mathbf{y}^* - X^*\hat{\boldsymbol{\beta}}$ and $\bar{y}^* = \Sigma_{t=1}^T y_t^*/T$. There are two main problems with this measure. First, if the transformed matrix X^* does not contain a constant, R^2 will not lie between zero and one. Second, we are now measuring the explained variation in a transformed $\mathbf{y}$. The first of these problems can be overcome by measuring the weighted variation in $\mathbf{y}$ around a *weighted mean.* This weighted mean is defined as

$$\bar{y}_w^* = \frac{\mathbf{j}'\boldsymbol{\Phi}^{-1}\mathbf{y}}{\mathbf{j}'\boldsymbol{\Phi}^{-1}\mathbf{j}} = \frac{\mathbf{j}'\boldsymbol{\Phi}^{-1}\hat{\mathbf{y}}}{\mathbf{j}'\boldsymbol{\Phi}^{-1}\mathbf{j}} \tag{2.3.15}$$

and the new definition of R^2 that results is

$$R^2 = 1 - \frac{\hat{\mathbf{e}}'\boldsymbol{\Phi}^{-1}\hat{\mathbf{e}}}{(\mathbf{y} - \mathbf{j}\bar{y}_w^*)'\boldsymbol{\Phi}^{-1}(\mathbf{y} - \mathbf{j}\bar{y}_w^*)} \tag{2.3.16}$$

This value will lie between zero and one and can be interpreted as the proportion of weighted variation in $\mathbf{y}$ explained by the regression. Also, as in the scalar covariance matrix case, this value will be monotonically related to the F statistic used to test the null hypothesis that all coefficients except the intercept are zero. The expressions in (2.3.14) and (2.3.16) will be equal if X^* has a constant column in exactly the same position as X.

The relevant question for the applied worker is which of the alternative R^2's is the "best" one to report? We do not have any strong recommendations on this point. However, we do feel that the method of calculation should be mentioned and that it is better not to report an R^2 at all than to report an ambiguous number.

2.4 SUMMARY

The statistical models and the classical statistical inference we have reviewed provide much of the basis for applied econometric work. However, these special case statistical models are not sufficient as a basis for modeling many economic data generation processes and the sampling theory approach to inference is not in many cases an efficient way of learning from economic data. In order to cope with the special characteristics of economic data we can (1) change and enrich the range of statistical models, (2) change the amount of information used, and (3) change the measure of performance or the basis for inference. In order to more effectively learn from economic data, we consider the following possibilities in the chapters ahead.

1. Classical sampling theory, as discussed in this chapter, is a collection of statistical techniques that do not involve formal considerations of nonsample information or possible loss and it evaluates the precision of the technique by its long-term accuracy over repeated samples. In most cases little consideration is given to the use to be made of the inferences. In contrast to this approach, in Chapter 3 a decision theoretic approach to inference is proposed and sample plus other relevant nonsample information are considered along with the losses or statistical consequences that would be incurred in choosing a decision or rule. A range of nontraditional, nonlinear-biased estimators are considered and, under a squared error loss measure, compared to the conventional rules developed in this chapter.
2. In some cases it may be possible to summarize the nonsample information about a parameter vector in terms of a subjective probability distribution. In Chapter 4, Bayes' theorem is used to provide a basis for combining prior and sample information to form a posterior distribution which is then used as a basis for inference. The Bayes principle leads to choice rules that minimize average loss.
3. For a range of statistical models it is not possible to establish finite sample properties for classes of corresponding estimators. In these cases we must consider the sampling properties of estimation rules as the sample size increases. Thus in Chapter 5 we will be concerned with the property of consistency and the concepts of probability limits and asymptotic distributions to illustrate the large sample properties of estimators.
4. Much of the material in this book is concerned with statistical models that are linear in the parameters although not necessarily linear in the outcome vector $\mathbf{y}$ and the design matrix X. In applied work, by exploiting various transformations, this specification will provide an adequate approximation in most situations. However, in some instances, to adequately reflect the sample data a statistical model that is nonlinear in the parameters is necessary. Consequently, in Chapter 6 estimation and inference for statistical models that are nonlinear in the parameters are considered and alter-

native computational procedures are compared and discussed in Appendix B.

5. Economic data are generated by systems of economic relations that are stochastic, simultaneous and dynamic. Seldom do we know the dimensions of the leads and lags underlying the data generation process. Therefore, in Chapters 7, 9, 10, and 16 we discuss the possibilities for identifying the time structure of the variable generation scheme and approximating it empirically. The simultaneous interdependent nature of economic data is discussed in Chapters 14 and 15 and statistical models and estimators are proposed to cope with the special characteristics of this data generation process.
6. In the statistical models considered in this chapter we have assumed the covariance matrix for the random error vector $\mathbf{e}$ is a known symmetric positive definite matrix or is a special-case scalar identity form. In applied work the nature of the process by which the random variable is generated is seldom known and, when this happens, in a strict sense the Aitken estimator is no longer applicable. Therefore, in Chapters 8 and 11 procedures are analyzed for identifying the nature of the stochastic process and for mitigating the impact of uncertainty relative to the stochastic assumptions.
7. In much of applied work the disturbances may be multiplicative instead of additive, nonnormal in nature and possibly related over sets of regression equations. These and other problems of this nature are considered in Chapters 12 and 20.
8. In the statistical models discussed, we have assumed that the data are consistent with one (fixed) parameter vector and we have not considered, for example, that the parameter vector can vary within a sample period or over individuals or the implications of aggregation over micro units with possibly different microparameter vectors. In Chapters 13 and 19 the models are extended to handle estimation and inference for variable parameter statistical models and when the data sample consists of both time series and cross-sectional data.
9. The statistical models discussed assume errors in the equations but no errors in the variables. Seldom if ever are economic relations exactly determined and economic variables measured without error. Therefore, in Chapter 17 we consider the statistical implications of errors in the variables and discuss alternative procedures for mitigating this problem.
10. Not all observed or treatment variables are continuous in nature. Some are qualitative in nature and can take on only the values zero or one. Others, for example, are truncated and can take on only values between zero and one. In Chapter 18 variants of these types of variables are considered; estimation and inference implications are evaluated and the procedure to use for each particular problem is identified.
11. The models previously discussed assume that the variables in the design matrix are correctly specified. Unfortunately, there is usually uncertainty in the mind of the applied researcher about the correct set of explanatory

variables, the functional form of the relationship, the way the variables should be scaled, and whether the model should be specified as linear or nonlinear in the parameters. Seldom, in actual practice, are these statistical model ingredients known, and thus some criterion must be used as a basis for choosing among the alternatives. In Chapter 21 several alternative search criteria are considered and the applicability of each is assessed.

12. In the specification of the statistical models we have assumed that the design matrix was of full column rank. With economic data in many cases this assumption is not fulfilled. Therefore, in Chapter 22 the statistical implications of collinearity are identified and procedures for mitigating its impact are evaluated.

The above chapters result because for many applied problems (1) the traditional statistical models must be changed or extended, (2) the amount and types of information available vary, and (3) the appropriate criterion for estimator performance depends on the problem considered.

2.5 EXERCISES

In the preceding sections we specified a general linear statistical model and on the basis of alternative specifications demonstrated, within a sampling theory context, linear and quadratic rules that yielded estimates of the unknown parameters $\boldsymbol{\beta}$ and σ^2; these estimates satisfied certain criteria, such as unbiasedness and minimum variance. To aid in understanding the sampling theory basis for inference, the meaning of statistical properties such as unbiasedness along with the restrictions and the inferential reach of the model and the sampling theory estimators (decision rules), we make use of the following sampling model within the context of a Monte Carlo sampling experiment.

2.5.1 Sampling Experiment One

Let

$$\mathbf{y} = X\boldsymbol{\beta} + \mathbf{e} = \mathbf{x}_1\beta_1 + \mathbf{x}_2\beta_2 + \mathbf{x}_3\beta_3 + \mathbf{e} = \mathbf{x}_1 10.0 + \mathbf{x}_2 0.4 + \mathbf{x}_3 0.6 + \mathbf{e} \tag{2.5.1}$$

where $\mathbf{y}$ is a (20×1) vector of observations, X is a (20×3) design matrix, $\boldsymbol{\beta} = (10, 0.4, 0.6)'$ and $\mathbf{e}$ is a (20×1) random vector with mean vector zero and covariance matrix $\sigma^2 I_{20} = 0.0625 I_{20}$.

Using a random number generator for a normal distribution, with mean zero and covariance $\sigma^2 I_{20} = .0625 I_{20}$, generate 100 samples of size 20. In conjunction with the known parameter vector and design matrix X (2.5.2), produce 100 samples of size 20 of the observed vector $\mathbf{y}$. Thus, the model is constructed from the following sampling process. Randomly select the observation y_1 from the distribution $f(y; x_1 = x_{11}, x_2 = x_{12}, x_3 = x_{13})$. Then we select a second observation y_2 at random from the distribution $f(y; x_1 = x_{21}, x_2 = x_{22}, x_3 = x_{23})$ and repeat this process until 20 values of y are drawn for each of the 100 samples.

The design matrix used is

$$
X = \begin{array}{c} \mathbf{x}_1 \quad\ \mathbf{x}_2 \quad\quad \mathbf{x}_3 \\ \begin{bmatrix} 1 & 0.693 & 0.693 \\ 1 & 1.733 & 0.693 \\ 1 & 0.693 & 1.386 \\ 1 & 1.733 & 1.386 \\ 1 & 0.693 & 1.792 \\ 1 & 2.340 & 0.693 \\ 1 & 1.733 & 1.792 \\ 1 & 2.340 & 1.386 \\ 1 & 2.340 & 1.792 \\ 1 & 0.693 & 0.693 \\ 1 & 0.693 & 1.386 \\ 1 & 1.733 & 0.693 \\ 1 & 1.733 & 1.386 \\ 1 & 0.693 & 1.792 \\ 1 & 2.340 & 0.693 \\ 1 & 1.733 & 1.792 \\ 1 & 2.340 & 1.386 \\ 1 & 2.340 & 1.792 \\ 1 & 1.733 & 1.386 \\ 1 & 0.693 & 0.693 \end{bmatrix} \end{array} \qquad (2.5.2)
$$

2.5.1a Individual Exercises

Exercise 2.1

Using the least squares rule and five of the samples, compute estimates of β_1, β_2, β_3, and σ^2 for each sample. Compute the estimated covariance matrix for each sample and compare it with the true covariance matrix $\sigma^2(X'X)^{-1}$.

Exercise 2.2

Using the true parameters as the hypothesis, compute t-test statistics for β_2 and β_3 for each sample in Exercise 2.1 and interpret. Repeat the tests under the hypotheses that $\beta_2 = 0$ and $\beta_3 = 0$.

Exercise 2.3

Using the true parameter value of σ^2 as the hypothesis, that is, $\sigma^2 = 0.0625$, test the compatibility of the estimates of σ^2 obtained in Exercise 2.1 and the hypothesis.

Exercise 2.4

Using the true parameters for β_1, β_2, and β_3 as the hypothesis, compute the F-test statistic for each of the five data samples and interpret. Repeat the test under the hypothesis $\beta_1 = \beta_2 = \beta_3 = 0$ and interpret.

Exercise 2.5
Choose a significance level and develop and interpret interval estimates for β_1, β_2, β_3, and σ^2 for each of the five data samples.

Exercise 2.6
Compute the mean of b_1, b_2, b_3, and $\hat{\sigma}^2$ for the five samples and compare these averages with the true parameters. Compute the mean variance for each of the b's for the five samples and compare with the true variances.

Exercise 2.7
Divide the observations for each sample and the rows of the design matrix in half and from the 5 samples you have used create 10 samples of size 10. Compute least squares estimates of the β's and σ^2. Compare these estimates with the estimates from the 5 samples (Exercise 2.1) and especially note their relative sampling variability as the sample size decreases.

2.5.1b Group Exercises

Exercise 2.8
Compute the average values for the estimates of β_1, β_2, β_3, and σ^2 for all 100 samples and compare these averages with the true parameters. Compute the average variances of the estimates of the β's and σ^2 for all 100 samples and compare these averages with the true variances. Compute the average total squared loss

$$\sum_{i=1}^{100} (\mathbf{b}_i - \boldsymbol{\beta})'(\mathbf{b}_i - \boldsymbol{\beta})/100$$

Exercise 2.9
Construct an empirical frequency distribution of all 100 samples for β_1, β_2, β_3, and σ^2 and interpret.

Exercise 2.10
Construct an empirical distribution of all 100 samples for the t- and F-test statistics. Construct and interpret the empirical distribution for the random variable $\hat{\sigma}_i^2/\sigma^2$, for $i = 1, 2, \ldots, 100$.

Exercise 2.11
Use the Kolmogorov–Smirnov D statistic or some other appropriate statistic to test the agreement between the empirical and theoretical (normal, t, χ^2 and F) distributions of the estimates and test statistics.

Exercise 2.12
Using the design matrix (2.5.2) and a random number generator on the computer you have access to, for a uniform distribution with mean zero and variance $\sigma^2 = 0.0625$, generate 100 samples of size 20, estimate the parameters and compare these results with those obtained in Exercise 2.8 and 2.10.

2.5.2 Sampling Experiment Two

To illustrate the statistical implications of the nonscalar identity case, develop and analyze a Monte Carlo experiment involving 100 samples of size 20 using the model

$$\mathbf{y} = X\boldsymbol{\beta} = 10.0\mathbf{x}_1 + 0.4\mathbf{x}_2 + 0.6\mathbf{x}_3 + \mathbf{e} \tag{2.5.3}$$

where X is given in (2.5.2) and $\mathbf{e}$ is a normal random vector with mean zero and covariance matrix

$$E[\mathbf{ee}'] = \sigma^2\boldsymbol{\Psi} = \frac{\sigma^2}{1-\rho^2}\begin{bmatrix} 1 & \rho & \rho^2 & \cdots & \rho^{T-1} \\ \rho & 1 & \rho & \cdots & \rho^{T-2} \\ \rho^2 & \rho & 1 & \cdots & \rho^{T-3} \\ \vdots & \vdots & \vdots & & \vdots \\ \rho^{T-1} & \rho^{T-2} & \rho^{T-3} & \cdots & 1 \end{bmatrix} \tag{2.5.4}$$

with $\sigma^2 = 1.0$ and $\rho = 0.8$. Using the experimental design given by (2.5.2), (2.5.3), and (2.5.4), develop 100 samples of data of size 20.

2.5.2a Individual Exercises

Exercise 2.13
Calculate the covariance matrices for the least squares estimator and the generalized least squares estimator and comment on the results.

Exercise 2.14
Calculate the mean of the least squares error variance estimator

$$\hat{\sigma}^2 = \frac{(\mathbf{y} - X\mathbf{b})'(\mathbf{y} - X\mathbf{b})}{T - K}$$

Exercise 2.15
Select five samples from the Monte Carlo data and for each sample compute values for the following estimators.

(*a*) The least squares estimator $\mathbf{b}$.
(*b*) The generalized least squares estimator $\hat{\boldsymbol{\beta}}$.
(*c*) The least squares error variance estimator $\hat{\sigma}^2$.
(*d*) The generalized least squares error variance estimator $\hat{\sigma}_g^2$.

Comment on the results.

Exercise 2.16

In Exercise 2.15 your computer program is likely to have provided estimated covariance matrices for $\mathbf{b}$ and $\hat{\boldsymbol{\beta}}$. Using the element β_2 as an example, compare the various estimates of $\text{var}(b_2)$ and $\text{var}(\hat{\beta}_2)$ with each other and with the relevant values from Exercise 2.13.

Exercise 2.17

Use the results in Exercise 2.15 and 2.16 to calculate t values that would be used to test

(*a*) $H_0: \beta_2 = 0$ against $H_1: \beta_2 \neq 0$.
(*b*) $H_0: \beta_2 = 0.4$ against $H_1: \beta_2 \neq 0.4$.

Since we have two estimators and five samples this involves, for each hypothesis, the calculation of 10 t values. Keeping in mind the validity of each null hypothesis, comment on the results.

2.5.2b Group Exercises

Exercise 2.18

Repeat Exercise 2.15 for all 100 samples and use the results to estimate the means of $\mathbf{b}$, $\hat{\boldsymbol{\beta}}$, $\hat{\sigma}^2$, and $\hat{\sigma}_g^2$ as well as the mean square error matrices of $\mathbf{b}$ and $\hat{\boldsymbol{\beta}}$. Are all these estimates reasonably close to their population counterparts?

Exercise 2.19

Use all 100 samples to estimate the means of the variance estimators $\text{var}(b_2)$ and $\text{var}(\hat{\beta}_2)$. Comment on the results and their implications for testing hypotheses about β_2.

Exercise 2.20

Repeat Exercise 2.17 for all 100 samples and calculate the proportion of Type I and Type II errors that are obtained when a 5% significance level is used. Comment.

Exercise 2.21

Construct empirical distributions for b_2, $\hat{\beta}_2$, and the two t statistics used in Exercise 2.20 to test the null hypothesis $\beta_2 = 0.4$. Comment.

2.6 REFERENCES

Detailed discussions of point and interval estimation and hypothesis testing, within a classical sampling theory framework may be found in the following books and journals articles.

Goldberger, A. S. (1964) *Econometric Theory,* Wiley, New York.
Graybill, F. A. (1961) *An Introduction to Linear Statistical Models,* McGraw-Hill, New York.
Intriligator, M. (1977) *Econometric Models, Techniques and Applications,* McGraw-Hill, New York.
Johnston, J. (1984) *Econometric Methods,* 3rd ed., McGraw-Hill, New York.
Judge, G. G., R. C. Hill, W. E. Griffiths, H. Lütkepohl, and T. C. Lee (1982) *Introduction to the Theory and Practice of Econometrics,* John Wiley, New York.
Kmenta, J. (1971) *Elements of Econometrics,* Macmillan, New York.
Lindgren, B. W. (1976) *Statistical Theory,* 3rd ed., Macmillan, New York.
Maddala, G. S. (1977) *Econometrics,* McGraw-Hill, New York.
Rao, C. R. (1973) *Linear Statistical Inference and Its Applications,* Wiley, New York.
Theil, H. (1971) *Principles of Econometrics,* Wiley, New York.
Zellner, A. (1962) "An Efficient Method of Estimating Seemingly Unrelated Regressions and Tests for Aggregation Bias," *Journal of the American Statistical Association,* 57, 348–368.

Chapter 3

Statistical Decision Theory and Biased Estimation

In Chapter 2, interest focused on the analysis of variants of the traditional linear statistical model within a classical sampling theory framework. Within this context, sample information in the form of observed values of the random variable y was used in conjunction with estimation rules in making inferences about the unknown location and scale parameters $\boldsymbol{\beta}$, σ^2. Consequently, statistical properties such as unbiasedness and minimum variance were specified and estimation rules were evaluated in terms of their accuracy within repeated samples or their long-run repetitive precision. Measuring how estimation rules perform in a long series of identical experiments means that even before an experiment is run we can evaluate its precision or accuracy.

Under this scenario, inferences are generally made without regard to the uses to which they are to be put and little emphasis was placed on the possible consequences of the alternative rules other than whether or not they satisfied certain statistical properties. In addition, classical statistical procedures emphasize the use of sample information in making inferences about the unknown parameters and to a large extent ignore any nonsample information that may exist about the individual parameters or relationships among the unknown parameters. Recognizing the restrictions implied by classical analysis for econometric practice, in this chapter we consider an approach to statistical inference that involves a formal consideration of both sample and nonsample information and the possible loss or statistical consequences of alternative rule choices. This gives a new basis for evaluating the classical estimation rules and permits us to enlarge the set of estimators that may be useful in learning from economic data.

In Section 1 the basic concepts of statistical decision theory are reviewed and alternative decision rules and principles are considered. In Section 2 a range of biased estimators that involve various types of nonsample information are evaluated within a decision theoretic framework. In Section 3 the statistical implications of making a preliminary test of significance based on the data at hand is considered and the corresponding pretest estimator is evaluated. In Section 4 nontraditional estimators are considered which, under conditions normally fulfilled in practice and a range of loss functions, are superior to the best linear unbiased rules of Chapter 2. An overview of the topics to be considered is given in Table 3.1.

TABLE 3.1 ***BASIS FOR DETERMINING ESTIMATOR PERFORMANCE AND ALTERNATIVE STATISTICAL MODELS AND ESTIMATORS USING SAMPLE AND NONSAMPLE INFORMATION***

		Sample Information and the Linear Statistical Model $y = X\beta + e$		Statistical Decision Theory
Exact prior information $R\beta = r$	Stochastic prior information $R\beta + v = r$		Inequality prior information $R\beta \geq r$	Basic concepts (Section 3.1.1)
Restricted least squares estimator (Section 3.2.1)	Aitken stochastic restricted estimator (Section 3.2.2a)	Least squares and Aitken estimators and inference (Chapter 2)	Inequality restricted estimators (Section 3.2.3)	Choice of decision rule (Section 3.1.2)
Estimator sampling performance (Section 3.2.1a)	Estimator sampling performance (Section 3.2.2b)	Stein-rule estimators and sampling performance (Sections 3.4.1 to 3.4.3)	Sampling performance (Section 3.2.3c)	Measure space (Section 3.1.3)
General linear hypotheses (Section 3.2.1e)	Compatibility tests (Section 3.2.2c)		Hypothesis tests and pretest estimator sampling performance (Section 3.2.3d)	Some linear model examples (Section 3.1.4)
Pretest estimators and estimator performance (Section 3.3.1)			Inequality pretest estimator (Section 3.3.2)	
Stein-like pretest estimator and sampling performance (Section 3.4.4)			Stein inequality estimators and sampling performance (Section 3.4.5)	

3.1 STATISTICAL DECISION THEORY

Concern with the implications of scarcity has led economists over time to develop a general theory of choice. Within this context Marschak once remarked, "Information is useful if it helps us make the right decisions." Consequently, as economists, a primary reason for interest in efficient procedures for learning from data is to gain information so that we may (1) better understand economic processes and institutions structurally and quantitatively and (2) use this descriptive information prescriptively as a basis for action or choice. Given these descriptive and prescriptive objectives, it would seem that a decision framework, based on the analysis of losses due to incorrect decisions (parameter estimates) can and should be used.

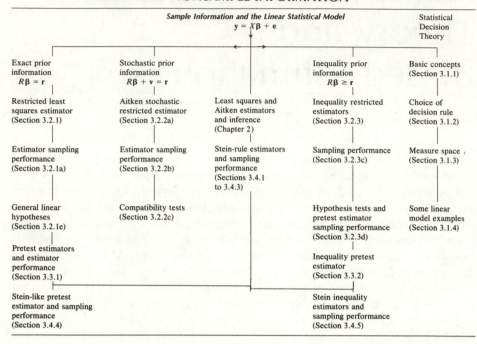

From the standpoint of classical statistics, where inferences are made without regard to the uses to which they are to be put, any two estimators may have the same precision matrix, but if one is biased while the other is unbiased, then one would choose the unbiased rule, which is right on average. Alternatively, if two rules (estimators) are unbiased but one has a smaller sampling variation than the other in the sense of (2.1.7), then the more precise estimator would be chosen. The problem, of course, with the classical properties approach to gauging estimator performance comes when one estimator is biased but has a smaller sampling variability than a competing estimator that is unbiased. How, indeed, does the investigator choose? Why should the analyst be interested in a rule that is "right" on average? Is there, in the above example, some trade-off for decision purposes between bias and variance, or in other words could a decision maker tolerate a rule that misses the mark on the average if it brought gains in terms of reduced sampling variability? In many respects, the sampling theorists and much of econometric literature is preoccupied with the concept of unbiasedness and the attainment of this goal in either small or large samples.

In this book, many of the choices between alternative estimators and procedures will be based on decision-theoretic concepts. In the sections to follow, some of the basic definitions and concepts of statistical decision theory are discussed, and the basis for estimator evaluation and choice is specified.

3.1.1 Basic Concepts

Statistical decision theory, as the name implies, is concerned with the problem of making decisions based on statistical knowledge. Since the knowledge is statistical in nature it involves uncertainties that we will consider to be unknown parameter values. The objective is to combine the sample information with other relevant information in order to make the "best" decision. These other types of nonsample information include (1) knowledge of the possible consequences of the decisions that can be expressed as the loss that would be incurred, over the range of the parameter space, if a particular decision rule is used, and (2) prior or nonsample information that reflects knowledge other than that derived from the statistical investigation.

A problem in decision theory has three ingredients: (1) the parameter space $\mathcal{B}$ that reflects the possible states of nature relative to the unknown parameter vector $\boldsymbol{\beta}$, (2) a set of all possible decisions or actions $\mathcal{A}$ and particular actions a and (3) a loss function $L(\boldsymbol{\beta},a)$ defined for all $(\boldsymbol{\beta},a) \epsilon (\mathcal{B} \times \mathcal{A})$.

When we experiment to obtain information about $\boldsymbol{\beta}$, the design is such that the observations $\mathbf{y}$ are distributed according to some probability distribution that has $\boldsymbol{\beta}$ as the unknown parameter vector. In this context, the loss incurred depends on the outcome of an observable random variable $\mathbf{y}$ through the function δ used to assign an action for a given $\mathbf{y}$. As noted above, the distribution of $\mathbf{y}$ depends on $\boldsymbol{\beta}$, the true state of nature. The function $\delta(\mathbf{y})$ is called a decision rule and the loss associated with this rule is denoted as $L(\boldsymbol{\beta},\delta(\mathbf{y}))$.

Since the T-dimensional sample vector $\mathbf{y}$ is random, it is important for decision purposes to consider the average losses involving actions taken under the various outcomes for $\mathbf{y}$. In other words since the estimator $\delta(\mathbf{y}) = \hat{\boldsymbol{\beta}}$ is random, as it depends on $\mathbf{y}$, the loss incurred in not knowing the parameter vector will also be random. The average losses or the expected value of the loss function $L(\boldsymbol{\beta},\hat{\boldsymbol{\beta}})$, where $\boldsymbol{\beta}$ is the true parameter is called a risk function $\rho(\boldsymbol{\beta},\delta(\mathbf{y})) = \rho(\boldsymbol{\beta},\hat{\boldsymbol{\beta}})$ and is designated by

$$\rho(\boldsymbol{\beta},\hat{\boldsymbol{\beta}}) = E[L(\boldsymbol{\beta},\hat{\boldsymbol{\beta}})] = \int_{\mathbf{y}} L(\boldsymbol{\beta},\hat{\boldsymbol{\beta}})f(\mathbf{y}|\boldsymbol{\beta})d\mathbf{y} \qquad (3.1.1)$$

where $f(\mathbf{y}|\boldsymbol{\beta})$ is the joint density of $\mathbf{y}$ conditional on $\boldsymbol{\beta}$ and $\int_{\mathbf{y}}$ is the multiple integral over all possible values of the random vector $\mathbf{y}$. Thus for each $\boldsymbol{\beta}$, $\rho(\boldsymbol{\beta},\hat{\boldsymbol{\beta}})$ is the expected loss over $\mathbf{y}$ that is incurred in using the decision rule or estimator $\delta(\mathbf{y}) = \hat{\boldsymbol{\beta}}$. We assume that the loss function is defined for each possible value of $L(\boldsymbol{\beta},\hat{\boldsymbol{\beta}})$ and that this function reflects the loss incurred corresponding to each combination of $\boldsymbol{\beta}$ and $\hat{\boldsymbol{\beta}}$. In other words, the value of the loss function of $\hat{\boldsymbol{\beta}}$ at $\boldsymbol{\beta}$ measures the loss incurred if the action (rule) is $\hat{\boldsymbol{\beta}}$ and the state of nature is $\boldsymbol{\beta}$. As an example, we may represent a linear loss function as $L(\boldsymbol{\beta},\hat{\boldsymbol{\beta}}) = |\boldsymbol{\beta} - \hat{\boldsymbol{\beta}}|$, where the possible states of nature are represented by the set of real numbers.

3.1.2 The Choice of a Decision Rule

Given a framework for defining loss or risk associated with each action and state of nature, the central problem of decision theory is how to choose a decision rule or, alternatively, how to choose among the alternative decision rules. Intuitively, it would seem that we should choose a rule that makes the risk of not knowing $\boldsymbol{\beta}$ as small as possible, that is, as a general criterion we should choose a rule that minimizes the risk for each value of $\boldsymbol{\beta}$ in $\mathcal{B}$. In general, there is no *one* rule with minimum risk for all $\boldsymbol{\beta}$ in $\mathcal{B}$. This means that typically there is no estimator $\hat{\boldsymbol{\beta}}_0$ such that for every other estimator $\hat{\boldsymbol{\beta}}$, $\rho(\boldsymbol{\beta},\hat{\boldsymbol{\beta}}_0) \leq \rho(\boldsymbol{\beta},\hat{\boldsymbol{\beta}})$, for every $\boldsymbol{\beta}$. This proposition is expressed graphically in Figure 3.1 for the measure space $\lambda = \boldsymbol{\beta}'\boldsymbol{\beta}$, where each element of the $\boldsymbol{\beta}$ vector may take on values between $-\infty$ and ∞. In Figure 3.1, over the range of the parameter space from the origin to $\lambda = \boldsymbol{\beta}'\boldsymbol{\beta} = a$, the estimator $\hat{\boldsymbol{\beta}}_2$ has the lowest risk. At point a the risk functions for $\hat{\boldsymbol{\beta}}_2$ and $\hat{\boldsymbol{\beta}}_3$ cross and $\hat{\boldsymbol{\beta}}_3$ has the smallest risk over the remaining range of the parameter space.

The situation represented by the alternative risk functions in Figure 3.1 is typical of what happens in practice. Consequently, in order to choose among

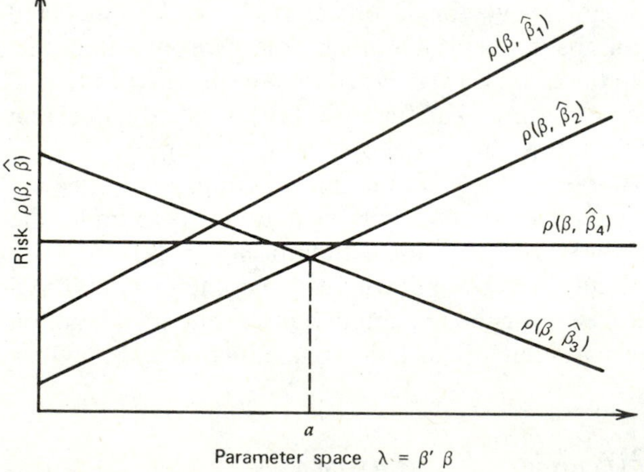

Figure 3.1 Risk functions for four alternative estimators.

possible estimators, it is common to add criteria to that of minimizing the risk. The classical approach to estimation consists of a list of desired properties, such as unbiasedness, invariance, minimum variance unbiasedness, and sufficiency. Opinion as to which criteria are most important is not always unanimous. Ideally, imposing new criteria that estimators should satisfy should not result in estimators that are unsatisfactory under the overall criterion of minimizing the risk. In particular, a desirable property of resultant estimators is admissibility.

In this context an estimator $\hat{\boldsymbol{\beta}}$ is said to *dominate an estimator* $\hat{\boldsymbol{\beta}}_0$ if for all $\boldsymbol{\beta}$,

$$\rho(\boldsymbol{\beta},\hat{\boldsymbol{\beta}}) \leq \rho(\boldsymbol{\beta},\hat{\boldsymbol{\beta}}_0) \tag{3.1.2}$$

If $\rho(\boldsymbol{\beta},\hat{\boldsymbol{\beta}}) < \rho(\boldsymbol{\beta},\hat{\boldsymbol{\beta}}_0)$ for some $\boldsymbol{\beta}$ and $\rho(\boldsymbol{\beta},\hat{\boldsymbol{\beta}}) \leq \rho(\boldsymbol{\beta},\hat{\boldsymbol{\beta}}_0)$, for all $\boldsymbol{\beta}$, the estimator $\hat{\boldsymbol{\beta}}$ is said to *strictly dominate* $\hat{\boldsymbol{\beta}}_0$. Under this definition the estimator $\hat{\boldsymbol{\beta}}_2$ in Figure 3.1 is said to strictly dominate $\hat{\boldsymbol{\beta}}_1$. However, note that $\hat{\boldsymbol{\beta}}_2$ does not dominate $\hat{\boldsymbol{\beta}}_3$ and $\hat{\boldsymbol{\beta}}_4$ does not dominate $\hat{\boldsymbol{\beta}}_2$.

An estimator is called *admissible* if it is not strictly dominated by any other estimator. We may say that an estimator $\hat{\boldsymbol{\beta}}_1$ is *inadmissible* if there is another estimator, $\hat{\boldsymbol{\beta}}_2$, such that $\rho(\boldsymbol{\beta},\hat{\boldsymbol{\beta}}_2) \leq \rho(\boldsymbol{\beta},\hat{\boldsymbol{\beta}}_1)$ for all $\boldsymbol{\beta}$ and, for some $\boldsymbol{\beta}$, the strict inequality holds. These results of course imply that an inadmissible estimator or rule should not be used. Unfortunately, there is usually a large class of admissible estimators for any one problem.

As we noted in the sampling theory approach, one important way of limiting the class of estimators or rules is to require that the estimator be *unbiased* and thus require that $E[\hat{\boldsymbol{\beta}}] = \boldsymbol{\beta}$. Furthermore, because of tractability, the requirement that $\hat{\boldsymbol{\beta}}$ be a *linear* function of $\mathbf{y}$ is sometimes imposed and in fact many of the estimators used in econometric work are restricted to the *linear unbiased* class. Unfortunately, as we will see in the chapters to come, requiring this property sometimes results in *inadmissible* estimators. The question of why one should be interested in a property of unbiasedness that requires absolute accuracy on the average has been asked many times. One might question whether it has been properly answered. Certainly, the typical response—"It is conventional"—is not an adequate reply.

Another restriction sometimes used in estimator choice, which tries to protect against the worst state of nature, is the *minimax criterion*. Under this criterion an estimator $\hat{\boldsymbol{\beta}}_0$ is said to be minimax, within the class of estimators D, if the maximum risk of $\hat{\boldsymbol{\beta}}_0$ is equal to or less than that for all other estimators $\hat{\boldsymbol{\beta}}$, that is,

$$\max_{\boldsymbol{\beta}} \rho(\boldsymbol{\beta},\hat{\boldsymbol{\beta}}_0) \leq \max_{\boldsymbol{\beta}} \rho(\boldsymbol{\beta},\hat{\boldsymbol{\beta}}) \tag{3.1.3}$$

for all $\hat{\boldsymbol{\beta}}$ in D. In the class of estimators demonstrated in Figure 3.1 the estimator $\hat{\boldsymbol{\beta}}_4$ is a minimax estimator since, for all $\boldsymbol{\beta}$, it minimizes the maximum risk and thus reflects a desire to act conservatively even in the face of a nature as a neutral opponent.

Another frequently used basis for choosing among estimators is the Bayes criterion. We noted that many admissible estimators have risks that are superior for different values of $\boldsymbol{\beta}$. In the Bayesian approach, the objective is to make proper use of nonsample or prior information $g(\boldsymbol{\beta})$ about $\boldsymbol{\beta}$. Since the prior $g(\boldsymbol{\beta})$ supposedly reflects which $\boldsymbol{\beta}$'s are the likely ones to appear, it seems reasonable to weight the risk functions $\rho(\boldsymbol{\beta},\hat{\boldsymbol{\beta}})$ by $g(\boldsymbol{\beta})$ and average, that is, take the expectations over $\boldsymbol{\beta}$. In using the Bayes principle, a multivariate distribution on the $\boldsymbol{\beta}$ space is assigned with probability density function $g(\boldsymbol{\beta})$. Under this specification the Bayes solution is to choose the estimator that minimizes the average risk with respect to the prior density $g(\boldsymbol{\beta})$, that is, the estimator $\hat{\boldsymbol{\beta}}_g$ is said to be Bayes if

$$E[\rho(\boldsymbol{\beta},\hat{\boldsymbol{\beta}}_g)] = \int_{\boldsymbol{\beta}} \rho(\boldsymbol{\beta},\hat{\boldsymbol{\beta}}_g)\mathbf{g}(\boldsymbol{\beta})d\boldsymbol{\beta} \leq E[\rho(\boldsymbol{\beta},\hat{\boldsymbol{\beta}})] \tag{3.1.4}$$

for all $\hat{\boldsymbol{\beta}}$ in D.

3.1.3 The Measure Space

Thus far we have not discussed the specific form of the loss or risk function that is to be used in evaluating estimator performance. Although there are many alternatives, for expository purposes we will at this point discuss only the squared error loss and risk matrix (generalized mean square error) measures.

3.1.3a Squared Error Loss

Since it seems reasonable, for a range of decision problems, to penalize outcomes far away from the true parameter vector $\boldsymbol{\beta}$ more than those close to it, a frequently used criterion for measuring the performance of an estimator, say $\hat{\boldsymbol{\beta}}$, is the weighted squared error loss function,

$$L(\boldsymbol{\beta},\hat{\boldsymbol{\beta}}) = (\hat{\boldsymbol{\beta}} - \boldsymbol{\beta})'W(\hat{\boldsymbol{\beta}} - \boldsymbol{\beta}) \tag{3.1.5}$$

with a corresponding risk function

$$\rho(\boldsymbol{\beta},\hat{\boldsymbol{\beta}}) = E[(\hat{\boldsymbol{\beta}} - \boldsymbol{\beta})'W(\hat{\boldsymbol{\beta}} - \boldsymbol{\beta})] \tag{3.1.6}$$

where W is a known symmetric positive definite $(K \times K)$ weight matrix. If $W = I_K$, the squared error loss for each parameter is weighted equally.

It should be noted that if we work with the reparameterized orthonormal statistical model where

$$\mathbf{y} = XS^{-1/2}S^{1/2}\boldsymbol{\beta} + \mathbf{e} = Z\boldsymbol{\theta} + \mathbf{e} \tag{3.1.7}$$

$S^{-1/2}X'XS^{-1/2} = Z'Z = I_K$ and $S^{1/2}\mathbf{b} = \hat{\boldsymbol{\theta}}$ with covariance $\Sigma_{\hat{\boldsymbol{\theta}}} = \sigma^2 I_K$ is the least squares estimator, then under the squared error loss criterion the least squares estimator has risk

$$\rho(\boldsymbol{\theta},\hat{\boldsymbol{\theta}}) = E[(\hat{\boldsymbol{\theta}} - \boldsymbol{\theta})'(\hat{\boldsymbol{\theta}} - \boldsymbol{\theta})] = \sigma^2 \operatorname{tr} I_K = \sigma^2 K \qquad (3.1.8)$$

Furthermore, writing the unweighted, squared error loss risk function in the $\boldsymbol{\theta}$ parameter space as

$$\begin{aligned}\rho(\boldsymbol{\theta},\hat{\boldsymbol{\theta}}) &= E[(\hat{\boldsymbol{\theta}} - \boldsymbol{\theta})'(\hat{\boldsymbol{\theta}} - \boldsymbol{\theta})] = E[(S^{1/2}\mathbf{b} - S^{1/2}\boldsymbol{\beta})'(S^{1/2}\mathbf{b} - S^{1/2}\boldsymbol{\beta})] \\ &= E[(\mathbf{b} - \boldsymbol{\beta})'S^{1/2}S^{1/2}(\mathbf{b} - \boldsymbol{\beta})] = E[(\mathbf{b} - \boldsymbol{\beta})'S(\mathbf{b} - \boldsymbol{\beta})] \qquad (3.1.9)\end{aligned}$$

yields a weighted loss function in the $\boldsymbol{\beta}$ space with weight matrix $X'X = S$.

Alternatively, an unweighted, squared error loss risk function in the $\boldsymbol{\beta}$ space results in the following weighted risk function in the $\boldsymbol{\theta}$ space:

$$\begin{aligned}E[(\mathbf{b} - \boldsymbol{\beta})'(\mathbf{b} - \boldsymbol{\beta})] &= E[(S^{-1/2}\hat{\boldsymbol{\theta}} - S^{-1/2}\boldsymbol{\theta})'(S^{-1/2}\hat{\boldsymbol{\theta}} - S^{-1/2}\boldsymbol{\theta})] \\ &= E[(\hat{\boldsymbol{\theta}} - \boldsymbol{\theta})'S^{-1}(\hat{\boldsymbol{\theta}} - \boldsymbol{\theta})] \qquad (3.1.10)\end{aligned}$$

In some of the following chapters, we will find it more convenient or analytically tractable to investigate the weighted risk function in the $\boldsymbol{\theta}$ space rather than its unweighted counterpart in the $\boldsymbol{\beta}$ space.

3.1.3b Generalized Mean Squared Error

The generalized mean squared error or risk matrix, which is another criterion that may be used to measure the performance of estimators, may be defined in terms of an estimator $\hat{\boldsymbol{\beta}}$ as

$$\begin{aligned}R(\boldsymbol{\beta},\hat{\boldsymbol{\beta}}) = \text{MSE}(\hat{\boldsymbol{\beta}},\boldsymbol{\beta}) &= E[(\hat{\boldsymbol{\beta}} - \boldsymbol{\beta})(\hat{\boldsymbol{\beta}} - \boldsymbol{\beta})'] \\ &= E[(\hat{\boldsymbol{\beta}} - E[\hat{\boldsymbol{\beta}}])(\hat{\boldsymbol{\beta}} - E[\hat{\boldsymbol{\beta}}])'] + (E[\hat{\boldsymbol{\beta}}] - \boldsymbol{\beta})(E[\hat{\boldsymbol{\beta}}] - \boldsymbol{\beta})' \\ &= \text{cov}(\hat{\boldsymbol{\beta}}) + (\text{bias } \hat{\boldsymbol{\beta}})(\text{bias } \hat{\boldsymbol{\beta}})', \qquad (3.1.11)\end{aligned}$$

which in words is the covariance matrix for $\hat{\boldsymbol{\beta}}$, plus the bias squared matrix for $\hat{\boldsymbol{\beta}}$. The diagonal elements of (3.1.11) are the mean square errors for each element of $\hat{\boldsymbol{\beta}}$ and the trace of the mean square error matrix is equal to the squared error loss criterion of (3.1.6) when $W = I$, that is

$$\operatorname{tr} E[(\hat{\boldsymbol{\beta}} - \boldsymbol{\beta})(\hat{\boldsymbol{\beta}} - \boldsymbol{\beta})'] = E[(\hat{\boldsymbol{\beta}} - \boldsymbol{\beta})'(\hat{\boldsymbol{\beta}} - \boldsymbol{\beta})] \qquad (3.1.12)$$

In using the generalized mean squared error or risk criterion, an estimator $\hat{\boldsymbol{\beta}}$ is equal to or superior to an estimator $\hat{\boldsymbol{\beta}}_0$ if the mean squared error for every linear combination of elements of $\hat{\boldsymbol{\beta}}$ is equal to or less than the mean squared error of the same combination of elements of $\boldsymbol{\beta}_0$, for all values of $\boldsymbol{\beta}$. This means that

$$E[(\hat{\boldsymbol{\beta}}_0 - \boldsymbol{\beta})(\hat{\boldsymbol{\beta}}_0 - \boldsymbol{\beta})'] - E[(\hat{\boldsymbol{\beta}} - \boldsymbol{\beta})(\hat{\boldsymbol{\beta}} - \boldsymbol{\beta})'] = \Delta \tag{3.1.13}$$

where Δ is a positive semidefinite matrix and therefore $\boldsymbol{\gamma}'\Delta\boldsymbol{\gamma} \geq 0$ for *any* K-dimensional real vector $\boldsymbol{\gamma} \neq \mathbf{0}$ and for all $\boldsymbol{\beta}$.

The risk matrix for the least squares estimator is

$$E[(\mathbf{b} - \boldsymbol{\beta})(\mathbf{b} - \boldsymbol{\beta})'] = \sigma^2(X'X)^{-1} \tag{3.1.14}$$

Since the least squares estimator is unbiased, it has a null bias matrix. If in (3.1.13) we let $\hat{\boldsymbol{\beta}} = \mathbf{b}$ and $\hat{\boldsymbol{\beta}}_0$ be all other linear unbiased estimators, the conclusion of the Gauss-Markov theorem is stated.

By making use of these criteria, the least squares or generalized least squares estimators of Chapter 2 are best linear unbiased.

3.1.4 Some Examples

To give the decision theoretic concepts an operational flavor, let us use the orthonormal K mean version of the linear statistical model that is $\mathbf{y} = Z\boldsymbol{\theta} + \mathbf{e}$ where $Z'Z = I_K$ and $\mathbf{e} \sim N(\mathbf{0},\sigma^2 I_T)$. The maximum likelihood estimator that uses only sample information is $\tilde{\boldsymbol{\theta}} = Z'\mathbf{y}$ and $\tilde{\boldsymbol{\theta}} \sim N(\boldsymbol{\theta},\sigma^2 I_K)$. Suppose, based on this sampling process, we want to choose a linear estimator $\bar{\boldsymbol{\theta}} = A\mathbf{y}$ that minimizes expected squared error loss, which is,

$$\rho(\boldsymbol{\theta},\bar{\boldsymbol{\theta}}) = E[L(\boldsymbol{\theta},\bar{\boldsymbol{\theta}})] = E[(\bar{\boldsymbol{\theta}} - \boldsymbol{\theta})'(\bar{\boldsymbol{\theta}} - \boldsymbol{\theta})] \tag{3.1.15}$$

Given this measure of performance, one criterion is to find, for the linear estimator $\bar{\boldsymbol{\theta}} = A\mathbf{y}$, the matrix A, which minimizes expected squared error loss or risk. That is, find the matrix A that minimizes

$$\begin{aligned} E[(\bar{\boldsymbol{\theta}} - \boldsymbol{\theta})'(\bar{\boldsymbol{\theta}} - \boldsymbol{\theta})] &= E[((\bar{\boldsymbol{\theta}} - E[\bar{\boldsymbol{\theta}}]) + (E[\bar{\boldsymbol{\theta}}] - \boldsymbol{\theta}))'((\bar{\boldsymbol{\theta}} - E[\bar{\boldsymbol{\theta}}]) \\ &\qquad + (E[\bar{\boldsymbol{\theta}}] - \boldsymbol{\theta}))] \\ &= E[(\bar{\boldsymbol{\theta}} - E[\bar{\boldsymbol{\theta}}])'(\bar{\boldsymbol{\theta}} - E[\bar{\boldsymbol{\theta}}]) + (E[\bar{\boldsymbol{\theta}}] - \boldsymbol{\theta})'(E[\bar{\boldsymbol{\theta}}] - \boldsymbol{\theta})] \end{aligned} \tag{3.1.16}$$

which is the sum of the variances of the elements of $\bar{\boldsymbol{\theta}}$, plus the sum of the squared bias for each element of $\bar{\boldsymbol{\theta}}$. For $\bar{\boldsymbol{\theta}} = A\mathbf{y}$ and $\mathbf{y} = Z\boldsymbol{\theta} + \mathbf{e}$, the risk with the appropriate substitutions in (3.1.16) becomes

$$E[(\bar{\boldsymbol{\theta}} - \boldsymbol{\theta})'(\bar{\boldsymbol{\theta}} - \boldsymbol{\theta})] = \sigma^2 \operatorname{tr} AA' + \boldsymbol{\theta}'(AZ - I_K)'(AZ - I_K)\boldsymbol{\theta} \tag{3.1.17}$$

where $\sigma^2 \operatorname{tr} AA'$ is the sum of the diagonal elements of the covariance matrix $\sigma^2 AA'$ for $\bar{\boldsymbol{\theta}}$, which, given the choice of A, is a fixed number. The only way to minimize (3.1.16) or (3.1.17) for all $\boldsymbol{\theta}$ is to choose A such that the second expression on the right-hand side of (3.1.17) is as small as possible.

One way of looking at the problem is to assume that nature or some opponent chooses the $\boldsymbol{\theta}$ vector and that we must choose A such that we can protect against an "unfavorable" outcome for nature's choice of $\boldsymbol{\theta}$. To guard against a large possible loss, we could choose A such that $AZ = I_K$ and thus make the last expression on the right-hand side of (3.1.17) equal to zero. This suggests that $A = Z'$ and leads to the unbiased linear (least squares) estimator $\tilde{\boldsymbol{\theta}} = Z'\mathbf{y}$ with covariance $\sigma^2(Z'Z)^{-1}$ and risk $E[(\tilde{\boldsymbol{\theta}} - \boldsymbol{\theta})'(\tilde{\boldsymbol{\theta}} - \boldsymbol{\theta})] = \sigma^2 \operatorname{tr}(Z'Z)^{-1} = \sigma^2 K$. Consequently, under a squared error loss criterion, the choice of a linear rule that minimizes the maximum expected loss (minimax decision rule) leads to an unbiased linear decision rule that is identical to the least squares rule $\tilde{\boldsymbol{\theta}}$ that minimizes the quadratic form $(\mathbf{y} - Z\boldsymbol{\theta})'(\mathbf{y} - Z\boldsymbol{\theta})$.

Continuing with the use of the orthonormal K mean statistical model, let us consider the development of the risk functions for a family of estimators $\delta_c(\tilde{\boldsymbol{\theta}}) = c\tilde{\boldsymbol{\theta}}$, where c is a scalar and $\tilde{\boldsymbol{\theta}}$ is the maximum likelihood estimator. Under a squared error loss measure, the family of risk functions may be specified as

$$\begin{aligned} E[L(\boldsymbol{\theta},\delta_c(\tilde{\boldsymbol{\theta}})] &= E[(c\tilde{\boldsymbol{\theta}} - \boldsymbol{\theta})'(c\tilde{\boldsymbol{\theta}} - \boldsymbol{\theta})] \\ &= E[(c\tilde{\boldsymbol{\theta}} - E[c\tilde{\boldsymbol{\theta}}])'(c\tilde{\boldsymbol{\theta}} - E[c\tilde{\boldsymbol{\theta}}])] \\ &\quad + E[(E[c\tilde{\boldsymbol{\theta}}] - \boldsymbol{\theta})'(E[c\tilde{\boldsymbol{\theta}}] - \boldsymbol{\theta})] \\ &= E[(c\tilde{\boldsymbol{\theta}} - c\boldsymbol{\theta})'(c\tilde{\boldsymbol{\theta}} - c\boldsymbol{\theta})] + E[(c\boldsymbol{\theta} - \boldsymbol{\theta})'(c\boldsymbol{\theta} - \boldsymbol{\theta})] \\ &= c^2E[(\tilde{\boldsymbol{\theta}} - \boldsymbol{\theta})'(\tilde{\boldsymbol{\theta}} - \boldsymbol{\theta})] + (c - 1)^2\boldsymbol{\theta}'\boldsymbol{\theta} \\ &= c^2\sigma^2K + (c - 1)^2\boldsymbol{\theta}'\boldsymbol{\theta} \end{aligned} \qquad (3.1.18)$$

First consider the risk function for the estimator when $c = 1$. In this case the risk over all $\boldsymbol{\theta}$ is $\rho(\boldsymbol{\theta},\delta_1(\tilde{\boldsymbol{\theta}})) = \sigma^2K$, the risk of the least squares estimator, which as shown in (3.1.17) is a minimax decision rule and as we will show later in this chapter when $K \leq 2$ this estimator is admissible. The risk function for the estimator $\tilde{\boldsymbol{\theta}}$ is given in Figure 3.2.

Now consider the case of $c > 1$. In this case

$$\rho(\boldsymbol{\theta},\delta_{c>1}(\tilde{\boldsymbol{\theta}})) = c^2\sigma^2K + (c - 1)^2\boldsymbol{\theta}'\boldsymbol{\theta} > \sigma^2K \qquad (3.1.19)$$

Therefore, the least squares estimator strictly dominates the family of estimators defined when $c > 1$ and thus demonstrates their inadmissibility.

Next consider the family of estimators when $0 < c < 1$. For this range of c all of the risk functions cross somewhere in the parameter space and no one choice of c dominates any other including the outcome of $c = 1$. The characteristics of these risk functions are in general similar to those shown in Figure 3.2, when $c = 0.6$. As in the case when $c = 1$ if $K \leq 2$ all of the estimators $0 < c < 1$ are admissible. The risks for the estimators in this range are unbounded.

Next let us consider the trivial estimator when $c = 0$ and thus $c\tilde{\boldsymbol{\theta}} = \mathbf{0}$. This means that regardless of the outcomes for the random vector $\mathbf{y}$ we choose $\boldsymbol{\theta}$ to be a null vector. This estimator has a risk of zero at the origin. It is equal to $\boldsymbol{\theta}'\boldsymbol{\theta}$

otherwise and therefore has an unbounded risk. The estimator is admissible and this indicates that although admissibility may be a gem of great value for decision rules, it does not assure us that the estimator is a meaningful one. A graph of the risk function when $c = 0$ is given in Figure 3.2.

When considering a decision rule such as $\delta_c(\tilde{\boldsymbol{\theta}}) = c\tilde{\boldsymbol{\theta}}$ it seems appropriate to ask if there is a particular value of c that minimizes risk over the range of the parameter space. To investigate this question for the risk function (3.1.18), we may find the value of c which minimizes risk by solving

$$\begin{aligned} \frac{d\rho(\boldsymbol{\theta},\delta_c(\tilde{\boldsymbol{\theta}}))}{dc} &= \frac{d(c^2\sigma^2K + (c-1)^2\boldsymbol{\theta}'\boldsymbol{\theta})}{dc} \\ &= 2c\sigma^2K + 2c\boldsymbol{\theta}'\boldsymbol{\theta} - 2\boldsymbol{\theta}'\boldsymbol{\theta} = 0 \\ &= c(\sigma^2K + \boldsymbol{\theta}'\boldsymbol{\theta}) - \boldsymbol{\theta}'\boldsymbol{\theta} = 0 \end{aligned} \tag{3.1.20}$$

which implies that the minimal risk is achieved when

$$c = \boldsymbol{\theta}'\boldsymbol{\theta}/(\sigma^2K + \boldsymbol{\theta}'\boldsymbol{\theta}) \tag{3.1.21}$$

Unfortunately in this case the choice of c depends on the unknown parameter vector $\boldsymbol{\theta}$ and the unknown scalar σ^2. Consequently this information is of little or no use to us. As we will see later in the book some researchers have used an estimator that replaces the unknown parameters by their sample maximum likelihood counterparts.

Finally, for this family of risk functions, let us consider the Bayes principle (3.1.4) in selecting an estimator. The best decision rule, using the Bayes princi-

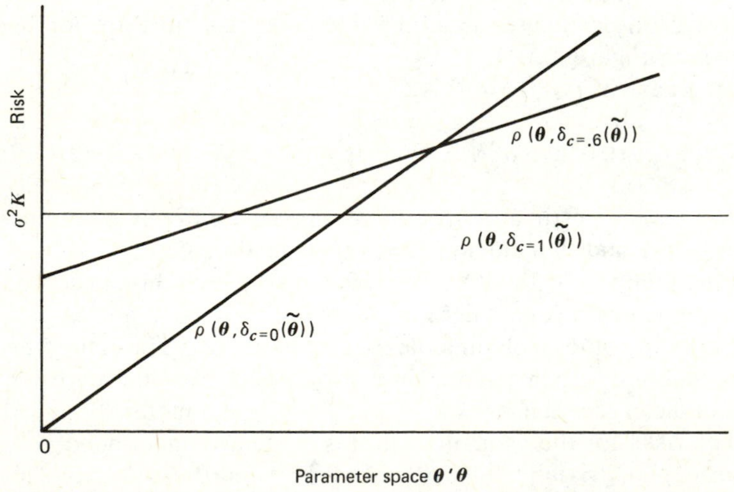

Figure 3.2 Characteristics of the risk functions for the estimators $\delta_c(\tilde{\boldsymbol{\theta}})$ when $c = 0$, $c = .6$, and $c = 1$.

ple, is the one that minimizes over all $\delta_c(\tilde{\boldsymbol{\theta}})$

$$E_{g(\boldsymbol{\theta})}[\rho(\boldsymbol{\theta},\delta_c(\tilde{\boldsymbol{\theta}}))] \tag{3.1.22}$$

where $g(\boldsymbol{\theta})$ represents the density of the random variables over which the expectation is being taken. For the orthonormal statistical model used in the above examples let the prior information be represented by the joint density $g(\boldsymbol{\theta}) \sim N(\mathbf{0},\tau^2 I_K)$. In this case the $\delta_c(\tilde{\boldsymbol{\theta}})$ decision rules have Bayes risks

$$\begin{aligned} E_{g(\boldsymbol{\theta})}[\rho(\boldsymbol{\theta},\delta_c(\tilde{\boldsymbol{\theta}}))] &= E_{g(\boldsymbol{\theta})}[c^2\sigma^2 K + (c-1)^2\boldsymbol{\theta}'\boldsymbol{\theta}] \\ &= c^2\sigma^2 K + (c-1)^2 E_{g(\boldsymbol{\theta})}[\boldsymbol{\theta}'\boldsymbol{\theta}] \\ &= c^2\sigma^2 K + (c-1)^2\tau^2 K \end{aligned} \tag{3.1.23}$$

In order to find the c that minimizes the average risk, that is the c that makes (3.1.23) a minimum, we solve

$$\frac{d(E_{g(\boldsymbol{\theta})}[\rho(\boldsymbol{\theta},\delta_c(\tilde{\boldsymbol{\theta}}))])}{dc} = 2c\sigma^2 K - 2(1-c)\tau^2 K = 0 \tag{3.1.24}$$

Solving for the optimum c we have

$$c_\beta = \tau^2/(\sigma^2 + \tau^2) \tag{3.1.25}$$

The corresponding Bayes risk of $\delta_{c\beta}(\tilde{\boldsymbol{\theta}})$, when c_β is substituted in (3.1.23), is

$$\begin{aligned} E_{g(\boldsymbol{\theta})}[\rho(\boldsymbol{\theta},\delta_c(\boldsymbol{\theta}))] &= \left(\frac{\tau^2}{\sigma^2+\tau^2}\right)^2 \sigma^2 K + \left(1 - \frac{\tau^2}{\sigma^2+\tau^2}\right)^2 \tau^2 K \\ &= \frac{\tau^2 K\sigma^2}{\sigma^2+\tau^2} \end{aligned}$$

In the sections and chapters to follow, the basic definitions and concepts relating to statistical theory are used to gauge the sampling performance of a range of traditional and nontraditional estimators that use various forms of nonsample information. The Bayesian approach to inference will be discussed in some detail in Chapter 4. Those interested in a more complete discussion of statistical decision theory should see Berger (1980), Ferguson (1967), and DeGroot (1970).

3.2 ESTIMATORS THAT COMBINE SAMPLE AND NONSAMPLE INFORMATION

In the previous section we noted that in decision theory an attempt is made to combine sample information with at least two other types of information or knowledge. One type deals with knowledge of the possible consequences of the decisions and the other is knowledge other than that derived from the statistical investigation. In this section we analyze *within a decision theoretic context* the statistical implications of using both sample and various kinds of nonsample information.

3.2.1 Exact Nonsample Information

There may be instances in applied work when the investigator has exact information on a particular parameter or linear combination of parameters. For example, in estimating a log-linear production function, information may be available that the firm is operating under the condition of constant returns to scale. Alternatively, in estimating a demand relation, information may be available from consumer theory on the homogeneity condition or information concerning the income response coefficient may be available from previous empirical work.

If information of this type is available, it may be stated in the form of the following set of linear relations or linear equality restrictions:

$$R\boldsymbol{\beta} = \mathbf{r} \tag{3.2.1}$$

where $\mathbf{r}$ is a $(J \times 1)$ vector of known elements and R is a $(J \times K)$ known prior information design matrix that expresses the structure of the information on the individual parameters β_i or some linear combination of the elements of the $\boldsymbol{\beta}$ vector. Information concerning the parameters such as β_1 equal to some scalar k, the sum of the coefficients equal to unity and β_2 equal to β_3 may be specified in the $R\boldsymbol{\beta} = \mathbf{r}$ format as

$$\begin{bmatrix} 1 & 0 & 0 & 0 & \dots & 0 \\ 1 & 1 & 1 & 1 & \dots & 1 \\ 0 & 1 & -1 & 0 & \dots & 0 \end{bmatrix} \begin{bmatrix} \beta_1 \\ \beta_2 \\ \vdots \\ \beta_K \end{bmatrix} = \begin{bmatrix} k \\ 1 \\ 0 \end{bmatrix} \tag{3.2.2}$$

where $J = 3$. If the first J elements of the coefficient vector were specified to be equal to the vector $\mathbf{k}_J$, then this information could be specified as

$$[I_J, 0_{(K-J)}] \begin{bmatrix} \boldsymbol{\beta}_J \\ \boldsymbol{\beta}_{K-J} \end{bmatrix} = \mathbf{k}_J \tag{3.2.3}$$

where I_J is a Jth-order identity matrix and $\mathbf{k}_J$ is a $(J \times 1)$ known vector.

Given information in the form of (3.2.1), how do we combine it with the information contained in the sample observations $\mathbf{y}$? Because information on the individual parameters and combinations thereof is specified to be known with certainty, that is, no sampling variability from sample to sample, linear equality relations (3.2.1) may be taken as givens or restrictions in any estimation process. In the general linear statistical model of Chapter 2, when using the least squares rule, the least squares estimator $\mathbf{b}$ has mean vector $\boldsymbol{\beta}$ and covariance $\Sigma_{\mathbf{b}} = \sigma^2(X'X)^{-1}$. Consequently, the coefficients are not independent and the restrictions on particular coefficients or their combinations reflected by (3.2.1) condition the values that other coefficients may take on. Therefore, if one uses the least squares criterion applied to both the sample information and the nonsample information (3.2.1), we are faced with the problem of finding the vector $\mathbf{b}^*$ that minimizes the quadratic form

$$S(\boldsymbol{\beta}) = (\mathbf{y} - X\boldsymbol{\beta})'(\mathbf{y} - X\boldsymbol{\beta}) \tag{3.2.4}$$

subject to

$$R\boldsymbol{\beta} = \mathbf{r} \quad \text{or} \quad R\boldsymbol{\beta} - \mathbf{r} = \mathbf{0} \tag{3.2.1}$$

Since (3.2.1) appears as linear equality restrictions, classical Lagrangian procedures may be applied to yield the minimizing solution [Judge et al. (1982), pp. 553–554]

$$\begin{aligned} \mathbf{b}^* &= \mathbf{b} + (X'X)^{-1}R'[R(X'X)^{-1}R']^{-1}(\mathbf{r} - R\mathbf{b}) \\ &= \mathbf{b} + S^{-1}R'(RS^{-1}R')^{-1}(\mathbf{r} - R\mathbf{b}) \end{aligned} \tag{3.2.5}$$

which differs from the unrestricted least squares estimator by a linear function of the vector $\mathbf{r} - R\mathbf{b}$. The restricted least squares random vector $\mathbf{b}^*$ has mean

$$\begin{aligned} E[\mathbf{b}^*] &= \boldsymbol{\beta} + S^{-1}R'(RS^{-1}R')^{-1}(\mathbf{r} - R\boldsymbol{\beta}) \\ &= \boldsymbol{\beta} + S^{-1}R'(RS^{-1}R')^{-1}\boldsymbol{\delta} \end{aligned} \tag{3.2.6}$$

and is unbiased if $(\mathbf{r} - R\boldsymbol{\beta}) = \boldsymbol{\delta} = \mathbf{0}$, that is, if the restrictions are correct. If the restrictions are not correct, the restricted least squares estimator is biased by a linear function of the vector $\boldsymbol{\delta} = \mathbf{r} - R\boldsymbol{\beta}$.

The covariance matrix of the restricted least squares estimator is

$$\begin{aligned} E[(\mathbf{b}^* - E[\mathbf{b}^*])(\mathbf{b}^* - E[\mathbf{b}^*])'] = \Sigma_{\mathbf{b}^*} &= \sigma^2[S^{-1} - S^{-1}R'(RS^{-1}R')^{-1}RS^{-1}] \\ &= \sigma^2[S^{-1} - C] \end{aligned} \tag{3.2.7}$$

where $C = S^{-1}R'(RS^{-1}R')^{-1}RS^{-1}$ is a positive semidefinite matrix. This means, among other things, that the diagonal elements of the covariance matrix of the restricted least squares estimator (3.2.7) are equal to or less than the corresponding elements on the diagonal of the covariance matrix of the unrestricted least squares estimator. Furthermore, the difference between the covariance matrices is $\Sigma_{\mathbf{b}} - \Sigma_{\mathbf{b}^*} = \sigma^2 C$, where C is a positive semidefinite matrix. Therefore, if $\mathbf{b}^*$ is unbiased, it is the best within the class of unbiased estimators that are a linear function of both types of information $\mathbf{y}$ and $R\boldsymbol{\beta} = \mathbf{r}$.

If the restrictions are incorrect and $E[\mathbf{r} - R\mathbf{b}] = \boldsymbol{\delta} \neq \mathbf{0}$, then the restricted least squares estimator is biased and has the mean square error or risk matrix

$$\begin{aligned}\mathcal{R}(\boldsymbol{\beta},\mathbf{b}^*) &= E[(\mathbf{b}^* - \boldsymbol{\beta})(\mathbf{b}^* - \boldsymbol{\beta})'] \\ &= \sigma^2[S^{-1} - C] + S^{-1}R'(RS^{-1}R')^{-1}\boldsymbol{\delta}\boldsymbol{\delta}'(RS^{-1}R')^{-1}RS^{-1} \end{aligned} \quad (3.2.8)$$

which in words is equal to the covariance matrix for the restricted least squares estimator plus the bias matrix resulting from the products of the bias vector.

It is apparent from the restricted least squares covariance matrix (3.2.7) and the mean square error matrix (3.2.8) that if the nonsample information is correct, then using it in conjunction with the sample information will lead to an unbiased estimator that has a precision matrix superior to the unrestricted least squares estimator.

3.2.1a Performance Under Squared Error Loss

In applied work we can never be completely sure that our outside information is correct, or in other words we are sometimes not sure that the restrictions we impose are consistent with the real-world parameter system underlying the data generation process. Therefore, it is important to know the average loss experienced with different degrees of error for the vector $\boldsymbol{\delta} = R\boldsymbol{\beta} - \mathbf{r}$. For expository purposes let us assume the orthonormal linear statistical model, which has a design matrix X such that $X'X = I_K$. We also assume that the information design matrix R is of the form I_K, that is, individual restrictions are placed on each of the elements of the $\boldsymbol{\beta}$ vector. As a basis for evaluating estimator performance, we first consider the squared error loss criterion

$$\rho(\boldsymbol{\beta},\mathbf{b}^*) = E[(\mathbf{b}^* - \boldsymbol{\beta})'(\mathbf{b}^* - \boldsymbol{\beta})] = E[\mathrm{tr}(\mathbf{b}^* - \boldsymbol{\beta})(\mathbf{b}^* - \boldsymbol{\beta})'] \quad (3.2.9)$$

For the orthonormal special case assumed, the risk is

$$\rho(\boldsymbol{\beta},\mathbf{b}^*) = \sigma^2\mathrm{tr}[I_K - I_K] + \mathrm{tr}[\boldsymbol{\delta}\boldsymbol{\delta}'] = \boldsymbol{\delta}'\boldsymbol{\delta} \quad (3.2.10)$$

The covariance matrix of the restricted least squares estimator is a null matrix because each of the parameters of the $\boldsymbol{\beta}$ vector is constrained and thus does not vary from sample to sample. Therefore, the risk of the restricted least squares estimator is equal to the sum of squares of the bias or restriction errors $\boldsymbol{\delta}'\boldsymbol{\delta}$. The covariance matrix for the least squares estimator for the orthonormal statistical model is $\sigma^2 I_K$ and thus the risk under squared loss is

$$\rho(\boldsymbol{\beta},\mathbf{b}) = E[(\mathbf{b} - \boldsymbol{\beta})'(\mathbf{b} - \boldsymbol{\beta})] = \sigma^2 K \quad (3.2.11)$$

a scalar that depends on the sample information and is unrelated to the information and/or errors contained in the system of linear equality relations.

Since the least squares risk is $\sigma^2 K$, for every $\boldsymbol{\delta}'\boldsymbol{\delta}$, and the restricted least squares risk is $\boldsymbol{\delta}'\boldsymbol{\delta}$ and thus a function of $\boldsymbol{\delta}'\boldsymbol{\delta}$, the two risks are equal when

$$\boldsymbol{\delta}'\boldsymbol{\delta} = \sigma^2 K \tag{3.2.12}$$

or

$$\frac{(\boldsymbol{\beta} - \mathbf{r})'(\boldsymbol{\beta} - \mathbf{r})}{\sigma^2} = \frac{\boldsymbol{\delta}'\boldsymbol{\delta}}{\sigma^2} = K$$

or

$$\frac{\boldsymbol{\delta}'\boldsymbol{\delta}}{2\sigma^2} = \frac{K}{2}$$

When the nonsample information in the form of restrictions is correct, the risk gain of using the restricted least squares estimator is $\sigma^2 K$. These results are shown in Figure 3.3. As indicated in the figure under a squared error loss measure of performance, the restricted estimator can be very good or very bad (precisely wrong and unbounded risk). Its performance relative to the least squares estimator depends on the quality of the nonsample information. If the quality of the nonsample information is such that $\boldsymbol{\delta}'\boldsymbol{\delta}/2\sigma^2 < K/2$, then $\rho(\boldsymbol{\beta},\mathbf{b}^*) < \rho(\boldsymbol{\beta},\mathbf{b})$ and the restricted least squares estimator is the clear choice. However, if the restrictions are such that $\boldsymbol{\delta}'\boldsymbol{\delta}/2\sigma^2 > K/2$, then the restricted estimator is inferior to the least squares estimator over an infinite range of the parameter space.

3.2.1b Performance Under the General Mean Squared Error Criterion

Alternatively, consider, for the same information design matrix $R = I_K$, the estimator choice problem under a general mean squared error measure that considers all of the elements of the risk matrix $E[(\mathbf{b}^* - \boldsymbol{\beta})(\mathbf{b}^* - \boldsymbol{\beta})']$. Under this

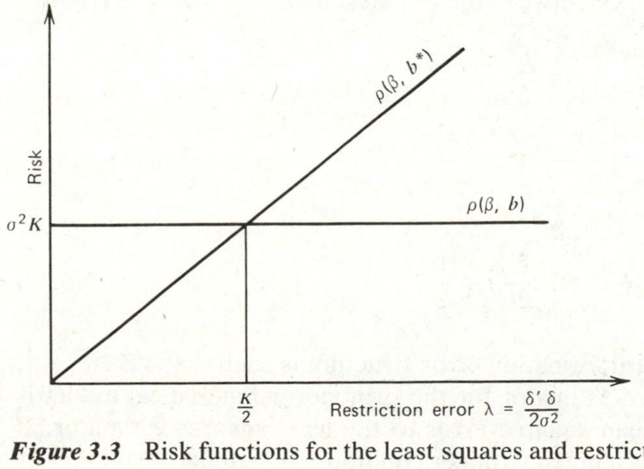

Figure 3.3 Risk functions for the least squares and restricted least squares estimators.

criterion we evaluate the difference between the risk matrix (covariance) for the unrestricted orthonormal least squares estimator $\sigma^2 I_K$ and that of the restricted least squares estimator $\boldsymbol{\delta\delta}'$ and evaluate the conditions under which the difference in risk matrices yields a positive semidefinite matrix. Thus we consider the characteristics of the difference matrix

$$\mathrm{E}[(\mathbf{b} - \boldsymbol{\beta})(\mathbf{b} - \boldsymbol{\beta})'] - E[(\mathbf{b}^* - \boldsymbol{\beta})(\mathbf{b}^* - \boldsymbol{\beta})'] = \sigma^2 I_K - \boldsymbol{\delta\delta}' \qquad (3.2.13)$$

Therefore, under the general mean squared or risk matrix criterion, the restricted least squares estimator $\mathbf{b}^*$ will be superior to the unrestricted least squares estimator $\mathbf{b}$, if for all $(K \times 1)$ vectors $\boldsymbol{\iota} \neq \mathbf{0}$.

$$\boldsymbol{\iota}'(\sigma^2 I_K - \boldsymbol{\delta\delta}')\boldsymbol{\iota} \geq 0 \qquad (3.2.14)$$

or

$$\boldsymbol{\iota}'\left(I_K - \frac{\boldsymbol{\delta\delta}'}{\sigma^2}\right)\boldsymbol{\iota} \geq 0$$

Since I_K is positive definite, this is equivalent to the requirement that

$$\frac{\boldsymbol{\iota}'\boldsymbol{\delta\delta}'\boldsymbol{\iota}}{\sigma^2 \boldsymbol{\iota}' I_K \boldsymbol{\iota}} \leq 1 \qquad (3.2.15)$$

and the maximum of the left side of (3.2.15) taken over all $(K \times 1)$ nonzero vectors is (Rao, 1973, p. 60)

$$\max_{\boldsymbol{\iota}} \frac{\boldsymbol{\iota}'\boldsymbol{\delta\delta}'\boldsymbol{\iota}}{\sigma^2 \boldsymbol{\iota}'\boldsymbol{\iota}} = \frac{\boldsymbol{\delta}'\boldsymbol{\delta}}{\sigma^2} \qquad (3.2.16)$$

This means that the difference between the two risk matrices (3.2.13) is positive semidefinite if and only if

$$\frac{\boldsymbol{\delta}'\boldsymbol{\delta}}{\sigma^2} \leq 1$$

or

$$\frac{\boldsymbol{\delta}'\boldsymbol{\delta}}{2\sigma^2} \leq \frac{1}{2} \qquad (3.2.17)$$

In other words, if the prior information error structure is such that $\boldsymbol{\delta}'\boldsymbol{\delta}/2\sigma^2 \leq \frac{1}{2}$, the restricted least squares estimator for the orthonormal statistical model is superior under general mean squared error to the least squares estimator. It should be noted that this is a much stronger condition for estimator superiority than the squared error loss criterion (3.2.9) and (3.2.11), that is, $\boldsymbol{\delta}'\boldsymbol{\delta}/2\sigma^2 \leq \frac{1}{2}$

versus $\boldsymbol{\delta}'\boldsymbol{\delta}/2\sigma^2 \leq K/2$. As developed in Judge and Bock (1978, p. 29), for general X and R design matrices under the risk matrix criterion, the restricted least squares rule is superior to the unrestricted least squares rule if

$$\boldsymbol{\iota}'\left(RS^{-1}R' - \frac{1}{\sigma^2}\boldsymbol{\delta}\boldsymbol{\delta}'\right)\boldsymbol{\iota} \geq \mathbf{0} \quad \text{or} \quad \frac{\boldsymbol{\delta}'(RS^{-1}R')^{-1}\boldsymbol{\delta}}{2\sigma^2} \leq \frac{1}{2} \tag{3.2.18}$$

This is the very reasonable or intuitive result that if the restrictions are "close to being correct" then the false, but not very false restrictions, are adding information that improves on least squares.

3.2.1c General Linear Hypotheses

Under the assumption of a normal error vector $\mathbf{e}$, if we consider the equality restrictions $R\boldsymbol{\beta} = \mathbf{r}$ as general linear hypotheses about the unknown coefficient vector $\boldsymbol{\beta}$, we may as in Chapter 2 use the likelihood ratio test to check the compatibility of the data, $\mathbf{b}$, and the general linear hypotheses $\mathbf{b}^*$. If we consider R to be any $(J \times K)$ hypothesis design matrix, where $J \leq K$, and R is of rank J, $R\mathbf{b} - \mathbf{r} = R(\mathbf{b} - \boldsymbol{\beta}) \sim N(\mathbf{0},\sigma^2 R(X'X)^{-1}R')$, use of the likelihood ratio procedure leads to the test statistic

$$\frac{(R\mathbf{b} - \mathbf{r})'[R(X'X)^{-1}R']^{-1}(R\mathbf{b} - \mathbf{r})}{J\hat{\sigma}^2}$$

which is distributed as an F random variable with J and $(T - K)$ degrees of freedom. The acceptance and rejection mechanism when using this test statistic is the same as in Chapter 2. For a development of this test statistic within the context of the restricted estimator $\mathbf{b}^*$ see Judge et al. (1982), pp. 560–562.

3.2.2 Stochastic Nonsample Information

There are many situations in applied work when assuming exact prior information is not appropriate or in fact this type of information does not exist. If uncertainty exists about the prior information specifications, one alternative is to make use of stochastic restrictions or hypotheses of the following form:

$$\mathbf{r} = R\boldsymbol{\beta} + \mathbf{v} \tag{3.2.19}$$

where R is again a known $(J \times K)$ prior information or hypothesis design matrix, $\mathbf{r}$ is a known or observable $(J \times 1)$ random vector and $\mathbf{v}$ is a $(J \times 1)$ unobservable, normally distributed random vector with mean vector $\boldsymbol{\delta}$ and covariance $\sigma^2\Omega$, with Ω known. The information in (3.2.19) may come from previous statistical investigations, where an unbiased estimate of a subset of $\boldsymbol{\beta}$ or linear combinations thereof, along with their variances and covariances, are available. Alternatively, prior information may be available that particular coefficients lie between certain upper and lower bounds that Nagar and Kakwani (1964) describe in the following way:

Let us suppose that prior information is available on the first two elements of $\boldsymbol{\beta}$. We may feel, for example, that almost certainly, say with 95% probability, β_1 lies between 0 and 1 and β_2 lies between $\frac{1}{4}$ and $\frac{3}{4}$. If we use "two times the σ rule," the range of β_1 is $\frac{1}{2} \pm 2\sqrt{\frac{1}{16}}$ and that of β_2 is $\frac{1}{2} \pm 2\sqrt{\frac{1}{64}}$ and, assuming for the moment that $\sigma^2 = 1$, we can write (for 3.2.19)

$$\begin{aligned} \tfrac{1}{2} &= \beta_1 + v_1 \qquad E[v_1] = 0 \qquad E[v_1^2] = \tfrac{1}{16} \\ \tfrac{1}{2} &= \beta_2 + v_2 \qquad E[v_2] = 0 \qquad E[v_2^2] = \tfrac{1}{64} \end{aligned}$$

Thus

$$\mathbf{r} = \begin{bmatrix} \frac{1}{2} \\ \frac{1}{2} \end{bmatrix}; \qquad R = \begin{bmatrix} 1 & 0 & 0 \cdots 0 \\ 0 & 1 & 0 \cdots 0 \end{bmatrix};$$

$$\mathbf{v} = \begin{bmatrix} v_1 \\ v_2 \end{bmatrix}; \qquad \Omega = \begin{bmatrix} \frac{1}{16} & 0 \\ 0 & \frac{1}{64} \end{bmatrix}.$$

Given the existence of this type of information or linear stochastic hypotheses, Theil and Goldberger considered the problem of how to combine this information with the sample information. They assumed that the random vector $\mathbf{e}$ associated with the sampling model $\mathbf{y} = X\boldsymbol{\beta} + \mathbf{e}$ was independent of the random vector $\mathbf{v}$ associated with the prior information and wrote the statistical model containing both types of information as

$$\begin{bmatrix} \mathbf{y} \\ \mathbf{r} \end{bmatrix} = \begin{bmatrix} X \\ R \end{bmatrix} \boldsymbol{\beta} + \begin{bmatrix} \mathbf{e} \\ \mathbf{v} \end{bmatrix} \tag{3.2.20a}$$

where $[\mathbf{e}',\mathbf{v}']'$ is a multivariate normal random vector with mean vector and covariance matrix

$$E\begin{bmatrix} \mathbf{e} \\ \mathbf{v} \end{bmatrix} = \begin{bmatrix} \mathbf{0} \\ \boldsymbol{\delta} \end{bmatrix}; \quad E\begin{bmatrix} \mathbf{e} \\ \mathbf{v} \end{bmatrix}\begin{bmatrix} \mathbf{e} \\ \mathbf{v} \end{bmatrix}' = \sigma^2 \begin{bmatrix} I_T & 0 \\ 0 & \Omega \end{bmatrix} \tag{3.2.20b}$$

3.2.2a The Estimator

If the covariance matrix (3.2.20b) for the random vector $[\mathbf{e}',\mathbf{v}']'$ is known, the Aitken estimator

$$\tilde{\boldsymbol{\beta}} = (\sigma^{-2}X'X + \sigma^{-2}R'\Omega^{-1}R)^{-1}(\sigma^{-2}X'\mathbf{y} + \sigma^{-2}R'\Omega^{-1}\mathbf{r}) \tag{3.2.21}$$

can be used and has mean

$$E[\tilde{\boldsymbol{\beta}}] = \boldsymbol{\beta} + (S + R'\Omega^{-1}R)^{-1}R'\Omega^{-1}\boldsymbol{\delta} \tag{3.2.22}$$

covariance matrix

$$E[(\tilde{\boldsymbol{\beta}} - E[\tilde{\boldsymbol{\beta}}])(\tilde{\boldsymbol{\beta}} - E[\tilde{\boldsymbol{\beta}}])'] = \sigma^2(S + R'\Omega^{-1}R)^{-1} = \sigma^2 W^{-1} \quad (3.2.23)$$

and mean square error or risk matrix

$$\begin{aligned} E[(\tilde{\boldsymbol{\beta}} - \boldsymbol{\beta})(\tilde{\boldsymbol{\beta}} - \boldsymbol{\beta})'] &= \sigma^2 W^{-1} + W^{-1}R'\Omega^{-1}\boldsymbol{\delta}\boldsymbol{\delta}'\Omega^{-1}RW^{-1} \\ &= \text{covariance} + \text{square of bias matrix} \quad (3.2.24) \end{aligned}$$

If the stochastic restrictions are unbiased, that is, $E[\mathbf{r} - R\boldsymbol{\beta}] = E[\mathbf{v}] = \boldsymbol{\delta} = \mathbf{0}$, the stochastic restricted estimator is unbiased and the Aitken estimator (3.2.21) is best linear unbiased out of the class of estimators making use of the sample information $\mathbf{y}$ and the stochastic prior information $\mathbf{r}$.

One difficulty with estimator (3.2.21) is that σ^2 is unknown. As it is written (3.2.21) does not depend explicitly on σ^2, which will cancel out. However, because the covariance of $\mathbf{v}$ is assumed to be $\sigma^2\Omega$, knowledge of σ^2 is required for proper specification of the prior information. To deal with this problem, Theil (1963) has suggested that σ^2 be replaced by an unbiased estimator based on the sample data, that is, $\hat{\sigma}^2 = (\mathbf{y} - X\mathbf{b})'(\mathbf{y} - X\mathbf{b})/(T - K)$. Now $\hat{\sigma}^2$ is stochastic, but it will differ from σ^2 to the order $1/\sqrt{T}$ in probability when the random vector $\mathbf{e}$ is normally distributed. Therefore, if σ^2 is replaced by $\hat{\sigma}^2$, the estimator is asymptotically unbiased if the stochastic prior information is correct on the average and has the asymptotic moment matrix given in (3.2.23). Theil generalized the model (3.2.20a) to allow for the possibility that the prior judgments on $R\boldsymbol{\beta}$ are positively correlated with the corresponding elements of the sample estimator.

3.2.2b Sampling Comparisons

If the stochastic prior information is correct on the average and $E[\mathbf{v}] = \boldsymbol{\delta} = \mathbf{0}$, we can evaluate the sampling performance of the least squares and stochastic restricted least squares estimators by comparing their covariance matrices. Consequently, using (A.5.3) of Appendix A we evaluate

$$\begin{aligned} E[(\mathbf{b} - \boldsymbol{\beta})(\mathbf{b} - \boldsymbol{\beta})'] &- E[(\tilde{\boldsymbol{\beta}} - E[\tilde{\boldsymbol{\beta}}])(\tilde{\boldsymbol{\beta}} - E[\tilde{\boldsymbol{\beta}}])'] \\ &= \sigma^2(X'X)^{-1} - \sigma^2[(X'X) + R'\Omega^{-1}R]^{-1} \\ &= \sigma^2 S^{-1} - \sigma^2[S + R'\Omega^{-1}R]^{-1} \\ &= \sigma^2 S^{-1}R'(\Omega + RS^{-1}R')^{-1}RS^{-1} \quad (3.2.25) \end{aligned}$$

which yields a difference matrix that is positive semidefinite. Therefore, the variance for each element of the coefficient vector for the stochastic restricted estimator is equal to or less than the variance of each corresponding element of the coefficient vector for the least squares estimator. That this should be true is easily seen if, following Judge and Bock (1978), we rewrite the statistical model (3.2.20a) in equivalent form as

$$\begin{bmatrix} \mathbf{y} \\ \Omega^{-1/2}\mathbf{r} \end{bmatrix} = \begin{bmatrix} X & 0 \\ 0 & \Omega^{-1/2} \end{bmatrix} \begin{bmatrix} \boldsymbol{\beta} \\ R\boldsymbol{\beta} + \boldsymbol{\delta} \end{bmatrix} + \begin{bmatrix} \mathbf{e} \\ \Omega^{-1/2}(\mathbf{v} - \boldsymbol{\delta}) \end{bmatrix} \tag{3.2.26}$$

subject to the restriction

$$[-R \quad I_J] \begin{bmatrix} \boldsymbol{\beta} \\ R\boldsymbol{\beta} + \boldsymbol{\delta} \end{bmatrix} = \mathbf{0} \tag{3.2.27}$$

Since the stochastic restricted estimator can be written as a restricted least squares estimator, we can use the results from Section 3.2.1 and Equation (3.2.7) to establish that the covariance matrix of the stochastic restricted estimator is superior to the unrestricted least squares estimator.

These results establish the superiority of the stochastic restricted estimator when the restrictions are correct on the average. When the restrictions are not correct, we must compare the covariance of the least squares estimator with the mean square error or risk matrix for the stochastic restricted estimator. In order for the stochastic restricted estimator to be superior to the least squares estimator, the difference matrix

$$E[(\mathbf{b} - \boldsymbol{\beta})(\mathbf{b} - \boldsymbol{\beta})'] - E[(\tilde{\boldsymbol{\beta}} - \boldsymbol{\beta})(\tilde{\boldsymbol{\beta}} - \boldsymbol{\beta})'] = \Delta \tag{3.2.28}$$

must be positive semidefinite. Making use of the mean square error matrix (3.2.24) and the least squares covariance matrix, we write (3.2.28) as

$$\begin{aligned} \mathcal{R}(\boldsymbol{\beta},\mathbf{b}) - \mathcal{R}(\boldsymbol{\beta},\tilde{\boldsymbol{\beta}}) &= \sigma^2 S^{-1} - \sigma^2 W^{-1} - W^{-1}R'\Omega^{-1}\boldsymbol{\delta}\boldsymbol{\delta}'\Omega^{-1}RW^{-1} \\ &= W^{-1}R'\Omega^{-1}[\sigma^2(RS^{-1}R' + \Omega) - \boldsymbol{\delta}\boldsymbol{\delta}']\Omega^{-1}RW^{-1} \end{aligned} \tag{3.2.29}$$

In order for the risk matrix of the stochastic restricted estimator to be superior to the least squares alternative, $\sigma^2(RS^{-1}R' + \Omega) - \boldsymbol{\delta}\boldsymbol{\delta}'$ must be positive semidefinite, or following Judge and Bock (1978),

$$\frac{\boldsymbol{\delta}'(RS^{-1}R' + \Omega)^{-1}\boldsymbol{\delta}}{2\sigma^2} \le \frac{1}{2} \tag{3.2.30}$$

Note the similarity between the above condition and that for the restricted least squares estimator (3.2.18).

Judge and Bock (1978) have shown that under the squared error loss criterion $\rho(\boldsymbol{\beta},\tilde{\boldsymbol{\beta}}) = E[(\tilde{\boldsymbol{\beta}} - \boldsymbol{\beta})'(\tilde{\boldsymbol{\beta}} - \boldsymbol{\beta})]$ the stochastic restricted estimator is superior (smaller risk) to the least squares estimator if

$$\frac{\boldsymbol{\delta}'(RS^{-1}R' + \Omega)^{-1}RS^{-2}R'(RS^{-1}R' + \Omega)^{-1}\boldsymbol{\delta}}{\sigma^2} < \operatorname{tr}\left([RS^{-1}R' + \Omega]^{-2}RS^{-1}R'\right) \tag{3.2.31}$$

If a weighted risk function is used where the weight matrix is $X'X = S$, the condition is the same except S^{-2} changes to S^{-1}.

Therefore, under all of the criteria, the superiority of the stochastic restricted estimator depends on the average specification error in the linear stochastic hypotheses. When the linear stochastic restrictions are correct, that is, $\boldsymbol{\delta} = \mathbf{0}$, the stochastic restricted estimator is superior to its least squares counterpart if $\Omega \neq 0$ and is known.

One weakness of the mixed estimator lies in assuming the random vector $\boldsymbol{\delta}$, representing the uncertainty of the prior information, has a zero mean vector, an assumption necessary for the estimator to be unbiased. Since the frequency and subjective interpretations of probability are different, the argument that prior judgments are equivalent to prior unbiased estimates seems unsatisfactory. As shown by Swamy and Mehta the estimator (3.2.21) may be less efficient than the least squares estimator based only on sample data if the stochastic prior information (3.2.19) is misspecified. The requirement that the prior covariance matrix Ω be known must in most cases be unreasonably demanding. In addition, the fixed $\boldsymbol{\beta}$ and random $\mathbf{r}$ and $\boldsymbol{\delta}$ in (3.2.19) does not fit any Bayesian axiom system and it would appear that no set of principles have been set down which would justify this specification.

3.2.2c Stochastic Linear Hypotheses

Since in applied research we are seldom sure that $\boldsymbol{\delta} = \mathbf{0}$, consider the following stochastic linear hypotheses about the stochastic nonsample information

$$E[\mathbf{r}] - R\boldsymbol{\beta} = \boldsymbol{\delta} = \mathbf{0} \tag{3.2.32}$$

or

$$E[\mathbf{r}] - R\boldsymbol{\beta}$$

where the random variable $\mathbf{r}$ is a normally distributed vector, with mean vector $R\boldsymbol{\beta} + \boldsymbol{\delta}$ and covariance matrix $\sigma^2\Omega$, that is independent of the least squares estimator $\mathbf{b}$. The stochastic prior and sample information provide two separate estimates of $R\boldsymbol{\beta}$, that is, $\mathbf{r}$ and $R\mathbf{b}$, and Theil (1963) has proposed that we test the compatibility of the two estimates by the test statistic

$$u_1 = \frac{(\mathbf{r} - R\mathbf{b})'(RS^{-1}R' + \Omega)^{-1}(\mathbf{r} - R\mathbf{b})}{\sigma^2} \tag{3.2.33a}$$

which, when σ^2 is known and $\boldsymbol{\delta} = \mathbf{0}$, has a central chi-square distribution with J degrees of freedom. If $\boldsymbol{\delta} \neq \mathbf{0}$, then u_1 is distributed as a noncentral chi square with noncentrality parameter $\lambda = \boldsymbol{\delta}'(RS^{-1}R' + \Omega)^{-1}\boldsymbol{\delta}/2\sigma^2$. If σ^2 is unknown and replaced by $\hat{\sigma}^2$, the test statistic

$$u_2 = \frac{(\mathbf{r} - R\mathbf{b})'(RS^{-1}R' + \Omega)^{-1}(\mathbf{r} - R\mathbf{b})}{J\hat{\sigma}^2} \tag{3.2.33b}$$

is distributed as an F random variable with J and $(T - K)$ degrees of freedom and noncentrality parameter λ.

3.2.3 Inequality-Restricted Nonsample Information

In this section we recognize that in applied work there exists in many cases nonsample information concerning the nonnegativity or nonpositivity of a parameter or linear combination of parameters, or that a parameter or linear combination of parameters lies between certain upper and lower bounds or that functions are monotonic, convex or quasi convex. Production functions, utility functions, behavioral coefficients, and marginal productivities are obvious examples. When information of this form is available, it can be represented within the context of this section by the following system of linear inequality constraints:

$$R\boldsymbol{\beta} \geq \mathbf{r} \tag{3.2.34a}$$

or

$$R\boldsymbol{\beta} - \boldsymbol{\delta} = \mathbf{r} \tag{3.2.34b}$$

where $\boldsymbol{\delta} \geq \mathbf{0}$. The prior information design matrix R and the real vector $\mathbf{r}$ can accommodate individual or linear combinations of inequality restrictions for a mixed system such as $\mathbf{r}_1 \leq R_1\boldsymbol{\beta} \leq \mathbf{r}_2$ by letting

$$R = \begin{bmatrix} R_1 \\ -R_1 \end{bmatrix} \quad \text{and} \quad \mathbf{r} = \begin{bmatrix} \mathbf{r}_1 \\ -\mathbf{r}_2 \end{bmatrix}$$

3.2.3a The Inequality-Restricted Estimator

Given information of this type, we can combine the information contained in both the sample and inequality restrictions and estimate the unknown K-dimensional coefficient vector $\boldsymbol{\beta}$ by minimizing the quadratic form

$$S(\boldsymbol{\beta}) = (\mathbf{y} - X\boldsymbol{\beta})'(\mathbf{y} - X\boldsymbol{\beta}) = \mathbf{y}'\mathbf{y} - 2\boldsymbol{\beta}'X'\mathbf{y} + \boldsymbol{\beta}'X'X\boldsymbol{\beta} \tag{3.2.35}$$

subject to the system of linear inequality constraints

$$R\boldsymbol{\beta} \geq \mathbf{r} \tag{3.2.36}$$

This is a quadratic programming problem that can be solved by several algorithms [see Judge and Takayama (1966) and Liew (1976)]. Because of the inequality structure of the constraint set, the classical Lagrangian approach that we used in solving for the equality-restricted least squares estimator is no longer applicable. Fortunately we can reduce this problem to a programming formulation by making use of the Kuhn-Tucker conditions (1951) for nonlinear inequality-restricted problems. Within this framework the necessary or optimality conditions can be derived by the direct application of Kuhn-Tucker conditions. The first step is to formulate the Lagrangian function

$$q = (\mathbf{y} - X\boldsymbol{\beta})'(\mathbf{y} - X\boldsymbol{\beta}) + 2\boldsymbol{\lambda}'(\mathbf{r} - R\boldsymbol{\beta}) \tag{3.2.37}$$

where $\boldsymbol{\lambda}$ is a Jth-order vector of Lagrangian multipliers. Given (3.2.37), the Kuhn-Tucker (1951) conditions are

$$\left.\frac{\partial q}{\partial \boldsymbol{\beta}}\right|_{(\mathbf{b}^+,\boldsymbol{\lambda}^+)} = -2X'(\mathbf{y} - X\mathbf{b}^+) - 2R'\boldsymbol{\lambda}^+ = \mathbf{0} \tag{3.2.38a}$$

and

$$\left.\frac{\partial q}{\partial \boldsymbol{\lambda}}\right|_{(\mathbf{b}^+,\boldsymbol{\lambda}^+)} = 2(\mathbf{r} - R\mathbf{b}^+) \leq \mathbf{0} \tag{3.2.38b}$$

along with

$$\boldsymbol{\lambda}^{+\prime}(\mathbf{r} - R\mathbf{b}^+) = 0 \tag{3.2.38c}$$

and

$$\boldsymbol{\lambda}^+ \geq \mathbf{0} \tag{3.2.38d}$$

where $\boldsymbol{\lambda}^+$ is the Kuhn-Tucker vector of multipliers associated with the constraints $R\boldsymbol{\beta} \geq \mathbf{r}$.

If we make use of (3.2.38a) the inequality-restricted least squares estimator may be partially expressed as

$$\begin{aligned} \mathbf{b}^+ &= (X'X)^{-1}X'\mathbf{y} + (X'X)^{-1}R'\boldsymbol{\lambda}^+ \\ &= \mathbf{b} + (X'X)^{-1}R'\boldsymbol{\lambda}^+ \end{aligned} \tag{3.2.39}$$

If *all* of the restrictions are redundant and $R\mathbf{b} \geq \mathbf{r}$, all of the elements of $\boldsymbol{\lambda}^+$ are zero and from (3.2.39) the inequality restricted solution reduces to the least squares solution. Alternatively, if *all* of the restrictions are binding all of the elements of $\boldsymbol{\lambda}^+$ are positive and (3.2.39) reduces to

$$\mathbf{b}^+ = \mathbf{b} + (X'X)^{-1}R'(R(X'X)^{-1}R')^{-1}(\mathbf{r} - R\mathbf{b}) = \mathbf{b}^*$$

the restricted least squares estimator. These results mean that for J independent restrictions, the inequality-restricted estimator is defined by a choice rule that, for each sample of data, selects among at most the 2^J different restricted and unrestricted estimators. For example, if the restrictions are of lower- and upper-bound types, that is, $r_0 \leq R_1\boldsymbol{\beta} \leq r_1$, then $J = 2$ and there are at most $2^J = 4$ possible solutions of which three are feasible:

1. Neither constraint is binding.
2. The lower-bound constraint is binding.
3. The upper-bound constraint is binding.

The fourth case, that both constraints are binding, is excluded as a solution in this situation, since it is not possible unless $r_0 = R_1\boldsymbol{\beta} = r_1$. If the two bounds coincide, $r_0 = r_1$, then there will be only one constraint and the solution will be either the restricted or unrestricted estimator. If we assume that $r_0 \neq r_1$, then as Klemn and Sposito have suggested, the solution can be expressed in the following closed form:

$$\begin{aligned}
\mathbf{b}^+ &= \mathbf{b}, && \text{if } r_0 \leq R_1\mathbf{b} \leq r_1 \\
&= \mathbf{b} + (X'X)^{-1}R_1'(R_1(X'X)^{-1}R_1')^{-1}(r_0 - R_1\mathbf{b}), && \text{if } r_0 > R_1\mathbf{b} \\
&= \mathbf{b} + (X'X)^{-1}R_1'(R_1(X'X)^{-1}R_1')^{-1}(r_1 - R_1\mathbf{b}), && \text{if } r_1 < R_1\mathbf{b}
\end{aligned} \tag{3.2.40}$$

The solution for the Lagrange multipliers is $\lambda_1^+ = \lambda_2^+ = 0$ for case 1; $\lambda_1^+ = (r_0 - R_1\mathbf{b})(R_1(X'X)^{-1}R_1')^{-1} > 0$ and $\lambda_2^+ = 0$ for case 2; and $\lambda_1^+ = 0$ and $\lambda_2^+ = (R_1\mathbf{b} - r_1)(R_1(X'X)^{-1}R_1')^{-1} > 0$ for case 3.

3.2.3b A Framework for Evaluating the Sampling Properties

Given a rule for combining sample and inequality form nonsample information, it is important for decision purposes to know the sampling properties of the inequality-restricted estimator and how its sampling performance compares with other estimators under a squared error loss measure. To examine the sampling properties we use the normal linear statistical model $\mathbf{y} = X\boldsymbol{\beta} + \mathbf{e}$ where the maximum likelihood estimator $\mathbf{b} = (X'X)^{-1}X'\mathbf{y} = S^{-1}X'\mathbf{y}$ is a normally distributed random vector with mean $\boldsymbol{\beta}$, covariance $\sigma^2 S^{-1}$ and risk $E[(\mathbf{b} - \boldsymbol{\beta})'(\mathbf{b} - \boldsymbol{\beta})] = \sigma^2 \operatorname{tr} S^{-1}$. For expository purposes let us consider nonsample information involving a single general linear inequality $\mathbf{c}'\boldsymbol{\beta} \geq r$, where $\mathbf{c}'$ is a $(1 \times K)$ known vector and r is a known scalar. For an evaluation of the sampling properties involving an orthonormal linear statistical model and the case when $\mathbf{c}'$ is a unit vector, see Judge et al. (1980, pp. 82–87) and Judge et al. (1982, pp. 570–574).

If we use the equality restriction $r = \mathbf{c}'\boldsymbol{\beta} = \delta = 0$ and the normal linear statistical model, the exact restricted estimator is $\mathbf{b}^* = \mathbf{b} - S^{-1}\mathbf{c}(\mathbf{c}'S^{-1}\mathbf{c})^{-1}(\mathbf{c}'\mathbf{b} - r)$, where $\mathbf{b}^*$ is a normally distributed vector with mean $E(\mathbf{b}^*) = \boldsymbol{\beta} - S^{-1}\mathbf{c}(\mathbf{c}'S^{-1}\mathbf{c})^{-1}\delta$, covariance

$$\begin{aligned}
E[(\mathbf{b}^* - E(\mathbf{b}^*))(\mathbf{b}^* - E(\mathbf{b}^*))'] &= \sigma^2[S^{-1} - S^{-1}\mathbf{c}(\mathbf{c}'S^{-1}\mathbf{c})^{-1}\mathbf{c}'S^{-1}] \\
&= \sigma^2(S^{-1} - H\mathbf{c}'S^{-1})
\end{aligned}$$

where H is defined in the obvious way and the mean square error or risk matrix $E[(\mathbf{b}^* - \boldsymbol{\beta})(\mathbf{b}^* - \boldsymbol{\beta})'] = \sigma^2(S^{-1} - H\mathbf{c}'S^{-1}) + H\delta\delta'H'$.

For purposes of analysis it is important to note that $S^{-1/2}\mathbf{c}(\mathbf{c}'S^{-1}\mathbf{c})^{-1}\mathbf{c}'S^{-1/2}$ is a symmetric idempotent matrix of rank one and that an orthonormal matrix Q exists such that

$$QS^{-1/2}\mathbf{c}(\mathbf{c}'S^{-1}\mathbf{c})^{-1}\mathbf{c}'S^{-1/2}Q' = \begin{bmatrix} 1 & \mathbf{0}' \\ \mathbf{0} & 0 \end{bmatrix}$$

Furthermore, if we let $\mathbf{h}' = \mathbf{c}'S^{-1/2}Q'$ then

$$\mathbf{h}(\mathbf{h}'\mathbf{h})^{-1}\mathbf{h}' = QS^{-1/2\prime}\mathbf{c}(\mathbf{c}'S^{-1}\mathbf{c})^{-1}\mathbf{c}'S^{-1/2}Q' = \begin{bmatrix} 1 & \mathbf{0}' \\ \mathbf{0} & 0 \end{bmatrix}$$

and

$$\mathbf{h}' = [h_1, \mathbf{h}'_{K-1}] = \mathbf{h}'\mathbf{h}(\mathbf{h}'\mathbf{h})^{-1}\mathbf{h}' = [h_1, \mathbf{h}'_{K-1}] \begin{bmatrix} 1 & \mathbf{0}' \\ \mathbf{0} & 0 \end{bmatrix} = [h_1, \mathbf{0}']$$

Given these results, we may reparameterize the statistical model as follows:

$$\mathbf{y} = XS^{-1/2}Q'QS^{1/2}\boldsymbol{\beta} + \mathbf{e} = Z\boldsymbol{\theta} + \mathbf{e} \tag{3.2.41}$$

where $\boldsymbol{\theta} = QS^{1/2}\boldsymbol{\beta}$, $Z = XS^{-1/2}Q'$, $Z'Z = QS^{-1/2}X'XS^{-1/2}Q' = QQ' = I_K$ and

$$\mathbf{c}'\boldsymbol{\beta} = \mathbf{c}'S^{-1/2}Q'QS^{1/2}\boldsymbol{\beta} = [h_1, \mathbf{0}']\boldsymbol{\theta} = h_1\theta_1 \geq h_1h_1^{-1}r = h_1r_0 \tag{3.2.42a}$$

The hypothesis or restriction error may be represented as

$$h_1\theta_1 + h_1h_1^{-1}\delta = h_1\theta_1 + h_1\delta_0 = h_1h_1^{-1}r = h_1r_0 \tag{3.2.42b}$$

with $-\infty < h_1\delta_0 < \infty$.

The maximum likelihood estimator in the orthonormal $\boldsymbol{\theta}$ space, which uses only sample information is $\mathbf{w} = (Z'Z)^{-1}Z'\mathbf{y} = Z'\mathbf{y}$, and the random vector $\mathbf{w}$ is distributed $N(\boldsymbol{\theta}, \sigma^2 I_K)$ and $\mathbf{b} = S^{-1/2}Q'\mathbf{w}$. The equality-restricted estimator is $\mathbf{w}^* = (r_0, \mathbf{w}'_{(K-1)})$ with mean $(r_0, \boldsymbol{\theta}_{K-1})'$, covariance $\sigma^2 \begin{bmatrix} 0 & \mathbf{0}' \\ \mathbf{0} & I_{K-1} \end{bmatrix}$ and risk $\sigma^2(K - 1) + \delta^2$.

Suppose that instead of the equality restriction, our information is of the form of the inequality $\mathbf{c}'\boldsymbol{\beta} \geq r$ or $\delta = r - \mathbf{c}'\boldsymbol{\beta} = h_1(r_0 - \theta_1) \leq 0$. Assuming h_1 positive and using the information that $r - \mathbf{c}'\boldsymbol{\beta} = r_0 - \theta_1 \leq 0$, the inequality-restricted maximum likelihood estimator, based on the information in (3.2.41) and (3.2.42) is defined by a rule that selects, for each sample of data, between two different estimators: one restricted and the other unrestricted. In the $\boldsymbol{\theta}$ space, the inequality-restricted estimator $\boldsymbol{\theta}^+$ may be expressed as

$$\boldsymbol{\theta}^+ = \begin{bmatrix} I_{(-\infty,r_0)}(w_1)r_0 + I_{[r_0,\infty)}(w_1)w_1 \\ \mathbf{w}_{(K-1)} \end{bmatrix} \tag{3.2.43}$$

where $I_{(a,b)}(w_1)$ is an indicator function that takes the value one when w_1 falls in the interval (a,b) and is zero otherwise.

Using $I_{[r_0,\infty)}(w_1) = 1 - I_{[-\infty,r_0)}(w_1)$, the estimator in (3.2.43) may be rewritten as

$$\boldsymbol{\theta}^+ = \begin{bmatrix} w_1 \\ \mathbf{w}_{(K-1)} \end{bmatrix} - \begin{bmatrix} I_{(-\infty,r_0)}(w_1)(w_1 - r_0) \\ \mathbf{0}_{(K-1)} \end{bmatrix} \tag{3.2.44}$$

and the inequality-restricted estimator $\mathbf{b}^+ = S^{-\frac{1}{2}}Q'\boldsymbol{\theta}^+$ is

$$\mathbf{b}^+ = \mathbf{b} - S^{-1/2}Q' \begin{bmatrix} I_{(-\infty,r)}(\mathbf{c}'\mathbf{b}) & \mathbf{0}' \\ \mathbf{0} & 0 \end{bmatrix} QS^{-1/2}\mathbf{c}(\mathbf{c}'S^{-1}\mathbf{c})^{-1}\mathbf{c}'[\mathbf{b} - S^{-1}\mathbf{c}(\mathbf{c}'S^{-1}\mathbf{c})^{-1}r] \tag{3.2.45}$$

Since $r_0 = \theta_1 + \delta_0$, if we let $u_1 = (w_1 - \theta_1)\,\sigma^{-1}$, a normal random variable with mean zero and variance one, then we rewrite (3.2.44) as

$$\boldsymbol{\theta}^+ = \begin{bmatrix} w_1 \\ \mathbf{w}_{(K-1)} \end{bmatrix} - \begin{bmatrix} I_{(-\infty,\delta_0\sigma^{-1})}(u_1)(\sigma(u_1) - \delta_0) \\ \mathbf{0}_{(K-1)} \end{bmatrix} = \begin{bmatrix} w_1 - d \\ \mathbf{w}_{(K-1)} \end{bmatrix} \tag{3.2.46}$$

where $d = I_{(-\infty,\delta_0\sigma^{-1})}(u_1)(\sigma(u_1) - \delta_0)$. In evaluating the mean and risk of (3.2.46), the following lemmas taken from Judge and Yancey (1978) are useful.

Lemma 1 If u is a normal random variable with mean zero and variance 1, then
if $\delta_0 \leq 0$, $E[I_{(-\infty,\delta\sigma^{-1})}(u)\delta_0] = (\delta_0/2)P(\chi^2_{(1)} \geq \delta_0^2\sigma^{-2})$;
if $\delta_0 > 0$, $E[I_{(-\infty,\delta\sigma^{-1})}(u)\delta_0] = \delta_0 - (\delta_0/2)P(\chi^2_{(1)} \geq \delta_0^2\sigma^{-2})$.

Lemma 2 If u is a normal random variable with mean zero and variance 1, then
$E[I_{(-\infty,\delta_0\sigma^{-1})}(u)u] = -(1/\sqrt{2\pi})P(\chi^2_{(2)} \geq \delta_0^2\sigma^{-2})$,

Lemma 3 If $I_{(-\infty,\delta_0\sigma^{-1})}(u)$ and u are as defined above, then:
If $\delta_0 \leq 0$, $E[a_1 I_{(-\infty,\delta_0\sigma^{-1})}(u)u^2] = a_1(\frac{1}{2})P(\chi^2_{(3)} \geq \delta_0^2/\sigma^2)$.
If $\delta_0 > 0$, $E[a_1 I_{(-\infty,\delta_0\sigma^{-1})}(u)u^2] = a_1 - a_1(\frac{1}{2})P(\chi^2_{(3)} \geq \delta_0^2/\sigma^2)$.

In our notation $\chi^2_{(\cdot)}$ is a chi-square random variable with $(\cdot)$ degrees of freedom.

3.2.3c The Mean and Risk of the Inequality-Restricted Estimator

Using these lemmas the mean of the K parameter inequality-restricted estimator (3.2.46) for $\delta_0 \leq 0$ is

$$E[\boldsymbol{\theta}^+] = \begin{bmatrix} \theta_1 \\ \boldsymbol{\theta}_{(K-1)} \end{bmatrix} + \begin{bmatrix} (\sigma/\sqrt{2\pi})P(\chi^2_{(2)} \geq \delta_0^2\sigma^{-2}) + \delta_0 2^{-1}P(\chi^2_{(1)} \geq \delta_0^2\sigma^{-2}) \\ \mathbf{0}_{(K-1)} \end{bmatrix} \tag{3.2.47}$$

and for $\delta_0 > 0$,

$$E[\boldsymbol{\theta}^+] = \begin{bmatrix} \theta_1 \\ \boldsymbol{\theta}_{(K-1)} \end{bmatrix} + \begin{bmatrix} (\sigma/\sqrt{2\pi})P(\chi^2_{(2)} \geq \delta_0^2\sigma^{-2}) + \delta_0 - \delta_0 2^{-1}P(\chi^2_{(1)} \geq \delta_0^2\sigma^{-2}) \\ \mathbf{0}_{(K-1)} \end{bmatrix} \tag{3.2.48}$$

Consequently, for $-\infty < \delta_0 \leq 0$, as the vector $\delta_0 \rightarrow -\infty$, the $E[\boldsymbol{\theta}^+] \rightarrow \boldsymbol{\theta}$. Alternatively, as $\delta_0 \rightarrow 0$ the

$$E[\boldsymbol{\theta}^+] \rightarrow \begin{bmatrix} \theta_1 \\ \boldsymbol{\theta}_{(K-1)} \end{bmatrix} + \begin{bmatrix} (\sigma/\sqrt{2\pi}) \\ \mathbf{0}_{(K-1)} \end{bmatrix} \tag{3.2.49}$$

Finally for $0 \leq \delta_0 < \infty$ as $\delta_0 \rightarrow \infty$, which implies $r_0 \rightarrow \infty$, the $E[\theta_1^+]$ is asymptotic to the line $f(\delta_0) = \theta_1 + \delta_0$, or in other words asymptotic to the mean of the *equality*-restricted estimator $\boldsymbol{\theta}^*$. The characteristics of the bias function are shown in Figure 3.4.

In evaluating the sampling performance of the inequality-restricted estimator $\mathbf{b}^+$, we use the weighted risk function

$$\rho(\boldsymbol{\beta},\mathbf{b}^+) = E[L(\boldsymbol{\beta},\mathbf{b}^+)] = E[(\mathbf{b}^+ - \boldsymbol{\beta})'W(\mathbf{b}^+ - \boldsymbol{\beta})] \tag{3.2.50}$$

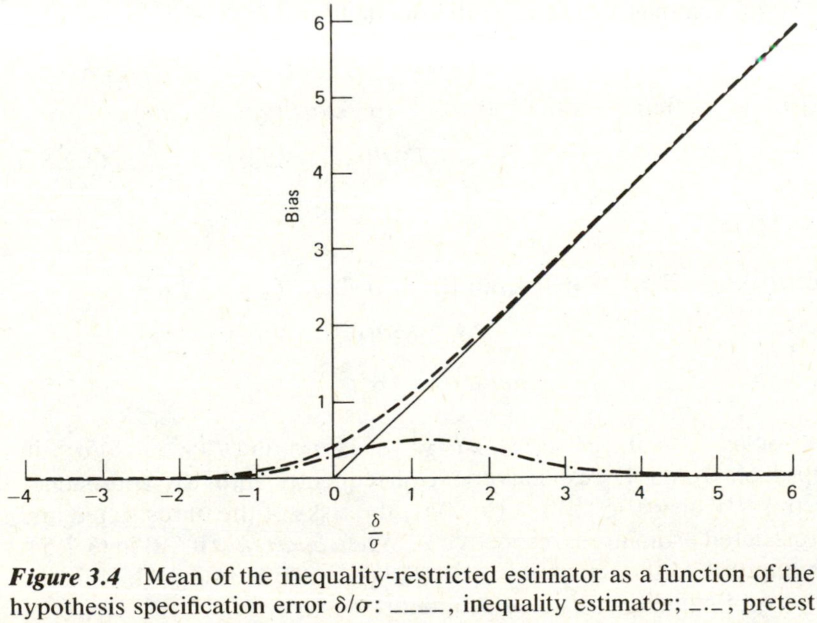

Figure 3.4 Mean of the inequality-restricted estimator as a function of the restriction hypothesis specification error δ/σ: ____, inequality estimator; _._, pretest estimator.

where W is a known positive definite weight matrix. Analysis of the arbitrarily *weighted* loss function for $\boldsymbol{\beta}$ implies the following arbitrarily weighted risk function for $\boldsymbol{\theta}$:

$$
\begin{aligned}
E[(\mathbf{b}^+ - \boldsymbol{\beta})'W(\mathbf{b}^+ - \boldsymbol{\beta})] &= E[(\boldsymbol{\theta}^+ - \boldsymbol{\theta})'QS^{-1/2}WS^{-1/2}Q'(\boldsymbol{\theta}^+ - \boldsymbol{\theta})] \\
&= E[(\boldsymbol{\theta}^+ - \boldsymbol{\theta})'A(\boldsymbol{\theta}^+ - \boldsymbol{\theta})] \\
&= \sigma^2 \mathrm{tr}(S^{-1}W) - 2E[u_1 a_1 d] - 2E[\mathbf{u}'_{(K-1)}\mathbf{a}_3 d] + E[d^2 a_1]
\end{aligned}
\tag{3.2.51}
$$

where, in line with the partitioned parameter space, $A = \begin{bmatrix} a_1 & \mathbf{a}_3' \\ \mathbf{a}_3 & A_2 \end{bmatrix}$. Consequently, the inequality-restricted estimator may be evaluated either in terms of the $\boldsymbol{\beta}$ or $\boldsymbol{\theta}$ space by using the appropriately weighted risk function.

Since $(u_1, \mathbf{u}'_{(K-1)})$ is a vector of *independent* standard normal random variables and remembering $d = I_{(-\infty,\delta_0\sigma^{-1})}(u_1)(\sigma(u_1) - \delta_0)$, the risk function $\rho(\mathbf{b}^+,\boldsymbol{\beta})$ becomes

$$
\begin{aligned}
E[(\mathbf{b}^+ - \boldsymbol{\beta})'W(\mathbf{b}^+ - \boldsymbol{\beta})] &= \rho(\mathbf{b},\boldsymbol{\beta}) - 2\sigma^2 E[a_1 I_{(-\infty,\delta_0\sigma^{-1})}(u_1)u_1^2] \\
&\quad + 2E[\delta_0 a_1 I_{(-\infty,\delta_0\sigma^{-1})}(u_1)u_1] \\
&\quad + \sigma^2 E[I_{(-\infty,\delta_0\sigma^{-1})}(u_1)u_1^2 a_1] \\
&\quad - 2E[I_{(-\infty,\delta_0\sigma^{-1})}(u_1)u_1]a_1\delta_0 \\
&\quad + E[I_{(-\infty,\delta_0\sigma^{-1})}(u_1)]\delta_0^2 a_1
\end{aligned}
\tag{3.2.52}
$$

Making use of Lemmas 1, 2, and 3, the inequality-restricted estimator risk function may be expressed, when $\delta_0 \leq 0$, as

$$
\begin{aligned}
E[(\mathbf{b}^+ - \boldsymbol{\beta})'W(\mathbf{b}^+ - \boldsymbol{\beta})] &= \rho(\mathbf{b},\boldsymbol{\beta}) - (\sigma^2/2)a_1 P(\chi^2_{(3)} \geq \delta_0^2/\sigma^2) \\
&\quad + a_1(\delta_0^2/2)P(\chi^2_{(1)} \geq \delta_0^2/\sigma^2)
\end{aligned}
\tag{3.2.53}
$$

and when $\delta_0 > 0$ as

$$
\begin{aligned}
E[(\mathbf{b}^+ - \boldsymbol{\beta})'W(\mathbf{b}^+ - \boldsymbol{\beta})] &= \rho(\mathbf{b},\boldsymbol{\beta}) + (\sigma^2/2)a_1 P(\chi^2_{(3)} \geq \delta_0^2/\sigma^2) \\
&\quad - (a_1/2)\delta_0^2 P(\chi^2_{(1)} \geq \delta_0^2/\sigma^2) \\
&\quad + a_1(\delta_0^2 - \sigma^2)
\end{aligned}
\tag{3.2.54}
$$

As $\delta_0 \to -\infty$ or as $\delta_0 \to 0$, the terms $\delta_0^2 P(\chi^2_{(\cdot)} \geq \delta_0^2/\sigma^2)$ and $P(\chi^2_{(\cdot)} \geq \delta_0^2/\sigma^2)$ in (3.2.53) approach 0 and 1, respectively. Consequently, $\rho(\mathbf{b}^+,\boldsymbol{\beta})$ approaches $\rho(\mathbf{b},\boldsymbol{\beta}) = \sigma^2 \mathrm{tr}\, S^{-1}W$ or $\sigma^2\mathrm{tr}(S^{-1}W) - (\sigma^2/2)a_1$, the risks of the unrestricted and inequality-restricted estimators, respectively. When $\delta_0 \to \infty$, $\rho(\mathbf{b}^+,\boldsymbol{\beta})$ in (3.2.54) becomes asymptotic to the line $f(\delta_0) = \sigma^2\mathrm{tr}(S^{-1}W) - (\sigma^2 - \delta_0^2)a_1$, which is the risk of the general equality-restricted estimator.

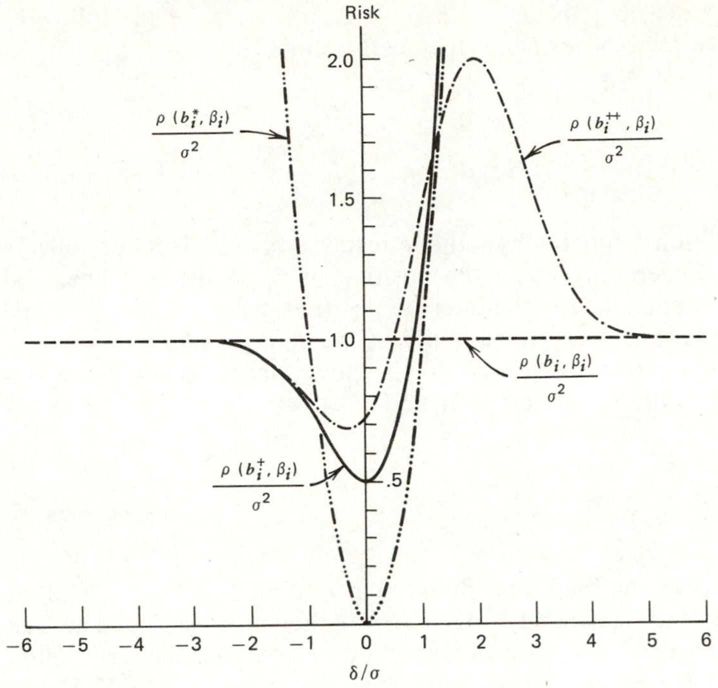

Figure 3.5 Risk functions for the maximum likelihood, equality-restricted, inequality-restricted, and inequality-pretest estimators.

If the *direction* of the inequality is correct (i.e., $\delta_0 < 0$), the risk is, over the range of the parameter space, equal to or less than the maximum likelihood risk $\sigma^2 \text{tr}(S^{-1}W)$. Alternatively, if the *direction* of the inequality is incorrect (i.e., $\delta_0 \geq 0$), then the inequality estimator risk is uniformly inferior to the equality estimator risk, and as δ_0 goes to infinity the risk function is unbounded.

Risk functions for the equality-restricted **b***, inequality-restricted $\mathbf{b}^+$, and maximum likelihood **b** estimators are given in Figure 3.5. In plotting the risks the functions have been standardized so that the maximum likelihood risk is one. These results indicate that when the direction of the inequality is correct, the inequality-restricted estimator offers a viable and, under squared error loss, superior rule to the conventional estimators using only sample information.

3.2.3d Hypothesis Testing

In applied work the underlying sampling process by which the data are generated is seldom known and thus there is uncertainty concerning the appropriate statistical sampling model. Given this uncertainty, for example, about the unknown parameter vector $\boldsymbol{\beta}$, the investigator usually procedes by specifying a linear hypothesis and then makes statistical tests concerning the compatibility of the sample information and the linear hypotheses. As a basis for developing a hypothesis testing framework with inequality hypotheses and a one-sided interval estimator, consider the orthonormal version of the linear statistical model where $X'X = I_K$ and $\mathbf{b} \sim N(\boldsymbol{\beta}, \sigma^2 I_K)$. Since the elements of **b** are normally and independently distributed, that is, $b_i \sim N(\beta_i, \sigma^2)$, consider the following null and alternative hypotheses about the coefficient β_i:

$$H_0\colon \beta_i \geq r_i$$
$$H_a\colon \beta_i < r_i \tag{3.2.55}$$

In contrast to traditional equality hypothesis testing, this specification reflects the investigators' uncertainty about the position of β_i on the real line, and postulates that β_i is contained in the interval $r_i \leq \beta_i < \infty$.

As a basis for checking the compatibility of the sample information and a linear inequality hypothesis for β_i, when σ^2 is known, let us follow Judge and Yancey (1978) and consider the test statistic

$$\frac{b_i - r_i}{\sigma} = u_i \tag{3.2.56}$$

which is distributed as a normal random variable with mean $\delta_i/\sigma = (r_i - \beta_i)/\sigma$ and variance 1. If it is assumed that $\delta_i = r_i - \beta_i = 0$, then u_i is a standard normal (0, 1) random variable and the test structure could be formulated in terms of δ_i, with $H_0\colon \delta_i \leq 0$ and $H_a\colon \delta_i > 0$. Consequently, by using test statistic (3.2.56) we make use of the following test mechanism.

1. Reject the hypothesis if $(b_i - r_i)/\sigma = u_i < c_i$ and use the maximum likelihood estimator b_i, where c_i is the critical value of the test from the standard normal table.
2. Accept the hypothesis if $u_i = (b_i - r_i)/\sigma \geq c_i$ and use the inequality-restricted estimator $b_i^+ = I_{(-\infty, r_i)}(b_i)r_i + I_{[r_i, \infty)}(b_i)b_i$.

By accepting the null hypothesis H_0, we take b_i^+ as the estimate of β_i and by rejecting H_0, the maximum likelihood estimate b_i is used. If the variance σ^2 is unknown the central t distribution with $(T - K)$ degrees of freedom is used as a basis for determining the critical value c_i for a given α level of the test for the one-sided likelihood ratio test.

If two or more inequality hypotheses are involved, a more satisfactory approach is to test the entire set of inequality hypotheses simultaneously. In this context, a sequence of one-at-a-time tests leaves unknown the α level of the joint result.

As an illustration of the problem of joint hypotheses, let us follow Yancey, Judge, and Bock (1981) and suppose that the hypothesis is $H_0\colon \beta_1 \geq 0$ and $\beta_2 \geq 0$ and the alternative hypothesis H_a, is that at least one $\beta_i < 0$. Since we are working with the orthonormal linear statistical model, the remaining $K - 2$ elements of $\boldsymbol{\beta}$ can be ignored. With unknown variance the likelihood ratio test is: reject H_0 if

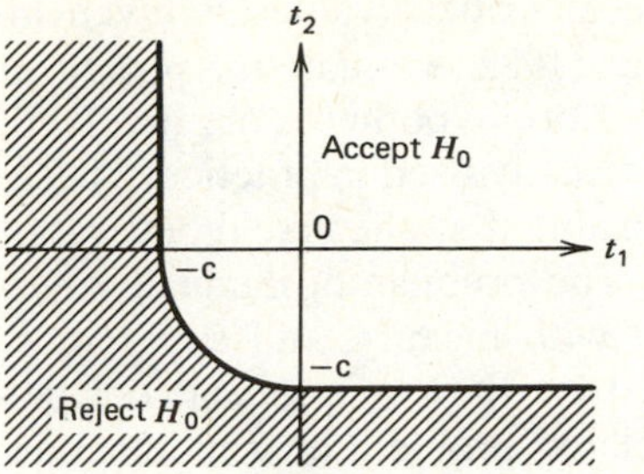

Figure 3.6 Acceptance and rejection regions for two inequality hypotheses.

$$t_1^2 \geq c^2/2 \quad \text{if} \quad t_2 > 0, \quad t_1 < 0, \tag{1}$$
$$t_2^2 \geq c^2/2 \quad \text{if} \quad t_1 > 0, \quad t_2 < 0, \tag{2}$$
$$t_1^2 + t_2^2 \geq c^2/2 \quad \text{if} \quad t_1 < 0 \quad \text{and} \quad t_2 < 0, \tag{3}$$

where $t_i = b_i/\hat{\sigma}$ is distributed as a central t with ν degrees of freedom, the b_i are elements of $\mathbf{b}$, and $c^2/2 \geq 0$ is the critical value of the test.

The acceptance and rejection regions for H_0 are shown in Figure 3.6. Given α, c^2 is determined by noting that t_1 and t_2 have a bivariate t distribution with $\nu = T - K$ degrees of freedom, and that in the second and fourth orthants, moving clockwise from the positive orthant $P(t_i \leq c_i, t_j \geq 0) = (\frac{1}{4})P(F_{(1,T-K)} \geq c^2)$, where $t_i^2 = F_{(1,T-K)}$ is distributed as an F random variable with one and $(T - K)$ degrees of freedom. To obtain the probability of rejection in the southwest orthant, we note that

$$P(t_1^2 + t_2^2 > c^2, t_1 \leq 0, t_2 \leq 0) = \tfrac{1}{4}P\left(F_{(2,T-K)} \geq \frac{c^2}{2}\right)$$

Consequently, given α for the joint test, the c^2 is determined such that

$$\alpha = \tfrac{1}{2}P(F_{(1,T-K)} \geq c^2) + \tfrac{1}{4}P\left(F_{(2,T-K)} \geq \frac{c^2}{2}\right)$$

If the variance is known, the t's and F's are replaced by standard normal and $\chi^2_{(\cdot)}$ random variables.

One-sided confidence regions can be constructed that are counterparts to the inequality hypotheses using the same distribution theory used for hypothesis testing. For example, if $\boldsymbol{\beta}$ is a (2×1) vector and $\mathbf{b}$ is $(0.4, 0.7)'$ and $\hat{\sigma} = 1.1$, from a sample of size 18, a one-sided 95% confidence region with $c^2/2 = 2.46$ is the union of the regions $\beta_1 \geq b_1 - c\,\hat{\sigma} = -1.33$ for $\beta_2 > b_2$, $\beta_2 \geq -1.03$ for $\beta_1 \geq b_1$ and $(\beta_1 - 0.4)^2 + (\beta_2 - 0.7)^2 \leq 2.98$, when $\beta_1 < b_1$ and $\beta_2 < b_2$. If Figure 3.6 were relabeled with (b_1, b_2) as the origin, t_1 as β_1, t_2 as β_2, the complement of the critical region would be the one-sided confidence region just described. As Yancey, Judge, and Bock (1981) note, the inequality hypothesis testing results can be generalized to the case involving joint testing of three or more hypotheses. Also, the test extends to include combinations of inequality and equality hypotheses in a single test. An abridged table of critical values is given in Yancey, et al. (1981). Yancey, Bohrer, and Judge (1982) evaluate the power of the inequality likelihood ratio tests when two or more hypotheses are involved and compare its power with that of other tests normally used in practice. These power function evaluations lead to the conclusion that the likelihood ratio inequality test is best among those considered. The problem of inequality hypothesis testing when $\mathbf{b}$ is multivariate normal with mean $\boldsymbol{\beta}$ and covariance matrix $\sigma^2\boldsymbol{\Phi}$, with $\boldsymbol{\Phi}$ known, has been analyzed by Barlow et al. (1972) and Gourieroux, Holly, and Monfort (1982). The related problem of simultaneous confidence bounds has been studied by Bohrer and Francis (1972). The analysis of more general equality and inequality constraints is treated in Chapter 6.

3.3 PRETEST ESTIMATORS

In much of the work concerned with measurement in the sciences, there is uncertainty as to the statistical model that best captures the most significant features of the process being modeled. Thus, there is uncertainty as to the agreement between the stochastic sampling model that is consistent with the way the data were generated and the statistical model that is employed for estimation and inference purposes. This situation is especially acute in the social sciences, where many plausible or theoretically acceptable models exist to describe or explain human behavior and much of the sample data are nonexperimentally or passively generated. Just as few economic variables are free of measurement error and few economic relations are nonstochastic, few statistical models are specified correctly and many of these specification errors imply bias-variance trade-offs when the least squares rule is used.

For example, consider the problem of an investigator who has a single data set and wants to estimate the parameters of a linear model that are known to lie in a high-dimensional parameter space Θ_1. However, prior information may exist suggesting that the relationship may be characterized by a lower-dimensional parameter space $\Theta_2 \subset \Theta_1$. Under this uncertainty, if the Θ_1-dimensional parameter space is estimated by least squares, the result, from the possibly overspecified model, will be unbiased but have large variance and thus may make a poor showing in terms of mean square error. Alternatively, the Θ_2-dimensional parameter space may incorrectly specify the statistical model and thus if estimated by least squares will be biased; this bias may or may not outweigh the reduction in variance if evaluated in a mean square error context. If this uncertainty about the dimension of the parameter space is represented in the form of general linear hypotheses, this leads to pretest estimators whose sampling performance over a range of statistical models and hypothesis designs we discuss in the following sections.

3.3.1 The Conventional Pretest Estimator

In applied work when there is uncertainty about the proper equality restrictions, hypotheses are specified in the form of (3.2.1) and one proceeds by making tests of the compatibility of the sample information **b** and the linear hypotheses $R\boldsymbol{\beta} = \mathbf{r}$. That is, questions such as the inclusion or exclusion of a variable or the choice of functional form are introduced in the form of general linear restrictions or hypotheses and then conventional test procedures are used for decision or choice purposes.

To see the sampling implications of this test mechanism, again let us for expository purposes consider the orthonormal statistical model where $X'X = I_K$, a hypothesis design matrix of the form $R = I_K$ and the likelihood ratio test procedures (Section 2.1.3b) of Chapter 2. To test the null hypothesis that $\boldsymbol{\beta} = \mathbf{r}$ against the hypothesis $\boldsymbol{\beta} \neq \mathbf{r}$, it is conventional to use the test statistic

$$u = \frac{(\mathbf{b} - \mathbf{r})'(\mathbf{b} - \mathbf{r})}{K\hat{\sigma}^2} \tag{3.3.1}$$

where u is distributed as a central F random variable with K and $(T - K)$ degrees of freedom if the hypotheses (restrictions) are correct and $\hat{\sigma}^2$ is the estimated scale parameter from the unrestricted model. Of course, if the restrictions are incorrect and $E[\mathbf{b} - \mathbf{r}] = (\boldsymbol{\beta} - \mathbf{r}) \neq \mathbf{0}$, then u (3.3.1) is distributed as a noncentral F with noncentrality parameter $\lambda = (\boldsymbol{\beta} - \mathbf{r})'(\boldsymbol{\beta} - \mathbf{r})/2\sigma^2 = \boldsymbol{\delta}'\boldsymbol{\delta}/2\sigma^2$. However, since the noncentrality parameter is unknown when testing, the hypotheses are assumed correct and the central F distribution is used as the null distribution. Consequently, the null hypothesis is rejected if $u \geq F^{\alpha}_{(K,T-K)} = c$, where c is determined for a given level of the test α by

$$\int_c^{\infty} dF_{(K,T-K)} = P[F_{(K,T-K)} \geq c] = \alpha$$

By accepting the null hypothesis, we take the restricted least squares estimator $\mathbf{b}^*$ as our estimate of $\boldsymbol{\beta}$; by rejecting the null hypothesis $\boldsymbol{\beta} - \mathbf{r} = \boldsymbol{\delta} = \mathbf{0}$, we use the unrestricted least squares estimator **b**. Thus the estimator that results is dependent on a preliminary test of significance and the estimator used by an applied worker is therefore of the following form.

$$\hat{\hat{\boldsymbol{\beta}}} = \begin{cases} \mathbf{b}^* & \text{if } u < c \\ \mathbf{b} & \text{if } u \geq c \end{cases} \tag{3.3.2}$$

Alternatively, the estimator may be written as

$$\begin{aligned} \hat{\hat{\boldsymbol{\beta}}} &= I_{(0,c)}(u)\mathbf{b}^* + I_{[c,\infty)}(u)\mathbf{b} \\ &= I_{(0,c)}(u)\mathbf{b}^* + [1 - I_{(0,c)}(u)]\mathbf{b} \\ &= \mathbf{b} - I_{(0,c)}(u)(\mathbf{b} - \mathbf{b}^*) = \mathbf{b} - I_{(0,c)}(u)(\mathbf{b} - \mathbf{r}) \end{aligned} \tag{3.3.3}$$

where $I_{(0,c)}(u)$ and $I_{[c,\infty)}(u)$ are indicator functions that take the values $I_{(0,c)}(u) = 1$ and $I_{[c,\infty)}(u) = 0$ if the argument u falls within the interval zero to c and $I_{(0,c)}(u) = 0$ and $I_{[c,\infty)}(u) = 1$ when $u \geq c$. Therefore, in a repeated sampling context, the data, the linear hypotheses, and the level of significance all determine the combination of the two estimators that are chosen on the average. From an applied standpoint one thing that becomes apparent from the above conditions is the impact of the level of significance on the outcome for the pretest estimator. If the level of significance α is equal to zero, then the pretest estimator in terms of (3.3.3) is

$$\hat{\hat{\boldsymbol{\beta}}} = I_{[0,\infty)}(u)\mathbf{b}^* + I_{(\cdot)}(u)\mathbf{b} = \mathbf{b}^* \tag{3.3.4}$$

and the restricted estimator is always chosen. Alternatively, if the level of significance α is equal to one, then the pretest estimator is

$$\hat{\hat{\boldsymbol{\beta}}} = I_{(\cdot)}(u)\mathbf{b}^* + I_{[0,\infty)}(u)\mathbf{b} = \mathbf{b} \tag{3.3.5}$$

and the least squares estimator is always chosen. *Therefore the choice of α, which is usually made in a cavalier way in applied work, has a crucial role to play in determining the sampling performance of the pretest estimator.*

3.3.1a Sampling Performance

Since this search-type estimator is used in much applied work, the sampling properties of the pretest estimator are of paramount importance. This conclusion is in contrast to the sampling properties most often discussed or alluded to in applied papers, namely the properties of the least squares estimator or one of its conventional variants.

Given the importance of the result, let us investigate the sampling performance of the pretest estimator under the squared error loss criterion. The risk function may be written using (3.3.3) and following Judge and Bock (1978, p. 70) as

$$\begin{aligned}
\rho(\boldsymbol{\beta}, \hat{\hat{\boldsymbol{\beta}}}) &= E[(\hat{\hat{\boldsymbol{\beta}}} - \boldsymbol{\beta})'(\hat{\hat{\boldsymbol{\beta}}} - \boldsymbol{\beta})] \\
&= E[(\mathbf{b} - \boldsymbol{\beta} - I_{(0,c)}(u)(\mathbf{b} - \mathbf{r}))'(\mathbf{b} - \boldsymbol{\beta} - I_{(0,c)}(u)(\mathbf{b} - \mathbf{r}))] \\
&= E[(\mathbf{b} - \boldsymbol{\beta})'(\mathbf{b} - \boldsymbol{\beta})] - E[I_{(0,c)}(u)(\mathbf{b} - \boldsymbol{\beta})'(\mathbf{b} - \boldsymbol{\beta})] + E[I_{(0,c)}(u)]\boldsymbol{\delta}'\boldsymbol{\delta} \\
&= \sigma^2 K + (2\boldsymbol{\delta}'\boldsymbol{\delta} - \sigma^2 K)P\left[\frac{\chi^2_{(K+2,\lambda)}}{\chi^2_{(T-K)}} \leq \frac{cK}{T-K}\right] \\
&\quad -\boldsymbol{\delta}'\boldsymbol{\delta}P\left[\frac{\chi^2_{(K+4,\lambda)}}{\chi^2_{(T-K)}} \leq \frac{cK}{T-K}\right]
\end{aligned} \tag{3.3.6}$$

or compactly

$$\rho(\boldsymbol{\beta}, \hat{\hat{\boldsymbol{\beta}}}) = \sigma^2 K + (2\boldsymbol{\delta}'\boldsymbol{\delta} - \sigma^2 K)l(2) - \boldsymbol{\delta}'\boldsymbol{\delta}l(4)$$

where $1 > l(2) > l(4) > 0$. From the risk function (3.3.6) the following results are clear.

1. If the restrictions are correct and $\boldsymbol{\delta} = \mathbf{0}$, the risk of the pretest estimator is $\sigma^2 K[1 - l(2)]$, where $1 > (1 - l(2)) > 0$ for $0 < c < \infty$. Therefore, the pretest estimator risk is less than that of the least squares estimator at the origin, and the decrease in risk depends on the level of significance α and correspondingly the critical value of the test c.
2. As the hypothesis error $\boldsymbol{\beta} - \mathbf{r} = \boldsymbol{\delta}$ and thus $\boldsymbol{\delta}'\boldsymbol{\delta}/2\sigma^2$ increases and approaches infinity, $l(\cdot)$ and $\boldsymbol{\delta}'\boldsymbol{\delta}l(\cdot)$ approach zero. Therefore, the risk of the pretest estimator approaches $\sigma^2 K$, the risk of the unrestricted least squares estimator.
3. As the hypothesis error grows, the risk of the pretest estimator increases, obtains a maximum after crossing the risk of the least squares estimator, and then monotonically decreases to approach $\sigma^2 K$, the risk of the least squares estimator.
4. The pretest estimator risk function defined on the $\boldsymbol{\delta}'\boldsymbol{\delta}/2\sigma^2$ parameter space crosses the risk function of the least squares estimator within the bounds $K/4 \le \boldsymbol{\delta}'\boldsymbol{\delta}/2\sigma^2 \le K/2$.

The sampling characteristics of the preliminary test estimator are summarized in Figure 3.7.

From these results we see that the pretest estimator does well relative to the least squares estimator if the hypotheses are correctly specified. However, in the $\boldsymbol{\delta}'\boldsymbol{\delta}/2\sigma^2$ parameter space representing the range of hypothesis errors, the pretest estimator is inferior to the least squares estimator over an infinite range of the parameter space. As also depicted in Figure 3.7, there is a range of the parameter space where the pretest estimator has risk that is inferior to (greater than) both the unrestricted and restricted least squares estimators. No one estimator depicted in Figure 3.7 dominates the other competitors. In addition,

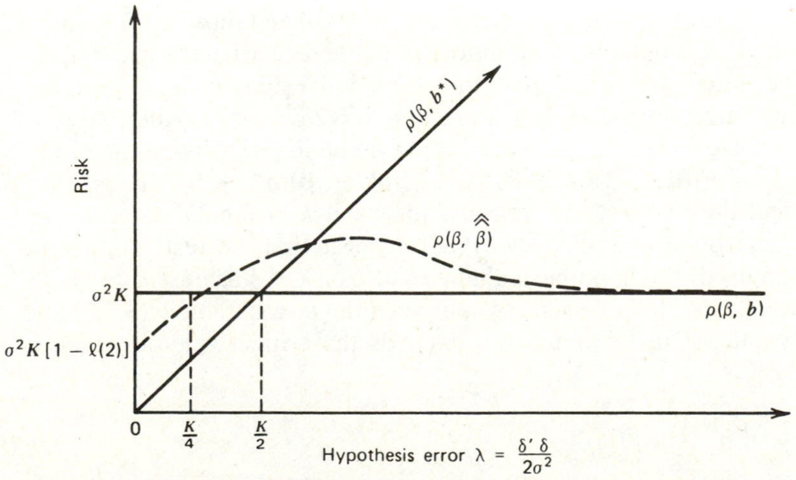

Figure 3.7 Risk functions for the least squares and restricted least squares estimators and typical risk function for the pretest estimator.

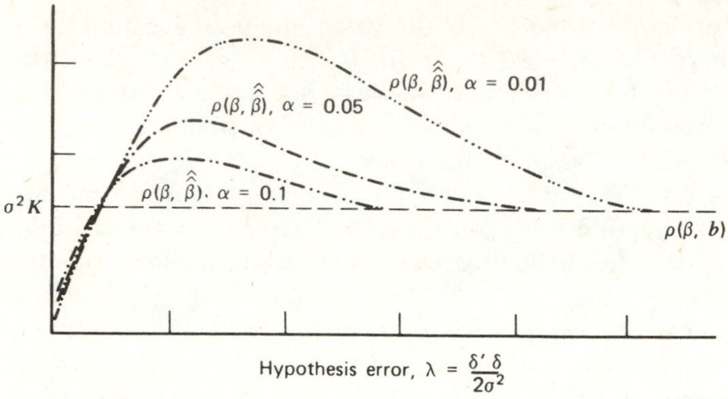

Figure 3.8 Impact of choice of the critical value of the test on the value of the pretest risk function.

in applied problems one seldom knows the hypothesis errors and thus the correct λ. Consequently, the choice of the estimator is unresolved.

Let us note again that the form of the pretest estimator in (3.3.3) implies, for evaluation purposes, the probabilities of ratios of random variables $l(2)$ and $l(4)$ being less than a constant that depends on the critical value of the test c or α, the level of statistical significance. Thus, as $\alpha \to 0$, the probabilities $l(\cdot) \to 1$ and the risk of the pretest estimator approaches that of the restricted least squares estimator $\mathbf{b}^*$. In contrast, as $\alpha \to 1$ and thus $l(\cdot)$ approaches zero, the risk of the pretest estimator approaches that of the least squares estimator $\mathbf{b}$. The impact of the choice of c or α, which has a crucial impact on the performance of the pretest estimator, is portrayed in Figure 3.8.

3.3.1b Mean Squared Error Norm

In traditional hypothesis testing the assumption is made that the hypotheses are correct and the tests are based on the hypothesis $\boldsymbol{\delta} = \mathbf{0}$ and thus $\lambda = \boldsymbol{\delta}'\boldsymbol{\delta}/2\sigma^2 = 0$. In comparing risk functions of the unrestricted and restricted least squares estimators, we noted in (3.2.12) that the restricted estimator was superior, under a squared error loss criterion when $\lambda = \boldsymbol{\delta}'\boldsymbol{\delta}/2\sigma^2 \leq K/2$. Alternatively, under the generalized mean square criterion we noted in (3.2.17) that the difference matrix $\Delta = E[(\mathbf{b} - \boldsymbol{\beta})(\mathbf{b} - \boldsymbol{\beta})'] - E[(\mathbf{b}^* - \boldsymbol{\beta})(\mathbf{b}^* - \boldsymbol{\beta})']$ is positive semidefinite and the restricted estimator superior if $\lambda = \boldsymbol{\delta}'\boldsymbol{\delta}/2\sigma^2 \leq \frac{1}{2}$. Therefore, Toro-Vizcarrondo and Wallace (1968) suggest that we test, depending on the criterion used, the hypothesis that $\lambda \leq K/2$ or $\lambda \leq \frac{1}{2}$ against $\lambda > (\cdot)$. To use one of these tests, the investigator computes the test statistic u (3.3.1) and rejects the hypothesis if the value of u exceeds the critical value c which is determined by

$$\int_c^\infty dF_{(K,T-K,\lambda=K/2 \text{ or } \lambda=1/2)} = \alpha$$

where α is the significance level of the test and $F_{(K,T-K,\lambda=(\cdot))}$ denotes a noncentral F distribution with noncentrality parameter $\lambda = \frac{1}{2}$ or $\lambda = K/2$. This test mechanism again leads to a preliminary test estimator that has the general characteristics of the traditional pretest estimator that was previously discussed.

3.3.1c The Optimal Level of Significance

Finally, let us note again that regardless of whether one applies the traditional or Toro-Vizcarrondo and Wallace tests the selection of the critical value c or α, the level of the test, is critical to determining the sampling properties of the resulting two-stage estimators. Since the investigator is unsure of the degree of hypothesis specification error, and thus the appropriate point in the λ parameter space for evaluating risk, the best of worlds would be to have a rule that mixes the unrestricted and restricted estimators so as to minimize risk regardless of the relevant specification error $\lambda = \boldsymbol{\delta}'\boldsymbol{\delta}/2\sigma^2$. This means that the risk function traced out by the cross-hatched area in Figure 3.9 is relevant. Unfortunately, the risk of the pretest estimator, regardless of the choice of α, is always equal to or greater than the minimum risk function for some range of the parameter space. Given this result, one criterion for choosing the α level might be to choose the critical value c that would minimize the maximum regret for not being on the risk function reflected by the boundary of the shaded area. Sawa and Hiromatsu considered this criterion and obtained minimax regret critical values for the pretest estimator; for example, for a single hypothesis an optimum value of c is 1.8. Brook, using an alternative regret function, developed optimal minimax regret critical values of c, for multiple hypotheses, of around 2. Another alternative criterion for choosing α is to minimize the average regret over the whole parameter space; from work of Toyoda and Wallace, under this criterion, the least squares estimator is always chosen unless the number of hypotheses is 5 or more. When the number of linear hypotheses is greater than 5, a critical value of $c = 2.0$ is suggested.

Alternatively, if the investigator has some information over and above the uniform probability density function for λ used by Toyoda and Wallace, then the minimum average risk criterion might form the basis for making a choice of the optimum α or c. This topic will be considered further when we discuss

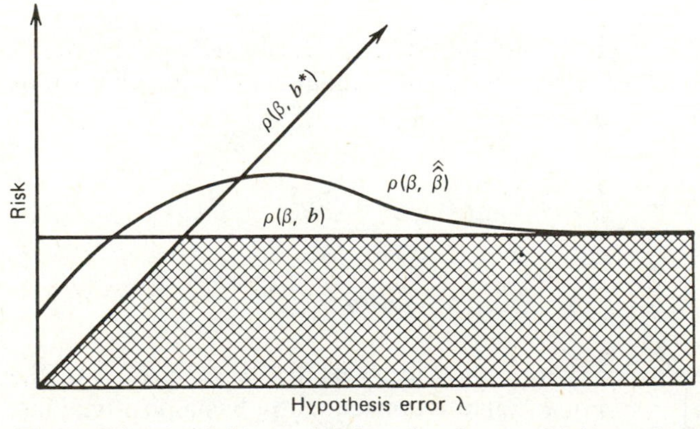

Figure 3.9 A minimum risk function for combining estimators.

Bayesian estimation and inference in Chapter 4. Perhaps it would be useful to note here that $\lambda = \boldsymbol{\delta}'\boldsymbol{\delta}/2\sigma^2$ is a composite of possible specification hypothesis errors on each of the K parameters. If an investigator has information on a prior density, it is more likely to exist on the individual parameters than on the λ parameter space.

It should be noted that we have considered in this section the orthonormal statistical model and a hypothesis design matrix of $R = I_K$. This was done for expository purposes. Judge and Bock (1978) have shown for the general case and for other criteria of performance that only the conditions, and not the general results, change.

3.3.2 Inequality Pretest Estimator

Let us consider again the testing of inequality hypotheses that was considered in Section 3.2.3d. For expository purpose let us again consider the orthonormal statistical model, where $b_i \sim N(\beta_i, \sigma^2)$, the null hypothesis is $H_0: \beta_i \geq r_i$ and the test statistic is $u_i = (b_i - r_i)/\sigma$. We noted in Section 3.2.3d that by accepting the null hypothesis H_0 we use b_i^+ the inequality estimator of β_i and if we reject H_0 the maximum likelihood estimator b_i is used. Consequently, when a preliminary test of the inequality hypothesis is made and a decision is taken based on the data at hand, the following pretest estimator results.

$$\begin{aligned} b_i^{++} &= I_{(-\infty,c_i)}(u_i)b_i + I_{[c_i,\infty)}(u_i)[I_{(-\infty,r_i)}(b_i)r_i + I_{[r_i,\infty)}(b_i)b_i] \\ &= b_i + I_{(-\infty,r_i)}(b_i)r_i - I_{(-\infty,c_i)}(u_i)I_{(-\infty,r_i)}(b_i)r_i \\ &\quad + I_{(-\infty,c_i)}(u_i)I_{(-\infty,r_i)}(b_i)b_i - I_{(-\infty,r_i)}(b_i)b_i \end{aligned} \tag{3.3.7}$$

Letting $\beta_i + \delta_i = r_i$ or $\delta_i = r_i - \beta_i$, we can define $w_i = (b_i - \beta_i)/\sigma$ and $d_i = c_i + \delta_i/\sigma$ and rewrite the pretest estimator as

$$\begin{aligned} b_i^{++} &= b_i + \sigma[I_{(-\infty,d_i)}(w_i) - I_{(-\infty,\delta_i/\sigma)}(w_i)]w_i \\ &\quad + [I_{(-\infty,\delta_i/\sigma)}(w_i) - I_{(-\infty,d_i)}(w_i)]\delta_i \end{aligned} \tag{3.3.8}$$

3.3.2a Mean of the Inequality Pretest Estimator

When $-\infty < \delta_i < 0$ and r_i is, in line with the null hypothesis, actually less than β_i, the mean of the inequality-restricted pretest estimator is by making use of Lemmas one and two of Section 3.2.3b

$$\begin{aligned} E[b_i^{++}] &= \beta_i + \frac{\sigma}{\sqrt{2\pi}}\left[P\left(\chi^2_{(2)} \geq \frac{\delta_i^2}{\sigma^2}\right) - P(\chi^2_{(2)} \geq d_i^2)\right] \\ &\quad + \frac{\delta_i}{2}\left[P\left(\chi^2_{(1)} \geq \frac{\delta_i^2}{\sigma^2}\right) - P(\chi^2_{(1)} \geq d_i^2)\right] \end{aligned} \tag{3.3.9}$$

For any given critical value of c_i for $-\infty < c_i < 0$, if $r_i - \beta_i = \delta_i = 0$, the $E[b_i^{++}] = \beta_i + (\sigma/\sqrt{2\pi})[1 - P(\chi^2_{(2)} \geq c_i^2)]$ and consequently has a positive bias. However, as $\delta_i \to -\infty$, the $E[b^{++}] = \beta_i$ and the pretest estimator is unbiased, since the maximum likelihood estimator b_i will always be used. Furthermore,

1. If $c_i = 0$ and $\delta_i = 0$, then $E[b_i^{++}] = \beta_i$.
2. If $c_i \to -\infty$ and $\delta_i = 0$, then $E[b_i^{++}] = \beta_i + (\sigma/\sqrt{2\pi})$.
3. If $c_i \to -\infty$ and $\delta_i \to -\infty$, then $E[b_i^{++}] = \beta_i$.

When $0 \le \delta_i < \infty$, which means that $-\infty < c_i < 0$, since r_i is actually greater than β_i and $d_i > 0$, the mean of the inequality-restricted estimator is

$$E[b_i^{++}] = \beta_i + \frac{\sigma}{\sqrt{2\pi}}\left\{P\left[\chi^2_{(2)} \ge \frac{\delta_i^2}{\sigma^2}\right] - P[\chi^2_{(2)} \ge d_i^2]\right\} + \delta_i - \frac{\delta_i}{2}\left\{P\left[\chi^2_{(1)} \ge \frac{\delta_i^2}{\sigma^2}\right] + P[\chi^2_{(1)} \ge d_i^2]\right\} \quad (3.3.10)$$

Note that if $c_i \to -\infty$, the inequality-restricted estimator b_i^+ results. With $c_i < 0$ and fixed and $\delta_i = 0$, then $E[b_i^{++}] = \beta_i + (\sigma/\sqrt{2\pi})\{1 - P[\chi^2_{(2)} \ge c_i^2]\}$.

For $c_i < 0$, $\delta_i > 0$ and $d_i > 0$, the mean of the pretest estimator is

$$E[b_i^{++}] = \beta_i - \frac{\delta_i}{2}\left\{P\left[\chi^2_{(1)} \ge \frac{\delta_i^2}{\sigma^2}\right] - P[\chi^2_{(1)} \ge d_i^2]\right\} + \frac{\sigma}{\sqrt{2\pi}}\left\{P\left[\chi^2_{(2)} \ge \frac{\delta_i^2}{\sigma^2}\right] - P[\chi^2_{(2)} \ge d_i^2]\right\} \quad (3.3.11)$$

For a fixed $c_i < 0$ if $\delta_i \to \infty$, then $E[b_i^{++}] = \beta_i$. The unbiased outcome for $\delta_i \to \infty$ results because the hypothesis (inequality restriction) is *rejected* all of the time and the maximum likelihood estimate is used for each sample.

For a given c_i the bias as a function of δ_i is given in Figure 3.4. *These results imply that for any $c_i < 0$ the bias of the inequality pretest estimator in the δ_i^2/σ^2 space is equal to or less than that of the inequality-restricted estimator.*

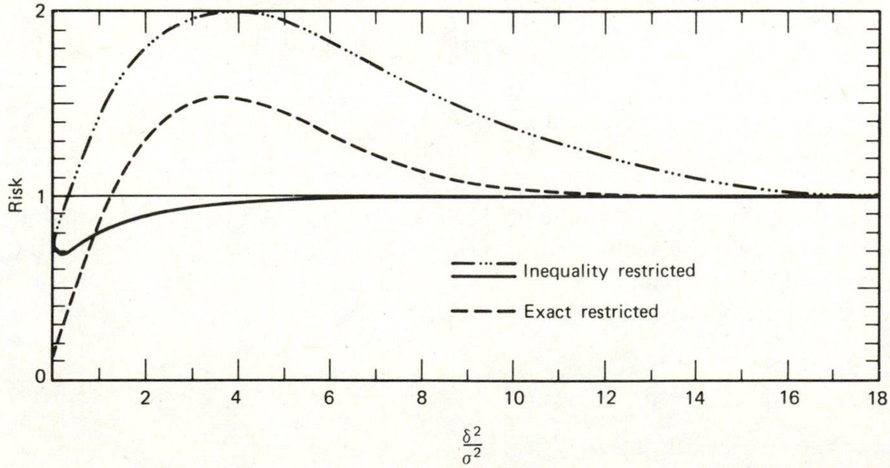

Figure 3.10 Risk functions for the inequality pretest and traditional pretest estimators, using critical values for the .05 significance level.

3.3.2b Risk of the Inequality Pretest Estimator

Given the test statistic and the test decision rule, the risk of the pretest estimator under squared error loss is

$$\begin{aligned}E[b_i^{++} - \beta_i]^2 = \rho(b_i^{++},\beta_i) &= E[(b_i - \beta_i)^2] + \sigma^2[\mathrm{I}_{(-\infty,d_i)}(w_i)w_i - I_{(-\infty,\delta_i/\sigma)}(w_i)w_i]^2 \\ &+ \delta_i^2[I_{(-\infty,\delta_i/\sigma)}(w_i) - I_{(-\infty,d_i)}(w_i)]^2 \\ &+ 2\sigma^2 w_i[I_{(-\infty,d_i)}(w_i)w_i - I_{(-\infty,\delta_i/\sigma)}(w_i)w_i] \\ &= \sigma^2 + \frac{\sigma^2}{2}\left\{P[\chi^2_{(3)} \geq d_i^2] - P\left[\chi^2_{(3)} \geq \frac{\delta_i^2}{\sigma^2}\right]\right\} \\ &+ \frac{\delta_i^2}{2}\left\{P\left[\chi^2_{(1)} \geq \frac{\delta_i^2}{\sigma^2}\right] - P[\chi^2_{(1)} \geq d_i^2]\right\}\end{aligned} \tag{3.3.12}$$

for $-\infty < c_i < 0$ and $-\infty < \delta_i < 0$. When $\delta_i \rightarrow 0$, the

$$\rho(b_i^{++},\beta_i) \rightarrow \sigma^2 + (\sigma^2/2)[P(\chi^2_{(3)} \geq c_i^2) - 1]$$

and the risk of the pretest estimator is equal to or less than that of the maximum likelihood estimator. As the critical value $c_i \rightarrow 0$, the $\rho(b_i^{++},\beta_i) \rightarrow \sigma^2$, the maximum likelihood risk. As $c_i \rightarrow -\infty$ and $\delta_i \rightarrow 0$, the $\rho(b_i^{++},\beta_i) \rightarrow \sigma^2/2$, the risk of the inequality-restricted estimator. Alternatively, for any c_i as $\delta_i \rightarrow -\infty$, the $\rho(b_i^{++},\beta_i) \rightarrow \sigma^2$, the maximum likelihood risk.

Next, consider the case when $0 \leq \delta_i < \infty$ and $c_i + \delta_i/\sigma \leq 0$. If we use the lemmas developed by Judge and Yancey (1978), the pretest risk may be rewritten as

$$\begin{aligned}\rho(b_i^{++},\beta_i) &= \sigma^2 + \sigma^2 E[I_{(-\infty,d_i)}(w_i)w_i^2 - (1 - I_{(\delta_i/\sigma,\infty)}(w_i))w_i^2] \\ &+ \delta_i^2 E[(1 - I_{(\delta_i/\sigma,\infty)}(w_i))w_i^2 - I_{(-\infty,d_i)}(w_i)w_i^2] \\ &= \frac{\sigma^2}{2}\left\{P[\chi^2_{(3)} \geq d_i^2] + P\left[\chi^2_{(3)} \geq \frac{\delta_i^2}{\sigma^2}\right]\right\} + \delta_i^2 \\ &- \frac{\delta_i^2}{2}\left\{P\left[\chi^2_{(1)} \geq \frac{\delta_i^2}{\sigma^2}\right] + P[\chi^2_{(1)} \geq d_i^2]\right\}\end{aligned} \tag{3.3.13}$$

When $\delta_i = 0$ and $-\infty < c_i \leq 0$, the $\rho(b_i^{++},\beta_i) = (\sigma^2/2)[1 + P(\chi^2_{(3)} \geq c_i^2)]$, which is in agreement with the result of (3.3.12). As $c_i \rightarrow 0$, the $\rho(b_i^{++},\beta_i) \rightarrow \sigma^2$, the maximum likelihood risk.

For any fixed δ_i, when $c_i \rightarrow -\infty$,

$$\rho(b_i^{++},\beta_i) \rightarrow \delta_i^2\left\{1 - \frac{1}{2}P\left[\chi^2_{(1)} \geq \frac{\delta_i^2}{\sigma^2}\right] + \frac{\sigma^2}{2}P\left[\chi^2_{(3)} \geq \frac{\delta_i^2}{\sigma^2}\right]\right\} \tag{3.3.14}$$

When $-\infty < c_i \leq 0$ and $c_i + \delta_i/\sigma > 0$, the risk function for the pretest estimator may be written as

$$\rho(b_i^{++},\beta_i) = \sigma^2 + \frac{\delta_i^2}{2}\left\{ P[\chi^2_{(1)} \geq d_i^2] - P\left[\chi^2_{(1)} \geq \frac{\delta_i^2}{\sigma^2}\right]\right\}$$

$$+ \frac{\sigma^2}{2}\left\{P\left[\chi^2_{(3)} \geq \frac{\delta_i^2}{\sigma^2}\right] - P[\chi^2_{(3)} \geq d_i^2]\right\} \qquad (3.3.15)$$

Since $P[\chi^2_{(1)} \geq d_i^2] \geq P[\chi^2_{(1)} \geq \delta_i^2/\sigma^2]$, the inequality pretest risk is less than the maximum likelihood risk when $\delta_i^2 < \sigma^2$, greater when $\delta_i^2 > \sigma^2$, and equal when $\delta_i^2 = \sigma^2$. *As* $\delta_i \rightarrow \infty$, the $\rho(b_i^{++},\beta_i) \rightarrow \sigma^2$, the maximum likelihood risk. The characteristics of the inequality pretest risk function are portrayed in Figure 3.10.

3.3.2c Pretest Estimator Comparisons

Given the inequality pretest results of Section (3.3.2b), an important question is how the inequality pretest risks compare with the risk for the traditional pretest estimator given in Section 3.3.1. This story is well reflected in Figure 3.10, where the two estimators are compared for a significance level of $\alpha = .05$. At the origin where the hypotheses are correct, the risk for the inequality-restricted pretest is greater than that for the equality-restricted pretest estimator. When the *directions* of the inequality hypotheses are correct, the traditional pretest estimator risk function crosses the inequality pretest estimator risk function in the neighborhood of the origin and the risk remains equal to or greater than the inequality pretest estimator over the remainder of the δ_i^2/σ^2 parameter space. When the direction of the inequality hypothesis is incorrect, the inequality pretest estimator is dominated by the traditional pretest estimator.

3.3.2d Summary Remarks

The analytical results of this section suggest the following conclusions.

1. For any critical value $c < 0$, the bias of the inequality-restricted pretest estimator in the δ/σ space is always equal to or less than that of the inequality-restricted estimator.

2. For any critical value $c < 0$, when the direction of the inequality restriction is correct, the risk of the inequality-restricted pretest estimator when σ^2 is known is equal to or less than the risk of the maximum likelihood estimator for every value of the δ/σ parameter space. As $c \rightarrow 0$ the risk of the inequality-restricted estimator approaches the maximum likelihood risk. As $c \rightarrow -\infty$, the pretest estimator risk approaches the corresponding inequality-restricted estimator risk.

3. If the *direction* of the linear hypothesis is correct ($\delta < 0$), the risk of the inequality-restricted estimator as $\delta \rightarrow -\infty$ approaches that of the equality-restricted or maximum likelihood estimator as c approaches $-\infty$ or zero, respectively.

4. When σ^2 is unknown, the t random variable with $(T - K)$ degrees of freedom is used as the test statistic, and, in general, the bias, risk, and variance results for the inequality pretest estimator are similar to the known σ^2 case.
5. When the direction of the inequality hypothesis is correct, the risk of the inequality pretest estimator is less than the traditional pretest estimator risk over almost the entire parameter space. When the direction of the inequality hypothesis is incorrect, the traditional pretest estimator dominates the inequality pretest estimator under a squared error loss measure.

3.4 STEIN RULES

In the preceding sections of this chapter we have investigated, under a squared error loss measure, the sampling performance of variants of the maximum likelihood estimator and the corresponding pretest estimators and have noted over at least part of the parameter space the unsatisfactory nature of these rules. In this section we consider some nontraditional rules for combining sample and various types of nonsample information. In particular we consider variants of two stage rules that have been proposed by James and Stein (1961), Baranchik (1964, 1973), Sclove, Morris, and Radhakrishnan (1972), and Judge, Yancey, and Bock (1984). In investigating the sampling performance of these estimators let us continue to use the orthonormal linear statistical model and a squared error loss measure.

3.4.1 The James and Stein Rule

In a 1955 paper, Stein considered the problem of estimating the unknown coefficient vector $\boldsymbol{\beta}$ for the orthonormal linear statistical model and showed that if the number of parameters was strictly greater than 2, it was possible to uniformly improve on the conventional maximum likelihood (least squares) estimator under a squared error loss measure of performance. Thus Stein was able to prove under squared error loss the inadmissibility of the traditional least squares rule, that is, there is an estimator $\boldsymbol{\beta}^*$ such that $\rho(\boldsymbol{\beta},\boldsymbol{\beta}^*) \leq \rho(\boldsymbol{\beta},\mathbf{b})$, for every value of $\boldsymbol{\beta}$, with strict inequality holding for some $\boldsymbol{\beta}$. If for the K-dimensional $\boldsymbol{\beta}$ vector, $K \leq 2$, then the least squares estimator is admissible. Following this work, James and Stein (1961) demonstrated a nonlinear estimator that dominated the least squares-maximum likelihood estimator.

Let us first consider a simple version of the James and Stein estimator based on the orthonormal linear statistical model $\mathbf{y} = X\boldsymbol{\beta} + \mathbf{e}$ or its K mean counterpart $X'\mathbf{y} = \boldsymbol{\beta} + X'\mathbf{e}$, where $X'X = I_K$, $\mathbf{e} \sim N(\mathbf{0},I_T)$ and $R\boldsymbol{\beta} = I_K\boldsymbol{\beta} = \mathbf{r} = \mathbf{0}$. Within this context the James and Stein estimator, which is a function of the maximum likelihood estimator $\mathbf{b}$, has the form

$$\boldsymbol{\beta}^* = (1 - a/\mathbf{b}'\mathbf{b})\mathbf{b} \tag{3.4.1}$$

where at this point a is an unspecified scalar. The mean of $\boldsymbol{\beta}^*$ is

$$E[\boldsymbol{\beta}^*] = E[\mathbf{b}] - E[(a/\mathbf{b}'\mathbf{b})\mathbf{b}]$$
$$= \boldsymbol{\beta} - aE[1/\chi^2_{(K+2,\lambda)}]\boldsymbol{\beta} \qquad (3.4.2)$$

where $\chi^2_{(K+2,\lambda)}$ is a noncentral chi-square random variable with noncentrality parameter $\lambda = \boldsymbol{\beta}'\boldsymbol{\beta}/2$ and a theorem given by Judge and Bock (1978, p. 321) is used in the evaluation. Consequently, the James and Stein rule is biased with bias $aE[1/\chi^2_{(K+2,\lambda)}]\boldsymbol{\beta}$. Bock, Judge, and Yancey (1984) provide a simple form for the exact evaluation of $E[(\chi^2_{(K,\lambda)})^{-m}]$.

The risk of the James and Stein estimator under a squared error loss measure is

$$\begin{aligned}\rho(\boldsymbol{\beta},\boldsymbol{\beta}^*) &= E[(\boldsymbol{\beta}^* - \boldsymbol{\beta})'(\boldsymbol{\beta}^* - \boldsymbol{\beta})]\\ &= E[(\mathbf{b} - \boldsymbol{\beta})'(\mathbf{b} - \boldsymbol{\beta})] - 2a + 2a\boldsymbol{\beta}'E[\mathbf{b}/\mathbf{b}'\mathbf{b}] + a^2E[1/\mathbf{b}'\mathbf{b}]\\ &= K - 2aE[\chi^2_{(K+2,\lambda)}/\chi^2_{(K-2,\lambda)}] + 2a\boldsymbol{\beta}'\boldsymbol{\beta}E[1/\chi^2_{(K+2,\lambda)}] + a^2E[1/\chi^2_{(K,\lambda)}]\\ &= K - a[2(K-2) - a]E[1/\chi^2_{(K,\lambda)}]\end{aligned} \qquad (3.4.3)$$

when theorems in Judge and Bock (1978, p. 322) are used in the evaluation. This result means that $\rho(\boldsymbol{\beta},\boldsymbol{\beta}^*) \leq \rho(\boldsymbol{\beta},\mathbf{b})$ for all $\boldsymbol{\beta}$ if $0 \leq a \leq 2(K-2)$. By differentiation of (3.4.3) with respect to a the value of a that minimizes the risk of $\boldsymbol{\beta}^*$ is $a = K - 2$. Therefore, the optimal (minimum risk) James and Stein estimator is

$$\boldsymbol{\beta}^* = (1 - (K-2)/\mathbf{b}'\mathbf{b})\mathbf{b} \qquad (3.4.4)$$

and this rule demonstrates the inadmissibility of the maximum likelihood estimator. When $\boldsymbol{\beta} = \mathbf{0}$ or $\lambda = \boldsymbol{\beta}'\boldsymbol{\beta}/2 = 0$ the risk of the James and Stein estimator is 2. The risk of $\boldsymbol{\beta}^*$ increases to the risk of the maximum likelihood estimator ($\rho(\boldsymbol{\beta},\mathbf{b}) = K$) as $\boldsymbol{\beta}'\boldsymbol{\beta} \to \infty$. Thus for values of $\boldsymbol{\beta}$ close to the origin the gain in risk is considerable. The characteristics of the risk function for the James and Stein estimator are depicted in Figure 3.11.

The James and Stein estimator (3.4.4) shrinks the maximum likelihood estimates toward a null mean vector. A more general formulation which makes the arbitrary origin of the above case more explicit considers a mean vector $\boldsymbol{\beta}_0 = \mathbf{r} = \mathbf{b}^*$ and an estimator of the form

$$\boldsymbol{\beta}_0^* = [1 - (K-2)/(\mathbf{b} - \mathbf{r})'(\mathbf{b} - \mathbf{r})](\mathbf{b} - \mathbf{r}) + \mathbf{r} \qquad (3.4.5)$$

This estimator has bias and risk characteristics consistent with the conventional James and Stein estimator, that is, a risk of 2 when $\lambda = \boldsymbol{\delta}'\boldsymbol{\delta}/2 = 0$ and a risk of K as $\lambda = \boldsymbol{\delta}'\boldsymbol{\delta}/2 \to \infty$ where $\boldsymbol{\delta} = \mathbf{r} - \boldsymbol{\beta}$.

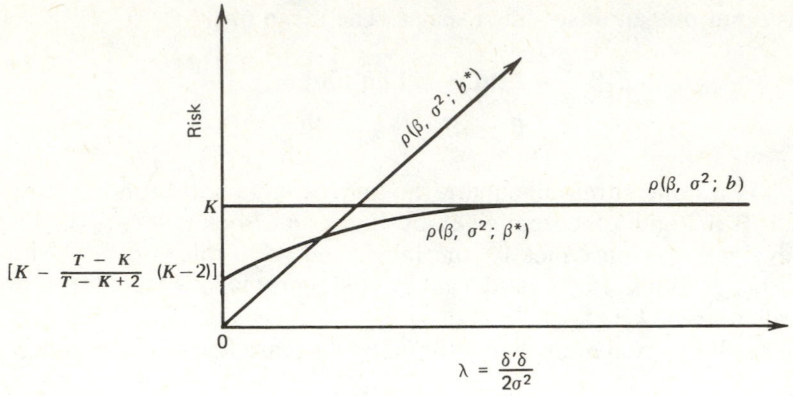

Figure 3.11 The risk characteristics of the Stein rule and least squares rule.

If $E[\mathbf{ee}'] = \sigma^2 I_T$ and σ^2 is unknown, the optimal James and Stein estimator may be written as

$$\boldsymbol{\beta}_s^* = \{1 - [(K - 2)/(T - K + 2)](s/\mathbf{b}'\mathbf{b})\}\mathbf{b} \tag{3.4.6}$$

and has risk

$$\rho(\boldsymbol{\beta},\sigma^2;\boldsymbol{\beta}_s^*) = K - [(K - 2)^2(T - K)/(T - K + 2)]E[1/\chi^2_{(K,\lambda)}] \tag{3.4.7}$$

where $s/\sigma^2 = (T - K)\hat{\sigma}^2/\sigma^2$ has a $\chi^2_{(T-K)}$ distribution that is independent of $\mathbf{b}$. Consequently at the origin where $\boldsymbol{\beta} = \mathbf{0}$ the risk is $K - (T - K)(K - 2)/(T - K + 2)$ and the risk increases to K, the maximum likelihood risk as $\boldsymbol{\beta}'\boldsymbol{\beta}/\sigma^2 \to \infty$. The evaluation of the mean of (3.4.6) may be developed as in (3.4.2). The covariance is developed by Judge and Bock (1978, pp. 178–179) and its generalization to an arbitrary vector $\mathbf{r}$ proceeds as in (3.4.5) above.

3.4.2 A Reformulated Rule

To see that the Stein rule is but another type of pretest estimator for combining the unrestricted and restricted least squares estimators, remember that $s/\sigma^2 = (T - K)\hat{\sigma}^2/\sigma^2$ is distributed as a central $\chi^2_{(T-K)}$ random variable and $(\mathbf{b} - \mathbf{r})'(\mathbf{b} - \mathbf{r})/\sigma^2$ is distributed as a noncentral $\chi^2_{(K,\lambda)}$ random variable. Therefore, if we divide each of these independent chi-square random variables by their corresponding degrees of freedom, we can write the generalized Stein-rule estimator with unknown variance as

$$\boldsymbol{\beta}_s^* = (1 - a_1/u)(\mathbf{b} - \mathbf{r}) + \mathbf{r} \tag{3.4.8}$$

where $a_1 = (K - 2)(T - K)/(K(T - K + 2))$ and $u = (\mathbf{b} - \mathbf{r})'(\mathbf{b} - \mathbf{r})/K\hat{\sigma}^2$, the likelihood ratio statistic of Chapter 2, has an F distribution with K and $(T - K)$ degrees of freedom and noncentrality parameter $\boldsymbol{\delta}'\boldsymbol{\delta}/2\sigma^2$. Of course, if $\mathbf{r} = \mathbf{b}^* =$

$\mathbf{0}$, the Stein rule is reduced to

$$\boldsymbol{\beta}_s^* = \left(1 - \frac{a_1}{u}\right)\mathbf{b} = \mathbf{b} - \frac{a_1}{u}\mathbf{b} \tag{3.4.9}$$

where $u = \mathbf{b}'\mathbf{b}/K\hat{\sigma}^2$. Therefore, the Stein rules specified in (3.4.8) and (3.4.9) provide, under a squared error loss measure, a superior way of using the test statistic u to combine the least squares and restricted least squares estimators. If the test statistic $u = a_1$, then the Stein rule becomes the restricted least squares estimator. As $a_1/u \to 0$ or, in other words, as the test statistic becomes larger relative to the scalar a_1, the Stein rule approaches the least squares estimator. The ratio a_1/u determines how much the least squares estimator is adjusted toward the restricted (hypothesis) estimator. However, contrary to the traditional pre-test estimator (3.3.3) the James and Stein rule is minimax.

3.4.3 A Positive Stein Rule

Although the James and Stein rule is minimax it is not admissible. Therefore, alternative superior rules exist. We begin our search for a better rule by noting that in (3.4.9), when $u < a_1$, the Stein rule changes the sign of the least squares estimates $\mathbf{b}$. Some may agree on adjusting the magnitudes of the least squares estimates, but a change of sign is a somewhat different matter. As it turns out, the estimator

$$\begin{aligned} \boldsymbol{\beta}_s^{**} &= I_{[a_1,\infty)}(u)\left[1 - \frac{a_1}{u}\right](\mathbf{b} - \mathbf{r}) + \mathbf{r} \\ &= [1 - \min(1, a_1/u)](\mathbf{b} - \mathbf{r}) + \mathbf{r} \end{aligned} \tag{3.4.10}$$

uniformly improves on the James and Stein rule and is minimax when $0 \leq a_1 \leq 2(K - 2)$. Therefore, if $a_1 \leq u < \infty$, the Stein-rule estimator is used and, if $u < a_1$, the restricted least squares (hypothesis) estimator is used. Consequently, if $\mathbf{r} = \mathbf{0}$, either $\mathbf{0}$ or the Stein-rule estimate is used; therefore, the estimator has been called the Stein positive-rule estimator. Thus we have another way of combining prior and sample information, and this positive-rule estimator confirms the inadmissibility of the James and Stein rules and demonstrates a superior alternative. Unlike the James and Stein rules, there is no single value of a_1 that is optimal. The proof of these propositions is given in Judge and Bock (1978, pp. 181–197).

The implications of the Stein-rule results were neatly summarized in the following remarks by Lindley in his discussion of a paper by Efron and Morris (1973):

> . . . the result of Stein's undermines the most important practical technique in statistics. . . . The next time you do an analysis of variance or fit a regression surface (a line is all right!) remember you are for sure, using an unsound procedure. Unsound, that is, by the criteria you have presumably been using to justify the procedure. . . .

The results for Sections 3.4.1, 3.4.2, and 3.4.3 have been extended to include a general design matrix X and these and results relating to a minimax-admissible estimator are given by Judge and Bock (1978). In general, the minimax Stein result holds and only the conditions change.

One disadvantage of the Stein-type estimators is that much of the risk gains occurs near the origin, that is, when the shrink vector $\mathbf{r}$ is correct. To remedy this deficiency Efron and Morris (1972) proposed a "limited translation" estimator and Stein (1981) proposed an estimator where the shrinkage is determined on a component by component basis. For an evaluation of these estimators see Bohrer and Yancey (1984) and Dey and Berger (1983). For an empirical Bayes interpretation of the Stein-like estimators see Section 4.3.3.

3.4.4 A Stein-like Pretest Estimator

Since the Stein rule combines the least squares and restricted least squares estimators, the next step is to compare these risk results with the traditional pretest estimator rule

$$\hat{\hat{\boldsymbol{\beta}}} = I_{(0,c)}(u)\mathbf{r} + I_{[c,\infty)}(u)\mathbf{b} = \mathbf{r} + I_{[c,\infty)}(u)(\mathbf{b} - \mathbf{r}) \tag{3.4.11}$$

which uses the likelihood ratio test statistic and the level of the test α or the critical value c to determine the mixture of the two estimators. Since the Stein-rule estimator is uniformly superior to the least squares estimator, it seems intuitive that if in (3.4.11) we replace the least squares estimator by the James and Stein or Stein positive-rule estimator, that is, respecify the pretest estimator as

$$\begin{aligned}\hat{\hat{\boldsymbol{\beta}}}_s^* &= I_{(0,c)}(u)\mathbf{r} + I_{[c,\infty)}(u)\boldsymbol{\beta}_s^* \\ &= I_{(0,c)}(u)\mathbf{r} + I_{[c,\infty)}(u)\left[\left(1 - \frac{a_1}{u}\right)(\mathbf{b} - \mathbf{r}) + \mathbf{r}\right] \\ &= \mathbf{r} + I_{[c,\infty)}(u)\left(1 - \frac{a_1}{u}\right)(\mathbf{b} - \mathbf{r}) \qquad (3.4.12)\end{aligned}$$

that this pretest estimator might be superior to the traditional pretest estimator. This is, in fact, the modified Stein-rule estimator proposed by Sclove, Morris, and Radhakrishnan (1972) and the theorems proved by them verify that the Stein pretest estimator (3.4.12) dominates (uniformly superior to) the traditional pretest estimator (3.4.11). If $0 \leq c \leq a_1$, the Stein-rule pretest estimator is a minimax estimator. Also, when $c > a_1$, the Stein-rule pretest estimator can no longer be a minimax substitute for the pretest (3.4.11); however, for comparable c values for both estimators the Stein rule continues to dominate under a squared error loss measure. These results are shown in Figure 3.12.

The problem of the optimal choice of the level of the test α and thus the critical value c still remains. However, it should be noted that by adding the Stein-rule estimators we have changed the minimum risk function reflected by Figure 3.9. Since the Stein-rule family, under squared error loss and conditions

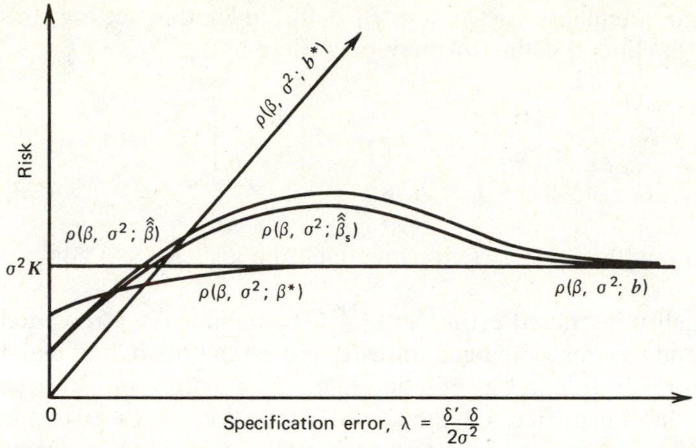

Figure 3.12 Typical risk functions for the traditional and Stein-rule pretest estimators.

normally fulfilled in practice, dominates the least squares estimator, as is shown in Figure 3.13, it cuts a corner off the minimum risk estimator previously discussed.

All of these results have been extended to cover a general design matrix X and hypothesis design matrix R. For a discussion of these Stein-rule generalizations see Judge and Bock (1978). As noted for the other estimators in this section, the general results hold and only the conditions change.

3.4.5 Stein-like Inequality Estimators

Consider the orthonormal statistical model where the unknown coefficient vector $\boldsymbol{\beta}$ has dimension K and the variance σ^2 is known and equal to one. Assume that nonsample information is available on one of the parameters, say the first,

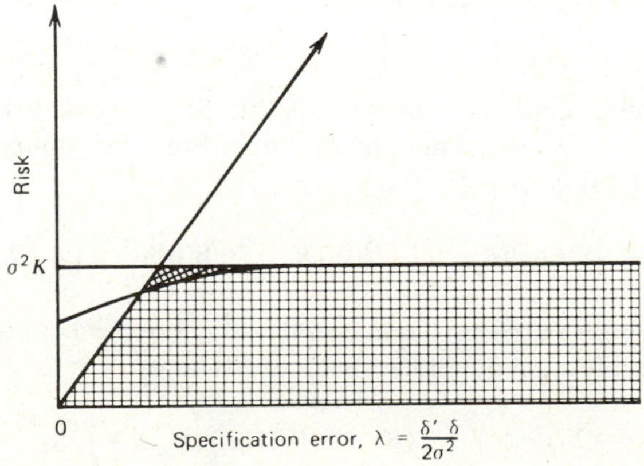

Figure 3.13 Minimum risk function that optimally combines b, b^*, and β^*.

in the form of a single inequality restriction, $\beta_1 \geq 0$. Under this setting, the inequality maximum likelihood estimator may be written as

$$\begin{aligned}\mathbf{b}^+ &= I_{(-\infty,0)}(b_1)\begin{bmatrix}0\\ \mathbf{b}_{(K-1)}\end{bmatrix} + I_{[0,\infty)}(b_1)\begin{bmatrix}b_1\\ \mathbf{b}_{(K-1)}\end{bmatrix}\\ &= I_{(-\infty,0)}(b_1)\mathbf{b}_0 + I_{[0,\infty)}(b_1)\mathbf{b} \qquad (3.4.13)\end{aligned}$$

where $\mathbf{b}_0 = (0,\mathbf{b}'_{(K-1)})'$ and $\mathbf{b}_{(K-1)}$ is a vector involving the last $(K - 1)$ components of $\mathbf{b}$.

Since (1) the inequality restricted estimator (3.4.13) combines, in a repeated sampling sense, the equality restricted and unrestricted estimators $\mathbf{b}_0$ and $\mathbf{b}$ and (2) for conditions normally fulfilled in practice (e.g., $K \geq 3$) the unrestricted Stein rule dominates the unrestricted estimator $\mathbf{b}$, a question arises as to the sampling properties of the estimator that results when the Stein rule $\boldsymbol{\beta}^*$, shrunk toward $\mathbf{0}$, is substituted for the unrestricted estimator $\mathbf{b}$ and the $\mathbf{b}_{(K-1)}$ components of $\mathbf{b}_0$ in (3.4.13). This means that in the case of one restriction and $K \geq 3$, a Stein inequality restricted estimator may be written as

$$\begin{aligned}\mathbf{b}_s^+ &= I_{(-\infty,0)}(b_1)\begin{bmatrix}0\\ (1 - c_1/\mathbf{b}'_{(K-1)}\mathbf{b}_{(K-1)})\mathbf{b}_{(K-1)}\end{bmatrix} + I_{[0,\infty)}(b_1)\left[(1 - c_2/\mathbf{b}'\mathbf{b})\begin{pmatrix}b_1\\ \mathbf{b}_{(K-1)}\end{pmatrix}\right]\\ &= \mathbf{b}^+ - I_{(-\infty,0)}(b_1)(c_1/\mathbf{b}_0'\mathbf{b}_0)\mathbf{b}_0 - I_{[0,\infty)}(b_1)(c_2/\mathbf{b}'\mathbf{b})\mathbf{b} \qquad (3.4.14)\end{aligned}$$

This Stein-like inequality estimator has mean

$$E[\mathbf{b}_s^+] = E[\mathbf{b}^+] - E[I_{(-\infty,0)}(b_1)(c_1/\mathbf{b}_0'\mathbf{b}_0)\mathbf{b}_0] - E[I_{[0,\infty)}(b_1)(c_2/\mathbf{b}'\mathbf{b})\mathbf{b}] \qquad (3.4.15)$$

and is thus a biased estimator of $\boldsymbol{\beta}$.

Using (3.4.14) and theorems by Judge, Yancey, and Bock (1982) we may express the risk of the Stein inequality estimator as

$$\begin{aligned}\rho(\mathbf{b}_s^+,\boldsymbol{\beta}) &= \rho(\mathbf{b}^+,\boldsymbol{\beta}) + E[I_{(-\infty,0)}(b_1)]c_1[c_1 - 2(K - 3)]E[1/\chi^2_{(K-1,\lambda_0)}]\\ &\quad + E[I_{[0,\infty)}(b_1)c_2\{c_2 - 2(K - 2)\}(1/\mathbf{b}'\mathbf{b})] \qquad (3.4.16)\end{aligned}$$

where $\lambda_0 = \boldsymbol{\beta}_0'\boldsymbol{\beta}_0/2$ and $\boldsymbol{\beta}_0 = (0, \boldsymbol{\beta}'_{(K-1)})'$.

The choice of c_1 and c_2, which minimizes the risk for the Stein inequality estimator, are $c_1 = K - 3$ and $c_2 = K - 2$. Thus the optimum Stein inequality estimator in the context of (3.4.14) is

$$\mathbf{b}_s^+ = \mathbf{b}^+ - I_{(-\infty,0)}(b_1)[(K - 3)/\mathbf{b}_0'\mathbf{b}_0]\mathbf{b}_0 - I_{[0,\infty)}(b_1)[(K - 2)/\mathbf{b}'\mathbf{b}]\mathbf{b} \qquad (3.4.17)$$

From (3.4.16), the risk difference between the maximum likelihood inequality restricted estimator and the Stein inequality restricted estimator is

$$\begin{aligned}\rho(\mathbf{b}_s^+,\boldsymbol{\beta}) - \rho(\mathbf{b}^+,\boldsymbol{\beta}) &= E[I_{(-\infty,0)}(b_1)]c_1[c_1 - 2(K - 3)]E[1/\chi^2_{(K-1,\lambda_0)}]\\ &\quad + E[I_{[0,\infty)}(b_1)c_2[c_2 - 2(K - 2)](1/\mathbf{b}'\mathbf{b})] \qquad (3.4.18)\end{aligned}$$

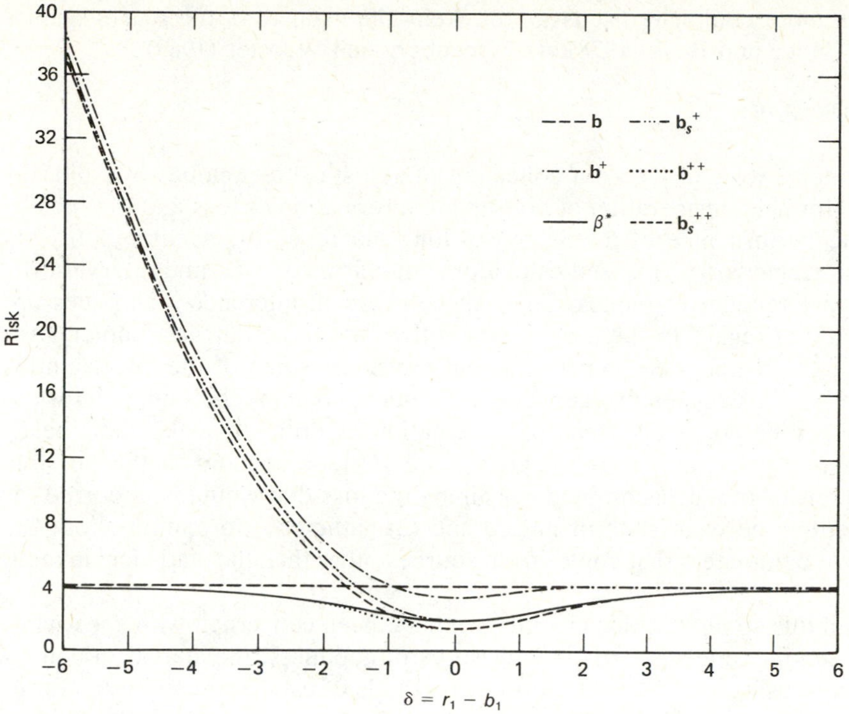

Figure 3.14 Risk functions for conventional, Stein and inequality-restricted estimators.

The right-hand side of (3.4.18) is negative if $0 \le c_1 < 2(K - 3)$ and $0 < c_2 < 2(K - 2)$. The fact that under these conditions the right-hand side of (3.4.18) is negative implies that the Stein inequality estimator $\mathbf{b}_s^+$ dominates or is uniformly superior to the inequality maximum likelihood restricted estimator $\mathbf{b}^+$ and therefore demonstrates its inadmissibility. The risk characteristics of the maximum likelihood estimator $\mathbf{b}$, the inequality estimator $\mathbf{b}^+$, the James and Stein and positive rule estimators $\boldsymbol{\beta}^*$ and $\boldsymbol{\beta}^{**}$ and the inequality James and Stein and positive rule estimators $\mathbf{b}_s^+$ and $\mathbf{b}_s^{++}$ are shown in Figure 3.14. If the direction of the inequality restriction is correct, the inequality Stein estimators are risk superior to their conventional Stein counterparts.

3.4.6 Some Remarks

The results of the preceding subsections suggest that, under a squared error loss measure, the Stein rules are uniformly superior to traditional equality and inequality maximum likelihood and pretest estimators. They can be recommended on the grounds of simplicity, generalizability, efficiency, and robustness.

In many cases, the choice between estimators rests on the trade off between bias and precision. In the world of Stein rules, the data determine the compromise between these two extremes.

For a more complete discussion of Stein-like estimators the reader should look at Judge and Bock (1978) and Greenberg and Webster (1983).

3.5 SUMMARY

In Chapter 2 we considered a collection of statistical techniques that did not involve formal consideration of nonsample information or loss and that evaluated the performance of a rule by its long-run repetitive accuracy. In this classical framework, unbiased estimators, significance tests, and interval estimation are familiar examples. Since these classical inference techniques are used without regard to the uses to which they are to be put, in Chapter 3 we turned to statistical decision theory that considers some of the uncertainties involved in the decision problem and attempts to combine the sample information with other relevant types of information in order to make the "best" decision. In particular, in the approach we (1) took account of the possible consequences of a decision by determining the loss that would be incurred for each action and each state of nature and (2) gathered information about the unknown parameters that comes from sources other than the statistical investigation.

Within this context in this chapter, we have been concerned with specifying and evaluating, under alternative measures of goodness, the statistical consequences of using several nontraditional methods of estimation and hypothesis testing and assessing the implications of the results for econometric theory and practice. Much of the literature concerned with estimation and inference from a sample of economic data deals with a situation when the statistical model is correctly specified and any nonsample information about the parameters is specified exactly. Thus, in econometric practice, it is customary to assume that the statistical model employed for purposes of estimation and inference is consistent with the sampling process whereby the sample observations were generated and the nonsample information is correct. In this event, statistical theory provides techniques for obtaining point and interval estimates of the population parameters and for hypothesis testing.

Under this scenario for the traditional linear statistical model with normal, independent, and identically distributed errors, it is customary to use the maximum likelihood-least squares estimator when estimating the unknown location parameters. From the sampling theory point of view, this approach is justified since it leads to minimum variance among unbiased estimators and, under squared error loss, the least squares estimator is minimax. These are impressive results and go a long way toward explaining the popularity of the least squares estimator, which is really best in a class of one. These results also suggest that if improvement in estimator performance is to be achieved, one must go outside of the traditional sampling theory rules and consider a range of alternative estimators that are biased and possibly nonlinear.

Despite its popularity, the statistical implications of remaining in the linear unbiased family of rules may in many cases be rather severe. One indication of the possibly questionable stature of the least squares rule occurred when Stein

(1955) showed, under conditions normally fulfilled in practice, that there were other minimax estimators. James and Stein (1961) exhibited an estimator that, under squared error loss, dominates the least squares estimator and thus demonstrates its inadmissibility. This result means that the unbiased least squares rule may have an inferior mean square error when compared to some biased estimators.

Another difficulty with the conventional estimator arises when the investigator has information about the unknown parameters that is over and above that contained in the sample observations. Assuming this fortunate event, we have in this chapter reviewed three alternative ways to take account of this nonsample information for purposes of estimation and inference.

We first considered nonsample information about the unknown parameters in the form of equality constraints and noted the gain in precision when this information was combined with the sample information. We also noted that if this information was incorrect that the estimators were biased and we therefore raised questions concerning the trade-off of bias for variance. Under a squared error loss measure, we investigated the sampling performance of the equality-restricted estimator and the traditional pretest estimator that use linear equality hypotheses and noted their unsatisfactory performance over a large range of the parameter space. In addition we noted that the Stein pretest estimator dominated the traditional pretest estimator and thus demonstrated its inadmissibility.

Alternatively, the nonsample information may be available in the form of linear stochastic restrictions. In this case, there is a sampling theory estimator available, but this estimator has many of the characteristics of the equality-restricted estimator and pretest estimator. In addition, one weakness of the stochastic prior information estimator lies in assuming that the random vector representing the uncertainty of the prior information has a mean of zero, that is, the prior information is unbiased. Additional assumptions regarding a known covariance matrix of the stochastic prior information seem unreasonably demanding.

Inequality restrictions offer another alternative for representing prior information. If the direction of the inequality restriction(s) is correct, the inequality-restricted estimator under squared error loss is uniformly superior to the maximum likelihood estimator. Also, when the direction of the inequality restriction is correct, the inequality-restricted pretest estimator is superior to the traditional pretest estimator over practically the entire parameter space. If the direction of the inequality is incorrect, as the specification error grows, the risk of the inequality-restricted estimator approaches that of the restricted least squares estimator. If the direction of the inequality is incorrect, the inequality-restricted pretest estimator is dominated by the traditional pretest estimator. Therefore, if the applied worker is sure of the direction of the inequality, for example, the parameters are nonnegative or nonpositive, then the inequality estimator not only performs well relative to other alternatives but is uniformly superior to the least squares estimator, which is used by most applied workers, and the James and Stein estimator, which, under a squared error loss measure, should be used by most applied workers. Inequality pretest estimators are risk superior to the maximum likelihood estimator if the direction of the restriction is correct. If the direction is not correct the risk performance is much like that of the equality pretest estimator. Stein-like inequality estimators dominate the traditional inequality estimator under squared error loss, and when the direction of the restriction is correct they are risk superior to the Stein estimators. These and other attributes give the inequality estimation and hypothesis testing framework great appeal in applied work in economics.

3.6 EXERCISES

Using the statistical model and the sample observations from the sampling experiment described in Section 2.5.1 of Chapter 2, complete the following exercises involving equality-restricted, stochastic-restricted, inequality-restricted, and Stein-rule estimators.

Exercise 3.1

Develop restricted least squares estimates of the $\boldsymbol{\beta}$ parameter vector, using 100 samples of data, a restricted least squares estimator and the restriction

$$R\boldsymbol{\beta} = [0 \quad 1 \quad 1]\begin{bmatrix} \beta_1 \\ \beta_2 \\ \beta_3 \end{bmatrix} = 1$$

Compare the mean vector and covariance for the 100 samples and compare the sampling results with those results from using an unrestricted least squares estimator. Under a squared error loss measure, develop the risk for the restricted least squares estimates from the 100 samples and compare this empirical risk with the corresponding unrestricted least squares result.

Exercise 3.2

Consider the restriction in Exercise 3.1 as a general linear hypothesis and develop one hundred estimates of the $\boldsymbol{\beta}$ vector by using a pretest estimator with the $\alpha = .05$ level of significance. Under a squared error loss measure, determine the empirical risk for the pretest estimator and compare it with that of the unrestricted and restricted least squares estimators. Change the restriction or general linear hypothesis to $R\boldsymbol{\beta} = \beta_2 + \beta_3 = 10.0$ and develop the empirical risks for the unrestricted, restricted, and pretest estimators. Discuss the results.

Exercise 3.3

Using the stochastic restriction, $R\boldsymbol{\beta} + v = \beta_2 + \beta_3 + v = 1$, where v is assumed to be normal with mean zero and variance $\frac{1}{64}$, obtain 100 estimates of the $\boldsymbol{\beta}$ vector by using the stochastic restricted estimator under known and unknown variance σ^2. Develop the mean vector and covariance and contrast with the results from the unrestricted and restricted least squares estimators.

Exercise 3.4

Using the inequality restriction $R\boldsymbol{\beta} = \beta_2 + \beta_3 \geq 1$ and the corresponding inequality estimator, estimate the $\boldsymbol{\beta}$ vector for the 100 samples and compare and contrast the results with those from the unrestricted and restricted least squares estimators.

Exercise 3.5

Assuming σ^2 known and using the general linear inequality hypothesis $\beta_2 + \beta_3 \geq 1$, and the corresponding pretest estimator ($\alpha = .05$) develop pretest estimates for the 100 samples. Compute the corresponding empirical risk and compare and contrast with the empirical risks for the traditional pretest estimator of Exercise 3.2.

Exercise 3.6

For the design matrix given in Section 2.5.1 of Chapter 2 there exists a square nonsingular matrix P that will transform the positive definite matrix $X'X$ into an identity matrix, that is, by using a procedure such as Cholesky's decomposition method there is a P matrix such that $PX'XP' = I_K$. Verify that

$$P = \begin{bmatrix} .223607 & 0 & 0 \\ -.513617 & .331131 & 0 \\ -.585486 & -.028953 & .498237 \end{bmatrix}$$

is such a matrix and reparameterize the statistical model as follows:

$$\mathbf{y} = X\boldsymbol{\beta} + \mathbf{e} = XPP^{-1}\boldsymbol{\beta} + \mathbf{e} = Z\boldsymbol{\theta} + \mathbf{e}$$

where $\boldsymbol{\theta} = P^{-1}\boldsymbol{\beta}$.

Given the transformed design matrix Z, use the least squares rule to obtain 100 estimates of the $\boldsymbol{\theta}$ vector and compute the empirical risk for the least squares rule under squared error loss. Specify a James and Stein estimator for this orthonormal model, assuming σ^2 known and equal to 0.0625, which shrinks to the null vector; compute estimates of the parameter vector $\boldsymbol{\theta}$ for the 100 samples and the corresponding empirical risk under squared error loss and compare with the least squares risk. Repeat the estimation process shrinking to the true parameter vector and compute the risk and make the relevant risk comparisons.

Exercise 3.7

Within the context of Exercise 3.6 specify alternative positive Stein rule estimators, compute the alternative estimates of the $\boldsymbol{\theta}$ vector for the 100 samples and develop the corresponding empirical risk and compare and contrast them to those of Exercise 3.6.

3.7 REFERENCES

Baranchik, A. J. (1964) "Multiple Regression and Estimation of the Mean of a Multivariate Normal Distribution," Technical Report No. 51, Stanford University, California.

Baranchik, A. J. (1973) "Inadmissibility of Maximum Likelihood Estimators in Some Multiple Regression Problems with Three or More Variables," *The Annals of Statistics,* 1, 312–321.

Barlow, R. E., P. J. Bartholomew, J. M. Bremner, and H. D. Brunk (1972) *Statistical Inference Under Order Restrictions,* Wiley, New York.

Berger, J. (1980) *Statistical Decision Theory,* Springer-Verlag, New York.

Bock, M. E., T. A. Yancey, and G. G. Judge (1972) "The Statistical Consequences of Preliminary Test Estimators in Regression," *Journal of the American Statistical Association,* 68, 109–116.

Bock, M. E., G. G. Judge, and T. A. Yancey (1984), "A Simple Form for Inverse Moments of Noncentral Chi-square and F Random Variables and for Certain Confluent Hypergeometric Functions," *Journal of Econometrics,* forthcoming.

Bock, M. E., G. G. Judge, and T. A. Yancey (1973) "Some Comments on Estimation in Regression after Preliminary Tests of Significance," *Journal of Econometrics,* 1, 191–200.

Bohrer, R. and G. R. Francis (1972) "Sharp One Sided Confidence Bounds Over Positive Regions," *Annals of Mathematical Statistics,* 43, 1541–1548.

Bohrer, R. (1975) "One-Sided Multivariable Inference," *Applied Statistics,* 24, 3, 380–384.

Bohrer, R. and T. Yancey (1984) "Algorithms for Numerical Evaluation of Stein-Like and Limited Translation Estimators." *Journal of Econometrics,* forthcoming.

Chernoff, H. and L. E. Moses (1959) *Elementary Decision Theory,* Wiley, New York.

De Groot, M. H. (1970) *Optimal Statistical Decisions,* McGraw-Hill, New York.

Dey, D. K. and J. O. Berger (1983) "On Truncation of Shrinkage Estimators in Simultaneous Estimation of Normal Means" *Journal of the American Statistical Association,* 78, 865–869.

Efron, B. and C. Morris (1973) "Stein's Estimation Rule and Its Competitors—An Empirical Bayes Approach," *Journal of the American Statistical Association,* 68, 117–130.

Efron, B. and C. Morris (1972) "Limiting the Risk of Bayes and Empirical Bayes Estimators—Part II," *Journal of the American Statistical Association,* 67, 130–139.

Ferguson, T. S. (1967) *Mathematical Statistics: A Decision Theoretic Approach,* Academic Press, New York.

Gourieroux, C., A. Holly, and A. Monfort (1982) "Likelihood Ratio, Wald and Kuhn-Tucker Tests in Linear Models with Inequality Constraints," *Econometrica,* 50, 43–62.

Greenberg, E. and C. E. Webster (1983) *Advanced Econometrics: A Bridge to the Literature,* Wiley, New York.
Hill, R. C., G. G. Judge, and T. Fomby (1978) "On Testing the Adequacy of the Regression Model," *Technometrics,* 20, 491–494.
James, W. and C. Stein (1961) "Estimation with Quadratic Loss," *Proceedings of the Fourth Berkeley Symposium on Mathematical Statistics and Probability,* University of California Press, Berkeley, 361–379.
Judge, G. G. and T. Takayama (1966) "Inequality Restrictions in Regression Analysis," *Journal of the American Statistical Association,* 61, 166–181.
Judge, G. G. and M. E. Bock (1976) "A Comparison of Traditional and Stein Rule Estimators Under Weighted Squared Error Loss," *International Economic Review,* 17, 434–440.
Judge, G. G. and M. E. Bock (1978) *The Statistical Implications of Pre-Test and Stein Rule Estimators in Econometrics,* North-Holland, New York.
Judge, G. G. and T. A. Yancey (1978) "Some Sampling Properties of a Linear Inequality Restricted Estimator," University of Georgia, Discussion Paper 78-020.
Judge, G. G., W. E. Griffiths, R. C. Hill, and T. C. Lee (1980) *The Theory and Practice of Econometrics,* Wiley, New York.
Judge, G. G. and M. E. Bock (1983) "Biased Estimation," *Handbook of Econometrics,* North-Holland, Amsterdam, pp. 599–650.
Judge, G. G., R. C. Hill, W. E. Griffiths, H. Lütkepohl, and T. C. Lee (1982) *Introduction to the Theory and Practice of Econometrics,* Wiley, New York.
Judge, G. G. and T. A. Yancey (1981) "Sampling Properties of an Inequality Restricted Estimator," *Economics Letters,* 4, 327–333.
Judge, G. G., T. A. Yancey, and M. E. Bock (1984) "The Nonoptimality of the Inequality Restricted Estimator Under Squared Error Loss," *Journal of Econometrics,* forthcoming.
Kuhn, H. and A. Tucker (1951) "Non-Linear Programming," in *Second Berkeley Symposium Proceedings,* J. Neyman, ed., University of California Press, Berkeley, 481–492.
Leamer, E. E. (1978) *Specification Searches; Ad Hoc Inference with Nonexperimental Data,* Wiley, New York.
Liew, C. K. (1976) "Inequality Constrained Least Squares Estimation," *Journal of the American Statistical Association,* 71, 746–751.
Nagar, A. L. and N. C. Kakwani (1964) "The Bias and Moment Matrix of a Mixed Regression Estimator" *Econometrica,* 32, 174–182.
Rao, C. R. (1973) *Linear Statistical Inference and Its Applications,* 2nd ed. Wiley, New York.
Sclove, S. L., C. Morris, and R. Radhakrishnan (1972) "Non-Optimality of Preliminary-Test Estimators for the Multinormal Mean," *Annals of Mathematical Statistics,* 43, 1481–1490.
Stein, C. (1955) "Inadmissibility of the Usual Estimator for the Mean of a Multivariate Normal Distribution," *Proceedings of the Third Berkeley Symposium on Mathematical Statistics and Probability,* University of California Press, Berkeley, 197–206.

Stein, C. (1981) "Estimation of the Mean of a Multivariate Normal Distribution" *The Annals of Statistics,* 9, 1135–1151.

Theil, H. (1963) "On the Use of Incomplete Prior Information in Regression Analysis," *Journal of the American Statistical Associations,* 58, 401–414.

Toro-Vizcarrondo, C. and T. D. Wallace (1968) "A Test of the Mean Square Error Criterion for Restrictions in Linear Regression," *Journal of the American Statistical Association,* 63, 558–572.

Yancey, T. A., M. E. Bock, and G. G. Judge (1972) "Some Finite Sample Results of Theil's Mixed Regression Estimator," *Journal of the American Statistical Association,* 67, 176–180.

Yancey, T. A., G. G. Judge, and M. E. Bock (1981) "Testing Multiple Equality and Inequality Hypotheses in Economics," *Economics Letters,* 4, 249–255.

Yancey, T. A., R. Bohrer, and G. G. Judge (1982) "Power Function Comparisons in Inequality Hypothesis Testing," *Economics Letters,* 5, 161–167.

Chapter 4

The Bayesian Approach to Inference

4.1 BAYESIAN INFERENCE AND BAYES' THEOREM

In Chapters 2 and 3 we considered the classical and decision theory approaches to estimation and hypothesis testing for the parameters of the linear statistical model. We now turn to the Bayesian approach, and we begin by outlining some of the differences between the alternative approaches.

The term *classical* does not have the unanimous support of all statisticians, but it is usually used to describe inference with at least the following two characteristics.

1. Estimators and test procedures are evaluated in terms of their properties in repeated samples.
2. The probability of an event is defined in terms of the limit of the relative frequency of that event.

When estimating a parameter within the classical framework, an *unbiased* estimator is considered desirable because, as more and more samples are taken, the average value of the sample estimates tends toward the value of the unknown parameter. In the class of unbiased estimators a *minimum variance* unbiased estimator is preferred because, on average, it yields values that are closer (in terms of squared difference) to the real parameter than are those obtained from any other unbiased estimator. Biased estimators are also used if their mean squared error (variance plus bias squared) is low relative to that of other estimators. Methods for interval estimation and hypothesis testing are similarly evaluated in terms of their performance in a large number of repeated samples. Roughly speaking, evaluation takes place within a repeated sampling context because we like to have techniques with a high *probability* of giving the correct result, and probability is defined in terms of the limit of a relative frequency.

In a Bayesian framework probability is defined in terms of a *degree of belief*, and although the properties of estimators and tests in repeated samples are of some interest, they do not provide the main basis for inference and estimator choice. The probability of an event is given by an individual's belief in how likely or unlikely the event is to occur. This belief may depend on quantitative and/or qualitative information, but it does not necessarily depend on the relative frequency of the event in a large number of future hypothetical experiments. Also, because this definition of probability is subjective, different individuals may assign different probabilities to the same event. Another consequence, and one of the main features of Bayesian analysis, is that uncertainty about the value of an unknown parameter can be expressed in terms of a probability distribution. It is assumed that what are likely and unlikely values for a parameter can be formalized by assigning to that parameter a probability density function (if the parameter could be any value within a given range), or a discrete probability function (if the parameter could only be one of a finite or countably infinite number of possible values). In the classical framework, because a parameter is fixed in repeated samples, a probability distribution cannot be assigned to the parameter, or, more correctly, it would simply be the trivial distribution where the probability is equal to one at the true parameter value and zero elsewhere. See Leamer (1978, pp. 22–39) for further discussion on subjective probability, and for a comparison with other probability definitions.

The Bayesian subjective probability distribution on a parameter summarizes an individual's knowledge about that parameter. The knowledge may exist before observing any sample information, in which case the distribution is called a *prior distribution,* or it may be derived from both prior and sample information, in which case the distribution is called a *posterior distribution.* A distribution that is a posterior distribution in relation to some past sample can be regarded as a prior distribution when viewed in relation to a future sample. In either case, the subjective distribution is the source of all inferences about the unknown parameter, and, in contrast to the classical approach that concentrates on point estimates, attainment of the posterior distribution is often the final objective of any research investigation. The procedure that combines a prior distribution with sample information to form a posterior distribution is known as *Bayes' theorem.*

The decision theory approach to inference can be viewed within both the repeated sampling context used by classical statistics, or within the Bayesian approach. The main distinguishing feature of decision theory is an emphasis on the consequences of taking a particular action (choosing an estimator), and the introduction of a loss function to reflect these consequences. In the sampling theory context it is considered desirable to find an estimator that minimizes expected loss (risk), where expected loss is the average loss incurred in repeated samples, and, therefore, is based on the relative frequency approach to probability. This criterion is not sufficient to uniquely define an estimator, however, and so other criteria such as admissibility, minimaxity, or Bayes' principle are often introduced. This was the approach taken in Chapter 3. In that chapter we also saw how the decision theory framework can be used to introduce some types of prior information, and in two cases (Section 3.2.2 and the use of Bayes' principle) some notions of subjective probability were introduced. In the Bayesian approach to decision theory, an estimator is chosen so as to minimize expected loss where the expectation is taken with respect to the posterior distribution of the unknown parameter. Thus the approach is based mainly on subjective probability, and choosing a point estimate via a loss function is just one possible use of the posterior distribution. Further details of Bayesian point estimators and their relationship with sampling theory estimators will be given in Section 4.5. For additional discussion on the various approaches to inference and their advantages and disadvantages see Berger (1980, pp. 17–29).

We turn now to examine how, in the Bayesian framework, prior views are modified to form posterior views. The first step is to introduce some notation. Let $\boldsymbol{\theta}$ be a vector of parameters in which we are interested, and let $\mathbf{y}$ be a vector of sample observations from the joint density function $f(\mathbf{y}|\boldsymbol{\theta})$. The function $f(\mathbf{y}|\boldsymbol{\theta})$ is algebraically identical to the likelihood function for $\boldsymbol{\theta}$ and contains all the sample information about $\boldsymbol{\theta}$. If, in the sense discussed above, $\boldsymbol{\theta}$ is regarded as a random vector, we can write

$$h(\boldsymbol{\theta},\mathbf{y}) = f(\mathbf{y}|\boldsymbol{\theta})g(\boldsymbol{\theta}) = g(\boldsymbol{\theta}|\mathbf{y})f(\mathbf{y}) \tag{4.1.1}$$

where h is the joint density function for $\boldsymbol{\theta}$ and $\mathbf{y}$, g denotes a density function for $\boldsymbol{\theta}$, and f denotes a density function for $\mathbf{y}$. Obviously, f and g sometimes denote marginal distributions and sometimes denote conditional distributions, and hence they are not used consistently to denote the same functional form. Nevertheless, in each case the meaning should be clear.

Rearranging (4.1.1) yields

$$g(\boldsymbol{\theta}|\mathbf{y}) = \frac{f(\mathbf{y}|\boldsymbol{\theta})g(\boldsymbol{\theta})}{f(\mathbf{y})} \tag{4.1.2}$$

This expression is known as Bayes' theorem. The posterior density function for $\boldsymbol{\theta}$ is $g(\boldsymbol{\theta}|\mathbf{y})$, since it summarizes all the information about $\boldsymbol{\theta}$ after the sample $\mathbf{y}$ has been observed, and $g(\boldsymbol{\theta})$ is the prior density for $\boldsymbol{\theta}$, summarizing the nonsample information about $\boldsymbol{\theta}$. If we recognize that, with respect to $\boldsymbol{\theta}$, $f(\mathbf{y})$ can be regarded as a constant and that $f(\mathbf{y}|\boldsymbol{\theta})$ can be written as the likelihood function $\ell(\boldsymbol{\theta}|\mathbf{y})$, then (4.1.2) becomes

$$g(\boldsymbol{\theta}|\mathbf{y}) \propto \ell(\boldsymbol{\theta}|\mathbf{y})g(\boldsymbol{\theta}) \tag{4.1.3}$$

where $\propto$ denotes "proportional to." In words, (4.1.3) can be written as

Posterior information $\propto$ sample information $\times$ prior information

Throughout the remainder of this chapter we will be concerned with the application of Bayesian principles to the general linear model

$$\mathbf{y} = X\boldsymbol{\beta} + \mathbf{e} \tag{4.1.4}$$

where $\mathbf{y}$ is a $(T \times 1)$ vector of observations on a dependent variable, X is a $(T \times K)$ matrix of observations on K explanatory variables, $\mathbf{e}$ is a $(T \times 1)$ disturbance vector with the properties $e \sim N(0,\sigma^2 I)$, and β and σ are unknown parameters about which we seek information. In the framework of (4.1.3), $\theta = (\beta',\sigma)'$ and

$$g(\beta,\sigma|y) \propto \ell(\beta,\sigma|y)g(\beta,\sigma) \tag{4.1.5}$$

In Sections 4.2 and 4.3 we consider derivation of the posterior distribution $g(\beta,\sigma|y)$ from the sample information $\ell(\beta,\sigma|y)$ and the prior information $g(\beta,\sigma)$. A noninformative prior is considered in Section 4.2 and a number of informative priors are considered in Section 4.3. In Section 4.4 we consider Bayesian point estimation and how it relates to the sampling theory approach; prediction and interval estimation are dealt with in Sections 4.5 and 4.6, respectively. Posterior odds and their role in the comparison of hypotheses are dis-

TABLE 4.1   *TOPICS IN THE BAYESIAN APPROACH TO INFERENCE*

The Derivation of Posterior Densities $g(\beta,\sigma|y) \propto \ell(\beta,\sigma|y)g(\beta,\sigma)$

Noninformative Priors

Specification (Section 4.2.1)
Posterior Densities (Section 4.2.2)

Informative Priors

Natural Conjugate (Section 4.3.1)
Posterior Densities (Section 4.3.2)
g-Prior (Section 4.3.4)
Independent t-Gamma (Section 4.3.5)
Assessment of Priors (Section 4.3.6)

Point Estimation
Section 4.4

Hypothesis Testing
Section 4.7

Interval Estimation
Section 4.6

Predictive Densities
$f(\bar{y}|y)$
Section 4.5

Posterior Odds $\dfrac{P(H_0|y)}{P(H_1|y)}$
Section 4.7

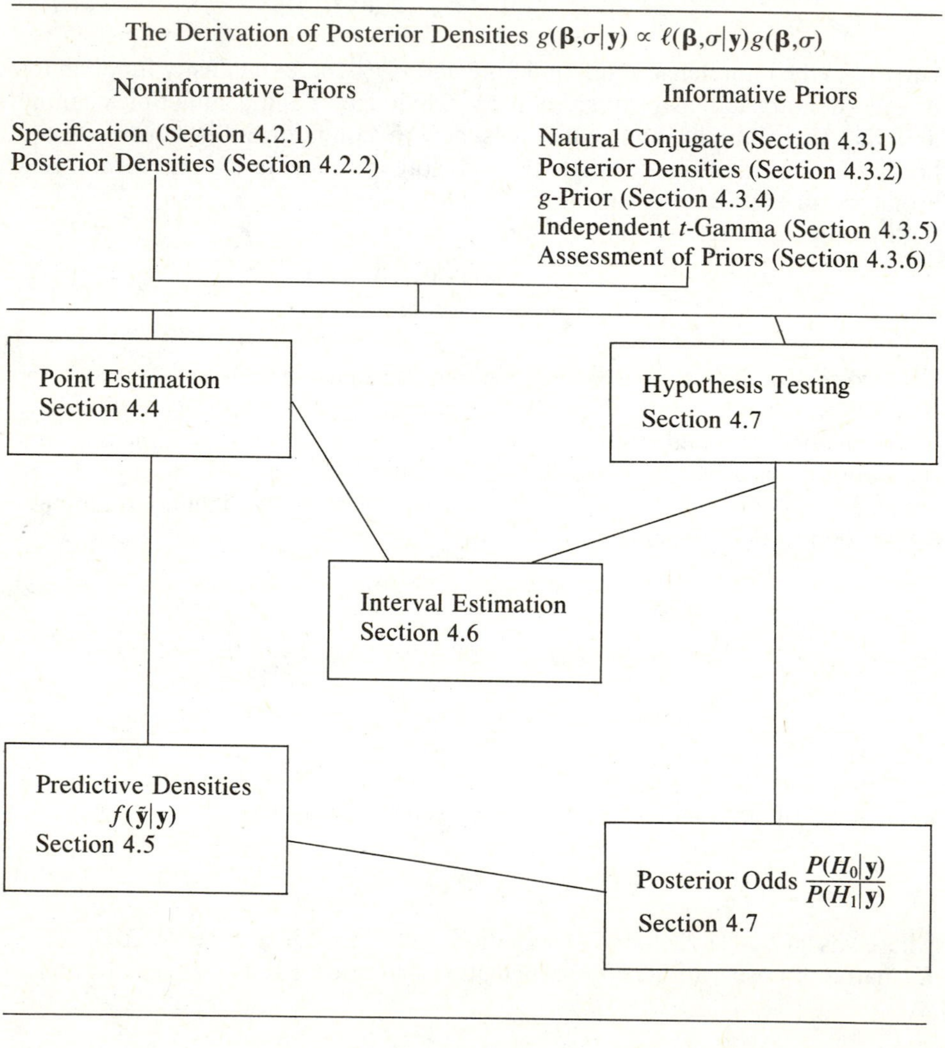

cussed in Section 4.7; concluding remarks are given in Section 4.8. These contents are summarized in Table 4.1.

The likelihood function that summarizes the sample information plays a basic role in Bayesian inference. From Chapter 2 it is given by

$$\ell(\boldsymbol{\beta},\sigma|\mathbf{y}) = (2\pi)^{-T/2}\sigma^{-T} \exp\left\{-\frac{1}{2\sigma^2}[(\mathbf{y} - X\boldsymbol{\beta})'(\mathbf{y} - X\boldsymbol{\beta})]\right\} \quad (4.1.6)$$

If we drop irrelevant constants and write this function in terms of the jointly sufficient statistic $(\mathbf{b}',\hat{\sigma}^2)$, where $\mathbf{b} = (X'X)^{-1}X'\mathbf{y}$, $\hat{\sigma}^2 = (\mathbf{y} - X\mathbf{b})'(\mathbf{y} - X\mathbf{b})/v$, and $v = T - K$, we obtain

$$\ell(\boldsymbol{\beta},\sigma|\mathbf{y}) \propto \sigma^{-T} \exp\left\{-\frac{1}{2\sigma^2}[v\hat{\sigma}^2 + (\boldsymbol{\beta} - \mathbf{b})'X'X(\boldsymbol{\beta} - \mathbf{b})]\right\} \quad (4.1.7)$$

This equation will be referred to throughout the chapter.

4.2 ANALYSIS WITH A NONINFORMATIVE PRIOR

4.2.1 Specification of the Noninformative Prior

The choice of a prior distribution depends on the opinions and knowledge of the researcher, and so it is impossible to choose a distribution that will necessarily be appropriate under all circumstances. The approach usually taken, therefore, is to consider broad classes of prior distributions that are likely to be useful in a variety of situations. In this section we discuss use of a *noninformative* prior, and, later in the chapter (Section 4.3), we consider classes of *informative* priors.

The most common noninformative prior for $\boldsymbol{\beta}$ and σ is

$$g(\boldsymbol{\beta},\sigma) \propto \sigma^{-1} \quad (4.2.1)$$

It is obtained by assuming each β_k and σ are a priori independent, with the marginal densities given by $g(\beta_k) \propto$ constant and $g(\sigma) \propto \sigma^{-1}$. We then have $g(\boldsymbol{\beta}) \propto$ constant and $g(\boldsymbol{\beta},\sigma) = g(\boldsymbol{\beta})g(\sigma) \propto \sigma^{-1}$.

The density $g(\sigma) \propto \sigma^{-1}$ is obtained by taking $g(\ln \sigma) =$ constant for $-\infty < \ln \sigma < \infty$ and transforming to $g(\sigma)$. Roughly speaking, $g(\beta_k)$ and $g(\ln \sigma)$ are noninformative priors because they are uniform densities and do not suggest that some values of the parameters are more likely than other values. However, it is natural to ask why, for example, $g(\ln \sigma) =$ constant was chosen instead of $g(\sigma) =$ constant, and whether there are any general rules that can be applied to specify noninformative priors. For details of such information we refer the reader to Jeffreys (1967), Zellner (1971, 1977), Box and Tiao (1973), Villegas (1977), and Berger (1980). Briefly, there are a number of desirable characteristics of noninformative priors as well as some information and invariance criteria for their specification. One rule that leads to priors and posteriors that are invariant under reparameterizations (such as considering the variance σ^2, or the precision $h = 1/\sigma^2$, instead of the standard deviation σ) treats scale and location parameters as a priori independent, and then takes the prior as proportional to the square root of the determinant of the information matrix. Another rule is (1) for a location parameter that can take any value on the real line take the prior as proportional to a constant and (2) for a scale parameter that must be positive, take the prior for the log of that parameter as proportional to a constant. See Jeffreys (1967) for more details about these rules. For our particular model both rules lead to the prior density in Equation 4.2.1 [see, e.g., Judge et al. (1982, Chapter 8)]. In other models different criteria can lead to different noninformative priors, but if the priors are all truly dominated by the likelihood function, the choice between them is likely to have little influence on the posterior distribution.

A property of $g(\boldsymbol{\beta},\sigma)$ that is not shared by conventional density functions is that it does not integrate to unity. We have

$$\int_{-\infty}^{\infty} g(\beta_k)d\beta_k = \infty \qquad \text{and} \qquad \int_0^{\infty} g(\sigma)d\sigma = \infty$$

and density functions with this property are termed improper. Improper priors are often used for representing ignorance. The fact that they are not integrable is of no consequence for making posterior inferences, providing that they lead (via Bayes' theorem) to posterior densities that are proper. Such is generally the case, although two exceptions can be found in Tiao and Tan (1965) and Griffiths et al. (1979).

One interpretation of noninformative priors like (4.2.1) is that they are locally uniform [Box and Tiao (1973)]. That is, they are assumed to hold over the region of the parameter space for which the likelihood function is appreciable, but outside this region they taper off to zero, and are therefore proper. This interpretation goes part way to overcoming some objections that have been raised concerning improper priors, but, pragmatically, it makes little difference whether the parameter range is finite or infinite; the resulting posterior distribution is essentially the same.

Three main reasons seem to have been put forward for using noninformative priors. First, there may be circumstances where we have very little information on the parameters (our knowledge is "vague" or "diffuse"), and we would like a prior distribution that reflects this lack of information. Second, although we might have substantial prior information, there may be occasions where it is considered more objective to present a posterior distribution that reflects only sample information, instead of "biasing" it with our own prior views. Finally, it is frequently very difficult to formulate an appropriate informative prior distribution, and, despite the consequential suboptimality, an easy way out of the difficulty is to use a noninformative prior.

There have been a number of objections to the use of noninformative priors. Some classicists object to the use of subjective distributions of any type, noninformative or informative, while, at the other extreme, some Bayesians argue that we are never completely ignorant about parameters of interest, and it is silly, therefore, not to take advantage of the additional information. Others argue that there are certain characteristics of improper priors that make them unattractive. For details see Hill (1980), Stone (1976), the discussion following the latter article, and the references therein. Two disadvantages of improper priors that are not shared by proper priors and that we mention later in this chapter are: (1) the specification of posterior odds is often difficult or ambiguous when improper priors are employed, and (2) improper priors can lead to estimators that are inadmissible.

4.2.2 Posterior Density Functions from a Noninformative Prior

Combining the likelihood in (4.1.7) with the noninformative prior $g(\boldsymbol{\beta},\sigma) \propto \sigma^{-1}$ leads to the joint posterior density

$$\begin{aligned} g(\boldsymbol{\beta},\sigma|\mathbf{y}) &\propto g(\boldsymbol{\beta},\sigma)\ell(\boldsymbol{\beta},\sigma|\mathbf{y}) \\ &\propto \sigma^{-(T+1)} \exp\left\{-\frac{1}{2\sigma^2}[\nu\hat{\sigma}^2 + (\boldsymbol{\beta}-\mathbf{b})'X'X(\boldsymbol{\beta}-\mathbf{b})]\right\} \end{aligned} \tag{4.2.2}$$

This joint density function summarizes all our postsample information about $\boldsymbol{\beta}$ and σ. If interest centers on only one or two parameters, however, it is likely to be a rather cumbersome way of presenting the information; and so it is useful to consider various marginal and conditional posterior densities. Also, an examination of the marginal and conditional densities provides some insights into the nature of the joint density in (4.2.2). With these points in mind we rewrite (4.2.2) as

$$g(\boldsymbol{\beta},\sigma|\mathbf{y}) = g(\boldsymbol{\beta}|\sigma,\mathbf{y}) \cdot g(\sigma|\mathbf{y}) \tag{4.2.3}$$

where

$$g(\boldsymbol{\beta}|\sigma,\mathbf{y}) = (2\pi)^{-K/2}\sigma^{-K}|X'X|^{1/2} \exp\left[-\frac{1}{2\sigma^2}(\boldsymbol{\beta}-\mathbf{b})'X'X(\boldsymbol{\beta}-\mathbf{b})\right] \tag{4.2.4}$$

and

$$g(\sigma|\mathbf{y}) = \frac{2}{\Gamma(\nu/2)}\left(\frac{\nu\hat{\sigma}^2}{2}\right)^{\nu/2}\frac{1}{\sigma^{\nu+1}}\exp\left(-\frac{\nu\hat{\sigma}^2}{2\sigma^2}\right) \tag{4.2.5}$$

Equation 4.2.4 shows that the conditional posterior density function for $\boldsymbol{\beta}$ given σ is multivariate normal with mean vector $\mathbf{b}$ and covariance $\sigma^2(X'X)^{-1}$. We are able to recognize this fact by examining the terms that contain $\boldsymbol{\beta}$ in the exponent of Equation (4.2.2). That part of the density function that determines its functional form ($\exp[-(\boldsymbol{\beta} - \mathbf{b})'X'X(\boldsymbol{\beta} - \mathbf{b})/2\sigma^2]$ in this case) is called the *kernel* of the density function, while the other part $[(2\pi)^{-K/2}\sigma^{-K}|X'X|^{1/2}]$ is the normalizing constant, introduced to make the function integrate to one. We find the normalizing constant by using known properties of the multivariate normal distribution. Note that, because the density in (4.2.4) is conditional on σ, the normalizing constant includes the term σ^{-K}. In (4.2.5) part of the term $\sigma^{-(v+1)}$ compensates for this introduction.

If, at the outset, we had assumed that σ was known, then our prior would simply be $g(\boldsymbol{\beta}) \propto$ constant and the posterior density for $\boldsymbol{\beta}$ would be the multivariate normal in (4.2.4). Marginal posterior densities for the individual elements in $\boldsymbol{\beta}$ would be the univariate normal densities derived from (4.2.4).

The marginal posterior density function for σ given in (4.2.5) is in the form of an *inverted-gamma* density function with parameters v and $\hat{\sigma}^2$, and it is recognizable through its kernel $\sigma^{-(v+1)}\exp(-v\hat{\sigma}^2/2\sigma^2)$. The term $[2/\Gamma(v/2)](v\hat{\sigma}^2/2)^{v/2}$ is the normalizing constant. See Zellner (1971) for details. Because of the decomposition in (4.2.3) through (4.2.5), the joint density function $g(\boldsymbol{\beta},\sigma|\mathbf{y})$ is often referred to as a *normal-gamma* distribution. The term "normal-gamma" is actually more in accordance with other presentations [e.g., DeGroot (1970)] where the analysis is in terms of a precision parameter $h = 1/\sigma^2$, and the marginal distribution for h is a gamma (not inverted) distribution.

In practice σ is unknown and so a posterior distribution for $\boldsymbol{\beta}$, which is more relevant than (4.2.4) is the marginal one obtained by integrating out the nuisance parameter σ. That is,

$$
\begin{aligned}
g(\boldsymbol{\beta}|\mathbf{y}) &= \int_0^\infty g(\boldsymbol{\beta},\sigma|\mathbf{y})d\sigma \\
&= \int_0^\infty g(\boldsymbol{\beta}|\sigma,\mathbf{y})g(\sigma|\mathbf{y})d\sigma \\
&\propto \int_0^\infty \sigma^{-(T+1)} \exp\left\{-\frac{1}{2\sigma^2}[v\hat{\sigma}^2 + (\boldsymbol{\beta} - \mathbf{b})'X'X(\boldsymbol{\beta} - \mathbf{b})]\right\} d\sigma \\
&\propto \left[1 + \frac{1}{v}(\boldsymbol{\beta} - \mathbf{b})'\frac{X'X}{\hat{\sigma}^2}(\boldsymbol{\beta} - \mathbf{b})\right]^{-(K+v)/2}
\end{aligned}
\tag{4.2.6}
$$

The second line in (4.2.6) shows that the marginal posterior density $g(\boldsymbol{\beta}|\mathbf{y})$ can be viewed as a weighted average of the conditional densities $g(\boldsymbol{\beta}|\sigma,\mathbf{y})$ with weights given by the marginal density for σ, $g(\sigma|\mathbf{y})$. The integral in (4.2.6) is solved by using properties of the gamma function [see, e.g., Judge et al. (1982, p. 86)]. From the kernel of $g(\boldsymbol{\beta}|\mathbf{y})$ given in the last line of (4.2.6) we can recognize that this density is a multivariate t with mean $\mathbf{b}$, covariance matrix $[v/(v - 2)]\hat{\sigma}^2(X'X)^{-1}$, and degrees of freedom parameter $v = T - K$. See Judge et al. (1982, p. 219) for the normalizing constant and properties of the multivariate t.

If we wish to present posterior information on a single parameter, say β_1, then its posterior density can be obtained by integrating $\beta_2, \beta_3, \ldots, \beta_K$ out of $g(\boldsymbol{\beta}|\mathbf{y})$. Alternatively, we can simply use known properties of the multivariate-t distribution. In either event we obtain

$$g(\beta_1|\mathbf{y}) \propto \left[1 + \frac{1}{v}\left(\frac{\beta_1 - b_1}{\hat{\sigma}\sqrt{a^{11}}}\right)^2\right]^{-(1+v)/2} \tag{4.2.7}$$

This density is a univariate t with mean b_1 and variance $[v/(v - 2)]\hat{\sigma}^2 a^{11}$, where b_1 is the first element in $\mathbf{b}$ and a^{11} is the first diagonal element in $(X'X)^{-1}$.

If interest centers on σ, then $\boldsymbol{\beta}$ is regarded as a nuisance parameter and we can use the marginal posterior for σ in (4.2.5). This density can also be obtained via the integral $g(\sigma|\mathbf{y}) = \int g(\boldsymbol{\beta},\sigma|\mathbf{y})d\boldsymbol{\beta}$.

To summarize, when we use a noninformative prior on $\boldsymbol{\beta}$ and σ and combine this with the likelihood function for the normal linear statistical model, the joint posterior density function for $(\boldsymbol{\beta}',\sigma)$ will be of the normal-gamma type. If we wish to make inferences about a single parameter, then its marginal posterior density function can be obtained by integrating out the remaining parameters. The marginal posterior for a single element of $\boldsymbol{\beta}$ is in the form of a univariate-t density, whereas the marginal posterior for σ is an inverted-gamma density.

Although the interpretation is different, these results are very similar to those we obtain using the sampling theory approach. For known σ the sampling theory result is $\mathbf{b} \sim N[\boldsymbol{\beta},\sigma^2(X'X)^{-1}]$ while the Bayesian counterpart is $(\boldsymbol{\beta}|\sigma) \sim N[\mathbf{b},\sigma^2(X'X)^{-1}]$. When σ is unknown, $[(\beta_1 - b_1)/\hat{\sigma}\sqrt{a^{11}}]$ has a (normalized) univariate t-distribution regardless of the approach. However, in the Bayesian approach β_1 is treated as the random variable, and in the sampling theory approach b_1 is the random variable. Finally, in the sampling theory approach $z = v\hat{\sigma}^2/\sigma^2$ follows a $\chi^2_{(v)}$ distribution, and, if we use this information to derive the density function for $\sigma = (v\hat{\sigma}^2/z)^{1/2}$, we obtain the density given in (4.2.5). These similarities between the two approaches are not surprising, given that we have used a noninformative prior distribution. As we see in Section 8.2.1f, however, there are occasions when we have a noninformative prior and the two approaches lead to different results.

4.3 ANALYSIS WITH INFORMATIVE PRIORS

When conducting economic research we are seldom completely ignorant concerning what are likely and unlikely values of the elements in the parameter vector $\boldsymbol{\beta}$. Our prior information may come from previous research, or from our knowledge of economic theory. In either case it is desirable to have a formal framework for incorporating this kind of prior information, and Bayesian analysis with an informative prior distribution provides such a framework. In this section, we derive the posterior distributions that correspond to a number of informative priors. We begin with what is known as the natural conjugate prior.

4.3.1 Specification of a Natural Conjugate Prior

In principle it does not matter what kind of density function has been used to frame prior information on $(\boldsymbol{\beta}',\sigma)$; it still can be combined with the likelihood function to form a posterior density function. Thus, in principle, we can choose the type of prior density function that best reflects our prior information. In practice, however, a number of various types of density functions can usually equally well represent our prior information, and, in terms of mathematical convenience, some of these will combine more easily with the likelihood function than others. Given these circumstances it is desirable to choose a prior distribution from a family of density functions that combines conveniently with the likelihood function and that is rich in the sense that it can represent a wide variety of prior opinions. In many instances natural conjugate priors have these properties. They are algebraically convenient because a natural conjugate prior leads to a posterior density with the same functional form, and hence the posterior density from one sample will be the natural conjugate prior for a future sample; and they are usually sufficiently flexible to represent a diversity of prior opinions. [There are some cases, however, where results can be quite sensitive to specification of the informative prior. See, e.g., Berger (1980, p. 85).]

To obtain the natural conjugate prior for a set of parameters we first write the likelihood function in terms of its sufficient statistics and then note its type of functional form when viewed as a function of the unknown parameters. The likelihood function for the model we are considering was written in terms of its sufficient statistics in Equation 4.1.7. When viewed as a function of $\boldsymbol{\beta}$ and σ, the $\ell(\boldsymbol{\beta},\sigma|\mathbf{y})$ is in the form of a normal-gamma function (see Section 4.2) because it can be written as

$$\ell(\sigma,\boldsymbol{\beta}|\mathbf{y}) \propto h_1(\boldsymbol{\beta}|\sigma,\mathbf{y}) \cdot h_2(\sigma|\mathbf{y}) \tag{4.3.1}$$

where

$$h_1(\boldsymbol{\beta}|\sigma,\mathbf{y}) = \exp\left[-\frac{1}{2\sigma^2}(\boldsymbol{\beta}-\mathbf{b})'X'X(\boldsymbol{\beta}-\mathbf{b})\right] \tag{4.3.2}$$

and

$$h_2(\sigma|\mathbf{y}) = \sigma^{-T}\exp\left(\frac{v\hat{\sigma}^2}{2\sigma^2}\right) \tag{4.3.3}$$

This suggests that the natural conjugate prior distribution for $(\boldsymbol{\beta}',\sigma)$ is one where the conditional distribution of $\boldsymbol{\beta}$ given σ is multivariate normal and the marginal distribution for σ is an inverted-gamma distribution. Thus for our informative prior we take

$$g(\boldsymbol{\beta}|\sigma) = (2\pi)^{-K/2}\sigma^{-K}|A|^{1/2} \exp\left[-\frac{1}{2\sigma^2}(\boldsymbol{\beta} - \bar{\boldsymbol{\beta}})'A(\boldsymbol{\beta} - \bar{\boldsymbol{\beta}})\right] \tag{4.3.4}$$

and

$$g(\sigma) = \frac{2}{\Gamma(\bar{v}/2)}\left(\frac{\bar{v}\bar{s}^2}{2}\right)^{\bar{v}/2}\frac{1}{\sigma^{\bar{v}+1}}\exp\left(-\frac{\bar{v}\bar{s}^2}{2\sigma^2}\right) \tag{4.3.5}$$

where the parameters $\bar{\boldsymbol{\beta}}$, A, $\bar{v}$, and $\bar{s}^2$ depend on our prior information. In particular,

$$E[\boldsymbol{\beta}|\sigma] = E[\boldsymbol{\beta}] = \bar{\boldsymbol{\beta}} \qquad \text{cov}[\boldsymbol{\beta}|\sigma] = \sigma^2 A^{-1}$$

$$E[\sigma] = \frac{\Gamma[(\bar{v}-1)/2]}{\Gamma(\bar{v}/2)}\left(\frac{\bar{v}}{2}\right)^{1/2}\bar{s} \qquad E[\sigma^2] = \frac{\bar{v}\bar{s}^2}{\bar{v}-2}$$

and the prior mode for σ is

$$\text{mode}(\sigma) = \left(\frac{\bar{v}}{\bar{v}+1}\right)^{1/2}\bar{s} \tag{4.3.6}$$

In (4.3.4) and (4.3.5) prior parameters take the place of the sufficient statistics that appear in (4.3.2) and (4.3.3), respectively. Also, for notation, a *single bar* over a symbol denotes a *prior parameter,* and, in later sections, a *double bar* denotes a *posterior parameter.*

Combining (4.3.4) and (4.3.5) and omitting the constants of proportionality gives the normal-gamma joint prior density

$$g(\boldsymbol{\beta},\sigma) \propto \sigma^{-K-v-1}\exp\left\{-\frac{1}{2\sigma^2}[vs^2 + (\boldsymbol{\beta} - \bar{\boldsymbol{\beta}})'A(\boldsymbol{\beta} - \bar{\boldsymbol{\beta}})]\right\} \tag{4.3.7}$$

The marginal prior density for $\boldsymbol{\beta}$ is obtained by integrating σ out of (4.3.7) and is the multivariate-*t* density

$$g(\boldsymbol{\beta}) \propto \left[1 + \frac{1}{\bar{v}}(\boldsymbol{\beta} - \bar{\boldsymbol{\beta}})'\frac{A}{\bar{s}^2}(\boldsymbol{\beta} - \bar{\boldsymbol{\beta}})\right]^{-(K+\bar{v})/2} \tag{4.3.8}$$

Correspondingly, each of the individual elements in $\boldsymbol{\beta}$ has a univariate-*t* prior density.

To prove that (4.3.7) is a natural conjugate prior we must show that the posterior density function derived from it will also be of the normal-gamma form; this proof is given in the next section. For an example of how prior information can be used to set values of the prior parameters $\bar{\boldsymbol{\beta}}$, A, $\bar{v}$, and $\bar{s}^2$, see Judge et al. (1982, p. 223).

4.3.2 Posterior Density Functions from a Natural Conjugate Prior

Using Bayes' theorem (4.1.5) to combine the natural conjugate prior (4.3.7) with the likelihood function, (4.1.6) yields the joint posterior density function

$$g(\boldsymbol{\beta},\sigma|\mathbf{y})$$
$$\propto \sigma^{-T-K-\bar{v}-1} \exp\left\{-\frac{1}{2\sigma^2}[\bar{v}\bar{s}^2 + (\boldsymbol{\beta} - \bar{\boldsymbol{\beta}})'A(\boldsymbol{\beta} - \bar{\boldsymbol{\beta}}) + (\mathbf{y} - X\boldsymbol{\beta})'(\mathbf{y} - X\boldsymbol{\beta})]\right\} \tag{4.3.9a}$$

$$= \sigma^{-T-K-\bar{v}-1} \exp\left\{-\frac{1}{2\sigma^2}\left[\bar{v}\bar{s}^2 + \begin{pmatrix} A^{1/2}\bar{\boldsymbol{\beta}} - A^{1/2}\boldsymbol{\beta} \\ \mathbf{y} - X\boldsymbol{\beta} \end{pmatrix}'\begin{pmatrix} A^{1/2}\bar{\boldsymbol{\beta}} - A^{1/2}\boldsymbol{\beta} \\ \mathbf{y} - X\boldsymbol{\beta} \end{pmatrix}\right]\right\} \tag{4.3.9b}$$

$$= \sigma^{-T-K-\bar{v}-1} \exp\left\{-\frac{1}{2\sigma^2}[\bar{v}\bar{s}^2 + (\boldsymbol{\omega} - W\boldsymbol{\beta})'(\boldsymbol{\omega} - W\boldsymbol{\beta})]\right\} \tag{4.3.9c}$$

where $A^{1/2}$ is a symmetric matrix such that $A = A^{1/2}A^{1/2}$,

$$\boldsymbol{\omega} = \begin{pmatrix} A^{1/2}\bar{\boldsymbol{\beta}} \\ \mathbf{y} \end{pmatrix} \qquad \text{and} \qquad W = \begin{pmatrix} A^{1/2} \\ X \end{pmatrix}$$

To simplify (4.3.9) it is convenient to define

$$\bar{\bar{\boldsymbol{\beta}}} = (W'W)^{-1}W'\boldsymbol{\omega} = (A + X'X)^{-1}(A\bar{\boldsymbol{\beta}} + X'X\mathbf{b}) \tag{4.3.10}$$

$$\begin{aligned} \bar{\bar{v}}\bar{\bar{s}}^2 &= \bar{v}\bar{s}^2 + (\boldsymbol{\omega} - W\bar{\bar{\boldsymbol{\beta}}})'(\boldsymbol{\omega} - W\bar{\bar{\boldsymbol{\beta}}}) \\ &= \bar{v}\bar{s}^2 + (\mathbf{y} - X\bar{\bar{\boldsymbol{\beta}}})'(\mathbf{y} - X\bar{\bar{\boldsymbol{\beta}}}) + (\bar{\boldsymbol{\beta}} - \bar{\bar{\boldsymbol{\beta}}})'A(\bar{\boldsymbol{\beta}} - \bar{\bar{\boldsymbol{\beta}}}) \\ &= \bar{v}\bar{s}^2 + \mathbf{y}'\mathbf{y} + \bar{\boldsymbol{\beta}}'A\bar{\boldsymbol{\beta}} - \bar{\bar{\boldsymbol{\beta}}}'(A + X'X)\bar{\bar{\boldsymbol{\beta}}} \end{aligned} \tag{4.3.11}$$

and

$$\bar{\bar{v}} = T + \bar{v} \tag{4.3.12}$$

Using these definitions and a decomposition similar to that used for deriving (4.1.7) from (4.1.6), we can write (4.3.9c) as

$$g(\boldsymbol{\beta},\sigma|\mathbf{y})$$
$$\propto \sigma^{-\bar{\bar{v}}-K-1} \exp\left\{-\frac{1}{2\sigma^2}[\bar{v}\bar{s}^2 + (\boldsymbol{\omega} - W\bar{\bar{\boldsymbol{\beta}}})'(\boldsymbol{\omega} - W\bar{\bar{\boldsymbol{\beta}}}) \right.$$
$$\left. + (\boldsymbol{\beta} - \bar{\bar{\boldsymbol{\beta}}})'W'W(\boldsymbol{\beta} - \bar{\bar{\boldsymbol{\beta}}})]\right\}$$

$$\propto \sigma^{-K} \exp\left[-\frac{1}{2\sigma^2}(\boldsymbol{\beta} - \bar{\bar{\boldsymbol{\beta}}})'(A + X'X)(\boldsymbol{\beta} - \bar{\bar{\boldsymbol{\beta}}})\right] \cdot \sigma^{-(\bar{\bar{v}}+1)} \exp\left(-\frac{\bar{\bar{v}}\bar{\bar{s}}^2}{2\sigma^2}\right)$$

$$\propto g(\boldsymbol{\beta}|\sigma,\mathbf{y}) \cdot g(\sigma|\mathbf{y}) \tag{4.3.13}$$

This function is of the normal-gamma type because the conditional posterior density function for $\boldsymbol{\beta}$, given σ, is multivariate normal with mean $\bar{\bar{\boldsymbol{\beta}}}$ and covariance matrix $\sigma^2(A + X'X)^{-1}$, and the marginal posterior density function for σ is inverted gamma with parameters $\bar{\bar{v}}$ and $\bar{\bar{s}}^2$.

The marginal posterior density for $\boldsymbol{\beta}$ is a multivariate-t distribution, and, along the lines described in Section 4.1.2, it is obtained by integrating σ out of (4.3.13). It is given by

$$g(\boldsymbol{\beta}|\mathbf{y}) \propto \left[1 + \frac{1}{\bar{\bar{v}}}(\boldsymbol{\beta} - \bar{\bar{\boldsymbol{\beta}}})' \frac{(A + X'X)}{\bar{\bar{s}}^2}(\boldsymbol{\beta} - \bar{\bar{\boldsymbol{\beta}}})\right]^{-(K+\bar{\bar{v}})/2} \tag{4.3.14}$$

The marginal posterior density for a single element from $\boldsymbol{\beta}$, say β_1, will have a univariate-t distribution with density function

$$g(\beta_1|\mathbf{y}) \propto \left[1 + \frac{1}{\bar{\bar{v}}}\left(\frac{\beta_1 - \bar{\bar{\beta}}_1}{\bar{\bar{s}}\sqrt{c^{11}}}\right)^2\right]^{-(1+\bar{\bar{v}})/2} \tag{4.3.15}$$

where $\bar{\bar{\beta}}_1$ is the first element in $\bar{\bar{\boldsymbol{\beta}}}$, and c^{11} is the first diagonal element in $(A + X'X)^{-1}$.

These posterior density functions represent our current state of knowledge (prior and sample) about the parameters and, if desired, they can be used to obtain point or interval estimates or to test hypotheses. Note from Equation 4.3.10 that the posterior mean $\bar{\bar{\boldsymbol{\beta}}}$ can be regarded as a matrix weighted average of the prior mean $\bar{\boldsymbol{\beta}}$ and the sampling theory estimator $\mathbf{b}$, with weights given by the inverses of the conditional covariance matrices σ^2A^{-1} and $\sigma^2(X'X)^{-1}$.

The properties of matrix-weighted averages have been studied by Chamberlain and Leamer (1976) and Leamer (1978, 1982). One property is that, except under special and unlikely circumstances, it will not be true that $\bar{\bar{\boldsymbol{\beta}}}$ lies between $\mathbf{b}$ and $\bar{\boldsymbol{\beta}}$, in the sense that each element in $\bar{\bar{\boldsymbol{\beta}}}$ lies between the corresponding elements from the other two vectors. This result is in contrast to the case of a simple weighted average (see Section 4.3.4). A simple illustrative example can be found in Judge et al. (1982, p. 230). For given values of $\mathbf{b}$, $\bar{\boldsymbol{\beta}}$ and $X'X$, Chamberlain and Leamer provide an ellipsoid bound that will contain $\bar{\bar{\boldsymbol{\beta}}}$ regardless of the value of the prior covariance matrix σ^2A^{-1}. Leamer (1982) extends this result by deriving ellipsoid bounds for cases where σ^2A^{-1} can be bounded from above and/or below. These ellipsoid bounds are useful because specification of A is often difficult, and because it is useful to be able to present posterior information that is relevant for a wide range of prior distributions.

Another point worth noting is that using a natural conjugate prior is equivalent to assuming that we have information from some previous hypothetical sample. If this hypothetical sample information is combined with our current sample and the combined sample is used in conjunction with a noninformative prior, we would get results identical to those just presented. In the hypothetical sample $X'X$ would be given by A, $X'\mathbf{y}$ by $A\bar{\boldsymbol{\beta}}$, $\hat{\sigma}^2$ by $\bar{s}^2$, and the degrees of freedom by $\bar{v}$.

When exact multicollinearity exists and $X'X$ is singular it is impossible to obtain a unique least squares estimator $\mathbf{b}$. Bayesian analysis with a natural conjugate prior can still proceed, however, and, providing that $A + X'X$ is nonsingular, the posterior mean $\bar{\bar{\boldsymbol{\beta}}}$ will be unique. (In Equation 4.3.10, $X'X\mathbf{b}$ can be replaced by $X'\mathbf{y}$.) In addition, a great deal of insight into the multicollinearity problem (both exact and nonexact collinearity) can be obtained by examining it within a Bayesian framework. For details see Zellner (1971, pp. 75–81), Leamer (1978, pp. 170–181), and Malinvaud (1980, p. 240).

4.3.3 Recursive Updating Formulae

As we obtain more sample information, it is desirable to update our posterior distributions to reflect this additional information. For the cases considered in Sections 4.2.2 and 4.3.2 this can be achieved using some convenient recursive formulae. In the context of Section 4.3.2 suppose that $\bar{\bar{\boldsymbol{\beta}}}_T$ is the posterior mean for $\boldsymbol{\beta}$ calculated from T observations, and that S_T is the matrix $(W'W)^{-1}$ based on T observations. Then, for an additional observation given by $(y_{T+1}, \mathbf{x}'_{T+1})$, it can be shown that

$$\bar{\bar{\boldsymbol{\beta}}}_{T+1} = \bar{\bar{\boldsymbol{\beta}}}_T + \frac{S_T\mathbf{x}_{T+1}(y_{T+1} - \mathbf{x}'_{T+1}\bar{\bar{\boldsymbol{\beta}}}_T)}{1 + \mathbf{x}'_{T+1}S_T\mathbf{x}_{T+1}} \tag{4.3.16}$$

and

$$S_{T+1} = S_T - \frac{S_T\mathbf{x}_{T+1}\mathbf{x}'_{T+1}S_T}{1 + \mathbf{x}'_{T+1}S_T\mathbf{x}_{T+1}} \tag{4.3.17}$$

Once these quantities have been obtained it is straightforward to update the remaining posterior parameters given in Equations (4.3.11) and (4.3.12). Analogous results also hold for the posterior parameters derived from a noninformative prior (Section 4.2.2).

4.3.4 The *g*-Prior Distribution

Although procedures for specifying the prior parameters of a natural conjugate prior have been developed (see Section 4.3.6), the implementation of these procedures can be difficult, and, in particular, there are many instances when it is not straightforward to specify the prior precision matrix A. A special case of the natural conjugate prior that is relatively easy to specify is the g prior suggested by Zellner (1982a). In this case the prior precision matrix is given by $A = g_0X'X$, g_0 being a prior parameter. Since g_0 is only a scalar it is much easier to specify than the complete precision matrix A, and as Zellner demonstrates, the g prior arises naturally through application of the rational expectations hypothesis.

If an investigator has little knowledge about σ (a common situation), then the diffuse prior $g(\sigma) \propto \sigma^{-1}$ can be employed in addition to setting $A = g_0 X'X$, and the joint posterior density in (4.3.13) becomes

$$g(\boldsymbol{\beta},\sigma|\mathbf{y}) \propto \sigma^{-K} \exp\left[-\frac{1+g_0}{2\sigma^2}(\boldsymbol{\beta}-\bar{\bar{\boldsymbol{\beta}}})'X'X(\boldsymbol{\beta}-\bar{\bar{\boldsymbol{\beta}}})\right] \cdot \sigma^{-(\bar{\bar{v}}+1)} \exp\left(-\frac{\bar{\bar{v}}\bar{\bar{s}}^2}{2\sigma^2}\right) \tag{4.3.18}$$

where $\bar{\bar{v}} = T$,

$$\bar{\bar{v}}\bar{\bar{s}}^2 = (\mathbf{y} - X\bar{\bar{\boldsymbol{\beta}}})'(\mathbf{y} - X\bar{\bar{\boldsymbol{\beta}}}) + g_0(\bar{\boldsymbol{\beta}} - \bar{\bar{\boldsymbol{\beta}}})'X'X(\bar{\boldsymbol{\beta}} - \bar{\bar{\boldsymbol{\beta}}}) \tag{4.3.19}$$

and

$$\bar{\bar{\boldsymbol{\beta}}} = \frac{g_0\bar{\boldsymbol{\beta}} + \mathbf{b}}{1 + g_0} \tag{4.3.20}$$

Thus, the posterior mean for $\boldsymbol{\beta}$ becomes a simple weighted average of the prior mean $\bar{\boldsymbol{\beta}}$ and the least squares estimate $\mathbf{b}$, with the relative weights determined by g_0. Marginal posterior densities for $\boldsymbol{\beta}$ and σ can be obtained from (4.3.18) along the lines described in Section 4.3.2. See Zellner (1982a) for further results and for an evaluation of the sampling properties of the posterior mean.

4.3.5 An Independent *t*-Gamma Prior

The natural conjugate prior is a convenient informative prior because it combines nicely with the likelihood function, but it has been criticized on a number of grounds [see, e.g., Leamer (1978, pp. 79–80)]. First, because it treats prior information as a previous sample from the same process, it does not distinguish between prior and sample information, no matter how strong their apparent conflict. Second, it is often difficult to conceptualize prior information about $\boldsymbol{\beta}$ conditionally on σ. Rather than assume our prior information about $\boldsymbol{\beta}$ depends on σ, as the natural conjugate prior implies, it might be more realistic to consider independent prior distributions for $\boldsymbol{\beta}$ and σ. Third, if in (4.3.7), we let $\bar{v}$ and A approach zero to obtain the limiting natural conjugate prior that represents ignorance, we obtain $g(\boldsymbol{\beta},\sigma) \propto \sigma^{-K-1}$. This is in conflict with the usual diffuse prior $g(\boldsymbol{\beta},\sigma) \propto \sigma^{-1}$, and it leads to a posterior distribution with T instead of $T - K$ degrees of freedom.

An alternative prior that overcomes these objections [Dickey (1975), Leamer (1978)] is to treat $\boldsymbol{\beta}$ and σ independently with a multivariate-t prior for $\boldsymbol{\beta}$ and an inverted-gamma prior for σ. In this case we have $g(\boldsymbol{\beta},\sigma) = g(\boldsymbol{\beta})g(\sigma)$ where

$$g(\boldsymbol{\beta}) \propto \left[1 + \frac{1}{\upsilon^*}(\boldsymbol{\beta} - \bar{\boldsymbol{\beta}})'A(\boldsymbol{\beta} - \bar{\boldsymbol{\beta}})\right]^{-(K+\upsilon^*)/2} \tag{4.3.21}$$

$$g(\sigma) \propto \frac{1}{\sigma^{\bar{\upsilon}+1}} \exp\left[-\frac{\bar{\upsilon}\bar{s}^2}{2\sigma^2}\right] \tag{4.3.22}$$

and υ^*, $\bar{\boldsymbol{\beta}}$, A, $\bar{\upsilon}$, and $\bar{s}^2$ are prior parameters to be specified. Combining (4.3.21) and (4.3.22) with the likelihood function and integrating out σ yields

$$g(\boldsymbol{\beta}|\mathbf{y}) \propto \left[1 + \frac{1}{\bar{\bar{\upsilon}}}(\boldsymbol{\beta} - \mathbf{b})'\frac{X'X}{\bar{\bar{s}}^2}(\boldsymbol{\beta} - \mathbf{b})\right]^{-(K+\bar{\bar{\upsilon}})/2} \left[1 + \frac{1}{\upsilon^*}(\boldsymbol{\beta} - \bar{\boldsymbol{\beta}})'A(\boldsymbol{\beta} - \bar{\boldsymbol{\beta}})\right]^{-(K+\upsilon^*)/2} \tag{4.3.23}$$

where $\bar{\bar{\upsilon}} = \bar{\upsilon} + T - K$, $\bar{\bar{\upsilon}}\bar{\bar{s}}^2 = \upsilon\hat{\sigma}^2 + \bar{\upsilon}\bar{s}^2$, $\upsilon = T - K$, and $\upsilon\hat{\sigma}^2 = (\mathbf{y} - X\mathbf{b})'(\mathbf{y} - X\mathbf{b})$. This posterior density is in the form of the product of two multivariate-*t* functions. It can be shown that a density of this form is also obtained if we begin with a noninformative prior and combine two samples with different variances [see Zellner (1971) and Leamer (1978)]. Furthermore, the density in (4.3.23) is a member of a broader class of densities known as *poly-t densities*. Poly-*t* densities arise from a surprisingly large number of econometric models and their properties have been investigated by Dickey (1968, 1975), Drèze (1977), and Richard and Tompa (1980).

Our earlier objections to the natural conjugate prior and its corresponding posterior do not hold for the posterior $g(\boldsymbol{\beta}|\mathbf{y})$ in (4.3.23). If the sample and prior information are apparently in conflict, $g(\boldsymbol{\beta}|\mathbf{y})$ will be bimodal with modes reflecting this conflict. The problem of specifying prior views about $\boldsymbol{\beta}$ conditionally on σ has been overcome; and, as $\bar{\upsilon}$ and A approach zero, the limiting form of the product of (4.3.21) and (4.3.22) is $g(\boldsymbol{\beta},\sigma) \propto \sigma^{-1}$.

To conclude, we note that it is possible to broaden the class of natural conjugate priors to include $g(\boldsymbol{\beta},\sigma) \propto \sigma^{-1}$ as a limiting case, providing that we also allow for the possibility of other improper priors. The prior

$$g(\boldsymbol{\beta},\sigma) \propto \sigma^{-\mu} \exp\left\{-\frac{1}{2\sigma^2}[\eta + (\boldsymbol{\beta} - \bar{\boldsymbol{\beta}})'A(\boldsymbol{\beta} - \bar{\boldsymbol{\beta}})]\right\} \tag{4.3.24}$$

is equivalent to the proper natural conjugate prior if $\mu > K + 1$, it is improper if $\mu \leq K + 1$, and it is equal to $g(\boldsymbol{\beta},\sigma) \propto \sigma^{-1}$ if $A = 0$, $\eta = 0$, and $\mu = 1$.

4.3.6 Assessment of Informative Priors

Throughout this section we have assumed that an investigator can specify an appropriate prior distribution that adequately reflects available prior information on $\boldsymbol{\beta}$ and σ. In this regard, it is relatively easy to visualize how percentiles of a distribution could be used to specify a prior mean and variance for each of the elements in $\boldsymbol{\beta}$. It is much more difficult, however, even for the trained statistician, to conceptualize prior information in terms of the covariances of the elements in $\boldsymbol{\beta}$. Also, although it might be possible to get some idea about likely values for σ because of their implications for the prior covariance matrix $\text{cov}(\boldsymbol{\beta}|\sigma)$, it is not immediately obvious how to proceed.

These facts have led to research into the assessment or elicitation of prior density functions. We will not give details of the various suggestions, but we note that one possibility is to use elicited percentiles, as mentioned above, while another is to assess what is known as the prior predictive density for y for a number of settings of the explanatory variables and to use these to derive parameters such as $\bar{\boldsymbol{\beta}}$, A, $\bar{v}$, and $\bar{s}$. Methods for combining information from both approaches have also been suggested. For details we refer the reader to Dickey (1980), Kadane (1980), Kadane et al. (1980), Winkler (1967, 1977, 1980), and Zellner (1972).

4.4 POINT ESTIMATION

The posterior density function for a parameter summarizes all the information that a researcher has about that parameter; thus, once the equation of the posterior density has been derived this could be regarded as a reasonable point at which to conclude a study. Under some circumstances, however, a researcher needs to make a decision on just one value (or *point estimate*) of a parameter, and in this situation, we need some procedure for determining which value is best. In the Bayesian framework this procedure consists of (1), assuming that there is a loss function, $L(\boldsymbol{\theta},\hat{\boldsymbol{\theta}})$, that describes the consequences of basing a decision on the point estimate $\hat{\boldsymbol{\theta}}$ when $\boldsymbol{\theta}$ is the true parameter vector, and (2), choosing that value of $\hat{\boldsymbol{\theta}}$ that minimizes expected loss where the expectation is taken with respect to the posterior density function for $\boldsymbol{\theta}$.

Thus, the Bayesian estimator for $\boldsymbol{\theta}$ is that value of $\hat{\boldsymbol{\theta}}$, which minimizes

$$E_{\boldsymbol{\theta}|\mathbf{y}}[L(\boldsymbol{\theta},\hat{\boldsymbol{\theta}})] = \int L(\boldsymbol{\theta},\hat{\boldsymbol{\theta}})g(\boldsymbol{\theta}|\mathbf{y})d\boldsymbol{\theta} \tag{4.4.1}$$

For example, for the general quadratic loss function

$$L(\boldsymbol{\theta},\hat{\boldsymbol{\theta}}) = (\boldsymbol{\theta} - \hat{\boldsymbol{\theta}})'Q(\boldsymbol{\theta} - \hat{\boldsymbol{\theta}}) \tag{4.4.2}$$

where Q is a positive definite matrix, it can be readily shown [e.g., Judge et al. (1982, p. 232)] that the posterior mean $E[\boldsymbol{\theta}|\mathbf{y}]$ is the optimal Bayesian point estimate. In terms of the coefficient vector $\boldsymbol{\beta}$ for the general linear model $\mathbf{y} = X\boldsymbol{\beta} + \mathbf{e}$ where $E[\mathbf{e}] = \mathbf{0}$ and $E[\mathbf{ee}'] = \sigma^2 I$, use of a natural conjugate prior led to the posterior mean $\bar{\bar{\boldsymbol{\beta}}} = (A + X'X)^{-1}(A\bar{\boldsymbol{\beta}} + X'X\mathbf{b})$; with a diffuse prior the posterior mean was the least squares estimator $\mathbf{b} = (X'X)^{-1}X'\mathbf{y}$. For σ and σ^2 the posterior means when a natural conjugate prior is used are

$$E[\sigma|\mathbf{y}] = \frac{\Gamma[(\bar{\bar{v}} - 1)/2]}{\Gamma(\bar{\bar{v}}/2)}\left(\frac{\bar{\bar{v}}}{2}\right)^{1/2}\bar{\bar{s}} \quad \text{and} \quad E[\sigma^2|\mathbf{y}] = \frac{\bar{\bar{v}}\bar{\bar{s}}^2}{\bar{\bar{v}} - 2}$$

respectively. To obtain the corresponding posterior means when a diffuse prior is employed the parameters $\bar{\bar{v}}$ and $\bar{\bar{s}}$ are replaced by v and $\hat{\sigma}^2$, respectively.

Other loss functions are also sometimes of interest. If the loss function is *linear,* for example, the posterior median is optimal; in Section 4.4.2 we give the optimal point estimate for the reciprocal of a coefficient under a *relative squared error* loss function. The remainder of this section is made up as follows. In Section 4.4.1 we consider some sampling theory properties of Bayesian estimators. Point estimates for reciprocals and ratios of coefficients are considered in Section 4.4.2; in Section 4.4.3 we examine some specific sampling theory estimators from a Bayesian point of view; and some concluding remarks are given in Section 4.4.4.

4.4.1 Sampling Theory Properties of Bayesian Estimators

Let us now compare the Bayesian approach of obtaining estimators that minimize expected posterior loss with the decision theory approach employed within a sampling theory framework. This latter approach was discussed in Chapter 3. Reiterating briefly, in the sampling theory approach, we first assume, as we did for the Bayesian approach, that we have a loss function $L(\boldsymbol{\theta},\hat{\boldsymbol{\theta}})$ that reflects the consequences of choosing $\hat{\boldsymbol{\theta}}$ when $\boldsymbol{\theta}$ is the real parameter vector. Then we assume that a desirable estimator is one that minimizes expected loss where the expectation is taken with respect to $\mathbf{y}$. That is, we would like to choose an estimator where average loss is a minimum with the average calculated from the losses incurred in repeated samples. This average loss is known as the *risk function* and is given by

$$\rho(\boldsymbol{\theta},\hat{\boldsymbol{\theta}}) = E_{\mathbf{y}|\boldsymbol{\theta}}[L(\boldsymbol{\theta},\hat{\boldsymbol{\theta}})] = \int L(\boldsymbol{\theta},\hat{\boldsymbol{\theta}})f(\mathbf{y}|\boldsymbol{\theta})\, d\mathbf{y} \qquad (4.4.3)$$

The risk function depends on $\boldsymbol{\theta}$ and so it is impossible to find an estimator that minimizes risk over the whole parameter space. There are a number of ways of overcoming this problem, one of which is to introduce a prior density $g(\boldsymbol{\theta})$, and to find that estimator that minimizes *average risk,* defined as

$$E_{\boldsymbol{\theta}}[\rho(\boldsymbol{\theta},\hat{\boldsymbol{\theta}})] = \int\int L(\boldsymbol{\theta},\hat{\boldsymbol{\theta}})f(\mathbf{y}|\boldsymbol{\theta})g(\boldsymbol{\theta})d\mathbf{y}\, d\boldsymbol{\theta} \qquad (4.4.4a)$$

To see the relationship between this estimator (which is also called a Bayesian estimator), and one that minimizes expected posterior loss, we rewrite (4.4.4a) as

$$E_{\boldsymbol{\theta}}[\rho(\boldsymbol{\theta},\hat{\boldsymbol{\theta}})] = \int f(\mathbf{y})\, [\int L(\boldsymbol{\theta},\hat{\boldsymbol{\theta}})g(\boldsymbol{\theta}|\mathbf{y})\, d\boldsymbol{\theta}]\, d\mathbf{y} \qquad (4.4.4b)$$

where we have used the fact that $f(\mathbf{y}|\boldsymbol{\theta})g(\boldsymbol{\theta}) = g(\boldsymbol{\theta}|\mathbf{y})f(\mathbf{y})$ and we have changed the order of integration. The function in (4.4.4b) will be minimized (with respect to $\hat{\boldsymbol{\theta}}$) when the integral within the square brackets is minimized. This integral is equal to expected posterior loss, and hence the two estimators are identical, providing the step from (4.4.4a) to (4.4.4b) is legitimate.

The legitimacy of (4.4.4b) hinges on whether or not the integral in (4.4.4a) converges (average risk is finite). In some cases average risk is infinite, in which case it is not possible to interchange the order of integration, and an estimator that minimizes average risk does not exist. Nevertheless, we may still be able to obtain an estimator that minimizes expected posterior loss. Such situations typically arise when improper priors are used in conjunction with commonly used loss functions such as the quadratic. For example, for a quadratic loss function and the improper prior $g(\boldsymbol{\beta},\sigma) \propto \sigma^{-1}$, the estimator **b** minimizes expected posterior loss. Under these same assumptions, however, average risk is infinite. A similar situation can arise with proper prior densities and some other types of loss functions. See Berger (1980, p. 122) for an example.

The relevance of considering the sampling properties of Bayesian estimators has been questioned by some [e.g., Tiao and Box (1973)], but, nevertheless, it is generally considered desirable if, in addition to their favorable Bayesian qualities, Bayesian estimators also perform well from a sampling theory viewpoint. See, for example, Hill (1975), Zellner (1978), and Berger (1982). One property that is possessed by virtually all Bayesian estimators that minimize average risk is that they are admissible [see Berger (1980) for details and Chapter 3 for the definition of admissibility]. Thus, it follows from the above discussion that when average risk is finite, the Bayesian estimator that minimizes expected posterior loss will be admissible. If an improper prior is employed, however, average risk is unlikely to be finite (and is difficult to interpret anyway), and the minimum expected posterior loss estimator may not be admissible. For example, the estimator **b** is the posterior mean that results from the improper prior $g(\boldsymbol{\beta},\sigma) \propto \sigma^{-1}$, and it therefore minimizes expected posterior loss for the loss function $(\boldsymbol{\beta} - \hat{\boldsymbol{\beta}})'X'X(\boldsymbol{\beta} - \hat{\boldsymbol{\beta}})$. With respect to this loss function, and for $K \geq 3$, however, **b** is inadmissible because it is dominated by the Stein-rule estimator. See Chapter 3 and Judge and Bock (1978).

The sampling theory properties of $\bar{\bar{\boldsymbol{\beta}}} = (A + X'X)^{-1}(A\bar{\boldsymbol{\beta}} + X'X\mathbf{b})$, the posterior mean obtained from employing a natural conjugate prior, have been investigated and compared with those of **b**, by Giles and Rayner (1979). The bias of $\bar{\bar{\boldsymbol{\beta}}}$ is $W^{-1}A(\bar{\boldsymbol{\beta}} - \boldsymbol{\beta})$, where $W = A + X'X$; its mean square error matrix is

$$\text{MSE}(\bar{\bar{\boldsymbol{\beta}}}) = \sigma^2 W^{-1}X'XW^{-1} + W^{-1}A(\bar{\boldsymbol{\beta}} - \boldsymbol{\beta})(\bar{\boldsymbol{\beta}} - \boldsymbol{\beta})'AW^{-1} \tag{4.4.5}$$

and Giles and Rayner show that $\text{MSE}(\bar{\bar{\boldsymbol{\beta}}}) - \text{MSE}(\mathbf{b})$ is negative semidefinite if and only if

$$(\bar{\boldsymbol{\beta}} - \boldsymbol{\beta})'[(X'X)^{-1} + 2A^{-1}]^{-1}(\bar{\boldsymbol{\beta}} - \boldsymbol{\beta}) \leq \sigma^2 \tag{4.4.6}$$

This inequality will always hold if the prior information is unbiased in the sense that $\bar{\boldsymbol{\beta}} = \boldsymbol{\beta}$. When $\bar{\boldsymbol{\beta}} \neq \boldsymbol{\beta}$, whether or not (4.4.6) holds will depend on the magnitude of the prior bias relative to the precision of the sample and prior information.

The properties of Bayesian and sampling theory estimators have also been compared for a number of other models. See, for example, Fomby and Guilkey (1978), Surekha and Griffiths (1984), and Zellner (1971, Ch. 9).

4.4.2 Point Estimates for Reciprocals and Ratios of Regression Coefficients

Zellner (1978) considers minimum expected posterior loss (MELO) estimators for reciprocals and ratios of regression coefficients. In the case of a reciprocal, say $\theta_1 = 1/\beta_1$, it can be shown that, for the relative squared error loss function $L(\theta_1,\hat{\theta}_1) = (\theta_1 - \hat{\theta}_1)^2/\theta_1^2$, the estimator that minimizes expected posterior loss is

$$\hat{\theta}_1^* = \frac{1}{E[\beta_1]} \cdot \frac{1}{1 + \text{var}[\beta_1]/E[\beta_1]^2} \tag{4.4.7}$$

where $E[\cdot]$ and $\text{var}[\cdot]$ refer to the posterior moments of β_1.

For the ratio of two regression coefficients, say $\theta_2 = \beta_1/\beta_2$, and the loss function $L = \beta_2^2(\theta_2 - \hat{\theta}_2)^2$, the Bayesian estimator is

$$\hat{\theta}_2^* = \frac{E[\beta_1]}{E[\beta_2]} \cdot \frac{1 + \text{cov}[\beta_1,\beta_2]/E[\beta_1]E[\beta_2]}{1 + \text{var}[\beta_2]/E[\beta_2]^2} \tag{4.4.8}$$

where, again, $E[\cdot]$, $\text{var}[\cdot]$ and $\text{cov}[\cdot,\cdot]$ refer to the posterior moments.

We now consider some results relating to $\hat{\theta}_1^*$ and $\hat{\theta}_2^*$ for the special case where the diffuse prior $g(\boldsymbol{\beta},\sigma) \propto \sigma^{-1}$ is employed in conjunction with the normal general linear model $\mathbf{y} = X\boldsymbol{\beta} + \mathbf{e}$. In this case the posterior moments in (4.4.7) and (4.4.8) are $E[\beta_i] = b_i$, $\text{var}[\beta_i] = v\hat{\sigma}^2 a^{ii}/(v - 2)$ and $\text{cov}[\beta_i,\beta_j] = v\hat{\sigma}^2 a^{ij}/(v - 2)$ where b_i is the ith element of $\mathbf{b}$ and a^{ij} is the (i,j)th element of $(X'X)^{-1}$. Many of the following results also hold under more general circumstances [see Zellner (1978)].

1. The maximum likelihood (ML) estimators for θ_1 and θ_2 are given by $1/b_1$ and b_1/b_2, respectively. Thus, the estimators $\hat{\theta}_1^*$ and $\hat{\theta}_2^*$ can be viewed as the ML estimators multiplied by a factor that depends on the relative second-order posterior moments. In the case of the reciprocal (Equation 4.4.7), the additional factor lies between zero and 1 and so can be regarded as a "shrinking" factor. If the coefficient of variation of β_1 is small, and hence $\beta_1 = 0$ is an unlikely value, the shrinking factor will be close to 1, and $\hat{\theta}_1^*$ will be close to $1/b_1$. When the coefficient of variation is large and small values of β_1 are likely, $\hat{\theta}_1^*$ and $1/b_1$ can be quite different. In the ratio case the relationship between $\hat{\theta}_2^*$ and b_1/b_2 varies depending on $\text{cov}[\beta_1,\beta_2]/E[\beta_1]E[\beta_2]$, as well as on the coefficient of variation of β_2. See Zellner (1978) for details.

2. The posterior means for $1/\beta_1$ and β_1/β_2 do not exist and so optimal point estimates for these quantities do not exist relative to the quadratic loss function $L = (\theta - \hat{\theta})^2$. Analogously, the ML estimators $1/b_1$ and b_1/b_2 do not possess finite sample moments and have infinite risk relative to quadratic loss. [In the sampling theory approach, inference about $1/\beta_1$, for example, is usually based on the limiting distribution of $\sqrt{T}(b_1^{-1} - \beta_1^{-1})$, which is normal with mean zero and variance $\sigma^2\beta_1^{-4}a^{11}$. See Section 5.3.1.]

3. The estimators $\hat{\theta}_1^*$ and $\hat{\theta}_2^*$ possess at least finite second order moments and hence have finite risk relative to quadratic loss functions. Asymptotically, $\hat{\theta}_1^*$ and $\hat{\theta}_2^*$ have the same distribution as the ML estimators.

4. In some situations the posterior distributions of θ_1 and θ_2 (and the distributions of the ML estimators $1/b_1$ and b_1/b_2) will have more than one pronounced mode. This could occur, for example, in small sample situations where the posterior coefficients of variation of β_1 and β_2 are large. Under these circumstances the estimators $\hat{\theta}_1^*$ and $\hat{\theta}_2^*$ are undesirable because it is highly likely that the MELO estimate will lie between the two posterior modes. For some alternative strategies in this case see Zellner (1978, p. 156).

Further properties and details of the estimators $\hat{\theta}_1^*$ and $\hat{\theta}_2^*$, and their extension to simultaneous equations models, can be found in Zellner (1978), Zellner and Park (1979), and Park (1982). See also Chapter 15. Zaman (1981) discusses estimation of a reciprocal with respect to other loss functions and prior distributions.

4.4.3 Bayesian Interpretations of Some Sampling Theory Estimators

4.4.3a Ridge Regression

To overcome what is known as the multicollinearity problem, Hoerl and Kennard (1970) suggest the "ridge regression" estimator

$$\bar{\bar{\boldsymbol{\beta}}} = (X'X + kI)^{-1}X'\mathbf{y} \tag{4.4.9}$$

where k is a value that is chosen such that the coefficient estimates have "stabilized." See Chapter 22 for details. Suppose, in the Bayesian approach, we specify the natural conjugate prior $(\boldsymbol{\beta}|\sigma) \sim N(\bar{\boldsymbol{\beta}},\sigma^2A^{-1})$ and take the special case where $\bar{\boldsymbol{\beta}} = \mathbf{0}$ and $A^{-1} = k^{-1}I$. It is clear that this prior leads to the posterior mean $\bar{\bar{\boldsymbol{\beta}}}$ given in Equation (4.4.9). Thus the ridge regression estimator can be viewed as a Bayesian estimator under quadratic loss, with the prior for $\boldsymbol{\beta}$ such that each of its elements is (a priori) independent and identically distributed with zero mean. It is difficult to envisage an economic environment where such a prior is relevant. Lindley and Smith (1972) suggest an educational example of possible relevance, but they too are generally skeptical of the appropriateness of the assumption.

4.4.3b Bayesian Pretest Estimators and the Stein Rule

In Chapter 3, pretest estimators of the form

$$\hat{\hat{\boldsymbol{\beta}}} = \begin{cases} \mathbf{b}^* & \text{if} \quad u < c \\ \mathbf{b} & \text{if} \quad u \geq c \end{cases} \tag{4.4.10}$$

were considered, where $\mathbf{b}^*$ is the restricted estimator under the null hypothesis H_0: $\boldsymbol{\beta} = \mathbf{r}(= \mathbf{b}^*)$; $\mathbf{b} = (X'X)^{-1}X'\mathbf{y}$ is the unrestricted estimator under the alternative hypothesis H_1: $\boldsymbol{\beta} \neq \mathbf{r}$; and $u = (\mathbf{b} - \mathbf{r})'X'X(\mathbf{b} - \mathbf{r})/K\hat{\sigma}^2$ is the $F_{(K,T-K)}$ statistic used to test the hypothesis $\boldsymbol{\beta} = \mathbf{r}$. Let us consider an analogous Bayesian estimator.

In Section 4.7 we will see that, in the Bayesian framework, uncertainty concerning the hypotheses is handled by calculating what is known as the posterior odds ratio, which is equal to the ratio of the posterior probabilities on each hypothesis. When a point estimate is required and alternative hypotheses lead to different point estimates, an optimal Bayesian point estimate is obtained by minimizing expected loss averaged over the hypotheses, with the posterior probabilities used as weights. That is, for two hypotheses H_0 and H_1, the *Bayesian "pretest" estimator* is that value of $\hat{\boldsymbol{\beta}}$ that minimizes

$$E[L(\boldsymbol{\beta},\hat{\boldsymbol{\beta}})] = P(H_0|\mathbf{y})E[L(\boldsymbol{\beta},\hat{\boldsymbol{\beta}})|H_0] + P(H_1|\mathbf{y})E[L(\boldsymbol{\beta},\hat{\boldsymbol{\beta}})|H_1] \quad (4.4.11)$$

where $P(H_0|\mathbf{y})$ and $P(H_1|\mathbf{y})$ are the posterior probabilities. With quadratic loss, where the posterior means are optimal, the minimizing value for $\hat{\boldsymbol{\beta}}$ is a weighted average of the posterior means, or

$$\hat{\boldsymbol{\beta}}^* = P(H_0|\mathbf{y}) \cdot E[\boldsymbol{\beta}|H_0] + P(H_1|\mathbf{y}) \cdot E[\boldsymbol{\beta}|H_1] \quad (4.4.12)$$

In the context of the hypotheses H_0: $\boldsymbol{\beta} = \mathbf{r}$ and H_1: $\boldsymbol{\beta} \neq \mathbf{r}$, there is a set of reasonable prior assumptions such that $E[\boldsymbol{\beta}|H_0] = \mathbf{b}^*$ and $E[\boldsymbol{\beta}|H_1] = \mathbf{b}$. Taking these values as the posterior means and noting that $P(H_1|\mathbf{y}) = 1 - P(H_0|\mathbf{y})$, $\hat{\boldsymbol{\beta}}^*$ becomes

$$\begin{aligned}\hat{\boldsymbol{\beta}}^* &= P(H_0|\mathbf{y})\mathbf{b}^* + [1 - P(H_0|\mathbf{y})]\mathbf{b} \\ &= [1 - P(H_0|\mathbf{y})](\mathbf{b} - \mathbf{b}^*) + \mathbf{b}^* \end{aligned} \quad (4.4.13)$$

A major distinction between this Bayesian "pretest" estimator and the sampling theory pretest estimator in (4.4.10) is that the Bayesian estimator is a continuous function of the data, while the sampling theory estimator is discontinuous at c. If any given sample $\hat{\hat{\boldsymbol{\beta}}}$ will either be $\mathbf{b}^*$ *or* $\mathbf{b}$, whereas $\hat{\boldsymbol{\beta}}^*$ will be a weighted average of both $\mathbf{b}^*$ *and* $\mathbf{b}$. The greater the posterior probability $P(H_0|\mathbf{y})$, the greater will be the weight on the restricted estimator $\mathbf{b}^*$.

A sampling theory estimator that is also a continuous function of the data and that is similar in form to (4.4.13) is the Stein rule estimator. From (3.4.8) this estimator is

$$\boldsymbol{\beta}_s^* = \left(1 - \frac{a_1}{u}\right)(\mathbf{b} - \mathbf{b}^*) + \mathbf{b}^* \quad (4.4.14)$$

where optimally, $a_1 = (K - 2)(T - K)/[K(T - K + 2)]$. The similarities between (4.4.13) and (4.4.14) are clear. In (4.4.13) support for H_0 is reflected through high values of the posterior probability $P(H_0|\mathbf{y})$, whereas in (4.4.14) support for H_0 is reflected through low values of the F-statistic u.

The above interpretation, and other Bayesian interpretations of the Stein rule, are outlined in Zellner and Vandaele (1975). They show that the Stein rule is also similar in form to the posterior mean derived from a natural conjugate prior, and that it is closely related to the minimum MSE estimator from the class of estimators denoted by $\hat{\boldsymbol{\beta}} = q_0\mathbf{j} + q_1\mathbf{b}$, where $\mathbf{j}' = (1, 1, \ldots, 1)$, and q_0 and q_1 are arbitrary scalars. Leamer (1978, p. 169) provides a further Bayesian interpretation.

Another Bayesian estimator that is closely linked to the Stein rule is the empirical Bayes estimator. To examine this estimator and some of its variants we follow Section 3.4 and consider the orthonormal linear statistical model $\mathbf{y} = X\boldsymbol{\beta} + \mathbf{e}$ and its K-mean counterpart $X'\mathbf{y} = \boldsymbol{\beta} + X'\mathbf{e}$ where $X'X = I_K$ and $\mathbf{e} \sim N(\mathbf{0},I_T)$. Recall that, in this case, the maximum likelihood and least squares estimator is $\mathbf{b} = X'\mathbf{y} \sim N(\boldsymbol{\beta},I_K)$. Now suppose our prior density on $\boldsymbol{\beta}$ is the natural conjugate prior $\boldsymbol{\beta} \sim N(\mathbf{0},\tau^2 I_K)$, and that we are employing a quadratic loss function, so that we are interested in the posterior mean for $\boldsymbol{\beta}$ as our point estimate. From Equation 4.3.10, with $A = 1/\tau^2$, $\bar{\boldsymbol{\beta}} = \mathbf{0}$, and $X'X = I$, this posterior mean is

$$\bar{\bar{\boldsymbol{\beta}}} = (\tau^{-2}I + I)^{-1}\mathbf{b} = \left(\frac{\tau^2}{1 + \tau^2}\right)\mathbf{b}$$

$$= \left(1 - \frac{1}{1 + \tau^2}\right)\mathbf{b} \tag{4.4.15}$$

In the empirical Bayes approach, the prior parameter τ^2 is assumed to be unknown and is estimated from the marginal distribution for $\mathbf{b}$. To obtain this distribution, note that $\mathbf{b} = \boldsymbol{\beta} + X'\mathbf{e}$, then, from the joint distribution for $\boldsymbol{\beta}$ and $\mathbf{e}$, we have $\mathbf{b} \sim N[\mathbf{0},(1 + \tau^2)I_K]$. Consequently, $\mathbf{b}'\mathbf{b}/(1 + \tau^2) \sim \chi^2_{(K)}$, and, using the result that the expectation of the reciprocal of a chi-square random variable is 2 less than its degrees of freedom, we have $E[(1 + \tau^2)/\mathbf{b}'\mathbf{b}] = K - 2$, and

$$E\left[\frac{K - 2}{\mathbf{b}'\mathbf{b}}\right] = \frac{1}{1 + \tau^2} \tag{4.4.16}$$

From this result it seems reasonable to estimate the factor $1/(1 + \tau^2)$ with $(K - 2)/\mathbf{b}'\mathbf{b}$ in which case (4.4.15) becomes

$$\bar{\bar{\boldsymbol{\beta}}}_1 = \left(1 - \frac{K - 2}{\mathbf{b}'\mathbf{b}}\right)\mathbf{b} \tag{4.4.17}$$

This estimator is precisely the James and Stein estimator that was developed in Section 3.4.4.

In Equation 4.4.15, it is clear that $1/(1 + \tau^2) \leqq 1$. However, it is feasible for its estimator, $(K - 2)/\mathbf{b}'\mathbf{b}$, to be greater than 1. Consequently, it seems reasonable that we might be able to improve on (4.4.17) by using the alternative estimator $\min\{1,(K - 2)/\mathbf{b}'\mathbf{b}\}$. This yields

$$\bar{\bar{\boldsymbol{\beta}}}_2 = \left(1 - \min\left\{1, \frac{K - 2}{\mathbf{b}'\mathbf{b}}\right\}\right) \mathbf{b} \tag{4.4.18}$$

which is equivalent to the Stein positive-rule estimator introduced in Section 3.4.3, and which, as noted in that section, is uniformly superior to $\bar{\bar{\boldsymbol{\beta}}}_1$. See Efron and Morris (1972, 1973) and Judge and Bock (1978) for more details.

The James and Stein estimator is an improvement over the maximum likelihood estimator in the sense that it has good ensemble properties. That is, with respect to the *total* squared error loss function $(\bar{\bar{\boldsymbol{\beta}}}_1 - \boldsymbol{\beta})'(\bar{\bar{\boldsymbol{\beta}}}_1 - \boldsymbol{\beta})$, the James and Stein estimator has uniformly lower risk than the maximum likelihood estimator. However, it is possible for an individual component of $\bar{\bar{\boldsymbol{\beta}}}_1$ to have risk that is much more than that of the corresponding component in $\mathbf{b}$ [e.g., $E(\bar{\bar{\beta}}_{1,k} - \beta_k)^2 >> E(b_k - \beta_k)^2$]. To overcome this problem, Efron and Morris (1972) suggest a "limited translation empirical Bayes estimator," which is a compromise between the James and Stein and maximum likelihood estimators. For each component in $\boldsymbol{\beta}$ this estimator chooses the empirical Bayes (James and Stein) estimator unless it differs from the maximum likelihood estimator of that component by more than a prespecified amount. Specifically, $[1 - (K - 2)/\mathbf{b}'\mathbf{b}]b_k$ is chosen as the estimator for β_k unless $|[1 - (K - 2)/\mathbf{b}'\mathbf{b}]b_k - b_k| \geqq d\sqrt{(K - 2)/\mathbf{b}'\mathbf{b}}$ where d is a constant satisfying $0 \leqq d \leqq \sqrt{K - 2}$. The alternative estimator, which is chosen when the difference between the two estimators satisfies the above inequality, is $b_k - \text{sgn}(b_k)\, d\sqrt{(K - 2)/\mathbf{b}'\mathbf{b}}$. In compact notation, the limited translation empirical Bayes estimator can be written as

$$\hat{\beta}_k^T = \left(1 - \frac{K - 2}{\mathbf{b}'\mathbf{b}} \min\left\{1, d\sqrt{\frac{\mathbf{b}'\mathbf{b}}{b_k^2(K - 2)}}\right\}\right) b_k \tag{4.4.19}$$

$$k = 1, 2, \ldots, K$$

When $d = 0$, $\hat{\beta}_k^T = b_k$, and with $d = \sqrt{K - 2}$, $\hat{\beta}_k^T = \bar{\bar{\beta}}_{1,k}$. Thus the value of d controls the gain in component risk obtained by moving toward the maximum likelihood estimator relative to the loss in ensemble risk, which results when moving away from the James and Stein estimator. Efron and Morris (1972) show that substantial gains in component risk can be achieved with little sacrifice in ensemble risk. A modification of the Efron and Morris procedure, based on order statistics, has been suggested by Stein (1981). This estimator again concentrates on the individual components and is especially successful in lowering risk when the empirical distribution of the $|\beta_k|$ is long tailed.

In contrast to the empirical Bayes approach, a strict Bayesian assumes, in terms of the above analysis, that the relevant prior information is known with certainty. Naturally, the James and Stein estimator that uses an estimate of τ^2 will be inferior to the Bayes estimator with a correctly specified τ^2. However, correct specification of the prior information may be difficult, in which case a

Bayesian is likely to be interested in an estimator which, using Bayesian criteria, is robust under misspecifications of the prior. Berger (1982) suggested such an estimator. He shows that, by combining the Bayes and empirical Bayes (James and Stein) estimators, we can obtain an estimator that is both robust to prior misspecifications, and has good sampling theory properties. In the context of our discussion, his estimator is

$$\hat{\boldsymbol{\beta}}^{B} = \left(1 - \min\left\{\frac{K-2}{\mathbf{b}'\mathbf{b}}, \frac{1}{1+\tau^2}\right\}\right)\mathbf{b} \tag{4.4.20}$$

This estimator is equal to the Bayes estimator when the prior information is supported by the data in the sense that $\mathbf{b}'\mathbf{b}$ is small, and is equal to the James and Stein estimator if the data appear to contradict the prior information. Because it is robust from the Bayesian point of view, and it performs favorably relative to sampling theory estimators, it is likely to be a useful compromise for both the Bayesian and sampling theory camps. See Berger (1982) for more details.

4.4.4 Some Concluding Remarks on Point Estimation

We conclude this section with some general comments and references to related work.

1. The reader should not conclude from this section that point estimates are the usual goal of a research investigation. Point estimates can be valuable but they are generally a very inadequate means of reporting results. It is much more useful to report complete posterior distributions. This point has been emphasized on several occasions by Box and Tiao, and Zellner.
2. Many of the ad hoc sampling theory approaches to model selection and point estimation can be viewed within a Bayesian framework [Leamer (1978)].
3. In the Bayesian approach, uncertainty could exist with respect to the prior distribution, the likelihood function, and the loss function. These uncertainties have led to consideration of *robust* Bayesian techniques. For further details, see Berger (1980, 1982) and Ramsay and Novick (1980).
4. In the above subsection we alluded to the empirical Bayes approach to point estimation without discussing it in detail. For details and further references, see Deely and Lindley (1981) and Morris (1983).
5. One way of overcoming uncertainty about the values of prior parameters is to assign a further prior distribution to these parameters. The parameters of this additional prior distribution are often known as hyperparameters. For some work in this area see Lindley and Smith (1972), Smith (1973), Trivedi (1980), and Goel and DeGroot (1981).

4.5 PREDICTION

The prediction of future values of a random variable is a common problem in econometrics. In the context of the model being studied in this chapter, the problem is to predict N future values $\tilde{\mathbf{y}}$ that we assume are related to a known $(N \times K)$ matrix $\tilde{X}$ through the equation

$$\tilde{\mathbf{y}} = \tilde{X}\boldsymbol{\beta} + \tilde{\mathbf{e}} \tag{4.5.1}$$

where $\tilde{\mathbf{e}} \sim N(\mathbf{0},\sigma^2 I)$. A similar process is assumed to have generated the previous observations $\mathbf{y} = X\boldsymbol{\beta} + \mathbf{e}$, and $\mathbf{e}$ and $\tilde{\mathbf{e}}$ are assumed to be independent. That is, $E[\mathbf{e}\tilde{\mathbf{e}}'] = 0$.

The main objective in the Bayesian approach to prediction is to derive a predictive density function $f(\tilde{\mathbf{y}}|\mathbf{y})$ that does not depend on the unknown coefficients $\boldsymbol{\beta}$ and σ, and that contains all the information about $\tilde{\mathbf{y}}$, given knowledge of the past observations $\mathbf{y}$. Information on the future values $\tilde{\mathbf{y}}$ can be presented solely in terms of the complete predictive density, or, alternatively, point predictions can be obtained by setting up a loss function and minimizing expected loss with respect to $f(\tilde{\mathbf{y}}|\mathbf{y})$.

The derivation of $f(\tilde{\mathbf{y}}|\mathbf{y})$ involves two main steps. In the first step the joint density function $h(\tilde{\mathbf{y}},\boldsymbol{\beta},\sigma|\mathbf{y})$ is found by multiplying the likelihood function for the future observations, $f(\tilde{\mathbf{y}}|\boldsymbol{\beta},\sigma,\mathbf{y})$, by the posterior density for the parameters, $g(\boldsymbol{\beta},\sigma|\mathbf{y})$. That is

$$h(\tilde{\mathbf{y}},\boldsymbol{\beta},\sigma|\mathbf{y}) = f(\tilde{\mathbf{y}}|\boldsymbol{\beta},\sigma,\mathbf{y}) \cdot g(\boldsymbol{\beta},\sigma|\mathbf{y}) \tag{4.5.2}$$

To specify the likelihood function we note that, since $\mathbf{e}$ and $\tilde{\mathbf{e}}$ are independent, $f(\tilde{\mathbf{y}}|\boldsymbol{\beta},\sigma,\mathbf{y}) = f(\tilde{\mathbf{y}}|\boldsymbol{\beta},\sigma)$, and this density is given by

$$f(\tilde{\mathbf{y}}|\boldsymbol{\beta},\sigma) = (2\pi)^{-N/2}\sigma^{-N} \exp\left\{-\frac{1}{2\sigma^2}(\tilde{\mathbf{y}} - \tilde{X}\boldsymbol{\beta})'(\tilde{\mathbf{y}} - \tilde{X}\boldsymbol{\beta})\right\} \tag{4.5.3}$$

Specification of the posterior density in (4.5.2) will depend on the choice of prior for $\boldsymbol{\beta}$ and σ. If we take, for example, the diffuse prior $g(\boldsymbol{\beta},\sigma) \propto \sigma^{-1}$, then the posterior density is (see Equations 4.1.6, 4.1.7, and 4.2.2)

$$g(\boldsymbol{\beta},\sigma|\mathbf{y}) \propto \sigma^{-(T+1)} \exp\left[-\frac{1}{2\sigma^2}(\mathbf{y} - X\boldsymbol{\beta})'(\mathbf{y} - X\boldsymbol{\beta})\right] \tag{4.5.4}$$

and (4.5.2) becomes

$$h(\tilde{\mathbf{y}},\boldsymbol{\beta},\sigma|\mathbf{y})$$

$$\propto \sigma^{-(N+T+1)} \exp\left\{-\frac{1}{2\sigma^2}[(\mathbf{y} - X\boldsymbol{\beta})'(\mathbf{y} - X\boldsymbol{\beta}) + (\tilde{\mathbf{y}} - \tilde{X}\boldsymbol{\beta})'(\tilde{\mathbf{y}} - \tilde{X}\boldsymbol{\beta})]\right\} \tag{4.5.5}$$

The second step toward derivation of $f(\tilde{\mathbf{y}}|\mathbf{y})$ is to integrate $\boldsymbol{\beta}$ and σ out of (4.5.5). This yields [see Zellner (1971, p. 73) for details]

$$f(\tilde{\mathbf{y}}|\mathbf{y}) = \int\int h(\tilde{\mathbf{y}},\boldsymbol{\beta},\sigma|\mathbf{y})d\boldsymbol{\beta}\, d\sigma \propto [v + (\tilde{\mathbf{y}} - \tilde{X}\mathbf{b})'C(\tilde{\mathbf{y}} - \tilde{X}\mathbf{b})]^{-(v+N)/2} \quad (4.5.6)$$

where $C = [\hat{\sigma}^2(I + \tilde{X}(X'X)^{-1}\tilde{X}')]^{-1}$ and $\mathbf{b} = (X'X)^{-1}X'\mathbf{y}$. Equation 4.5.6 is in the form of a multivariate-t distribution with mean $E[\tilde{\mathbf{y}}|\mathbf{y}] = X\mathbf{b}$ and covariance matrix

$$\Sigma_{\tilde{\mathbf{y}}|\mathbf{y}} = \frac{v}{v-2}C^{-1} = \frac{v\hat{\sigma}^2}{v-2}(I + \tilde{X}(X'X)^{-1}\tilde{X}') \quad (4.5.7)$$

[See Judge et al. (1982, p. 144) for the analogous sampling theory result.] If desired, properties of the multivariate-t distribution can be used to obtain the marginal predictive densities for one or more of the elements in $\tilde{\mathbf{y}}$. Also, similar principles can be applied to establish predictive densities for other types of priors [see, for example, Dickey (1975)].

If a proper informative prior is used, it is also possible to derive the predictive density for a sample of observations when no previous sample is available. Predictive densities of this type are frequently used in the calculation of posterior odds (see Section 4.7). As an example, if we employ the natural conjugate prior in (4.3.7), namely,

$$g(\boldsymbol{\beta},\sigma) \propto \sigma^{-K-\bar{v}-1} \exp\left\{-\frac{1}{2\sigma^2}[\bar{v}\bar{s}^2 + (\boldsymbol{\beta} - \bar{\boldsymbol{\beta}})'A(\boldsymbol{\beta} - \bar{\boldsymbol{\beta}})]\right\} \quad (4.5.8)$$

in conjunction with the likelihood function

$$f(\mathbf{y}|\boldsymbol{\beta},\sigma) \propto \sigma^{-T} \exp\left[-\frac{1}{2\sigma^2}(\mathbf{y} - X\boldsymbol{\beta})'(\mathbf{y} - X\boldsymbol{\beta})\right] \quad (4.5.9)$$

then, along similar lines to those used above, it can be shown that

$$f(\mathbf{y}) = \int\int f(\mathbf{y}|\boldsymbol{\beta},\sigma)\cdot g(\boldsymbol{\beta},\sigma)d\sigma\, d\boldsymbol{\beta} \propto [\bar{v} + (\mathbf{y} - X\bar{\boldsymbol{\beta}})'C_0(\mathbf{y} - X\bar{\boldsymbol{\beta}})]^{-(\bar{v}+T)/2} \quad (4.5.10)$$

where $C_0 = [\bar{s}^2(I + XA^{-1}X')]^{-1}$. Again, this density is in the form of a multivariate t distribution. In Section 4.7 we will include its normalizing constant, and write it in a form that is more convenient for calculation of the posterior odds.

4.6 INTERVAL ESTIMATION

In the classical approach to inference we frequently summarize our knowledge about a parameter by expressing our research results in terms of a confidence interval for that parameter. In the Bayesian approach it is preferable to present the complete posterior density function, but, if this is too unwieldy, it may be useful to use an interval estimate as a summary measure.

To obtain a Bayesian interval estimate for a parameter θ, with a probability content of, for example, 0.95, we need two values, a and d, such that

$$P(a < \theta < d) = \int_a^d g(\theta|\mathbf{y})d\theta = .95 \tag{4.6.1}$$

Values a and d that satisfy (4.6.1) will not be unique, however, and so we need some criterion for choosing between alternative intervals. One possibility is to choose the most likely region by insisting that the value of the posterior density function for every point inside the interval is greater than that for every point outside the interval, which implies $g(a|\mathbf{y}) = g(d|\mathbf{y})$. An interval with this property is known as the *highest posterior density* (HPD) interval, and, if the posterior density is unimodal, it is equivalent to finding the shortest interval (minimizing $d - a$) such that (4.6.1) holds.

As an example consider the posterior density function for β_1 given in Equation 4.2.7. In this case $t = (\beta_1 - b_1)/\hat{\sigma}\sqrt{a^{11}}$ has a univariate t distribution with v degrees of freedom, a^{11} being the first diagonal element of $(X'X)^{-1}$. Thus, if $t_{\alpha/2}$ is the point such that $P(t > t_{\alpha/2}) = \alpha/2$, then

$$P\left(-t_{\alpha/2} < \frac{\beta_1 - b_1}{\hat{\sigma}\sqrt{a^{11}}} < t_{\alpha/2}\right) = 1 - \alpha \tag{4.6.2}$$

To obtain an HPD interval of probability content $(1 - \alpha)$, Equation 4.6.2 is rearranged to yield $P(a < \beta_1 < d) = 1 - \alpha$ where $a = b_1 - t_{\alpha/2}\,\hat{\sigma}\sqrt{a^{11}}$ and $d = b_1 + t_{\alpha/2}\,\hat{\sigma}\sqrt{a^{11}}$.

Note that this interval is identical to the $(1 - \alpha)\%$ confidence interval that would be obtained using the sampling theory approach. However, the interpretation is different. In the Bayesian framework the statement $P(a < \beta_1 < d) = 1 - \alpha$ means that there is a $(1 - \alpha)$ (subjective) probability that β_1 lies between a and d. In the sampling theory framework, this statement implies that, in any given sample, there is a $(1 - \alpha)$ probability of obtaining a and d such that $a < \beta_1 < d$. Also, if we had used the posterior density from an informative prior, our HPD interval would reflect both prior and sample information. See Judge et al. (1982, Ch. 8) for a numerical example.

Unlike the t distribution, the inverted gamma density $g(\sigma|\mathbf{y})$ is not symmetric, and so values a and d such that $P(\sigma < a) = P(\sigma > d) = \alpha/2$ will not yield the HPD interval for σ, because they will not have the property $g(a|\mathbf{y}) = g(d|\mathbf{y})$. Under these circumstances a and d can be found by numerically evaluating the ordinates and distribution function for $g(\sigma|\mathbf{y})$, or, alternatively, an approximate HPD interval can be found by using tabulated values of the χ^2 distribution. For example, to derive an approximate HPD interval from the posterior density $g(\sigma|\mathbf{y})$ in (4.2.5), we note that $v\hat{\sigma}^2/\sigma^2$ has a $\chi^2_{(v)}$ distribution and, therefore, we can write

$$P(\chi^2_{(1-\alpha/2)} < \frac{v\hat{\sigma}^2}{\sigma^2} < \chi^2_{(\alpha/2)}) = 1 - \alpha \tag{4.6.3}$$

where $P(\chi^2 > \chi^2_{(\alpha/2)}) = \alpha/2$, and $P(\chi^2 > \chi^2_{(1-\alpha/2)}) = 1 - \alpha/2$. Rearranging (4.6.3) yields $P(a < \sigma < d) = 1 - \alpha$ where $a = (v\hat{\sigma}^2/\chi^2_{(\alpha/2)})^{1/2}$ and $d = (v\hat{\sigma}^2/\chi^2_{(1-\alpha/2)})^{1/2}$. See Judge et al. (1982, Chapter 8) for numerical examples of both exact and approximate HPD intervals for σ.

It is worth pointing out that, if we had derived the posterior density functions and HPD intervals for, for example, σ^2, σ^{-2} or log σ, instead of for σ, the appropriate transformations of these intervals would not yield exactly the HPD for σ. However, the HPD interval for log σ will correspond after transformation to that of log σ^2. See Box and Tiao (1973) for details and for tables that can be used to construct HPD intervals for log σ^2.

We have restricted the discussion to one-dimensional HPD intervals. It is also possible to consider HPD intervals (regions) in more than one dimension. See Box and Tiao (1973) for details and for some examples.

4.6.1 Hypothesis Testing Using HPD Intervals

One method for testing hypotheses within the Bayesian framework is to accept or reject a point null hypothesis depending on whether or not the specified value under H_0 lies within an HPD interval with a preassigned probability content. For example, in terms of the HPD for β_1 given above, we would accept a null hypothesis of the form H_0: $\beta_1 = \beta_1^*$ if β_1^* lies in the interval $(b_1 - t_{\alpha/2}\hat{\sigma}\sqrt{a^{11}}, b_1 + t_{\alpha/2}\hat{\sigma}\sqrt{a^{11}})$; otherwise we would reject H_0.

This method for testing hypotheses is obviously similar to the sampling theory approach of rejecting a null hypothesis when the hypothesized value for a parameter falls outside a confidence interval. When a diffuse prior and the model of this chapter are employed, the results (but not the interpretations) are identical. There are other models, however, where the results are not identical. See, for example, an application by Tsurumi (1977). Furthermore, this method of testing hypotheses is usually suggested only for circumstances where a diffuse or vague prior is employed, and one of the hypotheses is a single point [Lindley (1965), Zellner (1971, Ch. 10)]. When a proper prior is employed, or both hypotheses are composite, hypothesis testing is generally carried out within a posterior odds framework. It is to this topic that we now turn.

4.7 POSTERIOR ODDS AND HYPOTHESIS TESTING

Suppose we have two hypotheses, H_0 and H_1, that we wish to test or compare. In the Bayesian posterior odds framework we begin by assigning prior probabilities to each of the hypotheses, say $P(H_0)$ and $P(H_1)$, and forming the *prior odds* ratio given by $P(H_0)/P(H_1)$. Then, based on prior density functions conditioned on each of the hypotheses, and likelihood functions conditioned on each of the hypotheses, the prior odds ratio is modified to form a *posterior odds* ratio, which is denoted by $K_{01} = P(H_0|\mathbf{y})/P(H_1|\mathbf{y})$. This ratio summarizes all the evidence (prior and sample) in favor of one hypothesis relative to another; its calculation is frequently regarded as the endpoint of any study of competing hypotheses. In contrast to the usual sampling theory approach, it is possible to give the odds in favor of one hypothesis relative to another, and, although possible, as in the nonnested model procedures of Chapter 21, it is not necessary to accept or reject each hypothesis. Thus, as Zellner (1971, Chapter 10) points out, it may be more appropriate to describe the Bayesian procedure as "comparing" rather than "testing" hypotheses. If a decision to accept or reject must be made, it can be handled by using a loss function that expresses the consequences of making the wrong decision and by minimizing expected loss where the expectation is with respect to the posterior probabilities on each hypothesis.

Let us turn to the problem of deriving an expression for the posterior odds $K_{01} = P(H_0|\mathbf{y})/P(H_1|\mathbf{y})$. If the two hypotheses are inequalities such as $H_0: \theta \geq c$ and $H_1: \theta < c$, where θ is a parameter and c is a constant, then K_{01} can easily be obtained from the posterior density function $g(\theta|\mathbf{y})$. Specifically, $P(H_0|\mathbf{y}) = \int_c^\infty g(\theta|\mathbf{y})d\theta$ and $P(H_1|\mathbf{y}) = \int_{-\infty}^c g(\theta|\mathbf{y})d\theta$. This approach can be readily extended to regions of more than one dimension, such as the linear inequality hypotheses H_0: $R\boldsymbol{\beta} > \mathbf{r}$ and H_1: $R\boldsymbol{\beta} \leq \mathbf{r}$, in the general linear model $\mathbf{y} = X\boldsymbol{\beta} + \mathbf{e}$. Also, if a proper prior for θ (or $\boldsymbol{\beta}$) is specified, then the prior odds $P(H_0)/P(H_1)$ can be found in a similar way. With an improper prior the prior odds will be indeterminate, but the posterior odds can still be calculated. See Zellner (1979) for further details, examples and references.

For other types of hypotheses, such as comparing a "sharp" hypothesis H_0: $R\boldsymbol{\beta} = \mathbf{r}$ with the alternative H_1: $R\boldsymbol{\beta} \neq \mathbf{r}$, or comparing alternative nonnested regression models, we proceed as follows. Consider the two hypotheses

$$H_0: \mathbf{y} = Z\boldsymbol{\gamma} + \mathbf{e}_0 \tag{4.7.1}$$

and

$$H_1: \mathbf{y} = X\boldsymbol{\beta} + \mathbf{e} \tag{4.7.2}$$

where X is of dimension $(T \times K)$, Z is of dimension $(T \times K_0)$, $\mathbf{e} \sim N(\mathbf{0},\sigma^2 I)$, $\mathbf{e}_0 \sim N(\mathbf{0},\sigma_0^2 I)$, and $\boldsymbol{\gamma}$ and $\boldsymbol{\beta}$ are unknown coefficient vectors. When comparing nonnested regression models, X and Z would typically be different regressor matrices, each one being relevant for a particular economic theory. The model in (4.7.1) could also represent hypotheses of the form H_0: $R\boldsymbol{\beta} = \mathbf{0}$, with $Z\boldsymbol{\gamma}$ being obtained by substituting the restrictions into $X\boldsymbol{\beta}$ and rearranging. For example, such a model would arise with the partitioning $X = [Z\ X^*]$, $\boldsymbol{\beta}' = (\boldsymbol{\gamma}',\boldsymbol{\beta}^{*\prime})$ and the hypothesis H_0: $\boldsymbol{\beta}^* = \mathbf{0}$. The more general hypothesis H_0: $R\boldsymbol{\beta} = \mathbf{r} \neq \mathbf{0}$ can also be handled; however, in this case, after substituting $R\boldsymbol{\beta} = \mathbf{r}$ into the equation $\mathbf{y} = X\boldsymbol{\beta} + \mathbf{e}$ and rearranging, the left hand side of (4.7.1) would be a linear function of some of the columns of X as well as $\mathbf{y}$. See Judge et al. (1982, p. 239) for an example. Finally, we note that, although the elements of each disturbance vector are assumed to be independent and identically distributed, the procedure can be extended for models with more general covariance matrices.

Using H_1 as an example, and assuming it is legitimate to attach probabilities to hypotheses, we can write

$$
\begin{aligned}
P(H_1,\mathbf{y},\boldsymbol{\beta},\sigma) &= P(H_1) \cdot g(\boldsymbol{\beta},\sigma|H_1) \cdot f(\mathbf{y}|\boldsymbol{\beta},\sigma,H_1) \\
&= P(H_1,\boldsymbol{\beta},\sigma|\mathbf{y}) \cdot f(\mathbf{y})
\end{aligned}
\tag{4.7.3}
$$

Thus

$$
P(H_1,\boldsymbol{\beta},\sigma|\mathbf{y}) = \frac{P(H_1) \cdot g(\boldsymbol{\beta},\sigma|H_1) \cdot f(\mathbf{y}|\boldsymbol{\beta},\sigma,H_1)}{f(\mathbf{y})}
\tag{4.7.4}
$$

and

$$
\begin{aligned}
P(H_1|\mathbf{y}) &= \frac{P(H_1)}{f(\mathbf{y})} \iint g(\boldsymbol{\beta},\sigma|H_1) \cdot f(\mathbf{y}|\boldsymbol{\beta},\sigma,H_1)d\sigma d\boldsymbol{\beta} \\
&= \frac{P(H_1)f(\mathbf{y}|H_1)}{f(\mathbf{y})}
\end{aligned}
\tag{4.7.5}
$$

After obtaining a similar expression for $P(H_0|\mathbf{y})$ we have

$$
K_{01} = \frac{P(H_0|\mathbf{y})}{P(H_1|\mathbf{y})} = \frac{P(H_0) \iint g(\boldsymbol{\gamma},\sigma_0|H_0)f(\mathbf{y}|\boldsymbol{\gamma},\sigma_0,H_0)d\sigma_0 d\boldsymbol{\gamma}}{P(H_1) \iint g(\boldsymbol{\beta},\sigma|H_1)f(\mathbf{y}|\boldsymbol{\beta},\sigma,H_1)d\sigma\, d\boldsymbol{\beta}}
\tag{4.7.6}
$$

Equation 4.7.6 shows, in Zellner's (1971) words, "that the posterior odds are equal to the prior odds $P(H_0)/P(H_1)$ times the ratio of *averaged* likelihoods with the prior densities $g(\boldsymbol{\gamma},\sigma_0|H_0)$ and $g(\boldsymbol{\beta},\sigma|H_1)$ serving as the weighting functions. This contrasts with the usual likelihood-ratio testing procedure which involves taking the ratio of *maximized* likelihood functions. . . ."

We usually assume that $g(\boldsymbol{\gamma},\sigma_0|H_0)$ and $g(\boldsymbol{\beta},\sigma|H_1)$ are proper priors; otherwise the weighting functions in (4.7.6) will not integrate to one and the interpretation just given is questionable. Furthermore, certain ambiguities can arise [see Leamer (1978, p. 111) for examples]. In many cases, however, it is reasonable to specify an improper prior for those parameters with identical assumptions under both hypotheses. For example, K_{01} will not be adversely affected by the assumptions $\sigma = \sigma_0$ and $g(\sigma|H_0) = g(\sigma|H_1) \propto \sigma^{-1}$, even although this means that $f(\mathbf{y}|H_0)$ and $f(\mathbf{y}|H_1)$ will be improper.

The integrals (or averaged likelihood functions) in the numerator and denominator of (4.7.6) are the predictive densities $f(\mathbf{y}|H_0)$ and $f(\mathbf{y}|H_1)$, and their ratio $f(\mathbf{y}|H_0)/f(\mathbf{y}|H_1)$ is known as the "Bayes factor." Assuming the two hypotheses H_0 and H_1 are exhaustive, the unconditional predictive density $f(\mathbf{y})$ can be obtained by averaging over the two hypotheses. That is, $f(\mathbf{y}) = f(\mathbf{y}|H_0) \cdot P(H_0)$

$+ f(\mathbf{y}|H_1) \cdot P(H_1)$. Also, it is worth noting that when there are more than two competing hypotheses, it is still possible to calculate the posterior odds for any *pair* of hypotheses.

Before turning to some special cases of the posterior odds ratio in (4.7.6) it is instructive to examine the sampling theory approach from a Bayesian viewpoint [Zellner (1971, p. 295)]. Let $L(H_0,\hat{H}_1)$ denote the loss incurred if H_1 is selected and H_0 is the true state, and let $L(H_1,\hat{H}_0)$ denote the loss incurred if H_0 is selected and H_1 is the true state. Assuming that the loss incurred from choosing a *correct* state is zero, H_0 will be the minimum expected loss choice when

$$E[L|\hat{H}_0] = P(H_1|\mathbf{y}) \cdot L(H_1,\hat{H}_0) < E[L|\hat{H}_1] = P(H_0|\mathbf{y}) \cdot L(H_0,\hat{H}_1) \quad (4.7.7)$$

Using (4.7.6) this inequality is equivalent to

$$\frac{f(\mathbf{y}|H_0)}{f(\mathbf{y}|H_1)} > \frac{P(H_1) \cdot L(H_1,\hat{H}_0)}{P(H_0) \cdot L(H_0,\hat{H}_1)} \quad (4.7.8)$$

Thus, H_0 will be accepted when the sample evidence, as measured by the "likelihood ratio" $f(\mathbf{y}|H_0)/f(\mathbf{y}|H_1)$, is sufficiently large. What is sufficiently large is determined by the ratio of prior expected losses. This is in contrast to the sampling theory approach where the selection of a critical value for the likelihood ratio is generally based on an *arbitrary* significance level. The result in (4.7.8) suggests that the sampling theory process of selecting a significance level could be made more rigorous by considering the prior odds of the hypotheses, as well as the losses incurred from a wrong decision.

A special case of (4.7.8) that is of interest is that where the prior odds are equal to unity, $P(H_0)/P(H_1) = 1$, and the loss function is symmetric, $L(H_1,\hat{H}_0) = L(H_0,\hat{H}_1)$. In this case H_0 is chosen if

$$\frac{P(H_0|\mathbf{y})}{P(H_1|\mathbf{y})} = \frac{f(\mathbf{y}|H_0)}{f(\mathbf{y}|H_1)} > 1 \quad (4.7.9)$$

4.7.1 Posterior Odds from Natural Conjugate Priors

We now consider the posterior odds in (4.7.6) for the special case where $g(\boldsymbol{\gamma},\sigma_0|H_0)$ and $g(\boldsymbol{\beta},\sigma|H_1)$ are natural conjugate priors. The predictive density from a natural conjugate prior was given in (4.5.10). When we view this expression as conditional on H_1 and include the normalizing constant it becomes

$$f(\mathbf{y}|H_1) = \frac{\Gamma[(\bar{v} + T)/2]\bar{v}^{\bar{v}/2}|I + XA^{-1}X'|^{-1/2}}{\pi^{T/2}\Gamma(\bar{v}/2)\bar{s}^{T}} \cdot \left[\bar{v} + (\mathbf{y} - X\bar{\boldsymbol{\beta}})' \frac{(I + XA^{-1}X')^{-1}}{\bar{s}^2} (\mathbf{y} - X\bar{\boldsymbol{\beta}})\right]^{-(\bar{v}+T)/2} \quad (4.7.10)$$

where $\bar{v}$, $\bar{s}$, $\bar{\boldsymbol{\beta}}$, and A are parameters from the natural conjugate prior. Letting

$$k_1 = \frac{\Gamma[(\bar{v} + T)/2](\bar{v}\bar{s}^2)^{\bar{v}/2}}{\Gamma(\bar{v}/2)\pi^{T/2}} \tag{4.7.11}$$

and using the results

$$|I + XA^{-1}X'| = |A + X'X| \cdot |A|^{-1} \tag{4.7.12}$$

and

$$(\mathbf{y} - X\bar{\boldsymbol{\beta}})'(I + XA^{-1}X')^{-1}(\mathbf{y} - X\bar{\boldsymbol{\beta}}) = v\hat{\sigma}^2 + Q_1 \tag{4.7.13}$$

where $\mathbf{b} = (X'X)^{-1}X'\mathbf{y}$, $v\hat{\sigma}^2 = (\mathbf{y} - X\mathbf{b})'(\mathbf{y} - X\mathbf{b})$, $v = T - K$ and

$$Q_1 = (\mathbf{b} - \bar{\boldsymbol{\beta}})'[A^{-1} + (X'X)^{-1}]^{-1}(\mathbf{b} - \bar{\boldsymbol{\beta}}) \tag{4.7.14}$$

(4.7.10) becomes

$$f(\mathbf{y}|H_1) = k_1(|A|/|A + X'X|)^{1/2}(\bar{v}\bar{s}^2 + v\hat{\sigma}^2 + Q_1)^{-(\bar{v}+T)/2} \tag{4.7.15}$$

A similar strategy can be followed for the predictive density conditional on H_0, to obtain

$$f(\mathbf{y}|H_0) = k_0(|B|/|B + Z'Z|)^{1/2}(\bar{v}_0\bar{s}_0^2 + v_0\hat{\sigma}_0^2 + Q_0)^{-(\bar{v}_0+T)/2} \tag{4.7.16}$$

where $\bar{v}_0$, $\bar{s}_0$, B, and $\bar{\boldsymbol{\gamma}}$ are the parameters of the natural conjugate prior for $(\boldsymbol{\gamma},\sigma_0)$; $\hat{\boldsymbol{\gamma}} = (Z'Z)^{-1}Z'\mathbf{y}$, $v_0\hat{\sigma}_0^2 = (\mathbf{y} - Z\hat{\boldsymbol{\gamma}})'(\mathbf{y} - Z\hat{\boldsymbol{\gamma}})$, $v_0 = T - K_0$, $Q_0 = (\hat{\boldsymbol{\gamma}} - \bar{\boldsymbol{\gamma}})'[B^{-1} + (Z'Z)^{-1}]^{-1}(\hat{\boldsymbol{\gamma}} - \bar{\boldsymbol{\gamma}})$ and $k_0 = \{\Gamma[(\bar{v}_0 + T)/2](\bar{v}_0\bar{s}_0^2)^{\bar{v}_0/2}\}/\{\Gamma(\bar{v}_0/2)\pi^{T/2}\}$. The posterior odds ratio can then be written as

$$K_{01} = \frac{P(H_0)k_0(|B|/|B + Z'Z|)^{1/2}(\bar{v}_0\bar{s}_0^2 + v_0\hat{\sigma}_0^2 + Q_0)^{-(\bar{v}_0+T)/2}}{P(H_1)k_1(|A|/|A + X'X|)^{1/2}(\bar{v}\bar{s}^2 + v\hat{\sigma}^2 + Q_1)^{-(\bar{v}+T)/2}} \tag{4.7.17}$$

[For an alternative derivation, see Judge et al. (1982, p. 238).]

From (4.7.17) we note the following.

1. The greater the prior odds $P(H_0)/P(H_1)$, the greater will be the posterior odds.
2. The term $|B|/|(B + Z'Z)|$ and its counterpart in the denominator are measures of the precision of the prior information on $\boldsymbol{\beta}$ relative to the precision of the posterior information. Other things equal, these terms mean that we will favor the hypothesis with more prior information.
3. Goodness-of-fit considerations are given by the residual sums of squares terms $v_0\hat{\sigma}_0^2$ and $v\hat{\sigma}^2$, and these have the expected effect on the posterior odds.

4. The terms Q_0 and Q_1 are measures of the compatibility of the prior and sample information. The further $\mathbf{b}$ deviates from $\bar{\boldsymbol{\beta}}$, for example, the greater will be Q_1 and, other things equal, the greater will be the posterior odds in favor of H_0.
5. The relative effect of the prior information on σ and σ_0 depends on the ratio k_0/k_1, as well as the last bracketed terms in both the numerator and denominator.

Equation 4.7.17 simplifies considerably if we assume the prior densities for σ and σ_0 are identical. In this case $\bar{v} = \bar{v}_0$, $\bar{s} = \bar{s}_0$, and the term k_0/k_1 drops out. Furthermore, if we assume the prior information on σ is diffuse, and represent this fact by setting $\bar{v} = \bar{v}_0 = 0$, then the terms $\bar{v}\bar{s}^2$ and $\bar{v}_0\bar{s}_0^2$ also drop out.

A hypothesis comparison of special interest is that of comparing the "sharp" hypothesis H_0: $\boldsymbol{\beta} = \bar{\boldsymbol{\beta}}$ with the alternative H_1: $\boldsymbol{\beta} \neq \bar{\boldsymbol{\beta}}$. In this case $\hat{\boldsymbol{\gamma}} = \bar{\boldsymbol{\gamma}} = \bar{\boldsymbol{\beta}}$, $Q_0 = 0$, $B^{-1} = 0$ and $|B|/|B + Z'Z| = 1$ (see Equation 4.7.12). In conjunction with the variance assumptions of the previous paragraph, this gives a posterior odds ratio of

$$
\begin{aligned}
K_{C1} &= \frac{P(H_0)|A + X'X|^{1/2}}{P(H_1)|A|^{1/2}} \left[\frac{v\hat{\sigma}^2 + Q_1}{(\mathbf{y} - X\bar{\boldsymbol{\beta}})'(\mathbf{y} - X\bar{\boldsymbol{\beta}})}\right]^{T/2} \\
&= \frac{P(H_0)|A + X'X|^{1/2}}{P(H_1)|A|^{1/2}} \left[\frac{v\hat{\sigma}^2 + Q_1}{v\hat{\sigma}^2 + (\mathbf{b} - \bar{\boldsymbol{\beta}})'X'X(\mathbf{b} - \bar{\boldsymbol{\beta}})}\right]^{T/2} \\
&= \frac{P(H_0)|A + X'X|^{1/2}}{P(H_1)|A|^{1/2}} \left[\frac{1 + Q_1/v\hat{\sigma}^2}{1 + (K/v)F}\right]^{T/2}
\end{aligned}
\tag{4.7.18}
$$

where $F = (\mathbf{b} - \bar{\boldsymbol{\beta}})'X'X(\mathbf{b} - \bar{\boldsymbol{\beta}})/K\hat{\sigma}^2$ is the sampling theory F statistic used to test the hypothesis H_0: $\boldsymbol{\beta} = \bar{\boldsymbol{\beta}}$; and $Q_1/v\hat{\sigma}^2$ is a similar ratio of quadratic forms, dependent on the prior precision matrix A. To gain some insights into the relationship between (4.7.18) and the conventional F statistic, we will consider two special cases of (4.7.18). However, first we note that if $P(H_0) = P(H_1)$, then as $A^{-1} \to 0$, the posterior odds approach unity ($K_{01} \to 1$). This result is reasonable because when $A^{-1} = 0$, the prior covariance matrix for $\boldsymbol{\beta}$ under H_1 is zero, and the two hypotheses coincide.

For the first special case of (4.7.18) we assume that $K = 1$ and that $X = (1, 1, \ldots, 1)'$. Thus, we are faced with the problem of using a random sample $\mathbf{y}$ from a normal distribution with mean β to test the hypothesis H_0: $\beta = \bar{\beta}$. Denoting A by the scalar τ and letting $\bar{y}$ be the sample mean we have $X'X = T$, $v\hat{\sigma}^2 = \Sigma_t(y_t - \bar{y})^2$, $Q_1 = \tau T(\bar{y} - \bar{\beta})^2/(T + \tau)$, and $F = T(\bar{y} - \bar{\beta})^2/\hat{\sigma}^2$. Then (4.7.18) becomes

$$
K_{01} = \frac{P(H_0)}{P(H_1)} \cdot \sqrt{1 + \frac{T}{\tau}} \left\{\frac{1 + [\tau/(T + \tau)](F/v)}{1 + (F/v)}\right\}^{T/2}
\tag{4.7.19}
$$

A property of this expression that is in general agreement with the sampling theory approach is the greater the F value, the lower will be the posterior odds in favor of H_0. Another property, and one that may be surprising, is that, for a given F value, the posterior odds in favor of H_0 are an increasing function of the sample size T. This result is in contrast to the fixed significance level sampling theory situation where the magnitude of F (or its right-hand tail probability) is the only measure of support for H_1. Although in some circumstances it might be desirable, a criticism of the fixed significance level sampling theory approach is that it treats Type I and Type II errors asymmetrically. As T increases the probability of a Type I error remains constant while the probability of a Type II error (for a given β) declines. For both errors to be treated symmetrically the significance level needs to be a decreasing function of sample size. The posterior odds formulation treats both errors symmetrically, and this is reflected by the fact that, for a fixed F value, K_{01} is an increasing function of T. This phenomenon is known as Lindley's paradox. For details see Lindley (1957), Zellner (1971, p. 304), Leamer (1978, p. 105), and Judge et al. (1982, p. 101).

With respect to the parameter τ, we note that as $\tau^{-1} \to 0$, $K_{01} \to 1$. This is a special case of the result $A^{-1} \to 0$ that was discussed earlier. The consequences of $\tau \to 0$ (or $A \to 0$) will be discussed briefly in Section 4.7.2.

A second special case of (4.7.18), which leads to a simplification similar to (4.7.19), is that obtained from the g prior discussed in Section 4.3.4 [Zellner (1982a)]. When we set $A = g_0 X'X$, Equation 4.7.18 becomes

$$K_{01} = \frac{P(H_0)}{P(H_1)} \left(\frac{1 + g_0}{g_0}\right)^{K/2} \left\{\frac{1 + [g_0/(1 + g_0)](KF/v)}{1 + (KF/v)}\right\}^{T/2} \tag{4.7.20}$$

As expected, K_{01} is a decreasing function of F, and approaches unity as $g \to \infty$.

There are, of course, many other special cases of models and hypotheses based on natural conjugate priors. As mentioned at the outset, nonnested hypotheses can be handled within the same framework; also, simplifications can be derived for more general sharp hypotheses such as H_0: $R\boldsymbol{\beta} = \mathbf{r}$, where $R \neq I$ and $\mathbf{r} \neq \boldsymbol{\beta}$.

4.7.2 Posterior Odds from Other Prior Densities

One of the properties of the posterior odds ratio in (4.7.18) is that as $A \to 0$, $K_{01} \to \infty$. Consequently, if we are faced with the problem of comparing a sharp hypothesis such as H_0: $\boldsymbol{\beta} = \mathbf{r}$, with an alternative H_1: $\boldsymbol{\beta} \neq \mathbf{r}$, and we have little prior information about $\boldsymbol{\beta}$ (given H_1), then the limiting case of the natural conjugate prior is an unsatisfactory way of representing this lack of information. Alternatively, even if we have substantial prior information, we may wish to give the posterior odds relative to a particular uninformative reference prior, in which case the limiting case of the natural conjugate prior is again unsatisfactory. A more suitable prior for this task has been investigated by Zellner and Siow (1980). Building on the earlier work of Jeffreys (1967), they suggest a multivariate Cauchy density for $g(\boldsymbol{\beta}|\sigma)$, and they derive and analyze the posterior odds for comparing H_0: $\boldsymbol{\beta} = \mathbf{0}$ with H_1: $\boldsymbol{\beta} \neq \mathbf{0}$. See Zellner and Siow (1980) for details.

Posterior odds for other combinations of alternative priors, models and hypotheses have been derived and applied by various authors. For details we refer the reader to Bernardo (1980), Dickey (1975), Gaver and Geisel (1974), Leamer (1978), Lempers (1971), Rossi (1980), Zellner (1971, 1979, 1982b), Zellner and Geisel (1970), Zellner and Richard (1973), and Zellner and Williams (1973); as well as the references cited by these authors.

4.8 SUMMARY

In this chapter we have outlined the Bayesian approach to inference with particular emphasis on the parameters $\boldsymbol{\beta}$ and σ in the general linear model $\mathbf{y} = X\boldsymbol{\beta} + \mathbf{e}$. The differences (and similarities) between the Bayesian approach and the sampling and decision theory approaches were discussed, and details of the posterior densities derived from a noninformative prior and from an assortment of informative priors were given. Point estimation was examined from a Bayesian point of view and some relationships with sampling theory point estimators were considered. Prediction, interval estimation, and comparing hypotheses were also examined within the Bayesian framework. In some sections of later chapters, the Bayesian approach is applied to other econometric models.

The Bayesian approach has a number of desirable features not possessed by the sampling theory approach. See, for example, Zellner (1971, 1975). The most compelling arguments in favor of its adoption relate to the fact that it is based on a simple and unified set of principles that can be applied in a wide variety of situations; and this unified set of principles provides a formal framework for incorporating prior information. In the sampling theory approach researchers frequently use prior information in an *ad hoc* manner. For example, samples or models that lead to estimates that do not agree with *a priori* expectations are often discarded. Null hypotheses and significance levels are frequently chosen arbitrarily. The Bayesian approach provides a logical and unified framework for handling such questions. Furthermore, many of the sampling theory "ad hockeries" can be given a logical Bayesian interpretation [see, e.g., Leamer (1978)]. Because of these and other reasons, the relative importance of both applied and theoretical Bayesian research has grown considerably in recent years. See Zellner (1981) for a description of the historical development of Bayesian econometrics and a list of the major factors that he feels have contributed to the growth of Bayesian analysis; in a later paper, Zellner (1982b) gives further details of Bayesian applications in econometrics. In many of the following chapters we look at a range of statistical models through both sampling theory and Bayesian eyes.

Given the useful way in which it allows for the incorporation of prior information, and the other advantages of the Bayesian approach, we recommend that applied researchers pay more attention to the possibility of employing Bayesian techniques, particularly where prior information is involved. It does appear likely that the current trend toward an increasing number of Bayesian applications will continue, but it is appropriate to point out two difficulties. First, the assessment of informative prior densities is often a difficult problem. For a vector $\boldsymbol{\beta}$ of moderate dimension, it is not straightforward to specify a prior covariance matrix that accurately captures one's prior information. However, as mentioned in Section 4.3.6, valuable research in this direction does exist, and reference informative priors such as the g prior [Zellner (1982a)] may prove to be useful. Furthermore, it is possible to examine the robustness of results to specification of the prior.

The second potential difficulty is a computational one. In the analyses of this chapter there were, for the most part, no computational difficulties; but with more complicated models, problems can arise. For example, if we assume $E[\mathbf{ee}'] = \sigma^2\boldsymbol{\Psi}(\boldsymbol{\theta})$ where $\boldsymbol{\Psi}(\boldsymbol{\theta})$ denotes a covariance matrix that is dependent on a fixed vector of parameters $\boldsymbol{\theta}$, then it is not always possible to analytically integrate $\boldsymbol{\theta}$ out of the joint posterior density $g(\boldsymbol{\beta},\boldsymbol{\theta}|\mathbf{y})$. Three alternatives that are possible under these circumstances are [Zellner and Rossi (1982)], as follows:

1. Use of an asymptotic expansion to obtain an approximation to $g(\boldsymbol{\beta}|\mathbf{y})$, [e.g., Lindley (1980)].
2. Numerical integration.
3. Monte Carlo numerical integration.

Numerical integration is computationally feasible as long as $\boldsymbol{\theta}$ is not of dimension greater than 2 or 3. See Zellner (1971, Appendix C) for details and programs for Simpson's Rule. For larger dimensions either an asymptotic expansion, Monte Carlo numerical integration, or some other approximation must be employed. Details of Monte Carlo numerical integration can be found in Kloek and van Dijk (1978), van Dijk and Kloek (1980), and Zellner and Rossi (1984). Thus, computational techniques are available for handling some of the more complicated models; however, where computer programs are not readily available for employing these techniques, the number of Bayesian applications is likely to be limited. See Press (1980) for details of computer programs that are available for Bayesian analysis.

For a general discussion of the role of Bayesian techniques in econometrics the reader is directed to articles by Zellner (1974) and Rothenberg (1974).

4.9 EXERCISES

Exercise 4.1

The following results are useful in Section 4.7. Prove that

(a) $|I + XA^{-1}X'| = |A + X'X| \cdot |A^{-1}|$

(b) $[A^{-1} + (X'X)^{-1}]^{-1} = X'X - X'X(A + X'X)^{-1}X'X$

(c) $(I + XA^{-1}X')^{-1} = I - X(A + X'X)^{-1}X'$

(d) $(\mathbf{y} - X\mathbf{b})'(\mathbf{y} - X\mathbf{b}) + (\mathbf{b} - \bar{\boldsymbol{\beta}})'[A^{-1} + (X'X)^{-1}]^{-1}(\mathbf{b} - \bar{\boldsymbol{\beta}})$
$= (\mathbf{y} - X\bar{\boldsymbol{\beta}})'(I + XA^{-1}X')^{-1}(\mathbf{y} - X\bar{\boldsymbol{\beta}})$

Exercise 4.2

Consider the general linear model $\mathbf{y} = X\boldsymbol{\beta} + \mathbf{e}$ with normally distributed first-order autoregressive errors $e_t = \rho e_{t-1} + v_t$, and the usual definitions and assumptions.

(a) If $\boldsymbol{\beta}$, ρ, and σ_v are treated as a priori independent with each marginal prior density proportional to the square root of the determinant of the relevant partition of the information matrix, the joint prior density is approximately

$$g(\boldsymbol{\beta},\rho,\sigma_v) \propto \frac{1}{\sigma_v(1-\rho^2)^{1/2}}$$

Prove this result.

(b) Suppose you were interested in predicting N future observations given by $\underset{(N\times 1)}{\tilde{\mathbf{y}}} = \underset{(N\times K)}{\tilde{X}} \boldsymbol{\beta} + \tilde{\mathbf{e}}$.

Outline the steps you would go through to derive the predictive posterior density function $g(\tilde{\mathbf{y}}|\mathbf{y})$. What form is the following distribution?

$$g(\tilde{\mathbf{y}}|\mathbf{y},\boldsymbol{\beta},\rho,\sigma_v)$$

Exercise 4.3

Suppose that $y_1, y_2, \ldots, y_T$ is a random sample from a Poisson distribution with mean λ, and that the prior distribution for λ is the gamma distribution

$$g(\lambda) \propto \lambda^{\alpha-1}e^{-\beta\lambda}$$

Find the posterior density for λ. What does this result tell you about the prior for λ?

Exercise 4.4

For the prior $g(\sigma)$ given in Equation 4.3.5, show that

(a) $E[\sigma] = \dfrac{\Gamma[(\bar{v}-1)/2]}{\Gamma(\bar{v}/2)}\left[\dfrac{\bar{v}}{2}\right]^{1/2}\bar{s}$

(b) the mode for σ is $\left(\dfrac{\bar{v}}{\bar{v}+1}\right)^{1/2}\bar{s}$

Exercise 4.5

Find the sampling theory mean and mean square error matrix for $\bar{\bar{\boldsymbol{\beta}}} = (A + X'X)^{-1}(A\bar{\boldsymbol{\beta}} + X'X\mathbf{b})$. Show that MSE($\mathbf{b}$) − MSE($\bar{\bar{\boldsymbol{\beta}}}$) is positive semidefinite if and only if

$$(\bar{\boldsymbol{\beta}} - \boldsymbol{\beta})'[(X'X)^{-1} + 2A^{-1}]^{-1}(\bar{\boldsymbol{\beta}} - \boldsymbol{\beta}) \leq \sigma^2$$

Exercise 4.6

Consider the model $\mathbf{y} = \mathbf{x}\beta + \mathbf{e}$ where $E[\mathbf{ee}'] = \sigma^2 I$, β is a scalar,

$$\mathbf{y} = (0 \quad -1 \quad 1 \quad 2 \quad 5 \quad 1 \quad 1 \quad -2 \quad -2 \quad -6)'$$

and

$$\mathbf{x} = (0 \quad 1 \quad 2 \quad 3 \quad 4 \quad 0 \quad -1 \quad -2 \quad -3 \quad -4)'$$

Also, suppose that your prior information about β and σ can be summarized via the densities

$$g(\beta|\sigma) \sim N(2,\sigma^2)$$
$$g(\sigma) \propto \sigma^{-3} \exp\{-1/\sigma^2\}$$

(a) What are the values of $\bar{v}$ and $\bar{s}^2$ in the prior density for σ?
(b) Write down the joint prior density $g(\beta,\sigma)$.
(c) What is the least squares estimate for β?
(d) What is the conditional posterior density $g(\beta|\sigma,\mathbf{y})$? Give its mean and variance.
(e) Give the marginal posterior densities for β and σ. Include the normalizing constants. What are $E[\beta|\mathbf{y}]$ and $\text{var}[\beta|\mathbf{y}]$?
(f) Assuming prior odds of unity, find the posterior odds in favor of H_0: $\beta = 1$ against the alternative, H_1: $\beta \neq 1$. [Assume that $g(\sigma|H_0) = g(\sigma|H_1)$.]

Exercise 4.7

Given that $(v\hat{\sigma}/\sigma^2)$ has a $\chi^2_{(v)}$ distribution, show that the density function for σ is that given in Equation 4.2.5.

Exercise 4.8

Consider the posterior density function $g(\boldsymbol{\beta},\sigma|\mathbf{y})$ derived from a natural conjugate prior. See Section 4.3.2. Show that if $\bar{v} = 0$ and $A = g_0 X'X$, then the expressions for $g(\boldsymbol{\beta},\sigma|\mathbf{y})$, $\bar{\bar{v}}\bar{\bar{s}}^2$ and $\bar{\bar{\boldsymbol{\beta}}}$ are given by Equations 4.3.18, 4.3.19, and 4.3.20, respectively.

Exercise 4.9

Show that the "poly-t" density in (4.3.23) is obtained by combining (4.3.21) and (4.3.22) with the likelihood function, and integrating out σ.

Exercise 4.10

Show that (a) the MELO estimator $\hat{\theta}_1^*$ in (4.4.7) is optimal with respect to the loss function $L = (\theta_1 - \hat{\theta}_1)^2/\theta_1^2$; and (b) the MELO estimator $\hat{\theta}_2^*$ in (4.4.8) is optimal with respect to the loss function $L = \beta_2^2(\theta_2 - \hat{\theta}_2)^2$.

Exercise 4.11

Derive the predictive density $f(\tilde{\mathbf{y}}|\mathbf{y})$ given in Equation 4.5.6.

4.10 REFERENCES

Berger, J. O. (1980) *Statistical Decision Theory: Foundations, Concepts and Methods,* Springer-Verlag, New York.

Berger, J. O. (1982) "Bayesian Robustness and the Stein Effect," *Journal of the American Statistical Association,* 77, 358–368.

Bernardo, J. M. (1980) "A Bayesian Analysis of Classical Hypothesis Testing," in J. M. Bernardo, M. H. DeGroot, D. V. Lindley, and A. F. M. Smith, eds., *Bayesian Statistics,* Proceedings of the First International Meeting held in Valencia, Spain, May, 1979.

Box, G. E. P. and G. C. Tiao (1973) *Bayesian Inference in Statistical Analysis,* Addison-Wesley, Reading, Mass.

Chamberlain, G. and E. E. Leamer (1976) "Matrix Weighted Averages and Posterior Bounds," *Journal of the Royal Statistical Society,* Series B, 38, 73–84.

Deely, J. J. and D. V. Lindley (1981) "Bayes Empirical Bayes," *Journal of the American Statistical Association,* 76, 833–841.

DeGroot, M. H. (1970) *Optimal Statistical Decisions,* McGraw-Hill, New York.

Dickey, J. M. (1968) "Three Multidimensional-Integral Identities with Bayesian Applications," *Annals of Mathematical Statistics,* 39, 1615–1627.

Dickey, J. M. (1975) "Bayesian Alternatives to the F-test and Least-Squares Estimates in the Normal Linear Model," in S. E. Fienberg and A. Zellner, eds., *Studies in Bayesian Econometrics and Statistics in Honor of Leonard J. Savage,* Amsterdam: North-Holland Publishing Co., 515–554.

Dickey, J. M. (1980) "Beliefs about Beliefs, a Theory for Stochastic Assessments of Subjective Probabilities," in J. M. Bernardo et al. eds., *Bayesian Statistics,* Proceedings of the First International Meeting held in Valencia, Spain, May, 1979.

Drèze, J. (1977) "Bayesian Regression Analysis Using Poly-t Densities," *Journal of Econometrics,* 6, 329–354.

Efron, B. and C. Morris (1972) "Limiting Risk of Bayes and Empirical Bayes Estimators—Part II," *Journal of the American Statistical Association,* 67, 130–139.

Efron, B. and C. Morris (1973) "Stein's Estimation Rule and its Competitors—An Empirical Bayes Approach," *Journal of the American Statistical Association,* 68, 117–130.

Fomby, T. B. and D. K. Guilkey (1978) "On Choosing the Optimal Level of Significance for the Durbin-Watson Test and the Bayesian Alternative," *Journal of Econometrics,* 8, 203–213.

Gaver, K. M. and M. S. Geisel (1974) "Discriminating Among Alternative Models: Bayesian and Non-Bayesian Methods," in P. Zarembka, ed., *Frontiers of Econometrics,* Academic Press, New York, 49–77.

Giles, D. E. A. and A. C. Rayner (1979) "The Mean Squared Errors of the Maximum Likelihood and Natural-Conjugate Bayes Regression Estimators," *Journal of Econometrics,* 11, 319–334.

Goel, P. K. and M. H. DeGroot (1981) "Information About Hyperparameters in Hierarchical Models," *Journal of the American Statistical Association,* 76, 140–147.

Griffiths, W. E., R. G. Drynan, and S. Prakash (1979) "Bayesian Estimation of a Random Coefficient Model," *Journal of Econometrics,* 10, 201–220.

Hill, B. M. (1975) "On Coherence, Inadmissibility and Inference About Many Parameters in the Theory of Least Squares," in S. E. Fienberg and A. Zellner, eds., *Studies in Bayesian Econometrics and Statistics,* North-Holland, Amsterdam.

Hill, B. M. (1980) "On Finite Additivity, Non-Conglomerability, and Statistical Paradoxes," in J. M. Bernardo et al. eds., *Bayesian Statistics,* Proceedings of the First International Meeting, Valencia, Spain, May, 1979.

Hoerl, A. E. and R. W. Kennard (1970) "Ridge Regression: Biased Estimation and Applications for Nonorthogonal Problems," *Technometrics,* 12, 55–82.

Jeffreys, H. (1967) *Theory of Probability,* 3rd rev. ed., Oxford University, London.

Judge, G. G. and M. E. Bock (1978) *The Statistical Implications of Pre-Test and Stein-Rule Estimators in Econometrics,* North-Holland, Amsterdam.

Judge, G. G., R. C. Hill, W. E. Griffiths, H. Lütkepohl, and T. C. Lee (1982) *Introduction to the Theory and Practice of Econometrics,* Wiley, New York.

Kadane, J. B. (1980) "Predictive and Structural Methods for Eliciting Prior Distributions," in A. Zellner, ed., *Bayesian Analysis in Econometrics and Statistics: Essays in Honor of Harold Jeffreys,* North-Holland, Amsterdam.

Kadane, J. B., J. M. Dickey, R. L. Winkler, W. S. Smith, and S. C. Peters (1980) "Interactive Elicitation of Opinion for a Normal Linear Model," *Journal of the American Statistical Association,* 75, 845–54.

Kloek, T. and H. van Dijk (1978) "Bayesian Estimates of Equation System Parameters: An Application of Integration by Monte Carlo," *Econometrica,* 46, 1–19.

Leamer, E. E. (1978) *Specification Searches,* Wiley, New York.

Leamer, E. E. (1982) "Sets of Posterior Means with Bounded Variance Priors," *Econometrica,* 50, 725–736.

Lempers, F. B. (1971) *Posterior Probabilities of Alternative Linear Models,* Rotterdam University Press, Rotterdam.

Lindley, D. V. (1957) "A Statistical Paradox," *Biometrika,* 44, 187–192.

Lindley, D. V. (1965) *Introduction to Probability and Statistics from a Bayesian Viewpoint* (2 vols.), Cambridge University Press, Cambridge.

Lindley, D. V. (1980) "Approximate Bayesian Methods," in J. M. Bernardo et al., eds., *Bayesian Statistics,* Proceedings of the First International Meeting, Valencia, Spain, May, 1979, 223–237.

Lindley, D. V. and A. F. M. Smith (1972) "Bayes Estimates for the Linear Model," *Journal of the Royal Statistical Society,* Series B, 34, 1–41.

Malinvaud, E. (1980) *Statistical Methods in Econometrics,* 3rd ed., North-Holland, Amsterdam.

Morris, C. N. (1983) "Parametric Bayes Inference: Theory and Applications," *Journal of the American Statistical Association,* 78, 47–65.

Park, S. B. (1982) "Some Sampling Properties of Minimum Expected Loss (MELO) Estimators of Structural Coefficients," *Journal of Econometrics,* 18, 295–311.

Press, S. J. (1980) "Bayesian Computer Programs," in A. Zellner, ed., *Bayesian Analysis in Econometrics and Statistics: Essays in Honor of Harold Jeffreys,* North-Holland, Amsterdam, 429–442.

Ramsay, J. O. and M. R. Novick (1980) "PLU Robust Bayesian Decision Theory: Point Estimation," *Journal of the American Statistical Association,* 75, 901–907.

Richard, J. F. and H. Tompa (1980) "On the Evaluation of Poly-*t* Density Functions," *Journal of Econometrics,* 12, 335–351.

Rossi, P. E. (1980) "Testing Hypotheses in Multivariate Regression: Bayes vs. Non-Bayes Procedures," manuscript, Graduate School of Business, University of Chicago, presented at Econometric Society Meeting, August, 1980.

Rothenberg, T. (1974) "The Bayesian Approach and Alternatives in Econometrics," in S. Fienberg and A. Zellner, eds., *Studies in Bayesian Econometrics and Statistics,* North-Holland, Amsterdam, 55–67.

Smith, A. F. M. (1973) "A General Bayesian Linear Model," *Journal of the Royal Statistical Society,* Series B, 35, 67–75.

Stein, C. M. (1981) "Estimation of the Mean of a Multivariate Normal Distribution," *The Annals of Statistics,* 9, 1135–1151.

Stone, M. (1976) "Strong Inconsistency from Uniform Priors," *Journal of the American Statistical Association,* 71, 114–125.

Surekha, K. and W. E. Griffiths (1984) "A Monte Carlo Comparison of Some Bayesian and Sampling Theory Estimators in Two Heteroscedastic Error Models," *Communications in Statistics,* B13, forthcoming.

Tiao, G. C. and G. E. P. Box (1973) "Some Comments on Bayes Estimators," *American Statistician,* 27, 12–14.

Tiao, G. C. and W. Y. Tan (1965) "Bayesian Analysis of Random-Effect Models in the Analysis of Variance, I. Posterior Distribution of Variance-Components," *Biometrika,* 52, 37–53.

Trivedi, P. K. (1980) "Small Samples and Collateral Information: An Application of the Hyperparameter Model," *Journal of Econometrics,* 12, 301–318.

Tsurumi, H. (1977) "A Bayesian Test of a Parameter Shift and an Application," *Journal of Econometrics,* 6, 371–380.

van Dijk, H. K. and T. Kloek (1980) "Further Experience in Bayesian Analysis Using Monte Carlo Integration," *Journal of Econometrics,* 14, 307–328.

Villegas, C. (1977) "On the Representation of Ignorance," *Journal of the American Statistical Association,* 72, 651–654.

Winkler, R. L. (1967) "The Assessment of Prior Distributions in Bayesian Analysis," *Journal of the American Statistical Association,* 62, 776–800.

Winkler, R. L. (1977) "Prior Distributions and Model-Building in Regression Analysis," in A. Aykac and C. Brumat, eds., *New Developments in the Applications of Bayesian Methods,* North-Holland, Amsterdam.

Winkler, R. L. (1980) "Prior Information, Predictive Distributions, and Bayesian Model-Building," in A. Zellner, ed., *Bayesian Analysis in Economet-*

rics and Statistics: Essays in Honor of Harold Jeffreys, North-Holland, Amsterdam.

Zaman, A. (1981) ''Estimators Without Moments: The Case of the Reciprocal of a Normal Mean,'' *Journal of Econometrics,* 15, 289–298.

Zellner, A. (1971) *An Introduction to Bayesian Analysis in Econometrics,* Wiley, New York.

Zellner, A. (1972) ''On Assessing Informative Prior Distributions for Regression Coefficients,'' manuscript H. G. B. Alexander Research Foundation, Graduate School of Business, University of Chicago.

Zellner, A. (1974) ''The Bayesian Approach and Alternatives in Econometrics,'' in S. E. Fienberg and A. Zellner, eds., *Studies in Bayesian Econometrics and Statistics in Honor of Leonard J. Savage,* North-Holland, Amsterdam. 39–54.

Zellner, A. (1977) ''Maximal Data Information Prior Distributions,'' in A. Aykac and C. Brumat, eds., *New Developments in the Applications of Bayesian Methods,* North-Holland, Amsterdam.

Zellner, A. (1978) ''Estimation of Functions of Population Means and Regression Coefficients Including Structural Coefficients: A Minimum Expected Loss (MELO) Approach,'' *Journal of Econometrics,* 8, 127–158.

Zellner, A. (1979) ''Posterior Odds Ratios for Regression Hypotheses: General Considerations and Some Specific Results,'' invited paper presented at Econometric Society Meeting, Atlanta, Georgia.

Zellner, A. (1981) ''The Current State of Bayesian Econometrics,'' invited address, Canadian Conference on Applied Statistics, April 29–May 1, 1981, to appear in Conference Proceedings Volume.

Zellner, A. (1982a) ''On Assessing Prior Distributions and Bayesian Regression Analysis with g-Prior Distributions,'' revised version of paper presented to the Econometric Society Meeting, Denver, Colorado, September, 1980.

Zellner, A. (1982b) ''Applications of Bayesian Analysis in Econometrics,'' paper presented at the Institute of Statisticians International Conference on Practical Bayesian Statistics, St. John's College, Cambridge, July, 1982.

Zellner, A. and M. S. Geisel (1970) ''Analysis of Distributed Lag Models with Applications to Consumption Function Estimation,'' *Econometrica,* 38, 865–888.

Zellner, A. and S. B. Park (1979) ''Minimum Expected Loss (MELO) Estimators for Functions of Parameters and Structural Coefficients of Econometric Models,'' *Journal of the American Statistical Association,* 74, 185–193.

Zellner, A. and J. F. Richard (1973) ''Use of Prior Information in the Analysis and Estimation of Cobb-Douglas Production Function Models,'' *International Economic Review,* 14, 107–119.

Zellner, A. and P. E. Rossi (1984) ''Bayesian Analysis of Dichotomous Quantal Response Models,'' *Journal of Econometrics,* forthcoming.

Zellner, A. and A. Siow (1980) ''Posterior Odds Ratios for Selected Regression Hypotheses,'' in J. M. Bernardo et al., eds., *Bayesian Statistics,* Proceedings of the First International Meeting, Valencia, Spain, May, 1979, 585–603.

Zellner, A. and W. Vandaele (1975) ''Bayes-Stein Estimators for k-Means,

Regression and Simultaneous Equation Models,'' in S. E. Fienberg and A. Zellner, eds., *Studies in Bayesian Econometrics and Statistics in Honor of Leonard J. Savage,* North-Holland, Amsterdam, 627–653.

Zellner, A. and A. Williams (1973) ''Bayesian Analysis of the Federal Reserve-MIT-Penn Model's Almon Lag Consumption Function,'' *Journal of Econometrics,* 1, 267–299.

PART TWO

INFERENCE IN GENERAL STATISTICAL MODELS AND TIME SERIES

In the next three chapters we leave the conventional worlds discussed in Part I and now consider tools for analyzing situations when (1) it is not possible to derive exact sampling distributions, (2) the statistical models are nonlinear, and (3) the economic data can be modeled within a time series discrete stochastic process context. In each case the basic concepts and definitions are developed and the statistical implications are evaluated. Numerical optimization procedures useful in analyzing nonlinear statistical models are discussed in Appendix B at the end of the book. Multivariate time series models are considered in Part V.

Chapter 5

Some Asymptotic Theory and Other General Results for the Linear Statistical Model

In Chapters 2 and 3, and to a minor extent in Chapter 4, we were concerned with the sampling theory properties of estimators for $\boldsymbol{\beta}$ and σ^2 in the general linear statistical model $\mathbf{y} = X\boldsymbol{\beta} + \mathbf{e}$. We assumed that the disturbance covariance matrix was either $E[\mathbf{ee}'] = \sigma^2 I$, or $E[\mathbf{ee}'] = \sigma^2 \boldsymbol{\Psi}$ with $\boldsymbol{\Psi}$ known, that the regressor matrix X was nonstochastic, and, for the most part, that $\mathbf{e}$ was normally distributed. Under these assumptions we were able to derive the *exact* (finite sample) distribution of various estimators and test statistics and to compare estimators on the basis of criteria such as unbiasedness, minimum variance, and minimum squared error loss. Unfortunately, circumstances are not always such that it is possible to derive exact sampling distributions. If $\boldsymbol{\Psi}$ is unknown and has to be estimated, or X is stochastic, or $\mathbf{e}$ is not normally distributed, it is frequently too difficult to derive the probability distributions, and sometimes also the moments, of potentially useful statistics. As an alternative, we can consider the properties of such statistics as the sample size approaches infinity. These properties, known as asymptotic properties, are often much easier to derive, and, providing the sample size is large enough, they can provide useful approximations to finite sample properties. In addition, even if an estimator has known and desirable finite sample properties, it is usually considered an advantage if that estimator also possesses desirable asymptotic properties.

To make some of these ideas more explicit, let the least squares estimator $\mathbf{b} = (X'X)^{-1}X'\mathbf{y}$, based on a sample of size T, be denoted by $\mathbf{b}_T$. Also, suppose that, instead of being multivariate normal, the probability distribution of $\mathbf{y}$ is unknown. Then, it is clear that we cannot derive the form of the distribution function for $\mathbf{b}_T$, say $F_T(\mathbf{b})$. Thus, although we might be able to derive the mean and covariance matrix for $\mathbf{b}_T$, we would not know what probability distribution should be used for interval estimation and hypothesis testing. To overcome this problem we can consider the properties of the sequence of random vectors $\{\sqrt{T}(\mathbf{b}_T - \boldsymbol{\beta})\}$, and the nature of the corresponding sequence of distribution functions $\{F_T[\sqrt{T}(\mathbf{b}_T - \boldsymbol{\beta})]\}$ as $T \to \infty$. Under certain conditions we can find a distribution function that is the limit of the sequence of distribution functions, and this limiting distribution can then be used as an approximate distribution function for $\sqrt{T}(\mathbf{b}_T - \boldsymbol{\beta})$ for finite values of T. We cannot, in general, say how good such an approximation will be; it will depend on the magnitude of T, the distribution of $\mathbf{y}$ and the limiting behavior of X. However, in the absence of any finite sample properties, such "asymptotic approximations" are frequently our best source of information on which to base inferences. Thus, in this chapter we consider the limiting behavior of certain functions of estimators, the limiting behavior of their corresponding distribution functions, and a number of other related concepts such as the limiting behavior of the moments of various estimators. All these topics come under the general heading of asymptotic theory.

Rather than introduce the asymptotic theory concepts in isolation, we try, as much as possible, to illustrate the concepts with estimators and hypothesis tests from the general linear statistical model. In Section 5.1 we consider the consistency of the least squares estimator $\mathbf{b} = (X'X)^{-1}X'\mathbf{y}$ and its associated variance estimator $\hat{\sigma}^2 = (\mathbf{y} - X\mathbf{b})'(\mathbf{y} - X\mathbf{b})/(T - K)$, and introduce concepts such as convergence in probability, convergence almost surely, and order in probability. In Section 5.2 we briefly consider the finite sample properties of least squares when $\mathbf{e}$ is not normally distributed, but still has finite variance. This section serves as a lead into Section 5.3, where the asymptotic distribution of $\mathbf{b}$ is investigated, and concepts such as convergence in distribution are introduced. In Section 5.4 we discuss the asymptotic properties of least squares when the regressor matrix X is no longer nonstochastic, and we introduce the instrumental variables technique. The asymptotic properties of estimators for $\boldsymbol{\beta}$, which are based on an estimate of the unknown covariance matrix $\boldsymbol{\Psi}$, are the subject of Section 5.5, and in Section 5.6 we discuss the maximum likelihood estimation technique and its desirable asymptotic properties. Three useful testing procedures (likelihood ratio, Wald, and Lagrange multiplier) are described and compared in Section 5.7. Finally, in Section 5.8 we give a summary of a number of asymptotic theory results, including those which were introduced earlier in the chapter.

5.1 CONSISTENCY OF LEAST SQUARES

In this section we are concerned with certain aspects of the limiting behavior of the least squares (LS) estimator $\mathbf{b}_T$ in the general linear model $\mathbf{y} = X\boldsymbol{\beta} + \mathbf{e}$. For convenience we will drop the subscript T and simply denote the LS estimator by $\mathbf{b}$. The notation introduced in Chapters 2 to 4 still holds. We assume:

1. The regressor matrix X is nonstochastic.
2. The random vector $\mathbf{e}$ has mean $\mathbf{0}$, covariance matrix $E[\mathbf{ee}'] = \sigma^2 I$, and is not necessarily normally distributed.

Since we can write the least squares estimator as

$$\mathbf{b} = \boldsymbol{\beta} + (X'X)^{-1}X'\mathbf{e} \tag{5.1.1}$$

and we wish to make statements about how, and in what sense, $\mathbf{b}$ converges to $\boldsymbol{\beta}$ as $T \to \infty$, it is clear that we must investigate the convergence properties of $X'X$ and $X'\mathbf{e}$. With this point in mind we first consider $X'X$.

5.1.1 The Convergence of $X'X/T$

The strongest assumption usually made about $X'X$ is that

$$\lim_{T\to\infty} \left(\frac{X'X}{T}\right) = Q \tag{5.1.2}$$

where Q is a finite nonsingular matrix. This assumption implies that, as T increases, the elements of $X'X$ do not increase at a greater rate than T, and that the explanatory variables are not linearly dependent in the limit. Let us consider examples that violate each of these conditions.

If X is $(T \times 2)$ with $x_{t1} = 1$ for all t and $x_{t2} = t$ then

$$X'X = \begin{bmatrix} T & T(T+1)/2 \\ T(T+1)/2 & T(T+1)(2T+1)/6 \end{bmatrix} \tag{5.1.3}$$

From (5.1.3) it is clear that lim $(X'X/T)$ is not finite, and so, in this case, the assumption that Q is finite does not hold. However, in Section 5.3.5, which is concerned with "Asymptotically Uncooperative Regressors," most of the asymptotic properties in this chapter can be derived under less restrictive assumptions about X. This fact is important because, in economics, our explanatory variables are frequently trended.

The assumption that Q is nonsingular is more critical. For an example where this condition is violated [Dhrymes (1978)], let $x_{t1} = 1$ for all t and $x_{t2} = \lambda^t$, where $|\lambda| < 1$. Then

$$X'X = \begin{bmatrix} T & \dfrac{\lambda - \lambda^{T+1}}{1-\lambda} \\ \dfrac{\lambda - \lambda^{T+1}}{1-\lambda} & \dfrac{\lambda^2 - \lambda^{2(T+1)}}{1-\lambda^2} \end{bmatrix} \tag{5.1.4}$$

and

$$\lim_{T\to\infty} \left(\frac{X'X}{T}\right) = \begin{bmatrix} 1 & 0 \\ 0 & 0 \end{bmatrix} \tag{5.1.5}$$

Thus although $X'X$ is nonsingular for all finite T, $X'X/T$ is singular in the limit, and so (5.1.2) is violated.

5.1.2 The Order of Magnitude of a Sequence

Assumption (5.1.2) is a convenient vehicle for introducing the concept of the order of magnitude of a sequence. The fact that the elements of $T^{-1}X'X$ converge to finite limits implies that $T^{-1}X'X$ is bounded (in the sense that the sequences of the elements within $T^{-1}X'X$ are bounded), and under these circumstances we say that $X'X$ is at most of order T. We write it as

$$X'X = O(T) \tag{5.1.6}$$

More formally, we say that the sequence $\{a_T\}$ is *at most of order* T^k, and write it as $a_T = O(T^k)$ if there exists a real number N such that

$$T^{-k}|a_T| \leq N \tag{5.1.7}$$

for all T. This definition extends to vectors and matrices by applying the condition to every element in the relevant vector or matrix. Note that, although (5.1.2) implies (5.1.6), the converse is not necessarily true.

A related concept and its associated notation is introduced in the following definition. A sequence $\{a_T\}$ is *of smaller order than* T^k, and is written as $a_T = o(T^k)$, if

$$\lim_{T\to\infty} T^{-k}a_T = 0 \tag{5.1.8}$$

For example, if (5.1.2) holds, and we extend the above definition to matrices; then $X'X = o(T^2)$ because $\lim T^{-2}X'X = \lim T^{-1}Q = 0$. Also, note that if $a_T = O(T^k)$, then $a_T = o(T^{k+\delta})$ where $\delta > 0$.

It is frequently useful to employ results from the algebra associated with orders of magnitudes of sequences, and so we will briefly state some of these results. Consider the sequences $\{a_T\}$ and $\{b_T\}$ such that $a_T = O(T^k)$ and $b_T = O(T^j)$. The following results hold

$$\begin{aligned} a_T b_T &= O(T^{k+j}) \\ |a_T|^s &= O(T^{ks}); \qquad s > 0 \\ a_T + b_T &= O(\max\{T^k, T^j\}). \end{aligned}$$

The above results are also true if O is replaced by o. In addition, if $a_T = O(T^k)$ and $b_T = o(T^j)$, then

$$a_T b_T = o(T^{k+j}).$$

Before we can return to an evaluation of the asymptotic properties of **b**, there are a number of other asymptotic theory concepts that are needed, or that it is convenient to introduce. We begin with the concepts of convergence in probability and almost sure convergence.

5.1.3 Convergence in Probability and Almost Sure Convergence

The sequence of random variables $z_1, z_2, \ldots, z_T, \ldots$ *converges in probability* to the random variable z if, for all $\varepsilon > 0$,

$$\lim_{T\to\infty} P[|z_T - z| > \varepsilon] = 0 \tag{5.1.9}$$

This definition is extended to a sequence of random vectors $\mathbf{z}_1, \mathbf{z}_2, \ldots, \mathbf{z}_T, \ldots$ by interpreting $|\mathbf{z}_T - \mathbf{z}|$ as the Euclidean distance $[(\mathbf{z}_T - \mathbf{z})'(\mathbf{z}_T - \mathbf{z})]^{1/2}$, and to a sequence of random matrices by viewing a matrix as a vector whose elements have been rearranged. The random variable (or vector) z is called the *probability limit* of z_T, and is written as

$$\text{plim } z_T = z \tag{5.1.10}$$

or, alternatively, as

$$z_T \xrightarrow{p} z \tag{5.1.11}$$

The above definition implies that if we consider the sequence of probabilities $\{P[|z_T - z| > \varepsilon]\}$, then there exists a T, say T_0, such that, for $T > T_0$, each probability in the sequence is arbitrarily small. This is in contrast to the stronger convergence concept of almost sure convergence, where, for $T > T_0$, the probability of the union of the events $|z_{T_0+1} - z| > \varepsilon$, $|z_{T_0+2} - z| > \varepsilon, \ldots$ is arbitrarily small. More formally, the random variable z_T *converges almost surely* to the random variable z if

$$P(\lim_{T\to\infty} |z_T - z| > \varepsilon) = 0 \tag{5.1.12}$$

and we write this result as

$$z_T \xrightarrow{\text{a.s.}} z \tag{5.1.13}$$

The extension to vectors is analogous to that for convergence in probability. Almost sure convergence implies convergence in probability, but, as an example given by Greenberg and Webster (1983, pp. 4–6) illustrates, the converse is not necessarily true. In econometrics we deal mainly with convergence in probability, although there are instances where it is easier to prove almost sure convergence.

An important theorem for working with probability limits is *Slutsky's theorem* [see Greenberg and Webster (1983, p. 8)]. It states that, if $\mathbf{g}(\cdot)$ is a continuous (vector) function, then

$$\text{plim}[\mathbf{g}(\mathbf{z}_T)] = \mathbf{g}[\text{plim}(\mathbf{z}_T)] \tag{5.1.14}$$

Circumstances frequently arise where we have knowledge of an expectation, say $E(\mathbf{z}_T)$, but, because $E[\mathbf{g}(\mathbf{z}_T)] \neq \mathbf{g}[E(\mathbf{z}_T)]$, it is too difficult to evaluate $E[\mathbf{g}(\mathbf{z}_T)]$. Instead, if we know plim $\mathbf{z}_T$, and we are prepared to settle for large sample results, we can use Slutsky's theorem to evaluate plim$[\mathbf{g}(\mathbf{z}_T)]$.

5.1.4 Order in Probability

When discussing the limit of an algebraic sequence we introduced the concept of order of magnitude of a sequence. Associated with sequences of random variables and probability limits we have a similar concept known as order in probability. The sequence of random variables $\{z_T\}$ is *at most of order in probability* T^k, and we write

$$z_T = O_p(T^k) \tag{5.1.15}$$

if, for every $\varepsilon > 0$, there exists a real number N such that

$$P[T^{-k}|z_T| \geq N] \leq \varepsilon \tag{5.1.16}$$

for all T. Also, we say that $\{z_T\}$ is of *smaller order in probability than* T^k and write

$$z_T = o_p(T^k) \tag{5.1.17}$$

if

$$\text{plim } T^{-k} z_T = 0 \tag{5.1.18}$$

These definitions also hold for vectors and matrices by applying the conditions to every element in the relevant vector or matrix. The concepts in (5.1.15) and (5.1.17) can be related by noting that if $z_T = O_p(T^k)$, then $z_T = o_p(T^j)$ if $j > k$. The algebra for O_p and o_p is identical to that given for O and o in Section 5.1.2.

For an example let us return to the least squares estimator $\mathbf{b} = \boldsymbol{\beta} + (X'X)^{-1}X'\mathbf{e}$ and investigate the order in probability of the term $X'\mathbf{e}$. To simplify the discussion we will assume there is only one explanatory variable whose observations are contained in the vector $\mathbf{x}$, and therefore, we are interested in the order in probability of the scalar $\mathbf{x}'\mathbf{e}$. It is straightforward to extend the analysis to each element of the vector $X'\mathbf{e}$.

If (5.1.2) holds, that is, $\lim T^{-1}\,\mathbf{x}'\mathbf{x} = q$ is a finite nonzero constant, then, as described in (5.1.6), $\mathbf{x}'\mathbf{x} = O(T)$, and there exists a number N_1 such that

$$T^{-1}\mathbf{x}'\mathbf{x} \leq N_1 \tag{5.1.19}$$

Also, we have $E[\mathbf{x}'\mathbf{e}] = 0$ and $E[(\mathbf{x}'\mathbf{e})^2] = \sigma^2(\mathbf{x}'\mathbf{x})$. To proceed further we introduce a version of *Chebyshev's inequality,* that is, if z is a random variable with mean μ and finite variance, then, for every $\delta > 0$,

$$P[|z - \mu| \geq \delta] \leq \frac{E[(z - \mu)^2]}{\delta^2} \tag{5.1.20}$$

Applying this result to $\mathbf{x}'\mathbf{e}$ and using (5.1.19), we have, for any $N_2 > 0$

$$P[|\mathbf{x}'\mathbf{e}| \geq T^{1/2}N_2] \leq \frac{\sigma^2(\mathbf{x}'\mathbf{x})}{TN_2^2} \leq \frac{\sigma^2 N_1}{N_2^2} \tag{5.1.21}$$

or

$$P[T^{-1/2}|\mathbf{x}'\mathbf{e}| \geq N_2] \leq \frac{\sigma^2 N_1}{N_2^2} \tag{5.1.22}$$

If, for a given $\varepsilon > 0$ we choose N_2 such that $\sigma^2 N_1/N_2^2 \leq \varepsilon$, that is, $N_2 \geq \sigma(N_1/\varepsilon)^{1/2}$, we can write

$$P[T^{-1/2}|\mathbf{x}'\mathbf{e}| \geq N_2] \leq \varepsilon \tag{5.1.23}$$

Then, from the definition of order in probability in (5.1.15) and (5.1.16), we have

$$\mathbf{x}'\mathbf{e} = O_p(T^{1/2}) \tag{5.1.24}$$

Furthermore, from (5.1.24) we can write

$$\mathbf{x}'\mathbf{e} = o_p(T) \tag{5.1.25}$$

which, from (5.1.17) and (5.1.18), implies

$$\text{plim } T^{-1}\mathbf{x}'\mathbf{e} = 0 \tag{5.1.26}$$

This last result will be useful for establishing the property of consistency for the least squares estimator $\mathbf{b}$, and for the least squares variance estimator $\hat{\sigma}^2 = (\mathbf{y} - X\mathbf{b})'(\mathbf{y} - X\mathbf{b})/(T - K)$. Before turning to these problems it is worth stating the result in (5.1.24) in more general terms [Fuller (1976)].

If $\{z_T\}$ is a sequence of random variables such that

$$E[(z_T - E[z_T])^2] = O(T^k) \qquad \text{and} \qquad E[z_T] = O(T^{k/2})$$

then $z_T = O_p(T^{k/2})$.

5.1.5 Consistency

A special case of convergence in probability is where the probability limit of a sequence of random vectors (or variables) is equal to a vector of constants. That is, for the sequence $\{\mathbf{z}_T\}$, we can write $\mathbf{z}_T \xrightarrow{p} \mathbf{k}$ or plim $\mathbf{z}_T = \mathbf{k}$ where $\mathbf{k}$ is a vector of constants. This special case is of particular interest if $\mathbf{z}_T$ is an estimator for some unknown parameter vector $\boldsymbol{\theta}$. If plim $\mathbf{z}_T = \boldsymbol{\theta}$, then $\mathbf{z}_T$ is called a *consistent estimator* for $\boldsymbol{\theta}$. The property of consistency is considered a desirable one because it implies that, by taking T sufficiently large, we can ensure that the probability that $\mathbf{z}_T$ assumes values outside an arbitrarily small neighborhood of $\boldsymbol{\theta}$ is very small.

Another type of consistency, but one that is encountered less frequently in econometrics, is known as *strong consistency*. An estimator $\mathbf{z}_T$ is called strongly consistent for a parameter vector $\boldsymbol{\theta}$ if $\mathbf{z}_T \xrightarrow{\text{a.s.}} \boldsymbol{\theta}$.

Let us now demonstrate that the least squares estimator is consistent. From (5.1.1) we have

$$\mathbf{b} = \boldsymbol{\beta} + \left(\frac{X'X}{T}\right)^{-1} \frac{X'\mathbf{e}}{T}$$

and

$$\begin{aligned}
\text{plim}\, \mathbf{b} &= \boldsymbol{\beta} + \text{plim}\left(\frac{X'X}{T}\right)^{-1} \frac{X'\mathbf{e}}{T} \\
&= \boldsymbol{\beta} + \text{plim}\left(\frac{X'X}{T}\right)^{-1} \text{plim}\left(\frac{X'\mathbf{e}}{T}\right) \quad \text{from Slutsky's theorem} \\
&= \boldsymbol{\beta} + \left(\lim \frac{X'X}{T}\right)^{-1} \text{plim}\left(\frac{X'\mathbf{e}}{T}\right) \\
&= \boldsymbol{\beta} + Q^{-1}\mathbf{0} \quad \text{from (5.1.2) and (5.1.26)} \\
&= \boldsymbol{\beta}
\end{aligned} \tag{5.1.27}$$

In going from plim $(X'X/T)^{-1}$ to $(\lim X'X/T)^{-1}$, we have used Slutsky's theorem and the fact that the probability limit of a nonstochastic sequence is simply equal to its (nonprobabilistic) limit.

To show that the least squares variance estimator is consistent we first state *Khinchine's theorem*. If $z_1, z_2, \ldots, z_T$ are independent and identically distributed (i.i.d.) random variables with finite mean μ, then plim $T^{-1} \sum_{t=1}^{T} q_t = \mu$. An important feature of this theorem is that it does not require the existence of moments of higher order than the mean. Now consider the i.i.d. random variables, $e_1^2, e_2^2, \ldots, e_T^2$, which have mean $E[e_t^2] = \sigma^2$. From Khinchine's theorem it follows that

$$\text{plim}\, T^{-1}\mathbf{e}'\mathbf{e} = \sigma^2 \tag{5.1.28}$$

To prove plim $\hat{\sigma}^2 = \sigma^2$ consider

$$\hat{\sigma}^2 = \frac{\hat{\mathbf{e}}'\hat{\mathbf{e}}}{T - K}$$

$$= \frac{1}{T-K}\mathbf{e}'(I - X(X'X)^{-1}X')\mathbf{e}$$

$$= \frac{T}{T-K}\left[\frac{\mathbf{e}'\mathbf{e}}{T} - \frac{\mathbf{e}'X}{T}\left(\frac{X'X}{T}\right)^{-1}\frac{X'\mathbf{e}}{T}\right] \tag{5.1.29}$$

Then, using Slutsky's theorem and the fact that plim $[T/(T-K)] = 1$,

$$\begin{aligned}\text{plim }\hat{\sigma}^2 &= \text{plim }\frac{\mathbf{e}'\mathbf{e}}{T} - \text{plim }\frac{\mathbf{e}'X}{T}\text{ plim }\left(\frac{X'X}{T}\right)^{-1}\text{ plim }\frac{X'\mathbf{e}}{T}\\ &= \sigma^2 - 0 \cdot Q^{-1} \cdot 0\\ &= \sigma^2\end{aligned} \tag{5.1.30}$$

where the second to last equality is based on (5.1.2), (5.1.26), and (5.1.28).

5.1.6 Convergence in Quadratic Mean

A concept closely allied with consistency is that of convergence in quadratic mean. We say that the sequence of random vectors $\mathbf{z}_1, \mathbf{z}_2, \ldots, \mathbf{z}_T, \ldots$ converges in quadratic mean to the random vector $\mathbf{z}$ if $E[\mathbf{z}_T\mathbf{z}_T']$ and $E[\mathbf{z}\mathbf{z}']$ exist for all T and if

$$\lim_{T\to\infty} E[(\mathbf{z}_T - \mathbf{z})'(\mathbf{z}_T - \mathbf{z})] = 0 \tag{5.1.31}$$

As was the case for convergence in probability, a special case of convergence in quadratic mean occurs when $\mathbf{z}$, instead of being a random vector, is a vector of unknown parameters, say $\boldsymbol{\theta}$, and $\mathbf{z}_T$ is an estimator for $\boldsymbol{\theta}$. Under these circumstances we can write

$$\begin{aligned}E[(\mathbf{z}_T - \boldsymbol{\theta})'(\mathbf{z}_T - \boldsymbol{\theta})] &= (E[\mathbf{z}_T] - \boldsymbol{\theta})'(E[\mathbf{z}_T] - \boldsymbol{\theta})\\ &\quad + E[(\mathbf{z}_T - E[\mathbf{z}_T])'(\mathbf{z}_T - E[\mathbf{z}_T])]\\ &= \sum_{i=1}^{K} \text{bias}^2(z_{iT}) + \sum_{i=1}^{K} \text{var}(z_{iT})\end{aligned} \tag{5.1.32}$$

where z_{iT} is the ith element of $\mathbf{z}_T$ that is assumed to be K dimensional. Thus, from (5.1.32) $\mathbf{z}_T$ converges to $\boldsymbol{\theta}$ in quadratic mean if and only if the bias and variance of $\mathbf{z}_T$ approach zero as $T \to \infty$.

This result, and the fact that Chebyshev's inequality can be used to prove that convergence in quadratic mean implies convergence in probability [see, for example, Dhrymes (1974)], are frequently used to prove an estimator is consistent. For example, an alternative method for proving that the least squares estimator $\mathbf{b}$ is consistent is to demonstrate that its bias and covariance matrix approach zero as $T \to \infty$. Since $\mathbf{b}$ is unbiased its bias is zero for all T, and the limit of its covariance matrix is

$$\lim \sigma^2(X'X)^{-1} = \lim \frac{\sigma^2}{T} \lim \left(\frac{X'X}{T}\right)^{-1} = 0 \cdot Q^{-1} = 0$$

Let us also consider the maximum likelihood estimator for σ^2 when $\mathbf{e}$ is normally distributed. This estimator is given by $\tilde{\sigma}^2 = (\mathbf{y} - X\mathbf{b})'(\mathbf{y} - X\mathbf{b})/T$ and has bias and variance given respectively by

$$\text{bias}(\tilde{\sigma}^2) = E[\tilde{\sigma}] - \sigma^2 = -\frac{K}{T}\sigma^2 \rightarrow 0 \text{ as } T \rightarrow \infty$$

and

$$\text{var}(\tilde{\sigma}^2) = \frac{2(T - K)\sigma^4}{T^2} \rightarrow 0 \text{ as } T \rightarrow \infty$$

Thus, although $\tilde{\sigma}^2$ is a biased estimator, it is nevertheless consistent.

It is worth emphasizing that although convergence in quadratic mean implies convergence in probability, the converse is not true. Consequently, if lim $(E[\mathbf{z}_T] - \boldsymbol{\theta}) = \mathbf{0}$ and lim $E[(\mathbf{z}_T - E[\mathbf{z}_T])'(\mathbf{z}_T - E[\mathbf{z}_T])] = 0$, then these conditions are sufficient to prove that $\mathbf{z}_T$ is a consistent estimator for $\boldsymbol{\theta}$ (plim $\mathbf{z}_T = \boldsymbol{\theta}$), but *they are not necessary*. It is possible to find consistent estimators whose bias and variance do not approach zero as $T \rightarrow \infty$. For an example of a consistent estimator whose bias and variance do not have zero limits see Judge et al. (1982, p. 270). Also, in a more general form of the same example, Dhrymes (1974, p. 88) shows that it is possible to have a consistent estimator whose mean does not exist. As a further illustration consider the proof of consistency of $\hat{\sigma}^2$ given in (5.1.30). This proof does not require knowledge of the variance of $\hat{\sigma}^2$, and holds even if this variance does not exist.

Since we have indicated that convergence in quadratic mean and convergence almost surely are both stronger forms of convergence than convergence in probability, can the three convergence concepts be completely ordered? The answer is no. Convergence in quadratic mean does not imply convergence almost surely, and convergence almost surely does not imply convergence in quadratic mean. For an example, see Lukacs (1968, pp. 32–34).

5.2 FINITE SAMPLE PROPERTIES OF LEAST SQUARES WITH NONNORMAL ERRORS

When the error vector $\mathbf{e}$ is not normally distributed interval estimates and hypothesis tests for $\boldsymbol{\beta}$ must be based on what is known as the asymptotic distribution of the least squares estimator. We will take up this question in Section 5.3. In this section, to demonstrate the need to consider the asymptotic distribution, we will briefly state some of the finite sample properties of **b** when **e** is nonnormal. We retain the assumption that $E[\mathbf{ee}'] = \sigma^2 I$, with σ^2 finite. When the variance does not exist, the robust estimation procedures discussed in Chapter 20 are likely to be more suitable.

The existence of nonnormal errors has the following implications for the finite sample properties of least squares statistics.

1. Instead of being minimum variance from within the class of *all* unbiased estimators, the least squares estimator **b** is only minimum variance from within the class of linear unbiased estimators. More efficient nonlinear unbiased estimators may exist.
2. The variance estimator $\hat{\sigma}^2 = (\mathbf{y} - X\mathbf{b})'(\mathbf{y} - X\mathbf{b})/(T - K)$ is still unbiased but is no longer minimum variance from within the class of all unbiased estimators for σ^2.
3. The respective distributions of **b** and $(T - K)\hat{\sigma}^2/\sigma^2$ are no longer normal and $\chi^2_{(T-K)}$.

Consequently, the F statistic

$$F = \frac{(R\mathbf{b} - R\boldsymbol{\beta})'[R(X'X)^{-1}R']^{-1}(R\mathbf{b} - R\boldsymbol{\beta})/J}{\hat{\sigma}^2} \tag{5.2.1}$$

no longer has the $F_{(J,T-K)}$ distribution, and it is therefore no longer valid (in finite samples) for testing a set of J linear restrictions given by $R\boldsymbol{\beta} = \mathbf{r}$.

5.3 THE ASYMPTOTIC DISTRIBUTION OF THE LEAST SQUARES ESTIMATOR

It is sometimes argued that, because each element of the error vector **e** is made up of the sum of a large number of individual influences, then from a central limit theorem (discussed later in this section), it is reasonable to assume that **e** is normally distributed. This argument may be valid under some circumstances, but it would be reassuring if there was some justification for test statistics such as (5.2.1) even when **e** is not normally distributed. Thus, in this section we investigate how large sample (asymptotic) theory can be used to make inferences about $\boldsymbol{\beta}$, without invoking the normality assumption. We begin by introducing the concept of convergence in distribution followed by a statement of the relevant central limit theorems.

5.3.1 Convergence in Distribution

We state the definition of convergence in distribution in terms of a random vector $\mathbf{z}_T$. A scalar random variable can be regarded as a special case of this definition.

The sequence of random vectors $\mathbf{z}_1, \mathbf{z}_2, \ldots, \mathbf{z}_T, \ldots$ with corresponding distribution functions $F_1(\mathbf{z}), F_2(\mathbf{z}), \ldots, F_T(\mathbf{z}), \ldots$ *converges in distribution* to the random vector $\mathbf{z}$ with distribution function $F(\mathbf{z})$ if, and only if, at all continuity points of F, and for every $\varepsilon > 0$, there exists a T_0 such that

$$|F_T(\mathbf{z}) - F(\mathbf{z})| < \varepsilon \qquad \text{for} \qquad T > T_0$$

This result is often denoted by $\mathbf{z}_T \xrightarrow{d} \mathbf{z}$. The distribution given by $F(\mathbf{z})$ is called the asymptotic (or limiting) distribution of $\mathbf{z}_T$.

The usefulness of this concept lies in our ability to approximate an unknown distribution function $F_T(\mathbf{z})$ with a known asymptotic distribution $F(\mathbf{z})$. Circumstances frequently exist where the finite sample distribution of an estimator or test statistic is unknown or is too difficult to evaluate, but where it is still possible to derive the form of the asymptotic distribution of such an estimator or test statistic. The asymptotic distribution can then serve as an approximation to the finite sample distribution.

Let us consider a number of properties of convergence in distribution. First, convergence in distribution is a weaker form of convergence than convergence in probability. That is,

$$\mathbf{z}_T \xrightarrow{p} \mathbf{z} \qquad \text{implies} \qquad \mathbf{z}_T \xrightarrow{d} \mathbf{z}$$

but the converse is not necessarily true. To appreciate this point note that, if $\mathbf{z}_T \xrightarrow{p} \mathbf{z}$, then, for large T, the probability that $\mathbf{z}_T$ differs from $\mathbf{z}$ is very small, and so we would expect them to have approximately the same distribution. However, it is possible for completely unrelated (e.g., independent) random variables to have approximately the same distribution. Thus, if $\mathbf{z}_T \xrightarrow{d} \mathbf{z}$, then $\mathbf{z}_T$ and $\mathbf{z}$ will have approximately the same distribution, but any realization of $\mathbf{z}_T$ need not have a bearing on a realization of $\mathbf{z}$.

When $\mathbf{z} = \boldsymbol{\theta}$ is a vector of constants the converse does hold. That is, it is also true that

$$\mathbf{z}_T \xrightarrow{d} \boldsymbol{\theta} \qquad \text{implies} \qquad \mathbf{z}_T \xrightarrow{p} \boldsymbol{\theta}$$

In this case the limiting distribution of $\mathbf{z}_T$ is degenerate since it collapses to the single point $\boldsymbol{\theta}$.

Another important result is that the moments of the asymptotic distribution of a random variable are not necessarily equal to the limits of the moments of that random variable's finite sample distribution. That is, in terms of the first two moments, $\mathbf{z}_T \xrightarrow{d} \mathbf{z}$ does *not* necessarily imply that $\lim E[\mathbf{z}_T] = E[\mathbf{z}]$ and $\lim E[\mathbf{z}_T\mathbf{z}_T'] = E[\mathbf{z}\mathbf{z}']$. For example, in simultaneous equation estimation (Chapter 15), we frequently encounter estimators that do not possess finite moments of any order but that, nevertheless, possess asymptotic distributions with well-defined moments. As another example, consider a random sample $(y_1, y_2, \ldots, y_T)$ from a normal distribution with mean $\mu \neq 0$ and variance σ^2. As an estimator for μ^{-1}, the inverse of the sample mean $\bar{y}_T^{-1}$ is a natural choice. To establish its statistical properties we note that, from Khinchine's theorem, plim $\bar{y}_T = \mu$, and then, from Slutsky's theorem, plim $\bar{y}_T^{-1} = \mu^{-1}$. Also, because

$\sqrt{T}(\bar{y}_T - \mu) \sim N(0,\sigma^2)$ for all T, it follows that

$$\sqrt{T}(\bar{y}_T - \mu) \xrightarrow{d} N(0,\sigma^2)$$

Then, using the scalar version of a theorem that is given in Section 5.3.4,

$$\sqrt{T}(\bar{y}_T^{-1} - \mu^{-1}) \xrightarrow{d} N(0,\sigma^2\mu^{-4})$$

Thus the mean of the asymptotic distribution of $\bar{y}_T^{-1}$ is μ^{-1}, but $\lim E[\bar{y}_T^{-1}] \neq \mu^{-1}$ because it can be shown that $E[\bar{y}_T^{-1}]$ does not exist. Note that this example also demonstrates that an estimator can be consistent ($\text{plim } \bar{y}_T^{-1} = \mu^{-1}$), without its bias and variance going to zero as $T \to \infty$ ($E[\bar{y}_T^{-1}]$ and $\text{var}[\bar{y}_T^{-1}]$ do not exist). For further examples see Greenberg and Webster (1983, pp. 57–60).

There are certain conditions under which the limits of the moments of a sequence of random variables are equal to moments of the limiting distribution. In particular, in terms of a scalar random variable z_T, if $z_T \xrightarrow{d} z$, and if $E[z_T^m]$, $E[z^m]$ and $\lim E[z_T^m]$ are all finite, then for all $n < m$, $\lim E[z_T^n] = E[z^n]$. See, for example, Rao (1965, p. 100).

One particular expectation that always exists, and that is often useful for finding the limiting distribution of a random variable, is the characteristic function. For a scalar random variable it is defined as

$$\phi_T(u) = E[\exp(iuz_T)] \tag{5.3.1}$$

where $i = \sqrt{-1}$. It can be shown that if $\phi_T(u)$ is the characteristic function of z_T, and $\phi(u)$ is the characteristic function of z, then $z_T \xrightarrow{d} z$ implies that $\lim \phi_T(u) = \phi(u)$. The converse also holds. Specifically, if $\phi_T(u)$ is the characteristic function of z_T and it converges to a function $\phi(u)$ that is continuous at $u = 0$, and if $\phi(u)$ is the characteristic function of z, then it follows that $z_T \xrightarrow{d} z$. Thus, if for a given random variable z_T we find $\lim \phi_T(u) = \phi(u)$, and we can recognize $\phi(u)$ as the characteristic function of a random variable z, then it follows that the limiting distribution of z_T is identical to the distribution of z. This procedure is often used to establish central limit theorems such as those that appear in the next section.

Before turning to the central limit theorems let us consider how we might approach the problem of finding the asymptotic distribution of $\mathbf{b} = \boldsymbol{\beta} + (X'X)^{-1}X'\mathbf{e}$. In Section 5.1 we established that $(\mathbf{b} - \boldsymbol{\beta}) = (X'X/T)^{-1}(X'\mathbf{e}/T) \xrightarrow{p} \mathbf{0}$ because $(X'X/T)^{-1}$ converges to a constant matrix and $\text{plim } X'\mathbf{e}/T = \mathbf{0}$. It therefore follows that $\mathbf{b} \xrightarrow{d} \boldsymbol{\beta}$. This conclusion is not useful for making inferences about $\boldsymbol{\beta}$, however, because it implies that the asymptotic distribution of $\mathbf{b}$ collapses to a single point. To investigate a possible alternative we first state the following result. If $\mathbf{z}_T$ is a random vector that does not possess a limiting distribution, but $T^{-k}\mathbf{z}_T$ does have a well-defined limiting distribution, then $\mathbf{z}_T = O_p(T^k)$.

In our case the difficulty arose because $T^{-1}X'\mathbf{e}$ has a degenerate limiting distribution. However, we showed earlier that $X'\mathbf{e} = O_p(T^{1/2})$. Thus, instead of considering $T^{-1}X'\mathbf{e}$, from the above result it seems reasonable to consider the limiting distribution of $T^{-1/2}X'\mathbf{e}$. We follow this strategy in the next subsection. We indicate how a central limit theorem can be used to establish the limiting distribution of $T^{-1/2}X'\mathbf{e}$, and, from this result, we derive the limiting distribution of

$$\sqrt{T}(\mathbf{b} - \boldsymbol{\beta}) = \left(\frac{X'X}{T}\right)^{-1} \frac{X'\mathbf{e}}{\sqrt{T}} \tag{5.3.2}$$

5.3.2 Central Limit Theorems

The multivariate version of a central limit theorem that is usually given in introductory statistics courses, and that can be proved using the characteristic function approach just described, is known as the Lindeberg-Lévy central limit theorem. It states:

If $\mathbf{z}_1, \mathbf{z}_2, \ldots, \mathbf{z}_T$ are independent, identically distributed random vectors with mean vector $\boldsymbol{\mu}$ and covariance matrix $\boldsymbol{\Sigma}_\mathbf{z}$, then

$$T^{-1/2} \sum_{t=1}^{T} (\mathbf{z}_t - \boldsymbol{\mu}) \xrightarrow{d} N(\mathbf{0}, \boldsymbol{\Sigma}_\mathbf{z}) \tag{5.3.3}$$

This theorem is not directly relevant for us, however, because each of the elements in the vector $X'\mathbf{e}$ is not a sum of T identically distributed random variables. For example, the kth element of $X'\mathbf{e}$ is

$$\mathbf{x}_k'\mathbf{e} = x_{1k}e_1 + x_{2k}e_2 + \ldots + x_{Tk}e_T$$

which is the sum of T independent random variables with zero means, but with different variances $x_{1k}^2\sigma^2, x_{2k}^2\sigma^2, \ldots, x_{Tk}^2\sigma^2$.

To accommodate this situation we need a more general central limit theorem, and one possibility is the following multivariate version of a theorem given by Greenberg and Webster (1983).

If $\mathbf{z}_1, \mathbf{z}_2, \ldots, \mathbf{z}_T$ are independently distributed random vectors with mean vector $\boldsymbol{\mu}$ and covariance matrices $V_1, V_2, \ldots, V_T$ and the third moments of the $\mathbf{z}_t$ exist, then

$$T^{-1/2} \sum_{t=1}^{T} (\mathbf{z}_t - \boldsymbol{\mu}) \xrightarrow{d} N(\mathbf{0}, \boldsymbol{\Sigma}) \tag{5.3.4}$$

where

$$\boldsymbol{\Sigma} = \lim T^{-1} \sum_{t=1}^{T} V_t \tag{5.3.5}$$

To apply this theorem to $T^{-1/2}X'\mathbf{e}$ we let $\mathbf{x}_t$ be a $(K \times 1)$ vector equal to the tth row of X and let $\mathbf{z}_t = \mathbf{x}_t e_t$. Then $V_t = \sigma^2\mathbf{x}_t\mathbf{x}_t'$, and

$$\bar{\Sigma} = \lim T^{-1} \sum_{t=1}^{T} \sigma^2 \mathbf{x}_t \mathbf{x}_t' = \sigma^2 \lim T^{-1} X'X = \sigma^2 Q \tag{5.3.6}$$

where the limit assumption about $T^{-1}X'X$ in (5.1.2) has been used. For the third moments of the $\mathbf{z}_t$ to exist we need to assume that the third moment of e_t exists and that the elements x_{tk} are uniformly bounded. Then it follows that

$$T^{-1/2} \sum_{t=1}^{T} \mathbf{x}_t e_t = T^{-1/2} X'\mathbf{e} \xrightarrow{d} N(\mathbf{0}, \sigma^2 Q) \tag{5.3.7}$$

Assuming that the third moment of e_t exists was a convenient way of establishing (5.3.7), but it is a stricter condition than is necessary. A condition that is both necessary and sufficient for the sum of T independent but not identically distributed random variables to have a normal limiting distribution is given by the Lindeberg-Feller central limit theorem. See, for example, Theil (1971), Dhrymes (1974), Schmidt (1976), and Greenberg and Webster (1983). Schmidt demonstrates how the Lindeberg-Feller condition can be used to establish (5.3.7), while Theil uses the characteristic function approach to establish (5.3.7) directly.

5.3.3 The Least Squares Estimator and Related Statistics

To move from the limiting distribution of $T^{-1/2}X'\mathbf{e}$ to that of $\sqrt{T}(\mathbf{b} - \boldsymbol{\beta})$ we state the following theorem. If the random vector $\mathbf{z}_T$ converges in distribution to $\mathbf{z}$ and the random matrix A_T converges in probability to a matrix of constants C then

$$A_T \mathbf{z}_T \xrightarrow{d} C\mathbf{z} \tag{5.3.8}$$

Applying this result to (5.3.2) we have

$$\left(\frac{X'X}{T}\right)^{-1} \frac{X'\mathbf{e}}{\sqrt{T}} \xrightarrow{d} Q^{-1}\mathbf{q} \tag{5.3.9}$$

where $\mathbf{q} \sim N(\mathbf{0}, \sigma^2 Q)$. Since $Q^{-1}\mathbf{q} \sim N(\mathbf{0}, \sigma^2 Q^{-1} Q Q^{-1})$, it follows that

$$\sqrt{T}(\mathbf{b} - \boldsymbol{\beta}) \xrightarrow{d} N(\mathbf{0}, \sigma^2 Q^{-1}) \tag{5.3.10}$$

Note that, in (5.3.9), we use the result plim $(X'X/T) = Q$. This result holds because we are, in fact, making the stronger assumption that X is nonstochastic and that lim $(X'X/T) = Q$. This point should also be kept in mind in what follows.

The next step is to investigate how the asymptotic distribution in (5.3.10) can be used to make inferences about $\boldsymbol{\beta}$. For this purpose the following theorem is useful.

If $\mathbf{g}$ is a continuous vector function and $\mathbf{z}_T \xrightarrow{d} \mathbf{z}$ then

$$\mathbf{g}(\mathbf{z}_T) \xrightarrow{d} \mathbf{g}(\mathbf{z}) \tag{5.3.11}$$

Now suppose that we are interested in J linear combinations of the elements of $\boldsymbol{\beta}$ and that these functions are given by $R\boldsymbol{\beta}$ where R is a $(J \times K)$ matrix of rank J. Then, from (5.3.11) we have

$$\sqrt{T}(R\mathbf{b} - R\boldsymbol{\beta}) \xrightarrow{d} N(0,\sigma^2 RQ^{-1}R') \tag{5.3.12}$$

and

$$\frac{T(R\mathbf{b} - R\boldsymbol{\beta})'(RQ^{-1}R')^{-1}(R\mathbf{b} - R\boldsymbol{\beta})}{\sigma^2} \xrightarrow{d} \chi^2_{(J)} \tag{5.3.13}$$

Furthermore, using a result analogous to (5.3.8), it is possible to replace Q and σ^2 with consistent estimators without changing the asymptotic distribution in (5.3.13). For this purpose we use $(X'X/T)$ and $\hat{\sigma}^2$, respectively. Strictly speaking, $X'X/T$ is not an "estimator" for Q because X is nonstochastic, but, as mentioned above, it does satisfy the required condition that plim $(X'X/T) = Q$. Thus, we have

$$\lambda_1 = \frac{(R\mathbf{b} - R\boldsymbol{\beta})'[R(X'X)^{-1}R']^{-1}(R\mathbf{b} - R\boldsymbol{\beta})}{\hat{\sigma}^2} \xrightarrow{d} \chi^2_{(J)} \tag{5.3.14}$$

and this statistic can be used to construct interval estimates and test hypotheses about $R\boldsymbol{\beta}$. When $J = 1$ a result that is equivalent to (5.3.14) is

$$\omega = \frac{R\mathbf{b} - R\boldsymbol{\beta}}{\hat{\sigma}\sqrt{R(X'X)^{-1}R'}} \xrightarrow{d} N(0,1) \tag{5.3.15}$$

The statistic ω is the familiar "t statistic" that is used for interval estimates when $\mathbf{e}$ is normally distributed. However, in this case, the finite sample distribution of ω is unknown, and its large sample (approximate) distribution is a normal distribution. Consequently, from a theoretical point of view, we should employ the normal rather than the t distribution when $\mathbf{e}$ is not normally distributed. From a practical standpoint, however, it is quite possible that the t distribution is a better approximation in finite samples, and in large samples it makes no difference because the t distribution converges to the standard normal distribution.

An analogous situation exists with the statistic λ_1 in (5.3.14) and the conventional F statistic given by

$$\lambda_2 = \frac{(R\mathbf{b} - R\boldsymbol{\beta})'[R(X'X)^{-1}R']^{-1}(R\mathbf{b} - R\boldsymbol{\beta})}{J\hat{\sigma}^2} \tag{5.3.16}$$

When $\mathbf{e}$ is normally distributed, $\lambda_2 \sim F_{(J,T-K)}$. However, when $\mathbf{e}$ is not normally distributed, the finite sample distribution of λ_2 is not known and so, theoretically, we should use λ_1, which approximately follows a $\chi^2_{(J)}$ distribution. In practice, the statistic λ_2, which will reject a true null hypothesis less frequently, may provide a better finite sample approximation. As $T \to \infty$ the choice between λ_1 and λ_2 makes little difference because $JF_{(J,T-K)} \xrightarrow{d} \chi^2_{(J)}$. For some further discussion on the use of the F test when the disturbances are nonnormal, see Arnold (1980).

If we wish to make inferences about the error variance σ^2, it is necessary to investigate the asymptotic distribution of $\hat{\sigma}^2$. It can be shown [Schmidt (1976)] that, if the fourth moment of e_t exists, say μ_4, then

$$\sqrt{T}(\hat{\sigma}^2 - \sigma^2) \xrightarrow{d} N(0,\mu_4 - \sigma^4) \tag{5.3.17}$$

To make (5.3.17) operational we need a consistent estimator for μ_4. We will not pursue this problem further, however, we note that an appropriate next step would be to investigate the necessary additional assumptions about X to show that $\hat{\mu}_4 = T^{-1} \Sigma_{t=1}^{T} \hat{e}_t^4$ is consistent.

5.3.4 Nonlinear Functions of the Least Squares Estimator

In economics we are often more interested in some particular nonlinear functions of the elements in $\boldsymbol{\beta}$ than in $\boldsymbol{\beta}$ itself. For example, the partial adjustment model which is studied in Chapter 10 leads to the following equation [see (10.2.9)] for estimation

$$\begin{aligned} y_t &= \alpha_0\gamma + \alpha_1\gamma x_t + (1 - \gamma)y_{t-1} + \gamma e_t \\ &= \beta_1 + \beta_2 x_t + \beta_3 y_{t-1} + e_t^* \end{aligned} \tag{5.3.18}$$

This model does not satisfy the assumptions of this section because the explanatory variable y_{t-1} is stochastic. Nevertheless, we will discover in Section 5.4, that if some additional assumptions are made, the asymptotic results of this section still hold. In particular, $\sqrt{T}(\mathbf{b} - \boldsymbol{\beta}) \xrightarrow{d} N(\mathbf{0},\sigma^2 Q^{-1})$, where Q is a matrix that is consistently estimated by $X'X/T$, and the three columns in X are, respectively, a column of ones, a column of the x_t's, and a column containing the lagged values of the dependent variable. Now suppose, instead of being interested in $\boldsymbol{\beta}$, we are interested in α_0, α_1, and γ, which we will write as $g_1(\boldsymbol{\beta})$, $g_2(\boldsymbol{\beta})$, and $g_3(\boldsymbol{\beta})$, respectively. We then have

$$\mathbf{g}(\boldsymbol{\beta}) = \begin{bmatrix} g_1(\boldsymbol{\beta}) \\ g_2(\boldsymbol{\beta}) \\ g_3(\boldsymbol{\beta}) \end{bmatrix} = \begin{bmatrix} \alpha_0 \\ \alpha_1 \\ \gamma \end{bmatrix} = \begin{bmatrix} \beta_1/(1 - \beta_3) \\ \beta_2/(1 - \beta_3) \\ 1 - \beta_3 \end{bmatrix} \tag{5.3.19}$$

and to construct interval estimates and test hypotheses about $(\alpha_0,\alpha_1,\gamma)$ we need the asymptotic distribution of $\mathbf{g}(\mathbf{b})$. The following theorem is useful in this regard.

If $\sqrt{T}(\mathbf{b} - \boldsymbol{\beta}) \xrightarrow{d} N(\mathbf{0},\sigma^2 Q^{-1})$ and $\mathbf{g}$ is a J-dimensional vector function with at least two continuous derivatives, then

$$\sqrt{T}[\mathbf{g}(\mathbf{b}) - \mathbf{g}(\boldsymbol{\beta})] \xrightarrow{d} N\left[\mathbf{0},\sigma^2 \left(\frac{\partial \mathbf{g}}{\partial \boldsymbol{\beta}'}\right) Q^{-1} \left(\frac{\partial \mathbf{g}'}{\partial \boldsymbol{\beta}}\right)\right] \tag{5.3.20}$$

where

$$\frac{\partial \mathbf{g}'}{\partial \boldsymbol{\beta}} = \begin{bmatrix} \frac{\partial g_1}{\partial \beta_1} & \frac{\partial g_2}{\partial \beta_1} & \cdots & \frac{\partial g_J}{\partial \beta_1} \\ \frac{\partial g_1}{\partial \beta_2} & \frac{\partial g_2}{\partial \beta_2} & \cdots & \frac{\partial g_J}{\partial \beta_2} \\ \vdots & \vdots & \ddots & \vdots \\ \frac{\partial g_1}{\partial \beta_K} & \frac{\partial g_2}{\partial \beta_K} & \cdots & \frac{\partial g_J}{\partial \beta_K} \end{bmatrix} \tag{5.3.21}$$

Note that our notation is such that $(\partial \mathbf{g}'/\partial \boldsymbol{\beta})' = \partial \mathbf{g}/\partial \boldsymbol{\beta}'$.

Applying this theorem to our example we have

$$\frac{\partial \mathbf{g}}{\partial \boldsymbol{\beta}'} = \begin{bmatrix} (1 - \beta_3)^{-1} & 0 & \beta_1(1 - \beta_3)^{-2} \\ 0 & (1 - \beta_3)^{-1} & \beta_2(1 - \beta_3)^{-2} \\ 0 & 0 & -1 \end{bmatrix} \tag{5.3.22}$$

and the asymptotic covariance matrix for $\sqrt{T}[\mathbf{g}(\mathbf{b}) - \mathbf{g}(\boldsymbol{\beta})]$ is obtained by pre and post multiplying $\sigma^2 Q^{-1}$ by (5.3.22) and its transpose, respectively. A χ^2 statistic analogous to that in (5.3.13) can be constructed, and this statistic is made operational by replacing Q^{-1} by $(X'X/T)^{-1}$, σ^2 by $\hat{\sigma}^2$, and by evaluating $\partial \mathbf{g}/\partial \boldsymbol{\beta}'$ at $\mathbf{b}$. These substitutions do not alter the asymptotic distribution of the statistic, which now can be written as

$$\frac{[\mathbf{g}(\mathbf{b}) - \mathbf{g}(\boldsymbol{\beta})]'[F'(X'X)^{-1}F]^{-1}[\mathbf{g}(\mathbf{b}) - \mathbf{g}(\boldsymbol{\beta})]}{\hat{\sigma}^2} \xrightarrow{d} \chi^2_{(J)} \tag{5.3.23}$$

where

$$F = \left.\frac{\partial \mathbf{g}'}{\partial \boldsymbol{\beta}}\right|_{\mathbf{b}} \tag{5.3.24}$$

Equation 5.3.23 can be used to test hypotheses about $\mathbf{g}(\boldsymbol{\beta})$, or, if we are interested in a single element from $\mathbf{g}(\boldsymbol{\beta})$, we could use the normal distribution counterpart of (5.3.23). For example, if we are interested in testing an hypothesis about α_1 we could use the fact that

$$\frac{\hat{\alpha}_1 - \alpha_1}{s_{\hat{\alpha}_1}} \xrightarrow{d} N(0,1) \tag{5.3.25}$$

where $\hat{\alpha}_1 = b_2(1 - b_3)$ and

$$s^2_{\hat{\alpha}_1} = \hat{\sigma}^2 \mathbf{f}_2'(X'X)^{-1}\mathbf{f}_2 = \hat{\sigma}^2[(1 - b_3)^{-2}a^{22} + b_2^2(1 - b_3)^{-4}a^{33} + 2b_2(1 - b_3)^{-3}a^{23}]$$

where a^{ij} is the (i,j)th element of $(X'X)^{-1}$, and $\mathbf{f}_2$ is the second column of F.

5.3.5 Asymptotically Uncooperative Regressors

An assumption that was made early in this chapter and that has been used throughout is that $\lim(X'X/T) = Q$ is a finite nonsingular matrix. The purpose of this section is to demonstrate that one aspect of this assumption—that the elements of Q are finite—is not critical, and that the test statistics that we have derived will still be valid under some less restrictive assumptions. Following Schmidt (1976) we give these circumstances the title of asymptotically uncooperative regressors.

We begin by considering the diagonal elements of $X'X$ given by

$$d^2_{Tk} = \sum_{t=1}^{T} x^2_{tk} \quad ; \quad k = 1, 2, \ldots, K \tag{5.3.26}$$

and we assume that $\lim d^2_{Tk} = \infty$. That is, the sum of squares of each regressor approaches infinity with T. This is certainly a reasonable assumption for all regressors that violate the assumption that $\lim X'X/T$ is finite, as well as those for which $\lim X'X/T$ is finite but nonzero. It precludes regressors of the form λ^t where $|\lambda| < 1$.

If we let $D_T = \text{diag.}\,(d_{T1}, d_{T2}, \ldots, d_{TK})$, then, from (5.3.26), it can be shown that [Schmidt (1976, p. 86)]

$$\lim D_T^{-1}X'XD_T^{-1} = C \text{ is finite} \tag{5.3.27}$$

In addition, we will assume that C is nonsingular. These assumptions are sufficient to establish that the least squares estimator is consistent. We know that $\mathbf{b}$ has mean $\boldsymbol{\beta}$ and covariance matrix $\sigma^2(X'X)^{-1}$, and, therefore, that $\mathbf{b}$ will be consistent if $\lim(X'X)^{-1} = 0$. We have

$$\begin{aligned}
\lim(X'X)^{-1} &= \lim D_T^{-1}(D_T^{-1}X'XD_T^{-1})^{-1}D_T^{-1} \\
&= \lim D_T^{-1} \lim(D_T^{-1}X'XD_T^{-1})^{-1} \lim D_T^{-1} \\
&= 0 \cdot C^{-1} \cdot 0 \\
&= 0
\end{aligned} \tag{5.3.28}$$

For the limiting distribution of **b** we consider the limiting distribution of

$$
\begin{aligned}
D_T(\mathbf{b} - \boldsymbol{\beta}) &= D_T(X'X)^{-1}X'\mathbf{e} \\
&= (D_T^{-1}X'XD_T^{-1})^{-1}D_T^{-1}X'\mathbf{e}
\end{aligned}
\tag{5.3.29}
$$

Using the central limit theorem given by Equations 5.3.4 and 5.3.5, it can be shown that

$$
\sum_{t=1}^{T} D_T^{-1}\mathbf{x}_t e_t = D_T^{-1}X'\mathbf{e} \xrightarrow{d} N(\mathbf{0},\sigma^2 C)
\tag{5.3.30}
$$

providing we make the additional assumption $\lim(x_{Tk}^2/d_{Tk}^2) = 0$ [Anderson (1971, pp. 23–25)]. Together with the other assumptions this one implies that, in the limit, the largest squared value of each regressor is negligible relative to the sum of squares of all values. It takes the place of our earlier assumption (above Equation 5.3.7) that the elements x_{tk} are uniformly bounded. From (5.3.29), (5.3.30), and the fact that $D_T^{-1}X'XD_T^{-1} \xrightarrow{p} C$ we now have

$$
D_T(\mathbf{b} - \boldsymbol{\beta}) \xrightarrow{d} N(\mathbf{0},\sigma^2 C^{-1})
\tag{5.3.31}
$$

The central limit theorem we have used assumes the existence of the third moment of e_t, a much stronger condition than is required. For details of how to prove the same result under less restrictive assumptions about the distribution of e_t, see Anderson (1971, pp. 23–25). The assumptions we have made about X are sometimes referred to as the *Grenander conditions*. They will be used in later chapters and may be summarized as

1. $\lim d_{Tk}^2 = \lim \Sigma_{t=1}^{T} x_{tk}^2 = \infty$
2. $\lim(x_{Tk}^2/d_{Tk}^2) = 0$.
3. $\lim D_T^{-1}X'XD_T^{-1} = C$ is finite and nonsingular.

Before leaving this section it is useful to examine the implications of (5.3.31) for making inferences about $\boldsymbol{\beta}$. From (5.3.31) we have

$$
\frac{(\mathbf{b} - \boldsymbol{\beta})'D_T C D_T(\mathbf{b} - \boldsymbol{\beta})}{\sigma^2} \xrightarrow{d} \chi^2_{(K)}
\tag{5.3.32}
$$

Replacing C and σ^2 with the consistent estimators $D_T^{-1}X'XD_T^{-1}$ and $\hat{\sigma}^2$, respectively, yields (see Problem 5.1)

$$
\frac{(\mathbf{b} - \boldsymbol{\beta})'X'X(\mathbf{b} - \boldsymbol{\beta})}{\hat{\sigma}^2} \xrightarrow{d} \chi^2_{(K)}
\tag{5.3.33}
$$

This statistic is identical to the special case of Equation 5.3.14 with $R = I$. If we had begun by considering the linear combinations $R\boldsymbol{\beta}$, it would have also been possible to show that the more general result holds, that is,

$$\lambda_1 = \frac{(R\mathbf{b} - R\boldsymbol{\beta})'[R(X'X)^{-1}R']^{-1}(R\mathbf{b} - R\boldsymbol{\beta})}{\hat{\sigma}^2} \xrightarrow{d} \chi^2_{(J)} \qquad (5.3.34)$$

Thus, our traditional test statistics are valid when the assumption of finite $\lim(X'X/T)$ is violated, but to prove their validity, instead of using the scalar $\sqrt{T}$, we must choose an appropriate matrix function D_T to standardize the distribution of $(\mathbf{b} - \boldsymbol{\beta})$.

5.3.6 Other Approximation Methods and Some Terminology

In Section 5.3 we have been concerned with the problem of using a limiting distribution as a method for carrying out approximate finite sample inference. We saw that, under certain conditions, $\sqrt{T}(\mathbf{b} - \boldsymbol{\beta}) \xrightarrow{d} N(\mathbf{0},\sigma^2Q^{-1})$, and that this result leads us to test statistics such as λ_1 in (5.3.34). A common and imprecise way of referring to the limiting distribution of $\sqrt{T}(\mathbf{b} - \boldsymbol{\beta})$ is to say that $\mathbf{b}$ is asymptotically normal with mean $\boldsymbol{\beta}$ and covariance matrix σ^2Q^{-1}/T. Alternatively, we often replace Q^{-1}/T with $(X'X)^{-1}$ and say $\mathbf{b}$ is asymptotically normal with mean $\boldsymbol{\beta}$ and covariance matrix $\sigma^2(X'X)^{-1}$. Such usage is imprecise, because, strictly speaking, the limiting distribution of $\mathbf{b}$ is degenerate on the single point $\boldsymbol{\beta}$. It has covariance matrix zero. However, when making inferences about $\boldsymbol{\beta}$, with statistics such as λ_1, we do behave as if the covariance matrix for $\mathbf{b}$ is $\sigma^2(X'X)^{-1}$. As a consequence, σ^2Q^{-1}/T (and sometimes $\sigma^2(X'X)^{-1}$) is frequently called the *asymptotic covariance matrix* of $\mathbf{b}$. This term is particularly ambiguous because it could also describe the limit of the finite sample covariance matrix for $\mathbf{b}$, that is, $\lim E[(\mathbf{b} - \lim E[\mathbf{b}])(\mathbf{b} - \lim E[\mathbf{b}])']$. As we discussed in Section 5.3.1, in general these two definitions need not be the same. Throughout this book the term asymptotic covariance matrix will generally refer to the approximate covariance matrix obtained from a limiting distribution, rather than the limit of a finite sample covariance matrix. Although there are a number of instances where finite sample moments are approximated by their limits, most finite sample approximations in econometrics are based on limiting distributions. For details of other approximation methods, including asymptotic expansions of moments, density functions, distribution functions and characteristic functions, see Greenberg and Webster (1983), Phillips (1980, 1982, 1983), Rothenberg (1982), Sargan (1976) and Taylor (1983).

5.4 STOCHASTIC REGRESSORS

So far, one of the assumptions we have employed for the general linear model $\mathbf{y} = X\boldsymbol{\beta} + \mathbf{e}$ is that the regressor matrix is nonstochastic. In economics, however, where we seldom have the luxury of setting the values of the explanatory variables, this assumption will frequently be violated. It is worthwhile, therefore, to examine the implications of stochastic regressors for our usual least squares procedures, and since we require a number of asymptotic theory concepts, this chapter is a convenient place for such an examination. The assumptions in each subsection are progressively more complicated. In Section 5.4.1 we consider a model where the stochastic X matrix is completely independent of the disturbance vector $\mathbf{e}$, in Section 5.4.2 correlation between the regressors and past values of the disturbance is permitted, and in Section 5.4.3 contemporaneous correlation between X and $\mathbf{e}$ is assumed to exist. We assume throughout that $E[\mathbf{ee}'] = \sigma^2 I$.

5.4.1 Independent Stochastic Regressors

In this section we assume that the regressor matrix X is stochastic but completely independent of the disturbance vector $\mathbf{e}$. Under these circumstances the finite sample properties of Chapter 2 will still hold, providing we treat them as conditional on X. To appreciate this point note that the properties in Chapter 2 were derived from the marginal distribution of $\mathbf{e}$. When X is stochastic and we wish to obtain results conditional on X, the properties need to be derived from the conditional distribution of $\mathbf{e}|X$. Since $f(\mathbf{e}) = f(\mathbf{e}|X)$ when X and $\mathbf{e}$ are independent, it follows that, conditional on X, $E[\mathbf{b}] = \boldsymbol{\beta}$ and $E[(\mathbf{b} - \boldsymbol{\beta})(\mathbf{b} - \boldsymbol{\beta})'] = \sigma^2(X'X)^{-1}$; and if $\mathbf{e}$ is assumed to be normally distributed, the usual test statistics also hold conditional on X.

We are more likely, however, to be interested in unconditional inferences than in those restricted to the particular sample values of X. Unconditionally, we can say that the least squares estimator $\mathbf{b}$ will still be unbiased and have covariance matrix given by $\sigma^2 E[(X'X)^{-1}]$, providing that the expectations $E[(X'X)^{-1}X']$ and $E[(X'X)^{-1}]$ exist. See Judge et al. (1982) or Schmidt (1976) for details. Note, however, that unless something is known about the form of the distribution of X, it may be difficult to establish whether these expectations exist. Furthermore, because $\mathbf{b}$ is a nonlinear function of X and $\mathbf{e}$, it will not follow a normal distribution even if X and $\mathbf{e}$ are both normally distributed. Consequently, our usual test statistics do not hold in finite samples.

What about asymptotic properties? First we need to replace the assumption that $\lim(X'X/T)$ is finite and nonsingular with the stochastic assumption that

$$\text{plim}\left(\frac{X'X}{T}\right) = Q \tag{5.4.1}$$

is finite and nonsingular. Then, providing that

$$\text{plim}\left(\frac{X'\mathbf{e}}{T}\right) = \mathbf{0} \tag{5.4.2}$$

consistency of $\mathbf{b}$ can be established just as it was for the nonstochastic regressor case in Section 5.1.

Also, if $\mathbf{x}_t$ is a $(K \times 1)$ vector equal to the tth row of X, and $\mathbf{x}_1, \mathbf{x}_2, \ldots, \mathbf{x}_T$ are independent identically distributed random vectors with $E[\mathbf{x}_t\mathbf{x}_t'] = Q$, then it follows that $\mathbf{x}_1 e_1, \mathbf{x}_2 e_2, \ldots, \mathbf{x}_T e_T$ are independent identically distributed random vectors with

$$E[\mathbf{x}_t e_t] = \mathbf{0} \qquad \text{and} \qquad E[e_t^2 \mathbf{x}_t\mathbf{x}_t'] = \sigma^2 Q \tag{5.4.3}$$

and the central limit theorem in (5.3.3) is relevant. Its application yields

$$T^{-1/2} \sum_{t=1}^{T} \mathbf{x}_t e_t = T^{-1/2} X'\mathbf{e} \xrightarrow{d} N(\mathbf{0}, \sigma^2 Q) \tag{5.4.4}$$

Then, (5.4.1), (5.4.2), and (5.4.4), and the various theorems in Section 5.3, can be used exactly as before to establish the asymptotic validity of our usual test statistics. We need to use the result that $\operatorname{plim}(X'X/T) = Q$ rather than $\lim(X'X/T) = Q$, but this fact is of no consequence because in all our previous derivations the finite nonstochastic limit was a stronger condition than was required.

It should be emphasized that, to establish (5.4.4), we assumed that the $\mathbf{x}_t$ are independent and that both their first and second moments exist. These assumptions are sufficient to establish (5.4.3), and Khinchine's theorem can then be used to establish (5.4.1) and (5.4.2). However, as Schmidt (1976) notes, there may be circumstances where the existence of $E[\mathbf{x}_t]$ and $E[\mathbf{x}_t\mathbf{x}_t']$ are fairly strong assumptions. For example, if $x_t = 1/\omega_t$, where ω_t is normally distributed, then x_t has no moments.

The assumption that the $\mathbf{x}_t$ are independent is not critical. Although the central limit theorems we have discussed are not directly relevant for serially correlated $\mathbf{x}_t$'s, it is still possible to prove that the assumptions (5.4.1) through (5.4.3) imply (5.4.4). See, for example, Pollock (1979, p. 335). Alternatively, if all the moments of e_t exist, (5.4.4) can be established using the Mann-Wald theorem, presented in the next section.

Finally, it is possible to show that the least squares estimator will also be the maximum likelihood estimator if the vector $\mathbf{e}$ is normally distributed, and if the distribution of X does not depend on $\boldsymbol{\beta}$ or σ^2. In terms of probability density functions the likelihood function can be written as

$$f(\mathbf{y}, X) = f(\mathbf{y}|X) f(X)$$

Thus, the log-likelihood function will contain the terms $\log f(\mathbf{y}|X)$ and $\log f(X)$, and, because it does not contain $\boldsymbol{\beta}$ and σ^2, the term $\log f(X)$ will not enter into the maximization process. Furthermore, if $\mathbf{e}$ is normally distributed, then $f(\mathbf{y}|X)$ will be a normal distribution, and so the least squares estimator for $\boldsymbol{\beta}$ will also be the maximum likelihood estimator. Properties of maximum likelihood estimators are discussed in Section 5.6.

5.4.2 Partially Independent Stochastic Regressors

In this section we move from the model where the stochastic regressors are totally independent of the disturbance vector to the case where they are partially independent in the sense that the tth observation on the regressors is independent of the tth and succeeding values of the disturbance term, but it is not independent of past values of the disturbance term. The most common model with these properties is the linear model with lagged values of the dependent variable as explanatory variables. That is, a model where the tth observation is given by

$$y_t = \sum_{i=1}^{p} y_{t-i}\gamma_i + \mathbf{z}_t'\boldsymbol{\alpha} + e_t \tag{5.4.5}$$

and where the $\mathbf{z}_t$ are assumed to be nonstochastic, $\boldsymbol{\beta}' = (\gamma_1, \gamma_2, \ldots, \gamma_p, \boldsymbol{\alpha}')$ is a vector of unknown parameters, and the e_t are i.i.d. random variables with zero mean and variance σ^2. This model is discussed in more detail in Chapters 7 and 10, the case where $\boldsymbol{\alpha} = \mathbf{0}$ being considered in Chapter 7.

It is clear that we can write (5.4.5) in the form

$$\mathbf{y} = X\boldsymbol{\beta} + \mathbf{e} \tag{5.4.6}$$

where X contains both the lagged values of y and the nonstochastic regressors, and has tth row given by

$$\mathbf{x}_t' = (y_{t-1}, y_{t-2}, \ldots, y_{t-p}, \mathbf{z}_t') \tag{5.4.7}$$

Furthermore,

$$E[\mathbf{x}_t e_{t+s}] = \mathbf{0} \qquad \text{for} \qquad s \geq 0 \tag{5.4.8}$$

but

$$E[\mathbf{x}_t e_{t-s}] \neq \mathbf{0} \qquad \text{for} \qquad s > 0 \tag{5.4.9}$$

To illustrate that (5.4.9) is true, note that one of the components of $\mathbf{x}_t$ will be y_{t-1}, that y_{t-1} will be partly determined by e_{t-1}, and it therefore can be shown that $E[y_{t-1}e_{t-1}] \neq 0$. Also, because y_{t-1} depends on y_{t-2}, which depends in turn on e_{t-2}, we can show that $E[y_{t-1}e_{t-2}] \neq 0$; and this process can be continued for all past values of the disturbance.

The conditions in (5.4.8) and (5.4.9) define the partially independent stochastic regressor model and, in terms of the complete X matrix, they imply

$$E[X'\mathbf{e}] = E[\mathbf{x}_1 e_1] + E[\mathbf{x}_2 e_2] + \ldots + E[\mathbf{x}_T e_T] = \mathbf{0} \tag{5.4.10}$$

However, $E[(X'X)^{-1}X'\mathbf{e}] \neq \mathbf{0}$ because, in general, each element in $(X'X)^{-1}$ will be a function of the values of the regressors at every point in time. As a result, the least squares estimator $\mathbf{b} = \boldsymbol{\beta} + (X'X)^{-1}X'\mathbf{e}$ will be biased. Asymptotically the situation is more promising, essentially because we are able to write $\text{plim}[(X'X)^{-1}X'\mathbf{e}] = \text{plim}[(X'X/T)^{-1}]\ \text{plim}(X'\mathbf{e}/T)$. To examine the asymptotic properties of **b** we state the following version of a theorem proved by Mann and Wald (1943) and outlined by Harvey (1981, p. 48).

If the stochastic regressor matrix X and the disturbance vector **e** satisfy the following conditions.

1. $\text{plim}(X'X/T) = Q$ is finite and nonsingular.
2. $E[\mathbf{e}] = \mathbf{0}$, $E[\mathbf{ee}'] = \sigma^2 I$, and **e** has finite moments of every order.
3. $E[\mathbf{x}_t e_t] = \mathbf{0}$ for $t = 1, 2, \ldots, T$.

Then

$$\text{plim}\ T^{-1}X'\mathbf{e} = \mathbf{0} \tag{5.4.11}$$

and

$$T^{-1/2}X'\mathbf{e} \xrightarrow{d} N(\mathbf{0},\sigma^2 Q) \tag{5.4.12}$$

If the conditions of this theorem hold it is straightforward to show, along the lines of the earlier sections, that **b** is consistent, and that

$$\sqrt{T}(\mathbf{b} - \boldsymbol{\beta}) \xrightarrow{d} N(\mathbf{0},\sigma^2 Q^{-1}) \tag{5.4.13}$$

Thus, the least squares estimator and our usual test procedures are valid asymptotically. Also, if **e** is normally distributed, it is possible to show (see Chapter 7 or 10) that **b** is the maximum likelihood estimator conditional on $y_0, y_{-1}, \ldots, y_{-p+1}$. For details on how to obtain the unconditional maximum likelihood estimator see Chapter 10. Finally, it is possible, and more conventional, to give conditions on $\boldsymbol{\gamma}' = (\gamma_1, \gamma_2, \ldots, \gamma_p)$ and $\mathbf{z}_t$, which are sufficient for $\text{plim}(X'X/T)$ to be finite and nonsingular. See Chapters 7 and/or 10 or Schmidt (1976, p. 97).

5.4.3 General Stochastic Regressor Models and Instrumental Variable Estimation

Sometimes we encounter models where the tth observation on some stochastic regressors, say $\mathbf{x}_t$, is not even independent of the current disturbance e_t. Three common examples are:

1. The model in (5.4.5) with the additional assumption that the e_t are serially correlated (Chapter 10).

2. The errors in variables model (Chapter 17).
3. Simultaneous equations models (Chapters 14 and 15).

In all three cases, $E[X'\mathbf{e}] \neq \mathbf{0}$ and $\text{plim}(X'\mathbf{e}/T) \neq \mathbf{0}$, and so the least squares estimator is inconsistent. See Judge et al. [1982, p. 277] for some discussion.

An alternative, more general method of estimation that (under appropriate conditions) leads to consistent and asymptotically normal estimates is what is known as instrumental variable estimation. Many of the estimators that we later develop for the three models specified above can be viewed as special cases of instrumental variable estimators.

To introduce the instrumental variable estimator, we assume there exists a $(T \times K)$ matrix of (possibly stochastic) variables Z, which are correlated with X in the sense that

$$\text{plim}\,\frac{Z'X}{T} = \Sigma_{zx} \tag{5.4.14}$$

exists and is nonsingular, and which are contemporaneously uncorrelated with the disturbance in the sense that

$$E[\mathbf{z}_t e_t] = \mathbf{0} \tag{5.4.15}$$

where $\mathbf{z}_t'$ is the tth row of Z. Furthermore, we assume that

$$\text{plim}\left(\frac{Z'Z}{T}\right) = \Sigma_{zz} \tag{5.4.16}$$

exists and is nonsingular, and that e_t has finite moments of every order. Under these conditions it is possible to show that the instrumental variables estimator defined as

$$\boldsymbol{\beta}^{IV} = (Z'X)^{-1}Z'\mathbf{y} \tag{5.4.17}$$

is consistent, and that

$$\sqrt{T}(\boldsymbol{\beta}^{IV} - \boldsymbol{\beta}) \xrightarrow{d} N[\mathbf{0},\sigma^2\Sigma_{zx}^{-1}\Sigma_{zz}\Sigma_{zx}^{-1\prime}] \tag{5.4.18}$$

To prove (5.4.17) and (5.4.18) we first note that Z satisfies the conditions of the Mann-Wald theorem and so

$$\text{plim}\; T^{-1}Z'\mathbf{e} = \mathbf{0} \tag{5.4.19}$$

and

$$T^{-1/2}Z'\mathbf{e} \xrightarrow{d} N(\mathbf{0},\sigma^2\Sigma_{zz}). \tag{5.4.20}$$

Then, consistency of $\boldsymbol{\beta}^{IV} = \boldsymbol{\beta} + (Z'X)^{-1}Z'\mathbf{e}$ follows because

$$\begin{aligned}\text{plim } \boldsymbol{\beta}^{IV} &= \boldsymbol{\beta} + \text{plim}\left(\frac{Z'X}{T}\right)^{-1}\frac{Z'\mathbf{e}}{T}\\ &= \boldsymbol{\beta} + \Sigma_{zx}^{-1}\cdot \mathbf{0}\\ &= \boldsymbol{\beta}\end{aligned} \tag{5.4.21}$$

For asymptotic normality we note that

$$\sqrt{T}(\boldsymbol{\beta}^{IV} - \boldsymbol{\beta}) = \left(\frac{Z'X}{T}\right)^{-1}\frac{Z'\mathbf{e}}{\sqrt{T}} \tag{5.4.22}$$

Then, using (5.4.20), (5.4.14), and the theorem in (5.3.8) the result in (5.4.18) follows.

If we wish to construct interval estimates or test hypotheses about $\boldsymbol{\beta}$, we can, along the lines of Section 5.3.3, use (5.4.18) to derive an asymptotic χ^2 statistic. In this statistic we need to replace Σ_{zx}, Σ_{zz} and σ^2 by their respective consistent estimators $(Z'X/T)$, $(Z'Z/T)$ and $\hat{\sigma}^2 = (\mathbf{y} - X\boldsymbol{\beta}^{IV})'(\mathbf{y} - X\boldsymbol{\beta}^{IV})/T$. It is straightforward to prove consistency of $\hat{\sigma}^2$ providing we also assume plim$(X'X/T)$ and plim$(X'\mathbf{e}/T)$ are finite. Finally, we note that $\boldsymbol{\beta}^{IV}$ is not necessarily efficient in an asymptotic sense because there will be many sets of instrumental variables that fulfill the requirement of being uncorrelated with the stochastic term and correlated with the stochastic regressors. For details on how to combine a larger set of instrumental variables efficiently, see Harvey (1981, p. 80); examples are given in Section 11.2.1 and Chapter 15.

5.5 ESTIMATION WITH AN UNKNOWN DISTURBANCE COVARIANCE MATRIX

In this section we consider the model

$$\mathbf{y} = X\boldsymbol{\beta} + \mathbf{e} \qquad \text{E}[\mathbf{e}] = \mathbf{0} \qquad E[\mathbf{ee}'] = \Phi = \sigma^2\boldsymbol{\Psi} \tag{5.5.1}$$

and we return to our earlier assumption of a nonstochastic X, but we now assume that both σ^2 and $\boldsymbol{\Psi}$ are unknown. Previously, we had either assumed that $\boldsymbol{\Psi}$ was known (Chapter 2), or that $\boldsymbol{\Psi} = I$ (earlier sections of this chapter). With known $\boldsymbol{\Psi}$, the generalized least squares (GLS) estimator for $\boldsymbol{\beta}$,

$$\hat{\boldsymbol{\beta}} = (X'\boldsymbol{\Psi}^{-1}X)^{-1}X'\boldsymbol{\Psi}^{-1}\mathbf{y} \tag{5.5.2}$$

is the minimum variance estimator within the class of all linear unbiased estimators, and if $\mathbf{e}$ is also normally distributed, then $\hat{\boldsymbol{\beta}}$ is also the maximum likelihood (ML) estimator and is minimum variance from within the class of all unbiased estimators. When $\boldsymbol{\Psi}$ is unknown, which is the usual situation in practice, the GLS estimator is clearly infeasible, and an alternative estimation procedure must be employed. Three common procedures are least squares (LS), estimated (or feasible) generalized least squares (EGLS), and maximum likelihood (ML) estimation. In Sections 5.5.1 and 5.5.2 we consider some aspects of LS estimation; EGLS estimation is considered in Section 5.5.3; and ML estimation is taken up in Section 5.6.

5.5.1 Least Squares Estimation

If $E[\mathbf{ee}'] = \sigma^2\Psi$ and we use the LS estimator $\mathbf{b} = (X'X)^{-1}X'\mathbf{y}$, it can be shown that

$$E[\mathbf{b}] = \boldsymbol{\beta} \quad \text{and} \quad \Sigma_{\mathbf{b}} = \sigma^2(X'X)^{-1}X'\Psi X(X'X)^{-1} \tag{5.5.3}$$

Hence $\mathbf{b}$ is unbiased. However, for Ψ known, $\mathbf{b}$ is not minimum variance because the difference

$$\begin{aligned} \Sigma_{\mathbf{b}} - \Sigma_{\hat{\boldsymbol{\beta}}} &= \sigma^2(X'X)^{-1}X'\Psi X(X'X)^{-1} - \sigma^2(X'\Psi^{-1}X)^{-1} \\ &= \sigma^2 A\Psi A' \end{aligned} \tag{5.5.4}$$

where $A = (X'X)^{-1}X' - (X'\Psi^{-1}X)^{-1}X'\Psi^{-1}$, is a positive semidefinite matrix.

The LS and GLS estimators will be identical and hence the difference in (5.5.4) will be the null matrix, if $\Psi = I$ or, more generally, if and only if it is possible to write $X = Q\Gamma$, where Q, a $(T \times K)$ matrix, contains K of the characteristic vectors of Ψ and Γ is a $(K \times K)$ nonsingular matrix [Zyskind (1967)]. In general, there is no reason why X and Ψ should be related and so one would not expect this latter condition to hold. McElroy (1967) has shown that it will hold for all X with a constant term if and only if the e_t are equicorrelated. In this case, $\Psi = (1 - \rho)I + \rho\mathbf{jj}'$, where $0 \leq \rho < 1$ and $\mathbf{j}$ is a vector of 1's. Balestra (1970) extends this result by examining the structure of Ψ required for $\mathbf{b}$ to be BLUE for other types of X matrices. Some examples he considers are X with a time trend and "error components models" with dummy variables. Further results on BLUE when the covariance matrix is incorrectly specified are given by Mathew (1983).

Thus, although there are times when $\mathbf{b}$ will be as efficient as $\hat{\boldsymbol{\beta}}$, this in general will not be true. The loss in efficiency will depend on X and Ψ and is discussed further in later chapters where specific assumptions are made about Ψ. For the general case a lower bound on the efficiency, measured by the ratio of the generalized variances and expressed in terms of the characteristic roots of Ψ, has been derived by Watson (1955). His proof has been corrected by Bloomfield and Watson (1975) and Knott (1975).

The possible inefficiency of $\mathbf{b}$ is not the only consequence of using LS when $\Psi \neq I$. Another danger is an incorrect assessment of the reliability of $\mathbf{b}$. When LS is used, any tests and confidence intervals for $\boldsymbol{\beta}$ should be based on $\sigma^2(X'X)^{-1}X'\Psi X(X'X)^{-1}$, not on $\sigma^2(X'X)^{-1}$. If we let $\hat{\sigma}^2 = (\mathbf{y} - X\mathbf{b})'(\mathbf{y} - X\mathbf{b})/(T - K)$ and $\hat{\sigma}^2(X'X)^{-1}$ is incorrectly used to estimate the covariance $\Sigma_{\mathbf{b}}$, its bias is given by

$$E[\hat{\sigma}^2(X'X)^{-1}] - \Sigma_{\mathbf{b}} = \sigma^2(X'X)^{-1}\left\{\frac{\text{tr}[M\Psi]}{T-K} I - X'\Psi X(X'X)^{-1}\right\} \quad (5.5.5)$$

where $M = I - X(X'X)^{-1}X'$. The first term in (5.5.5) arises because $E[\hat{\sigma}^2] = \sigma^2 \text{ tr}[M\Psi]/(T-K)$ whereas the second is a result of incorrectly assuming that $\Sigma_{\mathbf{b}} = \sigma^2(X'X)^{-1}$. The bias clearly depends on the structure of X and Ψ but, in general, it can lead to misleading inferences about $\boldsymbol{\beta}$, and it will only be zero when $\Psi = I$. For a detailed analysis of the bias, and further references, see Greenwald (1983).

It is possible, under certain conditions, to obtain a consistent estimator of the complete covariance matrix $\sigma^2(X'X)^{-1}X'\Psi X(X'X)^{-1}$ without specifying the precise structure of Ψ. For details of such a procedure when Ψ is diagonal, see Section 11.2.1, and, for the more general case where the e_t can be serially correlated, see Domowitz (1982).

5.5.2 Least Squares, BLUS, and Recursive Residuals

As we shall see in the next section, an estimated generalized least squares estimator is obtained by using the GLS estimator $\hat{\boldsymbol{\beta}}$, with Ψ replaced by an estimate $\hat{\Psi}$. As such, EGLS estimators are generally two-step estimators. In the first step, the least squares estimator $\mathbf{b}$ and its corresponding residuals are found, and the residuals are used to estimate Ψ. This estimate of Ψ is used in the second step to obtain the EGLS estimator denoted by $\hat{\hat{\boldsymbol{\beta}}}$.

Estimation of Ψ based on the observable least squares residuals

$$\hat{\mathbf{e}} = \mathbf{y} - X\mathbf{b} = [I - X(X'X)^{-1}X']\mathbf{e} \quad (5.5.6)$$

rather than the unobservable disturbance vector $\mathbf{e}$, is asymptotically justified because it is possible to prove that each $\hat{e}_t$ converges in probability and distribution to its corresponding disturbance e_t. To demonstrate this result we assume that $\lim T^{-1}X'X = Q$ and $\lim T^{-1}X'\Psi X = V_0$ are both finite and nonsingular, and consider the mean and variance of $\hat{e}_t - e_t$. Specifically, if we let $\mathbf{x}_t'$ be the $(1 \times K)$ tth row of X we have

$$E[\hat{e}_t - e_t] = -\mathbf{x}_t'(X'X)^{-1}X'E[\mathbf{e}] = 0 \quad (5.5.7)$$

and

$$\begin{aligned} E[(\hat{e}_t - e_t)^2] &= \mathbf{x}_t'(X'X)^{-1}X'E[\mathbf{e}\mathbf{e}']X(X'X)^{-1}\mathbf{x}_t \\ &= \sigma^2\mathbf{x}_t'(X'X)^{-1}X'\Psi X(X'X)^{-1}\mathbf{x}_t \\ &= \frac{\sigma^2}{T}\mathbf{x}_t'\left(\frac{X'X}{T}\right)^{-1}\frac{X'\Psi X}{T}\left(\frac{X'X}{T}\right)^{-1}\mathbf{x}_t \end{aligned} \quad (5.5.8)$$

Since $\mathbf{x}_t$ remains fixed as $T \to \infty$, from (5.5.7) and (5.5.8) we have that the bias and variance of $(\hat{e}_t - e_t)$ approach zero as $T \to \infty$, and therefore that plim $(\hat{e}_t - e_t) = 0$. It then follows that $\hat{e}_t \xrightarrow{p} e_t$ and hence that $\hat{e}_t \xrightarrow{d} e_t$.

The finite sample properties of the LS residual vector

$$\hat{\mathbf{e}} = \mathbf{y} - X\mathbf{b} = (I - X(X'X)^{-1}X')\mathbf{e} = M\mathbf{e} \tag{5.5.9}$$

are sometimes considered undesirable because

$$E[\hat{\mathbf{e}}\hat{\mathbf{e}}'] = \sigma^2 M \Psi M \tag{5.5.10}$$

This covariance matrix will not be equal to $\sigma^2 I$ even if $\Psi = I$. Consequently, test statistics for the null hypothesis H_0: $\Psi = I$ (the e_t are independent and identically distributed) cannot be based on the assumption that, under H_0, the $\hat{e}_t$ will be independent and identically distributed. This fact complicates the formulation of appropriate tests and has led to the development of alternative types of residual vectors, say $\tilde{\mathbf{e}}$, which have the property that $E[\tilde{\mathbf{e}}\tilde{\mathbf{e}}'] = \sigma^2 I$ when $E[\mathbf{e}\mathbf{e}'] = \sigma^2 I$. Two such types of residuals are BLUS and recursive residuals, and we will describe them briefly in the following two subsections. Their possible use in testing for heteroscedasticity and autocorrelation is described in Sections 11.3.3 and 8.4.2c, respectively.

5.5.2a BLUS Residuals

In the model $\mathbf{y} = X\boldsymbol{\beta} + \mathbf{e}$, $E[\mathbf{e}] = \mathbf{0}$, $E[\mathbf{e}\mathbf{e}'] = \sigma^2 I$, the LS residuals $\hat{\mathbf{e}} = \mathbf{y} - X\mathbf{b}$ have covariance matrix $E[\hat{\mathbf{e}}\hat{\mathbf{e}}'] = \sigma^2 M$. The development of BLUS residuals was motivated by a desire to have a set of residuals that is (1) a linear function of $\mathbf{y}$, say $\tilde{\mathbf{e}} = B\mathbf{y}$; (2) unbiased, $E[\tilde{\mathbf{e}}] = \mathbf{0}$; and (3) homoscedastic and nonautocorrelated, $E[\tilde{\mathbf{e}}\tilde{\mathbf{e}}'] = \sigma^2 I$, when $\mathbf{e}$ is homoscedastic and nonautocorrelated. A vector satisfying these conditions is LUS: linear, unbiased, and possessing a "scalar covariance matrix." To choose B, note that M is idempotent of rank $(T - K)$ and hence has $(T - K)$ characteristic roots of unity and K characteristic roots of zero. If B is of dimension $[(T - K) \times T]$ and contains characteristic vectors corresponding to the $(T - K)$ unit roots, then it can be shown that $BX = 0$, $BB' = I$, $B'B = M$, $\tilde{\mathbf{e}} = B\mathbf{y} = B\mathbf{e} = B\hat{\mathbf{e}}$, and $E[\tilde{\mathbf{e}}\tilde{\mathbf{e}}'] = \sigma^2 BMB' = \sigma^2 I_{T-K}$ [Theil (1971, Chapter 5)]. Thus this B satisfies the LUS conditions and it is clear that $\tilde{\mathbf{e}}$ cannot be of order greater than $(T - K)$.

However, because of the multiplicity of the unit root, B is not unique. One way of obtaining a unique B is to first partition the observations as

$$\begin{bmatrix} \mathbf{y}_0 \\ \mathbf{y}_1 \end{bmatrix} = \begin{bmatrix} X_0 \\ X_1 \end{bmatrix} \boldsymbol{\beta} + \begin{bmatrix} \mathbf{e}_0 \\ \mathbf{e}_1 \end{bmatrix} \tag{5.5.11}$$

where X_0 is $(K \times K)$, X_1 is $[(T - K) \times K]$ and $\mathbf{y}_0$, $\mathbf{y}_1$, $\mathbf{e}_0$, and $\mathbf{e}_1$ are conformable, then we find a LUS residual vector such that $E[(\tilde{\mathbf{e}} - \mathbf{e}_1)'(\tilde{\mathbf{e}} - \mathbf{e}_1)]$ is a minimum. For a given partitioning this is the BLUS residual vector and it is "best" in the sense that $E[(\tilde{\mathbf{e}} - \mathbf{e}_1)'(\tilde{\mathbf{e}} - \mathbf{e}_1)]$ is a minimum. A convenient way to calculate it is

$$\tilde{\mathbf{e}} = \hat{\mathbf{e}}_1 - X_1 X_0^{-1} \left[\sum_{h=1}^{H} \frac{d_h}{1 + d_h} \mathbf{q}_h \mathbf{q}_h' \right] \hat{\mathbf{e}}_0 \tag{5.5.12}$$

where $\hat{\mathbf{e}}' = [\hat{\mathbf{e}}_0', \hat{\mathbf{e}}_1']$, and $d_1^2, d_2^2, \ldots, d_K^2$ and $\mathbf{q}_1, \mathbf{q}_2, \ldots, \mathbf{q}_K$ are the characteristic roots and vectors, respectively, of $X_0(X'X)^{-1}X_0'$. The K roots of $X_0(X'X)^{-1}X_0'$ will all be positive and less than or equal to one. Only the H roots which are strictly less than one, and their corresponding characteristic vectors, appear in (5.5.12). The number H is equal to the rank of X_1.

When using BLUS residuals, we need to decide on the appropriate partitioning in (5.5.11) or, if more than one partitioning is to be considered, the appropriate subset of the $\binom{T}{T-K}$ possibilities. See Theil (1971, p. 217) for some criteria upon which to partition.

Early references to the development of BLUS residuals can be found in Theil (1971, Chapter 5). For later developments and details of BLU residuals with a fixed covariance matrix and BAUS residuals (best augmented unbiased residuals with a scalar covariance matrix), see Abrahamse and Koerts (1971), Abrahamse and Louter (1971), Grossman and Styan (1972), Dubbelman, Abrahamse and Koerts (1972), Farebrother (1977), Dent and Styan (1978), and Dubbelman (1978).

5.5.2b Recursive Residuals

A vector of recursive residuals, $\mathbf{e}^*$, is also a member of the class of LUS residuals. That is, it is of dimension $(T - K)$, it is a linear function of $\mathbf{y}$, it is unbiased, and if $E[\mathbf{ee}'] = \sigma^2 I_T$ it possesses a scalar covariance matrix, $E[\mathbf{e}^*\mathbf{e}^{*\prime}] = \sigma^2 I_{T-K}$. It does not possess the minimum variance property of the BLUS residual vector but, given a particular partitioning such as in (5.5.11), it is unique and easy to calculate.

Let X_j be a $(j \times K)$ matrix containing the first j rows of X, and let $\mathbf{x}_j'$ be the jth row of X. Thus

$$X_{j+1} = \begin{bmatrix} X_j \\ \mathbf{x}_{j+1}' \end{bmatrix}$$

Also, assume that $j \geq K$, let $\mathbf{y}_j = (y_1, y_2, \ldots, y_j)'$, $S_j = (X_j'X_j)^{-1}$, and $\mathbf{b}_j$ be the LS estimate of $\boldsymbol{\beta}$ based on the first j observations. That is, $\mathbf{b}_j = S_j X_j' \mathbf{y}_j$. Then a vector of $(T - K)$ recursive residuals is given by

$$e_j^* = \frac{y_j - \mathbf{x}_j'\mathbf{b}_{j-1}}{(1 + \mathbf{x}_j' S_{j-1} \mathbf{x}_j)^{1/2}} = \frac{y_j - \mathbf{x}_j'\mathbf{b}_j}{(1 - \mathbf{x}_j' S_j \mathbf{x}_j)^{1/2}}, \qquad j = K+1, K+2, \ldots, T \tag{5.5.13}$$

A convenient way to calculate the $\mathbf{b}_j$ and S_j is via the recursive formulas:

$$\mathbf{b}_j = \mathbf{b}_{j-1} + \frac{S_{j-1}\mathbf{x}_j(y_j - \mathbf{x}_j'\mathbf{b}_{j-1})}{1 + \mathbf{x}_j' S_{j-1}\mathbf{x}_j} \tag{5.5.14}$$

and

$$S_j = S_{j-1} - \frac{S_{j-1}\mathbf{x}_j\mathbf{x}_j' S_{j-1}}{1 + \mathbf{x}_j' S_{j-1}\mathbf{x}_j} \tag{5.5.15}$$

As is the case with BLUS residuals, a different set of recursive residuals is obtained for each possible partitioning of the form (5.5.11). This is achieved by simply reordering the observations. For more information see Phillips and Harvey (1974); Brown, Durbin, and Evans (1975); and Farebrother (1978).

5.5.3 Estimated Generalized Least Squares

When we have the model $\mathbf{y} = X\boldsymbol{\beta} + \mathbf{e}$, with $E[\mathbf{e}] = \mathbf{0}$, $E[\mathbf{ee}'] = \sigma^2\boldsymbol{\Psi}$, and $\boldsymbol{\Psi}$ unknown, an alternative to the least squares estimator is the estimated generalized least squares (EGLS) estimator

$$\hat{\hat{\boldsymbol{\beta}}} = (X'\hat{\boldsymbol{\Psi}}^{-1}X)^{-1}X'\hat{\boldsymbol{\Psi}}^{-1}\mathbf{y} \tag{5.5.16}$$

This estimator is obtained by taking the GLS estimator $\hat{\boldsymbol{\beta}} = (X'\boldsymbol{\Psi}^{-1}X)^{-1} X'\boldsymbol{\Psi}^{-1}\mathbf{y}$ and replacing the unknown covariance matrix $\boldsymbol{\Psi}$ with an estimator $\hat{\boldsymbol{\Psi}}$.

In the most general case $\boldsymbol{\Psi}$ contains $[(T(T + 1)/2) - 1]$ different unknown parameters—the number of diagonal elements plus half the off-diagonal elements, less one, one being subtracted because the constant σ^2 has been factored out of $\Phi = \sigma^2\boldsymbol{\Psi}$. This large number of unknown parameters cannot be satisfactorily estimated with only T observations, and so, to restrict the number of unknown parameters in $\boldsymbol{\Psi}$, it is customary to make some further assumptions about the structure of this matrix. Specifically, it is usually assumed that the elements in $\boldsymbol{\Psi}$ are functions of an $(H \times 1)$ vector $\boldsymbol{\theta}$, where $H < T$ and H remains constant as T increases. Then the problem of estimating $\boldsymbol{\Psi}$ reduces to one of estimating $\boldsymbol{\theta}$. The nature of the assumed matrix function $\boldsymbol{\Psi}(\boldsymbol{\theta})$ will depend on what assumptions seem reasonable for the problem at hand, or it may depend on some preliminary hypothesis tests. For example, each of the topics heteroscedasticity (Chapter 11), autocorrelation (Chapter 8), disturbance related sets of regression equations (Chapter 12), and models for combining time series and cross-section data (Chapter 13) is based on a different assumption about the dependence of $\boldsymbol{\Psi}$ on $\boldsymbol{\theta}$. The choice of an estimator for $\boldsymbol{\Psi}$ will depend on the function $\boldsymbol{\Psi}(\boldsymbol{\theta})$, and so alternative estimators are discussed under the chapter headings just mentioned. However, most EGLS estimators do have some common characteristics and we consider these in the following subsection.

5.5.3a Properties of Estimated Generalized Least Squares Estimators

Evaluation of the finite sample properties of the EGLS estimator

$$\hat{\hat{\boldsymbol{\beta}}} = (X'\hat{\Psi}^{-1}X)^{-1}X'\hat{\Psi}^{-1}\mathbf{y} = \boldsymbol{\beta} + (X'\hat{\Psi}^{-1}X)^{-1}X'\hat{\Psi}^{-1}\mathbf{e} \qquad (5.5.17)$$

is, in general, a difficult problem, because $\hat{\Psi}$ and $\mathbf{e}$ will be correlated. Consequently, inferences about $\boldsymbol{\beta}$ need to be based on the asymptotic distribution of $\hat{\hat{\boldsymbol{\beta}}}$, and for specific functions $\Psi(\boldsymbol{\theta})$, Monte Carlo experiments are often used to check the accuracy of the asymptotic theory in finite samples. There are, however, two general results about the finite sample properties of $\hat{\hat{\boldsymbol{\beta}}}$ that can be stated.

First, if $\mathbf{e}$ is symmetrically distributed around zero, and if $\hat{\Psi}$ is an even function of $\hat{\mathbf{e}}$ (i.e., $\hat{\Psi}(\hat{\mathbf{e}}) = \hat{\Psi}(-\hat{\mathbf{e}})$), then it follows (Kakwani, 1967) that $\hat{\hat{\boldsymbol{\beta}}}$ will be an unbiased estimator for $\boldsymbol{\beta}$, providing that the mean of $\hat{\hat{\boldsymbol{\beta}}}$ exists.

For the second result we define

$$\hat{\hat{\mathbf{e}}} = \mathbf{y} - X\hat{\hat{\boldsymbol{\beta}}} \qquad (5.5.18)$$

$$\hat{\hat{\sigma}}^2 = \frac{\hat{\hat{\mathbf{e}}}'\hat{\Psi}^{-1}\hat{\hat{\mathbf{e}}}}{T - K} \qquad (5.5.19)$$

and let $\hat{\boldsymbol{\theta}}$ be the estimator of $\boldsymbol{\theta}$ (the unknown parameters in Ψ) obtained from the least squares residuals. Then, under not very restrictive conditions on the estimator $\hat{\boldsymbol{\theta}}$, it is possible to show (Breusch, 1980) that the exact distributions of $(\hat{\hat{\boldsymbol{\beta}}} - \boldsymbol{\beta})/\sigma$, $\hat{\hat{\sigma}}^2/\sigma^2$, $\hat{\boldsymbol{\theta}}$, and $\hat{\hat{\mathbf{e}}}/\sigma$ do not depend on the parameters $\boldsymbol{\beta}$ and σ^2. This result is an important one for the design of Monte Carlo experiments. It means that in such experiments, although we need to consider a number of points in the $\boldsymbol{\theta}$-parameter space, only one point in the parameter space for $(\boldsymbol{\beta},\sigma^2)$ needs to be considered.

For the asymptotic properties of $\hat{\hat{\boldsymbol{\beta}}}$ we first investigate the asymptotic properties of the GLS estimator $\hat{\boldsymbol{\beta}} = (X'\Psi^{-1}X)^{-1}X'\Psi^{-1}\mathbf{y}$, and then give sufficient conditions for the EGLS and GLS estimators to have the same asymptotic distribution. Consistency and asymptotic normality of $\hat{\boldsymbol{\beta}}$ are established by placing the same conditions on the transformed variables PX (where P is such that $P\Psi P' = I$) as were placed on X in Sections 5.1 and 5.3. Thus, we assume that the elements in PX are bounded and that

$$\lim_{T\to\infty} \left(\frac{X'\Psi^{-1}X}{T}\right) = V \qquad (5.5.20)$$

is a finite nonsingular matrix. Along the lines of the earlier sections it then follows that $\hat{\boldsymbol{\beta}}$ and

$$\hat{\sigma}_g^2 = \frac{(\mathbf{y} - X\hat{\boldsymbol{\beta}})'\Psi^{-1}(\mathbf{y} - X\hat{\boldsymbol{\beta}})}{T - K} \qquad (5.5.21)$$

are consistent estimators, and that

$$\sqrt{T}(\hat{\boldsymbol{\beta}} - \boldsymbol{\beta}) \xrightarrow{d} N(\mathbf{0}, \sigma^2 V^{-1}). \tag{5.5.22}$$

Now $\sqrt{T}(\hat{\hat{\boldsymbol{\beta}}} - \boldsymbol{\beta})$ will converge in probability and distribution to $\sqrt{T}(\hat{\boldsymbol{\beta}} - \boldsymbol{\beta})$ if

$$\begin{aligned}
\text{plim}[\sqrt{T}(\hat{\hat{\boldsymbol{\beta}}} - \boldsymbol{\beta}) - \sqrt{T}(\hat{\boldsymbol{\beta}} - \boldsymbol{\beta})] \\
&= \text{plim}\left[\left(\frac{X'\hat{\boldsymbol{\Psi}}^{-1}X}{T}\right)^{-1}\frac{X'\hat{\boldsymbol{\Psi}}^{-1}\mathbf{e}}{\sqrt{T}} - \left(\frac{X'\boldsymbol{\Psi}^{-1}X}{T}\right)^{-1}\frac{X'\boldsymbol{\Psi}^{-1}\mathbf{e}}{\sqrt{T}}\right] \\
&= \mathbf{0}
\end{aligned} \tag{5.5.23}$$

Sufficient conditions for (5.5.23) to hold are that

$$\text{plim}\left(\frac{X'\hat{\boldsymbol{\Psi}}^{-1}X}{T}\right) = \text{plim}\left(\frac{X'\boldsymbol{\Psi}^{-1}X}{T}\right)$$

and

$$\text{plim}\left(\frac{X'\hat{\boldsymbol{\Psi}}^{-1}\mathbf{e}}{\sqrt{T}}\right) = \text{plim}\left(\frac{X'\boldsymbol{\Psi}^{-1}\mathbf{e}}{\sqrt{T}}\right)$$

or, equivalently

$$\text{plim } T^{-1}X'(\hat{\boldsymbol{\Psi}}^{-1} - \boldsymbol{\Psi}^{-1})X = 0 \tag{5.5.24}$$

and

$$\text{plim } T^{-1/2}X'(\hat{\boldsymbol{\Psi}}^{-1} - \boldsymbol{\Psi}^{-1})\mathbf{e} = \mathbf{0} \tag{5.5.25}$$

Thus, (5.5.24) and (5.5.25) are a common way (e.g, Schmidt, 1976 and Theil, 1971) of stating sufficient conditions for

$$\sqrt{T}(\hat{\hat{\boldsymbol{\beta}}} - \boldsymbol{\beta}) \xrightarrow{d} N(\mathbf{0}, \sigma^2 V^{-1}) \tag{5.5.26}$$

In practice these conditions should be checked out for any specific function $\boldsymbol{\Psi}(\boldsymbol{\theta})$ and the corresponding estimator $\hat{\boldsymbol{\theta}}$. Most of the cases we study are such that (5.5.24) and (5.5.25) hold if $\hat{\boldsymbol{\theta}}$ is a consistent estimator for $\boldsymbol{\theta}$. However, as an example given by Schmidt (1976, p. 69) demonstrates, consistency of $\hat{\boldsymbol{\theta}}$ will not, in general, be sufficient for (5.5.26) to hold. For a set of sufficient conditions which can be used as an alternative to (5.5.24) and (5.5.25), see Fuller and Battese (1973).

One reason for using an EGLS estimator is that, under appropriate conditions, it is asymptotically more efficient than the LS estimator. For further details see Exercise 5.4.

The next task is to find a statistic that can be used for testing the hypothesis $R\boldsymbol{\beta} = \mathbf{r}$ where R is a $(J \times K)$ known matrix and $\mathbf{r}$ a $(J \times 1)$ known vector. Working in this direction, we noted that, from (5.5.20) and (5.5.24), $(X'\hat{\Psi}^{-1}X/T)$ is a consistent estimator for V, and, if we add the additional condition that

$$\text{plim } T^{-1}\mathbf{e}'(\hat{\Psi}^{-1} - \Psi^{-1})\mathbf{e} = 0 \tag{5.5.27}$$

then it is possible to use this condition along with (5.5.24) and (5.5.25) to prove that $\text{plim}(\hat{\hat{\sigma}}^2 - \sigma_g^2) = 0$. It then follows that $\hat{\hat{\sigma}}^2$ is a consistent estimator for σ^2, and, using results on convergence in probability and distribution given in Section 5.3, we have

$$\lambda_1 = \frac{(\hat{\hat{\boldsymbol{\beta}}} - \boldsymbol{\beta})'R'[R(X'\hat{\Psi}^{-1}X)^{-1}R']^{-1}R(\hat{\hat{\boldsymbol{\beta}}} - \boldsymbol{\beta})}{\hat{\hat{\sigma}}^2} \xrightarrow{d} \chi^2_{(J)} \tag{5.5.28}$$

This result can be used to test $R\boldsymbol{\beta} = \mathbf{r}$, or, alternatively, the argument presented in Section 5.3.3 can be used to justify using $\lambda_2 = \lambda_1/J$ and the $F_{(J,T-K)}$ distribution. Also, if in (5.5.28) we assume that the null hypothesis is true and replace $R\boldsymbol{\beta}$ with $\mathbf{r}$, then λ_1 is often referred to as the Wald test statistic. More general forms of this statistic will be discussed in Section 5.7.

5.6 MAXIMUM LIKELIHOOD ESTIMATION

As was discussed in Section 2.12 of Chapter 2, maximum likelihood (ML) estimation is one method for obtaining estimators for a statistical model where a specific distributional assumption is made about the vector of sample observations. Maximum likelihood estimators are popular because the criterion of finding those parameter values most likely to have produced the sample observations is an intuitively pleasing one, and because under fairly general conditions ML estimators have a number of desirable asymptotic properties. These properties are considered in Section 5.6.1 and, in Section 5.6.2, we examine some aspects of ML estimation for the linear model with unknown disturbance covariance matrix.

5.6.1 Properties of Maximum Likelihood Estimators

To state the properties of ML estimators we assume that $\mathbf{z}_1, \mathbf{z}_2, \ldots, \mathbf{z}_T$ are independent identically distributed random vectors each with density function $f(\mathbf{z}_t|\boldsymbol{\gamma})$, which depends on the vector of unknown parameters $\boldsymbol{\gamma}$; and we denote the log-likelihood function by

$$L(\boldsymbol{\gamma}) = \sum_{t=1}^{T} \ln f(\mathbf{z}_t|\boldsymbol{\gamma}) \tag{5.6.1}$$

The maximum likelihood estimator $\tilde{\boldsymbol{\gamma}}$ is that value of $\boldsymbol{\gamma}$ for which $L(\boldsymbol{\gamma})$ is a maximum. Under some regularity conditions stated below it is possible to show that:

1. $\tilde{\boldsymbol{\gamma}}$ is a consistent estimator for $\boldsymbol{\gamma}$.
2. $\tilde{\boldsymbol{\gamma}}$ is asymptotically normal in the sense that

$$\sqrt{T}(\tilde{\boldsymbol{\gamma}} - \boldsymbol{\gamma}) \xrightarrow{d} N[\mathbf{0}, \lim(I(\boldsymbol{\gamma})/T)^{-1}] \tag{5.6.2}$$

   where $I(\boldsymbol{\gamma})$ is the information matrix.

$$I(\boldsymbol{\gamma}) = -E\left[\frac{\partial^2 L}{\partial \boldsymbol{\gamma} \partial \boldsymbol{\gamma}'}\right] \tag{5.6.3}$$

3. $\tilde{\boldsymbol{\gamma}}$ is asymptotically efficient relative to all other consistent uniformly asymptotically normal estimators. That is, if $\hat{\boldsymbol{\gamma}}$ is another estimator with the property

$$\sqrt{T}(\hat{\boldsymbol{\gamma}} - \boldsymbol{\gamma}) \xrightarrow{d} N(0, W)$$

   where W is positive definite, then $W - \lim[I(\boldsymbol{\gamma})/T]^{-1}$ is positive semidefinite. [It is necessary to restrict the class of estimators $\hat{\boldsymbol{\gamma}}$ to those for which convergence to normality is uniform. Otherwise, it is always possible to construct another estimator whose variance is smaller in at least one point in the parameter space, and the same elsewhere. See Dhrymes (1974, p. 128) for an example.]

Proofs of these results as well as the regularity conditions sufficient to establish the results can be found in a number of textbooks such as Theil (1971), Dhrymes (1974), and Pollock (1979). Briefly, regularity conditions under which a consistent root of $\partial L/\partial \boldsymbol{\gamma} = \mathbf{0}$ exists and has the above properties are:

1. The range of $\mathbf{z}_t$ does not depend on $\boldsymbol{\gamma}$.
2. The expression $\int \Pi_{t=1}^{T} f(\mathbf{z}_t|\boldsymbol{\gamma}) d\mathbf{z}_1 \ldots d\mathbf{z}_T$ is twice differentiable under the integral.
3. The derivatives of $\ln f$ with respect to $\boldsymbol{\gamma}$ exist up to the third order for almost all $\mathbf{z}$, and for all $\boldsymbol{\gamma}$ belonging to a region A that contains the true parameter vector as an interior point.
4. The covariance matrix of $\partial L/\partial \boldsymbol{\gamma}$ is finite and positive definite everywhere in A.
5. The third derivatives of L are bounded by integrable functions of $\mathbf{z}$. That is, $|\partial^3 L/\partial \gamma_i^3| \leq H_i(\mathbf{z})$ and $E[H_i(\mathbf{z})] < M$ for all $\boldsymbol{\gamma}$ in A and a finite constant M.

To show that the consistent root of $\partial L/\partial \boldsymbol{\gamma} = \mathbf{0}$ is unique and corresponds to the global maximum of the likelihood function, some further conditions are usually imposed [see, for example, Dhrymes (1974, p. 120)]. An intermediate result that is ensured by the above conditions and that is useful in other contexts is that

$$E\left[\frac{\partial L}{\partial \boldsymbol{\gamma}}\right] = \mathbf{0} \quad \text{and} \quad E\left[\left(\frac{\partial L}{\partial \boldsymbol{\gamma}}\right)\left(\frac{\partial L}{\partial \boldsymbol{\gamma}}\right)'\right] = -E\left[\frac{\partial^2 L}{\partial \boldsymbol{\gamma} \partial \boldsymbol{\gamma}'}\right] \tag{5.6.4}$$

With respect to finite sample properties, in Chapter 2 we noted that the inverse of the information matrix is often known as the Cramér-Rao lower bound and that all unbiased estimators for $\boldsymbol{\gamma}$ will have a variance at least as great as this lower bound. Thus, if the variance of an unbiased estimator is equal to the Cramér-Rao lower bound it necessarily must be a minimum variance unbiased estimator (MVUE). It is also possible to prove (Dhrymes, 1974) that if $f(\mathbf{z}_t|\boldsymbol{\gamma})$ admits a set of (jointly) sufficient statistics for $\boldsymbol{\gamma}$, then (1) an unbiased estimator that is a function of the sufficient statistics will also be a MVUE, and (2) the ML estimator for $\boldsymbol{\gamma}$ will be a function of the sufficient statistics. Taken together, these last two results imply that if the density function admits sufficient statistics, then any ML estimator that is unbiased will also be a MVUE. Alternatively, if the ML estimator is biased but we can obtain an unbiased estimator through a one-to-one transformation of the ML estimator, then the resulting estimator will be a MVUE. These results could be regarded as a finite sample justification for using the ML technique, but the justification is not a strong one for the following reasons.

First, the distribution may not admit any sufficient statistics (of fixed dimension). Second, an unbiased estimator for $\boldsymbol{\gamma}$ may not exist or it may be too difficult to evaluate the mean of the ML estimator $\tilde{\boldsymbol{\gamma}}$. Third, the variance of a MVUE is not necessarily equal to the Cramér-Rao lower bound. It will often be greater because estimators that attain the Cramér-Rao lower bound frequently do not exist. Consequently, even if it is possible to find an unbiased ML estimator that is a MVUE, it may be too difficult to derive its finite sample variance, and there is no guarantee that the Cramér-Rao lower bound (which will frequently be easier to derive) will be equal to the variance.

Asymptotically the situation is much brighter. The condition in (5.6.2) shows that (subject to the regularity conditions) ML estimators always attain the Cramér-Rao lower bound asymptotically. Consequently, ML estimators are asymptotically efficient, and the Cramér-Rao lower bound can be used as a large sample approximation to the covariance matrix of the ML estimator.

Along the lines of previous sections, (5.6.2) can be used to construct an asymptotic χ^2 statistic for testing hypotheses about $\boldsymbol{\gamma}$. Details of this and other statistics are given in Section 5.7, but one item of interest at this point is the question of possible estimators for $\lim(I(\boldsymbol{\gamma})/T)$. This quantity can be replaced by a consistent estimator without changing the asymptotic distribution of test statistics for $\boldsymbol{\gamma}$. Alternative estimators that are often used for $\lim(I(\boldsymbol{\gamma})/T)$ are

1. $$-\frac{1}{T} E\left[\frac{\partial^2 L}{\partial \boldsymbol{\gamma} \partial \boldsymbol{\gamma}'}\right]_{\boldsymbol{\gamma}=\tilde{\boldsymbol{\gamma}}} \tag{5.6.5}$$

2. $$\frac{1}{T} E\left[\left(\frac{\partial L}{\partial \gamma}\right)\left(\frac{\partial L}{\partial \gamma}\right)'\right]_{\gamma=\tilde{\gamma}} \tag{5.6.6}$$

3. $$-\frac{1}{T}\left[\frac{\partial^2 L}{\partial \gamma \partial \gamma'}\right]_{\gamma=\tilde{\gamma}} \tag{5.6.7}$$

4. $$\frac{1}{T}\left[\sum_{t=1}^{T}\left(\frac{\partial \ln f(\mathbf{z}_t|\gamma)}{\partial \gamma}\right)\left(\frac{\partial \ln f(\mathbf{z}_t|\gamma)}{\partial \gamma}\right)'\right]_{\gamma=\tilde{\gamma}} \tag{5.6.8}$$

Estimators (1) and (2) are, of course, identical (see Equation 5.6.4), but, depending on the circumstances, one may be easier to compute than the other. The estimator in (2) has the advantage that only first rather than second derivatives are involved, but it has the disadvantage that the expectation of the first derivatives is often harder to find. Estimators (3) and (4) also require second and first derivatives, respectively, but not their expectations. Consequently, estimators (3) and (4) will often be easier to use than (1) or (2), and this will be particularly so if the computer program employed calculates numerical rather than analytical derivatives, and therefore avoids the problem of finding (and programming) explicit expressions for the derivatives. Which estimator yields the best finite sample approximation is an open question and is likely to depend on the model being studied. Also, in some cases additional conditions may be necessary to ensure the consistency of each estimator. Dhrymes (1974) has proved that (3) will always be consistent if $f(\mathbf{z}_t|\gamma)$ admits sufficient statistics; estimator (4) was suggested by Berndt, Hall, and Hausman (1974).

One difficulty with the discussion so far is that, at the outset, we assumed the $\mathbf{z}_t$ were independent identically distributed random vectors. In econometrics this assumption is frequently violated. For example, in a heteroscedastic error model the observations will no longer be identically distributed and in an autocorrelated error model the observations will no longer be independent. Fortunately, the results we have given do extend to these other cases, providing some additional assumptions are employed where necessary. With the exception of the next subsection, we defer details of other cases to the relevant chapters. Further discussion and examples can be found in Cox and Hinkley (1974, Ch. 9), Crowder (1976), and Pagan (1979).

5.6.2 Linear Models with Unknown Disturbance Covariance Matrix

Let us now consider ML estimation of $\boldsymbol{\beta}$, σ^2 and $\boldsymbol{\theta}$ in the model

$$\mathbf{y} = X\boldsymbol{\beta} + \mathbf{e}, \qquad \mathbf{e} \sim N[\mathbf{0},\sigma^2\boldsymbol{\Psi}(\boldsymbol{\theta})] \tag{5.6.9}$$

where the usual notation holds, and we have written $\boldsymbol{\Psi}(\boldsymbol{\theta})$ to emphasize that the unknown disturbance covariance matrix $\boldsymbol{\Psi}$ depends on the $(H \times 1)$ vector of parameters $\boldsymbol{\theta}$. This model is clearly an example of one where the observations (y_t's) are not independent and identically distributed. To find ML estimators, we set up the log-likelihood function that, excluding constants, is given by

$$L = -\frac{T}{2}\ln\sigma^2 - \frac{1}{2}\ln|\mathbf{\Psi}| - \frac{1}{2\sigma^2}(\mathbf{y} - X\boldsymbol{\beta})'\mathbf{\Psi}^{-1}(\mathbf{y} - X\boldsymbol{\beta}) \tag{5.6.10}$$

As was shown in Chapter 2, maximization of L with respect to $\boldsymbol{\beta}$ and σ^2, conditional on $\boldsymbol{\theta}$, yields

$$\tilde{\boldsymbol{\beta}}(\boldsymbol{\theta}) = [X'\mathbf{\Psi}^{-1}(\boldsymbol{\theta})X]^{-1}X'\mathbf{\Psi}^{-1}(\boldsymbol{\theta})\mathbf{y} \tag{5.6.11}$$

and

$$\tilde{\sigma}^2(\boldsymbol{\theta}) = \frac{[\mathbf{y} - X\tilde{\boldsymbol{\beta}}(\boldsymbol{\theta})]'\mathbf{\Psi}^{-1}(\boldsymbol{\theta})[\mathbf{y} - X\tilde{\boldsymbol{\beta}}(\boldsymbol{\theta})]}{T} \tag{5.6.12}$$

We have used the notation $\tilde{\boldsymbol{\beta}}(\boldsymbol{\theta})$, $\tilde{\sigma}^2(\boldsymbol{\theta})$, and $\mathbf{\Psi}(\boldsymbol{\theta})$ to emphasize the dependence of these quantities on $\boldsymbol{\theta}$. Substituting (5.6.11) and (5.6.12) back into (5.6.10), and ignoring constants, yields the concentrated log-likelihood function

$$L(\boldsymbol{\theta}) = -T\ln\{[\mathbf{y} - X\tilde{\boldsymbol{\beta}}(\boldsymbol{\theta})]'\mathbf{\Psi}^{-1}(\boldsymbol{\theta})[\mathbf{y} - X\tilde{\boldsymbol{\beta}}(\boldsymbol{\theta})]\} - \ln|\mathbf{\Psi}(\boldsymbol{\theta})| \tag{5.6.13}$$

The maximum likelihood estimator for $\boldsymbol{\theta}$, say $\tilde{\boldsymbol{\theta}}$, is that value of $\boldsymbol{\theta}$ for which $L(\boldsymbol{\theta})$ is a maximum, or, equivalently, that value of $\boldsymbol{\theta}$ for which

$$S(\boldsymbol{\theta}) = |\mathbf{\Psi}(\boldsymbol{\theta})|^{1/T}[\mathbf{y} - X\tilde{\boldsymbol{\beta}}(\boldsymbol{\theta})]'\mathbf{\Psi}^{-1}(\boldsymbol{\theta})[\mathbf{y} - X\tilde{\boldsymbol{\beta}}(\boldsymbol{\theta})] \tag{5.6.14}$$

is a minimum. If we define $\tilde{\mathbf{\Psi}} = \mathbf{\Psi}(\tilde{\boldsymbol{\theta}})$, then the maximum likelihood estimators for $\boldsymbol{\beta}$ and σ^2 (not conditional on $\boldsymbol{\theta}$) are given by

$$\tilde{\boldsymbol{\beta}} = \tilde{\boldsymbol{\beta}}(\tilde{\boldsymbol{\theta}}) = (X'\tilde{\mathbf{\Psi}}^{-1}X)^{-1}X'\tilde{\mathbf{\Psi}}^{-1}\mathbf{y} \tag{5.6.15}$$

and

$$\tilde{\sigma}^2 = \tilde{\sigma}^2(\tilde{\boldsymbol{\theta}}) = \frac{(\mathbf{y} - X\tilde{\boldsymbol{\beta}})'\tilde{\mathbf{\Psi}}^{-1}(\mathbf{y} - X\tilde{\boldsymbol{\beta}})}{T} \tag{5.6.16}$$

Thus, the ML estimator for $\boldsymbol{\beta}$ is of the same form as an EGLS estimator, but instead of using an estimate of $\mathbf{\Psi}$ based on least squares residuals, it uses an estimate of $\mathbf{\Psi}$ obtained by maximizing (5.6.13) with respect to $\boldsymbol{\theta}$. Maximization of (5.6.13) does not, in general, yield a closed form solution for $\tilde{\boldsymbol{\theta}}$, the first-order conditions being given by [see, for example, Magnus (1978)]

$$\tilde{\sigma}^2 \operatorname{tr}\left(\frac{\partial\mathbf{\Psi}^{-1}}{\partial\theta_h}\cdot\mathbf{\Psi}\right)_{\boldsymbol{\theta}=\tilde{\boldsymbol{\theta}}} = (\mathbf{y} - X\tilde{\boldsymbol{\beta}})'\left(\frac{\partial\mathbf{\Psi}^{-1}}{\partial\theta_h}\right)_{\boldsymbol{\theta}=\tilde{\boldsymbol{\theta}}}(\mathbf{y} - X\tilde{\boldsymbol{\beta}}) \qquad h = 1, 2, \ldots, H \tag{5.6.17}$$

where $\partial\Psi^{-1}/\partial\theta_h$ is a $(T \times T)$ matrix of partial derivatives of each element in Ψ^{-1} with respect to θ_h. Consequently, we need to resort to numerical methods to find the maximum of (5.6.13), the minimum of (5.6.14), or a solution to (5.6.17). For details of such techniques see Chapter 6, Appendix B, and Oberhofer and Kmenta (1974).

Since the ML estimator $\tilde{\boldsymbol\beta}$ is also an EGLS estimator, the properties of EGLS estimators discussed in Section 5.5.3a hold for the ML estimator. However, in the ML case we know in addition that $\tilde{\boldsymbol\beta}$ is asymptotically efficient, and we can make statements about the asymptotic distributions of $\tilde\sigma^2$ and $\tilde{\boldsymbol\theta}$. Using the notation $\boldsymbol\gamma' = (\boldsymbol\beta',\sigma^2,\boldsymbol\theta')$ it is possible to show [see, for example, Breusch (1980)] that

$$I(\boldsymbol\gamma) = \begin{bmatrix} \sigma^{-2}(X'\Psi^{-1}X) & \mathbf{0} & 0 \\ \mathbf{0} & \frac{1}{2}T\sigma^{-4} & \frac{1}{2}\sigma^{-2}(\text{vec }\Psi^{-1})'A \\ 0 & \frac{1}{2}\sigma^{-2}A'(\text{vec }\Psi^{-1}) & \frac{1}{2}A'(\Psi^{-1} \otimes \Psi^{-1})A \end{bmatrix} \tag{5.6.18}$$

where $A = A(\boldsymbol\theta) = \partial \text{ vec}(\Psi(\boldsymbol\theta)/\partial\boldsymbol\theta')$, and the operator vec$(\cdot)$ stacks the columns of a matrix as a vector.

Although $\Psi \neq I$, and thus the elements in the vector $\mathbf{y}$ are not independent and identically distributed, under appropriate conditions [see Magnus (1978)], it is possible to show that $\tilde{\boldsymbol\gamma}$ is consistent, that

$$\sqrt{T}(\tilde{\boldsymbol\gamma} - \boldsymbol\gamma) \xrightarrow{d} N[\mathbf{0},\lim\,(I(\boldsymbol\gamma)/T)^{-1}] \tag{5.6.19}$$

and that $\tilde{\boldsymbol\gamma}$ will be asymtotically efficient in the sense described earlier. Details of test statistics based on (5.6.19) are given in the next section. For some specific examples where the quantities in $I(\boldsymbol\gamma)$ are evaluated, see Magnus (1978).

5.7 THE WALD, LIKELIHOOD RATIO, AND LAGRANGE MULTIPLIER TESTS

In this section we focus attention on three alternative tests for testing hypotheses about the $(K + H + 1)$-dimensional vector $\boldsymbol\gamma = (\boldsymbol\beta',\sigma^2,\boldsymbol\theta')'$ in the model

$$\mathbf{y} = X\boldsymbol\beta + \mathbf{e}, \quad \mathbf{e} \sim N[\mathbf{0},\sigma^2\Psi(\boldsymbol\theta)] \tag{5.7.1}$$

The three tests are the Wald (W), likelihood ratio (LR), and Lagrange multiplier (LM) tests, and each is a possible procedure for testing a general null hypothesis of the form

$$H_0\colon \mathbf{g}(\boldsymbol\gamma) = \mathbf{0} \tag{5.7.2}$$

against the alternative

$$H_1\colon \mathbf{g}(\boldsymbol\gamma) \neq \mathbf{0} \tag{5.7.3}$$

where $\mathbf{g}$ is a J-dimensional vector function.

To introduce the Wald test we note that, from (5.6.19) and a result analogous to (5.3.20),

$$\sqrt{T}[\mathbf{g}(\tilde{\boldsymbol{\gamma}}) - \mathbf{g}(\boldsymbol{\gamma})] \xrightarrow{d} N[\mathbf{0}, \lim TF'I(\boldsymbol{\gamma})^{-1}F] \tag{5.7.4}$$

where $\tilde{\boldsymbol{\gamma}}$ is the unrestricted maximum likelihood estimator for $\boldsymbol{\gamma}$, F is the $[(K + H + 1) \times J]$ matrix $\partial \mathbf{g}'(\boldsymbol{\gamma})/\partial \boldsymbol{\gamma}$, and $I(\boldsymbol{\gamma})$ is the information matrix. Then, assuming H_0 is true, we have

$$\lambda_{\text{W}} = [\mathbf{g}(\tilde{\boldsymbol{\gamma}})]'[\tilde{F}'I(\tilde{\boldsymbol{\gamma}})^{-1}\tilde{F}]^{-1}[g(\tilde{\boldsymbol{\gamma}})] \xrightarrow{d} \chi^2_{(J)} \tag{5.7.5}$$

where $\tilde{F}$ is the matrix F evaluated at $\boldsymbol{\gamma} = \tilde{\boldsymbol{\gamma}}$, and $I(\tilde{\boldsymbol{\gamma}})$ is a consistent estimator for $I(\boldsymbol{\gamma})$ based on $\tilde{\boldsymbol{\gamma}}$. The statistic λ_{W}, used in conjunction with a critical value from the $\chi^2_{(J)}$ distribution, is known as the Wald test.

For the LM test we need the restricted ML estimator $\boldsymbol{\gamma}_R$, which can be obtained by maximizing the constrained likelihood, or by solving the first order conditions from the Lagrangian function

$$\phi(\boldsymbol{\gamma},\boldsymbol{\eta}) = L(\boldsymbol{\gamma}) + \boldsymbol{\eta}'\mathbf{g}(\boldsymbol{\gamma}) \tag{5.7.6}$$

where $L(\boldsymbol{\gamma})$ is the log-likelihood function, and $\boldsymbol{\eta}$ is a J-dimensional vector of Lagrange multipliers. The first-order conditions are given by

$$\mathbf{d}_R + F_R\boldsymbol{\eta}_R = \mathbf{0} \tag{5.7.7}$$

where

$$\mathbf{d}_R = \left.\frac{\partial L}{\partial \boldsymbol{\gamma}}\right|_{\boldsymbol{\gamma}=\boldsymbol{\gamma}_R} \qquad F_R = \left.\frac{\partial \mathbf{g}'}{\partial \boldsymbol{\gamma}}\right|_{\boldsymbol{\gamma}=\boldsymbol{\gamma}_R} \tag{5.7.8}$$

and $\boldsymbol{\eta}_R$ is the optimal solution for $\boldsymbol{\eta}$. Furthermore, if the null hypothesis is true, we would expect $\boldsymbol{\gamma}_R$ to be close to $\tilde{\boldsymbol{\gamma}}$ and $\mathbf{d}_R$ to be close to zero. This idea provides the underlying motivation for the test. Under suitable regularity conditions, it is possible to show that

$$\frac{\mathbf{d}}{\sqrt{T}} = \frac{1}{\sqrt{T}}\frac{\partial L}{\partial \boldsymbol{\gamma}} \xrightarrow{d} N\left[\mathbf{0}, \lim \frac{I(\boldsymbol{\gamma})}{T}\right] \tag{5.7.9}$$

If H_0 is true, it then follows that

$$\lambda_{\text{LM}} = \mathbf{d}_R'I(\boldsymbol{\gamma}_R)^{-1}\mathbf{d}_R \xrightarrow{d} \chi^2_{(J)} \tag{5.7.10}$$

where $I(\boldsymbol{\gamma}_R)$ is a consistent estimator of the information matrix based on the restricted estimator $\boldsymbol{\gamma}_R$. The statistic λ_{LM} used in conjunction with a critical value of the $\chi^2_{(J)}$ distribution is known as the LM test. This terminology is used because, from (5.7.7), λ_{LM} can also be written in terms of $\boldsymbol{\eta}_R$ as

$$\lambda_{LM} = \boldsymbol{\eta}_R' F_R' I(\boldsymbol{\gamma}_R)^{-1} F_R \boldsymbol{\eta}_R \tag{5.7.11}$$

From (5.7.5) and (5.7.11) it is clear that the LM test is based only on the restricted ML estimator, while the Wald test is based only on the unrestricted ML estimator. The LR test uses both the restricted and unrestricted estimators and is based on the statistic

$$\lambda_{LR} = 2[L(\tilde{\boldsymbol{\gamma}}) - L(\boldsymbol{\gamma}_R)] \xrightarrow{d} \chi^2_{(J)} \tag{5.7.12}$$

In general, λ_W, λ_{LM}, and λ_{LR} are asymptotically equivalent in the sense that they all have the same asymptotic distribution, and they all lead to tests that have the same asymptotic power characteristics. However, in finite samples the three statistics will not yield identical values, and so it is possible for the tests to yield conflicting conclusions. As Breusch and Pagan (1980) note, in the absence of any information on the finite sample properties of the tests, the choice between them is likely to depend on computational convenience. In particular, when the structure of the problem is such that the restricted ML estimates are easier to compute, λ_{LM} is likely to be computationally more convenient than the other two. If the unrestricted estimates are easier to compute λ_W is likely to be preferable. Because it requires both restricted and unrestricted estimates, λ_{LR} is likely to be computationally more demanding than both λ_W and λ_{LM}.

The precise form of each statistic will depend on the model being examined and the hypothesis being tested. For example, special cases arise if the restrictions being tested are only on $\boldsymbol{\beta}$, say of the linear form $R\boldsymbol{\beta} = \mathbf{r}$, or if a special structure for $\boldsymbol{\Psi}$ is assumed and the restrictions pertain only to the vector $\boldsymbol{\theta}$. In this regard, examples relating to the parameter vector $\boldsymbol{\theta}$ are given in the chapters on heteroscedasticity, autocorrelation, disturbance related sets of regression equations, and models for combining time series and cross-sectional data. See also Breusch and Pagan (1980) and references therein. One general result on tests of the form H_0: $\mathbf{g}(\boldsymbol{\theta}) = \mathbf{0}$ is worth noting at this point. Breusch (1980) shows that the exact distribution of the Wald, LR, and LM tests does not depend on the parameters $(\boldsymbol{\beta},\sigma^2)$ regardless of whether the hypothesis is correct or not. Consequently, if a Monte Carlo experiment is used to evaluate the finite sample powers of the three tests for testing hypotheses about $\boldsymbol{\theta}$, only different values of $\boldsymbol{\theta}$ need to be considered in the experimental design. Changing $\boldsymbol{\beta}$ and σ^2 will not change the powers of the tests.

5.7.1 Testing a Set of Linear Restrictions on $\boldsymbol{\beta}$

In the remainder of this section, we consider the special form of the three statistics for testing the set of linear restrictions H_0: $R\boldsymbol{\beta} = \mathbf{r}$ against the alternative H_1: $R\boldsymbol{\beta} \neq \mathbf{r}$. The results hold regardless of the structure of $\boldsymbol{\Psi}$ (providing our assumptions of this section still hold), and so are generally applicable for the models in many of the subsequent chapters. We begin by assuming σ^2 and

Ψ are known. Under these conditions the statistics λ_W, λ_{LM}, and λ_{LR} are identical and can be written as

$$\lambda_W = \lambda_{LM} = \lambda_{LR} = \frac{(R\tilde{\beta} - \mathbf{r})'[R(X'\Psi^{-1}X)^{-1}R']^{-1}(R\tilde{\beta} - \mathbf{r})}{\sigma^2} \tag{5.7.13a}$$

$$= \frac{\eta_R' R(X'\Psi^{-1}X)^{-1}R'\eta_R}{\sigma^2} \tag{5.7.13b}$$

$$= \frac{\hat{\mathbf{e}}^{*\prime}\Psi^{-1}\hat{\mathbf{e}}^* - \tilde{\mathbf{e}}'\Psi^{-1}\tilde{\mathbf{e}}}{\sigma^2} \tag{5.7.13c}$$

where $\tilde{\beta} = (X'\Psi^{-1}X)^{-1}X'\Psi^{-1}\mathbf{y}$ is the ML estimator for β when Ψ is known, $\eta_R = [R(X'\Psi^{-1}X)^{-1}R']^{-1}(\mathbf{r} - R\tilde{\beta})$ is the optimal value of the Lagrange multiplier vector, $\beta_R = \tilde{\beta} + (X'\Psi^{-1}X)^{-1}R'[R(X'\Psi^{-1}X)^{-1}R']^{-1}(\mathbf{r} - R\tilde{\beta})$ is the restricted ML estimator for β when Ψ is known, and $\tilde{\mathbf{e}} = \mathbf{y} - X\tilde{\beta}$ and $\hat{\mathbf{e}}^* = \mathbf{y} - X\beta_R$ are the residual vectors corresponding to $\tilde{\beta}$ and β_R, respectively. Because the three statistics are identical they obviously have the same (finite sample) $\chi^2_{(J)}$ distribution where J is the number of rows in R.

When Ψ and σ^2 are unknown, one way of approaching the problem is to find estimators for Ψ and σ^2 and to substitute these for the corresponding true parameters in (5.7.13). With an appropriate choice of estimators the resulting statistic will have an asymptotic $\chi^2_{(J)}$ distribution and could therefore provide the basis for an approximate test. Two possible estimators for Ψ and σ^2 that could be used are the unrestricted ML estimators, and the ML estimators obtained assuming the restriction H_0: $R\beta = \mathbf{r}$ is correct. If we let $(\tilde{\Psi}_0,\tilde{\sigma}_0^2)$ be the ML estimator for (Ψ,σ^2) under H_0 and $(\tilde{\Psi}_1,\tilde{\sigma}_1^2)$ be the ML estimator under the alternative hypothesis, then it can be shown that, when (Ψ,σ^2) is unknown, the Wald statistic λ_W is obtained by substituting $(\tilde{\Psi}_1,\tilde{\sigma}_1^2)$ for (Ψ,σ^2) in (5.7.13), while the Lagrange multiplier statistic λ_{LM} is obtained by substituting $(\tilde{\Psi}_0,\tilde{\sigma}_0^2)$ for (Ψ,σ^2) in (5.7.13). Since (5.7.13) is also the likelihood ratio test for known (Ψ,σ^2), λ_W can be viewed as the LR test conditional on $(\Psi = \tilde{\Psi}_1,\sigma^2 = \tilde{\sigma}_1^2)$ and λ_{LM} can be viewed as the LR test conditional on $(\Psi = \tilde{\Psi}_0,\sigma^2 = \tilde{\sigma}_0^2)$.

We can write λ_W and λ_{LM} in terms of restricted and unrestricted residual sums of squares as

$$\lambda_W = \frac{\hat{\mathbf{e}}_1^{*\prime}\tilde{\Psi}_1^{-1}\hat{\mathbf{e}}_1^* - \tilde{\mathbf{e}}_1'\tilde{\Psi}_1^{-1}\tilde{\mathbf{e}}_1}{\tilde{\mathbf{e}}_1'\tilde{\Psi}_1^{-1}\tilde{\mathbf{e}}_1/T} \tag{5.7.14}$$

and

$$\lambda_{LM} = \frac{\hat{\mathbf{e}}_0^{*\prime}\tilde{\Psi}_0^{-1}\hat{\mathbf{e}}_0^* - \tilde{\mathbf{e}}_0'\tilde{\Psi}_0^{-1}\tilde{\mathbf{e}}_0}{\hat{\mathbf{e}}_0^{*\prime}\tilde{\Psi}_0^{-1}\hat{\mathbf{e}}_0^*/T} \tag{5.7.15}$$

where $\hat{\mathbf{e}}_0^*$ and $\tilde{\mathbf{e}}_0$ are the residuals from the restricted and unrestricted models, respectively, conditional on $\Psi = \tilde{\Psi}_0$; and $\hat{\mathbf{e}}_1^*$ and $\tilde{\mathbf{e}}_1$ are the residuals from the restricted and unrestricted models, respectively, conditional on $\Psi = \tilde{\Psi}_1$. Whereas λ_W uses only $\tilde{\Psi}_1$ and λ_{LM} uses only $\tilde{\Psi}_0$, the LR test statistic for unknown (Ψ, σ^2) uses both $\tilde{\Psi}_1$ and $\tilde{\Psi}_0$. It can be written as

$$\lambda_{LR} = T[\ln(\hat{\mathbf{e}}_0^{*\prime}\tilde{\Psi}_0^{-1}\hat{\mathbf{e}}_0^*|\tilde{\Psi}_0|^{1/T}) - \ln(\tilde{\mathbf{e}}_1^{\prime}\tilde{\Psi}_1^{-1}\tilde{\mathbf{e}}_1|\tilde{\Psi}_1|^{1/T})] \tag{5.7.16}$$

Thus, λ_{LR} can also be written in terms of residual sums of squares, but in this case the determinants $|\tilde{\Psi}_0|$ and $|\tilde{\Psi}_1|$ also appear. In λ_W and λ_{LM} the equivalent determinants cancel out because each statistic depends only on one covariance matrix estimator. Like λ_W and λ_{LM}, λ_{LR} has an asymptotic $\chi^2_{(J)}$ distribution.

To put λ_{LR} in a form more comparable to λ_W and λ_{LM} we can transform it as

$$T(e^{\lambda_{LR}} - 1) = \frac{\hat{\mathbf{e}}_0^{*\prime}\tilde{\Psi}_0^{-1}\hat{\mathbf{e}}_0^*|\tilde{\Psi}_0|^{1/T} - \tilde{\mathbf{e}}_1^{\prime}\tilde{\Psi}_1^{-1}\tilde{\mathbf{e}}_1|\tilde{\Psi}_1|^{1/T}}{\tilde{\mathbf{e}}_1^{\prime}\tilde{\Psi}_1^{-1}\tilde{\mathbf{e}}_1|\tilde{\Psi}_1|^{1/T}/T} \tag{5.7.17}$$

Then, using results on inequalities related to logarithms (Savin, 1976; Berndt and Savin, 1977), or from the properties of conditional and unconditional maximized likelihood functions (Breusch, 1979), it is possible to show that

$$\lambda_W \geq \lambda_{LR} \geq \lambda_{LM} \tag{5.7.18}$$

These inequalities imply that, although the three tests are asymptotically equivalent, their finite sample distributions will not be the same. In particular, rejection of H_0 can be favored by selecting λ_W a priori, while acceptance of H_0 can be favored by selecting λ_{LM} a priori. Furthermore, the finite sample sizes of the tests will differ. If, for example, a (large sample) 5% significance level is employed and the LR test correctly states the probability of a Type 1 error as .05, then the probability of a Type 1 error will be less than .05 for the LM test, and greater than .05 for the Wald test. This source of conflict has led to research into "correcting" the tests so that their sizes are comparable in finite samples. Evans and Savin (1982) consider the case where $\Psi = I$, and Rothenberg (1984) investigates the more general case where Ψ is unknown. Using Edgeworth-type expansions to derive approximate power functions for his size-corrected tests, Rothenberg shows that when $J = 1$ the tests will have approximately the same power, but for $J > 1$ the power functions cross, and so there is no obvious reason for preferring one test over another.

One question we have not yet considered is the relationship between the three statistics and the traditional F statistic used to test the null hypothesis H_0: $R\boldsymbol{\beta} = \mathbf{r}$ when Ψ is known but σ^2 is unknown. This statistic is given by

$$\lambda_F = \frac{(\hat{\mathbf{e}}^{*\prime}\Psi^{-1}\hat{\mathbf{e}}^* - \tilde{\mathbf{e}}^{\prime}\Psi^{-1}\tilde{\mathbf{e}})/J}{\tilde{\mathbf{e}}^{\prime}\Psi^{-1}\tilde{\mathbf{e}}/(T - K)} \tag{5.7.19}$$

Under H_0, λ_F has an exact $F_{(J,T-K)}$ distribution. When Ψ is unknown we can, as described above, use λ_{LM}, λ_W, or λ_{LR}, each of which has an asymptotic $\chi^2_{(J)}$ distribution. However, instead of using one of these statistics and a critical value from the $\chi^2_{(J)}$ distribution, a common applied procedure is to use either (λ_{LM}/J) or (λ_W/J) in conjunction with a critical value from the $F_{(J,T-K)}$ distribution. This procedure is a common one because, when $\mathbf{\Psi}$ is unknown, both (λ_{LM}/J) and (λ_W/J) can be viewed as "estimates" of λ_F. Also, it can be argued that such a procedure is justified because $F_{(J,T-K)} \xrightarrow{d} \chi^2_{(J)}/J$. See, for example, Theil (1971, p. 402) and Section 5.3.

Further relevant work on the Wald, LR, and LM tests is that of Breusch (1980), Buse (1982), Gourieroux, Holly, and Monfort (1982), and Ullah and Zinde-Walsh (1982). Breusch shows that the exact distributions of λ_W, λ_{LR}, and λ_{LM} depend on $(\boldsymbol{\beta},\sigma^2)$ only through $(R\boldsymbol{\beta} - \mathbf{r})/\sigma$ and hence do not depend on $(\boldsymbol{\beta},\sigma^2)$ when the hypothesis is correct. This result is likely to be useful information for the design of Monte Carlo experiments which investigate the finite sample power of the tests. As a teaching device, Buse gives a diagrammatic explanation of the relationship between the three tests. Gourieroux et al. show how the tests can be modified when the alternative hypothesis is $R\boldsymbol{\beta} \geq \mathbf{r}$ rather than $R\boldsymbol{\beta} = \mathbf{r}$; and Ullah and Zinde-Walsh examine the robustness of the statistics when the disturbances follow a multivariate t distribution.

5.8 SUMMARY

In this section we give a convenient summary of a number of asymptotic theory concepts that have been used in this chapter or that will be used in later chapters of the book. A more complete summary of useful results can be found in Serfling (1980).

5.8.1. A sequence $\{a_T\}$ is at most of order T^k, and is written as $a_T = O(T^k)$ if there exists a real number N such that $T^{-k}|a_T| \leq N$ for all T.

5.8.2. A sequence $\{a_T\}$ is of smaller order than T^k, and is written as $a_T = o(T^k)$ if $\lim T^{-k}a_T = 0$.

5.8.3. If $a_T = O(T^k)$ and $b_T = O(T^j)$ then (1) $a_Tb_T = O(T^{k+j})$, (2) $|a_T|^s = O(T^{ks})$ for $s > 0$, and (3) $a_T + b_T = O(\max\{T^k,T^j\})$.

5.8.4. The results in 5.8.3. also hold if O is replaced by o.

5.8.5. If $a_T = O(T^k)$ and $b_T = o(T^j)$, then $a_Tb_T = o(T^{k+j})$.

5.8.6. The sequence of random variables $\{z_T\}$ converges in probability to the random variable z if, for all $\varepsilon > 0$, $\lim P[|z_T - z| < \varepsilon] = 1$. This is also written as $\text{plim } z_T = z$ or $z_T \xrightarrow{p} z$.

5.8.7. The sequence of random variables $\{z_T\}$ converges almost surely to the random variable z if $P[\lim|z_T - z| < \varepsilon] = 1$ and this result is written as $z_T \xrightarrow{\text{a.s.}} z$.

5.8.8. The sequence of random variables $\{z_T\}$ converges in quadratic mean (or mean square error) to the random variable z if $\lim E[(z_T - z)^2] = 0$, and this result is written as $z_T \xrightarrow{\text{q.m.}} z$.

5.8.9. The sequence of random variables $\{z_T\}$ with corresponding sequence of distribution functions $\{F_T(z)\}$ converges in distribution to the random variable z with distribution function $F(z)$ if, and only if, at all continuity points of F, and for every $\varepsilon > 0$, there exists a T_0 such that

$$|F_T(z) - F(z)| < \varepsilon \quad \text{for} \quad T > T_0.$$

This result is written as $z_T \xrightarrow{d} z$.

5.8.10. Definitions 5.8.6 through 5.8.9 can also be formulated for random vectors and matrices.

5.8.11. The following relationships hold between the different types of convergence.

$$z_T \xrightarrow{\text{a.s.}} z \Rightarrow z_T \xrightarrow{p} z \Rightarrow z_T \xrightarrow{d} z$$

$$z_T \xrightarrow{\text{q.m.}} z \Rightarrow z_T \xrightarrow{p} z \Rightarrow z_T \xrightarrow{d} z$$

5.8.12. If θ is a constant then

$$z_T \xrightarrow{p} \theta \Leftrightarrow z_T \xrightarrow{d} \theta$$

5.8.13. Slutsky's theorem: $\text{plim}[\mathbf{g}(\mathbf{z}_T)] = \mathbf{g}[\text{plim}(\mathbf{z}_T)]$ where $\mathbf{g}$ is a continuous function.

5.8.14. The sequence of random variables $\{z_T\}$ is at most of order in probability T^k, and is written as $z_T = O_p(T^k)$, if, for every $\varepsilon > 0$, there exists a real number N such that $P[T^{-k}|z_T| \geq N] \leq \varepsilon$ for all T.

5.8.15. The sequence of random variables $\{z_T\}$ is of smaller order in probability than T^k, and is written as $z_T = o_p(T^k)$, if $\text{plim } T^{-k}z_T = 0$.

5.8.16. The algebra for O_p and o_p is the same as that given in 5.8.3 through 5.8.5.

5.8.17. If $\text{plim } z_T = \theta$, then z_T is called a consistent estimator for θ.

5.8.18. Khinchine's theorem. If $z_1, z_2, \ldots, z_T$ are i.i.d. random variables with finite mean μ, then $\text{plim } T^{-1}\Sigma_{t=1}^{T} z_t = \mu$.

5.8.19. If z_T is an estimator for θ with $\lim(E[z_T] - \theta) = 0$ and $\lim \text{var}(z_T) = 0$, then $\text{plim } z_T = \theta$.

5.8.20. If $z_T \xrightarrow{d} z$, and if $E[z_T^m]$, $E[z^m]$ and $\lim E[z_T^m]$ are all finite, then $\lim E[z_T^n] = E[z^n]$ for all $n < m$.

5.8.21. If $\phi_T(u)$ is the characteristic function of z_T and $\phi(u)$ is the characteristic function of z, then

$$z_t \xrightarrow{d} z \Leftrightarrow \lim \phi_T(u) = \phi(u)$$

5.8.22. If $\mathbf{z}_1, \mathbf{z}_2, \ldots, \mathbf{z}_T$ are i.i.d. random vectors with mean $\boldsymbol{\mu}$ and covariance matrix $\boldsymbol{\Sigma}_\mathbf{z}$ then

$$T^{-1/2} \sum_{t=1}^{T} (\mathbf{z}_t - \boldsymbol{\mu}) \xrightarrow{d} N(\mathbf{0}, \boldsymbol{\Sigma}_\mathbf{z}).$$

5.8.23. If $\mathbf{z}_1, \mathbf{z}_2, \ldots, \mathbf{z}_T$ are independently distributed random vectors with mean $\boldsymbol{\mu}$ and covariance matrices $V_1, V_2, \ldots, V_T$, and the third moments of the $\mathbf{z}_T$ exist, then

$$T^{-1/2} \sum_{t=1}^{T} (\mathbf{z}_t - \boldsymbol{\mu}) \xrightarrow{d} N(\mathbf{0}, \boldsymbol{\Sigma})$$

where $\boldsymbol{\Sigma} = \lim T^{-1}\Sigma_{t=1}^{T} V_t$.

5.8.24. Mann and Wald theorem. If, in the general linear model $\mathbf{y} = X\boldsymbol{\beta} + \mathbf{e}$, the (possibly) stochastic regressor matrix X and the disturbance vector $\mathbf{e}$ satisfy the conditions (1) $\text{plim}(X'X/T) = Q$ is finite and nonsingular; (2) $E[\mathbf{e}] = \mathbf{0}$, $E[\mathbf{ee}'] = \sigma^2 I$, and $\mathbf{e}$ has finite moments of every order; and (3) $E[\mathbf{x}_t e_t] = \mathbf{0}$ for $t = 1, 2, \ldots, T$, then $\text{plim}\; T^{-1}X'\mathbf{e} = \mathbf{0}$ and $T^{-1/2}X'\mathbf{e} \xrightarrow{d} N(\mathbf{0}, \sigma^2 Q)$.

5.8.25. If $\mathbf{z}_T \xrightarrow{d} \mathbf{z}$ and $A_T \xrightarrow{p} C$ where A_T is a random matrix and C a matrix of constants, then $A_T\mathbf{z}_T \xrightarrow{d} C\mathbf{z}$.

5.8.26. If $\mathbf{z}_T \xrightarrow{d} \mathbf{z}$, then $\mathbf{g}(\mathbf{z}_T) \xrightarrow{d} \mathbf{g}(\mathbf{z})$ where $\mathbf{g}$ is a continuous function.

5.8.27. Let $\{z_T\}$ and $\{x_T\}$ be sequences of random variables and c be a constant. Then

1. $|z_T - x_T| \xrightarrow{p} 0$ and $x_T \xrightarrow{d} x \Rightarrow z_T \xrightarrow{d} x$

2. $z_T \xrightarrow{d} z$ and $x_T \xrightarrow{p} c \Rightarrow z_T \pm x_T \xrightarrow{d} z \pm c$

$$z_T x_T \xrightarrow{d} cz \text{ if } c \neq 0$$

$$z_T x_T \xrightarrow{p} 0 \text{ if } c = 0$$

$$(z_T/x_T) \xrightarrow{d} (z/c) \text{ if } c \neq 0$$

5.8.28. If $z_T = O_p(T^{-\delta})$ with $\delta > 0$, then $z_T = o_p(1)$.

5.8.29. If $z_T \xrightarrow{d} z$ then $z_T = O_p(1)$.

5.8.30. If $z_T \xrightarrow{d} z$ then $z_T + o_p(1) \xrightarrow{d} z$.

5.8.31. If $\{z_T\}$ is such that $E[(z_T - E[z_T])^2] = O(T^k)$ and $E[z_T] = O(T^{k/2})$ then $z_T = O_p(T^{k/2})$.

5.8.32. If $\{z_T\}$ is a sequence of random variables such that

$$z_T = \theta + O_p(T^{-\delta}), \qquad \delta > 0$$

and $g(z)$ is a function with s continuous derivatives at $z = \theta$ then

$$g(z_T) = g(\theta) + g^{(1)}(\theta)(z_T - \theta) + \cdots + \frac{1}{(s-1)!} g^{(s-1)}(\theta)(z_T - \theta)^{s-1} + O_p(T^{-s\delta}).$$

5.8.33. The result in 5.8.32 holds if O_p is replaced by o_p.

5.8.34. If, in the context of the general linear model $\mathbf{y} = X\boldsymbol{\beta} + \mathbf{e}$, $\sqrt{T}(\mathbf{b} - \boldsymbol{\beta}) \xrightarrow{d} N(\mathbf{0},\sigma^2 Q^{-1})$, and $\mathbf{g}$ is a vector function with at least two continuous derivatives, then

$$\sqrt{T}[\mathbf{g}(\mathbf{b}) - \mathbf{g}(\boldsymbol{\beta})] \xrightarrow{d} N\left[\mathbf{0},\sigma^2 \left(\frac{\partial \mathbf{g}}{\partial \boldsymbol{\beta}'}\right) Q^{-1} \left(\frac{\partial \mathbf{g}'}{\partial \boldsymbol{\beta}}\right)\right].$$

5.9 EXERCISES

Exercise 5.1

Prove that the least squares variance estimator $\hat{\sigma}^2 = (\mathbf{y} - X\boldsymbol{\beta})'(\mathbf{y} - X\boldsymbol{\beta})/(T - K)$ is consistent under the assumptions in Section 5.3.5.

Exercise 5.2

Consider a simple model with one explanatory variable that is a linear trend. That is

$$\mathbf{y} = \mathbf{x}\beta + \mathbf{e}$$

where $\mathbf{x} = (1, 2, \ldots, T)'$.

(a) Prove that the least squares estimator $b = (\mathbf{x}'\mathbf{x})^{-1}\mathbf{x}'\mathbf{y}$ is consistent.

(b) Show that $\mathbf{x}'\mathbf{e} = O_p(T^{3/2})$.

(c) Show that

$$\frac{\mathbf{x}'\mathbf{e}}{T^{3/2}} \xrightarrow{d} N\left(0, \frac{\sigma^2}{3}\right)$$

and that

$$\frac{T^{3/2}(b - \beta)}{\hat{\sigma}\sqrt{3}} \xrightarrow{d} N(0,1)$$

(d) Show that the Grenander conditions hold for this model. (See Section 5.3.5.)

Exercise 5.3

Prove that the estimator $\hat{\sigma}^2 = (\mathbf{y} - X\boldsymbol{\beta}^{IV})'(\mathbf{y} - X\boldsymbol{\beta}^{IV})/T$ is consistent under the assumptions outlined in Section 5.4.3.

Exercise 5.4

Consider the linear model $\mathbf{y} = X\boldsymbol{\beta} + \mathbf{e}$ where $E[\mathbf{ee}'] = \sigma^2\boldsymbol{\Psi}$, and where $\lim T^{-1}X'X = Q$, $\lim T^{-1}X'\boldsymbol{\Psi}X = V_0$ and $\lim T^{-1}X'\boldsymbol{\Psi}^{-1}X = V$ are all finite and nonsingular. Furthermore, assume that the result in Equation 5.5.26 holds. Show that

(a) $\sqrt{T}(\mathbf{b} - \boldsymbol{\beta}) \xrightarrow{d} N(\mathbf{0},\sigma^2 Q^{-1}V_0 Q^{-1})$
(b) The EGLS estimator $\hat{\hat{\boldsymbol{\beta}}}$ is asymptotically more efficient than $\mathbf{b}$ in the sense that the covariance matrix of the limiting distribution of $\sqrt{T}(\mathbf{b} - \boldsymbol{\beta})$ exceeds that of the limiting distribution of $\sqrt{T}(\hat{\hat{\boldsymbol{\beta}}} - \boldsymbol{\beta})$ by a positive semidefinite matrix. (*Hint*. Consider the class of all linear consistent estimators for $\boldsymbol{\beta}$ and show that $\hat{\boldsymbol{\beta}}$ is "best" from within this class. Note that $\hat{\hat{\boldsymbol{\beta}}}$ has the same limiting distribution as $\hat{\boldsymbol{\beta}}$.)

Exercise 5.5
Given the conditions outlined in Section 5.5.3a, show that the estimator $\hat{\hat{\sigma}}^2 = (\mathbf{y} - X\hat{\hat{\boldsymbol{\beta}}})'\hat{\Psi}^{-1}(\mathbf{y} - X\hat{\hat{\boldsymbol{\beta}}})/(T - K)$ is a consistent estimator for σ^2.

Exercise 5.6
Derive the information matrix given in Equation 5.6.18.

Exercise 5.7
Prove the equivalence of Equations 5.7.13a, 5.7.13b, and 5.7.13c.

Exercise 5.8
Use data of your own choice to find LS estimates for β_1, β_2, and β_3 for the partial adjustment model given in Section 5.3.4. Find the asymptotic covariance matrix for $(\alpha_0,\alpha_1,\gamma)'$ and construct asymptotic confidence intervals for these parameters.

Exercise 5.9
For a linear model and data of your own choice, split the sample into two groups and consider the corresponding model

$$\begin{pmatrix} \mathbf{y}_1 \\ \mathbf{y}_2 \end{pmatrix} = \begin{pmatrix} X_1 & 0 \\ 0 & X_2 \end{pmatrix} \begin{pmatrix} \boldsymbol{\beta}_1 \\ \boldsymbol{\beta}_2 \end{pmatrix} + \begin{pmatrix} \mathbf{e}_1 \\ \mathbf{e}_2 \end{pmatrix}$$

where the covariance matrix for $(\mathbf{e}_1',\mathbf{e}_2')'$ is assumed to be

$$\begin{pmatrix} \sigma_1^2 I & 0 \\ 0 & \sigma_2^2 I \end{pmatrix}$$

and $\sigma_1^2 \neq \sigma_2^2$.

(a) Test the hypothesis $\boldsymbol{\beta}_1 = \boldsymbol{\beta}_2$ using the Wald test and the LM test.
(b) Use the likelihood ratio test to test the joint hypothesis $\boldsymbol{\beta}_1 = \boldsymbol{\beta}_2$ and $\sigma_1^2 = \sigma_2^2$.

5.10 REFERENCES

Abrahamse, A. P. J. and J. Koerts (1971) "New Estimators of Disturbances in Regression Analysis," *Journal of the American Statistical Association*, 66, 71–74.

Abrahamse, A. P. J. and A. S. Louter (1971) "On a New Test for Autocorrelation in Least Squares Regression," *Biometrika,* 58, 53–60.

Anderson, T. W. (1971) *The Statistical Analysis of Time Series,* Wiley, New York.

Arnold, S. F. (1980) "Asymptotic Validity of F Tests for the Ordinary Linear Model and the Multiple Correlation Model," *Journal of the American Statistical Association,* 75, 890–894.

Balestra, P. (1970) "On the Efficiency of Ordinary Least Squares in Regression Models," *Journal of the American Statistical Association,* 65, 1330–1337.

Berndt, E. K., B. H. Hall, and J. A. Hausman (1974) "Estimation and Inference in Non-linear Structural Models," *Annals of Economic and Social Measurement,* 3, 653–665.

Berndt, E. R., and N. E. Savin (1977) "Conflict Among Criteria for Testing Hypotheses in the Multivariate Regression Model," *Econometrica,* 45, 1263–1278.

Bloomfield, P. and G. S. Watson (1975) "The Inefficiency of Least Squares," *Biometrika,* 62, 121–128.

Breusch, T. S. (1979) "Conflict Among Criteria for Testing Hypotheses: Extension and Comment," *Econometrica,* 47, 203–208.

Breusch, T. S. (1980) "Useful Invariance Results for Generalized Regression Models," *Journal of Econometrics,* 13, 327–340.

Breusch, T. S. and A. R. Pagan (1980) "The Lagrange Multiplier Test and Its Applications to Model Specification in Econometrics," *Review of Economic Studies,* 47, 239–254.

Brown, R. L., J. Durbin, and J. M. Evans (1975) "Techniques for Testing the Constancy of Regression Relationships Over Time," *Journal of the Royal Statistical Society,* Series B, 37, 149–192.

Buse, A. (1982) "The Likelihood Ratio, Wald, and Lagrange Multiplier Tests: An Expository Note," *The American Statistician,* 36, 153–157.

Cox, D. R. and D. V. Hinkley (1974) *Theoretical Statistics,* Chapman and Hall, London.

Crowder, M. J. (1976) "Maximum Likelihood Estimation for Dependent Observations," *Journal of the Royal Statistical Society,* Series B, 38, 45–53.

Dent, W. T. and G. P. H. Styan (1978) "Uncorrelated Residuals from Linear Models," *Journal of Econometrics,* 7, 211–225.

Dhrymes, P. J. (1974) *Econometrics, Statistical Foundations and Applications,* Springer-Verlag, New York.

Dhrymes P. J. (1978) *Introductory Econometrics,* Springer-Verlag, New York.

Domowitz, J. (1982) "The Linear Model with Stochastic Regressors and Heteroscedastic Dependent Errors," Discussion Paper No. 543, Center for Mathematical Studies in Economics and Management Science, Northwestern University, Evanston, Illinois.

Dubbelman, C. (1978) *Disturbances in the Linear Model,* Martinus Nijhoff, The Hague.

Dubbelman, C., A. P. J. Abrahamse, and J. Koerts (1972) "A New Class of

Disturbance Estimators in the General Linear Model,'' *Statistica Neerlandica,* 26, 127–142.

Evans, G. B. A. and N. E. Savin (1982) ''Conflict Among the Criteria Revisited: The W, LR and LM Tests,'' *Econometrica,* 50, 737–748.

Farebrother, R. W. (1977) ''A Note on the BLUS Predictor,'' unpublished, University of Manchester, England.

Farebrother, R. W. (1978) ''An Historical Note on Recursive Residuals,'' unpublished, University of Manchester, England.

Fuller, W. A. (1976) *Introduction to Statistical Time Series,* Wiley, New York.

Fuller, W. A. and G. E. Battese (1973) ''Transformations for Estimation of Linear Models with Nested-error Structure,'' *Journal of the American Statistical Association,* 68, 626–632.

Gourieroux, C., A. Holly, and A. Monfort (1982) ''Likelihood Ratio Test, Wald Test, and Kuhn-Tucker Test in Linear Models with Inequality Constraints on the Regression Parameters,'' *Econometrica,* 50, 63–80.

Greenberg, E. and C. E. Webster (1983) *Advanced Econometrics: A Bridge to the Literature,* Wiley, New York.

Grossman, S. I. and G. P. H. Styan (1972) ''Optimality Properties of Theil's BLUS Residuals,'' *Journal of the American Statistical Association,* 67, 672–673.

Harvey, A. C. (1981) *The Econometric Analysis of Time Series,* Halsted Press, New York.

Judge, G. G., R. C. Hill, W. E. Griffiths, H. Lütkepohl, and T. C. Lee (1982) *Introduction to the Theory and Practice of Econometrics,* Wiley, New York.

Kakwani, N. C. (1967) ''The Unbiasedness of Zellner's Seemingly Unrelated Regression Equations Estimators,'' *Journal of the American Statistical Association,* 62, 141–142.

Knott, M. (1975) ''On the Minimum Efficiency of Least Squares,'' *Biometrika,* 62, 129–132.

Lukacs, E. (1968) *Stochastic Convergence,* D. C. Heath, Lexington, Mass.

McElroy, F. W. (1967) ''A Necessary and Sufficient Condition That Ordinary Least-Squares Estimators Be Best Linear Unbiased,'' *Journal of the American Statistical Association,* 62, 1302–1304.

Magnus, J. (1978) ''Maximum Likelihood Estimation of the GLS Model with Unknown Parameters in the Disturbance Covariance Matrix,'' *Journal of Econometrics,* 7, 281–312.

Mann, H. B. and A. Wald (1943) ''On the Statistical Treatment of Linear Stochastic Difference Equations,'' *Econometrica,* 11, 173–220.

Mathew, T. (1983) ''Linear Estimation with an Incorrect Dispersion Matrix in Linear Models with a Common Linear Part'', *Journal of the American Statistical Association,* 78, 468–471.

Oberhofer, W. and J. Kmenta (1974) ''A General Procedure for Obtaining Maximum Likelihood Estimates in Generalized Regression Models,'' *Econometrica,* 42, 579–590.

Pagan, A. (1979) ''Some Identification and Estimation Results for Regression

Models with Stochastically Varying Coefficients,'' *Journal of Econometrics,* 13, 341–363.

Phillips, G. D. A. and A. C. Harvey (1974) ''A Simple Test for Serial Correlation in Regression Analysis,'' *Journal of the American Statistical Association,* 69, 935–939.

Phillips, P. C. B. (1980) ''The Exact Distribution of Instrumental Variable Estimators in an Equation Containing n+1 Endogenous Variables,'' *Econometrica,* 48, 861–878.

Phillips, P. C. B. (1982) ''Best Uniform and Modified Padé Approximants to Probability Densities in Econometrics'', in W. Hildenbrand, ed., *Advances in Econometrics,* New York: Cambridge University Press, 123–168.

Phillips, P. C. B. (1983) ''ERA's: A New Approach to Small Sample Theory'', *Econometrica,* 51, 1505–1526.

Pollock, D. S. G. (1979) *The Algebra of Econometrics,* Wiley, New York.

Rao, C. R. (1965) *Linear Statistical Inference and Its Applications,* Wiley, New York.

Rothenberg, T. J. (1984) ''Hypothesis Testing in Linear Models When the Error Covariance Matrix Is Nonscalar,'' *Econometrica,* 52, forthcoming.

Sargan, J. D. (1976) ''Econometric Estimators and the Edgeworth Approximation,'' *Econometrica,* 44, 421–448.

Savin, N. E. (1976) ''Conflict Among Testing Procedures in a Linear Regression Model with Autoregressive Disturbances,'' *Econometrica,* 44, 1303–1315.

Schmidt, P. (1976) *Econometrics,* Marcel Dekker, New York.

Serfling, R. J. (1980) *Approximation Theorems for Mathematical Statistics,* Wiley, New York.

Taylor, W. E. (1983) ''On the Relevance of Finite Sample Distribution Theory'', *Econometric Reviews,* 2, 1–84.

Theil, H. (1971) *Principles of Econometrics,* Wiley, New York.

Ullah, A. and V. Zinde-Walsh (1982) ''On the Robustness of LM, LR and W Tests in Regression Models,'' Working Paper, Department of Economics, University of Western Ontario.

Watson, G. S. (1955) ''Serial Correlation in Regression Analysis I,'' *Biometrika,* 42, 327–341.

Zyskind, G. (1967) ''On Canonical Forms, Non-negative Covariance Matrices and Best and Simple Least Squares Linear Estimators in Linear Models,'' *The Annals of Mathematical Statistics,* 38, 1092–1109.

Chapter 6

Nonlinear Statistical Models

6.1 INTRODUCTION

The usual approach to parameter estimation in linear econometric models is to specify an *objective function,* such as the sum of squares function or the maximum likelihood function, which is to be minimized or maximized with respect to the unknown parameters. For a given sample of data, the parameter vector leading to the optimal value of the objective function is then used as the estimate. By using the first-order conditions for an optimum of the objective function, the optimization problem for the traditional linear statistical model can, for either of the above criteria, be reduced to the problem of solving a system of linear equations. This is computationally convenient and moreover, as discussed in Chapters 2 and 5, leads to certain optimal properties of the resulting estimators. Apart from these advantages the following are reasons for the popularity of linear models in econometrics.

1. In many economic situations, linearity appears to be a reasonable approximation to reality.
2. Many nonlinear models can be transformed into linear models.

Unfortunately, for many applied problems, these conditions are not always fulfilled and nonlinear specifications cannot be avoided. An example is the constant elasticity of substitution (CES) production function of the form

$$\ln Q_t = \beta_0 + \beta_1 \ln[\beta_2 L_t^{\beta_3} + (1 - \beta_2)K_t^{\beta_3}] + e_t \qquad (6.1.1)$$

with $0 < \beta_2 < 1$, $0 \neq \beta_3 < 1$, $\beta_1 < 0$ or >1. In this model Q_t is the output, L_t the labor input, K_t the capital input, and e_t a random error. For the interpretation of the parameters see Chiang (1974, pp. 417–419).

The CES production function model is of the general form

$$y_t = f(\mathbf{x}_t, \boldsymbol{\beta}) + e_t, \qquad t = 1, 2, \ldots, T \qquad (6.1.2)$$

where y_t is an endogenous variable, $\mathbf{x}_t$ is an $(N \times 1)$ vector of explanatory variables, and f is a function that is known up to a K vector of parameters $\boldsymbol{\beta}$, for a given $\mathbf{x}_t$. Unless otherwise mentioned we will assume throughout this chapter that the errors e_t are independently, identically distributed (i.i.d.). To simplify the notation we will often write $f_t(\boldsymbol{\beta})$ for $f(\mathbf{x}_t,\boldsymbol{\beta})$ and as a more compact notation for (6.1.2) we use

$$\mathbf{y} = \mathbf{f}(X,\boldsymbol{\beta}) + \mathbf{e} \tag{6.1.3}$$

or

$$\mathbf{y} = \mathbf{f}(\boldsymbol{\beta}) + \mathbf{e} \tag{6.1.4}$$

where $\mathbf{y} = (y_1, y_2, \ldots, y_T)'$, $X' = (\mathbf{x}_1, \mathbf{x}_2, \ldots, \mathbf{x}_T)$, $\mathbf{e} = (e_1, e_2, \ldots, e_T)'$ and $\mathbf{f}(X,\boldsymbol{\beta}) = \mathbf{f}(\boldsymbol{\beta}) = [f_1(\boldsymbol{\beta}), \ldots, f_T(\boldsymbol{\beta})]'$. It will be assumed in the following that all required derivatives of $\mathbf{f}(\cdot)$ exist and are continuous.

To estimate the unknown parameters, an objective function is specified and an optimal value of the unknown coefficient vector is computed as the estimate. Least squares (LS) and maximum likelihood (ML) estimation are considered in Section 6.2. In general, a system of *nonlinear normal equations* has to be solved to find the solution of the optimization problem, and a closed form expression of the resulting estimator can usually not be given. A brief account of the computational aspects of this problem is given in Section 6.3. The use of nonsample information in the form of equality or inequality constraints is discussed in Section 6.4, and confidence regions and hypothesis testing are considered in Sections 6.5 and 6.6, respectively. A summary and some concluding remarks are given in Section 6.7. The topics of this chapter are depicted in a flow diagram in Table 6.1. Throughout we will give references for extensions of the material discussed. General reference sources and discussions of nonlinear regression and related topics are, for instance, Amemiya (1983), Bunke et al. (1977), Bard (1974), and Goldfeld and Quandt (1972). For an introductory treatment see Judge et al. (1982, Chapter 24).

6.2 ESTIMATION

Suppose the underlying model is of the form (6.1.4). In the following, the true parameter vector will be denoted by $\boldsymbol{\beta}^*$ whereas $\boldsymbol{\beta}$ is just some vector in the parameter space. Similarly, the true variance of the errors in (6.1.4) will be denoted by $\overset{*}{\sigma}{}^2$. Thus, $\mathbf{e} \sim (\mathbf{0},\overset{*}{\sigma}{}^2 I)$. Two estimation methods, least squares (LS) and maximum likelihood (ML), will be considered subsequently. Under our assumptions the ML estimator will be identical to the LS estimator.

6.2.1 Least Squares Estimation

As in the linear model case, the LS principle is intuitively appealing for estimating the parameters of the nonlinear statistical model (6.1.4). The nonlinear LS estimator $\mathbf{b}$ is chosen to minimize

$$S(\boldsymbol{\beta}) = [\mathbf{y} - \mathbf{f}(\boldsymbol{\beta})]'[\mathbf{y} - \mathbf{f}(\boldsymbol{\beta})] \tag{6.2.1}$$

TABLE 6.1 ***NONLINEAR STATISTICAL MODEL ESTIMATION AND INFERENCE***

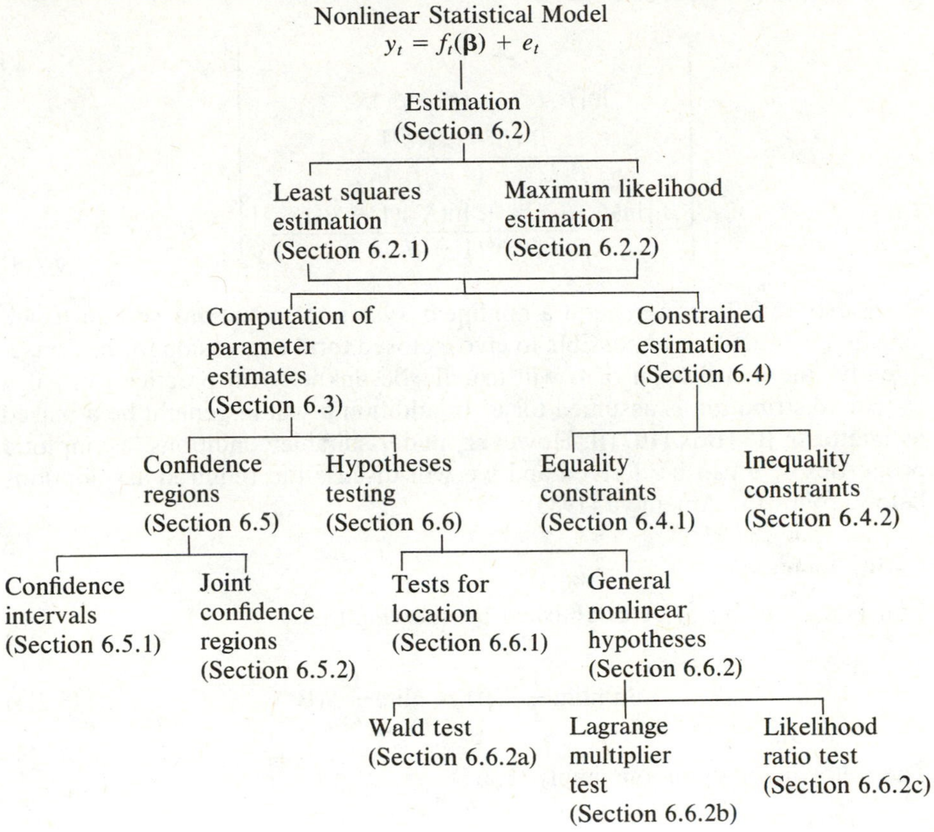

and the corresponding normal equations are

$$\left.\frac{\partial S}{\partial \boldsymbol{\beta}}\right|_{\mathbf{b}} = -2Z(\mathbf{b})'[\mathbf{y} - \mathbf{f}(\mathbf{b})] = \mathbf{0} \tag{6.2.2}$$

where $\partial S/\partial \boldsymbol{\beta} = [\partial S/\partial \beta_1, \ldots, \partial S/\partial \beta_K]'$ and

$$Z(\boldsymbol{\beta}) = \left.\frac{\partial \mathbf{f}}{\partial \boldsymbol{\beta}'}\right|_{\boldsymbol{\beta}} = \begin{bmatrix} \left.\frac{\partial f_1}{\partial \beta_1}\right|_{\boldsymbol{\beta}} & \cdots & \left.\frac{\partial f_1}{\partial \beta_K}\right|_{\boldsymbol{\beta}} \\ \vdots & \ddots & \vdots \\ \left.\frac{\partial f_T}{\partial \beta_1}\right|_{\boldsymbol{\beta}} & \cdots & \left.\frac{\partial f_T}{\partial \beta_K}\right|_{\boldsymbol{\beta}} \end{bmatrix} \tag{6.2.3}$$

is the $(T \times K)$ matrix of first derivatives of $\mathbf{f}$ with respect to the parameters. For instance, for the CES production function model (6.1.1) the tth row of $Z(\boldsymbol{\beta})$ is given by the (1×4) vector

$$\begin{bmatrix} 1 \\ \ln[\beta_2 L_t^{\beta_3} + (1-\beta_2)K_t^{\beta_3}] \\ \dfrac{\beta_1(L_t^{\beta_3} - K_t^{\beta_3}]}{\beta_2 L_t^{\beta_3} + (1-\beta_2)K_t^{\beta_3}} \\ \dfrac{\beta_1[\ln(L_t)\beta_2 L_t^{\beta_3} + \ln(K_t)(1-\beta_2)K_t^{\beta_3}]}{\beta_2 L_t^{\beta_3} + (1-\beta_2)K_t^{\beta_3}} \end{bmatrix} \tag{6.2.4}$$

Obviously (6.2.2) is in general a nonlinear system of equations so that it will usually be difficult or impossible to give a closed form expression for $\mathbf{b}$. Consequently, the distribution of $\mathbf{b}$ will usually be unknown in practice even if a specific distribution is assumed for $\mathbf{e}$. In addition $\mathbf{b}$ will in general be a biased estimator of $\boldsymbol{\beta}^*$ [Box (1971)]. However, under suitable conditions, asymptotic properties of $\mathbf{b}$ can be derived and we will discuss the required assumptions below, following Amemiya (1983).

6.2.1a Consistency

Consistency of $\mathbf{b}$ can be established by showing that

$$\min_{\boldsymbol{\beta}} \operatorname{plim} \frac{1}{T} S(\boldsymbol{\beta}) = \operatorname{plim} \frac{1}{T} S(\boldsymbol{\beta}^*) \tag{6.2.5}$$

The following assumptions imply (6.2.5).

1. The parameter space $\mathcal{B}$ is compact.
2. $(1/T)\mathbf{f}(\boldsymbol{\beta}_1)'\mathbf{f}(\boldsymbol{\beta}_2)$ converges uniformly in $\boldsymbol{\beta}_1, \boldsymbol{\beta}_2 \in \mathcal{B}$.
3. $\lim (1/T)[\mathbf{f}(\boldsymbol{\beta}^*) - \mathbf{f}(\boldsymbol{\beta})]'[\mathbf{f}(\boldsymbol{\beta}^*) - \mathbf{f}(\boldsymbol{\beta})]$ exists and is nonzero if $\boldsymbol{\beta} \neq \boldsymbol{\beta}^*$.

For a linear model with $\mathbf{f}(\boldsymbol{\beta}) = X\boldsymbol{\beta}$ the latter assumption becomes

$$\lim \frac{1}{T}(\boldsymbol{\beta}^* - \boldsymbol{\beta})'X'X(\boldsymbol{\beta}^* - \boldsymbol{\beta})$$

exists and is nonzero for $\boldsymbol{\beta} \neq \boldsymbol{\beta}^*$. In other words, $\lim X'X/T$ exists and is nonsingular, which is one of the conditions for the consistency of the linear LS estimator given in Chapter 5.

Amemiya partitions the sum of squares function as

$$\frac{1}{T} S(\boldsymbol{\beta}) = \frac{1}{T}\mathbf{e}'\mathbf{e} + \frac{2}{T}[\mathbf{f}(\boldsymbol{\beta}^*) - \mathbf{f}(\boldsymbol{\beta})]'\mathbf{e} + \frac{1}{T}[\mathbf{f}(\boldsymbol{\beta}^*) - \mathbf{f}(\boldsymbol{\beta})]'[\mathbf{f}(\boldsymbol{\beta}^*) - \mathbf{f}(\boldsymbol{\beta})] \tag{6.2.6}$$

where $\mathbf{e} = \mathbf{y} - \mathbf{f}(\boldsymbol{\beta}^*)$. The first term on the right-hand side is, of course, independent of the nonlinear specification (6.1.4) so that

$$\text{plim}\, \frac{1}{T}\mathbf{e}'\mathbf{e} = \overset{*}{\sigma}{}^2 \tag{6.2.7}$$

(see Section 5.1.5). Using Chebyshev's inequality

$$P\left\{\frac{1}{T}[\mathbf{f}(\boldsymbol{\beta}^*) - \mathbf{f}(\boldsymbol{\beta})]'\mathbf{e} > \varepsilon^2\right\} < \frac{\overset{*}{\sigma}{}^2}{\varepsilon^2 T^2}[\mathbf{f}(\boldsymbol{\beta}^*) - \mathbf{f}(\boldsymbol{\beta})]'[\mathbf{f}(\boldsymbol{\beta}^*) - \mathbf{f}(\boldsymbol{\beta})] \tag{6.2.8}$$

it follows that the plim of the second term on the right-hand side of (6.2.6) goes to zero by assumption 2. The third term of (6.2.6) is minimized for $\boldsymbol{\beta} = \boldsymbol{\beta}^*$ by assumption 3 above, thus (6.2.5) holds and we have established the consistency of $\mathbf{b}$. In fact, it is possible to prove strong consistency of $\mathbf{b}$, that is, $\mathbf{b} \xrightarrow{\text{a.s.}} \boldsymbol{\beta}^*$.

6.2.1b The Asymptotic Distribution of b

In order to show that $\sqrt{T}(\mathbf{b} - \boldsymbol{\beta}^*)$ is asymptotically normally distributed, Amemiya makes the following additional assumption.

4. $\boldsymbol{\beta}^*$ is an interior point of $\mathscr{B}$, $\lim (1/T)Z(\boldsymbol{\beta}^*)'Z(\boldsymbol{\beta}^*) = Q$ exists and is nonsingular and

$$\frac{1}{T}Z(\boldsymbol{\beta})'Z(\boldsymbol{\beta}) \quad \text{and} \quad \frac{1}{T}\sum_{t=1}^{T}\left(\frac{\partial^2 f_t}{\partial\beta_i\partial\beta_j}\bigg|_{\boldsymbol{\beta}}\right)^2, \qquad i,j = 1, \ldots, K,$$

converge uniformly in $\boldsymbol{\beta}$ in an open neighborhood of $\boldsymbol{\beta}^*$.

Using a first order Taylor expansion of the gradient of the sum of squares function at $\boldsymbol{\beta}^*$ gives

$$\frac{\partial S}{\partial\boldsymbol{\beta}}\bigg|_{\mathbf{b}} = \frac{\partial S}{\partial\boldsymbol{\beta}}\bigg|_{\boldsymbol{\beta}^*} + \left(\frac{\partial^2 S}{\partial\boldsymbol{\beta}\partial\boldsymbol{\beta}'}\bigg|_{\bar{\boldsymbol{\beta}}}\right)(\mathbf{b} - \boldsymbol{\beta}^*) \tag{6.2.9}$$

where $\bar{\boldsymbol{\beta}}$ lies on the line segment between $\mathbf{b}$ and $\boldsymbol{\beta}^*$. Since $\mathbf{b}$ minimizes S, we know that $[\partial S/\partial\boldsymbol{\beta}|_{\mathbf{b}}] = \mathbf{0}$ so that (6.2.9) implies

$$\sqrt{T}(\mathbf{b} - \boldsymbol{\beta}^*) = -\left(\frac{1}{T}\frac{\partial^2 S}{\partial\boldsymbol{\beta}\partial\boldsymbol{\beta}'}\bigg|_{\bar{\boldsymbol{\beta}}}\right)^{-1}\left(\frac{1}{\sqrt{T}}\frac{\partial S}{\partial\boldsymbol{\beta}}\bigg|_{\boldsymbol{\beta}^*}\right) \tag{6.2.10}$$

Using a central limit theorem, (see Section 5.3.2),

$$\frac{1}{\sqrt{T}} \frac{\partial S}{\partial \boldsymbol{\beta}}\bigg|_{\boldsymbol{\beta}^*} = \frac{-2}{\sqrt{T}} Z(\boldsymbol{\beta}^*)'\mathbf{e} \xrightarrow{d} N(\mathbf{0}, 4\overset{*}{\sigma}{}^2 Q) \tag{6.2.11}$$

Furthermore, given assumptions 1 to 4, the second term on the right-hand side of

$$\frac{1}{T} \frac{\partial^2 S}{\partial \boldsymbol{\beta} \partial \boldsymbol{\beta}'}\bigg|_{\bar{\boldsymbol{\beta}}} = \frac{1}{T}\left\{2Z(\bar{\boldsymbol{\beta}})'Z(\bar{\boldsymbol{\beta}}) - 2\sum_{t=1}^{T} [y_t - f_t(\bar{\boldsymbol{\beta}})] \left(\frac{\partial^2 f_t}{\partial \boldsymbol{\beta} \partial \boldsymbol{\beta}'}\bigg|_{\bar{\boldsymbol{\beta}}}\right)\right\} \tag{6.2.12}$$

can be shown to vanish asymptotically and the first term converges to $2Q$. Thus, in summary,

$$\sqrt{T}(\mathbf{b} - \boldsymbol{\beta}^*) \xrightarrow{d} N(\mathbf{0}, \overset{*}{\sigma}{}^2 Q^{-1}) = N(\mathbf{0}, \overset{*}{\sigma}{}^2[\lim Z(\boldsymbol{\beta}^*)'Z(\boldsymbol{\beta}^*)/T]^{-1}) \tag{6.2.13}$$

The above assumptions also guarantee that

$$\text{plim } Z(\mathbf{b})'Z(\mathbf{b})/T = Q \tag{6.2.14}$$

so that

$$\hat{\sigma}^2[Z(\mathbf{b})'Z(\mathbf{b})]^{-1} \tag{6.2.15}$$

can be used as an estimator of the asymptotic covariance matrix of $\mathbf{b}$. In (6.2.15),

$$\hat{\sigma}^2 = S(\mathbf{b})/(T - K) \tag{6.2.16}$$

is a consistent estimator for the variance $\overset{*}{\sigma}{}^2$ and is often preferred over

$$\tilde{\sigma}^2 = S(\mathbf{b})/T \tag{6.2.17}$$

although the two are, of course, asymptotically equivalent. For a derivation of the asymptotic distribution of $\tilde{\sigma}^2$ see Schmidt (1979). Different sets of assumptions have been given to derive the consistency and asymptotic normality of the nonlinear LS estimator and we will briefly discuss some of the other assumptions in the following.

6.2.1c Comments on the Assumptions for Consistency and Asymptotic Normality

Requiring the parameter space $\mathcal{B}$ to be compact is not very restrictive since, in practice, using numerical optimization algorithms, it will only be possible to compute the estimate in a bounded set. Note however that a corresponding assumption is not useful for linear models and this leads Malinvaud (1980, Chapter 9) to replace the assumption of a compact parameter space by the condition that, for all positive numbers c, the set

$$\left\{\boldsymbol{\beta}\left|\frac{1}{T}\,\mathbf{f}(\boldsymbol{\beta})'\mathbf{f}(\boldsymbol{\beta}) \le c\right.\right\} \tag{6.2.18}$$

is bounded uniformly for all T greater than some fixed integer.

As we mentioned earlier, assumption 3 corresponds to the assumption that lim $X'X/T$ exists and is nonsingular in the linear model case. In Chapter 5, we pointed out that this assumption is not necessary to obtain consistency and, in fact, it will often be violated in practice if some of the exogenous variables are trending. Therefore, it is important to note that assumption 3 can also be modified for nonlinear models [e.g., Wu (1981)]. Furthermore, attempts have been made to replace assumption 3 by conditions on the exogenous variables [e.g., Jennrich (1969), Malinvaud (1970), and Bierens (1981)].

6.2.1d Approximating the Functional Form

White (1981) assumes that the y_t are related by an unknown function g to a vector of observed and unobserved random variables $\mathbf{z}_t$, that is, $y_t = g(\mathbf{z}_t)$. The investigator will usually postulate an approximate functional form $h(\mathbf{z}_t,\boldsymbol{\beta})$ instead of $g(\mathbf{z}_t)$. In general, $h(\mathbf{z}_t,\boldsymbol{\beta}) \neq g(\mathbf{z}_t)$ so that the notion of a true parameter value is out of place. Assume, however, that $\boldsymbol{\beta}^*$ minimizes the prediction mean square error, that is

$$E[g(\mathbf{z}) - h(\mathbf{z},\boldsymbol{\beta}^*)]^2 = \min_{\boldsymbol{\beta}} E[g(\mathbf{z}) - h(\mathbf{z},\boldsymbol{\beta})]^2 \tag{6.2.19}$$

where the expectation is taken with respect to the distribution of $\mathbf{z}$. White (1981) gives conditions for the LS estimator of $\boldsymbol{\beta}^*$ obtained by minimizing

$$\sum_{t=1}^{T} [y_t - h(\mathbf{z}_t,\boldsymbol{\beta})]^2$$

to be strongly consistent, that is, $\mathbf{b} \overset{\text{a.s.}}{\to} \boldsymbol{\beta}^*$, and $\sqrt{T}\,(\mathbf{b} - \boldsymbol{\beta}^*)$ to be asymptotically normally distributed [see also Domowitz and White (1982)].

If the functional form of the relationship between y_t and the exogenous variables $\mathbf{x}_t$ is unknown and the investigator is not prepared to specify an approximate functional form, nonparametric methods can be employed to estimate the unknown function. For such methods, see Grossman (1982) and Wecker and Ansley (1983) and the references given in these articles.

6.2.2 Maximum Likelihood Estimation

To set up the likelihood function the distribution of the error terms has to be known. In practice, normality is assumed most often and we will only consider this case. More precisely, it will be assumed that

$$\mathbf{e} \sim N(\mathbf{0},\overset{*}{\sigma}{}^2 I) \tag{6.2.20}$$

For this case, the likelihood function is

$$\ell(\boldsymbol{\beta},\sigma^2) = \frac{1}{(2\pi\sigma^2)^{T/2}} \exp\left\{-\frac{[\mathbf{y} - \mathbf{f}(\boldsymbol{\beta})]'[\mathbf{y} - \mathbf{f}(\boldsymbol{\beta})]}{2\sigma^2}\right\} \tag{6.2.21}$$

and the log likelihood is

$$\ln \ell(\boldsymbol{\beta},\sigma^2) = \text{constant} - \frac{T}{2} \ln \sigma^2 - \frac{S(\boldsymbol{\beta})}{2\sigma^2} \tag{6.2.22}$$

Hence the ML estimator $\tilde{\boldsymbol{\beta}}$ is identical to the LS estimator $\mathbf{b}$. From the discussion in Section 6.2.1 it should be obvious that the normality assumption (6.2.20) is not sufficient to guarantee the usual desirable properties of the ML estimator. In addition to (6.2.20), conditions analogous to assumptions 1 to 4 have to be imposed in order for the ML estimator $\tilde{\boldsymbol{\theta}}$ of $\boldsymbol{\theta}^* = (\boldsymbol{\beta}^{*\prime},\overset{*}{\sigma}{}^2)'$ to be consistent and

$$\sqrt{T}\,(\tilde{\boldsymbol{\theta}} - \boldsymbol{\theta}^*) \xrightarrow{d} N(\mathbf{0}, \lim TI(\boldsymbol{\theta}^*)^{-1}) \tag{6.2.23}$$

where

$$I(\boldsymbol{\theta}^*) = -E\left[\left.\frac{\partial^2 \ln \ell}{\partial\boldsymbol{\theta}\partial\boldsymbol{\theta}'}\right|_{\boldsymbol{\theta}^*}\right] = \begin{bmatrix} \frac{1}{\overset{*}{\sigma}{}^2}[Z(\boldsymbol{\beta}^*)'Z(\boldsymbol{\beta}^*)] & \mathbf{0} \\ \mathbf{0}' & \frac{T}{2\overset{*}{\sigma}{}^4} \end{bmatrix} \tag{6.2.24}$$

[see Judge et al. (1982, Chapter 24)]. The term lim $TI(\boldsymbol{\theta}^*)^{-1}$ is the Cramér-Rao lower bound so that $\tilde{\boldsymbol{\theta}}$ is an asymptotically efficient estimator. The block-diagonal structure of (6.2.24) results, of course, from the special assumptions imposed on the considered model. Occasionally, models arise where $I(\boldsymbol{\theta}^*)$ is not block diagonal. For discussion of an example, see Theil and Laitinen (1979).

The asymptotic covariance matrix in (6.2.23) can be consistently estimated by $TI(\tilde{\boldsymbol{\theta}})^{-1}$. Alternative estimators that may provide a better approximation to the variance-covariance matrix of $\tilde{\boldsymbol{\beta}}$ are considered by Clarke (1980). Note that the ML estimator of $\overset{*}{\sigma}{}^2$ is $\tilde{\sigma}^2$ in (6.2.17) as in the linear model case. The ML estimator is a sufficient statistic if such a statistic exists. However, for nonlinear models such a statistic exists only under rather special conditions [see Hartley (1964)]. For a further discussion of the properties of the ML estimator see Goldfeld and Quandt (1972).

White (1982) considers the problem of misspecified models in the context of ML estimation and Gallant and Holly (1980) discuss a situation where the true parameter vector may vary with the sample size. As $T \to \infty$ the sequence of true parameter values is assumed to converge to a vector $\boldsymbol{\beta}^*$. Gallant and Holly give conditions for the ML estimator to have the usual desirable properties in this case. Their framework is actually much more general than the present discussion as they consider nonlinear simultaneous equations models. Burguete, Gallant, and Souza (1982) consider an even more general situation by allowing the parameter vector to be infinite dimensional. They also discuss various estimation procedures. Robust estimation in the context of nonlinear models is discussed by Bierens (1981) and Grossmann (1982) where further references can be found. In the next section we consider some issues related to the numerical computation of the LS estimates.

6.3 COMPUTATION OF PARAMETER ESTIMATES

In the foregoing paragraphs, we have seen that estimation of the parameters of a nonlinear statistical model involves solving a nonlinear system of normal equations or optimizing a nonlinear objective function. Unlike the linear model case the optimum cannot generally be given as a closed form expression. Hence iterative optimization algorithms have to be employed. Various algorithms are considered in Appendix B so that a detailed discussion at this point can be avoided. There are, however, some problems that deserve to be noted here.

Suppose that the objective function to be minimized is $H(\boldsymbol{\beta})$, where $\boldsymbol{\beta}$ is again a $(K \times 1)$ vector. The general form of the nth iteration is

$$\boldsymbol{\beta}_{n+1} = \boldsymbol{\beta}_n + \boldsymbol{\xi}_n \tag{6.3.1}$$

where $\boldsymbol{\xi}_n$ is the *step* carried out in the parameter space from the point $\boldsymbol{\beta}_n$ that was obtained in the $(n - 1)$th iteration. The first obvious problem is to find a starting vector $\boldsymbol{\beta}_1$. Clearly, it is desirable to choose $\boldsymbol{\beta}_1$ as close to the optimum $\mathbf{b}$ as possible to avoid an unnecessary number of iterations. We will see shortly that using a consistent estimate as starting vector is advantageous. In some cases, methods are available to obtain such consistent initial estimates. For example, in estimating time series or distributed lag models consistent initial estimates can be derived (see Chapters 7 and 10).

For the general nonlinear model (6.1.2), Hartley and Booker (1965) described a possible method for finding a consistent initial estimator. They partition the sample into K nonoverlapping subsets of m observations each and compute the average $\bar{y}_i$, $i = 1, 2, \ldots, K$. Accordingly, the $f_i(\boldsymbol{\beta})$ are averaged giving K functions $\bar{f}_i(\boldsymbol{\beta})$. Then $\boldsymbol{\beta}_1$ is chosen as solution of the system of K equations $\bar{y}_i = \bar{f}_i(\boldsymbol{\beta})$, $i = 1, \ldots, K$. This, of course, is also a nonlinear system of equations that needs to be solved iteratively. For a discussion of the consistency conditions of this estimator see Jennrich (1969) and Amemiya (1983). Gallant (1975a) suggests using K representative sample values to compute an initial estimate. This procedure cannot claim consistency of the resulting $\boldsymbol{\beta}_1$.

Using one of the gradient methods described in Appendix B, the step $\boldsymbol{\xi}_n$ is of the general form

$$\boldsymbol{\xi}_n = -P_n \left[\left. \frac{\partial H}{\partial \boldsymbol{\beta}} \right|_{\boldsymbol{\beta}_n} \right] \tag{6.3.2}$$

where P_n is a positive definite matrix. Thus, the first iteration is

$$\boldsymbol{\beta}_2 = \boldsymbol{\beta}_1 - P_1 \left[\frac{\partial H}{\partial \boldsymbol{\beta}} \bigg|_{\boldsymbol{\beta}_1} \right] \tag{6.3.3}$$

It can be shown that, under suitable conditions, $\boldsymbol{\beta}_2$ has the same asymptotic distribution as the optimizing vector $\mathbf{b}$ [Amemiya (1983); Fuller (1976, Chapter 5)]. From (6.3.3) we get

$$\sqrt{T}(\boldsymbol{\beta}_2 - \boldsymbol{\beta}^*) = \sqrt{T}(\boldsymbol{\beta}_1 - \boldsymbol{\beta}^*) - \sqrt{T}P_1 \left[\frac{\partial H}{\partial \boldsymbol{\beta}} \bigg|_{\boldsymbol{\beta}_1} \right] \tag{6.3.4}$$

Using a first-order Taylor expansion of $\partial H/\partial \boldsymbol{\beta}$,

$$\left[\frac{\partial H}{\partial \boldsymbol{\beta}} \bigg|_{\boldsymbol{\beta}_1} \right] = \left[\frac{\partial H}{\partial \boldsymbol{\beta}} \bigg|_{\boldsymbol{\beta}^*} \right] + \left[\frac{\partial^2 H}{\partial \boldsymbol{\beta} \partial \boldsymbol{\beta}'} \bigg|_{\bar{\boldsymbol{\beta}}} \right] (\boldsymbol{\beta}_1 - \boldsymbol{\beta}^*) \tag{6.3.5}$$

where $\bar{\boldsymbol{\beta}}$ is on the line segment between $\boldsymbol{\beta}_1$ and $\boldsymbol{\beta}^*$, and substituting in (6.3.4) gives

$$\sqrt{T}(\boldsymbol{\beta}_2 - \boldsymbol{\beta}^*) = \sqrt{T} \left(I - P_1 \left[\frac{\partial^2 H}{\partial \boldsymbol{\beta} \partial \boldsymbol{\beta}'} \bigg|_{\bar{\boldsymbol{\beta}}} \right] \right) (\boldsymbol{\beta}_1 - \boldsymbol{\beta}^*) - TP_1 \frac{1}{\sqrt{T}} \left[\frac{\partial H}{\partial \boldsymbol{\beta}} \bigg|_{\boldsymbol{\beta}^*} \right] \tag{6.3.6}$$

Thus, if the initial estimator of $\boldsymbol{\beta}_1$ is consistent, $S(\boldsymbol{\beta})$ is the objective function and P_1 is chosen such that

$$\operatorname{plim} \frac{1}{T} P_1^{-1} = \operatorname{plim} \frac{1}{T} \left[\frac{\partial^2 S}{\partial \boldsymbol{\beta} \partial \boldsymbol{\beta}'} \bigg|_{\bar{\boldsymbol{\beta}}} \right] = \operatorname{plim} \frac{1}{T} \left[\frac{\partial^2 S}{\partial \boldsymbol{\beta} \partial \boldsymbol{\beta}'} \bigg|_{\boldsymbol{\beta}^*} \right] \tag{6.3.7}$$

then the assumptions of Section 6.2.1 ensure that $\sqrt{T}(\boldsymbol{\beta}_2 - \boldsymbol{\beta}^*)$ and $\sqrt{T}(\mathbf{b} - \boldsymbol{\beta}^*)$ have the same asymptotic distribution [see (6.2.10)].

This discussion implies that many of the optimization procedures presented in Appendix B provide estimators asymptotically equivalent to the LS estimator if only one iteration is carried out. For instance, for the Newton-Raphson algorithm

$$P_1 = \left[\frac{\partial^2 S}{\partial \boldsymbol{\beta} \partial \boldsymbol{\beta}'} \bigg|_{\boldsymbol{\beta}_1} \right]^{-1} \tag{6.3.8}$$

and it follows from Section 6.2.1 that it satisfies (6.3.7). For the Gauss method

$$P_1 = \tfrac{1}{2}[Z(\boldsymbol{\beta}_1)'Z(\boldsymbol{\beta}_1)]^{-1} \tag{6.3.9}$$

and it is argued in Section 6.2.1 that, after multiplying (6.3.9) and (6.3.8) by T, the two resulting matrices are asymptotically equivalent [see (6.2.12)]. Consequently, starting with a consistent estimator $\boldsymbol{\beta}_1$ the Newton-Raphson and the Gauss methods asymptotically provide an LS estimator in one iteration. On the other hand, for the steepest decent algorithm $P_1 = I$, so that one iteration of this method does not suffice to obtain an estimator asymptotically equivalent to **b**.

6.4 ESTIMATION UNDER CONSTRAINTS

Often nonsample information on the parameter values is available that can be used to improve the estimators or to reduce the computational burden. In the following we will discuss the consequences of having nonsample information in the form of equality constraints or inequality constraints. The results of this section are also relevant for linear models with nonlinear constraints.

6.4.1 Equality Constraints

Suppose that the true parameters $\boldsymbol{\beta}^*$ are known to fulfill equality constraints given in the form

$$\mathbf{q}(\boldsymbol{\beta}) = \mathbf{0} \tag{6.4.1}$$

where $\mathbf{q}(\boldsymbol{\beta})$ is a function with values in the J-dimensional Euclidean space. We will assume that $\mathbf{q}(\cdot)$ is at least twice continuously differentiable and $[\partial\mathbf{q}/\partial\boldsymbol{\beta}'|_{\boldsymbol{\beta}}]$ has rank J in a neighborhood of the true parameter vector $\boldsymbol{\beta}^*$. This condition implies that one out of two equivalent constraints is removed. This assumption will be met in almost all practical situations and covers, for instance, the case of linear constraints $R\boldsymbol{\beta} = \mathbf{r}$, where R is a $(J \times K)$ matrix and $\mathbf{r}$ a $(J \times 1)$ vector. In this case, $\mathbf{q}(\boldsymbol{\beta}) = R\boldsymbol{\beta} - \mathbf{r}$. For the CES production function (6.1.1), it is often assumed that $\beta_3^* = 1/\beta_1^*$. Thus

$$\mathbf{q}(\boldsymbol{\beta}) = \beta_1 - \frac{1}{\beta_3} \tag{6.4.2}$$

which is sufficiently often differentiable where defined.

For the case where equality restrictions of the type (6.4.1) are available and assumptions 1 to 4 of Section 6.2.1 are satisfied, the restricted LS estimator $\mathbf{b}^*$ is consistent and asymptotically normally distributed, that is,

$$\sqrt{T}(\mathbf{b}^* - \boldsymbol{\beta}^*) \xrightarrow{d} N(\mathbf{0}, \Sigma_R) \tag{6.4.3}$$

where

$$\Sigma_R = \Sigma - \Sigma \left[\frac{\partial\mathbf{q}'}{\partial\boldsymbol{\beta}}\bigg|_{\boldsymbol{\beta}^*}\right]\left(\left[\frac{\partial\mathbf{q}}{\partial\boldsymbol{\beta}'}\bigg|_{\boldsymbol{\beta}^*}\right]\Sigma\left[\frac{\partial\mathbf{q}'}{\partial\boldsymbol{\beta}}\bigg|_{\boldsymbol{\beta}^*}\right]\right)^{-1}\left[\frac{\partial\mathbf{q}}{\partial\boldsymbol{\beta}'}\bigg|_{\boldsymbol{\beta}^*}\right]\Sigma \tag{6.4.4}$$

and

$$\underset{\sim}{\Sigma} = \overset{*}{\sigma}^2 \lim \left[\frac{Z(\boldsymbol{\beta}^*)'Z(\boldsymbol{\beta}^*)}{T}\right]^{-1} \tag{6.4.5}$$

is the asymptotic covariance matrix of the unrestricted LS estimator. This result can be shown by specifying a Lagrangian function [see (6.4.6)] and considering a first-order Taylor expansion of its gradient. For the details see Lütkepohl (1983). From (6.4.4) it follows that $\underset{\sim}{\Sigma} - \underset{\sim}{\Sigma}_R$ is positive semidefinite so that the restricted LS estimator is asymptotically superior to its unrestricted counterpart under asymptotic mean square error loss.

The constrained LS estimator can be computed by introducing a vector $\boldsymbol{\eta} = (\eta_1, \eta_2, \ldots, \eta_J)'$ of Lagrange multipliers and the constraints are incorporated in the minimization procedure by defining the Lagrangian function

$$S_R(\boldsymbol{\beta},\boldsymbol{\eta}) = S(\boldsymbol{\beta}) + \boldsymbol{\eta}'\mathbf{q}(\boldsymbol{\beta}) \tag{6.4.6}$$

It can be shown that a constrained minimum of $S(\boldsymbol{\beta})$ is obtained at a stationary point of $S_R(\boldsymbol{\beta},\boldsymbol{\eta})$. Thus we have to find a solution to $[\partial S_R/\partial\mathbf{v}|_{\mathbf{v}}] = \mathbf{0}$, where $\mathbf{v}' = (\boldsymbol{\beta}',\boldsymbol{\eta}')$. This can be done by minimizing

$$\hat{S}_R(\mathbf{v}) = \left[\frac{\partial S_R}{\partial \mathbf{v}}\bigg|_{\mathbf{v}}\right]'\left[\frac{\partial S_R}{\partial \mathbf{v}}\bigg|_{\mathbf{v}}\right]$$

Note that this method increases the number of parameters in the objective function and thereby may increase the minimization difficulties. This problem can be avoided if the restrictions are given or can be written in the form

$$\boldsymbol{\beta} = \mathbf{g}(\boldsymbol{\alpha}) \tag{6.4.7}$$

where $\boldsymbol{\alpha}$ is a M-dimensional vector. For instance, for the constraint (6.4.2) we can define $\boldsymbol{\alpha} = (\beta_0, \beta_1, \beta_2)'$ and

$$\mathbf{g}(\boldsymbol{\alpha}) = \begin{bmatrix} \beta_0 \\ \beta_1 \\ \beta_2 \\ 1/\beta_1 \end{bmatrix} \tag{6.4.8}$$

In this case the original model $\mathbf{y} = \mathbf{f}(\boldsymbol{\beta}^*) + \mathbf{e}$ can be redefined as

$$\mathbf{y} = \mathbf{f}(\mathbf{g}(\boldsymbol{\alpha}^*)) + \mathbf{e} = \mathbf{f} \circ \mathbf{g}(\boldsymbol{\alpha}^*) + \mathbf{e} \tag{6.4.9}$$

and the LS estimator of $\boldsymbol{\alpha}^*$ can be computed. Assuming that the function $f_t \circ \mathbf{g}(\cdot)$ has the properties assumed for f_t in Section 6.2.1 and $\boldsymbol{\alpha}^*$ is an interior point of the compact set of possible parameter vectors $\boldsymbol{\alpha}$, the LS estimator $\mathbf{a}$ is consistent and, by the chain rule

$$\left.\frac{\partial \mathbf{f} \circ \mathbf{g}}{\partial \boldsymbol{\alpha}}\right|_{\alpha} = \left[\left.\frac{\partial \mathbf{f}}{\partial \boldsymbol{\beta}'}\right|_{\mathbf{g}(\alpha)}\right] \cdot \left[\left.\frac{\partial \mathbf{g}}{\partial \boldsymbol{\alpha}'}\right|_{\alpha}\right] = Z(\mathbf{g}(\boldsymbol{\alpha})) \left[\left.\frac{\partial \mathbf{g}}{\partial \boldsymbol{\alpha}'}\right|_{\alpha}\right] \tag{6.4.10}$$

we get

$$\sqrt{T}(\mathbf{a} - \boldsymbol{\alpha}^*) \xrightarrow{d} N\left(\mathbf{0}, \overset{*}{\sigma}{}^2 \lim\left(\left[\left.\frac{\partial \mathbf{g}}{\partial \boldsymbol{\alpha}'}\right|_{\alpha^*}\right]' \frac{Z'(\boldsymbol{\beta}^*)'Z(\boldsymbol{\beta}^*)}{T} \left[\left.\frac{\partial \mathbf{g}}{\partial \boldsymbol{\alpha}'}\right|_{\alpha^*}\right]\right)^{-1}\right) \tag{6.4.11}$$

and consequently, by a result given in Chapter 5,

$$\sqrt{T}(\mathbf{b}^* - \boldsymbol{\beta}^*) \xrightarrow{d}$$

$$N\left(\mathbf{0}, \overset{*}{\sigma}{}^2 \lim \left[\left.\frac{\partial \mathbf{g}}{\partial \boldsymbol{\alpha}'}\right|_{\alpha^*}\right]\left(\left[\left.\frac{\partial \mathbf{g}}{\partial \boldsymbol{\alpha}'}\right|_{\alpha^*}\right]' \frac{Z(\boldsymbol{\beta}^*)'Z(\boldsymbol{\beta}^*)}{T} \left[\left.\frac{\partial \mathbf{g}}{\partial \boldsymbol{\alpha}'}\right|_{\alpha^*}\right]\right)^{-1} \left[\left.\frac{\partial \mathbf{g}}{\partial \boldsymbol{\alpha}'}\right|_{\alpha^*}\right]'\right) \tag{6.4.12}$$

Rothenberg (1973) discusses equality constraints of the above type in the context of maximum likelihood estimation.

6.4.2 Inequality Constraints

If the nonsample information is given in the form of inequality constraints

$$\mathbf{q}(\boldsymbol{\beta}) \geq \mathbf{0} \tag{6.4.13}$$

where $\mathbf{q}(\boldsymbol{\beta})$ is a function with values in the J-dimensional Euclidean space, this information can also be used to improve the LS estimator of $\boldsymbol{\beta}$. The inequality sign "$\geq$" between vectors means that all components of the left-hand vector are greater than or equal to the corresponding components of the right-hand vector. If the true parameter vector $\boldsymbol{\beta}^*$ is in the interior of the constrained parameter space and if the constrained parameter space has the same dimension as $\mathcal{B}$, the inequality constrained LS estimator has the same *asymptotic* distribution as the unrestricted LS estimator $\mathbf{b}$. This result is an immediate consequence of the discussion in Section 6.2.1 since, provided $\mathbf{q}(\cdot)$ is continuous, (6.4.13) implies that the constrained parameter space, say $\mathcal{R}$, is compact if $\mathcal{B}$ is compact so that assumptions 1 to 4 are satisfied. The case where the true parameter vector is on the boundary of the restricted region is more difficult to deal with. Some results are given by Chant (1974). Even if the true parameter vector is in the interior of the restricted region it is possible to improve on the *small sample* performance of the LS estimator by taking the inequality restrictions into account. We will discuss this possibility now.

Suppose that the constrained parameter space $\mathcal{R}$ is a convex subset of the unconstrained parameter space $\mathcal{B}$, which, for simplicity, is also assumed to be convex. Note that by assumption 1 in Section 6.2.1, $\mathcal{B}$ is a bounded set. The assumption here is that in addition to the restrictions that are required to specify $\mathcal{B}$ further constraints are available to reduce the feasible parameter space to the convex set $\mathcal{R}$. For example, $\mathcal{R}$ will be convex if $\mathbf{q}(\boldsymbol{\beta})$ is *quasi convex,* that is, for vectors $\boldsymbol{\beta}_1, \boldsymbol{\beta}_2 \in \mathcal{B}$ the condition $\mathbf{q}(\boldsymbol{\beta}_1) \leq \mathbf{q}(\boldsymbol{\beta}_2)$ implies for $0 \leq \lambda \leq 1$ that $\mathbf{q}(\lambda\boldsymbol{\beta}_1 + (1 - \lambda)\boldsymbol{\beta}_2) \leq \mathbf{q}(\boldsymbol{\beta}_2)$ so that a linear function is quasi convex. As an alternative to the restricted LS estimator, for any positive semidefinite $(K \times K)$ matrix W, we can define an estimator $\mathbf{b}_W$ such that

$$(\mathbf{b}_W - \mathbf{b})'W(\mathbf{b}_W - \mathbf{b}) = \min\{(\boldsymbol{\beta} - \mathbf{b})'W(\boldsymbol{\beta} - \mathbf{b})|\boldsymbol{\beta} \in \bar{\mathcal{R}}\} \tag{6.4.14}$$

where $\bar{\mathcal{R}}$ is the topological closure of the constrained parameter space. $\mathcal{R}$ being convex guarantees that $\mathbf{b}_W$ is well defined. If $\mathbf{b}$ satisfies the constraints or is on the boundary of $\mathcal{R}$, that is, $\mathbf{b} \in \bar{\mathcal{R}}$, then $\mathbf{b}_W = \mathbf{b}$, whereas, for $\mathbf{b}$ outside of $\bar{\mathcal{R}}$, the restricted estimator $\mathbf{b}_W$ will depend on W. It follows from results due to Rothenberg (1973) that

$$E[(\mathbf{b}_W - \boldsymbol{\beta}^*)'W(\mathbf{b}_W - \boldsymbol{\beta}^*)] \leq E[(\mathbf{b} - \boldsymbol{\beta}^*)'W(\mathbf{b} - \boldsymbol{\beta}^*)] \tag{6.4.15}$$

so that, under squared error loss, $\mathbf{b}_W$ is at least as good as the LS estimator $\mathbf{b}$. If W is positive definite and there is a positive probability for $\mathbf{b}$ to assume values outside $\mathcal{R}$, the inequality sign in (6.4.15) can be replaced by a strict inequality and thus, in this case, the restricted estimator is superior to the LS estimator independent of the sample size.

It may seem to be more plausible to incorporate the inequality constraints directly in the LS optimization algorithm rather than computing the LS estimator first and then minimizing the quadratic form $(\boldsymbol{\beta} - \mathbf{b})'W(\boldsymbol{\beta} - \mathbf{b})$ over $\bar{\mathcal{R}}$. However, the restricted LS estimator may in fact be inferior to the unrestricted estimator in small samples [Rothenberg (1973)] and, as mentioned earlier, nothing is gained in terms of large sample performance if $\boldsymbol{\beta}^*$ is in the interior of $\bar{\mathcal{R}}$. Also, note that, in this case, Rothenberg's restricted estimator does not dominate $\mathbf{b}$ *asymptotically*. This result is a consequence of the consistency of $\mathbf{b}$ which implies that the probability of $\mathbf{b}$ falling outside $\bar{\mathcal{R}}$ vanishes as $T \to \infty$. The inequality restricted LS estimator and Rothenberg's estimator can be computed using the methods described in Appendix B.

Of course, it is also possible to use a Bayesian approach in the nonlinear model case if the nonsample information can be summarized in a prior density $p_0(\boldsymbol{\beta})$. In this situation, if the error distribution is known, the posterior pdf is proportional to

$$p^*(\boldsymbol{\beta}) = \ell(\boldsymbol{\beta})p_0(\boldsymbol{\beta}) \tag{6.4.16}$$

where $\ell(\boldsymbol{\beta})$ is the likelihood function. If $p_0(\boldsymbol{\beta})$ is continuous and $p_0(\tilde{\boldsymbol{\beta}}) \neq 0$, the maximum posterior distribution estimator is asymptotically equivalent to the maximum likelihood estimator $\tilde{\boldsymbol{\beta}}$. For a further discussion of Bayesian methods see Bard (1974, Chapter IV, Section C).

6.5 CONFIDENCE REGIONS

As we have seen in the foregoing, only asymptotic properties of the parameter estimators for nonlinear models are generally available. Therefore the usual interval estimators or confidence regions are also only approximately or asymptotically correct. The discussion of Section 6.2.1 indicates that the interval estimates considered for linear models can be generalized to the nonlinear model case. Throughout this and the following section we assume that assumptions 1 to 4 of Section 6.2.1 guaranteeing consistency and asymptotic normality of the LS estimator are satisfied.

6.5.1 Confidence Intervals

From (6.2.13) it follows that an asymptotic $(1 - \alpha)100\%$ confidence interval for β_i^* is given by

$$(b_i - z_{\alpha/2}\sqrt{\tilde{\sigma}^2 z^{ii}}\,,\ b_i + z_{\alpha/2}\sqrt{\tilde{\sigma}^2 z^{ii}}\,) \tag{6.5.1}$$

where β_i^* and b_i are the ith coordinate of $\boldsymbol{\beta}^*$ and $\mathbf{b}$, respectively; $z_{\alpha/2}$ is the critical value of a normal distribution with mean zero and variance one; and z^{ii} is the ith diagonal element of $[Z(\mathbf{b})'Z(\mathbf{b})]^{-1}$. Thus $\sqrt{\tilde{\sigma}^2 z^{ii}}$ is an estimate of the asymptotic standard deviation of b_i. If the sample size is small $z_{\alpha/2}$ could be replaced by the critical value of a t distribution, since all results are only valid asymptotically and asymptotically the t distribution converges to the normal distribution. Also, $\hat{\sigma}^2$ may be used in (6.5.1) instead of $\tilde{\sigma}^2$.

To illustrate we use the output, labor, and capital data given in Table 6.2. The labor and capital data are random samples from a uniform distribution on the interval (0,1) and $\ln Q_t$ is computed by adding an error e_t, generated from a normal distribution with mean zero and standard deviation .25, to $-.5 \ln (.3L_t^{-2} + .7K_t^{-2})$ for each $t = 1, 2, \ldots, 30$. Thus $\beta_0^* = 0$, $\beta_1^* = -0.5$, $\beta_2^* = .3$, $\beta_3^* = -2$, and $\overset{*}{\sigma}{}^2 = .0625$. The LS estimates and 95% confidence intervals computed according to (6.5.1) are given in Table 6.3.

If the empirical investigator is not prepared to approximate the small sample distribution of $\mathbf{b}$ by its asymptotic distribution, *conservative confidence intervals* can be established, using Chebyshev's inequality

$$\Pr\left(|b_i - E[b_i]| \le \frac{\sigma_i}{\sqrt{\alpha}}\right) \ge 1 - \alpha \tag{6.5.2}$$

where b_i may be any estimator for β_i^* and σ_i is the standard deviation of b_i. Thus, if b_i is unbiased

$$\Pr\left(b_i - \frac{\sigma_i}{\sqrt{\alpha}} \le \beta_i^* \le b_i + \frac{\sigma_i}{\sqrt{\alpha}}\right) \ge 1 - \alpha \tag{6.5.3}$$

TABLE 6.2 *DATA FOR CES PRODUCTION FUNCTION*

t	L_t	K_t	$\ln Q_t$
1	0.228	0.802	−1.359
2	0.258	0.249	−1.695
3	0.821	0.771	0.193
4	0.767	0.511	−0.649
5	0.495	0.758	−0.165
6	0.487	0.425	−0.270
7	0.678	0.452	−0.473
8	0.748	0.817	0.031
9	0.727	0.845	−0.563
10	0.695	0.958	−0.125
11	0.458	0.084	−2.218
12	0.981	0.021	−3.633
13	0.002	0.295	−5.586
14	0.429	0.277	−0.773
15	0.231	0.546	−1.315
16	0.664	0.129	−1.678
17	0.631	0.017	−3.879
18	0.059	0.906	−2.301
19	0.811	0.223	−1.377
20	0.758	0.145	−2.270
21	0.050	0.161	−2.539
22	0.823	0.006	−5.150
23	0.483	0.836	−0.324
24	0.682	0.521	−0.253
25	0.116	0.930	−1.530
26	0.440	0.495	−0.614
27	0.456	0.185	−1.151
28	0.342	0.092	−2.089
29	0.358	0.485	−0.951
30	0.162	0.934	−1.275

and therefore we can use

$$\left(b_i - \frac{\sigma_i}{\sqrt{\alpha}}, b_i + \frac{\sigma_i}{\sqrt{\alpha}}\right) \tag{6.5.4}$$

as a $(1 - \alpha)100\%$ confidence interval for β_i^*. This procedure, however, has some obvious disadvantages. First, the resulting confidence intervals are much wider than those in (6.5.1). Suppose, for example, that $\alpha = .05$, then the standard deviation in (6.5.4) is multiplied by a factor $1/\sqrt{.05} = 4.47$ whereas $z_{\alpha/2}$ in (6.5.1) is 1.96. Furthermore, an unbiased estimator b_i is needed. If the sample size is so small that we are not willing to assume normality of the LS estimator, then it is difficult to justify the assumption that this estimator is unbiased.

TABLE 6.3 *ESTIMATION RESULTS FOR CES PRODUCTION FUNCTION*

β	True Parameter Values	LS Estimates	95% Confidence Regions
β_0	0.0	0.124	(−0.0214, 0.2704)
β_1	−0.5	−0.336	(−0.8431, 0.1704)
β_2	0.3	0.337	(0.0833, 0.5901)
β_3	−2.0	−3.011	(−5.1735, 0.8481)

Hence we have to use a procedure to reduce the bias. Bard (1974, p. 187) explains a possible method, which is due to Quenouille. In the following section joint confidence regions for all the parameters $\boldsymbol{\beta}^*$ are considered.

6.5.2 Joint Confidence Regions

We will now assume that the model errors are normally distributed, that is, $\mathbf{e} \sim N(\mathbf{0},\overset{*}{\sigma}{}^2 I)$. The following three statistics have been suggested to compute approximate joint confidence regions for $\boldsymbol{\beta}^*$.

$$F_1 = \frac{[S(\boldsymbol{\beta}) - S(\mathbf{b})]/K}{S(\mathbf{b})/(T-K)} \tag{6.5.5}$$

$$F_2 = \frac{(\boldsymbol{\beta} - \mathbf{b})'[\partial^2 S/\partial\boldsymbol{\beta}\partial\boldsymbol{\beta}'|_{\mathbf{b}}](\boldsymbol{\beta} - \mathbf{b})/2K}{S(\mathbf{b})/(T-K)} \tag{6.5.6}$$

$$F_3 = \frac{(\boldsymbol{\beta} - \mathbf{b})'Z(\mathbf{b})'Z(\mathbf{b})(\boldsymbol{\beta} - \mathbf{b})/K}{S(\mathbf{b})/(T-K)} \tag{6.5.7}$$

All three statistics are asymptotically distributed as $F_{(K,T-K)}$ if $\boldsymbol{\beta} = \boldsymbol{\beta}^*$ and thus, approximate $(1-\alpha)100\%$ confidence regions are given by $F_i \leq F_{\alpha(K,T-K)}$, $i = 1, 2, 3$. While all three statistics are identical for the linear model case (see Chapter 2), this does not hold for the nonlinear model (6.1.2). The confidence contours provided by F_1 are in general not ellipsoids. Joint confidence regions for the production function example are depicted in Figure 6.1.

Using a second-order Taylor expansion,

$$S(\boldsymbol{\beta}) = S(\mathbf{b}) + \left[\frac{\partial S}{\partial\boldsymbol{\beta}}\bigg|_{\mathbf{b}}\right]'(\boldsymbol{\beta} - \mathbf{b}) + \frac{1}{2}(\boldsymbol{\beta} - \mathbf{b})'\left[\frac{\partial^2 S}{\partial\boldsymbol{\beta}\partial\boldsymbol{\beta}'}\bigg|_{\bar{\boldsymbol{\beta}}}\right](\boldsymbol{\beta} - \mathbf{b}) \tag{6.5.8}$$

where $\bar{\boldsymbol{\beta}}$ is between $\boldsymbol{\beta}$ and $\mathbf{b}$, and consequently,

$$S(\boldsymbol{\beta}) - S(\mathbf{b}) = \frac{1}{2}(\boldsymbol{\beta} - \mathbf{b})'\left[\frac{\partial^2 S}{\partial\boldsymbol{\beta}\partial\boldsymbol{\beta}'}\bigg|_{\bar{\boldsymbol{\beta}}}\right](\boldsymbol{\beta} - \mathbf{b}) \tag{6.5.9}$$

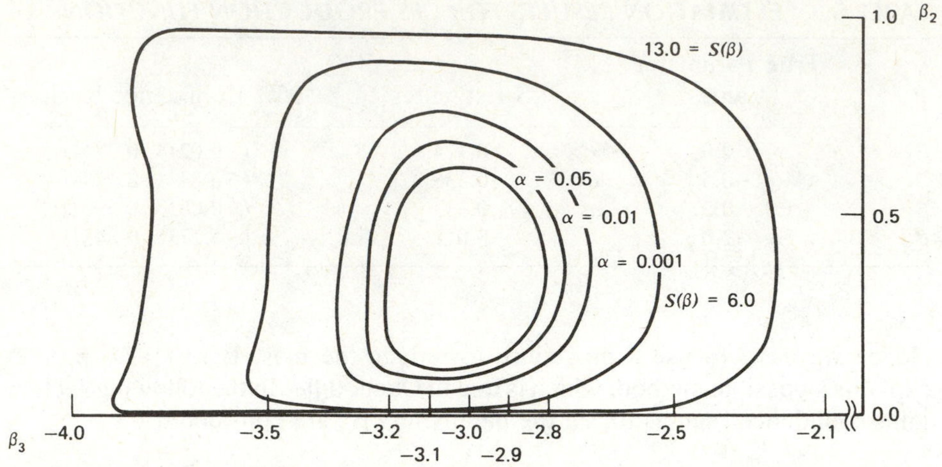

Figure 6.1 Exact confidence contours for the CES production function parameters with approximate confidence levels for the parameters β_2^* and $\beta_3^*(\beta_0 = .1245,\ \beta_1 = -.3363)$.

since $(\partial S/\partial \boldsymbol{\beta})|_{\mathbf{b}} = \mathbf{0}$ is the first-order condition for a minimum of $S(\boldsymbol{\beta})$; the numerator of F_2 in (6.5.6) is seen to be an approximation to the numerator of F_1 in (6.5.5). Unlike F_1, the statistic F_2 provides confidence ellipsoids. One example is given in Figure 6.2.

In (6.5.7), the expression $(\partial^2 S/\partial \boldsymbol{\beta} \partial \boldsymbol{\beta}'|_{\mathbf{b}})/2$ is further approximated by $Z(\mathbf{b})'Z(\mathbf{b})$ which is justified in large samples since, under the assumptions of

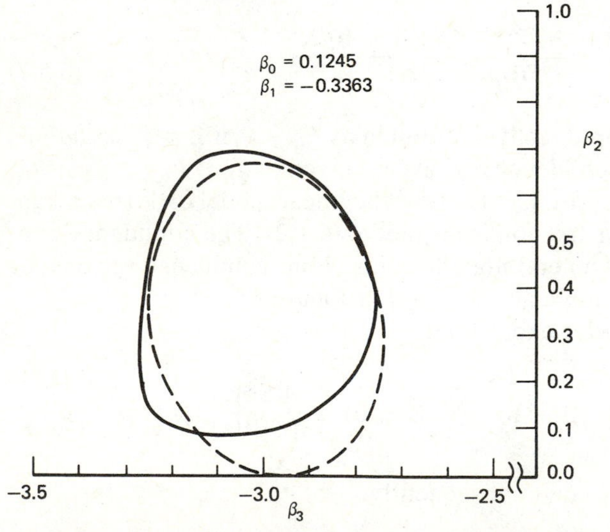

Figure 6.2 Confidence contours for significance levels $\alpha = .01$. Key: __ __ __, confidence region from (6.5.6); _____, confidence region from (6.5.5).

Section 6.2.1, the second term on the right-hand side of (6.2.12) becomes small as $T \to \infty$. The statistic F_3 also provides confidence ellipsoids.

Since $F_1 = F_2 = F_3$ for linear models, it is plausible that the accuracy of the confidence regions will depend on the functional form of the model. In particular, if the deviations from linearity are only slight the confidence regions can be expected to be good approximations to the actual confidence regions. This problem is discussed in detail by Beale (1960).

Another method to obtain confidence regions is suggested by Hartley (1964), who defines a statistic

$$F_4 = \frac{[\mathbf{y} - \mathbf{f}(\boldsymbol{\beta})]'W(W'W)^{-1}W'[\mathbf{y} - \mathbf{f}(\boldsymbol{\beta})]/K}{[\mathbf{y} - \mathbf{f}(\boldsymbol{\beta})]'[I - W(W'W)^{-1}W'][\mathbf{y} - \mathbf{f}(\boldsymbol{\beta})]/(T - K)} \tag{6.5.10}$$

Replacing $\boldsymbol{\beta}$ by $\boldsymbol{\beta}^*$, F_4 is $F_{(K,T-K)}$ distributed for any *fixed* $(T \times K)$ matrix W of rank K. Whereas for a linear model one would choose $W = X$, the choice of W has a degree of arbitrariness in the case of a nonlinear model and the problem arises of choosing W to obtain reasonable confidence regions. For details, see Hartley's article.

Conservative joint $(1 - \alpha)100\%$ confidence regions can be derived from the following version of Chebyshev's inequality

$$\Pr\left[(\mathbf{b} - \boldsymbol{\beta}^*)'\boldsymbol{\Sigma}_{\mathbf{b}}^{-1}(\mathbf{b} - \boldsymbol{\beta}^*) \leq \frac{K}{\alpha}\right] \geq 1 - \alpha \tag{6.5.11}$$

[Bard (1974), Section 7-10]. Here $\mathbf{b}$ may be any unbiased estimator for $\boldsymbol{\beta}^*$ and $\boldsymbol{\Sigma}_{\mathbf{b}}$ is the variance-covariance matrix of $\mathbf{b}$. The drawbacks of this procedure have already been discussed in Section 6.5.1.

The above statistics can also be used to compute joint confidence regions for subsets of the parameters and, of course, they can be used for hypothesis testing as discussed in the next section. In addition, the Wald, the Lagrange multiplier, and the likelihood ratio statistic presented in the following section can also be used to obtain confidence regions.

6.6 TESTING HYPOTHESES

Throughout this section we will assume that the model errors are normally distributed, that is, $\mathbf{e} \sim N(\mathbf{0}, \overset{*}{\sigma}{}^2 I)$, and the assumptions of Section 6.2.1 are satisfied so that the LS and ML estimators are identical and have the properties stated in Section 6.2. In fact, for much of what follows $\mathbf{e}$ need not be normally distributed if the ML estimator is used and is assumed to have suitable properties [e.g., Gallant and Holly (1980)]. Moreover, some results hold for the LS estimator if the assumptions of Section 6.2.1 are satisfied and the distribution of $\mathbf{e}$ is unknown.

6.6.1 Tests for Location

In order to test the hypothesis

$$H_0: \beta_i^* = c \qquad \text{against} \qquad H_a: \beta_i^* \neq c \tag{6.6.1}$$

where c is a constant, the asymptotic normality of the ML or LS estimator can be used. For example, considering the confidence intervals in Table 6.3, it follows that H_0: $\beta_0^* = 0$ cannot be rejected at the .05 level of significance.

Similarly, the hypothesis

$$H_0: \boldsymbol{\beta}^* = \boldsymbol{\upsilon} \tag{6.6.2}$$

where $\boldsymbol{\upsilon}$ is a $(K \times 1)$ vector, is rejected if $\boldsymbol{\upsilon}$ is not in the joint confidence region for all elements of $\boldsymbol{\beta}^*$. Any of the statistics given in (6.5.5) to (6.5.7) can be used to test (6.6.2). Also, these statistics can easily be modified to test for the location of a subvector of $\boldsymbol{\beta}^*$. Suppose $\boldsymbol{\beta}$ is partitioned into subvectors $\boldsymbol{\beta}_1$ and $\boldsymbol{\beta}_2$ with dimensions J and $K - J$, respectively, so that $\boldsymbol{\beta}' = (\boldsymbol{\beta}_1', \boldsymbol{\beta}_2')$. Then the hypothesis

$$H_0: \boldsymbol{\beta}_1^* = \boldsymbol{\omega} \tag{6.6.3}$$

where $\boldsymbol{\omega}$ is a $(J \times 1)$ vector, can be tested using

$$F_1 = \frac{[S(\mathbf{b}^*) - S(\mathbf{b})]/J}{S(\mathbf{b})/(T - K)} \tag{6.6.4}$$

where $\mathbf{b}^*$ is the restricted ML (LS) estimator computed under the constraint $\boldsymbol{\beta}_1^* = \boldsymbol{\omega}$. In this case F_1 is distributed as $F_{(J,T-K)}$.

Another test designed for testing the location of a subvector of $\boldsymbol{\beta}^*$ is described by Gallant (1975a,b) who attributes it to Hartley. It can be used to test (6.6.3) if the model is linear in $\boldsymbol{\beta}_2$. Choose a regressor z_t' such that the regression matrix has full rank and estimate the model

$$y_t = f_t\left(\begin{bmatrix} \boldsymbol{\omega} \\ \boldsymbol{\beta}_2 \end{bmatrix}\right) + z_t\boldsymbol{\delta} + e_t \tag{6.6.5}$$

If the restrictions for the parameters are correct, then δ should be zero. Therefore, $\hat{H}_0$: $\delta = 0$ is tested in the usual manner and H_0 is rejected if $\hat{H}_0$ is rejected. Since under H_0 the model is linear this test has a small-sample justification. Of course, a crucial problem is to find a regressor z_t' to give good power against the alternative. The test can be generalized to cover the case where the model is nonlinear in the nuisance parameters [Gallant (1977)].

6.6.2 Testing General Nonlinear Hypotheses

In this section we discuss tests of a more general hypothesis of the form

$$H_0\colon \mathbf{q}(\boldsymbol{\beta}^*) = \mathbf{0} \qquad \text{against} \qquad H_a\colon \mathbf{q}(\boldsymbol{\beta}^*) \neq \mathbf{0} \tag{6.6.6}$$

where $\mathbf{q}(\boldsymbol{\beta}^*)$ is a J-dimensional vector. For the CES production function, a reasonable hypothesis is

$$H_0\colon \beta_3^* = \frac{1}{\beta_1^*} \qquad \text{or} \qquad \mathbf{q}(\boldsymbol{\beta}^*) = \beta_1^* - \frac{1}{\beta_3^*} = 0 \tag{6.6.7}$$

Clearly, $\mathbf{q}(\boldsymbol{\beta})$ cannot be an arbitrary function. For example, in the model

$$y_t = \beta_0 + \beta_1 x_{t1}^{\beta_2} + e_t \tag{6.6.8}$$

we cannot test $H_0\colon \beta_2^* = 0$, that is, $\mathbf{q}(\boldsymbol{\beta}^*) = \beta_2^*$, since in this case β_0 and β_1 are no longer identifiable if H_0 is true [see Judge et al. (1982, Chapter 24)]. This violates an assumption on which the validity of the asymptotic properties of the estimator is based. We will assume in the following that $\mathbf{q}(\boldsymbol{\beta})$ satisfies the assumptions of Section 6.4.1; that is, $\mathbf{q}(\boldsymbol{\beta})$ is at least twice continuously differentiable, and $[\partial\mathbf{q}/\partial\boldsymbol{\beta}'|_{\boldsymbol{\beta}}]$ has full rank in a neighborhood of $\boldsymbol{\beta}^*$. Detailed formal conditions for model and constraints are given in Gallant and Holly (1980) and Rao (1973) [see also Chapter 5].

6.6.2a Wald Test

The test statistic

$$\lambda_W = T\mathbf{q}(\mathbf{b})' \left(\left[\frac{\partial \mathbf{q}}{\partial \boldsymbol{\beta}'}\bigg|_{\beta} \right] \hat{\boldsymbol{\Sigma}} \left[\frac{\partial \mathbf{q}}{\partial \boldsymbol{\beta}'}\bigg|_{\beta} \right]' \right)^{-1} \mathbf{q}(\mathbf{b}) \tag{6.6.9}$$

has an asymptotic central χ^2 distribution with J degrees of freedom if H_0 is true. This result follows by noting that $\sqrt{T}(\mathbf{b} - \boldsymbol{\beta}^*) \xrightarrow{d} N(\mathbf{0}, \boldsymbol{\Sigma}_{\mathbf{b}})$ implies

$$\sqrt{T}(\mathbf{q}(\mathbf{b}) - \mathbf{q}(\boldsymbol{\beta}^*)) = \sqrt{T}\mathbf{q}(\mathbf{b}) \xrightarrow{d} N\left(\mathbf{0}, \left[\frac{\partial \mathbf{q}}{\partial \boldsymbol{\beta}'}\bigg|_{\boldsymbol{\beta}^*} \right] \boldsymbol{\Sigma}_{\mathbf{b}} \left[\frac{\partial \mathbf{q}}{\partial \boldsymbol{\beta}'}\bigg|_{\boldsymbol{\beta}^*} \right]' \right)$$

provided the restrictions are correct and thus $\mathbf{q}(\boldsymbol{\beta}^*) = \mathbf{0}$ (see Chapter 5). As ML estimator of the variance-covariance matrix

$$\hat{\boldsymbol{\Sigma}} = \tilde{\sigma}^2 \left[\frac{Z(\mathbf{b})'Z(\mathbf{b})}{T} \right]^{-1} \tag{6.6.10}$$

can be used in (6.6.9). A test based on λ_W rejects H_0 if $\lambda_W > \chi^2_{(J,\alpha)}$. Note that this test does not require the computation of the constrained ML estimator.

For the CES example with $\mathbf{q}(\boldsymbol{\beta}) = \beta_1 - (1/\beta_3)$ we get $[\partial\mathbf{q}/\partial\boldsymbol{\beta}'|_{\boldsymbol{\beta}}] = [0, 1, 0, 1/\beta_3^2]$ and, consequently, for the hypothesis $\mathbf{q}(\boldsymbol{\beta}^*) = 0$ we have $\lambda_W = .0018 < \chi^2_{(1,.05)} = 3.84$. Thus we cannot reject the null hypothesis (6.6.7) at the .05 level.

6.6.2b Lagrange Multiplier Test

The Lagrange multiplier test statistic

$$\lambda_{LM} = \tilde{\boldsymbol{\eta}}' \left[\frac{\partial\mathbf{q}}{\partial\boldsymbol{\beta}'}\bigg|_{\boldsymbol{\beta}_R}\right] \tilde{\Sigma}_R \left[\frac{\partial\mathbf{q}}{\partial\boldsymbol{\beta}'}\bigg|_{\boldsymbol{\beta}_R}\right]' \tilde{\eta} \tag{6.6.11}$$

is asymptotically distributed as a χ^2 random variable with J degrees of freedom. In (6.6.11) $\tilde{\boldsymbol{\eta}}$ is the vector of Lagrange multipliers at the stationary point of $S_R(\boldsymbol{\beta},\boldsymbol{\eta})$ in (6.4.6), where the likelihood function obtains its constrained optimum. Here $\mathbf{b}^*$ is the constrained ML estimator and $\tilde{\Sigma}_R = S(\mathbf{b}^*)[Z(\mathbf{b}^*)'Z(\mathbf{b}^*)]^{-1}/T$. Clearly, $\tilde{\boldsymbol{\eta}}$ has to satisfy

$$\frac{\partial \ln \ell}{\partial\boldsymbol{\beta}}\bigg|_{\mathbf{b}^*} + \left[\frac{\partial\mathbf{q}}{\partial\boldsymbol{\beta}'}\bigg|_{\mathbf{b}^*}\right]' \tilde{\boldsymbol{\eta}} = \mathbf{0} \tag{6.6.12}$$

since this is a necessary condition for a stationary point of $S_R(\boldsymbol{\beta},\boldsymbol{\eta})$. Thus

$$\begin{aligned}\lambda_{LM} &= \left[\frac{\partial \ln \ell}{\partial\boldsymbol{\beta}}\bigg|_{\mathbf{b}^*}\right]' \tilde{\Sigma}_R \left[\frac{\partial \ln \ell}{\partial\boldsymbol{\beta}}\bigg|_{\mathbf{b}^*}\right] \\ &= \frac{[\mathbf{y} - \mathbf{f}(X,\mathbf{b}^*)]'Z(\mathbf{b}^*)[Z(\mathbf{b}^*)'Z(\mathbf{b}^*)]^{-1}Z(\mathbf{b}^*)'[\mathbf{y} - \mathbf{f}(X,\mathbf{b}^*)]}{S(\mathbf{b}^*)/T}\end{aligned} \tag{6.6.13}$$

which is the Rao efficient score test statistic [Rao (1973), Section 6e.3]. This is preferable to (6.6.11) if we incorporate our constraints directly in the likelihood function (see Section 6.4.1) and, consequently, we do not have to estimate $\tilde{\boldsymbol{\eta}}$. For this test only the constrained parameter estimator is required. For the CES production function we computed the constrained estimates of β_0^*, β_1^* and β_2^*. The value of the test statistic $\lambda_{LM} = .093$ is, like the Wald test statistic, considerably lower than the critical value $\chi^2_{(1,.05)}$.

6.6.2c Likelihood Ratio Test

The likelihood ratio test involves both constrained and unconstrained estimators. The null hypothesis is rejected if

$$\lambda_{LR} = 2[\ln \ell(\mathbf{b},\tilde{\sigma}^2) - \ln \ell(\mathbf{b}^*,\sigma_R^2)] \tag{6.6.14}$$

exceeds $\chi^2_{(J,\alpha)}$ for a prespecified significance level α [e.g., Rao (1973), Section 6e.3]. Under H_0, σ_R^2 is the ML estimator of $\overset{*}{\sigma}{}^2$. Equivalently, (6.6.14) can be written as

$$\lambda_{LR} = T[\ln S(\mathbf{b}^*) - \ln S(\mathbf{b})] \tag{6.6.15}$$

and thus, for our example, $\lambda_{LR} = .0827 < \chi^2_{(1,.05)}$.

Gallant and Holly (1980) and Burguete, Gallant, and Souza (1982) consider the above three test statistics under much more general assumptions and also determine the asymptotic distributions under a sequence of alternatives. Under their assumptions and the specific alternatives considered, all three test statistics are asymptotically distributed as a noncentral χ^2. These results are important to evaluate the power of the tests against these alternatives. See also Schmidt (1982) and the references given there. Using Edgeworth expansions Cavanagh (1982) shows that, in general, for nonlinear models with nonscalar identity error covariance matrix the power functions of the three tests cross so that none is uniformly most powerful.

6.6.3 Some Comments on Testing Hypotheses

Having presented a range of alternative test statistics it is natural to ask which one is preferable in a particular situation. Posed in this generality the question is difficult to answer. The likelihood ratio test requires the numerical minimization of two different objective functions; therefore, higher computation costs may be a reason for avoiding it. If the null hypothesis is true, some parameter estimates may be highly correlated. This in turn can increase the numerical estimation difficulties. Consequently, the Lagrange multiplier test, using only constrained estimates, may be most appropriate in this case. On the other hand, if the restrictions cannot be incorporated directly into the objective function then unconstrained optimization might be easier and the Wald test can be used.

Additional statistics are available if the location of $\boldsymbol{\beta}^*$ is to be tested. Hartley's test can only be applied for specific models and hypotheses and, furthermore, it depends on the ability of the user to find a regressor z_t that give good power against the alternative hypothesis. Monte Carlo experiments have been carried out to compare the performance of some of the statistics [e.g., Gallant (1975c)]. However, such studies suffer from their limited generality due to the wide range of different nonlinear functions.

In this section we have only considered tests for the parameter vector $\boldsymbol{\beta}^*$. Hypotheses on $\overset{*}{\sigma}{}^2$ can be constructed using the asymptotic distribution of $\tilde{\sigma}^2$. For details see Schmidt (1979, 1982).

6.7 SUMMARY

In this chapter we have extended the basic linear model of Chapter 2 by allowing the functional relationship between the dependent and the independent (exogenous) variables to be nonlinear in the parameters and the variables. The LS and ML principle can be used for estimating the parameters as in the linear model case. However, the small sample properties of the estimators can in general not be derived and we have concentrated on asymptotic properties.

Conditions for consistency and asymptotic normality of the LS estimator have been given and under the special assumptions of this chapter the ML estimator is identical to the LS estimator if the errors are assumed normally distributed.

In general, the sum of squares function will be such that a closed form solution for the minimum cannot be given. Consequently, iterative optimization methods have to be applied. If a consistent initial estimator is available to start the iteration, some of the algorithms provide estimators that are asymptotically equivalent to the LS estimator after one iteration.

Nonsample information should be taken into account to improve the estimators and help to simplify the numerical optimization of the objective function. Under general conditions the equality restricted LS estimator outperforms the unconstrained LS estimator asymptotically. On the other hand, inequality constraints do not have an impact on the *asymptotic* distribution of the LS estimator as long as the true parameter vector is in the interior of the feasible region. It is possible, though, to improve on the *small sample* performance of the nonlinear LS estimator if inequality constraints are available using Rothenberg's restricted estimator.

As in the linear model case, interval estimates can be established for nonlinear specifications. In general they will only be asymptotically valid. The asymptotic normal distribution of the LS estimator can be used to set up confidence intervals for the individual parameters. If the errors are assumed normally distributed, several approximate F statistics are available to determine approximate joint confidence regions for the model parameters. Depending on the statistic used, the confidence regions may not be ellipsoids. The approximate F statistics can also be used to test for the location of the parameter vector or portions thereof. The Wald, Lagrange multiplier, and likelihood ratio tests have been discussed for testing general nonlinear hypotheses. All three test statistics are χ^2 distributed under the null hypothesis.

The assumptions made in this chapter are rather restrictive and will be relaxed to some extent in later chapters. In Chapter 8 models with autocorrelated errors are considered and in Chapter 11 non-identically distributed, heteroscedastic errors are discussed. To generalize on the functional form of the model, rather than considering (6.1.2), one could investigate specifications of the type

$$g(y_t,\mathbf{x}_t,\boldsymbol{\beta}) = e_t \tag{6.7.1}$$

Under suitable assumptions for the function g and the error terms, similar results as for the model (6.1.2) hold. This type of model will be considered in the more general framework of nonlinear simultaneous equations in Chapter 15. Of course, the specification (6.7.1) includes models with nonscalar identity covariance error structure. For instance, if in (6.1.3) the error term is $\mathbf{u} \sim (\mathbf{0},\overset{*}{\sigma}{}^2\boldsymbol{\Psi})$, where $\boldsymbol{\Psi}$ is a positive definite $(T \times T)$ matrix, then a $(T \times T)$ matrix P exists so that $P\boldsymbol{\Psi}P' = I$. Premultiplying (6.1.3) by P gives

$$P\mathbf{y} - P\mathbf{f}(X,\boldsymbol{\beta}) = P\mathbf{u} = \mathbf{e}$$

which is a model of the type (6.7.1).

Among the remaining problems related to nonlinear statistical models is the lack of knowledge about the small sample performance of the estimators and test statistics. The Monte Carlo experiments that have been carried out in order to evaluate small sample properties suffer from their limited generality.

Despite all potential numerical problems related to the iterative optimization of the objective function, models nonlinear in the parameters and variables are now widely employed. For instance, CES production functions have been estimated by Bodkin and Klein (1967), Tsurumi (1970), Weitzman (1970), and Mizon (1977), among others, and nonlinear regression methods will be used later in this book, for example, when considering time series models in Chapter 7, infinite distributed lag models in Chapter 10, qualitative and limited dependent variables in Chapter 18 and models with nonnormal errors in Chapter 20.

6.8 EXERCISES

Most of the results in this chapter are only valid for large sample sizes. In econometrics, however, we typically work with small or moderate samples. Therefore, the small-sample and asymptotic distribution of the estimators or test statistics may differ substantially in practice. Also the values of the asymptotically equivalent test statistics given in Section 16.6 will usually differ in small samples. The reader is invited to explore the small-sample properties of some of the estimators and test statistics by solving the following exercises.

The model under consideration is assumed to be

$$y_t = f(\mathbf{x}_t, \boldsymbol{\beta}) + e_t, \qquad t = 1, 2, \ldots, 20 \tag{6.8.1}$$

where $f(\mathbf{x}_t, \boldsymbol{\beta}) = \beta_0 + \beta_1(x_{t1}^{\beta_2} + \beta_3 x_{t2})$ and the e_t are independently, normally distributed errors with mean zero and variance $\overset{*}{\sigma}{}^2 = 1$. It is left to the reader to give an economic interpretation to this model. The true parameter values are $\beta_0^* = 5$, $\beta_1^* = 2$, $\beta_2^* = 2$, and $\beta_3^* = .5$; and $x_{t1} = L_t$, and $x_{t2} = K_t$, $t = 1, 2, \ldots, 20$. The values for L_t and K_t are given in Table 6.2. We give the gradient and Hessian matrix of $f(\mathbf{x}_t, \boldsymbol{\beta})$ and thus provide all necessary derivatives for constructing the gradient and Hessian of the sum of squared errors objective function.

$$\left.\frac{\partial f}{\partial \boldsymbol{\beta}}\right|_{\boldsymbol{\beta}} = \begin{bmatrix} 1 \\ x_{t1}^{\beta_2} + \beta_3 x_{t2} \\ \beta_1 \ln (x_{t1}) x_{t1}^{\beta_2} \\ \beta_1 x_{t2} \end{bmatrix}' \tag{6.8.2}$$

$$\left.\frac{\partial^2 f}{\partial \boldsymbol{\beta} \partial \boldsymbol{\beta}'}\right|_{\boldsymbol{\beta}} = \begin{bmatrix} 0 & 0 & 0 & 0 \\ \cdot & 0 & \ln (x_{t1}) x_{t1}^{\beta_2} & x_{t2} \\ \cdot & \cdot & \beta_1 [\ln (x_{t1})]^2 x_{t1}^{\beta_2} & 0 \\ \cdot & \cdot & \cdot & 0 \end{bmatrix} \tag{6.8.3}$$

6.8.1 Individual Exercises

Exercise 6.1
Generate a sample of 20 values of y for the model (6.8.1) and compute LS/ML estimates for $\boldsymbol{\beta}^*$ and $\overset{*}{\sigma}{}^2$. Apply different starting values for the numerical optimization algorithm of your choice. Compute also the approximate covariance matrix of $\mathbf{b}$.

Exercise 6.2
Choose a significance level α and construct confidence intervals for the estimates.

Exercise 6.3
Generate another sample of size 20, combine it with the one used in Exercise 6.1, and repeat the estimation with the sample of size 40. Compare the results and interpret.

Exercise 6.4
Using a sample of size 20, compute LS estimates that satisfy

(a) $b_1 = b_2$
(b) $b_1 = 1/b_3$
(c) $b_1 = b_2$ and $b_1 = 1/b_3$

Exercise 6.5
Use the test statistics λ_W, λ_{LM}, and λ_{LR}, given in Section 6.6.2; to test the following null hypotheses:

(a) H_0: $\beta_1^* = \beta_2^*$.
(b) H_0: $\beta_1^* = 1/\beta_3^*$.
(c) H_0: $\beta_1^* = \beta_2^*$ and $\beta_1^* = 1/\beta_3^*$.

Compare the values of the test statistics and interpret.

Exercise 6.6
Using the three F statistics (6.5.5) to (6.5.7), test the following hypotheses

(a) H_0: $\boldsymbol{\beta}^* = (5, 2, 2, .5)'$.
(b) H_0: $\boldsymbol{\beta}^* = (3, 1, 2, .5)'$.

Compare the test values and interpret.

Exercise 6.7
Repeat all tests in Exercises 6.5 and 6.6 using a sample of size 40.

6.8.2 Joint or Class Exercises

Exercise 6.8
Compute the average values of the estimates of $\boldsymbol{\beta}^*$ and $\overset{*}{\sigma}{}^2$ from 100 samples and compare with the true values.

Exercise 6.9
Construct empirical frequency distributions for **b** and $\tilde{\sigma}^2$ and interpret.

Exercise 6.10
Use the Kolmogorov-Smirnov D statistic or some other appropriate statistic to test the agreement between the empirical and theoretical asymptotic distributions.

Exercise 6.11
Use the computed test statistics for the tests in Exercises 6.5 and 6.6 from 100 samples to perform a small-sample comparison of the asymptotically equivalent tests.

Exercise 6.12
Repeat Exercise 6.11 with 100 samples of size 40. Compare the results.

It is hoped that the Monte Carlo experiment described in Exercises 6.8 to 6.12 will contribute to the understanding of the problems related to nonlinear models. But it should be kept in mind that we are dealing here with a very special case that should not lead to generalizations. Although an investigation of the small-sample properties of estimators for other nonlinear models could be performed in a similar way, the wide variety of possible specifications hinders the derivation of general results by Monte Carlo experiments of this type.

6.9 REFERENCES

Amemiya, T. (1983) ''Nonlinear Regression Models,'' in Z. Griliches and M. D. Intriligator, eds., *Handbook of Econometrics,* North-Holland, Amsterdam, 333–390.

Bard, Y. (1974) *Nonlinear Parameter Estimation,* Academic Press, New York.

Beale, E. M. L. (1960) ''Confidence Regions in Non-linear Estimation,'' *Journal of the Royal Statistical Society* B, 22, 41–88.

Bierens, H. J. (1981) *Robust Methods and Asymptotic Theory in Nonlinear Econometrics,* Lecture Notes in Economics and Mathematical Systems 192, Springer, Berlin.

Bodkin, R. G. and L. R. Klein (1967) ''Nonlinear Estimation of Aggregate Production Functions,'' *Review of Economics and Statistics,* 49, 28–44.

Box, M. J. (1971) ''Bias in Nonlinear Estimation,'' *Journal of the Royal Statistical Society* B, 33, 171–201.

Bunke, H., K. Henschke, R. Struby, and C. Wisotzki (1977) ''Parameter Estimation in Nonlinear Regression Models,'' *Mathematische Operationsforschung und Statistik, Series Statistics,* 8, 23–40.

Burguete, J. F., A. R. Gallant, and G. Souza (1982) ''On the Unification of the Asymptotic Theory of Nonlinear Econometric Models,'' *Econometric Reviews,* 1, 151–190.

Cavanagh, C. L. (1982) ''Hypothesis Testing in Nonlinear Models,'' paper presented at the Econometric Society European Meeting, Dublin.

Chant, D. (1974), "On Asymptotic Tests of Composite Hypotheses in Nonstandard Conditions," *Biometrika,* 61, 291–298.

Chiang, A. C. (1974) *Fundamental Methods of Mathematical Economics,* 2nd ed., McGraw-Hill, New York.

Clarke, G. P. Y. (1980) "Moments of the Least Squares Estimators in a Nonlinear Regression Model," *Journal of the Royal Statistical Society* B, 42, 227–237.

Domowitz, I. and H. White (1982) "Misspecified Models with Dependent Observations," *Journal of Econometrics,* 20, 35–58.

Fuller, W. A. (1976) *Introduction to Statistical Time Series,* Wiley, New York.

Gallant, A. R. (1975a) "Nonlinear Regression," *The American Statistician,* 29, 73–81.

Gallant, A. R. (1975b) "The Power of the Likelihood Ratio Test of Location in Nonlinear Regression Models," *Journal of the American Statistical Association,* 70, 198–203.

Gallant, A. R. (1975c) "Testing a Subset of the Parameters of a Non-linear Regression Model," *Journal of the American Statistical Association,* 70, 927–932.

Gallant, A. R. (1977) "Testing a Nonlinear Regression Specification: A Nonregular Case," *Journal of the American Statistical Association,* 72, 523–530.

Gallant, A. R. and A. Holly (1980) "Statistical Inference in an Implicit, Nonlinear, Simultaneous Equation Model in the Context of Maximum Likelihood Estimation," *Econometrica,* 48, 697–720.

Goldfeld, S. M. and R. E. Quandt (1972) *Nonlinear Methods in Econometrics,* North-Holland, Amsterdam.

Grossmann, W. (1982) "Statistical Estimation of Nonlinear Regression Functions," *Mathematische Operationsforschung und Statistik, Series Statistics,* 13, 455–471.

Hartley, H. O. (1964) "Exact Confidence Regions for the Parameters in Nonlinear Regression Laws," *Biometrika,* 51, 347–353.

Hartley, H. O. and A. Booker (1965) "Non-linear Least Squares Estimation," *The Annals of Mathematical Statistics,* 36, 638–650.

Jennrich, R. I. (1969) "Asymptotic Properties of Non-linear Least Squares Estimators," *The Annals of Statistics,* 2, 633–643.

Judge, G. G., R. C. Hill, W. E. Griffiths, H. Lütkepohl, T. C. Lee (1982) *Introduction to the Theory and Practice of Econometrics,* Wiley, New York.

Lütkepohl, H. (1983) "Nonlinear Least Squares Estimation under Nonlinear Equality Constraints," *Economics Letters,* 13, 191–196.

Malinvaud, E. (1970) "The Consistency of Nonlinear Regressions," *The Annals of Mathematical Statistics,* 41, 956–969.

Malinvaud, E. (1980) *Statistical Methods of Econometrics,* 3rd ed., North-Holland, Amsterdam.

Mizon, G. E. (1977) "Inferential Procedures in Nonlinear Models: An Application in a UK Industrial Cross Section Study of Factor Substitution and Returns to Scale," *Econometrica,* 45, 1221–1242.

Rao, C. R. (1973) *Linear Statistical Inference and Its Applications,* 2nd ed., Wiley, New York.

Rothenberg, T. J. (1973) *Efficient Estimation with A Priori Information,* Yale University Press, New Haven.

Schmidt, W. H. (1979) "Asymptotic Results for Estimation and Testing Variances in Regression Models," *Mathematische Operationsforschung und Statistik, Series Statistics,* 10, 209–236.

Schmidt, W. H. (1982) "Testing Hypotheses in Nonlinear Regressions (with Discussion)," *Mathematische Operationsforschung und Statistik, Series Statistics,* 13, 3–19.

Theil, H. and K. Laitinen (1979) "Maximum Likelihood Estimation of the Rotterdam Model Under Two Different Conditions," *Economics Letters,* 2, 239–244.

Tsurumi, H. (1970) "Nonlinear Two-Stage Least Squares Estimation of CES Production Functions Applied to the Canadian Manufacturing Industries, 1926–1939, 1946–1967," *Review of Economics and Statistics,* 52, 200–207.

Wecker, W. E. and C. F. Ansley (1983) "The Signal Extraction Approach to Nonlinear Regression and Spline Smoothing," *Journal of the American Statistical Association,* 78, 81–89.

Weitzman, M. L. (1970) "Soviet Postwar Economic Growth and Capital-Labor Substitution," *American Economic Review,* 60, 676–692.

White, H. (1981) "Consequences and Detection of Misspecified Nonlinear Regression Models," *Journal of the American Statistical Association,* 76, 419–433.

White, H. (1982) "Maximum Likelihood Estimation of Misspecified Models," *Econometrica,* 50, 1–25.

Wu, C.-F. (1981) "Asymptotic Theory of Nonlinear Least Squares Estimation," *The Annals of Statistics,* 9, 501–513.

Chapter 7

Time Series

7.1 INTRODUCTION

Given a set of time series data $y_1, y_2, \ldots, y_T$ we have assumed in the preceding chapters that each associated random variable y_t consists of a mean, say μ_t, and a zero mean random part e_t. The mean was usually assumed to be a function of some other variables, for instance, $\mu_t = \mathbf{x}_t'\boldsymbol{\beta}$ in the simple linear statistical model in Chapteı 2, or $\mu_t = f(\mathbf{x}_t, \boldsymbol{\beta})$ in the nonlinear statistical model of Chapter 6. This presumes that a theory is available suggesting what other variables summarized in $\mathbf{x}_t$ have an impact on the observed value of y_t. This assumption is not always realistic since sometimes no adequate theory is available or a particular researcher is not ready to accept the existing theories. In such a situation the given time series is often analyzed without relating it to other variables. In the case when forecasting is the objective such specifications have been used with some success. Also, in conventional econometric models an analysis of the residuals is often made in an attempt to improve estimator performance. Consequently, time series analysis is also relevant in the context of econometric modeling if the original sample consists of time series data, and thus, the residuals are also a time series. This possibility will be discussed in greater detail in some of the following chapters.

The chapter is organized as follows: In Section 7.2 a range of useful time series models is introduced and the use of these models for forecasting is discussed in Section 7.3. Estimation and model specification is discussed in Sections 7.4 and 7.5, respectively. Spectral analysis, which is a rather different approach to time series analysis, is introduced in Section 7.6. Data transformations, such as trend and seasonal adjustment are treated in Section 7.7. A summary and conclusions are given in Section 7.8. The content of this chapter is summarized in Table 7.1. For the reader without some basic knowledge of the subject, studying a more detailed introduction [e.g., Judge et al. (1982)] may be useful before reading this chapter. Much of the material introduced below will be useful in some of the later chapters.

7.2 STOCHASTIC PROCESSES

Given a sample $y_1, y_2, \ldots, y_T$, we assume that these observations are realizations of random variables also denoted by $y_1, y_2, \ldots, y_T$, respectively. These random variables are a subsequence of an infinite sequence y_t, $t = 0, \pm 1, \pm 2, \ldots$ which is called a *stochastic process* or, more precisely, a *discrete stochastic process* since the time index t assumes integer values only. This general framework is, for example, useful to investigate the post sample development

TABLE 7.1 ***TIME SERIES TOPICS***

- Time series
  - Stochastic processes (Section 7.2)
    - Time domain analysis
      - Autoregressive processes (Section 7.2.1)
      - Moving average processes (Section 7.2.2)
      - ARIMA processes (Section 7.2.3)
      - Seasonal ARIMA processes (Section 7.2.4)
        - Forecasting (Section 7.3)
        - Estimation (Section 7.4)
        - Specification (Section 7.5)
          - Box-Jenkins approach (Section 7.5.1)
          - AR order selection (Section 7.5.2)
    - Frequency domain analysis (Section 7.6)
  - Data transformations (Section 7.7)
    - Box-Cox transformation (Section 7.7.1)
    - Seasonal and trend adjustment (Section 7.7.2)

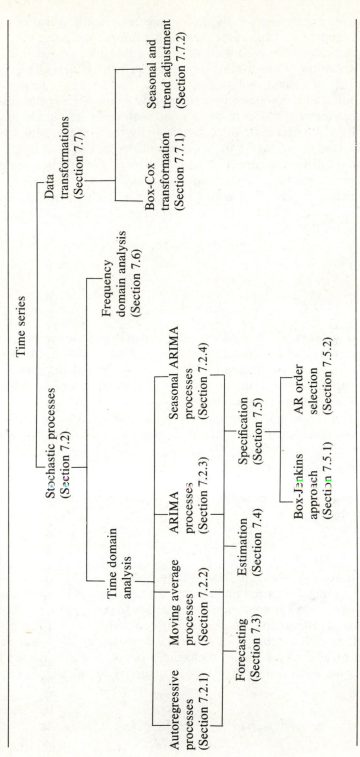

of a variable or, more generally, to investigate certain features of the distribution of a random variable associated with a future time point.

The relationship between a set of random variables is summarized in their joint distribution. Thus a stochastic process can be described by the joint distributions of all finite subsequences $y_t, y_{t+1}, \ldots, y_{t+k}$. In practice, these distributions can rarely be determined merely on the basis of the available data and consequently we have to be satisfied with investigating the first few moments of the distributions. In economics only the first two moments (means, variances, and covariances) are usually considered. But even this is not possible without further assumptions. A convenient and in practice useful assumption is the stationarity of a stochastic process.

A stochastic process y_t is called *stationary* if the first two moments of the joint distributions of the finite subsequences are finite and do not change through time, that is,

1. $E[y_t] = \mu < \infty$ for all t.
2. $E[(y_t - \mu)^2] < \infty$ for all t.
3. $E[(y_t - \mu)(y_{t+k} - \mu)] = \gamma_k$ for all t, k.

The first condition says that all the random variables have the same finite mean μ and 3 implies that the covariance between y_t and y_{t+k} depends only on k but not on the particular time point t. Of course, for $k = 0$ this condition implies that the variances $\text{var}(y_t)$ are constant $(=\gamma_0)$ for all t. From 2 it follows that all variances and covariances are finite.

Note, that this kind of stationarity is sometimes called *covariance stationarity* or *weak stationarity* and a stochastic process is called *strictly stationary* if the multivariate distribution of $(y_t, \ldots, y_{t+k})$ is identical to that of the time shifted set $(y_s, \ldots, y_{s+k})$ for all t, s, and k. Since the normal distribution is completely determined by its first and second moments, a stationary normally distributed process is strictly stationary. Such a process is often called a *Gaussian process*.

Examples of stationary processes have been discussed in previous chapters. For instance, if as assumed in Chapter 2, the y_t are independent and identically distributed with zero mean, the process is called *white noise*. Clearly, such a process is stationary and, in fact, strictly stationary.

The foregoing discussion implies that the covariances between the elements of a stochastic process are an important device to describe the structure of such a process. In general, the covariance between y_t and y_{t+k}, $E[(y_t - E[y_t])(y_{t+k} - E[y_{t+k}])]$, is called *autocovariance* since it measures the linear relationship between members of a single stochastic process. For a stationary stochastic process with mean μ the covariance structure is completely described by the sequence

$$\gamma_k = E[(y_t - \mu)(y_{t+k} - \mu)], \qquad k = 0, 1, 2, \ldots \tag{7.2.1}$$

since $\gamma_k = \gamma_{-k}$ as is easily checked. This sequence is called the *autocovariance function* of the process y_t. Since it depends essentially upon the unit of measurement of the underlying variable it is useful to normalize the γ_k by dividing by $\gamma_0 = \text{var}(y_t)$. This results in the *autocorrelation function* of y_t,

$$\rho_k = \frac{\gamma_k}{\gamma_0}, \qquad k = 1, 2, \ldots \tag{7.2.2}$$

Obviously, $\rho_0 = 1$ and is therefore often not reported. Since $\gamma_0 > |\gamma_k|$, $k = 1, 2, \ldots$, the ρ_k all lie between -1 and 1.

As we will see later, another important tool to describe the stochastic properties of a stationary stochastic process are the *partial autocorrelations*. The kth partial autocorrelation coefficient measures the correlation between y_t and y_{t-k} given $y_{t-1}, \ldots, y_{t-k+1}$.

To illustrate the foregoing concepts we will now discuss some particular stochastic processes. We will make use of the lag operator, L, and therefore remind the reader that this operator is defined so that $Ly_t = y_{t-1}$. That is, the time index is shifted backward by one period. Of course, applying L repeatedly n times gives $L^n y_t = y_{t-n}$. For a more detailed discussion of the following material and the lag operator see Judge et al. (1982, Chapter 25).

7.2.1 Autoregressive Processes

A finite-order *autoregressive process of order p* or briefly, AR(p), has the form

$$y_t = \theta_1 y_{t-1} + \theta_2 y_{t-2} + \ldots + \theta_p y_{t-p} + v_t \tag{7.2.3}$$

or

$$(1 - \theta_1 L - \theta_2 L^2 - \ldots - \theta_p L^p) y_t = v_t \tag{7.2.4}$$

In (7.2.3) and (7.2.4) v_t is white noise as defined above and we assume $\sigma_v^2 = \text{var}(v_t)$. An AR process may or may not be stationary. Consider, for instance, the special case

$$y_t = y_{t-1} + v_t \tag{7.2.5}$$

Obviously,

$$\begin{aligned} y_t &= y_{t-2} + v_{t-1} + v_t = y_{t-3} + v_{t-2} + v_{t-1} + v_t \\ &= \ldots = y_{t-n} + v_{t-n+1} + v_{t-n+2} + \ldots + v_t \end{aligned}$$

for any positive integer n. Since the v_t are uncorrelated the variance of their sum is the sum of their variances and hence,

$$\begin{aligned} \text{var}(y_t) &= \text{var}(y_{t-n}) + \text{var}(v_{t-n+1}) + \ldots + \text{var}(v_t) \\ &= \text{var}(y_{t-n}) + n\sigma_v^2 \end{aligned} \tag{7.2.6}$$

which cannot be finite since $n\sigma_v^2 \rightarrow \infty$ as $n \rightarrow \infty$. This violates a requirement for stationarity.

It can be shown that (7.2.3) is stationary with mean zero if the solutions of

$$1 - \theta_1 z - \theta_2 z^2 - \ldots - \theta_p z^p = 0 \tag{7.2.7}$$

are all outside the complex unit circle. That is, if $z = z_1 + iz_2$ solves (7.2.7), the modulus $|z| = \sqrt{z_1^2 + z_2^2} > 1$. For instance, for $p = 1$ and thus, $y_t = \theta_1 y_{t-1} + v_t$, the stationarity condition amounts to requiring $|\theta_1| < 1$ since $1 - \theta_1 z = 0$ implies $z = 1/\theta_1$. For this to exceed 1, θ_1 has to be less than 1.

Let us now assume that the AR process (7.2.3) fulfills the stationarity condition. An elegant way to determine the autocorrelations ρ_k of this process is to left-multiply (7.2.3) by y_{t-k}, take expectations and divide by the variance γ_0 of y_t. That is,

$$\frac{E[y_{t-k}y_t]}{\gamma_0} = \theta_1 \frac{E[y_{t-k}y_{t-1}]}{\gamma_0} + \ldots + \theta_p \frac{E[y_{t-k}y_{t-p}]}{\gamma_0}$$

or

$$\rho_k = \theta_1 \rho_{k-1} + \ldots + \theta_p \rho_{k-p} \qquad \text{for } k > 0 \tag{7.2.8}$$

These difference equations are known as *Yule-Walker equations*. The general solution is

$$\rho_k = \psi_1 \lambda_1^k + \psi_2 \lambda_2^k + \ldots + \psi_p \lambda_p^k \qquad \text{for } k \geq 0 \tag{7.2.9}$$

where the λ_i, $i = 1, 2, \ldots, p$ are the roots of the equation

$$z^p - \theta_1 z^{p-1} - \ldots - \theta_p = 0 \tag{7.2.10}$$

Initial conditions to determine $\psi_1, \psi_2, \ldots, \psi_p$ can be obtained by using $\rho_0 = 1$ together with the first $p - 1$ Yule-Walker equations.

The stationarity condition (7.2.7) can be stated equivalently by requiring the λ_i, $i = 1, 2, \ldots, p$, that is, the roots of (7.2.10), to be *inside* the complex unit circle. By virtue of (7.2.9), this implies that the autocorrelations ρ_k of a finite-order autoregressive process taper off to zero as k goes to infinity.

The kth partial autocorrelation coefficient of an AR process y_t measures the correlation not accounted for by an AR($k - 1$). Thus, denoting the jth coefficient of an AR(k) by ψ_{kj}, the coefficient ψ_{kk} is the kth partial autocorrelation coefficient. As we have seen above, this coefficient can be determined by using the Yule-Walker equations of order k. Recall that for an AR(p)

$$\rho_j = \theta_1 \rho_{j-1} + \ . \ . \ . + \theta_p \rho_{j-p} \qquad \text{for } j > 0$$

Replacing p by k and solving

$$\rho_j = \psi_{k1} \rho_{j-1} + \ . \ . \ . + \psi_{kk} \rho_{j-k} \qquad (j = 1, 2, \ . \ . \ . \ , k) \tag{7.2.11}$$

yields values $\psi_{k1}, \ . \ . \ . \ , \psi_{kk}$ the last of which is the kth partial autocorrelation coefficient. Of course, $\psi_{kk} = 0$ for $k > p$.

Thus, the autocorrelations of a stationary AR(p) process taper off whereas the partial autocorrelations have a cutoff point at lag p.

So far we have only discussed finite-order AR processes. It is not difficult to generalize the concept by allowing the order to be infinite. That is, we may consider

$$\begin{aligned} y_t &= \theta_1 y_{t-1} + \theta_2 y_{t-2} + \ . \ . \ . + v_t = \sum_{i=1}^{\infty} \theta_i y_{t-i} + v_t \\ &= (\theta_1 L + \theta_2 L^2 + \ . \ . \ .) y_t + v_t = \left(\sum_{i=1}^{\infty} \theta_i L^i \right) y_t + v_t \end{aligned} \tag{7.2.12}$$

Here and in the following section we mean by an infinite sum of random variables, $\Sigma_{i=1}^{\infty} \theta_i y_{t-i}$, the random variable y that satisfies

$$E \left[\sum_{i=1}^{n} \theta_i y_{t-i} - y \right]^2 \rightarrow 0 \qquad \text{as } n \rightarrow \infty \tag{7.2.13}$$

That is, y is the *mean square limit* of $\Sigma_{i=1}^{n} \theta_i y_{t-i}$.

Infinite-order AR processes are not only a theoretical construct but can also prove to be of value for practical purposes. For example, if the order of a process under consideration is unknown it may be convenient to avoid order constraints prior to the analysis. The stationarity of an infinite AR requires that the AR weights θ_n approach zero as n approaches infinity. Thus an infinite AR can be approximated by a finite AR of sufficiently high order. In the next subsection we will see that rather simple processes can have an infinite AR representation.

7.2.2 Moving Average Processes

Moving average (MA) processes are another important family of stationary processes. Their general form is

$$\begin{aligned} y_t &= v_t + \alpha_1 v_{t-1} + \ . \ . \ . + \alpha_q v_{t-q} \\ &= (1 + \alpha_1 L + \ . \ . \ . + \alpha_q L^q) v_t \end{aligned} \tag{7.2.14}$$

where v_t is again white noise with variance $\sigma_v^2 < \infty$. To indicate the order of this MA process we use the symbol MA(q) analogous to the AR case. The mean of the MA(q) process (7.2.14) is, assuming $E[v_t] = 0$,

$$E[y_t] = E[v_t] + \alpha_1 E[v_{t-1}] + \ldots + \alpha_q E[v_{t-q}] = 0$$

and the autocovariance function is for $k \geq 0$

$$\begin{aligned}
\gamma_k &= E[y_t y_{t+k}] \\
&= E[(v_t + \alpha_1 v_{t-1} + \ldots + \alpha_q v_{t-q})(v_{t+k} + \alpha_1 v_{t+k-1} + \ldots + \alpha_q v_{t+k-q})] \\
&= E\left[\left(\sum_{i=0}^{q} \alpha_i v_{t-i}\right)\left(\sum_{j=0}^{q} \alpha_j v_{t+k-j}\right)\right], \qquad \text{where } \alpha_0 = 1 \\
&= E\left[\sum_{i=0}^{q}\sum_{j=0}^{q} \alpha_i \alpha_j v_{t-i} v_{t+k-j}\right] = \sum_{i=0}^{q}\sum_{j=0}^{q} \alpha_i \alpha_j E[v_{t-1} v_{t+k-j}] \\
&= \begin{cases} \sigma_v^2 \sum_{i=0}^{q-k} \alpha_i \alpha_{i+k} & \text{for } k = 0, 1, \ldots, q \\ 0 & \text{for } k > q \end{cases}
\end{aligned} \tag{7.2.15}$$

This demonstrates the stationarity of an MA(q).

According to (7.2.15) the variance of an MA(q) is

$$\gamma_0 = \sigma_v^2(1 + \alpha_1^2 + \alpha_2^2 + \ldots + \alpha_q^2) \tag{7.2.16}$$

This formula also generalizes to MA processes of infinite order of the form

$$y_t = v_t + \alpha_1 v_{t-1} + \alpha_2 v_{t-2} + \ldots \tag{7.2.17}$$

The process y_t is stationary if

$$\gamma_0 = \sigma_v^2(1 + \alpha_1^2 + \alpha_2^2 + \ldots) \tag{7.2.18}$$

is finite. In fact, according to *Wold's decomposition theorem,* in some sense the converse is also true. That is, the nondeterministic part of any stationary stochastic process can be represented in the form of an infinite MA process. More precisely, any stationary stochastic process can be decomposed into a deterministic part and a nondeterministic part. The two components are uncorrelated and the nondeterministic part can be represented by an MA process [e.g., T. W. Anderson (1971, Section 7.6.3)]. Here a process is called *deterministic* if it can be predicted without error at any point in time. Thus, once it is started it is determined for all times. For example, the process $y_t = a \cos \omega t$, where a is a random variable, is deterministic. Once a has assumed a value it keeps this value for all t since it is independent of t and thus y_t is determined for all t. A process is called nondeterministic if it does not contain any deterministic components.

Wold's decomposition theorem implies that a stationary AR process has an MA representation. For instance, the MA representation of an AR(1) process $y_t = \theta_1 y_{t-1} + v_t$, $|\theta_1| < 1$, is easy to find. Successive substitution for y_{t-1}, y_{t-2}, etc., gives

$$\begin{aligned} y_t &= \theta_1(\theta_1 y_{t-2} + v_{t-1}) + v_t \\ &= v_t + \theta_1 v_{t-1} + \theta_1^2 v_{t-2} + \ldots \\ &= (1 + \theta_1 L + \theta_1^2 L^2 + \ldots)v_t \\ &= \frac{1}{1 - \theta_1 L} v_t \end{aligned} \tag{7.2.19}$$

This notation is of course only meaningful if the inverse of the operator $(1 - \theta_1 L)$ exists or in other words, if y_t satisfies the stationarity condition.

Conversely, many MA processes have AR representations. For instance, if $|\alpha_1| < 1$ in an MA(1) process,

$$y_t = v_t - \alpha_1 v_{t-1} = (1 - \alpha_1 L)v_t$$

we have

$$\frac{1}{1 - \alpha_1 L} y_t = v_t$$

or

$$(1 + \alpha_1 L + \alpha_1^2 L^2 + \ldots)y_t = v_t$$

or

$$y_t = -\alpha_1 y_{t-1} - \alpha_1^2 y_{t-2} - \ldots + v_t$$

Like AR operators, not all MA operators have an inverse, that is, not every MA process can be written as AR process. To guarantee invertibility of an MA(q) the solutions of the equation

$$1 + \alpha_1 z + \ldots + \alpha_q z^q = 0 \tag{7.2.20}$$

have to be outside the complex unit circle. Obviously, this *invertibility condition* is similar to the stationarity condition for AR processes given in (7.2.7). It is worth noting that, for any noninvertible MA process for which (7.2.20) has no roots on the unit circle, there exists an equivalent invertible MA process with identical autocovariance structure. A reason why the invertible representation is to be preferred is that it provides more efficient forecasts [see Harvey (1981, Section 6.4)]. If there are roots on the unit circle an invertible representation cannot be given. However, in this case there is a unique representation with all roots lying on or outside the complex unit circle. Unless otherwise noted, all MA processes considered in the following will be assumed to be invertible.

From the above discussion it follows that a finite-order invertible MA process has nonzero partial autocorrelations at all lags. Since the coefficients θ_k of the AR representation of an invertible MA(q) approach zero as $k \to \infty$, the partial autocorrelations also die out with growing k.

7.2.3 ARMA and ARIMA Processes

As a generalization of the previously mentioned processes, autoregressive schemes with moving average error terms of the form

$$y_t = \theta_1 y_{t-1} + \theta_2 y_{t-2} + \ldots + \theta_p y_{t-p} + v_t + \alpha_1 v_{t-1} + \ldots + \alpha_q v_{t-q} \tag{7.2.21}$$

have been considered. This process is called an *autoregressive-moving average process of order* (p,q) or briefly ARMA(p,q). Alternatively, (7.2.21) can be written as

$$(1 - \theta_1 L - \ldots - \theta_p L^p) y_t = (1 + \alpha_1 L + \ldots + \alpha_q L^q) v_t \tag{7.2.22}$$

To guarantee both stationarity and invertibility of this process we require that

$$\theta_p(z) = 1 - \theta_1 z - \ldots - \theta_p z^p \neq 0 \qquad \text{for } |z| \leq 1 \tag{7.2.23}$$

and

$$\alpha_q(z) = 1 + \alpha_1 z + \ldots + \alpha_q z^q \neq 0 \qquad \text{for } |z| \leq 1 \tag{7.2.24}$$

As an example of a nonstationary AR process we considered $y_t = y_{t-1} + v_t$ in Section 7.2.1. In this case, it is easy to transform y_t such that a stationary process results by simply considering the first differences $z_t = y_t - y_{t-1} = (1 - L)y_t$. More generally, if the AR operator $\theta(L)$ of the ARMA process y_t has unit roots [i.e., $\theta(1) = 0$], these can be eliminated by differencing. Assuming d unit roots, we get a general process

$$\theta_p(L)(1 - L)^d y_t = \alpha_q(L) v_t \tag{7.2.25}$$

where v_t is as usual zero mean white noise. Such a process is called an *autoregressive-integrated-moving average process* or briefly ARIMA(p,d,q) if $\theta_p(L)$ and $\alpha_q(L)$ have degree p and q, respectively.

It turns out that, in practice, a trend can often be eliminated by differencing and an ARMA model can then be fitted to the differenced data. The empirical autocorrelations of a time series showing this kind of nonstationarity typically die out at less than exponential speed. The asymptotic behavior of ARIMA processes is considered by Stigum (1975).

7.2.4 Seasonal ARIMA Processes

If the data shows a strong seasonal pattern, this indicates a high correlation between values observed during the same season in consecutive years. For example, for monthly data the random variables attached to the January of consecutive years may have a high correlation whereas the June figures may not be correlated with the January figures. In such a case, modeling the data generation process by an ARIMA process of the type considered above may require an unnecessarily large number of parameters. To cope with this problem Box and Jenkins (1976) suggest using multiplicative seasonal ARIMA models. Their general form is

$$\theta_p(L)\theta_P^s(L^s)(1 - L^s)^D(1 - L)^d y_t = \alpha_q(L)\alpha_Q^s(L^s)v_t \tag{7.2.26}$$

where $\theta_p(L)$, $\alpha_q(L)$ are as before, s is the seasonal period,

$$\theta_P^s(L^s) = 1 - \theta_1^s L^s - \ldots - \theta_P^s L^{sP} \tag{7.2.27}$$

$$\alpha_Q^s(L^s) = 1 + \alpha_1^s L^s + \ldots + \alpha_Q^s L^{sQ} \tag{7.2.28}$$

and D is the number of times the seasonal difference operator $(1 - L^s)$ is applied. For instance, for quarterly data $s = 4$ and assuming $p = P = Q = 1$ and $q = D = d = 0$ we get a process

$$(1 - \theta_1 L)(1 - \theta_1^s L^4)y_t = (1 + \alpha_1^s L^4)v_t$$

or

$$(1 - \theta_1 L - \theta_1^s L^4 + \theta_1\theta_1^s L^5)y_t = (1 + \alpha_1^s L^4)v_t$$

which can be regarded as an ARMA(5,4) process. However, writing it as a general ARMA(5,4) process would require nine instead of only three parameters. In Chapter 8 ARMA and seasonal ARMA processes will be used for modeling the error process of an econometric model and some special processes are discussed in more detail.

7.2.5 Nonlinear and Nonstationary Processes

By concentrating on ARIMA processes that are linear time series models we have neglected some important problems. First, it is not universally true that linear models are the optimal choice, and thus, nonlinear time series models have also been considered in the context of economic data analysis. References on nonlinear time series models include Granger and Andersen (1978), Engle (1982), Nicholls and Quinn (1982), and Priestley (1980, 1981, Chapter 11). The latter contains a number of further references on the topic.

Second, the only nonstationarities we have allowed for arise from unit roots in the AR operator. This is clearly restrictive since all roots in and on the complex unit circle cause nonstationarities. O. D. Anderson and de Gooijer (1982) consider AR processes with roots on the unit circle that are not equal to one. Other nonstationarities can arise from structural changes at a particular point in time resulting in a different covariance structure before and after that time point. Alternatively, the covariance structure may evolve smoothly through time or be subject to stochastic changes. Publications on nonstationary time series models include Granger and Newbold (1977, Section 9.4), Priestley (1965, 1981, Chapter 11).

7.3 FORECASTING ARIMA PROCESSES

If the generation process of a time series is known, this process can be used to predict future values of the variable of interest. Usually an attempt is made to derive forecasts that are optimal in some sense. Therefore, a loss function is set up that depends on the forecasting error that we make in predicting future values of the variable of interest. A fairly common loss function is the expected squared forecasting error.

More formally, the objective is to investigate the properties of the random variables y_{T+h} when realizations of the y_t are only available for $t \leq T$. Let us denote the forecast h time periods ahead by $y_T(h)$. From the above discussion it follows that the minimization of the expected quadratic forecasting error $E[(y_{T+h} - y_T(h))^2]$ is a meaningful objective. Note that a quadratic cost function implies that the costs are equal for over and understating the future values of the random variable by the same amount. This is certainly not always realistic. However, in many situations of practical relevance, the mean squared forecasting error can still be justified as a cost function. For a more detailed discussion concerning the choice of a cost function the reader is referred to Granger and Newbold (1977, Section 4.2). In the following we will give forecasting formulas for ARIMA processes.

Let us assume that y_t is a stationary ARMA process with MA representation

$$y_t = v_t + \alpha_1 v_{t-1} + \alpha_2 v_{t-2} + \cdots \tag{7.3.1}$$

As mentioned above, the objective is to find $y_T(h) = f(y_T, y_{T-1}, \ldots)$ such that

$$E[(y_{T+h} - y_T(h))^2] \leq E[(y_{T+h} - a)^2] \tag{7.3.2}$$

for any a. For practical reasons we will require f to be a linear function and rather than using the information set $\{y_t | t \leq T\}$ we can equivalently use $\{v_t | t \leq T\}$ since y_t is assumed stationary. The equivalence of the two information sets relies on the assumption that they consist of an infinite number of past values so that, for example, for an AR(1) process, $y_t = \theta_1 y_{t-1} + v_t$, the tth value can be computed as

$$y_t = v_t + \theta_1 v_{t-1} + \theta_1^2 v_{t-2} + \ldots$$

Of course, in practice only finite samples are available. However, if the sample size is sufficiently large, the assumption of an infinite information set is of little consequence as long as the MA operator has no roots close to the unit circle. For a more detailed discussion see Fuller (1976, Section 2.9).

Suppose that $\bar{y}_T(h)$ is any linear h-step forecast based on $\{v_t | t \leq T\}$, say

$$\bar{y}_T(h) = \beta_0 v_T + \beta_1 v_{T-1} + \ldots \tag{7.3.3}$$

then the forecasting error is

$$\begin{aligned} y_{T+h} - \bar{y}_T(h) = {} & v_{T+h} + \alpha_1 v_{T+h-1} + \ldots + \alpha_{h-1} v_{T+1} + \alpha_h v_T + \ldots \\ & - \beta_0 v_T - \beta_1 v_{T-1} - \ldots \end{aligned}$$

and thus, the mean squared forecasting error is

$$\begin{aligned} E[(y_{T+h} - \bar{y}_T(h))^2] = {} & E[(v_{T+h} + \alpha_1 v_{T+h-1} + \ldots + \alpha_{h-1} v_{T+1})^2] \\ & + E[(\alpha_h - \beta_0) v_T + (\alpha_{h+1} - \beta_1) v_{T-1} + \ldots]^2 \end{aligned}$$

Clearly, this expression is minimized if $\beta_0 = \alpha_h$, $\beta_1 = \alpha_{h+1}, \ldots$ and the optimal predictor is

$$y_T(h) = \alpha_h v_T + \alpha_{h+1} v_{T-1} + \ldots \tag{7.3.4}$$

In fact, to compute this forecast, it is not necessary to convert to the MA representation of the process y_t. For example, for a stationary ARMA(p,q) process

$$y_t = \theta_1 y_{t-1} + \ldots + \theta_p y_{t-p} + v_t + \alpha_1 v_{t-1} + \ldots + \alpha_q v_{t-q}$$

the optimal h-step forecast is

$$y_T(h) = \theta_1 \bar{y}_{T+h-1} + \ldots + \theta_p \bar{y}_{T+h-p} + \alpha_h v_T + \alpha_{h+1} v_{T-1} + \ldots + \alpha_q v_{T-q+h} \tag{7.3.5}$$

where $\bar{y}_t = y_t$ for $t \leq T$ and $\bar{y}_{T+j} = y_T(j)$ for $j = 1, \ldots, h - 1$.

If y_t is Gaussian, the optimal linear predictor is the conditional expected value given $y_T, y_{T-1}, \ldots$, that is,

$$y_T(h) = E[y_{T+h} | y_T, y_{T-1}, \ldots] \tag{7.3.6}$$

which implies that it has minimum mean squared error from within the class of all predictors, not just those that are linear. However, this result does not hold in general. Fuller (1976, Chapter 2) gives the following example of an AR(1) process $y_t = \theta y_{t-1} + v_t$, where $|\theta| < 1$,

$$v_t = \begin{cases} e_t, & t = 0, \pm 2, \pm 4, \ldots \\ \dfrac{e_{t-1}^2 - 1}{\sqrt{2}}, & t = \pm 1, \pm 3, \ldots \end{cases}$$

and the e_t are independent $N(0,1)$ random variables. It is easy to see that v_t is uncorrelated but not independent white noise. The optimal *linear* one-step forecast of y_{T+1} is $y_T(1) = \theta y_T$ [see (7.3.5)]. However, assuming T is even, a better forecast is

$$E[y_{T+1}|y_T, y_{T-1}, \ldots] = \theta y_T + \frac{e_T^2 - 1}{\sqrt{2}}$$

For a Gaussian process, approximate $(1 - \alpha)100\%$ confidence bounds for the h-step ahead point forecast $y_T(h)$ can be obtained using

$$y_T(h) \pm z_{\alpha/2}\sqrt{E[(y_T(h) - y_{T+h})^2]} \tag{7.3.7}$$

where $z_{\alpha/2}$ is the critical point of the normal distribution.

For ARIMA processes, that is, processes that have an ARMA representation after differencing a sufficient number of times, forecasts can be obtained as follows. Suppose y_t is an ARIMA process such that $z_t = (1 - L)y_t = y_t - y_{t-1}$ is an ARMA process. Then

$$\begin{aligned} y_{T+h} &= z_{T+h} + y_{T+h-1} = z_{T+h} + z_{T+h-1} + y_{T+h-2} = \ldots \\ &= z_{T+h} + z_{T+h-1} + \ldots + z_{T+1} + y_T \end{aligned}$$

Thus, an h-step ahead forecast of y_{T+h} can be computed as

$$\begin{aligned} y_T(h) &= z_T(h) + z_T(h-1) + \ldots + z_T(1) + y_T \\ &= z_T(h) + y_T(h-1) \end{aligned} \tag{7.3.8}$$

where the optimal forecasts $z_T(k)$ $(k = 1, 2, \ldots, h)$ of the ARMA process z_t are obtained as above. Similar formulas can be derived if the difference operator has to be applied more than once to obtain a stationary ARMA process or if the seasonal difference operator is applied.

In practice, the parameters of the process are not generally precisely known but will be estimated from a given set of data. Fuller and Hasza (1981) and Yamamoto (1976, 1980) derive the forecasting error for ARMA processes taking into account the variability in the parameter estimators. For further references see also Chapter 8, Section 8.3.

7.4 ESTIMATION OF ARMA PROCESSES

Usually the orders as well as the parameters of an ARMA process are unknown and have to be determined from the available data. In this section we assume that the orders are known so that only the parameters need to be estimated. In the next chapter various special processes will be assumed to represent the error term of a regression model and for these processes the estimation problem is treated in detail in a more general framework of regression models with autocorrelated errors. Therefore, we will only give a brief account of estimating ARMA processes in this section.

Assuming that the y_t are generated by a stationary Gaussian ARMA(p,q) process (7.2.21) the likelihood function can be shown to be of the form

$$\ell = \frac{1}{\sqrt{2\pi\sigma_v^2}} h(\theta_1, \ldots, \theta_p, \alpha_1, \ldots, \alpha_q) \exp - \left\{ \frac{\sum_{t=-\infty}^{T} (E_c[v_t])^2}{2\sigma_v^2} \right\} \tag{7.4.1}$$

[e.g., Newbold (1974), Granger and Newbold (1977)], where $h(\cdot)$ is a function of the parameters that does not depend on the data and $E_c[v_t]$ is the conditional expected value of v_t given the sample $y_1, y_2, \ldots, y_T$. The function $h(\cdot)$ is negligible for large T and thus minimizing the sum of squares

$$S = \sum_{t=-\infty}^{T} (E_c[v_t])^2 \tag{7.4.2}$$

results in estimators that are *asymptotically* equivalent to the exact ML estimators. For example, for a pure AR process

$$y_t = \theta_1 y_{t-1} + \theta_2 y_{t-2} + \ldots + \theta_p y_{t-p} + v_t \tag{7.4.3}$$

we get

$$E_c[v_t] = y_t - \theta_1 y_{t-1} - \ldots - \theta_p y_{t-p} \tag{7.4.4}$$

for $T \geq t > p$. Replacing all presample values by their expected value of zero the conditional sum of squares given these presample values becomes

$$S_c = \sum_{t=1}^{T} (y_t - \theta_1 y_{t-1} - \ldots - \theta_p y_{t-p})^2 \tag{7.4.5}$$

where $y_0 = y_{-1} = \ldots = y_{1-p} = 0$. Minimization of S_c yields estimates asymptotically equivalent to the LS estimates from (7.4.2) and thus, to the exact ML estimates. Another asymptotically equivalent estimator results from minimizing

$$S^* = \sum_{t=p+1}^{T} (y_t - \theta_1 y_{t-1} - \ldots - \theta_p y_{t-p})^2 \tag{7.4.6}$$

That is, $y_1, y_2, \ldots, y_p$ are regarded as presample values. Both (7.4.5) and (7.4.6) allow us to use a linear least squares routine for estimating a pure AR model if only large sample properties of the estimators are of interest.

If the mean μ of the y_t is nonzero, then the sample mean can be subtracted from the data before estimation of the remaining parameters. Alternatively, the y_t's in (7.4.3) can be replaced by $y_t - \mu$ giving a regression equation

$$y_t = \bar{\mu} + \theta_1 y_{t-1} + \ldots + \theta_p y_{t-p} + v_t \tag{7.4.7}$$

where

$$\bar{\mu} = \mu - \theta_1 \mu - \theta_2 \mu - \ldots - \theta_p \mu \tag{7.4.8}$$

If the model constructed for the data generating process involves an MA component, then the estimation problem is computationally more complicated. For expository purposes consider the MA(1) model

$$y_t = v_t - \alpha_1 v_{t-1} \tag{7.4.9}$$

Assuming $|\alpha_1| < 1$, this can be written as the infinite AR process

$$y_t + \alpha_1 y_{t-1} + \alpha_1^2 y_{t-2} + \ldots = v_t \tag{7.4.10}$$

Replacing all unknown initial conditions in (7.4.10) by zero we find the conditional LS estimate of α_1 by minimizing

$$S_c = \sum_{t=1}^{T} (y_t + \alpha_1 y_{t-1} + \alpha_1^2 y_{t-2} + \ldots \alpha_1^{t-1} y_1)^2 \tag{7.4.11}$$

This, however, is a nonlinear least squares problem and requires a numerical minimization. For this simple case, a grid search is a possible strategy to find the minimum since there is only one parameter known to be between minus one and one. To compute S_c the v_t can be conveniently obtained recursively using $v_t = y_t + \alpha_1 v_{t-1}$ and setting $v_0 = 0$. For higher-order models a numerical minimization algorithm is usually preferable. Some of these algorithms are discussed in Appendix B at the end of the book.

Estimation packages for ARMA models are now available in many computer centers and can considerably simplify the estimation problem for the user. Usually initial estimates for the parameters have to be supplied as starting values for the optimization algorithms and the success of the procedure in finding the optimum depends to some extent on the choice of these values. Initial estimates of the parameters of the autoregressive representation can be obtained by substituting the sample autocorrelations in the Yule-Walker equations and solving for the AR parameters. Initial estimates of the ARMA parameters can then be obtained from the AR estimates. For example, the ARMA(1,1) process $y_t = \theta_1 y_{t-1} + v_t + \alpha_1 v_{t-1}$ has the AR representation

$$(1 + \phi_1 L + \phi_2 L^2 + \ldots)y_t = \frac{1 - \theta_1 L}{1 + \alpha_1 L} y_t$$
$$= (1 + (-\theta_1 - \alpha_1)L + (\alpha_1^2 + \theta_1\alpha_1)L^2 + \ldots)y_t$$
$$= v_t$$

so that $\phi_1 = -\theta_1 - \alpha_1$ and $\phi_2 = \alpha_1^2 + \theta_1\alpha_1$. These two equations can be solved for α_1 and θ_1 and thus, replacing ϕ_1 and ϕ_2 by their initial estimates, we get initial estimates for α_1 and θ_1.

For a stationary, invertible Gaussian process the ML estimates are consistent, asymptotically efficient and normally distributed. The inverse of the information matrix

$$I(\tilde{\mathbf{v}}) = -E\left[\left.\frac{\partial^2 \ln \ell}{\partial \mathbf{v} \partial \mathbf{v}'}\right|_{\mathbf{v}=\tilde{\mathbf{v}}}\right] \tag{7.4.12}$$

can be used as an estimator of the asymptotic covariance matrix of the ML estimator $\tilde{\mathbf{v}} = (\tilde{\theta}_1, \ldots, \tilde{\theta}_p, \tilde{\alpha}_1, \ldots, \tilde{\alpha}_q)'$. Of course, in (7.4.12) $\ln \ell$ is the logarithm of the likelihood function. For a further discussion of ML estimation of ARMA processes see, Chapter 8 or Newbold (1974), Ali (1977), T. W. Anderson (1977), Ansley (1979), Ljung and Box (1979), Harvey (1981), and Priestley (1981).

As we have seen above, various asymptotically equivalent estimation procedures are available and the applied researcher has to make a choice as to which one to use for a particular problem at hand. This decision will often depend on the available software. If different estimation algorithms are available, the choice should be based on the small-sample properties of the resulting estimators. Ansley and Newbold (1980) performed a large-scale Monte Carlo study comparing ML, exact LS, and conditional LS estimators. They found that out of the set of these three asymptotically equivalent estimation rules ML is usually preferable in samples of the size typically available for economic variables. Approximations of the sample distribution of the parameter of an AR(1) model using Edgeworth expansions are considered by Phillips (1977, 1978) and Maekawa (1983). For a more extensive summary of small-sample results, see Chapter 8.

The asymptotic efficiency of the least squares estimates relies on the assumption that the process y_t is Gaussian. If the normality assumption is relaxed, it can be shown that under suitable conditions the estimators are still consistent and asymptotically normally distributed [e.g., Fuller (1976, Chapter 8), Hannan (1970)]. However, if the process is not Gaussian and outliers occur, robust estimation methods can be advantageous [e.g., Martin, Samorov, and Vandaele (1981), Birch and Martin (1981), and Martin (1980)]. Estimation when the model is slightly misspecified was, for instance, considered by Ploberger (1982). Stigum (1974), Dickey and Said (1981), Rao (1978), Fuller (1976), Hasza and Fuller (1979, 1982), Fuller, Hasza, and Goebel (1981), and Lai and Wei (1983) discuss estimation when the AR operator has a root on or in the unit circle (and thus, the process is nonstationary). A number of further references on this topic can be found in the article by Fuller, Hasza, and Goebel (1981).

7.5 SPECIFICATION OF ARIMA PROCESSES

One of the more difficult problems in modeling the generation process of a given time series is the specification of an adequate model. If the model is chosen from the class of ARIMA processes, the AR and MA order as well as the order of differencing have to be specified before the parameters can be estimated. Various methods have been suggested for that purpose. Perhaps the most popular one is the Box-Jenkins approach sketched as follows.

7.5.1 The Box-Jenkins Approach

The method proposed by Box and Jenkins (1976) is customarily partitioned in three stages: identification, estimation, and diagnostic checking. At the identification stage a *tentative* ARIMA model is specified for the data generating process on the basis of the autocorrelations ρ_k and partial autocorrelations ψ_{kk}. For a given sample $y_1, \ldots, y_T$, the former can be estimated by

$$r_k = \frac{\sum_{t=1}^{T-k} (y_t - \bar{y})(y_{t+k} - \bar{y})}{\sum_{t=1}^{T} (y_t - \bar{y})^2} \tag{7.5.1}$$

where $\bar{y}$ is the sample mean. An alternative, asymptotically equivalent estimate for ρ_k is

$$\bar{r}_k = \frac{T}{T-k} r_k \tag{7.5.2}$$

An estimate of the kth partial autocorrelation coefficient ψ_{kk} can be obtained by using the Yule-Walker equations, that is, by replacing the ρ_j in (7.2.11) by estimates. Alternatively, ψ_{kk} can be estimated by LS using the linear model

$$y_t^* = \psi_{k1} y_{t-1}^* + \cdots + \psi_{kk} y_{t-k}^* + v_t \tag{7.5.3}$$

where $y_t^* = y_t - \bar{y}$. To identify integers p, d, q the following results can be used.

1. If the autocorrelations do not die out rapidly, this indicates nonstationarity and differencing (usually not more than once or twice) is suggested until stationarity is obtained. Then an ARMA model is identified for the differenced series.
2. For an MA(q) process the autocorrelations $\rho_k = 0$ for $k > q$ and the partial autocorrelations taper off.

3. For an AR(p) the partial autocorrelations $\psi_{kk} = 0$ for $k > p$ and the autocorrelations taper off.
4. If neither the autocorrelations nor the partial autocorrelations have a cutoff point, an ARMA model may be adequate. The AR and the MA degree have to be inferred from the particular pattern of the autocorrelations and partial autocorrelations.

Also, if a seasonal ARIMA model is adequate this has to be inferred from the autocorrelations and partial autocorrelations. However, the specification of a tentative ARIMA model by visually inspecting the estimates of these quantities requires some experience and a more detailed exposition and examples can be found in Box and Jenkins (1976), O. D. Anderson (1976), Judge et al. (1982, Chapter 25), and Nelson (1973).

Once the orders of the tentative model are specified, its parameters can be estimated as discussed in Section 7.4. Finally, the adequacy of the model may be checked for example by analyzing the residuals or by overfitting the obtained model. For an overview of possible tests for model adequacy in the present context see Newbold (1981a). If the model is rejected at the checking stage, the model building cycle has to be restarted with a new identification round.

The Box-Jenkins procedure involves a subjective element at the identification stage that can be advantageous since it permits nonsample information to be taken into account that may exclude a range of models for a particular time series. On the other hand, this feature makes the procedure relatively difficult to apply and there has been a search for methods that allow an automatic fitting of ARIMA models or at least aid in the choice of an adequate process for a given time series. The *corner method* [Beguin, Gourieroux, and Monfort (1980)] and the S-array and R-array procedures [Gray, Kelley, and McIntire (1978), Woodward and Gray (1981)] belong to this class. In the following section we present some other methods for the special case of fitting pure AR models. Most of the methods have been extended to ARMA model building.

7.5.2 AR Order Selection

In this section we assume the basic model to be a stationary Gaussian AR(p) process

$$y_t = \theta_1 y_{t-1} + \ . \ . \ . + \theta_p y_{t-p} + v_t \tag{7.5.4}$$

where v_t is white noise as before and it is assumed that some upper bound for p, say m, is given for a particular time series under study. In the following section we present some methods and criteria for estimating p. Some of the criteria are listed in Table 7.2. and are further discussed in Chapter 21 in the context of selecting the regressors for a linear model.

TABLE 7.2 ***ESTIMATING THE ORDER OF AN AUTOREGRESSIVE PROCESS***

General estimation rule: Choose $\hat{p}$ such that $\Psi(\hat{p}) = \min\{\Psi(k) | k = 1, \ldots, m\}$

Criteria
$\Psi(k)$

$$\text{FPE}(k) = \frac{T+k}{T-k}\tilde{\sigma}_k^2$$

$$\text{FPE}^{\beta}(k) = \frac{1 + k/T^{\beta}}{1 - k/T}\tilde{\sigma}_k^2 \qquad 0 < \beta < 1$$

$$\text{FPE}_{\alpha}(k) = \left(1 + \frac{\alpha k}{T}\right)\tilde{\sigma}_k^2 \qquad \alpha > 0$$

$$\text{AIC}(k) = \ln \tilde{\sigma}_k^2 + \frac{2k}{T}$$

$$\text{SC}(k) = \ln \tilde{\sigma}_k^2 + \frac{k \ln T}{T}$$

$$\text{CAT}(k) = \frac{1}{T}\sum_{j=1}^{k} \frac{T-j}{T}\tilde{\sigma}_j^{-2} - \frac{T-k}{T}\tilde{\sigma}_k^{-2}$$

$$\Phi(k) = \ln \tilde{\sigma}_k^2 + \frac{2kc_T \ln \ln T}{T}, \qquad \lim_{T\to\infty} \sup c_T > 1$$

$$S_T(k) = (T + 2k)\tilde{\sigma}_k^2$$

7.5.2a Sequential Testing

A more traditional way to determine an adequate p is to test sequentially

$$\begin{aligned} H_1&: \theta_m = 0 \\ H_2&: \theta_m = \theta_{m-1} = 0 \\ &\text{etc.} \end{aligned} \tag{7.5.5}$$

The likelihood ratio test statistic

$$\Lambda_i = T(\ln \tilde{\sigma}_{m-i}^2 - \ln \tilde{\sigma}_m^2) \tag{7.5.6}$$

which is asymptotically $\chi^2_{(i)}$ distributed, can be used to test H_i. Here $\tilde{\sigma}_k^2$ is the ML estimate of the residual variance when an AR(k) is fitted to the data, that is,

$$\tilde{\sigma}_k^2 = \frac{1}{T}(\text{sum of squares of errors of AR}(k)) \tag{7.5.7}$$

where T is the sample size actually used for estimation.

Alternatively Quenouille's (1947) statistic

$$Q_i = T \sum_{k=m-i+1}^{m} \hat{\psi}_{kk}^2 \tag{7.5.8}$$

which is asymptotically $\chi^2_{(i)}$ distributed under the null hypothesis [T. W. Anderson (1971, p. 221)] could be used. Here $\hat{\psi}_{kk}$ is an estimate of the kth partial autocorrelation computed as LS estimate of the kth coefficient of an AR(k).

If any of the hypotheses in (7.5.5) is wrong, then all succeeding ones are also false and the testing procedure terminates if one of the hypotheses is rejected. The estimated value of p will depend on the significance level chosen. Therefore it is important to note that the Type I error of the kth test in a sequence of tests will differ from the significance level of the kth individual test. Following T. W. Anderson (1971, Section 3.2.2) the kth test in the sequence has a Type I error

$$\alpha_k = \begin{cases} \eta_k & \text{if } k = 1 \\ \eta_k(1 - \alpha_{k-1}) + \alpha_{k-1} & \text{if } k = 2, \ldots, m \end{cases} \tag{7.5.9}$$

where η_k is the significance level of the kth individual test. For further discussion of sequential testing see also Hannan (1970).

Note that using a testing procedure to determine the AR order implies that the resulting parameter estimators are actually pretest estimators. We pointed out in Chapter 3 that the sampling properties of pretest estimators are unknown in general. However, in the present case, asymptotic properties is all we can derive anyway and the asymptotic properties of the parameter estimators are not affected if the AR order is estimated consistently. Therefore, it is of interest that Pötscher (1982) gives conditions for consistent estimation of the AR order using Lagrange multiplier tests. In fact, Pötscher discusses testing procedures in the more general context of ARMA model fitting.

7.5.2b FPE

Since forecasting is the ultimate objective of many time series analyses it seems natural to choose p to minimize the prediction error. Based on this idea, Akaike (1969, 1970a) developed his *final prediction error* (FPE) criterion given by

$$\text{FPE}(k) = \frac{T + k}{T - k} \tilde{\sigma}_k^2 \tag{7.5.10}$$

Using this criterion, an estimate $\hat{p}$ is chosen such that

$$\text{FPE}(\hat{p}) = \min\{\text{FPE}(k) | k = 1, \ldots, m\} \tag{7.5.11}$$

Note that this criterion is equivalent to Amemiya's (1980) PC proposed for selection of regressors (see Chapter 21).

Modifications of the FPE criterion are suggested by Akaike (1970b) who considers

$$\mathrm{FPE}^{\beta}(k) = \frac{1 + k/T^{\beta}}{1 - k/T}\,\tilde{\sigma}_k^2, \qquad 0 < \beta < 1 \tag{7.5.12}$$

and McClave (1975) and Bhansali and Downham (1977) who investigate

$$\mathrm{FPE}_{\alpha}(k) = \left(1 + \frac{\alpha k}{T}\right)\tilde{\sigma}_k^2, \qquad \alpha > 0 \tag{7.5.13}$$

Increasing α reduces the probability of fitting too high an order. For $\alpha \leq 1$ the asymptotic probability of overfitting is substantial. The two criteria (7.5.12) and (7.5.13) are related by

$$\mathrm{FPE}^{\beta}(k) = \mathrm{FPE}_{\alpha}(k) + \mathrm{O}\left(\frac{1}{T^{\beta+1}}\right) \tag{7.5.14}$$

[see Bhansali and Downham (1977)] and moreover

$$\mathrm{FPE}(k) = \mathrm{FPE}_{2}(k) + \mathrm{O}\left(\frac{1}{T^{2}}\right) \tag{7.5.15}$$

An extension of the FPE criterion to the case of ARMA model fitting is given by Howrey (1978).

7.5.2c AIC

Another criterion proposed by Akaike (1973, 1974a) for AR order estimation is based on an extension of the maximum likelihood principle. Suppose we have a random sample $y_1, \ldots, y_T$ from a population characterized by a pdf $g(y)$ that is known to be contained in a class of densities

$$\mathfrak{D} = \{f(y|\boldsymbol{\theta})|\boldsymbol{\theta} \in \mathfrak{R}^i, \qquad i = 1, \ldots, m\} \tag{7.5.16}$$

where $\mathfrak{R}^i$ is the i-dimensional Euclidean space. The Kullback-Leibler mean information for discriminating between $g(y)$ and a member $f(y|\boldsymbol{\theta}) \in \mathfrak{D}$ is

$$I(g(\cdot), f(\cdot|\boldsymbol{\theta})) = \int [\ln g(y) - \ln f(y|\boldsymbol{\theta})]g(y)\, dy \tag{7.5.17}$$

This quantity is greater than zero unless $g(y) = f(y|\boldsymbol{\theta})$ almost everywhere. Thus, minimizing I is a meaningful objective. Obviously, this is a generalization of the ML principle, where the class of densities is constrained to a set of the type $\{f(y|\boldsymbol{\theta})|\boldsymbol{\theta} \in \mathfrak{R}^n\}$, that is, the considered densities differ only through their parameter vector and not its dimension.

Minimizing (7.5.17) requires that the unknown quantities be replaced by estimates. Akaike (1973) shows that minimizing

$$-2 \ln(\text{maximum likelihood}) + 2(\text{number of parameters}) \tag{7.5.18}$$

instead of (7.5.17) is reasonable. This result carries over to the more general case where the sample consists of realizations of an AR process. Assuming a Gaussian process *Akaike's information criterion* (AIC) reduces to

$$\text{AIC}(k) = \ln \tilde{\sigma}_k^2 + \frac{2k}{T} \tag{7.5.19}$$

The optimal AR order $\hat{p}$ is chosen such that

$$\text{AIC}(\hat{p}) = \min\{\text{AIC}(k) | k = 1, \ldots, m\} \tag{7.5.20}$$

AIC is closely related to the FPE criterion. In particular, it is easy to show that

$$\ln \text{FPE}(k) = \text{AIC}(k) + O\left(\frac{1}{T^2}\right) \tag{7.5.21}$$

Consequently the two criteria are asymptotically equivalent.

Shibata (1976) has shown that, for a finite-order AR process, AIC (and hence FPE) asymptotically overestimates the order with positive probability. Thus, an estimator of the AR order based on AIC will not be consistent. An extension to ARMA model fitting is considered by Akaike (1974b), Kitagawa (1977), and Ozaki (1977).

7.5.2d SC

Using Bayesian arguments, Schwarz (1978) derives yet another criterion. Assuming an a priori probability of the true model being k for $k \leq m$ and an a priori conditional distribution of the parameters given the AR(k) is the true model, Schwarz suggests choosing the a posteriori most probable model. This procedure leads to an order estimation criterion

$$-2 \ln(\text{maximum likelihood}) + (\ln T)(\text{number of parameters})$$

which is to be minimized. Thus, for a Gaussian process, $\hat{p}$ is chosen so as to minimize

$$\text{SC}(k) = \ln \tilde{\sigma}_k^2 + \frac{k \ln T}{T} \tag{7.5.22}$$

in order to determine the order of an AR process. Later we will see that the resulting estimator for the AR order is consistent. For a further discussion of

SC see Akaike (1978), Rissanen (1978), and Stone (1979). An extension to modeling ARMA processes is discussed by Hannan and Rissanen (1982).

7.5.2e CAT

Another criterion for estimating the order of an AR process was suggested by Parzen (1974). It is assumed that the process of interest is as given in (7.5.4) with possibly infinite order p and interest centers on the *transfer function*

$$\theta(z) = 1 - \theta_1 z - \theta_2 z^2 - \ldots \tag{7.5.23}$$

In this situation, Parzen proposes to choose the AR order $\hat{p}$ for a given sample of size T such that the overall mean square error of $\hat{\theta}_{\hat{p}}(z)$ as an estimate of $\theta(z)$ is minimized. As an estimate of the MSE he suggests the *criterion autoregressive transfer function* (CAT)

$$\text{CAT}(k) = \frac{1}{T}\sum_{j=1}^{k}\frac{1}{\hat{\sigma}_j^2} - \frac{1}{\hat{\sigma}_k^2} \tag{7.5.24}$$

where

$$\hat{\sigma}_k^2 = \frac{T}{T-k}\tilde{\sigma}_k^2 \tag{7.5.25}$$

For further discussion of this criterion see Parzen (1977, 1979).

7.5.2f Consistent Order Estimation

If the true order p of the data generating process is finite, the asymptotic theory for the parameter estimators discussed in Section 7.4 remains valid if p is estimated consistently. As we mentioned earlier, AIC and FPE do not provide consistent estimation rules. However, Hannan and Quinn (1979) have shown that choosing $\hat{p}$ such that

$$\Phi(\hat{p}) = \min\{\Phi(k)|k = 1, \ldots, m\} \tag{7.5.26}$$

where

$$\Phi(k) = \ln \tilde{\sigma}_k^2 + \frac{2kc_T \ln \ln T}{T} \tag{7.5.27}$$

and c_T is a quantity that depends on the sample size, results in an estimator $\hat{p}$ that converges almost surely (and hence in probability) to p for $T \rightarrow \infty$ if and only if

$$\lim_{T\rightarrow\infty} \sup c_T > 1 \tag{7.5.28}$$

This result implies that SC is a consistent estimation rule. For an extension of (7.5.27) to ARMA model fitting, see Hannan (1980).

7.5.2g Asymptotically Efficient Order Selection

Suppose now that the order of the considered AR process (7.5.4) is infinite, that is, $p = \infty$. Moreover, assume that

$$\sum_{n=1}^{\infty} |\theta_n| < \infty \tag{7.5.29}$$

and the sequence $\{m_T\}$ is such that

$$m_T \rightarrow \infty, \frac{m_T}{\sqrt{T}} \rightarrow 0 \qquad \text{as } T \rightarrow \infty \tag{7.5.30}$$

Shibata (1980) shows that in this situation estimating the AR order $\hat{p}$ such that

$$S_T(\hat{p}) = \min\{S_T(k)|k = 1, \ldots, m_T\} \tag{7.5.31}$$

where

$$S_T(k) = (T + 2k)\tilde{\sigma}_k^2 \tag{7.5.32}$$

results in an asymptotically efficient estimator of p in the sense that, asymptotically as $T \rightarrow \infty$, the one-step expected quadratic forecasting error is minimized. Note that here the maximum AR order is a function of the sample size T. Clearly $S_T(k)$ is equivalent to $FPE_2(k)$ given in (7.5.13) and FPE and AIC are asymptotically equivalent to $S_T(k)$ and thus, they share the optimality properties of the latter. Algebraic and Monte Carlo comparisons of the above criteria are reported, for example, by Bora-Senta and Kounias (1980) and Lütkepohl (1982).

7.6 FREQUENCY DOMAIN ANALYSIS

Using the models introduced in Section 7.2 to represent the generation process of a given time series can be regarded as an attempt to summarize the autocovariance structure of the data generation process in a convenient form. In the following we discuss an alternative way to summarize the autocovariance characteristics of a stochastic process. The spectrum or spectral density will be introduced for that purpose and we will try to provide an intuitive basis for some of the concepts underlying spectral analysis. A similar exposition can be found for example in Granger and Newbold (1977) and Harvey (1981). Spectral methods can be used in estimating regression models with autocorrelated disturbances as discussed in Chapter 8 and will also be useful in estimating distributed lag relationships in Chapter 10. Furthermore, spectral methods are used when multiple time series are discussed in Chapter 16.

7.6.1 The Spectrum of a Stochastic Process

In Figure 7.1 the graph of a time series is depicted that might well appear to be based on some real-life data, yet it is generated as a sum of m terms of the general form

$$a_j \cos(\omega_j t + h_j) \tag{7.6.1}$$

This term represents a periodic function with *amplitude* a_j, *frequency* ω_j (number of cycles per unit measured in radians), *phase* h_j and *wavelength* $2\pi/\omega_j$. Suppose that all the $a_j, j = 1, \ldots, m$, are independent random variables with zero mean, $E[a_j] = 0$, and the $h_j, j = 1, \ldots, m$, are independent random variables uniformly distributed over the interval $(-\pi,\pi)$. Furthermore, we assume independence of a_k and h_j for all k,j. The h_j are confined to the interval $(-\pi,\pi)$ since $\cos(\omega_j t + 2\pi + h_j) = \cos(\omega_j t + h_j)$. Also, we may assume that ω_j is in the interval $(-\pi,\pi)$ since

$$\cos[(\omega_j + 2\pi)t + h_j] = \cos(\omega_j t + h_j)$$

for integer t.

To investigate the properties of stochastic processes consisting of cosine terms of the form (7.6.1) we begin with the most simple case

$$y_t = a \cos(\omega t + h) \tag{7.6.2}$$

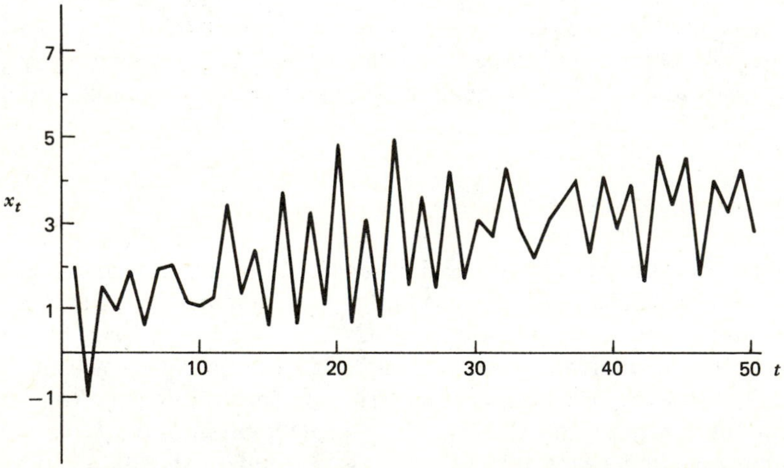

Figure 7.1 Time series generated as a sum of cosine terms: $x_t = 10\cos(.01t - 1.5) + \cos(.05t - 1) + .5\cos t + 2\cos(3t + 3) + \cos[(\pi/2)t] + .5\cos(\pi t)$.

where ω is a known constant and a and h have the aforementioned properties; that is, they are independent, $E[a] = 0$ and $h \sim U(-\pi,\pi)$. Obviously y_t has zero mean,

$$E[y_t] = E[a]E[\cos(\omega t + h)] = 0 \tag{7.6.3}$$

and

$$\begin{aligned}
E[y_t y_{t+k}] &= E[a^2 \cos(\omega t + h) \cos(\omega(t + k) + h)] \\
&= E[a^2]E[\cos(\omega t + h + \omega(t + k) + h) + \cos \omega k]/2 \\
&\quad \left\{\text{since } \cos A \cos B = \frac{1}{2}[\cos(A + B) + \cos(A - B)]\right\} \\
&= \frac{\sigma_a^2}{2}\left[\int_{-\pi}^{\pi} \frac{1}{2\pi} \cos(2\omega t + \omega k + 2h)dh + \cos \omega k \int_{-\pi}^{\pi} \frac{1}{2\pi}\, dh\right] \\
&= \frac{\sigma_a^2}{2} \cos \omega k = \gamma_k
\end{aligned} \tag{7.6.4}$$

since the first integral is zero as we are integrating over two cosine waves. In (7.6.4), $\sigma_a^2 = \text{var}(a)$. For $k = 0$ we get the variance of y_t,

$$\sigma_y^2 = \sigma_a^2/2 \tag{7.6.5}$$

and the autocorrelations of y_t are $\rho_k = \cos \omega k$.

Since the mean of y_t is constant for all t, the variance is finite and the autocovariance structure is independent of t, the process y_t is stationary. However, the autocorrelations ρ_k do not approach zero as k goes to infinity and thus y_t cannot be a stationary ARMA process. Such a process is nondeterministic, whereas y_t is deterministic in the sense that, given the infinite past of the process, the value of y_t can be predicted without error. Suppose we know $y_{t-1} = a \cos[\omega(t - 1) + h]$ and $y_{t-2} = a \cos[\omega(t - 2) + h]$. Using only these two values we can determine a and h and consequently, we can compute $y_s = a \cos(\omega s + h)$ for all $s \geq t$ since ω is assumed to be known.

Similarly, a process

$$y_t = a_1 \cos(\omega_1 t + h_1) + \ldots + a_m \cos(\omega_m t + h_m) \tag{7.6.6}$$

where the a_j and h_j have the properties as in (7.6.1), is deterministic. Using

$$\cos(\omega_j t + h_j) = \cos(\omega_j t) \cos h_j - \sin(\omega_j t)\sin h_j \tag{7.6.7}$$

this process can be written as

$$y_t = \sum_{j=1}^{m} \cos(\omega_j t) a_j \cos h_j - \sin(\omega_j t) a_j \sin h_j$$
$$= \sum_{j=1}^{m} \cos(\omega_j t) u_j - \sum_{j=1}^{m} \sin(\omega_j t) v_j \quad (7.6.8)$$

where $u_j = a_j \cos h_j$ and $v_j = a_j \sin h_j$ are random variables with the following properties:

$$E[u_j] = E[v_j] = 0 \quad (7.6.9a)$$
$$E[u_j u_k] = 0, \quad j \neq k \quad (7.6.9b)$$
$$E[v_j v_k] = 0, \quad j \neq k \quad (7.6.9c)$$
$$E[u_j v_k] = 0, \quad \text{for all } j,k \quad (7.6.9d)$$

Properties (7.6.9b) and (7.6.9c) follow since a_j and a_k are independent for $j \neq k$ and (7.6.9d) follows by the same argument if $j \neq k$ and by noting that

$$E[u_j v_j] = E[a_j^2] E[\cos h_j \sin h_j]$$
$$= \sigma_{a_j}^2 \int_{-\pi}^{\pi} (\cos h \sin h) f(h)\, dh$$
$$= \frac{\sigma_{a_j}^2}{2\pi} \int_{-\pi}^{\pi} \cos h \sin h\, dh$$
$$= \frac{\sigma_{a_j}^2}{2\pi} \left[\frac{1}{2} \sin^2 h\right]_{-\pi}^{\pi} = 0 \quad (7.6.10)$$

where $\sigma_{a_j}^2 = \text{var}(a_j)$, $f(h) = 1/2\pi$ is the density of $h_j \sim U(-\pi,\pi)$ and

$$\int \cos h \sin h\, dh = \tfrac{1}{2} \sin^2 h + \text{constant}$$

has been used.

The process (7.6.6) involves only a finite number of frequencies, and to generalize this process to be composed of all frequencies in the interval $[-\pi,\pi]$ we attach random variables $du(\omega)$ and $dv(\omega)$ to each frequency between $-\pi$ and π, and instead of summing up we take integrals. That is, we define

$$y_t = \int_{-\pi}^{\pi} \cos \omega t\, du(\omega) - \int_{-\pi}^{\pi} \sin \omega t\, dv(\omega) \quad (7.6.11)$$

Analogous to (7.6.9) we require that

$$E[du(\omega)] = E[dv(\omega)] = 0, \quad \text{for all } \omega$$
$$E[du(\omega) du(\lambda)] = 0, \quad \text{if } \omega \neq \lambda$$

$$E[dv(\omega)dv(\lambda)] = 0, \qquad \text{if } \omega \neq \lambda$$
$$E[du(\omega)dv(\lambda)] = 0, \qquad \text{for all } \omega,\lambda \tag{7.6.12}$$

It can be shown that any discrete stationary stochastic process can be represented in the form (7.6.11). Since this process potentially involves an infinite number of random variables, namely $du(\omega)$, $dv(\omega)$, $\omega \in [-\pi,\pi]$, knowledge of the past values of the process is in general not sufficient to predict future values without error. Thus, the process y_t in (7.6.11) is in general not deterministic. In fact, it may be purely nondeterministic and can have the same covariance structure as the AR, MA, and ARMA processes considered in Section 7.2. Before we investigate this possibility we will introduce a notational simplification.

Defining $dz(\omega) = du(\omega) + i\, dv(\omega)$ and noting that $\cos \omega t + i \sin \omega t = e^{i\omega t}$, (7.6.11) can be written as

$$y_t = \int_{-\pi}^{\pi} e^{i\omega t}\, dz(\omega) \tag{7.6.13}$$

From (7.6.12) it follows that

$$E[dz(\omega)] = 0 \text{ for all } \omega \qquad \text{and} \qquad E[dz(\omega)\overline{dz(\lambda)}] = 0 \text{ for } \omega \neq \lambda \tag{7.6.14}$$

where the overbar denotes complex conjugation. The last term is, of course, the covariance of $dz(\omega)$ and $dz(\lambda)$ since for complex random variables x, y the covariance is defined to be $E[(x - E[x])\overline{(y - E[y])}]$.

This notation makes it easy to evaluate the autocovariances of y_t. Of course,

$$E[y_t] = \int_{-\pi}^{\pi} e^{i\omega t}\, E[dz(\omega)] = 0 \tag{7.6.15}$$

Thus, we get as autocovariances of y_t

$$\begin{aligned}\gamma_k = E[y_t \bar{y}_{t-k}] &= E\left[\int_{-\pi}^{\pi} e^{i\omega t}\, dz(\omega) \overline{\int_{-\pi}^{\pi} e^{i\lambda(t-k)}\, dz(\lambda)}\right] \\ &= \int_{-\pi}^{\pi} e^{i\omega t}\, e^{-i\lambda(t-k)}\, E[dz(\omega)\overline{dz(\lambda)}] \\ &= \int_{-\pi}^{\pi} e^{i\omega k}\, E[dz(\omega)\overline{dz(\omega)}] \end{aligned} \tag{7.6.16}$$

where (7.6.14) and $\overline{e^{i\lambda t}} = e^{-i\lambda t}$ have been used.

To give this an even more convenient form we note that by the Riesz-Fischer Theorem [e.g., Sargent (1979, p. 229)], for a sequence of complex numbers $\{c_k\}_{k=-\infty,\ldots,\infty}$ with

$$\sum_{k=-\infty}^{\infty} |c_k|^2 < \infty \tag{7.6.17}$$

there exists a complex valued function $f(\omega)$ defined on the interval $[-\pi,\pi]$ such that

$$f(\omega) = \frac{1}{2\pi} \sum_{k=-\infty}^{\infty} c_k e^{-i\omega k} \tag{7.6.18}$$

$$\int_{-\pi}^{\pi} |f(\omega)|^2 \, d\omega < \infty \tag{7.6.19}$$

and

$$c_k = \int_{-\pi}^{\pi} e^{i\omega k} f(\omega) d\omega \tag{7.6.20}$$

Thus, if the γ_k satisfy the condition (7.6.17) (for instance, if y_t is a stationary ARMA process) then there exists a function $f_y(\omega)$ such that

$$E[dz(\omega)\overline{dz(\omega)}] = f_y(\omega)d\omega \tag{7.6.21}$$

and hence,

$$\gamma_k = \int_{-\pi}^{\pi} e^{i\omega k} f_y(\omega) d\omega \tag{7.6.22}$$

For $k = 0$ we get the variance of y_t,

$$\sigma_y^2 = \gamma_0 = \int_{-\pi}^{\pi} f_y(\omega) d\omega \tag{7.6.23}$$

This formula shows that $f_y(\omega)d\omega$ can be interpreted as the contribution of the frequencies $(\omega, \omega + d\omega)$ to the total variance of the process.

It follows from the symmetry of the autocovariances ($\gamma_k = \gamma_{-k}$) that $f_y(\omega)$ is a real valued function since, by (7.6.18),

$$\begin{aligned} f_y(\omega) &= \frac{1}{2\pi} \sum_{k=-\infty}^{\infty} \gamma_k e^{-i\omega k} \\ &= \frac{1}{2\pi} \left[\gamma_0 + \sum_{k=1}^{\infty} \gamma_k (e^{-i\omega k} + e^{i\omega k})\right] \\ &= \frac{1}{2\pi} \left(\gamma_0 + 2 \sum_{k=1}^{\infty} \gamma_k \cos \omega k\right) \end{aligned} \tag{7.6.24}$$

Furthermore, by (7.6.21), $f_y(\omega)$ assumes only nonnegative values. In this respect, it bears some similarity to a probability density function and is therefore called the *spectral density function* or *power spectral density function* or *spectrum* of the process y_t. Note that slightly different definitions of this function are given by some authors [e.g., Kendall, Stuart, and Ord (1983), Chatfield (1975)]. Of course, dividing $f(\omega)$ by $\gamma_0(=\sigma_y^2)$ results in a function with the very properties of a probability density function.

From (7.6.24) it also follows that $f_y(\omega)$ is symmetric about zero. Therefore, in practice, the spectral density function of a stochastic process is often only reported for frequencies between 0 and π. To illustrate the foregoing theory let us determine the spectral density of some processes considered in previous sections.

Suppose y_t is white noise (e.g., $y_t = v_t$). Then, $\gamma_k = 0$ for $k \neq 0$. Hence, by (7.6.24),

$$f_v(\omega) = f_y(\omega) = \frac{1}{2\pi}\gamma_0 = \frac{\sigma_y^2}{2\pi} = \frac{\sigma_v^2}{2\pi} \tag{7.6.25}$$

Thus, the spectral density of y_t is a constant function. In other words, all frequencies between $-\pi$ and π contribute equally to the variance of y_t. This, by the way, explains the name "white noise" for this kind of process.

As another example consider an MA(1) process

$$y_t = v_t + \alpha v_{t-1}, \qquad \sigma_v^2 = 1 \tag{7.6.26}$$

The autocovariances of this process are

$$\gamma_k \begin{cases} = 1 + \alpha^2 & \text{if } k = 0 \\ = \alpha & \text{if } k = \pm 1 \\ = 0 & \text{otherwise} \end{cases}$$

Consequently, by (7.6.24),

$$f_y(\omega) = \frac{1}{2\pi}(1 + \alpha^2 + 2\alpha \cos \omega) \tag{7.6.27}$$

This function is depicted in Figure 7.2 for two different values of α.

If y_t is a first-order autoregressive process,

$$y_t = \theta y_{t-1} + v_t \tag{7.6.28}$$

the autocovariance function is

$$\gamma_k = \sigma_y^2 \theta^k \tag{7.6.29}$$

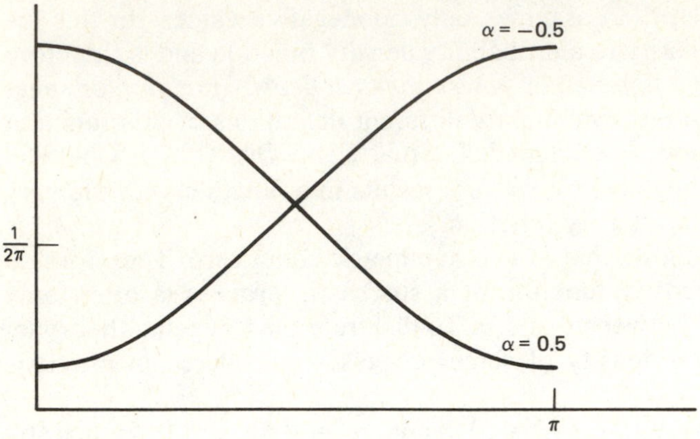

Figure 7.2 Spectral densities of MA(1) processes.

and thus,

$$\begin{aligned}
f_y(\omega) &= \frac{1}{2\pi}\left(\sigma_y^2 + \sigma_y^2 \sum_{k=1}^{\infty} \theta^k e^{-i\omega k} + \sigma_y^2 \sum_{k=1}^{\infty} \theta^k e^{i\omega k}\right) \\
&= \frac{\sigma_y^2}{2\pi}\left(1 + \frac{\theta e^{-i\omega}}{1 - \theta e^{-i\omega}} + \frac{\theta e^{i\omega}}{1 - \theta e^{i\omega}}\right) \\
&= \frac{\sigma_y^2}{2\pi} \frac{(1 - \theta e^{-i\omega})(1 - \theta e^{i\omega}) + \theta e^{-i\omega}(1 - \theta e^{i\omega}) + \theta e^{i\omega}(1 - \theta e^{-i\omega})}{1 + \theta^2 - \theta(e^{-i\omega} + e^{i\omega})} \\
&= \frac{\sigma_y^2}{2\pi} \frac{1 - \theta^2}{1 + \theta^2 - 2\theta \cos \omega} \qquad (7.6.30)
\end{aligned}$$

This function is depicted in Figure 7.3 for $\theta = .5$ and $\theta = -.5$. The following result provides a convenient tool for deriving the spectral density of more general stochastic processes.

Suppose

$$y_t = \alpha(L)x_t \qquad (7.6.31)$$

where

$$\alpha(L) = \sum_{n=0}^{\infty} \alpha_n L^n$$

and x_t is a stationary process with spectral density $f_x(\omega)$. Then the spectral density of y_t is

$$\begin{aligned}
f_y(\omega) &= |\alpha(e^{i\omega})|^2 f_x(\omega) \\
&= \alpha(e^{-i\omega})\alpha(e^{i\omega}) f_x(\omega) \qquad (7.6.32)
\end{aligned}$$

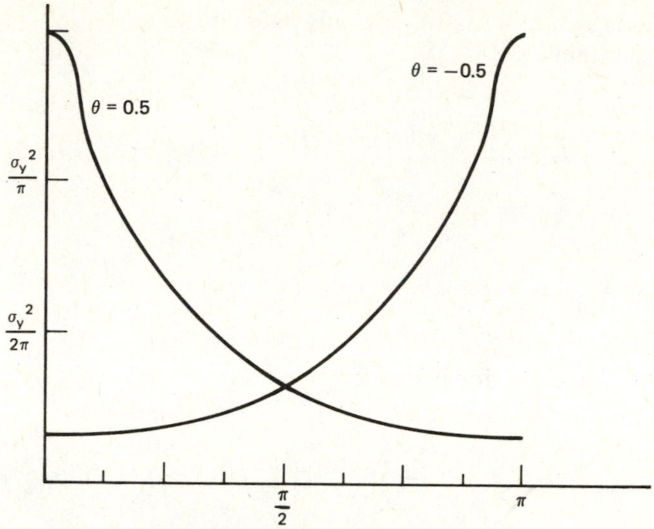

Figure 7.3 Spectral densities of AR(1) processes.

Since the spectral density of a white-noise process v_t is $f_v(\omega) = \sigma_v^2/2\pi$ this result implies that the spectrum of a stationary ARMA(p,q) process $\theta(L)y_t = \alpha(L)v_t$ or $y_t = \theta^{-1}(L)\alpha(L)v_t$ is

$$f_y(\omega) = |\alpha(e^{i\omega})/\theta(e^{i\omega})|^2 \frac{\sigma_v^2}{2\pi} \tag{7.6.33}$$

These examples suggest possible uses of the spectrum. For instance, if the residuals of an econometric model or a time series model are hypothesized to be white noise, the spectrum of the residual process should be flat and thus can be used to check the white-noise hypothesis. Furthermore, in Section 7.5 we have mentioned that the specification of an ARMA process can be quite tricky, since the orders have to be determined from the data. Thus, it may be difficult in practice to represent the correlation structure of a data generating process by an ARMA model. It will be shown in the following that the spectrum can be estimated without a preliminary specification of a particular process.

7.6.2 Estimation of the Spectrum

In order to estimate the spectral density $f_y(\omega)$ of a process y_t at a particular frequency ω it seems natural to use (7.6.24) and replace the autocovariances γ_k by estimates $\hat{\gamma}_k$ giving

$$\hat{f}_y(\omega) = \frac{1}{2\pi}\left(\hat{\gamma}_0 + 2\sum_{k=1}^{\infty} \hat{\gamma}_k \cos \omega k\right) \tag{7.6.34}$$

Having only T observations $y_1, \ldots, y_T$ we can only estimate $\gamma_0, \ldots, \gamma_{T-1}$. As estimates one can use either

$$c_k = \frac{1}{T}\sum_{t=1}^{T-k}(y_t - \bar{y})(y_{t+k} - \bar{y}) \tag{7.6.35}$$

or

$$\bar{c}_k = \frac{1}{T-k}\sum_{t=1}^{T-k}(y_t - \bar{y})(y_{t+k} - \bar{y}) \tag{7.6.36}$$

Replacing $\hat{\gamma}_k$ by 0 for $k \geq$ T we get, for instance,

$$\bar{f}_y(\omega) = \frac{1}{2\pi}\left(c_0 + 2\sum_{k=1}^{T-1} c_k \cos \omega k\right) \tag{7.6.37}$$

Unfortunately, this estimate is not consistent as its variance does not shrink to zero with growing sample size. This is essentially a consequence of estimating too many parameters from the given data. For example, c_{T-1} will always be computed using only two observations regardless of the size of T.

To overcome this problem various estimators of the spectral density have been proposed. Their general form is

$$\tilde{f}_y(\omega) = \frac{1}{2\pi}\left(\lambda_0 c_0 + 2\sum_{k=1}^{M_T} \lambda_k c_k \cos \omega k\right) \tag{7.6.38}$$

where the sequence $\lambda_0, \lambda_1, \ldots, \lambda_{M_T}$ is called a *lag window* and $M_T < T$ is the *truncation point*. For example, for the *Parzen window*

$$\lambda_k = \begin{cases} 1 - 6\left(\dfrac{k}{M_T}\right)^2 + 6\left(\dfrac{k}{M_T}\right)^3 & 0 \leq k \leq M_T/2 \\ 2(1 - k/M_T)^3 & M_T/2 \leq k \leq M_T \end{cases} \tag{7.6.39}$$

This sequence implies that the weight given to c_k decreases with increasing k and thus, the estimates based on fewer observations are less important in the sum in (7.6.38). The estimator of $f_y(\omega)$ based on the Parzen window is consistent provided M_T is chosen such that $M_T \rightarrow \infty$ and $M_T/T \rightarrow 0$ as $T \rightarrow \infty$. Various other "windows" are suggested in the literature. Many of them are discussed in Hannan (1970, Chapter 5, Section 4), Priestley (1981, Section 6.2), and Neave (1972). Estimated spectral densities of a number of time series are depicted in Nerlove (1964, 1972) and Granger (1966) discusses the "typical spectral shape" of economic time series.

So far, we have presented the spectrum as a tool to gain knowledge about certain features of a stochastic process, more precisely, about its frequency structure. For many economic time series it may seem difficult to interpret the frequency structure of a process. There are, however, situations where a decomposition of an economic time series into regular cycles is useful and meaningful, particularly when the seasonal characteristics of a time series are studied (see Section 7.7).

7.6.3 Some Literature on Spectral Analysis

The foregoing discussion of spectral analysis aims only at transmitting some basic ideas of the subject. The interested reader may find the following literature helpful for enriching his or her knowledge on the topic. Introductory expositions are given by Jenkins and Watts (1968), Bloomfield (1976), Chatfield (1975), Granger and Newbold (1977), Priestley (1981), and Nerlove, Grether, and Carvalho (1979). More advanced treatments of the topic are contained in Fuller (1976), Hannan (1970), and Brillinger (1975). Spectral analysis methods especially for econometrics are discussed by Dhrymes (1971, 1974).

7.7 DATA TRANSFORMATIONS AND ADJUSTMENTS

Time series are often subjected to transformations before being analyzed. Usually transformations or adjustments are carried out if the investigator feels that a particular model for the data generation process is more appropriately fitted after the data have been transformed in a certain way. In the following paragraphs, we will first briefly introduce the Box-Cox transformations and then discuss trend removal and seasonal adjustment.

7.7.1 The Box-Cox Transformation

Taking logarithms is a rather popular instantaneous data transformation. It is but one of a class of transformations suggested by Box and Cox (1964). Denoting the original time series by y_t the transformed series is

$$x_t = \frac{y_t^\lambda - 1}{\lambda} \tag{7.7.1}$$

where λ is a number between zero and one. Transformations of this type are often used to stabilize the variance of a time series. The boundary cases correspond to a logarithmic transformation ($\lambda = 0$) and a simple mean reduction ($\lambda = 1$). The choice of λ can be based on the data, that is, the optimal λ may be estimated from the data. The estimation can be carried out simultaneously with other parameters in a completely specified time series model for y_t. A discussion of practical experience with the Box-Cox transformation in the context of time series analysis is given by Nelson and Granger (1979) and Poirier (1980) and a discussion of the Box-Cox transformation for the variables of a regression model is given in Chapter 20. A general discussion of instantaneous data transformations is given by Granger and Newbold (1976).

7.7.2 Trend and Seasonal Component

Many economic time series have a trend and a seasonal component and we have seen in Section 7.2 how to take care of these components in the context of ARIMA models. However, it cannot be expected that every trend can be adequately dealt with by differencing or that all possible seasonal components can be satisfactorily captured in a seasonal ARIMA model. Furthermore, building a univariate time series model is not always the ultimate objective and sometimes the investigator may wish to remove the trend or seasonal component before a data set is used in some other analysis or the analyst is merely interested in the trend or seasonal component. Therefore procedures have been introduced for trend removal and seasonal adjustment. Many of these procedures rest on the assumption that the time series y_t consists of three components, the trend τ_t, the seasonal s_t, and the irregular part z_t. A simple additive structure

$$y_t = \tau_t + s_t + z_t \tag{7.7.2}$$

and the multiplicative form

$$y_t = \tau_t s_t z_t \tag{7.7.3}$$

are the most popular models. For the latter case, a logarithmic transformation can be used to obtain an additive model. Various different specifications and methods have been proposed for modeling the three components. Recent contributions include Nerlove, Grether, and Carvalho (1979), Schlicht (1981), Harvey (1982), and Hillmer and Tiao (1982).

A major problem in separating the three components results from the lack of precise and generally acceptable definitions of the trend and seasonal. The trend is usually thought of as representing the long-term movements of the time series whereas the seasonal could be described as "reflecting the regular periodic fluctuations which recur every year with about the same timing and with the same intensity." [Kallek (1978, p. 5)]. It must be admitted that more precise definitions have been proposed in the literature [e.g., Granger (1978)]. However, people who use time series often have a good idea of what they mean by a seasonal or trend component without reference to a specific definition. Thus, confronting them with a seasonally adjusted series they may be able to say, based on criteria such as the autocorrelation function, the spectrum, or simply the plot of the series, whether the adjustment procedure used has been successful in removing the seasonal component or not. It is much more difficult however, to make people specify what exactly they want an adjustment procedure to remove or in other words, what exactly the seasonal component is in a particular series. The subjective nature of trend and seasonality explains the existence of a substantial number of adjustment procedures. Before we introduce the basic foundations of some of them, we will discuss a number of desirable properties of such procedures in the following paragraphs.

7.7.2a Some Desirable Properties of Seasonal Adjustment Procedures

Despite the difficulties in giving a general, precise definition of seasonality and trend there are some intuitively appealing properties that have been identified as being desirable for an adjustment procedure. In the following we present some of these "desirable properties" for a seasonal adjustment procedure. Similar properties are relevant for methods of trend removal.

1. ***Linearity.*** The seasonally adjusted series y_t^a, say, should be a linear function of the original series y_t. In other words,

$$\mathbf{y}^a = S\mathbf{y} \tag{7.7.4}$$

where $\mathbf{y}^a = (y_1^a, \ldots, y_T^a)'$, $\mathbf{y} = (y_1, \ldots, y_T)'$ and S is a matrix. This property at least makes sense if the seasonal part is thought to be added to the nonseasonal components of the series as in (7.7.2). It implies, for instance, that the seasonal adjustment does not depend on the unit of measurement (e.g., dollars or millions of dollars if the GNP is considered). That is, it does not matter whether y_t is adjusted and then multiplied by a constant c or cy_t is adjusted. Also, linearity guarantees that the seasonal adjustment is invariant under linear aggregation since for two time series x_t and y_t we get $(x_t + y_t)^a = x_t^a + y_t^a$.

   Similarly, it may seem plausible to require an adjustment procedure to be product preserving since some economic variables are products of other economic quantities. For instance, y_t may be the amount spent for a particular good in period t and thus, it may be computed as the product of the price, p_t, times the quantity sold, x_t. In this situation a seasonal adjustment procedure is product preserving if

$$y_t^a = (p_t x_t)^a = p_t^a x_t^a \tag{7.7.5}$$

   Unfortunately, as Lovell (1963) pointed out, there is no adjustment procedure that is both product preserving and linear.

2. ***Idempotency.*** This property guarantees that an adjustment procedure leaves a series unchanged that was previously adjusted by the same method. That is, if $\mathbf{y}^a = f(\mathbf{y})$, then

$$f(\mathbf{y}^a) = f(f(\mathbf{y})) = \mathbf{y}^a \tag{7.7.6}$$

   Properties (7.7.4) and (7.7.6) taken together imply $\mathbf{y}^a = S\mathbf{y}$, where S is an idempotent matrix (i.e., $S^2 = S$). If an adjustment procedure is not idempotent it either leaves some seasonality in the data or else removes nonseasonal parts, since otherwise there wouldn't be anything to remove in the second round.

3. ***Orthogonality.*** This requirement ensures that the removed part of the series is empirically uncorrelated with what is left after the adjustment. The

idea underlying this criterion is that the seasonal part is thought to be uncorrelated with the rest of the series. Thus, if the removed part $\mathbf{y} - \mathbf{y}^a$ is correlated with the seasonally adjusted series $\mathbf{y}^a$, then either some seasonality is still in $\mathbf{y}^a$ or part of the nonseasonal component is in $\mathbf{y} - \mathbf{y}^a$. Formally this can be expressed by requiring $\sum_{t=1}^{T}(y_t - y_t^a)y_t^a = 0$ or, using vectors,

$$(\mathbf{y} - \mathbf{y}^a)'\mathbf{y}^a = 0 \tag{7.7.7}$$

Together with (7.7.4) and (7.7.6) this means

$$(\mathbf{y} - S\mathbf{y})'S\mathbf{y} = \mathbf{y}'(I - S')S\mathbf{y} = \mathbf{y}'(S - S'S)\mathbf{y} = 0 \tag{7.7.8}$$

This condition is clearly fulfilled if S is symmetric and idempotent since in this case $S - S'S = S - S^2 = S - S = 0$.

4. ***Stability.*** A seasonal adjustment procedure is said to be stable if it requires minimum revisions once new data become available. This is important for a decision maker who cannot be interested in basing a decision on a value that turns out to be substantially out of target once some more values become available.
5. ***Rapid Response to Changes in the Seasonal Component.*** The importance of this property is evident. Of course, if the seasonal pattern changes at some point in time the adjustment procedure should detect this and take the changes into account in the adjustment process.
6. ***No Dips at Seasonal Frequencies of the Spectrum of the Adjusted Series.*** Typically much of the variation of a seasonal time series is due to the seasonality so that the spectrum has peaks at the seasonal frequencies $\omega_k = 2\pi k/s$, $k = 1, 2, \ldots, s/2$, where s is the seasonal period that is here assumed to be an even integer. It seems desirable that a seasonal adjustment procedure should only remove the extra power at seasonal frequencies.

For a further discussion of these and other "desirable properties" of seasonal adjustment procedures see Lovell (1963), Maddala (1977, Chapter 15), Granger (1978), and Burman (1979). It is worth noting that the given properties do not suffice to characterize a seasonal adjustment procedure since the identity ($y_t^a = y_t$) satisfies them all.

7.7.2b Seasonal and Trend Adjustment Procedures

Out of the wide range of seasonal adjustment procedures we will only mention a few here. Subtracting seasonal means is one possibility. For instance, for monthly data the average of all January figures is subtracted from the individual January observations and so on for all months. Then the overall mean of the original series is added to the resulting figures. This simple procedure has some of the desirable properties listed above. In particular, it is linear, idempotent, and symmetric. It does not respond rapidly to changes in the seasonal pattern, however, and, therefore, may lead to quite unsatisfactory results.

Moving average methods are another rather popular tool for seasonal adjustment. For quarterly data one may for example replace y_t by

$$y_t^a = \tfrac{1}{4}(\tfrac{1}{2}y_{t-2} + y_{t-1} + y_t + y_{t+1} + \tfrac{1}{2}y_{t+2}) \tag{7.7.9}$$

Usually considerably more complicated moving averages are applied for seasonal adjustment. These procedures are linear but in general not idempotent or orthogonal. The stability and the response to changes in the seasonal structure will depend on the length of the particular moving average used and on the treatment of the first and last values of the series that obviously cannot be subjected to a symmetric moving average as in (7.7.9).

One of the most widely used seasonal adjustment procedures—the Census X-11 method—is based on moving averages. However, outliers, that is, values that are in some sense unusual compared with the rest of the series, are removed at various stages. Therefore the procedure is in general not linear. Despite much criticism of the method, its widespread use seems to suggest that it removes from the data what many regard as being the seasonal component. For a more detailed discussion see, for example, Shiskin, Young, and Musgrave (1967), Shiskin and Plewes (1978), Kallek (1978), Cleveland and Tiao (1976), Dagum (1975, 1978), and Wallis (1981).

For modeling a trend, smooth curves such as polynomials, exponential, or logarithmic curves are sometimes used. For these and other possible trend curves see, for example, Granger (1980). The problem inherent in this approach is, of course, the choice of the curve that is most suitable for a particular time series under consideration.

Moving average procedures can also be used for trend removal. For instance, for a nonseasonal series y_t the trend may be defined as

$$\tau_t = \tfrac{1}{5}(y_{t-2} + y_{t-1} + y_t + y_{t+1} + y_{t+2}) \tag{7.7.10}$$

Kendall (1976), Kendall, Stuart, and Ord (1983), and T. W. Anderson (1971) provide a more detailed discussion of this approach. Various other methods for trend and seasonal adjustment have been suggested and the reader is referred to the papers in Zellner (1978) for a further discussion of the subject.

7.7.2c Some Comments on Seasonal Adjustment

In the foregoing we have ignored some interesting problems in the context of seasonal adjustment that deserve to be pointed out here. First, for many time series there are reasons why the seasonal component cannot be expected to be stable over time. Of particular importance are calendar effects or holiday effects (e.g., Easter moves from March to April or the first to the second quarter of the year) or trading day variations (e.g., the number of working days during particular months varies from year to year). These problems have been recognized by time series analysts [e.g., Liu (1980), Cleveland and Grupe (1981), and Cleveland, Devlin, and Terpenning (1982)].

Second, if a time series is observed monthly but interest centers on the corresponding quarterly series, then the question arises whether it is preferable to seasonally adjust the monthly series and then aggregate to obtain quarterly data or aggregate prior to the adjustment. For a discussion of the aggregation problem in the context of seasonal series see, for example, Geweke (1978), Wei (1978), Lee and Wei (1979, 1980).

Third, there are series for which a pure additive or a pure multiplicative model is not adequate and a mixture is preferable. This problem is discussed, for instance, by Durbin and Murphy (1975) and Durbin and Kenny (1978).

7.8 SUMMARY

If time series data for a single variable are available, information on the generation process of the data can be used to forecast future values of the variable. In this chapter we introduced the class of ARIMA models to summarize the correlation structure of the data generation process. If the realizations of a variable are known to be generated by a particular ARIMA process, optimal forecasts can be obtained using this process. The mean squared forecasting error has been used for measuring the forecasting precision. Forecasting on the basis of ARIMA models implies linear forecasting functions. Since an optimal linear forecast may be inferior to a nonlinear forecast, some references to recent research on nonlinear time series models have been given.

If a particular ARIMA process is identified as being the generation process of a given set of data, estimation of the unknown parameters is theoretically straightforward. However, optimizing the sum of squares or likelihood function requires in general nonlinear optimization methods.

The specification of an adequate ARIMA process for a given set of data is often a rather difficult exercise. The Box-Jenkins approach to solving this problem involves inspecting the sample autocorrelations and partial autocorrelations. A proper interpretation of these quantities can be quite difficult and various automatic specification methods have been proposed that are based on optimizing criteria such as the asymptotic forecasting error or the entropy.

The spectrum or spectral density offers a rather different way to summarize the correlation structure of a stochastic process. Using a spectral approach the process can be thought of as being composed of sine and cosine waves with frequencies between $-\pi$ and π. The spectral density can be interpreted as a function that relates the frequencies to their contribution to the variance of a stationary stochastic process. This function completely characterizes the correlation structure of a stationary process and estimation of the spectrum does not require a preliminary specification of a particular candidate in the class of considered processes.

Often the given data are transformed prior to an analysis. We have briefly discussed the Box-Cox transformations as well as trend and seasonal adjustment. The latter transformations are usually based on the idea that a time series consists of a trend component representing the long-term movements, a seasonal component reflecting the regular fluctuations within a year and an irregular component that contains all other parts of the series. A major problem in using this notion of a time series arises from the subjective nature of the terms "trend" and "seasonal component."

If data series for related variables are available it seems natural to use this additional information to improve the forecasts of a variable of interest. This, of course, is the idea underlying many econometric analyses. However, econometric modeling requires the availability of nonsample information in the form of an economic theory. If a suitable theory is not available it is still possible to jointly analyze related time series and possibly improve the forecasts for the involved variables. A discussion of multiple time series analysis is given in Chapter 16 and special dynamic models relating economic variables are discussed in Chapters 9 and 10.

If an economic theory is available that can be entertained to relate some economic variables it is still possible that time series analysis methods can be used to advantage. For instance, if an econometric model of the type $y_t = \mathbf{x}_t'\boldsymbol{\beta} + e_t$ is specified and the y_t consist of time series data, then the residuals also constitute a time series. If the e_t are correlated so that $E[e_t e_s] \neq 0$ for $t \neq s$, then this dependence can be used to improve the parameter estimates as well as the forecasts of post sample y_t. The linear statistical model with autocorrelated error terms is discussed in detail in the next chapter.

The discussion of the present chapter has been biased toward ARIMA forecasting models because they will play a role in some parts of the remainder of this book. We acknowledge, however, that there are numerous other forecasting methods that may be preferable in many situations of practical interest. For a survey and a large scale comparison of such methods see Makridakis et al. (1982) and the references given in that article.

It has not been the objective of this chapter to provide a complete overview of the current state of time series analysis and in particular we have not tried to give a complete bibliography of the relevant literature. The interested reader can find considerably more references for example in Brillinger (1975), Kendall, Stuart, and Ord (1983), Priestley (1981), and Newbold (1981b).

7.9 EXERCISES

In this chapter, asymptotic properties of the estimators were given. The following exercises contain some sampling experiments that can help to relate the asymptotic theory to the small-sample properties of the estimators. The sampling experiments will be based on the models

$$y_t = \theta y_{t-1} + v_t \tag{7.9.1}$$

and

$$y_t = v_t + \alpha v_{t-1} \tag{7.9.2}$$

with $\alpha = \theta = .5$ and v_t is assumed to be Gaussian (normally distributed) white noise with variance $\sigma_v^2 = 1$.

7.9.1 Individual Exercises

Exercise 7.1
Generate five samples of size 30 using (7.9.1) and (7.9.2) and estimate the first five autocorrelations and partial autocorrelations. Compare the estimates to the theoretical values.

Exercise 7.2
Repeat Exercise 7.1 with samples of size 100. Compare the estimates to those obtained in Exercise 7.1. What are the consequences for using the Box-Jenkins model building procedure?

Exercise 7.3
Use the samples of Exercise 7.1 and 7.2 to estimate the parameters θ and α of the models (7.9.1) and (7.9.2) by conditional least squares. Compare the estimates to the actual parameter values and interpret.

Exercise 7.4
Use the samples of Exercise 7.2 and estimate the AR order of the models using the sequential testing procedures of Section 7.5.2a.

Exercise 7.5
Repeat Exercise 7.4 using the estimation criteria listed in Table 7.2. Compare the results and interpret.

Exercise 7.6
Use the Parzen window to estimate the spectral densities of the processes (7.9.1) and (7.9.2) from the data generated in Exercise 7.2. Compare the estimates to the theoretical spectral densities and interpret.

7.9.2 Class Exercises

We will assume now that at least 100 samples for each process and each sample size ($T = 30$, $T = 100$) have been considered by the students of a class.

Exercise 7.7
Use the estimates obtained in Exercises 7.1 and 7.2 for each of the two processes and each of the two sample sizes to construct empirical frequency distributions for the estimated autocorrelation and partial autocorrelation coefficients.

Exercise 7.8
Use the estimates of θ and α obtained in Exercise 7.3 to construct empirical frequency distributions for sample size 30 and sample size 100. Interpret the results.

Exercise 7.9
Use the estimates for the AR order obtained in Exercises 7.4 and 7.5, to construct frequency distributions for each of the different criteria and interpret.

7.10 REFERENCES

Akaike, H. (1969) "Fitting Autoregressive Models for Prediction," *Annals of the Institute of Statistical Mathematics,* 21, 243–247.

Akaike, H. (1970a) "Statistical Predictor Identification," *Annals of the Institute of Statistical Mathematics,* 22, 203–217.

Akaike, H. (1970b) "A Fundamental Relation Between Predictor Identification and Power Spectrum Estimation," *Annals of the Institute of Statistical Mathematics,* 22, 219–223.

Akaike, H. (1973) "Information Theory and an Extension of the Maximum Likelihood Principle," in B. N. Petrov and F. Csáki, eds., *2nd International Symposium on Information Theory,* Akadémiai Kiadó, Budapest, 267–281.

Akaike, H. (1974a) "A New Look at the Statistical Model Identification," *IEEE Transactions on Automatic Control,* AC-19, 716–723.

Akaike, H. (1974b) "Markovian Representation of Stochastic Processes and its Application to the Analysis of Autoregressive Moving Average Processes," *Annals of the Institute of Statistical Mathematics,* 26, 363–387.

Akaike, H. (1978) "A Bayesian Analysis of the Minimum AIC Procedure," *Annals of the Institute of Statistical Mathematics,* 30, 9–14.

Ali, M. M. (1977) "Analysis of Autoregressive-Moving Average Models: Estimation and Prediction," *Biometrika,* 64, 535–545.

Amemiya, T. (1980) "Selection of Regressors," *International Economic Review,* 21, 331–354.

Anderson, O. D. (1976) *Time Series Analysis and Forecasting: The Box-Jenkins Approach,* Butterworths, London.

Anderson, O. D. and J. G. de Gooijer (1982) "The Covariances Between Sampled Autocovariances and Between Serial Correlations for Finite Realizations from ARIMA Time Series Models," in O. D. Anderson, ed., *Time Series Analysis: Theory and Practice 1,* North-Holland, Amsterdam, 7–22.

Anderson, T. W. (1971) *The Statistical Analysis of Time Series,* Wiley, New York.

Anderson, T. W. (1977) "Estimation for Autoregressive Moving Average Models in the Time and Frequency Domains," *The Annals of Statistics,* 5, 842–865.

Ansley, C. F. (1979) "An Algorithm for the Exact Likelihood of a Mixed Autoregressive-Moving Average Process," *Biometrika,* 66, 59–65.

Ansley, C. F. and P. Newbold (1980) "Finite Sample Properties of Estimators for Autoregressive Moving Average Models," *Journal of Econometrics,* 13, 159–183.

Beguin, J.-M., C. Gourieroux, and A. Monfort (1980) "Identification of a Mixed Autoregressive-Moving Average Process: The Corner Method," in O. D. Anderson, ed., *Time Series,* North-Holland, Amsterdam, 423–436.

Bhansali, R. J. and D. Y. Downham (1977) "Some Properties of the Order of an

Autoregressive Model Selected by a Generalization of Akaike's EPF Criterion," *Biometrika,* 64, 547–551.

Birch, J. B. and R. D. Martin (1981) "Confidence Intervals for Robust Estimates of the First Order Autoregressive Parameter," *Journal of Time Series Analysis,* 2, 205–220.

Bloomfield, P. (1976) *Fourier Analysis of Time Series: An Introduction,* Wiley, New York.

Bora-Senta, E. and S. Kounias (1980) "Parameter Estimation and Order Determination of Autoregressive Models," in O. D. Anderson, ed., *Analyzing Time Series,* North-Holland, Amsterdam, 93–108.

Box, G. E. P. and D. R. Cox (1964) "An Analysis of Transformations," *Journal of the Royal Statistical Society,* Series B, 26, 211–243.

Box, G. E. P. and G. M. Jenkins (1976) *Time Series Analysis, Forecasting and Control,* Holden Day, San Francisco.

Brillinger, D. R. (1975) *Time Series: Data Analysis and Theory,* Holt, Rinehart and Winston, New York.

Burman, J. P. (1979) "Seasonal Adjustment—A Survey," in S. Makridakis and S. C. Wheelwright, eds., *Forecasting, Studies in the Management Sciences,* Vol. 12, North-Holland, Amsterdam, 45–57.

Chatfield, C. (1975) *The Analysis of Time Series: Theory and Practice,* Chapman and Hall, London.

Cleveland, W. P. and M. R. Grupe (1981) "Modelling Time Series when Calendar Effects are Present," paper presented at the Conference on Applied Time Series Analysis of Economic Data, Arlington, Va.

Cleveland, W. P. and G. C. Tiao (1976) "Decomposition of Seasonal Time Series: A Model for the Census X-11 Program," *Journal of the American Statistical Association,* 71, 581–587.

Cleveland, W. S., S. J. Devlin, and I. J. Terpenning (1982) "The SABL Seasonal and Calendar Adjustment Procedures," in O. D. Anderson, ed., *Time Series Analysis: Theory and Practice 1,* North-Holland, Amsterdam, 539–564.

Dagum, E. B. (1975) "Seasonal Factor Forecasts from ARIMA Models," *Proceedings of the International Statistical Institute's 40th Session, Contributed Papers,* Vol. 3, 206–219, Warsaw.

Dagum, E. B. (1978) "Modelling, Forecasting and Seasonally Adjusting Economic Time Series with the X-11 ARIMA Method," *The Statistician,* 27, 203–216.

Dhrymes, P. J. (1971) *Distributed Lags: Problems of Estimation and Formulation,* Holden-Day, San Francisco.

Dhrymes, P. J. (1974) *Econometrics: Statistical Foundations and Applications,* Springer, New York.

Dickey, D. A. and W. A. Fuller (1979) "Distribution of the Estimators for Autoregressive Time Series with Unit Root," *Journal of the American Statistical Association,* 74, 427–431.

Dickey, D. A. and S. E. Said (1981) "Testing ARIMA(p,1,q) versus ARMA(p+1,q)," *American Statistical Association, Proceedings of the Business and Economic Statistics Section,* 318–322.

Durbin, J. and P. B. Kenny (1978) "Seasonal Adjustment Behaves Neither Purely Multiplicatively nor Purely Additively," in A. Zellner, ed., *Seasonal Analysis of Economic Time Series,* U.S. Department of Commerce, Bureau of the Census, Washington, D.C., 173–188.

Durbin, J. and M. J. Murphy (1975) "Seasonal Adjustment Based on a Mixed Additive-Multiplicative Model," *Journal of the Royal Statistical Society,* Series A, 138, 385–410.

Engle, R. F. (1982) "Autoregressive Conditional Heteroscedasticity with Estimates of the Variance of United Kingdom Inflation," *Econometrica,* 50, 987–1007.

Fuller, W. A. (1976) *Introduction to Statistical Time Series,* Wiley, New York.

Fuller, W. A. and D. P. Hasza (1981) "Properties of Predictors for Autoregressive Time Series," *Journal of the American Statistical Association,* 76, 155–161.

Fuller, W. A., D. P. Hasza, and J. J. Goebel (1981) "Estimation of Parameters of Stochastic Difference Equations," *The Annals of Statistics,* 9, 531–543.

Geweke, J. (1978) "The Temporal and Sectoral Aggregation of Seasonally Adjusted Time Series," in A. Zellner, ed., *Seasonal Analysis of Economic Time Series,* U.S. Government Printing Office, Washington, D.C., 411–427.

Granger, C. W. J. (1966) "The Typical Spectral Shape of an Economic Variable," *Econometrica,* 34, 150–161.

Granger, C. W. J. (1978) "Seasonality: Causation, Interpretation, and Implications," in A. Zellner, ed., *Seasonal Analysis of Economic Time Series,* U.S. Department of Commerce, Bureau of the Census, Washington, D.C., 33–46.

Granger, C. W. J. (1980) *Forecasting in Business and Economics,* Academic Press, New York.

Granger, C. W. J. and A. P. Andersen (1978) *An Introduction to Bilinear Time Series Models,* Vandenhoeck and Ruprecht, Göttingen.

Granger, C. W. J. and P. Newbold (1976) "Forecasting Transformed Series," *Journal of the Royal Statistical Society,* Series B, 38, 189–203.

Granger, C. W. J. and P. Newbold (1977) *Forecasting Economic Time Series,* Academic Press, New York.

Gray, H. L., G. D. Kelley, and D. D. McIntire (1978) "A New Approach to ARMA Modeling," *Communications in Statistics,* B7, 1–77.

Hannan, E. J. (1970) *Multiple Time Series,* Wiley, New York.

Hannan, E. J. (1980) "The Estimation of the Order of an ARMA Process," *The Annals of Statistics,* 8, 1071–1081.

Hannan, E. J. and B. G. Quinn (1979) "The Determination of the Order of an Autoregression," *Journal of the Royal Statistical Society,* Series B, 41, 190–195.

Hannan, E. J. and J. Rissanen (1982) "Recursive Estimation of Mixed Autoregressive-Moving Average Order," *Biometrika,* 69, 81–94.

Harvey, A. C. (1981) *Time Series Models,* Allan, Oxford.

Harvey, A. C. (1982) "An Alternative Framework for Time Series Model Building and its Implications for Econometrics," paper presented at the European Meeting of the Econometric Society, Dublin.

Hasza, D. P. and W. A. Fuller (1979) "Estimation for Autoregressive Processes with Unit Roots," *The Annals of Statistics,* 7, 1106–1120.

Hasza, D. P. and W. A. Fuller (1982) "Testing For Nonstationary Parameter Specifications in Seasonal Time Series Models," *The Annals of Statistics,* 10, 1209–1216.

Hillmer, S. C. and G. C. Tiao (1982) "An ARIMA-Model-Based Approach to Seasonal Adjustment," *Journal of the American Statistical Association,* 77, 63–70.

Howrey, E. P. (1978) "Comments on 'Estimating Structural Models of Seasonality' by Robert F. Engle" in A. Zellner, ed., *Seasonal Analysis of Economic Time Series,* U.S. Department of Commerce, Bureau of the Census, Washington, D.C., 298–302.

Jenkins, G. M. and D. G. Watts (1968) *Spectral Analysis and its Applications,* Holden Day, San Francisco.

Judge, G. G., R. C. Hill, W. E. Griffiths, H. Lütkepohl, and T. C. Lee (1982) *Introduction to the Theory and Practice of Econometrics,* Wiley, New York.

Kallek, S. (1978) "An Overview of the Objectives and Framework of Seasonal Adjustment," in A. Zellner, ed., *Seasonal Analysis of Economic Time Series,* U.S. Department of Commerce, Bureau of the Census, Washington, D.C., 3–25.

Kendall, M. (1976) *Time-Series,* 2nd ed., Griffin, London.

Kendall, M., A. Stuart, and J. K. Ord (1983) *The Advanced Theory of Statistics,* Vol. 3, 4th ed., Griffin, London.

Kitagawa, G. (1977) "On a Search Procedure for the Optimal AR-MA Order," *Annals of the Institute of Statistical Mathematics,* 29, 319–332.

Lai, T. L. and C. Z. Wei (1983) "Asymptotic Properties of General Autoregressive Models and Strong Consistency of Least Squares Estimates of their Parameters," *Journal of Multivariate Analysis,* 13, 1–23.

Lee, R. M. and W. W. S. Wei (1979) "The Census X-11 Program and Quarterly Seasonal Adjustments," *ASA Proceedings of the Business and Economic Statistics Section,* 366–370.

Lee, R. M. and W. W. S. Wei (1980) "Model Based Seasonal Adjustment and Temporal Aggregation," *ASA Proceedings of the Business and Economic Statistics Section,* 427–431.

Liu, L. (1980) "Analysis of Time Series with Calendar Effects," *Management Science,* 26, 106–112.

Ljung, G. M. and G. E. P. Box (1979) "The Likelihood Functions of Stationary Autoregressive-Moving Average Models," *Biometrika,* 66, 265–270.

Lovell, M. C. (1963) "Seasonal Adjustment of Economic Time Series and Multiple Regression Analysis," *Journal of the American Statistical Association,* 58, 993–1010.

Lütkepohl, H. (1982) "Comparison of Criteria for Estimating the Order of a Vector Autoregressive Process," working paper, Universität Osnabrück.

Maddala, G. S. (1977) *Econometrics,* McGraw-Hill, New York.

Maekawa, K. (1983) "An Approximation to the Distribution of the Least

Squares Estimator in an Autoregressive Model with Exogenous Variables," *Econometrica,* 51, 229–238.

Makridakis, S., A. Andersen, R. Carbone, R. Fildes, M. Hibon, R. Lewandowski, J. Newton, E. Parzen, and R. Winkler (1982) "The Accuracy of Extrapolation (Time Series) Methods: Results of a Forecasting Competition," *Journal of Forecasting,* 1, 111–153.

Martin, R. D. (1980) "Robust Estimation of Autoregressive Models," in D. R. Brillinger and G. C. Tiao, eds., *Directions in Time Series.*

Martin, R. D., A. Samorov, and W. Vandaele (1981) "Robust Methods for ARIMA Models," paper presented at the Conference on Applied Time Series Analysis of Economic Data, Arlington, Va.

McClave, J. (1975) "Subset Autoregression," *Technometrics,* 17, 213–220.

Neave, H. R. (1972) "Comparison of Lag Window Generators," *Journal of the American Statistial Association,* 67, 152–158.

Nelson, C. R. (1973) *Applied Time Series for Managerial Forecasting,* Holden-Day, San Francisco.

Nelson, H. L. and C. W. J. Granger (1979) "Experience with Using the Box-Cox Transformation when Forecasting Economic Time Series," *Journal of Econometrics,* 10, 57–69.

Nerlove, M. (1964) "Spectral Analysis of Seasonal Adjustment Procedures," *Econometrica,* 32, 241–286.

Nerlove, M. (1972) "On the Structure of Serial Dependence in Some U.S. Price Series," in O. Eckstein, ed., *The Econometrics of Price Determination,* Board of Governors of the Federal Reserve System, Washington, D.C., 60–112.

Nerlove, M., D. M. Grether, and J. L. Carvalho (1979) *Analysis of Economic Time Series,* Academic Press, New York.

Newbold, P. (1974) "The Exact Likelihood Function for a Mixed Autoregressive-Moving Average Process," *Biometrika,* 61, 423–426.

Newbold, P. (1981a) "Model Checking in Time Series Analysis," paper presented at the Conference on Applied Time Series Analysis of Economic Data, Arlington, Va.

Newbold, P. (1981b) "Some Recent Developments in Time Series Analysis," *International Statistical Review,* 49, 53–66.

Nicholls, D. F. and B. G. Quinn (1982) *Random Coefficient Autoregressive Models: An Introduction,* Springer, New York.

Ozaki, T. (1977) "On the Order Determination of ARIMA Models," *Applied Statistics,* 26, 290–301.

Parzen, E. (1974) "Some Recent Advances in Time Series Modeling," *IEEE Transactions on Automatic Control,* AC-19, 723–730.

Parzen, E. (1977) "Multiple Time Series: Determining the Order of Approximating Autoregressive Schemes," in P. R. Krishnaiah, ed., *Multivariate Analysis—IV,* North-Holland, Amsterdam, 283–295.

Parzen, E. (1979) "Forecasting and Whitening Filter Estimation," in S. Makridakis and S. C. Wheelwright, eds., *Forecasting, Studies in Management Sciences,* Vol. 12, North-Holland, Amsterdam, 149–165.

Phillips, P. C. B. (1977) "Approximations to Some Finite Sample Distributions Associated with a First-Order Stochastic Difference Equation," *Econometrica,* 45, 463–485.

Phillips, P. C. B. (1978) "Edgeworth and Saddlepoint Approximations in the First-Order Noncircular Autoregression," *Biometrika,* 65, 91–98.

Ploberger, W. (1982) "The Asymptotic Behavior of a Class of Prediction-Error Estimators for Linear Models," Report No. 7, Institut für Ökonometrie und Operations Research, Technische Universität Wien.

Poirier, D. J. (1980) "Experience with using the Box-Cox Transformation when Forecasting Economic Time Series," *Journal of Econometrics,* 14, 277–280.

Pötscher, B. M. (1982) "Order Estimation of ARMA Systems by the Lagrange Multiplier Test," Report No. 5, Institut für Ökonometrie und Operations Research, Technische Universität Wien.

Priestley, M. B. (1965) "Evolutionary Spectra and Non-Stationary Processes," *Journal of the Royal Statistical Society,* Series B, 27, 204–237.

Priestley, M. B. (1980) "State-Dependent Models: A General Approach to Nonlinear Time Series Analysis," *Journal of Time Series Analysis,* 1, 47–71.

Priestley, M. B. (1981) *Spectral Analysis and Time Series,* Vols. I and II, Academic Press, London.

Quenouille, M. H. (1947) "A Large-Sample Test for the Goodness of Fit of Autoregressive Schemes," *Journal of the Royal Statistical Society,* 110, 123–129.

Rao, M. M. (1978) "Asymptotic Distribution of an Estimator of the Boundary Parameter of an Unstable Process," *The Annals of Statistics,* 6, 185–190.

Rissanen, J. (1978) "Modeling by Shortest Data Description," *Automatica,* 14, 465–471.

Sargent, T. J. (1979) *Macroeconomic Theory,* Academic Press, New York.

Schlicht, E. (1981) "A Seasonal Adjustment Principle and a Seasonal Adjustment Method Derived from this Principle," *Journal of the American Statistical Association,* 76, 374–378.

Schwarz, G. (1978) "Estimating the Dimension of a Model," *The Annals of Statistics,* 6, 461–464.

Shibata, R. (1976) "Selection of the Order on an Autoregressive Model by Akaike's Information Criterion," *Biometrika,* 63, 117–126.

Shibata, R. (1980) "Asymptotically Efficient Selection of the Order of the Model for Estimating Parameters of a Linear Process," *The Annals of Statistics,* 8, 147–164.

Shiskin, J. and T. J. Plewes (1978) "Seasonal Adjustment of the U.S. Unemployment Rate," *The Statistician,* 27, 181–202.

Shiskin, J., A. H. Young, and J. C. Musgrave (1967) "The X-11 Variant of the Census Method II Seasonal Adjustment Program," Technical Paper No. 15, U.S. Bureau of the Census, Washington, D.C.

Stigum, B. P. (1974) "Asymptotic Properties of Dynamic Stochastic Parameter Estimates (III)," *Journal of Multivariate Analysis,* 4, 351–381.

Stigum, B. P. (1975) "Asymptotic Properties of Autoregressive Integrated

Moving Average Processes,'' *Stochastic Processes and their Applications,* 3, 315–344.

Stone, M. (1979) ''Comments on Model Selection Criteria of Akaike and Schwarz,'' *Journal of the Royal Statistical Society,* Series B, 41, 276–278.

Wallis, K. F. (1981) ''Models for X-11 and 'X-11 Forecast' Procedures for Preliminary and Revised Seasonal Adjustments,'' paper presented at the Conference on Applied Time Series Analysis of Economic Data, Arlington, Va.

Wei, W. W. S. (1978) ''Some Consequences of Temporal Aggregation in Seasonal Time Series Models,'' in A. Zellner, ed., *Seasonal Analysis of Economic Time Series,* U.S. Government Printing Office, Washington, D.C., 433–444.

Woodward, W. A. and H. L. Gray (1981) ''On the Relationship Between the S Array and the Box-Jenkins Method of ARMA Model Identification,'' *Journal of the American Statistical Association,* 76, 579–587.

Yamamoto, T. (1976) ''Asymptotic Mean Square Prediction Error for an Autoregressive Model with Estimated Coefficients,'' *Applied Statistics,* 25, 123–127.

Yamamoto, T. (1980) ''On the Treatment of Autocorrelated Errors in the Multiperiod Prediction of Dynamic Simultaneous Equation Models,'' *International Economic Review,* 21, 735–748.

Zellner, A., ed. (1978) *Seasonal Analysis of Economic Time Series,* U.S. Department of Commerce, Bureau of the Census, Washington, D.C.

PART THREE

DYNAMIC SPECIFICATIONS

In this part of the book we return to the study of the general linear statistical model $\mathbf{y} = X\boldsymbol{\beta} + \mathbf{e}$ and we examine the special problems and estimation procedures that arise when using time series data. Economic behavior is seldom instantaneous, and so, when using time series data, an important part of model specification is the incorporation of appropriate lags. Lags can arise in a number of ways. In Chapter 8 we investigate estimation, prediction, and hypothesis testing for models where each element in the disturbance vector $\mathbf{e}$ depends on past values of itself or on current and past values of other disturbances. Such models come under the general title of autocorrelation and involve an assumption that $\mathbf{e}$ represents T (consecutive) realizations on a stochastic process (see Chapter 7). Lags are also introduced if the X matrix contains lagged values of one or more explanatory variables. In Chapter 9 we study finite distributed lag models that are characterized by explanatory variables with a finite number of lags, and that often involve restrictions on the coefficients of the lagged variables. When the number of lags is infinite, it is necessary to transform the model so that only a finite number of parameters is involved. This can sometimes be achieved by permitting lagged values of the dependent variable to appear as part of the X matrix. The special estimation problems that arise in this case are studied in Chapter 10 under the title of infinite distributed lags.

Chapter 8

Autocorrelation

8.1 EXISTENCE OF AUTOCORRELATION AND THE USE OF LEAST SQUARES

For the model $\mathbf{y} = X\boldsymbol{\beta} + \mathbf{e}$, where $\mathbf{y}$ is a $(T \times 1)$ vector of observations on a dependent variable, X is a $(T \times K)$ nonstochastic design matrix and $\mathbf{e}$ is a random vector with $E[\mathbf{e}] = \mathbf{0}$ and $E[\mathbf{ee}'] = \Phi = \sigma^2\boldsymbol{\Psi}$, autocorrelation exists if the disturbance terms corresponding to different observations are correlated, that is, if $\boldsymbol{\Psi}$ is not diagonal. Although this can occur with cross-sectional data that are based on some kind of natural ordering or are not drawn from a random sample of cross-sectional units, it is generally associated with time series data. Thus, we are usually concerned with the correlations between disturbances taken from different time periods. The number of these (unknown) correlations is equal to $T(T - 1)/2$ (half the number of off-diagonal elements in $\boldsymbol{\Psi}$), and so, for estimation to be tractable some kind of restrictions need to be placed on $\boldsymbol{\Psi}$. A common assumption that leads to a reduction in the number of parameters is that the e_t are observations from a particular stationary stochastic process. (See Chapter 7.)

The stationarity assumption implies that the first two moments of $\mathbf{e}$ do not depend on t. This enables us to write

$$\Phi = \sigma_e^2 \begin{bmatrix} 1 & \rho_1 & \rho_2 & \cdots & \rho_{T-1} \\ \rho_1 & 1 & \rho_1 & \cdots & \rho_{T-2} \\ \rho_2 & \rho_1 & 1 & \cdots & \rho_{T-3} \\ \vdots & \vdots & \vdots & & \vdots \\ \rho_{T-1} & \rho_{T-2} & \rho_{T-3} & \cdots & 1 \end{bmatrix} \tag{8.1.1}$$

where $\rho_s = E[e_t e_{t-s}]/\sigma_e^2 = E[e_t e_{t+s}]/\sigma_e^2$ for $s = 1, 2, \ldots$, is the correlation between two disturbances s periods apart (the autocorrelation coefficient) and the variance of e_t, σ_e^2 has been subscripted to distinguish it from σ_v^2, which is to be introduced as follows.

The number of unknown parameters in the matrix Φ is further reduced if the autocorrelation can be captured by a *particular* process, such as one of the autoregressive or moving average processes outlined in Chapter 7. For example, the most commonly assumed process in both theoretical and empirical work is the first-order autoregressive process [AR(1)],

$$e_t = \rho e_{t-1} + v_t \tag{8.1.2}$$

where, for stationarity $|\rho| < 1$, and the v_t are random variables with $E[v_t] = 0$, $E[v_t^2] = \sigma_v^2$, and $E[v_t v_s] = 0$ for $t \neq s$. Under (8.1.2) it can be shown [e.g., Judge et al. (1982, p. 436)] that the autocorrelation coefficients are given by

$$\rho_s = \rho^s \tag{8.1.3}$$

and that

$$\sigma_e^2 = \frac{\sigma_v^2}{1 - \rho^2} \tag{8.1.4}$$

Thus, with an AR(1) process, the number of unknown parameters in Φ is reduced to two, σ_v^2 and ρ. From Equation 8.1.3 we see that the correlation between different disturbances declines geometrically as the time between the disturbances (s) increases. The largest impact of v_t is felt immediately, and, through (8.1.2), there is some carryover into subsequent periods with the carryover gradually dying off. In fact, it can be shown that the total disturbance in any period, e_t, is a geometrically declining function of all past values of the v_t, that is,

$$e_t = v_t + \rho v_{t-1} + \rho^2 v_{t-2} + \cdot \cdot \cdot \tag{8.1.5}$$

Autocorrelation in the e_t, whether it is an AR(1) or some other process, is frequently a reasonable assumption when using time series data. The disturbance e_t contains the influence of all factors other than those explicitly included in X. These explanatory variables may be omitted because of ignorance of the correct model specification or because they are not measurable. In either case it is quite likely that the total effect of any changes in these omitted factors will not be immediate but distributed over time. This will lead to a vector of e_t that is autocorrelated. Alternatively, if we note that e_t represents a number of omitted economic time series and that most economic time series are highly autocorrelated, then it is clear that the e_t will be autocorrelated.

However, as noted by Maddala (1977, p. 291), we must be careful with the "omitted variable" interpretation of autocorrelation. If correlation in the residuals results from misspecification of X, it is likely that other assumptions, namely that $E[\mathbf{e}] = \mathbf{0}$, that X and $\mathbf{e}$ are uncorrelated, and that the e_t are homoscedastic, are likely to be violated. We need to assume that the total effect of the factors represented by e_t averages out to zero and also that it is uncorrelated with X.

Because of this association between the misspecification of X and autocorrelated errors, we should exercise caution when autocorrelation is diagnosed. It may mean that the errors can be reasonably represented by some stochastic process, and experience suggests this is quite often the case, but it could also mean that the X matrix should be respecified.

For a long time the AR(1) process was the only autocorrelation process considered in econometrics. This neglect of other processes probably occurred because most data were annual data for which the AR(1) process was a reasonable representation and because, without a computer, estimation of other possible processes is an onerous task. However, over the last decade, with the use of more frequently observed data and the virtual elimination of computational constraints, the other specifications outlined in Chapter 7 have been considered. These include autoregressive processes of finite order greater than one, moving-average processes, and combined autoregressive moving-average processes. They have the following form.

1. An autoregressive process of order p, AR(p),

$$e_t = \theta_1 e_{t-1} + \theta_2 e_{t-2} + \ldots + \theta_p e_{t-p} + v_t \tag{8.1.6}$$

2. A moving-average process of order q, MA(q),

$$e_t = v_t + \alpha_1 v_{t-1} + \ldots + \alpha_q v_{t-q} \tag{8.1.7}$$

3. A combined autoregressive moving-average process of order (p,q), ARMA(p,q),

$$e_t = \theta_1 e_{t-1} + \theta_2 e_{t-2} + \ldots + \theta_p e_{t-p} + v_t + \alpha_1 v_{t-1} + \ldots + \alpha_q v_{t-q} \tag{8.1.8}$$

The θ_i and α_j are unknown parameters while the v_t are random disturbances such that $E[v_t] = 0$, $E[v_t^2] = \sigma_v^2$, and $E[v_t v_s] = 0$ for $t \neq s$.

Processes of order higher than one are likely to be relevant when using monthly or quarterly data. For example, with quarterly data a fourth- or eighth-order process could be considered while, for monthly data, a twelfth-order process might be reasonable. The choice among an AR, MA, or ARMA process is often not straightforward. In some instances [Nicholls, Pagan, and Terrell (1975)], theory suggests that a particular type of process would be appropriate but, in most cases, any one of the three might be reasonable and the applied worker should entertain this possibility. For details of the properties of the various stochastic processes see Chapter 7 and Judge et al. (1982, Chapter 25).

The major distinction between the models considered in this chapter and those in Chapter 7 is the presence of the term $X\boldsymbol{\beta}$. In Chapter 7 we assumed that an *observable* random variable y_t followed the assumptions of one of the stochastic processes, and we were concerned with estimation of the parameters of that stochastic process. In this chapter, however, we assume that the *unobservable* disturbances satisfy the assumptions of a particular stochastic process, and estimation of the parameters of that process is of secondary importance relative to estimation of $\boldsymbol{\beta}$. Generally, the models in Chapter 7 can be viewed as special cases of those in this chapter, obtained by setting $\boldsymbol{\beta} = \mathbf{0}$.

It is also useful to keep in mind that the models in this chapter are special cases of a general model outlined in Chapter 10. In terms of one explanatory variable the general model is (Equation 10.1.2)

$$y_t = \frac{\gamma(L)}{\phi(L)} x_t + \frac{\alpha(L)}{\theta(L)} v_t \tag{8.1.9}$$

where $\gamma(L)$, $\phi(L)$, $\alpha(L)$, and $\theta(L)$ are finite-order polynomials in the lag operator L. The special cases with which we are currently concerned are obtained by setting $\gamma(L) = \gamma_0$, $\phi(L) = 1$, and by considering different orders for the polynomials $\alpha(L)$ and $\theta(L)$ in the disturbance specification $e_t = [\alpha(L)/\theta(L)]v_t$. We assume throughout that X (or x_t in Equation 8.1.9) is nonstochastic. Note, however, that lagged values of the dependent variable do become involved if we multiply both sides of (8.1.9) by $\theta(L)$ (where $\theta(L) \neq 1$). The case where lagged values of y_t occur through multiplication of both sides by $\phi(L) \neq 1$ is treated in Chapter 10.

The plan of this chapter is as follows. First, in Section 8.1.1, we discuss the consequences of using least squares (LS) when autocorrelation exists. Then, under various alternative assumptions, other methods of estimation are reviewed in Section 8.2. In Sections 8.2.1 to 8.2.4 we consider generalized least squares, nonlinear least squares, and maximum likelihood estimation of models with autoregressive errors of various orders; in Sections 8.2.5 to 8.2.7 this is extended to moving-average and autoregressive moving-average errors. Prediction is discussed in Section 8.3, and in Section 8.4 we describe methods for testing for various forms of autocorrelation. Some recommendations are given and the properties of pretest estimators are discussed in Section 8.5. An overview of the contents of the chapter is given in Table 8.1.

8.1.1 LS Estimation Under Autocorrelation

Since least squares (LS) requires less computation and, through testing procedures, we may not always be able to detect the presence of autocorrelation, it is worth studying the consequences of using LS when $\mathbf{\Psi}(\neq I)$ results from an autocorrelation process. There are two main consequences.

1. The LS estimator $\mathbf{b} = (X'X)^{-1}X'\mathbf{y}$ will be unbiased, but it will not in general be efficient.
2. The LS variance estimator $\hat{\sigma}^2(X'X)^{-1}$, with $\hat{\sigma}^2$ given by $(\mathbf{y} - X\mathbf{b})'(\mathbf{y} - X\mathbf{b})/(T - K)$, will be a biased estimator of $\sigma^2(X'X)^{-1}X'\mathbf{\Psi}X(X'X)^{-1}$. Consequently, the usual LS test statistics will not be valid [Judge et al. (1982, Section 10.6) and Section 5.5 of this text].

8.1.1a Efficiency

The efficiency of $\mathbf{b}$ relative to the generalized least squares (GLS) estimator $\hat{\boldsymbol{\beta}} = (X'\mathbf{\Psi}^{-1}X)^{-1}X'\mathbf{\Psi}^{-1}\mathbf{y}$ will depend on both $\mathbf{\Psi}$ and X, and so comparisons are usually made in terms of special assumptions about both these matrices. The most common is that $\mathbf{\Psi}$ is derived from an AR(1) process and that X consists of one column that follows an independent AR(1) process with parameter, say λ [Fuller (1976, p. 420); Malinvaud (1970, p. 526)]. In this case the ratio of the

TABLE 8.1 *ALTERNATIVE AUTOCORRELATION ERROR MODELS AND ESTIMATORS FOR THE GENERAL LINEAR STATISTICAL MODEL*

$$\mathbf{y} = X\boldsymbol{\beta} + \mathbf{e},\ E[\mathbf{e}] = \mathbf{0},\ E[\mathbf{ee}'] = \Phi = \sigma^2\Psi$$

Error Models				
First-order autoregressive errors (Section 8.2.1)	Second-and higher-order autoregressive errors (Sections 8.2.2–8.2.4)	First-order moving-average errors (Section 8.2.5)	Higher-order moving-average errors (Section 8.2.6)	Autoregressive moving-average errors (Section 8.2.7)
Estimators				
Generalized least squares Estimated generalized least squares Nonlinear least squares Maximum likelihood Bayesian	Generalized least squares Estimated generalized least squares Nonlinear least squares Maximum likelihood	Generalized least squares Nonlinear least squares Maximum likelihood Bayesian	Nonlinear least squares Maximum likelihood	Nonlinear least squares Maximum likelihood Frequency domain techniques (Section 8.2.8)

Tests		
Durbin–Watson Locally optimal tests Von Neumann ratio Durbin h statistic (Section 8.4.2)	Sample autocorrelations Dynamic specification Adequacy of fit Wald, LR, and LM tests (Section 8.4.1)	Periodogram of residuals Sign change test Generalizations of Durbin–Watson statistic Locally optimal tests Godfrey–Breusch test (Section 8.4.3)
Predictors		
Optimal prediction with AR errors (Section 8.3.1)	Optimal prediction with MA errors (Section 8.3.2)	Prediction MSEs (Section 8.3.3)

asymptotic variance of LS to that of GLS is given by

$$\omega = \frac{(1 - \rho^2)(1 - \rho\lambda)}{(1 + \rho^2 - 2\rho\lambda)(1 + \rho\lambda)]} \tag{8.1.10}$$

where ρ is defined in (8.1.2). For a low degree of autocorrelation in the disturbances and a "fairly smooth" X, this relative efficiency can be quite reasonable, for example, if $\rho = .3$ and $\lambda = .9$, $\omega = .95$. On the other hand, if ρ is moderate or high and X more erratic, the efficiency of LS can be extremely poor, such as when $\rho = .8$ and $\lambda = .5$, $\omega = .18$.

For more general $\mathbf{\Psi}$ and X it is not as easy to assess the situation, but some results do exist. In particular, if it is possible to write $X = Q\Gamma$, where Q contains K of the characteristic vectors of $\mathbf{\Psi}$ and Γ is a $(K \times K)$ nonsingular matrix, then $\mathbf{b} = (X'X)^{-1}X'\mathbf{y} = (X'\mathbf{\Psi}^{-1}X)^{-1}X'\mathbf{\Psi}^{-1}\mathbf{y} = \hat{\boldsymbol{\beta}}$, and so the LS estimator is fully efficient. Chipman (1965) has investigated the implications of this condition for an AR(1) process. From details of the AR(1) process (which is outlined in Section 8.2.1), we can write

$$\mathbf{\Psi}^{-1} = (1 + \rho^2)I - 2\rho\Theta + \rho(1 - \rho)C \tag{8.1.11}$$

where

$$2\Theta = \begin{bmatrix} 1 & 1 & 0 & \dots & 0 & 0 \\ 1 & 0 & 1 & \dots & 0 & 0 \\ 0 & 1 & 0 & \dots & 0 & 0 \\ \vdots & \vdots & \vdots & & \vdots & \vdots \\ 0 & 0 & 0 & \dots & 0 & 1 \\ 0 & 0 & 0 & \dots & 1 & 1 \end{bmatrix} \tag{8.1.12}$$

and $C = \text{diag}\,(1,0, \dots, 0,1)$. If it is reasonable to omit C and assume that $\mathbf{\Psi}^{-1}$ can be approximated by $W^{-1} = (1 + \rho^2)I - 2\rho\Theta$, then the efficiency question can be framed in terms of the characteristic vectors of W. These are $(\mathbf{q}_1, \mathbf{q}_2, \dots, \mathbf{q}_T)$ with the elements of $\mathbf{q}_j' = (q_{1j}, q_{2j}, \dots, q_{Tj})$ given by

$$q_{i1} = \frac{1}{\sqrt{T}} \quad \text{and} \quad q_{ij} = \sqrt{\frac{2}{T}} \cos \frac{(2i - 1)(j - 1)\pi}{2T}, \qquad j = 2, 3, \dots, T$$

See Anderson (1971).

Writing X as a linear transformation of K of the $\mathbf{q}_j$'s implies that successive observations on each variable can be represented by a Fourier series in K frequencies with the same set of frequencies for each variable. This will not hold in general, but the behavior of some economic variables is often fairly smooth, in which case it may be reasonable to approximate X with the characteristic vectors representing the *K lowest* frequencies. Chipman (1965) provides some empirical evidence on this hypothesis. In a later paper (Chipman 1979), in which the regression model takes the form of a simple linear trend implying that X can be approximately written as a linear transformation of two of the characteristic vectors of W, he shows that for $0 \leq \rho < 1$, the LS estimator is always at least 75% as efficient as the GLS estimator.

Krämer (1980) also provides evidence suggesting that when the disturbances follow an AR(1) process, LS will frequently be almost as efficient as GLS. Using a relative trace (squared error loss) criterion Krämer shows that, if the model contains a constant term, or if the explanatory variables are centered around zero, then there is very little to lose by using LS instead of GLS.

Some results for a covariance matrix $\boldsymbol{\Psi}$ from an arbitrary stationary stochastic process have been given by Grenander and Rosenblatt (1957), Watson and Hannan (1956), and Engle (1974b). Grenander and Rosenblatt give necessary and sufficient conditions for X such that $\mathbf{b}$ and $\hat{\boldsymbol{\beta}}$ have the same *asymptotic* covariance matrix. This class of X matrices includes polynomial and trigonometric polynomial functions of time. Watson and Hannan use spectral analysis to provide a lower bound on the loss of efficiency from an incorrect choice of the process generating $\boldsymbol{\Psi}$; and Engle argues that, from a practical standpoint, a more relevant comparison is the relative efficiency of two misspecifications. He shows that LS may often be better than assuming another incorrect truncation of the actual process and illustrates this with an example of assuming an AR(1) process when an AR(2) process is appropriate.

8.1.1b Bias in Variance Estimation

Although there are instances when LS is almost as efficient as GLS, this is of little comfort if the reliability of $\mathbf{b}$ is not properly assessed, and indeed it will not be if the usual "formula" $\hat{\sigma}^2(X'X)^{-1}$ is used. This expression will be a biased estimator of $\sigma^2(X'X)^{-1}X'\boldsymbol{\Psi}X(X'X)^{-1}$ even when $\mathbf{b} = \hat{\boldsymbol{\beta}}$; this has implications for the width of confidence intervals and the results of hypothesis tests about $\boldsymbol{\beta}$.

There are two components to the bias. One occurs because $(X'X)^{-1} \neq (X'X)^{-1}X'\boldsymbol{\Psi}X(X'X)^{-1}$ and the other because $E[\hat{\sigma}^2] = \sigma^2 \operatorname{tr}[M\boldsymbol{\Psi}]/(T-K) \neq \sigma^2$, where $M = I - X(X'X)^{-1}X'$. To obtain some idea of the extent of this bias, a number of special cases has been examined in the literature. If $\mathbf{e}$ follows an AR(1) process and X contains only one column that also follows an independent AR(1) process (with parameter λ), the ratio of $(X'X)^{-1}X'\boldsymbol{\Psi}X(X'X)^{-1}$ to $(X'X)^{-1}$, which in this case is a scalar, is approximately $(1+\rho\lambda)/(1-\rho\lambda)$ while, also approximately [Maddala (1977, p. 282)],

$$(T-1)E[\hat{\sigma}^2] = \sigma^2\left(T - \frac{1+\rho\lambda}{1-\rho\lambda}\right) \tag{8.1.13}$$

If both ρ and λ are positive, the usual situation with economic time series, both these expressions indicate that LS procedures will underestimate the variances, and the extent of this underestimation can be substantial. This can lead to unjustified confidence in the reliability of the estimates.

Although this result comes from a very special case, only one explanatory variable and the assumption that both the explanatory variable and the error follow AR(1) processes with positive parameters, it seems to have led many textbooks to conclude generally that LS variance estimates will be biased downward in the presence of autocorrelation. This will not be true in general, as is clear from the above when ρ and λ have opposite signs. However, a more thorough analysis by Nicholls and Pagan (1977), still using only one explanatory variable but with alternative assumptions about it and the error process, indicates that understatement of the variances is the more likely situation, provided we have positive autocorrelation. But, in addition, they note that negative autocorrelation in the regressors and/or the disturbances could be quite likely if the regressors are the result of first difference transformations.

For general X and an AR(1) process, some results on the bias have been provided by Chipman (1965), Sathe and Vinod (1974), and Neudecker (1977a, 1978). For the case $E[\mathbf{ee}'] = \sigma_v^2 W$, where W^{-1} is the approximation to $\mathbf{\Psi}^{-1}$ defined below Equation 8.1.12, Chipman shows that the condition $X = Q\Gamma$, where Q contains the characteristic vectors of W corresponding to the K smallest characteristic roots, is sufficient for the variances to be underestimated by LS procedures. Sathe and Vinod tabulate upper and lower bounds on the bias for alternative T, K, and ρ while Neudecker, in a similar way, just considers the component given by $E[\hat{\sigma}^2]$.

One of the difficulties of using biased variance estimates is the possible reversal of hypothesis test decisions. If the F statistic used to test a set of linear restrictions on $\boldsymbol{\beta}$, say $R\boldsymbol{\beta} = \mathbf{r}$, is based on LS estimates, then the decision to accept or reject $R\boldsymbol{\beta} = \mathbf{r}$ may be different than it would be if based on a test statistic using an unbiased variance estimate. Granger and Newbold (1974) illustrate this with some simulation experiments. However, a decision based on an unbiased variance estimate can only reverse a least-squares-based decision if the least squares F (or t in the case of one restriction) value falls within two bounds. Kiviet (1980), correcting and extending earlier work by Vinod (1976), has tabulated these bounds for a number of autocorrelation processes. Thus, if one uses LS in an inappropriate situation, these tables can be used to assess the likelihood of making an incorrect test decision.

However, if a calculated value falls outside the range of "possible test decision reversal," this does not necessarily mean that it is not worthwhile for the applied worker to obtain a GLS estimate. The tables are constructed in terms of "appropriate" and "inappropriate" tests based on $\mathbf{b}$. A test based on $\hat{\boldsymbol{\beta}}$ is likely to be more powerful and could lead to a different decision.

Thus we conclude that there are frequently circumstances when autocorrelated disturbances exist and the LS estimator is relatively efficient. However, the use of LS can lead to poor assessments of the reliability of the estimates, and to invalid test statistics; it is therefore desirable to consider alternative methods of estimation. These alternative methods are discussed in the following section.

8.2 ESTIMATION UNDER ALTERNATIVE AUTOCORRELATION SPECIFICATIONS

In this section we are concerned with estimation of the linear model $\mathbf{y} = X\boldsymbol{\beta} + \mathbf{e}$, where the earlier definitions hold and the elements of the vector $\mathbf{e}$ are autocorrelated. Estimation under a number of alternative autocorrelation specifications will be considered; in each case the tth disturbance e_t will be some function of an uncorrelated homoscedastic (white noise) disturbance v_t, with variance σ_v^2. The exact function and the matrix Ψ will depend on the case under consideration but, in every case, we will write the covariance matrix for $\mathbf{e}$ as $E[\mathbf{ee}'] = \Phi = \sigma_v^2\Psi$.

If this covariance matrix is known, the generalized least squares (GLS) estimator $\hat{\boldsymbol{\beta}} = (X'\Psi^{-1}X)^{-1}X'\Psi^{-1}\mathbf{y}$ is best linear unbiased and is obtained by minimizing

$$\begin{aligned} S(\boldsymbol{\beta},\Psi) = (\mathbf{y} - X\boldsymbol{\beta})'\Psi^{-1}(\mathbf{y} - X\boldsymbol{\beta}) &= (P\mathbf{y} - PX\boldsymbol{\beta})'(P\mathbf{y} - PX\boldsymbol{\beta}) \\ &= (\mathbf{y}^* - X^*\boldsymbol{\beta})'(\mathbf{y}^* - X^*\boldsymbol{\beta}) \end{aligned} \tag{8.2.1}$$

where $\mathbf{y}^* = P\mathbf{y}$, $X^* = PX$ and P is such that $P\Psi P' = I$.

For most specifications considered, we are interested in:

1. The nature of P and the sum of squares being minimized in (8.2.1).
2. Estimation of the parameters upon which Ψ depends so that we can employ an estimated generalized least squares (EGLS) estimator, say $\hat{\hat{\boldsymbol{\beta}}} = (X'\hat{\Psi}^{-1}X)^{-1}X'\hat{\Psi}^{-1}\mathbf{y}$.
3. Nonlinear least squares (NLS) estimation of $\boldsymbol{\beta}$ and the parameters in Ψ such that (8.2.1) is a minimum.
4. Maximum likelihood (ML) estimation under normality.

If $\mathbf{y}$ has a multivariate normal distribution, its density is

$$f(\mathbf{y}) = (2\pi)^{-T/2}|\sigma_v^2\Psi|^{-1/2} \exp\left\{-\frac{(\mathbf{y} - X\boldsymbol{\beta})'\Psi^{-1}(\mathbf{y} - X\boldsymbol{\beta})}{2\sigma_v^2}\right\} \tag{8.2.2}$$

and so for ML estimation the log likelihood is, apart from a constant,

$$L = -\frac{T}{2}\ln\sigma_v^2 - \frac{1}{2}\ln|\Psi| - \frac{(\mathbf{y} - X\boldsymbol{\beta})'\Psi^{-1}(\mathbf{y} - X\boldsymbol{\beta})}{2\sigma_v^2} \tag{8.2.3}$$

Conditional on $\boldsymbol{\beta}$ and Ψ, the ML estimator for σ_v^2 is

$$\tilde{\sigma}_v^2 = (\mathbf{y} - X\boldsymbol{\beta})'\Psi^{-1}(\mathbf{y} - X\boldsymbol{\beta})/T \tag{8.2.4}$$

and substituting this into L and ignoring constants gives the concentrated log likelihood function

$$L(\boldsymbol{\beta},\boldsymbol{\Psi}) = -\frac{T}{2}\ln[(\mathbf{y}-X\boldsymbol{\beta})'\boldsymbol{\Psi}^{-1}(\mathbf{y}-X\boldsymbol{\beta})] - \frac{1}{2}\ln|\boldsymbol{\Psi}| \tag{8.2.5}$$

The maximum likelihood estimators for $\boldsymbol{\beta}$ and the unknown elements in $\boldsymbol{\Psi}$ are those values that maximize (8.2.5). After some rearranging, we can show that these values are equal to the values that minimize

$$\begin{aligned} S_L(\boldsymbol{\beta},\boldsymbol{\Psi}) &= |\boldsymbol{\Psi}|^{1/T}(\mathbf{y}-X\boldsymbol{\beta})'\boldsymbol{\Psi}^{-1}(\mathbf{y}-X\boldsymbol{\beta}) \\ &= |\boldsymbol{\Psi}|^{1/T}S(\boldsymbol{\beta},\boldsymbol{\Psi}) \end{aligned} \tag{8.2.6}$$

and so the difference between the objective function for the ML estimates (8.2.6), and that for the GLS estimator (8.2.1), is that the former contains the tth root of the determinant of $\boldsymbol{\Psi}$.

It is sometimes advantageous to concentrate $\boldsymbol{\beta}$ out of the likelihood function. Since $\hat{\boldsymbol{\beta}} = (X'\boldsymbol{\Psi}^{-1}X)^{-1}X'\boldsymbol{\Psi}^{-1}\mathbf{y}$ is the ML estimator for $\boldsymbol{\beta}$ conditional on $\boldsymbol{\Psi}$, ML estimates for the unknown elements in $\boldsymbol{\Psi}$ can be found by minimizing

$$S_L(\boldsymbol{\Psi}) = |\boldsymbol{\Psi}|^{1/T}(\mathbf{y}-X\hat{\boldsymbol{\beta}})'\boldsymbol{\Psi}^{-1}(\mathbf{y}-X\hat{\boldsymbol{\beta}}) \tag{8.2.7}$$

Substituting the ML estimate for $\boldsymbol{\Psi}$ into the expressions for $\hat{\boldsymbol{\beta}}$ and $\tilde{\sigma}_v^2$ gives the unconditional ML estimates for $\boldsymbol{\beta}$ and σ_v^2, respectively.

In what follows we review estimation techniques for models with AR, MA, and ARMA error processes. If, in each of the models, we set $\boldsymbol{\beta} = \mathbf{0}$ so that $y_t = e_t$, then the techniques are also relevant for the "pure" time series models discussed in Chapter 7.

8.2.1 Estimation with AR(1) Errors

By far the most popular autocorrelated error process assumed for the vector $\mathbf{e}$ is the first order autoregressive process. Under this assumption the model can be written as

$$y_t = \mathbf{x}_t'\boldsymbol{\beta} + e_t, \tag{8.2.8}$$

$$e_t = \rho e_{t-1} + v_t \tag{8.2.9}$$

where $E[v_t] = 0$, $E[v_t^2] = \sigma_v^2$, $E[v_t v_s] = 0$ for $t \neq s$, $|\rho| < 1$, and $\mathbf{x}_t'$ is a $(1 \times K)$ vector containing the tth observation on K explanatory variables. From (8.1.3) and (8.1.4) the covariance matrix $E[\mathbf{ee}'] = \boldsymbol{\Phi} = \sigma_v^2\boldsymbol{\Psi}$ can be written as

$$\boldsymbol{\Phi} = \sigma_v^2\boldsymbol{\Psi} = \frac{\sigma_v^2}{1-\rho^2}\begin{bmatrix} 1 & \rho & \rho^2 & \cdots & \rho^{T-1} \\ \rho & 1 & \rho & \cdots & \rho^{T-2} \\ \rho^2 & \rho & 1 & \cdots & \rho^{T-3} \\ \vdots & \vdots & \vdots & \ddots & \vdots \\ \rho^{T-1} & \rho^{T-2} & \rho^{T-3} & \cdots & 1 \end{bmatrix} \tag{8.2.10}$$

and its inverse is

$$\Phi^{-1} = \frac{1}{\sigma_v^2}\Psi^{-1} = \frac{1}{\sigma_v^2}\begin{bmatrix} 1 & -\rho & 0 & \cdots & 0 & 0 \\ -\rho & 1+\rho^2 & -\rho & \cdots & 0 & 0 \\ 0 & -\rho & 1+\rho^2 & \cdots & 0 & 0 \\ \vdots & \vdots & \vdots & \ddots & \vdots & \vdots \\ 0 & 0 & 0 & \cdots & 1+\rho^2 & -\rho \\ 0 & 0 & 0 & \cdots & -\rho & 1 \end{bmatrix} \tag{8.2.11}$$

8.2.1a GLS Estimation

When ρ is known, the GLS estimator $\hat{\boldsymbol{\beta}} = (X'\Psi^{-1}X)^{-1}X'\Psi^{-1}\mathbf{y}$ is most conveniently obtained by using $\hat{\boldsymbol{\beta}} = (X^{*\prime}X^*)^{-1}X^{*\prime}\mathbf{y}^*$, which is the LS estimator applied to the transformed model $\mathbf{y}^* = X^*\boldsymbol{\beta} + \mathbf{e}^*$, where $\mathbf{y}^* = P\mathbf{y}$, $X^* = PX$, $\mathbf{e}^* = P\mathbf{e}$, and

$$P = \begin{bmatrix} \sqrt{1-\rho^2} & 0 & 0 & \cdots & 0 & 0 \\ -\rho & 1 & 0 & \cdots & 0 & 0 \\ 0 & -\rho & 1 & \cdots & 0 & 0 \\ \vdots & \vdots & \vdots & \ddots & \vdots & \vdots \\ 0 & 0 & 0 & \cdots & 1 & 0 \\ 0 & 0 & 0 & \cdots & -\rho & 1 \end{bmatrix} \tag{8.2.12}$$

is such that $P'P = \Psi^{-1}$. The first observation of the transformed model is given by

$$\sqrt{1-\rho^2}\,y_1 = \sqrt{1-\rho^2}\,\mathbf{x}_1'\boldsymbol{\beta} + \sqrt{1-\rho^2}\,e_1 \tag{8.2.13}$$

while the remaining $(T-1)$ are given by

$$y_t - \rho y_{t-1} = (\mathbf{x}_t - \rho\mathbf{x}_{t-1})'\boldsymbol{\beta} + e_t - \rho e_{t-1}, \qquad t = 2, 3, \ldots, T \tag{8.2.14}$$

If the first column of X is a vector of ones, the first column of X^* will no longer be constant. Its first element will be $\sqrt{1-\rho^2}$, while the remaining elements will be $(1-\rho)$.

The sum of squares, which is minimized by the GLS estimator, Equation 8.2.1, can be written as

$$\begin{aligned}(\mathbf{y}^* - X^*\boldsymbol{\beta})'(\mathbf{y}^* - X^*\boldsymbol{\beta}) &= \mathbf{e}'P'P\mathbf{e} = (\sqrt{1-\rho^2}\,e_1)^2 + \sum_{t=2}^{T}(e_t - \rho e_{t-1})^2 \\ &= e_1^{*2} + \sum_{t=2}^{T} v_t^2 \end{aligned} \tag{8.2.15}$$

where $e_1^* = \sqrt{1-\rho^2}y_1 - \sqrt{1-\rho^2}\mathbf{x}_1'\boldsymbol{\beta}$ and $v_t = y_t - \rho y_{t-1} - (\mathbf{x}_t - \rho\mathbf{x}_{t-1})'\boldsymbol{\beta}$, $t = 2, 3, \ldots, T$.

Early work using this model [Cochrane and Orcutt (1949)] ignored (8.2.13) and based the regression on the $(T-1)$ observations in (8.2.14) or, equivalently, minimized the sum of squares $\Sigma_{t=2}^{T} v_t^2$. This gives an approximate GLS estimator $\hat{\boldsymbol{\beta}}_0 = (X_0^{*\prime}X_0^*)^{-1}X_0^{*\prime}\mathbf{y}_0^*$, where $X_0^* = P_0X$; $\mathbf{y}_0^* = P_0\mathbf{y}$; and P_0, of dimension $[(T-1) \times T]$, is the matrix P with its first row removed. Such an analysis is conditional on y_1, and it may be more appropriate if we do not view the process as having been in operation for a long period into the past. However, if y_1 is a legitimate observation on the process, ignoring it will result in a loss in efficiency which can be considerable if the explanatory variables are trended or if there is strong multicollinearity. See Kadiyala (1968), Poirier (1978), Maeshiro (1979), Chipman (1979), Park and Mitchell (1980), Doran (1981) and Krämer (1982).

Estimated Gen Least Squares

8.2.1b EGLS Estimation

When ρ is unknown, the usual situation, we can either use LS, the dangers of which were discussed in Section 8.1, or use some means of estimating both $\boldsymbol{\beta}$ and ρ. Given an estimator for ρ, say $\hat{\rho}$, we can use this estimator in place of the actual parameter in the transformations in (8.2.13) and (8.2.14). The application of LS to the transformed variables yields the EGLS estimator $\hat{\boldsymbol{\beta}} = (X'\hat{\boldsymbol{\Psi}}^{-1}X)^{-1}X'\hat{\boldsymbol{\Psi}}^{-1}\mathbf{y}$, where $\hat{\boldsymbol{\Psi}}$ is the matrix in (8.2.11) with ρ replaced by $\hat{\rho}$. A number of alternative $\hat{\rho}$'s have been suggested or used in the literature. A list of some of these alternatives follows.

1. *The Sample Correlation Coefficient.* In this case the estimator is

$$r_1 = \frac{\Sigma_{t=2}^{T} \hat{e}_t\hat{e}_{t-1}}{\Sigma_{t=1}^{T} \hat{e}_t^2} \tag{8.2.16}$$

where the disturbances (e_t's), because they are unobservable, have been replaced by the LS residuals $\hat{e}_t = y_t - \mathbf{x}_t'\mathbf{b}$, $t = 1, 2, \ldots, T$. When the variables are transformed using r_1 in place of ρ in the transformation matrix P_0, the resulting approximate EGLS estimator for $\boldsymbol{\beta}$ is known as the Cochrane–Orcutt (1949) two-step procedure. When both (8.2.13) and (8.2.14) are used (the complete transformation matrix P), the estimator is often termed the Prais–Winsten (1954) estimator.

We can also regard r_1 as an estimator of ρ in the linear regression $\hat{e}_t = \rho\hat{e}_{t-1} + \hat{v}_t$ except, in this case, the summation in the denominator of (8.2.16) would not include $\hat{e}_1$. Theil (1971) gives another modification of r_1, namely

$$r_1^* = \frac{(T-K)\Sigma_{t=2}^{T} \hat{e}_t\hat{e}_{t-1}}{(T-1)\Sigma_{t=1}^{T} \hat{e}_t^2} \tag{8.2.17}$$

2. ***The Durbin–Watson Statistic.*** This statistic,

$$d = \frac{\sum_{t=2}^{T}(\hat{e}_t - \hat{e}_{t-1})^2}{\sum_{t=1}^{T}\hat{e}_t^2}$$

is often used to test for the existence of autocorrelation (see Section 8.4), is calculated by most LS computer programs, and can easily be modified to yield an estimator for ρ that is approximately equal to r_1, namely

$$\hat{\rho} = 1 - \tfrac{1}{2}d \tag{8.2.18}$$

3. ***The Theil–Nagar Modification.*** Theil and Nagar (1961) suggest that the estimator

$$\rho^* = \frac{T^2(1 - d/2) + K^2}{T^2 - K^2} \tag{8.2.19}$$

will be an improvement over $\hat{\rho}$ if the explanatory variables in X are fairly smooth in the sense that their first and second differences are small when compared to their corresponding ranges. This is based on an approximation to the mean and variance of d.

4. ***The Durbin Estimator.*** Still another alternative is provided by Durbin (1960). We can rewrite (8.2.14) as

$$\begin{aligned} y_t &= \rho y_{t-1} + \mathbf{x}_t'\boldsymbol{\beta} - \rho\mathbf{x}_{t-1}'\boldsymbol{\beta} + v_t \\ &= \rho y_{t-1} + \beta_1(1 - \rho) + \mathbf{x}_t^{0\prime}\boldsymbol{\beta}^0 - \rho\mathbf{x}_{t-1}^{0\prime}\boldsymbol{\beta}^0 + v_t \end{aligned} \tag{8.2.20}$$

where $\mathbf{x}_t' = (1, \mathbf{x}_t^{0\prime})$ and $\boldsymbol{\beta}' = (\beta_1, \boldsymbol{\beta}^{0\prime})$. As a consequence an estimate for ρ is given by the coefficient of y_{t-1} in a regression of y_t on y_{t-1}, a constant, $\mathbf{x}_t^0$, and $\mathbf{x}_{t-1}^0$.

At this point it is natural to ask: Which estimator for ρ leads to the most efficient EGLS estimator for $\boldsymbol{\beta}$? Before discussing evidence on this, we will outline how nonlinear least squares and maximum likelihood estimates for $\boldsymbol{\beta}$ and ρ can be obtained.

8.2.1c NLS Estimation

As mentioned in Equation 8.2.15, the GLS estimator $\hat{\boldsymbol{\beta}} = (X'\boldsymbol{\Psi}^{-1}X)^{-1}X'\boldsymbol{\Psi}^{-1}\mathbf{y}$ is obtained by finding that $\boldsymbol{\beta}$ that minimizes

$$\begin{aligned} (\mathbf{y} - X\boldsymbol{\beta})'P'P(\mathbf{y} - X\boldsymbol{\beta}) &= e_1^{*2} + \sum_{t=2}^{T} v_t^2 \\ &= (1 - \rho^2)(y_1 - \mathbf{x}_1'\boldsymbol{\beta})^2 + \sum_{t=2}^{T} [y_t - \rho y_{t-1} - (\mathbf{x}_t - \rho\mathbf{x}_{t-1})'\boldsymbol{\beta}]^2 \end{aligned}$$

Similarly, given an estimate for ρ, say $\hat{\rho}$, and corresponding matrices $\hat{P}$ and $\hat{\Psi}$ such that $\hat{P}'\hat{P} = \hat{\Psi}^{-1}$, we obtain the EGLS estimator $\hat{\hat{\beta}} = (X'\hat{\Psi}^{-1}X)^{-1}X'\hat{\Psi}^{-1}\mathbf{y}$ by finding that β that minimizes $(\mathbf{y} - X\beta)'\hat{P}'\hat{P}(\mathbf{y} - X\beta)$. Nonlinear least squares (NLS) estimates are obtained by simultaneously finding both β and ρ that minimize $e_1^{*2} + \Sigma_{t=2}^T v_t^2$. In this case the estimator for β will still be of the same form,

$$\hat{\hat{\beta}} = (X'\hat{\Psi}^{-1}X)^{-1}X'\hat{\Psi}^{-1}\mathbf{y}$$

but the estimator for ρ need not correspond to any of those given in Section 8.2.1b.

Also, some slight modifications of NLS are often used. These differ in their treatment of the first observation, namely

1. Find β and ρ, which minimize $\Sigma_{t=2}^T v_t^2$.
2. Find β, ρ, and $\bar{e}_0$, which minimize $\Sigma_{t=1}^T v_t^2$, where $v_1 = y_1 - \mathbf{x}_1'\beta - \rho\bar{e}_0$.
3. Set $\bar{e}_0 = 0$ and find β and ρ, which minimize $\Sigma_{t=1}^T v_t^2$.

The first two are identical [Pagan (1974)] and, in effect, treat the first observation as fixed. Also, under the assumption of normality, they are often referred to as ML estimators [Kmenta (1971), Hildreth and Lu (1960), Cochrane and Orcutt (1949)]. However, since they are based on the joint density $f(y_2, y_3, \ldots, y_T|y_1)$, they are only ML estimators conditional on y_1. The unconditional likelihood function based on all T observations, $f(y_1, y_2, \ldots, y_T)$, includes e_1^{*2} as well as an additional term that depends only on ρ. See Equations 8.2.22 to 8.2.29.

The third modification, setting $\bar{e}_0 = 0$, fixes e_0 at its expectation and is equivalent to assuming that the first observation was not generated by an autoregressive process. All the procedures are asymptotically equivalent, and so the use of any particular one has usually been based on convenience rather than on statistical properties.

Whatever sum of squares is chosen, it can be minimized using either iterative or search techniques. One iterative technique for minimizing $\Sigma_{t=2}^T v_t^2$ [Cochrane and Orcutt (1949)] is to estimate ρ using r_1 in (8.2.16), obtain the corresponding $\hat{\hat{\beta}}_0$ (first observation treated as fixed), reestimate ρ by applying LS to (8.2.14) rewritten as

$$(y_t - \mathbf{x}_t'\hat{\hat{\beta}}_0) = \rho(y_{t-1} - \mathbf{x}_{t-1}'\hat{\hat{\beta}}_0) + v_t \tag{8.2.21}$$

reestimate β, and so on until convergence. There is no guarantee, however, that this procedure will locate a global minimum. Sargan (1964) has shown that convergence to at least a local minimum will always occur, but Dufour et al. (1980) give examples where multiple minima exist.

Other iterative techniques such as Gauss-Newton or the Davidon-Fletcher-Powell algorithms can also be used. For an AR(p) process, Pagan (1974) gives a detailed account of how the Gauss-Newton algorithm can be used to minimize $\Sigma_{t=p+1}^T v_t^2$.

To ensure location of a global minimum, a search technique [Hildreth and Lu (1960)] can be employed. For this technique we select a number of values of ρ over the interval from -1 to $+1$ and, for each value the GLS estimator $\hat{\boldsymbol{\beta}}$ and the corresponding sum of squares, $(\mathbf{y}^* - X^*\hat{\boldsymbol{\beta}})'(\mathbf{y}^* - X^*\hat{\boldsymbol{\beta}})$ are calculated. The required estimates are those that lead to the smallest sum of squares. They can usually be located by implementing the procedure in two steps. In the first, the neighborhood of the minimum is located by taking values of ρ at fairly wide intervals, say .05; while in the second, the values of ρ are restricted to this neighborhood and taken at increments sufficiently small to achieve the desired degree of accuracy.

8.2.1d ML Estimation

Let us now consider maximum likelihood estimation under the assumption of normality. The likelihood function is given by

$$\ell(\boldsymbol{\beta},\sigma_v^2,\rho|\mathbf{y}) = f(y_1)\cdot f(y_2|y_1)\ldots f(y_T|y_{T-1}) \tag{8.2.22}$$

where

$$f(y_1) = (2\pi)^{-1/2}\sqrt{\frac{1-\rho^2}{\sigma_v^2}}\cdot\exp\left[-\frac{1-\rho^2}{2\sigma_v^2}(y_1 - \mathbf{x}_1'\boldsymbol{\beta})^2\right] \tag{8.2.23}$$

and

$$f(y_t|y_{t-1}) = (2\pi\sigma_v^2)^{-1/2}\exp\left[-\frac{1}{2\sigma_v^2}(y_t - \rho y_{t-1} - \mathbf{x}_t'\boldsymbol{\beta} + \rho\mathbf{x}_{t-1}'\boldsymbol{\beta})^2\right] \tag{8.2.24}$$

where $t = 2, 3, \ldots, T$. Thus

$$\ell(\boldsymbol{\beta},\sigma^2,\rho|\mathbf{y}) = \frac{\sqrt{1-\rho^2}}{(2\pi\sigma_v^2)^{T/2}}\exp\left\{-\frac{1}{2\sigma_v^2}\left[(y_1\sqrt{1-\rho^2} - \mathbf{x}_1'\boldsymbol{\beta}\sqrt{1-\rho^2})^2 + \sum_{t=2}^{T}(y_t - \rho y_{t-1} - \mathbf{x}_t'\boldsymbol{\beta} + \rho\mathbf{x}_{t-1}'\boldsymbol{\beta})^2\right]\right\} \tag{8.2.25}$$

and, ignoring the constant 2π, the log of the likelihood function is equal to

$$L = -\frac{T}{2}\ln\sigma_v^2 + \frac{1}{2}\ln(1-\rho^2) - \frac{1}{2\sigma_v^2}(\mathbf{y}^* - X^*\boldsymbol{\beta})'(\mathbf{y}^* - X^*\boldsymbol{\beta}) \tag{8.2.26}$$

where $\mathbf{y}^* = P\mathbf{y}$, $X^* = PX$ and P is defined in (8.2.12). Deriving (8.2.26) in this way emphasizes the dependence of y_t on y_{t-1}. Alternatively, by noting that

$$-\ln|\boldsymbol{\Psi}| = \ln|\boldsymbol{\Psi}^{-1}| = \ln|P|^2 = \ln(1-\rho^2) \tag{8.2.27}$$

we could have obtained the concentrated log-likelihood function

$$L(\rho,\boldsymbol{\beta}) = -\frac{T}{2}\ln(\mathbf{y}^* - X^*\boldsymbol{\beta})'(\mathbf{y}^* - X^*\boldsymbol{\beta}) + \frac{1}{2}\ln(1-\rho^2)$$

$$= -\frac{T}{2}\ln\left(e_1^{*2} + \sum_{t=2}^{T} v_t^2\right) + \frac{1}{2}\ln(1-\rho^2) \tag{8.2.28}$$

directly from (8.2.5). Maximum likelihood estimates $\tilde{\boldsymbol{\beta}}$ and $\tilde{\rho}$ are found by maximizing (8.2.28) or, alternatively, by minimizing

$$S_L(\boldsymbol{\beta},\rho) = (1-\rho^2)^{-1/T}(\mathbf{y}^* - X^*\boldsymbol{\beta})'(\mathbf{y}^* - X^*\boldsymbol{\beta}) \tag{8.2.29}$$

As in the case of NLS estimates, they can be found using either an iterative or a search procedure. The ML estimator for $\boldsymbol{\beta}$ is of the EGLS type, but the ML estimate of ρ upon which it is based can be different from the NLS estimate because (8.2.28) contains the term $\frac{1}{2}\ln(1-\rho^2)$ as well as the sum of squares term. However, when the sample size is large and ρ is not too close to 1, the sum of squares term will dominate the other and the two sets of estimates will essentially be the same. Because $\frac{1}{2}\ln(1-\rho^2)$ does not depend on T, they are asymptotically equivalent.

Specific algorithms for maximizing (8.2.28) have been outlined by Hildreth and Dent (1974) and Beach and MacKinnon (1978a). The former first substitutes $\tilde{\boldsymbol{\beta}}$ into $L(\rho,\boldsymbol{\beta})$ so that it is only a function of ρ. It then uses a search procedure over ρ to locate the neighborhood of the minimum and, within this neighborhood, locates $\tilde{\rho}$ by using an iterative procedure that finds a smaller neighborhood with each iteration. The Beach-MacKinnon algorithm is a modification of the Cochrane-Orcutt iterative procedure to allow for the additional terms e_1^{*2} and $\frac{1}{2}\ln(1-\rho^2)$. They claim that it is computationally more efficient than using a search procedure.

8.2.1e Properties

If the general conditions given in Section 5.5.2 hold, then

$$\sqrt{T}(\hat{\hat{\boldsymbol{\beta}}} - \boldsymbol{\beta}) \xrightarrow{d} N(\mathbf{0},\sigma^2 V^{-1}) \tag{8.2.30}$$

where $\hat{\hat{\boldsymbol{\beta}}}$ can be any of the above estimators for $\boldsymbol{\beta}$, and $V = \lim T^{-1}X'\Psi^{-1}X$. Conditions more specific to the AR(1) process are given by Hildreth (1969), Theil (1971, pp. 405–407), and Magnus (1978). From (8.2.30) and the results in Chapter 5 approximate tests of hypotheses about $\boldsymbol{\beta}$ can be based on the assumption that $\hat{\hat{\boldsymbol{\beta}}}$ is normally distributed with mean $\boldsymbol{\beta}$ and covariance matrix $\hat{\sigma}_v^2(X'\hat{P}'\hat{P}X)^{-1}$, where $\hat{P}$ is based on a consistent estimator for ρ and

$$\hat{\sigma}_v^2 = \frac{(\mathbf{y} - X\hat{\hat{\boldsymbol{\beta}}})'\hat{P}'\hat{P}(\mathbf{y} - X\hat{\hat{\boldsymbol{\beta}}})}{T-K} \tag{8.2.31}$$

is a consistent estimator for σ_v^2. Furthermore, by deriving the information matrix, we can show that the ML estimators $\tilde{\rho}$ and $\tilde{\sigma}_v^2$ have respective asymptotic variances $(1 - \rho^2)/T$ and $2\sigma^4/T$, and that they are (asymptotically) independent as well as independent of the ML estimator $\tilde{\boldsymbol{\beta}}$.

Because the alternative estimators for $\boldsymbol{\beta}$ all have the same asymptotic distribution, and their small-sample properties are difficult to derive analytically, any choice between estimators that is based on sampling properties has been based on Monte Carlo evidence.

Such evidence has been provided by Griliches and Rao (1969), Hildreth and Lu (1969), Hildreth and Dent (1974), Beach and MacKinnon (1978a), Spitzer (1979), Park and Mitchell (1980), and Harvey (1981a), but, as is frequently the case with Monte Carlo studies, the evidence does not suggest a clear-cut choice. Some of the contradictory conclusions are resolved by Taylor (1981) who, using analytical approximations, shows that the conclusions of any Monte Carlo study will depend heavily on the specification of X, and on whether the results are conditional on a given X or unconditional with respect to the distribution of a stochastic X. Despite the uncertainties that remain it does seem clear that, when estimating $\boldsymbol{\beta}$, it is desirable to include the initial transformed observation (Equation 8.2.13), and that the ML estimator seldom performs poorly relative to the other estimators.

The efficiency of various estimators for $\boldsymbol{\beta}$ will depend to a large extent on the accuracy with which ρ is estimated. The studies by Hildreth and Dent (1974), Beach and MacKinnon (1978a), and Griffiths and Beesley (1984) all found a substantial bias in the ML estimator for ρ. Consequently, it is possible that an adjusted ML estimator for ρ, such as the one suggested by Hildreth and Dent, may lead to a more efficient estimator for $\boldsymbol{\beta}$.

Another related finding that has emerged from the Monte Carlo studies, particularly those of Park and Mitchell (1980) and Griffiths and Beesley (1984), is that $\hat{\sigma}_v^2(X'\hat{\boldsymbol{\Psi}}^{-1}X)^{-1}$ can be a very poor approximation to the finite sample covariance matrix for any $\hat{\hat{\boldsymbol{\beta}}}$. This fact, and the fact that most estimators for $\boldsymbol{\beta}$ will be relatively efficient, mean that future research directed toward methods for more accurate assessment of the reliability of $\hat{\hat{\boldsymbol{\beta}}}$ is likely to be much more profitable than further efficiency comparisons. For an evaluation of some efforts in this direction see Ullah et al. (1983) and Miyazaki and Griffiths (1984).

8.2.1f Bayesian Estimation

Before turning to higher-order AR processes, we briefly consider a Bayesian approach to estimation of the general linear model with AR(1) errors. We begin with the noninformative prior density

$$g(\boldsymbol{\beta},\rho,\sigma_v) \propto (1 - \rho^2)^{-1/2}\sigma_v^{-1} \tag{8.2.32}$$

which results from the application of Jeffreys' rule. See, for example, Fomby and Guilkey (1978). Combining this with the likelihood (Equation 8.2.25) yields the joint posterior density

$$g(\boldsymbol{\beta},\rho,\sigma_v|\mathbf{y}) \propto \sigma_v^{-(T+1)} \exp\left[-\frac{(\mathbf{y}^* - X^*\boldsymbol{\beta})'(\mathbf{y}^* - X^*\boldsymbol{\beta})}{2\sigma_v^2}\right] \tag{8.2.33}$$

where $\mathbf{y}^* = P\mathbf{y}$, $X^* = PX$ and P is the transformation matrix defined in Equation 8.2.12. Integrating σ_v out of (8.2.33) and rearranging gives, for the joint posterior density for $\boldsymbol{\beta}$ and ρ,

$$g(\boldsymbol{\beta},\rho|\mathbf{y}) \propto (RSS)^{-T/2}\left[1 + \frac{(\boldsymbol{\beta} - \hat{\boldsymbol{\beta}})'X^{*\prime}X^*(\boldsymbol{\beta} - \hat{\boldsymbol{\beta}})}{RSS}\right]^{-T/2} \tag{8.2.34}$$

where $\hat{\boldsymbol{\beta}} = (X^{*\prime}X^*)^{-1}X^{*\prime}\mathbf{y}^*$ and $RSS = (\mathbf{y}^* - X^*\hat{\boldsymbol{\beta}})'(\mathbf{y}^* - X^*\hat{\boldsymbol{\beta}})$. Note that both $\hat{\boldsymbol{\beta}}$ and RSS depend on ρ.

From (8.2.34) it is clear that the density $g(\boldsymbol{\beta}|\rho,\mathbf{y})$ is a multivariate t distribution with mean $\hat{\boldsymbol{\beta}}$. Thus, if ρ were known, the Bayesian estimator with quadratic loss is the GLS estimator. When ρ is unknown, the Bayesian estimator will be the mean of the density $g(\boldsymbol{\beta}|\mathbf{y})$, which is obtained by integrating ρ out of (8.2.34). Unfortunately, this integration is not analytically tractable, and we must resort to numerical methods.

To implement these methods, we first note that

$$E[\boldsymbol{\beta}|\mathbf{y}] = \iint \boldsymbol{\beta} g(\boldsymbol{\beta},\rho|\mathbf{y})\, d\boldsymbol{\beta}\, d\rho = \iint \boldsymbol{\beta} g(\boldsymbol{\beta}|\rho,\mathbf{y})g(\rho|\mathbf{y})\, d\boldsymbol{\beta}\, d\rho = \int \hat{\boldsymbol{\beta}} g(\rho|\mathbf{y})\, d\rho \tag{8.2.35}$$

where, after the first two equalities, the second integral is a K-dimensional one. The last equality indicates that the Bayesian estimator (with quadratic loss) is a weighted average of GLS estimators with weights given by the marginal posterior for ρ. Since it uses all values of ρ in this way, it is an intuitively more satisfying estimator than an EGLS estimator, which uses just one point estimate of ρ. The density $g(\rho|\mathbf{y})$ is obtained by integrating $\boldsymbol{\beta}$ out of (8.2.34) and is given by

$$g(\rho|\mathbf{y}) \propto (RSS)^{-(T-K)/2}|X^{*\prime}X^*|^{-1/2} \tag{8.2.36}$$

Thus, to obtain the Bayesian estimator $E[\boldsymbol{\beta}|\mathbf{y}]$, we first numerically integrate (8.2.36) to find the normalizing constant for $g(\rho|\mathbf{y})$, and then numerically integrate (8.2.35). More specifically, the Bayesian estimator for the kth element of $\boldsymbol{\beta}$, β_k is given by

$$E[\beta_k|\mathbf{y}] = \frac{\int_{-1}^{1} \hat{\beta}_k(RSS)^{-(T-K)/2}|X^{*\prime}X^*|^{-1/2}\, d\rho}{\int_{-1}^{1} (RSS)^{-(T-K)/2}|X^{*\prime}X^*|^{-1/2}\, d\rho} \tag{8.2.37}$$

where $\hat{\beta}_k$ is the kth element of $\hat{\boldsymbol{\beta}}$.

If one is interested in the shape of the posterior density $g(\beta_k|\mathbf{y})$, as well as its mean, this can be analyzed by applying bivariate numerical integration to

If one is interested in the shape of the posterior density $g(\beta_k|\mathbf{y})$, as well as its mean, this can be analyzed by applying bivariate numerical integration to

$$g(\beta_k, \rho|\mathbf{y}) \propto (RSS)^{-(T-K+1)/2}|X^{*\prime}X^*|^{-1/2}c_{kk}^{-1/2} \cdot \left[1 + \frac{(\beta_k - \hat{\beta}_k)^2}{c_{kk} \cdot (RSS)}\right]^{-(T-K+1)/2} \tag{8.2.38}$$

where c_{kk} is the kth diagonal element of $(X^{*\prime}X^*)^{-1}$.

There are some differences between the above approach and the original contribution of Zellner and Tiao (1964). Zellner and Tiao (ZT) do not assume that the AR(1) process is necessarily stationary; they treat the initial observation differently, and they consider a model where X does not contain a constant term. If, in the ZT approach, X does contain a constant, then some difficulties occur at $|\rho| = 1$ and the posterior $g(\rho|\mathbf{y})$ is improper [O'Brien (1970)]. However, if $|\rho| < 1$, and the first observation is retained in the likelihood function, these problems do not occur. Another consequence of Zellner and Tiao's treatment of the first observation is that it enabled them to derive an analytical expression for $g(\boldsymbol{\beta}|\mathbf{y})$.

Other relevant work is that of Drèze (1977), Richard (1975), Fomby and Guilkey (1978), and Griffiths and Dao (1980). Drèze shows how an approximation to $g(\boldsymbol{\beta}|\mathbf{y})$ can be written as a "ratio-form poly-t density," which is amenable to analysis via two-dimensional numerical integration; Richard considers higher-order AR processes and some alternative prior densities. In terms of sampling theory properties, a Monte Carlo experiment by Fomby and Guilkey suggests that the Bayesian estimator is superior to both an EGLS estimator and a pretest estimator based on the Durbin-Watson test; Griffiths and Dao give the Bayesian counterpart of the pretest estimator.

8.2.2 Estimation with AR(2) Errors

A much more flexible autocorrelated error process is obtained if we assume the errors follow a second-order autoregressive scheme. In this case the model can be written as

$$y_t = \mathbf{x}_t'\boldsymbol{\beta} + e_t, \tag{8.2.39}$$

$$e_t = \theta_1 e_{t-1} + \theta_2 e_{t-2} + v_t \tag{8.2.40}$$

where $E[v_t] = 0$, $E[v_t v_s] = 0$ for $t \neq s$, and $E[v_t^2] = \sigma_v^2$. This process will be stationary if $\theta_1 + \theta_2 < 1$, $\theta_2 - \theta_1 < 1$ and $-1 < \theta_2 < 1$. The elements of the covariance matrix $E[\mathbf{ee}'] = \Phi = \sigma_v^2\Psi$ can be found from the variance

$$\sigma_e^2 = \frac{(1 - \theta_2)\sigma_v^2}{(1 + \theta_2)[(1 - \theta_2)^2 - \theta_1^2]} \tag{8.2.41}$$

and the autocorrelation coefficients

$$\rho_1 = \frac{\theta_1}{1 - \theta_2} \tag{8.2.42}$$

$$\rho_2 = \theta_2 + \frac{\theta_1^2}{1 - \theta_2} \tag{8.2.43}$$

and

$$\rho_s = \theta_1 \rho_{s-1} + \theta_2 \rho_{s-2}, \qquad s > 2 \tag{8.2.44}$$

The inverse of $\mathbf{\Psi}$ is given by

$$\mathbf{\Psi}^{-1} = \begin{bmatrix} 1 & -\theta_1 & -\theta_2 & 0 & \cdots & 0 & 0 \\ -\theta_1 & 1 + \theta_1^2 & -\theta_1 + \theta_1\theta_2 & -\theta_2 & \cdots & 0 & 0 \\ -\theta_2 & -\theta_1 + \theta_1\theta_2 & 1 + \theta_1^2 + \theta_2^2 & -\theta_1 + \theta_1\theta_2 & \cdots & 0 & 0 \\ 0 & -\theta_2 & -\theta_1 + \theta_1\theta_2 & 1 + \theta_1^2 + \theta_2^2 & \cdots & 0 & 0 \\ \vdots & \vdots & \vdots & \vdots & & \vdots & \vdots \\ 0 & 0 & 0 & 0 & \cdots & 1 + \theta_1^2 & -\theta_1 \\ 0 & 0 & 0 & 0 & \cdots & -\theta_1 & 1 \end{bmatrix} \tag{8.2.45}$$

8.2.2a GLS Estimation

A matrix P such that $P'P = \mathbf{\Psi}^{-1}$ is given by

$$P = \begin{bmatrix} \sigma_v/\sigma_e & 0 & 0 & 0 & \cdots & 0 & 0 \\ -\rho_1\sqrt{1 - \theta_2^2} & \sqrt{1 - \theta_2^2} & 0 & 0 & \cdots & 0 & 0 \\ -\theta_2 & -\theta_1 & 1 & 0 & \cdots & 0 & 0 \\ 0 & -\theta_2 & -\theta_1 & 1 & \cdots & 0 & 0 \\ \vdots & \vdots & \vdots & \vdots & & \vdots & \vdots \\ 0 & 0 & 0 & 0 & \cdots & 1 & 0 \\ 0 & 0 & 0 & 0 & \cdots & -\theta_1 & 1 \end{bmatrix} \tag{8.2.46}$$

where

$$\frac{\sigma_v}{\sigma_e} = \left\{\frac{(1 + \theta_2)[(1 - \theta_2)^2 - \theta_1^2]}{1 - \theta_2}\right\}^{1/2} \tag{8.2.47}$$

and ρ_1, in terms of θ_1 and θ_2, is given in Equation 8.2.42. Thus, if θ_1 and θ_2 were known, the GLS estimator $\hat{\boldsymbol{\beta}} = (X'\mathbf{\Psi}^{-1}X)^{-1}X'\mathbf{\Psi}^{-1}\mathbf{y}$ can be obtained by applying LS to the transformed model $\mathbf{y}^* = X^*\boldsymbol{\beta} + \mathbf{e}^*$, where $\mathbf{y}^* = P\mathbf{y}$, $X^* = PX$ and

$\mathbf{e}^* = P\mathbf{e}$. Its mean and covariance matrix are $E[\hat{\boldsymbol{\beta}}] = \boldsymbol{\beta}$ and $\Sigma_{\hat{\beta}} = (X'\Phi^{-1}X)^{-1} = \sigma_v^2(X^{*\prime}X^*)^{-1}$.

One can gain more insight into the nature of the transformed model by writing out the individual elements of $\mathbf{y}^* = X^*\boldsymbol{\beta} + \mathbf{e}^*$ and by examining $\mathbf{e}^{*\prime}\mathbf{e}^*$, the sum of squares being minimized. The transformed model is given by

$$\left(\frac{\sigma_v}{\sigma_e}\right)y_1 = \left(\frac{\sigma_v}{\sigma_e}\right)\mathbf{x}_1'\boldsymbol{\beta} + \left(\frac{\sigma_v}{\sigma_e}\right)e_1 \tag{8.2.48}$$

$$\sqrt{1-\theta_2^2}(y_2 - \rho_1 y_1) = \sqrt{1-\theta_2^2}(\mathbf{x}_2 - \rho_1\mathbf{x}_1)'\boldsymbol{\beta} + \sqrt{1-\theta_2^2}(e_2 - \rho_1 e_1) \tag{8.2.49}$$

$$y_t - \theta_1 y_{t-1} - \theta_2 y_{t-2} = (\mathbf{x}_t - \theta_1\mathbf{x}_{t-1} - \theta_2\mathbf{x}_{t-2})'\boldsymbol{\beta} + e_t - \theta_1 e_{t-1} - \theta_2 e_{t-2} \tag{8.2.50}$$

where $t = 3, 4, \ldots, T$; and the sum of squares by

$$\begin{aligned}\mathbf{e}'P'P\mathbf{e} &= \left[\frac{\sigma_v}{\sigma_e}e_1\right]^2 + [\sqrt{1-\theta_2^2}(e_2 - \rho_1 e_1)]^2 + \sum_{t=3}^{T}(e_t - \theta_1 e_{t-1} - \theta_2 e_{t-2})^2 \\ &= e_1^{*2} + e_2^{*2} + \sum_{t=3}^{T} v_t^2\end{aligned} \tag{8.2.51}$$

where $e_1^* = (\sigma_v/\sigma_e)y_1 - (\sigma_v/\sigma_e)\mathbf{x}_1'\boldsymbol{\beta}$,

$$e_2^* = \sqrt{1-\theta_2^2}(y_2 - \rho_1 y_1) - \sqrt{1-\theta_2^2}(\mathbf{x}_2 - \rho_1\mathbf{x}_1)'\boldsymbol{\beta}$$

and

$$v_t = y_t - \theta_1 y_{t-1} - \theta_2 y_{t-2} - (\mathbf{x}_t - \theta_1\mathbf{x}_{t-1} - \theta_2\mathbf{x}_{t-2})'\boldsymbol{\beta}, \qquad t = 3, 4, \ldots, T$$

As in the AR(1) case, we can obtain an approximate GLS estimator $\hat{\boldsymbol{\beta}}_0 = (X_0^{*\prime}X_0^*)^{-1}X_0^{*\prime}\mathbf{y}_0^*$, where $X_0^* = P_0X$, $\mathbf{y}_0^* = P_0\mathbf{y}$ and P_0, of dimension $[(T-2) \times T]$, is given by P with its first two rows deleted. This is the estimator obtained by ignoring e_1^{*2} and e_2^{*2} and minimizing $\Sigma_{t=3}^T v_t^2$. It effectively only uses $(T-2)$ observations.

8.2.2b EGLS Estimation

In practice we need to estimate θ_1 and θ_2 and base the transformations (8.2.48) to (8.2.50) on these estimates. If $\hat{P}$ is the matrix P with θ_1 and θ_2 replaced by some estimated values $\hat{\theta}_1$ and $\hat{\theta}_2$, then the resulting EGLS estimator for $\boldsymbol{\beta}$ is $\hat{\hat{\boldsymbol{\beta}}} = (X'\hat{P}'\hat{P}X)^{-1}X'\hat{P}'\hat{P}\mathbf{y}$.

To estimate θ_1 and θ_2, we can first obtain the LS residuals $\hat{\mathbf{e}} = \mathbf{y} - X\mathbf{b}$ and then use these to obtain the sample autocorrelation coefficients

$$r_s = \frac{\sum_{t=s+1}^{T} \hat{e}_t \hat{e}_{t-s}}{\sum_{t=1}^{T} \hat{e}_t^2} \qquad s = 1, 2 \tag{8.2.52}$$

which are estimators for ρ_1 and ρ_2. They can, however, contain considerable small-sample bias, an indication of which is given by Malinvaud (1970, p. 517). Estimators for θ_1 and θ_2 are obtained by solving (8.2.42) and (8.2.43) for θ_1 and θ_2 in terms of ρ_1 and ρ_2 and substituting the sample counterparts. This yields

$$\hat{\theta}_1 = \frac{r_1(1 - r_2)}{(1 - r_1^2)} \tag{8.2.53}$$

$$\hat{\theta}_2 = \frac{(r_2 - r_1^2)}{(1 - r_1^2)} \tag{8.2.54}$$

Alternatively, we can estimate θ_1 and θ_2 directly by applying LS to the equation

$$\hat{e}_t = \theta_1 \hat{e}_{t-1} + \theta_2 \hat{e}_{t-2} + \hat{v}_t \qquad t = 3, 4, \ldots, T \tag{8.2.55}$$

These two procedures are almost identical, differing only through the end terms of the summations of the squares and cross-products of the $\hat{e}_t$'s.

8.2.2c NLS Estimation

Nonlinear LS estimators for θ_1, θ_2, and $\boldsymbol{\beta}$ are those values that minimize $e_1^{*2} + e_2^{*2} + \sum_{t=3}^{T} v_t^2$. Since e_1^{*2} and e_2^{*2} differ in nature from the v_t^2, $t = 3, 4, \ldots, T$, other asymptotically equivalent procedures, similar to the modifications outlined for the AR(1) process, are often used. These are

1. Find $\boldsymbol{\beta}$, θ_1, and θ_2, which minimize $\sum_{t=3}^{T} v_t^2$.
2. Find $\boldsymbol{\beta}$, θ_1, θ_2, $\bar{e}_0$, and $\bar{e}_{-1}$, which minimize $\sum_{t=1}^{T} v_t^2$, where $v_1 = y_1 - \mathbf{x}_1'\boldsymbol{\beta} - \theta_1 \bar{e}_0 - \theta_2 \bar{e}_{-1}$, and $v_2 = y_2 - \theta_1 y_1 - (\mathbf{x}_2 - \theta_1 \mathbf{x}_1)'\boldsymbol{\beta} - \theta_2 \bar{e}_0$.
3. Set $\bar{e}_{-1} = \bar{e}_0 = 0$ and find $\boldsymbol{\beta}$, θ_1, and θ_2, which minimize $\sum_{t=1}^{T} v_t^2$.

As before, treating e_0 and e_{-1} as parameters to be estimated (case 2), is identical to ignoring the first two observations (case 1) [Pagan (1974)]. Under the assumption of normality, either procedure yields ML estimates *conditional on* y_1 *and* y_2.

Also, we can again employ either an iterative or a search technique to minimize the chosen sum of squares. For $\sum_{t=3}^{T} v_t^2$ the Cochrane-Orcutt iterative procedure can be extended in an obvious manner but, for $e_1^{*2} + e_2^{*2} + \sum_{t=3}^{T} v_t^2$ we would need to use some other algorithm such as one of those described in Appendix B. To carry out a search procedure, we specify values for θ_1 and θ_2, and then calculate $\hat{\boldsymbol{\beta}}$ and the resulting sum of squares $(\mathbf{y}^* - X^*\hat{\boldsymbol{\beta}})'(\mathbf{y}^* - X^*\hat{\boldsymbol{\beta}})$. This is repeated for new values of θ_1 and θ_2 until a sufficient number of points has been taken to ensure that the minimum sum of squares has been located.

The values of θ_1 and θ_2 can be restricted to the stationary region, but such a procedure could still be computationally expensive.

8.2.2d ML Estimation

If, in addition to the earlier assumptions, we assume that e_t is normally distributed, we can follow a similar procedure to that outlined in Equations 8.2.22 to 8.2.29 for the AR(1) process. In this case

$$|\Psi^{-1}| = (1 + \theta_2)^2[(1 - \theta_2)^2 - \theta_1^2] \tag{8.2.56}$$

and the concentrated log-likelihood function is

$$L(\theta_1,\theta_2,\boldsymbol{\beta}) = -\frac{T}{2}\ln(\mathbf{y}^* - X^*\boldsymbol{\beta})'(\mathbf{y}^* - X^*\boldsymbol{\beta}) + \frac{1}{2}\ln\{(1 + \theta_2)^2[(1 - \theta_2)^2 - \theta_1^2]\} \tag{8.2.57}$$

Nonlinear LS estimates of θ_1, θ_2, and $\boldsymbol{\beta}$ will differ from the ML ones because of the presence of the second term in (8.2.57). Beach and MacKinnon (1978b) outline an efficient algorithm for maximizing (8.2.57) or, alternatively, we could use one of the procedures outlined in Appendix B. In the context of a distributed lag model with geometrically declining weights, Schmidt (1971) uses a search procedure, searching over θ_1, θ_2, and the "distributed lag parameter."

8.2.2e Properties

Under the conditions in Section 5.5.2 the above estimators for $\boldsymbol{\beta}$ will be asymptotically normally distributed with mean $\boldsymbol{\beta}$ and covariance matrix $\sigma_v^2(X'P'PX)^{-1}$. To use this result to test hypotheses about $\boldsymbol{\beta}$, we replace P by $\hat{P}$ (which is based on one of the above estimators for θ_1 and θ_2) and σ_v^2 by $\hat{\sigma}_v^2 = (\mathbf{y} - X\hat{\hat{\boldsymbol{\beta}}})'\hat{P}'\hat{P}(\mathbf{y} - X\hat{\hat{\boldsymbol{\beta}}})/(T - K)$. There is little evidence on which of the above estimators performs best in small samples. However, conventional wisdom [see Beach and MacKinnon (1978b)], suggests the ML estimator is likely to be better provided that the model specification is correct. Also, if y_1 and y_2 are legitimate observations from the AR(2) process, minimizing $e_1^{*2} + e_2^{*2} + \Sigma_{t=3}^T v_t^2$ should be more efficient than minimizing $\Sigma_{t=3}^T v_t^2$.

8.2.3 Estimation with Higher-Order AR Errors

In the previous section we outlined how the general linear model with AR(1) errors can be extended to that with AR(2) errors. If we have sufficient observations, this extension readily generalizes to errors that follow any finite-order AR process. However, the expression for the transformation matrix P becomes progressively more complicated. A general expression for Ψ^{-1} is given by Wise (1955) while Fuller (1976, p. 423) defines the required P matrix. Pagan (1974) gives details of how the Gauss-Newton algorithm can be used to minimize

$\Sigma_{t=p+1}^{T} v_t^2$, where p is the order of the process and Pagan and Byron (1978) summarize the various modifications of NLS and ML estimation. See also Harvey (1981a, pp. 203–206).

8.2.4 A Particular AR(4) Process

Thomas and Wallis (1971) suggest that when quarterly data are being used, a fourth-order process may be appropriate. However, instead of a general fourth-order process, they suggest that only the disturbances in corresponding quarters of each year should be correlated. This leads to the specification

$$e_t = \rho e_{t-4} + v_t \tag{8.2.58}$$

whose covariance matrix is

$$\sigma_v^2 \mathbf{\Psi}_4 = \sigma_v^2(\mathbf{\Psi}_1 \otimes I_4) \tag{8.2.59}$$

where $\mathbf{\Psi}_1$ is of dimension $(T/4 \times T/4)$ and has the same structure as $\mathbf{\Psi}$ obtained from an AR(1) process. See Equation 8.2.10. The structure of $\mathbf{\Psi}_4$ is such that $E[e_t e_{t-s}] = 0$ unless s is a multiple of 4 in which case it is $\sigma_e^2 \rho^{s/4}$. Also, $\sigma_e^2 = \sigma_v^2/(1 - \rho^2)$.

The appropriate matrix for transforming the data is $P_4 = P_1 \otimes I_4$, where P_1 is the P defined in (8.2.12) and the transformed elements of $\mathbf{y}^* = P_4\mathbf{y}$, for example, are

$$y_t^* = y_t\sqrt{1 - \rho^2}, \qquad t = 1, 2, 3, 4 \tag{8.2.60}$$

$$y_t^* = y_t - \rho y_{t-4}, \qquad t = 5, 6, \ldots, T \tag{8.2.61}$$

Least squares estimates are given by minimizing the sum of squares

$$\mathbf{e}'P_4'P_4\mathbf{e} = \mathbf{e}^{*\prime}\mathbf{e}^* = \sum_{t=1}^{4} e_t^{*2} + \sum_{t=5}^{T} v_t^2 \tag{8.2.62}$$

where

$$e_t^* = \sqrt{1 - \rho^2}e_t = \sqrt{1 - \rho^2}(y_t - \mathbf{x}_t'\boldsymbol{\beta}), \qquad t = 1, 2, 3, 4$$

and

$$v_t = e_t - \rho e_{t-4} = y_t - \rho y_{t-4} - (\mathbf{x}_t - \rho\mathbf{x}_{t-4})'\boldsymbol{\beta}, \qquad t = 5, 6, \ldots, T$$

We can employ either an EGLS, NLS, or ML estimator. For an EGLS estimator we can estimate ρ from LS applied to $\hat{e}_t = \rho\hat{e}_{t-4} + \hat{v}_t$, $t = 5, 6, \ldots, T$, where $\hat{e}_t = y_t - \mathbf{x}_t'\mathbf{b}$. Nonlinear LS estimates of $\boldsymbol{\beta}$ and ρ are such that (8.2.62) is a minimum while, under normality, the concentrated likelihood function from which ML estimates can be found is

$$L(\rho,\boldsymbol{\beta}) = -\frac{T}{2}\ln(\mathbf{y}^* - X^*\boldsymbol{\beta})'(\mathbf{y}^* - X^*\boldsymbol{\beta}) + 2\ln(1-\rho^2) \tag{8.2.63}$$

8.2.5 Estimation with MA(1) Errors

Although the most popular autocorrelated error specification in econometrics has been the autoregressive one, there are many instances when moving-average errors are justified by economic theory [Nicholls, Pagan, and Terrell (1975)], and, in addition, models with MA or ARMA errors are often better representations of the data generating process. We begin a study of the alternative models by considering the general linear model with MA(1) disturbances. It is given by

$$y_t = \mathbf{x}_t'\boldsymbol{\beta} + e_t \tag{8.2.64}$$

and

$$e_t = v_t + \alpha v_{t-1} \tag{8.2.65}$$

where $E[v_t] = 0$, $E[v_t^2] = \sigma_v^2$, $E[v_t v_s] = 0$ for $t \neq s$ and we assume the process is invertible, that is $|\alpha| < 1$. The invertibility assumption means that the MA process can be alternatively written as an infinite order AR process and it must hold if the ML and various approximate NLS estimators (described below) are to have the same asymptotic distribution. It should be kept in mind, however, that $\alpha = 1$ is a legitimate MA model that may arise in practice when overdifferencing has taken place. For further details see Chapter 7, Davidson (1981) and Harvey (1981b, Chapter 5 and 1981c).

The covariance matrix for $\mathbf{e}$ is $E[\mathbf{ee}'] = \sigma_v^2\Psi$ where $\sigma_e^2 = \sigma_v^2(1+\alpha^2)$; the autocorrelations are $\rho_1 = \alpha/(1+\alpha^2)$ and $\rho_s = 0$ for $s > 1$; and

$$\Psi = \begin{bmatrix} 1+\alpha^2 & \alpha & 0 & \cdots & 0 & 0 \\ \alpha & 1+\alpha^2 & \alpha & \cdots & 0 & 0 \\ 0 & \alpha & 1+\alpha^2 & \cdots & 0 & 0 \\ \vdots & \vdots & \vdots & & \vdots & \vdots \\ 0 & 0 & 0 & \cdots & 1+\alpha^2 & \alpha \\ 0 & 0 & 0 & \cdots & \alpha & 1+\alpha^2 \end{bmatrix} \tag{8.2.66}$$

For known α the GLS estimator that minimizes $(\mathbf{y} - X\boldsymbol{\beta})'\Psi^{-1}(\mathbf{y} - X\boldsymbol{\beta}) = \mathbf{e}'\Psi^{-1}\mathbf{e}$ is given by $\hat{\boldsymbol{\beta}} = (X'\Psi^{-1}X)^{-1}X'\Psi^{-1}\mathbf{y}$.

8.2.5a GLS, NLS, and ML Estimation

To compute the GLS estimator, or the NLS and ML estimators when α is unknown, a transformation matrix P such that $P'P = \Psi^{-1}$ is required. The structure of Ψ^{-1} is cumbersome [Pesaran (1973), Shaman (1973), Balestra (1980)], and so we will not describe it here. However, we will describe the transformation matrix suggested by Balestra (1980). Note that a matrix P satisfying $P'P = \Psi^{-1}$ is not unique, and alternatives include the matrix suggested by Pesaran (1973) and the matrix implicit in the Kalman filtering algorithm (Harvey, 1981b, p. 112).

Following Balestra, we define

$$a_s = 1 + \alpha^2 + \ldots + \alpha^{2s} \tag{8.2.67}$$

and

$$Q = \begin{bmatrix} 1 & 0 & 0 & 0 & \ldots & 0 \\ c & a_1 & 0 & 0 & \ldots & 0 \\ c^2 & a_1 c & a_2 & 0 & \ldots & 0 \\ c^3 & a_1 c^2 & a_2 c & a_3 & \ldots & 0 \\ \vdots & \vdots & \vdots & \vdots & \ddots & \vdots \\ c^{T-1} & a_1 c^{T-2} & a_2 c^{T-3} & a_3 c^{T-4} & \ldots & a_{T-1} \end{bmatrix} \tag{8.2.68}$$

where $c = -\alpha$. Then it can be shown that

$$Q\Psi Q' = D = \text{diag}(a_0 a_1, a_1 a_2, a_2 a_3, \ldots, a_{T-1} a_T) \tag{8.2.69}$$

and so an appropriate transformation matrix is given by

$$P = D^{-1/2} Q \tag{8.2.70}$$

Thus, the GLS estimator $\hat{\boldsymbol{\beta}} = (X^{*\prime}X^*)^{-1}X^{*\prime}\mathbf{y}^*$ can be found by minimization of

$$S(\boldsymbol{\beta},\alpha) = \mathbf{e}^{*\prime}\mathbf{e}^* = (\mathbf{y}^* - X^*\boldsymbol{\beta})'(\mathbf{y}^* - X^*\boldsymbol{\beta}) \tag{8.2.71}$$

where $\mathbf{e}^* = P\mathbf{e}$, $\mathbf{y}^* = P\mathbf{y}$ and $X^* = PX$. Alternatively, if α is unknown, NLS estimates for $\boldsymbol{\beta}$ and α can be found by numerically minimizing (8.2.71) with respect to both $\boldsymbol{\beta}$ and α. The transformed residuals $\mathbf{e}^* = P\mathbf{e}$ (or the variables $\mathbf{y}^*$ and X^*) can be conveniently calculated via the simple recursive expressions

$$\begin{aligned} e_1^* &= (a_0/a_1)^{1/2} e_1 \\ e_2^* &= (a_1/a_2)^{1/2} e_2 - \alpha(a_0/a_2)^{1/2} e_1^* \\ &\vdots \\ e_T^* &= (a_{T-1}/a_T)^{1/2} e_T - \alpha(a_{T-2}/a_T)^{1/2} e_{T-1}^* \end{aligned} \tag{8.2.72}$$

This transformation can be related to that of the Kalman filtering algorithm [see Appendix C and Harvey (1981b, p. 112) for details] by multiplying the tth equation in (8.2.72) by $(a_t/a_{t-1})^{1/2}$. Specifically, it can be shown that

$$\left(\frac{a_t}{a_{t-1}}\right)^{1/2} e_t^* = e_t - \alpha \left(\frac{a_{t-2}}{a_{t-1}}\right)^{1/2} e_{t-1}^* \tag{8.2.73}$$

is the prediction error that occurs if e_t is predicted at time $t - 1$. The term $\alpha(a_{t-2}/a_{t-1})^{1/2}e_{t-1}^*$ is the minimum mean square error predictor of e_t at time $t - 1$ and $E[(a_t/a_{t-1})e_t^{*2}] = \sigma_v^2(a_t/a_{t-1})$ is the variance of the prediction error.

For ML estimation under the assumption of normally distributed errors, we note that

$$|\Psi| = \frac{1 - \alpha^{2T+2}}{1 - \alpha^2} \tag{8.2.74}$$

and so ML estimators for $\boldsymbol{\beta}$ and α (see Equation 8.2.6) are obtained by numerically minimizing

$$S_L(\boldsymbol{\beta},\alpha) = [(1 - \alpha^{2T+2})/(1 - \alpha^2)]^{1/T}(\mathbf{y}^* - X^*\boldsymbol{\beta})'(\mathbf{y}^* - X^*\boldsymbol{\beta}) \tag{8.2.75}$$

Any one of a number of iterative procedures (see Chapter 6 and Appendix B) can be used to find the minimum of (8.2.71) or (8.2.75). For an example of an algorithm specifically designed for the MA(1) model see Balestra (1980). Alternatively, a search procedure that calculates $S(\boldsymbol{\beta},\alpha)$ or $S_L(\boldsymbol{\beta},\alpha)$ for a number of preassigned values of α in the interval $[-1,1]$ can be employed. Note that, for $\alpha = \pm 1$, $|\Psi| = T + 1$. Although we are assuming that the process is strictly invertible and hence that $|\alpha| \neq 1$, it is still possible (and, as we shall see later, quite probable) for one of the endpoints to be a minimizing value. See Sargan and Bhargava (1983b) for some details on estimation when $\alpha = 1$.

8.2.5b Approximations

Instead of finding estimators that minimize $S(\boldsymbol{\beta},\alpha) = \mathbf{e}^{*\prime}\mathbf{e}^*$ or $S_L(\boldsymbol{\beta},\alpha) = |\Psi|^{1/T}\mathbf{e}^{*\prime}\mathbf{e}^*$, approximate procedures with fewer computations are frequently used. In particular, a common alternative is to replace the transformed observations implied by (8.2.72) with

$$v_t = e_t - \alpha v_{t-1} \qquad t = 1, 2, \ldots, T \tag{8.2.76}$$

where v_0 is set equal to zero. This approximate transformation is equivalent to replacing the transformation matrix P given by (8.2.68) through (8.2.70) with the matrix

$$P_0 = \begin{bmatrix} 1 & 0 & 0 & \cdots & 0 \\ c & 1 & 0 & \cdots & 0 \\ c^2 & c & 1 & \cdots & 0 \\ \vdots & \vdots & \vdots & & \vdots \\ c^{T-1} & c^{T-2} & c^{T-3} & \cdots & 1 \end{bmatrix} \tag{8.2.77}$$

Approximate NLS and approximate ML estimators are obtained by numerically minimizing $S^*(\boldsymbol{\beta},\alpha) = \mathbf{e}'P_0'P_0\mathbf{e}$, and $S_L^*(\boldsymbol{\beta},\alpha) = |\boldsymbol{\Psi}|^{1/T}\mathbf{e}'P_0'P_0\mathbf{e}$, respectively. For large T, $a_{T-1} \approx a_T$, particularly if $|\alpha|$ is not close to unity, and so the approximation will have its greatest effect on the early observations. Also, as $T \to \infty$ the difference between all four criterion functions (S, S_L, S^*, and S_L^*) diminishes. In the following section on the properties of the various estimators we refer to the estimators that minimize S^* and S_L^* as conditional LS and conditional ML (conditional on $v_0 = 0$), while the estimators that minimize S and S_L will be referred to as unconditional LS and unconditional ML, respectively. Strictly speaking, however, S_L^* is not the criterion function for conditional ML estimation. As we will see in Section 8.2.6 on the general MA(q) error model, the determinant of the covariance matrix in the conditional density $f(\mathbf{y}|v_0)$ is equal to unity. If the conditioning value is $v_0 = 0$, conditional ML is identical to conditional LS. Nevertheless, S_L^* is still a valid approximate ML criterion function, and in the next section it is convenient to refer to it as the "conditional ML" function.

8.2.5c Properties

In terms of asymptotic properties there is no basis for choice between the conditional and unconditional LS and ML estimators. Under certain conditions—see Pierce (1971)—these estimators will all have an asymptotic normal distribution, will be consistent, and will have a covariance matrix that can be estimated using the inverse of the matrix of second derivatives of the log likelihood function, or the approximation being used in the NLS or ML algorithm. Based on these estimates, approximate tests on the coefficients can be carried out in the usual way.

The small sample properties of the various estimators have been investigated using both Monte Carlo experiments [see, for example, Dent and Min (1978), Ansley and Newbold (1980), and Harvey's review (1981b, pp. 135–139)], and the analytical properties of the criterion functions [see, for example, Davidson (1981) and Osborn (1982)]. Most of these studies are concerned with the properties of estimators for α in the pure time series model where $\boldsymbol{\beta} = \mathbf{0}$, rather than with the properties of various estimators for $\boldsymbol{\beta}$. The main results can be summarized as follows.

1. The equivalent of the likelihood function, S_L, will always have a global minimum within the region $-1 \leq \alpha \leq 1$ and necessarily has stationary points at $\alpha = \pm 1$. For small-sample sizes, one of these stationary points is frequently the global minimum. Thus, in any given study, there is a high probability that $\tilde{\alpha} = \pm 1$ will be the maximum likelihood estimator for α [Davidson (1981), Cryer and Ledolter (1981)], and this result is true even if the true value of $|\alpha|$ is not close to one (say less than .8). However, the probability is greater the closer $|\alpha|$ is to unity and the smaller the sample size. The results of Sargan and Bhargava (1983b) and Griffiths and Beesley (1984) confirm that the probability will also be high when the model has an X component (i.e., when $\boldsymbol{\beta} \neq \mathbf{0}$). In general the distribution of the ML estimator $\tilde{\alpha}$ tends to be bimodal with a well-behaved distribution in the interval $[-1,1]$, and a spike at ± 1.

2. The conditional function S_L^* will always have a minimum within the region $-1 < \alpha < 1$, but the least squares functions S and S^* do not necessarily possess unconstrained minima within the corresponding closed interval $-1 \leq \alpha \leq 1$ [Davidson (1981)]. In terms of the *expected values* of the criterion functions, it can be shown [Osborn (1982)] that $E[S_L]$ is the only expected function that has a stationary point at the true value of α, that $E[S^*]$ always has a minimum within the region $-1 < \alpha < 1$, and that $E[S]$ frequently has no unconstrained minimum within this region, particularly if T is small and $|\alpha|$ close to unity.

3. If we consider the values of α that minimize the expected criterion functions $E[S]$, $E[S^*]$ and $E[S_L]$, it can be shown [Osborn (1982)] that the conditional LS minimizing value will be between zero and the true value of α, while the unconditional LS minimizing value will be between the true value of α and the invertibility boundary (or it will be a constrained minimum on the boundary). These results are not surprising given the nature of the functions discussed in the first two points, and they go a long way to explaining the results of many Monte Carlo studies. In particular, most Monte Carlo studies have found that unconditional LS leads to more (constrained) coefficient estimates at ± 1 than does ML, which in turn gives more boundary estimates than conditional LS. Conditional ML has no boundary estimates. Consequently, when the various estimators are evaluated in terms of their mean square errors [Davidson (1981), Dent and Min (1978)], conditional ML and conditional LS are preferable for true values of α away from the invertibility boundary, while ML performs best for values of α approaching ± 1. Unconditional LS is best for extreme cases near ± 1 but otherwise it is worse and it does not appear to be recommended by any authors.

4. If $\hat{\sigma}^2_{\text{ML}}$, $\hat{\sigma}^2_{\text{ULS}}$, and $\hat{\sigma}^2_{\text{CLS}}$ represent the alternative estimators for σ_v^2 obtained from ML, unconditional and conditional LS, respectively, then it can be shown that $\hat{\sigma}^2_{\text{ML}} \geq \hat{\sigma}^2_{\text{ULS}}$ and $\hat{\sigma}^2_{\text{CLS}} > \hat{\sigma}^2_{\text{ULS}}$. Furthermore, *on average* we would expect $\hat{\sigma}^2_{\text{CLS}} \geq \hat{\sigma}^2_{\text{ML}} \geq \hat{\sigma}^2_{\text{ULS}}$. See Osborn (1982). Thus, it is reasonable to hypothesize that conditional LS will lead to overstatement of the variance, while unconditional LS will underestimate the variance.

5. Because of the prevalence of boundary estimates for α when sample size is small, extreme caution must be exercised when making inferences about α.

A question that is not addressed in the above results is the relative performance of the various estimators in terms of efficiency of estimating $\boldsymbol{\beta}$ when the model contains an X component and $\boldsymbol{\beta} \neq \mathbf{0}$. In this case the unconditional LS and ML estimators for $\boldsymbol{\beta}$ will be of the form $\hat{\hat{\boldsymbol{\beta}}} = (X'\hat{\Psi}^{-1}X)^{-1}X'\hat{\Psi}^{-1}\mathbf{y}$, while the conditional LS and ML estimators will be of the form $\hat{\hat{\boldsymbol{\beta}}}_0 = (X'\hat{P}_0'\hat{P}_0X)^{-1} X'\hat{P}_0'\hat{P}_0\mathbf{y}$. Since $\hat{\hat{\boldsymbol{\beta}}}_0$ is based on an approximate transformation rather than the more efficient GLS transformation, there is likely to be a loss of efficiency from estimating $\boldsymbol{\beta}$ via one of the conditional procedures, and this loss of efficiency will not necessarily be reflected in the relative efficiencies of the various estimators for α. In view of this fact, and that in some circumstances with known α the approximation can be considerably worse than GLS [Balestra (1980), Park and Heikes (1983)], we can conclude that in terms of estimating $\boldsymbol{\beta}$, unconditional LS and ML are likely to be preferable to the conditional estimators. Combining this conclusion with the results on relative efficiency of the various estimators for α (see point 3 above), it seems reasonable to recommend the unconditional ML estimator over the other three alternatives. One strategy that has not been investigated but that may prove even better is to use the fully transformed estimator $\hat{\hat{\boldsymbol{\beta}}} = (X'\hat{\Psi}^{-1}X)^{-1}X'\hat{\Psi}^{-1}\mathbf{y}$, with $\hat{\Psi}$ based on either a conditional LS or a conditional ML estimate of α.

We conclude this section with a few comments on two-step EGLS estimation. In a linear model with AR errors, a common estimation procedure is to use the LS residuals to estimate the autoregressive parameters, and then to use these estimates to compute an EGLS esimator for $\boldsymbol{\beta}$. A similar procedure can be followed for the linear model with MA(1) errors. For example, one possible estimator for α is based on the sample autocorrelation coefficient derived from LS residuals,

$$r_1 = \frac{\sum_{t=2}^{T}\hat{e}_t\hat{e}_{t-1}}{\sum_{t=1}^{T}\hat{e}_t^2}$$

Solving $\rho_1 = \alpha/(1 + \alpha^2)$ for α and substituting r_1 for ρ_1 yields

$$\hat{\alpha} = \frac{1 - (1 - 4r_1^2)^{1/2}}{2r_1} \tag{8.2.78}$$

Note that $\hat{\alpha}$ is only meaningful if $|r_1| < .5$. The invertibility condition requires $|\alpha| < 1$, which in turn implies $|\rho_1| < .5$. This estimator is easy to construct but, because it ignores information contained in the other sample autocorrelations, it is inefficient relative to the NLS and ML estimators. Because of this inefficiency, in this section we have concentrated on the NLS and ML techniques. For further information on the estimator in (8.2.78) and other related results see Fuller (1976, pp. 343–356), Durbin (1959), McClave (1973), and Mentz (1977).

8.2.5d Bayesian Estimation

For Bayesian estimation of the general linear model with MA(1) errors, we shall use the uninformative prior

$$g(\boldsymbol{\beta},\alpha,\sigma_v) \propto \frac{1}{\sigma_v}, \qquad |\alpha| < 1 \tag{8.2.79}$$

This prior combines the commonly used diffuse one $g(\boldsymbol{\beta},\sigma_v) \propto 1/\sigma_v$ with the assumption that α is a priori independent of $\boldsymbol{\beta}$ and σ_v with prior $g(\alpha) = \frac{1}{2}$, $|\alpha| < 1$. One might object to calling the prior $g(\alpha) = \frac{1}{2}$ uninformative, in which case an alternative prior, such as one based on the square root of the determinant of the information matrix [e.g., Zellner (1971, p. 47)], could be used. The latter would add an additional term to the following results, but it would not change the essential features of the analysis.

Combining (8.2.79) with the likelihood and integrating out σ_v yields the joint posterior density

$$g(\boldsymbol{\beta},\alpha|\mathbf{y}) \propto \left[\frac{1-\alpha^{2T+2}}{1-\alpha^2}\right]^{-1/2} (\text{RSS})^{-T/2}\left[1+\frac{(\boldsymbol{\beta}-\hat{\boldsymbol{\beta}})'X^{*\prime}X^*(\boldsymbol{\beta}-\hat{\boldsymbol{\beta}})}{\text{RSS}}\right]^{-T/2} \tag{8.2.80}$$

where $\hat{\boldsymbol{\beta}} = (X^{*\prime}X^*)^{-1}X^{*\prime}\mathbf{y}^*$, $\text{RSS} = (\mathbf{y}^* - X^*\hat{\boldsymbol{\beta}})'(\mathbf{y}^* - X^*\hat{\boldsymbol{\beta}})$, and the transformed variables $\mathbf{y}^*$ and X^* are defined in (8.2.70) and (8.2.71). Both $\hat{\boldsymbol{\beta}}$ and RSS depend on α.

From (8.2.80) it is clear that $g(\boldsymbol{\beta}|\alpha,\mathbf{y})$ is a multivariate t distribution with mean $\hat{\boldsymbol{\beta}}$, the GLS estimator. To find the Bayesian quadratic loss estimator for $\boldsymbol{\beta}$, which is not conditional on α, we can consider each β_k in turn after first integrating the remaining $(K-1)$ β_k's out of (8.2.80). This gives

$$g(\beta_k,\alpha|\mathbf{y}) \propto \left[\frac{1-\alpha^{2T+2}}{1-\alpha^2}\right]^{-1/2} \text{RSS}^{-(T-K+1)/2}|X^{*\prime}X^*|^{-1/2}c_{kk}^{-1/2}$$
$$\times\left[1+\frac{(\beta_k-\hat{\beta}_k)^2}{c_{kk}\cdot\text{RSS}}\right]^{-(T-K+1)/2} \tag{8.2.81}$$

where c_{kk} is the kth diagonal element of $(X^{*\prime}X^*)^{-1}$ and $\hat{\beta}_k$ is the kth element of $\hat{\boldsymbol{\beta}}$. Information about $g(\beta_k|\mathbf{y})$ can be obtained by applying bivariate numerical integration to (8.2.81).

To obtain information about α, we can integrate β_k out of (8.2.81) and then apply univariate numerical integration to

$$g(\alpha|\mathbf{y}) \propto \left[\frac{1-\alpha^{2T+2}}{1-\alpha^2}\right]^{-1/2} \text{RSS}^{-(T-K)/2}|X^{*\prime}X^*|^{-1/2} \tag{8.2.82}$$

8.2.6 Estimation with Higher-Order MA Errors

We now consider estimation of the parameters of the general linear model with qth order MA errors. The first-order model that we discussed in the previous section could, of course, also be considered within this framework. One difference is that, in the MA(1) case, it is possible to derive more explicit closed form expressions for the various criterion functions. The general model can be written as

$$y_t = \mathbf{x}_t'\boldsymbol{\beta} + e_t, \tag{8.2.83}$$

$$e_t = v_t + \sum_{j=1}^{q} \alpha_j v_{t-j} \tag{8.2.84}$$

where $E[v_t] = 0$, $E[v_t^2] = \sigma_v^2$, $E[v_t v_s] = 0$ for $t \neq s$ and we assume the α_j's are such that the invertibility condition holds. See Chapter 7. The covariance matrix $E[\mathbf{ee}'] = \Phi = \sigma_v^2 \Psi$ is such that $\sigma_e^2 = (1 + \alpha_1^2 + \alpha_2^2 + \ldots + \alpha_q^2)\sigma_v^2$, and the autocorrelations are given by

$$\begin{aligned} \rho_s &= \frac{\alpha_s + \alpha_1 \alpha_{s+1} + \ldots + \alpha_{q-s}\alpha_q}{1 + \alpha_1^2 + \ldots + \alpha_q^2} \qquad s = 1, 2, \ldots, q \\ &= 0, \qquad s > q \end{aligned} \tag{8.2.85}$$

Following Pagan and Nicholls (1976), who were influenced by Phillips (1966), we can write (8.2.84) in matrix notation as

$$\mathbf{e} = M\mathbf{v} + \bar{M}\bar{\mathbf{v}} \tag{8.2.86}$$

where $\mathbf{e}' = (e_1, e_2, \ldots, e_T)$, $\mathbf{v}' = (v_1, v_2, \ldots, v_T)$, $\bar{\mathbf{v}}' = (v_0, v_{-1}, \ldots, v_{-(q-1)})$,

$$\underset{(T \times T)}{M} = \begin{bmatrix} 1 & 0 & \ldots & & & & 0 \\ \alpha_1 & 1 & \ldots & & & & 0 \\ \vdots & \ddots & \ddots & & & & \\ \alpha_q & & & \ddots & & & \vdots \\ 0 & \ddots & & & \ddots & & \\ & & \ddots & & & \ddots & \\ \vdots & & & \ddots & & 1 & 0 \\ 0 & 0 & \ldots & 0 & \alpha_q & \ldots & \alpha_1 & 1 \end{bmatrix} \tag{8.2.87}$$

and

$$\underset{(T \times q)}{\bar{M}} = \begin{bmatrix} \alpha_1 & \alpha_2 & \ldots & \alpha_q \\ \alpha_2 & & \cdot^{\cdot^{\cdot}} & 0 \\ \vdots & \cdot^{\cdot^{\cdot}} & & \\ \alpha_q & & & \vdots \\ 0 & & & \\ \vdots & & & \\ 0 & 0 & \ldots & 0 \end{bmatrix} \tag{8.2.88}$$

A convenient way to write the covariance matrix for **e** is

$$E[\mathbf{ee}'] = E[(M\mathbf{v} + \bar{M}\bar{\mathbf{v}})(M\mathbf{v} + \bar{M}\bar{\mathbf{v}})'] = \sigma_v^2(MM' + \bar{M}\bar{M}') = \sigma_v^2\mathbf{\Psi} \tag{8.2.89}$$

This expression will be used below.

8.2.6a NLS and ML Estimation

For nonlinear least squares estimation of $\boldsymbol{\beta}$ and $\boldsymbol{\alpha} = (\alpha_1, \alpha_2, \ldots, \alpha_q)'$ we need to find those values of $\boldsymbol{\beta}$ and $\boldsymbol{\alpha}$ that minimize $\mathbf{e}'\mathbf{\Psi}^{-1}\mathbf{e}$. For this purpose a number of alternative and computationally more convenient expressions for $\mathbf{e}'\mathbf{\Psi}^{-1}\mathbf{e}$, as well as a number of approximations, have been considered.

One approach is to minimize

$$\mathbf{v}'\mathbf{v} + \bar{\mathbf{v}}'\bar{\mathbf{v}} \tag{8.2.90}$$

with respect to $\boldsymbol{\beta}$, $\boldsymbol{\alpha}$, and $\bar{\mathbf{v}}$. It can be shown [Pagan and Nicholls (1976)] that this minimization problem is equivalent to minimizing $\mathbf{e}'\mathbf{\Psi}^{-1}\mathbf{e}$ with respect to $\boldsymbol{\beta}$ and $\boldsymbol{\alpha}$; and it is convenient computationally because the successive residuals in the sum of squares can be calculated recursively as

$$\begin{aligned}
v_{-q+1} &= \bar{v}_{-q+1} \\
&\ \ \vdots \\
v_0 &= \bar{v}_0 \\
v_1 &= y_1 - \mathbf{x}_1'\boldsymbol{\beta} - \sum_{j=1}^{q} \alpha_j \bar{v}_{1-j} \\
v_t &= y_t - \mathbf{x}_t'\boldsymbol{\beta} - \sum_{j=1}^{t-1} \alpha_j v_{t-j} - \sum_{j=t}^{q} \alpha_j \bar{v}_{t-j}, \qquad t = 2, 3, \ldots, q \\
v_t &= y_t - \mathbf{x}_t'\boldsymbol{\beta} - \sum_{j=1}^{q} \alpha_j v_{t-j}, \qquad t = q+1, q+2, \ldots, T
\end{aligned} \tag{8.2.91}$$

Some modifications of (8.2.90) that have been used are

1. Minimize $\mathbf{v}'\mathbf{v}$ with respect to $\boldsymbol{\beta}$, $\boldsymbol{\alpha}$, and $\bar{\mathbf{v}}$.
2. Set $\bar{\mathbf{v}} = \mathbf{0}$ and minimize $\mathbf{v}'\mathbf{v}$ (cf. Equation 8.2.76).
3. The "backcasting method" of Box and Jenkins (1970, p. 213).

If the v_t are normally distributed, the first of these is equivalent to ML estimation conditional on $\bar{\mathbf{v}}$ [Phillips (1966), Trivedi (1970), Hendry and Trivedi (1972)]. To illustrate this, we can substitute (8.2.89) into $\mathbf{y} = X\boldsymbol{\beta} + \mathbf{e}$ to yield

$$\mathbf{y} = X\boldsymbol{\beta} + \bar{M}\bar{\mathbf{v}} + M\mathbf{v} \tag{8.2.92}$$

Conditional on $\bar{\mathbf{v}}$, we find that $\mathbf{y}$ has a multivariate normal distribution with mean $E[\mathbf{y}] = X\boldsymbol{\beta} + \bar{M}\bar{\mathbf{v}}$ and covariance matrix $E[(\mathbf{y} - X\boldsymbol{\beta} - \bar{M}\bar{\mathbf{v}})(\mathbf{y} - X\boldsymbol{\beta} - \bar{M}\bar{\mathbf{v}})'] = \sigma_v^2 MM'$. Its density is

$$f(\mathbf{y}|\bar{\mathbf{v}}) = (2\pi\sigma_v^2)^{-T/2}|MM'|^{-1/2} \times \exp\left[-\frac{1}{2\sigma_v^2}(\mathbf{y} - X\boldsymbol{\beta} - \bar{M}\bar{\mathbf{v}})'M'^{-1}M^{-1}(\mathbf{y} - X\boldsymbol{\beta} - \bar{M}\bar{\mathbf{v}})\right] \tag{8.2.93}$$

Now $|M| = 1$ and $\mathbf{v} = M^{-1}(\mathbf{y} - X\boldsymbol{\beta} - \bar{M}\bar{\mathbf{v}})$, so (8.2.93) can be written as

$$f(\mathbf{y}|\bar{\mathbf{v}}) = (2\pi\sigma_v^2)^{-T/2}\exp\left(-\frac{\mathbf{v}'\mathbf{v}}{2\sigma_v^2}\right) \tag{8.2.94}$$

Substituting the ML estimator $\tilde{\sigma}_v^2 = \mathbf{v}'\mathbf{v}/T$ into (8.2.94) yields a concentrated log likelihood function which, ignoring constants, is $L = -(T/2)\ln(\mathbf{v}'\mathbf{v})$. Thus minimizing $\mathbf{v}'\mathbf{v}$ with respect to $\boldsymbol{\beta}$, $\boldsymbol{\alpha}$ and $\bar{\mathbf{v}}$ yields, conditional on $\bar{\mathbf{v}}$, ML estimators for $\boldsymbol{\beta}$ and $\boldsymbol{\alpha}$.

Instead of minimizing (8.2.90), exact NLS estimates can also be found by minimizing an alternative function that does not depend on the presample disturbances $\bar{\mathbf{v}}$ and that is based on a simplification of $\mathbf{e}'\boldsymbol{\Psi}^{-1}\mathbf{e}$. To derive this simplification we note that, from (8.2.89)

$$\boldsymbol{\Psi} = M(I + M^{-1}\bar{M}\bar{M}'M'^{-1})M' \tag{8.2.95}$$

and letting $C = M^{-1}\bar{M}$ we have

$$\begin{aligned}\boldsymbol{\Psi}^{-1} &= M'^{-1}(I_T + CC')^{-1}M^{-1} \\ &= M'^{-1}[I_T - C(I_q + C'C)^{-1}C']M^{-1}\end{aligned} \tag{8.2.96}$$

The sum of squares can now be written as

$$\mathbf{e}'\boldsymbol{\Psi}^{-1}\mathbf{e} = \boldsymbol{\delta}'\boldsymbol{\delta} - \boldsymbol{\delta}'C(I_q + C'C)^{-1}C'\boldsymbol{\delta} \tag{8.2.97}$$

where $\boldsymbol{\delta} = M^{-1}\mathbf{e}$. For computing NLS estimates for $\boldsymbol{\beta}$ and $\boldsymbol{\alpha}$ from (8.2.97) we note that, since M is a lower triangular matrix, $\boldsymbol{\delta} = M^{-1}\mathbf{e}$ and $C = M^{-1}\bar{M}$ can be readily calculated recursively; in addition the inverse $(I_q + C'C)^{-1}$ is only of order q. The approximate procedure of setting $\bar{\mathbf{v}} = \mathbf{0}$ and minimizing $\mathbf{v}'\mathbf{v}$ in (8.2.90) is equivalent to ignoring the second term in (8.2.97) and minimizing $\boldsymbol{\delta}'\boldsymbol{\delta}$. It is often called conditional least squares.

To derive another form of (8.2.97), which frequently appears in the literature and which is useful for illustrating the relationship between (8.2.90) and (8.2.97), we rewrite (8.2.89) as

$$\begin{pmatrix}\bar{\mathbf{v}} \\ \mathbf{v}\end{pmatrix} = \begin{pmatrix}0 \\ M^{-1}\end{pmatrix}\mathbf{e} + \begin{pmatrix}I_q \\ C\end{pmatrix}\bar{\mathbf{v}} = W\mathbf{e} + Z\bar{\mathbf{v}} \tag{8.2.98}$$

It can be shown that

$$\Psi^{-1} = M'^{-1}[I_T - C(I_q + C'C)^{-1}C']M^{-1}$$
$$= W'(I_T - Z(Z'Z)^{-1}Z')W \quad (8.2.99)$$

and that the minimum mean square error predictor for $\bar{\mathbf{v}}$ given $\mathbf{e}$ is

$$\hat{\bar{\mathbf{v}}} = E[\bar{\mathbf{v}}|\mathbf{e}] = -(Z'Z)^{-1}Z'W\mathbf{e} \quad (8.2.100)$$

The link between minimizing $\mathbf{v}'\mathbf{v} + \bar{\mathbf{v}}'\bar{\mathbf{v}}$ and $\mathbf{e}'\Psi^{-1}\mathbf{e}$ can be made by replacing $\bar{\mathbf{v}}$ by $\hat{\bar{\mathbf{v}}}$. This yields

$$\begin{aligned}\mathbf{v}'\mathbf{v} + \hat{\bar{\mathbf{v}}}'\hat{\bar{\mathbf{v}}} &= \mathbf{e}'W'W\mathbf{e} + \hat{\bar{\mathbf{v}}}'Z'Z\hat{\bar{\mathbf{v}}} + 2\hat{\bar{\mathbf{v}}}'Z'W\mathbf{e} \\ &= \mathbf{e}'W'W\mathbf{e} - \mathbf{e}'W'Z(Z'Z)^{-1}Z'W\mathbf{e} \\ &= \mathbf{e}'W'[I_T - Z(Z'Z)^{-1}Z']W\mathbf{e} \\ &= \mathbf{e}'\Psi^{-1}\mathbf{e} \end{aligned} \quad (8.2.101)$$

If desirable it is also possible to concentrate $\boldsymbol{\beta}$ out of the sum of squares function. See, for example, Davidson (1981).

A further computational procedure that can be viewed as an alternative to (8.2.90) or (8.2.97) is to factor Ψ as $\Psi = LDL'$ where L is a lower triangular matrix with diagonal elements equal to unity and D is a diagonal matrix [Phadke and Kedem (1978)]. In this decomposition computational gains can be achieved if advantage is taken of the "band matrix" structure of Ψ. Nonlinear LS estimates are obtained by minimizing

$$\mathbf{e}^{*\prime}\mathbf{e}^* = \mathbf{e}'\Psi^{-1}\mathbf{e} = \mathbf{e}'L'^{-1}D^{-1}L^{-1}\mathbf{e} \quad (8.2.102)$$

Note that, if $P = D^{-1/2}L^{-1}$, this procedure is equivalent to finding P such that $P'P = \Psi^{-1}$. The Kalman filter algorithm [Harvey and Phillips (1979)] can be viewed as a systematic framework for the decomposition $\Psi = LDL'$.

For maximum likelihood estimation under the assumption of normally distributed disturbances, values of $\boldsymbol{\beta}$ and $\boldsymbol{\alpha}$ that minimize $|\Psi|^{-1/T}\mathbf{e}'\Psi^{-1}\mathbf{e}$ need to be found. In this procedure the sum of squares function can be computed using any of the above methods (or an approximation), while the determinant $|\Psi|$ can be calculated from

$$|\Psi| = |Z'Z| = |I_q + C'C| \quad (8.2.103)$$

or from the product of the diagonal elements of D in the decomposition $\Psi = LDL'$.

To obtain estimates for $\boldsymbol{\beta}$ and $\boldsymbol{\alpha}$ one of the above methods for computing a value of either the NLS or ML objective function (or an approximation) needs to be used in conjunction with an optimization algorithm. A number of possible algorithms are described in Chapter 6 and Appendix B. In addition, Pagan and Nicholls (1976) suggest an algorithm that is a Newton-Raphson, Gauss-Newton hybrid and that is useful for illustrating the difference between algorithms for ML, NLS, and conditional NLS estimators. For details see the article by Pagan and Nicholls or the first edition of this book [Judge et al. (1980, p. 204)]. Other suggestions are those of Osborn (1976), Dent and Min (1978) and Phadke and Kedem (1978). Pagan (1974) has provided the analytical derivatives for conditional ML and conditional NLS estimation; Godolphin and deGooijer (1982) suggest an approximate procedure based on the first-order conditions of the likelihood function.

8.2.6b Properties

Much of the discussion on estimator properties for the MA(1) model also holds for the general case, but many of the analytical results no longer necessarily hold in small samples. The main conclusions can be summarized as follows.

1. Under appropriate conditions the alternative estimators will all have the same desirable asymptotic properties as the maximum likelihood estimator.
2. The likelihood function possesses at least two stationary points on the invertibility boundary, and hence, in small samples, it is quite likely that the ML estimates will occur at the boundary [Davidson (1981)].
3. Unconditional LS appears to lead to a large number of boundary estimates.
4. In Monte Carlo experiments using a model with no X component, conditional LS and (unconditional) ML perform best, with ML being better for parameter values close to the invertibility boundary [e.g., Ansley and Newbold (1980)].
5. If we consider efficiency in the estimation of $\boldsymbol{\alpha}$, and the fact that an approximate procedure (such as conditional LS) may lead to an efficiency loss in the estimation of $\boldsymbol{\beta}$, the preferred estimation technique is ML.

8.2.7 Estimation with ARMA Errors

Sometimes it is reasonable to model the error process as a combined autoregressive moving-average process. In these circumstances, using the general ARMA(p,q) case, we write the model as

$$y_t = \mathbf{x}_t'\boldsymbol{\beta} + e_t,$$

$$e_t = \sum_{i=1}^{p} \theta_i e_{t-i} + v_t + \sum_{j=1}^{q} \alpha_j v_{t-j} \qquad (8.2.104)$$

where $E[v_t] = 0$, $E[v_t^2] = \sigma_v^2$, $E[v_t v_s] = 0$ for $t \neq s$ and $\boldsymbol{\beta}$, $\boldsymbol{\theta} = (\theta_1, \theta_2, \ldots, \theta_p)'$, $\boldsymbol{\alpha} = (\alpha_1, \alpha_2, \ldots, \alpha_q)'$ and σ_v^2 are parameters to be estimated. We assume that the process is stationary and that the invertibility condition holds. Let the covariance matrix for $\mathbf{e}$ be given by $E[\mathbf{ee}'] = \Phi = \sigma_v^2\boldsymbol{\Psi}$. The structure of $\boldsymbol{\Psi}$ is a rather complex one. See Box and Jenkins (1970, p. 74) for the general case. As an example, for the ARMA(1,1) case, $e_t = \theta e_{t-1} + v_t + \alpha v_{t-1}$, the elements of $\boldsymbol{\Psi}$ are given by

$$\boldsymbol{\Psi}_{tt} = \frac{1 + \alpha^2 + 2\alpha\theta}{1 - \theta^2}$$

and

$$\boldsymbol{\Psi}_{ts} = \frac{(\theta + \alpha)(1 + \theta\alpha)\theta^{|t-s|-1}}{1 - \theta^2}, \qquad t \neq s \tag{8.2.105}$$

8.2.7a NLS and ML Estimation

With the exception of the ARMA(1,1) case [Tiao and Ali (1971)], and even in this case the algebra is tedious, it is not straightforward to derive a matrix P such that $P\boldsymbol{\Psi}P' = I$. Hence direct minimization of $\mathbf{e}'\boldsymbol{\Psi}^{-1}\mathbf{e}$ is difficult. However, as with the model with pure MA errors, we can find alternative sums of squares that are simpler and lead to the same results, or, we can approximate $\mathbf{e}'\boldsymbol{\Psi}^{-1}\mathbf{e}$ via various treatments of the presample disturbances.

To consider these approximations, suppose that we wish to minimize $\Sigma_{t=1}^{T} v_t^2$. Given a set of parameter values $(\boldsymbol{\beta},\boldsymbol{\theta},\boldsymbol{\alpha})$, the residuals in this sum of squares can be calculated recursively using

$$v_t = e_t - \sum_{i=1}^{p} \theta_i e_{t-i} - \sum_{j=1}^{q} \alpha_j v_{t-j}$$

and

$$e_t = y_t - \mathbf{x}_t'\boldsymbol{\beta}, \qquad t = 1, 2, \ldots, T \tag{8.2.106}$$

provided that we are given values of $\bar{\mathbf{e}}' = (e_0, e_{-1}, \ldots, e_{1-p})$ and $\bar{\mathbf{v}}' = (v_0, v_{-1}, \ldots, v_{1-q})$. Some asymptotically equivalent treatments of $\bar{\mathbf{e}}$ and $\bar{\mathbf{v}}$ [Pierce (1971)] are

1. Minimize $\Sigma_{t=1}^{T} v_t^2$ with $\bar{\mathbf{e}}$ and $\bar{\mathbf{v}}$ set equal to $\mathbf{0}$.
2. Minimize $\Sigma_{t=p+1}^{T} v_t^2$ with $v_p, v_{p-1}, \ldots, v_{p-q+1}$ all set equal to zero; this permits calculation of the e_t for the early observations.
3. Minimize $\Sigma_{t=1}^{T} v_t^2$ with respect to $\boldsymbol{\beta}$, $\boldsymbol{\theta}$, $\boldsymbol{\alpha}$, $\bar{\mathbf{e}}$, and $\bar{\mathbf{v}}$, the last two vectors being treated as unknown parameters.

None of these procedures is exactly identical to minimizing $\mathbf{e}'\boldsymbol{\Psi}^{-1}\mathbf{e}$ with respect to $\boldsymbol{\beta}$, $\boldsymbol{\theta}$, and $\boldsymbol{\alpha}$, but they are all computationally superior, particularly the first two. The task of minimizing $\mathbf{e}'\boldsymbol{\Psi}^{-1}\mathbf{e}$ can be lessened somewhat by using an alternative, but equivalent, sum of squares. For $t = 1, 2, \ldots, T$,

Equation 8.2.104 can be written as

$$\begin{aligned} D\mathbf{e} &= \bar{D}\bar{\mathbf{e}} + M\mathbf{v} + \bar{M}\bar{\mathbf{v}} \\ &= M\mathbf{v} + N\bar{\mathbf{w}} \end{aligned} \tag{8.2.107}$$

where M and $\bar{M}$ are as defined in Equations 8.2.87 and 8.2.88; D has the same structure as M except that the α_j's are replaced by $-\theta_i$'s and there are p (not q) θ_i's; $\bar{D}$ has the same structure as $\bar{M}$ with α_j's replaced by $+\theta_j$'s; $N = (\bar{M},\bar{D})$; and $\bar{\mathbf{w}}' = (\bar{\mathbf{v}}',\bar{\mathbf{e}}')$. If we use (8.2.107), the covariance matrix $\sigma_v^2\,\mathbf{\Psi}$ can be written as

$$\begin{aligned} \sigma_v^2\mathbf{\Psi} = E[\mathbf{ee}'] &= D^{-1}E[(M\mathbf{v} + N\bar{\mathbf{w}})(M\mathbf{v} + N\bar{\mathbf{w}})']D'^{-1} \\ &= \sigma_v^2 D^{-1}(MM' + N\Omega N')D'^{-1} \end{aligned} \tag{8.2.108}$$

where $E[\bar{\mathbf{w}}\bar{\mathbf{w}}'] = \sigma_v^2\Omega$ and $\bar{\mathbf{w}}$ and $\mathbf{v}$ are uncorrelated. The exact structure of Ω will depend on the order of the process—see Newbold (1974) for the ARMA(1,1) case.

Extending the work of Pagan and Nicholls (1976), we can show that minimizing

$$\mathbf{v}'\mathbf{v} + \bar{\mathbf{w}}'\Omega^{-1}\bar{\mathbf{w}} \tag{8.2.109}$$

with respect to $\boldsymbol{\beta}$, $\boldsymbol{\theta}$, $\boldsymbol{\alpha}$, and $\bar{\mathbf{w}}$ is equivalent to minimizing $\mathbf{e}'\mathbf{\Psi}^{-1}\mathbf{e}$ with respect to $\boldsymbol{\beta}$, $\boldsymbol{\theta}$, and $\boldsymbol{\alpha}$. We still need to find a matrix H such that $H'H = \Omega^{-1}$, but since Ω is only of order $(p + q)$, this is a considerably easier task than finding P such that $P'P = \mathbf{\Psi}^{-1}$. See Newbold (1974) for an example.

For an alternative procedure that eliminates the presample disturbances $\bar{\mathbf{w}}$ and involves factorization of a matrix that is only of order max(p,q) we proceed as we did for the MA case, and derive a simplified expression for $\mathbf{e}'\mathbf{\Psi}^{-1}\mathbf{e}$. [See Ali (1977), Ljung and Box (1979), Kohn (1981), and a correction to Ali's paper made by Ansley (1979).] Working in this direction, we first note that, if $p \geq q$, we can write

$$N = (\bar{M},\bar{D}) = \begin{bmatrix} \bar{M}^* & \bar{D}^* \\ 0 & 0 \end{bmatrix} = \begin{bmatrix} N^* \\ 0 \end{bmatrix} \tag{8.2.110}$$

where $\bar{M}^*$ is $(p \times q)$, $\bar{D}^*$ is $(p \times p)$ and, consequently, N^* is $[p \times (p + q)]$. If $q > p$, we could similarly define N^* as a $[q \times (p + q)]$ matrix. From (8.2.110) we can conveniently write

$$N\Omega N' = \begin{bmatrix} N^*\Omega N^{*\prime} & 0 \\ 0 & 0 \end{bmatrix} = \begin{pmatrix} S \\ 0 \end{pmatrix}(S' \quad 0') = BB' \tag{8.2.111}$$

where S is a $(p \times p)$ lower triangular matrix obtained by factorization of $N^*\Omega N^{*\prime}$ and $B' = (S',0')$. Then,

$$\Psi = D^{-1}(MM' + BB')D'^{-1}$$
$$= D^{-1}M(I_T + M^{-1}BB'M'^{-1})M'D'^{-1} \qquad (8.2.112)$$

and, letting $C = M^{-1}B$,

$$\Psi^{-1} = D'M'^{-1}(I_T + CC')^{-1}M^{-1}D$$
$$= D'M'^{-1}[I_T - C(I_p + C'C)^{-1}C']M^{-1}D \qquad (8.2.113)$$

from which we can write

$$\mathbf{e}'\Psi^{-1}\mathbf{e} = \boldsymbol{\delta}'\boldsymbol{\delta} - \boldsymbol{\delta}'C(I_p + C'C)^{-1}C'\boldsymbol{\delta} \qquad (8.2.114)$$

where $\boldsymbol{\delta} = M^{-1}D\mathbf{e}$. This expression is a convenient one computationally because the lower triangular nature of M permits recursive calculation of $\boldsymbol{\delta}$ and C, and the largest inverse is only of order p. Furthermore, for ML estimation we note that, because $|M| = |D| = 1$,

$$|\Psi| = |I_T + CC'| = |I_p + C'C| \qquad (8.2.115)$$

An example of $|\Psi|$ is given by the ARMA(1,1) case $e_t = \theta e_{t-1} + v_t + \alpha v_{t-1}$, where

$$|\Psi| = 1 + \frac{(1 - \alpha^{2T})(\alpha + \theta)^2}{(1 - \alpha^2)(1 - \theta)^2} \qquad (8.2.116)$$

For further information on NLS and ML estimation of the general ARMA case see Newbold (1974), Osborn (1976), Ali (1977), Dent (1977), Ansley (1979), Ljung and Box (1979), Harvey and Phillips (1979), and Pearlman (1980). These authors are generally concerned with alternative expressions for $\mathbf{e}'\Psi^{-1}\mathbf{e}$ and $|\Psi|$, and with the computational efficiency of alternative optimization algorithms. Monte Carlo experiments to investigate the finite sample properties of a number of the asymptotically equivalent estimation procedures (ML, NLS, and various approximations) have been carried out for the pure time series model ($\boldsymbol{\beta} = \mathbf{0}$) by Dent and Min (1978) and Ansley and Newbold (1980).

None of the estimators performs best under all circumstances, but, in terms of overall performance, Ansley and Newbold recommend the ML estimator.

8.2.7b Some Extensions

The various models we have considered in Section 8.2 have been extended in a number of ways. One extension is the consideration of models with composite disturbances where each disturbance component satisfies different assumptions. For some details of work in this area see Pagan (1973), Revankar (1980), Anderson and Hsiao (1982), and King (1982a). Estimation and hypothesis testing in models with lagged values of the dependent variable and moving average errors where the v_t are heteroscedastic have been considered by Cragg (1982).

8.2.8 Regression in the Frequency Domain

The estimation procedures discussed so far all require specification of the nature of the autocorrelation process. In practice, however, there will be some degree of uncertainty with respect to choice of the process. Given these circumstances, we can use one or more of the testing procedures mentioned in Section 8.4, or, alternatively, we can use a technique such as regression within the frequency domain that does not require specification of the form of the autocorrelation process. The techniques suggested by Amemiya (1973) provide another alternative.

To carry out regression within the frequency domain, a Fourier transformation is applied to the model $\mathbf{y} = X\boldsymbol{\beta} + \mathbf{e}$. Either a complex finite Fourier transform [Engle (1974a), Engle and Gardner (1976)] or a real finite Fourier transform [Harvey (1978, 1981b)] can be employed. The transformed model from the latter transformation is given by

$$\mathbf{y}^* = X^*\boldsymbol{\beta} + \mathbf{e}^* \tag{8.2.117}$$

where $\mathbf{y}^* = Z\mathbf{y}$, $X^* = ZX$, $\mathbf{e}^* = Z\mathbf{e}$ and Z is the $(T \times T)$ orthogonal matrix with elements for $s = 1, 2, \ldots, T$ defined by

$$\begin{aligned}
z_{ts} &= T^{-1/2}, && t = 1\\
z_{ts} &= (2/T)^{1/2}\cos[\pi t(s-1)/T], && t = 2, 4, 6, \ldots, T-2 \\
& && \text{(or } T-1 \text{ if } T \text{ is odd)}\\
z_{ts} &= (2/T)^{1/2}\sin[\pi(t-1)(s-1)/T], && t = 3, 5, 7, \ldots, T-1 \\
& && \text{(or } T \text{ if } T \text{ is odd)}\\
z_{ts} &= T^{-1/2}(-1)^{s+1}, && t = T \text{ (if } T \text{ is even)}
\end{aligned} \tag{8.2.118}$$

If $\mathbf{e}$ is generated by a stationary stochastic process, such as any one of the stationary stochastic processes considered in the previous sections, and it has a covariance matrix denoted by $\sigma^2\Omega$, then it can be shown that the covariance matrix for $\mathbf{e}^*$

$$E[\mathbf{e}^*\mathbf{e}^{*\prime}] = \sigma^2 Z\Omega Z' = \sigma^2\Omega^* \tag{8.2.119}$$

will be approximately diagonal, with the approximation becoming negligible as $T \to \infty$. Furthermore, the diagonal elements of Ω^* will be proportional to the spectral density of the original disturbance, $f_e(\omega_j)$, evaluated at the frequencies $\omega_j = 2\pi j/T$, $j = -T/2, -T/2 + 1, \ldots, T/2 - 1$ (or $j = -(T-1)/2, -(T-3)/2, \ldots, (T-1)/2$ if T is odd). See Chapter 7 and Harvey (1981b) for the definitions of these various concepts.

If the $f_e(\omega_j)$ are known and we ignore the approximation, we have converted the problem of autocorrelation into one of heteroscedasticity and the GLS estimator can be obtained via weighted least squares. See Chapter 11. When the $f_e(\omega_j)$ are unknown (which, of course, will usually be the case) consistent estimates can be conveniently found from the LS residuals obtained from the transformed model (8.2.117). See Harvey (1978, 1981b) for details. The EGLS estimator $\hat{\hat{\boldsymbol{\beta}}} = (X^{*\prime}\hat{\Omega}^{*-1}X^*)^{-1}X^{*\prime}\hat{\Omega}^{*-1}\mathbf{y}^*$, with $\hat{\Omega}^*$ based on the estimates of $f_e(\omega_j)$, will be consistent and asymptotically efficient. The small-sample properties of this estimator, however, are not outstanding. This fact is not surprising since the estimator does not utilize information on the form of the autocorrelated error process. Relevant Monte Carlo evidence has been provided by Engle and Gardner (1976) and Gallant and Goebel (1976) who find that, in many circumstances, it is better to use a time domain estimator that makes an incorrect assumption about the form of autocorrelation than to employ the frequency domain estimator.

Regression in the frequency domain has been suggested for purposes other than correcting for autocorrelation. In particular, if $E[\mathbf{ee}'] = \sigma^2 I$, then $E[\mathbf{e}^*\mathbf{e}^{*\prime}] = \sigma^2 I$, and a restricted estimator that omits transformed observations corresponding to some of the frequencies has been suggested. This technique is known as *band spectrum regression*. For further details as well as reasons for its implementation, see Engle (1974a, 1976) and Harvey (1978, 1981b).

8.3 PREDICTION IN MODELS WITH AUTOCORRELATED ERRORS

Frequently, the general linear model is used not only to obtain information about unknown parameters, but also to predict future values of the dependent variable. In this section we outline a framework for prediction and give "best linear unbiased predictors" for some specific cases.

The model can be written as

$$\mathbf{y} = X\boldsymbol{\beta} + \mathbf{e} \tag{8.3.1}$$

where $E[\mathbf{e}] = \mathbf{0}$, $E[\mathbf{ee}'] = \Phi = \sigma_v^2\Psi$, the usual definitions hold, and we emphasize that $\mathbf{y}$ is a $(T \times 1)$ vector of *past* observations on the dependent variable. In general, the elements in $\mathbf{e}$ are assumed to be autocorrelated.

The problem is to find an appropriate predictor for N future observations given by

$$\bar{\mathbf{y}} = \bar{X}\boldsymbol{\beta} + \bar{\mathbf{e}} \tag{8.3.2}$$

where $\bar{\mathbf{y}}$, $\bar{X}$, and $\bar{\mathbf{e}}$ are of dimensions $(N \times 1)$, $(N \times K)$, and $(N \times 1)$, respectively, and

$$E\left[\begin{pmatrix}\mathbf{e}\\ \bar{\mathbf{e}}\end{pmatrix}(\mathbf{e}'\bar{\mathbf{e}}')\right] = \sigma_v^2\begin{bmatrix}\Psi & V\\ V' & \bar{\Psi}\end{bmatrix} \tag{8.3.3}$$

In Equations 8.3.2 and 8.3.3

1. $\bar{\mathbf{y}}$ is the vector of unknown future observations.
2. $\bar{X}$ is the matrix of future explanatory variables that are assumed known.
3. $\sigma_v^2\bar{\Psi}$ is the covariace matrix of the future disturbances $\bar{\mathbf{e}}$.
4. $\sigma_v^2 V$ is a matrix of covariances between the past and future disturbances.

If the variances and covariances are known, the best linear unbiased predictor (BLUP) for $\bar{\mathbf{y}}$ is [Goldberger (1962) and Theil (1971, p. 280)]

$$\hat{\bar{\mathbf{y}}} = \bar{X}\hat{\boldsymbol{\beta}} + V'\Psi^{-1}(\mathbf{y} - X\hat{\boldsymbol{\beta}}) \tag{8.3.4}$$

where $\hat{\boldsymbol{\beta}} = (X'\Psi^{-1}X)^{-1}X'\Psi^{-1}\mathbf{y}$ is the generalized least squares estimator. This predictor is best linear unbiased in the sense that, with respect to repeated sampling from the joint distribution of $(\mathbf{y}',\bar{\mathbf{y}}')'$, it is unbiased, $E[\hat{\bar{\mathbf{y}}} - \bar{\mathbf{y}}] = \mathbf{0}$, and the prediction error of any other predictor of $\bar{\mathbf{y}}$, which is also linear in $\mathbf{y}$ and unbiased, has a covariance matrix that exceeds that of $(\hat{\bar{\mathbf{y}}} - \bar{\mathbf{y}})$ by a positive semidefinite matrix.

The covariance matrix of the prediction error (or alternatively the mean square error of the predictor) is [Theil (1971, p. 288)]

$$\sigma_v^2[\bar{X}C\bar{X}' + \bar{\Psi} - V'(\Psi^{-1} - \Psi^{-1}XCX'\Psi^{-1})V - \bar{X}CX'\Psi^{-1}V - V'\Psi^{-1}XC\bar{X}'] \tag{8.3.5}$$

where $C = (X'\Psi^{-1}X)^{-1}$.

Note that the BLUP in (8.3.4) is made up of two components. The first, $\bar{X}\hat{\boldsymbol{\beta}}$, is an estimate of the nonstochastic component of the future observations and the second, $V'\Psi^{-1}(\mathbf{y} - X\hat{\boldsymbol{\beta}})$, is an estimate of the future disturbances. This latter estimate is based on the sample residuals and the covariance between the past and future disturbances.

8.3.1 AR Errors

For the AR(1) case, where $e_t = \rho e_{t-1} + v_t$, and Ψ is given by Equation 8.2.5, the tth element of $\hat{\bar{\mathbf{y}}}$ reduces to

$$\hat{y}_{T+t} = \bar{\mathbf{x}}'_{T+t}\hat{\boldsymbol{\beta}} + \rho^t(y_T - \mathbf{x}'_T\hat{\boldsymbol{\beta}}) \tag{8.3.6}$$

where $\bar{\mathbf{x}}_{T+t}$ is the tth row of $\bar{X}$ and $\mathbf{x}'_T$ is the last row of X. In this case, the last residual in the sample is the only one that contains information about the future disturbances and, because of the term ρ^t, the importance of this information declines as we predict further into the future.

For a model with AR(2) errors, $e_t = \theta_1 e_{t-1} + \theta_2 e_{t-2} + v_t$, the last *two* sample residuals contain relevant information and the BLUP for the $(T + 1)$th observation is given by

$$\hat{y}_{T+1} = \bar{\mathbf{x}}'_{T+1}\hat{\boldsymbol{\beta}} + \theta_1\hat{e}_T + \theta_2\hat{e}_{T-1} \tag{8.3.7}$$

where $\hat{e}_t = y_t - \mathbf{x}_t\hat{\boldsymbol{\beta}}$. For predictions more than one period into the future, the second component gets progressively more complicated, but we can simplify matters by defining $\hat{\hat{y}}_{T+t} = \bar{\mathbf{x}}'_{T+t}\hat{\boldsymbol{\beta}} + \hat{\hat{e}}_{T+t}$, where

$$\hat{\hat{e}}_{T+t} = \begin{cases} \theta_1\hat{e}_T + \theta_2\hat{e}_{T-1} & \text{if } t = 1 \\ \theta_1\hat{\hat{e}}_{T+1} + \theta_2\hat{e}_T & \text{if } t = 2 \\ \theta_1\hat{\hat{e}}_{T+t-1} + \theta_2\hat{\hat{e}}_{T+t-2} & \text{if } t = 3, 4, \ldots \end{cases} \tag{8.3.8}$$

and proceeding recursively. This yields predictions identical to those that would be obtained from (8.3.4) and the extension to higher-order AR errors is straightforward.

8.3.2 MA Errors

When we have a model with MA(1) errors, $e_t = v_t + \alpha v_{t-1}$, the e_t's more than one period apart are uncorrelated so that the sample residuals do not contain any information about disturbances more than one period into the future. Consequently,

$$\hat{\hat{y}}_{T+t} = \bar{\mathbf{x}}'_{T+t}\hat{\boldsymbol{\beta}} \qquad \text{for } t > 1 \tag{8.3.9}$$

In terms of (8.3.4) this occurs because only the first row in V' contains nonzero elements.

However, for predicting $\bar{e}_{T+1}$, *all* the sample residuals contain some information.

Using the definitions for P, a_t, $\mathbf{y}^*$ and X^* given in Section 8.2.5a we have

$$\begin{aligned} \hat{\hat{y}}_{T+1} &= \bar{\mathbf{x}}'_{T+1}\hat{\boldsymbol{\beta}} + (0, 0, \ldots, 0, \alpha)P'P(\mathbf{y} - X\hat{\boldsymbol{\beta}}) \\ &= \bar{\mathbf{x}}'_{T+1}\hat{\boldsymbol{\beta}} + [0, 0, \ldots, 0, \alpha(a_{T-1}/a_T)^{1/2}](\mathbf{y}^* - X^*\hat{\boldsymbol{\beta}}) \\ &= \bar{\mathbf{x}}'_{T+1}\hat{\boldsymbol{\beta}} + \alpha(a_{T-1}/a_T)^{1/2}\hat{e}_T^* \end{aligned} \tag{8.3.10}$$

where $\hat{e}_T^*$ is the last sample residual from the transformed model. Note, from Equation 8.2.72, that it will be a function of all the untransformed residuals $\hat{\mathbf{e}} = \mathbf{y} - X\hat{\boldsymbol{\beta}}$.

An alternative procedure that approximates the BLUP and is less demanding computationally is to set $\hat{v}_0 = 0$, then recursively obtain

$$\hat{v}_t = y_t - \mathbf{x}'_t\hat{\boldsymbol{\beta}} - \alpha\hat{v}_{t-1}, \qquad t = 1, 2, \ldots, T \tag{8.3.11}$$

The approximate BLUP is defined as

$$\hat{\hat{y}}_{T+1} = \bar{\mathbf{x}}'_{T+1}\hat{\boldsymbol{\beta}} + \alpha\hat{v}_T \tag{8.3.12}$$

For MA errors of higher order and ARMA errors this approximation readily generalizes, and for most practical purposes it is sufficiently accurate. The exact procedure in (8.3.4) is computationally more involved, but it can be implemented using one or more of the simplifications in Sections 8.2.6 and 8.2.7. For example, for the MA(q) model the elements in V can be calculated from (8.2.85) and the inverse of $\boldsymbol{\Psi}$ can be found using (8.2.96) or (8.2.102). Alternatively, the BLUP can be calculated by computing estimates of the presample disturbances from Equation 8.2.100 (with $\mathbf{e}$ replaced by the GLS residual $\mathbf{y} - X\hat{\boldsymbol{\beta}}$), and then by recursive substitution into the qth order extension of (8.3.11). The Kalman filter algorithm [Harvey (1981b)] is another possible alternative.

8.3.3 Mean Square Error of Predictions

In addition to providing point predictions from each of the autocorrelated error models, it is important to be able to assess the reliability of these predictions. For this purpose we need the mean square error (MSE) of the predictors, or, equivalently, the covariance matrix of the prediction errors. If the autocorrelation parameters (the parameters in V and $\boldsymbol{\Psi}$) are known, the mean square error of each of the predictors can be found by appropriate simplification of (8.3.5). For example, in the AR(1) error case the tth diagonal element of (8.3.5) becomes

$$\begin{aligned}\text{MSE}(\hat{\hat{y}}_{T+t}) = {} & \sigma_v^2[(1 - \rho^{2t})/(1 - \rho^2)] \\ & + \sigma_v^2(\mathbf{x}_{T+t} - \rho^t\mathbf{x}_T)'(X'\boldsymbol{\Psi}^{-1}X)^{-1}(\mathbf{x}_{T+t} - \rho^t\mathbf{x}_T) \qquad (8.3.13)\end{aligned}$$

In practice, however, V and $\boldsymbol{\Psi}$, and hence parameters such as ρ, θ_1, θ_2, and α, will be unknown and will need to be replaced by estimates. The EGLS estimator will replace the GLS estimator for $\boldsymbol{\beta}$, and in the MA and ARMA cases, estimates of the presample disturbances will be functions of the estimated parameters. Under these circumstances the predictor $\hat{\hat{\mathbf{y}}}$ is no longer best linear unbiased, the MSE matrix in (8.3.5) does not reflect all the uncertainty in the predictions, and we are forced to rely on asymptotic properties. For example, in the AR(1) case it can be shown [Baillie (1979)] that the asymptotic MSE of the predictor based on estimated parameters (say $\hat{\hat{y}}^*_{T+t}$) is given by

$$\text{AMSE}(\hat{\hat{y}}^*_{T+t}) \approx \text{MSE}(\hat{\hat{y}}_{T+t}) + \sigma_v^2 t^2 \rho^{2(t-1)}/T \qquad (8.3.14)$$

We can view the last term in (8.3.14) as the MSE contribution attributable to estimation of ρ. The situation is not always this simple, however. For further details on the asymptotic MSE for predictors with estimated parameters, as well as some finite sample results and some results on misspecification we refer the reader to Ansley and Newbold (1981), Baillie (1979, 1980), Bhansali (1981), Fuller and Hasza (1980, 1981), Phillips (1979), Spitzer and Baillie (1983) and Yamamoto (1976, 1979). Nicholls and Pagan (1982) build on work by Salkever (1976) and Fuller (1980) to show how predictions and their standard errors can be obtained with standard econometric computer packages.

8.4 TESTING FOR THE EXISTENCE AND TYPE OF AUTOCORRELATION

Because, in practice, we seldom know if a disturbance is autocorrelated or, if it is, we are always uncertain about what is a reasonable assumption concerning the form of the autocorrelation, some test procedures are required. We shall consider in turn (1) some general tests that can be used to test for any type of autocorrelation and that have asymptotic validity, (2) tests designed specifically to test for AR(1) errors, and (3) tests designed as alternatives to those in case 2 for cases when the errors may not be AR(1). For further details, and an excellent survey of the literature on testing for autocorrelation, see King (1983c).

8.4.1 General Large-Sample Tests

8.4.1a Using Sample Autocorrelations

A given AR, MA, or ARMA process can be described by the behavior of its autocorrelation function $\rho_s = E[e_t e_{t-s}]/E[e_t^2]$, $s = 1, 2, \ldots$. In particular, for an AR process ρ_s gradually dies out while that for an MA process becomes zero after a finite point. See Section 7.5.1 and Box and Jenkins (1970, Chapter 3) for details. We can estimate the ρ_s with the sample autocorrelations

$$r_s = \frac{\sum_{t=1}^{T-s} \hat{e}_t \hat{e}_{t+s}}{\sum_{t=1}^{T} \hat{e}_t^2}$$

where the $\hat{e}_t$ are the LS residuals $\hat{e}_t = y_t - \mathbf{x}_t'\mathbf{b}$, and then use these to make some judgment about the ρ_s and hence the type of process. The legitimacy of such an approach depends on the condition that each $\hat{e}_t$ converges in probability to the corresponding e_t. Unfortunately, in small samples the $\hat{e}_t$ will be correlated even if the e_t are not; also, the r_s may exhibit substantial small-sample bias [Malinvaud (1970, p. 519)]. Nevertheless, if the sample is sufficiently large, they may yield some useful information.

An approximate expression for the variance of the r_s has been provided by Bartlett (1946) and, if ρ_s is essentially zero for lags s greater than some value p, this expression can be estimated using

$$\widehat{\text{var}}(r_s) = \frac{1}{T}\left(1 + 2\sum_{i=1}^{p} r_i^2\right), \qquad s > p \tag{8.4.1}$$

Under a null hypothesis of no autocorrelation $\rho = 0$ and each r_s, $s = 1, 2, \ldots$, has a standard error $T^{-1/2}$. Thus a reasonable first step would be to compare each r_s with $T^{-1/2}$. The largest s taken would depend on the type and number of observations. If we have at least 40 observations and quarterly data, it would seem reasonable to take values up to r_8. As a second step we could select p as the first lag at which a correlation was "significant" and then use

(8.4.1) to test for significant correlations at lags longer than p. For example, if r_1 were significant, $r_2, r_3, \ldots$ could be tested using the standard error $T^{-1/2}(1 + 2r_1^2)^{1/2}$.

This type of procedure is certainly not conclusive, and it is frequently not easy to discriminate between AR and MA processes. However, it may detect correlations that are often overlooked by standard regression tests such as the Durbin–Watson. If, based on the r_s, a number of autocorrelation assumptions seem reasonable, each of the resulting models could be estimated and we could attempt to discriminate between models on the basis of other criteria such as the significance of the θ_i's and/or α_j's, the value of the likelihood function, and the a priori validity of the coefficient estimates. See Pagan (1974) for two examples.

8.4.1b Wald, Likelihood Ratio, and Lagrange Multiplier Tests

Once a particular model has been estimated, a Wald test can be used to judge its relevance by comparing estimates of the θ_i and α_j with their asymptotic standard errors. A possible strategy, although one which is rather ad hoc, is to drop coefficients that are insignificant and to reestimate the model accordingly.

A more rigorous testing procedure for selection of the order of an AR or MA model is to carry out a sequence of likelihood ratio tests. For details, see Section 7.5.2 and Anderson (1971), and for some examples, Fisher (1970) and Kenward (1975). The sequential testing procedure does not generalize in a straightforward manner to combined ARMA processes. However, having decided on a particular AR or MA process, we can always carry out an additional test to check whether a combined process might be more suitable. Also, the likelihood ratio test can be used to test restrictions over and above those involved in the choice of order for a process. For example, Wallis (1972) suggests that, when using quarterly data, an appropriate model may be a "combined AR(1)-AR(4)" one given by

$$(1 - \theta_1 L)(1 - \theta_4 L^4)e_t = v_t \tag{8.4.2}$$

This is equivalent to the fifth-order process $e_t = \sum_{i=1}^{5} \theta_i e_{t-i} + v_t$, where $\theta_2 = \theta_3 = 0$ and $\theta_5 = -\theta_1\theta_4$. These restrictions can be readily tested using the likelihood ratio test.

Lagrange multiplier (LM) tests can also be used to shed light on the choice of an autocorrelation process. If the null hypothesis is $\theta_p = 0$, and the alternative is the restricted AR(p) process $e_t = \theta_p e_{t-p} + v_t$, $\theta_p \neq 0$, then the LM test statistic Tr_p^2 has a $\chi^2_{(1)}$ distribution, asymptotically. Note that this is equivalent to the sample autocorrelation test mentioned in Section 8.4.1a. Furthermore, it can be shown that the LM test statistic for the analogous restricted MA(p) process, is also Tr_p^2. For the more general alternative, such as $e_t = \sum_{j=1}^{p} \theta_j e_{t-j} + v_t$ in the AR(p) case, and the null hypothesis $\theta_1 = \theta_2 = \ldots = \theta_p = 0$, the LM test statistic $T\sum_{j=1}^{p} r_j^2$ has a $\chi^2_{(p)}$ distribution, asymptotically. See Breusch and Pagan (1980) for more details, and Godfrey (1981) for some discussion on the question of why identical LM test statistics are sometimes appropriate for quite different alternative hypotheses. In some finite sample power comparisons, Godfrey shows that the LM test performs favorably relative to the LR test, despite the fact that the alternative hypothesis for the LM test is less clearly defined.

If one of the above "search procedures" is used to choose a particular model, it must be kept in mind that reported standard errors, and so forth, are conditional on the chosen model being the "correct one." Unconditional variances are not readily derived and can be quite higher. See the comments in Section 8.5.

8.4.1c Adequacy of Fit

Once the chosen model has been estimated, sample autocorrelations calculated from the residuals should not show any significant correlations. Their asymptotic distribution and an "adequacy of fit" statistic are considered by Pierce (1971). The latter statistic is $T\Sigma_{k=1}^{s} r_k^2$ which, if the ARMA(p,q) model is "adequate," has an approximate $\chi^2_{(s-p-q)}$ distribution. Also, it is closely related to the LM test statistic [Breusch and Pagan (1980)].

A number of other goodness-of-fit statistics have been suggested in the literature for choosing the order of an AR process. These statistics are reviewed in Section 7.5.2 in the context of the pure time series model.

8.4.1d Discriminating Between Dynamics and Autocorrelation

When considering regression with time series errors, one of the problems of model selection is discriminating between distributed lag models with a lagged dependent variable; and models with AR errors, where the transformed model contains a lagged dependent variable. For example, the transformed version of the AR(1) error model with one explanatory variable can be written as

$$y_t = \beta_1(1 - \rho) + \rho y_{t-1} + \beta_2 x_t - \beta_2 \rho x_{t-1} + v_t \tag{8.4.3}$$

This model can be considered a special case of the more general model

$$y_t = \gamma_1 + \gamma_2 y_{t-1} + \gamma_3 x_t + \gamma_4 x_{t-1} + v_t \tag{8.4.4}$$

where, in both cases, we assume that v_t is a white noise disturbance. Equation 8.4.4 reduces to (8.4.3) if the restriction $\gamma_4 = -\gamma_2\gamma_3$ is imposed. Thus, it can be argued that an appropriate model selection strategy is to begin with a model such as (8.4.4), test whether the restriction $\gamma_4 = -\gamma_2\gamma_3$ is reasonable, and, if so, model the dynamics of the system with an AR(1) error term. Such a strategy goes part way to overcoming the problem of whether a test that rejects a null hypothesis of zero autocorrelation in the model $y_t = \beta_1 + \beta_2 x_2 + e_t$ is indicative of autocorrelation or some other specification error. For details of this and other approaches to discriminating between dynamics and autocorrelation, see Sargan (1964, 1980), Kenward (1975), Hendry (1974, 1980), Hendry and Anderson (1977), Hendry and Mizon (1978), Mizon and Hendry (1980), and the discussion in Harvey (1981a). Kiviet (1981) outlines some dangers of the approach. The formulation of a general research strategy for dynamic models is discussed by Hendry and Richard (1982).

8.4.2 Testing for AR(1) Errors

8.4.2a The Durbin–Watson Test

The most popular test for first-order autoregressive errors is the Durbin–Watson (DW) test [Durbin and Watson (1950, 1951, 1971)] which is based on the statistic

$$d = \frac{\sum_{t=2}^{T}(\hat{e}_t - \hat{e}_{t-1})^2}{\sum_{t=1}^{T}\hat{e}_t^2} = \frac{\hat{\mathbf{e}}'A\hat{\mathbf{e}}}{\hat{\mathbf{e}}'\hat{\mathbf{e}}} = \frac{\mathbf{e}'MAM\mathbf{e}}{\mathbf{e}'M\mathbf{e}} \tag{8.4.5}$$

where $\hat{e}_t$ is an element of $\hat{\mathbf{e}} = \mathbf{y} - X\mathbf{b}$, $M = I - X(X'X)^{-1}X'$ and

$$A = \begin{bmatrix} 1 & -1 & 0 & \dots & 0 \\ -1 & 2 & -1 & \dots & 0 \\ 0 & -1 & 2 & \dots & 0 \\ \vdots & \vdots & \vdots & & \vdots \\ 0 & 0 & 0 & \dots & 1 \end{bmatrix} \tag{8.4.6}$$

For testing $H_0: \rho = 0$ against the alternative $H_1: \rho > 0$ the DW test rejects H_0 if $d < d^*$, d^* being the critical value of d for a specified significance level. If the alternative hypothesis is one of negative autocorrelation, the critical region is of the form $d > d^{**}$. It is assumed that the disturbances are normally distributed, although it can be shown [King, (1981a)] that some of the optimal properties of the DW test hold for a wider class of distributions.

A disadvantage of the DW test is that the distribution of d, and hence the critical value d^* (or d^{**}), depend on the X matrix in the model under consideration. Thus, tabulation of significance points which are relevant for all problems is impossible. Durbin and Watson partially overcame this difficulty by finding two other statistics d_L and d_U, whose distributions do not depend on X, and which have the property $d_L \leq d \leq d_U$. For different significance levels, and given values of T and K, they used the distributions of d_L and d_U to tabulate critical values d_L^* and d_U^* [Durbin and Watson (1951)]; and they used the inequality relationships between d, d_L, and d_U to establish a bounds test. In the bounds test for H_0: $\rho = 0$ against the alternative H_1: $\rho > 0$ the null hypothesis is rejected if $d < d_L^*$, it is accepted if $d > d_U^*$, and the test is regarded as inconclusive if $d_L^* < d < d_U^*$. If the alternative hypothesis is $H_1: \rho < 0$, the null hypothesis is rejected if $d > 4 - d_L^*$, it is accepted if $d < 4 - d_U^*$, and the test is regarded as inconclusive if $4 - d_U^* < d < 4 - d_L^*$.

In instances where d falls within the inconclusive region the exact critical value d^* can be found numerically, providing appropriate computer software [e.g., SHAZAM, White (1978)] is available. Numerical methods for finding d^* include the Imhof (1961) technique used by Koerts and Abrahamse (1969) and techniques given by Pan Jei-jian (1968) and L'Esperance, Chall, and Taylor (1976). If an appropriate computer program is not available, or the associated computational costs are too expensive, the $a + bd_U$ approximation [Durbin and Watson (1971)] can be employed. This approximation is relatively cheap computationally and also quite accurate. The value d^* is found from

$$d^* = a + bd_U^* \tag{8.4.7}$$

where a and b are chosen such that $E[d] = a + bE[d_U]$ and $\text{var}[d] = b^2 \text{var}[d_U]$. The quantities $E[d_U]$ and $\text{var}[d_U]$, for different values of T and K, are tabulated in Judge et al. (1982); while $E[d]$ and $\text{var}[d]$ can be calculated from

$$E[d] = \frac{P}{T - K} \tag{8.4.8}$$

$$\text{var}[d] = \left[\frac{2}{(T - K)(T - K + 2)}\right] (Q - PE[d]) \tag{8.4.9}$$

where

$$P = 2(T - 1) - \text{tr}[X'AX(X'X)^{-1}] \tag{8.4.10}$$

and

$$Q = 2(3T - 4) - 2\,\text{tr}[X'A^2X(X'X)^{-1}] + \text{tr}\{[X'AX(X'X)^{-1}]^2\} \tag{8.4.11}$$

The critical value bounds originally tabulated by Durbin and Watson (1951) have been extended by Savin and White (1977), and also appear in most textbooks [e.g., Judge et al. (1982)]. These bounds are constructed under the assumption that X contains a constant term. It is also possible to derive critical value bounds, some of which are much narrower, for other types of X matrices. The X matrices for which additional critical value bounds have been published include regressions with no intercept [Farebrother (1980), King (1981b)], regressions with a trend and/or seasonal dummy variables [King (1981c)], regressions with a trend and/or monthly dummy variables [King (1983b)], and polynomial trend models [Bartels et al. (1982)].

The DW test has a number of optimal properties. In particular, it is approximately uniformly most powerful similar (UMPS), and approximately uniformly most powerful invariant (UMPI), if X can be written as a linear transformation of K of the characteristic vectors of the matrix A (defined in Equation 8.4.6). Furthermore, it is approximately locally best invariant (LBI) in the neighborhood of $\rho = 0$ for any X matrix. See Anderson (1948) and Durbin and Watson (1950) for details on the UMPS property and King (1981a) for details on the UMPI and LBI properties.

The condition that the X matrix can be written as a linear transformation of K of the characteristic vectors of A will not hold in general and is precisely the condition under which least squares (LS) is almost fully efficient [Chipman (1965)]. Consequently, as Chipman points out, when LS is relatively inefficient and we badly need to detect serial correlation, the DW may have very low power. Approximate bounds on the power have been calculated by Tillman (1975). These values make it clear that the power can be quite low for some X matrices, but with the exception of two test statistics recently investigated by King (1981a, 1982b), and described below, the DW has generally compared favorably with other tests that have been suggested. It is worth noting that even when LS is fully efficient, it is still worthwhile detecting serial correlation because of its effect on variance estimation and confidence intervals for $\boldsymbol{\beta}$.

King (1981a) notes that the theoretical considerations used by Durbin and Watson (1950) to derive the test statistic d could just as easily have led to an alternative, closely related statistic, given by

$$d' = \frac{\hat{\mathbf{e}}'A_0\hat{\mathbf{e}}}{\hat{\mathbf{e}}'\hat{\mathbf{e}}} = d + \frac{\hat{e}_1^2 + \hat{e}_T^2}{\hat{\mathbf{e}}'\hat{\mathbf{e}}} \tag{8.4.12}$$

where A_0 is identical to A, except that the top left and bottom right elements are equal to 2 instead of unity. A test with critical region $d' < d'^*$ is both an approximate UMPS and an approximate UMPI test for H_0: $\rho = 0$ against H_1: $\rho > 0$, providing X can be written as a linear transformation of K of the characteristic vectors of A_0. Furthermore, it is a LBI test in the neighborhood of $\rho = 0$ for any X matrix; and it is exactly related to the first-order sample autocorrelation coefficient, $r = \Sigma_{t=2}^T \hat{e}_t\hat{e}_{t-1}/\Sigma_{t=1}^T \hat{e}_t^2$, through the expression $d' = 2(1 - r)$. See King (1981a) for details. King tabulates critical values for a bounds test based on d' and, in an empirical investigation of the power of d' relative to that of d, he finds that d' is more powerful than d if (1) $0 < \rho < .5$ and the alternative hypothesis is one of positive autocorrelation; and (2) $-1 < \rho < 0$ and the alternative hypothesis is one of negative autocorrelation. Thus, in King's words, "it appears that for the typical problem of testing for positive autoregressive disturbances, Durbin and Watson's choice of test statistic is correct. However, there are situations where it is preferable to use d' in place of d."

8.4.2b King's Locally Optimal Bounds Test and the Berenblut–Webb Test

Building on his earlier results described in the previous section, King (1982b) suggests a test that is locally most powerful invariant in the neighborhood of $\rho = \rho_1$, where ρ_1 is a prespecified central value of ρ under H_1: $\rho > 0$ (or H_1: $\rho < 0$). His test statistic is

$$s(\rho_1) = \frac{\hat{\mathbf{e}}^{*\prime}\hat{\mathbf{e}}^*}{\hat{\mathbf{e}}'\hat{\mathbf{e}}} \tag{8.4.13}$$

where $\hat{\mathbf{e}}^* = \mathbf{y}^* - X^*\hat{\boldsymbol{\beta}}$ are the transformed GLS residuals obtained under the assumption $\rho = \rho_1$ and $\hat{\mathbf{e}} = \mathbf{y} - X\mathbf{b}$ are the LS residuals. A null hypothesis of H_0: $\rho = 0$ is rejected in favor of the alternative H_1: $\rho > 0$ if $s(\rho_1)$ is less than a critical value $s^*(\rho_1)$. King shows that this test is approximately UMPI in similar circumstances to the DW test; he tabulates critical values for bounds tests using $s(.5)$, $s(.75)$ and $s(-.5)$; and, in an empirical investigation, he compares the powers of $s(.5)$, $s(.75)$, $s(-.5)$ and $s(-.75)$ with those of d, d', and a statistic g proposed by Berenblut and Webb (1973).

The Berenblut–Webb statistic is designed for testing for AR(1) errors when the process is not necessarily stationary, that is, values of $|\rho| \geq 1$ are possible. It is given by $g = RSS^*/\hat{\mathbf{e}}'\hat{\mathbf{e}}$ where RSS^* is the residual sum of squares from a regression of the first differences of $\mathbf{y}$ on the first differences of X without a constant term. Thus, it is roughly equivalent to $s(1)$. Provided that the *original* equation contains a constant term, g and the Durbin–Watson bounds can be used to test for serial correlation in exactly the same way as the Durbin–Watson statistic is used. The test based on g possesses a number of desirable properties and, in the examples considered by Berenblut and Webb, its power was always greater than that of the Durbin–Watson test for $\rho > .7$, and was frequently greater for $\rho > .5$.

King's power comparisons show that $s(\rho_1)$, with ρ_1 set at either .5 or .75, is likely to be a very useful alternative to both the DW and Berenblut–Webb tests. There were very few instances when $s(\rho_1)$ had lower power than the DW, and, although the power advantage was limited for some design matrices typically found in economic applications, there were some X's for which the power difference was quite large. Furthermore, these were the circumstances under which LS is likely to be relatively inefficient. As expected, the g test did perform slightly better than $s(\rho_1)$ for ρ close to one, but the difference was not great. Overall, King recommends using $s(.5)$ for testing against H_1: $\rho > 0$ and $s(-.5)$ for testing against H_1: $\rho < 0$. Further work involving the Berenblut-Webb test has been carried out by Sargan and Bhargava (1983a) who investigate the problem of testing the null hypothesis $\rho = 1$ against the alternative $|\rho| < 1$.

8.4.2c Tests based on a Transformation of LS Residuals

An alternative to the Durbin–Watson test is to transform the LS residuals to a new vector of residuals whose distribution does not depend on X and to use a test based on this new vector. Two examples are the vectors of BLUS and recursive residuals discussed in Chapter 5. Under the null hypothesis of no serial correlation each of these vectors will have mean zero and covariance $\sigma^2 I_{T-K}$, and thus the independence of residuals can be tested using the von Neumann ratio. See Theil (1971, Chapter 5) and Phillips and Harvey (1974) for details of the BLUS and recursive residual procedures, respectively, and also for references to earlier work and tabulation of significant points for the von Neumann ratio.

Further alternatives have been suggested by Abrahamse and Koerts (1971), Abrahamse and Louter (1971), Neudecker (1977b), Durbin (1970b), and Sims (1975). Under the assumption that the variables in X are "slowly changing over time," Abrahamse et al. recommend the residuals

$$\mathbf{v} = L(L'ML)^{-1/2}L'M\mathbf{y} \tag{8.4.14}$$

where L, of order $(T \times (T - K))$, contains the characteristic vectors corresponding to the $T - K$ largest roots of A. Under the null hypothesis, $\mathbf{v} \sim N(\mathbf{0},\sigma^2 LL')$ and $\mathbf{v}'A\mathbf{v}/\mathbf{v}'\mathbf{v}$ has the same probability distribution as the Durbin–Watson upper bound. Based on a similar assumption about X, Durbin proposed a transformation that leads to residuals which again can be tested via d_U. Sims modified this transformation to yield a set of residuals that are more likely to resemble the LS residual vector, and which, computationally, can be obtained as easily as those of Durbin. See Sims (1975, p. 164) for computational details and Dent and Cassing (1978) for some Monte Carlo results.

Studies that have compared the power of these various alternatives with that of the DW statistic [Koerts and Abrahamse (1969); Abrahamse and Koerts (1969); Abrahamse and Louter (1971); Phillips and Harvey (1974); L'Esperance and Taylor (1975); Dubbelman, Louter, and Abrahamse (1978)] have generally concluded that the DW is the best test, provided that we have an accurate method for dealing with the inconclusive region.

8.4.2d Testing for AR(1) Errors when X Contains a Lagged Dependent Variable

In the presence of a lagged dependent variable the DW statistic is likely to have reduced power and is biased toward 2 [Nerlove and Wallis (1966), Durbin (1970a)]. For these circumstances, Durbin (1970a) utilized the theory on the Lagrange multiplier test to develop the "h statistic"

$$h = r_1 \sqrt{\frac{T}{1 - T\hat{V}(b_1)}} \tag{8.4.15}$$

where r_1 is the first-order autocorrelation coefficient calculated from the LS residuals (and which could be replaced by $1 - \frac{1}{2}d$), and $\hat{V}(b_1)$ is the LS estimate of the variance of the coefficient of y_{t-1}. Under the null hypothesis of no serial correlation, h is asymptotically normal with zero mean and unit variance and, for testing against the alternative of AR(1) errors, it is valid even if X contains lags of y that are greater than one.

It is clear that h cannot be calculated if $T\hat{V}(b_1) > 1$. For this case Durbin suggests an asymptotically equivalent test, namely, regress $\hat{e}_t$ on $\hat{e}_{t-1}$ and X, where X includes the relevant lagged y's, and test the significance of the coefficient of $\hat{e}_{t-1}$ using standard LS procedures. Durbin also indicates how to extend the test for testing against higher-order AR schemes, and Sargan (1964) has given a test for an AR(2) alternative when the null hypothesis is an AR(1) scheme. The statistic for the latter test does not require estimation of the AR(2) model and has a slight error, which is noted in Durbin's (1970a) paper.

Because the test based on Durbin's *h* statistic is an asymptotic one, a number of Monte Carlo studies [Maddala and Rao (1973), Kenkel (1974, 1975, 1976), Park (1975, 1976), Spencer (1975), McNown and Hunter (1980), and Inder (1984)] have been undertaken to evaluate its small-sample performance. The results from these studies are not in complete agreement, and there are instances where the power of Durbin's *h* test is quite low, and where the finite sample size of the test is quite different from its asymptotic size. However, there does not yet seem to be an operational alternative that is clearly superior to the *h* test.

8.4.3 Some Tests for Alternatives Other Than AR(1) Errors

8.4.3a Durbin's Test Based on the Periodogram of Residuals

As an alternative to the Durbin–Watson statistic when one wishes to detect autocorrelation that may arise from any nonindependent process, Durbin (1969) suggests a test based on the cumulative periodogram of LS residuals. It is based on a modification of the Kolmogorov-Smirnov statistic and is another "bounds test," the bounds being tabulated by Durbin.

8.4.3b Geary's Sign Change Test

Geary (1970) recommends a nonparametric test in which the number of sign changes in the residuals is counted and the proportion is tested, using the binomial distribution, to see if it differs significantly from one-half. Cumulative probabilities required for the test are provided by Geary. Since the residuals will not be independent, even if there is no autocorrelation, the test is only asymptotically valid. Comparisons of the relative performance of the Geary and Durbin–Watson tests, for detecting AR(1) errors [Habibagahi and Pratschke (1972), Harrison (1975), Schmidt and Guilkey (1975)] have shown the Durbin–Watson test to be greatly superior, unless the sample size is large. (Harrison, Schmidt, and Guilkey point out that Habibagahi and Pratschke had overstated the case for the Geary test). Belsley (1973, 1974) points out that one should not expect the Geary test to compete very well with the Durbin–Watson test on the latter's home ground and that its usefulness is likely to lie in its ease of computation and its ability to detect correlation from nonnormal processes and processes such as $e_t = \rho e_{t-i} + v_t$, $i \neq 1$. However, Tillman (1974) presents some asymptotic results and Smith (1976) some empirical evidence that cast doubt on the ability of Geary's test to detect other than AR(1) errors. Furthermore, both theoretical results [King (1981a)] and empirical evidence [Gastwirth and Selwyn (1980); Bartels and Goodhew (1981)] suggest that the Durbin–Watson test is quite robust with respect to departures from normality.

8.4.3c Some Generalizations of the Durbin–Watson Statistic

Wallis (1972) suggests that the assumption $e_t = \rho e_{t-4} + v_t$ is likely to be a reasonable one when quarterly data are used; for testing with this as an alternative he recommends d_4, where

$$d_j = \frac{\sum_{t=j+1}^{T}(\hat{e}_t - \hat{e}_{t-j})^2}{\sum_{t=1}^{T}\hat{e}_t^2}, \quad j = 1, 2, \ldots \tag{8.4.16}$$

Like the Durbin–Watson test this is a bounds test, and Wallis tabulates two sets of bounds, one for when the equation contains seasonal dummy variables and one for when it does not. Further sets of critical values are provided by King and Giles (1977) and Giles and King (1978). For the case when y_{t-1} is one of the regressors, Wallis shows that d_4 will be biased toward 2, but not too greatly, and hence it still could be useful. He gives some examples where autocorrelation is detected by d_4 but not by d_1. An alternative test, similar in nature to that described in Section 8.4.2b, has been suggested by King (1983e).

For testing against an alternative of an autoregressive process of order no greater than some a priori level, say q, Vinod (1973) recommends using $d_1, d_2, \ldots, d_q$ to test a sequence of hypotheses. If all the hypotheses are accepted, we conclude that autocorrelation does not exist. If the jth hypothesis is rejected, we stop and conclude that an autoregressive process of order at least j is appropriate. Tables of the bounds for d_1, d_2, d_3 and d_4, with and without dummies, are provided by Vinod.

A further test and the relevant bounds are given by Schmidt (1972). For testing the null hypothesis $\theta_1 = \theta_2 = 0$, when the alternative is $e_t = \theta_1 e_{t-1} + \theta_2 e_{t-2} + v_t$, he suggests using $d_1 + d_2$.

8.4.3d Testing for MA(1) Errors

For testing the null hypothesis H_0: $\alpha = 0$ against the alternative H_1: $\alpha > 0$ (or H_1: $\alpha < 0$) in the MA(1) error model, King (1983d) points out that the test based on the modified DW statistic d' (see Section 8.4.2a) is locally best invariant, and that the DW test is approximately locally best invariant. In addition, extending his earlier work on testing for AR(1) errors (Section 8.4.2b), he suggests a statistic given by

$$r(\alpha_0) = \frac{\hat{\mathbf{e}}^{*\prime}\hat{\mathbf{e}}^*}{\hat{\mathbf{e}}'\hat{\mathbf{e}}} \tag{8.4.17}$$

where $\hat{\mathbf{e}}^* = \mathbf{y}^* - X^*\hat{\boldsymbol{\beta}}$ is the vector of GLS residuals calculated under the assumption that $\alpha = \alpha_0$ (see Section 8.2.5), and $\hat{\mathbf{e}} = \mathbf{y} - X\mathbf{b}$ is the vector of least squares residuals. He shows that, when α_0 is fixed and positive (negative), the test that rejects H_0 for small values of $r(\alpha_0)$ is a most powerful invariant test in the neighborhood of $\alpha = \alpha_0$ against the alternative H_1: $\alpha > 0$ (H_1: $\alpha < 0$). As was the case for the DW test and the other tests described in Sections 8.4.2a, 8.4.2b, and 8.4.3c, the critical values of this test will depend on the matrix X

and so it is impossible to tabulate critical values that are relevant for all problems. To alleviate this problem King tabulates critical values which can be used for bounds tests with $r(.5)$ and $r(-.5)$. Also, in some empirical power comparisons, he finds that the tests based on $r(\pm.5)$ are always more powerful than the DW test when $|\alpha| \geq .3$.

8.4.3e Additional Remarks

The optimal properties of the DW test for detecting MA(1) errors have been reflected in the earlier empirical power comparisons of Blattberg (1973) and Smith (1976). In addition, these authors found that the DW test has quite high power when the errors follow an AR(2) process; and it has long been recognized [see, e.g., Praetz (1979) and Weber and Monarchi (1982)] that the DW test will detect other types of misspecification such as incorrect functional form and omitted variables. These observations raise questions concerning an appropriate strategy when a "significant" value of the DW statistic is obtained, and the effects of incorrectly assuming an AR(1) process when some other form of misspecification is present. For discriminating between alternative types of autocorrelation some of the techniques outlined in Section 8.4.1 can be used and, in addition, King (1983a) has suggested a finite sample test for testing AR(1) errors against the alternative of MA(1) errors. The effect of incorrectly assuming AR(1) errors on the efficiency of estimation of $\boldsymbol{\beta}$ has been investigated in Monte Carlo experiments by Griffiths and Beesley (1984) and Weber and Monarchi (1982); Thursby (1981) has suggested a strategy for discriminating between AR(1) errors and misspecification in the form of incorrect functional form or omitted variables.

8.4.3f Testing for General AR or MA Errors when X Contains a Lagged Dependent Variable

We conclude this section with a description of the Lagrange multiplier test, suggested by Godfrey (1978a) and Breusch (1978) for testing for the existence of AR or MA errors of any order whether or not X contains lagged values of the dependent variable. If X does contain lagged values of the dependent variable, then, like Durbin's h-statistic test outlined in Section 8.4.2d, this test is relevant for distributed lag models, which are discussed in Chapter 10.

The null hypothesis for the test is that the e_t are uncorrelated and the alternative hypotheses considered are

$$e_t = \theta_1 e_{t-1} + \theta_2 e_{t-2} + \ldots + \theta_q e_{t-q} + v_t \qquad (8.4.18)$$

and

$$e_t = v_t + \alpha_1 v_{t-1} + \ldots + \alpha_q v_{t-q} \qquad (8.4.19)$$

Thus we are testing for the existence of either AR(q) or MA(q) errors. The statistic for both these alternative hypotheses is the same, and so while it may help to identify the order of the process it does not enable one to discriminate between the two types of autocorrelation. Godfrey and Breusch show that under the null hypothesis,

$$\ell = \frac{\hat{\mathbf{e}}'\hat{E}[\hat{E}'\hat{E} - \hat{E}'X(X'X)^{-1}X'\hat{E}]^{-1}\hat{E}'\hat{\mathbf{e}}}{\hat{\sigma}^2} \tag{8.4.20}$$

has an asymptotic $\chi^2_{(q)}$ distribution where

1. $\hat{\mathbf{e}} = \mathbf{y} - X\mathbf{b}$ is the LS residual vector.
2. $\hat{E} = (\hat{\mathbf{e}}_1, \hat{\mathbf{e}}_2, \ldots, \hat{\mathbf{e}}_q)$.
3. $\hat{\mathbf{e}}_j = (0, \ldots, 0, \hat{e}_1, \ldots, \hat{e}_{T-j})'$.
4. $\hat{\sigma}^2 = \hat{\mathbf{e}}'\hat{\mathbf{e}}/T$.

This test is a convenient one because it is based only on least squares quantities. Fitts (1973) provides an alternative for the MA(1) case, but his test requires nonlinear estimation. Also of likely interest are test statistics which test the null hypothesis that an assumed autocorrelation structure is correct, against the alternative hypothesis that some higher-order process is appropriate. Godfrey (1978b) provides statistics for a number of these cases and Sargan and Mehta (1983) outline a sequential testing procedure which can be used to select the order of an AR disturbance.

8.5 RECOMMENDATIONS AND SOME COMMENTS ON PRETESTING

Given the array of models, tests, and estimation techniques discussed in Sections 8.2 and 8.4, the applied worker will be concerned with which of these should be chosen and what research strategy should be followed. As always, it is impossible to give a blanket recommendation that is appropriate for all situations. However, based on reported results the following steps appear reasonable.

1. Use the Durbin–Watson statistic (d_1) [or preferably King's $s(.5)$ statistic], the large sample tests in Section 8.4.1, and, if considered necessary, higher-order d_j statistics to select what seems to be a reasonable autocorrelation assumption or assumptions. If one is using the conventional 5% significance level, the exact significance point of the DW [or $s(.5)$] should be used. It is better to use the upper critical bound of one of these tests than to regard the inconclusive region as an indication of no autocorrelation. Also, one should keep in mind that a low DW can be indicative of other forms of misspecification such as omitted variables or incorrect functional form.

2. If autocorrelation exists, estimate the chosen function(s) via ML if possible, otherwise use NLS or conditional NLS. In most cases, if the number of observations is sufficiently great, there should be little difference between these techniques.

3. If possible, and desirable, discriminate further between models on the basis of standard error and/or likelihood ratio tests.

This strategy is designed to find a model that "best represents reality" and, given that the selected model is the "real one," it is also designed to estimate it in the most efficient manner. The problem with such an approach is that the reported coefficient estimates and their reliability are conditional on the final model being the "correct one." They ignore the fact that a number of other models have been rejected and that one of these could be "correct." Ideally, the reported reliability of the results should take this into account. Unfortunately, it is very difficult to study the unconditional sampling properties of estimates generated from search procedures or strategies such as the one suggested here and such studies are in their infancy. Thus, given the current state of the art, the best bet appears to be to carry out a limited, but hopefully effective, search procedure, and to report both the procedure followed and the final set of estimates. It may also be useful to report estimates from two or more competing models. However, one should keep in mind the sense in which the results are suboptimal and also other possible strategies.

In connection with testing for AR(1) errors one possible alternative strategy is to use a Durbin–Watson significance level which is considerably higher than the conventional .05 level, say 0.35 or 0.4. Such a strategy is suggested by Monte Carlo evidence on the efficiency of pre-test estimators [Judge and Bock (1978, Chapter 7); Schmidt (1971); Fomby and Guilkey (1978); Peck (1976); Giles and King (1984)], and by the fact that when X is such that LS is very inefficient, the DW has low power [Chipman (1965)]. In terms of the effects of pretesting on hypothesis tests for $\boldsymbol{\beta}$ the Monte Carlo support for a high significance level is not as strong [Nakamura and Nakamura (1978); Giles and King (1984)], but a level above 0.05 can produce some gains. Monte Carlo results on pretest estimators where the errors follow either an AR(1) or an MA(1) scheme have been provided by Griffiths and Beesley (1984).

We have assumed throughout that the autocorrelation process generating the disturbances is stationary. Newbold and Davies (1978) argue that nonstationary processes are quite likely and that tests of the hypothesis $\boldsymbol{\beta} = \mathbf{0}$, which assume stationarity, are particularly unrealistic. They condemn applied econometricians who consider only an AR(1) scheme and give Monte Carlo results to show how, in the presence of an alternative process, this can lead to incorrect inferences. The question of nonstationary disturbances is worthy of future research. It is likely to depend heavily on the specification of X. The suggestion that alternatives to an AR(1) process should be considered is a good one, and it is one to which applied econometricians seem to be paying increasing attention.

Before concluding it is worthwhile mentioning some results obtained for models containing errors that are both autocorrelated and heteroscedastic. Harrison and McCabe (1975) provide Monte Carlo evidence, and Epps and Epps (1977) give both asymptotic results and Monte Carlo evidence which suggest that the Durbin–Watson and Geary tests are robust in the presence of heteroscedasticity. Epps and Epps go on to consider the performance of the Goldfeld–Quandt and Glejser tests for heteroscedasticity when both problems are present. They find both tests to be invalid but that a useful approximate procedure is to first test for autocorrelation and, if necessary, correct for it using a Cochrane–Orcutt transformation, and then use the transformed model to test for heteroscedasticity. It should be pointed out that the usefulness of this procedure was judged by the performance of the tests not by the efficiency of the resulting estimators. Lagrange multiplier statistics for simultaneously testing for both heteroscedasticity and autocorrelation (as well as normality and functional form) have been considered by Jarque and Bera (1980) and Bera and Jarque (1982). See also King and Evans (1983).

8.6 EXERCISES

8.6.1 General Exercises

Exercise 8.1

Calculate the covariance matrices and compute the relative efficiency of the LS estimator $\mathbf{b}$, the GLS estimator $\hat{\boldsymbol{\beta}}$, and the approximate GLS estimator $\hat{\boldsymbol{\beta}}_0$ in the AR(1) error model

$$y_t = \beta_1 + \beta_2 t + e_t, \qquad t = 1, 2, \ldots, 10$$
$$e_t = .8e_{t-1} + v_t$$

where the v_t are independent and identically distributed random variables with zero mean and unit variance. To reduce the computational load we note that

$$X'\Psi X = \begin{bmatrix} 150.8194 & 829.5064 \\ 829.5064 & 5020.2833 \end{bmatrix}$$

Exercise 8.2

Prove that minimizing S_L in (8.2.6) is equivalent to maximizing the log-likelihood in (8.2.5).

Exercise 8.3

Show that (8.2.34) is obtained when σ_v is integrated out of (8.2.33); and that (8.2.36) results from integrating $\boldsymbol{\beta}$ out of (8.2.34).

Exercise 8.4

For the AR(2) error model, prove that $P'P = \Psi^{-1}$ where P is the transformation matrix in (8.2.46) and Ψ^{-1} is defined in (8.2.45).

Exercise 8.5

Prove that the transformed residuals given for the MA(1) error model in (8.2.72) are obtained from the transformation $P\mathbf{e}$ where P is defined in (8.2.70). Relate this transformation to that obtained using the Kalman filter [Harvey (1981b, p. 112)].

Exercise 8.6

Prove that, for the MA(q) error model, $|\Psi| = |I_q + C'C|$. See Equation 8.2.103.

Exercise 8.7

Prove that, in the ARMA error model, minimizing $\mathbf{v}'\mathbf{v} + \bar{\mathbf{w}}'\Omega^{-1}\bar{\mathbf{w}}$ with respect to $\boldsymbol{\beta}$, $\boldsymbol{\theta}$, $\boldsymbol{\alpha}$, and $\bar{\mathbf{w}}$ is equivalent to minimizing $\mathbf{e}'\boldsymbol{\Psi}^{-1}\mathbf{e}$ with respect to $\boldsymbol{\beta}$, $\boldsymbol{\theta}$, and $\boldsymbol{\alpha}$. See Section 8.2.7 for the various definitions.

Exercise 8.8

Prove that, in the AR(1) error model, the general expression for the BLUP in (8.3.4) reduces to (8.3.6), and the expression for its MSE in (8.3.5) reduces to (8.3.13).

Exercise 8.9

Prove that the predictor in (8.3.4) is a BLUP and that its MSE is given by (8.3.5).

Exercise 8.10

(a) Prove that the DW statistic can be written as

$$d = \frac{\sum_{i=1}^{T-K} \theta_i z_i^2}{\sum_{i=1}^{T-K} z_i^2} \qquad (8.6.1)$$

where the z_i are independent standard normal random variables and $\theta_1, \theta_2, \ldots, \theta_{T-K}$ are the nonzero characteristic roots of MAM. See Equations 8.4.5 and 8.4.6.

(b) Show that

$$E[d] = \frac{1}{T-K} \sum_{i=1}^{T-K} \theta_i = \bar{\theta} \qquad (8.6.2)$$

and

$$\text{var}[d] = \frac{2}{(T-K)(T-K+2)} \left[\sum_{i=1}^{T-K} \theta_i^2 - (T-K)\bar{\theta}^2 \right] \qquad (8.6.3)$$

and that these two expressions are equivalent to

$$E[d] = \frac{P}{T-K} \qquad (8.6.4)$$

and

$$\text{var}[d] = \frac{2}{(T-K)(T-K+2)} [Q - P \cdot E[d]] \qquad (8.6.5)$$

where P and Q are defined in (8.4.10) and (8.4.11).

8.6.2 Individual Exercises Using Monte Carlo Data

For the remaining problems generate 100 samples of $\mathbf{y}$, each of size 21, from the model

$$y_t = \beta_1 + \beta_2 x_{t2} + \beta_3 x_{t3} + e_t \tag{8.6.6}$$

where $e_t = \rho e_{t-1} + v_t$ and the v_t are independent normal random variables with zero mean and variance $E[v_t^2] = \sigma_v^2$. Use the first 20 observations for estimation and the last one for prediction purposes. Some suggested parameter values are $\beta_1 = 10$, $\beta_2 = 1$, $\beta_3 = 1$, $\rho = .8$, and $\sigma_v^2 = 6.4$, and a suggested design matrix is

$$X = \begin{bmatrix} 1.00 & 14.53 & 16.74 \\ 1.00 & 15.30 & 16.81 \\ 1.00 & 15.92 & 19.50 \\ 1.00 & 17.41 & 22.12 \\ 1.00 & 18.37 & 22.34 \\ 1.00 & 18.83 & 17.47 \\ 1.00 & 18.84 & 20.24 \\ 1.00 & 19.71 & 20.37 \\ 1.00 & 20.01 & 12.71 \\ 1.00 & 20.26 & 22.98 \\ 1.00 & 20.77 & 19.33 \\ 1.00 & 21.17 & 17.04 \\ 1.00 & 21.34 & 16.74 \\ 1.00 & 22.91 & 19.81 \\ 1.00 & 22.96 & 31.92 \\ 1.00 & 23.69 & 26.31 \\ 1.00 & 24.82 & 25.93 \\ 1.00 & 25.54 & 21.96 \\ 1.00 & 25.63 & 24.05 \\ 1.00 & 28.73 & 25.66 \end{bmatrix} \tag{8.6.7}$$

and $\mathbf{x}'_{T+1} = [1.00 \quad 20.00 \quad 20.00]$.

Exercise 8.11

Calculate the covariance matrices for the following estimators.

(a) The generalized least squares estimator

$$\hat{\boldsymbol{\beta}} = (X'\Psi^{-1}X)^{-1}X'\Psi^{-1}\mathbf{y}$$

(b) The approximate generalized least squares estimator (see Section 8.2.1a)

$$\hat{\boldsymbol{\beta}}_0 = (X'P_0'P_0X)^{-1}X'P_0'P_0\mathbf{y}$$

(c) The least squares estimator

$$\mathbf{b} = (X'X)^{-1}X'\mathbf{y}$$

(d) The "generalized least squares estimator" which incorrectly assumes the errors are MA(1) with $\alpha = 0.8$.

Comment on the relative efficiency of the four estimators.

Exercise 8.12

Select five samples from the Monte Carlo data and, for each sample, compute values for the following estimators.

(a) The least squares estimator **b**.
(b) The estimator $\rho^* = 1 - d/2$, where d is the Durbin–Watson statistic.
(c) The approximate estimated generalized least squares estimator for $\boldsymbol{\beta}$ that uses ρ^*, call it $\hat{\hat{\boldsymbol{\beta}}}_0$.
(d) The estimated generalized least squares estimator for $\boldsymbol{\beta}$ that uses ρ^*, call it $\hat{\hat{\boldsymbol{\beta}}}$.
(e) The maximum likelihood estimator for $\boldsymbol{\beta}$ under the assumption the errors follow an MA(1) error process, call it $\tilde{\boldsymbol{\beta}}$.

Compare the various estimates with each other and with the true parameter values.

Exercise 8.13

The computer programs used in Exercise 8.12 to obtain values of the estimators $\mathbf{b}$, $\hat{\hat{\boldsymbol{\beta}}}_0$, $\hat{\hat{\boldsymbol{\beta}}}$ and $\tilde{\boldsymbol{\beta}}$ are also likely to yield estimates of the covariance matrices of these estimators. In all four cases, however, the variance estimates could be biased. Explain why. Also, taking the parameter β_3 as an example, compare the various estimates of $\text{var}(b_3)$, $\text{var}(\hat{\hat{\beta}}_{03})$, $\text{var}(\hat{\hat{\beta}}_3)$ and $\text{var}(\tilde{\beta}_3)$ with the relevant answers in Exercise 8.11.

Exercise 8.14

Use the results in Exercise 8.12 and 8.13 to calculate t values that would be used to test

(a) H_0: $\beta_3 = 0$ against H_1: $\beta_3 \neq 0$
(b) H_0: $\beta_3 = 1$ against H_1: $\beta_3 \neq 1$

Since we have four estimators and five samples this involves, for each hypothesis, the calculation of 20 t values. Keeping in mind the validity or otherwise of each null hypothesis, comment on the results.

Exercise 8.15

Given that $\mathbf{x}'_{T+1} = (1\ 20\ 20)$, for each of the five samples calculate values for the following two predictors:

(a) $y^*_{T+1} = \mathbf{x}'_{T+1}\hat{\hat{\boldsymbol{\beta}}}$
(b) $\hat{y}_{T+1} = \mathbf{x}'_{T+1}\hat{\hat{\boldsymbol{\beta}}} + \rho^*(y_T - \mathbf{x}'_T\hat{\hat{\boldsymbol{\beta}}})$

Compare these predictions with the realized values.

Exercise 8.16

Calculate the mean and variance of the DW statistic for the X matrix used to generate your data. Use this information and the mean and variance of the Durbin–Watson upper bound [see Table 6 in Judge et al. (1982)] to find an approximate critical value for the Durbin–Watson test. Use a 5% significance level.

Exercise 8.17

Using the same five samples that were used in Exercises 8.12 to 8.13, an alternative hypothesis of positive autocorrelation, and a 5% significance level, test for autocorrelation using

(a) The Durbin–Watson test (use the critical value obtained in Exercise 8.16).
(b) King's locally optimal bounds test with $\rho_1 = .5$.

8.6.3 Group Exercises Using Monte Carlo Data

Exercise 8.18

Repeat Exercise 8.12 for all 100 samples and use the results to estimate the mean and mean square error matrix for each estimator. For example, for **b**, estimates of its mean and mean square error matrix are given, respectively, by

$$\frac{1}{100}\sum_{i=1}^{100}\mathbf{b}(i) \qquad \text{and} \qquad \frac{1}{100}\sum_{i=1}^{100}[(\mathbf{b}(i) - \boldsymbol{\beta})(\mathbf{b}(i) - \boldsymbol{\beta})']$$

where $\mathbf{b}(i)$ is the least squares estimator from the ith sample. Use these results and those of Exercise 8.11 to answer the following questions.

(a) Do any of the estimators appear to be biased?
(b) By comparing the estimated mean and mean square error of **b** with the true ones, comment on the extent of the sampling error in the Monte Carlo experiment.
(c) Is $\sigma^2(X'\Psi^{-1}X)^{-1}$ a good approximation of the finite sample mean square error matrix of (a) $\hat{\hat{\boldsymbol{\beta}}}$; and (b) $\hat{\hat{\boldsymbol{\beta}}}_0$?
(d) What are the efficiency consequences of incorrectly assuming the errors follow an MA(1) error process?

Exercise 8.19

Use all 100 samples to estimate the means of the variance estimators $\text{var}(b_3)$, var($\hat{\hat{\beta}}_{03}$), var($\hat{\hat{\beta}}_3$) and var($\tilde{\beta}_3$) that were obtained in Exercise 8.13. Comment on the results, particularly with respect to your answers to Exercise 8.11.

Exercise 8.20
Repeat Exercise 8.14 for all 100 samples and calculate the proportion of Type I and Type II errors obtained when a 5% significance level is used. Comment.

Exercise 8.21
Repeat Exercise 8.15 for all 100 samples and calculate

$$\text{MSE}(y^*_{T+1}) = \frac{1}{100}\sum_{i=1}^{100}[y^*_{T+1}(i) - y_{T+1}(i)]^2$$

and

$$\text{MSE}(\hat{y}_{T+1}) = \frac{1}{100}\sum_{i=1}^{100}[\hat{y}_{T+1}(i) - y_{T+1}(i)]^2$$

where i refers to the ith sample. Comment on the results and compare the value of MSE($\hat{y}_{T+1}$) with the value obtained from the asymptotic expression in (8.3.14).

Exercise 8.22
Use all 100 samples to construct empirical distributions for ρ^* and the ML estimator for α. Comment.

8.7 REFERENCES

Abrahamse, A. P. J. and J. Koerts (1969) "A Comparison of the Power of the Durbin–Watson Test and the BLUS Test," *Journal of the American Statistical Association,* 64, 938–948.

Abrahamse, A. P. J. and J. Koerts (1971) "New Estimates of Disturbances in Regression Analysis," *Journal of the American Statistical Association,* 66, 71–74.

Abrahamse, A. P. J. and A. S. Louter (1971) "On a New Test for Autocorrelation in Least Squares Regression," *Biometrika,* 58, 53–60.

Ali, M. M. (1977) "Analysis of Autoregressive-Moving Average Models: Estimation and Prediction," *Biometrika,* 64, 535–545.

Amemiya, T. (1973) "Generalized Least Squares with an Estimated Autocovariance Matrix," *Econometrica,* 41, 723–732.

Anderson, T. W. (1948) "On the Theory of Testing Serial Correlation," *Skandinarisk Aktuarietidskrift,* 31, 88–116.

Anderson, T. W. (1971) *The Statistical Analysis of Time Series,* Wiley, New York.

Anderson, T. W. and C. Hsiao (1982) "Formulation and Estimation of Dynamic Models Using Panel Data," *Journal of Econometrics,* 18, 47–82.

Ansley, C. F. (1979) "An Algorithm for the Exact Likelihood of a Mixed Autoregressive-Moving Average Process," *Biometrika,* 66, 59–65.

Ansley, C. F. and P. Newbold (1980) "Finite Sample Properties of Estimators for Autoregressive Moving Average Models," *Journal of Econometrics,* 13, 159–183.

Ansley, C. F. and P. Newbold (1981) "On the Bias in Estimates of Forecast Mean Squared Error," *Journal of the American Statistical Association,* 76, 569–578.

Baillie, R. T. (1979) "The Asymptotic Mean Squared Error of Multistep Prediction from the Regression Model with Autoregressive Errors," *Journal of the American Statistical Association,* 74, 175–184.

Baillie, R. T. (1980) "Predictions from ARMAX Models," *Journal of Econometrics,* 12, 365–374.

Balestra, P. (1980) "A Note on the Exact Transformation Associated with the First-Order Moving Average Process," *Journal of Econometrics,* 14, 381–394.

Bartels, R., G. Bornholt, and K. Hanslow (1982) "The Polynomial Trend Model with Autocorrelated Residuals," *Communications in Statistics,* 11, 1393–1402.

Bartels, R. and J. Goodhew (1981) "The Robustness of the Durbin–Watson Test," *The Review of Economics and Statistics,* 63, 136–139.

Bartlett, M. S. (1946) "On the Theoretical Specification of Sampling Properties of Autocorrelated Time Series," *Journal of the Royal Statistical Society,* Series B, 8, 27–41.

Beach, C. M. and J. G. MacKinnon (1978a) "A Maximum Likelihood Procedure for Regression with Autocorrelated Errors," *Econometrica,* 46, 51–58.

Beach, C. M. and J. G. MacKinnon (1978b) "Full Maximum Likelihood Estimation of Second-Order Autoregressive Error Models," *Journal of Econometrics,* 7, 187–198.

Belsley, C. A. (1973) "The Relative Power of the τ-Test: A Furthering Comment," *Review of Economics and Statistics,* 55, 132.

Belsley, C. A. (1974) "The τ-Test and High-Order Serial Correlation: A Reply," *Review of Economics and Statistics,* 56, 417–418.

Bera, A. K. and C. M. Jarque (1982) "Model Specification Tests: A Simultaneous Approach," *Journal of Econometrics,* 20, 59–82.

Berenblut, I. I. and G. I. Webb (1973) "A New Test for Autocorrelated Errors in the Linear Regression Model," *Journal of the Royal Statistical Society,* Series B, 35, 33–50.

Bhansali, R. J. (1981) "Effects of Not Knowing the Order of an Autoregressive Process on the Mean Squared Error of Predition-1," *Journal of the American Statistical Association,* 76, 588–597.

Blattberg, R. C. (1973) "Evaluation of the Power of the Durbin–Watson Statistic for Non-First Order Serial Correlation Alternatives," *The Review of Economics and Statistics,* 55, 508–515.

Box, G. E. P. and G. M. Jenkins (1970), *Time Series Analysis, Forecasting and Control,* Holden Day, San Francisco.

Breusch, T. S. (1978) "Testing for Autocorrelation in Dynamic Linear Models," *Australian Economic Papers,* 17, 334–355.

Breusch, T. S. and A. R. Pagan (1980) "The Lagrange Multiplier Test and its Applications to Model Specification in Econometrics," *Review of Economic Studies,* 47, 239–253.

Chipman, J. S. (1965) "The Problem of Testing for Serial Correlation in Regression Analysis: The Story of a Dilemma," Technical Report 4, University of Minnesota, Minneapolis.

Chipman, J. S. (1979) "Efficiency of Least Squares Estimation of Linear Trend When Residuals Are Autocorrelated," *Econometrica,* 47, 115–128.

Cochrane, D. and G. H. Orcutt (1949) "Application of Least Squares Regressions to Relationships Containing Autocorrelated Error Terms," *Journal of the American Statistical Association,* 44, 32–61.

Cragg, J. G. (1982) "Estimation and Testing in Time-Series Regression Models with Heteroscedastic Disturbances," *Journal of Econometrics,* 20, 135–157.

Cryer, J. D. and J. Ledolter (1981) "Small-Sample Properties of the Maximum Likelihood Estimator in the First-Order Moving Average Model," *Biometrika,* 68, 691–694.

Davidson, James E. H. (1981) "Problems with the Estimation of Moving Average Processes," *Journal of Econometrics,* 16, 295–310.

Dent, W. T. (1977) "Computation of the Exact Likelihood Function of an ARIMA Process," *Journal of Statistical Computation and Simulation,* 5, 193–206.

Dent, W. T. and S. Cassing (1978) "On Durbin's and Sims' Residuals in Autocorrelation Tests," *Econometrica,* 46, 1489–1492.

Dent, W. T. and A. S. Min (1978) "A Monte Carlo Study of Autoregressive Integrated Moving Average Processes," *Journal of Econometrics,* 7, 23–55.

Doran, H. E. (1981) "Omission of an Observation from a Regression Analysis," *Journal of Econometrics,* 16, 367–374.

Drèze, J. (1977) "Bayesian Regression Analysis Using Poly-*t* Densities," *Journal of Econometrics,* 6, 329–354.

Dubbelman, C., A. S. Louter, and A. P. J. Abrahamse (1978) "On Typical Characteristics of Economic Time Series and the Relative Qualities of Five Autocorrelation Tests," *Journal of Econometrics,* 8, 295–306.

Dufour, J.-M., M. J. I. Gaudry, and T. C. Lieu (1980) "The Cochrane–Orcutt Procedure: Numerical Examples of Multiple Admissible Minima," *Economics Letters,* 6, 43–48.

Durbin, J. (1959) "Efficient Estimation of Parameters in Moving-Average Models," *Biometrika,* 46, 306–316.

Durbin, J. (1960) "Estimation of Parameters in Time-Series Regression Models," *Journal of the Royal Statistical Society,* Series B, 22, 139–153.

Durbin, J. (1969) "Tests for Serial Correlation in Regression Analysis Based on the Periodogram of Least Squares Residuals," *Biometrika,* 56, 1–15.

Durbin, J. (1970a) "Testing for Serial Correlation in Least-Squares Regression When Some of the Regressors Are Lagged Dependent Variables," *Econometrica,* 38, 410–421.

Durbin, J. (1970b) "An Alternative to the Bounds Test for Testing for Serial Correlation in Least Squares Regression," *Econometrica,* 38, 422–429.

Durbin, J. and G. S. Watson (1950) "Testing for Serial Correlation in Least Squares Regression I," *Biometrika,* 37, 409–428.

Durbin, J. and G. S. Watson (1951) "Testing for Serial Correlation in Least Squares Regression II," *Biometrika,* 38, 159–178.

Durbin, J. and G. S. Watson (1971) "Testing for Serial Correlation in Least Squares Regression III," *Biometrika,* 58, 1–19.

Engle, R. F. (1974a) "Band Spectrum Regression," *International Economic Review,* 15, 1–11.

Engle, R. F. (1974b) "Specifications of the Disturbance Term for Efficient Estimation," *Econometrica,* 42, 135–146.

Engle, R. F. (1976) "Interpreting Spectral Analyses in Terms of Time Domain Models," *Annals of Economic and Social Measurement,* 5, 89–110.

Engle, R. F. and R. Gardner (1976) "Some Finite Sample Properties of Spectral Estimators of a Linear Regression," *Econometrica,* 46, 149–166.

Epps, T. W. and M. L. Epps (1977) "The Robustness of Some Standard Tests for Autocorrelation and Heteroskedasticity When Both Problems Are Present," *Econometrica,* 45, 745–753.

Farebrother, R. W. (1980) "The Durbin–Watson Test for Serial Correlation When There is No Intercept in the Regression," *Econometrica,* 48, 1553–1563.

Fisher, G. R. (1970) "Quarterly Dividend Behavior," in K. Hilton and D. F. Heathfield, eds., *The Econometric Study of the United Kingdom,* Macmillan, London, 149–184.

Fitts, J. (1973) "Testing for Autocorrelation in the Autoregressive Moving Average Error Model," *Journal of Econometrics,* 1, 363–376.

Fomby, T. B. and D. K. Guilkey (1978) "On Choosing the Optimal Level of Significance for the Durbin–Watson Test and the Bayesian Alternative," *Journal of Econometrics,* 8, 203–214.

Fuller, W. A. (1976) *Introduction to Statistical Time Series,* Wiley, New York.

Fuller, W. A. (1980) "The Use of Indicator Variables in Computing Predictions," *Journal of Econometrics,* 12, 231–243.

Fuller, W. A. and D. P. Hasza (1980) "Predictors for the First-Order Autoregressive Process," *Journal of Econometrics,* 13, 139–157.

Fuller, W. A. and D. P. Hasza (1981) "Properties of Predictors for Autoregressive Time Series," *Journal of the American Statistical Association,* 76, 155–161.

Gallant, A. R. and J. J. Goebel (1976) "Nonlinear Regression With Autocorrelated Errors," *Journal of the American Statistical Association,* 71, 961–967.

Gastwirth, J. L. and M. R. Selwyn (1980) "The Robustness Properties of Two Tests for Serial Correlation," *Journal of the American Statistical Association,* 75, 138–141.

Geary, R. C. (1970) "Relative Efficiency of Count of Sign Changes for Assessing Residual Autoregression in Least Squares Regression," *Biometrika,* 57, 123–127.

Giles, D. E. A. and M. L. King (1978) "Fourth-Order Autocorrelation: Further Significance Points for the Wallis Test," *Journal of Econometrics,* 8, 255–260.

Godfrey, L. G. (1978a) "Testing Against General Autoregressive and Moving Average Error Models When the Regressors Include Lagged Dependent Variables," *Econometrica,* 46, 1293–1302.

Godfrey, L. G. (1978b) "Testing for Higher Order Serial Correlation in Regression Equations When the Regressors Include Lagged Dependent Variables," *Econometrica,* 46, 1303–1310.

Godfrey, L. G. (1981) "On the Invariance of the Lagrange Multiplier Test with Respect to Certain Changes in the Alternative Hypothesis," *Econometrica,* 49, 1443–1456.

Godolphin, E. J. and J. J. de Gooijer (1982) "On the Maximum Likelihood Estimation of the Parameters of a Gaussian Moving Average Process," *Biometrika,* 69, 443–451.

Goldberger, A. S. (1962) "Best Linear Unbiased Prediction in the Generalized Linear Regression Model," *Journal of the American Statistical Association,* 57, 369–375.

Granger, C. W. J. and P. Newbold (1974) "Spurious Regessions in Econometrics," *Journal of Econometrics,* 2, 111–120.

Grenander, U. and M. Rosenblatt (1957) *Statistical Analysis of Stationary Time Series,* Wiley, New York.

Griffiths, W. E. and D. Dao (1980) "A Note on a Bayesian Estimator in an Autocorrelation Error Model," *Journal of Econometrics,* 12, 390–392.

Griffiths, W. E. and P. A. A. Beesley (1984) "The Small Sample Properties of Some Preliminary Test Estimators in a Linear Model with Autocorrelated Errors," *Journal of Econometrics,* forthcoming.

Griliches, Z. and P. Rao (1969) "Small Sample Properties of Several Two-Stage Regression Methods in the Context of Autocorrelated Errors," *Journal of the American Statistical Association,* 64, 253–272.

Habibagahi, H. and J. L. Pratschke (1972) "A Comparison of the Power of the von Neumann Ratio, Durbin–Watson and Geary Tests," *Review of Economics and Statistics,* 54, 179–185.

Harrison, M. J. (1975) "The Power of the Durbin–Watson and Geary Tests: Comment and Further Evidence," *Review of Economics and Statistics,* 57, 377–379.

Harrison, M. J. and B. P. M. McCabe (1975) "Autocorrelation with Heteroscedasticity: A Note on the Robustness of Durbin–Watson, Geary, and Henshaw Tests," *Biometrika,* 62, 214–216.

Harvey, A. C. (1978) "Linear Regression in the Frequency Domain," *International Economic Review,* 19, 507–512.

Harvey, A. C. (1981a) *The Econometric Analysis of Time Series,* Halsted, New York.

Harvey, A. C. (1981b) *Time Series Models,* Halsted, New York.

Harvey, A. C. (1981c) "Finite Sample Prediction and Overdifferencing," *Journal of Time Series Analysis,* 2, 221–232.

Harvey, A. C. and G. D. A. Phillips (1979) "Maximum Likelihood Estimation of Regression Models with Autoregressive-Moving Average Disturbances," *Biometrika,* 66, 49–58.

Hendry, D. F. (1974) "Stochastic Specification in an Aggregate Demand Model of the United Kingdom," *Econometrica,* 42, 559–578.

Hendry, D. F. (1980) "Predictive Failure and Econometric Modelling in Macroeconomics: The Transactions Demand for Money," in P. Ormerod, ed., *Modelling the Economy,* Heinemann Educational Books.

Hendry, D. F. and G. J. Anderson (1977) "Testing Dynamic Specification in Small Simultaneous Systems: An Application to a Model of Building Society Behavior in the United Kingdom," in M. D. Intrilligator, ed., *Frontiers of Quantitative Economics*-IIIA, North-Holland, Amsterdam, 361–383.

Hendry, D. F. and G. E. Mizon (1978) "Serial Correlation as a Convenient Simplification not a Nuisance: A Comment on a Study of the Demand for Money by the Bank of England," *Economic Journal,* 88, 549–563.

Hendry, D. F. and J.-F. Richard (1982) "On the Formulation of Empirical Models in Dynamic Econometrics," *Journal of Econometrics,* 20, 3–34.

Hendry, D. F. and P. K. Trivedi (1972) "Maximum Likelihood Estimation of Difference Equations with Moving Average Errors: A Simulation Study," *Review of Economic Studies,* 39, 117–146.

Hildreth, C. (1969) "Asymptotic Distribution of Maximum Likelihood Estimators in a Linear Model with Autoregressive Disturbances," *Annals of Mathematical Statistics,* 40, 583–594.

Hildreth, C. and W. Dent (1974) "An Adjusted Maximum Likelihood Estimator in W. Sellekaert, ed., *Econometrics and Economic Theory: Essays in Honor of Jan Tinbergen,* Macmillan, London, 3–25.

Hildreth, C. and J. Y. Lu (1960) "Demand Relations with Autocorrelated Disturbances," Michigan State University Agricultural Experiment Station Technical Bulletin 276, East Lansing, Mich.

Hildreth, C. and J. Y. Lu (1969) "A Monte Carlo Study of the Regression Model with Autoregressive Disturbances," Rand Memorandum RM5728PR.

Imhof, J. P. (1961) "Computing the Distribution of Quadratic Forms in Normal Variables," *Biometrika,* 48, 419–426.

Inder, B. A. (1984) "Finite-Sample Power of Tests for Autocorrelation in Models Containing Lagged Dependent Variables," *Economics Letters,* 14, 179–185.

Jarque, C. M. and A. K. Bera (1980) "Efficient Tests for Normality, Homoscedasticity and Serial Independence of Regression Residuals," *Economics Letters,* 6, 255–259.

Judge, G. G. and M. E. Bock (1978) *The Statistical Implications of Pre-Test and Stein-Rule Estimators in Econometrics,* North-Holland, Amsterdam.

Judge, G. G., W. E. Griffiths, R. C. Hill, and T. C. Lee (1980) *The Theory and Practice of Econometrics,* 1st ed., Wiley, New York.

Judge, G. G., R. C. Hill, W. E. Griffiths, H. Lütkepohl, and T. C. Lee (1982) *Introduction to the Theory and Practice of Econometrics,* Wiley, New York.

Kadiyala, K. R. (1968) "A Transformation Used to Circumvent the Problem of Autocorrelation," *Econometrica,* 36, 93–96.

Kenkel, J. L. (1974) "Some Small Sample Properties of Durbin's Tests for Serial Correlation in Regression Models Containing Lagged Dependent Variables," *Econometrica,* 42, 763–769.

Kenkel, J. L. (1975) "Small Sample Tests for Serial Correlation in Models Containing Lagged Dependent Variables," *Review of Economics and Statistics,* 57, 383–386.

Kenkel, J. L. (1976) "Comment on the Small Sample Power of Durbin's *h* Test," *Journal of the American Statistical Association,* 71, 96–97.

Kenward, L. R. (1975) "Autocorrelation and Dynamic Methodology with an Application to Wage Determination Models," *Journal of Econometrics,* 3, 179–187.

King, M. L. (1981a) "The Alternative Durbin–Watson Test: An Assessment of Durbin and Watson's Choice of Test Statistic," *Journal of Econometrics,* 17, 51–66.

King, M. L. (1981b) "The Durbin–Watson Bounds Test and Regressions Without an Intercept," *Australian Economic Papers,* 20, 161–170.

King, M. L. (1981c) "The Durbin–Watson Test for Serial Correlation: Bounds for Regressions with Trend and/or Seasonal Dummy Variables," *Econometrica,* 49, 1571–1581.

King, M. L. (1982a) "Testing for a Serially Correlated Component in Regression Disturbances," *International Economic Review,* 23, 577–582.

King, M. L. (1982b) "A Locally Optimal Bounds Test for Autoregressive Disturbances," Monash University, Department of Econometrics and Operations Research Working Paper No. 21/82, Melbourne, Australia.

King, M. L. (1983a) "Testing for Autoregressive Against Moving Average Errors in the Linear Regression Model," *Journal of Econometrics,* 21, 35–52.

King, M. L. (1983b) "The Durbin–Watson Test for Serial Correlation: Bounds for Regressions Using Monthly Data," *Journal of Econometrics,* 21, 357–366.

King, M. L. (1983c) "Testing for Autocorrelation in Linear Regression Models: A Survey," forthcoming in M. L. King and D. E. A. Giles, eds., *Specification Analysis in the Linear Model: Essays in Honour of Donald Cochrane.*

King, M. L. (1983d) "Testing for Moving Average Regression Disturbances," *Australian Journal of Statistics,* 25, 23–34.

King, M. L. (1983e) "A New Test for Fourth-Order Autoregressive Disturbances," *Journal of Econometrics,* forthcoming.

King, M. L. and M. A. Evans (1983) "A Joint Test for Serial Correlation and Heteroscedasticity," Working paper, Monash University, Melbourne.

King, M. L. and D. E. A. Giles (1977) "A Note on Wallis' Bounds Test and Negative Autocorrelation," *Econometrica,* 45, 1023–1026.

King, M. L. and D. E. A. Giles (1984) "Autocorrelation Pre-Testing in the Linear Model: Estimation, Testing and Prediction," *Journal of Econometrics,* forthcoming.

Kiviet, J. F. (1980) "Effects of ARMA Errors on Tests for Regression Coefficients: Comments on Vinod's Article; Improved and Additional Results," *Journal of the American Statistical Association,* 75, 353–358.

Kiviet, J. F. (1981) "On the Rigour of Some Specification Tests for Modelling Dynamic Relationships," working paper, University of Amsterdam.

Kmenta, J. (1971) *Elements of Econometrics,* Macmillan, New York.

Koerts, J. and A. P. J. Abrahamse (1968) "On the Power of the BLUS Procedure," *Journal of the American Statistical Association,* 63, 1227–1236.

Koerts, J. and A. P. J. Abrahamse (1969) *On the Theory and Application of the General Linear Model,* Rotterdam University Press, Rotterdam.

Kohn, R. (1981) "A Note on an Alternative Derivation of the Likelihood of an Autoregressive Moving Average Process," *Economics Letters,* 7, 233–236.

Krämer, W. (1980) "Finite Sample Efficiency of Ordinary Least Squares in the Linear Regression Model with Autocorrelated Errors," *Journal of the American Statistical Association,* 75, 1005–1009.

Krämer, W. (1982) "Note on Estimating Linear Trend When Residuals are Autocorrelated," *Econometrica,* 50, 1065–1067.

L'Esperance, W. L. and D. Taylor (1975) "The Power of Four Tests of Autocorrelation in the Linear Regression Model," *Journal of Econometrics,* 3, 1–21.

L'Esperance, W. L., D. Chall, and D. Taylor (1976) "An Algorithm for Determining the Distribution Function of the Durbin–Watson Statistic," *Econometrica,* 44, 1325–1346.

Ljung, G. M. and G. E. P. Box (1979) "The Likelihood Function of Stationary Autoregressive-Moving Average Models," *Biometrika,* 66, 265–270.

McClave, J. T. (1973) "On the Bias of Autoregressive Approximations to Moving Averages," *Biometrika,* 60, 599–605.

McNown, R. F. and K. R. Hunter (1980) "A Test for Autocorrelation in Models with Lagged Dependent Variables," *The Review of Economics and Statistics,* 62, 313–317.

Maddala, G. S. (1977) *Econometrics,* McGraw-Hill, New York.

Maddala, G. S. and A. S. Rao (1973) "Tests for Serial Correlation in Regression Models with Lagged Dependent Variables and Serially Correlated Errors," *Econometrica,* 41, 761–774.

Maeshiro, A. (1979) "On the Retention of the First Observations in Serial Correlation Adjustment of Regression Models," *International Economic Review,* 20, 259–265.

Magnus, J. R. (1978) "Maximum Likelihood Estimation of the GLS Model with Unknown Parameters in the Disturbance Covariance Matrix," *Journal of Econometrics,* 7, 281–312.

Malinvaud, E. (1970) *Statistical Methods in Econometrics,* North-Holland, Amsterdam.

Mentz, R. P. (1977) "Estimation in the First-Order Moving Average Model Through the Finite Autoregressive Approximation: Some Asymptotic Results," *Journal of Econometrics,* 6, 225–236.

Miyazaki, S. and W. E. Griffiths (1984) "The Properties of Some Covariance Matrix Estimators in Linear Models with AR(1) Errors," *Economics Letters,* 14, 351–356.

Mizon, G. E. and D. F. Hendry (1980) "An Empirical and Monte Carlo Analysis of Tests of Dynamic Specification,'' *Review of Economic Studies,* 47, 21–45.

Nakamura, A. and M. Nakamura (1978) ''On the Impact of the Tests for Serial Correlation upon the Test of Significance for the Regression Coefficient,'' *Journal of Econometrics,* 7, 199–210.

Nerlove, M. and K. F. Wallis (1966) ''Use of the Durbin–Watson Statistic in Inappropriate Situations,'' *Econometrica,* 34, 235–238.

Neudecker, H. (1977a) ''Bounds for the Bias of the Least Squares Estimator of σ^2 in the Case of a First-Order Autoregressive Process (Positive Autocorrelation),'' *Econometrica,* 45, 1257–1262.

Neudecker, H. (1977b) ''Abrahamse and Koerts New Estimator of Disturbances in Regression Analysis,'' *Journal of Econometrics,* 5, 129–132.

Neudecker, H. (1978) ''Bounds for the Bias of the LS Estimator of σ^2 in the Case of a First-Order (Positive) Autoregressive Process When the Regression Contains a Constant Term,'' *Econometrica,* 46, 1223–1226.

Newbold, P. (1974) ''The Exact Likelihood for a Mixed ARMA Process,'' *Biometrika,* 61, 423–426.

Newbold, P. and N. Davies (1978) ''Error Mis-Specification and Spurious Regressions,'' *International Economic Review,* 19, 513–520.

Nicholls, D. F. and A. R. Pagan (1977) ''Specification of the Disturbance for Efficient Estimation—An Extended Analysis,'' *Econometrica,* 45, 211–217.

Nicholls, D. F. and A. R. Pagan (1982) ''Estimating Predictions, Prediction Errors and Their Standard Deviations Using Constructed Variables,'' working paper, Australian National University, Canberra.

Nicholls, D. F., A. R. Pagan, and R. D. Terrell (1975) ''The Estimation and Use of Models with Moving Average Disturbance Terms: A Survey,'' *International Economic Review,* 16, 113–134.

O'Brien, R. J. (1970) ''Serial Correlation in Econometric Models,'' in K. Hilton and D. F. Heathfield, eds., *The Econometric Study of the United Kingdom,* Macmillan, London.

Osborn, D. R. (1976) ''Maximum Likelihood Estimation of Moving Average Processes,'' *Annals of Economic and Social Measurement,* 3, 75–87.

Osborn, D. R. (1982) ''On the Criteria Functions Used for the Estimation of Moving Average Processes,'' *Journal of the American Statistical Association,* 77, 388–392.

Pagan, A. (1973) ''Efficient Estimation of Models with Composite Disturbance Terms,'' *Journal of Econometrics,* 1, 329–340.

Pagan, A. (1974) ''A Generalized Approach to the Treatment of Autocorrelation,'' *Australian Economic Papers,* 13, 267–280.

Pagan, A. R. and R. P. Byron (1978) ''A Synthetic Approach to the Estimation of Models with Autocorrelated Disturbance Terms,'' in A. R. Bergstrom et al., eds., *Stability and Inflation,* Wiley, New York.

Pagan, A. R. and D. F. Nicholls (1976) ''Exact Maximum Likelihood Estimation of Regression Models with Finite Order Moving Average Errors,'' *Review of Economic Studies,* 43, 383–388.

Pan Jei-jian (1968) ''Distributions of the Noncircular Serial Correlation Coeffi-

cients," *Selected Translations in Mathematical Statistics, 7, Institute of Mathematical Statistics* and the *American Mathematical Society.*
Park, C. Y. and R. G. Heikes (1983) "A Note on Balestra's (1980) Approximate Estimator for the First-Order Moving Average Process," *Journal of Econometrics,* 21, 387–388.
Park, R. E. and B. M. Mitchell (1980) "Estimating the Autocorrelated Error Model with Trended Data," *Journal of Econometrics,* 13, 185–201.
Park, S. (1975) "On the Small-Sample Power of Durbin's h Test," *Journal of the American Statistical Association,* 70, 60–63.
Park, S. (1976) "Rejoinder," *Journal of the American Statistical Association,* 71, 97–98.
Pearlman, J. G. (1980) "An Algorithm for the Exact Likelihood of a High-Order Autoregressive Moving Average Process," *Biometrika,* 67, 232–233.
Peck, J. K. (1976) "The Estimation of a Dynamic Equation Following a Preliminary Test for Autocorrelation," Cowles Foundation Discussion Paper No. 404R, Yale University, New Haven, Conn.
Pesaran, M. H. (1973) "Exact Maximum Likelihood Estimation of a Regression Equation with a First-Order Moving-Average Error," *Review of Economic Studies,* 40, 529–536.
Phadke, M. S. and G. Kedem (1978) "Computation of the Exact Likelihood Function of Multivariate Moving Average Models," *Biometrika,* 65, 511–519.
Phillips, A. W. (1966) "The Estimation of Systems of Difference Equations with Moving Average Disturbances," Econometrics Society Meeting, San Francisco, reprinted in A. E. Bergstrom et al., eds., *Stability and Inflation,* Wiley, New York.
Phillips, G. D. A. and A. C. Harvey (1974) "A Simple Test for Serial Correlation in Regression Analysis," *Journal of the American Statistical Association,* 69, 935–939.
Phillips, P. C. B. (1979) "The Sampling Distribution of Forecasts from a First-Order Autoregression," *Journal of Econometrics,* 9, 241–261.
Pierce, D. A. (1971) "Distribution of Residual Autocorrelations in the Regression Model with Autoregressive—Moving Average Errors," *Journal of the Royal Statistical Society,* Series B, 33, 140–146.
Poirier, D. J. (1978) "The Effect of the First Observation in Regression Models with First-Order Autoregressive Disturbances," *Applied Statistics,* 27, 67–68.
Praetz, P. D. (1979) "The Detection of Omitted Variables by Durbin–Watson Statistics in Multiple Regression Models," *Australian Journal of Statistics,* 21, 129–138.
Prais, S. J. and C. B. Winsten (1954) "Trend Estimators and Serial Correlation," Cowles Commission Discussion Paper No. 383, Chicago.
Revankar, N. S. (1980) "Analysis of Regressions Containing Serially Correlated and Serially Uncorrelated Error Components," *International Economic Review,* 21, 185–200.
Richard, J. F. (1975) "Bayesian Analysis of the Regression Model When the

Disturbances Are Generated by an Autoregressive Process," in Ahmet Aykac and Carlo Brumat, eds., *New Developments in the Applications of Bayesian Methods,* North-Holland, Amsterdam.

Salkever, D. S. (1976) "The Use of Dummy Variables to Compute Predictions, Prediction Errors and Confidence Intervals," *Journal of Econometrics,* 4, 393–397.

Sargan, J. D. (1964) "Wages and Prices in the United Kingdom: A Study in Econometric Methodology" in P. E. Hart, G. Mills, and J. K. Whitaker, eds., *Econometric Analysis for National Economic Planning,* Butterworths, London, 25–54.

Sargan, J. D. (1980) "Some Tests of Dynamic Specification for a Single Equation," *Econometrica,* 48, 879–897.

Sargan, J. D. and A. Bhargava (1983a) "Testing Residuals from Least Squares Regression for Being Generated by the Gaussian Random Walk," *Econometrica,* 51, 153–174.

Sargan, J. D. and A. Bhargava (1983b) "Maximum Likelihood Estimation of Regression Models with First Order Moving Average Errors when the Root Lies on the Unit Circle," *Econometrica,* 51, 799–820.

Sargan, J. D. and F. Mehta (1983) "A Generalization of the Durbin Significance Test and its Application to Dynamic Specification," *Econometrica,* 51, 1551–1569.

Sathe, S. T. and H. D. Vinod (1974) "Bounds on the Variance of Regression Coefficients due to Heteroscedastic or Autoregressive Errors," *Econometrica,* 42, 333–340.

Savin, N. E. and K. J. White (1977) "The Durbin–Watson Test for Serial Correlation with Extreme Sample Sizes or Many Regressors," *Econometrica,* 45, 1989–1996.

Schmidt, P. (1971) "Estimation of a Distributed Lag Model with Second Order Autoregressive Disturbances: A Monte Carlo Experiment," *International Economic Review,* 12, 372–380.

Schmidt, P. (1972) "A Generalization of the Durbin–Watson Test," *Australian Economic Papers,* 11, 203–209.

Schmidt, P. and D. K. Guilkey (1975) "Some Further Evidence on the Power of the Durbin–Watson and Geary Tests," *Review of Economics and Statistics,* 57, 379–382.

Shaman, P. (1973) "On the Inverse of the Covariance Matrix for an Autoregressive-Moving Average Process," *Biometrika,* 60, 193–196.

Sims, C. A. (1975) "A Note on Exact Tests for Serial Correlation," *Journal of the American Statistical Association,* 70, 162–165.

Smith, V. K. (1976) "The Estimated Power of Several Tests for Autocorrelation with Non-First-Order Alternatives," *Journal of the American Statistical Association,* 71, 879–883.

Spencer, B. G. (1975) "The Small Sample Bias of Durbin's Tests for Serial Correlation When One of the Regressors Is the Lagged Dependent Variable and the Null Hypothesis Is True," *Journal of Econometrics,* 3, 249–254.

Spitzer, J. J. (1979) "Small-Sample Properties of Nonlinear Least Squares and

Maximum Likelihood Estimators in the Context of Autocorrelated Errors," *Journal of the American Statistical Association,* 74, 41–47.
Spitzer, J. J. and R. T. Baillie (1983) "Small-Sample Properties of Predictions from the Regression Model with Autoregressive Errors," *Journal of the American Statistical Association,* 78, 258–263.
Taylor, William E. (1981) "On the Efficiency of the Cochrane–Orcutt Estimator," *Journal of Econometrics,* 17, 67–82.
Theil, H. (1971) *Principles of Econometrics,* Wiley, New York.
Theil, H. and A. L. Nagar (1961) "Testing the Independence of Regression Disturbances," *Journal of the American Statistical Association,* 56, 793–806.
Thomas, J. J. and K. F. Wallis (1971) "Seasonal Variation in Regression Analysis," *Journal of the Royal Statistical Society,* Series A, 134, 67–72.
Thursby, J. G. (1981) "A Test Strategy for Discriminating Between Autocorrelation and Misspecification in Regression Analysis," *The Review of Economics and Statistics,* 63, 117–123.
Tiao, G. C. and M. M. Ali (1971) "Analysis of Correlated Random Effects: Linear Model with Two Random Components," *Biometrika,* 58, 37–51.
Tillman, J. A. (1974) "The Relative Power of the τ-Test: A Comment," *The Review of Economics and Statistics,* 56, 416–417.
Tillman, J. A. (1975) "The Power of the Durbin–Watson Test," *Econometrica,* 43, 959–973.
Trivedi, P. L. (1970) "Inventory Behavior in U. K. Manufacturing, 1956–67," *Review of Economic Studies,* 37, 517–527.
Ullah, A., V. K. Srivastrava, L. Magee, and A. Srivastava (1983) "Estimation of Linear Regression Model with Autocorrelated Disturbances," *Journal of Time Series Analysis,* 4, 127–135.
Vinod, H. D. (1973) "Generalization of the Durbin–Watson Statistic for Higher Order Autoregressive Processes," *Communications in Statistics,* 2, 115–144.
Vinod, H. D. (1976) "Effects of ARMA Errors on the Significance Tests for Regression Coefficients," *Journal of the American Statistical Association,* 71, 929–933.
Wallis, K. F. (1972) "Testing for Fourth-Order Autocorrelation in Quarterly Regression Equations," *Econometrica,* 40, 617–636.
Watson, G. S. and E. J. Hannan (1956) "Serial Correlation in Regression Analysis II," *Biometrika,* 43, 436–445.
Weber, J. E. and D. E. Monarchi (1982) "Performance of the Durbin–Watson Test and WLS Estimation when the Disturbance Term Includes Serial Dependence in Addition to First-Order Autocorrelation," *Journal of the American Statistical Association,* 77, 117–128.
White, K. J. (1978) "A General Computer Program for Econometric Models—SHAZAM," *Econometrica,* 46, 239–240.
Wise, J. (1955) "Autocorrelation Function and the Spectral Density Function," *Biometrika,* 42, 151–159.
Yamamoto, T. (1976) "Asymptotic Mean Square Prediction Error for an

Autoregressive Model with Estimated Coefficients," *Applied Statistics*, 25, 123–127.

Yamamoto, T. (1979) "On the Prediction Efficiency of the Generalized Least Squares Model with an Estimated Variance Covariance Matrix," *International Economic Review*, 20, 693–705.

Zellner, A. (1971) *An Introduction to Bayesian Inference in Econometrics*, Wiley, New York.

Zellner, A. and G. C. Tiao (1964) "Bayesian Analysis of the Regression Model with Autocorrelated Errors," *Journal of the American Statistical Association*, 59, 763–778.

Chapter 9

Finite Distributed Lags

9.1 INTRODUCTION

In many situations there is an obvious time lag between a decision made by some economic agent and the completion of the action initiated thereby. For instance, if a company decides to carry out an investment project, some time will elapse before it is completed. Taken together, all capital x_t appropriated at a time t by all firms of a particular region will induce payments y to be made in periods $t + 1$, $t + 2$, and so on. In other words, the capital expenditures y_t of period t depend on the capital appropriations of earlier time periods, x_{t-1}, $x_{t-2}, \ldots$.

Examples of consumer lag behavior are also numerous. A higher income may cause a family to seek a new apartment but not until the present lease expires. If a person is promoted to a higher salary bracket, he or she may also move from the Chevrolet to the Pontiac class, but may want to wait for the new model. Also, a higher income may cause the household to graduate to a larger size of refrigerator, but if the present one is new, it will probably not be replaced at once. Thus, because of habit persistence and lags in consumer behavior, current consumption (y_t) is often hypothesized as a function of "lagged" income (x_{t-1}).

A more general hypothesis is that the lagged effect of a change in an independent variable is not felt all at once at a single point in time, but the impact is distributed over a number of future points in time. That is, the dependent variable y_t depends on lagged values of the independent variable. The length of the lag may sometimes be known a priori, but usually it is unknown and in many cases it is assumed to be infinite. The structure of the lag effect may take on a variety of shapes. For example, it may decline gradually or have a very small impact immediately following the cause, and rise fast, reaching its peak impact after a short interval and then tapering off slowly. These lagged effects arise from habit persistence, institutional or technological constraints, and/or expectational effects that link anticipations with experience.

With lag behavior in the firm and household, the resulting market equilibrium will also be dynamic. For example, the equilibrium price in a cobweb model is a distributed lag function. A distributed lag will also result from the market in which producers never learn, expecting the price of the previous period and thus always being disappointed. The market models with changing stocks under different assumptions of price settings by merchants will also result in a distributed lag function for equilibrium price. For a range of examples, see Allen (1959). It is thus clear that in order to describe or model how economic data are generated, time lags must often be included in the relations of an economic model.

Generally, if we only consider one dependent and one explanatory variable we get a model of the form

$$y_t = \alpha + \beta_0 x_t + \beta_1 x_{t-1} + \ldots + e_t \tag{9.1.1}$$

and we assume that the variable x at all times is independent of the stochastic process e_t. At this point allowing an infinite number of lagged x_t in the model is a matter of convenience since it does not force us to specify a maximal lag at this stage. Also we will see in Chapter 10 that there may be theoretical reasons for postulating an infinite lag length.

In order to keep the discussion simple we assume in this chapter that e_t is a normally distributed white noise process with zero mean. To assume a specific process has implications for the estimation and interpretation of the relationship postulated in (9.1.1). Furthermore, it will be assumed that $\beta_n = 0$ for $n > n^*$ so that (9.1.1) is a finite distributed lag model with lag length n^*. More general types of distributed lag models will be considered in Chapter 10.

The organization of the present chapter is as follows: In the next section the general problem of estimating lag weights and lag lengths without assuming any constraints for the former is considered. It will be pointed out that constraining the lag weights can improve the estimation accuracy, and various restricted lag formulations will be discussed in Sections 9.3 to 9.7. A summary is given in Section 9.8. A visual representation of this chapter is presented in Table 9.1.

9.2 UNCONSTRAINED LAGS

In this section the estimation of a model of the general form

$$y_t = \sum_{i=0}^{n^*} \beta_i x_{t-i} + e_t \tag{9.2.1}$$

will be discussed. The β_i are the unknown distributed lag coefficients or weights, the x_{t-i} are lagged values of the explanatory variable, $n^*(<\infty)$ is the lag length and e_t is independent white noise. The x_t will be assumed to be nonstochastic for convenience. We will first repeat some estimation results when n^* is assumed to be known and then investigate joint estimation of the lag length n^* and the lag weights.

9.2.1 Estimation When the Lag Length Is Known

Assuming that T observations on y_t and x_t and n^* presample values of x_t are available the model (9.2.1) can be written in matrix notation as

$$\mathbf{y} = X\boldsymbol{\beta} + \mathbf{e} \tag{9.2.2}$$

TABLE 9.1 ***FINITE DISTRIBUTED LAGS***

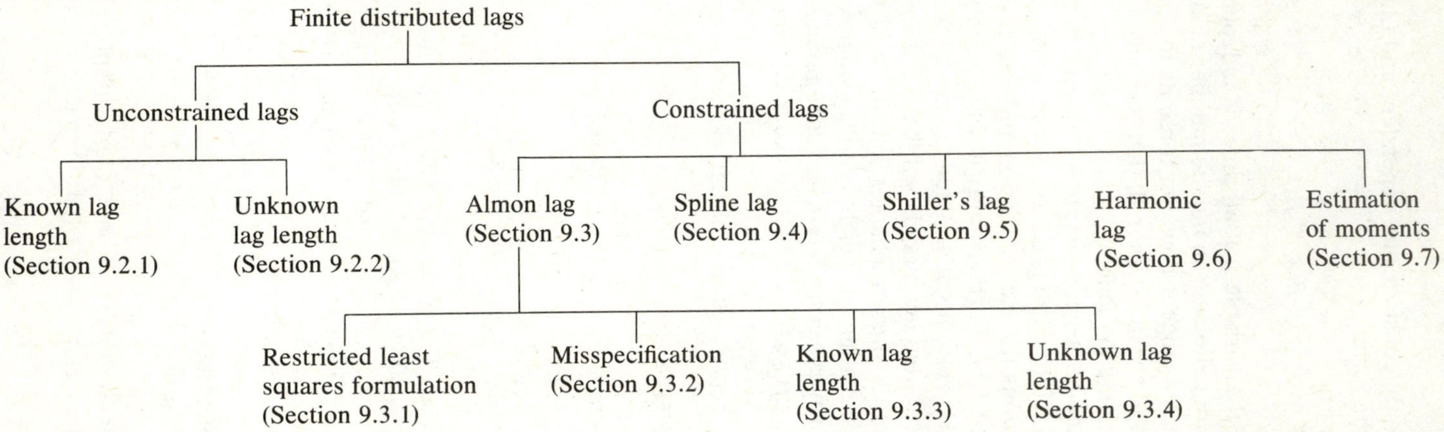

where

$$X = \begin{bmatrix} x_1 & x_0 & \cdots & x_{-n^*+1} \\ x_2 & x_1 & \cdots & x_{-n^*+2} \\ \vdots & \vdots & \vdots & \vdots \\ x_T & x_{T-1} & \cdots & x_{T-n^*} \end{bmatrix} \tag{9.2.3}$$

$\mathbf{y}' = (y_1, \ldots, y_T)$, $\boldsymbol{\beta}' = (\beta_0, \ldots, \beta_{n^*})$, and $\mathbf{e}' = (e_1, \ldots, e_T)$. If the vector of random variables $\mathbf{e}$ is normally distributed with mean vector zero and covariance matrix $\sigma^2 I$, then the least squares estimator $\mathbf{b} = (X'X)^{-1}X'\mathbf{y}$ is best unbiased with an $N(\boldsymbol{\beta},\sigma^2(X'X)^{-1})$ distribution.

To investigate the asymptotic distribution of $\mathbf{b}$ we make the following assumptions:

1. $d_T^2 = x_1^2 + x_2^2 + \ldots + x_T^2 \underset{T\to\infty}{\longrightarrow} \infty$ (9.2.4a)

2. $\lim_{T\to\infty} \frac{x_T^2}{d_T^2} = 0$ (9.2.4b)

3. $R = \lim_{T\to\infty} D_T^{-1}X'XD_T^{-1}$ (9.2.4c)

where $D_T = \text{diag.}(d_T, \ldots, d_T) = d_T I_{n^*+1}$, is finite and nonsingular.

These conditions are sometimes referred to as *Grenander conditions*. They are not very restrictive and are discussed in more detail in Chapter 5. If we assume that the Grenander conditions are satisfied, then the least squares estimator $\mathbf{b}$ is consistent and $D_T(\mathbf{b} - \boldsymbol{\beta})$ is asymptotically normally distributed with variance-covariance matrix $\sigma^2 R^{-1}$; that is,

$$D_T(\mathbf{b} - \boldsymbol{\beta}) \xrightarrow{d} N(\mathbf{0},\sigma^2 R^{-1}) \tag{9.2.5}$$

(see Chapter 5). Now we are ready to investigate the estimation problem with unknown lag length.

9.2.2 Estimation of the Lag Length

If the lag length n^* is unknown the number of regressors to be used in the linear model (9.2.1) is unknown. Using $n \neq n^*$ regressors implies biased ($n < n^*$) or inefficient ($n > n^*$) estimators for the lag weights. To estimate the lag length, the criteria for model selection discussed in Chapter 21 can be employed. Here we will only discuss some possible candidates reformulated for the present situation. For example, Akaike's (1973) information criterion assumes the form

$$\text{AIC}(n) = \ln \tilde{\sigma}_n^2 + \frac{2n}{T} \tag{9.2.6}$$

where $\tilde{\sigma}_n^2$ is the maximum likelihood estimator for σ^2 evaluated under the assumption that $n = n^*$ and an estimate $\hat{n}$(AIC) of n^* is chosen so that AIC assumes its minimum for $n = \hat{n}$. That is, $\hat{n} = \hat{n}_T(\text{AIC})$ is chosen such that

$$\text{AIC}(\hat{n}_T(\text{AIC})) = \min\{\text{AIC}(n) | n = 0, 1, \ldots, N_T\} \tag{9.2.7}$$

where N_T is the maximum lag length the investigator is prepared to consider if a sample of size T is available.

Other suggested criteria that could be minimized instead of AIC are

$$\text{PC}(n) = \tilde{\sigma}_n^2 \frac{T + n + 1}{T - n + 1} \tag{9.2.8}$$

$$\text{SC}(n) = \ln \tilde{\sigma}_n^2 + \frac{n \ln T}{T} \tag{9.2.9}$$

$$\text{CAT}(n) = \frac{\sum_{j=0}^{n} \tilde{\sigma}_j^{-2}(T - j - 1)}{T^2} - \frac{\tilde{\sigma}_n^{-2}(T - n - 1)}{T} \tag{9.2.10}$$

$$C_p(n) = \tilde{\sigma}_n^2 + \frac{2n\hat{\sigma}^2}{T} \tag{9.2.11}$$

and

$$\text{BEC}(n) = \tilde{\sigma}_n^2 + \frac{n\tilde{\sigma}_{N_T}^2 \ln T}{T - N_T - 1} \tag{9.2.12}$$

where $\hat{\sigma}^2 = T\tilde{\sigma}_{N_T}^2/(T - N_T - 1)$ in (9.2.11). To investigate the properties of the resulting estimators we follow Geweke and Meese (1981) and define

$$X_n = \begin{bmatrix} x_1 & x_0 & \cdots & x_{-n+1} \\ x_2 & x_1 & \cdots & x_{-n+2} \\ \vdots & \vdots & & \vdots \\ x_T & x_{T-1} & \cdots & x_{T-n} \end{bmatrix} \tag{9.2.13}$$

We assume that $X_n'X_n$ is nonsingular for $n < T$ and also

$$R_n = \lim_{T\to\infty} D_T^{-1} X_n' X_n D_T^{-1} \tag{9.2.14}$$

exists and is nonsingular. Here $D_T = \text{diag.}(d_T, \ldots, d_T)$ is an $((n + 1) \times (n + 1))$ matrix and d_T is as defined in (9.2.4a). Furthermore we define $\boldsymbol{\beta}_n' = (\beta_0, \ldots, \beta_n)$ and maintain the assumption that the error vector of $\mathbf{y} = X\boldsymbol{\beta} + \mathbf{e} = X_n\boldsymbol{\beta}_n + \mathbf{e}$ is normally distributed with zero mean and covariance matrix $\sigma^2 I$ for $n \geq n^*$. In addition, the conditions (9.2.4) are assumed to hold.

Geweke and Meese show that under these assumptions, if $T \to \infty$ and $N_T \to \infty$, the probability that $\hat{n}_T$ is less than n^* vanishes for all the forementioned criteria, that is, $P\{\hat{n}_T < n^*\} \to_{T\to\infty} 0$. In other words, the probability of underestimating the true lag length becomes zero if T is large. On the other hand, for all criteria but SC and BEC the probability of overestimating the true lag length does not vanish, that is, $P\{\hat{n}_T > n^*\} > 0$ if $\hat{n}_T = \hat{n}_T(\text{AIC})$, $\hat{n}_T(\text{PC})$, $\hat{n}_T(\text{CAT})$, or $\hat{n}_T(C_p)$. Of the above criteria SC and BEC lead to a consistent estimator for n^*. To be precise, $P\{\hat{n}_T = n^*\} \to 1$ for $T \to \infty$ if $\hat{n}_T = \hat{n}_T(\text{SC})$ or $\hat{n}_T(\text{BEC})$. Using these estimators for the lag length the *asymptotic* distribution of the estimator of the lag weights will be the same as if n^* were known.

Geweke and Meese (1981) also give upper bounds for $P\{\hat{n}_T(\text{AIC}) \leq n^* + j\}$ and $P\{\hat{n}_T(\text{SC}) \leq n^* + j\}$ for various nonnegative integers j and sample sizes T, and they perform Monte Carlo experiments to investigate the small sample behavior of the different estimators. Their results indicate that for $T \geq 100$ the small sample results are close to the theoretical asymptotic results.

Note that the above results do not imply that the inconsistent criteria such as AIC and C_p are necessarily useless for estimating the lag length. In fact, Shibata (1981) proves some optimality properties of these criteria. Assuming that the true lag length is infinite, he shows that, under weak conditions, PC, AIC, and C_p choose the finite lag model that asymptotically minimizes the sum of squared errors of prediction.

As an alternative to the above model-selection procedures, sequential tests could be used to estimate the lag length. We only mention an interesting variant suggested by Pagano and Hartley (1981). They propose to use an orthogonal reparameterization of the model. For the details see their paper.

9.2.3 Some Problems

In economic applications the lag length is occasionally quite substantial—for example, if an order-delivery relationship is considered. If, in such a situation, x_t is a variable that does not change much or moves regularly around its mean, the columns of the regression matrix in (9.2.3) may be nearly linearly dependent; that is, $X'X$ may be nearly singular. This is the typical multicollinearity situation considered in Chapter 22. In the context of distributed lag estimation various procedures to cope with this problem have been proposed. Generally speaking, the dimension of the parameter space is reduced by assuming that the lag weights β_i are values of a function $f(i)$ that depends on less than $n^* + 1$ parameters. For instance, if the lag coefficients decline arithmetically as in Figure 9.1, we have

$$\beta_i = f(i) = \begin{cases} (n^* + 1 - i)\alpha & i = 0, 1, \ldots, n^* \\ 0 & \text{otherwise} \end{cases} \tag{9.2.15}$$

which depends only on the parameter α. This lag function was actually suggested by Fisher (1937). He regarded this as a computationally simple specifica-

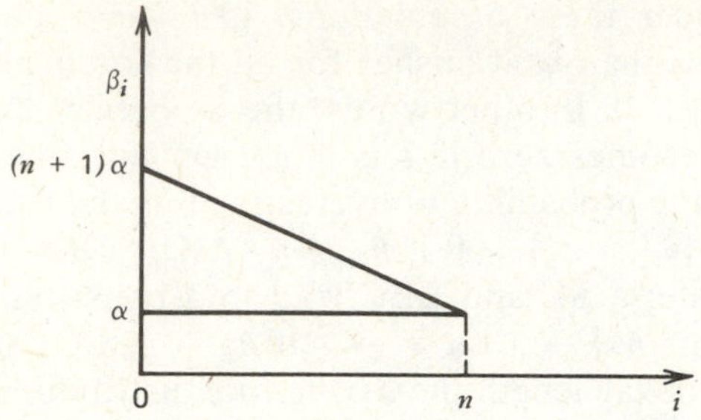

Figure 9.1 An arithmetic distributed lag.

tion and a very rough approximation to the actual lag scheme. Another example is due to DeLeeuw (1962). He used the inverted-V lag, which is defined by

$$\beta_i = f(i) = \begin{cases} (i + 1)\alpha & 0 \le i \le s \\ (n^* - i + 1)\alpha & s + 1 \le i \le n^* \\ 0 & \text{otherwise} \end{cases} \qquad (9.2.16)$$

(see Figure 9.2). We will not elaborate on these lag schemes because they are relatively inflexible. Instead, we will concentrate on more general attempts to overcome the multicollinearity problem in the following sections.

9.3 THE ALMON DISTRIBUTED LAG

A rather popular method of reducing the effect of multicollinearity in the present context is proposed by Almon (1965). She suggests using the fact that for any real numbers $\beta_0, \beta_1, \ldots, \beta_{n^*}$ a polynomial $P(z)$ of order not greater than n^* can be found such that $P(i) = \beta_i$, $i = 0, 1, \ldots, n^*$. The polynomial degree may be substantially lower than n^*, especially if we do not require an exact equality between $P(i)$ and β_i but are satisfied with an approximate fit.

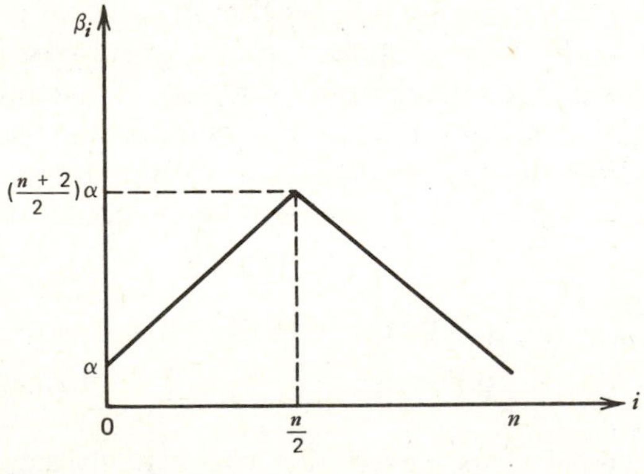

Figure 9.2 The inverted V lag.

In the Almon procedure it is assumed that the lag weights can be represented by a polynomial of degree $q < n^*$,

$$\beta_i = \alpha_0 + \alpha_1 i + \ldots + \alpha_q i^q \tag{9.3.1}$$

or

$$\boldsymbol{\beta} = H\boldsymbol{\alpha} \tag{9.3.2}$$

where $\boldsymbol{\alpha}' = (\alpha_0, \alpha_1, \ldots, \alpha_q)$ and

$$H = \begin{bmatrix} 1 & 0 & 0 & \ldots & 0 \\ 1 & 1 & 1 & \ldots & 1 \\ 1 & 2 & 2^2 & \ldots & 2^q \\ \vdots & \vdots & \vdots & & \vdots \\ 1 & n^* & n^{*2} & \ldots & n^{*q} \end{bmatrix} \tag{9.3.3}$$

The parameters $\boldsymbol{\alpha}$ may be estimated by substituting (9.3.2) into (9.2.2) to obtain

$$\mathbf{y} = XH\boldsymbol{\alpha} + \mathbf{e} = Z\boldsymbol{\alpha} + \mathbf{e} \tag{9.3.4}$$

and applying least squares. The estimator $\hat{\boldsymbol{\alpha}} = (Z'Z)^{-1}Z'\mathbf{y}$ is distributed $N(\boldsymbol{\alpha},\sigma^2(Z'Z)^{-1})$. An estimator of $\boldsymbol{\beta}$ is $\hat{\boldsymbol{\beta}} = H\hat{\boldsymbol{\alpha}}$, which is distributed

$$N(\boldsymbol{\beta},\sigma^2 H(Z'Z)^{-1}H')$$

if the model is correct.

This model has been widely used in applied econometric work because of the flexibility of the polynomial lag shape, the economy in terms of the number of parameters that must be estimated and the ease of estimation. However, the method is beset with difficulties and an extensive body of literature has developed proposing methods to cope with them. The estimators generated by these procedures, unfortunately, have sampling distributions and properties that are unknown as they often follow complicated pretesting schemes. These consequences are sometimes ignored in the literature. In the following the restricted least squares nature of the Almon lag is presented and the consequences of model misspecification noted, procedures suggested for operating when the polynomial degree and/or lag length are unknown are reviewed, and recommendations are given.

9.3.1 A Restricted Least Squares Formulation

The specification of the finite polynomial distributed lag presented above represents what Cooper (1972) calls the direct approach. A more explicit formulation of the restricted least squares nature of the Almon model is useful when discussing its properties. The relation $\boldsymbol{\beta} = H\boldsymbol{\alpha}$ implies that

$$\boldsymbol{\alpha} = H^{+}\boldsymbol{\beta} = (H'H)^{-1}H'\boldsymbol{\beta} \tag{9.3.5}$$

where H^{+} is the generalized inverse of H. It follows that

$$\begin{aligned} \mathbf{0} &= \boldsymbol{\beta} - H\boldsymbol{\alpha} \\ &= \boldsymbol{\beta} - HH^{+}\boldsymbol{\beta} \\ &= (I - H(H'H)^{-1}H')\boldsymbol{\beta} \end{aligned} \tag{9.3.6}$$

The estimator $\hat{\boldsymbol{\beta}} = H\hat{\boldsymbol{\alpha}}$, where $\hat{\boldsymbol{\alpha}} = (Z'Z)^{-1}Z'\mathbf{y}$, is equivalent to the restricted least squares estimator (Section 3.2) obtained by estimating (9.2.1) subject to $n^* - q$ independent linear homogeneous restrictions of the form $R\boldsymbol{\beta} = \mathbf{0}$ from the $n^* + 1$ equations (9.3.6).

There are several other ways to formulate the model and each simply represents the choice of a different, but equivalent, restriction matrix R. They are all equivalent, since each represents a nonsingular transformation of the restriction matrix R which does not affect the results for the lag weights. The first is from Almon's original work in which Lagrangian interpolation polynomials [Apostol (1962)] were employed. Almon noted that if the $n^* + 1$ lag weights β_i were to lie upon a polynomial of degree q, they could be calculated as linear combinations of any $q + 1$ points on the polynomial; that is

$$\boldsymbol{\beta} = Q'\boldsymbol{\beta}_1 \tag{9.3.7}$$

where Q is a $((q + 1) \times (n^* + 1))$ matrix of Lagrangian interpolation coefficients whose (k,m)th element is

$$Q_{km} = \prod_{\substack{j=1 \\ j \neq k}}^{q+1} \frac{m - j}{k - j} \tag{9.3.8}$$

and $\boldsymbol{\beta}_1$ contains $q + 1$ elements of $\boldsymbol{\beta}$, here chosen to be $\beta_0, \ldots, \beta_q$. The coefficients Q_{km} have the property that $Q_{km} = \delta_{km}$, $k, m = 1, \ldots, q + 1$, where δ_{km} is the Kronecker delta. Using these properties, Q may be partitioned as $Q = [I_{q+1} : Q_R']$ which leads to $n^* - q$ restrictions [Hill and Johnson (1976)]

$$R\boldsymbol{\beta} = [Q_R : -I_{n*-q}]\boldsymbol{\beta} = \mathbf{0} \tag{9.3.9}$$

These restrictions may equivalently be imposed by substituting (9.3.7) into (9.2.2) to obtain

$$\mathbf{y} = XQ'\boldsymbol{\beta}_1 + \mathbf{e} = P\boldsymbol{\beta}_1 + \mathbf{e} \tag{9.3.10}$$

Then $\boldsymbol{\beta}$ may be estimated as $\tilde{\boldsymbol{\beta}} = Q'\tilde{\boldsymbol{\beta}}_1$, where $\tilde{\boldsymbol{\beta}}_1 = (P'P)^{-1}P'\mathbf{y}$. Again, if the restrictions (9.3.9) are correct, $\tilde{\boldsymbol{\beta}}$ is best linear and unbiased with covariance matrix $\sigma^2 Q'(P'P)^{-1}Q$. As a practical matter, *although the direct approach is expositionally more convenient, the Almon approach represented by* (9.3.10) *appears to produce less computational error* [Cooper (1972), Trivedi and Pagan (1979)] as $Z = XH$ may be near singular and $Z'Z$ difficult to invert.

Furthermore the Almon approach is advantageous if there are particular restrictions for any of the lag weights; for example, if a lag coefficient is known to be zero such a constraint can easily be imposed in the above setting. Especially when *endpoint constraints* ($\beta_{-1} = \beta_{n^*+1} = 0$) are imposed this possibility may be of interest. If the lag model is known to be of the form (9.2.1), then the endpoint constraints represent nonsample information that Almon (1965) used in her pioneering study. Note, however, that these constraints may imply restrictions for the possible lag shapes the researcher has no intention to impose. These undesirable effects on the estimates of the lag weights are demonstrated by Dhrymes (1971, pp. 231–234), Trivedi (1970), and Schmidt and Waud (1973).

Shiller (1973) has pointed out an alternative way to derive the restriction matrix. If $f(i)$ is a polynomial in i of degree q, then $(1 - L)^{q+1}f(i) = 0$, where $Lf(i) = f(i - 1)$. Thus, since $\beta_i = f(i)$, we get $(1 - L)^{q+1}\beta_i = 0$ for $i = q + 1, \ldots, n^*$ and a $((n^* - q) \times (n^* + 1))$ restriction matrix can be derived by setting the $(i, i + j)$th element equal to the coefficient of L^j in the expansion of $(1 - L)^{q+1}$, $i = 1, \ldots, n^* - q$; $j = 0, \ldots, q + 1$, with all remaining elements being zero. A different way to derive the constraints for the lag coefficients is used in Judge et al. (1982, Chapter 27).

9.3.2 Effects of Misspecifying the Polynomial Degree and/or Lag Length

In the analysis presented above it has been presumed that the Almon distributed lag model has been specified correctly, implying that the polynomial degree q and lag length n^* are known a priori. Unfortunately, these parameters are seldom if ever known in applications. Several studies have investigated the effects of misspecifying the lag length or polynomial degree in an Almon lag model. See, for example, Frost (1975), Schmidt and Waud (1973), Trivedi (1970), Teräsvirta (1976), Harper (1977), Griffiths and Kerrison (1978), Schmidt and Sickles (1975), Trivedi and Pagan (1979), and Thomas (1977).

Studies of the consequences of applying incorrect restrictions to a linear model show that [from Trivedi and Pagan (1979)]:

1. If the assumed polynomial degree is correct, but the assumed lag length is greater than the true lag length, the polynomial distributed lag estimator will generally be biased. It will definitely be biased if the difference between the assumed and true lag length is greater than the degree of the approximating polynomial.
2. If the assumed polynomial degree is correct, then understating the true lag length usually leads to bias in the polynomial distributed lag estimator.
3. If the assumed lag length is correct, but the assumed polynomial is of an order higher than the true polynomial, the polynomial distributed lag estimator is unbiased but inefficient.

4. If the assumed lag length is correct, but the assumed polynomial is of lower order than the true polynomial, then the polynomial distributed lag estimator is always biased.

These results have led researchers to adopt procedures using the sample data to obtain information about the polynomial degree and/or lag length. Some of these methods are reviewed below.

9.3.3 Procedures for Estimating the Polynomial Degree When the True Lag Length is Known

When the lag length n^* is known, the nested nature of the restrictions associated with increasing the polynomial degree q may be used to construct likelihood ratio tests for the "optimal" polynomial degree. Such procedures have been suggested by Teräsvirta (1976), Godfrey and Poskitt (1975), Trivedi and Pagan (1979), and Hill and Johnson (1976). Since a polynomial of degree q may be imposed on the lag weights by specifying $n^* - q$ linear homogeneous restrictions of the form $R\boldsymbol{\beta} = \mathbf{0}$ on the model $\mathbf{y} = X\boldsymbol{\beta} + \mathbf{e}$, these restrictions may be viewed as hypotheses and tested under a variety of norms. If the linear hypotheses are $R\boldsymbol{\beta} = \mathbf{0}$, the appropriate test statistic is

$$u = \frac{\mathbf{b}'R'[R(X'X)^{-1}R']^{-1}R\mathbf{b}}{(n^* - q)\hat{\sigma}^2} \tag{9.3.11}$$

which is distributed as a noncentral F random variable with $n^* - q$ and $T - n^* - 1$ degrees of freedom and noncentrality parameter

$$\lambda = \frac{\boldsymbol{\beta}'R'[R(X'X)^{-1}R']^{-1}R\boldsymbol{\beta}}{2\sigma^2} \tag{9.3.12}$$

Under alternative measures of goodness the test statistic u has different distributions under the null hypothesis. The various norms, hypotheses, and test procedures are summarized in Table 9.2.

A possible testing procedure, when the lag length n^* is known, is to select a maximum polynomial degree that is felt to be greater than the true degree [if no notion of a maximum degree is held, one may choose a polynomial of degree n^*, which corresponds to the unrestricted model (9.2.1)], sequentially lower the polynomial degree by one, thus *adding* one restriction; and then choose as the best polynomial degree that which produces the *last acceptable hypothesis under the adopted norm and test procedure*. When carrying out this sequential procedure, care should be taken with respect to the level of Type I error chosen for each individual test. Trivedi and Pagan (1979) state that the significance

TABLE 9.2 ***LIKELIHOOD RATIO TEST PROCEDURES UNDER ALTERNATIVE NORMS FOR THE ALMON POLYNOMIAL DEGREE GIVEN LAG LENGTH***

Norm	Noncentrality Parameter Under the Null Hypotheses	Test Procedure
Classical hypothesis test of truth or falsity of restrictions $R\boldsymbol{\beta} = \mathbf{0}$	$\lambda = 0$	Calculate u, compare it to the critical value $c = F_{(n^*-q, T-n^*-1, \alpha)}$. If $u \geq c$, reject H_0 and conclude that $\mathbf{b}$ is better than $\hat{\boldsymbol{\beta}}$
Generalized mean square error [Toro-Vizcarrondo and Wallace (1968)]. $\hat{\boldsymbol{\beta}}$ better than $\mathbf{b}$ iff $\text{MSE}(\mathbf{d}'\hat{\boldsymbol{\beta}}) \leq \text{MSE}(\mathbf{d}'\mathbf{b})$ for all $\mathbf{d} \neq \mathbf{0}$	$\lambda \leq \frac{1}{2}$	Calculate u, compare it to the critical value $c = F_{(n^*-q, T-n^*-1, \frac{1}{2}, \alpha)}$, tabulated in Wallace and Toro-Vizcarrondo (1969). If $u \geq c$, reject H_0 and conclude that $\mathbf{b}$ is better than $\hat{\boldsymbol{\beta}}$.
Squared error loss [Wallace (1972) and Yancey, Judge, and Bock (1973)]. $\hat{\boldsymbol{\beta}}$ is better than $\mathbf{b}$ iff $\text{tr MSE}(\hat{\boldsymbol{\beta}}) \leq \text{tr MSE}(\mathbf{b})$	$\lambda \leq \frac{1}{2} d_L$ $\text{tr}\{(X'X)^{-1}R'(R(X'X)^{-1}R']^{-1}R(X'X)^{-1}\}$, where d_L is the largest characteristic root of expression under the trace operator	Calculate u, compare it to the critical value $c = F_{(n^*-q, T-n^*-1, \lambda, \alpha)}$, which must be calculated in each application. If $u \geq c$, reject H_0 and conclude that $\mathbf{b}$ is better than $\hat{\boldsymbol{\beta}}$
Weighted squared error loss [Wallace (1972)]. $\hat{\boldsymbol{\beta}}$ is better than $\mathbf{b}$ iff $E(X\hat{\boldsymbol{\beta}} - X\boldsymbol{\beta})'(X\hat{\boldsymbol{\beta}} - X\boldsymbol{\beta}) \leq$ $E(X\mathbf{b} - X\boldsymbol{\beta})'(X\mathbf{b} - X\boldsymbol{\beta})$ or $E(\hat{\boldsymbol{\beta}} - \boldsymbol{\beta})'X'X(\hat{\boldsymbol{\beta}} - \boldsymbol{\beta}) \leq$ $E(\mathbf{b} - \boldsymbol{\beta})'X'X(\mathbf{b} - \boldsymbol{\beta})$	$\lambda \leq \dfrac{n^* - q - 1}{2}$	Calculate u, compare it to the critical value $c = F_{(n^*-q, T-n^*-1, \lambda, \alpha)}$ tabulated in Goodnight and Wallace (1972). If $u \geq c$, reject H_0 and conclude that $\mathbf{b}$ is better than $\hat{\boldsymbol{\beta}}$.

level of the kth test in the series is

$$1 - \prod_{j=1}^{k} (1 - \gamma_j) \tag{9.3.13}$$

where γ_j is the significance level of the jth individual test in the series. If all the γ_j are equal, the probability of rejecting the null hypothesis where it is true will rise as the order of the polynomial is reduced. Following the suggestion of Anderson (1971), one might make γ_j very small for high values of q so that if a higher-order polynomial is not required, the probability of deciding on a high order is small, and values of γ_j larger for low values of q in such a way that the level of significance at lower polynomial degrees is acceptable. It should be noted that *any* of these procedures produce pretest estimators (see Chapter 3, Section 3.3) whose distributions and properties are currently unknown.

Amemiya and Morimune (1974), Schmidt and Sickles (1975), and Trivedi and Pagan (1979) offer quite a different approach to the problem. They suggest adopting a norm and estimating the value of loss under different model specifications. Amemiya and Morimune (1974) adopt the norm $\text{tr}[\text{MSE}(\tilde{\boldsymbol{\beta}})X'X]$, where $\text{MSE}(\tilde{\boldsymbol{\beta}}) = E(\tilde{\boldsymbol{\beta}} - \boldsymbol{\beta})(\tilde{\boldsymbol{\beta}} - \boldsymbol{\beta})'$. It can be shown that this norm equals

$$E[(\tilde{\boldsymbol{\beta}} - \boldsymbol{\beta})'X'X(\tilde{\boldsymbol{\beta}} - \boldsymbol{\beta})]$$

the weighted squared error loss function that is also interpretable as the mean square error of $X\tilde{\boldsymbol{\beta}}$ as a predictor of $X\boldsymbol{\beta}$. Schmidt and Sickles (1975) calculate values of this norm using the unrestricted least squares estimates of $\boldsymbol{\beta}$ and σ^2 in place of the true but unknown values. The polynomial degree *could* be chosen by selecting the one that minimizes this value. However, there is no necessity for adopting their ad hoc procedure when under the chosen norm straightforward mean square error tests can be carried out as shown above. Alternatively, the model selection criteria discussed in Section 9.2.2 and/or Chapter 21 can be used to estimate the polynomial degree.

What, then, is the best procedure for an applied worker faced with such a situation to follow from a sampling theory point of view? Available results offer very little comfort and apply only to investigators who are interested in point estimation, not interval estimation or hypothesis testing.

1. If the purpose of the point estimation is prediction, the positive rule variant of the Stein-rule estimator (see Chapter 3) is known to dominate the least squares estimator under the mean square error of prediction loss function. Naturally, the smaller the specification error associated with the set of restrictions selected to combine with the sample data, the greater the gain over least squares.

If some pretesting is to be carried out several points must be recalled: (a) the properties of estimators produced from more than one test are unknown, (b) the critical value of the pretest (see Chapter 3) greatly affects the risk function of the pretest estimator, and (c) under the mean square error of prediction loss function the modified pretest estimator (3.4.12) is known to dominate the traditional pretest estimator (3.4.11).

2. If point estimation is carried out under squared error loss, estimators from the family of estimators proposed by Judge and Bock (1978, Chapter 10) are known to dominate least squares. The corresponding positive part rules (see Chapter 3) dominate these rules in turn [see also Trivedi (1978)].

To summarize, recall that prior information may be used in conjunction with sample information in one of two ways: the prior information may be used to improve sample estimators *or* one can use the sample to test the validity of the information. For a given sample these are usually mutually exclusive problems. In the procedures used above the purposes are mixed by trying out various sets of hypotheses and finally imposing one that does not appear to disagree "too much" with the sample information. This violates the basic statistical dichotomy and produces estimates whose properties are unknown. Investigators must make every available effort to adopt prior information developed from solid theoretical ground rather than "sift" the data for a suitable theory.

9.3.4 Procedures for Estimating the Lag Length and Polynomial Degree When Both Are Unknown

When the lag length n^* and the polynomial degree q are unknown, the problems discussed above are compounded. A possibility of utilizing a sequential testing procedure for jointly estimating n^* and q is noted by Hendry, Pagan, and Sargan (1982). Suppose that the true lag length n^* is known not to be greater than N. Then an adequate polynomial degree can be determined conditional on the lag length being N, using a sequential testing procedure as described in the previous section. Suppose Q is the polynomial degree corresponding to lag length N. If n^* is in fact less than N, then $\beta_N = 0$. In this case, reducing the lag length to $N - 1$, we can also reduce the polynomial degree by one since we have eliminated one root of the polynomial and the number of roots of a polynomial corresponds to its degree. Thus, $Q - 1$ is the polynomial degree for lag length $N - 1$, and so on. Hence a sequence of nested hypotheses can be set up as follows:

$$\begin{aligned} H_1&: \quad q = Q - 1,\ n^* = N - 1 \\ H_2&: \quad q = Q - 2,\ n^* = N - 2 \\ &\ \ \vdots \end{aligned} \tag{9.3.14}$$

The usual F test statistics can be used in this procedure.

Alternatively, one could use a two-step procedure and apply one of the methods introduced in Section 9.2.2 to estimate the lag length first and then determine the polynomial degree as in Section 9.3.3 [Pagano and Hartley (1981)]. Yet another possibility is to search over all possible pairs (n,q) using a suitable model specification criterion (see Chapter 21). Teräsvirta and Mellin (1983) have compared various of these criteria and procedures in this context in a Monte Carlo study. Their overall conclusion is that the purpose of the analysis should be taken into account when an estimation procedure is chosen. However, in their study model selection criteria like the one proposed by Schwarz (SC) and a procedure called TPEC did quite well in choosing the correct lag length and polynomial degree and in producing relatively low mean square errors. The idea underlying the TPEC procedure is to test, for all combinations of lag lengths n and polynomial degrees q, whether imposing the corresponding restrictions reduces a weighted squared error loss function as compared to the LS estimator of the unrestricted model. The F statistic is evaluated for any pair (n,q) and the most parsimonious model is chosen among the specifications with lowest F values. For more details the reader is referred to the paper by Teräsvirta and Mellin (1983).

As another means of shedding light on what might be appropriate values of n^* and q, Harper (1977) suggests using the specification error tests of Ramsey (1969, 1974) and Ramsey and Gilbert (1972). Since incorrect selection of n^* and q results in a model with a disturbance that has a nonzero mean, the specification error tests RESET and RASET can be adopted. These tests are designed to detect a nonzero mean of the disturbances of a regression model. Further discussions and modifications of these tests are given by Ramsey and Schmidt (1976), Thursby and Schmidt (1977), and Thursby (1979).

Finally, although it is true that the above procedures will produce point estimates for n^*, q, and the corresponding lag weight vector, recall that the exact small sample properties of the resulting estimators are unknown. It is by no means clear that an unrestricted estimator necessarily produces inferior estimates of the lag weights. Teräsvirta (1980) gives some general guidelines when the imposition of polynomial constraints may result in improved estimation accuracy. Briefly, if the error variance of the model is large, the sample size T is small, and the lag function is rather smooth, the use of a polynomial lag may be advantageous.

9.4 POLYNOMIAL SPLINE DISTRIBUTED LAGS

As a generalization Corradi and Gambetta (1976) and Poirier (1976) suggest that rather than a polynomial lag one may wish to consider a spline lag. To illustrate we discuss a cubic spline that is a set of cubic polynomials joined together smoothly by requiring their first and second derivatives to be equal at the points where they join. Such functions have a long history of use in curve fitting applications because of their flexibility. The method presumes that the function generating the weights can be approximated by the function

$$\beta_i = I_{[0,i_1]}(i)g_1(i) + I_{[i_1,i_2]}(i)g_2(i) + I_{[i_2,n*]}(i)g_3(i) \qquad (9.4.1)$$

where $I_{[\cdot]}(i)$ is an indicator function that is one if the argument i is in the stated interval and zero otherwise, i_j are points in the interval $[0,n^*]$ and the $g_j(i)$ are cubic polynomials

$$g_j(i) = a_j i^3 + b_j i^2 + c_j i + d_j \tag{9.4.2}$$

Although three cubics are presented here, there may be any number in general and the intervals they cover may be varied at will, but intervals of equal length are usually adopted. The restrictions required to join these cubics smoothly are

$$\begin{aligned} g_1(i_1) &= g_2(i_1);\ g_1'(i_1) = g_2'(i_1);\ g_1''(i_1) = g_2''(i_1) \\ g_2(i_2) &= g_3(i_2);\ g_2'(i_2) = g_3'(i_2);\ g_2''(i_2) = g_3''(i_2) \end{aligned} \tag{9.4.3}$$

These 6 restrictions are imposed upon the model

$$\mathbf{y} = X\boldsymbol{\beta} + \mathbf{e} = XH^*\boldsymbol{\alpha}^* + \mathbf{e} = Z^*\boldsymbol{\alpha}^* + \mathbf{e} \tag{9.4.4}$$

where $\boldsymbol{\beta} = H^*\boldsymbol{\alpha}^*$, H^* is an $((n^* + 1) \times 12)$ matrix that relates the lag weights $\boldsymbol{\beta}$ to the vector $\boldsymbol{\alpha}^* = [\boldsymbol{\alpha}_1', \boldsymbol{\alpha}_2', \boldsymbol{\alpha}_3']'$ where $\boldsymbol{\alpha}_j = [a_j\ b_j\ c_j\ d_j]'$, $j = 1, 2, 3$. The 12 coefficients of $\boldsymbol{\alpha}^*$ are subjected to 6 linear and homogeneous restrictions which may be written $R\boldsymbol{\alpha}^* = \mathbf{0}$. The cubic spline coefficients are then estimated by applying restricted least squares and estimates of the β_i's are obtained from $\hat{\boldsymbol{\beta}} = H^*\hat{\boldsymbol{\alpha}}^*$. The usual test procedures can be applied straightforwardly to test the smoothness restrictions.

Splines are flexible and relatively easy to apply, but they involve the same difficulties as the usual Almon lags, namely that the lag length is unknown, and it is not clear how flexible the function should be, which under these circumstances is equivalent to asking how many polynomials should be joined together and what their degree should be.

9.5 SHILLER'S DISTRIBUTED LAG

Shiller (1973, 1975) considers a different approach in generalizing the Almon lag. His notion is that investigators have adopted polynomial lag models in the past not really because it was felt that the lag weights fell on a polynomial of a particular degree but because such an assumption produces a smooth and simple curve. He suggests putting prior distributions on linear combinations of coefficients, which eliminate any jagged shapes. Taylor (1974) has shown that the Bayes estimator of the distributed lag weights produced by imposing "smoothness" priors is equivalent to the imposition of *stochastic,* rather than exact, restrictions of the form (9.3.9). The stochastic restrictions (see Chapter 3) may be written

$$\mathbf{0} = R\boldsymbol{\beta} + \mathbf{v} \tag{9.5.1}$$

and when combined with model (9.2.2) give

$$\begin{bmatrix} \mathbf{y} \\ \mathbf{0} \end{bmatrix} = \begin{bmatrix} X \\ R \end{bmatrix} \boldsymbol{\beta} + \begin{bmatrix} \mathbf{e} \\ \mathbf{v} \end{bmatrix} \tag{9.5.2}$$

where $E(\mathbf{ee}') = \sigma^2 I$. $E(\mathbf{ev}') = 0$ and $E(\mathbf{vv}') = (\sigma^2/k^2)I$.

The parameter k is specified a priori and the best linear unbiased estimator of $\boldsymbol{\beta}$ is

$$\hat{\boldsymbol{\beta}}^* = [X'X + k^2R'R]^{-1}X'\mathbf{y} \tag{9.5.3}$$

The value of k one adopts of course reflects the strength with which the exact polynomial restrictions are held. As $k \to \infty$ the estimator $\hat{\boldsymbol{\beta}}^*$ approaches the corresponding Almon estimator, and as $k \to 0$, $\hat{\boldsymbol{\beta}}^*$ approaches the ordinary least squares estimator $\mathbf{b}$. Fomby (1979) has noted that the stochastic restrictions may be *tested* under the generalized mean square error norm for MSE improvement by employing the procedures suggested by Judge, Yancey, and Bock (1973) and Yancey, Judge, and Bock (1974). As with pretests involved with exact restrictions, however, the pretest estimator thus produced is inferior to the least squares estimator under both risk matrix and squared error loss functions for a large range of the parameter space. (See Chapter 3.) For a generalization of Shiller's approach, see Corradi (1977).

9.6 THE HARMONIC LAG

Hamlen and Hamlen (1978) note that occasionally when the Almon technique is being used, a polynomial of low degree is insufficient to represent the lag structure adequately. In such a case the multicollinearity problem may not be mitigated and also there is a potential for roundoff errors as there may be a substantial range between the smallest and the largest variable in the transformed regressor matrix Z in (9.3.4). To cope with these difficulties they propose the use of trigonometric functions. In this approach the lag weights are written as

$$\beta_j = \bar{\beta} + \sum_{k=0}^{q} (A_k \sin \theta_{jk} + B_k \cos \theta_{jk}) \quad \text{for } j = 1, 2, \ldots, n^* \tag{9.6.1}$$

where

$$\theta_{jk} = \frac{2\pi}{n^* + 1} \cdot j \cdot k \tag{9.6.2}$$

$\bar{\beta}$ is a constant equivalent to the mean of the series $\beta_j, j = 1, 2, \ldots, n^*$, n^* is the number of lags, and q is the number of harmonics (sine and cosine terms in pairs) with $q \leq n^*$. Compactly, (9.6.1) can be written as

$$\boldsymbol{\beta} = H\boldsymbol{\alpha} \tag{9.6.3}$$

where

$$\boldsymbol{\alpha}' = (\bar{\beta} + B_0 \quad A_1 \quad A_2 \quad \ldots \quad A_q \quad B_1 \quad B_2 \quad \ldots \quad B_q) \tag{9.6.4}$$

and

$$H = \begin{bmatrix} 1 & 0 & \cdots & 0 & 0 & \cdots & 0 \\ 1 & \sin\theta_{11} & \cdots & \sin\theta_{1q} & \cos\theta_{11} & \cdots & \cos\theta_{1q} \\ 1 & \sin\theta_{21} & \cdots & \sin\theta_{2q} & \cos\theta_{21} & \cdots & \cos\theta_{2q} \\ \vdots & \vdots & \ddots & \vdots & \vdots & \ddots & \vdots \\ 1 & \sin\theta_{n*1} & \cdots & \sin\theta_{n*q} & \cos\theta_{n*1} & \cdots & \cos\theta_{n*q} \end{bmatrix} \tag{9.6.5}$$

Like the Almon lag, the parameters $\boldsymbol{\alpha}$ may be estimated by substituting (9.6.3) into (9.2.2) to obtain

$$\mathbf{y} = XH\boldsymbol{\alpha} + \mathbf{e} = Z\boldsymbol{\alpha} + \mathbf{e} \tag{9.6.6}$$

and applying least squares. The estimator

$$\hat{\boldsymbol{\alpha}} = (Z'Z)^{-1}Z'\mathbf{y} \tag{9.6.7}$$

is distributed $N(\boldsymbol{\alpha},\sigma^2(Z'Z)^{-1})$. An estimator of $\boldsymbol{\beta}$ is $\hat{\boldsymbol{\beta}} = H\hat{\boldsymbol{\alpha}}$, which is distributed $N(\boldsymbol{\beta},\sigma^2 H(Z'Z)^{-1}H')$ *if the model is correct.*

In their paper about the harmonic alternatives to the Almon polynomial technique, Hamlen and Hamlen (1978) offer no theoretical basis upon which to decide, a priori, when the polynomial or the harmonics of the same degree should be used to maximize the efficiency of the estimators and minimize the risk of specification error. The relationship between the Almon lag and the harmonic lag is discussed by Morey (1981).

9.7 ESTIMATION OF THE MOMENTS OF THE LAG DISTRIBUTION

Hatanaka and Wallace (1980) show that in some circumstances the first few moments

$$\mu_j = \sum_{i=0}^{n^*} i^j \beta_i, \qquad j = 0, 1, \ldots \tag{9.7.1}$$

of the lag distribution can be estimated more precisely than the lag weights β_i. Thus, if interest focuses on the long-run response μ_0 or the mean lag μ_1, say, it may be preferable to estimate these moments directly using

$$\boldsymbol{\mu} = W\boldsymbol{\beta} \tag{9.7.2}$$

where $\boldsymbol{\mu}' = (\mu_0, \ldots, \mu_{n*})$ and $W = H'$ when q is replaced by n^* in (9.3.3). Since W is invertible we can substitute $W^{-1}\boldsymbol{\mu}$ for $\boldsymbol{\beta}$ in (9.2.2) and get

$$\mathbf{y} = XW^{-1}\boldsymbol{\mu} + \mathbf{e} = Z\boldsymbol{\mu} + \mathbf{e} \tag{9.7.3}$$

where of course $Z = XW^{-1}$. Under our standard assumptions for $\mathbf{e}$ the least squares estimator $\hat{\boldsymbol{\mu}} = (Z'Z)^{-1}Z'\mathbf{y}$ for $\boldsymbol{\mu}$ is distributed as $N(\boldsymbol{\mu},\sigma^2(Z'Z)^{-1})$.

Hatanaka and Wallace show that the variance of $\hat{\mu}_i$ is less than that of $\hat{\mu}_j$ if $i < j$. In particular, the long-run response μ_0 and the mean lag μ_1 are estimated most accurately. Clearly these "moments" are not the moments of a proper distribution since $\mu_0 = \Sigma_{i=0}^{n^*}\beta_i$ may not equal one. However, the μ_i can be used to compute the moments of the distribution $\rho_i = \beta_i/\mu_0$, $i = 0, 1, \ldots, n^*$. Let us denote the moments of this distribution by $M_1, M_2, \ldots$; that is, $M_j = \Sigma_{i=0}^{n^*} i^j \rho_i$. Silver and Wallace (1980) suggest a method due to Pearson to identify a particular lag distribution on the basis of M_1, M_2, M_3, and M_4.

9.8 SUMMARY

The difficulties faced by investigators who attempt to estimate intertemporal effects associated with economic phenomena are substantial and not by any means resolved at this point. In this chapter we have considered models where the effect of a change in an independent variable persists over time but which is assumed negligible after a finite length of time. The most immediate difficulty is, of course, that if the effect lasts only a finite length of time, it is usually the case that this lag length is unknown. The consequences of misspecifying the lag length in a distributed lag regression model may be severe.

Even if the true length is known, however, which implies that usual regression procedures may be used under classical assumptions, maximum likelihood estimators may be imprecise due to multicollinearity. As a result investigators have considered constrained estimators in the hope that better estimates of the lag parameters will be obtained. Unfortunately, as pointed out in Chapter 3, the resulting estimators are superior to least squares only over a portion of the parameter space. If pretests of the associated restrictions are performed, the resulting estimator has, by now, well-known statistical consequences. The recommendations for this situation are the same as those in Chapter 3. If point estimates of the lag coefficients are desired, using the positive part rule yields an estimator that is superior to least squares over the entire parameter space. The problem of what restrictions to impose, however, remains.

Finally, it must be remembered that the analysis of this chapter is based on assumptions that will rarely be met in practice and consequently the procedures presented are to some extent of only pedagogical value. First, we have assumed that there is just one explanatory variable. Most of the above procedures can be extended to models with more than one lagged explanatory variable. The techniques may however become more cumbersome and the mentioned problems will be compounded. Second, we have presumed that the lag length is indeed finite and we will see in the next chapter that there are good reasons for rejecting this assumption in many situations of practical relevance as there are economic theories that lead to infinite lag distributions. Third, it has been assumed that the error terms of the basic model (9.2.1) are independent. This is a rather heroic assumption in a dynamic framework where intertemporal dependencies between the variables are explicitly postulated. Pagano and Hartley (1981) demonstrate the potentially severe consequences of ignoring residual autocorrelation in a distributed lag analysis. The independence assumption will be relaxed in much of the next chapter. Fourth, it has been assumed that the process x_t is independent of the error process. In practice this also is a rather severe constraint as it excludes situations with feedback between y and x. Dynamic models with feedback between the variables are considered in Chapter 16. Fifth, as in previous chapters the parameters of the model are assumed time invariant. Models with time varying coefficients are treated in Chapter 19.

9.9 EXERCISES

Generate 100 samples $\mathbf{y}$ of size 20 from the model

$$y_t = 5 + 5x_t + 8x_{t-1} + 9x_{t-2} + 8x_{t-3} + 5x_{t-4} + e_t$$

where e_t are independently distributed normal random variables with mean zero and variance 100. The values of $(x_1, x_2, \ldots, x_{24})$ are 2795, 2444, 2206, 2633, 2335, 2381, 2616, 2590, 2878, 2418, 2708, 3029, 2648, 3127, 3495, 3777, 3923, 4408, 4621, 4099, 4793, 5187, 5207, and 5688.

9.9.1 Individual Exercises

Exercise 9.1
Using five samples of data compute the least squares estimates of the coefficients for each of the five samples assuming that the lag length is $n^* = 4$. Compute the sample means and variances of these estimates and compare them to their theoretical counterparts.

Exercise 9.2
Use AIC (9.2.6) and SC (9.2.9) and a maximum lag of $N_T = 6$ to estimate the lag length for the five samples of Exercise 9.1. Interpret your results.

Exercise 9.3
Using the five data samples and the true lag length $n^* = 4$, impose the Almon constraint that the lag coefficients fall on a polynomial of degree $q = 2$. Com-

pute the restricted least squares estimates of the coefficients, their sample means and variances, and compare them to their theoretical counterparts.

Exercise 9.4

Repeat Exercise 9.3 under the following three alternative hypotheses:

(a) $n^* = 4, q = 3$
(b) $n^* = 6, q = 2$
(c) $n^* = 3, q = 2$

Exercise 9.5

Using the five samples of data from the previous exercises compute the least squares estimates for the coefficients of a distributed lag model with lag length $n = 6$ for each of the five samples, and compute the sample means and sample variances. Impose a set of restrictions that implies a lag length $n = 5$ and a polynomial of degree two. Compute the positive part rule discussed in Chapter 3 which combines these restrictions with the sample data for the five samples, their sample means and variances.

9.9.2 Joint or Class Exercises

Exercise 9.6

Using the specified statistical model and all 100 samples of data, compute the least squares estimates of the coefficients assuming a lag length of $n^* = 4$. Compute the sample means and variances of the estimates and the squared error loss.

Exercise 9.7

Estimate the lag length for all 100 samples using AIC and SC and a maximum lag $N_T = 6$. Construct a frequency distribution for each of the two criteria and interpret.

Exercise 9.8

Using the 100 samples and assuming a lag length of $n^* = 4$ and a polynomial lag distribution of degree two, compute the appropriate restricted least squares estimates, and their sample means, variances, and squared error loss.

Exercise 9.9

Using the 100 samples generated above, compute the least squares estimates of a distributed lag model with lag length $n = 6$, their sample means, variances, and squared error loss. Impose a set of restrictions on the model that implies a lag length $n = 5$ and a polynomial lag distribution of degree two. Compute the corresponding restricted least squares estimates, and their sample means, variances, and squared error loss. Compute the positive part rule of Chapter 3 that combines these restrictions with the sample data for the 100 samples, and their sample means, variances, and squared error loss.

9.10 REFERENCES

Akaike, H. (1973) "Information Theory and an Extension of the Maximum Likelihood Principle," in B. N. Petrov and F. Csáki, eds., *2nd International Symposium on Information Theory,* Akadémiai Kiadó, Budapest, 267–281.

Allen, R. G. D. (1959) *Mathematical Economics,* 2nd ed., Macmillan, London.

Almon, S. (1965) "The Distributed Lag Between Capital Appropriations and Expenditures," *Econometrica,* 33, 178–196.

Amemiya, T. and K. Morimune (1974) "Selecting the Optimal Order of Polynomial in the Almon Distributed Lag," *Review of Economics and Statistics,* 56, 378–386.

Anderson, T. W. (1971) *The Statistical Analysis of Time Series,* Wiley, New York.

Apostol, T. (1962) *Calculus, Volume 2,* Wiley, New York.

Cooper, J. D. (1972) "Two Approaches to Polynomial Distributed Lag Estimation: An Expository Note and Comment," *American Statistician,* 26, 32–35.

Corrado, C. (1977) "Smooth Distributed Lag Estimation and Smoothing Spline Functions in Hilbert Spaces," *Journal of Econometrics,* 5, 211–219.

Corrado, C. and G. Gambetta (1976) "The Estimation of Distributed Lags by Spline Functions," *Empirical Economics,* 1, 41–51.

DeLeeuw, F. (1962) "The Demand for Capital Goods by Manufacturers: A Study of Quarterly Time Series," *Econometrica,* 30, 407–423.

Dhrymes, P. J. (1971) *Distributed Lags: Problems of Estimation and Formulation,* Holden-Day, San Francisco.

Fisher, I. (1937) "Note on a Short-Cut Method for Calculating Distributed Lags," *Bulletin de l'Institut International de Statistique,* 29, 323–328.

Fomby, T. B. (1979) "Mean Square Error Evaluation of Shiller's Smoothness Priors," *International Economic Review,* 20, 203–216.

Frost, P. A. (1975) "Some Properties of the Almon Lag Technique When One Searches for Degree of Polynomial and Lag," *Journal of the American Statistical Association,* 70, 606–612.

Geweke, J. and R. Meese (1981) "Estimating Regression Models of Finite but Unknown Order," *International Economic Review,* 22, 55–70.

Godfrey, L. G. and D. S. Poskitt (1975) "Testing the Restrictions of the Almon Lag Technique," *Journal of the American Statistical Association,* 70, 105–108.

Goodnight, J. and T. D. Wallace (1972) "Operational Techniques and Tables for Making Weak MSE Tests for Restrictions in Regressions," *Econometrica,* 40, 699–709.

Griffiths, W. E. and R. F. Kerrison (1978) "Using Specification Error Tests to Choose Between Alternative Polynomial Lag Distributions: An Application to Investment Functions," working paper, University of New England, Armidale, Australia.

Hamlen, S. S. and W. A. Hamlen, Jr. (1978) "Harmonic Alternatives to the Almon Polynomial Technique," *Journal of Econometrics,* 6, 57–66.

Harper, C. P. (1977) "Testing for the Existence of a Lagged Relationship Within Almon's Method," *Review of Economics and Statistics,* 50, 204–210.

Hatanaka, M. and T. D. Wallace (1980) "Multicollinearity and the Estimation of Low Order Moments in Stable Lag Distributions," in: J. Kmenta and J. Ramsey, eds., *Evaluation of Econometric Models,* Academic Press, New York.

Hendry, D. F., A. R. Pagan and J. D. Sargan (1982) "Dynamic Specification," forthcoming in *Handbook of Econometrics,* Z. Griliches and M. D. Intriligator, eds., North-Holland, Amsterdam.

Hill, R. C. and S. R. Johnson (1976) "Almon Lags, Restricted Least Squares and the Choice of Optimal Polynomials," working paper, University of Georgia, Athens.

Judge, G. G. and M. E. Bock (1978) *The Statistical Implications of Pre-Test and Stein-Rule Estimators in Econometrics,* North-Holland, Amsterdam.

Judge, G. G., R. C. Hill, W. E. Griffiths, H. Lütkepohl and T. C. Lee (1982) *Introduction to the Theory and Practice of Econometrics,* Wiley, New York.

Judge, G. G., T. A. Yancey and M. E. Bock (1973) "Properties of Estimators After Preliminary Test of Significance When Stochastic Restrictions Are Used in Regression," *Journal of Econometrics,* 1, 29–48.

Morey, M. J. (1981) "On the Correspondence Between the Almon Polynomial and a Harmonic Alternative Due to Hamlen and Hamlen," working paper, Department of Economics, Indiana University, Bloomington, Indiana.

Pagano, M. and M. J. Hartley (1981) "On Fitting Distributed Lag Models Subject to Polynomial Restrictions," *Journal of Econometrics,* 16, 171–198.

Poirier, D. J. (1976) *The Economics of Structural Change with Special Emphasis on Spline Functions,* North-Holland, Amsterdam.

Ramsey, J. B. (1969) "Tests for Specification Errors in Classical Linear Least Squares Regression Analysis," *Journal of the Royal Statistical Society, Series B,* 31, 350–371.

Ramsey, J. B. (1974) "Classical Model Selection Through Specification Error Tests," in Paul Zarembka, ed., *Frontiers in Econometrics,* Academic Press, New York, 13–47.

Ramsey, J. B. and R. Gilbert (1972) "A Monte Carlo Study of Some Small Sample Properties of Tests for Specification Error," *Journal of the American Statistical Association,* 67, 180–186.

Ramsey, J. B. and P. Schmidt (1976) "Some Further Results on the Use of OLS and BLUS Residuals in Specification Error Tests," *Journal of the American Statistical Association,* 71, 389–390.

Schmidt, P. and R. Sickles (1975) "On the Efficiency of the Almon Lag Technique," *International Economic Review,* 16, 792–795.

Schmidt, P. and R. N. Waud (1973) "The Almon Lag Technique and the Monetary versus Fiscal Policy Debate," *Journal of the American Statistical Association,* 68, 11–19.

Shibata, R. (1981) "An Optimal Selection of Regression Variables," *Biometrika,* 68, 45–54.

Shiller, R. J. (1973) "A Distributed Lag Estimator Derived from Smoothness Priors," *Econometrica,* 41, 775–788.

Shiller, R. J. (1975) "Alternative Prior Representations of 'Smoothness' for Distributed Lag Estimation," working paper 89, National Bureau of Economic Research.

Silver, J. L. and T. D. Wallace (1980) "The Lag Relationship Between Wholesale and Consumer Prices: An Application of the Hatanaka-Wallace Procedure," *Journal of Econometrics,* 12, 375–387.

Taylor, W. E. (1974) "Smoothness Priors and Stochastic Prior Restrictions in Distributed Lag Estimation," *International Economic Review,* 15, 803–804.

Teräsvirta, T. (1976) "A Note on Bias in the Almon Distributed Lag Estimator," *Econometrica,* 44, 1317–1322.

Teräsvirta, T. (1980) "The Polynomial Distributed Lag Revisited," *Empirical Economics,* 5, 69–81.

Teräsvirta, T. and I. Mellin (1983) "Estimation of Polynomial Distributed Lag Models," Research Report No. 41, Department of Statistics, University of Helsinki.

Thursby, J. G. (1979) "Alternative Specification Error Tests: A Comparative Study," *Journal of the American Statistical Association,* 74, 222–225.

Thursby, J. G. and P. Schmidt (1977) "Some Properties of Tests for Specification Error in a Linear Regression Model," *Journal of the American Statistical Association,* 72, 635–641.

Thomas, J. J. (1977) "Some Problems in the Use of Almon's Technique in the Estimation of Distributed Lags," *Empirical Economics,* 2, 175–193.

Toro-Vizcarrondo, C. and T. D. Wallace (1968) "A Test of the Mean Square Error Criterion for Restrictions in Linear Regression," *Journal of the American Statistical Association,* 63, 558–572.

Trivedi, P. K. (1970) "A Note on the Application of Almon's Method of Calculating Distributed Lag Coefficients," *Metroeconomica,* 22, 281–286.

Trivedi, P. K. (1978) "Estimation of a Distributed Lag Model Under Quadratic Loss," *Econometrica,* 46, 1181–1192.

Trivedi, P. K. and A. R. Pagan (1979) "Polynomial Distributed Lags: A Unified Treatment," *Economic Studies Quarterly,* 30, 37–49.

Wallace, T. D. (1972) "Weaker Criteria and Tests for Linear Restrictions in Regression," *Econometrica,* 40, 689–698.

Wallace, T. D. and C. E. Toro-Vizcarrondo (1969) "Tables for the Mean Square Error Test for Exact Linear Restrictions in Regression," *Journal of the American Statistical Association,* 64, 1649–1663.

Yancey, T. A., G. G. Judge, and M. E. Bock (1973) "Wallace's Mean Squared Error Criterion for Testing Linear Restrictions in Regression: A Tighter Bound," *Econometrica,* 41, 1203–1206.

Yancey, T. A., G. G. Judge, and M. E. Bock (1974) "A Mean Square Error Test When Stochastic Restrictions Are Used in Regression," *Communications in Statistics,* 3, 755–769.

Chapter 10

Infinite Distributed Lags

10.1 INTRODUCTION

10.1.1 The General Model

In Chapter 9 we considered a special case of a dynamic model of the general form

$$\begin{aligned} y_t &= \beta_0 x_t + \beta_1 x_{t-1} + \beta_2 x_{t-2} + \ldots + e_t \\ &= (\beta_0 + \beta_1 L + \beta_2 L^2 + \ldots) x_t + e_t \\ &= \beta(L) x_t + e_t \end{aligned} \tag{10.1.1}$$

where y_t is the dependent variable, x_t is an explanatory variable, and e_t is a zero mean stationary stochastic process as defined in Chapter 7. As this model contains an infinite number of parameters, some further assumptions are necessary to obtain a tractable specification. Therefore, throughout much of this chapter, we will assume that our model has the form

$$y_t = \frac{\gamma(L)}{\phi(L)} x_t + \frac{\alpha(L)}{\theta(L)} v_t \tag{10.1.2}$$

where v_t is Gaussian white noise; that is, $v_t \sim N(0,\sigma_v^2)$ and v_t is independent of v_s for $s \neq t$, and

$$\begin{aligned} \gamma(L) &= \gamma_0 + \gamma_1 L + \ldots + \gamma_r L^r \\ \phi(L) &= 1 + \phi_1 L + \ldots + \phi_m L^m \\ \alpha(L) &= 1 + \alpha_1 L + \ldots + \alpha_q L^q \\ \theta(L) &= 1 + \theta_1 L + \ldots + \theta_p L^p \end{aligned}$$

are finite-order polynomials in the lag operator L, defined such that $L^k x_t = x_{t-k}$ (see Section 7.2). The model (10.1.2) implies that $\beta(L) = \gamma(L)/\phi(L)$. For this expression to be meaningful $\phi(L)$ has to be such that the random variable $\phi^{-1}(L)\gamma(L)x_t$ is well defined. Therefore, we require that

$$\phi(z) \neq 0 \qquad \text{for} \qquad |z| \leq 1 \tag{10.1.3}$$

Furthermore, we assume that

$$\alpha(z) \text{ and } \theta(z) \neq 0 \qquad \text{for} \qquad |z| \leq 1 \tag{10.1.4}$$

so that $e_t = [\alpha(L)/\theta(L)]v_t$ is an ARMA(p,q) process (see Chapter 7). The zero-order coefficients of $\phi(L)$, $\alpha(L)$, $\theta(L)$ are set at one so that the representation (10.1.2) is unique if we further require that no cancellation is possible in $\gamma(L)/\phi(L)$ and $\alpha(L)/\theta(L)$. An intercept term is deleted for convenience. It would make the presentation somewhat more cumbersome without contributing to a clarification of the major problems involved in the analysis of the model. The reader may assume that y_t and x_t have been mean adjusted.

If $p = q = 0$—that is, if $e_t = v_t$ is white noise—then

$$y_t = \frac{\gamma(L)}{\phi(L)} x_t + v_t \tag{10.1.5}$$

and it makes sense to regard (10.1.2) as a structural form equation that describes the response of y to changes in the exogenous variable x. Alternatively, (10.1.2) may be thought of as a reduced form equation corresponding to a structural form

$$\phi(L)y_t = \gamma(L)x_t + v_t \tag{10.1.6}$$

where $\phi(L) = \theta(L)$ and q is assumed to be zero. Clearly there is a considerable difference between the specifications (10.1.5) and (10.1.6). Another useful representation of the general form (10.1.2) is

$$A(L)y_t = B(L)x_t + C(L)v_t \tag{10.1.7}$$

where $A(L) = \phi(L)\theta(L)$, $B(L) = \theta(L)\gamma(L)$, and $C(L) = \phi(L)\alpha(L)$ are all finite-order operators.

Note that, as it stands, the model in (10.1.2) is not very useful for forecasting y_t unless something can be said about the future development of x_t. Where assumptions regarding the exogenous variable are necessary we will assume in the following that x_t is an ARMA process of the form

$$\eta(L)x_t = \psi(L)w_t \tag{10.1.8}$$

where w_t is white noise, independent of the process v_t, and $\eta(L)$ and $\psi(L)$ are finite-order invertible polynomials in the lag operator (see Chapter 7). The presumption of v_t and w_t being independent implies the type of exogeneity of x_t that is needed for the analysis of this chapter. While many of the results below remain valid without the exogeneity assumption, care has to be exercised in interpreting (10.1.2) if such an assumption is not made. For instance,

$$\sum_{i=0}^{\infty} \beta_i = \beta(1) = \frac{\gamma(1)}{\phi(1)} \tag{10.1.9}$$

is often interpreted as the long-run response of y to a unit change in x. This interpretation is not valid if there is feedback between x and y since in this case a change in x induces a change in y, which in turn implies further movement in x and so on. More general models, where feedback is permitted, are treated in Chapter 16. Often relationships with more than two variables are of interest. To keep the discussion at a simple level we will concentrate on the two variable case in this chapter. This restriction is also removed in Chapter 16.

10.1.2 Some Special Cases

A number of special cases of (10.1.2) have been investigated and applied in recent years. We will briefly discuss them here as examples. A theoretical justification for some of these models will be given in Section 10.2.1.

Clearly, if $m = p = q = 0$, then (10.1.2) is precisely the finite distributed lag model considered in Chapter 9. For a further discussion of the relationship between the lag function in (10.1.2) and finite lags, see Pagan (1978). If $r = m = 0$, we have a simple regression model with autocorrelated errors as discussed in Chapter 8.

For the *geometric lag* model [Koyck (1954), Nerlove (1956), Cagan (1956)] the lag function has the form

$$\beta(L) = \alpha(1 + \lambda L + \lambda^2 L^2 + \ldots) = \frac{\alpha}{1 - \lambda L} \tag{10.1.10}$$

where $0 < \lambda < 1$. That is, $\gamma(L) = \alpha$ and $\phi(L) = 1 - \lambda L$. The error term e_t can have different structures.

The *Pascal lag* was proposed and applied by Solow (1960) and has the form

$$\beta(L) = \frac{\alpha(1 - \lambda)^m}{(1 - \lambda L)^m} \tag{10.1.11}$$

where again $0 < \lambda < 1$ and m is a positive integer. For $m = 1$ the lag structure reduces to a geometric lag with geometrically declining lag weights β_i. If m is greater than one, the lag weights increase first and then taper off. Such a lag shape is often regarded as plausible in practical applications.

Also the *discounted polynomial lag* proposed by Schmidt (1974a) can be regarded as an attempt to give more flexibility to the geometric lag specification. Its general form is

$$\beta(L) = \sum_{i=0}^{\infty} \lambda^i \left(\sum_{j=0}^{r} p_j i^j \right) L^i \tag{10.1.12}$$

with $0 < \lambda < 1$. This operator can be shown to equal

$$\frac{\gamma(L)}{(1 - \lambda L)^{r+1}} \tag{10.1.13}$$

where $\gamma(L)$ has degree r [see, e.g., Burt (1980), Lütkepohl (1982a)]. For $r = 0$ we have again the simple geometric lag. It will be seen below that the parameters of this model are relatively easy to estimate.

The general form of (10.1.2) with $\alpha(L) = \theta(L) = 1$ is often referred to as the *rational distributed lag model* and was introduced in this context by Jorgenson (1966) who also investigates the special version

$$\beta(L) = \frac{\gamma(L)}{\prod_{j=1}^{r} (\exp(j) - L)} \tag{10.1.14}$$

Note that both the numerator and the denominator polynomial have the same degree.

Usually the above lag structures are regarded as being approximations to the "true" lag structure $\beta(L)$. It was pointed out by Sims (1972) that such approximations have to be interpreted carefully. In particular, a lag structure capable of uniformly approximating the true lag weights arbitrarily well will not necessarily provide a long-run response arbitrarily close to the true response. Furthermore, Sims gives an example where true and approximate lag weights are only an ε-distance apart, but the standard error of forecast diverges to infinity with growing sample size. Thus, tighter approximation properties than just a uniform approximation of the lag coefficients are in general required to justify the use of a particular lag model. Sims shows that the rational lags fulfill such requirements under quite general conditions for the true lag structure and the exogenous variable. A similar result for the discounted polynomial lag is given by Schmidt and Mann (1977) and Lütkepohl (1980).

In the next section suggestions for choosing an adequate model for a given set of economic variables are discussed. Estimation problems are considered in Section 10.3 and checking the adequacy of a fitted model is considered in Section 10.4. Some alternative infinite lag specifications are presented in Section 10.5 and some problems related to the interpretation of the lag weights are treated in Section 10.6. Conclusions are given in Section 10.7. A guide for this chapter is presented in Table 10.1.

10.2 MODEL SPECIFICATION

The major problem in working with a lag model of the type (10.1.2) is the specification of the operators $\gamma(L)$, $\phi(L)$, $\alpha(L)$, and $\theta(L)$. In particular selecting the orders r, m, p, and q is often a difficult exercise. Roughly there are two approaches to specifying a lag model: (1) a theory-based approach and (2) a data-based approach. Both possibilities will be considered in turn in the following.

10.2.1 Theory-based Model Specification

Various theories lead to specific distributed lag models. Some examples will be presented below to illustrate how economists have specified distributed lag

TABLE 10.1 ***INFINITE DISTRIBUTED LAG MODELS***

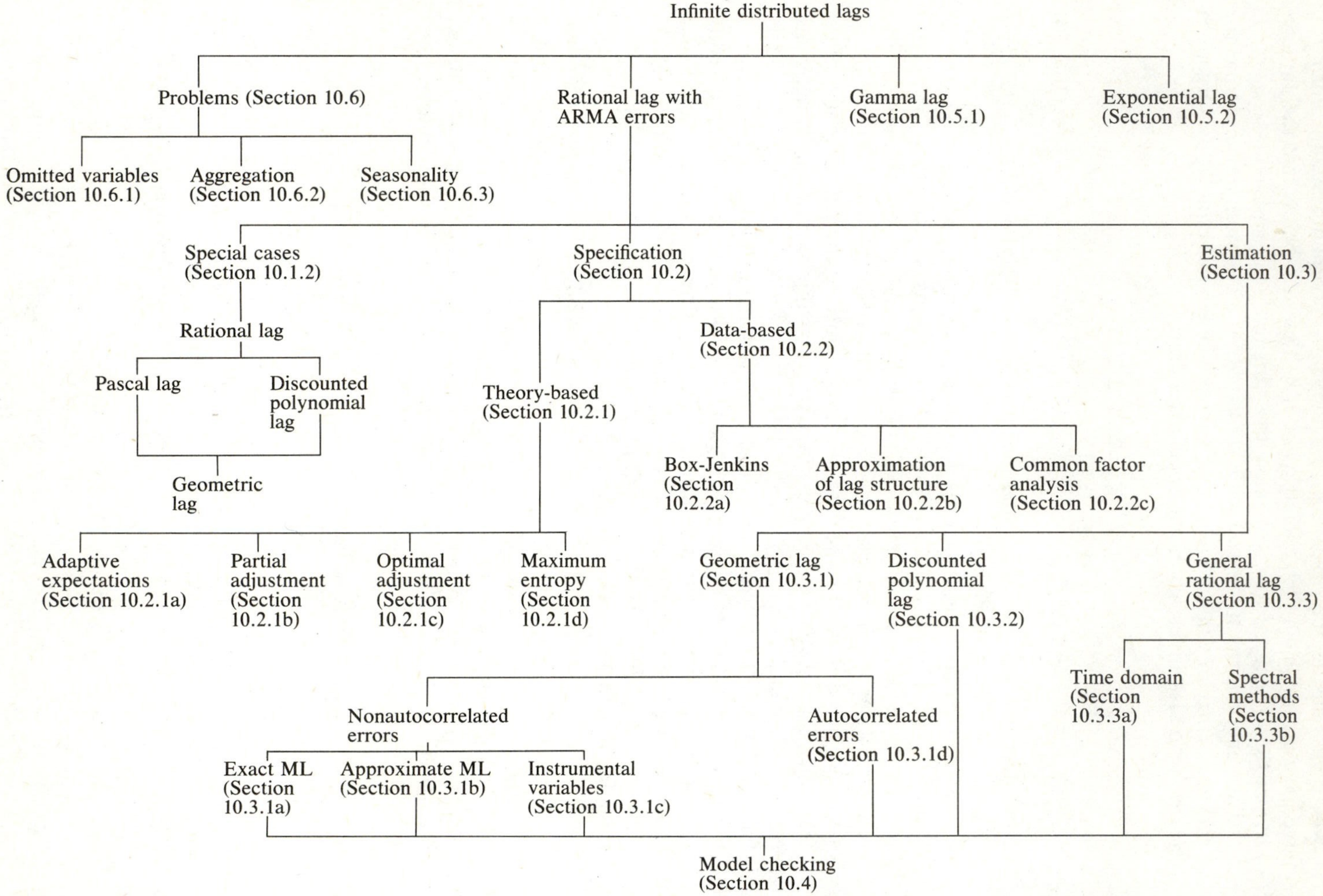

models in the past. For other examples, see, for example, Nerlove's (1972) survey and Just (1977).

10.2.1a Adaptive Expectations

The adaptive expectations model was suggested by Cagan (1956). In this model, the quantity supplied, y_t, may depend on the unobservable expected price x_t^*—that is,

$$y_t = \alpha_0 + \alpha_1 x_t^* + e_t \tag{10.2.1}$$

The expectations x_t^* are revised in proportion to the error associated with the previous level of expectations:

$$x_t^* - x_{t-1}^* = \lambda(x_{t-1} - x_{t-1}^*) \tag{10.2.2}$$

where $0 < \lambda < 1$ is the coefficient of expectations, x_{t-1} is the actual observable price, e_t is the stochastic term, and α_0 and α_1 are parameters. If we solve the above difference equation for x_t^*, we have

$$x_t^* = \sum_{i=0}^{\infty} \lambda(1 - \lambda)^i x_{t-1-i} \tag{10.2.3}$$

which implies a geometrically declining distributed lag form for expected prices as a function of all past prices. If we substitute (10.2.3) into (10.2.1) we have the geometric distributed lag function

$$y_t = \alpha_0 + \alpha_1 \sum_{i=0}^{\infty} \lambda(1 - \lambda)^i x_{t-1-i} + e_t \tag{10.2.4}$$

Koyck (1954) showed that an equation of the above form can be reduced by lagging it once, multiplying through by $(1 - \lambda)$ and subtracting it from the original equation, to yield a simple form

$$y_t = \alpha_0 \lambda + \alpha_1 \lambda x_{t-1} + (1 - \lambda) y_{t-1} + e_t^* \tag{10.2.5}$$

where $e_t^* = e_t - (1 - \lambda)e_{t-1}$. Using lag operator notation gives

$$[1 - (1 - \lambda)L]y_t = \alpha_0 \lambda + (\alpha_1 \lambda L)x_t + [1 - (1 - \lambda)L]e_t$$

or

$$y_t = \alpha_0 + \frac{\alpha_1 \lambda L}{1 - (1 - \lambda)L} x_t + e_t \tag{10.2.6}$$

which is obviously a model of the type (10.1.2) (if the intercept term is neglected). Assuming that e_t is Gaussian white noise, this model is completely specified and can be estimated by the methods presented in Section 10.3.

10.2.1b Partial Adjustment

The partial adjustment model was proposed by Nerlove (1956). The basic idea is that the current value of the independent variable determines the "desired" value of the dependent variable:

$$y_t^* = \alpha_0 + \alpha_1 x_t + v_t \tag{10.2.7}$$

but only some fixed fraction (γ) of the desired adjustment is accomplished in one period:

$$y_t - y_{t-1} = \gamma(y_t^* - y_{t-1}) \tag{10.2.8}$$

where $0 < \gamma < 1$ is the *coefficient of adjustment*. Combining (10.2.7) and (10.2.8) gives

$$y_t = \alpha_0\gamma + \alpha_1\gamma x_t + (1 - \gamma)y_{t-1} + \gamma v_t \tag{10.2.9}$$

or

$$y_t = \alpha_0 + \frac{\alpha_1\gamma}{1 - (1 - \gamma)L} x_t + \frac{\gamma}{1 - (1 - \gamma)L} v_t \tag{10.2.10}$$

Again we have a completely specified model provided the standard assumptions for v_t are made.

10.2.1c Optimal Adjustment

In the above theories the way the lags are introduced is somewhat dissatisfying since it results from ad hoc assumptions. For instance, it is not stated why the simple adjustment mechanism is reasonable in the partial adjustment model. To provide a deeper reasoning one would like to base the theory on some kind of optimizing behavior. One attempt in this direction was made by McLaren (1979). He assumes that an individual's desired level y^* of a variable y depends linearly on another variable x—that is,

$$y_t^* = \alpha x_t \tag{10.2.11}$$

The cost for not being in the static optimum in period t is assumed to be

$$C_1(t) = (y_t^* - y_t)^2 \tag{10.2.12}$$

and the adjustment cost is

$$C_2(t) = c(y_t - y_{t-1})^2 \tag{10.2.13}$$

Assuming an infinite planning horizon and a discount rate r, the individual has to solve the following optimization problem at time 0:

$$\text{minimize} \sum_{t=0}^{\infty} (1 + r)^{-t}[C_1(t) + C_2(t)] \tag{10.2.14}$$

Given that x_t is an ARMA process as in (10.1.8) with moving average representation

$$x_t = \frac{\psi(L)}{\eta(L)} w_t \tag{10.2.15}$$

McLaren shows that (10.2.14) is solved by choosing

$$y_t = \xi(L)x_t \tag{10.2.16}$$

where

$$\xi(z) = \frac{\alpha\eta(z)}{\mu(z)\psi(z)} \left[\frac{\psi(z)}{\eta(z)\mu(z^{-1})}\right]_+ \tag{10.2.17}$$

Here $[\ ]_+$ is an operator extracting only the nonnegative powers of the Laurent expansion of the term in brackets and $\mu(z) = K(1 - vz)$, where K and v are constants depending on c. It can be shown that $\xi(L)$ has a representation as a quotient of two finite-order polynomials in the lag operator [see McLaren (1979)]. However, the actual lag structure is only determined conditional on the structure of x_t. Furthermore, there is no error term in (10.2.16). It is noted by Lütkepohl (1984) that aggregating over individuals will lead to a general rational lag model with ARMA error term as in (10.1.2). There are also other economic theories that lead to models with lagged variables. Notably the rational expectations hypothesis belongs to this class. Rational expectations models are treated in a more general setting in Chapter 16.

10.2.1d Maximum Entropy

A particular lag distribution can also be justified by other than specific economic theories. Theil and Fiebig (1981) show how the maximum entropy (ME) principle can be used to specify a lag distribution. If the task is to estimate some true distribution, the most noninformative distribution should be chosen out of the class of all distributions that satisfy the constraints from prior knowledge. The entropy is used as a measure of noninformativeness. This is the principle of maximum entropy.

Assuming that the lag coefficients are $\beta_0, \beta_1, \ldots$ as in (10.1.1), we define a distribution

$$p_i = \frac{\beta_i}{\sum_{i=0}^{\infty} \beta_i} \tag{10.2.18}$$

For this distribution, the entropy takes the form

$$H = -\sum_{i=0}^{\infty} p_i \ln p_i \tag{10.2.19}$$

It turns out that if the mean lag is known to be μ, then the ME distribution is

$$p_i = \frac{1}{1+\mu}\left(\frac{\mu}{1+\mu}\right)^i$$

[see Theil and Fiebig (1981)]. Substituting $\lambda/(1-\lambda)$ for μ gives

$$p_i = (1-\lambda)\lambda^i \tag{10.2.20}$$

so that the relevant distribution is Koyck's geometric lag distribution and on substitution (10.1.1) becomes

$$\begin{aligned} y_t &= \alpha(1-\lambda)\sum_{i=0}^{\infty} \lambda^i x_{t-i} + e_t \\ &= \frac{\alpha(1-\lambda)}{1-\lambda L} x_t + e_t \end{aligned} \tag{10.2.21}$$

The above examples show that economic and other theories are usually only able to specify a part of the model. The rest will have to be derived from the data. Consequently, a joint theory- and data-based approach is called for. In the next section we take the extreme viewpoint that the only prior information about the relationship between x and y is the exogeneity of x and the stationarity conditions (10.1.3) and (10.1.4) are assumed to hold. Of course, these are already quite strong assumptions in some sense, but no economic theories will be used to justify a particular lag and error structure. Viewing an economic theory as a set of constraints to be observed in the statistical analysis, we will more or less assume in the following section that such constraints do not exist.

10.2.2 Data-Based Model Specification

If economic theory does not provide a model for the relationship between two variables x and y, statistical tools may be applied to fill the gap. That is, if the model (10.1.2) is hypothesized, the operators $\gamma(L)$, $\phi(L)$, $\alpha(L)$, and $\theta(L)$ and, specifically, their orders have to be determined with statistical techniques. In the following discussion we will discuss possibilities to determine the lag structure and the error structure of a general model like (10.1.1). We will first assume that the model has the special form (10.1.2).

10.2.2a The Box-Jenkins Approach for Specifying Transfer Function Models

In their influential book Box and Jenkins (1976) not only develop a procedure for specifying univariate ARIMA models (see Chapter 7), but also describe a technique applicable for the specific model (10.1.2), where x_t is assumed to be an exogenous ARMA process. The assumption of no feedback between x and y is essential in their procedure. We will also assume that x_t and y_t are stationary processes for which the conditions (10.1.3) and (10.1.4) are satisfied. Box and Jenkins suggest to specify the orders of the involved operators roughly in the following steps:

Step 1 Specify a univariate ARMA model $\eta(L)x_t = \psi(L)w_t$. For a discussion of this procedure see Chapter 7.

Step 2 Define a process

$$z_t = \frac{\eta(L)}{\psi(L)} y_t \tag{10.2.22}$$

and multiply (10.1.2) by $\eta(L)/\psi(L)$ to get

$$z_t = \frac{\gamma(L)}{\phi(L)} w_t + \frac{\eta(L)\alpha(L)}{\psi(L)\theta(L)} v_t \tag{10.2.23}$$

Step 3 Multiplying (10.2.23) by w_{t-k}, taking expectations, and dividing by the variance σ_w^2 of w_t gives

$$\begin{aligned} \xi_k &= \frac{\operatorname{cov}(z_t, w_{t-k})}{\sigma_w^2} \\ &= \operatorname{corr}(z_t, w_{t-k}) \frac{\sigma_z}{\sigma_w} \end{aligned} \tag{10.2.24}$$

where σ_z is the standard deviation of z_t and ξ_k is the kth coefficient of the series

$$\frac{\gamma(L)}{\phi(L)} = \sum_{k=0}^{\infty} \xi_k L^k \tag{10.2.25}$$

since v_t and w_t are independent white noise processes by assumption. Thus, the cross-correlations between z_t and w_t can be used to determine the orders of $\gamma(L)$ and $\phi(L)$. A description of how exactly this is done is beyond the scope of this presentation and the reader is referred to Box and Jenkins (1976) and Granger and Newbold (1977) for details.

Step 4 Identify a univariate ARMA model for the series

$$s_t = y_t - \frac{\gamma(L)}{\phi(L)} x_t \tag{10.2.26}$$

to obtain the orders of $\alpha(L)$ and $\theta(L)$.

The above outline is only meant to give a rough impression of what is involved in a purely data-based specification of a model like (10.1.2). The successful application of the above technique requires some experience and for examples the reader may consult Box and Jenkins (1976) and Granger and Newbold (1977).

An alternative specification scheme is proposed and discussed for example by Haugh and Box (1977) and Granger and Newbold (1977). They "prewhiten" y_t and x_t; that is, they build a univariate ARMA model for each of the two variables first and then they construct a bivariate model for the two resulting residual series. In a final step the univariate models are amalgamated with the bivariate residual model. This approach can be generalized to the case of a feedback relationship between x and y.

10.2.2b Approximating the Lag Structure

The techniques for model specification sketched in the foregoing are admittedly difficult to handle. Therefore, alternative strategies have been proposed and applied.

In Section 10.1.2 we mentioned that not only the rational lags but also the discounted polynomial lag structures can approximate any reasonable lag scheme to any desired degree of accuracy in a relevant sense. Thus, instead of using (10.1.2) one could assume that in the model (10.1.1)

$$\beta(L) = \sum_{i=0}^{\infty} \lambda^i p(i) L^i \qquad (10.2.27)$$

where $0 < \lambda < 1$ and $p(i) = \Sigma_{j=0}^{r} p_j i^j$. Such a model has the advantage that only the polynomial degree r has to be determined in order to specify the lag structure instead of the two orders r and m in the case of a rational lag. We will see in the next section that varying the polynomial degree r comes down to varying the number of regressors in the regression model used for estimating the parameters. Therefore, the usual criteria for model selection such as AIC and PC (see Chapter 9 or Chapter 21) may be used to determine r.

If e_t is not white noise but a (nondeterministic) stationary stochastic process, it is known to have a possibly infinite-order moving average representation, say

$$\begin{aligned} e_t &= v_t + \mu_1 v_{t-1} + \mu_2 v_{t-2} + \cdots \\ &= (1 + \mu_1 L + \mu_2 L^2 + \cdots) v_t \\ &= \mu(L) v_t \end{aligned} \qquad (10.2.28)$$

(see Chapter 7). In (10.1.2) $\mu(L)$ is approximated by $\alpha(L)/\theta(L)$ and similarly a discounted polynomial approximation could be used. However, for estimation purposes it turns out to be advantageous to multiply $y_t = \beta(L)x_t + \mu(L)v_t$ by $\mu^{-1}(L)$ (assuming that the latter exists). This results in a specification of the general form

$$y_t = \delta(L) y_{t-1} + v(L) x_t + v_t \qquad (10.2.29)$$

where

$$\delta(L) = \frac{1}{L}[1 - \mu^{-1}(L)] \quad \text{and} \quad v(L) = \mu^{-1}(L)\beta(L)$$

Now the operators $\delta(L)$ and $v(L)$ can be approximated by operators

$$\sum_{i=0}^{\infty} \lambda^i p_1(i)L^i \quad \text{and} \quad \sum_{i=0}^{\infty} \lambda^i p_2(i)L^i$$

respectively, where $p_1(i)$ and $p_2(i)$ are polynomials of finite but unknown degrees that have to be determined. After the model has been fitted, the lag coefficients can be recovered by noting that

$$\beta(L) = [1 - L\delta(L)]^{-1}v(L) \tag{10.2.30}$$

Another strategy for specifying the lag model (10.1.1) is to approximate the infinite lag by a lag of finite length. For this purpose also the criteria discussed in Chapter 9 can be used. Shibata (1981) derives asymptotic optimality conditions for some of them. However, such a strategy may lead to unsatisfactory results if the sample size is small since such models may involve a considerable number of parameters. Below we will discuss a procedure for finding a more parsimonious specification.

10.2.2c Common Factor Analysis

Assuming that the model is actually of the form

$$\xi(L)y_t = v(L)x_t + v_t \tag{10.2.31}$$

with finite-order operators

$$\xi(L) = 1 + \xi_1 L + \ldots + \xi_n L^n = (1 - \psi_1 L) \ldots (1 - \psi_n L) \tag{10.2.32a}$$

$$v(L) = 1 + v_1 L + \ldots + v_s L^s = (1 - \omega_1 L) \ldots (1 - \omega_s L) \tag{10.2.32b}$$

and v_t is white noise as usual, the following procedure is useful to reduce the number of parameters to be estimated. In (10.2.32) the ψ_i and ω_i are the roots of $\xi(L)$ and $v(L)$, respectively. If k of the ψ_i are equal to k of the ω_i, then $\xi(L) = \zeta(L)\bar{\xi}(L)$ and $v(L) = \zeta(L)\bar{v}(L)$, where $\zeta(L)$ consists of the k common factors of $\xi(L)$ and $v(L)$. Using this notation and assuming that $\zeta(L)$ is invertible, (10.2.31) can be rewritten as

$$\bar{\xi}(L)y_t = \bar{v}(L)x_t + \frac{v_t}{\zeta(L)} \tag{10.2.33}$$

Note that there are $n + s$ parameters in (10.2.31), whereas (10.2.33) contains only $(n - k) + (s - k) + k = n + s - k$ parameters. Thus, (10.2.33) is a more parsimonious specification of (10.2.31).

In order to specify a model of the type (10.2.33) a sequence of nested tests can be carried out. Initially the orders of $\xi(L)$ and $v(L)$ in (10.2.31) are specified so as to be at least as great as the true orders of these operators. Then a sequence of tests for common roots of $\xi(L)$ and $v(L)$ is carried out and finally the roots are sequentially tested to be zero. Sargan (1980) suggests using the Wald test since it requires only the estimation of the unconstrained model. For details see Sargan's article or Harvey (1981, Chapter 8). The procedure is briefly called COMFAC analysis and was applied by Hendry and Mizon (1978) and Mizon and Hendry (1980).

10.2.3 Conclusions

As indicated earlier, the data-based and the theory-based approaches to model specification should not be used as substitutes, but should be integrated into one strategy for model construction. The model set-up must be general enough to include an adequate model, but constraints from economic theory should be used where available. This is of particular importance as there are often alternative specifications fitting the data equally well so that a purely data-based approach cannot discriminate among these specifications. Also, it is often difficult to extract a simple, parsimoniously parameterized structure from the data and any aid from economic theory or institutional knowledge should be gratefully accepted. On the other hand, not all economic theories are adequate, and if they are at variance with the data they must be reconsidered taking into account the empirical evidence.

Sometimes competing economic theories are available that lead to different models for a set of economic variables. In such a nonnested case a general model may be set up as in Chapter 21 that includes the various competitors and an adequate submodel can be determined by testing different sets of restrictions. As an example Hendry and Richard (1983) consider the following simple model:

$$y_t = \beta_0 x_t + \beta_1 x_{t-1} + \lambda y_{t-1} + v_t \tag{10.2.34}$$

where v_t is Gaussian white noise and x_t is exogenous. Hendry and Richard list nine special cases of (10.2.34) obtained by placing constraints on the parameters β_0, β_1, and λ.

1. If $\beta_1 = \lambda = 0$, (10.2.34) reduces to a simple, nondynamic, linear regression model.
2. For $\beta_0 = \beta_1 = 0$, y_t is an autoregressive process of order one.
3. With the constraint $\beta_0 = \lambda = 0$ (10.2.34) turns into a leading indicator model, where x is an indicator that leads y by one period.
4. If y and x are logarithms of the original variables, the restrictions $\lambda = 1$ and

$\beta_0 = -\beta_1$ imply a static linear regression model for the growth rates of the two variables.

5. For $\lambda = 0$, (10.2.34) is a finite distributed lag model with lag length 1.
6. Constraining β_1 to be zero results in a partial adjustment model (see Section 10.2.1b).
7. A simple regression model with AR(1) error term is implied by $\beta_1/\beta_0 = -\lambda$. This can be seen by rewriting (10.2.34) as

$$(1 - \lambda L)y_t = \beta_0(1 + \frac{\beta_1}{\beta_0} L)x_t + v_t \tag{10.2.35}$$

and dividing by $(1 - \lambda L)$.

8. The restriction $\beta_0 + \beta_1 + \lambda = 1$ gives an "error correction mechanism" of the type

$$y_t - y_{t-1} = \beta_0(x_t - x_{t-1}) + (1 - \lambda)(x_{t-1} - y_{t-1}) + v_t \tag{10.2.36}$$

where y_t is obtained from y_{t-1} by adding a random shock v_t, a portion of the change in x and a portion of the deviation from the equilibrium value $(x_{t-1} = y_{t-1})$ of the previous period.

9. For $\beta_0 = 0$, (10.2.34) is called a "dead-start" model for obvious reasons.

This example shows how "small" changes in a model can make a great difference for its interpretation. If there is uncertainty as to which interpretation is appropriate in a particular case, a framework such as the above makes it easy to use the data to settle the matter by testing constraints for the general specification (10.2.34). Of course, sometimes there may not be sufficient information in the data to obtain a definite model even if one starts from a specification as simple as (10.2.34). This problem is aggravated if the starting point is a more general specification involving more lags of x and y like the model (10.1.2), and the applied researcher should avoid interpreting the lack of evidence against a specific model due to insufficient information as evidence in favor of this model. In Section 10.3 we will assume that a model has been specified so that we can proceed to parameter estimation.

10.3 ESTIMATION OF RATIONAL DISTRIBUTED LAG MODELS WITH ARMA ERRORS

Estimating the parameters of a dynamic model of the type (10.1.2), we cannot hope in general to derive small sample properties of the resulting estimators. Therefore, it is usually attempted to find estimators with optimal asymptotic properties and maximum likelihood (ML) estimation is the obvious choice. Since exact ML estimates are sometimes difficult to compute, asymptotically equivalent procedures have been proposed. We will first consider the estimation problem for simple geometric lag models and look at more general cases in Sections 10.3.2 and 10.3.3.

10.3.1 Estimation of Geometric Lag Models

In this section we will discuss estimation of the model

$$y_t = \alpha \sum_{i=0}^{\infty} \lambda^i x_{t-i} + e_t = f_t(\alpha,\lambda) + e_t, \qquad t = 1, \ldots, T \tag{10.3.1}$$

under alternative assumptions for e_t. Here $f_t(\alpha,\lambda)$ is defined in the obvious way and $0 < \lambda < 1$.

10.3.1a Exact Maximum Likelihood When the Disturbances Are Not Autocorrelated

If the e_t are a Gaussian white noise process—that is, the e_t are independent and identically normally distributed with zero mean and variance σ_e^2—it is easy to see that ML and LS (least squares) estimation are equivalent (see Chapter 6). Therefore, instead of maximizing the likelihood function, we can minimize

$$\begin{aligned} S(\alpha,\lambda) &= \sum_{t=1}^{T} (y_t - f_t(\alpha,\lambda))^2 \\ &= \sum_{t=1}^{T} \left(y_t - \alpha \sum_{i=0}^{\infty} \lambda^i x_{t-i}\right)^2 \end{aligned} \tag{10.3.2}$$

An obvious problem results since the x_t are unknown for $t \leq 0$. One way to proceed in this case was suggested by Klein (1958). The model (10.3.1) is rewritten as

$$\begin{aligned} y_t &= \alpha \sum_{i=0}^{t-1} \lambda^i x_{t-i} + \lambda^t \alpha \sum_{i=0}^{\infty} \lambda^i x_{-i} + e_t \\ &= \alpha \sum_{i=0}^{t-1} \lambda^i x_{t-i} + \lambda^t \eta_0 + e_t \end{aligned} \tag{10.3.3}$$

Here η_0 is independent of t and can be regarded as a further parameter in the model. This parameter contains all presample values of the exogenous variable x and can be estimated together with the other parameters. Thus, we have a nonlinear LS problem as discussed in Chapter 6. However, (10.3.3) is linear for each fixed λ, and furthermore this parameter is known to lie between zero and one so that a search procedure can be easily adopted to obtain LS (ML) estimates.

It follows from results in Chapter 6 that if x_t is nonstochastic and

$$\lim_{T\to\infty} \frac{1}{T} \sum_{t=1}^{T} x_t^2 \tag{10.3.4}$$

exists and is finite, the ML estimators $\tilde{\alpha}$, $\tilde{\lambda}$, and $\tilde{\sigma}_e^2$ are consistent, asymptotically efficient, and normally distributed; that is,

$$\sqrt{T}\left(\begin{bmatrix}\tilde{\alpha}\\ \tilde{\lambda}\\ \tilde{\sigma}_e^2\end{bmatrix}-\begin{bmatrix}\alpha\\ \lambda\\ \sigma_e^2\end{bmatrix}\right)\xrightarrow{d} N(\mathbf{0},\Omega) \tag{10.3.5}$$

where

$$\tilde{\sigma}_e^2 = \frac{S(\tilde{\alpha},\tilde{\lambda})}{T}$$

$$\Omega = \begin{bmatrix}\sigma_e^2 \lim T[Z(\alpha,\lambda)'Z(\alpha,\lambda)]^{-1} & 0\\ 0 & 2\sigma_e^4\end{bmatrix} \tag{10.3.6}$$

and $Z(\alpha,\lambda)$ is the $(T \times 2)$ matrix with tth row

$$\left[\frac{\partial f_t(\alpha,\lambda)}{\partial\alpha}, \frac{\partial f_t(\alpha,\lambda)}{\partial\lambda}\right] = \left[\sum_{i=0}^{\infty} \lambda^i x_{t-i}, \ \alpha \sum_{i=1}^{\infty} i\lambda^{i-1}x_{t-i}\right] \tag{10.3.7}$$

A consistent estimator of Ω can be obtained by replacing all parameters by their ML estimators and setting all presample values of x_t in $Z(\alpha,\lambda)$ at zero. Here it has been used that $\lambda^t\eta_0$, the so-called *truncation remainder,* vanishes asymptotically as $t \to \infty$, so that it does not affect the asymptotic distribution of the other parameters. Replacing presample values of x_t by zero means simply deleting the truncation remainder.

Although its treatment does not matter asymptotically, there has been discussion on what to do with $\lambda^t\eta_0$ in small samples [e.g., Pesaran (1973), Schmidt (1975), Schmidt and Guilkey (1976), Glejser (1977)]. Note that η_0 cannot be estimated consistently [e.g., Dhrymes (1971a)], the reason being that the associated "regressor" λ^t approaches zero too fast as the sample size increases. Also, it is perhaps worth noting that x_t may actually be stochastic; for instance, it may be a stationary ARMA process. In that case it suffices to replace the limit in (10.3.4) by the almost sure limit. Furthermore, similar results can be derived if x_t is trending [see Dhrymes (1971a)]. Before we consider a more general version of the geometric lag model, we will discuss alternative ways to obtain estimators that are asymptotically equivalent to the ML estimators derived in the foregoing.

10.3.1b Approximate Maximum Likelihood When the Disturbances Are Not Autocorrelated

Although it is not difficult to compute exact ML estimators for the simple model (10.3.1) as discussed in Section 10.3.1a, we will now consider an approximate ML procedure that is theoretically easy to generalize to cope with more general models. Note that, using lag operator notation (10.3.1) can be written as

$$y_t = \frac{\alpha x_t}{1 - \lambda L} + e_t$$

or, premultiplying by $(1 - \lambda L)$ and rearranging,

$$y_t = \lambda y_{t-1} + \alpha x_t + e_t - \lambda e_{t-1} \tag{10.3.8}$$

Thus we get a sum of squares function

$$S^*(\alpha,\lambda) = \mathbf{e}'\mathbf{e} = \sum_{t=2}^{T} (y_t - \lambda y_{t-1} - \alpha x_t + \lambda e_{t-1})^2 \tag{10.3.9}$$

where $\mathbf{e}' = (e_2, \ldots, e_T)$. This function can be evaluated recursively starting with e_2, if e_1 is assumed to be zero. Minimizing (10.3.9) is equivalent to ML estimation when y_1 is assumed fixed. Hence, the LS estimates will be asymptotically equivalent to the exact ML estimates.

The function $S^*(\alpha,\lambda)$ can be minimized with respect to α and λ using an iterative optimization method. Employing the Gauss algorithm is one possibility. As discussed in Appendix B the nth iteration has the general form

$$\boldsymbol{\beta}_{n+1} = \boldsymbol{\beta}_n - \left[\left(\frac{\partial \mathbf{e}}{\partial \boldsymbol{\beta}'}\right)'\left(\frac{\partial \mathbf{e}}{\partial \boldsymbol{\beta}'}\right)\right]^{-1}\left(\frac{\partial \mathbf{e}}{\partial \boldsymbol{\beta}'}\right)'\mathbf{e} \tag{10.3.10}$$

where $\boldsymbol{\beta}_n = (\alpha_n, \lambda_n)'$ and all derivatives are evaluated at $\boldsymbol{\beta}_n$. Thus the Gauss method requires only first partial derivatives and these can also be determined recursively since, from (10.3.8),

$$\frac{\partial e_t}{\partial \alpha} = -x_t + \lambda \frac{\partial e_{t-1}}{\partial \alpha}$$

and

$$\frac{\partial e_t}{\partial \lambda} = -y_{t-1} + e_{t-1} + \lambda \frac{\partial e_{t-1}}{\partial \lambda}$$

As noted in Chapter 6, if only asymptotic results are of interest, it is not necessary to iterate until convergence. It suffices to perform one iteration provided consistent initial estimates for α and λ are available. These can be obtained by computing an instrumental variable estimator for the linear specification (10.3.8). In the next section we consider instrumental variable estimation.

10.3.1c Instrumental Variable Estimation

Since the first regressor in Equation 10.3.8,

$$y_t = \lambda y_{t-1} + \alpha x_t + u_t \tag{10.3.11}$$

is correlated with the error term $u_t = e_t - \lambda e_{t-1}$, it is known that the LS estimator of λ will be inconsistent [see Chapter 5, Judge et al. (1982, Chapter 27) or

Doran and Griffiths (1978)]. However, the instrumental variable technique can be used to obtain consistent estimators.

To obtain useful instruments recall that an instrumental variable should be correlated with the associated regressor but uncorrelated with the error term. For example, as instrument for y_{t-1} in (10.3.11), we may use x_{t-1} so that we get as instrumental variable estimator

$$\begin{bmatrix} \hat{\alpha} \\ \hat{\lambda} \end{bmatrix} = (Z'X)^{-1}Z'\mathbf{y} \tag{10.3.12}$$

where

$$\mathbf{y} = \begin{bmatrix} y_2 \\ \vdots \\ y_T \end{bmatrix}, \quad X = \begin{bmatrix} x_2 & y_1 \\ x_3 & y_2 \\ \vdots & \vdots \\ x_T & y_{T-1} \end{bmatrix}, \quad \text{and} \quad Z = \begin{bmatrix} x_2 & x_1 \\ x_3 & x_2 \\ \vdots & \vdots \\ x_T & x_{T-1} \end{bmatrix} \tag{10.3.13}$$

[see Liviatan (1963)].

10.3.1d Autocorrelated Disturbances e_t

We will now assume that the errors e_t in (10.3.1) follow an AR(1) process so that

$$e_t = \rho e_{t-1} + v_t \tag{10.3.14}$$

where $-1 < \rho < 1$ and v_t is Gaussian white noise with variance σ_v^2. This case can be treated as discussed in Chapter 8. Writing (10.3.1) as

$$\mathbf{y} = \mathbf{f}(\alpha,\lambda) + \mathbf{e} \tag{10.3.15}$$

where $\mathbf{y} = (y_1, \ldots, y_T)'$, $\mathbf{f}(\alpha,\lambda) = [f_1(\alpha,\lambda), \ldots, f_T(\alpha,\lambda)]'$, and $\mathbf{e} = (e_1, \ldots, e_T)'$, we can premultiply by

$$P = \begin{bmatrix} \sqrt{1-\rho^2} & 0 & \cdots & 0 & 0 \\ -\rho & 1 & \cdots & 0 & 0 \\ 0 & -\rho & \cdots & 0 & 0 \\ \vdots & \vdots & \ddots & \vdots & \vdots \\ 0 & 0 & \cdot & 1 & 0 \\ 0 & 0 & \cdots & -\rho & 1 \end{bmatrix} \tag{10.3.16}$$

to obtain the model

$$\mathbf{y}^* = \mathbf{f}^*(\alpha,\lambda,\rho) + \mathbf{e}^* \tag{10.3.17}$$

where $\mathbf{y}^* = P\mathbf{y}$, $\mathbf{f}^*(\alpha,\lambda,\rho) = P\mathbf{f}(\alpha,\lambda)$, $\mathbf{e}^* = P\mathbf{e} = (\sqrt{1-\rho^2}e_1, v_2, \ldots, v_T)'$. Estimating the parameters in (10.3.17) by LS—that is, by minimizing $\mathbf{e}^{*\prime}\mathbf{e}^*$—results in estimated generalized least squares (EGLS) estimates which are asymptotically equivalent to the ML estimates. To obtain exact ML estimates,

$$(1-\rho^2)^{-1/T}\mathbf{e}^{*\prime}\mathbf{e}^* \tag{10.3.18}$$

can be minimized (see Section 8.2.1d). If the explanatory variables x_t satisfy the condition (10.3.4), the ML estimators are consistent, asymptotically efficient, and normally distributed,

$$\sqrt{T}\left(\begin{bmatrix}\tilde{\alpha}\\ \tilde{\lambda}\\ \tilde{\rho}\\ \tilde{\sigma}_v^2\end{bmatrix} - \begin{bmatrix}\alpha\\ \lambda\\ \rho\\ \sigma_v^2\end{bmatrix}\right) \xrightarrow{d} N(\mathbf{0},\Omega^*) \tag{10.3.19}$$

where

$$\tilde{\sigma}_v^2 = \frac{[\mathbf{y}^* - \mathbf{f}^*(\tilde{\alpha},\tilde{\lambda},\tilde{\rho})]'[\mathbf{y}^* - \mathbf{f}^*(\tilde{\alpha},\tilde{\lambda},\tilde{\rho})]}{T} \tag{10.3.20}$$

and

$$\Omega^{*^{-1}} = \begin{bmatrix} \sigma_v^{-2}\lim T^{-1}\left[\frac{\partial\mathbf{f}}{\partial(\alpha,\lambda)}\right]' P'P\left[\frac{\partial\mathbf{f}}{\partial(\alpha,\lambda)}\right] & 0 & 0\\ 0 & \frac{1}{1-\rho^2} & 0\\ 0 & 0 & \frac{1}{2\sigma_v^4}\end{bmatrix} \tag{10.3.21}$$

Thus, $\tilde{\alpha}$ and $\tilde{\lambda}$ are asymptotically independent of the parameters that characterize the error process. The asymptotic covariance matrix Ω^* can be estimated consistently by replacing all parameters by their ML estimates and the presample values of x_t by zero. As in the case with nonautocorrelated errors similar results can be derived under more general conditions for x_t [Dhrymes (1971a)].

As indicated above there are different ways to compute asymptotically equivalent estimates. For fixed λ and ρ minimizing

$$\mathbf{e}^{*\prime}\mathbf{e}^* = [\mathbf{y}^* - \mathbf{f}^*(\alpha,\lambda,\rho)]'[\mathbf{y}^* - \mathbf{f}^*(\alpha,\lambda,\rho)] \tag{10.3.22}$$

is a linear least squares problem so that LS estimates for α can be computed conditionally on a range of (λ,ρ) combinations, where $0 < \lambda < 1$ and $-1 < \rho < 1$. The values for α, λ, and ρ that jointly minimize (10.3.22) are chosen as estimates. Essentially the same procedure can be used to find the minimum of (10.3.18) [see Dhrymes (1971a), Zellner and Geisel (1970)]. Note, however, that in either case $\mathbf{f}^*(\alpha,\lambda,\rho)$ contains the presample values of x_t, $t \le 0$, that are usually not available in practice. They can be replaced by zero or estimated via the truncation remainder term (see Section 10.3.1a). Again this term cannot be estimated consistently.

An alternative way to compute approximate ML estimates results from writing the model in lag operator notation as

$$y_t = \frac{\alpha x_t}{1 - \lambda L} + \frac{v_t}{1 - \rho L}$$

and premultiplying by $(1 - \lambda L)(1 - \rho L) = 1 - (\lambda + \rho)L + \lambda\rho L^2$. Thus we get

$$y_t = (\lambda + \rho)y_{t-1} - \lambda\rho y_{t-2} + \alpha x_t - \alpha\rho x_{t-1} + v_t - \lambda v_{t-1}$$

and minimizing

$$\sum_{t=3}^{T} v_t^2 = \sum_{t=3}^{T} (y_t - (\lambda + \rho)y_{t-1} + \lambda\rho y_{t-2} - \alpha x_t + \alpha\rho x_{t-1} + \lambda v_{t-1})^2 \tag{10.3.23}$$

is equivalent to ML estimation when the first two observations, y_1 and y_2, are assumed to be fixed and $v_2 = 0$. If the Gauss algorithm is used to find the minimum of (10.3.23), the nth iteration is

$$\boldsymbol{\beta}_{n+1} = \boldsymbol{\beta}_n - \left[\left(\frac{\partial \mathbf{v}}{\partial \boldsymbol{\beta}'}\right)'\left(\frac{\partial \mathbf{v}}{\partial \boldsymbol{\beta}'}\right)\right]^{-1}\left(\frac{\partial \mathbf{v}}{\partial \boldsymbol{\beta}'}\right)'\mathbf{v} \tag{10.3.24}$$

where $\boldsymbol{\beta}_n = (\alpha_n, \lambda_n, \rho_n)'$ is the parameter vector obtained in the $(n - 1)$st iteration, $\mathbf{v} = (v_3, v_4, \ldots, v_T)'$ and all derivatives are evaluated at $\boldsymbol{\beta}_n$ and can be determined recursively as in Section 10.3.1b. If the starting vector $\boldsymbol{\beta}_1$ contains consistent estimates of α, λ, and ρ, asymptotically efficient estimates are obtained in one iteration of the Gauss algorithm; that is, $\boldsymbol{\beta}_2$ will be an asymptotically efficient estimate (see Chapter 6).

As in the case of independent disturbances instrumental variable estimation of $y_t = \lambda y_{t-1} + \alpha x_t + u_t$, where $u_t = e_t - \lambda e_{t-1}$, provides consistent estimates $\hat{\lambda}$ and $\hat{\alpha}$ of λ and α (see Section 10.3.1c). These estimates can be used to compute residuals

$$\hat{e}_t = y_t - \hat{\alpha} \sum_{i=0}^{t-1} \hat{\lambda}^i x_{t-i} \tag{10.3.25}$$

and a consistent estimate

$$\hat{\rho} = \frac{\sum_{t=2}^{T} \hat{e}_t \hat{e}_{t-1}}{\sum_{t=2}^{T} \hat{e}_t^2} \tag{10.3.26}$$

The estimates $\hat{\lambda}$, $\hat{\alpha}$, and $\hat{\rho}$ can be used as initial values for the Gauss or some other iterative algorithm. Note that the truncation remainder has been omitted in computing $\hat{e}_t$ in (10.3.25). From an asymptotic point of view this simplification is of no consequence. However, in small samples it may be preferable to take account of the truncation remainder when computing the $\hat{e}_t$. For details see Amemiya and Fuller (1967) and for a different development of the two-step procedure see Hatanaka (1974).

A number of authors have discussed the above and other estimation procedures for the geometric lag model. These include Koyck (1954), Cagan (1956), Taylor and Wilson (1964), Wallis (1967), Oi (1969), Dhrymes (1969, 1971b), Zellner and Park (1965), Harvey (1981), and Fomby and Guilkey (1983). More details are provided in Judge et al. (1980), and a summary of the earlier work on the subject is contained in Dhrymes (1971a).

10.3.2 Discounted Polynomial Lags

A similar simplification as in (10.3.3) for the geometric lag can be obtained for the discounted polynomial lag in (10.1.12). To illustrate we assume that (10.1.1) has the form

$$y_t = \sum_{i=0}^{\infty} \lambda^i p(i) x_{t-i} + e_t \tag{10.3.27}$$

where e_t is Gaussian white noise, $0 < \lambda < 1$, and

$$p(i) = \sum_{j=0}^{r} p_j i^j \tag{10.3.28}$$

Schmidt (1974a) shows that (10.3.27) can be rewritten as

$$y_t = \sum_{j=0}^{r} p_j s_{jt} + r_t + e_t \tag{10.3.29}$$

where

$$s_{jt} = \sum_{i=0}^{t-1} \lambda^i i^j x_{t-i}, \qquad j = 0, 1, \ldots, r \tag{10.3.30}$$

with 0^0 defined to be 1, and

$$r_t = \sum_{i=t}^{\infty} (\lambda^i \sum_{j=0}^{r} p_j i^j x_{t-i}) = \lambda^t \sum_{j=0}^{r} \eta_j t^j \tag{10.3.31}$$

The η_j contain the presample values of x and can be treated as further parameters in the model. Alternatively, the r_t can be replaced by zero without affecting the *asymptotic* properties of the parameter estimators. To reduce their impact in small samples, it may be advantageous to treat the first few observations as presample values if the r_t are replaced by zero since these terms have the most significant impact at the beginning of the sample period.

For a fixed λ, (10.3.29) is a linear regression model and the polynomial coefficients p_j can be estimated efficiently by linear least squares. If λ is not treated as a constant but as a further parameter in the model, a search procedure is suggested. That is, the linear least squares problem is solved for a range of different λ values between zero and one, and the one that minimizes the error sum of squares is chosen as estimate for λ. The resulting estimators of the polynomial coefficients and λ are the ML estimators that are consistent, asymptotically normally distributed, and efficient, provided the model is correct. The variances of the asymptotic distribution are given by Schmidt and Mann (1977). Note however that, as in the geometric lag model, the η_j cannot be estimated consistently. This is again due to the fast convergence of the associated "regressors" to zero and is usually of no consequence since these parameters are rarely of interest.

In many situations a model of this type will only be regarded as an approximation to the "true" structure. In this case Lütkepohl (1980) points out that even with some fixed λ the model is general enough to provide arbitrarily good approximations to all reasonable lag structures if an appropriate polynomial degree r has been chosen (see Section 10.2.2b). This assumption not only simplifies the estimation problem for the p_j, but also makes it easy to obtain the distribution of the resulting lag coefficients that are in the case of a constant λ linearly related to the p_j:

$$\beta_i = \lambda^i(p_0 + p_1 i + \ldots + p_r i^r) \qquad (10.3.32)$$

If the error term in the original lag model (10.1.1) is not white noise, it is preferable to transfer to the version (10.2.29) and then approximate the operators $\delta(L)$ and $v(L)$ as explained in Section 10.2.2b. A similar transformation as above can then be used to obtain a linear model with a finite set of parameters that can be estimated by linear least squares if the discount factor λ is fixed. For details see Lütkepohl (1982a).

Of course, the infinite lag operators $\delta(L)$ and $v(L)$ in (10.2.29) could also be approximated by finite lags. This possibility is considered by Sims (1971a) and Shibata (1981). As pointed out earlier, the disadvantage of this procedure is that a substantial number of parameters may be required to obtain an adequate approximation.

Various estimation procedures have been investigated for other than the above mentioned special case models. For instance, Solow (1960), Chetty (1971), Maddala and Rao (1971), Schmidt (1973), and Guthrie (1976) consider estimation of the Pascal distributed lag [see (10.1.11)] and maximum likelihood procedures for rational distributed lag models with white noise error term are considered by Dhrymes, Klein, and Steiglitz (1970) and Maddala and Rao

(1971). In Section 10.3.3 we will discuss the estimation of general models of the type (10.1.2).

10.3.3 General Rational Lag Models with ARMA Errors

10.3.3a Time Domain Estimation

To discuss ML estimation of (10.1.2) we write the model as

$$\phi(L)\theta(L)y_t = \theta(L)\gamma(L)x_t + \phi(L)\alpha(L)v_t$$

or

$$\begin{aligned} y_t &= -\frac{1}{L}(\phi(L)\theta(L) - 1)y_{t-1} + \theta(L)\gamma(L)x_t + \phi(L)\alpha(L)v_t \\ &= \psi_1 y_{t-1} + \ldots + \psi_{m+p}y_{t-(m+p)} + \eta_0 x_t + \eta_1 x_{t-1} + \ldots + \eta_{r+p}x_{t-(r+p)} \\ &\quad + v_t + \xi_1 v_{t-1} + \ldots + \xi_{m+q}v_{t-(m+q)} \end{aligned} \tag{10.3.33}$$

where the ψ_i, η_i, and ξ_i are determined by the coefficients of $\phi(L)$, $\theta(L)$, $\gamma(L)$, and $\alpha(L)$. Assuming that v_t is Gaussian white noise and that, for $h = \max(m + p, r + p)$, the $y_1, y_2, \ldots, y_h$ are fixed and $v_t = 0$ for $t \leq h$, then, instead of maximizing the likelihood function, it follows from (10.3.33) that we can equivalently minimize the sum of squares function

$$\begin{aligned} \mathbf{v}'\mathbf{v} &= \sum_{t=h+1}^{T} (y_t - \psi_1 y_{t-1} - \ldots - \psi_{m+p}y_{t-(m+p)} - \eta_0 x_t - \ldots - \eta_{r+p}x_{t-(r+p)} \\ &\qquad - \xi_1 v_{t-1} - \ldots - \xi_{m+q}v_{t-(m+q)})^2 \\ &= \sum_{t=h+1}^{T} [\phi(L)\theta(L)y_t - \theta(L)\gamma(L)x_t - \frac{1}{L}(\phi(L)\alpha(L) - 1)v_{t-1}]^2 \end{aligned} \tag{10.3.34}$$

where $\mathbf{v} = (v_{h+1}, \ldots, v_T)'$. This is a nonlinear optimization problem and the Gauss algorithm is one candidate for solving it as in the special case considered in Section 10.3.1d. The nth iteration has exactly the form (10.3.24) if $\boldsymbol{\beta}$ is specified to be the vector of all parameters,

$$\boldsymbol{\beta} = (\gamma_0, \gamma_1, \ldots, \gamma_r, \phi_1, \ldots, \phi_m, \theta_1, \ldots, \theta_p, \alpha_1, \ldots, \alpha_q)'$$

Under general conditions this procedure provides consistent, asymptotically efficient, and normally distributed estimators in one iteration if consistent estimators are used as starting values. The asymptotic covariance matrix is the inverse information matrix.

As in the case of the simple geometric lag model, consistent starting values can be obtained by instrumental variable estimation. Premultiplying (10.1.2) by $\phi(L)$ gives the linear model

$$y_t = -\phi_1 y_{t-1} - \ldots - \phi_m y_{t-m} + \gamma_0 x_t + \gamma_1 x_{t-1} + \ldots + \gamma_r x_{t-r} + u_t \tag{10.3.35}$$

Of course, the $u_t = [\phi(L)\alpha(L)/\theta(L)]v_t$ are in general autocorrelated and thus correlated with some of the regressors so that consistent estimation by linear least squares is not possible and instrumental variable techniques are suggested. Theoretically x_{t-r-i} could be used as an instrument for y_{t-i}. However, Dhrymes (1971a, p. 250) notes that in practice this may not be a good way to obtain initial estimates $\hat{\phi}_i$ and $\hat{\gamma}_i$ as economic time series are often highly autocorrelated so that the matrix of instruments may be ill conditioned. Dhrymes suggests to use the principal components of a matrix of lagged x variables.

Once consistent estimates $\hat{\phi}(L)$ and $\hat{\gamma}(L)$ are available, residuals

$$\hat{e}_t = y_t - \frac{\hat{\gamma}(L)}{\hat{\phi}(L)} x_t \tag{10.3.36}$$

where presample values of x_t are set at zero, can be computed. These can be used to obtain initial estimates of $\alpha(L)$ and $\theta(L)$ by methods described in Chapter 7.

Algorithms especially designed for estimating the parameters of models like (10.1.2) exist in many computing centers, and rather than trying to write one's own routine it is usually preferable to make use of this service where available.

10.3.3b Spectral Methods

Application of the ML procedure of the preceding section requires that the error process $e_t = [\alpha(L)/\theta(L)]v_t$ is specified. Since we are often mainly interested in the lag distribution $\gamma(L)/\phi(L)$, it may be preferable to use an estimation technique that avoids a preliminary specification of the degrees of $\alpha(L)$ and θ(L). Hannan (1963, 1965) has proposed to use spectral methods for this purpose. An extensive discussion of the properties of the resulting estimators is given by Dhrymes (1971a, Chapter 10). He shows that generalized least squares (GLS) estimation is asymptotically equivalent to minimizing

$$S = \frac{1}{2\pi} \sum_{j=-s+1}^{s} \left[\frac{\hat{f}_y(\omega_j) - 2\beta(\omega_j)\hat{f}_{xy}(\omega_j) + |\beta(\omega_j)|^2 \hat{f}_x(\omega_j)}{\hat{f}_e(\omega_j)} \right] \tag{10.3.37}$$

where $\beta(\omega) = \gamma(\omega)/\phi(\omega)$, $\omega_j = j\pi/s$, $\hat{f}_y(\cdot)$, $\hat{f}_x(\cdot)$, and $\hat{f}_e(\cdot)$ are consistent estimates of the spectral densities of y_t, x_t, and e_t, respectively, and $\hat{f}_{xy}(\cdot)$ is the cross-spectral density of x_t and y_t. The number s depends upon the sample size T and can for example be chosen to be approximately $\sqrt{T}$. Recall that the spectral density of a stationary stochastic process x_t with autocovariance function $\gamma_k(x) = E[x_t x_{t+k}]$ is

$$f_x(\omega) = \frac{1}{2\pi} \sum_{k=-\infty}^{\infty} \gamma_k(x) e^{-i\omega k} \tag{10.3.38}$$

(see Chapter 7). Similarly, the cross-spectral density of two jointly stationary processes x_t and y_t with cross-covariances $\gamma_k(x,y) = \text{cov}(x_{t+k}, y_t)$ is

$$f_{xy}(\omega) = \frac{1}{2\pi} \sum_{k=-\infty}^{\infty} \gamma_k(x,y) e^{-i\omega k} \tag{10.3.39}$$

The estimation of spectral densities is briefly discussed in Secion 7.6 and will not be repeated here. For a more detailed presentation of spectral methods see Dhrymes (1971a). Sims (1974a) also discusses another (though inefficient) estimation method due to Hannan (1963, 1965) and its equivalence to time-domain estimation methods. For an application of spectral methods in a distributed lag analysis see Cargill and Meyer (1972) and for a Monte Carlo comparison with other procedures see Cargill and Meyer (1974).

10.3.4 Some Comments

For the estimators resulting from the procedures discussed in the foregoing in general only *large sample* properties are known. To investigate the small sample properties, a number of Monte Carlo experiments have been carried out. Many of them are based on a geometric distributed lag model of the type

$$y_t = \alpha x_t + \lambda y_{t-1} + e_t \tag{10.3.40}$$

where e_t is a Gaussian AR(1) process, $e_t = \rho e_{t-1} + v_t$. The results of the sampling experiments depend on the sample size, the parameters λ and ρ and the exogenous variable x_t. This is reflected in the different conclusions from the various studies. Dhrymes's (1971a) results overall favor ML estimation. This is in line with results by Sargent (1968), who mentions, however, that the performance of the ML estimator is fairly sensitive to misspecification of the error structure. Maddala and Rao (1973) found that for a trending variable their ML procedure often provided estimates inferior to LS, whereas Gaab (1974) concludes that linear least squares estimation of α and λ gives poor results as compared to other procedures. Comparing generalized least squares and ordinary least squares, Maeshiro (1980) finds that the latter may be superior even for moderate sized samples if the exogenous variable is trended. Tse (1982) uses Edgeworth expansions to approximate the small sample distribution of λ under the assumption that e_t is not autocorrelated.

In this section we have focused on estimating models with only one explanatory variable. However, the methods can be readily extended to allow for more exogenous variables [e.g., Dhrymes (1971a)]. Other extensions of the above results include the possibility of a heteroscedastic error term [e.g., Cragg (1982)].

10.4 MODEL CHECKING

After a model has been fitted to a given set of data, some checks for the adequacy of the model should be carried out. This procedure is routine in a static linear regression analysis where t values and F values as well as the Durbin-Watson statistic are examined. Similar checks are useful for a dynamic model. Clearly one should check the significance of individual parameters and, if possible, reduce the model size in accordance with the principle of parsimony. Also a residual analysis can be useful. However, for a dynamic model something more should be done than just a test against *first-order* autocorrelation like the Durbin-Watson test for nondynamic regression models.

Assuming that the fitted model has the general form (10.1.2) and the exogenous variable x is generated by the ARMA process (10.1.8), Box and Jenkins (1976) suggest to inspect the residual autocorrelations and the cross-correlations between the residuals of (10.1.2) and (10.1.8). Estimating the residual autocorrelations of (10.1.2) by

$$r_k(v) = \frac{\sum_{t=1}^{T-k} v_t v_{t+k}}{\sum_{t=1}^{T} v_t^2} \tag{10.4.1}$$

and assuming that they are calculated from the true model errors, where the true parameters are assumed to be known, these quantities are approximately normally distributed with mean zero and variance $1/T$. Thus, a rough check of the model adequacy would be to compare the $r_k(v)$ with $\pm 2/\sqrt{T}$, the bounds of an approximate 95% confidence interval around zero. Also, the user of this check should look for possible patterns of the correlogram that may indicate nonwhite residuals.

It is clear, however, that this check of the model adequacy is very crude since in practice the autocorrelations are computed from the estimation residuals; that is, $r_k(\hat{v})$, say, is used instead of $r_k(v)$. As a consequence these quantities will be correlated and $1/T$ will be a poor approximation to their variance, at least for small k. In fact, $1/T$ may overstate the true asymptotic variance considerably for small k, and, thus, an uncritical comparison with $\pm 2/\sqrt{T}$ may give the wrong impression of a correctly specified model when it is actually inadequate. Therefore, it is preferable to use tests based on exact asymptotic distributions.

One candidate is a portmanteau test based on the statistic

$$Q = T^*[r_1^2(\hat{v}) + \ldots + r_K^2(\hat{v})] \tag{10.4.2}$$

which is asymptotically distributed as χ^2 with $K - p - q$ degrees of freedom if the model is correctly specified. Note that the asymptotic distribution of Q does not depend on the distributed lag function $\beta(L) = \gamma(L)/\phi(L)$. The multiplicative constant T^* is the number of residuals used in computing the $r_k(\hat{v})$. It is not necessarily equal to the sample size as some residuals at the beginning of the sample period may not be available if allowance is made for starting up values. Also, it may be advantageous to adjust for degrees of freedom. The number of autocorrelation coefficients K should be chosen large enough so that the coefficients of $v(L) = \alpha(L)/\theta(L)$ are negligible for lags greater than K [see Box and Jenkins (1976)]. Breusch and Pagan (1980) point out the close relationship between the portmanteau test and a Lagrange multiplier (LM) test (see also Section 8.4.1b).

An LM statistic can also be used to test the significance of k extra parameters in $\alpha(L)$ or $\theta(L)$. In this case, under the null hypothesis of the original model being correct, the LM statistic is χ^2 distributed with k degrees of freedom. For details see Harvey (1981, Chapter 5) or Newbold (1981).

To check the distributed lag function $\beta(L)$, it is suggested to examine the cross-correlations

$$r_k(\hat{w},\hat{v}) = \frac{\sum_{t=1}^{T-k} \hat{w}_t \hat{v}_{t+k}}{\left(\sum_{t=1}^{T} \hat{w}_t^2\right)^{1/2}\left(\sum_{t=1}^{T} \hat{v}_t^2\right)^{1/2}} \tag{10.4.3}$$

where the caret (ˆ) denotes estimation residuals as previously discussed. Again a first crude check could be to compare these quantities with $\pm 2/\sqrt{T}$, and again it is important to keep in mind that $1/T$ may overstate the true asymptotic variance considerably. As a further check the statistic

$$S = T^*[r_0^2(\hat{w},\hat{v}) + \ldots + r_K^2(\hat{w},\hat{v})] \tag{10.4.4}$$

can be used. It is asymptotically χ^2 distributed with $K + 1 - (r + m + 1) = K - r - m$ degrees of freedom if the model is specified correctly. Note that the asymptotic distribution does not depend on the error term specification [e.g., Granger and Newbold (1977, Section 7.7)]. For a survey of checks for model adequacy in the present context see Newbold (1981).

The ultimate objective of many analyses of economic data is the prediction of the dependent variable y. Therefore, it is plausible to judge a model by its forecasting performance [see Harvey (1981, Chapter 5)]. If (10.1.2) together with (10.1.8) is the true model, the optimal (linear minimum mean square error) forecasts can be obtained by converting to the representation (10.2.29). Then we get optimal h-step forecasts $y_t(h)$ of y_t as

$$y_t(h) = \delta(L)\hat{y}_{t+h-1} + v(L)\hat{x}_{t+h} \tag{10.4.5}$$

where $\hat{x}_s = x_s$ for $s \leq t$ and $\hat{x}_{t+h} = x_t(h)$, the optimal h-step forecast of x_t (see Chapter 7), for $h \geq 1$ and similarly for $\hat{y}_s$. This formula can be used for recursively calculating the $y_t(h)$ starting with $h = 1$. A more detailed discussion of forecasting with dynamic models will be given in a more general framework in Chapter 16. It should be understood that the model specification has to be reexamined if the model fails to pass any of the adequacy checks.

10.5 ALTERNATIVE DISTRIBUTED LAG MODELS

In certain situations the use of the rational lag model including its special case versions is not satisfactory—for instance, if nonsample information is available that cannot be easily accounted for in the specification (10.1.2). For example, it is not easy to constrain the lag weights to be all nonnegative in the general rational lag model. Therefore, alternative lag distributions have been proposed that make it easier to allow for certain prior information. We will present two of these lag models below. It will be assumed throughout this section that the error term is Gaussian white noise. This assumption is imposed for ease of presentation. If, in practice, it is not satisfied, a model for the error term can be constructed based on the estimation residuals obtained from the procedures introduced below.

10.5.1 Gamma Distributed Lags

In the gamma distributed lag proposed by Tsurumi (1971), the β's are assumed to fall on a multiple of the density of a gamma distribution defined by

$$f(x) = \frac{\gamma^s}{\Gamma(s)} x^{s-1} \exp(-\gamma x), \qquad x \geq 0, \gamma > 0, s > 0 \tag{10.5.1}$$

where $\Gamma(\cdot)$ is the gamma function. Specifically, it is assumed that

$$\beta_i = \alpha i^{s-1} \exp(-i) \qquad \text{for} \qquad i = 0, 1, \ldots \tag{10.5.2}$$

where α and s are parameters to be estimated. The distributed lag model, when this scheme is substituted, becomes

$$y_t = \alpha \sum_{i=0}^{\infty} i^{s-1} \exp(-i) x_{t-i} + e_t \tag{10.5.3}$$

Some gamma distributions are shown in Figure 10.1, where β_0 is zero for $s \neq 1$. They show intuitively plausible, unimodal lag schemes, which is the reason for using the gamma lag.

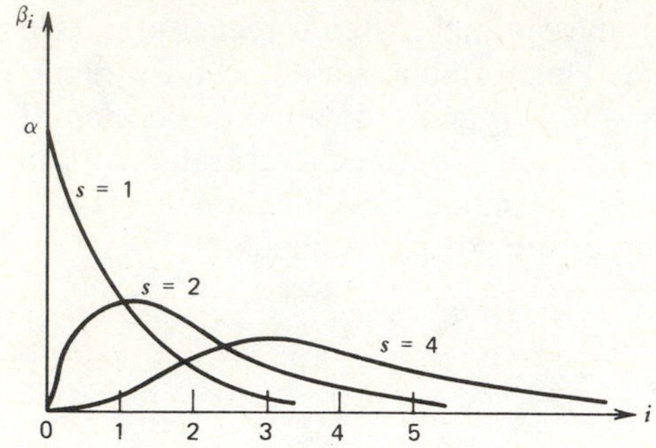

Figure 10.1 Gamma distributions.

If β_0 is known to be zero, the lag model can be written as

$$y_t = \alpha \sum_{i=1}^{\infty} i^{s-1} \exp(-i)x_{t-i} + e_t \tag{10.5.4}$$

and for estimation Tsurumi truncates the infinite sum at m and writes

$$y_t = \alpha \sum_{i=1}^{m} i^{s-1} \exp(-i)x_{t-i} + \alpha\eta_t + e_t \tag{10.5.5}$$

where

$$\eta_t = \sum_{i=m+1}^{\infty} i^{s-1} \exp(-i)x_{t-i} \tag{10.5.6}$$

which is dependent on t. Tsurumi argues that if m is reasonably large, treating η_t as a constant parameter to be estimated will not entail serious error. Regarding the choice of m, Tsurumi suggests choosing an m that minimizes the estimate of the residual variance, which is obtained by dividing $T - m$ into the sum of squared errors.

To allow for a nonzero β_0, Schmidt (1974b) suggests replacing i^{s-1} by $(i + 1)^{s-1}$ — that is,

$$\beta_i = \alpha(i + 1)^{s-1} \exp(-i) \quad \text{for } i = 0, 1, \ldots \tag{10.5.7}$$

Schmidt further suggests making use of a more flexible two-parameter (s and γ) distribution

$$\beta_i = \alpha(i + 1)^{s-1} \exp(-\gamma i) \quad \text{for } i = 0, 1, \ldots \tag{10.5.8}$$

Considering the search method used in obtaining maximum likelihood estimates, Schmidt points out the inconvenience of s having an infinite range. He suggests replacing the exponent $s - 1$ with $\delta/(1 - \delta)$, where $0 \le \delta < 1$. Thus the lag parameter specification would be

$$\beta_i = \alpha(i + 1)^{\delta/(1-\delta)} \exp(-\gamma i) \quad \text{for } i = 0, 1, \ldots \tag{10.5.9}$$

Here the discount factor $\exp(-\gamma i)$ may be replaced by λ^i so that

$$\beta_i = \alpha(i + 1)^{\delta/(1-\delta)}\lambda^i \quad \text{for } i = 0, 1, \ldots \tag{10.5.10}$$

with parameters $0 \le \delta < 1$ and $0 \le \lambda < 1$. The above specification reduces to the geometric lag model when $\delta = 0$.

In estimation, the distributed lag function is written as

$$y_t = \alpha Z_t + \eta_t^* + e_t \tag{10.5.11}$$

where

$$Z_t = \sum_{i=0}^{t-1} (\beta_i/\alpha)x_{t-i} \tag{10.5.12}$$

$$\eta_t^* = \sum_{i=t}^{\infty} \beta_i x_{t-i} \tag{10.5.13}$$

and β_i is specified in (10.5.10). Note that η_t^* is different from, but consistent with, the "truncation remainder" of (10.3.3). Schmidt acknowledges the time-dependent nature of η_t^* but argues that it is asymptotically negligible and that its omission will not affect the asymptotic properties of the resulting estimates. If η_t^* is dropped from the equation and the e_t are assumed to be identically and independently normally distributed, the maximum likelihood estimates of δ, λ, and thus α are also the least squares estimates, since the estimation of α is linear, given δ and λ (hence Z_t). Schmidt suggests to search over δ and λ and then pick the values that minimize the sum of squared errors. For the asymptotic variances of the estimates, the inverse of the information matrix can be used. The information matrix is given by Schmidt (1974b).

A theoretical justification for using the gamma lag is provided by Theil and Fiebig (1981). They note that this distribution arises as a maximum entropy distribution (see Section 10.2.1e). Theil and Stern mentioned the gamma distribution as a plausible lag distribution as early as 1960 [Theil and Stern (1960)].

10.5.2 Exponential Lags

Although the gamma lag is quite flexible, there are many intuitively appealing lag structures that cannot be approximated very well by a member of this class of lag schemes. Viewing this problem, Lütkepohl (1981) proposes a class of infinite lag models that avoid sign changes in the lag weights and can approximate any possible lag structure to any desired degree of accuracy. We may call this family of lag models exponential lag models, since the lag weights are of the form

$$\beta_i = \alpha \exp[p(i)] \quad \text{for } i = 0, 1, 2, \ldots \tag{10.5.14}$$

where α is a constant and

$$p(i) = \sum_{k=1}^{m} p_k i^k \tag{10.5.15}$$

is a polynomial in i of degree m. In this model, the sign of the lag weights is determined by the sign of α, and p_m, the parameter of the leading term, is restricted to be negative so that the sum of the lag weights, that is, the total lag response, will be finite. The exponential lag models include the simple geometric lag because, when $m = 1$, $\exp(p_1 i) = (\exp p_1)^i = \lambda^i$, where $\lambda = \exp p_1$ and $0 < \exp p_1 < 1$ for $p_1 < 0$. For $m = 2$, the lag scheme is proportional to a truncated normal density function with mean $-p_1/(2p_2)$ and variance $-1/2p_2$ (with $p_2 < 0$).

In estimation, we write the distributed lag model as

$$y_t = \alpha \sum_{i=0}^{\infty} [\exp p(i)] x_{t-i} + e_t, \quad t = 1, \ldots, T \tag{10.5.16}$$

with $p(i)$ as in (10.5.15). We maintain the assumption of independently, identically, normally distributed e_t. In order to find the maximum likelihood estimates, it suffices to minimize the sum of squared errors

$$S = (\mathbf{y} - \mathbf{f})'(\mathbf{y} - \mathbf{f}) \tag{10.5.17}$$

where $\mathbf{y} = (y_1, \ldots, y_T)'$ and

$$\mathbf{f} = \left[\alpha \sum_{i=0}^{\infty} (\exp p(i)) x_{1-i}, \ldots, \alpha \sum_{i=0}^{\infty} (\exp p(i)) x_{T-i}\right]' \tag{10.5.18}$$

The presample values of x can be replaced by zero—that is, $x_t = 0$ for $t \leq 0$—without affecting the asymptotic distribution of the parameter estimates.

Of course, in small samples the treatment of the presample values has an impact on the parameter estimates. One possibility to reduce this impact is to replace $\mathbf{y}$ by $\mathbf{y}(T_0) = (y_{T_0}, \ldots, y_T)'$ and $\mathbf{f}$ by

$$\mathbf{f}(T_0) = \left[\alpha \sum_{i=0}^{T_0-1} (\exp p(i)) x_{T_0-i}, \ldots, \alpha \sum_{i=0}^{T-1} (\exp p(i)) x_{T-i}\right]' \tag{10.5.19}$$

where T_0 is some positive number. Since $\exp p(i)$ approaches zero as i goes to infinity, it is clear that the impact of the initial conditions declines with increasing T_0, which, on the other hand, reduces the degrees of freedom. Thus, the choice of T_0 will depend on the size of the available sample. It should be clear, however, that T_0 has no impact on the asymptotic properties of the estimators and asymptotic properties is all we can derive since the considered model is nonlinear in the parameters.

Alternatively, the impact of the presample values of x can be mitigated by replacing them by "back forecasts" [see Box and Jenkins (1976, Section 6.4.3)]. For a stationary process x_t the presample values could simply be replaced by the mean of the observed x_t. The minimization of (10.5.17) can be accomplished by using a nonlinear least squares algorithm (see Appendix B).

A crucial problem in setting up an exponential lag model is the choice of the polynomial order m. Lütkepohl suggests using model selection criteria or sequential testing procedures for this purpose.

10.5.3 Some Further Remarks

It is worth noting that one of the earliest suggested infinite lag distributions is the *log normal distribution* [see Fisher (1937)]. This lag distribution seems to have attracted little attention by later authors although it also has an intuitively plausible unimodular shape.

In closing this section we remind the reader that after having fitted any of the above lag schemes, it is imperative that the model adequacy be checked. Some of the techniques described in Section 10.4 lend themselves for this purpose.

10.6 PROBLEMS RELATED TO THE INTERPRETATION OF THE LAG WEIGHTS

As shown in Section 10.2.1 there are some economic theories that lead to specific lag distributions. However, Nerlove's (1972) observation that current empirical research on lags in economic behavior is not soundly based on economic theory and that the theoretical research on distributed lags is not very strongly empirically oriented, seems still valid. Therefore, lag distributions are often based purely on the data or on ad hoc assumptions rather than on sound economic theory. There are some problems that have to be recognized when empirical distributions are interpreted. Some of these problems will be addressed in the following discussion.

10.6.1 Omitted Variables

If "important" variables are neglected in the model, the lag distribution cannot be interpreted as the response function of y to a unit increase in x in general. Since allowance is made for an autocorrelated error term, this does not mean that the model is incorrectly specified. However, it is important to note that omitting variables may induce feedback between x and y so that x is no longer exogenous in a model like (10.1.1). This violates one of our basic assumptions and can lead to problems in the course of specifying a model.

On the other hand, omitting important variables may also induce a one-way causal bivariate system where feedback actually exists between the variables.

This situation is particularly troublesome since it means that the bivariate empirical model implies exogeneity of x in the bivariate system; whereas in the actual system, involving other variables as well, fluctuations in y have an impact on x. An example of this problem occurring in practice is given by Lütkepohl (1982b). We emphasize, however, that if the generation process of the *bivariate* system is correctly specified, it is still useful for forecasting purposes even though superior forecasts may be obtained from a higher dimensional system. It will be easier to treat the problem of omitted variables in a more general multiple time-series setting, and we will return to this problem in Chapter 16 where also the related problem of measurement errors is considered [see also Grether and Maddala (1973)].

10.6.2 Aggregation Over Time

The problem of temporal aggregation of distributed lag models is more easily and more adequately treated in the context of multiple time series, and we will do so in Chapter 16. Here we will only summarize some results that are of particular importance in a distributed lag analysis. We will assume that the basic, disaggregate model is a discrete time model. Results on temporal aggregation in continuous time can be found in Sims (1971b) and Geweke (1978).

First, there may be a considerable change in the lag structure if a distributed lag relationship is temporally aggregated, and, thus, the lag coefficients cannot be interpreted as the long-run response of y to a unit change in x even if the "true" model for the aggregated data has been specified. It is even possible that temporal aggregation induces feedback between x and y [Tiao and Wei (1976)]. Also, if the aggregation period becomes large, the strength of the correlation between variables associated with different time periods diminishes and the relationship between the aggregated variables x and y approaches a nondynamic structure with growing period of aggregation [Tiao and Wei (1976), Mundlak (1961)]. This phenomenon also makes it difficult to unravel the disaggregate structure from an estimated aggregated model. A related problem is that of estimating the parameters of the original model from aggregated data. This problem is discussed by Wei (1978) who shows that a loss of estimation efficiency will result from using temporally aggregated data.

If a model is constructed for the aggregated data generation process, such a model may be used for prediction. However, depending on the structure of the original process, as discussed in Chapter 16, forecasting with the aggregated model will in general be less efficient than aggregating forecasts from the original model. Earlier discussions of the consequences of temporal aggregation in the context of distributed lag analyses include Ironmonger (1959), Nerlove (1959), Mundlak (1961), Bryan (1967), and Engle and Liu (1972).

10.6.3 Seasonality

When quarterly data or monthly data are used, the dependent variable in a distributed lag model may exhibit a pronounced seasonal pattern that cannot be explained by the seasonal changes of the independent variables. To circumvent the problem, one can either seasonally adjust the data series (see Chapter 7) or account for the seasonality directly within the distributed lag model.

If seasonally adjusted data are used, the error term in the distributed lag model may become a high-order moving-average process and the lag function is distorted in general [Wallis (1974), Sims (1974b)]. In addition, the least squares estimates with adjusted data will not be fully efficient [Thomas and Wallis (1971)]. Applying a purely data-based modeling strategy and specifying a non-seasonal model for the adjusted data as described in Section 10.2.2a may result in an inadequate model [Newbold (1980)].

Alternatively, one can incorporate the seasonal influences directly into a distributed lag relationship by making use of the variable distributed lag formulation introduced by Tinsley (1967). To illustrate a simple model of a variable lag parameter distribution, we assume a finite lag of the form

$$y_t = \beta_0(t)x_t + \beta_1(t-1)x_{t-1} + \beta_2(t-2)x_{t-2} + e_t \tag{10.6.1}$$

with the variable parameter $\beta_i(t)$ explained by an explanatory variable z_t:

$$\beta_0(t) = c_0 + d_0 z_t \tag{10.6.2}$$

$$\beta_1(t-1) = c_1 + d_1 z_{t-1} \tag{10.6.3}$$

and

$$\beta_2(t-2) = c_2 + d_2 z_{t-2} \tag{10.6.4}$$

Substitution of (10.6.2) through (10.6.4) into (10.6.1) results in

$$y_t = c_0 x_t + c_1 x_{t-1} + c_2 x_{t-2} + d_0 z_t x_t + d_1 z_{t-1} x_{t-1} + d_2 z_{t-2} x_{t-2} + e_t \tag{10.6.5}$$

To incorporate seasonal influences directly into a distributed lag relationship, dummy variables could be used instead of the explanatory variable z_t as Pesando (1972) proposed. In particular, the distributed lag weights are specified as

$$\beta_i = c_i + s_{1i} D_{1,t-i} + s_{2i} D_{2,t-i} + s_{3i} D_{3,t-i} \tag{10.6.6}$$

where D_1, D_2, and D_3 are seasonal dummy variables, and the c's and s's are parameters. If the above seasonally varying, distributed lag weights are substituted into a general finite lag function

$$y_t = \sum_{i=0}^{n} \beta_i x_{t-i} + e_t \tag{10.6.7}$$

we obtain

$$y_t = \sum_{i=0}^{n} c_i x_{t-i} + \sum_{j=1}^{3} \sum_{i=0}^{n} s_{ji} D_{j,t-i} x_{t-i} + e_t \tag{10.6.8}$$

Pesando (1972) estimated the relationship (10.6.8) by constraining the c's and s's to lie along low-order polynomials, thus employing four sets of Almon variables (Chapter 9) in actual regressions.

10.7 SUMMARY AND CONCLUSIONS

In this chapter we have discussed rather general infinite distributed lag models as well as a number of special cases. A summary of the considered models is given in Table 10.2. We have seen how rational distributed lag models with ARMA error term can arise from economic theories and we have sketched methods for specifying such models if no theory is available from which to derive a precise specification. In many cases it will be necessary to combine economic theory and sample information to obtain a reasonable model since some of the theories leading to distributed lag models are based on ad hoc assumptions that will not necessarily provide an acceptable description of the data generation process.

Once a model is specified, its parameters have to be estimated. We have mainly considered maximum likelihood methods and approximate maximum likelihood methods. For a general rational distributed lag model with ARMA errors, these methods lead to a nonlinear optimization problem. Available software can be used for its solution. In special cases the applied researcher may take advantage of the simplifications noted in Section 10.3.

After having fitted a particular model, its adequacy needs to be checked, and if inadequacies are detected modifications have to be made. This is an important step in all econometric analyses. Whereas in static linear regression models a test against first-order residual autocorrelation by using the usual Durbin-Watson statistic may be sufficient, tests against higher-order autocorrelation should accompany dynamic modeling. Some possible tests have been indicated in Section 10.4.

If nonsample information is available that cannot easily be incorporated in the general rational lag model, it may be useful to select the lag model from some other class of lag distributions. In Section 10.5 we have presented the gamma lag and the exponential lag for that purpose. The former can approximate a wide range of unimodal distributed lags with nonnegative or nonpositive lag coefficients, whereas the latter can approximate *any* reasonable distributed lag function without sign changes in the lag coefficients to any desired degree of accuracy.

If the specification of a lag model is based on sample information, the interpretation of the lag coefficients is usually difficult. Some sources for such problems are discussed in Section 10.6. In particular, the impact of omitted variables, temporal aggregation, and seasonality have been considered.

TABLE 10.2 *ALTERNATIVE INFINITE DISTRIBUTED LAG MODELS*

Lag Scheme	Lag Function	Remarks
Geometric	$\beta(L) = \dfrac{\alpha(1-\lambda)}{1-\lambda L}$	$0 < \lambda < 1$
Pascal	$\beta(L) = \dfrac{\alpha(1-\lambda)^m}{(1-\lambda L)^m}$	$0 < \lambda < 1$ m = positive integer; when $m = 1$, it is geometric
Discounted polynomial	$\beta(L) = \sum_{i=0}^{\infty} \lambda^i \sum_{j=0}^{r} p_j i^j L^i = \dfrac{\gamma(L)}{(1-\lambda L)^{r+1}}$	$0 \le \lambda < 1$, $\gamma(L)$ is a polynomial in the lag operator of order r
Rational	$\beta(L) = \dfrac{\gamma(L)}{\phi(L)}$	$\gamma(L)$ and $\phi(L)$ are polynomials in the lag operator L of order r and m, respectively
Gamma	$\beta(L) = \alpha \sum_{i=0}^{\infty} i^{s-1} \exp(-i) L^i$	
Exponential	$\beta(L) = \alpha \sum_{i=0}^{\infty} \exp\left(\sum_{k=1}^{n} p_k i^k\right) L^i$	$p_m < 0$

Although some of the models discussed in this chapter may appear to be rather general, there are some severe limitations that should be kept in mind when distributed lag analyses are carried out. First, we have only considered models with one explanatory variable. Theoretically, it is not difficult to generalize the model (10.1.1) or (10.1.2) to include more exogenous variables. However, the practical difficulties in sample-based model building may increase substantially.

Second, we have assumed that there is no feedback between x and y in (10.1.1). In other words, we have assumed that there is only one endogenous variable in the model. Clearly, in practice these restrictions may be rather severe and, in fact, exclude the majority of systems of economic variables. Therefore, in Chapter 16 a generalization to models with several or more endogenous and exogenous variables is presented.

We do not give a complete list of references relevant to infinite distributed lag models at the end of this chapter. Much of the earlier literature is summarized in Griliches's (1967) influential survey article. Other sources for further references include Dhrymes's (1971a) book and the surveys by Nerlove (1972), Sims (1974a), and Hendry, Pagan, and Sargan (1983).

10.8 EXERCISES

The following exercises are based on the geometric lag model

$$y_t = \alpha_0 + \alpha \sum_{i=0}^{\infty} \lambda^i x_{t-i} + e_t \qquad (10.8.1)$$

where $0 < \lambda < 1$, $e_t = \rho e_{t-1} + v_t$, $-1 < \rho < 1$, and v_t is zero mean Gaussian white noise with variance σ_v^2. Monte Carlo data should be generated using the transformed model

$$y_t = \alpha_0(1 - \lambda) + \alpha x_t + \lambda y_{t-1} + e_t - \lambda e_{t-1} \qquad (10.8.2)$$

with $\alpha_0 = 10$, $\alpha = 0.3$, $\lambda = 0.8$, $\rho = 0.6$, $y_0 = 53.3$, $e_0 = 2.84$, and $v_t \sim N(0,4)$. One hundred fixed values for the explanatory variable x_t are listed in Table 10.3.

10.8.1 Individual Exercises

Exercise 10.1

Generate a sample of size 100. Use the first 25 values to compute instrumental variable estimates for α_0, α, and λ with x_{t-1} as instrument for y_{t-1} (see Section 10.3.1c).

Exercise 10.2

Repeat Exercise 10.1 with a sample of size 50 and a sample of size 100.

TABLE 10.3 ***HYPOTHETICAL FIXED VALUES OF THE EXPLANATORY VARIABLE x***

51.30	71.40	109.80	270.50	392.30
50.00	72.10	116.30	279.90	399.90
45.60	77.80	121.30	284.60	405.60
40.90	79.50	125.30	290.70	411.10
38.80	80.10	133.10	296.60	419.60
40.10	80.50	147.70	300.50	426.70
41.10	80.20	161.20	310.30	430.90
41.50	81.40	170.50	315.70	438.70
43.00	84.30	181.50	321.40	445.60
42.20	86.60	195.40	322.20	450.00
41.60	87.30	199.00	329.50	455.10
42.00	88.70	205.10	336.80	461.80
44.10	89.60	211.20	340.90	469.30
48.80	90.60	219.80	346.80	475.50
51.80	91.70	225.70	351.70	481.30
52.70	92.90	231.60	359.20	490.10
53.90	94.50	240.10	368.80	495.30
58.50	97.20	248.90	370.50	500.60
66.90	100.00	255.30	380.60	505.80
72.10	104.20	261.40	385.50	510.30

Exercise 10.3
Repeat Exercises 10.1 and 10.2 using x_{t-3} as an instrument instead of x_{t-1}.

Exercise 10.4
Compute consistent estimates of ρ using the instrumental variable estimates for α_0, α, and λ obtained in Exercises 10.1 and 10.2.

Exercise 10.5
Making use of the results of Exercises 10.1, 10.2, and 10.4 improve the estimates with the two-step Gauss method.

Exercise 10.6
Assume that the e_t are not autocorrelated and use the first 25 sample values of your generated data to compute Klein's ML estimates for α_0, α, and λ.

10.8.2 Joint or Class Exercises

Exercise 10.7
Generate 100 samples of size 100 and repeat Exercises 10.1 and 10.2. Compute the means, variances, and mean square errors (MSE's) of the resulting estimators and construct frequency distributions.

Exercise 10.8

Making use of the results of Exercise 10.7, compute two-step Gauss estimators for all 100 samples and all three different sample sizes. Compute the means, variances, and MSE's of the estimates, and construct frequency distributions.

Exercise 10.9

Repeat Exercise 10.6 with all 100 samples of Exercise 10.7.

Exercise 10.10

Using results from Exercises 10.7–10.9, construct a table comparing the alternative estimators based on samples of different size. Rank the estimators in terms of MSE and in terms of their variances. What conclusions can you draw?

10.9 REFERENCES

Amemiya, T. and W. A. Fuller (1967) "A Comparative Study of Alternative Estimators in a Distributed Lag Model," *Econometrica,* 35, 509–529.

Box, G. E. P. and G. M. Jenkins (1976) *Time Series Analysis, Forecasting and Control,* Holden-Day, San Francisco.

Breusch, T. S. and A. R. Pagan (1980) "The Lagrange Multiplier Test and Its Applications to Model Specification in Econometrics," *Review of Economic Studies,* 48, 239–253.

Bryan, W. R. (1967) "Bank Adjustments to Policy: Alternative Estimates of the Lag," *American Economic Review,* 57, 855–864.

Burt, O. R. (1980) "Schmidt's LaGuerre Lag is a Pascal Rational Lag," mimeo, University of Kentucky, Lexington, Kentucky.

Cagan, P. (1956) "The Monetary Dynamics of Hyper Inflations," in M. Friedman, ed., *Studies in the Quantity Theory of Money,* University of Chicago Press, Chicago.

Cargill, T. F. and R. A. Meyer (1972) "A Spectral Approach to Estimating the Distributed Lag Relationship Between Long- and Short-Term Interest Rates," *International Economic Review,* 13, 223–238.

Cargill, T. F. and R. A. Meyer (1974) "Some Time and Frequency Domain Distributed Lag Estimators: A Comparative Monte Carlo Study," *Econometrica,* 42, 1031–1044.

Chetty, V. K. (1971) "Estimation of Solow's Distributed Lag Models," *Econometrica,* 39, 99–117.

Cragg, J. G. (1982) "Estimation and Testing in Time-Series Regression Models with Heteroscedastic Disturbances," *Journal of Econometrics,* 20, 135–157.

Dhrymes, P. J. (1969) "Efficient Estimation of Distributed Lags with Autocorrelated Errors," *International Economic Review,* 10, 47–67.

Dhrymes, P. J. (1971a) *Distributed Lags: Problems of Estimation and Formulation,* Holden-Day, San Francisco.

Dhrymes, P. J. (1971b) "On the Strong Consistency of Estimators for Certain Distributed Lag Models with Autocorrelated Errors," *International Economic Review,* 12, 329–343.

Dhrymes, P. J., L. R. Klein, and K. Steiglitz (1970) "Estimation of Distributed Lags," *International Economic Review,* 11, 235–250.

Doran, H. E. and W. E. Griffiths (1978) "Inconsistency of the OLS Estimator of the Partial Adjustment-Adaptive Expectation Model," *Journal of Econometrics,* 6, 133–146.

Engle, R. F. and T. C. Liu (1972) "Effects of Aggregation over Time on Dynamic Characteristics of an Econometric Model," in B. G. Hickman, ed., *Econometric Models of Cyclical Behavior,* Vol. 1, Studies in Income and Wealth, No. 36, National Bureau of Economic Research, Columbia University Press, New York.

Fisher, I. (1937) "Note on a Short-Cut Method for Calculating Distributed Lags," *Bulletin de l'Institut International de Statistique,* 29, 323–327.

Fomby, T. B. and D. K. Guilkey (1983) "An Examination of Two-Step Estimators for Models with Lagged Dependent and Autocorrelated Errors," *Journal of Econometrics,* 22, 291–300.

Gaab, W. (1974) Schätzung verteilter lags, Anton Hain, Meisenheim am Glan.

Geweke, J. (1978) "Temporal Aggregation in the Multiple Regression Model," *Econometrica,* 46, 643–661.

Glejser, H. (1977) "On Two New Methods to Deal with Truncation Remainders in Small Sample Distributed Lag Models with Autocorrelated Disturbances," *International Economic Review,* 18, 783–786.

Granger, C. W. J. and P. Newbold (1977) *Forecasting Economic Time Series,* Academic Press, New York.

Grether, D. M. and G. S. Maddala (1973) "Errors in Variables and Serially Correlated Disturbances in Distributed Lag Models," *Econometrica,* 41, 255–262.

Griliches, Z. (1967) "Distributed Lags: A Survey," *Econometrica,* 35, 16–49.

Guthrie, R. S. (1976) "A Note on the Bayesian Estimation of Solow's Distributed Lag Model," *Journal of Econometrics,* 4, 295–300.

Hannan, E. J. (1963) "Regression for Time Series," in M. Rosenblatt, ed., *Proceedings of a Symposium in Time Series Analysis,* Wiley, New York.

Hannan, E. J. (1965) "The Estimation of Relationships Involving Distributed Lags," *Econometrica,* 33, 206–224.

Harvey, A. C. (1981) *The Econometric Analysis of Time Series,* Philip Allan, Oxford.

Hatanaka, M. (1974) "An Efficient Two-Step Estimator for the Dynamic Adjustment Model with Autoregressive Errors," *Journal of Econometrics,* 2, 199–220.

Haugh, L. D. and G. E. P. Box (1977) "Identification of Dynamic Regression (Distributed Lag) Models Connecting Two Time Series," *Journal of the American Statistical Association,* 72, 121–130.

Hendry, D. F. and G. E. Mizon (1978) "Serial Correlation as a Convenient Simplification, Not a Nuisance: A Comment on a Study of the Demand for Money by the Bank of England," *The Economic Journal,* 88, 549–563.

Hendry, D. F., A. R. Pagan, and J. D. Sargan (1983) "Dynamic Specification," forthcoming in *Handbook of Econometrics,* North-Holland, Amsterdam.

Hendry, D. F. and J.-F. Richard (1983) "The Econometric Analysis of Economic Time Series," *International Statistical Review,* 51, 111–163.

Ironmonger, D. S. (1959) "A Note on the Estimation of Long-Run Elasticities," *Journal of Farm Economics,* 41, 626–632.

Jorgenson, D. W. (1966) "Rational Distributed Lag Functions," *Econometrica,* 34, 135–149.

Judge, G. G., W. E. Griffiths, R. C. Hill, and T. C. Lee (1980) *The Theory and Practice of Econometrics,* John Wiley, New York.

Judge, G. G., R. C. Hill, W. E. Griffiths, H. Lütkepohl and T. C. Lee (1982) *Introduction to the Theory and Practice of Econometrics,* Wiley, New York.

Just, R. E. (1977) "Existence of Stable Distributed Lags," *Econometrica,* 45, 1467–1480.

Klein, L. R. (1958) "The Estimation of Distributed Lags," *Econometrica,* 26, 553–565.

Koyck, L. M. (1954) *Distributed Lags and Investment Analysis,* North-Holland, Amsterdam.

Liviatan, N. (1963) "Consistent Estimation of Distributed Lags," *International Economic Review,* 4, 44–52.

Lütkepohl, H. (1980) "Approximation of Arbitrary Distributed Lag Structures by a Modified Polynomial Lag: An Extension," *Journal of the American Statistical Association,* 75, 428–430.

Lütkepohl, H. (1981) "A Model for Non-Negative and Non-Positive Distributed Lag Functions," *Journal of Econometrics,* 16, 211–219.

Lütkepohl, H. (1982a) "Discounted Polynomials for Multiple Time Series Model Building," *Biometrika,* 69, 107–115.

Lütkepohl, H. (1982b) "Non-Causality Due to Omitted Variables," *Journal of Econometrics,* 19, 367–378.

Lütkepohl, H. (1984) "The Optimality of Rational Distributed Lags: A Comment," *International Economic Review,* forthcoming.

Maddala, G. S. and A. S. Rao (1971) "Maximum Likelihood Estimation of Solow's and Jorgenson's Distributed Lag Models," *Review of Economics and Statistics,* 53, 80–88.

Maddala, G. S. and A. S. Rao (1973) "Tests for Serial Correlation in Regression Models with Lagged Dependent Variables and Serially Correlated Errors," *Econometrica,* 41, 761–774.

Maeshiro, A. (1980) "Small Sample Properties of Estimators of Distributed Lag Models," *International Economic Review,* 21, 721–733.

McLaren, K. R. (1979) "The Optimality of Rational Distributed Lags," *International Economic Review,* 20, 183–191.

Mizon, G. E. and D. F. Hendry (1980) "An Empirical Application and Monte Carlo Analysis of Tests of Dynamic Specification," *Review of Economic Studies,* 57, 21–45.

Mundlak, Y. (1961) "Aggregation over Time in Distributed Lag Models," *International Economic Review,* 2, 154–163.

Nerlove, M. (1956) "Estimates of the Elasticities of Supply of Selected Agricultural Commodities," *Journal of Farm Economics,* 38, 496–509.

Nerlove, M. (1959) "On the Estimation of Long-Run Elasticities: A Reply," *Journal of Farm Economics,* 41, 632–640.

Nerlove, M. (1972) "Lags in Economic Behavior," *Econometrica,* 40, 221–251.

Newbold, P. (1980) "A Note on Relations Between Seasonally Adjusted Variables," *Journal of Time Series Analysis,* 1, 31–35.

Newbold, P. (1981) "Model Checking in Time Series Analysis," paper presented at the Conference on Applied Time Series Analysis of Economic Data, Arlington, Va.

Oi, W. (1969) "A Bracketing Rule for the Estimation of Simple Distributed Lag Models," *Review of Economics and Statistics,* 51, 445–452.

Pagan, A. (1978) "Rational and Polynomial Lags: The Finite Connection," *Journal of Econometrics,* 8, 247–254.

Pesando, J. E. (1972) "Seasonal Variability in Distributed Lag Models," *Journal of the American Statistical Association,* 67, 311–312.

Pesaran, M. H. (1973) "The Small Sample Problem of Truncation Remainders in the Estimation of Distributed Lag Models with Autocorrelated Errors," *International Economic Review,* 14, 120–131.

Sargan, J. D. (1980) "Some Tests of Dynamic Specification for a Single Equation," *Econometrica,* 48, 879–897.

Sargent, T. J. (1968) "Some Evidence on the Small Sample Properties of Distributed Lag Estimators in the Presence of Autocorrelated Disturbances," *Review of Economics and Statistics,* 50, 87–95.

Schmidt, P. (1973) "On the Difference Between Conditional and Unconditional Asymptotic Distributions of Estimates in Distributed Lag Models with Integer-Valued Parameters," *Econometrica,* 41, 165–169.

Schmidt, P. (1974a) "A Modification of the Almon Distributed Lag," *Journal of the American Statistical Association,* 69, 679–681.

Schmidt, P. (1974b) "An Argument for the Usefulness of the Gamma Distributed Lag Model," *International Economic Review,* 15, 246–250.

Schmidt, P. (1975) "The Small Sample Effects of Various Treatments of Truncation Remainders in the Estimation of Distributed Lag Models," *Review of Economics and Statistics,* 57, 387–389.

Schmidt, P. and D. K. Guilkey (1976) "The Effects of Various Treatments of Truncation Remainders in Tests of Hypotheses in Distributed Lag Models," *Journal of Econometrics,* 4, 211-230.

Schmidt, P. and N. R. Mann (1977) "A Note on the Approximation of Arbitrary Distributed Lag Structures by a Modified Almon Lag," *Journal of the American Statistical Association,* 72, 442–443.

Shibata, R. (1981) "An Optimal Selection of Regression Variables," *Biometrika,* 68, 45–54.

Sims, C. A. (1971a) "Distributed Lag Estimation When the Parameter Space is Explicitly Infinite-Dimensional," *Annals of Mathematical Statistics,* 42, 1622–1636.

Sims, C. A. (1971b) "Discrete Approximations to Continuous Time Distributed Lags in Econometrics," *Econometrica,* 39, 545–563.

Sims, C. A. (1972) "The Role of Approximate Prior Restrictions in Distributed Lag Estimation," *Journal of the American Statistical Association,* 67, 169–175.

Sims, C. A. (1974a) "Distributed Lags," Chapter 5 in M. D. Intriligator and D. A. Kendrick, eds., *Frontiers in Quantitative Economics,* Vol. II, North-Holland, Amsterdam, 289–332.

Sims, C. A. (1974b) "Seasonality in Regression," *Journal of the American Statistical Association,* 69, 618–626.

Solow, R. M. (1960) "On a Family of Lag Distributions," *Econometrica,* 28, 393–406.

Taylor, L. D. and T. A. Wilson (1964) "Three-pass Least Squares: A Method of Estimating Models with a Lagged Dependent Variable," *Review of Economics and Statistics,* 46, 329–346.

Theil, H. and R. M. Stern (1960) "A Simple Unimodal Lag Distribution" *Metroeconomica,* 12, 111–119.

Theil, H. and D. Fiebig (1981) "A Maximum Entropy Approach to the Specification of Distributed Lags," *Economics Letters,* 7, 339–342.

Thomas, J. J. and K. F. Wallis (1971) "Seasonal Variation in Regression Analysis," *Journal of the Royal Statistical Society, Series A (General),* 134, 57–72.

Tiao, G. C. and W. S. Wei (1976) "Effects of Temporal Aggregation on the Dynamic Relationship of Two Time Series Variables," *Biometrika,* 63, 513–523.

Tinsley, P. A. (1967) "An Application of Variable Weight Distributed Lags," *Journal of the American Statistical Association,* 62, 1277–1289.

Tse, Y. K. (1982) "Edgeworth Approximations in First-Order Stochastic Difference Equations with Exogenous Variables," *Journal of Econometrics,* 20, 175–195.

Tsurumi, H. (1971) "A Note on Gamma Distributed Lags," *International Economic Review,* 12, 317–323.

Wallis, K. F. (1967) "Lagged Dependent Variables and Serially Correlated Errors: A Reappraisal of Three-Pass Least Squares," *Review of Economics and Statistics,* 49, 555–567.

Wallis, K. F. (1974) "Seasonal Adjustment and Relations Between Variables," *Journal of the American Statistical Association,* 69, 18–31.

Wei, W. W. S. (1978) "The Effect of Temporal Aggregation on Parameter Estimation in a Distributed Lag Model," *Journal of Econometrics,* 6, 237–246.

Zellner, A. and M. Geisel (1970) "Analysis of Distributed Lag Models with Application to Consumption Function Estimation," *Econometrica,* 38, 865–888.

Zellner, A. and C. J. Park (1965) "Bayesian Analysis of a Class of Distributed Lag Models," *Econometric Annals of the Indian Economic Journal,* 13, 432–444.

PART FOUR

SOME ALTERNATIVE COVARIANCE STRUCTURES

In Part Four we consider the statistical implications of (1) error variances that are possibly heteroscedastic and unknown, (2) sets of regression equations that may be disturbance related and the error covariance matrix is unknown, and (3) sample data that have both a cross section and time-series dimension. In the first chapter emphasis is placed on identifying heteroscedastic errors. When they exist we develop procedures for mitigating their impact. In the second chapter a statistical model consistent with disturbance related sets of regression equations is considered and the sampling performance of the corresponding estimators is evaluated. In the last chapter in Part Four we recognize that economic data may exist in both a time-series and cross-sectional form and concentrate on how statistically to make the best use of this type of sample information.

Chapter 11

Heteroscedasticity

11.1 EXISTENCE OF HETEROSCEDASTICITY AND THE USE OF LS AND GLS

For the general linear model $\mathbf{y} = X\boldsymbol{\beta} + \mathbf{e}$, $E[\mathbf{e}] = \mathbf{0}$, $E[\mathbf{ee}'] = \boldsymbol{\Phi} = \sigma^2\boldsymbol{\Psi}$, heteroscedasticity exists if the diagonal elements of $\boldsymbol{\Phi}$ are not all identical. If, in addition, $\mathbf{e}$ is free from autocorrelation, $\boldsymbol{\Phi}$ can be written as a diagonal matrix with the tth diagonal element given by σ_t^2. This assumption is likely to be a realistic one when using cross-sectional data on a number of microeconomic units such as firms or households. A common example is the estimation of household expenditure functions. In this case y_t represents expenditure by the tth household on some commodity group such as food, and the explanatory variables include total expenditure (or income) and household size. It is usually postulated that expenditure on some commodity is more easily explained by conventional variables for households with low incomes than it is for households with high incomes. Thus, if $\mathbf{x}_t'$ represents a row of X corresponding to the tth observation, the variance of y_t around $\mathbf{x}_t'\boldsymbol{\beta}$ is expected to be low for low incomes and high for high incomes, and this is introduced formally by relating σ_t^2 to the relevant x_{kt}, or more generally, to some function of $\mathbf{x}_t$. For example, see Prais and Houthakker (1955), and the discussion in Theil (1971, p. 245).

Heteroscedasticity also naturally arises (1) when the observations are based on average data, and (2) in a number of "random coefficient" models. To illustrate the first case, let y_{it} be the yield of a particular crop on the ith acre of the tth farm and let x_{1it} and x_{2it}, respectively, be the amount of labor and capital used on the ith acre of the tth farm. Suppose that it is reasonable to assume a production function either linear in the original or logarithms of the original units, say

$$y_{it} = \beta_0 + \beta_1 x_{1it} + \beta_2 x_{2it} + e_{it} \tag{11.1.1}$$

where $E[\mathbf{ee}'] = \sigma^2 I_N$, $\mathbf{e}' = (\mathbf{e}_1', \mathbf{e}_2', \ldots, \mathbf{e}_T')$, $\mathbf{e}_t' = (e_{1t}, e_{2t}, \ldots, e_{N_t t})$, N_t is the number of acres on the tth farm, and $N = \sum_{t=1}^{T} N_t$. Also, suppose that the only data available on $\mathbf{y}$, $\mathbf{x}_1$, and $\mathbf{x}_2$ is average farm data. This being the case, we average (11.1.1) over i and obtain

$$\bar{y}_t = \beta_0 + \beta_1\bar{x}_{1t} + \beta_2\bar{x}_{2t} + \bar{e}_t \tag{11.1.2}$$

where $\bar{y}_t = N_t^{-1}\sum_{i=1}^{N_t} y_{it}$ and the other averages are similarly defined. Now

$E[\bar{e}_t] = 0$ and

$$E[\bar{e}_t^2] = \frac{1}{N_t^2} E\left[\left(\sum_{i=1}^{N_t} e_{it}\right)^2\right] = \frac{N_t\sigma^2}{N_t^2} = \frac{\sigma^2}{N_t} \tag{11.1.3}$$

where the second equality is based on the fact that the e_{it} are uncorrelated and have constant variance. Thus, if estimation is based on (11.1.2), we have the problem of a heteroscedastic disturbance, where $\sigma_t^2 = \sigma^2/N_t$. However, we would expect the N_t to be known, which means that

$$\boldsymbol{\Psi}^{-1} = \text{diag}(N_1, N_2, \ldots, N_T) \tag{11.1.4}$$

is known and that generalized least squares (GLS) can be applied directly.

As another example of a heteroscedastic error model, consider the random coefficient model introduced by Hildreth and Houck (1968). In this case

$$y_t = \sum_{k=1}^{K} \beta_{kt} x_{kt} = \sum_{k=1}^{K} (\beta_k + v_{kt}) x_{kt} = \sum_{k=1}^{K} \beta_k x_{kt} + e_t \tag{11.1.5}$$

where $e_t = \sum_{k=1}^{K} v_{kt} x_{kt}$, $E[v_{kt}] = 0$, $E[v_{kt} v_{ls}] = 0$ for $k \neq l$ or $t \neq s$, and $E[v_{kt}^2] = \alpha_k$. This implies that $E[e_t] = 0$, $E[e_t e_s] = 0$ for $t \neq s$, and

$$\sigma_t^2 = E[e_t^2] = \sum_{k=1}^{K} \alpha_k x_{kt}^2.$$

Thus each coefficient, β_{kt}, is assumed to be a random variable with mean β_k, and estimation of the means $\boldsymbol{\beta}' = (\beta_1, \beta_2, \ldots, \beta_K)$ can be carried out in the framework of the general linear model with heteroscedasticity. The estimated generalized least squares (EGLS) estimator requires estimation of the α_k; this is discussed in Section 11.2.4.

Before examining some specific heteroscedastic structures, we shall discuss the use of least squares (LS) and GLS under the general assumption that

$$\boldsymbol{\Phi} = \text{diag}(\sigma_1^2, \sigma_2^2, \ldots, \sigma_T^2).$$

In this context GLS is often referred to as "weighted least squares." To demonstrate the reason for this title, note that the tth observation of $\mathbf{y} = X\boldsymbol{\beta} + \mathbf{e}$ can be written as

$$y_t = \mathbf{x}_t'\boldsymbol{\beta} + e_t \tag{11.1.6}$$

and the GLS estimator is given by

$$\begin{aligned}\hat{\boldsymbol{\beta}} &= (X'\Phi^{-1}X)^{-1}X'\Phi^{-1}\mathbf{y} \\ &= \left(\sum_{t=1}^{T} \sigma_t^{-2}\mathbf{x}_t\mathbf{x}_t'\right)^{-1} \sum_{t=1}^{T} \sigma_t^{-2}\mathbf{x}_t y_t \\ &= \left(\sum_{t=1}^{T} \mathbf{x}_t^*\mathbf{x}_t^{*\prime}\right)^{-1} \sum_{t=1}^{T} \mathbf{x}_t^* y_t^* \\ &= (X^{*\prime}X^*)^{-1}X^{*\prime}\mathbf{y}^* \end{aligned} \tag{11.1.7}$$

where $\mathbf{x}_t^* = \mathbf{x}_t/\sigma_t$, $y_t^* = y_t/\sigma_t$, $X^* = PX$, $\mathbf{y}^* = P\mathbf{y}$, $P = \text{diag}(\sigma_1^{-1}, \sigma_2^{-1}, \ldots, \sigma_T^{-1})$ and $P'P = \Phi^{-1}$. Thus GLS is LS applied to the transformed model $P\mathbf{y} = PX\boldsymbol{\beta} + P\mathbf{e}$ whose tth observation is

$$\frac{y_t}{\sigma_t} = \frac{\mathbf{x}_t'\boldsymbol{\beta}}{\sigma_t} + \frac{e_t}{\sigma_t} \tag{11.1.8}$$

Each of the observations is weighted by the inverse of the standard deviation of the corresponding e_t, and the GLS estimator is that $\boldsymbol{\beta}$ which minimizes $\Sigma(e_t/\sigma_t)^2$, the sum of squares of weighted residuals. More reliable observations (those with a relatively low σ_t) are weighted more heavily and play a greater part in the estimation process than those which are less reliable. In terms of the example discussed above, where average data were used, this implies that observations from large farms would be weighted more heavily than observations from small farms.

When σ_t^2 depends on unknown parameters, an estimated generalized least squares (EGLS) estimator for $\boldsymbol{\beta}$ can be used by replacing σ_t^2 in (11.1.7) with an estimate $\hat{\sigma}_t^2$. Methods of estimation for the σ_t^2 are discussed in Section 11.2.

If LS is used when $\Phi \neq \sigma^2 I$, the estimator $\mathbf{b} = (X'X)^{-1}X'\mathbf{y}$ will be inefficient and its variance estimator will be biased. Any evaluation of the extent of the inefficiency and variance bias will clearly depend on X, and on the nature and severity of the heteroscedasticity, and so must be carried out in terms of specific cases. For example, in the model $y_t = \beta x_t + e_t$, $E[e_t^2] = \sigma_t^2$, the loss of efficiency from using LS instead of GLS is given by

$$\Sigma_{\mathbf{b}} - \Sigma_{\hat{\boldsymbol{\beta}}} = \frac{\Sigma x_t^2\sigma_t^2}{(\Sigma x_t^2)^2} - \frac{1}{\Sigma(x_t/\sigma_t)^2} \tag{11.1.9}$$

When $\sigma_t^2 = \sigma^2$, this difference is zero and if $\sigma_t^2 = \sigma^2 x_t^2$ it is given by $(\sigma^2/(\Sigma x_t^2)^2)(\Sigma x_t^4 - (\Sigma x_t^2)^2/T)$ indicating, as one would suspect, that the greater the variation for x_t^2, the greater the loss in efficiency. The bias in the LS variance estimator for the model $y_t = \beta x_t + e_t$, $E[e_t^2] = \sigma_t^2$, is given by

$$E[\hat{\sigma}^2(X'X)^{-1}] - \Sigma_{\mathbf{b}} = \frac{-T}{(T-1)(\Sigma x_t^2)^2}\left(\Sigma x_t^2\sigma_t^2 - \frac{\Sigma x_t^2 \Sigma \sigma_t^2}{T}\right) \tag{11.1.10}$$

and hence depends on the degree of correlation between σ_t^2 and x_t^2. When this correlation is positive, as is frequently the case, the sampling variance of **b** will be underestimated. When there is no correlation, there will be no bias. For further examples see Theil (1951), Prais (1953), Geary (1966), Goldfeld and Quandt (1972), and Sathe and Vinod (1974). Some asymptotic properties of **b** are considered in Section 11.2.1.

The choice of an appropriate variance estimation method and an estimator for $\boldsymbol{\beta}$ depends upon what further assumptions are made about the variances (σ_t^2). A number of assumptions, and the possible techniques that can be used under each assumption, are reviewed in Section 11.2. In Section 11.3 tests for heteroscedasticity are discussed, and in Section 11.4 we make some recommendations on testing, modeling, and estimation.

11.2 ESTIMATION UNDER ALTERNATIVE HETEROSCEDASTIC SPECIFICATIONS

In this section we review some of the alternative heteroscedastic structures and associated inferential procedures that have appeared in the literature; each subsection contains details of those procedures relating to a specific set of assumptions about the σ_t^2. We begin with the case where there are no restrictions on the variances, and then consider various restrictive assumptions, such as the variances are constant over subsets of observations, or they are functionally related to a set of exogenous variables. See Table 11.1 for a summary. The questions we are generally concerned with are how to estimate the σ_t^2 or the parameters upon which they depend, how to test for a specific form of heteroscedasticity, and how to make inferences about $\boldsymbol{\beta}$. The broader question of how to test for the existence of heteroscedasticity of *any form* is considered in Section 11.3. A variety of estimators for $\boldsymbol{\beta}$ will be examined, but, given a set of estimates $(\hat{\sigma}_1^2, \hat{\sigma}_2^2, \ldots, \hat{\sigma}_T^2)$, we will frequently be concerned with EGLS estimators of the form

$$\hat{\hat{\boldsymbol{\beta}}} = \left(\sum_{t=1}^{T} \hat{\sigma}_t^{-2}\mathbf{x}_t\mathbf{x}_t'\right)^{-1} \sum_{t=1}^{T} \hat{\sigma}_t^{-2}\mathbf{x}_t y_t \tag{11.2.1}$$

The section concludes with some comments on heteroscedasticity and functional form.

11.2.1 No Restrictions on the Variance of Each y_t

Consider the model $\mathbf{y} = X\boldsymbol{\beta} + \mathbf{e}$, $E[\mathbf{e}] = \mathbf{0}$, $E[\mathbf{ee}'] = \boldsymbol{\Phi} = \text{diag}(\sigma_1^2, \sigma_2^2, \ldots, \sigma_T^2)$. Let a matrix A with each of its elements squared be denoted by $\dot{A}$. Thus $\dot{\boldsymbol{\sigma}} = (\sigma_1^2, \sigma_2^2, \ldots, \sigma_T^2)'$ contains the nonzero elements of $\boldsymbol{\Phi}$ and $\dot{\hat{\mathbf{e}}}$ contains the squares of the LS residuals $\hat{\mathbf{e}} = \mathbf{y} - X\mathbf{b}$. If there are no restrictions placed on the σ_t^2, there is only one observation corresponding to each variance, and so one should not be too optimistic about obtaining reliable estimates. However, following Rao (1970), it is possible to derive an estimator for $\dot{\boldsymbol{\sigma}}$ which is a "minimum norm quadratic unbiased estimator" (MINQUE). The quadratic form $\mathbf{y}'A\mathbf{y}$ is said to be a MINQUE of the linear function $\Sigma d_t\sigma_t^2$ if the Euclidean norm of A, which is equal to $(\text{tr}[AA])^{1/2}$, is a minimum subject to the conditions $AX = 0$ and $\Sigma a_{tt}\sigma_t^2 \equiv \Sigma d_t\sigma_t^2$. [See Rao (1970) for details and for reasons why such a criterion might be desirable.] The MINQUE of $\dot{\boldsymbol{\sigma}}$ is given by

$$\hat{\dot{\boldsymbol{\sigma}}} = \dot{M}^{-1}\dot{\hat{\mathbf{e}}} \tag{11.2.2}$$

where $M = I - X(X'X)^{-1}X'$ is an idempotent matrix of rank $(T - K)$. Unbiasedness can readily be demonstrated by noting that the diagonal elements of

$$E[\hat{\mathbf{e}}\hat{\mathbf{e}}'] = M\Phi M \tag{11.2.3}$$

can be written as

$$E[\dot{\hat{\mathbf{e}}}] = \dot{M}\dot{\boldsymbol{\sigma}} \tag{11.2.4}$$

Although M is singular, under quite wide conditions [Rao (1970)] $\dot{M}$ will be nonsingular and the estimator in (11.2.2) will exist. Since the rank of M is $(T - K)$, this implies that it is possible to write K of the $\hat{e}_t$'s as linear functions of the other $(T - K)$. This in turn implies that K of the $\hat{\sigma}_t^2$'s can be written as nonlinear functions of the other $(T - K)$ $\hat{\sigma}_t^2$'s or that there are K nonlinear restrictions on the elements of $\boldsymbol{\sigma}$. We expect some type of restrictions such as these, since we are estimating $(T + K)$ parameters with T observations.

There are two major problems with using the estimator in (11.2.2), namely, it is inconsistent and it can contain negative elements. Since the number of parameters increases with the number of observations, one cannot obtain a consistent estimator for $\dot{\boldsymbol{\sigma}}$, which implies that the asymptotic properties of $\hat{\hat{\boldsymbol{\beta}}}$, based on $\hat{\dot{\boldsymbol{\sigma}}}$, cannot be derived from those of $\hat{\boldsymbol{\beta}}$. Furthermore, $\hat{\dot{\boldsymbol{\sigma}}}$ is likely to contain negative elements and using these as weights in $\hat{\hat{\boldsymbol{\beta}}}$ has no clear interpretation. Some efforts have been directed toward alternative estimators that overcome the problem of negative estimates [Hartley and Jayatillake (1973); Horn, Horn, and Duncan (1975); and Horn and Horn (1975)] but, with the exception of unbiasedness [Hartley and Jayatillake (1973)] the properties of the resulting $\hat{\hat{\boldsymbol{\beta}}}$'s have not been investigated.

Given these circumstances, two potentially more profitable avenues are (1) to impose plausible restrictions on each of the σ_t^2, or (2) to use an alternative estimator whose asymptotic properties can be derived without further restrictions being placed on the σ_t^2. Various restrictions on the σ_t^2 are considered in Sections 11.2.2–11.2.6. In the remainder of this section we discuss the asymptotic properties of least squares and instrumental variables estimators that can be used without specifying a specific structure for the σ_t^2.

It is straightforward to show that the LS estimator $\mathbf{b} = (X'X)^{-1}X'\mathbf{y}$ has mean

TABLE 11.1 *ALTERNATIVE HETEROSCEDASTIC ERROR MODELS AND ESTIMATORS*

$\mathbf{y} = X\boldsymbol{\beta} + \mathbf{e},\ E[\mathbf{e}] = \mathbf{0},\ E[\mathbf{ee}'] = \boldsymbol{\Phi} = \text{diag}(\sigma_1^2, \sigma_2^2, \ldots, \sigma_T^2)$		
No restrictions on the variance of y_t. (Section 11.2.1)	Variances constant within subgroups of observations. $\boldsymbol{\Phi} = \begin{bmatrix} \sigma_1^2 I_{T_1} & & & \\ & \sigma_2^2 I_{T_2} & & \\ & & \ddots & \\ & & & \sigma_m^2 I_{T_m} \end{bmatrix}$ (Section 11.2.2)	Standard deviation of y_t is a linear function of exogenous variables. $\sigma_t^2 = (\mathbf{z}_t'\boldsymbol{\alpha})^2$ (Section 11.2.3)
Variance estimation: MINQUE Estimation of $\boldsymbol{\beta}$ 1. Least squares 2. Instrumental variables	Variance estimation: 1. Within each subgroup 2. Maximum likelihood 3. MINQUE	Estimation of $\boldsymbol{\alpha}$: 1. LS 2. GLS 3. Maximum likelihood

Variance of y_t is a linear function of exogenous variables.	Variance of y_t is proportional to a power of its expectation.	The log of the variance of y_t is a linear function of exogenous variables—"multiplicative heteroscedasticity."	Autoregressive conditional heteroscedasticity
$\sigma_t^2 = \mathbf{z}_t'\boldsymbol{\alpha}$	$\sigma_t^2 = \sigma^2(\mathbf{x}_t'\boldsymbol{\beta})^p$	$\sigma_t^2 = \exp\{\mathbf{z}_t'\boldsymbol{\alpha}\}$	$e_t = v_t(\alpha_0 + \alpha_1 e_{t-1}^2)^{1/2}$
(Section 11.2.4)	(Section 11.2.5)	(Section 11.2.6)	(Section 11.2.7)
Estimation of $\boldsymbol{\alpha}$: 1. LS and modified LS 2. GLS and modified GLS 3. MINQUE 4. Maximum likelihood	Estimation of $\boldsymbol{\beta}$: 1. EGLS based on **b** 2. Maximum likelihood	Estimation of $\boldsymbol{\alpha}$: 1. LS 2. Maximum likelihood	Estimation of $\boldsymbol{\alpha}$ and $\boldsymbol{\beta}$: Maximum likelihood
A special case: The Hildreth–Houck random coefficient model. $\sigma_t^2 = \dot{\mathbf{x}}_t'\boldsymbol{\alpha},\ \boldsymbol{\alpha} > \mathbf{0}$ (Section 11.2.4a)			

$\boldsymbol{\beta}$ and covariance matrix $(X'X)^{-1}X'\Phi X(X'X)^{-1}$, and, furthermore, under the usual assumptions (see Chapter 5)

$$\sqrt{T}(\mathbf{b} - \boldsymbol{\beta}) \xrightarrow{d} N(\mathbf{0}, Q^{-1}VQ^{-1}) \tag{11.2.5}$$

where $Q = \lim T^{-1}X'X$ and $V = \lim T^{-1}X'\Phi X$. The result in (11.2.5) can be used to test hypotheses and construct interval estimates for $\boldsymbol{\beta}$, providing that we can find a consistent estimator for V. Under appropriate conditions [Eicker (1967), White (1980), Nicholls and Pagan (1983)], it can be shown that such an estimator is given by

$$\hat{V} = T^{-1}X'\hat{\Phi}X = T^{-1}\sum_{t=1}^{T} \hat{e}_t^2 \mathbf{x}_t \mathbf{x}_t' \tag{11.2.6}$$

where $\hat{e}_t = y_t - \mathbf{x}_t'\mathbf{b}$, and $\hat{\Phi}$ is a diagonal matrix with tth diagonal element given by $\hat{e}_t^2$. Eicker considers the conditions for nonstochastic X; White allows for the possibility of stochastic but independent $\mathbf{x}_t'$; and Nicholls and Pagan consider the situation where $\mathbf{x}_t'$ can contain lagged values of y_t. See also Hsieh (1983). The results of White and Nicholls and Pagan are stated in terms of almost sure convergence (strong consistency).

Thus, although it is impossible to obtain consistent estimators for the σ_t^2 without further restrictions on these variances, it is nevertheless possible to obtain a consistent estimator of the limit of the weighted average $T^{-1}X'\Phi X = T^{-1}\sum_{t=1}^{T}\sigma_t^2\mathbf{x}_t\mathbf{x}_t'$. In addition, as an alternative to $\hat{V}$, a consistent estimator for V can be found by replacing $\hat{e}_t^2$ in (11.2.6) with the tth element of the MINQUE estimator $\hat{\boldsymbol{\sigma}}$ given in Equation (11.2.2).

From (11.2.5), (11.2.6), and the consistency of $\hat{V}$, we have

$$(R\mathbf{b} - R\boldsymbol{\beta})'[R(X'X)^{-1}X'\hat{\Phi}X(X'X)^{-1}R']^{-1}(R\mathbf{b} - R\boldsymbol{\beta}) \xrightarrow{d} \chi^2_{(J)} \tag{11.2.7}$$

where R is a known $(J \times K)$ matrix of rank J. This version of the Wald statistic can be used to test hypotheses of the form $R\boldsymbol{\beta} = \mathbf{r}$, or to construct confidence regions of the form $R\boldsymbol{\beta} \leq \mathbf{r}$. Thus, we are able to use LS to make inferences about $\boldsymbol{\beta}$ without specifying the precise nature of the heteroscedasticity. However, if it is possible to relate the σ_t^2 to a set of explanatory variables (as is assumed in many of the following subsections), we would expect to achieve a gain in asymptotic efficiency by using the appropriately defined EGLS estimator. The critical factor in any choice between LS and EGLS is likely to be the sensitivity of the EGLS estimator to a misspecification of the form of heteroscedasticity.

Another way of improving asymptotic efficiency relative to that of LS, and a way that does not require specification of the precise form of heteroscedasticity, is to use the instrumental variable type of estimator suggested by White (1982) and Cragg (1983). If we premultiply the linear model by the transpose of the $(T \times G)$ matrix $Z = [X \quad F]$, which contains the matrix X and some additional instrumental variables F, we obtain

$$Z'\mathbf{y} = Z'X\boldsymbol{\beta} + Z'\mathbf{e} \tag{11.2.8}$$

Application of GLS to (11.2.8) yields

$$\boldsymbol{\beta}^* = [X'Z(Z'\Phi Z)^{-1}Z'X]^{-1}X'Z(Z'\Phi Z)^{-1}Z'\mathbf{y} \tag{11.2.9}$$

and an obvious feasible alternative to $\boldsymbol{\beta}^*$ is

$$\hat{\boldsymbol{\beta}}^* = [X'Z(Z'\hat{\Phi}Z)^{-1}Z'X]^{-1}X'Z(Z'\hat{\Phi}Z)^{-1}Z'\mathbf{y} \tag{11.2.10}$$

where $\hat{\Phi}$ is defined below (11.2.6). White (1982) and Cragg (1983) provide conditions under which

$$\sqrt{T}(\hat{\boldsymbol{\beta}}^* - \boldsymbol{\beta}) \xrightarrow{d} N[\mathbf{0}, \lim T(X'Z(Z'\Phi Z)^{-1}Z'X)^{-1}] \tag{11.2.11}$$

and

$$(R\hat{\boldsymbol{\beta}}^* - R\boldsymbol{\beta})'\{R[X'Z(Z'\hat{\Phi}Z)^{-1}Z'X]^{-1}R'\}^{-1}(R\hat{\boldsymbol{\beta}}^* - R\boldsymbol{\beta}) \xrightarrow{d} \chi^2_{(J)} \tag{11.2.12}$$

(White actually considers a more general model where X can contain stochastic regressors that are not independent of $\mathbf{e}$, and where $\hat{\Phi}$ is based on the squares of the residuals from an instrumental variables estimator.) Noting that the GLS estimator $\hat{\boldsymbol{\beta}} = (X'\Phi^{-1}X)^{-1}X'\Phi^{-1}\mathbf{y}$ can be viewed as a regression of $\Phi^{-1/2}\mathbf{y}$ on $\Phi^{-1/2}X$, Cragg points out that the estimator $\boldsymbol{\beta}^*$ can be viewed as an instrumental variables estimator in which the instruments for $\Phi^{-1/2}X$ are its values predicted by its regression on $\Phi^{1/2}Z$. That is, the instruments are the values of $\Phi^{1/2}Z(Z'\Phi Z)^{-1}Z'X$ arising from regressions of the form $\Phi^{-1/2}X = \Phi^{1/2}Z\boldsymbol{\pi} + U$.

Cragg goes on to show that the greatest gain in (asymptotic) efficiency over the LS estimator is likely to occur if the columns of F are chosen to include those variables in $(\mathbf{x}_t' \otimes \mathbf{x}_t')$ not already included in X, as well as any other exogenous variables likely to influence the variances. This result suggests that the number of variables in F should be large. However, based on small sample evidence from a Monte Carlo experiment, Cragg recommends that the number of auxiliary variables should not be too large. His Monte Carlo experiment also showed that the gain in small sample efficiency from using $\hat{\boldsymbol{\beta}}^*$ instead of $\mathbf{b}$ can be substantial, but it did uncover some problems with small sample bias in the covariance estimators $[X'Z(Z'\hat{\Phi}Z)^{-1}Z'X]^{-1}$ and $(X'X)^{-1}X'\hat{\Phi}X(X'X)^{-1}$. Replacing the diagonal elements of $\hat{\Phi}$ with the MINQUE estimator $\hat{\boldsymbol{\sigma}}$ seemed to reduce this bias, but Cragg still concludes that, for his simple versions of the Wald statistics in (11.2.7) and (11.2.12), the χ^2-distribution is not a good finite sample approximation. One question not yet investigated, but relevant for the applied worker, is whether the White-Cragg estimator is more efficient than an EGLS estimator that makes an incorrect assumption about the form of heteroscedasticity.

11.2.2 Variances Constant Within Subgroups of Observations

In many instances it might be reasonable to assume that the variance is constant within subgroups of observations but that it varies from group to group. Suppose that there are m groups with T_i observations in the ith group, $\Sigma_{i=1}^{m} T_i = T$. This model can be written as

$$\begin{bmatrix} \mathbf{y}_1 \\ \mathbf{y}_2 \\ \vdots \\ \mathbf{y}_m \end{bmatrix} = \begin{bmatrix} X_1 \\ X_2 \\ \vdots \\ X_m \end{bmatrix} \boldsymbol{\beta} + \begin{bmatrix} \mathbf{e}_1 \\ \mathbf{e}_2 \\ \vdots \\ \mathbf{e}_m \end{bmatrix} \tag{11.2.13}$$

where $\mathbf{y}_i$ is $(T_i \times 1)$, X_i is $(T_i \times K)$, $\mathbf{e}_i$ is $(T_i \times 1)$, $E[\mathbf{e}_i\mathbf{e}_i'] = \sigma_i^2 I$, and $E[\mathbf{e}_i\mathbf{e}_j'] = 0$, $i \neq j$. Equation (11.2.13) can be viewed as a set of regression equations where the coefficient vector for each equation is restricted to be the same and where there is no correlation between the disturbances in different equations (Section 12.1). Alternatively, each of the X_i matrices may be a different set of replications of the explanatory variables in which case all rows in a given X_i would be identical, thus providing a natural way for grouping the data. Other possibilities of groups with constant variances are observations grouped according to geographical region or, with time series data, observations before and after some critical point in time.

For (11.2.13) the GLS estimator for $\boldsymbol{\beta}$ is given by

$$\hat{\boldsymbol{\beta}} = \left(\sum_{i=1}^{m} \sigma_i^{-2} X_i' X_i\right)^{-1} \sum_{i=1}^{m} \sigma_i^{-2} X_i' \mathbf{y}_i \tag{11.2.14}$$

For this estimator to be operational, we need to replace σ_i^2 with an estimator. If $T_i > K$, $i = 1, 2, \ldots, m$, one possibility is

$$\hat{\sigma}_i^2 = (T_i - K)^{-1}(\mathbf{y}_i - X_i\mathbf{b}_i)'(\mathbf{y}_i - X_i\mathbf{b}_i) \tag{11.2.15}$$

where $\mathbf{b}_i = (X_i'X_i)^{-1}X_i'\mathbf{y}_i$. Under appropriate conditions, this estimator will be consistent (with respect to each $T_i \to \infty$) and, with the added assumption of normality,

$$\hat{\hat{\boldsymbol{\beta}}} = \left(\sum_{i=1}^{m} \hat{\sigma}_i^{-2} X_i' X_i\right)^{-1} \sum_{i=1}^{m} \hat{\sigma}_i^{-2} X_i' \mathbf{y}_i \tag{11.2.16}$$

will be asymptotically efficient with asymptotic covariance matrix

$$\left(\sum_{i=1}^{m} \sigma_i^{-2} X_i' X_i\right)^{-1}$$

[Taylor (1977)]. Some finite sample results on the moments of $\hat{\hat{\boldsymbol{\beta}}}$, approximate for the general case and exact for $m = 2$, have been obtained by Taylor (1977, 1978). These results indicate that, in terms of mean square error, EGLS dominates LS over a large range of the (σ_1^2/σ_2^2) parameter space including rather small samples with a moderate degree of heteroscedasticity. The relative efficiency of $\hat{\hat{\boldsymbol{\beta}}}$ declines as m increases. Also, for $m = 2$, EGLS is almost as efficient as GLS indicating that there is little to gain from a perfect knowledge of the variances. Swamy and Mehta (1979) also give some results for the $m = 2$ case. They propose a new estimator and suggest that one should choose between $\mathbf{b}_1$, $\mathbf{b}_2$, $\mathbf{b}$, $\hat{\hat{\boldsymbol{\beta}}}$, and their estimator, with the choice depending on (1) the relative magnitudes of σ_1^2 and σ_2^2, (2) whether or not $X_2'X_2 - X_1'X_1$ is positive definite, and (3) the relative magnitudes of T_1, T_2, and K.

If the rows for a given X_i are identical, (11.2.15) reduces to

$$\hat{\sigma}_i^2 = (T_i - 1)^{-1} \sum_{j=1}^{T_i} (y_{ij} - \bar{y}_i)^2$$

where y_{ij} is the jth element of $\mathbf{y}_i$, $\bar{y}_i = \sum_{j=1}^{T_i} y_{ij}/T_i$ and, in this case, we only need the condition $T_i > 1$.

In (11.2.15) no allowance is made for the fact that each $\mathbf{b}_i$ is an estimate of the same $\boldsymbol{\beta}$. If we incorporate the additional information given by this restriction, it is likely that the resulting $\hat{\sigma}_i^2$'s will be more efficient, and, although there will be no difference asymptotically, this may lead to a $\hat{\hat{\boldsymbol{\beta}}}$ that is more efficient in finite samples. Estimation techniques that use all the information include the maximum likelihood estimator [Kmenta (1971, pp. 265–266), Hartley and Jayatillake (1973), Oberhofer and Kmenta (1974), Magnus (1978)], MINQUE and its modifications [Rao (1970, 1972), Rao and Subrahmaniam (1971), Brown (1978)], and the Bayesian approach [Drèze (1977)]. For example, in an iterative procedure to obtain ML estimates, first-round estimates of the σ_i^2 can be obtained from

$$\hat{\sigma}_i^2 = (T_i - K)^{-1}(\mathbf{y}_i - X_i\mathbf{b})'(\mathbf{y}_i - X_i\mathbf{b}) \tag{11.2.17}$$

where

$$\mathbf{b} = \left(\sum_{i=1}^{m} X_i'X_i\right)^{-1} \sum_{i=1}^{m} X_i'\mathbf{y}_i$$

is the LS estimator applied to the whole sample. These variance estimates are used to obtain an EGLS estimator $\hat{\hat{\boldsymbol{\beta}}}$ which then replaces $\mathbf{b}$ in (11.2.17) to give a second round of variance estimates. This process is continued until the estimates converge.

If, in the context of this model, we wish to test for homoscedasticity where $\sigma_1^2 = \sigma_2^2 = \ldots = \sigma_m^2 = \sigma^2$, the likelihood ratio test [Kmenta (1971, p. 268); Maddala (1977, p. 263)] or Bartlett's test (Section 11.3.3) could be used. When $m = 2$, the usual F test for equality of variances can be employed.

11.2.2a Some Properties of a Preliminary-Test Estimator

From an applied standpoint, an estimator more relevant than the EGLS estimator is the preliminary-test estimator, which is implicitly used when estimation is preceded by a test for heteroscedasticity. This estimator is equal to LS if homoscedasticity is accepted, and EGLS if homoscedasticity is rejected. Its properties have been investigated by Ohtani and Toyoda (1979) and Greenberg (1980) for the case where $m = 2$ and an F test is used. In particular, Greenberg (1980) uses Taylor's results (1977, 1978) to establish the finite sample moments for the pretest estimator

$$\boldsymbol{\beta}^* = I_{(0,c_1)}(F_{(\cdot)})\hat{\hat{\boldsymbol{\beta}}} + I_{[c_1,c_2)}(F_{(\cdot)})\mathbf{b} + I_{[c_2,\infty)}(F_{(\cdot)})\hat{\hat{\boldsymbol{\beta}}} \tag{11.2.18}$$

where the hypothesis of equal variances is accepted if $c_1 \leq F_{(\cdot)} \leq c_2$, and rejected otherwise. The EGLS estimator $\hat{\hat{\boldsymbol{\beta}}}$ is defined in (11.2.16). Under a squared error loss measure the characteristics of the risk functions for the EGLS estimator $\hat{\hat{\boldsymbol{\beta}}}$, the LS estimator $\mathbf{b}$ and the pretest estimator $\boldsymbol{\beta}^*$, relative to the GLS estimator with known variance $\hat{\boldsymbol{\beta}}$, are given in Figure 11.1 for various values of $\lambda = \sigma_1^2/\sigma_2^2$. Mandy (1984) has investigated the performance of the inequality pretest estimator when H_0: $\sigma_1^2 = \sigma_2^2$ and H_a: $\sigma_1^2 > \sigma_2^2$ and the characteristics of this pretest risk function are also illustrated in Figure 11.1. No estimator dominates over the whole range of the parameter space. However, unless λ is close to one performance of the EGLS estimator is superior to that

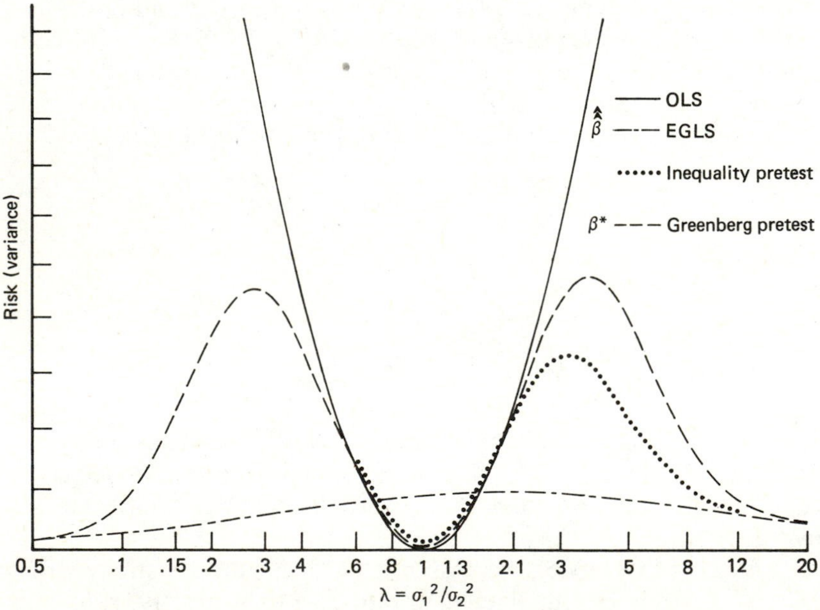

Figure 11.1 Risk characteristics of pretest and conventional estimators, double log scale.

of the pretest estimator $\boldsymbol{\beta}^*$. Again the problem of an optimum level of significance arises and is unresolved. Yancey, Judge and Miyazaki (1984), utilizing appropriate Stein estimators, have developed estimators that are uniformly superior to the pretest and EGLS estimators.

11.2.3 The Standard Deviation of y_t Is a Linear Function of Exogenous Variables

When economic data are being used, replications of a particular $\mathbf{x}_t$ are rare and it is often difficult to decide how to group the data to obtain constant variance within each group. An alternative approach is to relate σ_t^2 explicitly to $\mathbf{x}_t$. The models considered in this and the remaining subsections of Section 11.2 fall into this framework. In this subsection we assume that σ_t is a linear function of a set of explanatory variables. Hence we are considering the model

$$y_t = \mathbf{x}_t'\boldsymbol{\beta} + e_t, \qquad t = 1, 2, \ldots, T \tag{11.2.19}$$

$$E[e_t] = 0, \qquad E[e_t^2] = \sigma_t^2 = (\mathbf{z}_t'\boldsymbol{\alpha})^2, \quad E[e_te_s] = 0 \qquad (t \neq s) \tag{11.2.20}$$

where $\boldsymbol{\alpha}$ is an $(S \times 1)$ vector of unknown parameters and $\mathbf{z}_t = (1, z_{2t}, \ldots, z_{St})'$ is an $(S \times 1)$ vector of nonstochastic variables that may be identical to, or functions of, the variables in $\mathbf{x}_t$. The first element in $\mathbf{z}_t$ is assumed to be unity.

In the context of this model the GLS estimator for $\boldsymbol{\beta}$ is given by

$$\begin{aligned}\hat{\boldsymbol{\beta}} &= (X'\Phi^{-1}X)^{-1}X'\Phi^{-1}\mathbf{y} \\ &= \left(\sum_{t=1}^{T} (\mathbf{z}_t'\boldsymbol{\alpha})^{-2}\mathbf{x}_t\mathbf{x}_t'\right)^{-1} \sum_{t=1}^{T} (\mathbf{z}_t'\boldsymbol{\alpha})^{-2}\mathbf{x}_t y_t\end{aligned} \tag{11.2.21}$$

and it has mean $\boldsymbol{\beta}$ and covariance $(X'\Phi^{-1}X)^{-1} = (\Sigma_{t=1}^{T}(\mathbf{z}_t'\boldsymbol{\alpha})^{-2}\mathbf{x}_t\mathbf{x}_t')^{-1}$. When $\boldsymbol{\alpha}$ in (11.2.21) is replaced by an estimator, say $\hat{\boldsymbol{\alpha}}$, this defines an EGLS estimator $\hat{\hat{\boldsymbol{\beta}}}$. We will describe three possible estimators for $\boldsymbol{\alpha}$, a "LS estimator" $\hat{\boldsymbol{\alpha}}$, a "GLS estimator" $\hat{\hat{\boldsymbol{\alpha}}}$ and the ML estimator $\tilde{\boldsymbol{\alpha}}$. Corresponding to each of these is an EGLS estimator for $\boldsymbol{\beta}$. The one corresponding to $\tilde{\boldsymbol{\alpha}}$ will also be the ML estimator for $\boldsymbol{\beta}$.

By assumption, the standardized variables $\sigma_1^{-1}e_1, \sigma_2^{-1}e_2, \ldots, \sigma_T^{-1}e_T$ are independently and identically distributed with mean zero and variance one. Thus the expectation of the absolute value of one of the standardized variables can be written as $E[\sigma_t^{-1}|e_t|] = c$, where c is a constant that is independent of t and depends on the distribution of the $\sigma_t^{-1}|e_t|$. Also, $E[|e_t|] = c\sigma_t$ and, if the e_t are normally distributed, it can be shown that $c = (2/\pi)^{1/2}$. From these results and Equation (11.2.20) we can write

$$|\hat{e}_t| = c\mathbf{z}_t'\boldsymbol{\alpha} + v_t \tag{11.2.22}$$

where $\hat{e}_t$ is the LS residual $\hat{e}_t = y_t - \mathbf{x}_t'\mathbf{b}$ and v_t is a new "disturbance" $v_t = |\hat{e}_t| - E[|e_t|]$. Applying LS to (11.2.22) gives an estimator for $c\boldsymbol{\alpha}$,

$$c\hat{\boldsymbol{\alpha}} = \left(\sum_{t=1}^{T} \mathbf{z}_t\mathbf{z}_t'\right)^{-1} \sum_{t=1}^{T} \mathbf{z}_t|\hat{e}_t| = (Z'Z)^{-1}Z'|\hat{\mathbf{e}}| \tag{11.2.23}$$

where $Z' = (\mathbf{z}_1, \mathbf{z}_2, \ldots, \mathbf{z}_T)$ and $|\hat{\mathbf{e}}| = (|\hat{e}_1|, |\hat{e}_2|, \ldots, |\hat{e}_T|)'$. The fact that we have estimated $c\boldsymbol{\alpha}$ instead of $\boldsymbol{\alpha}$ is of no consequence for estimation of $\boldsymbol{\beta}$ because the EGLS estimator

$$\hat{\hat{\boldsymbol{\beta}}} = \left(\sum_{t=1}^{T} (\mathbf{z}_t'\hat{\boldsymbol{\alpha}})^{-2}\mathbf{x}_t\mathbf{x}_t'\right)^{-1} \sum_{t=1}^{T} (\mathbf{z}_t'\hat{\boldsymbol{\alpha}})^{-2}\mathbf{x}_t y_t$$

does not change if $\hat{\boldsymbol{\alpha}}$ is replaced by $c\hat{\boldsymbol{\alpha}}$. However, it does make a difference when the covariance matrix for $\hat{\hat{\boldsymbol{\beta}}}$ is estimated. In this case $\hat{\boldsymbol{\alpha}}$, not $c\hat{\boldsymbol{\alpha}}$, needs to be used.

The estimator $\hat{\boldsymbol{\alpha}}$ will not possess all the "good LS properties" because, in general, the v_t will be heteroscedastic and autocorrelated and will have nonzero means. However, under appropriate conditions [Harvey (1974), Theil (1971), Ch. 8], $|\hat{e}_t|$ will converge in distribution to $|e_t|$; $\hat{\boldsymbol{\alpha}}$ will be a consistent estimator for $\boldsymbol{\alpha}$; and the resulting EGLS estimator for $\boldsymbol{\beta}$ will have the same asymptotic properties as the GLS estimator.

Although asymptotically we cannot improve on the estimator $\hat{\hat{\boldsymbol{\beta}}}$ derived from $\hat{\boldsymbol{\alpha}}$, if we could find a more efficient estimator for $\boldsymbol{\alpha}$, we would intuitively expect the resulting new EGLS estimator for $\boldsymbol{\beta}$ to be better in finite samples. To find such an estimator, note that if $|\hat{e}_t|$ converges in distribution to $|e_t|$, then, asymptotically, the v_t will be independently distributed with zero mean and variance

$$E[v_t^2] = E[|e_t|^2] - (E[|e_t|])^2 = \sigma_t^2(1 - c^2) = (\mathbf{z}_t'\boldsymbol{\alpha})^2(1 - c^2) \tag{11.2.24}$$

This "asymptotic heteroscedasticity" of v_t suggests that we should apply a GLS estimator to (11.2.22). If we make use of $\hat{\boldsymbol{\alpha}}$ in (11.2.23), such an estimator is given by

$$\begin{aligned} c\hat{\hat{\boldsymbol{\alpha}}} &= (Z'\hat{\Phi}^{-1}Z)^{-1}Z'\hat{\Phi}^{-1}|\hat{\mathbf{e}}| \\ &= \left(\sum_{t=1}^{T} (\mathbf{z}_t'\hat{\boldsymbol{\alpha}})^{-2}\mathbf{z}_t\mathbf{z}_t'\right)^{-1} \sum_{t=1}^{T} (\mathbf{z}_t'\hat{\boldsymbol{\alpha}})^{-2}\mathbf{z}_t|\hat{e}_t| \end{aligned} \tag{11.2.25}$$

The properties of $\hat{\boldsymbol{\alpha}}$ and $\hat{\hat{\boldsymbol{\alpha}}}$ have not been fully investigated, but it seems reasonable to expect that under appropriate conditions both $\hat{\boldsymbol{\alpha}}$ and $\hat{\hat{\boldsymbol{\alpha}}}$ will be asymptotically normal with asymptotic covariance matrices

$$\Sigma_{\hat{\alpha}} = \left(\frac{1 - c^2}{c^2}\right)(Z'Z)^{-1}Z'\Phi Z(Z'Z)^{-1} \tag{11.2.26}$$

and $\Sigma_{\hat{\hat{\alpha}}} = ((1 - c^2)/c^2)(Z'\Phi^{-1}Z)^{-1}$; and so, in this sense, $\hat{\hat{\boldsymbol{\alpha}}}$ will be more efficient. Thus, although there is no difference asymptotically, it seems reasonable to expect an EGLS estimator for $\boldsymbol{\beta}$ based on $\hat{\hat{\boldsymbol{\alpha}}}$ to be more efficient than the corresponding one based on $\hat{\boldsymbol{\alpha}}$.

The estimator $\hat{\hat{\boldsymbol{\alpha}}}$ was suggested by Harvey (1974) while, for the purpose of testing for homoscedasticity, $\hat{\boldsymbol{\alpha}}$ was suggested by Glejser (1969). Now we indicate how some asymptotic tests can be carried out.

The e_t will be homoscedastic if $\boldsymbol{\alpha}^* = \mathbf{0}$, where $\boldsymbol{\alpha}^* = (\alpha_2, \alpha_3, \ldots, \alpha_S)'$ and $\boldsymbol{\alpha}' = (\alpha_1, \boldsymbol{\alpha}^{*\prime})$. Under this as the null hypothesis,

$$\mathbf{\Sigma}_{\hat{\alpha}} = \mathbf{\Sigma}_{\hat{\hat{\alpha}}} = \left(\frac{1 - c^2}{c^2}\right) \alpha_1^2 (Z'Z)^{-1} \tag{11.2.27}$$

and α_1^2 can be consistently estimated from the LS residuals, say $\hat{\alpha}_1^2 = \Sigma_{t=1}^T \hat{e}_t^2/T$. If $\hat{\boldsymbol{\alpha}}$ and $\hat{\hat{\boldsymbol{\alpha}}}$ are approximately normal, then under the null hypothesis,

$$g = \left(\frac{c^2}{1 - c^2}\right) \frac{\hat{\hat{\boldsymbol{\alpha}}}^{*\prime} D^{-1} \hat{\hat{\boldsymbol{\alpha}}}^*}{\hat{\alpha}_1^2} \tag{11.2.28}$$

and

$$g^* = \left(\frac{c^2}{1 - c^2}\right) \frac{\hat{\boldsymbol{\alpha}}^{*\prime} D^{-1} \hat{\boldsymbol{\alpha}}^*}{\hat{\alpha}_1^2} \tag{11.2.29}$$

will each have an approximate $\chi^2_{(S-1)}$ distribution, where D is the matrix $(Z'Z)^{-1}$ with its first row and column deleted and, if the e_t are normally distributed, $c = (2/\pi)^{1/2}$. The null hypothesis $\boldsymbol{\alpha}^* = \mathbf{0}$ is rejected if the chosen statistic (g or g^*) falls in the appropriate critical region. The statistic g^* is likely to be computationally more convenient than g because $c^2\hat{\boldsymbol{\alpha}}^{*\prime} D^{-1} \hat{\boldsymbol{\alpha}}^*$ is equal to the regression sum of squares of the regression of $|\hat{\mathbf{e}}|$ on Z [Goldberger (1964, p. 176)]. For a related testing procedure see Glejser (1969).

Maximum likelihood estimation provides another method for estimating $\boldsymbol{\alpha}$ and $\boldsymbol{\beta}$. If the e_t are normally distributed, the logarithm of the likelihood function is apart from a constant

$$L = -\sum_{t=1}^{T} \ln \mathbf{z}_t'\boldsymbol{\alpha} - \frac{1}{2} \sum_{t=1}^{T} \left(\frac{y_t - \mathbf{x}_t'\boldsymbol{\beta}}{\mathbf{z}_t'\boldsymbol{\alpha}}\right)^2 \tag{11.2.30}$$

Setting first derivatives of L (with respect to $\boldsymbol{\alpha}$ and $\boldsymbol{\beta}$) equal to zero yields equations nonlinear in $\boldsymbol{\alpha}$ and $\boldsymbol{\beta}$ so that nonlinear methods (Appendix B) are required to find the ML estimates. For an example, see Rutemiller and Bowers (1968) who, for their application, used the method of scoring. An asymptotic test for heteroscedasticity can be based on the likelihood ratio test statistic $u = (L_1 - L_0)/2$, where L_1 is (11.2.30) evaluated at the ML estimates of $\boldsymbol{\alpha}$ and $\boldsymbol{\beta}$ and L_0 is the same function evaluated at $\hat{\alpha}_1^2 = T^{-1}(\mathbf{y} - X\mathbf{b})'(\mathbf{y} - X\mathbf{b})$, $\boldsymbol{\alpha}^* = \mathbf{0}$ and $\mathbf{b} = (X'X)^{-1}X'\mathbf{y}$. The latter are ML estimates under the assumption $\boldsymbol{\alpha}^* = \mathbf{0}$. Under the null hypothesis $\boldsymbol{\alpha}^* = \mathbf{0}$, u will have an approximate $\chi^2_{(S-1)}$ distribution.

Maximum likelihood estimation may be computationally difficult and so as a further alternative Harvey (1974) suggests an estimator based on one iteration of the method of scoring and that has the same asymptotic distribution as the

ML estimator. Using a more general framework, Jobson and Fuller (1980) derive the properties of the nonlinear least squares estimator for $\boldsymbol{\alpha}$, which minimizes $\Sigma_t[\hat{e}_t^2 - (\mathbf{z}_t'\boldsymbol{\alpha})^2]^2$. With this estimator as a preliminary one, they too suggest an estimator that can be regarded as the result of one iteration in the method of scoring, and that has the same asymptotic properties as the ML estimator.

11.2.4 The Variance of y_t Is a Linear Function of Exogenous Variables

Another heteroscedastic error model that has received some attention in the literature [Hildreth and Houck (1968), Theil (1971), Goldfeld and Quandt (1972), Froehlich (1973), Harvey (1974), Raj (1975), Amemiya (1977)] occurs when σ_t^2 is assumed to be a linear function of a set of exogenous variables. In this case we have

$$y_t = \mathbf{x}_t'\boldsymbol{\beta} + e_t, \qquad t = 1, 2, \ldots, T \tag{11.2.31}$$

$$E[e_t] = 0, \qquad E[e_t^2] = \sigma_t^2 = \mathbf{z}_t'\boldsymbol{\alpha}, \quad E[e_t e_s] = 0 \qquad (t \neq s) \tag{11.2.32}$$

where, as in the previous subsection, $\boldsymbol{\alpha}$ is an $(S \times 1)$ vector of unknown parameters and $\mathbf{z}_t' = (1, z_{2t}, \ldots, z_{St})$ is the tth observation of S known nonstochastic variables. The GLS estimator for $\boldsymbol{\beta}$,

$$\begin{aligned}\hat{\boldsymbol{\beta}} &= (X'\Phi^{-1}X)^{-1}X'\Phi^{-1}\mathbf{y} \\ &= \left(\sum_{t=1}^{T} (\mathbf{z}_t'\boldsymbol{\alpha})^{-1}\mathbf{x}_t\mathbf{x}_t'\right)^{-1} \sum_{t=1}^{T} (\mathbf{z}_t'\boldsymbol{\alpha})^{-1}\mathbf{x}_t y_t\end{aligned} \tag{11.2.33}$$

has mean $\boldsymbol{\beta}$ and covariance $(X'\Phi^{-1}X)^{-1} = (\Sigma_{t=1}^{T}(\mathbf{z}_t'\boldsymbol{\alpha})^{-1}\mathbf{x}_t\mathbf{x}_t')^{-1}$. As with the previous case where $\sigma_t^2 = (\mathbf{z}_t'\boldsymbol{\alpha})^2$, a number of possible estimators for $\boldsymbol{\alpha}$, each of which can be used in (11.2.33) to give an EGLS estimator for $\boldsymbol{\beta}$, have been suggested.

From (11.2.32) we can write

$$\hat{e}_t^2 = \mathbf{z}_t'\boldsymbol{\alpha} + v_t \tag{11.2.34}$$

where $v_t = \hat{e}_t^2 - E[e_t^2]$ and $\hat{e}_t^2$ is the square of the LS residual $\hat{e}_t = y_t - \mathbf{x}_t'\mathbf{b}$. The application of LS to (11.2.34) [Goldfeld and Quandt (1972)] yields

$$\hat{\boldsymbol{\alpha}} = \left(\sum_{t=1}^{T} \mathbf{z}_t\mathbf{z}_t'\right)^{-1} \sum_{t=1}^{T} \mathbf{z}_t\hat{e}_t^2 = (Z'Z)^{-1}Z'\dot{\hat{\mathbf{e}}} \tag{11.2.35}$$

where $Z' = (\mathbf{z}_1, \mathbf{z}_2, \ldots, \mathbf{z}_T)$ and $\dot{\hat{\mathbf{e}}} = (\hat{e}_1^2, \hat{e}_2^2, \ldots, \hat{e}_T^2)'$. However, v_t in (11.2.34) has a nonzero mean and suffers from both heteroscedasticity and autocorrelation. Thus $\hat{\boldsymbol{\alpha}}$ will be biased and, relative to a GLS estimator for $\boldsymbol{\alpha}$, inefficient. The bias can readily be demonstrated by noting that

$$E[\dot{\hat{\mathbf{e}}}] = \dot{M}z\boldsymbol{\alpha} \tag{11.2.36}$$

and hence that $E[\hat{\boldsymbol{\alpha}}] = (Z'Z)^{-1}Z'\dot{M}Z\boldsymbol{\alpha}$, where $\dot{M}$ is the matrix $M = I - X(X'X)^{-1}X'$ with each of its elements squared. This suggests two possible unbiased estimators for $\boldsymbol{\alpha}$ [Hildreth and Houck (1968)]—namely,

$$\hat{\boldsymbol{\alpha}}(1) = (Z'\dot{M}\dot{M}Z)^{-1}Z'\dot{M}\dot{\hat{\mathbf{e}}} \tag{11.2.37}$$

and

$$\hat{\boldsymbol{\alpha}}(2) = (Z'\dot{M}Z)^{-1}Z'\dot{\hat{\mathbf{e}}} \tag{11.2.38}$$

The first estimator results from applying LS to

$$\dot{\hat{\mathbf{e}}} = \dot{M}Z\boldsymbol{\alpha} + \mathbf{w} \tag{11.2.39}$$

where, from (11.2.36), $E[\mathbf{w}] = \mathbf{0}$, while the second is a MINQUE [Froehlich (1973)].

Further estimators for $\boldsymbol{\alpha}$ can be defined by noting the covariance structure of v_t in (11.2.34), and $\mathbf{w}$ in (11.2.39) and applying GLS to each of these equations. For Equation (11.2.34), if $\hat{e}_t^2$ converges in distribution to e_t^2, asymptotically the v_t will have zero mean, be uncorrelated and have a variance proportional to $(\mathbf{z}_t'\boldsymbol{\alpha})^2$ [Harvey (1974), Amemiya (1977)]. Thus if, in an asymptotic sense, we apply GLS to (11.2.34), this gives the estimator

$$\hat{\hat{\boldsymbol{\alpha}}} = \left(\sum_{t=1}^{T} (\mathbf{z}_t'\hat{\boldsymbol{\alpha}})^{-2}\mathbf{z}_t\mathbf{z}_t'\right)^{-1} \sum_{t=1}^{T} (\mathbf{z}_t'\hat{\boldsymbol{\alpha}})^{-2}\mathbf{z}_t\hat{e}_t^2 \tag{11.2.40}$$

where $(\mathbf{z}_t'\hat{\boldsymbol{\alpha}})^2$ has been used to estimate the variance of v_t. This estimator will be asymptotically more efficient than $\hat{\boldsymbol{\alpha}}$ in (11.2.35).

For Equation (11.2.39), if the e_t are normally distributed, $\mathbf{w}$ will have an exact covariance matrix given by $2\dot{Q}$, where $Q = M\Phi M$, and application of GLS gives [Raj (1975)]

$$\hat{\hat{\boldsymbol{\alpha}}}(1) = (Z'\dot{M}\dot{\hat{Q}}^{-1}\dot{M}Z)^{-1}Z'\dot{M}\dot{\hat{Q}}^{-1}\dot{\hat{\mathbf{e}}} \tag{11.2.41}$$

where Q has been replaced by $\hat{Q} = M\hat{\Phi}M$ and $\hat{\Phi}$ has the tth diagonal element $(\mathbf{z}_t'\hat{\boldsymbol{\alpha}}(1))^2$. Theil (1971, p. 624), based on Theil and Mennes (1959), suggests ignoring the off-diagonal elements of $\dot{Q}$. This yields an estimator that is simpler and is asymptotically equivalent to $\hat{\hat{\boldsymbol{\alpha}}}(1)$. Also, the estimators $\hat{\hat{\boldsymbol{\alpha}}}$ and $\hat{\hat{\boldsymbol{\alpha}}}(1)$ can be regarded as special cases of nonlinear estimators investigated within a more general framework by Jobson and Fuller (1980).

Although the GLS estimators $\hat{\hat{\boldsymbol{\alpha}}}$ and $\hat{\hat{\boldsymbol{\alpha}}}(1)$ are asymptotically more efficient than their LS counterparts, they do not lead to EGLS estimators for $\boldsymbol{\beta}$ that are asymptotically more efficient. Under appropriate conditions [Hildreth and Houck (1968), Amemiya (1977)] the EGLS estimators for $\boldsymbol{\beta}$ will all have an asymptotic covariance matrix given by $(\Sigma_{t=1}^{T}(\mathbf{z}_t'\boldsymbol{\alpha})^{-1}\mathbf{x}_t\mathbf{x}_t')^{-1}$. However, one would hope that asymptotically more efficient estimators for $\boldsymbol{\alpha}$ do lead to EGLS estimators for $\boldsymbol{\beta}$ that are more efficient in finite samples. This needs to be verified with Monte Carlo studies. In the context of a random cofficient model, Raj (1975) uses a Monte Carlo experiment to compare the LS estimator $\mathbf{b}$ with $\hat{\hat{\boldsymbol{\beta}}}$ obtained using $\hat{\boldsymbol{\alpha}}(1)$, $\hat{\hat{\boldsymbol{\alpha}}}(1)$, and the Theil modification of $\hat{\hat{\boldsymbol{\alpha}}}(1)$. Based on mean square error the latter two estimators for $\boldsymbol{\beta}$ outperformed the other two for a large sample size ($T = 50$), but for $T = 10$ and 20, $\mathbf{b}$ was uniformly better than all the EGLS $\boldsymbol{\beta}$ estimators. This perhaps surprising result appears to be due to the fact that it is possible to obtain negative estimates of the σ_t^2; these negative estimates were retained in Raj's study. When the estimators are modified to exclude the possibility of a $\hat{\Phi}$ that is not positive definite [Hildreth and Houck (1968)], Monte Carlo results suggest that the $\hat{\hat{\boldsymbol{\beta}}}$'s compare favorably with $\mathbf{b}$ although they are not uniformly better. For modifications of $\hat{\boldsymbol{\alpha}}(1)$ and $\hat{\boldsymbol{\alpha}}(2)$, such evidence has been provided by Griffiths (1971) while Goldfeld and Quandt (1972) provide evidence on a modification of $\hat{\boldsymbol{\alpha}}$. Finite sample comparisons of $\hat{\boldsymbol{\alpha}}$ with $\hat{\boldsymbol{\alpha}}(1)$ or $\hat{\hat{\boldsymbol{\alpha}}}$ with $\hat{\hat{\boldsymbol{\alpha}}}(1)$ and the $\hat{\hat{\boldsymbol{\beta}}}$'s that result, have not, to our knowledge, been made.

If the e_t are normally distributed and if the conditions required for asymptotic normality of $\hat{\boldsymbol{\alpha}}$ and $\hat{\hat{\boldsymbol{\alpha}}}$ hold [Amemiya (1977)], a test for homoscedasticity, based on either $\hat{\boldsymbol{\alpha}}$ or $\hat{\hat{\boldsymbol{\alpha}}}$ and similar to (11.2.28) and (11.2.29) can be constructed. For example, if $\boldsymbol{\alpha}' = (\alpha_1, \boldsymbol{\alpha}^{*\prime})$, under the null hypothesis $\boldsymbol{\alpha}^* = \mathbf{0}$,

$$\Sigma_{\hat{\alpha}} = 2\alpha_1^2(Z'Z)^{-1} \tag{11.2.42}$$

and

$$g = \frac{\hat{\boldsymbol{\alpha}}^{*\prime}D^{-1}\hat{\boldsymbol{\alpha}}^*}{2\hat{\sigma}^4} \tag{11.2.43}$$

has an approximate $\chi^2_{(S-1)}$ distribution, where $\hat{\boldsymbol{\alpha}}' = (\hat{\alpha}_1, \hat{\boldsymbol{\alpha}}^{*\prime})$, $\hat{\sigma}^2 = \hat{\mathbf{e}}'\hat{\mathbf{e}}/T$, and D is the matrix $(Z'Z)^{-1}$ with its first row and column deleted. It is interesting to note that g is identical to the Breusch–Pagan statistic, which is discussed in Section 11.3 in connection with a wider class of models.

Numerical methods can be used to compute maximum likelihood estimates [Goldfeld and Quandt (1972)], and another test for homoscedasticity can be based on the likelihood ratio test. In this case the logarithm of the likelihood function is apart from a constant

$$L = -\frac{1}{2}\sum_{t=1}^{T} \ln \mathbf{z}_t'\boldsymbol{\alpha} - \frac{1}{2}\sum_{t=1}^{T} \frac{(y_t - \mathbf{x}_t'\boldsymbol{\beta})^2}{\mathbf{z}_t'\boldsymbol{\alpha}} \tag{11.2.44}$$

Both Harvey (1974) and Amemiya (1977) use the information matrix from this function to demonstrate the asymptotic efficiency of $\hat{\hat{\boldsymbol{\alpha}}}$ under normality.

11.2.4a A Special Case: The Hildreth–Houck Random Coefficient Model

If, in Equation 11.2.32, $\mathbf{z}_t = \dot{\mathbf{x}}_t$ so that $\sigma_t^2 = \dot{\mathbf{x}}_t'\boldsymbol{\alpha}$, and $\boldsymbol{\alpha}$ is interpreted as a vector of variances for the "random coefficients," we have the random coefficient model given in Equation (11.1.5) [Hildreth and Houck (1968)]. The techniques just described are equally relevant for this model, but, in addition to the constraint $\sigma_t^2 \geq 0$, we know that $\boldsymbol{\alpha} \geq \mathbf{0}$.

To incorporate this information on $\boldsymbol{\alpha}$, Hildreth and Houck (1968) suggest changing negative estimates to zero or using a quadratic programming estimator; Griffiths, Drynan, and Prakash (1979) illustrate how Bayesian methods can be applied. Monte Carlo evidence on the finite sample performance of alternative estimators has been provided by Froehlich (1973), Griffiths (1971), Raj (1975), and Dent and Hildreth (1977). The latter paper also investigates the efficiency of alternative numerical methods that can be used to obtain constrained maximum likelihood estimates. From these results it appears that one should avoid using negative $\hat{\alpha}_k$'s and that there is some gain from using constrained ML or a $\hat{\hat{\boldsymbol{\beta}}}$ based on a "restricted EGLS" estimator of $\boldsymbol{\alpha}$. The model is discussed further in Chapter 19.

11.2.5 The Variance of y_t Is Proportional to a Power of Its Expectation

Another heteroscedastic error model that has received considerable attention in the econometric literature is one where the variance of y_t is assumed to be proportional to a power of its expectation [Theil (1951, 1971), Prais (1953), Prais and Houthakker (1955), Kakwani and Gupta (1967), Amemiya (1973), Battese and Bonyhady (1981)]. In this case we have $\text{var}(y_t) = \sigma_t^2 = \sigma^2(\mathbf{x}_t'\boldsymbol{\beta})^p$, where, in the majority of studies, p is either assumed known or is explicitly set equal to 2. Considering the $p = 2$ case, we have the model

$$y_t = \mathbf{x}_t'\boldsymbol{\beta} + e_t, \quad t = 1, 2, \ldots, T \tag{11.2.45}$$

where

$$E[e_t] = 0, \qquad E[e_t^2] = \sigma_t^2 = \sigma^2(\mathbf{x}_t'\boldsymbol{\beta})^2, \qquad E[e_te_s] = 0 \quad (t \neq s) \tag{11.2.46}$$

The covariance matrix for $\mathbf{e}$ is

$$E[\mathbf{ee}'] = \Phi = \sigma^2\boldsymbol{\Psi} = \sigma^2 \operatorname{diag}((\mathbf{x}_1'\boldsymbol{\beta})^2, (\mathbf{x}_2'\boldsymbol{\beta})^2, \ldots, (\mathbf{x}_T'\boldsymbol{\beta})^2)$$

This can be regarded as a special case of the model $\sigma_t^2 = (\mathbf{z}_t'\boldsymbol{\alpha})^2$ [Equation (11.2.20)], where $\mathbf{z}_t = \mathbf{x}_t$ and $\boldsymbol{\alpha}$ is proportional to $\boldsymbol{\beta}$.

The GLS estimator $\hat{\boldsymbol{\beta}} = (X'\Phi^{-1}X)^{-1}X'\Phi^{-1}\mathbf{y}$ is not a feasible one because Φ depends on $\boldsymbol{\beta}$. However, one can first use the LS estimator $\mathbf{b} = (X'X)^{-1}X'\mathbf{y}$, and then use the resulting estimate in an EGLS estimator,

$$\hat{\hat{\boldsymbol\beta}} = (X'\hat{\Psi}^{-1}X)^{-1}X'\hat{\Psi}^{-1}\mathbf{y}$$

$$= \left(\sum_{t=1}^{T} (\mathbf{x}_t'\mathbf{b})^{-2}\mathbf{x}_t\mathbf{x}_t'\right)^{-1} \sum_{t=1}^{T} (\mathbf{x}_t'\mathbf{b})^{-2}\mathbf{x}_t y_t \tag{11.2.47}$$

Under appropriate conditions [Theil (1971), Amemiya (1973)] $\sqrt{T}(\hat{\hat{\boldsymbol\beta}} - \boldsymbol\beta)$ has a limiting normal distribution with mean $\mathbf{0}$ and covariance matrix $\lim T(X'\Phi^{-1}X)^{-1}$. A convenient estimator for the approximate covariance matrix for $\hat{\hat{\boldsymbol\beta}}$ is

$$\hat{\Sigma}_{\hat{\hat{\boldsymbol\beta}}} = \hat{\sigma}^2 \left(\sum_{t=1}^{T} (\mathbf{x}_t'\mathbf{b})^{-2}\mathbf{x}_t\mathbf{x}_t'\right)^{-1} \tag{11.2.48}$$

where

$$\hat{\sigma}^2 = (T - K)^{-1} \sum_{t=1}^{T} [(\mathbf{x}_t'\mathbf{b})^{-2}(y_t - \mathbf{x}_t'\hat{\hat{\boldsymbol\beta}})^2] \tag{11.2.49}$$

We say "convenient" because this would be the covariance matrix given by the transformed least squares computer run used to obtain $\hat{\hat{\boldsymbol\beta}}$. Asymptotically, there is no difference; but, in finite samples, we may be able to obtain a better estimator for $\Sigma_{\hat{\hat{\boldsymbol\beta}}}$ by substituting $\hat{\hat{\boldsymbol\beta}}$ for $\mathbf{b}$ in (11.2.48) and (11.2.49). This also raises the question of using the above results in an iterative fashion. Specifically, in (11.2.47) we could replace $\mathbf{x}_t'\mathbf{b}$ with $\mathbf{x}_t'\hat{\hat{\boldsymbol\beta}}$, use the new estimator for $\boldsymbol\beta$ to form another estimate of σ_t^2, and so on. See Prais (1953), Prais and Aitchison (1954), and Kakwani and Gupta (1967).

As an alternative to (11.2.47) we can make some specific distributional assumptions about $\mathbf{y}$ and use numerical methods to obtain ML estimates. If $\mathbf{y}$ has a multivariate normal distribution, then, in contrast to the other models studied, the ML estimator for $\boldsymbol\beta$ will not be of the "EGLS type." The dependence of Φ on $\boldsymbol\beta$ implies that both the sum of squares function $(\mathbf{y} - X\boldsymbol\beta)'\Phi^{-1}(\mathbf{y} - X\boldsymbol\beta)$, as well as the complete log-likelihood function, are no longer simple quadratic functions of $\boldsymbol\beta$. For each of three cases, y_t with normal, lognormal, and gamma distributions, Amemiya (1973) gives the logarithm of the likelihood function and its first- and second-order partial derivatives. Based on the Cramēr–Rao lower bound, he demonstrates that the EGLS estimator in (11.2.47) is asymptotically inefficient when y_t is normal or lognormally distributed, but efficient when y_t has the gamma distribution. The asymptotic inefficiency of $\hat{\hat{\boldsymbol\beta}}$ under the normality assumption is confirmed within a more general context by Jobson and Fuller (1980), who go on to suggest a nonlinear least squares estimator that is asymptotically equivalent to the ML estimator. Their estimator for $\boldsymbol\beta$ is one that utilizes information in both $\mathbf{y}$ and the least squares residuals. Specifically, it is a weighted nonlinear least squares procedure that is applied jointly to the two equations

$$y_t = \mathbf{x}_t'\boldsymbol{\beta} + e_t \tag{11.2.50}$$

and

$$\hat{e}_t^2 = (\mathbf{x}_t'\boldsymbol{\beta})^2 + v_t \tag{11.2.51}$$

Further results presented by Carroll and Ruppert (1982) show that, although the EGLS estimator is asymptotically not as efficient as the Jobson–Fuller estimator, it is more robust with respect to misspecification of the variance function.

The use of testing procedures to discriminate between the normal, lognormal and gamma distributions has been illustrated by Amemiya (1973) and Surekha and Griffiths (1982). Amemiya uses a classical nonnested hypothesis test, while Surekha and Griffiths calculate the posterior odds within a Bayesian framework. Test statistics used to test for heteroscedasticity of the form $\sigma_t^2 = \sigma^2(\mathbf{x}_t'\boldsymbol{\beta})^2$, without specification of the form of distribution, have been studied by Bickel (1978), Carroll and Ruppert (1981), and Hammerstorm (1981).

The more general variance specification, where $\sigma_t^2 = \sigma^2(\mathbf{x}_t'\boldsymbol{\beta})^p$ and p is an unknown parameter to be estimated, has been considered by Box and Hill (1974) and Battese and Bonyhady (1981). Assuming normality, Battese and Bonyhady use maximum likelihood methods to estimate the model for a number of household expenditure functions, and they demonstrate how a test for homoscedasticity ($p = 0$), or a test for $p = 2$, can be based on the asymptotic normality of the ML estimates and the Cramér–Rao lower bound.

11.2.6 The Log of the Variance of y_t Is a Linear Function of Exogenous Variables—Multiplicative Heteroscedasticity

Another heteroscedastic error model that has appeared in the literature is one called "multiplicative heteroscedasticity" [Harvey (1976)]. The assumptions of this model are

$$y_t = \mathbf{x}_t'\boldsymbol{\beta} + e_t, \qquad t = 1, 2, \ldots, T \tag{11.2.52}$$

$$E[e_t] = 0, \qquad E[e_t^2] = \sigma_t^2 = \exp\{\mathbf{z}_t'\boldsymbol{\alpha}\}, \quad E[e_te_s] = 0, \qquad t \neq s \tag{11.2.53}$$

where $\mathbf{z}_t$ is an $(S \times 1)$ vector containing the tth observation on S nonstochastic variables and $\boldsymbol{\alpha}$ is an $(S \times 1)$ vector of unknown parameters. The first element in $\mathbf{z}_t$ is assumed to be unity. As an example, if we consider the special case where $S = 2$, $\boldsymbol{\alpha}' = (\log k, \lambda)$ and $\mathbf{z}_t' = (1, \log x_{2t})$, we have $\sigma_t^2 = kx_{2t}^{\lambda}$, where the variance is proportional to a power of one of the explanatory variables [Geary (1966), Park (1966), Kmenta (1971)].

The GLS estimator for $\boldsymbol{\beta}$ is

$$\hat{\boldsymbol{\beta}} = \left[\sum_{t=1}^{T} \exp(-\mathbf{z}_t'\boldsymbol{\alpha})\mathbf{x}_t\mathbf{x}_t'\right]^{-1} \sum_{t=1}^{T} \exp(-\mathbf{z}_t'\boldsymbol{\alpha})\mathbf{x}_t y_t \tag{11.2.54}$$

To obtain an EGLS estimator for $\boldsymbol{\beta}$, an estimator for $\boldsymbol{\alpha}$ is required; one possibility is to obtain LS residuals $\hat{\mathbf{e}} = \mathbf{y} - X\mathbf{b}$, and set up the equation,

$$\ln \hat{e}_t^2 = \mathbf{z}_t'\boldsymbol{\alpha} + v_t \tag{11.2.55}$$

where $v_t = \ln(\hat{e}_t^2/\sigma_t^2)$. Applying LS to this equation yields

$$\hat{\boldsymbol{\alpha}} = \left(\sum_{t=1}^{T} \mathbf{z}_t\mathbf{z}_t'\right)^{-1} \sum_{t=1}^{T} \mathbf{z}_t \ln \hat{e}_t^2 \tag{11.2.56}$$

A problem with this estimator is that the v_t have nonzero means and are heteroscedastic and autocorrelated. However, if the e_t are normally distributed and if $\hat{e}_t$ converges in distribution to e_t, then, asymptotically, the v_t will be independent with mean and variance given by Harvey (1976):

$$E[v_t] = -1.2704 \quad \text{and} \quad E[v_t^2] - (E[v_t])^2 = 4.9348 \tag{11.2.57}$$

This implies that $\hat{\alpha}_1$, the first element in $\hat{\boldsymbol{\alpha}}$, will be inconsistent. However, this is of no consequence, since, in

$$\hat{\hat{\boldsymbol{\beta}}} = \left(\sum_{t=1}^{T} \exp(-\mathbf{z}_t'\hat{\boldsymbol{\alpha}})\mathbf{x}_t\mathbf{x}_t'\right)^{-1} \sum_{t=1}^{T} \exp(-\mathbf{z}_t'\hat{\boldsymbol{\alpha}})\mathbf{x}_t y_t \tag{11.2.58}$$

changing $\hat{\alpha}_1$ only changes the constant of proportionality. If we let $\hat{\boldsymbol{\alpha}}' = (\hat{\alpha}_1, \hat{\boldsymbol{\alpha}}^{*\prime})$, then $\hat{\boldsymbol{\alpha}}^*$ is consistent and $\hat{\hat{\boldsymbol{\beta}}}$ is asymptotically efficient.

The asymptotic covariance matrix for $\hat{\boldsymbol{\alpha}}$ is

$$\Sigma_{\hat{\boldsymbol{\alpha}}} = 4.9348(Z'Z)^{-1} \tag{11.2.59}$$

where $Z' = (\mathbf{z}_1, \mathbf{z}_2, \ldots, \mathbf{z}_T)$. Therefore, as a test for homoscedasticity $(\boldsymbol{\alpha}^* = \mathbf{0})$,

$$g = \frac{\hat{\boldsymbol{\alpha}}^{*\prime}D^{-1}\hat{\boldsymbol{\alpha}}^*}{4.9348} \tag{11.2.60}$$

will have an approximate $\chi^2_{(S-1)}$ distribution, where D is equal to $(Z'Z)^{-1}$ with its first row and column deleted and $\hat{\boldsymbol{\alpha}}^{*\prime}D^{-1}\hat{\boldsymbol{\alpha}}^*$ is equal to the regression sum of squares from (11.2.56).

The log of the likelihood function is, apart from a constant,

$$L = -\frac{1}{2}\sum_{t=1}^{T} \mathbf{z}_t'\boldsymbol{\alpha} - \frac{1}{2}\sum_{t=1}^{T} [\exp(-\mathbf{z}_t'\boldsymbol{\alpha})(y_t - \mathbf{x}_t'\boldsymbol{\beta})^2] \tag{11.2.61}$$

and, based on the inverse of the information matrix, the asymptotic covariance matrices for ML estimators $\tilde{\boldsymbol{\beta}}$ and $\tilde{\boldsymbol{\alpha}}$ can be derived as $\Sigma_{\tilde{\beta}} = (X'\Phi^{-1}X)^{-1}$ and $\Sigma_{\tilde{\alpha}} = 2(Z'Z)^{-1}$. This verifies that $\hat{\hat{\boldsymbol{\beta}}}$ is asymptotically efficient but indicates that $\hat{\boldsymbol{\alpha}}$ is not. Thus we may wish to improve on $\hat{\boldsymbol{\alpha}}$, hoping that, in finite samples, this will lead to a better estimator for $\boldsymbol{\beta}$. As an alternative to ML estimation, Harvey (1976) provides an estimator based on one iteration of the method of scoring. It has the same asymptotic distribution as $\tilde{\boldsymbol{\alpha}}$ and is given by

$$\hat{\hat{\boldsymbol{\alpha}}} = \hat{\boldsymbol{\alpha}} + \mathbf{d} + 0.2807(Z'Z)^{-1} \sum_{t=1}^{T} [\mathbf{z}_t \exp(-\mathbf{z}_t'\hat{\boldsymbol{\alpha}})\hat{e}_t^2] \tag{11.2.62}$$

where $\mathbf{d}$ is an $(S \times 1)$ vector with the first element equal to 0.2704 and the remaining elements equal to zero.

To test $\boldsymbol{\alpha}^* = \mathbf{0}$, Equation (11.2.60) can be used with $\hat{\boldsymbol{\alpha}}^*$ replaced by $\hat{\hat{\boldsymbol{\alpha}}}^*$ or $\tilde{\boldsymbol{\alpha}}^*$, and 4.9348 replaced by 2. This test will be asymptotically more powerful than the one based on $\hat{\boldsymbol{\alpha}}^*$. Alternatively, we can use the likelihood ratio test which, in this case, can be conveniently written as [Harvey (1976)]

$$u = T \ln s^2 - \sum_{t=1}^{T} \mathbf{z}_t'\tilde{\boldsymbol{\alpha}} \tag{11.2.63}$$

where $s^2 = T^{-1}(\mathbf{y} - X\mathbf{b})'(\mathbf{y} - X\mathbf{b})$. Under the null hypothesis u is approximately distributed as $\chi^2_{(S-1)}$.

A modification of Harvey's procedure is outlined by Just and Pope (1978), who consider asymptotically efficient estimation of the nonlinear model $y_t = \exp(\mathbf{x}_t'\boldsymbol{\beta}) + e_t$, where $E[e_t^2] = \sigma_t^2 = \exp(\mathbf{x}_t'\boldsymbol{\alpha})$. Griffiths and Anderson (1982) extend Just and Pope's procedure to a time series of cross-sectional data, and apply the extended procedure to production function estimation.

11.2.7 Autoregressive Conditional Heteroscedasticity

The assumption of heteroscedastic disturbances has traditionally been considered in the context of cross-section data. With time-series data the disturbance term is modeled with some kind of stochastic process, and most of the conventional stochastic processes assume homoscedasticity. (See Chapter 8.) Two exceptions are the heteroscedastic stochastic processes proposed by Engle (1982) and Cragg (1982); in this section we discuss the first of these two—namely, Engle's autoregressive conditional heteroscedasticity (ARCH) model.

Engle argues that, for many econometric models, it is unreasonable to assume that the conditional forecast variance $\text{var}[y_t|y_{t-1}]$ is constant, as it is for many stochastic processes, and that it is more realistic to assume that $\text{var}[y_t|y_{t-1}]$ depends on y_{t-1}. In support of his argument he cites examples from monetary theory and the theory of finance, as well as general examples where small and large forecast errors tend to cluster together. The simplest version of Engle's ARCH disturbance model is the first-order one, which can be written as

$$y_t = \mathbf{x}_t'\boldsymbol{\beta} + e_t \tag{11.2.64}$$

where

$$e_t = v_t(\alpha_0 + \alpha_1 e_{t-1}^2)^{1/2} \tag{11.2.65}$$

the v_t are independent normal random variables with zero mean and unit variance, and the parameters (α_0,α_1) are assumed to satisfy $\alpha_0 > 0$ and $\alpha_1 \geq 0$. Under these assumptions the conditional means and variances for e_t and y_t are

$$E[e_t|e_{t-1}] = 0, \quad \text{var}[e_t|e_{t-1}] = \alpha_0 + \alpha_1 e_{t-1}^2 \tag{11.2.66}$$

$$E[y_t|y_{t-1}] = \mathbf{x}_t'\boldsymbol{\beta}, \quad \text{var}[y_t|y_{t-1}] = \alpha_0 + \alpha_1 e_{t-1}^2 \tag{11.2.67}$$

and, furthermore, both $(e_t|e_{t-1})$ and $(y_t|y_{t-1})$ are normally distributed. However, the marginal (unconditional) densities for e_t and y_t will not be normal. The unconditional means are $E[e_t] = 0$ and $E[y_t] = \mathbf{x}_t'\boldsymbol{\beta}$, and, providing $0 \leq \alpha_1 < 1$, the unconditional variances can be derived as

$$\text{var}[y_t] = \text{var}[e_t] = \frac{\alpha_0}{1 - \alpha_1} \tag{11.2.68}$$

It can also be shown that the e_t are uncorrelated so that we have $E[\mathbf{e}] = \mathbf{0}$ and $E[\mathbf{ee}'] = \sigma^2 I$, where $\sigma^2 = \alpha_0/(1 - \alpha_1)$. Thus, it follows that the LS estimator $\mathbf{b} = (X'X)^{-1}X'\mathbf{y}$ is best linear unbiased, and that the usual estimator for the covariance matrix for $\mathbf{b}$ is valid. (We are assuming that X does not contain lagged values of $\mathbf{y}$.) However, by using maximum likelihood techniques it is possible to find a nonlinear estimator that is asymptotically more efficient than LS.

Conditional on an initial observation y_0, the likelihood function for $\boldsymbol{\alpha} = (\alpha_0,\alpha_1)'$ and $\boldsymbol{\beta}$ can be written as $f(\mathbf{y}) = \Pi_{t=1}^T f(y_t|y_{t-1})$. Using this result, and ignoring a constant factor, the log-likelihood function can be written as

$$\begin{aligned} L = &-\frac{1}{2}\sum_t \ln[\alpha_0 + \alpha_1(y_{t-1} - \mathbf{x}_{t-1}'\boldsymbol{\beta})^2] \\ &-\frac{1}{2}\sum_t \left\{\frac{(y_t - \mathbf{x}_t'\boldsymbol{\beta})^2}{\alpha_0 + \alpha_1(y_{t-1} - \mathbf{x}_{t-1}'\boldsymbol{\beta})^2}\right\} \end{aligned} \tag{11.2.69}$$

It is clear from this function that, although $(y_t|y_{t-1})$ is normally distributed, the vector $\mathbf{y}$ does not possess a multivariate normal distribution. A maximum likelihood estimator for $\boldsymbol{\alpha}$ and $\boldsymbol{\beta}$ can be found by numerically maximizing (11.2.69), or, alternatively, one can use an asymptotically equivalent estimator that is based on the scoring algorithm and that can be found using most least squares computer programs [Engle (1982)]. To find a value for this estimator we proceed as follows.

1. Find the LS estimate $\mathbf{b} = (X'X)^{-1}X'\mathbf{y}$ and the corresponding residuals $\hat{\mathbf{e}} = \mathbf{y} - X\mathbf{b}$. [We will assume that $(T + 1)$ observations $(y_0, y_1, \ldots, y_T)$ and $(\mathbf{x}_0, \mathbf{x}_1, \ldots, \mathbf{x}_T)$ are available, so that, in this step, $\hat{\mathbf{e}}$, X, and $\mathbf{y}$ will each have $(T + 1)$ rows.]

2. Find an initial estimator for $\boldsymbol{\alpha}$ as

$$\hat{\boldsymbol{\alpha}}^0 = (Z'Z)^{-1}Z'\dot{\hat{\mathbf{e}}} \tag{11.2.70}$$

where $\dot{\hat{\mathbf{e}}} = (\hat{e}_1^2, \hat{e}_2^2, \ldots, \hat{e}_T^2)'$, and Z is a $(T \times 2)$ matrix with tth row equal to $\mathbf{z}_t' = (1, \hat{e}_{t-1}^2)$.

3. Compute initial estimates of the conditional variances

$$h_t^0 = \mathbf{z}_t'\hat{\boldsymbol{\alpha}}^0, \qquad t = 1, 2, \ldots, T \tag{11.2.71}$$

4. Find an asymptotically efficient estimator for $\boldsymbol{\alpha}$ from

$$\hat{\boldsymbol{\alpha}}^1 = \hat{\boldsymbol{\alpha}}^0 + (Z^{*\prime}Z^*)^{-1}Z^{*\prime}(\dot{\hat{\mathbf{e}}}^* - \mathbf{j}) \tag{11.2.72}$$

where $\mathbf{j} = (1, 1, \ldots, 1)'$, and Z^* and $\dot{\hat{\mathbf{e}}}^*$ are respectively $(T \times 2)$ and $(T \times 1)$ with tth rows equal to

$$\mathbf{z}_t^{*\prime} = \frac{\mathbf{z}_t'}{h_t^0} = \left(\frac{1}{h_t^0}, \frac{\hat{e}_{t-1}^2}{h_t^0}\right) \qquad \text{and} \qquad \hat{e}_t^{*2} = \frac{\hat{e}_t^2}{h_t^0} \tag{11.2.73}$$

5. Given that $\hat{\boldsymbol{\alpha}}^1 = (\hat{\alpha}_0^1, \hat{\alpha}_1^1)'$, compute the following

$$h_t^1 = \mathbf{z}_t'\hat{\boldsymbol{\alpha}}^1, \quad t = 1, 2, \ldots, T \tag{11.2.74}$$

$$r_t = \{(h_t^1)^{-1} + 2\hat{e}_t^2(\hat{\alpha}_1^1)^2(h_{t+1}^1)^{-2}\}^{1/2}, \quad t = 1, 2, \ldots, T-1 \tag{11.2.75}$$

$$s_t = (h_t^1)^{-1} - \hat{\alpha}_1^1(h_{t+1}^1)^{-2}(\hat{e}_{t+1}^2 - h_{t+1}^1), \quad t = 1, 2, \ldots, T-1 \tag{11.2.76}$$

6. An asymptotically efficient estimator for $\boldsymbol{\beta}$ is given by

$$\hat{\boldsymbol{\beta}}^1 = \mathbf{b} + (X^{*\prime}X^*)^{-1}X^{*\prime}\hat{\mathbf{e}}^* \tag{11.2.77}$$

where X^* and $\hat{\mathbf{e}}^*$ are, respectively, $[(T - 1) \times K]$ and $[(T - 1) \times 1]$ with tth rows equal to $\mathbf{x}_t^{*\prime} = \mathbf{x}_t'r_t$ and $\hat{e}_t^* = \hat{e}_t s_t / r_t$.

If desirable, further sets of estimates for $\boldsymbol{\alpha}$ and $\boldsymbol{\beta}$ can be obtained by using (11.2.72) and (11.2.77) iteratively. For hypothesis testing and interval estimation it can be shown that $\boldsymbol{\alpha}^1$ and $\boldsymbol{\beta}^1$ are asymptotically normal with approximate covariance matrix estimators $2(Z^{*\prime}Z^*)^{-1}$ and $(X^{*\prime}X^*)^{-1}$, respectively. To test whether the disturbances do in fact follow an ARCH process Engle suggests a simplification of the Lagrange multiplier test. His proposed statistic is TR^2, where R^2 is the squared multiple correlation coefficient in the regression used to obtain $\hat{\boldsymbol{\alpha}}^0$; this statistic has an asymptotic $\chi^2_{(1)}$-distribution under the null hypothesis H_0: $\alpha_1 = 0$. For more details of the ARCH model and its estimation, as well as an application, see Engle (1982).

11.2.8 Some Comments on Functional Form and Heteroscedasticity

The applied worker who suspects the existence of heteroscedasticity is faced with the problem of choosing from the array of variance specifications that we have just presented, as well as choosing an appropriate functional form for $E[y_t]$. These two decisions are not independent, and in this subsection we discuss some of the issues involved. Further discussion will be given in Chapter 20 in connection with the Box–Cox transformation and the choice between a multiplicative and an additive disturbance.

Quite frequently, especially in the biometric literature, some type of transformation, such as a logarithmic transformation, is suggested as a possible means for rendering observations homoscedastic. To illustrate this, consider the model

$$y_t = \beta_1 x_{2t}^{\beta_2} x_{3t}^{\beta_3} e^{u_t} \tag{11.2.78}$$

where $u_t \sim N(0,\sigma^2)$. From the properties of the lognormal distribution the variances of e^{u_t} and y_t are $\text{Var}(e^{u_t}) = e^{\sigma^2}(e^{\sigma^2} - 1)$ and

$$\text{Var}(y_t) = (\beta_1 x_{2t}^{\beta_2} x_{3t}^{\beta_3})^2 e^{\sigma^2}(e^{\sigma^2} - 1)$$

Hence y_t is heteroscedastic. However, the log of (11.2.78) is

$$\ln y_t = \mathbf{x}_t'\boldsymbol{\beta} + u_t \tag{11.2.79}$$

where $\mathbf{x}_t' = (1, \ln x_{2t}, \ln x_{3t})$, $\boldsymbol{\beta}' = (\ln \beta_1, \beta_2, \beta_3)$, and $\ln y_t$ is both homoscedastic and a linear function of $\boldsymbol{\beta}$. Thus LS is the appropriate technique, and this is true because we assumed that u_t is homoscedastic, and that we have a constant elasticity model.

Suppose that we wish to retain the assumption of a heteroscedastic $\mathbf{y}$ that follows the lognormal distribution, but instead we assume that the slopes are constant, or at least they do not vary systematically with $\mathbf{x}_t$ and y_t. In this case the model becomes

$$y_t = (\mathbf{x}_t'\boldsymbol{\beta})e^{u_t} \tag{11.2.80}$$

where $u_t \sim N(0,\sigma^2)$ and $\mathbf{x}_t' = (1, x_{2t}, x_{3t})$. Taking logs of (11.2.80) gives

$$\ln y_t = \ln(\mathbf{x}_t'\boldsymbol{\beta}) + u_t \tag{11.2.81}$$

Thus, although $\ln y_t$ is homoscedastic, it is nonlinear in $\boldsymbol{\beta}$ and requires nonlinear estimation. Note that the slopes, $\partial y_t/\partial \mathbf{x}_t = \boldsymbol{\beta} e^{u_t}$, are not constant because they are random variables. However, unlike the constant elasticity model, they do not vary systematically with $\mathbf{x}_t$ and y_t.

Alternatively, if $\mathbf{y}$ is a normally distributed random vector, we could specify

$$y_t = \mathbf{x}_t'\boldsymbol{\beta} + u_t \tag{11.2.82}$$

where $u_t \sim N(0,\sigma_t^2)$ and where σ_t^2 is some function of $\mathbf{x}_t$ or another set of variables, $\mathbf{z}_t$. In this case y_t is heteroscedastic and the slopes are either constant or random [such as in (11.2.81)] depending on whether u_t is a function of $\mathbf{x}_t$ or some other variables. An appropriate estimation technique would be EGLS and taking logs of (11.2.82) would not make estimation any easier.

These are just three possible specifications in which y_t is heteroscedastic. They have been presented to point out that the appropriate method of estimation for a model with heteroscedastic $\mathbf{y}$ will depend not only on how the heteroscedasticity is modeled, but also on the choice of functional form and the distributional assumptions about $\mathbf{y}$. Because of the ease with which (11.2.78) can be estimated, it may be tempting to use this specification when, in fact, it is more appropriate to assume that $E[y_t]$ is a linear function of $\boldsymbol{\beta}$, such as in (11.2.80) or (11.2.82), and to model the heteroscedasticity in an alternative fashion. For a comparison of these alternatives, applied to household expenditure functions, see Battese and Bonyhady (1981).

One way of tackling uncertainty when choosing from functions such as (11.2.78), (11.2.80), and (11.2.82) is to use the flexible functional form implied by the Box–Cox transformation. See Chapter 20 for details, and Egy and Lahiri (1979) for an application where a flexible functional form is used in conjunction with a heteroscedastic disturbance. Also, the availability of the Box–Cox transformation, and the possible existence of uncertainty with respect to choice of a variance function, suggest that an even more flexible approach would be to apply the Box–Cox transformation to the functional specifications for both $E[y_t]$ and σ_t^2. For work in this direction see Gaudry and Dagenais (1979). These models are quite general, but, unless a large number of observations are available, reliable estimation is likely to be very difficult. Furthermore, Monte Carlo evidence provided by Surekha and Griffiths (1984) suggests that EGLS estimators for $\boldsymbol{\beta}$ are not very sensitive to misspecification of the functional form for σ_t^2.

11.3 GENERAL TESTS FOR HETEROSCEDASTICITY

In the previous section some alternative heteroscedastic structures were reviewed, and estimation techniques and hypotheses tests for each of these structures were presented assuming that the particular model discussed was correct. In a practical setting the major difficulty with using one of these estimators and/or hypothesis tests is that it presupposes knowledge of the particular form of heteroscedasticity that may exist. A more realistic situation is one in which an investigator would like to test for the existence of heteroscedasticity without specifying precisely the form it should take. Some tests that have been suggested for this purpose are summarized below. In addition to (or instead of) these tests we could, of course, use one of the tests given in Section 11.2. In this case, since each test is designed against a specific alternative, we would hope that the test being used is robust under alternative heteroscedastic specifications.

11.3.1 Breusch–Pagan Test

The first general test we consider is relevant for alternative hypotheses of the form

$$\sigma_t^2 = h(\mathbf{z}_t'\boldsymbol{\alpha}) \tag{11.3.1}$$

where h is a function independent of t, $\mathbf{z}_t$ is an $(S \times 1)$ nonstochastic vector with first element equal to unity, and $\boldsymbol{\alpha} = (\alpha_1, \boldsymbol{\alpha}^{*\prime})'$ is an $(S \times 1)$ vector of unknown coefficients. It is clear that (11.3.1) includes the specifications $\sigma_t^2 = (\mathbf{z}_t'\boldsymbol{\alpha})^2$, $\sigma_t^2 = \mathbf{z}_t'\boldsymbol{\alpha}$, and $\sigma_t^2 = \exp\{\mathbf{z}_t'\boldsymbol{\alpha}\}$. Note that it also includes the case of constant variances within subgroups of observations if, in $\sigma_t^2 = \mathbf{z}_t'\boldsymbol{\alpha}$, $\mathbf{z}_t$ contains appropriate dummy variables.

Since the first element in $\mathbf{z}_t$ is unity, a null hypothesis of homoscedasticity is equivalent to H_0: $\boldsymbol{\alpha}^* = \mathbf{0}$. Under the assumption that the e_t are normally distributed, Breusch and Pagan (1979) show that the Lagrange multiplier statistic for this null hypothesis does not depend on the function h, and is given by

$$\eta = \frac{\mathbf{q}'Z(Z'Z)^{-1}Z'\mathbf{q}}{2\hat{\sigma}^4} \tag{11.3.2}$$

where $\mathbf{q} = \dot{\hat{\mathbf{e}}} - \hat{\sigma}^2\mathbf{j}$, and has tth element equal to $q_t = \hat{e}_t^2 - \hat{\sigma}^2$; $\mathbf{j} = (1, 1, \ldots, 1)'$; $\dot{\hat{\mathbf{e}}} = (\hat{e}_1^2, \hat{e}_2^2, \ldots, \hat{e}_T^2)'$ is a vector of the squares of the least squares residuals $\hat{\mathbf{e}} = \mathbf{y} - X\mathbf{b}$, $Z' = (\mathbf{z}_1, \mathbf{z}_2, \ldots, \mathbf{z}_T)$, and $\hat{\sigma}^2 = \hat{\mathbf{e}}'\hat{\mathbf{e}}/T$. Under H_0, η is asymptotically distributed as $\chi^2_{(S-1)}$.

We can calculate η conveniently by noting that the numerator in (11.3.2) is equal to the regression or explained sum of squares for the regression of $\mathbf{q}$ on Z. To demonstrate this fact we recall that the explained sum of squares for a general regression of $\mathbf{y}$ on X is given by $\mathbf{y}'X(X'X)^{-1}X'\mathbf{y} - T^{-1}(\mathbf{j}'\mathbf{y})^2$. In our case we have $\mathbf{j}'\mathbf{q} = 0$, and so the result follows. Furthermore, since the explained sum of squares is not altered by adding a constant to the dependent variable, the numerator in (11.3.2) can also be found as the explained sum of squares from the regression of $\dot{\hat{\mathbf{e}}}$ on Z. In Section 11.2.4 where we studied the model $\sigma_t^2 = \mathbf{z}_t'\boldsymbol{\alpha}$, this regression was used to obtain the estimator $\hat{\boldsymbol{\alpha}} = (Z'Z)^{-1}Z'\dot{\hat{\mathbf{e}}}$; then, based on the asymptotic distribution of $\hat{\boldsymbol{\alpha}}$, a statistic identical to η was given in Equation (11.2.43). However, because of the Breusch–Pagan result, this statistic is now justified for a wider class of models. Similar comments apply to a paper by Godfrey (1978) where η is derived for the alternative hypothesis $\sigma_t^2 = \exp(\mathbf{z}_t'\boldsymbol{\alpha})$.

A statistic asymptotically equivalent to η, and also computationally convenient, can be obtained by considering the square of the multiple correlation coefficient (R^2) in the regression of $\hat{\mathbf{e}}$ on Z (or of $\mathbf{q}$ on Z). We can write

$$R^2 = \frac{\mathbf{q}'Z(Z'Z)^{-1}Z'\mathbf{q}}{\mathbf{q}'\mathbf{q}} = \frac{\mathbf{q}'Z(Z'Z)^{-1}Z'\mathbf{q}}{\Sigma_t(\hat{e}_t^2 - \hat{\sigma}^2)^2} \tag{11.3.3}$$

and we define the alternative statistic as

$$\eta^* = TR^2 = \frac{\mathbf{q}'Z(Z'Z)^{-1}Z'\mathbf{q}}{T^{-1}\Sigma_t(\hat{e}_t^2 - \hat{\sigma}^2)^2} \tag{11.3.4}$$

The denominator in η^* can be viewed as an estimator for the variance of e_t^2. When H_0 is true and the e_t are normally distributed

$$\text{var}[e_t^2] = E[e_t^2 - \sigma^2] = 2\sigma^4 \tag{11.3.5}$$

Thus, under appropriate convergence assumptions,

$$\text{plim } T^{-1}\Sigma_t(\hat{e}_t^2 - \hat{\sigma}^2)^2 = \text{plim } 2\hat{\sigma}^4 = 2\sigma^4 \tag{11.3.6}$$

which implies η and η^* are "asymptotically equivalent."

When the e_t are not normally distributed $\text{var}[e_t^2] \neq 2\sigma^4$, and the statistic η is no longer valid. It has asymptotically incorrect size and its power is extremely sensitive to the kurtosis of the distribution of e_t [Koenker (1981), Koenker and Bassett (1982)]. However, the statistic η^* is still an appropriate one. Koenker (1981) outlines the conditions under which plim $T^{-1}\Sigma(\hat{e}_t^2 - \hat{\sigma}^2)^2 = \text{var}(e_t^2)$ and the statistic η^* is asymptotically $\chi^2_{(S-1)}$ under H_0.

Studies of the finite sample properties of the test using η (under the assumption of normality) have shown that it is quite powerful when heteroscedasticity is present, but that its finite sample size is often incorrect. Godfrey (1978), Breusch and Pagan (1979), and Surekha and Griffiths (1983) all found that the test rejects the null hypothesis (when it is true) less frequently than indicated by the selected Type I error.

11.3.2 Bartlett Test

If we have m independent, normal random samples, where there are T_i observations in the ith sample and these have mean $\bar{y}_i$ and variance s_i^2, then the likelihood ratio test statistic for testing $\sigma_1^2 = \sigma_2^2 = \ldots = \sigma_m^2$ is

$$u = \sum_{i=1}^{m} \left(\frac{s_i^2}{s^2}\right)^{T_i/2} \tag{11.3.7}$$

where

$$T_i s_i^2 = \sum_{j=1}^{T_i} (y_{ij} - \bar{y}_i)^2, \qquad Ts^2 = \sum_{i=1}^{m} T_i s_i^2, \qquad \sum_{i=1}^{m} T_i = T$$

and the y_{ij}, $i = 1, 2, \ldots, m$; $j = 1, 2, \ldots, T_i$, are observations on the normal random variables [Kendall and Stuart, (1973, p. 245)].

To obtain an unbiased test and a modification of $-2 \ln u$, which, under the null hypothesis, is a closer approximation of a $\chi^2_{(m-1)}$ test, Bartlett (1937) replaces T_i by $T_i - 1$ and divides by a scaling constant. This leads to the statistic

$$M = \frac{(T - m) \ln \hat{\sigma}^2 - \Sigma_{i=1}^{m} (T_i - 1) \ln \hat{\sigma}_i^2}{1 + [1/3(m - 1)][\Sigma_{i=1}^{m} 1/(T_i - 1) - 1/(T - m)]} \tag{11.3.8}$$

where

$$(T_i - 1)\hat{\sigma}_i^2 = \sum_{j=1}^{T_i} (y_{ij} - \bar{y}_i)^2 \qquad \text{and} \qquad (T - m)\hat{\sigma}^2 = \sum_{i=1}^{m} (T_i - 1)\hat{\sigma}_i^2$$

To test for homogeneity of variances an approximate test can be based on the statistic M and critical values from the $\chi^2_{(m-1)}$-distribution, or, alternatively, if the number of observations is identical within each group, the exact critical values provided by Dyer and Keating (1980) can be used.

In the context of the heteroscedastic linear regression model, the assumptions necessary for the Bartlett test are met when the alternative hypothesis is the model given in Section 11.2.2, with the variances and explanatory variables constant within each group. If the explanatory variables vary within each group, the $\hat{\sigma}_i^2$ in (11.3.8) can be replaced by those based on the least squares residuals from separate within group regressions (Equation (11.2.15)). However, because the statistic u does not use the information that $\boldsymbol{\beta}$ is constant over all groups, in both these cases, it is not strictly the likelihood ratio test statistic.

Despite its apparent limited applicability, the statistic M has been widely used for testing for heteroscedasticity in general. Its usefulness in this regard is likely to depend on whether the observations can be placed in groups in which the variances are approximately constant, or, alternatively, whether they can be ordered according to nondecreasing variance.

Under the title "BAMSET," Ramsey (1969) suggests a modification of u based on the BLUS residuals defined in Chapter 5. He suggests replacing s_i^2 and s^2 in (11.3.7) with the alternative definitions

$$v_i s_i^2 = \sum_{j=1}^{v_i} \tilde{e}_j^2, \quad (T - K)s^2 = \sum_{j=1}^{T-K} \tilde{e}_j^2, \qquad \text{and} \qquad \sum_{i=1}^{m} v_i = T - K$$

where $\tilde{e}_j$ is the jth BLUS residual and each v_i is an integer approximately equal to $(T - K)/m$. Under the null hypothesis, $-2 \ln u$ is distributed asymptotically as $\chi^2_{(m-1)}$.

In this case the fact that $\boldsymbol{\beta}$ is constant within all groups, or for all observations, has been utilized, and the independence of the s_i^2 has been ensured by using BLUS residuals. If one is testing for heteroscedasticity in general, the choice of groups is completely arbitrary. Ramsey suggests $m = 3$ as a compromise between sufficient degrees of freedom and sufficient observations in each group. Some Monte Carlo evidence on the power of the test has been provided by Ramsey and Gilbert (1972).

11.3.3 Goldfeld–Quandt Test

Another possible test for heteroscedasticity is the one outlined by Goldfeld and Quandt (1965, 1972). As with the previous test, its performance will be best when it is possible to order the observations according to nondecreasing variance. That is, $\sigma_t^2 \geq \sigma_{t-1}^2$, $t = 2, 3, \ldots, T$. The steps for implementing the test are:

1. Omit r central observations.
2. Run two separate regressions, on the first and the last $(T - r)/2$ observations.
3. Calculate $R = S_2/S_1$, where S_1 and S_2 are the residual sums of squares from the first and second regressions, respectively.
4. Base a decision on the fact that, under homoscedasticity, R has the F distribution with $[(T - r - 2K)/2, (T - r - 2K)/2]$ degrees of freedom.

It is not essential that the two regressions be based on the same number of observations. If the number of observations does differ, then the degrees of freedom must be changed accordingly.

In contrast to the previous tests, this one is based on an exact finite sample distribution. It overcomes the problem of the lack of independence of LS residuals by running two separate regressions. Some central observations are omitted so that, under heteroscedasticity, residuals in the numerator correspond to relatively large variances and those in the denominator to relatively small variances. The omitted observations correspond to intermediate-sized variances. The optimum value of r is not obvious. Large values are likely to increase the power of the test through an increase in the value of the F statistic but decrease the power through a reduction in degrees of freedom. Goldfeld and Quandt (1965) suggest $r = 8$ for $T = 30$, and $r = 16$ for $T = 60$. However, in their later work (1972, Chapter 3) they use $r = 4$ for $T = 30$.

Instead of running two separate regressions to obtain independent sums of squares for the numerator and denominator of the F statistic, it is possible to use either BLUS residuals [Theil (1971, pp. 196–218)] or recursive residuals [Harvey and Phillips (1974)] from one regression. In both these cases the $(T - K)$ residuals are divided into two approximately equal groups and an F statistic similar to that used for the Goldfeld–Quandt test is calculated. Assuming that $(T - K)$ is even, this procedure leads to a statistic that, under homoscedasticity, has an $F_{[(T-K)/2,(T-K)/2]}$ distribution.

11.3.4 Szroeter's Class of Tests

Szroeter (1978) introduces a class of tests that includes those in the Section 11.3.3 as special cases. He assumes that the e_t are normally distributed and, as before, that the observations have been ordered such that $\sigma_t^2 \geq \sigma_{t-1}^2$, $t = 2, 3, \ldots, T$. The class is described by the test statistic

$$\tilde{h} = \frac{\Sigma_{t\varepsilon A} h_t \hat{e}_t^2}{\Sigma_{t\varepsilon A} \hat{e}_t^2} \tag{11.3.9}$$

where A is some nonempty subset of $\{1, 2, \ldots, T\}$; the $\hat{e}_t$ are a set of residuals; and the h_t are a set of nonstochastic scalars such that $h_t \leq h_s$ if $t < s$. Specification of these last three items defines a particular member of the class. That is, we need to specify the observations included in A, the type of residuals (e.g., LS or BLUS) and the set of h_t. For a given critical value c, the null hypothesis of homoscedasticity is rejected if

$$\tilde{h} > c \tag{11.3.10}$$

The statistic $\tilde{h}$ can be viewed as a weighted average of the h_t with weights given by the squares of the residuals $\hat{e}_t$. If heteroscedasticity does not exist we would not expect $\tilde{h}$ to be significantly greater than the simple average $\bar{h} = \Sigma_{t\varepsilon A} h_t / T_A$, where T_A is the number of elements in A. On the other hand, if heteroscedasticity does exist, then we would expect h_t and $\hat{e}_t^2$ to be positively correlated, in which case $\tilde{h}$ would be larger, and possibly "significantly larger," than $\bar{h}$. Szroeter gives the conditions under which a test defined by (11.3.9) and (11.3.10) is consistent; and, based on an asymptotic power function, he shows that a test will tend to be more powerful the higher the correlation between h_t and σ_t^2.

The distribution of $\tilde{h}$ and the critical value c will obviously depend upon the particular test chosen from the class defined by (11.3.9). However, in general, $\tilde{h}$ is given by the ratio of two quadratic forms in the normally distributed LS residuals, and so for any given test, and any given X matrix, the critical value can always be calculated using the Imhof procedure [Imhof (1961), Koerts and Abrahamse (1969)]. A similar situation arises with the Durbin–Watson test for autocorrelation. The Durbin–Watson statistic is equal to the ratio of two quadratic forms in the LS residuals, and for any given X matrix the exact critical value can be found using the Imhof or a related procedure. See Chapter 8. To avoid computation of a critical value for each particular problem, Szroeter suggests particular members of his class of tests that utilize existing tables. We shall briefly consider some of these, as well as some related suggestions made by other authors.

If $h_t = -1$ for $t = 1, 2, \ldots, (T - r)/2$ and $h_t = +1$ for $t = (T + r)/2 + 1, \ldots, T$ and we use LS residuals from two separate regressions with the middle r observations omitted, (11.3.9) and (11.3.10) can be shown to be equivalent to the Goldfeld–Quandt test. Also, similarly defining h_t and using BLUS or recursive residuals with K observations omitted, gives the tests suggested by Theil (1971) and Harvey and Phillips (1974), respectively.

An example of an alternative set of h_t, suggested by Szroeter for use with *BLUS or recursive residuals*, is

$$h_t = 2\left[1 - \cos\frac{\pi(t-K)}{T-K+1}\right], \qquad t = K+1, K+2, \ldots, T \tag{11.3.11}$$

where $A = \{K+1, K+2, \ldots, T\}$. In this case, for an α-percent significance level, the critical region can be written as $\tilde{h} > (T-K)V_u/(T-K+1)$, where V_u is the upper α-percent significance point from the distribution of the von Neumann (1941) ratio, treated as if we have $(T-K+1)$ observations. See Hart (1942) for the tabulated values.

If *LS residuals* from a single regression are used, the distribution of $\tilde{h}$ will depend on X, and hence general critical values cannot be tabulated. However, along similar lines to the Durbin–Watson test, it is possible to derive distributions that bound $\tilde{h}$ and do not depend on X. One of Szroeter's suggestions is to calculate $\tilde{h}$ using

$$h_t = 2\left[1 - \cos\frac{\pi t}{T+1}\right], \quad t = 1, 2, \ldots, T \tag{11.3.12}$$

It is then possible to construct a bounds test where we reject the null hypothesis if $\tilde{h} > 4 - d_L$, accept it if $\tilde{h} < 4 - d_U$, and otherwise treat the test as inconclusive. The values d_L and d_U are the Durbin–Watson lower and upper critical values, respectively, corresponding to $T + 1$ observations, $K + 1$ regressors, and the required significance level [Durbin and Watson (1951)]. The problem of the inconclusive region has been investigated further by Harrison (1980) and King (1981). Harrison demonstrates that the probability of obtaining an inconclusive result is quite high, and, to avoid the computational demands of finding the exact critical value via the Imhof procedure, he suggests a relatively simple approximation method. King notes that a narrower inconclusive region can be obtained by recognizing that most regression models contain a constant term. For this case he derives and tabulates new values h_L^* and h_U^*, which, in the context of the test described above, lead to critical value bounds of $4 - h_L^*$ and $4 - h_U^*$. Some examples are presented to demonstrate how the probability of obtaining a value in the narrower inconclusive region $(4 - h_U^*, 4 - h_L^*)$ can be considerably lower than that for the region $(4 - d_U, 4 - d_L)$.

Harrison and McCabe (1979) suggest another member of the Szroeter class of tests that uses LS residuals and that sets $h_t = 1$ for $t = 1, 2, \ldots, m$ and $h_t = 0$ for $t = m+1, m+2, \ldots, T$, with m approximately equal to $T/2$. Because this set of h_t is nonincreasing rather than nondecreasing, the critical region in this case is of the form $\tilde{h} < c$. Using existing F distribution tables, Harrison and McCabe indicate how critical values for a corresponding bounds test can be evaluated. They also suggest an approximation for the inconclusive region and carry out some small sample power comparisons.

A further bounds test that uses LS residuals and that is another member of the Szroeter class is that advocated by King (1982). He shows that setting $h_t = t$ leads to a test that is approximately locally best invariant under quite general conditions. To write the test in a form more convenient for the derivation of critical value bounds, he assumes the observations have been ordered according to nonincreasing rather than nondecreasing variances. This implies the critical region is of the form $\tilde{h} < c$. Also, he finds it is further convenient to write this critical region in the equivalent form

$$s = \frac{\sum_{t=1}^{T} \hat{e}_t^2(t-1)/T}{\sum_{t=1}^{T} \hat{e}_t^2} < c^* \tag{11.3.13}$$

When s is calculated on the basis of observations that are ordered according to nondecreasing variances, (11.3.13) can be written as $s > (T-1)/T - c^*$. King tabulates critical values for two bounding statistics s_L and s_U such that $s_L \leq s \leq s_U$, for regression models with and without a constant term.

Finally, Szroeter (1978) gives an asymptotic test that, under additional assumptions, can be used in both simultaneous equation and nonstochastic regressor models. Although it is only asymptotic, this test is relatively simple and it does not involve an inconclusive region. It may therefore be preferred to the various bounds tests. Specifically, Szroeter shows that, under the null hypothesis,

$$Q = \frac{T(\tilde{h} - \bar{h})}{\left[2 \sum_{t=1}^{T} (h_t - \bar{h})^2\right]^{1/2}} \xrightarrow{d} N(0,1) \tag{11.3.14}$$

where $\bar{h} = \Sigma_{t=1}^{T} h_t/T$. As a convenient and useful choice for h_t, Szroeter suggests $h_t = t$. King's (1982) results add support to this choice. In this case (11.3.14) simplifies to

$$Q = \left(\frac{6T}{T^2 - 1}\right)^{1/2} \left(\tilde{h} - \frac{T+1}{2}\right) \tag{11.3.15}$$

where $\tilde{h} = \Sigma \hat{e}_t^2 t / \Sigma \hat{e}_t^2$. Monte Carlo results on the finite sample power of this test have been provided by Surekha and Griffiths (1983). In the models they consider the test outperforms both the Breusch–Pagan and Goldfeld–Quandt tests.

For the applied worker the relevant question is which member of Szroeter's class of tests performs best. Unfortunately, there is no one member that will be best under all circumstances. The relative power of each test will depend on the alternative hypothesis. In particular, it will depend on how the σ_t^2 vary, the very question we are trying to answer. However, if we take into account

Szroeter's results on the desirability of choosing h_t so that the correlation between h_t and σ_t^2 is high, King's approximate locally best invariance property, and the Monte Carlo results of Surekha and Griffiths (1983), it does appear that $h_t = t$ is a good choice. This will be particularly so if the variances are monotonically related to one of the explanatory variables as is often hypothesized in economics. Furthermore, the choice $h_t = t$ leads to a test that is computationally very simple and easy to apply. For example, one particularly straightforward strategy is to use the bounds test recommended by King (1982), then, if this test is inconclusive, to employ the asymptotic test statistic in (11.3.15). For another class of tests which is an extension of King's (1982) work and which shows some promise in terms of its optimal power properties see Evans and King (1983a,b).

11.3.5 White's Test

A test based on the fact that heteroscedasticity leads to a least squares covariance matrix estimator that is inconsistent has been suggested by White (1980). To introduce this test let $\hat{\mathbf{e}} = (\hat{e}_1, \hat{e}_2, \ldots, \hat{e}_T)'$ be the vector of least squares residuals and let the least squares variance estimator be $\hat{\sigma}^2 = (T - K)^{-1}\hat{\mathbf{e}}'\hat{\mathbf{e}}$. When homoscedasticity exists, $\hat{V} = T^{-1}\Sigma\hat{e}_t^2\mathbf{x}_t\mathbf{x}_t'$ and $\tilde{V} = T^{-1}\hat{\sigma}^2X'X$ will both be consistent estimators of the same matrix. However, under heteroscedasticity, these estimators will tend to diverge, unless the heteroscedasticity is of a special type that is independent of X. [See White (1980, pp. 326–327) for a formal statement of the conditions under which heteroscedasticity does not lead to a divergence in $\hat{V}$ and $\tilde{V}$.] It is therefore possible to base a test on whether or not the difference $\hat{V} - \tilde{V}$ is statistically significant. The most simple version of a test statistic for this purpose is given by TR^2, where R^2 is the squared multiple correlation coefficient of the regression of $\hat{e}_t^2$ on the variables in $(\mathbf{x}_t' \otimes \mathbf{x}_t')$, with redundant variables deleted and a constant term included even if one does not appear in $\mathbf{x}_t$. Under the null hypothesis TR^2 has an asymptotic χ^2-distribution with degrees of freedom equal to the number of explanatory variables in the above auxiliary regression, excluding the constant. If there are no redundancies in $(\mathbf{x}_t' \otimes \mathbf{x}_t')$ other than the obvious ones, and $\mathbf{x}_t$ includes a constant, this number will be $K(K + 1)/2 - 1$. See White (1980) for details and for sufficient conditions for the asymptotic results to hold.

As White notes, this test could be regarded as a general one for misspecification as it is also likely to pick up other specification errors such as a misspecified mean function $E[y_t] = \mathbf{x}_t'\boldsymbol{\beta}$, or correlation between $\mathbf{x}_t$ and e_t in a stochastic regressor model. However, if the researcher feels relatively confident about the absence of these latter problems, the test can be regarded as one designed to detect heteroscedasticity. Note that the test is similar in form to other tests suggested in this section, particularly the Lagrange-multiplier test statistic. Hsieh (1983) has modified White's test for errors which can be both heteroscedastic and heterokurtic, and he has examined the small sample power of the tests in a Monte Carlo experiment. Extensions of the test for more complex models have been discussed by White (1982) and Cragg (1982).

11.3.6 Additional Nonparametric Tests

Goldfeld and Quandt (1965, 1972) suggest a "peak test" that does not depend on the assumption that the e_t are normally distributed. It involves comparing the absolute value of each residual with the values of preceding residuals. One that is greater constitutes a "peak," and the test is based on whether the number of peaks is significant. A probability distribution for the number of peaks under the null hypothesis of homoscedasticity is given in Goldfeld and Quandt (1972, pp. 120–122). This distribution is valid asymptotically for LS residuals and valid in finite samples for BLUS or recursive residuals, the latter having been advocated by Heyadat and Robson (1970). It is also possible to derive tests based on the rank correlation coefficient [Johnston (1972, p. 219), Horn (1981)], and on regression quantiles [Koenker and Bassett (1982)].

11.4 CONCLUDING REMARKS

In this section we make some recommendations for the researcher who wishes to estimate a function and allow for the possibility of heteroscedasticity. The questions of interest are how to test for heteroscedasticity, how to model the heteroscedasticity if it appears to be present, and how to estimate the chosen model. At the outset we must realize that there is no well-established "best way" to test for and model heteroscedasticity. The relative merits of alternative procedures will depend on the unknown underlying model and unknown parameter values. The best we can do is to suggest what we consider to be reasonable strategies to follow.

As Harrison (1980) and other authors have noted, testing for heteroscedasticity has been much less popular than testing for autocorrelation. Nevertheless, there are many occasions, particularly when using cross-sectional data, where the assumption of heteroscedastic errors is a reasonable one. Furthermore, the consequences of ignoring heteroscedasticity can be severe. It is desirable, therefore, to carry out routine testing for heteroscedasticity, just as the Durbin–Watson statistic is used for routine testing for autocorrelation. Toward this end, it would not be difficult to incorporate a member of Szroeter's class of tests (such as $h_t = t$) into standard computer packages. In addition, it is worth pointing out that tests such as the Goldfeld–Quandt test, the Lagrange-multiplier test, and White's test can be implemented using existing packages without much additional effort. With respect to choice of a test, when it is possible to order the observations according to nondecreasing variance, one of Szroeter's tests with increasing h_t's is likely to be a good choice. If the variance depends on more than one explanatory variable and the variables do not always move in the same direction, it is impossible to rank the observations according to nondecreasing variance. In this case the Breusch–Pagan test or alternatively the White test, could be used. Finally, if we have no a priori notions about how the variance might change, but we still wish to test for heteroscedasticity, any one of a number of tests (e.g., Bartlett, Goldfeld–Quandt) could be used. However, we should not be too optimistic about their power.

When testing for heteroscedasticity it should be kept in mind that a significant test statistic may be an indication of heteroscedasticity, but it could also be an indication of some other type of misspecification such as an omitted variable or an incorrect functional form. Available evidence [White (1980), Thursby (1982)] suggests that this will certainly be true for White's test and the Goldfeld–Quandt test. A testing strategy designed to discriminate between misspecification and heteroscedasticity has been suggested by Thursby (1982).

If testing suggests that heteroscedasticity is present, we need to choose an appropriate model. If we have strong a priori notions about the form of heteroscedasticity, the model should be chosen accordingly. Where uncertainty about model specification exists, a diagnostic check can be made using a test suggested by Godfrey (1979). However, unless the number of observations is large, and as long as $\mathbf{z}$ is specified correctly, it may be asking too much of the data to discriminate between models such as $\sigma_t^2 = (\mathbf{z}_t'\boldsymbol{\alpha})^2$, $\sigma_t^2 = \mathbf{z}_t'\boldsymbol{\alpha}$, and $\sigma_t^2 = \exp\{\mathbf{z}_t'\boldsymbol{\alpha}\}$. Many may work equally well, in which case the choice could be based on estimation convenience. In a Monte Carlo study using the variance specifications $\sigma_t^2 = (\mathbf{z}_t'\boldsymbol{\alpha})^2$ and $\sigma_t^2 = \exp\{\mathbf{z}_t'\boldsymbol{\alpha}\}$, Surekha and Griffiths (1984) found that the efficiency of EGLS estimators for $\boldsymbol{\beta}$ depended more on the choice of estimator and the sample size than it did on specification of the correct variance structure. Their results also indicate that the EGLS estimator for $\boldsymbol{\beta}$ based on (11.2.62) can perform poorly in small sample sizes ($T = 20$); and other studies [e.g., Griffiths (1971)] have shown that the specification $\sigma_t^2 = \mathbf{z}_t'\boldsymbol{\alpha}$ can lead to poor estimators for $\boldsymbol{\beta}$ if negative variance estimates are retained. In summary, a choice between variance structures such as $\sigma_t^2 = \mathbf{z}_t'\boldsymbol{\alpha}$, $\sigma_t^2 = (\mathbf{z}_t'\boldsymbol{\alpha})^2$, and $\sigma_t^2 = \exp\{\mathbf{z}_t'\boldsymbol{\alpha}\}$ is not likely to be very important providing estimators with poor properties are avoided. There are, of course, other variance structures such as $\sigma_t^2 = \sigma^2(\mathbf{x}_t'\boldsymbol{\beta})^2$, and the ARCH model, which could be chosen if a researcher regards them as more appropriate. In the absence of any prior knowledge concerning the form of heteroscedasticity, asymptotically invalid test statistics can be avoided by using White's (1980) least squares covariance matrix estimator.

Unless we have strong a priori reasons for believing that heteroscedasticity does (or does not) exist, the Monte Carlo results of Goldfeld and Quandt (1972) and Surekha and Griffiths (1984) suggest that it is reasonable to use a pretest estimator. That is, the conventional procedure of testing for heteroscedasticity and using LS if the test is negative and an alternative EGLS (or ML) estimator otherwise appears justified. For estimation of a specific model, most recommended estimators for $\boldsymbol{\beta}$ have identical asymptotic properties. Thus, apart from the estimators mentioned above that have exhibited some poor small sample properties, there is no clear basis for choice. It seems reasonable to use any EGLS estimator for $\boldsymbol{\beta}$ that is based on asymptotically efficient estimates of the variance parameters, or to use maximum likelihood estimation.

11.5 EXERCISES

11.5.1 General Exercises

Exercise 11.1

Given that the disturbance vector **e** is normally distributed, show that the covariance matrix for **w** in Equation 11.2.39 is given by $2\dot{Q}$, where $\dot{Q}$ is the matrix $Q = M\Phi M$ with each of its elements squared, and M and Φ are defined in Section 11.2.4.

Exercise 11.2

Derive the information matrix for the parameters of the model in Section 11.2.4, under the assumption of normality. Use the result to show that $\hat{\hat{\boldsymbol{\alpha}}}$ in (11.2.40) is asymptotically more efficient than $\hat{\boldsymbol{\alpha}}$ in (11.2.35).

Exercise 11.3

Prove that the statistic g in (11.2.43) is identical to the Lagrange-multiplier statistic η in (11.3.2).

Exercise 11.4

Derive the information matrix for the parameters of the model in Equation 11.2.46, for the normal, lognormal, and gamma distributions. Under what circumstances is EGLS asymptotically efficient?

Exercise 11.5

Consider the model in Equations 11.2.52 and 11.2.53 and assume that the e_t are normally distributed. Write down the likelihood function for $(\boldsymbol{\beta}', \boldsymbol{\alpha}')$ and derive the information matrix. Show that the estimator $\hat{\boldsymbol{\alpha}}$ (see Equation 11.2.56) is asymptotically inefficient relative to the maximum likelihood estimator but that the same is not true for the estimated generalized least squares estimator $\hat{\hat{\boldsymbol{\beta}}}$ defined in Equation 11.2.58.

Exercise 11.6

Prove that the Goldfeld–Quandt test (Section 11.3.3) is a member of Szroeter's class of tests (Section 11.3.4).

Exercise 11.7

Prove that (11.3.14) reduces to (11.3.15) when $h_t = t$.

11.5.2 Individual Exercises Using Monte Carlo Data

For the remaining exercises, generate 100 samples of **y**, each of size 20, from the model

$$y_t = \beta_1 + \beta_2 x_{t2} + \beta_3 x_{t3} + e_t \tag{11.5.1}$$

where the e_t's are normally and independently distributed with $E[e_t] = 0$, $E[e_t^2] = \sigma_t^2$, and

$$\sigma_t^2 = \exp\{\alpha_1 + \alpha_2 x_{t2}\} \tag{11.5.2}$$

Some suggested parameter values are $\beta_1 = 10$, $\beta_2 = 1$, $\beta_3 = 1$, $\alpha_1 = -2$, and $\alpha_2 = 0.25$; for a possible X matrix where the observations have been ordered according to the magnitude of x_{2t}, see Equation 8.6.7.

Exercise 11.8

Calculate the covariance matrices for the generalized least squares (GLS) estimator

$$\hat{\boldsymbol{\beta}} = \left(\sum_{t=1}^{T} \sigma_t^{-2}\mathbf{x}_t\mathbf{x}_t'\right)^{-1} \sum_{t=1}^{T} \sigma_t^{-2}\mathbf{x}_t y_t$$

and the least squares (LS) estimator

$$\mathbf{b} = \left(\sum_{t=1}^{T} \mathbf{x}_t\mathbf{x}_t'\right)^{-1} \sum_{t=1}^{T} \mathbf{x}_t y_t,$$

where $\mathbf{x}_t = (1, x_{2t}, x_{3t})'$. Comment on the results.

Exercise 11.9

Select five samples from those generated, and, for each sample, compute values for the following estimators:

1. The LS estimator $\mathbf{b}$.
2. The estimator

$$\hat{\boldsymbol{\alpha}}(1) = \left(\sum_{t=1}^{T} \mathbf{z}_t\mathbf{z}_t'\right)^{-1} \sum_{t=1}^{T} \mathbf{z}_t \ln \hat{e}_t^2$$

   where $\mathbf{z}_t = (1, x_{2t})'$ and $\hat{e}_t = y_t - \mathbf{x}_t'\mathbf{b}$.
3. The estimated generalized least squares (EGLS) estimator for $\boldsymbol{\beta}$ that uses $\hat{\boldsymbol{\alpha}}(1)$ obtained in (2), call it $\hat{\hat{\boldsymbol{\beta}}}(1)$.
4. The estimator

$$\hat{\boldsymbol{\alpha}}(2) = \hat{\boldsymbol{\alpha}}(1) + \mathbf{d} + 0.2807 \left[\sum_{t=1}^{T} \mathbf{z}_t\mathbf{z}_t'\right]^{-1} \sum_{t=1}^{T} \mathbf{z}_t \exp(-\mathbf{z}_t'\hat{\boldsymbol{\alpha}}(1))\hat{e}_t^2$$

   where $\mathbf{d} = (0.2704, 0)'$.
5. The EGLS estimator for $\boldsymbol{\beta}$ which uses $\hat{\boldsymbol{\alpha}}(2)$ obtained in (4), call it $\hat{\hat{\boldsymbol{\beta}}}(2)$. Compare the various estimates with each other and the true parameter values.

Exercise 11.10

With the exception of **b** all the estimators in Exercise 11.9 were *correctly* chosen in the sense that they are intended for a model with multiplicative heteroscedasticity, and this type of heteroscedasticity does exist. For each of the same five samples calculate values for the following estimators that incorrectly assume the existence of alternative types of heteroscedasticity.

1. The estimator

$$\hat{\hat{\boldsymbol{\beta}}}(3) = \left[\sum_{t=1}^{T} (\mathbf{z}_t'\hat{\boldsymbol{\eta}})^{-2}\mathbf{x}_t\mathbf{x}_t'\right]^{-1} \sum_{t=1}^{T} (\mathbf{z}_t'\hat{\boldsymbol{\eta}})^{-2}\mathbf{x}_t y_t$$

   where

$$\hat{\boldsymbol{\eta}} = c^{-1}\left(\sum_{t=1}^{T} \mathbf{z}_t\mathbf{z}_t'\right)^{-1} \sum_{t=1}^{T} \mathbf{z}_t|\hat{e}_t|.$$

   See Equation (11.2.23).
2. The estimator

$$\hat{\hat{\boldsymbol{\beta}}}(4) = \left[\sum_{t=1}^{T} (\mathbf{x}_t'\mathbf{b})^{-2}\mathbf{x}_t\mathbf{x}_t'\right]^{-1} \sum_{t=1}^{T} (\mathbf{x}_t'\mathbf{b})^{-2}\mathbf{x}_t y_t$$

   Comment on the estimates.

Exercise 11.11

Use the estimates obtained from **b** and $\hat{\hat{\boldsymbol{\beta}}}(i)$, $i = 1, 2, 3, 4$, to calculate 25 "*t*-values" that, in each case, would be used to test the null hypothesis $\beta_3 = 1.0$. Comment on the values.

Exercise 11.12

For each of the five samples compute values for

1. The Breusch–Pagan (BP) test statistic.
2. Szroeter's asymptotic test statistic in Equation 11.3.15. Comment on the test results for a 5% significance level.

Exercise 11.13

Define $\hat{\hat{\boldsymbol{\beta}}}(5)$ and $\hat{\hat{\boldsymbol{\beta}}}(6)$ as the following estimators:

$$\hat{\hat{\boldsymbol{\beta}}}(5) = \begin{cases} \mathbf{b} & \text{if the BP test accepted homoscedasticity} \\ \hat{\hat{\boldsymbol{\beta}}}(2) & \text{if the BP test rejected homoscedasticity} \end{cases}$$

$$\hat{\hat{\boldsymbol{\beta}}}(6) = \begin{cases} \mathbf{b} & \text{if Szroeter's test accepted homoscedasticity} \\ \hat{\hat{\boldsymbol{\beta}}}(2) & \text{if Szroeter's test rejected homoscedasticity} \end{cases}$$

For each of the five samples write down the values for $\hat{\hat{\boldsymbol{\beta}}}(5)$ and $\hat{\hat{\boldsymbol{\beta}}}(6)$.

11.5.3 Group Exercises Using Monte Carlo Data

Exercise 11.14

Let $\hat{\hat{\boldsymbol{\beta}}}_i(j)$ be the estimate obtained from the ith sample using the estimator $\hat{\hat{\boldsymbol{\beta}}}(j)$. From the 100 samples generated, calculate estimates of the means and mean square error matrices of all the estimators for $\boldsymbol{\beta}$ mentioned in the earlier problems. That is, find

$$\sum_{i=1}^{100} \frac{\hat{\hat{\boldsymbol{\beta}}}_i(j)}{100} \quad \text{and} \quad \sum_{i=1}^{100} \frac{[\hat{\hat{\boldsymbol{\beta}}}_i(j) - \boldsymbol{\beta}][\hat{\hat{\boldsymbol{\beta}}}_i(j) - \boldsymbol{\beta}]'}{100}$$

for $j = 1, 2, \ldots, 6$, and repeat the process for the least squares estimator $\mathbf{b}$.

Exercise 11.15

Along the lines of Exercise 11.14 estimate the means and mean square error matrices for $\hat{\boldsymbol{\alpha}}(1)$ and $\hat{\boldsymbol{\alpha}}(2)$.

Exercise 11.16

The following questions should be answered using the numerical results obtained in Exercises 11.4 and 11.15.

1. Do the estimators $\hat{\boldsymbol{\alpha}}(1)$ and $\hat{\boldsymbol{\alpha}}(2)$ appear to be unbiased?
2. Is $\hat{\boldsymbol{\alpha}}(2)$ more efficient than $\hat{\boldsymbol{\alpha}}(1)$ in finite samples?
3. With respect to the relative efficiency of $\hat{\hat{\boldsymbol{\beta}}}(1)$ and $\hat{\hat{\boldsymbol{\beta}}}(2)$, did the more efficient estimator of $\boldsymbol{\alpha}$ lead to an EGLS estimator for $\boldsymbol{\beta}$ that is more efficient?
4. Does knowledge of the correct form of heteroscedasticity enable more efficient estimation of $\boldsymbol{\beta}$?
5. Do any of the estimators for $\boldsymbol{\beta}$ appear biased?
6. Is EGLS estimation better than LS?
7. Is it worthwhile to carry out a preliminary test for heteroscedasticity and to choose an estimator based on the outcome of this test?
8. Has the Monte Carlo data accurately estimated the mean square error of $\mathbf{b}$?

Exercise 11.17

Using all 100 samples, construct empirical distributions for the t statistics obtained in Exercise 11.11. Comment on the shape of these distributions and the proportion of times the hypothesis $\beta_3 = 1.0$ was rejected at the 5% significance level. In terms of accurate interval estimation of β_3

1. Is EGLS estimation worth it?
2. Does knowledge of the correct form of heteroscedasticity help?

Exercise 11.18

Based on the results from the 100 samples, which test for heteroscedasticity, the Breusch–Pagan or the Szroeter test, is more powerful?

11.6 REFERENCES

Amemiya, T. (1973) "Regression Analysis When the Variance of the Dependent Variable is Proportional to the Square of its Expectation," *Journal of the American Statistical Association,* 68, 928–934.

Amemiya, T. (1977) "A Note on a Heteroscedastic Model," *Journal of Econometrics,* 6, 365–370; and "Corrigenda," *Journal of Econometrics,* 8, 275.

Bartlett, M. S. (1937) "Properties of Sufficiency and Statistical Tests," *Proceedings of the Royal Society, Series A,* 160, 268–282.

Battese, G. E. and B. P. Bonyhady (1981) "Estimation of Household Expenditure Functions: An Application of a Class of Heteroscedastic Regression Models," *The Economic Record,* 57, 80–85.

Bickel, P. J. (1978) "Using Residuals Robustly I: Tests for Heteroscedasticity, Nonlinearity," *Annals of Statistics,* 6, 266–291.

Box, G. E. P. and W. J. Hill (1974) "Correcting Inhomogeneity of Variances With Power Transformation Weighting," *Technometrics,* 16, 385–398.

Breusch, T. S. and A. R. Pagan (1979) "A Simple Test for Heteroscedasticity and Random Coefficient Variation," *Econometrica,* 47, 1287–1294.

Brown, K. G. (1978) "Estimation of Variance Components Using Residuals," *Journal of the American Statistical Association,* 73, 141–146.

Carroll, R. J. and D. Ruppert (1981) "On Robust Tests for Heteroscedasticity," *Annals of Statistics,* 9, 205–209.

Carroll, R. J. and D. Ruppert (1982) "A Comparison Between Maximum Likelihood and Generalized Least Squares in a Heteroscedastic Linear Model," *Journal of the American Statistical Association,* 77, 878–882.

Cragg, J. G. (1982) "Estimation and Testing in Time-Series Regression Models with Heteroscedastic Disturbances," *Journal of Econometrics,* 20, 135–157.

Cragg, J. G. (1983) "More Efficient Estimation in the Presence of Heteroscedasticity of Unknown Form," *Econometrica,* 51, 751–764.

Dent, W. and C. Hildreth (1977) "Maximum Likelihood Estimation in Random Coefficient Models," *Journal of the American Statistical Association,* 72, 69–72.

Drèze, J. (1977) "Bayesian Regression Analysis Using Poly-t Densities," *Journal of Econometrics,* 6, 329–354.

Durbin, J. and G. S. Watson (1951) "Testing for Serial Correlation in Least Squares Regression II," *Biometrika,* 38, 159–178.

Dyer, D. D. and J. P. Keating (1980) "On the Determination of Critical Values for Bartlett's Test," *Journal of the American Statistical Association,* 75, 313–319.

Egy, D. and K. Lahiri (1979) "On Maximum Likelihood Estimation of Functional Form and Heteroskedasticity," *Economics Letters,* 2, 155–159.

Eicker, F. (1967) "Limit Theorems for Regressions with Unequal and Dependent Errors," in L. Le Cam and J. Neyman, eds., *Proceedings of the Fifth Berkeley Symposium on Mathematical Statistics and Probability,* University of California Press, Berkeley, 1, 59–82.

Engle, R. F. (1982) "Autoregressive Conditional Heteroscedasticity with Esti-

mates of the Variance of United Kingdom Inflations," *Econometrica,* 50, 987–1008.
Evans, M. A. and M. L. King (1983a) "A Locally Optimal Test for Heteroscedastic Disturbances," working paper, Monash University, Melbourne.
Evans, M. A. and M. L. King (1983b) "A Further Class of Tests for Heteroscedasticity," working paper, Monash University, Melbourne.
Froehlich, B. R. (1973) "Some Estimators for a Random Coefficient Regression Model," *Journal of the American Statistical Association,* 68, 329–334.
Gaudry, M. J. I. and M. G. Dagenais (1979) "Heteroscedasticity and the Use of Box-Cox Transformations," *Economics Letters,* 2, 225–229.
Geary, R. C. (1966) "A Note on Residual Heterovariance and Estimation Efficiency in Regression," *American Statistician,* 20, (4), 30–31.
Glejser, H. (1969) "A New Test for Heteroscedasticity," *Journal of the American Statistical Association,* 64, 316–323.
Godfrey, L. G. (1978) "Testing for Multiplicative Heteroskedasticity," *Journal of Econometrics,* 8, 227–236.
Godfrey, L. G. (1979) "A Diagnostic Check of the Variance Model in Regression Equations with Heteroskedastic Disturbances," unpublished, University of York, England.
Goldberger, A. S. (1964) *Econometric Theory,* Wiley, New York.
Goldfeld, S. M. and R. E. Quandt (1965) "Some Tests for Homoscedasticity," *Journal of the American Statistical Association,* 60, 539–547.
Goldfeld, S. M. and R. E. Quandt (1972) *Nonlinear Methods in Econometrics,* North-Holland, Amsterdam.
Greenberg, E. (1980) "Finite Sample Moments of a Preliminary Test Estimator in the Case of Possible Heteroscedasticity," *Econometrica,* 48, 1805–1813.
Griffiths, W. E. (1971) "Generalized Least Squares with an Estimated Covariance Matrix—A Sampling Experiment," Econometric Society Meetings, New Orleans.
Griffiths, W. E. and J. R. Anderson (1982) "Using Time-Series and Cross-Section Data to Estimate a Production Function with Positive and Negative Marginal Risks," *Journal of the American Statistical Association,* 77, 529–536.
Griffiths, W. E., R. G. Drynan, and S. Prakash (1979) "Bayesian Estimation of a Random Coefficient Model," *Journal of Econometrics,* 10, 201–220.
Hammerstrom, T. (1981) "Asymptotically Optimal Tests for Heteroscedasticity in the General Linear Model," *Annals of Statistics,* 9, 368–380.
Harrison, M. J. (1980) "The Small Sample Performance of the Szroeter Bounds Test for Heteroscedasticity and a Simple Test for Use When Szroeter's Test is Inconclusive," *Oxford Bulletin of Economics and Statistics,* 42, 235–250.
Harrison, M. J. and B. P. M. McCabe (1979) "A Test for Heteroscedasticity Based on Ordinary Least Squares Residuals," *Journal of the American Statistical Association,* 74, 494–499.
Hart, B. I. (1942) "Significance Levels for the Ratio of the Mean-Square Successive Difference to the Variance," *Annals of Mathematical Statistics,* 13, 445–447.

Hartley, H. O. and K. S. E. Jayatillake (1973) "Estimation for Linear Models with Unequal Variances," *Journal of the American Statistical Association,* 68, 189–192.

Harvey, A. C. (1974) "Estimation of Parameters in a Heteroscedastic Regression Model," European Meeting of the Econometric Society, Grenoble, France.

Harvey, A. C. (1976) "Estimating Regression Models with Multiplicative Heteroscedasticity," *Econometrica,* 44, 461–465.

Harvey, A. C. and G. D. A. Phillips (1974) "A Comparison of the Power of Some Tests for Heteroscedasticity in the General Linear Model," *Journal of Econometrics,* 2, 307–316.

Heyadat, A. and D. S. Robson (1970) "Independent Stepwise Residuals for Testing Homoscedasticity," *Journal of the American Statistical Association,* 65, 1573–1581.

Hildreth, C. and J. P. Houck (1968) "Some Estimators for a Linear Model with Random Coefficients," *Journal of the American Statistical Association,* 63, 584–595.

Horn, P. (1981) "Heteroscedasticity of Residuals: A Non-Parametric Alternative to the Goldfeld–Quandt Peak Test," *Communications in Statistics A,* 10, 795–808.

Horn, S. D. and R. A. Horn (1975) "Comparison of Estimators of Heteroscedastic Variances in Linear Models," *Journal of the American Statistical Association,* 70, 872–879.

Horn, S. D., R. A. Horn, and D. B. Duncan (1975) "Estimating Heteroscedastic Variances in Linear Models," *Journal of the American Statistical Association,* 70, 380–385.

Hsieh, D. A. (1983) "A Heteroscedasticity-Consistent Covariance Matrix Estimator for Time Series Regressions," *Journal of Econometrics,* 22, 281–290.

Imhof, J. P. (1961) "Computing the Distribution of Quadratic Forms in Normal Variables," *Biometrika,* 48, 419–426.

Jobson, J. D. and W. A. Fuller (1980) "Least Squares Estimation when the Covariance Matrix and Parameter Vector are Functionally Related," *Journal of the American Statistical Association,* 75, 176–181.

Johnston, J. (1972) *Econometric Methods,* 2nd ed., McGraw-Hill, New York.

Just, R. E. and R. D. Pope (1978) "Stochastic Specification of Production Functions and Economic Implications," *Journal of Econometrics,* 7, 67–86.

Kakwani, N. C. and D. B. Gupta (1967) "Note on the Bias of the Prais and Aitchison's and Fisher's Iterative Estimators in Regression Analysis with Heteroskedastic Errors," *Review of the International Statistical Institute,* 35, 291–295.

Kendall, M. G. and A. Stuart (1973) *The Advanced Theory of Statistics,* Vol. 2: *Inference and Relationship,* Hafner, New York.

King, M. L. (1981) "A Note on Szroeter's Bounds Test," *Oxford Bulletin of Economics and Statistics,* 43, 315–321.

King, M. L. (1982) "A Bounds Test for Heteroscedasticity," working paper

No. 5/82, Department of Economics and Operations Research, Monash University, Australia.

Kmenta, J. (1971) *Elements of Econometrics,* Macmillan, New York.

Koenker, R. (1981) "A Note on Studentizing a Test for Heteroscedasticity," *Journal of Econometrics,* 17, 107–112.

Koenker, R. and G. Bassett, Jr. (1982) "Robust Tests for Heteroscedasticity Based on Regression Quantiles," *Econometrica,* 50, 43–61.

Koerts, J. and A. P. J. Abrahamse (1969) *On the Theory and Application of the General Linear Model,* Rotterdam University Press, Rotterdam, Netherlands.

Maddala, G. S. (1977) *Econometrics,* McGraw-Hill, New York.

Magnus, J. R. (1978) "Maximum Likelihood Estimation of the GLS Model with Unknown Parameters in the Disturbance Covariance Matrix," *Journal of Econometrics,* 7, 281–312.

Mandy, D. (1984) "The Moments of a Pre-Test Estimator Under Possible Heteroscedasticity," *Journal of Econometrics,* forthcoming.

Nicholls, D. F. and A. R. Pagan (1983) "Heteroscedasticity in Models with Lagged Dependent Variables," *Econometrica,* 51, 1233–1242.

Oberhofer, W. and J. Kmenta (1974) "A General Procedure for Obtaining Maximum Likelihood Estimates in Generalized Regression Models," *Econometrica,* 42, 579–590.

Ohtani, K. and T. Toyoda (1979) "Estimation of Regression Coefficients After A Preliminary Test for Homoscedasticity," *Journal of Econometrics,* 12, 151–159.

Park, R. E. (1966) "Estimation with Heteroscedastic Error Terms," *Econometrica,* 34, 888.

Prais, S. J. (1953) "A Note on Heteroscedastic Errors in Regression Analysis," *Review of the International Statistical Institute,* 21, 28–29.

Prais, S. J. and J. Aitchison (1954) "The Grouping of Observations in Regression Analysis," *Review of the International Statistical Institute,* 22, 1–22.

Prais, S. J. and H. S. Houthakker (1955) *The Analysis of Family Budgets,* Cambridge University Press, New York.

Ramsey, J. B. (1969) "Tests for Specification Error in Classical Linear Least Squares Regression Analysis," *Journal of the Royal Statistical Society* (*B*), 31, 250–271.

Ramsey, J. B. and R. Gilbert (1972) "Some Small Sample Properties of Tests for Specification Error," *Journal of the American Statistical Association,* 67, 180–186.

Rao, C. R. (1970) "Estimation of Heteroscedastic Variances in Linear Models," *Journal of the American Statistical Association,* 65, 161–172.

Rao, C. R. (1972) "Estimation of Variance and Covariance Components in Linear Models," *Journal of the American Statistical Association,* 67, 112–115.

Rao, J. N. K. and K. Subrahmaniam (1971) "Combining Independent Estimators and Estimation in Linear Regression with Unequal Variances," *Biometrics,* 27, 971–990.

Rutemiller, H. C. and D. A. Bowers (1968) "Estimation in a Heteroscedastic Regression Model," *Journal of the American Statistical Association,* 63, 552–557.

Sathe, S. T. and H. D. Vinod (1974) "Bounds on the Variance of Regression Coefficients due to Heteroscedastic or Autoregressive Errors," *Econometrica,* 42, 333–340.

Surekha, K. and W. E. Griffiths (1982) "A Bayesian Comparison of Some Distributional Assumptions in a Heteroscedastic Error Model," working paper, Indian Statistical Institute, Calcutta.

Surekha, K. and W. E. Griffiths (1983) "An Evaluation of the Power of Some Tests for Heteroscedasticity," working paper, Indian Statistical Institute, Calcutta.

Surekha, K. and W. E. Griffiths (1984) "A Monte Carlo Comparison of Some Bayesian and Sampling Theory Estimators in Two Heteroscedastic Error Models," *Communications in Statistics B,* 13, forthcoming.

Swamy, P. A. V. B. and J. S. Mehta (1979) "Estimation of Common Coefficients in Two Regression Equations," *Journal of Econometrics,* 10, 1–14.

Szroeter, J. (1978) "A Class of Parametric Tests for Heteroscedasticity in Linear Econometric Models," *Econometrica,* 46, 1311–1328.

Taylor, W. E. (1977) "Small Sample Properties of a Class of Two-Stage Aitken Estimators," *Econometrica,* 45, 497–508.

Taylor, W. E. (1978) "The Heteroscedastic Linear Model: Exact Finite Sample Results," *Econometrica,* 46, 663–675.

Theil, H. (1951) "Estimates and Their Sampling Variance of Parameters of Certain Heteroscedastic Distributions," *Review of the International Statistical Institute,* 19, 141–147.

Theil, H. (1971) *Principles of Econometrics,* Wiley, New York.

Theil, H. and L. B. M. Mennes (1959) "Multiplicative Randomness in Time Series Regression Analysis," Economic Institute of the Netherlands School of Economics Report 5901.

Thursby, J. G. (1982) "Misspecification, Heteroscedasticity, and the Chow and Goldfeld–Quandt Tests," *Review of Economics and Statistics,* 64, 314–321.

von Neumann, J. (1941) "Distribution of the Ratio of the Mean-Square Successive Difference to the Variance," *Annals of Mathematical Statistics,* 12, 367–395.

White, H. (1980) "A Heteroskedasticity-Consistent Covariance Matrix Estimator and a Direct Test for Heteroskedasticity," *Econometrica,* 48, 817–838.

White, H. (1982) "Instrumental Variables Regression with Independent Observations," *Econometrica,* 50, 483–499.

Yancey, T. A., G. G. Judge and S. Miyazaki (1984) "Some Improved Estimators in the Case of Possible Heteroscedasticity," *Journal of Econometrics,* 25, forthcoming.

Chapter 12

Disturbance-Related Sets of Regression Equations

In a number of the earlier chapters we considered the general linear model $\mathbf{y} = X\boldsymbol{\beta} + \mathbf{e}$, where $\mathbf{y}$ was a $(T \times 1)$ vector of observations on a dependent variable, X a $(T \times K)$ nonstochastic design matrix, $\mathbf{e}$ a $(T \times 1)$ unobservable random vector with $E[\mathbf{e}] = \mathbf{0}$ and $E[\mathbf{ee}'] = \Phi = \sigma^2\Psi$, and $\boldsymbol{\beta}$ a $(K \times 1)$ vector of unknown parameters. Under alternative assumptions about the covariance matrix for $\mathbf{e}$, a number of methods for estimating $\boldsymbol{\beta}$, and for testing hypotheses about $\boldsymbol{\beta}$ and Ψ, were examined. In this chapter we allow for some further extensions of the stochastic specification and discuss estimation and hypothesis testing for these extensions.

We consider a set of regression equations where each member of the set is an equation of the form $\mathbf{y} = X\boldsymbol{\beta} + \mathbf{e}$ and where there may be correlation between the disturbances in different equations. Such a specification is likely to be reasonable when estimating a number of related economic functions such as demand equations for a number of commodities, investment functions for a number of firms, or consumption functions for subsets of the population. For these cases the disturbances for different functions, at a given point in time, are likely to reflect some common unmeasurable or omitted factors, and so one would expect them to exhibit some correlation. This correlation between different disturbances at a given point in time is known as contemporaneous correlation and, in Section 12.1, we discuss estimation and hypothesis testing under this assumption. When there is a different number of observations on each equation, the estimation techniques can be modified and, in Section 12.2, some possible modifications are outlined. Because the observations on any one equation will frequently be observations over time, it is often reasonable to introduce, and extend, some of the time series assumptions made about the disturbance vector in a single equation. This leads to disturbances that are both contemporaneously and serially correlated; models with this property are discussed in Section 12.3. In Section 12.4 we make some comments on model specification, and in Section 12.5 we consider estimation when the disturbance covariance matrix is singular. The material in all these sections is summarized in Table 12.1. For an additional survey to the one provided in this chapter, see Srivastava and Dwivedi (1979).

TABLE 12.1 *DISTURBANCE RELATED SETS OF REGRESSION EQUATIONS*

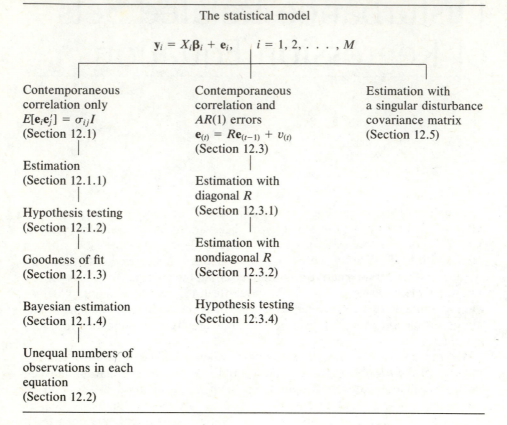

The statistical model

$$\mathbf{y}_i = X_i\boldsymbol{\beta}_i + \mathbf{e}_i, \qquad i = 1, 2, \ldots, M$$

Contemporaneous correlation only $E[\mathbf{e}_i\mathbf{e}_j'] = \sigma_{ij}I$ (Section 12.1)	Contemporaneous correlation and $AR(1)$ errors $\mathbf{e}_{(t)} = R\mathbf{e}_{(t-1)} + v_{(t)}$ (Section 12.3)	Estimation with a singular disturbance covariance matrix (Section 12.5)
Estimation (Section 12.1.1)	Estimation with diagonal R (Section 12.3.1)	
Hypothesis testing (Section 12.1.2)	Estimation with nondiagonal R (Section 12.3.2)	
Goodness of fit (Section 12.1.3)	Hypothesis testing (Section 12.3.4)	
Bayesian estimation (Section 12.1.4)		
Unequal numbers of observations in each equation (Section 12.2)		

12.1 SETS OF EQUATIONS WITH CONTEMPORANEOUSLY CORRELATED DISTURBANCES

The linear statistical model studied in the earlier chapters can be extended to the case where we have M such models

$$\mathbf{y}_i = X_i\boldsymbol{\beta}_i + \mathbf{e}_i, \qquad i = 1, 2, \ldots, M \tag{12.1.1}$$

where $\mathbf{y}_i$ and $\mathbf{e}_i$ are of dimension $(T \times 1)$, X_i is $(T \times K_i)$ and $\boldsymbol{\beta}_i$ is $(K_i \times 1)$. A convenient way to write these equations is

$$\begin{bmatrix} \mathbf{y}_1 \\ \mathbf{y}_2 \\ \vdots \\ \mathbf{y}_M \end{bmatrix} = \begin{bmatrix} X_1 & & & \\ & X_2 & & \\ & & \ddots & \\ & & & X_M \end{bmatrix} \begin{bmatrix} \boldsymbol{\beta}_1 \\ \boldsymbol{\beta}_2 \\ \vdots \\ \boldsymbol{\beta}_M \end{bmatrix} + \begin{bmatrix} \mathbf{e}_1 \\ \mathbf{e}_2 \\ \vdots \\ \mathbf{e}_M \end{bmatrix} \tag{12.1.2}$$

or, alternatively,

$$\mathbf{y} = X\boldsymbol{\beta} + \mathbf{e} \tag{12.1.3}$$

where the definitions of $\mathbf{y}$, X, $\boldsymbol{\beta}$, and $\mathbf{e}$ are obvious from (12.1.2) and where their dimensions are respectively $(MT \times 1)$, $(MT \times K)$, $(K \times 1)$, and $(MT \times 1)$ with $K = \Sigma_{i=1}^{M} K_i$. In this section it will be assumed that $E[\mathbf{e}_i] = \mathbf{0}$ and $E[\mathbf{e}_i\mathbf{e}_j'] = \sigma_{ij}I_T$ and hence that the covariance matrix of the joint disturbance vector is given by

$$\mathrm{E}[\mathbf{ee}'] = \Omega = \Sigma \otimes I \tag{12.1.4}$$

where

$$\Sigma = \begin{bmatrix} \sigma_{11} & \sigma_{12} & \cdots & \sigma_{1M} \\ \sigma_{12} & \sigma_{22} & \cdots & \sigma_{2M} \\ \vdots & \vdots & & \vdots \\ \sigma_{1M} & \sigma_{2M} & \cdots & \sigma_{MM} \end{bmatrix} \tag{12.1.5}$$

In many applications $\mathbf{y}_i$ and X_i will contain observations on variables for T different time periods and the subscript i will correspond to a particular economic or geographical unit such as a household, a firm, or a state. Hence the joint model in (12.1.3) can be regarded as one way in which time series and cross-sectional data can be combined. Other models for combining time series–cross-sectional data exist and are outlined in Chapter 13. These differ depending on the assumptions made about the coefficient and disturbance vectors in each equation.

If each observation in $\mathbf{y}_i$ and X_i represents a different point in time, the covariance assumption in (12.1.4) implies that the disturbances in different equations are correlated at a given point in time but are not correlated over time. As mentioned above, this is known as contemporaneous correlation, and for sets of economic relationships it is often likely to be a reasonable assumption.

12.1.1 Estimation

When the system in (12.1.2) is viewed as the single equation (12.1.3), we can estimate $\boldsymbol{\beta}$ and hence all the $\boldsymbol{\beta}_i$ via generalized least squares (GLS). If X is of rank K and Σ is known and of rank M, the GLS estimator exists and is given by

$$\hat{\boldsymbol{\beta}} = (X'\Omega^{-1}X)^{-1}X'\Omega^{-1}\mathbf{y} = (X'(\Sigma^{-1} \otimes I)X)^{-1}X'(\Sigma^{-1} \otimes I)\mathbf{y} \tag{12.1.6}$$

Written in detail, we find that $\hat{\boldsymbol{\beta}}$ becomes

$$\hat{\boldsymbol{\beta}} = \begin{bmatrix} \hat{\boldsymbol{\beta}}_1 \\ \hat{\boldsymbol{\beta}}_2 \\ \vdots \\ \hat{\boldsymbol{\beta}}_M \end{bmatrix} = \begin{bmatrix} \sigma^{11}X_1'X_1 & \sigma^{12}X_1'X_2 & \cdots & \sigma^{1M}X_1'X_M \\ \sigma^{12}X_2'X_1 & \sigma^{22}X_2'X_2 & \cdots & \sigma^{2M}X_2'X_M \\ \vdots & \vdots & \ddots & \vdots \\ \sigma^{1M}X_M'X_1 & \sigma^{2M}X_M'X_2 & \cdots & \sigma^{MM}X_M'X_M \end{bmatrix}^{-1} \begin{bmatrix} \sum_{i=1}^{M} \sigma^{1i}X_1'\mathbf{y}_i \\ \sum_{i=1}^{M} \sigma^{2i}X_2'\mathbf{y}_i \\ \vdots \\ \sum_{i=1}^{M} \sigma^{Mi}X_M'\mathbf{y}_i \end{bmatrix} \tag{12.1.7}$$

where σ^{ij} is the (i,j)th element of Σ^{-1}. Within the class of all estimators that are unbiased and linear functions of $\mathbf{y}$, this estimator is minimum variance and, if $\mathbf{y}$ is normally distributed, it is the maximum likelihood estimator and is minimum variance within the class of all unbiased estimators. It has mean $E[\hat{\boldsymbol{\beta}}] = \boldsymbol{\beta}$ and covariance matrix

$$E[(\hat{\boldsymbol{\beta}} - \boldsymbol{\beta})(\hat{\boldsymbol{\beta}} - \boldsymbol{\beta})'] = (X'\Omega^{-1}X)^{-1} = (X'(\Sigma^{-1} \otimes I)X)^{-1}$$

If interest centers on one equation, say the ith, and only estimators that are a function of $\mathbf{y}_i$ are considered, then the least squares (LS) estimator $\mathbf{b}_i = (X_i'X_i)^{-1}X_i'\mathbf{y}_i$ is the minimum variance, linear unbiased estimator. However, we can improve on this estimator by considering a wider class—namely, linear unbiased estimators that are a function of $\mathbf{y}$. Within this class $\hat{\boldsymbol{\beta}}_i$, the ith vector component of $\hat{\boldsymbol{\beta}}$, is better than $\mathbf{b}_i$ because it allows for the correlation between $\mathbf{e}_i$ and the other disturbance vectors, and because it uses information on explanatory variables that are included in the system but excluded from the ith equation. The possible gain in efficiency obtained by jointly considering all the equations led Zellner (1962) to give (12.1.2) the title "a set of seemingly unrelated regression equations."

Zellner notes that if $\sigma_{ij} = 0$ for $i \neq j$ or if $X_1 = X_2 = \ldots = X_M$ the estimators $\mathbf{b}_i$ and $\hat{\boldsymbol{\beta}}_i$ will be identical, and so there will be no gain in efficiency. Also, the efficiency gain tends to be higher when the explanatory variables in different equations are not highly correlated but the disturbance terms corresponding to different equations are highly correlated. Conditions that are both necessary and sufficient for $\mathbf{b}_i = \hat{\boldsymbol{\beta}}_i$ for all equations are given by Dwivedi and Srivastava (1978).

In addition, there are some conditions under which GLS applied to a subset of the system of equations yields an estimator identical to the corresponding subvector of the GLS estimator applied to the complete system [Schmidt (1978)]. If there is a subset of H equations in which some of the explanatory variables do not appear, but these variables, along with all other explanatory variables in the system, appear in the remaining $M - H$ equations, then the GLS estimator from the H equations is identical to the appropriate subvector of the GLS estimator of the whole system. As a simple example, consider the $M = 2$ case studied by Revankar (1974). In this case $\mathbf{y} = X\boldsymbol{\beta} + \mathbf{e}$ can be written as

$$\begin{bmatrix} \mathbf{y}_1 \\ \mathbf{y}_2 \end{bmatrix} = \begin{bmatrix} X_1 & 0 \\ 0 & X_2 \end{bmatrix} \begin{bmatrix} \boldsymbol{\beta}_1 \\ \boldsymbol{\beta}_2 \end{bmatrix} + \begin{bmatrix} \mathbf{e}_1 \\ \mathbf{e}_2 \end{bmatrix} \tag{12.1.8}$$

Now suppose X_2 is a subset of X_1, say $X_1 = (X_2, X_1^*)$, and consider estimation of $\boldsymbol{\beta}_2$. The GLS estimator of the second equation by itself is simply the LS estimator $\mathbf{b}_2 = (X_2'X_2)^{-1}X_2'\mathbf{y}_2$ and because X_2 is a subset of X_1, it is possible to show that $\mathbf{b}_2$ is identical to $\hat{\boldsymbol{\beta}}_2$, the second vector component of $\hat{\boldsymbol{\beta}} = [X'(\Sigma^{-1} \otimes I) X]^{-1}X'(\Sigma^{-1} \otimes I)\mathbf{y}$. Thus one cannot obtain a more efficient estimator of $\boldsymbol{\beta}_2$ by considering the whole system. This is not true for $\boldsymbol{\beta}_1$, however. For further results on this simple two equation model in the context of covariance analysis see Conniffe (1982a).

In most applications Σ is unknown, and so the estimator $\hat{\boldsymbol{\beta}}$ cannot be employed. However, one can utilize the estimated generalized least squares (EGLS) estimator

$$\hat{\hat{\boldsymbol{\beta}}} = [X'(\hat{\Sigma}^{-1} \otimes I)X]^{-1}X'(\hat{\Sigma}^{-1} \otimes I)\mathbf{y} \tag{12.1.9}$$

where the estimator $\hat{\Sigma}$ is based on LS residuals $\hat{\mathbf{e}}_i = \mathbf{y}_i - X_i\mathbf{b}_i$ and has elements given by

$$\hat{\sigma}_{ij} = T^{-1}\hat{\mathbf{e}}_i'\hat{\mathbf{e}}_j, \qquad i,j = 1, 2, \ldots, M \tag{12.1.10}$$

The estimator $\hat{\hat{\boldsymbol{\beta}}}$, defined by (12.1.9) and (12.1.10), is frequently referred to as Zellner's seemingly unrelated regression estimator or technique.

The presence of T in the divisor in (12.1.10) means that $\hat{\sigma}_{ij}$ will be biased and, because the number of explanatory variables in each equation can be different, one cannot carry out the usual single-equation procedure of "correcting for degrees of freedom." Two alternatives to using T are $(T - K_i)^{1/2}(T - K_j)^{1/2}$, and $T - K_i - K_j + \mathrm{tr}[(X_i'X_i)^{-1}X_i'X_j(X_j'X_j)^{-1}X_j'X_i]$. The first of these yields an estimator that is unbiased for $i = j$ and the second gives an unbiased estimator for all i and j [Zellner and Huang (1962)]. However, the latter can lead to an estimator for Σ that is not positive definite; therefore, it is unlikely that the resulting estimator for $\boldsymbol{\beta}$ will be an improvement over $\hat{\hat{\boldsymbol{\beta}}}$ [Theil (1971, p. 322)].

The choice of a divisor in (12.1.10) will not influence the asymptotic properties of the resulting EGLS estimator. In particular, if $\lim_{T\to\infty} T^{-1}X_i'X_j$ is finite and nonsingular for all i and j, then $\hat{\hat{\boldsymbol{\beta}}}$ is consistent and $\sqrt{T}(\hat{\hat{\boldsymbol{\beta}}} - \boldsymbol{\beta})$ has a limiting normal distribution with mean zero and covariance matrix $\lim T[X'(\Sigma^{-1} \otimes I)X]^{-1}$. Thus, $\hat{\hat{\boldsymbol{\beta}}}$ has the same asymptotic properties as the GLS estimator $\hat{\boldsymbol{\beta}}$. Furthermore, $T[X'(\hat{\Sigma}^{-1} \otimes I)X]^{-1}$ is a consistent estimator for $\lim T[X'(\Sigma^{-1} \otimes I)X]^{-1}$, and so, in finite samples, $[X'(\hat{\Sigma}^{-1} \otimes I)X]^{-1}$ can be treated as an approximate covariance matrix for $\hat{\hat{\boldsymbol{\beta}}}$.

Another estimator for $\boldsymbol{\beta}$ is defined by using (12.1.9) and (12.1.10) in an iterative procedure. A new set of variance estimates can be obtained from

$$\hat{\hat{\sigma}}_{ij} = T^{-1}(\mathbf{y}_i - X_i\hat{\hat{\boldsymbol{\beta}}}_i)'(\mathbf{y}_j - X_j\hat{\hat{\boldsymbol{\beta}}}_j) \tag{12.1.11}$$

where $\hat{\hat{\boldsymbol{\beta}}}' = (\hat{\hat{\boldsymbol{\beta}}}_1', \hat{\hat{\boldsymbol{\beta}}}_2', \ldots, \hat{\hat{\boldsymbol{\beta}}}_M')$; these can be used to form a new estimator for $\boldsymbol{\beta}$ and so on until convergence. When the disturbances follow a multivariate normal distribution, this estimator will be the maximum likelihood estimator [Dhrymes (1971), Oberhofer and Kmenta (1974), Magnus (1978)]. Its asymptotic properties are identical to those of $\hat{\boldsymbol{\beta}}$ in (12.1.9).

Telser (1964) has suggested another iterative estimator for $\boldsymbol{\beta}$ which emphasizes the across equation residual correlation by explicitly introducing the residuals of other equations as explanatory variables. To illustrate this procedure, consider the two-equation system in (12.1.8), without the restrictions on X_1. It is possible to define a vector $\mathbf{w}$ such that $\mathbf{e}_1 = \delta\mathbf{e}_2 + \mathbf{w}$, where $\delta = \sigma_{12}/\sigma_{22}$, and the elements of $\mathbf{w}$ are uncorrelated and identically distributed with mean zero and variance $(\sigma_{11} - \sigma_{12}^2/\sigma_{22})$; furthermore $\mathbf{w}$ will be uncorrelated with $\mathbf{e}_2$. Thus, we can write the first equation in the system as

$$\mathbf{y}_1 = X_1\boldsymbol{\beta}_1 + \delta\mathbf{e}_2 + \mathbf{w} \tag{12.1.12}$$

In the Telser iterative procedure, we replace $\mathbf{e}_2$ with the LS residuals $\hat{\mathbf{e}}_2 = \mathbf{y}_2 - X_2\mathbf{b}$, and then apply LS to (12.1.12). The resulting residuals, say $\mathbf{y}_1 - X_1\hat{\boldsymbol{\beta}}_1^*$, can then be used in the second equation counterpart of (12.1.12), and so on. This process converges to an estimator that has the same asymptotic properties as the Zellner EGLS estimator $\hat{\hat{\boldsymbol{\beta}}}$. Conniffe (1982b) shows that, in small samples, there are some circumstances where it is more efficient to use the Telser estimator based on one iteration, than to use the estimator $\hat{\hat{\boldsymbol{\beta}}}$.

Unless conditions are such that $\hat{\hat{\boldsymbol{\beta}}}' = \mathbf{b}' = (\mathbf{b}_1', \mathbf{b}_2', \ldots, \mathbf{b}_M')$, it is more efficient, asymptotically, to use $\hat{\hat{\boldsymbol{\beta}}}$ than to apply LS to each equation separately. However, because it does not follow that this will also be true in small samples, there has been some investigation into the finite sample properties of $\hat{\hat{\boldsymbol{\beta}}}$ [Zellner and Huang (1962); Zellner (1962, 1963); Kakwani (1967); Kmenta and Gilbert (1968); Kataoka (1974); Revankar (1974, 1976); Mehta and Swamy (1976); Hall (1977); Kariya (1981a); Binkley (1982); Conniffe (1982b)]. Also, further approximations to the asymptotic distribution have been considered [Srivastava (1970), Kakwani (1974), Phillips (1977)]. Derivation of the finite sample distribution is a difficult problem so that most of the exact results are derived under at least one of the following simplifying assumptions: (1) $M = 2$, (2) $X_i'X_j = 0$ for $i \neq j$; (3) the variables in one equation are a subset of those in another such as in (12.1.8); and (4) "unrestricted" residuals, those from LS applied to the system with every variable in every equation, are used to estimate the variances. As we would expect, the conclusions from the various studies are not precisely the same; but, in general, they indicate that $\hat{\hat{\boldsymbol{\beta}}}$ will be more efficient than $\mathbf{b}$, provided that the correlation between disturbances in different equations is not too low. Also, the iterative maximum likelihood estimator is not uniformly better than $\hat{\hat{\boldsymbol{\beta}}}$.

12.1.1a Stein-Like Estimators

In Chapter 3 we showed that there exists a family of Stein-rule estimators that dominate the maximum likelihood rule under squared error loss. In this section we extend the Stein-rule estimator to include sets of regression equations. We will assume throughout that $\mathbf{e}$ is normally distributed, and we begin by also assuming that Σ is known so that we can choose a matrix H such that $H(\Sigma \otimes I)H' = I_{TM}$. Then, the statistical model can be rewritten as $H\mathbf{y} = HX\boldsymbol{\beta} + H\mathbf{e}$ or $\dot{\mathbf{y}} = \dot{X}\boldsymbol{\beta} + \dot{\mathbf{e}}$.

This model conforms to the standard general linear statistical model considered previously in Chapter 3 and any of the family of minimax and positive-rule estimators discussed by Judge and Bock (1978) could be employed. Following Judge and Bock (1978, Chapter 10), if the Berger variant is used the corresponding Stein-rule estimator may be defined as

$$\boldsymbol{\beta}_{s1}(\hat{\boldsymbol{\beta}}) = \left[I_K - \frac{a\dot{X}'\dot{X}}{\hat{\boldsymbol{\beta}}'(\dot{X}'\dot{X})^2\hat{\boldsymbol{\beta}}}\right]\hat{\boldsymbol{\beta}} \tag{12.1.13}$$

where $\hat{\boldsymbol{\beta}}$ is the GLS estimator for $\boldsymbol{\beta}$. Under a squared error loss measure, this estimator is a minimax estimator and will dominate the GLS maximum likelihood estimator if $0 \leq a \leq 2(K - 2)$ with optimum value $a = K - 2$. The positive-rule counterpart of the above estimator will dominate both the Berger and maximum likelihood (GLS) estimators.

Also, if we assume the disturbance covariance matrix is $\sigma^2\Sigma_0 \otimes I_T$, where Σ_0 is a known nonsingular matrix, σ^2 is an unknown positive constant, and s is an estimate of σ^2 such that s/σ^2 has a chi-square distribution with $MT - K$ degrees of freedom and is independent of $\hat{\boldsymbol{\beta}}$, a corresponding extended Stein-rule estimator is

$$\boldsymbol{\beta}_{s2}(\hat{\boldsymbol{\beta}},s) = \left[I_K - \frac{as\dot{X}'\dot{X}}{\hat{\boldsymbol{\beta}}'(\dot{X}'\dot{X})^2\hat{\boldsymbol{\beta}}}\right]\hat{\boldsymbol{\beta}} \tag{12.1.14}$$

This estimator and its positive-part counterpart will be minimax and dominate the GLS (maximum likelihood) estimator under squared error loss if $0 \leq a \leq (K - 2)/(MT - K + 2)$.

To generalize the results for the model $\mathbf{y} = X\boldsymbol{\beta} + \mathbf{e}$, let us assume that Σ is an unknown positive definite diagonal matrix with diagonal elements σ_{ii}. Let $\mathbf{v} = (v_1, v_2, \ldots, v_M)'$ be a random vector independent of $\hat{\boldsymbol{\beta}}$ where v_i/σ_{ii} has a chi-square distribution with $(T - K_i)$ degrees of freedom, independent for $i = 1, 2, \ldots, M$. Further define a $(K \times K)$ block diagonal matrix W with blocks $W_i = (v_i/(T - K_i - 2))[X_i'X_i]^{-1}$. Also let

$$h = \min_{1\leq i\leq M} (T + K_i - 2)^{-1}v_i/\sigma_{ii} \qquad \text{and} \qquad \tau = E(h^{-1})$$

Given these specifications and definitions the Berger and Bock (1976)–James and Stein estimator for the set of regression equations is

$$\boldsymbol{\beta}_{s3}(\mathbf{b}, W) = \left[I_K - \frac{cW^{-1}}{\mathbf{b}'W^{-2}\mathbf{b}}\right]\mathbf{b} \tag{12.1.15}$$

where $\mathbf{b} = (X'X)^{-1}X'\mathbf{y}$ is the ML estimator for $\boldsymbol{\beta}$ when Σ is diagonal. From the proofs of Berger and Bock (1976) this estimator is a minimax estimator if $0 \leq c \leq 2(K - 2\tau)$ holds along with certain other conditions usually fulfilled in practice. Extension of this estimator to the positive-rule variant is direct.

In the general case where Σ is unknown and not necessarily diagonal, no corresponding estimator in the Stein-rule family currently exists. One tempting alternative is to estimate the variance-covariance matrix as Zellner has done and use this matrix, say $\tilde{W}$, to replace W in the Berger and Bock estimator. Unfortunately, no analytical results exist for the risk function for this estimator and the difficulty of obtaining such results is not to be underestimated. Some information on the performance of this estimator under squared error loss is given in a sampling experiment that is reported in Judge and Bock (1978, Ch. 11).

12.1.2 Hypothesis Testing

12.1.2a Linear Restrictions on the Coefficient Vector

We now consider a test procedure for testing a set of linear coefficient restrictions of the form $R\boldsymbol{\beta} = \mathbf{r}$, where R and $\mathbf{r}$ are known matrices of dimensions $(J \times K)$ and $(J \times 1)$, respectively. There are two main differences between this test procedure and the one outlined in Chapter 2 for the single equation case. First, the relevant test statistic will now depend on Σ, which, because it is unknown, needs to be replaced with an estimator $\hat{\Sigma}$. In the general case, this replacement implies that the test will only have a large sample justification. Second, it is now possible to test restrictions that relate the coefficients in one equation with the coefficients in other equations. This is of particular interest in economics. For example, if the coefficient vectors for each equation are all equal, $\boldsymbol{\beta}_1 = \boldsymbol{\beta}_2 = \cdots = \boldsymbol{\beta}_M$, the use of data aggregated over micro units does not lead to aggregation bias [Zellner (1962)]. Also, some aspects of economic theory, such as the Slutsky conditions in demand analysis, often suggest linear relationships between coefficients in different equations.

Under the assumptions that $\mathbf{e}$ is normally distributed, and the null hypothesis $R\boldsymbol{\beta} = \mathbf{r}$ is true, it can be shown that

$$g = (\mathbf{r} - R\hat{\boldsymbol{\beta}})'(RCR')^{-1}(\mathbf{r} - R\hat{\boldsymbol{\beta}}) \sim \chi^2_{(J)} \tag{12.1.16}$$

where $C = [X'(\Sigma^{-1} \otimes I)X]^{-1}$. When Σ is unknown and we replace $\hat{\boldsymbol{\beta}}$ with $\hat{\hat{\boldsymbol{\beta}}}$, and C with $\hat{C} = [X'(\hat{\Sigma}^{-1} \otimes I)X]^{-1}$, we have the result

$$\hat{g} = (\mathbf{r} - R\hat{\hat{\boldsymbol{\beta}}})'(R\hat{C}R')^{-1}(\mathbf{r} - R\hat{\hat{\boldsymbol{\beta}}}) \xrightarrow{d} \chi^2_{(J)} \tag{12.1.17}$$

Thus, an appropriate asymptotic test procedure is to reject H_0: $R\boldsymbol{\beta} = \mathbf{r}$ if $\hat{g}$ is greater than a prespecified critical value from the $\chi^2_{(J)}$-distribution.

In some cases it is more convenient to write g in terms of restricted and unrestricted residual sums of squares. Let

$$\hat{\boldsymbol{\beta}}^* = \hat{\boldsymbol{\beta}} + CR'(RCR')^{-1}(\mathbf{r} - R\hat{\boldsymbol{\beta}}) \tag{12.1.18}$$

be the restricted GLS estimator obtained by minimizing $(\mathbf{y} - X\boldsymbol{\beta})'(\Sigma^{-1} \otimes I)(\mathbf{y} - X\boldsymbol{\beta})$ subject to $R\boldsymbol{\beta} = \mathbf{r}$. It can be shown that (12.1.16) is equivalent to

$$g = (\mathbf{y} - X\hat{\boldsymbol{\beta}}^*)'(\Sigma^{-1} \otimes I)(\mathbf{y} - X\hat{\boldsymbol{\beta}}^*) - (\mathbf{y} - X\hat{\boldsymbol{\beta}})'(\Sigma^{-1} \otimes I)(\mathbf{y} - X\hat{\boldsymbol{\beta}}) \tag{12.1.19}$$

Thus, the test procedure can be viewed as a test of the significance of the increase in the residual sum of squares from the imposition of linear constraints. If, in (12.1.19), Σ is replaced by $\hat{\Sigma}$ and $\hat{\boldsymbol{\beta}}$ and $\hat{\boldsymbol{\beta}}^*$ are modified accordingly, the resulting expression is equal to $\hat{g}$ given in (12.1.17).

In addition, rather than use the expression in (12.1.18), it is often easier to obtain the restricted estimator $\hat{\boldsymbol{\beta}}^*$ by rewriting the model (12.1.2) to incorporate the restrictions. For example, if $K_1 = K_2 = \ldots = K_M = k$, and we wish to impose the restrictions $\boldsymbol{\beta}_1 = \boldsymbol{\beta}_2 = \ldots = \boldsymbol{\beta}_M$, (12.1.2) can be written as

$$\begin{bmatrix} \mathbf{y}_1 \\ \mathbf{y}_2 \\ \vdots \\ \mathbf{y}_M \end{bmatrix} = \begin{bmatrix} X_1 \\ X_2 \\ \vdots \\ X_M \end{bmatrix} \boldsymbol{\beta}_1 + \begin{bmatrix} \mathbf{e}_1 \\ \mathbf{e}_2 \\ \vdots \\ \mathbf{e}_M \end{bmatrix} \tag{12.1.20}$$

or, equivalently, as

$$\mathbf{y} = X^*\boldsymbol{\beta}_1 + \mathbf{e} \tag{12.1.21}$$

where X^* is of order $(MT \times k)$. The M vector components of $\hat{\boldsymbol{\beta}}^*$ will all be the same, and one of them can be obtained by applying GLS to (12.1.21). This yields

$$\hat{\boldsymbol{\beta}}_1^* = [X^{*\prime}(\Sigma^{-1} \otimes I)X^*]^{-1}X^{*\prime}(\Sigma^{-1} \otimes I)\mathbf{y} \tag{12.1.22}$$

and the restricted residual sum of squares can be written as

$$(\mathbf{y} - X\hat{\boldsymbol{\beta}}^*)'(\Sigma^{-1} \otimes I)(\mathbf{y} - X\hat{\boldsymbol{\beta}}^*) = (\mathbf{y} - X^*\hat{\boldsymbol{\beta}}_1^*)'(\Sigma^{-1} \otimes I)(\mathbf{y} - X^*\hat{\boldsymbol{\beta}}_1^*) \tag{12.1.23}$$

Discussion of the restricted estimator and the model in (12.1.21) raises the question of whether to estimate Σ using LS residuals from the restricted or the unrestricted model. In (12.1.10) we suggested using the unrestricted residuals

$\hat{\mathbf{e}} = (I - X(X'X)^{-1}X')\mathbf{y}$. However, since we are interested in the probability distribution of $\hat{g}$ when the null hypothesis $R\boldsymbol{\beta} = \mathbf{r}$ is true, it is equally valid to base $\hat{g}$ on an estimate of Σ that assumes that the null hypothesis is true. For example, using the restrictions incorporated into (12.1.20), such an estimate would be based on the residuals $\mathbf{e}^* = (I - X^*(X^{*\prime}X^*)^{-1}X^{*\prime})\mathbf{y}$.

If we employ ML estimators for $\boldsymbol{\beta}$ and Σ, then the question of whether to estimate Σ from the residuals of the restricted or the unrestricted model is equivalent to a choice between the Lagrange multiplier (LM) and Wald tests.

To illustrate the difference we will use the following notation (cf. Section 5.7):

1. $\tilde{\Sigma}$ and $\tilde{\Sigma}^*$ are, respectively, the unrestricted and restricted ML estimators for Σ.
2. $\tilde{\boldsymbol{\beta}}_U$ and $\tilde{\boldsymbol{\beta}}_U^*$ are, respectively, the unrestricted and restricted ML estimators for $\boldsymbol{\beta}$, conditional on the unrestricted covariance matrix estimator $\Sigma = \tilde{\Sigma}$.
3. $\tilde{\boldsymbol{\beta}}_R$ and $\tilde{\boldsymbol{\beta}}_R^*$ are, respectively, the unrestricted and restricted ML estimators for $\boldsymbol{\beta}$, conditional on the restricted covariance matrix estimator $\Sigma = \tilde{\Sigma}^*$.
4. S_0 is an $(M \times M)$ matrix with (i,j)th element equal to $(\mathbf{y}_i - X_i\tilde{\boldsymbol{\beta}}_{Ui}^*)'(\mathbf{y}_j - X_j\tilde{\boldsymbol{\beta}}_{Uj}^*)/T$.
5. S_1 is an $(M \times M)$ matrix with (i,j)th element equal to $(\mathbf{y}_i - X_i\tilde{\boldsymbol{\beta}}_{Ri})'(\mathbf{y}_j - X_j\tilde{\boldsymbol{\beta}}_{Rj})/T$.

Then, it can be shown that the Wald statistic for testing H_0: $R\boldsymbol{\beta} = \mathbf{r}$ is

$$\begin{aligned}\lambda_W &= (\mathbf{y} - X\tilde{\boldsymbol{\beta}}_U^*)'(\tilde{\Sigma}^{-1} \otimes I)(\mathbf{y} - X\tilde{\boldsymbol{\beta}}_U^*) - (\mathbf{y} - X\tilde{\boldsymbol{\beta}}_U)'(\tilde{\Sigma}^{-1} \otimes I)(\mathbf{y} - X\tilde{\boldsymbol{\beta}}_U)\\ &= T\,\mathrm{tr}(S_0\tilde{\Sigma}^{-1}) - TM \qquad (12.1.24)\end{aligned}$$

and the LM statistic is

$$\begin{aligned}\lambda_{LM} &= (\mathbf{y} - X\tilde{\boldsymbol{\beta}}_R^*)'(\tilde{\Sigma}^{*-1} \otimes I)(\mathbf{y} - X\tilde{\boldsymbol{\beta}}_R^*) - (\mathbf{y} - X\tilde{\boldsymbol{\beta}}_R)'(\tilde{\Sigma}^{*-1} \otimes I)(\mathbf{y} - X\tilde{\boldsymbol{\beta}}_R)\\ &= TM - T\,\mathrm{tr}(S_1\tilde{\Sigma}^{*-1}) \qquad (12.1.25)\end{aligned}$$

Both these statistics have an asymptotic $\chi^2_{(J)}$-distribution. For the special case where $X_1 = X_2 = \ldots = X_M$, we have $\tilde{\boldsymbol{\beta}}_R = \tilde{\boldsymbol{\beta}}_U$ and (12.1.25) becomes

$$\lambda_{LM} = TM - T\,\mathrm{tr}(\tilde{\Sigma}\tilde{\Sigma}^{*-1}) \qquad (12.1.26)$$

If, in addition, there are no cross-equation restrictions, and the restrictions on each equation are identical for all equations, we have $\tilde{\boldsymbol{\beta}}_R^* = \tilde{\boldsymbol{\beta}}_U^*$ and (12.1.24) becomes

$$\lambda_W = T\,\mathrm{tr}(\tilde{\Sigma}^*\tilde{\Sigma}^{-1}) - TM \qquad (12.1.27)$$

Similar simplifications can be obtained for g and $\hat{g}$ by rewriting each residual sum of squares in terms of the trace of the product of two matrices. For example, we can write $(\mathbf{y} - X\hat{\boldsymbol{\beta}})'(\Sigma^{-1} \otimes I)(\mathbf{y} - X\hat{\boldsymbol{\beta}}) = T \operatorname{tr}[S\Sigma^{-1}]$, where the (i,j)th element of S is given by $s_{ij} = (\mathbf{y}_i - X_i\hat{\boldsymbol{\beta}}_i)'(\mathbf{y}_j - X_j\hat{\boldsymbol{\beta}}_j)/T$. Finally, we note that the likelihood ratio test for H_0: $R\boldsymbol{\beta} = \mathbf{r}$ is given by

$$\lambda_{LR} = T \ln[|\tilde{\Sigma}^*|/|\tilde{\Sigma}|] \tag{12.1.28}$$

and it is possible to show that $\lambda_W \geq \lambda_{LR} \geq \lambda_{LM}$. Thus, although the three test statistics have the same asymptotic distribution, their finite sample distributions will not be the same. Rejection of H_0 can be favored by selecting λ_W a priori, while acceptance of H_0 can be favored by selecting λ_{LM} a priori. See Berndt and Savin (1977) for further details.

One difficulty with using a test procedure based on one of the above asymptotic test statistics is that it may not perform well in small samples. Some evidence of particularly bad small sample performance in the context of testing for homogeneity and symmetry in demand systems has been provided by Laitinen (1978), Meisner (1979), and Bera, Byron, and Jarque (1981). For the special case where $X_1 = X_2 = \ldots = X_M$ and the constraints are such that $R = I_M \otimes \mathbf{a}'$ (identical constraints on the coefficients of each equation), Laitinen shows that the exact distribution of $\hat{g}$ is the Hotelling T^2-distribution. [See, also, Malinvaud (1980, p. 230).] The critical values for the T^2-distribution are considerably higher than the corresponding ones for an asymptotic χ^2-distribution, implying that the latter test will tend to reject a correct null hypothesis more frequently than it should. In the more general situation of testing symmetry restrictions, an exact finite sample distribution is no longer available. However, using Monte Carlo methods, Meisner (1979) demonstrates that the problem of an excessive number of Type I errors still remains. Bera et al. (1981) show that even though the problem is not nearly as severe if the LM test is used instead of the Wald test, H_0 is still rejected more frequently than it should be. For some related results on the small sample efficiency of the restricted estimator and the accuracy of its estimated covariance matrix, see Fiebig and Theil (1983).

One possible procedure that may lead to a test with better finite sample properties is to use a statistic analogous to the F-statistic used to test a set of linear restrictions in the single equation case. For known Σ this statistic is given by

$$\lambda_F = \frac{(\mathbf{r} - R\hat{\boldsymbol{\beta}})(RCR')^{-1}(\mathbf{r} - R\hat{\boldsymbol{\beta}})/J}{(\mathbf{y} - X\hat{\boldsymbol{\beta}})'(\Sigma^{-1} \otimes I)(\mathbf{y} - X\hat{\boldsymbol{\beta}})/(MT - K)}$$

$$= \frac{g/J}{T \operatorname{tr}[S\Sigma^{-1}]/(MT - K)} \sim F_{(J, MT-K)} \tag{12.1.29}$$

where S is an $(M \times M)$ matrix with (i,j)th element equal to $(\mathbf{y}_i - X_i\hat{\boldsymbol{\beta}}_i)'(\mathbf{y}_j - X_j\hat{\boldsymbol{\beta}}_j)/T$. Now the denominator in (12.1.29) converges in probability to one, and so $J\lambda_F$ and g have the same asymptotic distribution—namely, $\chi^2_{(J)}$. The same result holds when Σ is replaced by $\hat{\Sigma}$, g becomes $\hat{g}$ and, correspondingly, λ_F

becomes $\hat{\lambda}_F$. Thus, from an asymptotic standpoint, the statistic in (12.1.29) leads us back to $\hat{g}$ and the $\chi^2_{(J)}$-distribution. However, it is possible that using $\hat{\lambda}_F$ in conjunction with the $F_{(J,MT-K)}$ distribution will lead to a better approximation in finite samples. Some justification for this procedure lies in the fact that $JF_{(J,MT-K)}$ converges in distribution to $\chi^2_{(J)}$. [See Theil (1971, p. 402).] Tests based on the F distribution will tend to reject H_0 less frequently than those based on the χ^2-distribution, and so this may go part way to overcoming some of the problems mentioned above. More research is obviously needed. For some examples see Theil (1971, p. 314–315, 335–345).

Related work on testing the equality of coefficient vectors in different equations has been carried out by Chow (1960), Fisher (1970), Toyoda (1974), Jayatissa (1977), Schmidt and Sickles (1977), Smith and Choi (1982), and Dufour (1982). Tests based on whether or not the restrictions $R\boldsymbol{\beta} = \mathbf{r}$ reduce mean square error, irrespective of their validity, have been studied by McElroy (1977b).

12.1.2b Testing for a Diagonal Covariance Matrix

Since the LS estimator $\mathbf{b} = (X'X)^{-1}X'\mathbf{y}$ is fully efficient when Σ is diagonal, it is useful to have test statistics for testing this hypothesis. Assuming normality, Breusch and Pagan (1980) have shown that the LM statistic for testing the null hypothesis of a diagonal Σ is given by

$$\lambda_{\text{LM}} = T \sum_{i=2}^{M} \sum_{j=1}^{i-1} r_{ij}^2 \tag{12.1.30}$$

where

$$r_{ij} = \frac{\hat{\sigma}_{ij}}{\sqrt{\hat{\sigma}_{ii}\hat{\sigma}_{jj}}} \tag{12.1.31}$$

and $\hat{\sigma}_{ij} = (\mathbf{y}_i - X_i\mathbf{b}_i)'(\mathbf{y}_j - X_j\mathbf{b}_j)/T$. Under H_0, λ_{LM} has an asymptotic $\chi^2_{[M(M-1)/2]}$ distribution. Note that $M(M-1)/2$ is half the number of off-diagonal elements in Σ.

For the two equation case Kariya (1981b) shows that the test with critical region $r_{12} > c$ is locally best invariant for one sided alternatives of the form H_1: $\sigma_{12} > 0$. He also derives the finite sample null distribution for r_{12}.

The likelihood ratio test can also be used to test the diagonality of Σ. It is possible to show that, apart from a constant, the maximized log-likelihood function is given by $(-T/2)\ln|\tilde{\Sigma}|$, and thus the likelihood ratio statistic can be written as

$$\lambda_{\text{LR}} = T\ln[|\tilde{\Sigma}^*|/|\tilde{\Sigma}|] \tag{12.1.32}$$

where $\tilde{\Sigma}^*$ is the constrained ML estimator for Σ. That is, $\tilde{\Sigma}^*$ is a diagonal matrix with variance estimates $\hat{\sigma}_{ii}$ based on the LS residuals. The matrix $\tilde{\Sigma}$ is the unconstrained ML estimator, but it may be adequate to approximate it with an estimator based on the residuals of the EGLS estimator $\hat{\hat{\boldsymbol{\beta}}}$. (See Equation 12.1.9.) Under H_0, λ_{LR} has an asymptotic $\chi^2_{[M(M-1)/2]}$ distribution.

12.1.3 Goodness of Fit Measures

When presenting applied econometric results it is customary to include some kind of goodness of fit measure that is a description of how well the model fits the data (or the data fit the model). As we discussed in Section 2.3, in the single equation case where X contains a constant term and $E[\mathbf{ee}'] = \sigma^2 I$, the coefficient of multiple determination or R^2 is an unambiguous measure. However, if X does not contain a constant, or $E[\mathbf{ee}'] = \sigma^2\boldsymbol{\Psi}$, there are a number of alternative possible measures, each with its own advantages and disadvantages. This is also true when considering a set of seemingly unrelated regression equations, and in this section we outline some of the possible "R^2 definitions" for this model.

One possibility for a measure of goodness of fit is the R^2 obtained by applying least squares to the whole system. If we measure the variation in $\mathbf{y}$ for a given equation around the mean for *that* equation, this definition is given by

$$R^2 = 1 - \frac{\hat{\mathbf{e}}'\hat{\mathbf{e}}}{\mathbf{y}'(I_M \otimes D_T)\mathbf{y}} \tag{12.1.33}$$

where $\hat{\mathbf{e}} = \mathbf{y} - X\mathbf{b}$ are the least squares residuals and $D_T = I_T - \mathbf{jj}'/T$, with $\mathbf{j} = (1, 1, \ldots, 1)'$. The matrix D_T transforms a given $\mathbf{y}_i$ from its original observations into deviations around its mean. Note that D_T is idempotent, and $[(I_M \otimes D_T)\mathbf{y}]'(I_M \otimes D_T)\mathbf{y} = \mathbf{y}'(I_M \otimes D_T)\mathbf{y}$. If R_i^2 is the coefficient of determination for the ith equation, it can be shown that [Dhrymes (1974)]

$$R^2 = \sum_{i=1}^{M} R_i^2 \frac{\mathbf{y}_i' D_T \mathbf{y}_i}{\mathbf{y}'(I_M \otimes D_T)\mathbf{y}} \tag{12.1.34}$$

and thus this definition is a weighted average of the coefficients for each equation with the weight of the ith equation given by that equation's proportion of the total dependent variable variation. Thus it has a certain amount of intuitive appeal. However, it is based on least squares residuals, not those of the efficient GLS estimator. Also, as Dhrymes points out, the ratio $R^2/(1 - R^2)$ cannot be expressed solely as a function of the observations and hence cannot be used to test the overall significance of the relationships, unless $\Sigma = \sigma^2 I$. The first problem can be overcome by using the GLS residuals $\tilde{\mathbf{e}} = \mathbf{y} - X\hat{\boldsymbol{\beta}}$ in place of $\hat{\mathbf{e}}$ in (12.1.33) but, as was the case with the single equation GLS approach, R^2 can then be negative.

Both problems can be overcome by using McElroy's (1977a) multiequation analog of Buse's (1973) result. This is

$$R_*^2 = 1 - \frac{\tilde{\mathbf{e}}'(\Sigma^{-1} \otimes I)\tilde{\mathbf{e}}}{\mathbf{y}'(\Sigma^{-1} \otimes D_T)\mathbf{y}} \tag{12.1.35}$$

Note that the denominator in the second term can be written as $\mathbf{y}'(\Sigma^{-1} \otimes D_T)\mathbf{y} = \mathbf{y}'(I \otimes D_T)'(\Sigma^{-1} \otimes I)(I \otimes D_T)\mathbf{y}$; therefore, the variation for a given equation is measured around the unweighted mean of $\mathbf{y}$ for that equation. The measure in (12.1.35) will be between zero and one, and it is monotonically related to the F statistic

$$F = \frac{R_*^2}{1 - R_*^2} \cdot \frac{MT - \Sigma_i K_i}{\Sigma_i K_i - M} \tag{12.1.36}$$

which is used to test the null hypothesis that all coefficients in the system are zero, with the exception of the intercepts in each equation. See Equation 12.1.29 for a general expression for the F test used to test any set of linear restrictions. However, one could still object to (12.1.35) on the grounds that it gives the proportion of explained variation in the transformed $\mathbf{y}$, not $\mathbf{y}$ in its original units. This is a legitimate objection but, as was the case with single-equation GLS, it is impossible to get a single measure that satisfies all the criteria.

For the case where $X_1 = X_2 = \ldots = X_M$ (or if these matrices are not equal, the system is estimated in its "unrestricted form"), some further measures have been provided by Hooper (1959), Glahn (1969), and Carter and Nagar (1977). See Dhrymes (1974, pp. 240–263) for a discussion on the relationship between canonical correlations, coefficients of vector correlation and alienation, and Hooper's measure. McElroy (1977a) points out the differences between the measures of Hooper, Glahn, and the one in (12.1.35).

If $E[\mathbf{ee}'] = \Omega \neq \Sigma \otimes I$, as occurs when the elements in each $\mathbf{e}_i$ are autocorrelated, the definition in (12.1.35) is no longer appropriate. Buse (1979) has extended his earlier work to allow for this case.

12.1.4 Bayesian Estimation

In this section we consider some aspects of Bayesian estimation of sets of regression equations. We begin by noting that, when $\mathbf{e}$ is normally distributed, the likelihood function can be written as

$$\begin{aligned} f(\mathbf{y}|\boldsymbol{\beta},\Sigma) &\propto |\Sigma|^{-T/2} \exp\{-\tfrac{1}{2}(\mathbf{y} - X\boldsymbol{\beta})'(\Sigma^{-1} \otimes I)(\mathbf{y} - X\boldsymbol{\beta})\} \\ &\propto |\Sigma|^{-T/2} \exp\{-\tfrac{1}{2} \operatorname{tr} A\Sigma^{-1}\} \end{aligned} \tag{12.1.37}$$

where A is an $(M \times M)$ matrix with (i,j)th element equal to $(\mathbf{y}_i - X_i\boldsymbol{\beta}_i)'(\mathbf{y}_j - X_j\boldsymbol{\beta}_j)$.

A commonly used noninformative or diffuse prior for $\boldsymbol{\beta}$ and Σ is given by $g(\boldsymbol{\beta},\Sigma) = g(\boldsymbol{\beta})g(\Sigma)$, where $g(\boldsymbol{\beta}) \propto$ constant and

$$g(\Sigma) \propto |\Sigma|^{-(M+1)/2} \tag{12.1.38}$$

When $M = 1$, (12.1.38) reduces to $g(\sigma_{11}) \propto \sigma_{11}^{-1}$, and, in addition, (12.1.38) can be viewed as the limiting form of an informative prior that is in the form of a

Wishart density. For further details and justification see Zellner (1971, Ch. 8) and references therein.

Combining (12.1.37) and (12.1.38) via Bayes' Theorem yields the joint posterior density

$$\begin{aligned} g(\boldsymbol{\beta},\Sigma|\mathbf{y}) &\propto |\Sigma|^{-(T+M+1)/2} \exp\{-\tfrac{1}{2}(\mathbf{y} - X\boldsymbol{\beta})'(\Sigma^{-1} \otimes I)(\mathbf{y} - X\boldsymbol{\beta})\} \\ &\propto |\Sigma|^{-(T+M+1)/2} \exp\{-\tfrac{1}{2} \operatorname{tr} A\Sigma^{-1}\} \end{aligned} \tag{12.1.39}$$

To analyze this density further we note that it can be written as $g(\boldsymbol{\beta},\Sigma|\mathbf{y}) = g(\boldsymbol{\beta}|\Sigma,\mathbf{y})g(\Sigma|\mathbf{y})$, where the conditional posterior density for $\boldsymbol{\beta}$ is given by

$$g(\boldsymbol{\beta}|\Sigma,\mathbf{y}) \propto \exp\{-\tfrac{1}{2}(\boldsymbol{\beta} - \hat{\boldsymbol{\beta}})'X'(\Sigma^{-1} \otimes I)X(\boldsymbol{\beta} - \hat{\boldsymbol{\beta}})\} \tag{12.1.40}$$

and the marginal posterior for Σ is given by

$$\begin{aligned} g(\Sigma|\mathbf{y}) &\propto |X'(\Sigma^{-1} \otimes I)X|^{-1/2}\Sigma^{-(T+M+1)/2} \\ &\qquad \exp\{-\tfrac{1}{2}(\mathbf{y} - X\hat{\boldsymbol{\beta}})'(\Sigma^{-1} \otimes I)(\mathbf{y} - X\hat{\boldsymbol{\beta}})\} \\ &\propto |X'(\Sigma^{-1} \otimes I)X|^{-1/2}\Sigma^{-(T+M+1)/2} \exp\{-\tfrac{1}{2} \operatorname{tr} S\Sigma^{-1}\} \end{aligned} \tag{12.1.41}$$

where S is an $M \times M$ matrix with (i,j)th element equal to $s_{ij} = (\mathbf{y}_i - X_i\hat{\boldsymbol{\beta}}_i)'(\mathbf{y}_j - X_j\hat{\boldsymbol{\beta}}_j)$, and $\hat{\boldsymbol{\beta}}' = (\hat{\boldsymbol{\beta}}_1', \hat{\boldsymbol{\beta}}_2', \ldots, \hat{\boldsymbol{\beta}}_M')$ is the GLS estimator $\hat{\boldsymbol{\beta}} = [X'(\Sigma^{-1} \otimes I)X]^{-1}X'(\Sigma^{-1} \otimes I)\mathbf{y}$. Furthermore, using the second expression in Equation 12.1.39, and properties of the inverted Wishart distribution [see Zellner (1971)], Σ can be integrated out of (12.1.39) to yield

$$g(\boldsymbol{\beta}|\mathbf{y}) \propto |A|^{-T/2} \tag{12.1.42}$$

The conditional posterior $g(\boldsymbol{\beta}|\Sigma,\mathbf{y})$ is a multivariate normal density with mean equal to the GLS estimator $\hat{\boldsymbol{\beta}}$. If we condition on an estimate for Σ based on LS residuals, say $\hat{\Sigma}$, then the mean becomes the Zellner EGLS estimator $\hat{\hat{\boldsymbol{\beta}}} = [X'(\hat{\Sigma}^{-1} \otimes I)X]^{-1}X'(\hat{\Sigma}^{-1} \otimes I)\mathbf{y}$.

Unfortunately, it is difficult to further analyze the marginal posterior densities for $\boldsymbol{\beta}$ and Σ unless we make additional assumptions about X or Σ, or use an approximation. One special case that does lead to tractable results is the traditional multivariate regression model where $X_1 = X_2 = \ldots = X_M = \bar{X}$ (say). In this case $X = I \otimes \bar{X}$, $\hat{\boldsymbol{\beta}} = \mathbf{b}$, and it is possible to write

$$A = (Y - \bar{X}B)'(Y - \bar{X}B) = S + (B - \hat{B})'\bar{X}'\bar{X}(B - \hat{B}) \tag{12.1.43}$$

where

$$\begin{aligned} Y &= (\mathbf{y}_1, \mathbf{y}_2, \ldots, \mathbf{y}_M), \\ B &= (\boldsymbol{\beta}_1, \boldsymbol{\beta}_2, \ldots, \boldsymbol{\beta}_M), \\ \hat{B} &= (\mathbf{b}_1, \mathbf{b}_2, \ldots, \mathbf{b}_M) = (X'X)^{-1}X'Y, \end{aligned}$$

and

$$S = (Y - \bar{X}\hat{B})'(Y - \bar{X}\hat{B})$$

The marginal posterior densities then become

$$g(\Sigma|\mathbf{y}) \propto \Sigma^{-(T+M-k+1)/2} \exp\{-\tfrac{1}{2} \operatorname{tr} S\Sigma^{-1}\} \tag{12.1.44}$$

and

$$g(\boldsymbol{\beta}|\mathbf{y}) \propto |S + (B - \hat{B})'\bar{X}'\bar{X}(B - \hat{B})|^{-T/2} \tag{12.1.45}$$

where k is the column dimension of $\bar{X}$. These densities are respectively, an inverted Wishart and a generalized multivariate t distribution. From them it is possible to derive the marginal posterior density for a submatrix of Σ, or a subvector of $\boldsymbol{\beta}$. For example, if we wish to make inferences about the ith subvector $\boldsymbol{\beta}_i$, it is possible to show that the marginal posterior density for $\boldsymbol{\beta}_i$ is in the multivariate-t form

$$g(\boldsymbol{\beta}_i|\mathbf{y}) \propto [s_{ii} + (\boldsymbol{\beta}_i - \mathbf{b}_i)'\bar{X}'\bar{X}(\boldsymbol{\beta}_i - \mathbf{b}_i)]^{-(T-M+1)/2} \tag{12.1.46}$$

Further details of the properties of the inverted Wishart and generalized t distributions can be found in Zellner (1971, Ch. 8). Zellner also indicates how some progress can be made on the more general model where the X_i's are not identical by treating it within the traditional multivariate framework with restrictions on the coefficients [see also Drèze (1977) and Zellner (1979)]; Zellner (1971) goes on to discuss informative priors and some restrictive aspects of a simple natural conjugate prior.

12.1.5 Extensions of the Model

There have been a number of other studies and extensions of the seemingly unrelated regressions model. These include the effects of misspecification [Rao (1974), Srivastava and Srivastava (1983)], the inclusion of random coefficients [Singh and Ullah (1974)], nonlinear equations with related disturbances [Gallant (1975)], the inclusion of error components [Avery (1977), Baltagi (1980), Prucha (1984), Verbon (1980)], the use of biased estimators with lower mean square error [Zellner and Vandaele (1971), Srivastava (1973)], estimation and inference for heteroscedastic systems of equations [Duncan (1983)], and estimation under inequality variance-covariance restrictions [Zellner (1979)].

12.2 SETS OF EQUATIONS WITH UNEQUAL NUMBERS OF OBSERVATIONS

In Section 12.1 we studied a set of equations where the number of observations on each equation was the same. However, this may not always be the case. If one were investigating investment functions for a number of firms, for example, it would not be surprising to find that the available data on different firms correspond to different time periods. Thus, in this section, we allow for the possibility that the available number of observations is different for different equations, and we investigate the implications for the estimation and hypothesis testing results in Section 12.1.

There are two main consequences. The GLS estimator of the vector containing the coefficients from all the equations can still be obtained in a straightforward manner, but it does not reduce to the same expression obtained when the numbers of observations are equal. Second, the choice of an estimator for the disturbance covariance becomes a problem. Following Schmidt (1977), we will illustrate these facts with a system of two seemingly unrelated regressions

$$\begin{bmatrix} \mathbf{y}_1 \\ \mathbf{y}_2 \end{bmatrix} = \begin{bmatrix} X_1 & 0 \\ 0 & X_2 \end{bmatrix} \begin{bmatrix} \boldsymbol{\beta}_1 \\ \boldsymbol{\beta}_2 \end{bmatrix} + \begin{bmatrix} \mathbf{e}_1 \\ \mathbf{e}_2 \end{bmatrix} \tag{12.2.1}$$

where there are T observations on the first equation and $(T + N)$ observations on the second equation. When (12.2.1) is written as

$$\mathbf{y} = X\boldsymbol{\beta} + \mathbf{e} \tag{12.2.2}$$

this implies that $\mathbf{y}$ and $\mathbf{e}$ are of dimension $(2T + N)$, X is $[(2T + N) \times (K_1 + K_2)]$, and $\boldsymbol{\beta}$ is $[(K_1 + K_2) \times 1]$. In line with the earlier assumptions it will be assumed that the vectors $(e_{1t}, e_{2t})'$ are independently and identically distributed with zero mean and covariance matrix

$$\Sigma = \begin{pmatrix} \sigma_{11} & \sigma_{12} \\ \sigma_{12} & \sigma_{22} \end{pmatrix} \tag{12.2.3}$$

This, in turn, implies that

$$E[\mathbf{ee}'] = \Omega = \begin{bmatrix} \sigma_{11}I_T & \sigma_{12}I_T & 0 \\ \sigma_{12}I_T & \sigma_{22}I_T & 0 \\ 0 & 0 & \sigma_{22}I_N \end{bmatrix} \neq \Sigma \otimes I_T \tag{12.2.4}$$

and the GLS estimator is

$$\hat{\boldsymbol{\beta}} = (X'\Omega^{-1}X)^{-1}X'\Omega^{-1}\mathbf{y} \neq [X'(\Sigma^{-1} \otimes I)X]^{-1}X'(\Sigma^{-1} \otimes I)\mathbf{y} \tag{12.2.5}$$

Thus, although the GLS estimator is readily attainable, it does not reduce to the expression given in (12.1.7). To obtain the corresponding expression, we can partition X_2 and $\mathbf{y}_2$ as

$$X_2 = \begin{bmatrix} X_2^* \\ X_2^0 \end{bmatrix} \quad \text{and} \quad \mathbf{y}_2 = \begin{bmatrix} \mathbf{y}_2^* \\ \mathbf{y}_2^0 \end{bmatrix}$$

where X_2^* and $\mathbf{y}_2^*$ contain T observations and X_2^0 and $\mathbf{y}_2^0$ contain N observations.

Then $\hat{\boldsymbol{\beta}}$ can be written as

$$\hat{\boldsymbol{\beta}} = \begin{bmatrix} \hat{\boldsymbol{\beta}}_1 \\ \hat{\boldsymbol{\beta}}_2 \end{bmatrix} = \begin{bmatrix} \sigma^{11}X_1'X_1 & \sigma^{12}X_1'X_2^* \\ \sigma^{12}X_2^{*\prime}X_1 & \sigma^{22}X_2^{*\prime}X_2^* + \dfrac{1}{\sigma_{22}}X_2^{0\prime}X_2^0 \end{bmatrix}^{-1} \times \begin{bmatrix} \sigma^{11}X_1'\mathbf{y}_1 + \sigma^{12}X_1'\mathbf{y}_2^* \\ \sigma^{12}X_2^{*\prime}\mathbf{y}_1 + \sigma^{22}X_2^{*\prime}\mathbf{y}_2^* + \dfrac{1}{\sigma_{22}}X_2^{0\prime}\mathbf{y}_2^0 \end{bmatrix} \tag{12.2.6}$$

where σ^{ij} is the (i,j)th element of Σ^{-1}. If the additional N observations $(X_2^0,\mathbf{y}_2^0)$ are ignored, this estimator becomes identical to $\hat{\boldsymbol{\beta}}$ in (12.1.7).

When Σ is unknown, the more usual case, $\hat{\boldsymbol{\beta}}$ is unobtainable so that an estimator for Σ must be found. Five possible estimators are discussed and evaluated in a Monte Carlo experiment by Schmidt (1977). To describe these estimators, we let $\hat{\mathbf{e}}_1$ and $\hat{\mathbf{e}}_2$ be the least squares residuals from the first and second equations, respectively, and let $\hat{\mathbf{e}}_2' = (\hat{\mathbf{e}}_2^{*\prime}, \hat{\mathbf{e}}_2^{0\prime})$ be partitioned conformably with $\mathbf{y}_2$. Also, define $S_{11} = \hat{\mathbf{e}}_1'\hat{\mathbf{e}}_1/T$, $S_{12} = \hat{\mathbf{e}}_1'\hat{\mathbf{e}}_2^*/T$, $S_{22}^* = \hat{\mathbf{e}}_2^{*\prime}\hat{\mathbf{e}}_2^*/T$, $S_{22}^0 = \hat{\mathbf{e}}_2^{0\prime}\hat{\mathbf{e}}_2^0/N$, and $S_{22} = \hat{\mathbf{e}}_2'\hat{\mathbf{e}}_2/(T + N)$.

The five estimators are

1. $\hat{\sigma}_{11} = S_{11}, \quad \hat{\sigma}_{22} = S_{22}^*, \quad \hat{\sigma}_{12} = S_{12}.$ (12.2.7)
2. $\hat{\sigma}_{11} = S_{11}, \quad \hat{\sigma}_{22} = S_{22}, \quad \hat{\sigma}_{12} = S_{12}.$ (12.2.8)
3. $\hat{\sigma}_{11} = S_{11}, \quad \hat{\sigma}_{22} = S_{22}, \quad \hat{\sigma}_{12} = S_{12}(S_{22}/S_{22}^*)^{1/2}.$ (12.2.9)
4. $\hat{\sigma}_{11} = S_{11} - (N/(T + N))(S_{12}/S_{22}^*)^2(S_{22}^* - S_{22}^0), \quad \hat{\sigma}_{22} = S_{22},$ $\hat{\sigma}_{12} = S_{12}(S_{22}/S_{22}^*)^{1/2}.$ (12.2.10)
5. Maximum likelihood estimation under the assumption that $(e_{1t},e_{2t})'$ has a bivariate normal distribution.

These estimators differ in the extent to which they utilize the additional N observations on y_2. The first ignores the extra observations; the second utilizes them in the estimation of σ_{22}, but this can lead to an estimate of Σ that is not positive definite; the third estimates both σ_{12} and σ_{22} with the extra observations; and the fourth and fifth use all the observations to estimate all the components in Σ.

All these estimators of Σ are consistent and lead to EGLS estimators of $\boldsymbol{\beta}$ that have the same asymptotic distribution as the GLS estimator. However, because the estimators in (4) and (5) use all the observations, in finite samples we might expect that they would lead to EGLS estimators for $\boldsymbol{\beta}$ that are better than those obtained from variance estimators (1) to (3). This point was investigated by Schmidt in his Monte Carlo study. Some of his general conclusions were:

1. As N increases for fixed T, the efficiency of the various estimators does not necessarily increase and the relative performance of estimators that use all the observations is not always better.
2. When σ_{12} is high, 0.925 in the experiment, the maximum likelihood estimator is best, but its superiority decreases with decreasing sample size.
3. For $T = 10$ and σ_{12} anything but high, the maximum likelihood estimator is particularly bad.
4. The second variance estimation procedure can yield an estimate of Σ that is singular, and the resulting EGLS estimator for $\boldsymbol{\beta}$ may not possess finite moments.

Although there seemed to be no clear advantages from using the extra observations (except when σ_{12} is high), Schmidt recommends using procedure (4) because the results from a single Monte Carlo study are necessarily limited, and, it is an intuitively more pleasing estimator. Also, there were no occasions when it did substantially worse than any of the other estimators.

The same problem, for a more general model, has been studied from the Bayesian point of view by Swamy and Mehta (1975). They investigated the model outlined in the next section, where the disturbances are assumed to follow a first-order autoregressive process.

12.3 SETS OF EQUATIONS WITH FIRST-ORDER AUTOREGRESSIVE DISTURBANCES

In this section we return to the assumption of equal numbers of observations for each equation and extend the model of Section 12.1 by allowing for the possible existence of first-order autoregressive disturbances. As mentioned earlier, a system of seemingly unrelated regressions will often consist of time series observations on a number of cross-sectional units, each cross-sectional unit being described by one equation from the system. In such a system each equation's disturbance vector represents a time series, and so these vectors are likely to exhibit serial correlation. In this section we consider a simple model that allows for this possibility, namely, one with first-order autoregressive disturbances.

The seemingly unrelated regressions (SUR) model we are considering is given by

$$\begin{bmatrix} \mathbf{y}_1 \\ \mathbf{y}_2 \\ \vdots \\ \mathbf{y}_M \end{bmatrix} = \begin{bmatrix} X_1 & & & \\ & X_2 & & \\ & & \ddots & \\ & & & X_M \end{bmatrix} \begin{bmatrix} \boldsymbol{\beta}_1 \\ \boldsymbol{\beta}_2 \\ \vdots \\ \boldsymbol{\beta}_M \end{bmatrix} + \begin{bmatrix} \mathbf{e}_1 \\ \mathbf{e}_2 \\ \vdots \\ \mathbf{e}_M \end{bmatrix} \tag{12.3.1}$$

or, more compactly, by

$$\mathbf{y} = X\boldsymbol{\beta} + \mathbf{e} \tag{12.3.2}$$

where $\mathbf{y}$ is of dimension $(MT \times 1)$, X_i is $(T \times K_i)$, X is $(MT \times K)$, where $K = \Sigma_{i=1}^{M} K_i$, $\boldsymbol{\beta}$ is $(K \times 1)$ and $\mathbf{e}$ is $(MT \times 1)$. It is assumed that $(e_{1t}, e_{2t}, \ldots, e_{Mt})'$ is generated by a stationary, first-order autoregressive [AR(1)] process represented by

$$\begin{bmatrix} e_{1t} \\ e_{2t} \\ \vdots \\ e_{Mt} \end{bmatrix} = \begin{bmatrix} \rho_{11} & \rho_{12} & \cdots & \rho_{1M} \\ \rho_{21} & \rho_{22} & \cdots & \rho_{2M} \\ \vdots & \vdots & & \vdots \\ \rho_{M1} & \rho_{M2} & \cdots & \rho_{MM} \end{bmatrix} \begin{bmatrix} e_{1,t-1} \\ e_{2,t-1} \\ \vdots \\ e_{M,t-1} \end{bmatrix} + \begin{bmatrix} v_{1t} \\ v_{2t} \\ \vdots \\ v_{Mt} \end{bmatrix} \tag{12.3.3}$$

or, in matrix notation, as

$$\mathbf{e}_{(t)} = R\mathbf{e}_{(t-1)} + \mathbf{v}_{(t)} \tag{12.3.4}$$

where the $\mathbf{v}_{(t)}$ are independent identically distributed random vectors with mean zero, $E[\mathbf{v}_{(t)}] = \mathbf{0}$, and covariance matrix

$$E[\mathbf{v}_{(t)}\mathbf{v}_{(t)}'] = \Sigma = \begin{bmatrix} \sigma_{11} & \sigma_{12} & \cdots & \sigma_{1M} \\ \sigma_{21} & \sigma_{22} & \cdots & \sigma_{2M} \\ \vdots & \vdots & & \vdots \\ \sigma_{M1} & \sigma_{M2} & \cdots & \sigma_{MM} \end{bmatrix} \tag{12.3.5}$$

That is, $E[v_{it}] = 0$ and $E[v_{it}v_{js}] = \sigma_{ij}$ for $t = s$ and zero otherwise. The AR(1) representation in (12.3.3) and (12.3.4) extends the single equation case by allowing the current disturbance for a given equation to depend on the previous period's disturbance in all equations. It is often referred to as a *vector autoregressive model* to distinguish it from the simpler case where R is diagonal and each e_{it} depends only on the previous disturbance in the ith equation. That is, $e_{it} = \rho_{ii}e_{i,t-1} + v_{it}$. The general process in (12.3.4) will be stationary if the roots of $|I - Rz| = 0$ are greater than one in absolute value.

Note the notational distinction between the vector definitions $\mathbf{e}_{(t)}$ and $\mathbf{v}_{(t)}$ and those given by $\mathbf{e}_i$ and $\mathbf{v}_i$. The $(M \times 1)$ vector $\mathbf{e}_{(t)}$ contains the tth disturbances from all equations, while the $(T \times 1)$ vector $\mathbf{e}_i$ contains all the disturbances for the ith equation; $\mathbf{v}_{(t)}$ and $\mathbf{v}_i$ are defined in a similar fashion. The assumptions we have made about $\mathbf{v}_{(t)}$ could also be written as

$$E[\mathbf{v}_i\mathbf{v}_j'] = \sigma_{ij}I_T \quad \text{and} \quad E[\mathbf{v}\mathbf{v}'] = \Sigma \otimes I_T \tag{12.3.6}$$

where $\mathbf{v}' = (\mathbf{v}_1', \mathbf{v}_2', \ldots, \mathbf{v}_M')$.

The complete covariance matrix $E[\mathbf{ee}'] = \Omega$ is complicated, but, fortunately, we do not need to specify it explicitly in order to estimate $\boldsymbol{\beta}$. Nevertheless, it is instructive to indicate how it can be derived. For this purpose we define $V_s = E[\mathbf{e}_{(t)}\mathbf{e}'_{(t-s)}]$ as the matrix of covariances for disturbances that are s-periods apart. Thus, $V_0 = E[\mathbf{e}_{(t)}\mathbf{e}'_{(t)}]$ gives the contemporaneous covariance matrix for the e_{it}. From (12.3.4) and the fact that $\mathbf{e}_{(t)}$ is stationary we can write

$$V_0 = RV_0R' + \Sigma \tag{12.3.7}$$

Solving this equation for the elements of V_0 gives [Guilkey and Schmidt (1973)]

$$\text{vec}(V_0) = (I - R \otimes R)^{-1}\,\text{vec}(\Sigma) \tag{12.3.8}$$

where vec(·) is obtained by stacking the columns of a matrix. For example,

$$\text{vec}(\Sigma) = (\sigma_{11}, \sigma_{21}, \ldots, \sigma_{M1}, \sigma_{12}, \ldots, \sigma_{M2}, \ldots, \sigma_{MM})'$$

Then, again using (12.3.4), the other elements of Ω can be found from

$$V_s = R^sV_0 \tag{12.3.9}$$

If we define $E[\mathbf{e}_i\mathbf{e}_j'] = \Omega_{ij}$, where

$$E[\mathbf{ee}'] = \Omega = \begin{bmatrix} \Omega_{11} & \Omega_{12} & \cdots & \Omega_{1M} \\ \Omega_{21} & \Omega_{22} & \cdots & \Omega_{2M} \\ \vdots & \vdots & & \vdots \\ \Omega_{M1} & \Omega_{M2} & \cdots & \Omega_{MM} \end{bmatrix} \tag{12.3.10}$$

then the diagonal elements of a given Ω_{ij} are identical and equal to the (i,j)th element of V_0; the matrix V_1 provides the elements adjacent to the diagonal in each Ω_{ij}; V_2 provides the elements two positions from the diagonal, and so on. Note that Ω_{ij} is not necessarily symmetric unless $i = j$. For details of the structure of these matrices in the case where R is diagonal see Exercise 12.4.

12.3.1 Estimation When *R* is Diagonal

We turn now to the problem of estimating $\boldsymbol{\beta}$, and we begin by considering the special case where R is diagonal and where, for the moment, R and Σ are assumed known. A diagonal R implies that (12.3.4) can be written as

$$e_{it} = \rho_{ii}e_{i,t-1} + v_{it} \tag{12.3.11}$$

so that, in this case, the value of the disturbance e_{it} does not depend on the lagged disturbances in other equations.

As long as MT is not too large, so that inversion of Ω is computationally feasible, we could derive Ω in the manner described above and estimate $\boldsymbol{\beta}$ via the generalized least squares (GLS) estimator

$$\hat{\boldsymbol{\beta}} = (X'\Omega^{-1}X)^{-1}X'\Omega^{-1}\mathbf{y} \tag{12.3.12}$$

This estimator is minimum variance within the class of all linear unbiased estimators and has a covariance matrix $(X'\Omega^{-1}X)^{-1}$. However, in practice MT could be quite large and in general, it is easier to transform the observations so that the GLS estimator $\hat{\boldsymbol{\beta}}$ can be obtained by applying the GLS-SUR estimator of Section 12.1 directly to the transformed observations. To do this, we need an $(MT \times MT)$ transformation matrix P such that

$$P\Omega P' = \Sigma \otimes I \tag{12.3.13}$$

This implies that $\Omega^{-1} = P'(\Sigma^{-1} \otimes I)P$ and that Equation 12.3.12 can be written as

$$\hat{\boldsymbol{\beta}} = (X^{*\prime}(\Sigma^{-1} \otimes I_T)X^*)^{-1}X^{*\prime}(\Sigma^{-1} \otimes I_T)\mathbf{y}^* \tag{12.3.14}$$

where $X^* = PX$ and $\mathbf{y}^* = P\mathbf{y}$ are the transformed observations. Note that Equation 12.3.14 is the form of the GLS-SUR estimator given in Section 12.1.

A matrix P, that satisfies (12.3.13) is

$$\underset{(MT \times MT)}{P} = \begin{bmatrix} P_{11} & 0 & \cdots & 0 \\ P_{21} & P_{22} & \cdots & 0 \\ \vdots & \vdots & \ddots & \vdots \\ P_{M1} & P_{M2} & \cdots & P_{MM} \end{bmatrix} \tag{12.3.15}$$

where

$$\underset{(T \times T)}{P_{ii}} = \begin{bmatrix} \alpha_{ii} & 0 & 0 & \cdots & 0 \\ -\rho_{ii} & 1 & 0 & \cdots & 0 \\ 0 & -\rho_{ii} & 1 & \cdots & 0 \\ \vdots & \vdots & \vdots & \ddots & \vdots \\ 0 & 0 & 0 & \cdots & 1 \end{bmatrix}, \qquad i = 1, 2, \ldots, M \tag{12.3.16}$$

$$\underset{(T \times T)}{P_{ij}} = \begin{bmatrix} \alpha_{ij} & 0 & \cdots & 0 \\ 0 & 0 & \cdots & 0 \\ \vdots & \vdots & \ddots & \vdots \\ 0 & 0 & \cdots & 0 \end{bmatrix}, \qquad i \neq j \tag{12.3.17}$$

and the elements of

$$\underset{(M \times M)}{A} = \begin{bmatrix} \alpha_{11} & 0 & \cdots & 0 \\ \alpha_{21} & \alpha_{22} & \cdots & 0 \\ \vdots & \vdots & \ddots & \vdots \\ \alpha_{M1} & \alpha_{M2} & \cdots & \alpha_{MM} \end{bmatrix} \tag{12.3.18}$$

are chosen such that $\Sigma = AV_0A'$.

We will return to the elements of A and how they are determined in a moment. First, note that the transformed observations in $\mathbf{y}^* = P\mathbf{y}$ (and it is similar for the variables in $X^* = PX$) are given by

$$y_{i1}^* = \sum_{j=1}^{i} \alpha_{ij} y_{j1}, \qquad i = 1, 2, \ldots, M \tag{12.3.19}$$

and

$$y_{it}^* = y_{it} - \rho_{ii} y_{i,t-1}, \qquad i = 1, 2, \ldots, M; t = 2, 3, \ldots, T \tag{12.3.20}$$

For all observations except the first, this transformation is the familiar one used for a single equation with AR(1) errors. This is clear from Equation 12.3.20 where each regression equation is transformed separately using the autoregressive parameter for the equation in question. However, from Equation 12.3.19, we can see that the transformed *first* observation for a given equation depends on the first observations in other equations.

To demonstrate that the above transformation satisfies the condition $P\Omega P' = \Sigma \otimes I$ we need to show that the transformed disturbance vector $\mathbf{e}^* = P\mathbf{e}$ is such that $E[\mathbf{e}^*\mathbf{e}^{*\prime}] = \Sigma \otimes I$, or, equivalently, that $E[\mathbf{e}_{(t)}^*\mathbf{e}_{(t)}^{*\prime}] = \Sigma$ and $E[\mathbf{e}_{(t)}^*\mathbf{e}_{(s)}^{*\prime}] = 0$ for $t \neq s$, where $\mathbf{e}_{(t)}^* = (e_{1t}^*, e_{2t}^*, \ldots, e_{Mt}^*)'$. Since

$$\mathbf{e}_{(t)}^* = \mathbf{e}_{(t)} - R\mathbf{e}_{(t-1)} = \mathbf{v}_{(t)} \qquad \text{for} \qquad t = 2, 3, \ldots, T \tag{12.3.21}$$

and the $\mathbf{v}_{(t)}$ possess the required properties, it is clear that the transformation is satisfactory for $t > 1$. To prove that it is also satisfactory for $t = 1$ we note that $\mathbf{e}_{(1)}^* = A\mathbf{e}_{(1)}$ and, therefore,

$$E[\mathbf{e}_{(1)}^*\mathbf{e}_{(1)}^{*\prime}] = AE[\mathbf{e}_{(1)}\mathbf{e}_{(1)}']A' = AV_0A' = \Sigma \tag{12.3.22}$$

Furthermore, $\mathbf{e}_{(1)}^*$ is independent of $\mathbf{v}_{(t)}$ $(t > 1)$ because $\mathbf{e}_{(1)}$ is independent of $\mathbf{v}_{(t)}$.

The elements of A can be found via triangular or Cholesky decomposition [Graybill (1969, p. 299)] of Σ and V_0. If H and B are lower triangular matrices such that $\Sigma = HH'$ and $V_0 = BB'$, then a lower triangular matrix A such that $\Sigma = AV_0A'$ is given by $A = HB^{-1}$. A closed form expression for A for the $M = 2$ case is given in Exercise 12.4. However, in general, it is easier to obtain A numerically than to derive closed form expressions such as this one.

Despite the fact that A can be obtained relatively easily numerically, it is clear that transformation of the first observation in each equation is a cumbersome procedure. Also, as we mention below, when the σ_{ij}'s and ρ_{ii}'s need to be estimated, it leads to an additional step in the estimation procedure. If one is prepared to ignore the first observation in each equation and use instead an approximate GLS estimator, the transformation procedure is simplified greatly. In this case P becomes an $(M(T-1) \times MT)$ block diagonal matrix, call it P_0, with ith diagonal block given by

$$\underset{(T-1)\times T}{P_{0ii}} = \begin{bmatrix} -\rho_{ii} & 1 & 0 & \cdots & 0 \\ 0 & -\rho_{ii} & 1 & \cdots & 0 \\ \vdots & \vdots & \vdots & & \vdots \\ 0 & 0 & 0 & \cdots & 1 \end{bmatrix} \tag{12.3.23}$$

Thus each equation can be transformed separately with its own ρ_{ii}; the transformed variables become $X_0^* = P_0 X$ and $\mathbf{y}_0^* = P_0\mathbf{y}$; and the approximate GLS estimator is given by

$$\hat{\boldsymbol{\beta}}_0 = (X_0^{*\prime}(\Sigma^{-1} \otimes I_{T-1})X_0^*)^{-1}X_0^{*\prime}(\Sigma^{-1} \otimes I_{T-1})\mathbf{y}_0^* \tag{12.3.24}$$

For known σ_{ij} and ρ_{ii} this estimator has covariance matrix given by

$$\Sigma_{\hat{\boldsymbol{\beta}}_0} = (X'P_0'(\Sigma^{-1} \otimes I_{T-1})P_0X)^{-1}$$

and because it ignores M observations, it will be less efficient than $\hat{\boldsymbol{\beta}}$.

It is worth pointing out the slight difference between the above approach and that of Parks (1967). He suggests two alternative estimators, both of which retain all observations and use a block diagonal transformation matrix. The first, like $\hat{\boldsymbol{\beta}}_0$, involves a straightforward transformation but, because it uses all observations, it is inconsistent with the assumption that the e_{it}'s possess stationary covariances. The second estimator overcomes this problem but at the cost of assuming that

$$E[v_{i1}v_{j1}] \neq \sigma_{ij} = E[v_{it}v_{jt}], \qquad t \neq 1$$

When σ_{ij} and ρ_{ii} are unknown and are replaced by estimates $\hat{\sigma}_{ij}$ and $\hat{\rho}_{ii}$, the GLS estimator $\hat{\boldsymbol{\beta}}$ becomes an estimated generalized least squares (EGLS) estimator $\hat{\hat{\boldsymbol{\beta}}}$ and the estimator $\hat{\boldsymbol{\beta}}_0$ becomes an approximate EGLS estimator $\hat{\hat{\boldsymbol{\beta}}}_0$. Both these new estimators ($\hat{\hat{\boldsymbol{\beta}}}$ and $\hat{\hat{\boldsymbol{\beta}}}_0$) have the same asymptotic properties and, in finite samples, $\hat{\hat{\boldsymbol{\beta}}}$ is not necessarily more efficient than $\hat{\hat{\boldsymbol{\beta}}}_0$.

To estimate $\boldsymbol{\beta}$ when the σ_{ij} and ρ_{ii} are unknown, the following procedure can be used.

1. Apply LS separately to each equation and estimate each ρ_{ii} from the corresponding residuals. That is,

$$\hat{\rho}_{ii} = \frac{\sum_{t=2}^{T} \hat{e}_{it}\hat{e}_{i,t-1}}{\sum_{t=2}^{T} \hat{e}_{i,t-1}^2}, \qquad i = 1, 2, \ldots, M \tag{12.3.25}$$

where $\hat{\mathbf{e}}_i = (\hat{e}_{i1}, \hat{e}_{i2}, \ldots, \hat{e}_{iT})' = \mathbf{y}_i - X_i\mathbf{b}_i = (I_T - X_i(X_i'X_i)^{-1}X_i')\mathbf{y}_i$.

2. Use $\hat{P}_{0ii}$, the matrix P_{0ii} with each ρ_{ii} replaced by $\hat{\rho}_{ii}$, to transform the observations on the ith equation. For the dependent variable, and it is similar for all the explanatory variables, this means that the transformed observations are given by

$$y_{it}^* = y_{it} - \hat{\rho}_{ii} y_{i,t-1}, \qquad i = 1, 2, \ldots, M; \qquad t = 2, 3, \ldots, T \tag{12.3.26}$$

where, in contrast to Equations 12.3.19 and 12.3.20 the "*" will now denote observations transformed with *estimated* values of ρ_{ii} and/or σ_{ij}. Note that we have only transformed $M(T - 1)$ observations.

3. Using, for each equation, the appropriate $(T - 1)$ transformed observations, re-estimate the equations separately and estimate the σ_{ij} from the residuals of these estimated equations. The residuals are given by

$$\hat{\mathbf{v}}_i = \mathbf{y}_{0i}^* - X_{0i}^*\mathbf{b}_i^* = (I_{T-1} - X_{0i}^*(X_{0i}^{*\prime}X_{0i}^*)^{-1}X_{0i}^{*\prime})\mathbf{y}_{0i}^* \tag{12.3.27}$$

where $\mathbf{y}_{0i}^* = \hat{P}_{0ii}\mathbf{y}_i$ and $X_{0i}^* = \hat{P}_{0ii}X_i$; and the estimated covariances by

$$\hat{\sigma}_{ij} = \frac{\hat{\mathbf{v}}_i'\hat{\mathbf{v}}_j}{T - 1} \tag{12.3.28}$$

4. Find $\hat{A}$, the matrix A (Equation 12.3.18) with each ρ_{ii} and σ_{ij} replaced by their corresponding estimates $\hat{\rho}_{ii}$ and $\hat{\sigma}_{ij}$. Based on $\hat{A}$, transform the initial observations according to Equation 12.3.19 and combine these M transformed observations with the other $M(T - 1)$ transformed observations that were obtained in step 2. If $\hat{P}$ denotes the complete $(MT \times MT)$ transformation matrix formed using $\hat{A}$ and $\hat{P}_{0ii}$, $(i = 1, 2, \ldots, M)$, the complete set of transformed observations is now given by $X^* = \hat{P}X$ and $\mathbf{y}^* = \hat{P}\mathbf{y}$.

5. Apply the SUR estimation technique to the transformed observations to obtain the EGLS estimator

$$\hat{\hat{\boldsymbol{\beta}}} = [X^{*\prime}(\hat{\Sigma}^{-1} \otimes I_T)X^*]^{-1}X^{*\prime}(\hat{\Sigma}^{-1} \otimes I_T)\mathbf{y}^* \tag{12.3.29}$$

where $\hat{\Sigma}$ is the matrix of estimated σ_{ij}'s.

If one is content with an approximate EGLS estimator that is based only on $M(T - 1)$ observations, step 4 could be omitted and step 5 replaced by

$$\hat{\hat{\boldsymbol{\beta}}}_0 = [X_0^{*\prime}(\hat{\Sigma}^{-1} \otimes I_{T-1})X_0^*]^{-1}X_0^{*\prime}(\hat{\Sigma}^{-1} \otimes I_{T-1})\mathbf{y}_0^* \tag{12.3.30}$$

where $X_0^* = \hat{P}_0X$ and $\mathbf{y}_0^* = \hat{P}_0\mathbf{y}$.

Under appropriate conditions [Parks (1967)] both estimators will be asymptotically efficient with an asymptotic covariance matrix consistently estimated by $[X^{*\prime}(\hat{\Sigma}^{-1} \otimes I_T)X^*]^{-1}$ or by $[X_0^{*\prime}(\hat{\Sigma}^{-1} \otimes I_{T-1})X_0^*]^{-1}$. Also, consistent estimates of the ρ_{ii} and σ_{ij} can be obtained in a number of other ways, all of which lead to asymptotically equivalent estimators for $\boldsymbol{\beta}$. For example, instead of using step 3, we could replace the residuals in (12.3.27) with those obtained from the regression in (12.3.25)—namely,

$$\tilde{v}_{it} = \hat{e}_{it} - \hat{\rho}_{ii}\hat{e}_{i,t-1}, \qquad i = 1, 2, \ldots, M; \quad t = 2, 3, \ldots, T \tag{12.3.31}$$

Another possible variation is, in step 1, to apply the SUR estimator to the untransformed data and to use the resulting residuals, instead of those from least squares, to estimate the ρ_{ii}. In addition, if nonlinear least squares and maximum likelihood estimation are considered, this leads to some further alternative estimators, which differ depending on the function being minimized and on the treatment of the initial observations. See, for example, Kmenta and Gilbert (1970) and Magnus (1978).

12.3.2 Estimation with Nondiagonal *R*

We turn now to the more general case where R is not necessarily diagonal. In this case a suitable transformation matrix P such that $P\Omega P' = \Sigma \otimes I$ is given by

$$P = \begin{bmatrix} P_{11} & P_{12} & \cdots & P_{1M} \\ P_{21} & P_{22} & \cdots & P_{2M} \\ \vdots & \vdots & \ddots & \vdots \\ P_{M1} & P_{M2} & \cdots & P_{MM} \end{bmatrix} \tag{12.3.32}$$

where

$$\underset{(T \times T)}{P_{ii}} = \begin{bmatrix} \alpha_{ii} & 0 & 0 & \cdots & 0 & 0 \\ -\rho_{ii} & 1 & 0 & \cdots & 0 & 0 \\ \vdots & \vdots & \vdots & & \vdots & \vdots \\ 0 & 0 & 0 & \cdots & -\rho_{ii} & 1 \end{bmatrix} \tag{12.3.33}$$

$$\underset{(T \times T)}{P_{ij}} = \begin{bmatrix} \alpha_{ij} & 0 & 0 & \cdots & 0 & 0 \\ -\rho_{ij} & 0 & 0 & \cdots & 0 & 0 \\ \vdots & \vdots & \vdots & & \vdots & \vdots \\ 0 & 0 & 0 & \cdots & -\rho_{ij} & 0 \end{bmatrix}, \qquad i \neq j \tag{12.3.34}$$

and the elements of

$$\underset{(M \times M)}{A} = \begin{bmatrix} \alpha_{11} & 0 & \cdots & 0 \\ \alpha_{21} & \alpha_{22} & \cdots & 0 \\ \vdots & \vdots & & \vdots \\ \alpha_{M1} & \alpha_{M2} & \cdots & \alpha_{MM} \end{bmatrix} \tag{12.3.35}$$

are chosen such that $\Sigma = AV_0A'$.

Using $\mathbf{y}^* = P\mathbf{y}$ as an example, the transformed observations have the form

$$y_{i1}^* = \sum_{j=1}^{i} \alpha_{ij} y_{j1}, \qquad i = 1, 2, \ldots, M \tag{12.3.36}$$

and

$$y_{it}^* = y_{it} - \rho_{i1} y_{1,t-1} - \rho_{i2} y_{2,t-1} - \cdots - \rho_{iM} y_{M,t-1},$$
$$i = 1, 2, \ldots, M; \quad t = 2, 3, \ldots, T \tag{12.3.37}$$

The transformation for the first observation from each equation is similar in form to that for the diagonal R case, and it involves both the ρ_{ij} and the σ_{ij}. For the remaining observations the diagonal R transformation is extended by including the previous period's observations from all equations; it depends only on the ρ_{ij}. Thus, if the first row in each of the submatrices P_{ij}, $i, j = 1, 2, \ldots, M$ is ignored, the transformation matrix depends only on the ρ_{ij} and is relatively straightforward. To include the first rows, we need to know both the σ_{ij} and ρ_{ij}; from these values we need to derive first V_0 and then A.

When the complete transformation matrix is employed we obtain the GLS estimator

$$\hat{\boldsymbol{\beta}} = [X^{*\prime}(\Sigma^{-1} \otimes I_T)X^*]^{-1}X^{*\prime}(\Sigma^{-1} \otimes I_T)\mathbf{y}^* \tag{12.3.38}$$

where $X^* = PX$ and $\mathbf{y}^* = P\mathbf{y}$. If the first observation in each equation is ignored by deleting the first row in each of the M^2 matrices P_{ij}, $i, j = 1, 2, \ldots, M$, we have an approximate GLS estimator

$$\hat{\boldsymbol{\beta}}_0 = [X_0^{*\prime}(\Sigma^{-1} \otimes I_{T-1})X_0^*]^{-1}X_0^{*\prime}(\Sigma^{-1} \otimes I_{T-1})\mathbf{y}_0^* \tag{12.3.39}$$

where $X_0^* = P_0X$, $\mathbf{y}_0^* = P_0\mathbf{y}$, and P_0 is the $[M(T-1) \times MT]$ matrix obtained by deleting the first row of each P_{ij}.

If R and Σ are known, $\hat{\boldsymbol{\beta}}_0$ is less efficient than $\hat{\boldsymbol{\beta}}$, but it is much more convenient. If $\hat{\boldsymbol{\beta}}_0$ is used, the matrices V_0 and A do not have to be derived and the transformation depends only on the elements of R, not on those of Σ.

When R and Σ are unknown and replaced by consistent estimates, the resulting estimators, which we denote by $\hat{\hat{\boldsymbol{\beta}}}$ and $\hat{\hat{\boldsymbol{\beta}}}_0$, are asymptotically equivalent. As in the previous section, there are a number of possible estimators for Σ and R. The estimation steps that follow are those suggested by Guilkey and Schmidt (1973), modified to include the initial observations.

1. Apply LS to each equation and obtain the LS residuals

$$\hat{\mathbf{e}}_i = \mathbf{y}_i - X_i\mathbf{b}_i = (I_T - X_i(X_i'X_i)^{-1}X_i')\mathbf{y}_i, \qquad i = 1, 2, \ldots, M \qquad (12.3.40)$$

2. For each equation regress $\hat{e}_{it}$ on $(\hat{e}_{1,t-1}, \hat{e}_{2,t-1}, \ldots, \hat{e}_{M,t-1})$. This yields estimates $\hat{\rho}_{i1}, \hat{\rho}_{i2}, \ldots, \hat{\rho}_{iM}$, $i = 1, 2, \ldots, M$, or, in matrix notation, $\hat{R}$.
3. Let $\hat{P}_0$ be the matrix P_0 with the ρ_{ij} replaced by the estimates obtained in step 2, and obtain the transformed variables $X_0^* = \hat{P}_0 X$, $\mathbf{y}_0^* = \hat{P}_0\mathbf{y}$.
4. Regress $\mathbf{y}_0^*$ on X_0^* and calculate the residuals $(\hat{v}_{12}, \hat{v}_{13}, \ldots, \hat{v}_{1T}, \hat{v}_{22}, \ldots, \hat{v}_{2T}, \ldots, \hat{v}_{M2}, \ldots, \hat{v}_{MT})$ from this regression.
5. Estimate Σ by $\hat{\Sigma}$ where its elements are given by

$$\hat{\sigma}_{ij} = \frac{\sum_{t=2}^{T} \hat{v}_{it}\hat{v}_{jt}}{T - 1} \qquad (12.3.41)$$

6. Use the elements of $\hat{\Sigma}$ and $\hat{R}$ to find estimates $\hat{V}_0$ and $\hat{A}$ of V_0 and A, respectively. (See Equation 12.3.8.)
7. From $\hat{P}_0$ and $\hat{A}$, form $\hat{P}$, an estimate of the complete transformation matrix and find the transformed variables $X^* = \hat{P}X$ and $\mathbf{y}^* = \hat{P}\mathbf{y}$. This is equivalent to using $\hat{A}$ to transform the observations corresponding to $t = 1$ and appropriately combining these transformed observations with X_0^* and $\mathbf{y}_0^*$.
8. Apply the SUR estimation technique to the transformed observations to obtain the EGLS estimator

$$\hat{\hat{\boldsymbol{\beta}}} = [X^{*\prime}(\hat{\Sigma}^{-1} \otimes I_T)X^*]^{-1}X^{*\prime}(\hat{\Sigma}^{-1} \otimes I_T)\mathbf{y}^* \qquad (12.3.42)$$

Two obvious possible modifications, both of which could be used are

1. Omit steps 6 and 7 and replace step 8 with an estimator based on $M(T - 1)$ transformed observations

$$\hat{\hat{\boldsymbol{\beta}}}_0 = [X_0^{*\prime}(\hat{\Sigma}^{-1} \otimes I_{T-1})X_0^*]^{-1}X_0^{*\prime}(\hat{\Sigma}^{-1} \otimes I_{T-1})\mathbf{y}_0^* \qquad (12.3.43)$$

2. Omit step 4 and use the residuals obtained in step 2,

$$\hat{v}_{it} = \hat{e}_{it} - \hat{\rho}_{i1}\hat{e}_{1,t-1} - \ldots - \hat{\rho}_{iM}\hat{e}_{M,t-1} \qquad (12.3.44)$$

in place of the $\hat{v}_{it}$ in Equation 12.3.41.

The estimators for β with or without the modifications, are all consistent and asymptotically efficient with an asymptotic covariance matrix that is consistently estimated by $[X^{*\prime}(\hat{\Sigma}^{-1} \otimes I_T)X^*]^{-1}$ or $[X_0^{*\prime}(\hat{\Sigma}^{-1} \otimes I_{T-1})X_0^*]^{-1}$.

An alternative estimation technique is that of maximum likelihood. Under the assumption of normally distributed disturbances, Beach and MacKinnon (1979) advocate maximum likelihood estimation that retains the initial observations and that, through the Jacobian term, constrains the parameter estimates to lie within the stationary region. However, as they point out, except in a very special case it is impossible to concentrate any parameters out of the likelihood function, and numerical maximization of the function with respect to all the parameters may prove to be computationally difficult.

12.3.3 Finite Sample Properties

Evidence on the finite sample properties of a number of the alternative estimators for β has been provided by Kmenta and Gilbert (1970), Guilkey and Schmidt (1973), Maeshiro (1980), and Doran and Griffiths (1983). This evidence is from specialized cases, and is mostly in the form of Monte Carlo results, and so generalization is difficult. In particular, any conclusions drawn will depend on the specification of X, R, and Σ, as well as the number of equations and the number of observations. In a two equation model with $T = 20$, 50, and 100, Guilkey and Schmidt found that the asymptotic properties of the estimators are a good guide to their finite sample performance. On the other hand, in a three equation model (where the number of unknown parameters is increased considerably), Doran and Griffiths found that, with $T = 20$, it is frequently better to base EGLS estimation on the assumption that R is diagonal, even when it is not. Maeshiro shows that, when Σ and R are known, the loss in efficiency from using $\hat{\beta}_0$ instead of $\hat{\beta}$ can be substantial. However, using a more general model with unknown Σ and R, Doran and Griffiths found that omitting the first transformed observation from each equation has little impact. Thus, there is no general consensus of opinion on finite sample properties. Further details can be found from the papers referred to above.

12.3.4 Hypothesis Testing

To test a set of linear restrictions of the form $R\beta = \mathbf{r}$, the procedure outlined in Section 12.1.2a can be followed with X replaced by either X^* or X_0^*. The $\hat{\rho}_{ij}$ introduce some added uncertainty but the test statistics still possess the same asymptotic distribution.

Also of interest are test statistics for testing what autoregressive disturbance specification might be appropriate. If we assume R is diagonal and wish to test H_0: $\rho_{11} = \rho_{22} = \ldots = \rho_{MM} = 0$, then one approach [followed by Parks (1969) in a systems of demand equations application] is to apply the Durbin–Watson test separately to each equation. However, since H_0 is a joint hypothesis, it is more appropriate to treat it as such and use a single statistic. One possibility is a slightly modified Lagrange multiplier statistic given by [see, e.g., Harvey (1982)]

$$q = T \sum_{j=1}^{M} \hat{\rho}_{jj}^{2} \tag{12.3.45}$$

Under H_0, q has an asymptotic $\chi^2_{(M)}$-distribution.

For the more general case where R is not diagonal, Guilkey (1974) has used the Wald and likelihood ratio principles to suggest two test statistics for testing $R = 0$ and also two statistics for testing whether R could be diagonal. If $R = 0$, the SUR technique outlined in Section 12.1.1 could be used and, if R is diagonal, the procedure given in Section 12.3.1 could be used. The statistics are outlined below.

For testing $R = 0$, the Wald test suggested by Guilkey [see also Hendry (1971) and Harvey (1982)] is

$$u = \text{vec}(\hat{R})'(\hat{\Sigma}^{-1} \otimes \hat{E}'_{-1}\hat{E}_{-1}) \text{ vec}(\hat{R}) \tag{12.3.46}$$

where $\hat{R}$ is the estimate of R obtained in step 2 of the estimation procedure described in Section 12.3.2, $\hat{\Sigma}$ is the estimate obtained using step 5 or some other consistent estimator, and $\hat{E}_{-1}$ is the $[(T-1) \times M]$ matrix of "explanatory variables" used in step 2. That is,

$$\hat{E}_{-1} = \begin{bmatrix} \hat{e}_{11} & \hat{e}_{21} & \cdots & \hat{e}_{M1} \\ \hat{e}_{12} & \hat{e}_{22} & \cdots & \hat{e}_{M2} \\ \vdots & \vdots & \ddots & \vdots \\ \hat{e}_{1,T-1} & \hat{e}_{2,T-1} & \cdots & \hat{e}_{M,T-1} \end{bmatrix} \tag{12.3.47}$$

Under the null hypothesis $R = 0$, u converges in distribution to a random variable with $\chi^2_{(M^2)}$-distribution.

The "likelihood ratio" can also be used to obtain a test statistic. We put "likelihood ratio" in quotation marks because, strictly speaking, we should be using maximum likelihood estimates. If $\hat{E}$ is the $((T-1) \times M)$ matrix obtained by deleting the first row of $\hat{E}_{-1}$ and adding the row $(\hat{e}_{1T}, \hat{e}_{2T}, \ldots, \hat{e}_{MT})$, and we define

$$\hat{\Sigma} = (T-1)^{-1}(\hat{E} - \hat{E}_{-1}\hat{R})'(\hat{E} - \hat{E}_{-1}\hat{R})$$

and $\hat{\Sigma}_0 = (T-1)^{-1}\hat{E}'\hat{E}$, then under the null hypothesis $R = 0$,

$$u^* = (T-1)(\ln|\hat{\Sigma}_0| - \ln|\hat{\Sigma}|) \tag{12.3.48}$$

converges in distribution to a $\chi^2_{(M^2)}$ random variable.

For testing the null hypothesis that R is diagonal, we begin by defining $\hat{\mathbf{r}}$ as the $[(M^2 - M) \times 1]$ vector obtained by deleting the diagonal elements of R and stacking the columns. Correspondingly, $\hat{W}$ is defined as the $[(M^2 - M) \times (M^2 - M)]$ matrix formed by deleting the M rows and columns of $\hat{\Sigma} \otimes (\hat{E}'_{-1}\hat{E}_{-1})^{-1}$ in corresponding positions. These positions are the first, $(M + 2)$th, $(2M + 3)$th, $(3M + 4)$th, . . . , and M^2th. Then, under the null hypothesis that the nondiagonal elements of R are zero

$$\bar{u} = \hat{\mathbf{r}}'\hat{W}^{-1}\hat{\mathbf{r}} \tag{12.3.49}$$

converges in distribution to a $\chi^2_{(M^2-M)}$ random variable.

Alternatively, using the "likelihood ratio," we obtain the statistic

$$\bar{u}^* = (T - 1)(\ln|\hat{\Sigma}_D| - \ln|\hat{\Sigma}|) \tag{12.3.50}$$

where

$$\hat{\Sigma} = (T - 1)^{-1}(\hat{E} - \hat{E}_{-1}\hat{R})'(\hat{E} - \hat{E}_{-1}\hat{R})$$
$$\hat{\Sigma}_D = (T - 1)^{-1}(\hat{E} - \hat{E}_{-1}\hat{R}^*)'(\hat{E} - \hat{E}_{-1}\hat{R}^*)$$

and $\hat{R}^*$ is an $(M \times M)$ diagonal matrix with an ith diagonal element given by

$$\hat{\rho}_{ii} = \frac{\sum_{t=2}^{T}\hat{e}_{it}\hat{e}_{i,t-1}}{\sum_{t=2}^{T}\hat{e}_{i,t-1}^2}$$

Under the null hypothesis that the nondiagonal elements of R are zero, $\bar{u}^*$ converges in distribution to a $\chi^2_{(M^2-M)}$ random variable.

In a Monte Carlo experiment that estimated the finite sample power of the above four tests (and one other one), Guilkey (1974) found that all the tests were satisfactory and equally good for $T \geq 50$ but rather poor for $T = 20$.

For the case where $X_1 = X_2 = \ldots = X_M$, Szroeter (1978) has provided exact tests for testing for first- or *higher-order*-vector autoregressive errors. His higher-order specification is not the general one

$$\mathbf{e}_{(t)} = R_1\mathbf{e}_{(t-1)} + R_2\mathbf{e}_{(t-2)} + \ldots + R_p\mathbf{e}_{(t-p)} + \mathbf{v}_{(t)}$$

where the $\mathbf{e}_{(t-i)}$ and $\mathbf{v}_{(t)}$ are $(M \times 1)$ vectors and the R_i are $(M \times M)$ matrices, but rather a multivariate generalization of the specification considered by Wallis (1972)—namely, $\mathbf{e}_{(t)} = R_p\mathbf{e}_{(t-p)} + \mathbf{v}_{(t)}$. The finite sample power of these tests has not been evaluated, but they seem worthy of consideration. If the X_i's are not identical, the tests could be used providing they were based on "unrestricted residuals," those obtained by including every explanatory variable in every equation.

Noting that the Durbin-Watson test is a useful device for detecting a number of forms of misspecification in single equation models (e.g., omitted variables, incorrect functional form, lack of a suitable dynamic structure), Harvey (1982) suggests that a test of the null hypothesis $R = 0$ is likely to be useful for detecting misspecification in sets of regression equations. Among other things, he considers the tests in (12.3.45) and (12.3.46), as well as a test for $R = 0$ when the alternative hypothesis is $R = \rho I$.

Finally, Guilkey (1975) has suggested a test for the case where each X_i may contain lagged dependent variables, and some errors in his paper have been corrected by Maritz (1978) and Breusch (1978).

12.3.5 Extensions of the AR(1) Error Model

So far we have restricted the discussion of disturbance-related sets of equations to those with disturbances possessing only contemporaneous correlation or both contemporaneous and serial correlation, where the latter is described by a first-order (vector) autoregressive process. Other possible specifications include autoregressive (AR) disturbances of order higher than one, moving-average (MA) disturbances, and autoregressive moving-average (ARMA) disturbances. As in the single equation case the methods described in the above sections can be extended to handle higher-order AR errors or, alternatively, we can use nonlinear least squares, maximum likelihood estimation or, depending on the treatment of the initial observations, an asymptotically equivalent modification of one of these techniques. With MA and ARMA errors a nonlinear procedure, either maximum likelihood estimation or a modification, is required, and computational difficulties may arise. For details of work in this area see Chapter 16, Byron (1977), Pagan and Byron (1978), Nicholls and Hall (1979), Hall (1979), and references given in these articles.

Another possible extension is to allow for the inclusion of lagged dependent variables as explanatory variables. When the e_{it} are not autocorrelated this extension introduces no real problems as long as appropriate assumptions concerning the stability of the system are made. However, if in addition the e_{it} are autocorrelated, then a number of the estimation procedures we have discussed will no longer possess desirable properties. For further details see Spencer (1979) and Wang et al. (1980).

12.4 RECOMMENDATIONS

In Section 12.5 we conclude this chapter with a discussion of some special features of estimation when the disturbance covariance matrix is singular. Before turning to this section we make a few brief remarks on model selection.

In the above sections we discussed estimation of a set of equations under alternative assumptions about the disturbance vectors. In practice the appropriate disturbance specification is unknown and so, before estimation, the researcher needs to choose what appears to be the most suitable set of assumptions. If, in this regard, some a priori information is available, then the set of assumptions should be chosen accordingly but, failing this, it seems reasonable to base the choice on the outcome of hypothesis tests and on the number of observations available. For example, suppose we have a set of 3 equations and only 20 observations. In this case, even if we regard a complete first-order-vector autoregressive disturbance as the most appropriate assumption, it is unlikely that all the parameters could be accurately estimated. This is borne out by the results of Doran and Griffiths (1983). Also, a null hypothesis stating that a simpler model exists is likely to be accepted and, in a sample of size 20, an estimated generalized least squares estimator based on the simpler model is likely to be just as efficient as an estimator based on the more complicated assumption. On the other hand, if 200 or 300 observations are available, it would seem appropriate to specify some multivariate autocorrelation process of order greater than one. In a sample of this size, even if no serial correlation existed, the more complicated assumption is unlikely to lead to much of a drop in efficiency.

Thus, as a general recommendation for a researcher estimating a set of equations, we suggest that possible contemporaneous correlation should always be allowed for and, if the number of observations is sufficient, some kind of autocorrelation process could also be assumed. The precise form of this latter assumption could be based on hypothesis tests as well as on the number of observations.

12.5 ESTIMATION WITH A SINGULAR DISTURBANCE COVARIANCE MATRIX

12.5.1 Some Illustrations

In linear regression, we often assume that the covariance matrix of the disturbance term is nonsingular, in which case the generalized least squares procedure is applicable. However, there are cases when the disturbance covariance matrix cannot be assumed nonsingular. An example is the estimation of the parameters of the linear expenditure system [Stone (1954)]:

$$\mathbf{y}_i = \gamma_i \mathbf{p}_i + \beta_i \left(\mathbf{m} - \sum_{j=1}^{M} \gamma_j \mathbf{p}_j \right) + \mathbf{e}_i, \qquad i = 1, 2, \ldots, M \quad (12.5.1)$$

where $\mathbf{y}_i$ is the T-vector of observations on the expenditure for the ith commodity, $\mathbf{m}$ is the T-vector of observations on total expenditure (income), $\mathbf{p}_j$ the T-vector of prices for the jth commodity, and $\mathbf{e}_i$ the T-vector of unobserved random disturbances. The γ_i and β_i are unknown scalar parameters to be estimated. The parameter γ_i is often interpreted as the subsistence level of expenditure and β_i is the budget share after fulfilling the subsistence expenditures. Thus the budget share β_i is subject to a constraint $\Sigma_{i=1}^{M} \beta_i = 1$. The constraint on the β_i's and the fact that total expenditure $\mathbf{m}$ is the sum of the $\mathbf{y}_i$'s imply that $\Sigma_{i=1}^{M} \mathbf{e}_i = \mathbf{0}$. Hence the disturbances are linearly dependent. If one tries to estimate the M equations jointly using the seemingly unrelated regression technique discussed above, one will be faced with a singular disturbance covariance matrix that cannot be inverted. One will note that the complete disturbance vector contains MT elements, and hence its covariance matrix is of order $(MT \times MT)$, but the rank of this matrix cannot be larger than $(M-1)T$ because of the linear dependence of the disturbance terms [Parks (1971)].

Another example that involves a singular disturbance covariance matrix is a system of linear probability models. Assume that the tth observation for the ith category or state proportion y_{it}, based on n_{it} cases, is given by

$$y_{it} = p_{it} + e_{it}, \qquad t = 1, 2, \ldots, T, \qquad i = 1, 2, \ldots, M \tag{12.5.2}$$

where p_{it} is the tth true proportion for the ith category and the e_{it} are assumed to be independently distributed, each with a multinomial distribution with mean zero, variances $p_{it}(1 - p_{it})/N_t$ and covariances $-p_{it}p_{jt}/N_t$. The total number of cases for each t is denoted by $N_t = \Sigma_i n_{it}$.

Assume now that the true proportions are related to explanatory variables, at least over a range, by a relationship that is linear in the parameters such that

$$\mathbf{p}_i = X_i \boldsymbol{\beta}_i, \qquad i = 1, 2, \ldots, M \tag{12.5.3}$$

where $\mathbf{p}_i$ is a T-vector of true proportions for the ith category, X_i is a $(T \times K_i)$ matrix of rank K_i containing observations on K_i nonstochastic variables, and $\boldsymbol{\beta}_i$ is a $(K_i \times 1)$ unknown coefficient vector. Given (12.5.2), Equation 12.5.3 may be rewritten as

$$\mathbf{y}_i = X_i \boldsymbol{\beta}_i + \mathbf{e}_i \tag{12.5.4}$$

where $\mathbf{e}_i$ is a T-vector of disturbances. The system of linear probability models is

$$\mathbf{y} = X\boldsymbol{\beta} + \mathbf{e} \tag{12.5.5}$$

where $\mathbf{y}' = (\mathbf{y}_1', \mathbf{y}_2', \ldots, \mathbf{y}_M')$, $\boldsymbol{\beta}' = (\boldsymbol{\beta}_1', \boldsymbol{\beta}_2', \ldots, \boldsymbol{\beta}_M')$, $\mathbf{e}' = (\mathbf{e}_1', \mathbf{e}_2', \ldots, \mathbf{e}_M')$, and X is a block diagonal matrix with X_i's on the diagonal. Since $\Sigma_i p_{it} = 1$, the covariance matrix of $\mathbf{e}$ is singular. This may be seen from the tth cross-sectional covariance matrix of $\mathbf{e}$, that is,

$$E[\mathbf{e}_t\mathbf{e}_t'] = \frac{1}{N_t}\begin{bmatrix} p_{1t}(1-p_{1t}) & -p_{1t}p_{2t} & \cdots & -p_{1t}p_{Mt} \\ -p_{2t}p_{1t} & p_{2t}(1-p_{2t}) & \cdots & -p_{2t}p_{Mt} \\ \vdots & \vdots & \ddots & \vdots \\ -p_{Mt}p_{1t} & -p_{Mt}p_{2t} & \cdots & p_{Mt}(1-p_{Mt}) \end{bmatrix} \tag{12.5.6}$$

The covariance $E[\mathbf{e}_t\mathbf{e}_t']$ is singular, since the sum of any row or column is zero. The total covariance matrix $E[\mathbf{e}\mathbf{e}']$ is $(MT \times MT)$ in dimension, but the rank is only $(M-1)T$. Also, note that if $X_1 = X_2 = \ldots = X_M$, the equations in

(12.5.5) are also linearly dependent. This dependence can be removed by deleting one of the M equations [Lee, Judge, and Zellner (1968)].

However, because the linear dependence of disturbances may imply linear constraints on the parameter vector, deleting equations is not always a desirable procedure. Unless the implied parameter restrictions are imposed or fulfilled automatically, discarding information will result in estimates that are inefficient. In the following section, we will discuss the procedure of utilizing the seemingly redundant information.

Another situation in which the singular disturbance covariance matrix could occur is the case of precise observations. Assume that $\mathbf{y}_1$ is a vector of observations with noise or errors and $\mathbf{y}_2$ is a vector of precise observations that have no errors. In this case, the model can be partitioned as

$$\begin{pmatrix} \mathbf{y}_1 \\ \mathbf{y}_2 \end{pmatrix} = \begin{pmatrix} X_1 \\ X_2 \end{pmatrix} \boldsymbol{\beta} + \begin{pmatrix} \mathbf{e} \\ \mathbf{0} \end{pmatrix} \tag{12.5.7}$$

If the number of precise observations in $\mathbf{y}_2$ is less than the number of unknown parameters in $\boldsymbol{\beta}$, then $\mathbf{y}_1$ must be used together with $\mathbf{y}_2$ to estimate $\boldsymbol{\beta}$. The total disturbance covariance matrix will be singular, since the covariance associated with $\mathbf{y}_2$ is a null matrix.

Alternatively, the regular regression model,

$$\mathbf{y} = X\boldsymbol{\beta} + \mathbf{e} \tag{12.5.8}$$

may have a nonsingular disturbance covariance matrix, but if we wish to incorporate some a priori restrictions $R\boldsymbol{\beta} = \mathbf{r}$ on the parameters and we write the model in the mixed form as

$$\begin{bmatrix} \mathbf{y} \\ \mathbf{r} \end{bmatrix} = \begin{bmatrix} X \\ R \end{bmatrix} \boldsymbol{\beta} + \begin{bmatrix} \mathbf{e} \\ \mathbf{0} \end{bmatrix} \tag{12.5.9}$$

then we have the same problem of a singular covariance matrix.

From the above examples, we can see that a singular covariance matrix will occur if a system of similar equations exhibits some dependency among equations, or some observations are precisely observed without errors, or some a priori restrictions on parameters are treated as additional observations. Conversely, a singular covariance problem may be viewed as the problem of parameter restrictions. In the following section we will transform the singular covariance matrix problem to a restricted least squares problem.

12.5.2 The Restricted Generalized Inverse Estimator

We will write our model as

$$\mathbf{y} = X\boldsymbol{\beta} + \mathbf{e} \tag{12.5.10}$$

where $E[\mathbf{e}] = \mathbf{0}$ and $E[\mathbf{ee}'] = \mathbf{\Psi}$, which is of order $(T \times T)$ and singular with rank $g < T$. The covariance matrix $\mathbf{\Psi}$ does not have an inverse and generalized least squares cannot be applied. Since $\mathbf{\Psi}$ is symmetric and positive semidefinite of order T, with rank g, it has $T - g$ zero characteristic roots and g positive characteristic roots. Let F be a $(T \times g)$ matrix whose columns are characteristic vectors of $\mathbf{\Psi}$ corresponding to the positive roots, and G be a $(T \times (T - g))$ matrix whose columns are characteristic vectors of $\mathbf{\Psi}$ corresponding to the zero roots. Then the augmented matrix $U = (F\ G)$ is orthogonal, that is,

$$U'U = \begin{bmatrix} F'F & F'G \\ G'F & G'G \end{bmatrix} = \begin{bmatrix} I_g & 0 \\ 0 & I_{T-g} \end{bmatrix} = I_T \tag{12.5.11}$$

The matrix U will diagonalize the covariance matrix $\mathbf{\Psi}$ into

$$U'\mathbf{\Psi}U = \Lambda = \begin{bmatrix} \lambda_1 & & & & & \\ & \lambda_2 & & & & \\ & & \ddots & & & \\ & & & \lambda_g & & \\ & & & & \ddots & \\ & & & & & 0 \end{bmatrix} = \begin{bmatrix} \Lambda_g & 0 \\ 0 & 0 \end{bmatrix} \tag{12.5.12}$$

where Λ_g is a diagonal matrix of characteristic roots λ_i, $i = 1, 2, \ldots, g$. Thus, if we transformed the model (12.5.10) by premultiplying by U', we have

$$U'\mathbf{y} = U'X\boldsymbol{\beta} + U'\mathbf{e} \tag{12.5.13}$$

which is equivalent to

$$\begin{bmatrix} F'\mathbf{y} \\ G'\mathbf{y} \end{bmatrix} = \begin{bmatrix} F'X \\ G'X \end{bmatrix} \boldsymbol{\beta} + \begin{bmatrix} F'\mathbf{e} \\ G'\mathbf{e} \end{bmatrix} \tag{12.5.14}$$

Note that the covariance matrix of $G'\mathbf{e}$ is $E[G'\mathbf{ee}'G] = G'\mathbf{\Psi}G = 0$, from (12.5.12). Therefore, $G'\mathbf{e}$ is a random vector whose elements are all equal to their expectation, which is zero. Thus the model (12.5.14) can be viewed as fitting the model

$$F'\mathbf{y} = F'X\boldsymbol{\beta} + F'\mathbf{e} \tag{12.5.15}$$

subject to the restrictions

$$G'\mathbf{y} = G'X\boldsymbol{\beta} \tag{12.5.16}$$

Since the covariance matrix of $F'\mathbf{e}$ is

$$E[F'\mathbf{ee}'F] = F'\Psi F = \Lambda_g \tag{12.5.17}$$

the restricted least squares estimator $\boldsymbol{\beta}^*$ of $\boldsymbol{\beta}$ is

$$\boldsymbol{\beta}^* = \hat{\boldsymbol{\beta}} + CX'G(G'X'CX'G)^{-1}(G'\mathbf{y} - G'X\hat{\boldsymbol{\beta}}) \tag{12.5.18}$$

where

$$\hat{\boldsymbol{\beta}} = CX'F\Lambda_g^{-1}F'\mathbf{y} \tag{12.5.19}$$

is the unconstrained estimator with covariance matrix

$$C = (X'F\Lambda_g^{-1}F'X)^{-1} \tag{12.5.20}$$

It is assumed that $F'X$ has full column rank K so that the inverse (12.5.20) exists. Also note that $F\Lambda_g^{-1}F'$ is the generalized inverse of $\Psi(=F\Lambda_g F')$ and may be denoted by Ψ^+. The generalized inverse Ψ^+ fulfills the following four conditions:

1. $$\Psi\Psi^+ = F\Lambda_g F'F\Lambda_g^{-1}F' = (\Psi\Psi^+)' \tag{12.5.21}$$
2. $$\Psi^+\Psi = F\Lambda_g^{-1}F'F\Lambda_g F' = (\Psi^+\Psi)' \tag{12.5.22}$$
3. $$\Psi\Psi^+\Psi = \Psi \tag{12.5.23}$$
4. $$\Psi^+\Psi\Psi^+ = \Psi^+ \tag{12.5.24}$$

There are cases when $G'X = 0$ and the constraint on the parameters in (12.5.16) vanishes. In this case, the restricted estimator $\boldsymbol{\beta}^*$ is the same as the unrestricted estimator $\hat{\boldsymbol{\beta}}$,

$$\boldsymbol{\beta}^* = \hat{\boldsymbol{\beta}} = (X'\Psi^+X)^{-1}X'\Psi^+\mathbf{y} \tag{12.5.25}$$

and the covariance matrix of $\boldsymbol{\beta}^*$ and $\hat{\boldsymbol{\beta}}$ is the same—namely,

$$C = (X'\Psi^+X)^{-1} \tag{12.5.26}$$

There are also cases when $G'X \neq 0$ but the unrestricted estimator $\hat{\boldsymbol{\beta}}$ automatically fulfills the restrictions (12.5.16). In this case the last factor of (12.5.18) is zero and the adjustment factor for $\boldsymbol{\beta}^*$ vanishes, making $\boldsymbol{\beta}^*$ identically equal to $\hat{\boldsymbol{\beta}}$. For an example, see the generalized inverse method of estimating transition probabilities [Lee, Judge, and Zellner (1977, Appendix A)].

A simple example of a singular covariance matrix is that obtained from a two-equation system of linear probability models (12.5.4). The tth cross-section disturbance covariance matrix is a (2×2) version of (12.5.6)—namely,

$$\mathbf{\Psi}_t = \frac{1}{N_t}\begin{bmatrix} p_{1t}p_{2t} & -p_{1t}p_{2t} \\ -p_{2t}p_{1t} & p_{2t}p_{1t} \end{bmatrix} \tag{12.5.27}$$

where $p_{1t} + p_{2t} = 1$. The characteristic roots are $2p_{1t}p_{2t}/N_t$ and 0. The associated characteristic vectors when normalized are

$$F = \sqrt{\tfrac{1}{2}}\begin{bmatrix} 1 \\ -1 \end{bmatrix} \qquad \text{for } \lambda_1 = 2p_{1t}p_{2t}/N_t \tag{12.5.28}$$

$$G = \sqrt{\tfrac{1}{2}}\begin{bmatrix} 1 \\ 1 \end{bmatrix} \qquad \text{for } \lambda_2 = 0 \tag{12.5.29}$$

The generalized inverse of $\mathbf{\Psi}_t$ is then

$$\mathbf{\Psi}_t^+ = F\Lambda_g^{-1}F' = N_t\begin{bmatrix} \dfrac{1}{4p_{1t}p_{2t}} & \dfrac{-1}{4p_{1t}p_{2t}} \\ \dfrac{-1}{4p_{1t}p_{2t}} & \dfrac{1}{4p_{1t}p_{2t}} \end{bmatrix} \tag{12.5.30}$$

12.5.3 Concluding Remarks

In the previous sections it was shown that a singular covariance matrix will occur if (1) we combine equations that are linearly dependent; (2) some observations are free of errors; or (3) some a priori restrictions on parameters are treated as additional observations. The orthogonal transformation procedure shows that the generalized inverse of the singular covariance matrix may be used in place of the ordinary inverse in the restricted least squares formula. The restriction is the linear combination of equations, the identity relating the precise observations, or the extraneous parameter restrictions. It can be shown, as Theil suggests (1971, p. 281) that if the singular covariance matrix is due to linear dependency among equations, as an alternative to dealing with the whole system, the dependent equations may be deleted. In this case, for the subsystem obtained after deleting the redundant equations, the condensed covariance matrix will be nonsingular and the regular procedure is applicable [Lee, Judge, and Zellner (1977, Section A.6)]. However, if the singular covariance matrix results from one of the last two cases, the equations relating to the precise observations become parameter restrictions and should not be discarded. If the number of precise observations, say J, exceeds the number of unknown parameters, K, then there are at least $(J - K)$ precise observations that are repeated. Even when $J < K$, some precise observations may be repetitive. Repetitive, precise observations duplicate parameter restrictions and may be discarded without changing the restricted generalized inverse estimator. For examples of deleting equations, see Kendall and Stuart (1958, pp. 355–356); Lee, Judge, and Zellner (1968, 1977); Parks (1971); and Theil (1971, pp. 275, 281). The deletion of redundant equations is in the spirit of preventing an artificial attempt to raise the number of degrees of freedom by adding linear combinations of existing observations. See Theil (1971, p. 281, Problem 7.3).

For some related work on estimation in linear models with a singular covariance matrix see Powell (1969), Rao (1973), and Don (1982).

12.6 EXERCISES

12.6.1 General Exercises

Exercise 12.1

Prove that the GLS estimator $\hat{\boldsymbol{\beta}} = (X'(\Sigma^{-1} \otimes I)X)^{-1}X'(\Sigma^{-1} \otimes I)\mathbf{y}$ is identical to the LS estimator $\mathbf{b} = (X'X)^{-1}X'\mathbf{y}$ when:

1. $X_1 = X_2 = \ldots = X_M = \bar{X}$.
2. Σ is diagonal.

Exercise 12.2

Prove that the two expressions for g in Equations 12.1.16 and 12.1.19 are identical.

Exercise 12.3

Derive the expressions for λ_W and λ_{LM} given in the last lines of Equations 12.1.24 and 12.1.25.

Exercise 12.4

Consider the SUR model with AR(1) errors studied in Section 12.3 where the matrix R is diagonal and given by

$$R = \begin{bmatrix} \rho_1 & & & \\ & \rho_2 & & \\ & & \ddots & \\ & & & \rho_M \end{bmatrix}$$

1. Show that

$$V_0 = \begin{bmatrix} \dfrac{\sigma_{11}}{1-\rho_1^2} & \dfrac{\sigma_{12}}{1-\rho_1\rho_2} & \cdots & \dfrac{\sigma_{1M}}{1-\rho_1\rho_M} \\ \dfrac{\sigma_{21}}{1-\rho_2\rho_1} & \dfrac{\sigma_{22}}{1-\rho_2^2} & \cdots & \dfrac{\sigma_{2M}}{1-\rho_2\rho_M} \\ \vdots & \vdots & \ddots & \vdots \\ \dfrac{\sigma_{M1}}{1-\rho_M\rho_1} & \dfrac{\sigma_{M2}}{1-\rho_M\rho_2} & \cdots & \dfrac{\sigma_{MM}}{1-\rho_M^2} \end{bmatrix}$$

and that

$$E[\mathbf{e}_i\mathbf{e}_j'] = \Omega_{ij} = \frac{\sigma_{ij}}{1-\rho_i\rho_j}\begin{bmatrix} 1 & \rho_j & \cdots & \rho_j^{T-1} \\ \rho_i & 1 & \cdots & \rho_j^{T-2} \\ \vdots & \vdots & & \vdots \\ \rho_i^{T-1} & \rho_i^{T-2} & \cdots & 1 \end{bmatrix}$$

2. For the case where $M = 2$, show that the matrix A satisfies the equation $\Sigma = AV_0A'$ when it has the following elements:

$$\alpha_{11} = \sqrt{1-\rho_1^2}$$

$$\alpha_{12} = 0$$

$$\alpha_{21} = \frac{\sigma_{12}\sqrt{1-\rho_1^2}}{\sigma_{11}}\left(1 - \left\{\frac{(\sigma_{11}\sigma_{22}-\sigma_{12}^2)(1-\rho_1^2)(1-\rho_2^2)}{\sigma_{11}\sigma_{22}(1-\rho_1\rho_2)^2 - \sigma_{12}^2(1-\rho_1^2)(1-\rho_2^2)}\right\}^{1/2}\right)$$

$$\alpha_{22} = \left\{\frac{(\sigma_{11}\sigma_{22}-\sigma_{12}^2)(1-\rho_2^2)(1-\rho_1\rho_2)^2}{\sigma_{11}\sigma_{22}(1-\rho_1\rho_2)^2 - \sigma_{12}^2(1-\rho_1^2)(1-\rho_2^2)}\right\}^{1/2}$$

Exercise 12.5
Show, for the SUR model with contemporaneous correlation only, that the maximized log-likelihood function is, apart from a constant, equal to $(-T/2)\ln|\tilde{\Sigma}|$.

Exercise 12.6
Consider the Bayesian approach in Section 12.1.4. Prove that the marginal posteriors $g(\Sigma|\mathbf{y})$ and $g(\boldsymbol{\beta}|\mathbf{y})$ are given by (12.1.41) and (12.1.42), respectively, and that they can be written as (12.1.44) and (12.1.45) when $X_1 = X_2 = \ldots = X_M = \bar{X}$.

Exercise 12.7
Consider a SUR-model with AR(1) errors where

$$\Sigma = \begin{bmatrix} 2 & 1 \\ 1 & 1 \end{bmatrix}, \quad R = \begin{bmatrix} 0.8 & 0.5 \\ -1.0 & 0.0 \end{bmatrix}, \quad M = 2, \quad \text{and} \quad T = 4$$

1. Prove that the error process is stationary.
2. Derive the complete covariance matrix Ω.
3. Find a transformation matrix P such that $P\Omega P' = \Sigma \otimes I_T$.

12.6.2 Exercises Using Monte Carlo Data

To give experience in estimation and hypothesis testing and more insight into the sampling properties of various estimators, we recommend generating some

Monte Carlo data from a set of regression equations, and using these data to answer the exercises in this section. As one possible model for generating the data we suggest

$$\begin{bmatrix} \mathbf{y}_1 \\ \mathbf{y}_2 \end{bmatrix} = \begin{bmatrix} X_1 & 0 \\ 0 & X_2 \end{bmatrix} \begin{bmatrix} \boldsymbol{\beta}_1 \\ \boldsymbol{\beta}_2 \end{bmatrix} + \begin{bmatrix} \mathbf{e}_1 \\ \mathbf{e}_2 \end{bmatrix} \tag{12.6.1}$$

where X is the design matrix for the familiar "General Electric-Westinghouse investment function example," which was used by Boot and de Witt (1960), Zellner (1962), and many others. Specifically,

$$X_1 = \begin{bmatrix} 1 & 1170.6 & 97.8 \\ 1 & 2015.8 & 104.4 \\ 1 & 2803.3 & 118.0 \\ 1 & 2039.7 & 156.2 \\ 1 & 2256.2 & 172.6 \\ 1 & 2132.2 & 186.6 \\ 1 & 1834.1 & 220.9 \\ 1 & 1588.0 & 287.8 \\ 1 & 1749.4 & 319.9 \\ 1 & 1687.2 & 321.3 \\ 1 & 2007.7 & 319.6 \\ 1 & 2208.3 & 346.0 \\ 1 & 1656.7 & 456.4 \\ 1 & 1604.4 & 543.4 \\ 1 & 1431.8 & 618.3 \\ 1 & 1610.5 & 647.4 \\ 1 & 1819.4 & 671.3 \\ 1 & 2079.7 & 726.1 \\ 1 & 2371.6 & 800.3 \\ 1 & 2759.9 & 888.9 \end{bmatrix}, \quad X_2 = \begin{bmatrix} 1 & 191.5 & 1.8 \\ 1 & 516.0 & 0.8 \\ 1 & 729.0 & 7.4 \\ 1 & 560.4 & 18.1 \\ 1 & 519.9 & 23.5 \\ 1 & 628.5 & 26.5 \\ 1 & 537.1 & 36.2 \\ 1 & 561.2 & 60.8 \\ 1 & 617.2 & 84.4 \\ 1 & 626.7 & 91.2 \\ 1 & 737.2 & 92.4 \\ 1 & 760.5 & 86.0 \\ 1 & 581.4 & 111.1 \\ 1 & 662.3 & 130.6 \\ 1 & 583.8 & 141.8 \\ 1 & 635.2 & 136.7 \\ 1 & 723.8 & 129.7 \\ 1 & 864.1 & 145.5 \\ 1 & 1193.5 & 174.8 \\ 1 & 1188.9 & 213.5 \end{bmatrix} \tag{12.6.2}$$

A possible set of parameter values and stochastic assumptions is

$$\boldsymbol{\beta}_1 = (\beta_{11}, \beta_{12}, \beta_{13})' = (-20, 0.04, 0.14)'$$

$$\boldsymbol{\beta}_2 = (\beta_{21}, \beta_{22}, \beta_{23})' = (10, 0.05, 0.06)'$$

$$\begin{bmatrix} e_{1t} \\ e_{2t} \end{bmatrix} = \begin{bmatrix} \rho_{11} & \rho_{12} \\ \rho_{21} & \rho_{22} \end{bmatrix} \begin{bmatrix} e_{1,t-1} \\ e_{2,t-1} \end{bmatrix} + \begin{bmatrix} v_{1t} \\ v_{2t} \end{bmatrix} \tag{12.6.3}$$

where

$$R = \begin{bmatrix} \rho_{11} & \rho_{12} \\ \rho_{21} & \rho_{22} \end{bmatrix} = \begin{bmatrix} 0.8 & -1.0 \\ 0.2 & -0.1 \end{bmatrix} \tag{12.6.4}$$

and $(v_{1t}, v_{2t})'$ is a normal random vector with mean zero and covariance matrix

$$E\left[\begin{pmatrix} v_{1t} \\ v_{2t} \end{pmatrix}(v_{1t}\ v_{2t})\right] = \Sigma = \begin{bmatrix} \sigma_{11} & \sigma_{12} \\ \sigma_{21} & \sigma_{22} \end{bmatrix} = \begin{bmatrix} 300 & 120 \\ 120 & 70 \end{bmatrix}$$

We recommend generating 50 samples of $\mathbf{y}_1$ and $\mathbf{y}_2$, each of size $T = 20$.

12.6.2a Individual Exercises

Exercise 12.8
Show that the autoregressive process described in Equations 12.6.3 and 12.6.4 is stationary.

Exercise 12.9
Calculate the contemporaneous disturbance covariance matrix

$$V_0 = E\left[\begin{pmatrix} e_{1t} \\ e_{2t} \end{pmatrix}(e_{1t}\ e_{2t})\right]$$

and find a lower triangular matrix A such that $\Sigma = AV_0A'$.

Exercise 12.10
Use A, obtained in Exercise 12.9 to find the transformation matrix P which is such that $P\Omega P' = \Sigma \otimes I_T$, where $\Omega = E[\mathbf{ee}']$. Use P to obtain the covariance matrix for the generalized least squares (GLS) estimator of $\boldsymbol{\beta}$, say $\hat{\boldsymbol{\beta}}_G$.

Exercise 12.11
If one incorrectly assumes that the model is less complicated than that in Equations 12.6.1–12.6.4, or does not transform the observations for $t = 1$, an estimator less efficient than the GLS will be obtained. Given that the model in Equations 12.6.1–12.6.4 is the correct one, find algebraic expressions and numerical values for the covariance matrices of the following estimators.

1. The GLS estimator obtained by assuming $R = 0$,

$$\hat{\boldsymbol{\beta}}_Z = (X'(\Sigma^{-1} \otimes I_T)X)^{-1}X'(\Sigma^{-1} \otimes I_T)\mathrm{y} \qquad (12.6.5)$$

2. The GLS estimator obtained by assuming

$$R = \begin{bmatrix} 0.8 & 0 \\ 0 & -0.1 \end{bmatrix}$$

$$\hat{\boldsymbol{\beta}}_P = (X'\bar{P}'(\Sigma^{-1} \otimes I_T)\bar{P}X)^{-1}X'\bar{P}'(\Sigma^{-1} \otimes I_T)\bar{P}\mathbf{y} \qquad (12.6.6)$$

where $\bar{P}$ is the transformation matrix obtained under the assumption that R = diagonal (0.8, −0.1). (Based on this assumption we first need to obtain the contemporaneous covariance matrix for $(e_{1t}, e_{2t})'$ and the transformation matrix for the initial observations, say $\bar{V}_0$ and $\bar{A}$, respectively.)

3. The approximate GLS estimator obtained by assuming R = diagonal (0.8, −0.1),

$$\hat{\boldsymbol{\beta}}_{PO} = (X'\bar{P}_0'(\Sigma^{-1} \otimes I_{T-1})\bar{P}_0 X)^{-1}X'\bar{P}_0'(\Sigma^{-1} \otimes I_{T-1})\bar{P}_0\mathbf{y} \quad (12.6.7)$$

where $\bar{P}_0$ is the (38×40) matrix obtained by deleting the first and twenty-first rows of $\bar{P}$.

4. The approximate GLS estimator obtained by correctly assuming R is given by Equation 12.6.4,

$$\hat{\boldsymbol{\beta}}_{GO} = (X'P_0'(\Sigma^{-1} \otimes I_{T-1})P_0 X)^{-1}X'P_0'(\Sigma^{-1} \otimes I_{T-1})P_0\mathbf{y} \quad (12.6.8)$$

where P_0 is the (38×40) matrix obtained by deleting the first and twenty-first rows of the matrix P that was obtained in Exercise 12.10.

Exercise 12.12

Using as a definition of efficiency the "weak mean squared error" criterion $E[(\hat{\boldsymbol{\beta}} - \boldsymbol{\beta})'(\hat{\boldsymbol{\beta}} - \boldsymbol{\beta})]$, rank the estimators $\hat{\boldsymbol{\beta}}_G$, $\hat{\boldsymbol{\beta}}_Z$, $\hat{\boldsymbol{\beta}}_P$, $\hat{\boldsymbol{\beta}}_{PO}$ and $\hat{\boldsymbol{\beta}}_{GO}$ according to their relative efficiency. Comment on this ranking.

Exercises 12.13–12.16

Each student selects five samples of $\mathbf{y}$ and calculates values for a number of estimators and test statistics for each of these samples. Exercises 12.17 to 12.19 use the combined set of answers from all students.

Exercise 12.13

Select five samples and for each of these samples compute values for the estimated GLS estimators $\hat{\hat{\boldsymbol{\beta}}}_Z$, $\hat{\hat{\boldsymbol{\beta}}}_{PO}$, $\hat{\hat{\boldsymbol{\beta}}}_P$, $\hat{\hat{\boldsymbol{\beta}}}_{GO}$, and $\hat{\hat{\boldsymbol{\beta}}}_G$. These are given by the estimators in Exercises 12.10 and 12.11 with the σ_{ij} and/or ρ_{ij} replaced by estimates. Compare these values with each other and the true parameter values.

Exercise 12.14

For each of the 25 estimates obtained in Exercise 12.13 calculate "t-test statistics" for the null hypothesis $\beta_{12} = 0.04$. In each case assume that the estimator used was appropriate for the model so that the asymptotic covariance matrices are estimated, respectively, by

$$[X'(\hat{\Sigma}^{-1} \otimes I_T)X]^{-1},\ [X'\hat{\bar{P}}_0'(\hat{\Sigma}^{-1} \otimes I_{T-1})\hat{\bar{P}}_0 X]^{-1},\ [X'\hat{\bar{P}}'(\hat{\Sigma}^{-1} \otimes I_T)\hat{\bar{P}}X]^{-1},$$
$$[X'\hat{P}_0'(\hat{\Sigma}^{-1} \otimes I_{T-1})\hat{P}_0 X]^{-1}, \quad \text{and} \quad [X'\hat{P}'(\hat{\Sigma}^{-1} \otimes I_T)\hat{P}X]^{-1}$$

Comment on the values.

Exercise 12.15

For each of the five samples selected in Exercise 12.13, use the restricted counterpart of the estimator $\hat{\hat{\boldsymbol\beta}}_{GO}$ to estimate $\boldsymbol\beta$ under the set of restrictions $\beta_{12} = \beta_{22}$, $\beta_{13} = \beta_{23}$. Under the null hypothesis that this set of restrictions is true, calculate the χ^2-test statistics obtained by appropriately modifying Equation 12.1.19.

Exercise 12.16

Again, for each of the five samples,

1. Use u in Equation 12.3.46 to test the hypothesis $R = 0$.
2. Use $\bar{u}$ in Equation 12.3.49 to test the hypothesis that R is diagonal.

12.6.2b Group or Class Exercises

Exercise 12.17

Let $\hat{\hat{\boldsymbol\beta}}_G(i)$ be the estimate from the ith sample obtained using the estimator $\hat{\hat{\boldsymbol\beta}}_G$. Calculate $\Sigma_{i=1}^{50}\ (\hat{\hat{\boldsymbol\beta}}_G(i) - \boldsymbol\beta)(\hat{\hat{\boldsymbol\beta}}_G(i) - \boldsymbol\beta)'/50$, which is an estimate of the mean square error matrix for $\hat{\hat{\boldsymbol\beta}}_G$. Repeat this process for estimators $\hat{\hat{\boldsymbol\beta}}_Z$, $\hat{\hat{\boldsymbol\beta}}_{PO}$, $\hat{\hat{\boldsymbol\beta}}_P$, and $\hat{\hat{\boldsymbol\beta}}_{GO}$.

Exercise 12.18

Compare the results of Exercise 12.17 with those in Exercises 12.10 and 12.11. Do the results suggest that the ranking obtained in Exercise 12.12 is still appropriate when the disturbance covariance matrix and autoregressive parameters are unknown?

Exercise 12.19

Using all 50 samples, construct empirical distributions for

1. The t statistics obtained in Exercise 12.14.
2. The χ^2 statistics obtained in Exercise 12.15.
3. The u statistics obtained in Exercise 12.16.
4. The $\bar{u}$ statistics obtained in Exercise 12.16.

Giving due consideration to the model that generated the data, and the truth or otherwise of each of the null hypotheses, comment on the shape of each of the above distributions and on the proportion of times each null hypothesis was rejected at the 5% level of significance.

12.7 REFERENCES

Avery, R. B. (1977) "Error Components and Seemingly Unrelated Regressions," *Econometrica,* 45, 199–209.

Baltagi, B. H. (1980) "On Seemingly Unrelated Regressions with Error Components," *Econometrica,* 48, 1547–1551.

Beach, C. M., and J. G. MacKinnon (1979) "Maximum Likelihood Estimation of Singular Equation Systems with Autoregressive Disturbances," *International Economic Review,* 20, 459–464.

Bera, A., R. P. Byron and C. M. Jarque (1981) "Further Evidence on Asymptotic Tests for Homogeneity and Symmetry in Large Demand Systems," *Economics Letters,* 8, 101–105.

Berger, J. O., and M. E. Bock (1976) "Combining Independent Normal Mean Estimation Problems with Unknown Variances," *Annals of Statistics,* 4, 642–648.

Berndt, E. R., and N. E. Savin (1977) "Conflict Among Criteria for Testing Hypotheses in the Multivariate Regression Model," *Econometrica,* 45, 1263–1278.

Binkley, J. K. (1982) "The Effect of Variable Correlation on the Efficiency of Seemingly Unrelated Regression in a Two-Equation Model," *Journal of the American Statistical Association,* 77, 890–895.

Boot, J. C. G., and G. M. deWitt (1960) "Investment Demand: An Empirical Contribution to the Aggregation Problem," *International Economic Review,* 1, 3–30.

Breusch, T. S. (1978) "Testing for Vector Autoregressive Disturbances in Simultaneous Systems with Lagged Endogenous Variables," Australian National University Working Papers in Economics and Econometrics, No. 57, Canberra, Australia.

Breusch, T. S., and A. R. Pagan (1980) "The Lagrange Multiplier Test and Its Applications to Model Specification in Econometrics," *Review of Economic Studies,* 47, 239–253.

Buse, A. (1973) "Goodness of Fit in Generalized Least Squares Estimation," *The American Statistician,* 27, 106–108.

Buse, A. (1979) "Goodness-of-Fit in the Seemingly Unrelated Regressions Model: A Generalization," *Journal of Econometrics,* 10, 109–114.

Byron, R. P. (1977) "Efficient Estimation and Inference in Large Econometric Systems," *Econometrica,* 45, 1499–1516.

Carter, R. A. L., and A. L. Nagar (1977) "Coefficients of Correlation for Simultaneous Equation Systems," *Journal of Econometrics,* 6, 39–50.

Chow, G. C. (1960) "Tests of Equality Between Sets of Coefficients in Two Linear Regressions," *Econometrica,* 28, 591–605.

Conniffe, D. (1982a) "Covariance Analysis and Seemingly Unrelated Regressions," *The American Statistician,* 36, 169–171.

Conniffe, D. (1982b) "A Note on Seemingly Unrelated Regressions," *Econometrica,* 50, 229–233.

Dhrymes, P. J. (1971) "Equivalence of Iterative Aitken and Maximum Likelihood Estimators for a System of Regression Equations," *Australian Economic Papers,* 10, 20–24.

Dhrymes, P. J. (1974) *Econometrics: Statistical Foundations and Applications,* 2nd ed., Springer-Verlag, New York.

Don, F. J. Henk (1982) "Restrictions on Variables," *Journal of Econometrics,* 18, 369–393 and "Corrigenda," *Journal of Econometrics,* 23, 291–292.

Doran, H. E., and W. E. Griffiths (1983) "On the Relative Efficiency of Estimators Which Include the Initial Observations in the Estimation of Seemingly Unrelated Regressions with First-Order Autoregressive Disturbances," *Journal of Econometrics,* 23, 165–191.

Drèze, J. (1977) "Bayesian Regression Analysis Using Poly-*t* Densities," *Journal of Econometrics,* 6, 329–354.

Dufour, J.-M. (1982) "Generalized Chow Tests for Structural Change: A Coordinate Free Approach," *International Economic Review,* 23, 565–575.

Duncan, G. M. (1983) "Estimation and Inference for Heteroscedastic Systems of Equations," *International Economic Review,* 24, 559–566.

Dwivedi, T. D., and V. K. Srivastava (1978) "Optimality of Least Squares in the Seemingly Unrelated Regression Equations Model," *Journal of Econometrics,* 7, 391–395.

Fiebig, D. G. and H. Theil (1983) "The Two Perils of Symmetry-Constrained Estimation of Demand Systems," *Economics Letters,* 13, 105–111.

Fisher, F. M. (1970) "Tests of Equality Between Sets of Coefficients in Two Linear Regressions: An Expository Note," *Econometrica,* 38, 361–366.

Gallant, A. R. (1975) "Seemingly Unrelated Nonlinear Regressions," *Journal of Econometrics,* 3, 35–50.

Glahn, H. (1969) "Some Relationships Derived from Canonical Correlation Theory," *Econometrica,* 37, 252–256.

Graybill, F. A. (1969) *Introduction to Matrices with Applications in Statistics,* Wadsworth, Belmont, Calif.

Guilkey, D. K. (1974) "Alternative Tests for a First-Order Vector Autoregressive Error Specification," *Journal of Econometrics,* 2, 95–104.

Guilkey, D. K. (1975) "A Test for the Presence of First-Order Vector Autoregressive Errors When Lagged Endogenous Variables are Present," *Econometrica,* 43, 711–718.

Guilkey, D. K., and P. Schmidt (1973) "Estimation of Seemingly Unrelated Regressions with Vector Autoregressive Errors," *Journal of American Statistical Association,* 68, 642–647.

Hall, A. D. (1977) "Further Finite Sample Results in the Context of Two Seemingly Unrelated Regression Equations," Australian National University Working Papers in Economics and Econometrics No. 39, Canberra, Australia.

Hall, A. D. (1982) "The Relative Efficiency of Time and Frequency Domain Estimates in SUR Systems," *Journal of Statistical Computation and Simulation,* 16, 81–96.

Harvey, A. C. (1982) "A Test of Misspecification for Systems of Equations," Discussion Paper No. A31, London School of Economics Econometrics Programme, London, England.

Hendry, D. F. (1971) "Maximum Likelihood Estimation of Systems of Simultaneous Regression Equations with Errors Generated by a Vector Autoregressive Process," *International Economic Review,* 12, 257–272.

Hooper, J. W. (1959) "Simultaneous Equations and Canonical Correlation Theory," *Econometrica,* 27, 245–256.

Jayatissa, W. A. (1977) "Tests of Equality Between Sets of Coefficients in Two Linear Regressions When Disturbance Variances are Unequal," *Econometrica,* 45, 1291–1292.

Judge, G. G., and M. E. Bock (1978) *The Statistical Implications of Pre-Test and Stein-Rule Estimators in Econometrics,* North-Holland, Amsterdam.

Kakwani, N. C. (1967) "The Unbiasedness of Zellner's Seemingly Unrelated Regression Equation Estimators," *Journal of the American Statistical Association,* 62, 141–142.

Kakwani, N. C. (1974) "A Note on the Efficiency of the Zellner's Seemingly Unrelated Regressions Estimator," *Annals of the Institute of Statistical Mathematics,* 26, 361–362.

Kariya, T. (1981a) "Bounds for the Covariance Matrices of Zellner's Estimator in the SUR Model and the 2SAE in a Heteroscedastic Model," *Journal of the American Statistical Association,* 76, 975–989.

Kariya, T. (1981b) "Tests for the Independence Between Two Seemingly Unrelated Regression Equations," *Annals of Statistics,* 9, 381–390.

Kataoka, Y. (1974) "The Exact Finite Sample Distribution of Joint Least Squares Estimators for Seemingly Unrelated Regression Equations," *Economic Studies Quarterly,* 25, 36–44.

Kmenta, J., and R. F. Gilbert (1968) "Small Sample Properties of Alternative Estimators of Seemingly Unrelated Regressions," *Journal of the American Statistical Association,* 63, 1180–1200.

Kmenta, J., and R. F. Gilbert (1970) "Estimation of Seemingly Unrelated Regressions with Autoregressive Disturbances," *Journal of the American Statistical Association,* 65, 186–196.

Laitinen, K. (1978) "Why is Demand Homogeneity so Often Rejected," *Economics Letters,* 1, 187–191.

Lee, T. C., G. G. Judge, and A. Zellner, (1968) "Maximum Likelihood and Bayesian Estimation of Transition Probabilities," *Journal of the American Statistical Association,* 63, 1162–1179.

Lee, T. C., G. G. Judge, and A. Zellner (1977) *Estimating the Parameters of the Markov Probability Model from Aggregate Time Series Data,* 2nd ed., North-Holland, Amsterdam.

Maeshiro, A. (1980) "New Evidence on the Small Sample Properties of Estimators of SUR Models with Autocorrelated Disturbances," *Journal of Econometrics,* 12, 177–187.

Magnus, J. R. (1978) "Maximum Likelihood Estimation of the GLS Model with Unknown Parameters in the Disturbance Covariance Matrix," *Journal of Econometrics,* 7, 281–312.

Malinvaud, E. (1980) *Statistical Methods of Econometrics,* 3rd ed., North-Holland, Amsterdam.

Maritz, A. (1978) "A Note of Correction to Guilkey's Test for Serial Independence in Simultaneous Equations Models," *Econometrica,* 46, 471.

McElroy, M. B. (1977a) "Goodness of Fit for Seemingly Unrelated Regressions: Glahn's $R^2_{y \cdot x}$ and Hooper's $\bar{r}^2$," *Journal of Econometrics,* 6, 381–387.

McElroy, M. B. (1977b) "Weaker MSE Criteria and Tests for Linear Restrictions in Regression Models with Non-Spherical Disturbances," *Journal of Econometrics,* 6, 389–394.

Meisner, J. F. (1979) "The Sad Fate of the Asymptotic Slutsky Asymmetry Test for Large Systems," *Economics Letters,* 2, 231–233.

Mehta, J. S., and P. A. V. B. Swamy (1976) "Further Evidence on the Relative Efficiencies of Zellner's Seemingly Unrelated Regressions Estimators," *Journal of the American Statistical Association,* 71, 634–639.

Nicholls, D. F., and A. D. Hall (1979) "The Exact Likelihood Function of Multivariate Autoregressive Moving Average Models," *Biometrika,* 66, 259–264.

Oberhofer, W., and J. Kmenta (1974) "A General Procedure for Obtaining Maximum Likelihood Estimates in Generalized Regression Models," *Econometrica,* 42, 579–590.

Pagan, A. R., and R. P. Byron (1978) "A Synthetic Approach to the Estimation of Models with Autocorrelated Disturbance Terms," in A. R. Bergstrom, ed., *Stability and Inflation: Essays in Honor of A. W. Phillips,* Wiley, New York.

Parks, R. W. (1967) "Efficient Estimation of a System of Regression Equations When Disturbances are Both Serially and Contemporaneously Correlated," *Journal of the American Statistical Association,* 62, 500–509.

Parks, R. W. (1969) "Systems of Demand Equations: An Empirical Comparison of Alternative Functional Forms," *Econometrica,* 37, 629–650.

Parks, R. W. (1971) "Maximum Likelihood Estimation of the Linear Expenditure System," *Journal of the American Statistical Association,* 66, 900–903.

Phillips, P. C. B. (1977) "An Approximation to the Finite Sample Distribution of Zellner's Seemingly Unrelated Regression Estimator," *Journal of Econometrics,* 6, 147–164.

Powell, A. A. (1969) "Aitken Estimators as a Tool in Allocating Predetermined Aggregates," *Journal of the American Statistical Association,* 64, 913–922.

Prucha, I. R. (1984) "On the Asymptotic Efficiency of Feasible Aitken Estimators for Seemingly Unrelated Regression Models with Error Components," *Econometrica,* 52, 203–208.

Rao, C. R. (1973) "Representations of Best Linear Unbiased Estimators in the Gauss-Markoff Model with a Singular Dispersion Matrix," *Journal of Multivariate Analysis,* 3, 276–292.

Revankar, N. S. (1974) "Some Finite Sample Results in the Context of Two Seemingly Unrelated Regression Equations," *Journal of the American Statistical Association,* 69, 187–190.

Revankar, N. S. (1976) "Use of Restricted Residuals in SUR Systems: Some Finite Sample Results," *Journal of the American Statistical Association,* 71, 183–188.

Schmidt, P. (1977) "Estimation of Seemingly Unrelated Regressions with Unequal Numbers of Observations," *Journal of Econometrics,* 5, 365–377.

Schmidt, P. (1978) "A Note on the Estimation of Seemingly Unrelated Regression Systems," *Journal of Econometrics,* 7, 259–261.

Schmidt, P., and P. Sickles (1977) "Some Further Evidence on the Use of the Chow Test Under Heteroskedasticity," *Econometrica,* 45, 1293–1298.

Singh, B., and A. Ullah (1974) "Estimation of Seemingly Unrelated Regressions with Random Coefficients," *Journal of the American Statistical Association,* 69, 191–195.

Smith, P. J., and S. C. Choi (1982) "Simple Tests to Compare Two Dependent Regression Lines," *Technometrics,* 24, 123–126.

Spencer, D. E. (1979) "Estimation of a Dynamic System of Seemingly Unrelated Regressions with Autoregressive Disturbances," *Journal of Econometrics,* 10, 227–241.

Srivastava, V. K. (1970) "The Efficiency of Estimating Seemingly Unrelated Regression Equations," *Annals of the Institute of Statistical Mathematics,* 22, 483–493.

Srivastava, V. K. (1973) "The Efficiency of an Improved Method of Estimating Seemingly Unrelated Regression Equations," *Journal of Econometrics,* 1, 341–350.

Srivastava, V. K., and T. D. Dwivedi (1979) "Estimation of Seemingly Unrelated Regression Equations: A Brief Survey," *Journal of Econometrics,* 10, 15–32.

Srivastava, S. K., and V. K. Srivastava (1983) "Estimation of the Seemingly Unrelated Regression Equation Model Under Specification Error," *Biometrika,* forthcoming.

Stone, R. (1954) "Linear Expenditure Systems and Demand Analysis: An Application to the Pattern of British Demand," *The Economic Journal,* 64, 511–527.

Swamy, P. A. V. B., and J. S. Mehta (1975) "On Bayesian Estimation of Seemingly Unrelated Regressions When Some Observations are Missing," *Journal of Econometrics,* 3, 157–169.

Szroeter, J. (1978) "Generalized Variance-Ratio Tests for Serial Correlation in Multivariate Regression Models," *Journal of Econometrics,* 8, 47–60.

Telser, L. G. (1964) "Iterative Estimation of a Set of Linear Regression Equations," *Journal of the American Statistical Association,* 59, 845–862.

Theil, H. (1971) *Principles of Econometrics,* Wiley, New York.

Toyoda, T. (1974) "Use of the Chow Test Under Heteroscedasticity," *Econometrica,* 42, 601–608.

Verbon, H. A. A. (1980) "Testing for Heteroscedasticity in a Model of Seemingly Unrelated Regression Equations with Variance Components (SUREVC)," *Economics Letters,* 5, 149–153.

Wallis, K. F. (1972) "Testing for Fourth-Order Autocorrelation in Quarterly Regression Equations," *Econometrica,* 40, 617–636.

Wang, J. H. K., M. Hidiroglou and W. A. Fuller (1980) "Estimation of Seemingly Unrelated Regressions with Lagged Dependent Variables and Autocorrelated Errors," *Journal of Statistical Computation and Simulation,* 10, 133–146.

Zellner, A. (1962) "An Efficient Method of Estimating Seemingly Unrelated

Regressions and Tests of Aggregation Bias,'' *Journal of the American Statistical Association,* 57, 348–368.

Zellner, A. (1963) ''Estimators for Seemingly Unrelated Regression Equations: Some Exact Finite Sample Results,'' *Journal of the American Statistical Association,* 58, 977–992. ''Corrigenda,'' (1972), 67, 255.

Zellner, A. (1971) *An Introduction to Bayesian Inference in Econometrics,* Wiley, New York.

Zellner, A. (1979) ''An Error-Components Procedure (ECP) for Introducing Prior Information about Covariance Matrices and Analysis of Multivariate Regression Models,'' *International Economic Review,* 20, 679–692.

Zellner, A., and D. S. Huang (1962) ''Further Properties of Efficient Estimators for Seemingly Unrelated Regression Equations,'' *International Economic Review,* 3, 300–313.

Zellner, A., and W. Vandaele (1971) ''Bayes-Stein Estimators for k-Means, Regression and Simultaneous Equations Models,'' in S. E. Fienberg and A. Zellner, eds., 1975, *Studies in Bayesian Econometrics and Statistics in Honor of Leonard J. Savage,* North-Holland, Amsterdam.

Chapter 13

Inference in Models That Combine Time Series and Cross-Sectional Data

13.1 INTRODUCTION

Estimation of relationships that combine time series and cross-sectional data is a problem frequently encountered in economics. Typically, one may possess several years of data on a number of firms, households, geographical areas, or biological units. The problem, when using these data to estimate a relationship, is to specify a model that will adequately allow for differences in behavior over cross-sectional units as well as any differences in behavior over time for a given cross-sectional unit. Once a model has been specified, there are the additional problems of the most efficient estimation procedure and how to test hypotheses about the parameters. This chapter is concerned with these problems. In the remainder of the introduction we give a classification of some of the alternative models that have been suggested in the literature and, in subsequent sections, we discuss estimation and hypothesis testing in specific models and make some recommendations about model choice.

In general, the models considered can be written as

$$y_{it} = \beta_{1it} + \sum_{k=2}^{K} \beta_{kit} x_{kit} + e_{it} \tag{13.1.1}$$

where $i = 1, 2, \ldots, N$ refers to a cross-sectional unit, hereafter referred to as an individual, and $t = 1, 2, \ldots, T$ refers to a given time period. Thus y_{it} is the value of the dependent variable for individual i at time t and x_{kit} is the value of the kth nonstochastic explanatory variable for individual i at time t. The stochastic term e_{it} is assumed to have mean zero, $E[e_{it}] = 0$, and constant variance, $E[e_{it}^2] = \sigma_e^2$. The β_{kit} are unknown parameters or response coefficients and, as the subscripts suggest, for the most general case they can be different for different individuals and in different time periods. However, in most cases more restrictive assumptions will be made and, in fact, this is a convenient way to classify the various models. In particular, in Sections 13.2 to 13.6 the following five cases will be considered.

1. All coefficients are constant and the disturbance is assumed to capture differences over time and individuals,

$$y_{it} = \beta_1 + \sum_{k=2}^{K} \beta_k x_{kit} + e_{it} \tag{13.1.2}$$

2. Slope coefficients are constant and the intercept varies over individuals,

$$y_{it} = \beta_{1i} + \sum_{k=2}^{K} \beta_k x_{kit} + e_{it} \tag{13.1.3}$$

3. Slope coefficients are constant and the intercept varies over individuals and time,

$$y_{it} = \beta_{1it} + \sum_{k=2}^{K} \beta_k x_{kit} + e_{it} \tag{13.1.4}$$

4. All coefficients vary over individuals,

$$y_{it} = \beta_{1i} + \sum_{k=2}^{K} \beta_{ki} x_{kit} + e_{it} \tag{13.1.5}$$

5. All coefficients vary over time and individuals,

$$y_{it} = \beta_{1it} + \sum_{k=2}^{K} \beta_{kit} x_{kit} + e_{it} \tag{13.1.6}$$

In cases 2 to 4 the models can be classified further depending upon whether the variable coefficients are assumed to be random or fixed. The fixed assumption leads to dummy variable models and the seemingly unrelated regression model while the random assumption leads to error components models and the Swamy random coefficient model. In case 5 we will assume, for the most part, that the coefficients are random. An overview of these assumptions and models, as well as their location in the Chapter, is given in Table 13.1. In each of the sections we will be interested in generalized least squares estimation of the response coefficients or their mean vector, the prediction of random components, variance estimators that can be used in an estimated generalized least squares estimator, hypothesis tests for misspecification, and various extensions of the models.

It should be emphasized that the simple classification given above is to some extent arbitrary, and that in the following sections, we concentrate on inference procedures for the basic models in each category. There are many other ways in which the various models could be classified, and there exists a large number of extended and more complex models, some of which do not fit neatly into one of our categories. We will make reference to many of these extensions later in the chapter. For further details we recommend the special journal issues edited by Mazodier (1978) and Heckman and Singer (1982), as well as the paper by

TABLE 13.1 *ALTERNATIVE MODELS FOR COMBINING TIME SERIES AND CROSS-SECTIONAL DATA*

The linear model

$$y_{it} = \beta_{1it} + \sum_{k=2}^{K} \beta_{kit} x_{kit} + e_{it}$$

- All coefficients constant, $\beta_{kit} = \beta_k$ and e_{it} heteroscedastic and autocorrelated (Section 13.2)
- Slope coefficients constant, intercept variable
  - Intercept varies over individuals only
    $\beta_{1it} = \beta_{1i}$
    $\beta_{kit} = \beta_k, k \neq 1$
    (Section 13.3)
    - β_{1i} fixed coefficients. Dummy variable model (Section 13.3.1)
    - β_{1i} random. Error components model (Section 13.3.2)
    - → β_{1i} fixed or random? (Section 13.3.3)
  - Intercept varies over individuals and time
    $\beta_{1it} = \bar{\beta}_1 + \mu_i + \lambda_t$
    $\beta_{kit} = \beta_k, k \neq 1$
    (Section 13.4)
    - μ_i, λ_t fixed coefficients. Dummy variable model (Section 13.4.1)
    - μ_i, λ_t random. Error components model (Section 13.4.2)
    - → μ_i, λ_t fixed or random? (Section 13.4.3)
- Slope coefficients variable
  - Coefficients vary over individuals
    $\beta_{kit} = \beta_{ki}$
    (Section 13.5)
    - β_{ki} fixed parameters. Seemingly unrelated regressions (Chapter 12)
    - β_{ki} random. Swamy random coefficient model (Section 13.5.1)
    - → β_{ki} fixed or random? (Section 13.5.2)
  - Coefficients vary over individuals and time
    $\beta_{kit} = \bar{\beta}_k + \mu_{ki} + \lambda_{kt}$
    (Section 13.6)
    - μ_{ki}, λ_{kt} random. Hsiao random coefficient model (Section 13.6.1)

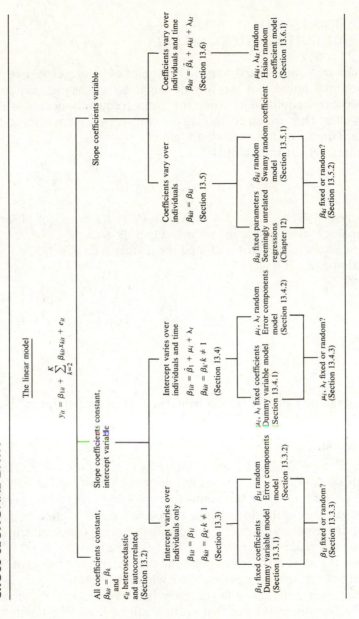

Chamberlain (1983). Other comparisons of different schemes of parameter variation can be found in Swamy (1971, 1974), Rosenberg (1973a), and Chapter 19.

13.2 MODELS WITH ALL COEFFICIENTS CONSTANT

In Chapters 8 and 11 we discussed the topics of heteroscedasticity and autocorrelation and noted that the former might be a reasonable assumption when using cross-sectional data while the latter frequently occurs when using time series data. Thus, when combining the two types of data, it seems reasonable to set up a model that captures both effects.

An example of such a model is

$$\mathbf{y}_i = X_i\boldsymbol{\beta} + \mathbf{e}_i, \qquad i = 1, 2, \ldots, N, \tag{13.2.1}$$

where $\mathbf{y}_i = (y_{i1}, y_{i2}, \ldots, y_{iT})'$, X_i is a $(T \times K)$ matrix of observations on K explanatory variables for the ith individual, $\boldsymbol{\beta} = (\beta_1, \beta_2, \ldots, \beta_K)'$ is a vector of parameters to be estimated, and the disturbance $\mathbf{e}_i = (e_{i1}, e_{i2}, \ldots, e_{iT})'$ is such that $E[\mathbf{e}_i] = \mathbf{0}$ and

$$E[\mathbf{e}_i\mathbf{e}_j'] = \frac{\sigma_{ij}}{1 - \rho_i\rho_j}\begin{bmatrix} 1 & \rho_j & \cdots & \rho_j^{T-1} \\ \rho_i & 1 & \cdots & \rho_j^{T-2} \\ \vdots & \vdots & & \vdots \\ \rho_i^{T-1} & \rho_i^{T-2} & \cdots & 1 \end{bmatrix} \tag{13.2.2}$$

This covariance matrix results from the first-order autoregressive process

$$e_{it} = \rho_i e_{i,t-1} + v_{it}, \qquad i = 1, 2, \ldots, N \tag{13.2.3}$$

where $E[v_{it}] = 0$, $E[v_{it}v_{jt}] = \sigma_{ij}$ and $E[v_{it}v_{js}] = 0$ for $t \neq s$. Thus this model assumes that (1) the coefficients are the same for all individuals, (2) the disturbance vector for a given individual follows a first-order autoregressive process, (3) the variance of the disturbance can be different for different individuals, and (4) the disturbances for different individuals are contemporaneously correlated.

In many circumstances these are likely to be a reasonable set of assumptions. Perhaps the most restrictive is that the coefficients are constant for all individuals. However, the more general case where the coefficients are not necessarily constant over individuals has already been extensively discussed in Section 12.3. In fact, the results of that section can be used to estimate the restricted model in Equation 13.2.1 and to test the hypothesis that the coefficients are the same for all individuals. See Sections 12.1.2a and 12.3 and also Kmenta (1971). If the first-order autoregressive scheme is regarded as too restrictive, alternative assumptions discussed in Chapter 12, such as first-order vector autoregressive errors or moving-average errors, can be made.

13.3 MODELS WITH CONSTANT SLOPE COEFFICIENTS AND AN INTERCEPT THAT VARIES OVER INDIVIDUALS

One of the most simple models used for combining time series and cross-sectional data is one where a varying intercept term is assumed to capture differences in behavior over individuals and where the slope coefficients are assumed to be constant. This model can be written as

$$y_{it} = \bar{\beta}_1 + \mu_i + \sum_{k=2}^{K} \beta_k x_{kit} + e_{it}, \qquad i = 1, 2, \ldots, N$$
$$t = 1, 2, \ldots, T \tag{13.3.1}$$

where $\beta_{1i} = \bar{\beta}_1 + \mu_i$ is the intercept for the ith individual, $\bar{\beta}_1$ is the "mean intercept," and μ_i represents the difference from this mean for the ith individual. The appropriate estimation procedure for (13.3.1) depends upon whether the μ_i are assumed to be random or fixed. If the μ_i are fixed (13.3.1) is the dummy variable or covariance model while if the μ_i are random it is an error components model. These two models are discussed in Sections 13.3.1 and 13.3.2, respectively, and in Section 13.3.3 we discuss the relevant issues for choice between the two models. Further discussion can be found, for example, in Maddala (1971), Nerlove (1971a), Swamy (1971), Mundlak (1978a), and Hausman and Taylor (1981). An introductory discussion may be found in Judge et al. (1982, pp. 477–487).

13.3.1 The Dummy Variable Model

For the ith individual, Equation 13.3.1 can be rewritten as

$$\mathbf{y}_i = (\bar{\beta}_1 + \mu_i)\mathbf{j}_T + X_{si}\boldsymbol{\beta}_s + \mathbf{e}_i, \tag{13.3.2}$$

where $\mathbf{y}_i = (y_{i1}, y_{i2}, \ldots, y_{iT})'$, $\mathbf{e}_i = (e_{i1}, e_{i2}, \ldots, e_{iT})'$, $\mathbf{j}_T = (1, 1, \ldots, 1)'$ and is of dimension $(T \times 1)$, and X_{si} contains values of the explanatory variables except for the constant and is of dimension $(T \times K')$, where $K' = K - 1$. In this section the intercepts $\beta_{1i} = \bar{\beta}_1 + \mu_i$ are assumed to be fixed parameters which, along with the slope coefficients $\boldsymbol{\beta}_s = (\beta_2, \beta_3, \ldots, \beta_K)'$, need to be estimated. We shall assume that $E[\mathbf{e}_i] = \mathbf{0}$, $E[\mathbf{e}_i\mathbf{e}_i'] = \sigma_e^2 I_T$ and that $E[\mathbf{e}_i\mathbf{e}_j'] = 0$ for $i \neq j$.

Under these assumptions the least squares estimator is best linear unbiased. To demonstrate its structure, we need to write the complete set of NT observations in the dummy variable form

$$\mathbf{y} = [I_N \otimes \mathbf{j}_T \quad X_s] \begin{pmatrix} \boldsymbol{\beta}_1 \\ \boldsymbol{\beta}_s \end{pmatrix} + \mathbf{e} \tag{13.3.3}$$

where $\mathbf{y}' = (\mathbf{y}_1', \mathbf{y}_2', \ldots, \mathbf{y}_N')$, $X_s' = (X_{s1}', X_{s2}', \ldots, X_{sN}')$, $\mathbf{e}' = (\mathbf{e}_1', \mathbf{e}_2', \ldots, \mathbf{e}_T')$, and $\boldsymbol{\beta}_1 = (\beta_{11}, \beta_{12}, \ldots, \beta_{1N})'$. To illustrate the dummy variables, note that, for $N = 3$,

$$I_N \otimes \mathbf{j}_T = \begin{bmatrix} 1 & 1 & \ldots & 1 & & & & & & & & \\ & & & & 1 & 1 & \ldots & 1 & & & & \\ & & & & & & & & \ddots & & & \\ & & & & & & & & & 1 & 1 & \ldots & 1 \end{bmatrix}'$$

Some least squares computer packages automatically insert a constant term in which case (13.3.3) is not convenient. This problem can be overcome by using the reparameterization

$$\mathbf{y} = \begin{bmatrix} \mathbf{j}_{NT} & \begin{pmatrix} I_{N-1} \\ \mathbf{0}' \end{pmatrix} \otimes \mathbf{j}_T & X_s \end{bmatrix} \begin{pmatrix} \boldsymbol{\delta} \\ \boldsymbol{\beta}_s \end{pmatrix} + \mathbf{e} \tag{13.3.4}$$

where $\boldsymbol{\delta} = (\delta_1, \delta_2, \ldots, \delta_N)'$, $\beta_{1N} = \delta_1$, $\beta_{1i} = \delta_1 + \delta_{i+1}$, $i = 1, 2, \ldots, N-1$, and the dummy variables, for $N = 3$, for example, are given by

$$\begin{bmatrix} \mathbf{j}_{NT} & \begin{pmatrix} I_{N-1} \\ \mathbf{0}' \end{pmatrix} \otimes \mathbf{j}_T \end{bmatrix} =$$

$$= \begin{bmatrix} 1 & 1 & \ldots & 1 & 1 & 1 & \ldots & 1 & \ldots & 1 & 1 & \ldots & 1 \\ 1 & 1 & \ldots & 1 & & & & & & & & & \\ & & & & \ddots & & & & & & & & \\ & & & & 1 & 1 & \ldots & 1 & & & & & \end{bmatrix}' \tag{13.3.5}$$

Least squares estimates of $(\boldsymbol{\beta}_1', \boldsymbol{\beta}_s')$ can be found from (13.3.3) or (13.3.4) and, of course, the results will be identical. If (13.3.4) is used and $\hat{\delta}_i$, $i = 1, 2, \ldots, N$ are the least squares estimates of the δ_i, then the least squares estimates of the β_{1i} are given by $b_{1i} = \hat{\delta}_1 + \hat{\delta}_{i+1}$, $i = 1, 2, \ldots, N-1$ and $b_{1N} = \hat{\delta}_1$. Estimates of the μ_i are given by

$$\hat{\mu}_i = b_{1i} - \sum_{j=1}^{N} \frac{b_{1j}}{N} \tag{13.3.6}$$

The application of least squares to (13.3.3) or (13.3.4) requires a matrix inversion of order $(N + K)$ and if N is large this could be computationally inconvenient. The problem can be overcome by considering, from either equation, the partitioned inverse that yields the least squares estimator for $\boldsymbol{\beta}_s$. After simplification this estimator becomes

$$\mathbf{b}_s = (X_s'(I_N \otimes D_T)X_s)^{-1}X_s'(I_N \otimes D_T)\mathbf{y}$$
$$= \left(\sum_{i=1}^{N} X_{si}'D_TX_{si}\right)^{-1} \sum_{i=1}^{N} X_{si}'D_T\mathbf{y}_i \tag{13.3.7}$$

where $D_T = I_T - \mathbf{j}_T\mathbf{j}_T'/T$ is the matrix that transforms the observations on each individual so that they are in terms of deviations around the mean for that individual. That is, $X_{si}'D_TX_{si} = X_{si}'D_T'D_TX_{si}$ because D_T is idempotent and the tth row of D_TX_{si} is given by

$$(x_{2it} - \bar{x}_{2i.}, \ldots, x_{kit} - \bar{x}_{ki.})$$

where the kth mean is $\bar{x}_{ki.} = \Sigma_{t=1}^T x_{kit}/T$. The transformation on $\mathbf{y}$ is similar.

If Equation 13.3.1 is averaged over time and the result subtracted from (13.3.1), we have

$$(y_{it} - \bar{y}_{i.}) = \sum_{k=2}^{K} \beta_k(x_{kit} - \bar{x}_{ki.}) + e_{it} - \frac{\Sigma_{t=1}^T e_{it}}{T} \tag{13.3.8}$$

where $\bar{y}_{i.} = \Sigma_{t=1}^T y_{it}/T$ and $\mathbf{b}_s$ can be viewed as the estimator obtained when least squares is applied to (13.3.8). This estimator only requires a matrix inversion of order K'; its covariance matrix is given by $\sigma_e^2(X_s'(I_N \otimes D_T)X_s)^{-1}$. Because it utilizes the variation of the variables within each group or individual, it is often known as the "within estimator." Furthermore, it plays an important role in the error components model of the next section.

If $\mathbf{b}_s$ is found from (13.3.8) rather than from (13.3.3) or (13.3.4), the least squares estimates of the intercepts can be found from

$$b_{1i} = \bar{y}_{i.} - \sum_{k=2}^{K} b_k \bar{x}_{ki.} \tag{13.3.9}$$

For testing hypotheses about the coefficients, the usual least squares procedures are appropriate. Of particular interest is the hypothesis $\beta_{11} = \beta_{12} = \ldots = \beta_{1N} = \bar{\beta}_1$, and this can be tested using the conventional F test that compares the restricted and unrestricted residual sums of squares. It is worth noting that a joint test such as this one is preferable to individual t tests on the coefficients of each dummy variable. If one follows the procedure of dropping dummy variables where t tests are insignificant, two different parameterizations of the same problem can lead to different dummy variables being omitted.

13.3.2 The Error Components Model

In this section we are again interested in using Equation 13.3.1 to model differences in individual behavior, but instead of assuming that the μ_i are fixed parameters, we assume that they are random variables with $E[\mu_i] = 0$, $E[\mu_i^2] = \sigma_\mu^2$, and $E[\mu_i\mu_j] = 0$ for $i \neq j$. The μ_i and e_{it} are assumed to be uncorrelated and, for the ith individual, the model is

$$\mathbf{y}_i = X_i\boldsymbol{\beta} + \mu_i\mathbf{j}_T + \mathbf{e}_i \tag{13.3.10}$$

where X_i is of dimension $(T \times K)$ and includes the constant term, $\boldsymbol{\beta} = (\bar{\beta}_1, \beta_2, \ldots, \beta_K)'$, and the covariance matrix for the composite disturbance is

$$\Phi_i = E[(\mu_i\mathbf{j}_T + \mathbf{e}_i)(\mu_i\mathbf{j}_T + \mathbf{e}_i)'] = \sigma_\mu^2\mathbf{j}_T\mathbf{j}_T' + \sigma_e^2 I_T \tag{13.3.11}$$

The assumption that the μ_i are random variables implies that the N individuals can be regarded as a *random sample* from some larger population, and it also implies that the μ_i and X_i are uncorrelated. This point will be taken up in Section 13.3.3.

Also, from (13.3.10) we can argue that our classification of models is, to some extent, arbitrary. We are regarding the error components model as one with a random intercept. It could also be regarded as one where all coefficients are constant and the disturbance covariance matrix is of the form given by (13.3.11). Alternatively, the intercept in the constant coefficient model in Section 13.2 could be redefined to include the disturbance and, as such, it would vary over time and individuals.

It is interesting to compare the error components covariance matrix with that of the model studied in Section 13.2. In Equation 13.3.11 the covariance matrix is identical for all individuals. Disturbances in different time periods for the same individual are correlated, but this correlation is constant over time and it is identical for all individuals. In Equation 13.2.2 the correlation declines as the disturbances become further apart in time and it can be different for different individuals.

13.3.2a GLS Estimation

If Equation 13.3.10 is rewritten to include all individuals, it becomes

$$\mathbf{y} = X\boldsymbol{\beta} + \boldsymbol{\mu} \otimes \mathbf{j}_T + \mathbf{e} \tag{13.3.12}$$

where $X' = (X_1', X_2', \ldots, X_N')$, $\boldsymbol{\mu} = (\mu_1, \mu_2, \ldots, \mu_N)'$, $\mathbf{y}' = (\mathbf{y}_1', \mathbf{y}_2', \ldots, \mathbf{y}_N')$, and $\mathbf{e}' = (\mathbf{e}_1', \mathbf{e}_2', \ldots, \mathbf{e}_N')$. The covariance matrix is block diagonal and given by

$$\Phi = E[(\boldsymbol{\mu} \otimes \mathbf{j}_T + \mathbf{e})(\boldsymbol{\mu} \otimes \mathbf{j}_T + \mathbf{e})'] = I_N \otimes \Phi_i \tag{13.3.13}$$

If σ_μ^2 and σ_e^2 are known, the generalized least squares (GLS) estimator for $\boldsymbol{\beta}$ is best linear unbiased and is given by

$$\hat{\boldsymbol{\beta}} = (X'\Phi^{-1}X)^{-1}X'\Phi^{-1}\mathbf{y} \tag{13.3.14}$$

If we partition this estimator as $\hat{\boldsymbol{\beta}}' = (\hat{\bar{\beta}}_1, \hat{\boldsymbol{\beta}}_s')$, then it is possible to show that $\hat{\boldsymbol{\beta}}_s$ is a matrix weighted average of the within estimator $\mathbf{b}_s$, which was described in Section 13.3.1, and another estimator which is known as the "between estimator.'' To demonstrate this, we first note that

$$\Phi^{-1} = I_N \otimes \Phi_i^{-1} = I_N \otimes \left(\frac{\mathbf{j}_T\mathbf{j}_T'}{T\sigma_1^2} + \frac{D_T}{\sigma_e^2}\right) \tag{13.3.15}$$

where $\sigma_1^2 = T\sigma_\mu^2 + \sigma_e^2$. Then, if this expression and the partitions $X = (\mathbf{j}_{NT}, X_s)$ and $X_i = (\mathbf{j}_T, X_{si})$ are substituted into (13.3.14), we obtain, after some algebra,

$$\hat{\boldsymbol{\beta}}_s = \left[\frac{X_s'Q_1X_s}{\sigma_1^2} + \frac{\Sigma_{i=1}^N X_{si}'D_TX_{si}}{\sigma_e^2}\right]^{-1}\left[\frac{X_s'Q_1\mathbf{y}}{\sigma_1^2} + \frac{\Sigma_{i=1}^N X_{si}'D_T\mathbf{y}_i}{\sigma_e^2}\right] \tag{13.3.16}$$

where

$$Q_1 = I_N \otimes \frac{\mathbf{j}_T\mathbf{j}_T'}{T} - \frac{\mathbf{j}_{NT}\mathbf{j}_{NT}'}{NT} \tag{13.3.17}$$

is an idempotent matrix such that

$$Q_1X_s = \begin{bmatrix} \bar{x}_{21.} - \bar{x}_{2..}, & \ldots, & \bar{x}_{K1.} - \bar{x}_{K..} \\ \bar{x}_{22.} - \bar{x}_{2..}, & \ldots, & \bar{x}_{K2.} - \bar{x}_{K..} \\ \vdots & & \vdots \\ \bar{x}_{2N.} - \bar{x}_{2..}, & \ldots, & \bar{x}_{KN.} - \bar{x}_{K..} \end{bmatrix} \otimes \mathbf{j}_T$$

and $\bar{x}_{k..} = \Sigma_{i=1}^N \Sigma_{t=1}^T x_{kit}/NT$. Thus Q_1, when multiplied by X or $\mathbf{y}$, has the effect of calculating the means for each individual ($\bar{x}_{ki.}$), expressing the individual means in terms of deviations from the overall mean, and repeating each of these N observations T times.

The between estimator is given by

$$\boldsymbol{\beta}_s^* = (X_s'Q_1X_s)^{-1}X_s'Q_1\mathbf{y} \tag{13.3.18}$$

and is obtained by applying least squares to

$$\bar{y}_{i.} = \bar{\beta}_1 + \sum_{k=2}^{K} \beta_k\bar{x}_{ki.} + \mu_i + \frac{\Sigma_{t=1}^T e_{it}}{T} \tag{13.3.19}$$

which is Equation 13.3.1 averaged over time. Note that $\boldsymbol{\beta}_s^*$ only utilizes the variation between individuals. Now $\hat{\boldsymbol{\beta}}_s$ can be written as

$$\hat{\boldsymbol{\beta}}_s = \left[\frac{X_s'Q_1X_s}{\sigma_1^2} + \frac{\Sigma_{i=1}^N X_{si}'D_TX_{si}}{\sigma_e^2}\right]^{-1}\left[\left(\frac{X_s'Q_1X_s}{\sigma_1^2}\right)\boldsymbol{\beta}_s^* + \left(\frac{\Sigma_{i=1}^N X_{si}'D_TX_{si}}{\sigma_e^2}\right)\mathbf{b}_s\right] \tag{13.3.20}$$

which is a matrix weighted average of $\boldsymbol{\beta}_s^*$ and $\mathbf{b}_s$. Under certain assumptions the weights are the inverses of the covariance matrices of the respective estimators.

Thus the generalized least squares estimator can be viewed as an efficient combination of the dummy variable estimator that utilizes variation within individuals and the estimator $\boldsymbol{\beta}_s^*$ that utilizes variation between individuals. For further discussion of this decomposition see Maddala (1971), Nerlove (1971a), Swamy (1971), and Arora (1973).

We have not yet mentioned the GLS estimator of the intercept obtained from partitioning (13.3.14). It is given by

$$\hat{\bar{\beta}}_1 = \bar{y}_{..} - \sum_{k=2}^{K} \hat{\beta}_k \bar{x}_{k..} \tag{13.3.21}$$

The expression for $\hat{\boldsymbol{\beta}}_s$ in Equation 13.3.20 is an informative one but, from the point of view of the applied worker, it may not be a very convenient one for calculation. To calculate $\hat{\boldsymbol{\beta}}$ via a standard least squares computer package, we need a transformation matrix P such that $P'P = c\Phi^{-1}$ where c is any scalar. Fuller and Battese (1973) suggest the transformation $P = I_N \otimes P_i$, where

$$P_i = I_T - \left(1 - \frac{\sigma_e}{\sigma_1}\right) \frac{\mathbf{j}_T \mathbf{j}_T'}{T} \tag{13.3.22}$$

$P_i'P_i = \sigma_e^2 \Phi_i^{-1}$ and hence $P'P = \sigma_e^2 \Phi^{-1}$. Multiplying both sides of (13.3.12) by P yields

$$y_{it} - \alpha \bar{y}_{i.} = (1 - \alpha)\bar{\beta}_1 + \sum_{k=2}^{K} \beta_k (x_{kit} - \alpha \bar{x}_{ki.}) + v_{it} \tag{13.3.23}$$

where $\alpha = 1 - \sigma_e/\sigma_1$ and the v_{it} are homoscedastic and uncorrelated. Assuming α is known, application of least squares to (13.3.23) yields the GLS estimator $\hat{\boldsymbol{\beta}}$. Methods for estimating α when it is unknown are discussed in Section 13.3.2c.

The matrices P_i and Φ_i^{-1} are found by considering the orthogonal matrix that diagonalizes Φ_i. This matrix is $C = (T^{-1/2}\mathbf{j}_T, C_1')'$, where C_1 is any $(T - 1) \times T$ matrix such that $C_1 \mathbf{j}_T = 0$, $C_1 C_1' = I_{T-1}$ and $C_1'C_1 = D_T$. The characteristic roots of Φ_i are σ_1^2 and σ_e^2 with multiplicity of 1 and $(T - 1)$, respectively. The transformation $I_N \otimes \mathbf{j}_T'/T^{1/2}$ leads to $\boldsymbol{\beta}_s^*$ while the use of $I_N \otimes C_1$ leads to $\mathbf{b}_s$. See Balestra and Nerlove (1966), Nerlove (1971a), Swamy (1971), Arora (1973), and Fuller and Battese (1973).

13.3.2b Prediction of Random Components

In addition to the estimation of $\boldsymbol{\beta}$ one may be interested in predicting the μ_i's. This is of interest because it describes how the behavior of different individuals varies as well as provides a basis for more efficient prediction of future observations on a given individual. The best linear unbiased predictor of μ_i [Lee and Griffiths (1979), Taub (1979)] is given by

$$\hat{\mu}_i = \left(\frac{\sigma_\mu^2}{\sigma_1^2}\right) \mathbf{j}_T'(\mathbf{y}_i - X_i \hat{\boldsymbol{\beta}}) \tag{13.3.24}$$

and it can be viewed as a proportion of the GLS residual allocated to $\hat{\mu}_i$, the precise proportion depending upon the relative variances σ_μ^2 and σ_e^2. It is best linear unbiased in the sense that $E[\hat{\mu}_i - \mu_i] = 0$, and that $E[(\hat{\mu}_i - \mu_i)^2]$ is smaller than the prediction error variance of any other predictor that is unbiased and a linear function of $\mathbf{y}$. The expectation is taken with respect to repeated sampling over both time and individuals.

Conditional on μ_i, $\hat{\mu}_i$ is a biased predictor because $E[\hat{\mu}_i|\mu_i] \neq \mu_i$. The bias, as well as a "best constrained predictor" that restricts the mean squared bias to be less than a predetermined value, have been considered by Battese and Fuller (1982).

Also, it is interesting to note that $\hat{\mu}_i$ is that value of μ_i obtained when the quadratic function

$$S = \frac{1}{\sigma_e^2} \sum_{i=1}^{N} (\mathbf{y}_i - X_i\boldsymbol{\beta} - \mu_i\mathbf{j}_T)'(\mathbf{y}_i - X_i\boldsymbol{\beta} - \mu_i\mathbf{j}_T) + \frac{1}{\sigma_\mu^2} \sum_{i=1}^{N} \mu_i^2 \tag{13.3.25}$$

is minimized with respect to $\boldsymbol{\beta}$ and the μ_i. This can be regarded as an extension of the Theil and Goldberger (1960) mixed estimation procedure [Lee and Griffiths (1979)].

13.3.2c Estimation of Variance Components

Both the GLS estimator for $\boldsymbol{\beta}$ and the predictor for μ_i depend on the variances σ_e^2 and σ_μ^2, which are generally unknown. In this section we indicate how they can be estimated. One method for obtaining unbiased estimators is to use the residuals from $\boldsymbol{\beta}_s^*$ to estimate σ_1^2 and the residuals from $\mathbf{b}_s$ to estimate σ_e^2. This yields [Maddala (1971), Swamy (1971), Arora (1973)]

$$\hat{\sigma}_1^2 = \frac{\mathbf{e}^{*\prime}\mathbf{e}^*}{N - K} \tag{13.3.26}$$

and

$$\hat{\sigma}_e^2 = \frac{\hat{\mathbf{e}}'\hat{\mathbf{e}}}{N(T - 1) - K'} \tag{13.3.27}$$

where $\mathbf{e}^* = Q_1\mathbf{y} - Q_1X_s\boldsymbol{\beta}_s^*$ are the residuals from the estimator $\boldsymbol{\beta}_s^*$ and $\hat{\mathbf{e}} = (I_N \otimes D_T)\mathbf{y} - (I_N \otimes D_T)X_s\mathbf{b}_s$ are the residuals from the estimator $\mathbf{b}_s$. An estimator for the variance of μ_i is

$$\hat{\sigma}_\mu^2 = \frac{\hat{\sigma}_1^2 - \hat{\sigma}_e^2}{T} \tag{13.3.28}$$

This estimator has the disadvantage that $\hat{\sigma}_\mu^2$ can be negative. If this occurs, we can set the negative estimate to zero or, as Maddala (1971) suggests, it may be an indication that time effects, which are discussed in Section 13.4, have been incorrectly omitted. Assuming that $\sigma_\mu^2 = 0$ leads to the least squares estimator.

A number of other variance estimators has been suggested. These include estimators based on least squares residuals [Wallace and Hussain (1969)], estimators based only on the residuals $\hat{\mathbf{e}}$ [Amemiya (1971)], the "fitting of constants" method [Henderson (1953), Fuller and Battese (1973)], MINQUE estimation [Rao (1970, 1972)] and maximum likelihood estimation [Amemiya (1971), Nerlove (1971a), Maddala (1971)]. When any of these variance estimates are used in place of the real variances in the GLS estimator for $\boldsymbol{\beta}$, we have an estimated generalized least squares (EGLS) estimator. Under appropriate conditions these EGLS estimators will possess the same asymptotic distribution as the GLS estimator. See, for example, Swamy (1971) and Fuller and Battese (1973).

The finite sample properties of various EGLS estimators as well as the between and within estimators have been investigated analytically by Swamy and Mehta (1979) and Taylor (1980), and in Monte Carlo studies by Arora (1973) and Maddala and Mount (1973). Taylor concludes that (i) the EGLS estimator is more efficient than the within estimator for all but the fewest degrees of freedom and its variance is never more than 17% above the Cramèr-Rao bound, (ii) the asymptotic approximation to the variance of the EGLS estimator is similarly within 17% of the true variance but remains significantly smaller for moderately large sample sizes, and (iii) more efficient estimators for the variance components do not necessarily yield more efficient EGLS estimators. Swamy and Mehta introduce some new estimators and outline criteria that one could use to choose between least squares, estimated generalized least squares, the within estimator, the between estimator, and their new estimators.

13.3.2d Testing the Specification

If all the $\mu_i = 0$ or, equivalently, $\sigma_\mu^2 = 0$ the individual components do not exist and the least squares estimator is best linear unbiased. To test this hypothesis we could, as mentioned in Section 13.3.1, use the dummy variable estimator and the F test based on the restricted and unrestricted residual sums of squares. An alternative, which requires only least squares estimation, is a test based on the Lagrange multiplier statistic [Breusch and Pagan (1980)]. Under the null hypothesis $\sigma_\mu^2 = 0$ Breusch and Pagan show that

$$\lambda_{\text{LM}} = \frac{NT}{2(T-1)}\left[\frac{\tilde{\mathbf{e}}'(I_N \otimes \mathbf{j}_T\mathbf{j}_T')\tilde{\mathbf{e}}}{\tilde{\mathbf{e}}'\tilde{\mathbf{e}}} - 1\right]^2 \tag{13.3.29}$$

is asymptotically distributed as $\chi^2_{(1)}$ where $\tilde{\mathbf{e}}$ is the vector of least squares residuals obtained by regressing $\mathbf{y}$ on X. Note that $\tilde{\mathbf{e}}'(I_N \otimes \mathbf{j}_T\mathbf{j}_T')\tilde{\mathbf{e}} = \Sigma_{i=1}^N(\Sigma_{t=1}^T\tilde{\mathbf{e}}_{it})^2$.

13.3.3 Fixed or Random Effects?

In Sections 13.3.1 and 13.3.2 we considered estimation of

$$\mathbf{y}_i = X_i\boldsymbol{\beta} + \mu_i\mathbf{j}_T + \mathbf{e}_i \tag{13.3.30}$$

where μ_i was first assumed to be fixed (Section 13.3.1) and then random (Section 13.3.2). If the choice between these two assumptions is clear, then the estimation procedure could be chosen accordingly. However, if the choice is not an obvious one, it is useful to consider the problem in terms of whether or not the μ_i are correlated with the X_i, and if so, the possible nature of the dependence of μ_i on X_i [Mundlak (1978a), Chamberlain (1978, 1979, 1983), Hausman and Taylor (1981)].

Mundlak (1978a) suggests that the μ_i can always be considered random, but, when using the dummy variable estimator, our inference is *conditional on the μ_i in the sample*. When the error components model is used, specific assumptions about the distribution of the μ_i are made, and, as a result, unconditional inference is possible. Because the conditional inference implied by the dummy variable estimator does not make any specific assumptions about the distribution of the μ_i, it can be used for a wider range of problems. However, if the restrictive distributional assumption of the error components model is correct, then, as expected, using this additional information leads to a more efficient estimator.

The relevant question then is whether it is reasonable to assume that the μ_i are i.i.d. $(0,\sigma_\mu^2)$ or whether they are a consequence of some other random process. Mundlak, Chamberlain, and others argue that it is more reasonable to assume that μ_i and X_i are correlated and hence that $E[\mu_i]$ will not be constant but some function of X_i. For example, if we are considering a production function where i refers to the ith firm, and the ith firm knows its value μ_i, then a simple profit maximization assumption will imply that X_i depends on μ_i. If μ_i and X_i are in fact correlated, the error components model is similar to an omitted variable misspecification and its GLS estimator, as well as the LS estimator $\mathbf{b} = (X'X)^{-1}X'\mathbf{y}$, will be biased. However, conditional on the μ_i in the sample, the dummy variable estimator will be best linear unbiased.

Thus, it would appear that a reasonable prescription is to use the error components model if the $\mu_i \sim$ i.i.d. $(0,\sigma_\mu^2)$ assumption is a reasonable one and N is sufficiently large for reliable estimation of σ_μ^2; otherwise, particularly when μ_i and X_i are correlated, or N is small, use the dummy variable (within) estimator. However, as noted by Chamberlain (1978) and Hausman and Taylor (1981), there are two possibly undesirable features of the within estimator when μ_i and X_i are correlated. First, if X_i contains some time invariant measurable variables, then it is impossible to separate these variables from the dummy variables. They will be eliminated when the within estimator $\mathbf{b}_s$ is obtained. This problem does not arise if the error components model is used, but, in this case, we would be faced with the problem of biased and inconsistent estimates.

The second problem with using the within estimator is that it may be less efficient than alternative consistent estimators that exploit information on the relationship between μ_i and X_i, and that do not ignore sample variation across individuals.

For the case where there are no time invariant variables in X_i, Mundlak (1978a) shows that there will be no efficiency loss from using the within estimator if $E(\mu_i)$ is linearly related to $\bar{\mathbf{x}}_i = (\bar{x}_{2i.}, \bar{x}_{3i.}, \ldots, \bar{x}_{Ki.})'$; in this case the unconditional GLS estimator is identical to the dummy variable estimator. However, as Lee (1978a) and others have pointed out, this is a fairly special case. The μ_i may be related to some other variables that are correlated with X_i, they may be related to only some of the components in $\bar{\mathbf{x}}_i$, or the relationship may be a nonlinear one. In these cases the two estimators are not identical. Some alternative estimation techniques that consider these aspects are those of Chamberlain (1978, 1983), Chamberlain and Griliches (1975) and Hausman and Taylor (1981). Chamberlain (1978) and Chamberlain and Griliches (1975) relate the individual effects to a set of exogenous variables in a factor analytic model. Hausman and Taylor (1981) do not assume any specification for the μ_i, but use knowledge about which vectors in X_i are correlated with the μ_i to develop an efficient instrumental variables estimator. They show that Mundlak's (1978a) specification where the GLS and within estimators are identical can be considered a special case.

A completely different approach particularly designed for small T and large N is that outlined by Chamberlain (1983). He shows that if μ_i and X_i are correlated, then this fact will be reflected in the values of the coefficients in a linear regression of y_{it} on all leads and lags of the explanatory variables. This essentially involves a multivariate specification with T dependent variables, KT explanatory variables, and N observations on each of the variables. Chamberlain suggests that it is too restrictive to assume that $E(\mu_i|X_i)$ is a linear function, and he goes on to formulate inference procedures based on the estimation of a minimum mean square error linear predictor. The estimates obtained can be used first to test whether μ_i and X_i are correlated, and, secondly, to test whether the coefficients obey certain restrictions that are implied by the specification. Evidence that the restrictions do not hold is suggestive of some type of specification error, such as random coefficients [Chamberlain (1982)], omitted variables, or serial correlation in the e_{it}. See also, Chamberlain (1979).

The foregoing discussion suggests that it would be convenient to have a statistical test to test the hypothesis that the μ_i and X_i are uncorrelated. In addition to the Chamberlain procedure, tests for this purpose have been developed by Hausman (1978) and Pudney (1978) and considered further by Hausman and Taylor (1981). Under the null hypothesis that the error components model is the correct specification, Hausman shows that

$$m = (\mathbf{b}_s - \hat{\boldsymbol{\beta}}_s)'(M_1 - M_0)^{-1}(\mathbf{b}_s - \hat{\boldsymbol{\beta}}_s) \tag{13.3.31}$$

has an asymptotic $\chi^2_{(K')}$-distribution, where $M_1 = \sigma_e^2[X_s'(I_N \otimes D_T)X_s]^{-1}$ is the covariance matrix for the dummy variable estimator $\mathbf{b}_s$ and

$$M_0 = \left[\frac{1}{\sigma_1^2} X_s' Q_1 X_s + \frac{1}{\sigma_e^2} (X_s'(I_N \otimes D_T)X_s)\right]^{-1}$$

is the covariance matrix for the generalized least squares estimator $\hat{\boldsymbol{\beta}}_s$. The unknown variances in $\hat{\boldsymbol{\beta}}_s$, M_0, and M_1 can be replaced by appropriately chosen estimates without affecting the asymptotic distribution of m. If the null hypothesis is true, then, asymptotically, $\mathbf{b}_s$ and $\hat{\boldsymbol{\beta}}_s$ differ only through sampling error. However, if μ_i and X_i are correlated, $\hat{\boldsymbol{\beta}}_s$ and $\mathbf{b}_s$ could differ widely and it is hoped that this will be reflected in the test. Rejection of the null hypothesis does suggest that $\mathbf{b}_s$ is the more appropriate estimator, but Hausman recommends carefully checking the specification because errors in variables problems, if present, may invalidate the dummy variable estimates.

Finally, we note that an approach for integrating the fixed and random effects into a combined model, which is a special case of a switching regressions model, and which is particularly relevant when a number of the individual effects are likely to be equal, has been outlined by Mundlak and Yahav (1981).

13.3.4 Extensions of the Model

In the previous section we discussed a number of extensions of the basic individual effects model, with particular emphasis on the question of fixed versus random effects. In this section we briefly mention a number of other extensions that have appeared in the literature. First, if X contains a vector of lagged values of the dependent variable, then a number of problems are introduced. In particular, if circumstances are such that T is small and N is large, we are likely to be interested in estimator properties as $N \to \infty$ for fixed T. In the traditional autoregressive model, however, we are concerned with estimator properties as $T \to \infty$. For details of this and other problems that occur when a lagged dependent variable is included, as well as some solutions, see Anderson and Hsiao (1981, 1982), Balestra and Nerlove (1966), Berzeg (1979), Bhargava and Sargan (1983), Chamberlain (1979, 1983), Maddala (1971), Nerlove (1967, 1971a), Nickell (1981), Sevestre and Trognon (1982), and Trognon (1978).

Another extension is the introduction of a more general disturbance covariance matrix. Such an extension could involve the introduction of heteroscedasticity and autocorrelation in the e_{it}, as well as a generalization of the stochastic specification for μ_i. Examples of studies along these lines are Bhargava et al. (1982), Glejser (1978), Hause (1977, 1980), Kiefer (1980), Lillard and Willis (1978), Lillard and Weiss (1979), McCurdy (1982) and Schmidt (1983). Note that, if $(\mu_i \mathbf{j}_T + \mathbf{e}_i)$ is regarded as a random drawing from a multivariate distribution with arbitrary covariance matrix Σ, then, providing N is large and T is small, it is possible to estimate Σ without making specific assumptions about the type of heteroscedasticity and autocorrelation in $\mathbf{e}_i$. This does assume, however, that the autocorrelation and variance parameters are identical for all individuals.

Other extensions include models with a discrete dependent variable [Chamberlain (1979, 1980, 1983), Heckman (1978), Flinn and Heckman (1982) and

Singer (1982)], models with a truncated dependent variable [Griliches et al. (1978), Hausman and Wise (1979), Kiefer and Neumann (1981), and Maddala (1978)], and the use of biased estimators with lower mean square error [Mundlak (1978a)].

13.4 MODELS WITH CONSTANT SLOPE COEFFICIENTS AND AN INTERCEPT THAT VARIES OVER INDIVIDUALS AND TIME

The analysis of the previous section can be extended so that the intercept, in addition to containing a component that is constant over time and varies from individual to individual, also contains a component that varies over time and is constant over individuals. This extended model is

$$y_{it} = \bar{\beta}_1 + \mu_i + \lambda_t + \sum_{k=2}^{K} \beta_k x_{kit} + e_{it}, \qquad i = 1, 2, \ldots, N$$

$$t = 1, 2, \ldots, T \qquad (13.4.1)$$

with intercept $\beta_{1it} = \bar{\beta}_1 + \mu_i + \lambda_t$. In a given time period, the time effects, λ_t, represent the influence of factors that are common to all individuals.

Our discussion in this section runs parallel to that of Section 13.3. If the μ_i and λ_t are fixed, Equation 13.4.1 is a dummy variable model, and if they are random it is an error components model. These two models are discussed in Sections 13.4.1 and 13.4.2, respectively, and, to help the applied worker choose between the two models, a statistical test is given in Section 13.4.3. For further discussion see Wallace and Hussain (1969), Swamy (1971), Nerlove (1971b), Swamy and Arora (1972), and Mundlak (1978a).

13.4.1 The Dummy Variable Model

When μ_i and λ_t are treated as fixed parameters, one of the μ_i and one of the λ_t are redundant and some restrictions such as $\Sigma_i \mu_i = 0$ and $\Sigma_t \lambda_t = 0$ need to be imposed. To estimate (13.4.1) using least squares, we need to reparameterize the equation so that the restrictions are incorporated. One such reparameterization is to define $\beta_{1i} = \bar{\beta}_1 + \mu_i$, $i = 1, 2, \ldots, N$ and $\lambda_t^* = \lambda_t - \lambda_T$, $t = 1, 2, \ldots, T - 1$, and write the model for the ith individual as

$$\mathbf{y}_i = \beta_{1i}\mathbf{j}_T + \begin{pmatrix} I_{T-1} \\ \mathbf{0}' \end{pmatrix} \boldsymbol{\lambda}^* + X_{si}\boldsymbol{\beta}_s + \mathbf{e}_i \qquad (13.4.2)$$

where $\boldsymbol{\lambda}^* = (\lambda_1^*, \lambda_2^*, \ldots, \lambda_{T-1}^*)'$. With all observations included, this becomes

$$\mathbf{y} = \left[I_N \otimes \mathbf{j}_T \quad \mathbf{j}_N \otimes \begin{pmatrix} I_{T-1} \\ \mathbf{0}' \end{pmatrix} \quad X_s \right] \begin{pmatrix} \boldsymbol{\beta}_1 \\ \boldsymbol{\lambda}^* \\ \boldsymbol{\beta}_s \end{pmatrix} + \mathbf{e} \tag{13.4.3}$$

where $\boldsymbol{\beta}_1 = (\beta_{11}, \beta_{12}, \ldots, \beta_{1N})'$, $\mathbf{y} = (\mathbf{y}_1', \mathbf{y}_2', \ldots, \mathbf{y}_N')'$, $X_s' = (X_{s1}', X_{s2}', \ldots, X_{sN}')$, and $\mathbf{e}' = (\mathbf{e}_1', \mathbf{e}_2', \ldots, \mathbf{e}_N')$. The matrix X_s contains observations on all the explanatory variables except for the constant. It is assumed that $E[\mathbf{e}] = \mathbf{0}$ and $E[\mathbf{ee}'] = \sigma_e^2 I_{NT}$, and hence that the least squares estimator for the $[(N + T - 1 + K') \times 1]$ parameter vector $(\boldsymbol{\beta}_1', \boldsymbol{\lambda}^{*\prime}, \boldsymbol{\beta}_s')'$ is best linear unbiased.

Before giving an expression for the least squares estimator, it is worthwhile illustrating the dummy variables. For $N = 3$,

$$\left[I_N \otimes \mathbf{j}_T \quad \mathbf{j}_N \otimes \begin{pmatrix} I_{T-1} \\ \mathbf{0}' \end{pmatrix} \right]'$$

$$= \left[\begin{array}{ccccccccccccccccc}
1 & 1 & \cdots & 1 & 1 & & & & & & & & & & & \\
 & & & & & 1 & 1 & \cdots & 1 & 1 & & & & & & \\
 & & & & & & & & & & \ddots & & & & & \\
 & & & & & & & & & & & 1 & 1 & \cdots & 1 & 1 \\
1 & & & & & 1 & & & & & \cdots & 1 & & & & \\
 & 1 & & & & & 1 & & & & & & 1 & & & \\
 & & \ddots & & & & & \ddots & & & & & & \ddots & & \\
 & & & 1 & 0 & & & & 1 & 0 & \cdots & & & & 1 & 0
\end{array} \right] \tag{13.4.4}$$

If an alternative parameterization is used, the dummy variables will have a different structure. In particular, to include a constant term, we could replace $I_N \otimes \mathbf{j}_T$ with

$$\left[\mathbf{j}_{NT} \quad \begin{pmatrix} I_{N-1} \\ \mathbf{0}' \end{pmatrix} \otimes \mathbf{j}_T \right]$$

See Equations 13.3.3 to 13.3.5.

Least squares estimates of the unknown parameters can be obtained directly from (13.4.3) or, if $N + T - 1 + K'$ is too large, by using results obtained by partitioning the least squares estimator. For the slope coefficients this partitioning leads to the estimator

$$\mathbf{b}_s = (X_s' Q X_s)^{-1} X_s' Q \mathbf{y} \tag{13.4.5}$$

The matrix

$$Q = I_{NT} - I_N \otimes \frac{\mathbf{j}_T \mathbf{j}_T'}{T} - \frac{\mathbf{j}_N \mathbf{j}_N'}{N} \otimes I_T + \frac{\mathbf{j}_{NT} \mathbf{j}_{NT}'}{NT} \tag{13.4.6}$$

is idempotent and transforms the observations on X_s and $\mathbf{y}$ such that QX_s, for example, is an $(NT \times K')$ matrix with the typical element given by

$$x_{kit} - \bar{x}_{ki.} - \bar{x}_{k.t} + \bar{x}_{k..} \tag{13.4.7}$$

where

$$\bar{x}_{ki\cdot} = \frac{\sum_{t=1}^{T} x_{kit}}{T}, \qquad \bar{x}_{k\cdot t} = \frac{\sum_{i=1}^{N} x_{kit}}{N}, \qquad \text{and} \qquad \bar{x}_{k\cdot\cdot} = \frac{\sum_{i=1}^{N}\sum_{t=1}^{T} x_{kit}}{NT}$$

If Equation 13.4.1 is averaged over t, averaged over i, and averaged over both t and i, we obtain, respectively,

$$\bar{y}_{i.} = \bar{\beta}_1 + \mu_i + \sum_{k=2}^{K} \bar{x}_{ki.}\beta_k + \frac{\Sigma_t e_{it}}{T} \tag{13.4.8}$$

$$\bar{y}_{.t} = \bar{\beta}_1 + \lambda_t + \sum_{k=2}^{K} \bar{x}_{k.t}\beta_k + \frac{\Sigma_i e_{it}}{N} \tag{13.4.9}$$

and

$$\bar{y}_{..} = \bar{\beta}_1 + \sum_{k=2}^{K} \bar{x}_{k..}\beta_k + \frac{\Sigma_i\Sigma_t e_{it}}{NT} \tag{13.4.10}$$

Subtracting (13.4.8) and (13.4.9) from (13.4.1) and (13.4.10) yields

$$y_{it} - \bar{y}_{i.} - \bar{y}_{.t} + \bar{y}_{..} = \sum_{k=2}^{K} (x_{kit} - \bar{x}_{ki.} - \bar{x}_{k.t} + \bar{x}_{k..})\beta_k + v_{it} \tag{13.4.11}$$

where v_{it} is defined in an obvious way. The estimator $\mathbf{b}_s$ in Equation 13.4.5 can be viewed as the least squares estimator obtained from Equation 13.4.11. It can also be interpreted as the GLS estimator obtained from (13.4.11), where $QQ = Q$ is the covariance matrix of the disturbance and Q is the generalized inverse of itself [Swamy and Arora (1972)]. The covariance matrix for $\mathbf{b}_s$ is $\sigma_e^2(X_s'QX_s)^{-1}$.

If $\boldsymbol{\beta}_s$ is estimated using (13.4.5), the remaining parameters in the model can be estimated from

$$\hat{\mu}_i = (\bar{y}_{i.} - \bar{y}_{..}) - \sum_{k=2}^{K} (\bar{x}_{ki.} - \bar{x}_{k..})b_k \tag{13.4.12}$$

$$\hat{\lambda}_t = (\bar{y}_{.t} - \bar{y}_{..}) - \sum_{k=2}^{K}(\bar{x}_{k.t} - \bar{x}_{k..})b_k \tag{13.4.13}$$

and

$$\hat{\bar{b}}_1 = \bar{y}_{..} - \sum_{k=2}^{K} \bar{x}_{k..} b_k \tag{13.4.14}$$

where b_k is an element of $\mathbf{b}_s$ and $\hat{\bar{b}}_1$ is an estimate of $\bar{\beta}_1$.

As mentioned in Section 13.3.1, to test hypotheses concerning whether or not the dummy variables should be included, we can use the F test, which compares the restricted and unrestricted residual sums of squares. For two applications of the above model see Hoch (1962) and Mundlak (1963). We turn now to the error components model.

13.4.2 The Error Components Model

Instead of assuming that the individual and time effects are fixed parameters, in this section we assume they are random variables such that $E[\mu_i] = 0$, $E[\lambda_t] = 0$, $E[\mu_i^2] = \sigma_\mu^2$, $E[\lambda_t^2] = \sigma_\lambda^2$, $E[\mu_i\mu_j] = 0$ for $i \neq j$, $E[\lambda_t\lambda_s] = 0$ for $t \neq s$, and λ_t, μ_i and e_{it} are uncorrelated for all i and t. Under these assumptions the observations on the ith individual are given by

$$\mathbf{y}_i = X_i\boldsymbol{\beta} + \mu_i\mathbf{j}_T + I_T\boldsymbol{\lambda} + \mathbf{e}_i \tag{13.4.15}$$

where $\boldsymbol{\lambda} = (\lambda_1, \lambda_2, \ldots, \lambda_T)'$ and the other symbols have their earlier definitions. In particular, $X_i = (\mathbf{j}_T, X_{si})$ includes a constant term. The covariance matrix for the composite disturbance is

$$\begin{aligned}\Phi_{ii} &= E[(\mu_i\mathbf{j}_T + I_T\boldsymbol{\lambda} + \mathbf{e}_i)(\mu_i\mathbf{j}_T + I_T\boldsymbol{\lambda} + \mathbf{e}_i)'] \\ &= \sigma_\mu^2\mathbf{j}_T\mathbf{j}_T' + \sigma_\lambda^2 I_T + \sigma_e^2 I_T \end{aligned}\tag{13.4.16}$$

and the covariance between disturbance vectors for two different individuals is

$$\begin{aligned}\Phi_{ij} &= E[(\mu_i\mathbf{j}_T + I_T\boldsymbol{\lambda} + \mathbf{e}_i)(\mu_j\mathbf{j}_T + I_T\boldsymbol{\lambda} + \mathbf{e}_j)'] \\ &= \sigma_\lambda^2 I_T \end{aligned}\tag{13.4.17}$$

When all NT observations are included, the model becomes

$$\mathbf{y} = X\boldsymbol{\beta} + \boldsymbol{\mu} \otimes \mathbf{j}_T + (\mathbf{j}_N \otimes I_T)\boldsymbol{\lambda} + \mathbf{e} \tag{13.4.18}$$

where $\boldsymbol{\mu} = (\mu_1, \mu_2, \ldots, \mu_N)'$ and the complete disturbance covariance matrix is

$$\begin{aligned}\Phi &= E[(\boldsymbol{\mu} \otimes \mathbf{j}_T + (\mathbf{j}_N \otimes I_T)\boldsymbol{\lambda} + \mathbf{e})(\boldsymbol{\mu} \otimes \mathbf{j}_T + (\mathbf{j}_N \otimes I_T)\boldsymbol{\lambda} + \mathbf{e})'] \\ &= \sigma_\mu^2(I_N \otimes \mathbf{j}_T\mathbf{j}_T') + \sigma_\lambda^2(\mathbf{j}_N\mathbf{j}_N' \otimes I_T) + \sigma_e^2 I_{NT} \end{aligned}\tag{13.4.19}$$

Unlike Φ in Section 13.3.2 this covariance matrix is not block diagonal. The disturbances corresponding to different individuals are contemporaneously correlated.

13.4.2a GLS Estimation

For estimating $\boldsymbol{\beta}$, the generalized least squares (GLS) estimator

$$\hat{\boldsymbol{\beta}} = (X'\Phi^{-1}X)^{-1}X'\Phi^{-1}\mathbf{y} \tag{13.4.20}$$

is best linear unbiased with covariance matrix $(X'\Phi^{-1}X)^{-1}$. If $\hat{\boldsymbol{\beta}}$ is partitioned as $\hat{\boldsymbol{\beta}}' = (\hat{\beta}_1, \hat{\boldsymbol{\beta}}_s')$, it is possible to show that the estimator of the slope coefficients $\hat{\boldsymbol{\beta}}_s$ is a matrix weighted average of three other estimators.

Direct multiplication shows that

$$\Phi^{-1} = \frac{Q}{\sigma_e^2} + \frac{Q_1}{\sigma_1^2} + \frac{Q_2}{\sigma_2^2} + \frac{Q_3}{\sigma_3^2} \tag{13.4.21}$$

where Q and Q_1, are defined in Equations 13.4.6 and 13.3.17, respectively,

$$Q_2 = \frac{\mathbf{j}_N\mathbf{j}_N'}{N} \otimes I_T - \frac{\mathbf{j}_{NT}\mathbf{j}_{NT}'}{NT} \tag{13.4.22}$$

$$Q_3 = \frac{\mathbf{j}_{NT}\mathbf{j}_{NT}'}{NT} \tag{13.4.23}$$

$\sigma_1^2 = \sigma_e^2 + T\sigma_\mu^2$, $\sigma_2^2 = \sigma_e^2 + N\sigma_\lambda^2$ and $\sigma_3^2 = \sigma_e^2 + T\sigma_\mu^2 + N\sigma_\lambda^2$. Partitioning (13.4.20) and using (13.4.21) yields, after some algebra,

$$\hat{\boldsymbol{\beta}}_s = \left[\frac{X_s'Q_1X_s}{\sigma_1^2} + \frac{X_s'Q_2X_s}{\sigma_2^2} + \frac{X_s'QX_s}{\sigma_e^2}\right]^{-1} \cdot \left[\left(\frac{X_s'Q_1X_s}{\sigma_1^2}\right)\boldsymbol{\beta}_s^* + \left(\frac{X_s'Q_2X_s}{\sigma_2^2}\right)\boldsymbol{\beta}_s^0 + \left(\frac{X_s'QX_s}{\sigma_e^2}\right)\mathbf{b}_s\right] \tag{13.4.24}$$

and $\hat{\beta}_1 = \bar{y}_{..} - \Sigma_{k=2}^K \bar{x}_{k..}\hat{\beta}_k$, where $\boldsymbol{\beta}_s^* = (X_s'Q_1X_s)^{-1}X_s'Q_1\mathbf{y}$, $\boldsymbol{\beta}_s^0 = (X_s'Q_2X_s)^{-1}X_s'Q_2\mathbf{y}$ and $\mathbf{b}_s$ is the dummy variable estimator.

The estimator $\boldsymbol{\beta}_s^*$ utilizes variation between individuals and is obtained by applying least squares to Equation 13.4.8, the estimator $\boldsymbol{\beta}_s^0$ utilizes variation over time and is obtained by applying least squares to Equation 13.4.9, and $\mathbf{b}_s$ is the dummy variable estimator that utilizes variation not explained by differences in individuals or time periods. The GLS estimator $\hat{\boldsymbol{\beta}}_s$ is an efficient matrix weighted average of these three estimators. For further details see Nerlove (1971b) and Swamy and Arora (1972).

As a convenient means for calculating the GLS estimator, Fuller and Battese (1974) suggest a transformation matrix P such that $P'P = \sigma_e^2\Phi^{-1}$. This leads to the transformed variables

$$x_{kit}^* = x_{kit} - \alpha_1 \bar{x}_{ki.} - \alpha_2 \bar{x}_{k.t} + \alpha_3 \bar{x}_{k..}$$

and

$$y_{it}^* = y_{it} - \alpha_1 \bar{y}_{i.} - \alpha_2 \bar{y}_{.t} + \alpha_3 \bar{y}_{..}$$

where $\alpha_1 = 1 - \sigma_e/\sigma_1$, $\alpha_2 = 1 - \sigma_e/\sigma_2$, and $\alpha_3 = \alpha_1 + \alpha_2 - 1 + \sigma_e/\sigma_3$. The least squares regression of y_{it}^* on the x_{kit}^* yields the GLS estimator $\hat{\boldsymbol{\beta}}$.

The orthogonal matrix that diagonalizes Φ and thus enables one to determine Φ^{-1} and P is [Nerlove (1971b)]

$$\begin{bmatrix} A_1 \\ A_2 \\ A_3 \\ A_4 \end{bmatrix} = \begin{bmatrix} N^{-1/2}\mathbf{j}_N' \otimes T^{-1/2}\mathbf{j}_T' \\ N^{-1/2}\mathbf{j}_N' \otimes C_1 \\ C_2 \otimes T^{-1/2}\mathbf{j}_T' \\ C_2 \otimes C_1 \end{bmatrix} \tag{13.4.25}$$

where C_1 and C_2 are such that $C_1C_1' = I_{T-1}$, $C_1'C_1 = D_T$, $C_2C_2' = I_{N-1}$, and $C_2'C_2 = D_N$. The characteristic roots of Φ are σ_3^2, σ_2^2, σ_1^2, and σ_e^2 with multiplicity 1, $(T - 1)$, $(N - 1)$, and $(N - 1)(T - 1)$. Swamy and Arora (1972) demonstrate how A_2, A_3, and A_4 lead to the estimators $\boldsymbol{\beta}_s^0$, $\boldsymbol{\beta}_s^*$, and $\mathbf{b}_s$, respectively. The inclusion of A_1 in any of these transformations permits estimation of the intercept term.

13.4.2b Predicting Random Components

Prediction of the random components μ_i and λ_t is sometimes of interest and, following Lee and Griffiths (1979), best linear unbiased predictors are given by

$$\hat{\mu}_i = \left(\frac{T\sigma_\mu^2}{\sigma_1^2}\right)\left(\bar{y}_{i.} - \hat{\hat{\beta}}_1 - \sum_{k=2}^{K} \hat{\hat{\beta}}_k \bar{x}_{ki.}\right) \tag{13.4.26}$$

and

$$\hat{\lambda}_t = \left(\frac{N\sigma_\lambda^2}{\sigma_2^2}\right)\left(\bar{y}_{.t} - \hat{\hat{\beta}}_1 - \sum_{k=2}^{K} \hat{\hat{\beta}}_k \bar{x}_{k.t}\right) \tag{13.4.27}$$

Prediction of the μ_i gives information on the future behavior of individuals and so it is likely to be of more interest than the prediction of λ_t, which gives information on past realizations. It can be shown that these predictors are obtained by minimizing an extended "residual sum of squares function" similar to that given in Equation 13.3.25. Also, further results and some computational suggestions can be found in Henderson (1975).

13.4.2c Estimation of Variance Components

The GLS estimator for $\boldsymbol{\beta}$ and the predictors for μ_i and λ_t depend on the unknown variances σ_e^2, σ_μ^2 and σ_λ^2. To replace these unknowns with estimates, any of the variance estimators mentioned in Section 13.3.2c, suitably modified for the time effects, can be employed. Swamy and Arora (1972) suggest the unbiased estimators

$$\hat{\sigma}_1^2 = \frac{\mathbf{e}^{*\prime}\mathbf{e}^*}{N - K} \tag{13.4.28}$$

$$\hat{\sigma}_2^2 = \frac{\mathbf{e}^{0\prime}\mathbf{e}^0}{T - K} \tag{13.4.29}$$

and

$$\hat{\sigma}_e^2 = \frac{\hat{\mathbf{e}}'\hat{\mathbf{e}}}{(N - 1)(T - 1) - K'} \tag{13.4.30}$$

where $\mathbf{e}^* = Q_1\mathbf{y} - Q_1X_s\boldsymbol{\beta}_s^*$ are the residuals from the estimator $\boldsymbol{\beta}_s^*$, $\mathbf{e}^0 = Q_2\mathbf{y} - Q_2X_2\boldsymbol{\beta}_s^0$ are the residuals from $\boldsymbol{\beta}_s^0$ and $\hat{\mathbf{e}} = Q\mathbf{y} - QX_s\mathbf{b}_s$ are the residuals from $\mathbf{b}_s$.

Some alternative variance estimators are those based only on least squares residuals [Wallace and Hussain (1969)], those based on the dummy variable residuals [Amemiya (1971)], and those derived from the fitting of constants method [Fuller and Battese (1974)].

Substitution of a set of variance estimates into $\hat{\boldsymbol{\beta}}$ leads to an estimated generalized least squares (EGLS) estimator, $\hat{\hat{\boldsymbol{\beta}}}$, and the properties of various EGLS estimators have been examined by Wallace and Hussain (1969), Swamy and Arora (1972), Fuller and Battese (1974) and Kelejian and Stephan (1983). Wallace and Hussain show that the dummy variable estimator is asymptotically efficient relative to the GLS estimator while Swamy and Arora, in terms of finite sample properties, indicate the conditions under which $\hat{\hat{\boldsymbol{\beta}}}$, with variance estimators $\hat{\sigma}_1^2$, $\hat{\sigma}_2^2$, and $\hat{\sigma}_e^2$, is likely to be better than the least squares and dummy variable estimators. Fuller and Battese consider a less restrictive set of assumptions and give the conditions under which an EGLS estimator is unbiased and asymptotically equivalent to the GLS estimator. Further aspects of the asymptotic distribution of the GLS and EGLS estimators are considered by Kelejian and Stephan. Baltagi (1981) carries out an extensive Monte Carlo experiment where he examines the finite sample properties of EGLS estimators, the performance of tests for the stability of cross-sectional regressions over time (and time series regressions over individuals), the performances of the Hausman specification test and the Lagrange multiplier test (see Sections 13.4.2d and 13.4.3), and the frequency of negative variance estimates.

13.4.2d Testing the Specifications

To test the hypotheses $\boldsymbol{\mu} = \mathbf{0}$, $\boldsymbol{\lambda} = \mathbf{0}$, or $\boldsymbol{\mu} = \boldsymbol{\lambda} = \mathbf{0}$, one can use the dummy variable estimator and the F test that compares restricted and unrestricted residual sums of squares. Another alternative is the Lagrange multiplier test for the hypothesis $\sigma_\mu^2 = \sigma_\lambda^2 = 0$. Breusch and Pagan (1980) show that, under the null hypothesis

$$\lambda_{LM} = \frac{NT}{2}\left\{\frac{1}{T-1}\left[\frac{\tilde{\mathbf{e}}'(I_N \otimes \mathbf{j}_T\mathbf{j}_T')\tilde{\mathbf{e}}}{\tilde{\mathbf{e}}'\tilde{\mathbf{e}}} - 1\right]^2 + \frac{1}{N-1}\left[\frac{\tilde{\mathbf{e}}'(\mathbf{j}_N\mathbf{j}_N' \otimes I_T)\tilde{\mathbf{e}}}{\tilde{\mathbf{e}}'\tilde{\mathbf{e}}} - 1\right]^2\right\} \tag{13.4.31}$$

is asymptotically distributed as $\chi^2_{(2)}$, where $\tilde{\mathbf{e}}$ is the vector of least squares residuals obtained by regressing $\mathbf{y}$ on X. Note that $\tilde{\mathbf{e}}'(I_N \otimes \mathbf{j}_T\mathbf{j}_T')\tilde{\mathbf{e}} = \Sigma_{i=1}^N(\Sigma_{t=1}^T \tilde{\mathbf{e}}_{it})^2$ and $\tilde{\mathbf{e}}'(\mathbf{j}_N\mathbf{j}_N' \otimes I_T)\tilde{\mathbf{e}} = \Sigma_{t=1}^T(\Sigma_{i=1}^N \tilde{\mathbf{e}}_{it})^2$.

13.4.3 Fixed or Random Effects?

The problem of choice between the fixed and random effects models can be examined within the same framework as that considered in Section 13.3.3 for the model with individual effects only. Specifically, it can be argued that μ_i and λ_t can always be regarded as random components, but when we treat them as fixed and use the dummy variable estimator our inference is conditional on the μ_i and λ_t in the sample. Such a procedure can always be employed, irrespective of the properties of μ_i and λ_t, and, in particular, irrespective of whether or not the μ_i and λ_t are correlated with the explanatory variables. The error components GLS estimator will suffer from omitted variable bias if the μ_i and λ_t are correlated with the explanatory variables, and it will not in general be efficient unless the required distributional assumptions for μ_i and λ_t hold. On the other hand, when these more restrictive assumptions do hold, the error components GLS estimator will be more efficient than the dummy variable estimator, and our inference is not conditional on the μ_i and λ_t in the sample.

Another possibility is to pursue a mixed approach where the λ_t (say) are treated as fixed and the μ_i are treated as random variables. Such an approach is likely to be particularly useful if T is small and if the researcher wishes to follow some of the more general specifications for μ_i and e_{it} mentioned in Sections 13.3.3 and 13.3.4. Note that if the dummy variables for time are included within X, then the model becomes one with individual effects only, and it can be handled within the framework of Section 13.3 provided T is not too large.

A null hypothesis of no correlation between the effects and the explanatory variables can be tested by comparing the dummy variable estimator with an EGLS estimator. Following Hausman (1978), if the null hypothesis is true,

$$m = (\mathbf{b}_s - \hat{\boldsymbol{\beta}}_s)'(M_1 - M_0)^{-1}(\mathbf{b}_s - \hat{\boldsymbol{\beta}}_s) \tag{13.4.32}$$

has an asymptotic $\chi^2_{(K')}$ distribution, where $M_1 = \sigma_e^2(X_s'QX_s)^{-1}$ is the covariance matrix for the dummy variable estimator $\mathbf{b}_s$, and

$$M_0 = [\sigma_1^{-2}(X_s'Q_1X_s) + \sigma_2^{-2}(X_s'Q_2X_s) + \sigma_e^{-2}(X_s'QX_s)]^{-1}$$

is the covariance matrix for the GLS estimator $\hat{\boldsymbol{\beta}}_s$. In (13.4.32) unknown variances can be replaced by appropriate estimates without changing the asymptotic distribution.

13.4.4 Extensions of the Model

As pointed out by Swamy (1974), the assumptions of the error components model discussed in this section could be regarded as fairly restrictive. They imply that the contemporaneous covariance between observations on two individuals is the same for every pair of individuals and that the covariance between two observations on a given individual is constant over time and the same for every individual. It may be preferable to use the model outlined in Section 13.2. Alternatively, an attempt could be made to generalize the error components model by allowing for more general forms of serial correlation. For research in this direction see Swamy and Mehta (1973), Revankar (1979), Lee (1978b), and Pudney (1978).

Another extension of models with individual and time components is into multivariate systems. Such an extension might be used, for example, if a researcher wishes to use time series and cross-sectional data to estimate a system of demand equations. For some work in this direction see Avery (1977), Baltagi (1980), Chamberlain and Griliches (1975), Jöreskog (1978), Magnus (1982), Prucha (1984), and Reinsel (1982).

Other extensions include error components models with heteroscedasticity [Mazodier and Trognon (1978)], nonlinear error components models with heteroscedasticity [Griffiths and Anderson (1982)], error components models where some of the individuals sampled in each period change from period to period [Biørn (1981)], and models with a lagged dependent variable [Swamy (1974)].

13.5 MODELS WITH SLOPE COEFFICIENTS THAT VARY OVER INDIVIDUALS

It is possible that different behavior over individuals will be reflected not only in a different intercept but also in different slope coefficients. When this is the case, our model can be written as

$$y_{it} = \sum_{k=1}^{K} \beta_{ki} x_{kit} + e_{it}, \qquad i = 1, 2, \ldots, N$$
$$t = 1, 2, \ldots, T \qquad (13.5.1)$$

where $x_{1it} \equiv 1$ and, in contrast to the previous two sections, we are no longer treating the constant term differently from the other explanatory variables. Our assumptions imply that the response of the dependent variable y_{it} to an explanatory variable x_{kit} is different for different individuals but, for a given individual, it is constant over time. When the response coefficients β_{ki} are fixed parameters, Equation 13.5.1 can be viewed as the "seemingly unrelated regressions model" and when the β_{ki} are random parameters, it is equivalent to the "Swamy random coefficient model." The seemingly unrelated regressions model was discussed extensively in Chapter 12, and so we will not discuss it further at this point. We begin with the Swamy random coefficient model in Section 13.5.1, and in Section 13.5.2 we discuss the problem of choice between the fixed and random assumptions.

13.5.1 The Swamy Random Coefficient Model

When the $(K \times 1)$ response vector for each individual, $\boldsymbol{\beta}_i$, can be regarded as a random vector drawn from a probability distribution with mean $\bar{\boldsymbol{\beta}}$ and covariance matrix Δ, the model in (13.5.1) becomes the random coefficient model introduced by Swamy (1970, 1971). For the ith individual this model can be written as

$$\mathbf{y}_i = X_i(\bar{\boldsymbol{\beta}} + \boldsymbol{\mu}_i) + \mathbf{e}_i, \qquad i = 1, 2, \ldots, N \tag{13.5.2}$$

where $\mathbf{y}_i$ and X_i contain observations on the dependent and explanatory variables, respectively, and

$$\boldsymbol{\beta}_i = \bar{\boldsymbol{\beta}} + \boldsymbol{\mu}_i \tag{13.5.3}$$

with $E[\boldsymbol{\mu}_i] = \mathbf{0}$, $E[\boldsymbol{\mu}_i\boldsymbol{\mu}_i'] = \Delta$, and $E[\boldsymbol{\mu}_i\boldsymbol{\mu}_j'] = 0$ for $i \neq j$.

For the seemingly unrelated regressions model studied in Chapter 12 a number of assumptions about $\mathbf{e}_i$, of varying degrees of complexity, were considered. Any of these could also be used for this model but, in general, we will consider the simple one, where $E[\mathbf{e}_i\mathbf{e}_i'] = \sigma_{ii}I$ and $E[\mathbf{e}_i\mathbf{e}_j'] = 0$ for $i \neq j$. This implies that the disturbances across individuals are heteroscedastic but uncorrelated and, if the $\boldsymbol{\beta}_i$ were fixed parameters, the least squares estimators $\mathbf{b}_i = (X_i'X_i)^{-1}X_i'\mathbf{y}_i$ would be best linear unbiased.

For this model we are interested in estimating the mean coefficient vector $\bar{\boldsymbol{\beta}}$, predicting each individual vector $\boldsymbol{\beta}_i$, estimating the variances upon which the generalized least squares (GLS) estimator for $\bar{\boldsymbol{\beta}}$ and the best linear unbiased predictor (BLUP) for $\boldsymbol{\beta}_i$ depend, and testing the hypothesis that $\Delta = 0$. Each of these items will be considered in turn.

13.5.1a GLS Estimation

To estimate $\bar{\boldsymbol{\beta}}$, we first write Equation 13.5.2 to include all NT observations. This yields

$$\mathbf{y} = X\bar{\boldsymbol{\beta}} + Z\boldsymbol{\mu} + \mathbf{e} \tag{13.5.4}$$

where $\mathbf{y}' = (\mathbf{y}_1', \mathbf{y}_2', \ldots, \mathbf{y}_N')$, $X' = (X_1', X_2', \ldots, X_N')$, $\boldsymbol{\mu}' = (\boldsymbol{\mu}_1', \boldsymbol{\mu}_2', \ldots, \boldsymbol{\mu}_N')$, $\mathbf{e}' = (\mathbf{e}_1', \mathbf{e}_2', \ldots, \mathbf{e}_N')$, and

$$Z = \begin{bmatrix} X_1 & & & \\ & X_2 & & \\ & & \ddots & \\ & & & X_N \end{bmatrix}$$

The covariance matrix for the composite disturbance is $\Phi = E[(Z\boldsymbol{\mu} + \mathbf{e})(Z\boldsymbol{\mu} + \mathbf{e})']$ and is block diagonal with ith diagonal block given by

$$\Phi_{ii} = X_i \Delta X_i' + \sigma_{ii} I \tag{13.5.5}$$

The GLS estimator for $\bar{\boldsymbol{\beta}}$ has its usual properties and is given by

$$\hat{\bar{\boldsymbol{\beta}}} = (X'\Phi^{-1}X)^{-1}X'\Phi^{-1}\mathbf{y} = \left(\sum_{j=1}^{N} X_j'\Phi_{jj}^{-1}X_j\right)^{-1} \sum_{i=1}^{N} X_i'\Phi_{ii}^{-1}\mathbf{y}_i = \sum_{i=1}^{N} W_i\mathbf{b}_i \tag{13.5.6}$$

where

$$W_i = \left\{\sum_{j=1}^{N} [\Delta + \sigma_{jj}(X_j'X_j)^{-1}]^{-1}\right\}^{-1} [\Delta + \sigma_{ii}(X_i'X_i)^{-1}]^{-1} \tag{13.5.7}$$

and

$$\mathbf{b}_i = (X_i'X_i)^{-1}X_i'\mathbf{y}_i \tag{13.5.8}$$

is the least squares estimator (predictor) of $\boldsymbol{\beta}_i$. The last equality in (13.5.8) is based on a matrix result that can be found, for example, in Rao (1965, p. 29); it shows that the GLS estimator is a matrix weighted average of the estimators $\mathbf{b}_i$, with weights inversely proportional to their covariance matrices. Also, the last expression in Equation 13.5.8 only requires a matrix inversion of order K, and so, if T is large, it is a convenient one for computational purposes. The covariance matrix for $\hat{\bar{\boldsymbol{\beta}}}$ is

$$(X'\Phi^{-1}X)^{-1} = \left(\sum_{j=1}^{N} X_j'\Phi_{jj}^{-1}X_j\right)^{-1} = \left\{\sum_{j=1}^{N} [\Delta + \sigma_{jj}(X_j'X_j)^{-1}]^{-1}\right\}^{-1} \tag{13.5.9}$$

Mundlak (1978b) has provided another interpretation of the GLS estimator. Making an analogy with the error components model, he shows that $\hat{\bar{\boldsymbol{\beta}}}$ can be written as a weighted average of a "between estimator" and a "within estimator."

13.5.1b Predicting Random Components

Prediction of the individual components $\boldsymbol{\beta}_i$ is of interest because it provides information on the behavior of each individual and also because it provides a basis for predicting future values of the dependent variable for a given individual.

If the class of unbiased predictors $\{\boldsymbol{\beta}_i^*\}$ is restricted to those for which $E[\boldsymbol{\beta}_i^*|\boldsymbol{\beta}_i] = \boldsymbol{\beta}_i$, then the BLUP for $\boldsymbol{\beta}_i$ is given by the least squares "estimator" $\mathbf{b}_i = (X_i'X_i)^{-1}X_i'\mathbf{y}_i$ [Swamy (1970, 1971)]. However, if the sampling properties of the class of predictors are considered in terms of repeated sampling over both time *and* individuals, then

$$\hat{\boldsymbol{\beta}}_i = \hat{\bar{\boldsymbol{\beta}}} + \Delta X_i'(X_i \Delta X_i' + \sigma_{ii} I)^{-1}(\mathbf{y}_i - X_i \hat{\bar{\boldsymbol{\beta}}}) \tag{13.5.10}$$

is the BLUP for $\boldsymbol{\beta}_i$ [Lee and Griffiths (1979)]. This predictor is unbiased in the sense that $E[\hat{\boldsymbol{\beta}}_i - \boldsymbol{\beta}_i] = \mathbf{0}$, where the expectation is an unconditional one, and it is best in the sense that $V^* - V$ is nonnegative definite, where V is the covariance matrix of the prediction error $(\hat{\boldsymbol{\beta}}_i - \boldsymbol{\beta}_i)$ and V^* is the covariance matrix of the prediction error from any other linear unbiased predictor.

The predictor $\hat{\boldsymbol{\beta}}_i$ can be viewed as an estimate of the mean, $\hat{\bar{\boldsymbol{\beta}}}$, plus a predictor for $\boldsymbol{\mu}_i$, where the latter is given by a weighted proportion of the GLS residual vector $\mathbf{y}_i - X_i\hat{\bar{\boldsymbol{\beta}}}$. Also, using the same matrix result mentioned earlier [Rao (1965, p. 29)], it can be written as

$$\hat{\boldsymbol{\beta}}_i = (\Delta^{-1} + \sigma_{ii}^{-1} X_i'X_i)^{-1}(\sigma_{ii}^{-1} X_i'X_i \mathbf{b}_i + \Delta^{-1}\hat{\bar{\boldsymbol{\beta}}}) \tag{13.5.11}$$

which is a matrix weighted average of $\mathbf{b}_i$ and $\hat{\bar{\boldsymbol{\beta}}}$. A Bayesian argument leads to the same predictor [Smith (1973), Leamer (1978, p. 274)], and it can also be obtained by minimizing the quadratic function

$$S = \sum_{i=1}^{N} \frac{(\mathbf{y}_i - X_i\boldsymbol{\beta}_i)'(\mathbf{y}_i - X_i\boldsymbol{\beta}_i)}{\sigma_{ii}} + \sum_{i=1}^{N} (\boldsymbol{\beta}_i - \bar{\boldsymbol{\beta}})'\Delta^{-1}(\boldsymbol{\beta}_i - \bar{\boldsymbol{\beta}}) \tag{13.5.12}$$

with respect to $\bar{\boldsymbol{\beta}}$ and the $\boldsymbol{\beta}_i$ [Lee and Griffiths (1979)]. Finally, it is interesting to note that the GLS estimator for the mean coefficient vector is a simple average of the BLUPs. That is, $\hat{\bar{\boldsymbol{\beta}}} = \sum_{i=1}^{N} \hat{\boldsymbol{\beta}}_i/N$.

13.5.1c Estimating Variances

Both the GLS estimator for $\bar{\boldsymbol{\beta}}$ and the BLUP for the $\boldsymbol{\beta}_i$ depend on the unknown variances Δ and σ_{ii} and hence, for them to be operational, estimates of the variances are required. Swamy (1970) shows how the least squares estimators $\mathbf{b}_i = (X_i'X_i)^{-1}X_i'\mathbf{y}_i$ and their residuals $\tilde{\mathbf{e}}_i = \mathbf{y}_i - X_i\mathbf{b}_i$ can be used to obtain the unbiased estimators

$$\hat{\sigma}_{ii} = \frac{\tilde{\mathbf{e}}_i'\tilde{\mathbf{e}}_i}{T - K} \tag{13.5.13}$$

and

$$\hat{\Delta} = \frac{S_b}{N-1} - \frac{1}{N}\sum_{i=1}^{N} \hat{\sigma}_{ii}(X_i'X_i)^{-1} \tag{13.5.14}$$

where

$$S_b = \sum_{i=1}^{N} \mathbf{b}_i\mathbf{b}_i' - \frac{1}{N}\sum_{i=1}^{N} \mathbf{b}_i \sum_{i=1}^{N} \mathbf{b}_i' \tag{13.5.15}$$

The estimated generalized least squares (EGLS) estimator for $\bar{\boldsymbol{\beta}}$ that uses these variance estimates is, under certain conditions [Swamy (1970)], consistent and asymptotically efficient. An estimate of the asymptotic covariance matrix is given by substituting $\hat{\sigma}_{ii}$ and $\hat{\Delta}$ into Equation 13.5.9. Conditions under which the EGLS estimator for $\bar{\boldsymbol{\beta}}$ has a finite mean and is unbiased are given by Rao (1982).

One difficulty with the estimator $\hat{\Delta}$ is that it may not be nonnegative definite. Swamy (1971) discusses this problem at length and suggests methods for adjusting it or constraining it such that it is nonnegative definite. This will, of course, destroy the unbiasedness property. However, unbiasedness should not be sacred, at least not as sacred as nonnegative definite covariance matrices, and so the easiest solution seems to be to use the natural sample quantity $\tilde{\Delta} = S_b/(N-1)$ as an estimator. This estimator will be nonnegative definite and consistent. In finite samples, which variance estimator leads to the more efficient EGLS estimator for $\bar{\boldsymbol{\beta}}$ is an open question. Under the assumption of normally distributed disturbances one can also use the maximum likelihood technique to estimate the parameters. This is outlined by Swamy (1971, 1973) and, for a more general model, by Rosenberg (1973b).

13.5.1d Testing the Specification

Of likely interest is a test for the null hypothesis

$$H_0\colon \boldsymbol{\beta}_1 = \boldsymbol{\beta}_2 = \ldots = \boldsymbol{\beta}_N = \bar{\boldsymbol{\beta}}$$

If this null hypothesis is true, the individual coefficient vectors are not random and they are all identical to the mean. In addition, the joint model in Equation 13.5.4 becomes a heteroscedastic error one, where the variances are constant within subgroups of observations. Swamy (1970) suggests the statistic

$$g = \sum_{i=1}^{N} \frac{(\mathbf{b}_i - \bar{\bar{\boldsymbol{\beta}}})'X_i'X_i(\mathbf{b}_i - \bar{\bar{\boldsymbol{\beta}}})}{\hat{\sigma}_{ii}} \tag{13.5.16}$$

where

$$\bar{\bar{\boldsymbol{\beta}}} = \left(\sum_{i=1}^{N} \hat{\sigma}_{ii}^{-1} X_i' X_i\right)^{-1} \sum_{i=1}^{N} \hat{\sigma}_{ii}^{-1} X_i' X_i \mathbf{b}_i$$

Under H_0, g has an asymptotic $\chi^2_{[K(N-1)]}$-distribution.

This test is valid irrespective of whether, under the alternative hypothesis, the $\boldsymbol{\beta}_i$ are regarded as fixed and different or random and different. An alternative test, based explicitly on the randomness assumption, is one for which the null hypothesis is $\Delta = 0$. Such a test is outlined in Swamy (1971).

13.5.1e Extensions of the Model

The assumptions that have been made about the $\mathbf{e}_i$ could be regarded as fairly restrictive. There is no correlation between the disturbances corresponding to different individuals and, in addition, there is no serial correlation. An alternative set of assumptions which relaxes these restrictions is that adopted by Parks (1967) for the fixed coefficient model and outlined earlier in Section 12.3. Parks assumes that the disturbance for each individual follows an AR(1) process and also that contemporaneous correlation exists. When these assumptions are introduced into the random coefficient model [Swamy (1973, 1974)], the covariance matrix $\Phi = E[(Z\boldsymbol{\mu} + \mathbf{e})(Z\boldsymbol{\mu} + \mathbf{e})']$ contains N^2 $(T \times T)$ blocks Φ_{ij}, which are given by

$$\Phi_{ii} = X_i \Delta X_i' + \Omega_{ii} \tag{13.5.17}$$

and

$$\Phi_{ij} = \Omega_{ij}, \qquad i \neq j \tag{13.5.18}$$

where

$$\Omega_{ij} = \frac{\sigma_{ij}}{1 - \rho_i \rho_j} \begin{bmatrix} 1 & \rho_j & \cdots & \rho_j^{T-1} \\ \rho_i & 1 & \cdots & \rho_j^{T-2} \\ \vdots & \vdots & \ddots & \vdots \\ \rho_i^{T-1} & \rho_i^{T-2} & \cdots & 1 \end{bmatrix} \tag{13.5.19}$$

Estimators for Δ, the σ_{ij}, and the ρ_i are given by Swamy (1974), and these can be used in an EGLS estimator for $\bar{\boldsymbol{\beta}}$. One possible problem with the EGLS estimator is that it requires a matrix inversion of order NT. A convenient transformation that enables its calculation on standard computer packages does not seem to be available.

Other extensions include instrumental variable estimation when X contains lagged values of the dependent variable [Swamy (1974)], estimation when the covariance matrix could be singular [Rosenberg (1973b)], and attempts to produce estimators that may be biased but which have lower mean square error [Swamy (1973, 1974)]. Applications can be found, for example, in Swamy (1971), Feige and Swamy (1974), and Hendricks et al. (1979).

13.5.2 Fixed or Random Coefficients?

The question concerning whether the $\boldsymbol{\beta}_i$ should be assumed fixed and different and the seemingly unrelated regressions framework used, or whether they should be assumed random and different and the random coefficient framework used, has been considered by Mundlak (1978b). Extending his work on the error components model [Mundlak (1978a)], he suggests that, in both cases, the coefficients can be regarded as random but, in the first case, our inference is conditional on the coefficients in the sample. The important consideration is likely to be whether the variable coefficients are correlated with the explanatory variables. If they are, then the assumptions of the Swamy random coefficient model are unreasonable and the GLS estimator of the mean coefficient vector will be biased. In these circumstances the fixed coefficient model can be used. If the variable coefficients are not correlated with the explanatory variables, then it might be reasonable to assume that they are random drawings from a probability distribution and the Swamy random coefficient model could be used. This model uses the additional information provided by the "random assumption," and so, if the assumption is reasonable, the estimates should be more efficient.

Wherever possible, any dependence of the coefficients on the explanatory variables should be modeled explicitly, and, as an example, Mundlak (1978b) considers estimation of the special case where $E[\boldsymbol{\beta}_i]$ is linearly related to the mean vector of the explanatory variables for the ith individual.

The "heterogeneity bias" that arises when least squares is applied to a model with random coefficients correlated with the explanatory variables has been considered further by Chamberlain (1982). He demonstrates that, as in the case of the error components model, heterogeneity bias is reflected by a full set of lags and leads in the regression of y_{it} on $x_{ki1}, x_{ki2}, \ldots, x_{kiT}$; conversely, under certain conditions, evidence of a contemporaneous relationship only is indicative of no heterogeneity bias. Based on the minimum mean square error linear predictor of y_{it} given $x_{ki1}, x_{ki2}, \ldots, x_{kiT}$, Chamberlain suggests an estimation technique which is particularly useful when T is small and N is large. If the coefficient estimates tend to exhibit a certain structure, then heterogeneity bias can be attributed to the correlation between the explanatory variables and a random intercept only. On the other hand, no evidence of this structure is an indication of correlation between the explanatory variables and all the random coefficients.

Under the assumptions that $E[\mathbf{e}_i\mathbf{e}_i'] = \sigma_e^2 I$ and $E[\mathbf{e}_i\mathbf{e}_j'] = 0$ for $i \neq j$, a test for the null hypothesis that the variable coefficients and the explanatory variables are uncorrelated has been provided by Pudney (1978). It is based on the sample covariance between the $\mathbf{b}_i = (X_i'X_i)^{-1}X_i'\mathbf{y}_i$ and the means of the explanatory variables for each individual, $\bar{\mathbf{x}}_i' = \mathbf{j}_T'X_i/T$, where $\mathbf{j}_T = (1, 1, \ldots, 1)'$. The sample covariance is given by

$$S_{xb} = \frac{1}{N}\left(\sum_{i=1}^{N} \mathbf{b}_i\bar{\mathbf{x}}_i' - \frac{1}{N}\sum_{i=1}^{N} \mathbf{b}_i \sum_{i=1}^{N} \bar{\mathbf{x}}_i'\right) \tag{13.5.20}$$

and the test statistic is

$$z = N\boldsymbol{\eta}'V^{-1}\boldsymbol{\eta} \tag{13.5.21}$$

where $\boldsymbol{\eta} = \text{vec}(S_{xb})$ and

$$V = \frac{1}{N}\sum_{i=1}^{N} (\bar{\mathbf{x}}_i \otimes I_K)(\hat{\Delta} + \hat{\sigma}_e^2(X_i'X_i)^{-1})(\bar{\mathbf{x}}_i' \otimes I_K) \tag{13.5.22}$$

Under the null hypothesis, z is asymptotically distributed (with respect to increasing N) as $\chi^2_{(K^2)}$.

Zellner (1966) has shown that a macro coefficient estimator will not possess aggregation bias if the coefficient vectors of the individual micro units satisfy the assumptions of the Swamy random coefficient model. In this sense the above test can be regarded as a test for aggregation bias. The test given in Equation 13.5.16 can also be regarded as a test for aggregation bias, but the null hypothesis in this case is a more restrictive one. Acceptance of the null hypothesis in Equation 13.5.16 suggests that aggregation bias does not exist because the coefficients are fixed and identical. For the test in Equation 13.5.21 acceptance of the null hypothesis does not imply that the coefficients are identical but that they can be regarded as random drawings from the same probability distribution.

13.6 MODELS WITH SLOPE COEFFICIENTS THAT VARY OVER TIME AND INDIVIDUALS

Just as it was possible to extend the error components model with individual effects to the Swamy random coefficient model where all coefficients could vary over individuals, it is possible to extend the error components model, with individual and time effects, so that all coefficients have a component specific to an individual and a component specific to a given time period. This model can be written as

$$y_{it} = \sum_{k=1}^{K} (\bar{\beta}_k + \mu_{ki} + \lambda_{kt})x_{kit} + e_{it}, \qquad i = 1, 2, \ldots, N; \quad t = 1, 2, \ldots, T \tag{13.6.1}$$

where $\beta_{kit} = \bar{\beta}_k + \mu_{ki} + \lambda_{kt}$ measures the response of the dependent variable to the kth explanatory variable for individual i in time period t. Each coefficient consists of a mean $\bar{\beta}_k$, an individual specific component μ_{ki} and a time specific component λ_{kt}.

As in the previous models, it is possible to assume that the μ_{ki} and λ_{kt} are either fixed parameters to be estimated or random variables. We will generally assume that they are random variables but, when convenient, we will indicate how they could be estimated as fixed parameters. Also, as Pudney (1978) points out, sometimes it may be reasonable and practical to assume that one of the components is fixed and the other random. For example, if T is small and N is large, and both components are random, any estimate of the variance of λ_{kt} is likely to be unreliable. In such circumstances it would be preferable to treat the λ_{kt} as fixed, include appropriate dummy variables, and thus use inference conditional on the λ_{kt} in the sample. If, in Equation 13.6.1, the time effects are removed by including dummy variables in the set of explanatory variables, the model becomes identical to the Swamy random coefficient model.

Before outlining how the parameters in Equation 13.6.1 can be estimated, we briefly mention some other models where the coefficients vary over time and individuals.

One alternative to (13.6.1) is the model

$$y_{it} = \sum_{k=1}^{K} (\bar{\beta}_k + \mu_{ki} + e_{kit})x_{kit} \tag{13.6.2}$$

We assume $x_{1it} \equiv 1$ and so, in this case, the disturbance e_{1it} replaces the disturbance e_{it} of the earlier model. In addition, the time effects λ_{kt} have been replaced by a random component e_{kit} which is not restricted to be the same for all individuals in a given time period. The estimation of this model has been discussed by Swamy and Mehta (1975, 1977); Pudney (1978); and Singh and Ullah (1974). The most general set of random assumptions are those adopted by Swamy and Mehta. In addition to all the disturbances having zero mean, they assume that

$$E[\boldsymbol{\mu}_i\boldsymbol{\mu}_j'] = \begin{cases} \Delta & \text{if } i = j. \\ 0 & \text{otherwise} \end{cases} \tag{13.6.3}$$

and

$$E[\mathbf{e}_{it}\mathbf{e}_{js}'] = \begin{cases} \Delta_{ii} & \text{if } i = j \text{ and } t = s \\ 0 & \text{otherwise} \end{cases} \tag{13.6.4}$$

where $\boldsymbol{\mu}_i = (\mu_{1i}, \mu_{2i}, \ldots, \mu_{Ki})'$ and $\mathbf{e}_{it} = (e_{1it}, e_{2it}, \ldots, e_{Kit})'$, and both Δ and the Δ_{ii} are not restricted to be diagonal. Pudney assumes that $\Delta_{ii} = \Delta_e$ for $i = 1, 2, \ldots, N$ while Singh and Ullah rewrite the model as

$$y_{it} = \sum_{k=1}^{K} (\beta_{ki} + e_{kit})x_{kit} \tag{13.6.5}$$

treat the β_{ki} as fixed parameters, and assume that $E[\mathbf{e}_{it}\mathbf{e}_{jt}'] = \Delta_{ij}$ with Δ_{ij} diagonal.

The above models all assume that the random coefficients vary around a constant mean. Models where the coefficients also change systematically over time have been analyzed by Rosenberg (1973c), Johnson and Rausser (1975), Harvey (1978), and Liu and Hanssens (1981).

13.6.1 The Hsiao Random Coefficient Model

Estimation and hypothesis testing for the model in Equation 13.6.1 have been discussed by Hsiao (1974, 1975); in this section, we outline some of his procedures. A special case of the Hsiao model where random coefficients are only associated with time invariant and individual invariant variables has been studied by Wansbeek and Kapteyn (1978, 1979, 1982).

For the ith individual, Equation 13.6.1 can be written as

$$\mathbf{y}_i = X_i\bar{\boldsymbol{\beta}} + X_i\boldsymbol{\mu}_i + \bar{Z}_i\boldsymbol{\lambda} + \mathbf{e}_i, \tag{13.6.6}$$

where $\mathbf{y}_i$ and X_i are of dimension $(T \times 1)$ and $(T \times K)$, respectively, and contain observations on the dependent and explanatory variables, $\boldsymbol{\mu}_i = (\mu_{1i}, \mu_{2i}, \ldots, \mu_{Ki})'$, $\boldsymbol{\lambda}' = (\boldsymbol{\lambda}_1', \boldsymbol{\lambda}_2', \ldots, \boldsymbol{\lambda}_T')$, $\boldsymbol{\lambda}_t = (\lambda_{1t}, \lambda_{2t}, \ldots, \lambda_{Kt})'$, $\mathbf{e}_i = (e_{i1}, e_{i2}, \ldots, e_{iT})'$,

$$\underset{(T \times TK)}{\bar{Z}_i} = \begin{bmatrix} \mathbf{x}_{i1}' & & & \\ & \mathbf{x}_{i2}' & & \\ & & \ddots & \\ & & & \mathbf{x}_{iT}' \end{bmatrix}$$

and $\mathbf{x}_{it}' = (x_{1it}, x_{2it}, \ldots, x_{Kit})$. Hsiao assumes that $E[\mathbf{e}_i] = \mathbf{0}$, $E[\boldsymbol{\mu}_i] = \mathbf{0}$, $E[\boldsymbol{\lambda}_t] = \mathbf{0}$, $E[\mathbf{e}_i\mathbf{e}_i'] = \sigma_e^2 I$, and $E[\mathbf{e}_i\mathbf{e}_j'] = 0$ for $i \neq j$; $E[\boldsymbol{\mu}_i\boldsymbol{\mu}_i'] = \Delta$ and $E[\boldsymbol{\mu}_i\boldsymbol{\mu}_j'] = 0$ for $i \neq j$; and $E[\boldsymbol{\lambda}_t\boldsymbol{\lambda}_t'] = A$ and $E[\boldsymbol{\lambda}_t\boldsymbol{\lambda}_s'] = 0$ for $t \neq s$. Furthermore, $\boldsymbol{\mu}_i$, $\boldsymbol{\lambda}_t$, and $\mathbf{e}_i$ are all uncorrelated, and A and Δ are diagonal with diagonal elements given by α_k and δ_k, respectively.

Rewriting (13.6.6) to include all NT observations yields

$$\mathbf{y} = X\bar{\boldsymbol{\beta}} + Z\boldsymbol{\mu} + \bar{Z}\boldsymbol{\lambda} + \mathbf{e} \tag{13.6.7}$$

where $\mathbf{y}' = (\mathbf{y}_1', \mathbf{y}_2', \ldots, \mathbf{y}_N')$, $X' = (X_1', X_2', \ldots, X_N')$, Z is block diagonal with X_i as the ith diagonal block, $\bar{Z}' = (\bar{Z}_1', \bar{Z}_2', \ldots, \bar{Z}_N')$, $\boldsymbol{\mu}' = (\boldsymbol{\mu}_1', \boldsymbol{\mu}_2', \ldots, \boldsymbol{\mu}_N')$, and $\mathbf{e}' = (\mathbf{e}_1', \mathbf{e}_2', \ldots, \mathbf{e}_N')$.

If $\boldsymbol{\mu}$ and $\boldsymbol{\lambda}$ are regarded as fixed parameters, $\bar{\boldsymbol{\beta}}$, $\boldsymbol{\mu}$, and $\boldsymbol{\lambda}$ can be estimated by applying least squares to (13.6.7), provided that we reparameterize to eliminate redundant parameters, and provided that NT is sufficiently large. The matrix $[X, Z, \bar{Z}]$ is of dimension $(NT \times (T + N + 1)K)$, and of rank $(T + N - 1)K$, and so $2K$ parameters are redundant. For estimation a convenient approach would be to drop $(\mu_{1N}, \mu_{2N}, \ldots, \mu_{KN}, \lambda_{1T}, \lambda_{2T}, \ldots, \lambda_{KT})$, eliminate the corresponding columns in Z and $\bar{Z}$, and redefine the other parameters accordingly. Note that we are assuming $NT > (T + N - 1)K$.

13.6.1a Estimation and Prediction with Known Variances

When $\boldsymbol{\mu}$ and $\boldsymbol{\lambda}$ are random, with the assumptions specified above, the covariance matrix for the composite disturbance is

$$\begin{aligned}\Phi &= E[(Z\boldsymbol{\mu} + \bar{Z}\boldsymbol{\lambda} + \mathbf{e})(Z\boldsymbol{\mu} + \bar{Z}\boldsymbol{\lambda} + \mathbf{e})'] \\ &= Z(I_N \otimes \Delta)Z' + \bar{Z}(I_T \otimes A)\bar{Z}' + \sigma_e^2 I_{NT} \qquad (13.6.8)\end{aligned}$$

and the GLS estimator $\hat{\bar{\boldsymbol{\beta}}} = (X'\Phi^{-1}X)^{-1}X'\Phi^{-1}\mathbf{y}$ is the best linear unbiased estimator for $\bar{\boldsymbol{\beta}}$, with covariance matrix $(X'\Phi^{-1}X)^{-1}$. Presumably, NT would have to be large before one would contemplate using this model so that inversion of Φ could be a problem. Hsiao (1974) shows that Φ^{-1} can be written as

$$\begin{aligned}\Phi^{-1} = I - ZGZ' &- \bar{Z}C\bar{Z}'(I - ZGZ') \\ &+ (I + \bar{Z}C\bar{Z}')Z(Z'\bar{Z}C\bar{Z}'Z - G^{-1})^{-1}Z'\bar{Z}C\bar{Z}'(I - ZGZ')\end{aligned}$$

where $C = [\bar{Z}'\bar{Z} + (I_T \otimes A^{-1})]^{-1}$ and $G = [Z'Z + (I_N \otimes \Delta^{-1})]^{-1}$. In this expression the largest order of inversion is reduced to max $\{NK, TK\}$, but this could still be quite large. Except for a special case [Wansbeek and Kapteyn (1982)], a convenient transformation matrix P such that $P'P = c\Phi^{-1}$, where c is a scalar, does not seem to be available.

If one is interested in predicting the random components associated with each individual, then, following Lee and Griffiths (1979), the predictor

$$\hat{\boldsymbol{\mu}} = (I_N \otimes \Delta)Z'\Phi^{-1}(\mathbf{y} - X\hat{\bar{\boldsymbol{\beta}}}) \qquad (13.6.9)$$

can be shown to be best linear unbiased.

13.6.1b Estimating Variances

Both $\hat{\bar{\boldsymbol{\beta}}}$ and $\boldsymbol{\mu}$ depend on Δ, A, and σ_e^2 and, typically, these variances will be unknown. Hsiao outlines how they can be estimated using the maximum likelihood technique or, alternatively, a technique suggested by Hildreth and Houck (1968). We will briefly describe the latter technique.

Equation 13.6.1 can be rewritten as

$$y_{it} = \sum_{k=1}^{K} \beta_{ki} x_{kit} + v_{it} \tag{13.6.10}$$

where $\beta_{ki} = \bar{\beta}_k + \mu_{ki}$ and $v_{it} = \Sigma_{k=1}^{K} \lambda_{kt} x_{kit} + e_{it}$. The variance of v_{it} is

$$\theta_{it} \equiv E[v_{it}^2] = \sum_{k=1}^{K} x_{kit}^2 \alpha_k + \sigma_e^2 \tag{13.6.11}$$

and if these elements are placed in a $(T \times 1)$ vector $\boldsymbol{\theta}_i$, we have

$$\boldsymbol{\theta}_i = \dot{X}_i \boldsymbol{\alpha}, \tag{13.6.12}$$

where $\dot{X}_i$ is X_i with each of its elements squared and $\boldsymbol{\alpha} = (\alpha_1 + \sigma_e^2, \alpha_2, \ldots, \alpha_K)'$.

Let $\tilde{\mathbf{e}}_i = \mathbf{y}_i - X_i \mathbf{b}_i$ be the residual vector from the least squares estimator, $\mathbf{b}_i = (X_i' X_i)^{-1} X_i' \mathbf{y}_i$, applied to the ith cross section and let $\dot{\tilde{\mathbf{e}}}_i$ be the squares of these residuals. Then,

$$E[\dot{\tilde{\mathbf{e}}}_i] = \dot{M}_i \boldsymbol{\theta}_i = F_i \boldsymbol{\alpha} \tag{13.6.13}$$

where $\dot{M}_i$ contains squares of the elements of $M_i = I - X_i(X_i'X_i)^{-1}X_i'$, and $F_i = \dot{M}_i \dot{X}_i$. Repeating this process for all cross sections gives

$$E[\dot{\tilde{\mathbf{e}}}] = F\alpha \tag{13.6.14}$$

where $\dot{\tilde{\mathbf{e}}}' = (\dot{\tilde{\mathbf{e}}}_1', \ldots, \dot{\tilde{\mathbf{e}}}_N')$ and $F' = (F_1', F_2', \ldots, F_N')$. Application of least squares to (13.6.14) yields the unbiased estimator $\hat{\boldsymbol{\alpha}} = (F'F)^{-1}F'\dot{\tilde{\mathbf{e}}}$.

Following the same procedure with respect to each time period will yield an unbiased estimator, $\hat{\boldsymbol{\delta}}$, for $\boldsymbol{\delta} = (\delta_1 + \sigma_e^2, \delta_2, \ldots, \delta_K)'$. Under certain conditions [Hildreth and Houck (1968)] these estimators will be consistent and, in addition, a consistent estimator for σ_e^2 is given by

$$\hat{\sigma}_e^2 = \sum_{i=1}^{N} \sum_{t=1}^{T} \frac{\tilde{e}_{it} e_{it}^*}{NT} \tag{13.6.15}$$

where the e_{it}^* are the residuals obtained by applying least squares separately to each time period. From $\hat{\boldsymbol{\alpha}}$, $\hat{\boldsymbol{\delta}}$, and $\hat{\sigma}_e^2$ we can derive estimates for δ_1 and α_1.

Hsiao (1974) gives sufficient conditions for the consistency and asymptotic efficiency of the estimated generalized least squares estimator for $\bar{\boldsymbol{\beta}}$ which depends on the above variance estimates, and he also indicates how one can test for the constancy of coefficients over time or individuals. Some of Hsiao's asymptotic results have been corrected and extended by Kelejian and Stephan (1983).

Various refinements of the above technique are available and are discussed in Chapters 11 and 19. One problem is that some of the variance estimates may be negative and, in this case, the easiest solution is to change the negative estimates to zero.

In empirical work the Hsiao model does not seem to have gained the same widespread acceptance that some of the other models have achieved. This may be because the estimation procedures are not easily handled on standard computer packages, because the assumptions are not considered realistic, or because we seldom have data sets where both N and T are sufficiently large. It would be preferable to relax the assumption that Δ and A are diagonal and, as Hsiao notes, in principle this can be handled within the same estimation framework. However, it would be computationally more difficult and the problem of $\hat{A}$ and $\hat{\Delta}$ being nonnegative definite would be magnified. Also, if there are a sufficient number of time series observations, it might be preferable to drop the λ_{kt} and model the "time effects" with an autocorrelated e_{it} [see Swamy (1974)].

13.7 RECOMMENDATIONS

In the previous sections we have presented an array of alternative models and estimators. The applied worker is faced with the problem of choice between these models, or, in other words, one must decide which set of assumptions is the most plausible for a particular problem. As always, it is impossible to give blanket recommendations that are suitable for every problem. However, the following issues are worth considering.

1. Are the slope coefficients likely to vary over individuals, or is it reasonable to capture individual differences through the intercept or appropriate modeling of the disturbance term?
2. If the coefficients or the intercept vary over individuals, are the differences likely to depend on the explanatory variables of the individuals? If so, a dummy variable model or the seemingly unrelated regressions model is likely to be preferable. Alternatively, one could use a model that treats the correlation between the individual effects and the explanatory variables more explicitly. If such correlation does not exist, then the random assumptions of the error components models or the Swamy random coefficient model might be reasonable.
3. For modeling changes over time which method is better?
   (a) Use the constant correlation structure of the error components model.
   (b) Assume that the disturbances follow an autoregressive or moving average process.
   (c) Use dummy variables for changes over time and regard inference as conditional on those changes in the sample?
4. How many observations are there? In models where the parameters are assumed to be random, the relative sizes of N and T will have an important bearing on the finite sample reliability of variance estimates. For example,

if N is small, it is unlikely that $\hat{\sigma}_\mu^2$ for the error components model or $\hat{\Delta}$ for the Swamy random coefficient model will be very reliable. Consequently, the estimated generalized least squares estimators for the slope coefficients are also likely to be unreliable and, for estimation, it may be better to treat the coefficients as fixed even when the random assumption is reasonable.

At various points in the chapter we gave a number of tests that could be used to help us choose between models. In general, for model choice, we recommend that applied workers combine a judicious use of some of these tests with their a priori answers to the above four questions.

13.8 EXERCISES

13.8.1 General Exercises

Exercise 13.1

Prove that the matrices Q, Q_1, Q_2, and Q_3 are idempotent. See Equations 13.3.17, 13.4.6, 13.4.22, and 13.4.23 for the definitions.

Exercise 13.2

Use results on the partitioned inverse of a matrix to derive the estimators given in Equations 13.3.7, 13.3.16, 13.4.5, and 13.4.24.

Exercise 13.3

Show that the inverse of $\Phi_i = \sigma_\mu^2 \mathbf{j}_T \mathbf{j}_T' + \sigma_e^2 I_T$ is

$$\Phi_i^{-1} = \frac{\mathbf{j}_T \mathbf{j}_T'}{T\sigma_1^2} + \frac{D_T}{\sigma_e^2}$$

where $\sigma_1^2 = T\sigma_\mu^2 + \sigma_e^2$ and $D_T = I_T - \mathbf{j}_T \mathbf{j}_T'/T$.

Exercise 13.4

Show that $P_i'P_i = \sigma_e^2 \Phi_i^{-1}$, where Φ_i^{-1} is given in Exercise 13.3,

$$P_i = I_T - \alpha \mathbf{j}_T \mathbf{j}_T'/T$$

and $\alpha = 1 - \sigma_e/\sigma_1$.

Exercise 13.5

Let $A = I_N \otimes D_T$. Show that (Section 13.3.2c):

1. $\hat{\mathbf{e}} = A\mathbf{y} - AX_s\mathbf{b}_s = (A - AX_s(X_s'AX_s)^{-1}X_s'A)\mathbf{e}$.
2. A has rank $N(T - 1)$.
3. $A - AX_s(X_s'AX_s)^{-1}X_s'A$ is idempotent of rank $N(T - 1) - K'$.
4. $\hat{\sigma}_e^2$ in Equation 13.3.27 is an unbiased estimator.

Exercise 13.6

In Chapter 8 (Equation 8.3.4) we showed that a general expression for a best linear unbiased predictor is

$$\hat{\bar{\mathbf{y}}} = \bar{X}\hat{\boldsymbol{\beta}} + V'\Psi^{-1}(\mathbf{y} - X\hat{\boldsymbol{\beta}})$$

See Equations 8.3.2 and 8.3.3 for the relevant definitions. By appropriately defining $\bar{\mathbf{y}}$, $\bar{X}$, and V for each case, derive the BLUP predictors given in Sections 13.3.2b, 13.4.2b, 13.5.1b, and 13.6.1a.

Exercise 13.7

Consider the following error components model,

$$y_{it} = \bar{\beta}_1 + \beta_2 x_{it} + \mu_i + e_{it}, \qquad i = 1, 2, 3, \quad t = 1, 2, 3, 4$$

where the assumptions of Section 13.3.2 hold and we have the following data:

	$i = 1$		$i = 2$		$i = 3$	
	y	x	y	x	y	x
$t = 1$	51.03	32.52	43.90	32.86	64.29	41.86
$t = 2$	27.75	18.71	23.77	18.52	42.16	28.33
$t = 3$	35.72	27.01	28.60	22.93	61.99	34.21
$t = 4$	35.85	18.66	27.71	25.02	34.26	15.69

Find values of:

1. The dummy variable estimator of the slope coefficient β_2.
2. Estimators for σ_e^2 and σ_μ^2 (if $\hat{\sigma}_\mu^2 < 0$, set $\hat{\sigma}_\mu^2 = 0$).
3. The estimated generalized least squares estimator for β_2.
4. The predictors $\hat{\mu}_1$, $\hat{\mu}_2$, $\hat{\mu}_3$ (see Equation 13.3.24).
5. The dummy variable estimator for μ_1, μ_2, and μ_3 (see Equation 13.3.6).

Exercise 13.8

Prove that the estimator $\hat{\Delta}$ (Equation 13.5.14) is unbiased.

13.8.2 Exercises Using Monte Carlo Data

For the remaining problems we recommend generating Monte Carlo data consisting of 50 samples from an error components model with individual effects. Specifically, we suggest

$$y_{it} = \beta_1 + \beta_2 x_{it} + \mu_i + e_{it}, \qquad \begin{array}{l} i = 1, 2, 3, 4 \\ t = 1, 2, \ldots, 10 \end{array} \tag{13.8.1}$$

where $\beta_1 = 10$ and $\beta_2 = 1$; the μ_i are i.i.d. $N(0,14)$; and the e_{it} are i.i.d. $N(0,16)$.

Values of the explanatory variable for the four individuals are

$$\mathbf{x}_1 = \begin{bmatrix} 38.46 \\ 35.32 \\ 3.78 \\ 35.34 \\ 20.83 \\ 36.72 \\ 41.67 \\ 30.71 \\ 23.70 \\ 39.53 \end{bmatrix}, \quad \mathbf{x}_2 = \begin{bmatrix} 32.52 \\ 18.71 \\ 27.01 \\ 18.66 \\ 25.58 \\ 39.19 \\ 47.70 \\ 27.01 \\ 33.57 \\ 27.32 \end{bmatrix}, \quad \mathbf{x}_3 = \begin{bmatrix} 32.86 \\ 18.52 \\ 22.93 \\ 25.02 \\ 35.13 \\ 27.29 \\ 16.99 \\ 12.56 \\ 26.76 \\ 41.42 \end{bmatrix}, \quad \mathbf{x}_4 = \begin{bmatrix} 41.86 \\ 28.33 \\ 34.21 \\ 15.69 \\ 29.70 \\ 23.03 \\ 14.80 \\ 21.53 \\ 32.86 \\ 42.25 \end{bmatrix}$$

13.8.2a Individual Exercises

Exercise 13.9
Calculate the variance of the following estimators for β_2:

1. The LS estimator $\bar{b}_2$.
2. The GLS estimator $\hat{\beta}_2$.
3. The dummy variable estimator b_2.

Comment on the relative efficiencies.

Exercise 13.10
Select five samples from those generated and, for each sample, compute values for the estimators $\hat{\sigma}_1^2$, $\hat{\sigma}_e^2$ and $\hat{\sigma}_\mu^2$ given in Equations 13.3.26 to 13.3.28. If $\hat{\sigma}_\mu^2 < 0$, set $\hat{\sigma}_\mu^2 = 0$ and $\hat{\sigma}_1^2 = \hat{\sigma}_e^2$. Comment on the values.

Exercise 13.11
For the same five samples compute values for the estimators $\bar{b}_2$, and b_2, and $\hat{\hat{\beta}}_2$, where $\hat{\hat{\beta}}_2$ is the EGLS estimator for β_2 that uses the variance estimates obtained in Exercise 13.10. Note that b_2 may already have been calculated in Exercise 13.10. Compare the estimates with each other and the true parameter values.

Exercise 13.12
For each of the five samples,

1. Use the g statistic in Equation 13.3.29 to test the hypothesis $\sigma_\mu^2 = 0$.
2. Use the m statistic in Equation 13.3.31 to test the hypothesis of no systematic misspecification.

In both cases use a 10% significance level.

Exercise 13.13
For the same five samples compute estimates for μ_1, μ_2, μ_3, and μ_4 from

1. The dummy variable estimator.
2. The predictor in (13.3.24) with σ_μ^2 and σ_e^2 replaced by $\hat{\sigma}_\mu^2$ and $\hat{\sigma}_e^2$.

Comment on the values.

Exercise 13.14

Incorrectly assume that the data are generated from the Swamy random coefficient model with the assumptions employed in Section 13.5.1. For each of five samples, find $\hat{\Delta}$, defined in Equations 13.5.14, and $\tilde{\Delta} = S_b/(N - 1)$, where S_b is defined in (13.5.15). Comment on the results and note how many times $\hat{\Delta}$ is not nonnegative definite.

Exercise 13.15

For the same five samples compute values for the two EGLS estimators for $(\bar{\beta}_1, \bar{\beta}_2)'$ which use, respectively, $\hat{\Delta}$ and $\tilde{\Delta}$. Call them $(\hat{\hat{\beta}}_1, \hat{\hat{\beta}}_2)'$ and $(\tilde{\bar{\beta}}_1, \tilde{\bar{\beta}}_2)'$ and comment on the values.

13.8.2b Group Exercises

Exercise 13.16

Use the 50 samples to estimate the mean square errors (MSEs) of the estimators $\tilde{b}_2$, b_2, and $\hat{\hat{\beta}}_2$. With respect to the answers in Exercise 13.9 are the MSE estimates of $\tilde{b}_2$ and b_2 accurate? Comment on, and suggest reasons for, the relative efficiencies of $\tilde{b}_2$, b_2, $\hat{\hat{\beta}}_2$.

Exercise 13.17

Use the 50 samples to estimate the MSEs of the prediction errors for the two predictors of μ_1, μ_2, μ_3, and μ_4 given in Exercise 13.3. Comment on the relative efficiency.

Exercise 13.18

Using all 50 samples, comment on the proportion of times each of the null hypotheses in Exercise 13.12 were rejected.

Exercise 13.19

From the results of all 50 samples, estimate the MSEs of the estimators $\hat{\hat{\beta}}_2$ and $\tilde{\bar{\beta}}_2$ given in Exercise 13.15. Based on the results and those in Exercise 13.16:

1. Do you think it is preferable to use a covariance matrix estimator that is always nonnegative definite?
2. Is there much loss, if any, from assuming a more complicated covariance structure than that which actually exists?

13.9 REFERENCES

Amemiya, T. (1971) "The Estimation of Variances in a Variance-Components Model," *International Economic Review,* 12, 1–13.

Anderson, T. W. and Hsiao, C. (1981) "Estimation of Dynamic Models with Error Components," *Journal of the American Statistical Association,* 76, 598–606.

Anderson, T. W. and Hsiao, C. (1982) "Formulation and Estimation of Dynamic Models Using Panel Data," *Journal of Econometrics,* 18, 67–82.

Arora, S. S. (1973) "Error Components Regression Models and Their Applications," *Annals of Economic and Social Measurement,* 2, 451–461.

Avery, R. B. (1977) "Error Components and Seemingly Unrelated Regressions," *Econometrica,* 45, 199–209.

Balestra, P. and Nerlove, M. (1966) "Pooling Cross-Section and Time Series Data in the Estimation of a Dynamic Model: The Demand for Natural Gas," *Econometrica,* 34, 585–612.

Baltagi, B. H. (1980) "On Seemingly Unrelated Regressions with Error Components," *Econometrica,* 48, 1547–1551.

Baltagi, B. H. (1981) "An Experimental Study of Alternative Testing and Estimation Procedures in a Two-Way Error Component Model," *Journal of Econometrics,* 17, 21–49.

Battese, G. E. and Fuller, W. A. (1982) "An Error Components Model for Prediction of County Crop Areas Using Survey and Satellite Data," University of New England Working Papers in Econometrics and Applied Statistics No. 15, Armidale, Australia.

Berzeg, K. (1979) "The Error Components Model: Conditions for the Existence of Maximum Likelihood Estimates." *Journal of Econometrics,* 10, 99–102.

Bhargava, A., Franzini, L., and Narendranathan, W. (1982) "Serial Correlation and the Fixed Effects Model," *Review of Economic Studies,* 49, 533–550.

Bhargava, A. and J. D. Sargan (1983) "Estimating Dynamic Random Effects Models from Panel Data Covering Short Time Periods," *Econometrica,* 51, 1635–1659.

Biørn, E. (1981) "Estimating Economic Relations from Incomplete Cross-Section/Time-Series Data," *Journal of Econometrics,* 16, 221–236.

Breusch, T. S., and Pagan, A. R. (1980) "The Lagrange Multiplier Test and Its Applications to Model Specification in Econometrics," *Review of Economic Studies,* 47, 239–253.

Chamberlain, G. (1978) "Omitted Variable Bias in Panel Data: Estimating the Returns to Schooling," *Annales de L'Insee,* 30/31, 49–82.

Chamberlain, G. (1979) "Heterogeneity, Omitted Variable Bias, and Duration Dependence," Harvard Institute of Economic Research Discussion Paper No. 691, Cambridge, Mass.

Chamberlain, G. (1980) "Analysis of Covariance with Qualitative Data," *Review of Economic Studies,* 47, 225–238.

Chamberlain, G. (1982) "Multivariate Regression Models for Panel Data," *Journal of Econometrics,* 18, 5–46.

Chamberlain, G. (1983) "Panel Data," in Z. Griliches and M. D. Intriligator, eds., *Handbook of Econometrics,* North-Holland, Amsterdam.

Chamberlain, G., and Griliches, Z. (1975) "Unobservables with a Variance-Components Structure: Ability, Schooling and the Economic Success of Brothers," *International Economic Review,* 16, 422–450.

Feige, E. L. and Swamy, P. A. V. B. (1974) "A Random Coefficient Model of the Demand for Liquid Assets," *Journal of Money, Credit, and Banking,* 6, 241–252.

Flinn, C. and Heckman, J. (1982) "New Methods for Analyzing Structural Models of Labor Force Dynamics," *Journal of Econometrics,* 18, 115–168.

Fuller, W. A., and Battese, G. E. (1973) "Transformations for Estimation of Linear Models with Nested Error Structure," *Journal of the American Statistical Association,* 68, 626–632.

Fuller, W. A. and Battese, G. E. (1974) "Estimation of Linear Models with Crossed-Error Structure," *Journal of Econometrics,* 2, 67–78.

Glejser, H. (1978) "Truncated Distributed Lags in Small Sample Panel Models," *Annales de L'Insee,* 30/31, 131–136.

Griliches, Z., Hall, B. H., and Hausman, J. A. (1978) "Missing Data and Self-Selection in Large Panels," *Annales de L'Insee,* 30/31, 137–176.

Griffiths, W. E. and Anderson, J. R. (1982) "Using Time-Series and Cross-Section Data to Estimate a Production Function with Positive and Negative Marginal Risks," *Journal of the American Statistical Association,* 77, 529–536.

Harvey, A. C. (1978) "The Estimation of Time-Varying Parameters from Panel Data," *Annales de L'Insee,* 30/31, 203–226.

Hause, J. (1977) "The Covariance Structure of Earnings and the On-the-Job Training Hypothesis," *Annals of Economic and Social Measurement,* 6, 335–365.

Hause, J. (1980) "The Fine Structure of Earnings and the On-the-Job Training Hypothesis," *Econometrica,* 48, 1013–1029.

Hausman, J. A. (1978) "Specification Tests in Econometrics," *Econometrica,* 46, 1251–1272.

Hausman, J. A. and Taylor, W. E. (1981) "Panel Data and Unobservable Individual Effects," *Econometrica,* 49, 1377–1398.

Hausman, J. A. and Wise, D. A. (1979) "Attrition Bias in Experimental and Panel Data: The Gary Income Maintenance Experiment," *Econometrica,* 47, 455–473.

Heckman, J. (1978) "Simple Statistical Models for Discrete Panel Data Developed and Applied to Test the Hypothesis of True State Dependence Against the Hypothesis of Spurious State Dependence," *Annales de L'Insee,* 30/31, 227–269.

Heckman, J., and Singer, B., eds., (1982) *Journal of Econometrics,* 18, No. 1.

Henderson, C. R. (1953) "Estimation of Variance and Covariance Components," *Biometrics,* 9, 226–252.

Henderson, C. R. (1975) "Best Linear Unbiased Estimation and Prediction Under a Selection Model," *Biometrics,* 31, 423–447.

Hendricks, W., Koenker, R., and Poirier, D. (1979) "Stochastic Parameter Models for Panel Data: An Application to the Connecticut Peak Load Pricing Experiment," *International Economic Review,* 20, 707–724.

Hildreth, C., and Houck, J. P. (1968) "Some Estimators for a Linear Model with Random Coefficients," *Journal of the American Statistical Association,* 63, 584–595.

Hoch, I. (1962) "Estimation of Production Function Parameters Combining Time-Series and Cross-Section Data," *Econometrica,* 30, 34–53.

Hsiao, C. (1974) "Statistical Inference for a Model with Both Random Cross Sectional and Time Effects," *International Economic Review,* 15, 12–30.

Hsiao, C. (1975) "Some Estimation Methods for a Random Coefficient Model," *Econometrica,* 43, 305–325.

Johnson, S. R., and Rausser, G. C. (1975) "An Estimating Method for Models with Stochastic, Time Varying Parameters," *American Statistical Association, Proceedings of the Business and Economic Statistics Section,* 356–361.

Jöreskog, K. G. (1978) "An Econometric Model for Multivariate Panel Data," *Annales de L'Insee,* 30/31, 355–366.

Judge, G. G., R. C. Hill, W. E. Griffiths, H. Lütkepohl and T. C. Lee (1982) *Introduction to the Theory and Practice of Econometrics,* Wiley, New York.

Kelejian, H. H., and Stephan, S. W. (1983) "Inference in Random Coefficient and Error Component Models: Some Corrections and Extensions of the Literature," *International Economic Review,* 24, 249–254.

Kiefer, N. M. (1980) "Estimation of Fixed Effect Models for Time Series of Cross-Sections with Arbitrary Intertemporal Covariance," *Journal of Econometrics,* 14, 195–202.

Kiefer, N. M., and Neumann, G. R. (1981) "Individual Effects in a Nonlinear Model; Explicit Treatment of Heterogeneity in the Empirical Job-Search Model," *Econometrica,* 49, 965–979.

Kmenta, J. (1971) *Elements of Econometrics,* Macmillan, New York.

Leamer, E. E. (1978) *Specification Searches: Ad Hoc Inference with Nonexperimental Data,* Wiley, New York.

Lee, L. F. (1978a) "On the Issues of Fixed Effects vs. Random Effects Econometric Models with Panel Data," University of Minnesota Center for Economic Research Discussion Paper No. 78-101, Minneapolis.

Lee, L. F. (1978b) "Estimation of Error Components Model with ARMA (p,q) Time Component—An Exact GLS Approach," University of Minnesota Center for Economic Research Discussion Paper No. 78-104, Minneapolis.

Lee, L. F., and Griffiths, W. E. (1979) "The Prior Likelihood and Best Linear Unbiased Prediction in Stochastic Coefficient Linear Models," University of New England Working Papers in Econometrics and Applied Statistics No. 1, Armidale, Australia.

Lillard, L., and Weiss, Y. (1979) "Components of Variation in Panel Earnings Data: American Scientists 1960–1970," *Econometrica,* 47, 437–454.

Lillard, L., and Willis, R. J. (1978) "Dynamic Aspects of Earnings Mobility," *Econometrica,* 46, 985–1012.

Liu, L. M., and Hanssens, D. M. (1981) "A Bayesian Approach to Time-Varying Cross-Sectional Regression Models," *Journal of Econometrics,* 15, 341–356.

MaCurdy, T. E. (1982) "The Use of Time Series Processes to Model the Error Structure of Earnings in a Longitudinal Data Analysis," *Journal of Econometrics,* 18, 83–114.

Maddala, G. S. (1971) "The Use of Variance Components in Pooling Cross Section and Time Series Data," *Econometrica,* 39, 341–358.

Maddala, G. S. (1978) "Selectivity Problems in Longitudinal Data," *Annales de L'Insee,* 30/31, 423–451.

Maddala, G. S., and Mount, T. D. (1973) "A Comparative Study of Alternative Estimators for Variance Components Models," *Journal of the American Statistical Association,* 68, 324–328.

Magnus, J. R. (1983) "Multivariate Error Components Analysis of Linear and Nonlinear Regression Models by Maximum Likelihood," *Journal of Econometrics* 19, 239–286.

Mazodier, P., ed. (1978) *Annales de L'Insee,* 30/31.

Mazodier, P., and Trognon, A. (1978) "Heteroscedasticity and Stratification in Error Components Models," *Annales de L'Insee,* 30/31, 451–482.

Mundlak, Y. (1963) "Estimation of Production and Behavioral Functions from a Combination of Cross-Section and Time-Series Data," in C. F. Christ, ed., *Measurement in Economics,* Stanford University Press, Stanford.

Mundlak, Y. (1978a) "On the Pooling of Time Series and Cross Section Data," *Econometrica,* 46, 69–85.

Mundlak, Y. (1978b) "Models with Variable Coefficients-Integration and Extension," *Annales de L'Insee,* 30/31, 483–510.

Mundlak, Y., and Yahav, J. A. (1981) "Random Effects, Fixed Effects, Convolution, and Separation," *Econometrica,* 49, 1399–1416.

Nerlove, M. (1967) "Experimental Evidence on the Estimation of Dynamic Economic Relations from a Time Series of Cross Sections," *Economic Studies Quarterly,* 18, 42–74.

Nerlove, M. (1971a) "Further Evidence on the Estimation of Dynamic Economic Relations from a Time Series of Cross Sections," *Econometrica,* 39, 359–382.

Nerlove, M. (1971b) "A Note on Error Components Models," *Econometrica,* 39, 383–396.

Nickell, S. (1981) "Biases in Dynamic Models with Fixed Effects," *Econometrica,* 49, 1417–1426.

Parks, R. W. (1967) "Efficient Estimation of a System of Regression Equations When Disturbances Are Both Serially and Contemporaneously Correlated," *Journal of the American Statistical Association,* 62, 500–509.

Prucha, I. R. (1984) "On the Asymptotic Efficiency of Feasible Aitken Estimators for Seemingly Unrelated Regression Models with Error Components," *Econometrica,* 52, 203–208.

Pudney, S. E. (1978) "The Estimation and Testing of Some Error Components Models," London School of Economics, mimeo.

Rao, C. R. (1965) *Linear Statistical Inference and Its Applications,* Wiley, New York.

Rao, C. R. (1970) "Estimation of Heteroscedastic Variances in Linear Models," *Journal of the American Statistical Association,* 65, 161–172.

Rao, C. R. (1972) "Estimation of Variance and Covariance Components in Linear Models," *Journal of the American Statistical Association,* 67, 112–115.

Rao, U. L. G. (1982) "A Note on the Unbiasedness of Swamy's Estimator for the Random Coefficient Regression Model,'' *Journal of Econometrics,* 18, 395–401.

Reinsel, G. (1982) ''Multivariate Repeated-Measurement of Growth Curve Models with Multivariate Random-Effects Covariance Structure,'' *Journal of the American Statistical Association,* 77, 190–195.

Revankar, N. S. (1979) ''Error Component Models with Serially Correlated Time Effects,'' *Journal of the Indian Statistical Association,* 17, 137–160.

Rosenberg, B. (1973a) ''A Survey of Stochastic Parameter Regression,'' *Annals of Economic and Social Measurement,* 2, 381–398.

Rosenberg, B. (1973b) ''Linear Regression with Randomly Dispersed Parameters,'' *Biometrika,* 60, 65–72.

Rosenberg, B. (1973c) ''The Analysis of a Cross Section of Time Series by Stochastically Convergent Parameter Regression,'' *Annals of Economic and Social Measurement,* 2, 399–428.

Schmidt, P. (1983) ''A Note on a Fixed Effect Model with Arbitrary Interpersonal Covariance,'' *Journal of Econometrics,* 22, 391–394.

Sevestre, P., and Trognon, A. (1982) ''A Note on Autoregressive Error Components Models,'' L'Insee Working Paper No. 8204, Paris, France.

Singer, B. (1982) ''Aspects of Non-Stationarity,'' *Journal of Econometrics,* 18, 169–190.

Singh, B., and Ullah, A. (1974) ''Estimation of Seemingly Unrelated Regressions with Random Coefficients,'' *Journal of the American Statistical Association,* 69, 191–195.

Smith, A. F. M. (1973) ''A General Bayesian Linear Model,'' *Journal of the Royal Statistical Society, Series B,* 35, 67–75.

Swamy, P. A. V. B. (1970) ''Efficient Inference in a Random Coefficient Regression Model,'' *Econometrica,* 38, 311–323.

Swamy, P. A. V. B. (1971) *Statistical Inference in Random Coefficient Regression Models,* Springer-Verlag, New York.

Swamy, P. A. V. B. (1973) ''Criteria, Constraints, and Multicollinearity in Random Coefficient Regression Models,'' *Annals of Economic and Social Measurement,* 2, 429–450.

Swamy, P. A. V. B. (1974) ''Linear Models with Random Coefficients,'' in P. Zarembka, ed., *Frontiers in Econometrics,* Academic Press, New York.

Swamy, P. A. V. B., and Arora, S. S. (1972) ''The Exact Finite Sample Properties of the Estimators of Coefficients in the Error Components Regression Model,'' *Econometrica,* 40, 253–260.

Swamy, P. A. V. B., and Mehta, J. S. (1973) ''Bayesian Analysis of Error Components Regression Models,'' *Journal of the American Statistical Association,* 68, 648–658.

Swamy, P. A. V. B., and Mehta, J. S. (1975) ''Bayesian and Non-Bayesian Analysis of Switching Regressions and of Random Coefficient Regression Models,'' *Journal of the American Statistical Association,* 70, 593–602.

Swamy, P. A. V. B., and Mehta, J. S. (1977) ''Estimation of Linear Models with Time and Cross-Sectionally Varying Coefficients,'' *Journal of the American Statistical Association,* 72, 890–898.

Swamy, P. A. V. B., and Mehta, J. S. (1979) "Estimation of Common Coefficients in Two Regression Equations," *Journal of Econometrics,* 10, 1–14.

Taub, A. J. (1979) "Prediction in the Context of the Variance-Components Model," *Journal of Econometrics,* 10, 103–108.

Taylor, W. E. (1980) "Small Sample Considerations in Estimation From Panel Data," *Journal of Econometrics,* 13, 203–223.

Theil, H., and Goldberger, A. S. (1960) "On Pure and Mixed Statistical Estimation in Economics," *International Economic Review,* 2, 65–78.

Trognon, A. (1978) "Miscellaneous Asymptotic Properties of Ordinary Least Squares and Maximum Likelihood Estimators in Dynamic Error Components Models," *Annales de L'Insee,* 30/31, 631–657.

Wallace, T. D., and Hussain, A. (1969) "The Use of Error Components Models in Combining Cross Section with Time Series Data," *Econometrica,* 37, 55–72.

Wansbeek, T. J., and Kapteyn, A. (1978) "The Separation of Individual Variation and Systematic Change in the Analysis of Panel Survey Data," *Annales de L'Insee,* 30/31, 659–680.

Wansbeek, T. J., and Kapteyn, A. (1979) "Estimators of the Covariance Structure of a Model for Longitudinal Data," in *Proceedings of the Econometric Society European Meeting, 1981,* E. Charatsis, ed., North-Holland, Amsterdam.

Wansbeek, T. J., and Kapteyn, A. (1982) "A Class of Decompositions of the Variance-Covariance Matrix of a Generalized Error Components Model," *Econometrica,* 50, 713–724.

Zellner, A. (1966) "On the Aggregation Problem: A New Approach to a Troublesome Problem," in K. A. Fox, et al., ed., *Economic Models, Estimation, and Risk Programming: Essays in Honor of Gerhard Tintner, 1969,* Springer-Verlag, New York.

PART FIVE

INFERENCE IN SIMULTANEOUS EQUATION MODELS

In previous chapters we have acknowledged the stochastic and dynamic nature of economic data. In Part Five we recognize the simultaneous aspect of the economic data generation process and specify a statistical model that is consistent with this type of sampling mechanism. Emphasis is directed to the identification requirements for a simultaneous equation system, and the possibilities for estimation and inference with this instantaneous feedback statistical model. The last chapter of Part Five, which is concerned with multiple time series and systems of dynamic simultaneous equations, in some respect generalizes the results of the first two chapters.

Chapter 14

Specification and Identification in Simultaneous Equations Models

14.1 INTRODUCTION

In the preceding chapters we have stressed the importance of understanding the sampling process by which the data were generated, and then adapting the statistical models and estimators to the peculiarities of the data and the objectives of the research. We have recognized that economic variables are in reality random variables whose properties can be described by probability distributions. We have further indicated the stochastic nature of the observed data and their relationships to stochastic nonobservable variables in the form of random errors in the variables or random errors in the equation. We have also noted that economic data are often passively generated in that the observed values come as a result of the existing economic structure, and thus there are limited possibilities for controlling some of the important economic variables and isolating relations and capturing the corresponding relevant parameters.

Most conceptual frameworks for understanding economic processes and institutions reflect the vision that in economics everything depends on everything else. This idea translates into the realization that economic data that are a product of the existing economic system must then be described as a system of simultaneous relations among the random economic variables and that these relations involve current and past (lagged) values of some of the variables.

This scenario led Marschak (1950) to comment that "economic data are generated by systems of relations that are in general stochastic, dynamic and simultaneous." He further noted that, although these properties of the data give rise to many unsolved problems in statistical inference, they constitute the basic ingredients underlying economic theory, and quantitative knowledge of them is needed for economic practice.

Previous chapters have emphasized the stochastic nature of economic variables and we have considered single and multiple equation models designed to explain their behavior. In Chapters 7–10 we have also considered the dynamic nature of economic variables. In this part of the book, Chapters 14–16, we are concerned with the simultaneous and interdependent nature of economic variables, and what this implies for the statistical model and our basis for parameter estimation and inference.

Up to this point we have lived in the simple world of one-way causality. That is, we have assumed that the explanatory variables in the design matrix have an impact on the values of the left-hand side random variable y, but there is no feedback in the other direction. While this model is appropriate for describing the data generation process in many circumstances, it is inconsistent with many others. In particular, it is usually inappropriate when modeling the generation of price and quantity data in one or more markets, since we know that the values of these variables are determined jointly or simultaneously by supply and demand. Another example arises if we consider a set of macroeconomic variables whose values are jointly determined by the equilibrium of a set of macroeconomic behavioral relations. The specification of simultaneous economic models is well documented in the economic and econometric literature and for a discussion of and motivation for the use of simultaneous equations models, the reader is encouraged to read Haavelmo (1943), Girshick and Haavelmo (1953), Marschak (1953), and Koopmans (1953). For an introductory discussion of the simultaneous equation statistical model and the problem of identification, see Chapter 12 in Judge et al. (1982).

The remainder of this chapter is devoted to formulating the simultaneous equation model as well as discussing basic issues. In particular, in Section 14.2 the statistical model is presented; the consequences of using ordinary least squares (LS) as an estimation rule for an equation in a simultaneous equation system are developed in Section 14.3. Section 14.4 contains a discussion of the reduced form of a simultaneous equation system and the use of LS for its estimation. In Section 14.5 the concept of identification is presented and Section 14.6 contains concluding remarks.

14.2 THE SIMULTANEOUS EQUATIONS STATISTICAL MODEL AND ASSUMPTIONS

To introduce the idea of simultaneity we must pay special attention to how the economic variables are classified. Basically, each equation in the model may contain the following types of variables:

Endogenous, or jointly determined variables, have outcome values determined through joint interaction with other variables within the system. Examples, within the context of a partial or general equilibrium system, include such variables as price, consumption, production, and income.

Exogenous variables affect the outcome of the endogenous variables, but their values are determined outside the system. The exogenous variables thus are assumed to condition the outcome values of the endogenous variables but are not reciprocally affected because no feedback relation is assumed. Examples in this category are weather-related variables, such as rainfall and temperature, and the world price of a commodity for a country model that involves only a minor part of the production or consumption of the commodity. Lagged

TABLE 14.1 ***SPECIFICATION AND IDENTIFICATION OF SIMULTANEOUS EQUATIONS MODELS***

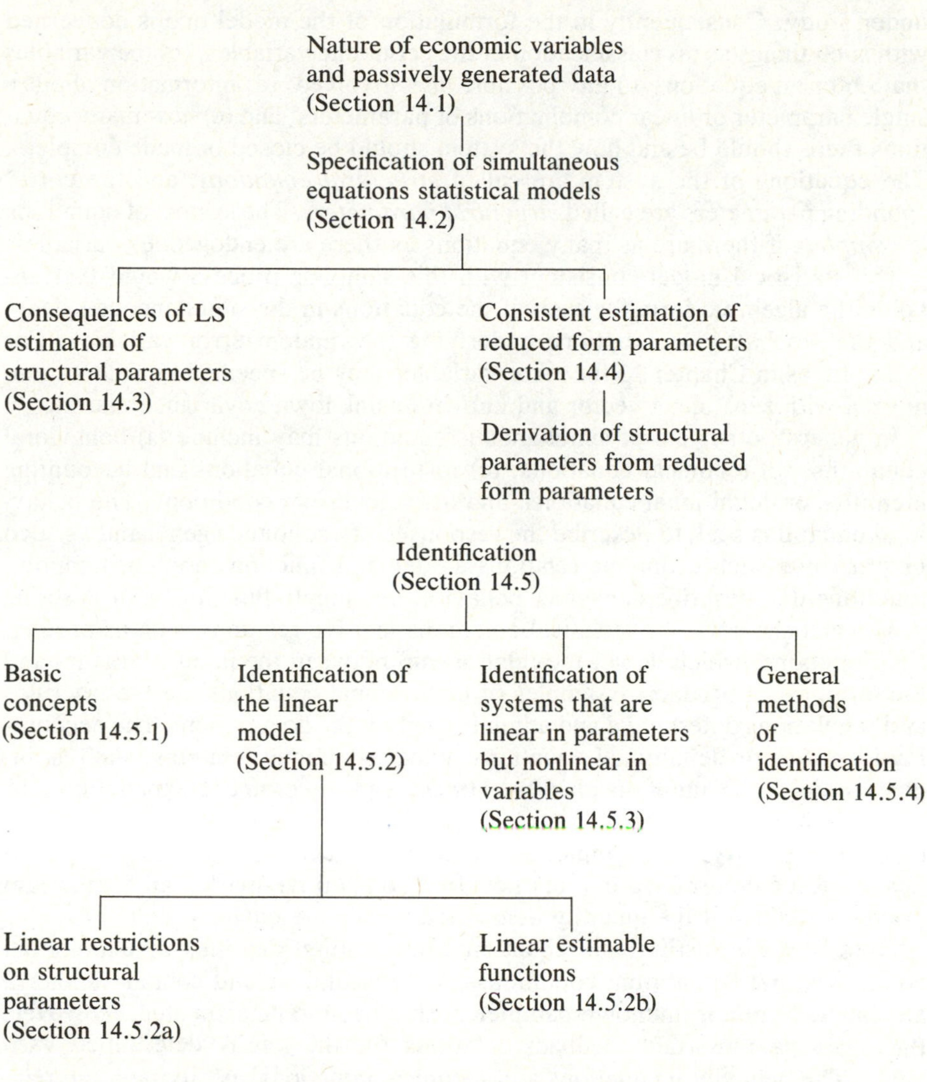

endogenous variables may be placed in the same category as the exogenous variables since for the current period the observed values are predetermined. The exogenous variables and variables that may involve any length of lag are called *predetermined variables*. For statistical purposes the relevant distinction is between jointly dependent variables and predetermined variables.

The final classification of variables involves the nonobservable random errors, or, as they were called in the early simultaneous equation literature, random shocks or disturbances. We have already talked about the various specifications for these random variables in the previous chapters.

An economic model expresses all the information available about the system under study. Consequently in the formulation of the model one is concerned with such things as (a) classification of the economic variables, (b) the variables that enter an equation, (c) any possible lags involved, (d) information about a single parameter or linear combinations of parameters, and (e) how many equations there should be and how the system should be closed or made complete. The equations of the system are called *structural equations,* and the corresponding parameters are called *structural parameters*. The system of equations is *complete* if there are as many equations as there are endogenous variables.

The statistical model consistent with this sampling process would then involve the algebraic form for each of the equations in the simultaneous system and the stochastic assumptions underlying the random error variables. For example, as in Chapter 12 the error variables may be specified as multivariate normal with zero mean vector and known or unknown covariance matrix.

In general, a system of simultaneous equations may include (a) behavioral equations, (b) technical equations, (c) institutional equations and accounting identities or definitional equations, and (d) equilibrium conditions. The behavioral equations seek to describe the responses of economic agents and as such may involve such economic relations as demand functions and consumption functions that describe consumer behavior and supply functions that describe producer behavior. The technical equations involve relations such as production functions, which depict the relationship between the input of factors and the output of a product. Examples of institutional equations are the tax rules and regulations determined and administered by the government. The accounting identities or definitional equations reflect economic relations, such as income equals consumption plus investment and government expenditure, or personal disposable income equals GNP minus tax, and so on. Equilibrium conditions specify, for example, the conditions under which prices and quantities are to be determined in a market. In a competitive market an equilibrium price is obtained if the quantity demanded equals the quantity supplied.

Note that the institutional equations, accounting identities or definitional equations, and equilibrium conditions are deterministic and contain neither a stochastic term nor unknown parameters that need to be estimated. However, they provide important feedback relations for the jointly determined variables. The behavioral equations and technical equations specify possible relationships among the endogenous and predetermined variables and contain stochastic disturbance terms as well as unknown parameters that are to be estimated. Let us note again these equations express the basic structural relationships among economic variables for the phenomena that are being modeled and as such are called *structural equations*.

With these definitions and concepts, let us specify a statistical model that is consistent with many economic systems. This model will be linear in both the variables and parameters. In Sections 14.5.2 and 14.5.3, generalizations of this model are considered.

In the model we represent the T observations on the M endogenous variables by the $(T \times 1)$ vectors $\mathbf{y}_1, \mathbf{y}_2, \ldots, \mathbf{y}_M$; the K exogenous and predetermined variables by the $(T \times 1)$ vectors $\mathbf{x}_1, \mathbf{x}_2, \ldots, \mathbf{x}_K$; and the M random error variables by the $(T \times 1)$ vectors $\mathbf{e}_1, \mathbf{e}_2, \ldots, \mathbf{e}_M$. A general linear statistical model reflecting the M equations that represent the relationships among the jointly endogenous variables, the exogenous and predetermined variables, and the random errors, may be stated as

$$\begin{aligned}
\mathbf{y}_1\gamma_{11} + \mathbf{y}_2\gamma_{21} + \cdots + \mathbf{y}_M\gamma_{M1} + \mathbf{x}_1\beta_{11} + \mathbf{x}_2\beta_{21} + \cdots + \mathbf{x}_K\beta_{K1} + \mathbf{e}_1 &= \mathbf{0} \\
\mathbf{y}_1\gamma_{12} + \mathbf{y}_2\gamma_{22} + \cdots + \mathbf{y}_M\gamma_{M2} + \mathbf{x}_1\beta_{12} + \mathbf{x}_2\beta_{22} + \cdots + \mathbf{x}_K\beta_{K2} + \mathbf{e}_2 &= \mathbf{0} \\
&\vdots \\
\mathbf{y}_1\gamma_{1M} + \mathbf{y}_2\gamma_{2M} + \cdots + \mathbf{y}_M\gamma_{MM} + \mathbf{x}_1\beta_{1M} + \mathbf{x}_2\beta_{2M} + \cdots + \mathbf{x}_K\beta_{KM} + \mathbf{e}_M &= \mathbf{0}
\end{aligned} \tag{14.2.1}$$

where the γ's and the β's are the structural parameters of the system that are unknown and are thus to be estimated from the data. In matrix notation the linear statistical model may be written compactly as

$$Y\Gamma + XB + \mathbf{E} = 0 \tag{14.2.2}$$

where 0 is a $(T \times M)$ matrix of zeros,

$$Y = \begin{bmatrix} y_{11} & y_{12} & \cdots & y_{1M} \\ y_{21} & y_{22} & \cdots & y_{2M} \\ \vdots & \vdots & \ddots & \vdots \\ y_{T1} & y_{T2} & \cdots & y_{TM} \end{bmatrix}_{(T \times M)} = (\mathbf{y}_1 \; \mathbf{y}_2 \; \ldots \; \mathbf{y}_M) \tag{14.2.3}$$

and

$$X = \begin{bmatrix} x_{11} & x_{12} & \cdots & x_{1K} \\ x_{21} & x_{22} & \cdots & x_{2K} \\ \vdots & \vdots & \ddots & \vdots \\ x_{T1} & x_{T2} & \cdots & x_{TK} \end{bmatrix}_{(T \times K)} = (\mathbf{x}_1 \; \mathbf{x}_2 \; \ldots \; \mathbf{x}_K) \tag{14.2.4}$$

are the sample values of the jointly dependent and the predetermined variables, respectively, and

$$\mathbf{E} = \begin{bmatrix} e_{11} & e_{12} & \cdots & e_{1M} \\ e_{21} & e_{22} & \cdots & e_{2M} \\ \vdots & \vdots & \ddots & \vdots \\ e_{T1} & e_{T2} & \cdots & e_{TM} \end{bmatrix}_{(T \times M)} = (\mathbf{e}_1 \; \mathbf{e}_2 \; \ldots \; \mathbf{e}_M) \tag{14.2.5}$$

is the matrix of unobservable values of the random error vectors. The matrix

$$\Gamma = \begin{bmatrix} \gamma_{11} & \gamma_{12} & \cdots & \gamma_{1M} \\ \gamma_{21} & \gamma_{22} & \cdots & \gamma_{2M} \\ \vdots & \vdots & & \vdots \\ \gamma_{M1} & \gamma_{M2} & \cdots & \gamma_{MM} \end{bmatrix}_{(M \times M)} = (\boldsymbol{\Gamma}_1\, \boldsymbol{\Gamma}_2 \ldots \boldsymbol{\Gamma}_M) \quad (14.2.6)$$

is the $(M \times M)$ matrix of coefficients of the current endogenous variables, where each column refers to the coefficients for a particular equation in (14.2.1).

$$B = \begin{bmatrix} \beta_{11} & \beta_{12} & \cdots & \beta_{1M} \\ \beta_{21} & \beta_{22} & \cdots & \beta_{2M} \\ \vdots & \vdots & & \vdots \\ \beta_{K1} & \beta_{K2} & \cdots & \beta_{KM} \end{bmatrix}_{(K \times M)} = (\mathbf{B}_1\, \mathbf{B}_2 \ldots \mathbf{B}_M) \quad (14.2.7)$$

is a $(K \times M)$ matrix of unknown coefficients of the exogenous-predetermined variables, and each column contains the coefficients of a particular equation in (14.2.1). It is important to note that Y and $\mathbf{E}$ are of the same order. Γ is a square matrix of order M, and B is of order $(K \times M)$, where, in general, K may or may not be equal to M.

The assumptions that define the statistical model are as follows.

Assumption 1 (Random Disturbances) The stochastic assumptions for the unobservable random error vectors $\mathbf{e}_1, \mathbf{e}_2, \ldots, \mathbf{e}_M$ are the same as those for the set of regression equations analyzed in Chapter 12. That is, we assume that the structural disturbances are generated by a stationary multivariate process with

$$E[\mathbf{e}_i] = \mathbf{0} \qquad \text{for} \quad i = 1, 2, \ldots, M \qquad (14.2.8)$$

and

$$E[\mathbf{e}_i\mathbf{e}_i'] = \sigma_{ii}I_T = \sigma_i^2 I_T \qquad \text{for} \quad i = 1, 2, \ldots, M \qquad (14.2.9)$$

and

$$E[\mathbf{e}_i\mathbf{e}_j'] = \sigma_{ij}I_T \qquad \text{for} \quad i \neq j \quad \text{and} \quad i,j = 1, 2, \ldots, M \quad (14.2.10)$$

or, compactly, as

$$E[\mathbf{e}_i\mathbf{e}_j'] = \sigma_{ij}I_T \qquad \text{for} \quad i,j = 1, 2, \ldots, M \qquad (14.2.11)$$

which, as in Chapter 12, implies that

$$E\left\{\begin{bmatrix} \mathbf{e}_1 \\ \mathbf{e}_2 \\ \vdots \\ \mathbf{e}_M \end{bmatrix}\begin{bmatrix} \mathbf{e}_1 \\ \mathbf{e}_2 \\ \vdots \\ \mathbf{e}_M \end{bmatrix}'\right\} = \begin{bmatrix} \sigma_{11}I & \sigma_{12}I & \cdots & \sigma_{1M}I \\ \sigma_{21}I & \sigma_{22}I & \cdots & \sigma_{2M}I \\ \vdots & \vdots & & \vdots \\ \sigma_{M1}I & \sigma_{M2}I & \cdots & \sigma_{MM}I \end{bmatrix} = \Sigma \otimes I_T \quad (14.2.12)$$

The unknown contemporaneous covariance matrix Σ is an $(M \times M)$ symmetric and positive semidefinite matrix. It may be of less than full rank because some of the equations may appear in the form of identities with null error vectors. In estimation the identities are substituted for so that the resulting system may be assumed to have an error covariance that is nonsingular.

In addition to the assumptions on the random disturbances, we make the following:

Assumption 2 (Completeness) The matrix Γ is nonsingular.

Assumption 3 (Limiting Behavior of Exogenous Variables) If the predetermined variables are purely exogenous (that is, they include only exogenous or lagged exogenous variables), we assume that

$$\lim_{T\to\infty} \frac{X'X}{T} = \Sigma_{xx} \quad (14.2.13)$$

is finite and nonsingular. If X contains lagged endogenous variables and $\mathbf{z}_t'$ denotes that part of the tth rows of X that includes only the exogenous variables, then we also assume

$$\lim_{T\to\infty} \frac{1}{T-k} \sum_{t=1}^{T-k} \mathbf{z}_t \mathbf{z}_{t+k}' \quad (14.2.14)$$

is finite for $k = 1, 2, \ldots$.

Assumption 4 (Stability in the Presence of Lagged Endogenous Variables) If the predetermined variables include lagged endogenous variables, write XB as

$$XB = X_0B_0 + Y_{-1}B_1 + Y_{-2}B_2 + \ldots + Y_{-P}B_P \quad (14.2.15)$$

where Y_{-P} is the $(T \times M)$ matrix of observations on Y, lagged P periods, B_P is the $M \times M$ matrix of corresponding coefficients, and P is the maximum lag present in the model. Then it is assumed that all the roots of the determinental equation

$$|B_0 + B_1z + \ldots + B_Pz^P| = 0 \quad (14.2.16)$$

are greater than one in absolute value. This assumption is motivated in greater detail in Chapter 16.

Two important consequences of these assumptions, that will be used later, are that

$$\text{plim}(\mathbf{E}'\mathbf{E}/T) = \Sigma \tag{14.2.17}$$

and

$$\text{plim}(X'\mathbf{E}/T) = 0. \tag{14.2.18}$$

Assumptions 3 and 4 also imply that plim $X'X/T$ is finite and nonsingular, even under the presence of lagged endogenous variables. For a proof of (14.2.18), see Schmidt (1976, p. 123).

14.3 CONSEQUENCES OF ORDINARY LEAST SQUARES ESTIMATION OF STRUCTURAL EQUATION PARAMETERS

The least squares estimator is biased and inconsistent for the parameters of a structural equation in a simultaneous equation system. To see this, consider the ith equation in (14.2.1) written as

$$Y\mathbf{\Gamma}_i + X\mathbf{B}_i + \mathbf{e}_i = \mathbf{0} \tag{14.3.1}$$

Some elements of $\mathbf{\Gamma}_i$ and $\mathbf{B}_i$ are generally known to be zero; also it is customary to select one endogenous variable to appear on the left-hand side of the equation. This is called selection of a normalization rule and is achieved by setting one coefficient, say γ_{ii}, to the value -1. Then, with rearrangement if necessary,

$$\mathbf{y}_i = Y_i\boldsymbol{\gamma}_i + Y_i^*\boldsymbol{\gamma}_i^* + X_i\boldsymbol{\beta}_i + X_i^*\boldsymbol{\beta}_i^* + \mathbf{e}_i$$

$$\mathbf{y}_i = Y_i\boldsymbol{\gamma}_i + X_i\boldsymbol{\beta}_i + \mathbf{e}_i$$

$$\mathbf{y}_i = (Y_i \quad X_i)\begin{bmatrix}\boldsymbol{\gamma}_i \\ \boldsymbol{\beta}_i\end{bmatrix} + \mathbf{e}_i$$

or compactly as

$$\mathbf{y}_i = Z_i\boldsymbol{\delta}_i + \mathbf{e}_i \tag{14.3.2}$$

where

$$\Gamma_i = \begin{bmatrix}-1 \\ \boldsymbol{\gamma}_i \\ \boldsymbol{\gamma}_i^*\end{bmatrix} = \begin{bmatrix}-1 \\ \boldsymbol{\gamma}_i \\ \mathbf{0}\end{bmatrix}, \qquad B_i = \begin{bmatrix}\boldsymbol{\beta}_i \\ \boldsymbol{\beta}_i^*\end{bmatrix} = \begin{bmatrix}\boldsymbol{\beta}_i \\ \mathbf{0}\end{bmatrix}, \qquad \boldsymbol{\delta}_i = \begin{bmatrix}\boldsymbol{\gamma}_i \\ \boldsymbol{\beta}_i\end{bmatrix}$$

$$Y = [\mathbf{y}_i \quad Y_i \quad Y_i^*], \qquad X = [X_i \quad X_i^*], \qquad Z_i = (Y_i \quad X_i)$$

and $M = m_i + m_i^*$, $K = k_i + k_i^*$. The matrix Y_i^* contains those m_i^* endogenous variables that do not appear in the ith equation; that is, their associated coefficients $\boldsymbol{\gamma}_i^*$ are zero. The matrix X_i^* contains those k_i^* predetermined variables that do not appear in the ith equation; that is, their associated coefficients $\boldsymbol{\beta}_i^*$ are zero.

The least squares estimator of $\boldsymbol{\delta}_i$ in (14.3.2) is

$$\hat{\boldsymbol{\delta}}_i = (Z_i'Z_i)^{-1}Z_i'\mathbf{y}_i. \tag{14.3.3}$$

It has expectation

$$\begin{aligned} E[\hat{\boldsymbol{\delta}}_i] &= E[(Z_i'Z_i)^{-1}Z_i'(Z_i\boldsymbol{\delta}_i + \mathbf{e}_i)] \\ &= \boldsymbol{\delta}_i + E[(Z_i'Z_i)^{-1}Z_i'\mathbf{e}_i] \end{aligned} \tag{14.3.4}$$

The last term in (14.3.4) does not vanish because Z_i contains endogenous variables that are jointly determined with $\mathbf{y}_i$ and thus not independent of $\mathbf{e}_i$. Consequently, $E[\hat{\boldsymbol{\delta}}_i] \neq \boldsymbol{\delta}_i$ and $\hat{\boldsymbol{\delta}}_i$ is biased.

Furthermore, as the sample size increases $\hat{\boldsymbol{\delta}}_i$ does not converge in probability to $\boldsymbol{\delta}_i$ since

$$\text{plim } \hat{\boldsymbol{\delta}}_i = \boldsymbol{\delta}_i + \text{plim}[Z_i'Z_i/T]^{-1} \text{ plim}[Z_i'\mathbf{e}_i/T] \neq \boldsymbol{\delta}_i$$

The last term, $\text{plim}[Z_i'\mathbf{e}_i/T]$ does not converge to the zero vector because $Z_i = (Y_i \quad X_i)$ contains Y_i, which is not independent of the error vector $\mathbf{e}_i$, a result that obtains no matter how large the sample size. Therefore, the use of the least squares rule on a structural equation containing two or more endogenous variables will yield biased and inconsistent parameter estimators.

14.4 REDUCED FORM EQUATIONS AND THEIR ESTIMATION

If the system of equations (14.2.2) is complete—that is, if Γ is nonsingular—then we can express the endogenous variables as a function of the predetermined variables plus random disturbances. This is called the *reduced form* of the simultaneous equations system. Specifically, if we post multiply (14.2.2) by Γ^{-1} and rearrange we obtain the reduced form

$$\begin{aligned} Y &= -XB\Gamma^{-1} - \mathbf{E}\Gamma^{-1} \\ &= X\Pi + V \end{aligned} \tag{14.4.1}$$

where

$$\Pi = -B\Gamma^{-1} = \begin{bmatrix} \pi_{11} & \pi_{12} & \cdots & \pi_{1M} \\ \pi_{21} & \pi_{22} & \cdots & \pi_{2M} \\ \vdots & \vdots & & \vdots \\ \pi_{K1} & \pi_{K2} & \cdots & \pi_{KM} \end{bmatrix} = (\boldsymbol{\pi}_1 \; \boldsymbol{\pi}_2 \; . \; . \; . \; \boldsymbol{\pi}_M) \tag{14.4.2}$$

is the $(K \times M)$ matrix of reduced form parameters and

$$V = -\mathbf{E}\Gamma^{-1} = \begin{bmatrix} v_{11} & v_{12} & \cdots & v_{1M} \\ v_{21} & v_{22} & \cdots & v_{2M} \\ \vdots & \vdots & & \vdots \\ v_{T1} & v_{T2} & \cdots & v_{TM} \end{bmatrix} = (\mathbf{v}_1 \ \mathbf{v}_2 \ \ldots \ \mathbf{v}_M) \qquad (14.4.3)$$

is the $(T \times M)$ matrix of reduced form disturbances.

The stochastic assumptions on V follow directly from those on $\mathbf{E}$. If $\mathbf{e}_t'$ is the tth row of $\mathbf{E}$ and $\mathbf{v}_t'$ the tth row of V, then

$$\mathbf{v}_t' = -\mathbf{e}_t'\Gamma^{-1} \qquad (14.4.4)$$

Since the vectors $\mathbf{e}_t$ have mean $E(\mathbf{e}_t) = \mathbf{0}$ and covariance matrix $E(\mathbf{e}_t\mathbf{e}_t') = \Sigma$, it follows that

$$E[\mathbf{v}_t] = E[-\mathbf{e}_t'\Gamma^{-1}]' = -(\Gamma^{-1})'E[\mathbf{e}_t] = \mathbf{0}$$

and

$$\begin{aligned} \text{var}(\mathbf{v}_t) = E[\mathbf{v}_t\mathbf{v}_t'] &= (\Gamma^{-1})'E(\mathbf{e}_t\mathbf{e}_t')(\Gamma^{-1}) \\ &= (\Gamma^{-1})'\Sigma\Gamma^{-1} = \Omega \end{aligned} \qquad (14.4.5)$$

Further, since $E(\mathbf{e}_t\mathbf{e}_s') = 0$, then $E(\mathbf{v}_t\mathbf{v}_s') = 0$, for $t \neq s$.

Individual reduced form equations can be taken from (14.4.1) as

$$\mathbf{y}_i = X\boldsymbol{\pi}_i + \mathbf{v}_i \qquad (14.4.6)$$

where $\mathbf{v}_i$ is the ith column of V. If X is nonstochastic, then

$$E(X'V) = E(-X'\mathbf{E}\Gamma^{-1}) = 0$$

so that $E(X'\mathbf{v}_i) = \mathbf{0}$. If X contains lagged endogenous variables, then $\text{plim}(X'V/T) = \text{plim}(-(X'\mathbf{E}/T)\Gamma^{-1}) = 0$ [see (14.2.18)]. In the former case, using standard proofs, the least squares estimator of the reduced form parameters for the ith equation,

$$\hat{\boldsymbol{\pi}}_i = (X'X)^{-1}X'\mathbf{y}_i \qquad (14.4.7)$$

or for the whole system

$$\hat{\Pi} = (X'X)^{-1}X'Y \qquad (14.4.8)$$

is unbiased and consistent, and in the latter case it is consistent. Note that joint estimation of the M reduced form equations in a seemingly unrelated regression format does not lead to an increase in efficiency in this case, even though $E(\mathbf{v}_i\mathbf{v}_j') = \omega_{ij}I$ since the matrix of explanatory variables for each equation (i.e., X) is identically the same.

We conclude that while OLS is not a consistent way to estimate the structural parameters, the reduced form parameters can be consistently estimated by least squares. This result is useful for several reasons. First, in cases where only predictions are desired, the estimated reduced form coefficients provide a basis for making those predictions. Specifically, if X_0 is a $(T_0 \times K)$ matrix of values for the predetermined variables for which predictions of the endogenous variables are desired, then

$$\hat{Y}_0 = X_0\hat{\Pi} \tag{14.4.9}$$

yields predicted values, such that $\text{plim}(\hat{Y}_0 - Y_0) = 0$. In Chapter 15 we will explore more efficient ways of estimating Π, which lead to more precise forecasts.

Second, since it is possible to consistently estimate the reduced form parameters, and since the relationship between the structural parameters and the reduced form parameters is known,

$$\Pi = -B\Gamma^{-1} \tag{14.4.10}$$

$$\Omega = (\Gamma^{-1})'\Sigma\Gamma^{-1} \tag{14.4.11}$$

the question arises as to whether values of the structural parameters can be uniquely derived from knowledge of the reduced form parameters and other information about the structural parameters. If this were possible, unique consistent estimates of the structural parameters could be derived from the estimates of the reduced form parameters. This question is the topic of the next section, which is concerned with the *identification problem*.

14.5 IDENTIFICATION

Economists are in general nonexperimental scientists. To a large extent it is not possible to control variables and isolate relationships by using careful experimental designs. Nevertheless, our goal is to learn about the unknown structure of the system that generates the data we observe. To make matters more manageable, economists construct models that purport to explain observed phenomena, and assume that they represent the structures that actually generated the data. The crux of the *identification* concept is the following: Statistical inference is concerned with characteristics of the distribution of observable random variables. Having assumed that our model represents the structure that truly generated the data, we have the problem of whether it is possible to draw inferences from the probability distribution of the observed random variables back to an underlying structure. In general, this is not possible, and thus the structure is not estimable, unless some nonsample, a priori information is also available. In this section, we explore the limits of observational information and examine the requirements for the nonsample information.

14.5.1 Basics

Certain concepts can be stated that will apply not only to the model developed earlier in this chapter, but also to more general models that will appear later on. Let $\mathbf{y}$ be a vector of observable random variables. A *structure* S is a complete specification of the probability density function of $\mathbf{y}$, say $f(\mathbf{y})$. The set of all possible structures, $\mathcal{S}$, is called a *model*. The identification problem then is that of making judgments about S given $\mathcal{S}$ and the observations $\mathbf{y}$. To make matters more precise, assume $\mathbf{y}$ is generated by the parametric probability density $f(\mathbf{y}|S) = f(\mathbf{y}|\boldsymbol{\alpha})$, where $\boldsymbol{\alpha}$ is a K-dimensional real vector. The function f is assumed known but $\boldsymbol{\alpha}$ is not. Hence a structure is described by a point in $\mathcal{R}^K$ and a model by a set of points in $\mathcal{R}^K$.

In general it is said that two structures $S = \boldsymbol{\alpha}$ and $S^* = \boldsymbol{\alpha}^*$ are *observationally equivalent* if $f(\mathbf{y}|\boldsymbol{\alpha}) = f(\mathbf{y}|\boldsymbol{\alpha}^*)$ for all $\mathbf{y}$. Here, however, we will view two structures as observationally equivalent if they produce identical first and second moments of f. For the normal distribution, recall that all information is contained in the first and second moments. Furthermore, the structure $S^0 = \boldsymbol{\alpha}^0$ in $\mathcal{S}$ is *globally identified* if there is no other feasible $\boldsymbol{\alpha}$ that is observationally equivalent.

Since a set of structures is simply a subset of $\mathcal{R}^K$, it is possible that there may be a number of observationally equivalent structures, but that they are isolated from one another. Consequently, a structure $S^0 = \boldsymbol{\alpha}^0$ is *locally identified* if there exists an open neighborhood containing $\boldsymbol{\alpha}^0$ such that no other $\boldsymbol{\alpha}$ in the open neighborhood is observationally equivalent to $\boldsymbol{\alpha}^0$.

14.5.2 Identification in the Linear Simultaneous Equations Model

In this section we consider the identification of the simultaneous equations model (14.2.2). We first discuss conditions under which two structures will be observationally equivalent, and then derive identification criteria that ensure that no two structures will be observationally equivalent.

One observation on all M simultaneous equations can be written as

$$\mathbf{y}_t'\Gamma + \mathbf{x}_t'B + \mathbf{e}_t' = \mathbf{0}', \qquad t = 1, \ldots, T, \tag{14.5.1}$$

where $\mathbf{y}_t'$, $\mathbf{x}_t'$, and $\mathbf{e}_t'$ are the tth rows of Y, X, and $\mathbf{E}$, respectively. Suppose $\mathbf{e}_t$ has density $P(\mathbf{e}_t|\Sigma)$, then the joint density of $\mathbf{e}_1, \mathbf{e}_2, \ldots, \mathbf{e}_T$ is

$$\prod_{t=1}^{T} P(\mathbf{e}_t|\Sigma) \tag{14.5.2}$$

Making a change of variables by substituting for $\mathbf{e}_t$ in (14.5.2) and multiplying by the Jacobian of the transformation and using (14.5.1), the joint density of $\mathbf{y}_1, \mathbf{y}_2, \ldots, \mathbf{y}_T$, conditional on the $\mathbf{x}_t$'s is

$$P(\mathbf{y}_1, \ldots, \mathbf{y}_T|\Gamma,B,\Sigma,X) = \|\Gamma\|^T \prod_{t=1}^{T} P(\mathbf{e}_t|\Sigma)$$

$$= \|\Gamma\|^T \prod_{t=1}^{T} P(-\mathbf{y}_t'\Gamma - \mathbf{x}_t'B|\Sigma) \qquad (14.5.3)$$

where $\|\cdot\|$ denotes the absolute value of the determinant of the argument.

If we postmultiply (14.5.1) by an arbitrary nonsingular $(M \times M)$ matrix F, each equation will be replaced by a linear combination of the original M equations in the structure. That is,

$$\mathbf{y}_t'(\Gamma F) + \mathbf{x}_t'(BF) + \mathbf{e}_t'F = \mathbf{y}_t'\Gamma^* + \mathbf{x}_t'B^* + \boldsymbol{\omega}_t' = \mathbf{0}' \qquad (14.5.4)$$

Since $\boldsymbol{\omega}_t' = \mathbf{e}_t'F$,

$$P(\boldsymbol{\omega}_t|F'\Sigma F) = \|F\|^{-1}P(\mathbf{e}_t|\Sigma) \qquad (14.5.5)$$

The density of $\mathbf{y}_1, \mathbf{y}_2, \ldots, \mathbf{y}_T$ for this new structure is

$$\|\Gamma F\|^T \cdot \prod_{t=1}^{T} P(\boldsymbol{\omega}_t|F'\Sigma F) = \|\Gamma\|^T \|F\|^T \|F\|^{-T} \prod_{t=1}^{T} P(\mathbf{e}_t|\Sigma)$$

$$= \|\Gamma\|^T \prod_{t=1}^{T} P(\mathbf{e}_t|\Sigma) \qquad (14.5.6)$$

the joint density which is identical to (14.5.3) determined from the original structure. Hence (14.5.1) and (14.5.4) are observationally equivalent. Note that by letting $F = \Gamma^{-1}$, one observationally equivalent structure is the reduced form of the simultaneous equation system. Consequently, all structures that could be created by postmultiplying the original structure by a nonsingular matrix have the same reduced form.

Given that we are defining observational equivalence by the first two moments of P, the conditions for observational equivalence can be stated as follows: Two structures $S = (\Gamma,B,\Sigma)$ and $S^* = (\Gamma^*,B^*,\Sigma^*)$ are observationally equivalent if and only if:

1. $B\Gamma^{-1} = B^*\Gamma^{*-1}$ and $(\Gamma^{-1})'\Sigma\Gamma^{-1} = (\Gamma^{*-1})'\Sigma^*(\Gamma^{*-1})$.
2. There exists a nonsingular matrix F such that

$$\begin{pmatrix}\Gamma^* \\ B^*\end{pmatrix} = \begin{pmatrix}\Gamma \\ B\end{pmatrix}F \quad \text{and} \quad \Sigma^* = F'\Sigma F$$

If there were no a priori restrictions on the parameters of the model (14.5.1), any nonsingular F would be *admissible* in the sense that the resulting transformed structure satisfies the restrictions of the model. Clearly this is a hopeless situation. If on the basis of economic theory, we can specify a set of a priori restrictions on the model, any transformed model must obey the same a priori restrictions if the transformation is to remain admissible.

14.5.2a Identification of a Single Equation Using Linear Restrictions on Structural Parameters

To make matters specific, assume for the moment that all a priori restrictions are in the form of linear restrictions on Γ, B, and Σ. Nonlinear restrictions are briefly discussed in Section 14.5.3. In this context, the identification question is, do the a priori restrictions on Γ, B, and Σ imply sufficient restrictions on the set of admissible transformation matrices F to make some or all of the coefficients in the original and transformed structures identical, and thus identified? This notion leads us to a definition of the identification of the ith equation as follows. The ith equation is identified if and only if all admissible transformations have the form

$$F = \begin{bmatrix} & 0 & \\ & \vdots & \\ \cdots & c_{ii} & \cdots \\ & \vdots & \\ & 0 & \end{bmatrix}$$

That is, the ith column of F must be a scalar multiple of the $(M \times 1)$ unit vector whose elements are all zero except a one in the ith row. Note that when Γ and B are post multiplied by such an F, their ith columns are only changed by a scalar multiple.

Extending this definition to the entire system, we have that the system is identified if and only if all the equations are identified, or equivalently, that the admissible transformation matrix is diagonal. In the instance where normalization rules are imposed, such as $\gamma_{ii} = -1$, then the only nonzero element of the ith column must be 1.

To determine conditions under which the ith equation is identified, let

$$A = \begin{bmatrix} \Gamma \\ B \end{bmatrix}$$

so that $\mathbf{a}_i$, the ith column of A, contains the parameters of the ith equation. Let R_i and $\mathbf{r}_i$ be $J \times (M + K)$ and $(J \times 1)$ matrices of constants, respectively, such that all prior information about the ith equation of the model including the normalization rule, can be written

$$R_i \mathbf{a}_i = \mathbf{r}_i \tag{14.5.7}$$

For example, if the a priori information is that $\gamma_{1i} = 0$, $\gamma_{2i} + \gamma_{3i} = 1$, and $\gamma_{ii} = -1$, then (14.5.7) is

$$\begin{bmatrix} 1 & 0 & 0 & 0 & \dots & 0 & \dots & 0 \\ 0 & 1 & 1 & 0 & \dots & 0 & \dots & 0 \\ 0 & 0 & 0 & 0 & \dots & 1 & \dots & 0 \end{bmatrix} \mathbf{a}_i = \begin{bmatrix} 0 \\ 1 \\ -1 \end{bmatrix} \tag{14.5.8}$$

If (14.5.7) is the only restriction available, then we can make the following observation: We know that the ith column of AF is $A\mathbf{f}_i$, where $\mathbf{f}_i$ is the ith column of F. Since F is admissible, the resulting structural coefficients satisfy the restrictions $R_i(A\mathbf{f}_i) = \mathbf{r}_i$. However, for the ith equation to be identified, $\mathbf{f}_i$ should be equal to $\mathbf{j}_i$, a unit vector whose elements are zero except a one in the ith row. Indeed $\mathbf{j}_i$ is a solution of $R_iA\mathbf{f}_i = \mathbf{r}_i$ because $R_iA\mathbf{j}_i = R_i\mathbf{a}_i = \mathbf{r}_i$ by (14.5.7). Therefore, for $(R_iA)\mathbf{f}_i = \mathbf{r}_i$ to have a unique solution of $\mathbf{f}_i = \mathbf{j}_i$, it requires that $\text{Rank}(R_iA) = M$. Now, we can formally state the following theorem:

THEOREM Rank Condition for Identification of a Single Equation

The ith equation is identified if and only if $\text{Rank}(R_iA) = M$.

Note that if the only restrictions are zero coefficient restrictions, then $\mathbf{r}_i = \mathbf{0}$ and the rank condition reduces to $\text{Rank}(R_iA) = M - 1$ so that the homogeneous equation $R_iA\mathbf{f}_i = \mathbf{0}$ has a unique solution up to scalar multiplication. By normalization the ith equation is identified. A necessary but not sufficient condition to achieve the rank condition can be stated in the following corollary:

COROLLARY Order Condition

A necessary condition for the identification of the ith equation is that J, the number of linear restrictions including normalization, must be greater than or equal to M. If R_i excludes the normalization rule, then the rank of R_iA must be $M - 1$ and the order of R_i must be $J > M - 1$.

If normalization is included in the restrictions, then this theorem and corollary lead to the following definitions.

1. The parameters of the ith equation are not identified, or *underidentified,* if $\text{Rank}(R_iA) < M$.
2. The parameters of the ith equation are *exactly,* or *just, identified* if $\text{Rank}(R_iA) = M$ and $\text{Rank}(R_i) = M$.
3. The parameters of the ith equation are *overidentified* if $\text{Rank}(R_iA) = M$ and $\text{Rank}(R_i) > M$.

It should be noted that restrictions on the system coefficients are not the only type of information that can be used to identify equations. It is possible that restrictions on the contemporaneous covariance matrix Σ can help reduce the number of admissible transformation matrices F. Let $\mathbf{\Sigma}_i$ denote the ith column of Σ, which contains the variance of the ith equation error and covariances of the ith equation error and other equation errors. Also let the g linear restrictions on $\mathbf{\Sigma}_i$ be

$$H_i\mathbf{\Sigma}_i = \mathbf{h}_i \tag{14.5.9}$$

where H_i is $(g \times M)$, and $\mathbf{h}_i$ is $(g \times 1)$. If F is any admissible transformation matrix, then

$$H_i\mathbf{\Sigma}_i^* = \mathbf{h}_i \tag{14.5.10}$$

where $\mathbf{\Sigma}_i^*$ is the ith column of $F'\Sigma F$. Since the ith column of $F'\Sigma F$ is $F'\Sigma\mathbf{f}_i$, the restrictions become

$$H_iF'\Sigma\mathbf{f}_i = \mathbf{h}_i \tag{14.5.11}$$

Combining the restrictions on both structural coefficients and error covariances, we can write

$$\begin{bmatrix} R_i & 0 \\ 0 & H_iF' \end{bmatrix}\begin{bmatrix} A \\ \Sigma \end{bmatrix}\mathbf{f}_i = \begin{bmatrix} \mathbf{r}_i \\ \mathbf{h}_i \end{bmatrix} \tag{14.5.12}$$

Thus, for $\mathbf{f}_i$ to have a unique solution of $\mathbf{f}_i = \mathbf{j}_i$, where $\mathbf{j}_i$ is the unit vector, it is necessary that

$$\text{Rank}\begin{bmatrix} R_i & 0 \\ 0 & H_iF' \end{bmatrix}\begin{bmatrix} A \\ \Sigma \end{bmatrix} = M \tag{14.5.13}$$

Since the above conditions must hold for all admissible F, including $F = I$, we can generalize the rank and order conditions as follows:

THEOREM Generalized Rank Condition for Identification of a Single Equation

For the ith equation to be identified, it is necessary that

$$\text{Rank}\begin{bmatrix} R_iA \\ H_i\Sigma \end{bmatrix} = M \tag{14.5.14}$$

COROLLARY Generalized Order Condition

A necessary condition for the identification of the ith equation is that $J + g$, the number of linear restrictions on the structural coefficients including normalization plus the number of restrictions on the covariances, must be greater than or equal to M.

Note that the generalized rank condition is necessary but not sufficient. For sufficiency, it is required that the unique solution of $\mathbf{f}_i$ in (14.5.12) be $\mathbf{j}_i$. This requires that $H_i F' \Sigma \mathbf{j}_i = \mathbf{h}_i$ holds for every admissible F in addition to the already known result $R_i A \mathbf{j}_i = \mathbf{r}_i$.

To form a useful sufficiency condition, we consider the case where the only restrictions on Σ are zero restrictions so that $\mathbf{h}_i = \mathbf{0}$ and H_i consists of only unit vectors. We also rearrange all the structural equations so that the ith equation is the first equation, and the equations whose equation errors are uncorrelated with the first equation error are arranged to appear at the end of the system. In this way, H_i becomes $H_i = (0 \quad I)$, and Σ may be partitioned according to H_i into

$$\Sigma = \begin{bmatrix} \Sigma_{11} & \Sigma_{12} \\ \Sigma_{21} & \Sigma_{22} \end{bmatrix} \tag{14.5.15}$$

where the first row of Σ_{12} and the first column of Σ_{21} contain all zeros. The admissible F matrix is also partitioned into

$$F = \begin{bmatrix} F_{11} & F_{12} \\ F_{21} & F_{22} \end{bmatrix} \tag{14.5.16}$$

corresponding to the partitioning of Σ. Under these arrangements, the relation $H_i F' \Sigma \mathbf{f}_i = \mathbf{h}_i$ can be simplified to

$$(0 \quad I) \begin{bmatrix} F'_{11} & F'_{21} \\ F'_{12} & F'_{22} \end{bmatrix} \begin{bmatrix} \Sigma_{11} & \Sigma_{12} \\ \Sigma_{21} & \Sigma_{22} \end{bmatrix} \mathbf{j}_i = \mathbf{0} \tag{14.5.17}$$

or

$$(F'_{12}\Sigma_{11} + F'_{22}\Sigma_{21} \quad F'_{12}\Sigma_{12} + F'_{22}\Sigma_{22})\mathbf{j}_i = \mathbf{0} \tag{14.5.18}$$

For this result to hold the first column of $F'_{12}\Sigma_{11} + F'_{22}\Sigma_{21}$ must be zero. In view of the partitioning, the first column of Σ_{21} is zero, and hence we require the first column of $F'_{12}\Sigma_{11}$ to be zero. (This condition alone is another necessary condition for identification.) The first column of $F'_{12}\Sigma_{11}$ will be zero when $F_{12} = 0$. In words, $F_{12} = 0$ means that every equation whose equation error is uncorrelated with the first equation error is identified with respect to every equation whose equation error is correlated with the first equation error. Therefore, we can state a sufficiency theorem as follows:

THEOREM

A sufficient condition for the ith equation to be identified is that:

1. The generalized rank condition holds.
2. Every equation whose equation error is uncorrelated with the ith equation

error is identified with respect to every equation whose equation error is correlated with the ith equation error.

A useful corollary can be stated as follows:

COROLLARY

A sufficient condition for the identification of the ith equation is that:

1. The generalized rank condition holds.
2. Every equation whose equation error is uncorrelated with the ith equation is identified.

Note that the necessary generalized rank and order conditions can be further extended to include restrictions involving all elements of $\begin{pmatrix} \mathbf{a}_i \\ \mathbf{\Sigma}_i \end{pmatrix}$; that is, elements of $\mathbf{a}_i$ are linearly related to elements of $\mathbf{\Sigma}_i$. Examples of such a priori knowledge are rare.

If R_i excludes the normalization rule and R_i and H_i include only homogeneous restrictions so that $\mathbf{r}_i = \mathbf{0}$ and $\mathbf{h}_i = \mathbf{0}$, then the rank of $\begin{pmatrix} R_i & 0 \\ 0 & H_i \end{pmatrix}\begin{pmatrix} A \\ \Sigma \end{pmatrix}$ must be $M - 1$ and the order of $\begin{pmatrix} R_i & 0 \\ 0 & H_i \end{pmatrix}$ must be $J + g \geq M - 1$. When there are no restrictions on the covariances, then $g = 0$, and the rank and order conditions reduce to those of R_iA and R_i as previously stated.

An example of zero restrictions on covariances is a *recursive system,* in which Γ is a triangular matrix *and* Σ is a diagonal matrix. In this case, for every structural equation, there are $M - 1$ zero covariances; therefore, $g = M - 1$ and $J \geq 1$ (at least for normalization). Thus $g + J \geq M$ and the generalized rank condition holds for every equation. Also because Γ is a triangular matrix, the $M - 1$ zero restrictions on the coefficients in $\mathbf{\Gamma}_1$ identify the first equation, which together with the generalized rank condition recursively identifies the subsequent equations.

Generalizing the idea of recursiveness, Hausman and Taylor (1983) show that, within the context of a single equation, covariance restrictions aid identification if and only if they imply that a set of endogenous variables is predetermined in the equation of interest. Although they do not establish necessary and sufficient conditions for identification within the context of the complete system, they show that if the system of equations is identifiable as a whole, covariance restrictions cause residuals to behave as instruments in the sense that the full system estimator can be treated as an instrumental variable estimator where the instruments include residuals uncorrelated with the equation error due to the covariance restrictions.

14.5.2b Identification of the System in Terms of "Linear Estimable Functions"

In this section, following Richmond (1974), we consider identification of the entire system of equations and of parametric functions. Since the matrix of reduced form parameters Π can be consistently estimated, assume that Π is known and let us consider under what conditions Γ and B can be uniquely determined. Let $\mathbf{\Gamma}_i$ and $\mathbf{B}_i$ denote the ith columns of Γ and B, respectively, and let $\mathbf{d} = (\Gamma_1' \; \Gamma_2' \; . \; . \; . \; \Gamma_M' \; \mathbf{B}_1' \; \mathbf{B}_2' \; . \; . \; . \; \mathbf{B}_M')'$ be the $(M(M + K) \times 1)$ vector formed by stacking the parameter vectors as indicated. Then, since $\Pi = -B\Gamma^{-1}$, it follows that

$$\Pi\Gamma + B = (\Pi \quad I_K)\begin{pmatrix}\Gamma \\ B\end{pmatrix} = 0 \tag{14.5.19}$$

or

$$(I_M \otimes \Pi \; \vdots \; I_M \otimes I_K)\mathbf{d} = \mathbf{0} \tag{14.5.20}$$

or

$$\Phi\mathbf{d} = \mathbf{0} \tag{14.5.21}$$

where Φ is the $(MK \times (M^2 + MK))$ matrix on the left-hand side of (14.5.20). Now assume that all prior information, including normalization rules and possible cross equation parameter constraints, may be written

$$R\mathbf{d} = \mathbf{r} \tag{14.5.22}$$

where R is $(J \times M(M + K))$ and $\mathbf{r}$ is $(J \times 1)$, and both are known. Combining (14.5.21) and (14.5.22), we have

$$W\mathbf{d} = \begin{bmatrix}\Phi \\ R\end{bmatrix}\mathbf{d} = \begin{bmatrix}\mathbf{0} \\ \mathbf{r}\end{bmatrix} = \mathbf{r}^* \tag{14.5.23}$$

Note that (14.5.23) is simply a system of $MK + J$ linear equations in $M^2 + MK$ variables $\mathbf{d}$. Identification means that this system must have full column rank. Thus the whole vector $\mathbf{d}$ is identified if and only if $\text{Rank}(W) = M^2 + MK$.

Now, let

$$Q = \begin{pmatrix}I_M \otimes \Gamma \\ I_M \otimes B\end{pmatrix} \tag{14.5.24}$$

Then

$$W = \begin{pmatrix}I_M \otimes \Pi & I_M \otimes I_K \\ R_1 & R_2\end{pmatrix} = \begin{pmatrix}0 & I_M \otimes I_K \\ RQ & R_2\end{pmatrix}\begin{pmatrix}I_M \otimes \Gamma^{-1} & 0 \\ I_M \otimes \Pi & I_M \otimes I_K\end{pmatrix} \tag{14.5.25}$$

where $R = (R_1 \quad R_2)$. Since Γ is nonsingular, the second partitioned matrix on the right-hand side of (14.5.25) is nonsingular, so

$$\text{Rank}(W) = \text{Rank}\begin{pmatrix} 0 & I_M \otimes I_K \\ RQ & 0 \end{pmatrix} \tag{14.5.26}$$

Since the vector $\mathbf{d}$ is identified if and only if rank$(W) = M^2 + MK$, it follows that $\mathbf{d}$ is identified if and only if Rank$(RQ) = M^2$.

In the present context, it is also possible to identify parametric functions of the parameters $\mathbf{d}$. Let $\mathbf{c}$ be an $((M^2 + MK) \times 1)$ vector of constants. Then, the parametric function $\mathbf{c}'\mathbf{d}$ is identified, given Π, if it has a unique value for every $\mathbf{d}$ satisfying (14.5.23). It can be shown that $\mathbf{c}'\mathbf{d}$ is identified if and only if

$$\text{Rank}\begin{pmatrix} RQ \\ \mathbf{c}'Q \end{pmatrix} = \text{Rank}(RQ) \tag{14.5.27}$$

For a proof, see Richmond (1974). The implication of (14.5.27) is that although an individual parameter is not identified when Rank$(RQ) < M^2$ the parametric function $\mathbf{c}'\mathbf{d}$ may be identified if the condition (14.5.27) holds.

14.5.3 Identification of Systems That are Linear in the Parameters But Nonlinear in the Variables

Simultaneous equations models that are linear in the parameters and nonlinear in the variables are frequently used in economics. The nonlinearities often arise because endogenous variables enter different equations in different forms. For example, the endogenous variable may appear in one equation and its natural logarithm, square, or reciprocal may appear in another. In such models, identification rules developed for the simultaneous equations model that is linear in the parameters and variables do not apply, so it is important to determine appropriate identification conditions.

One approach is to employ the general local identification concepts for the general nonlinear model of Rothenberg (1971) or Bowden (1973). These are discussed in Section 14.5.4. Their conditions depend on the likelihood function, and thus require the specification of a particular distribution for the errors. Conditions for identification in nonlinear models under weaker distributional assumptions about the errors have been developed by Fisher (1961, 1965, 1966), Kelejian (1971), and Brown (1983). Brown extends the work of Fisher and develops necessary and sufficient conditions for identification in models nonlinear in the variables. We will briefly present these conditions.

Write the tth observation for a simultaneous equation model that is nonlinear in the variables as (where for notational convenience the t subscript is suppressed and the model has been transposed)

$$A'\mathbf{q}(\mathbf{y},\mathbf{x}) = \mathbf{e} \tag{14.5.28}$$

where $\mathbf{y}$ is an $(M \times 1)$ vector of endogenous variables, $\mathbf{x}$ is a $(K \times 1)$ vector of exogenous variables, $\mathbf{e}$ is an $(M \times 1)$ vector of disturbances, $\mathbf{q}$ is an $(N \times 1)$ vector of known functions of $\mathbf{y}$ and $\mathbf{x}$, and A' is the $(M \times N)$ matrix of unknown coefficients. For simplicity, assume that constant terms are in the last column of A' so that the last element of $\mathbf{q}(\cdot)$ is the constant function $\mathbf{q}_N(\mathbf{y},\mathbf{x}) = 1$. All the other elements of $\mathbf{q}(\cdot)$ are linearly independent and continuously differentiable functions of $\mathbf{y}$ and $\mathbf{x}$.

It is assumed that equation (14.5.28) implicitly defines a single relevant $(M \times 1)$ vector-valued continuous function $\mathbf{G}(\mathbf{e},\mathbf{x})$ such that $\mathbf{y} = \mathbf{G}(\mathbf{e},\mathbf{x})$. This relationship may not be expressible in a closed form, but is analogous to the reduced form. See Fisher (1966, p. 131) and Brown (1983, p. 177) for more detail.

It is also assumed that the disturbances $\mathbf{e}$ are distributed independently of the exogenous variables $\mathbf{x}$ and that prior information on the coefficients of the ith equation can be written as a set of homogenous restrictions

$$R_i \mathbf{a}_i = \mathbf{0} \tag{14.5.29}$$

where R_i is a $(J_i \times N)$ matrix of known constants and $\mathbf{a}_i$ is the $(N \times 1)$ vector of coefficients for the ith equation.

Define $\tilde{Q}'$ to be an N-row matrix whose columns form a basis for the space generated by

$$\begin{aligned}\frac{\partial \mathbf{q}(\mathbf{G}(\mathbf{e},\mathbf{x}),\mathbf{x})}{\partial \mathbf{x}'} &= \frac{\partial \mathbf{q}(\cdot)}{\partial \mathbf{x}'} + \frac{\partial \mathbf{q}(\cdot)}{\partial \mathbf{y}'} \cdot \frac{\partial \mathbf{G}(\mathbf{e},\mathbf{x})}{\partial \mathbf{x}'} \\ &= \left[I_N - \frac{\partial \mathbf{q}(\cdot)}{\partial \mathbf{y}'} \left(A' \frac{\partial \mathbf{q}(\cdot)}{\partial \mathbf{y}'} \right)^{-1} A' \right] \frac{\partial \mathbf{q}}{\partial \mathbf{x}'}\end{aligned} \tag{14.5.30}$$

where the implicit function theorem is used to obtain

$$\frac{\partial \mathbf{G}(\mathbf{e},\mathbf{x})}{\partial \mathbf{x}'} = -\left(A' \frac{\partial \mathbf{q}(\cdot)}{\partial \mathbf{y}'} \right)^{-1} A' \frac{\partial \mathbf{q}(\cdot)}{\partial \mathbf{x}'} \tag{14.5.31}$$

Also define $\bar{\mathbf{q}}(\mathbf{x}) = E[\mathbf{q}(\mathbf{G}(\mathbf{e},\mathbf{x}), \mathbf{x})|\mathbf{x}]$, where the expectation is with respect to the distribution of $\mathbf{e}$ given the true structural parameter values. Then let $\bar{\mathbf{q}} = \bar{\mathbf{q}}(\mathbf{x}^0)$ for any choice of $\mathbf{x}^0$.

Under the assumptions stated above, the ith equation is identified if and only if the rank of the partitioned matrix $(\bar{\mathbf{q}} \vdots \tilde{Q}' \vdots R_i') = N - 1$. For the proof of this result see Brown (1983, p. 182). While the application of this condition is straightforward, determination of $\bar{\mathbf{q}}(\mathbf{x})$ is conceivably difficult. Brown shows, however, that if the intercept is unrestricted, then an equivalent necessary and sufficient condition is that the rank of $(\tilde{Q}' \vdots R_i')$ be $N - 2$. Brown also presents an alternative form of the identification condition that relates his work to Fisher's, and shows why Fisher's results are sufficient but not necessary for identification. He presents a simple example as well.

14.5.4 General Methods of Identification

The general problem of identification has been studied by several authors, including Fisher (1966), Rothenberg (1971), Bowden (1973), Wegge (1965), and Richmond (1974, 1976). In this section we state the general results that apply for nonlinear simultaneous equations subject to general nonlinear constraints, developed by Fisher, Rothenberg, and Richmond. Bowden generalizes the problem further, using information criteria, but we will not consider his results here.

Let $\mathbf{y}$ be an $(M \times 1)$ vector of real observable random variables and let the joint density of $\mathbf{y}$ be $f(\mathbf{y}|\boldsymbol{\alpha})$, where $\boldsymbol{\alpha}$ is a K-dimensional parameter vector in $\mathcal{A} \subset \mathcal{R}^K$. Let

$$I(\boldsymbol{\alpha}) = -E\left(\frac{\partial^2 \ln f}{\partial \boldsymbol{\alpha}\, \partial \boldsymbol{\alpha}'}\right)$$

be the information matrix. Furthermore suppose the structural parameters $\boldsymbol{\alpha}$ are known to satisfy the constraint equations

$$\boldsymbol{\psi}_i(\boldsymbol{\alpha}) = 0, \qquad i = 1, \ldots, J \tag{14.5.32}$$

where each $\boldsymbol{\psi}_i$ is a known function possessing continuous partial derivatives. Let $\mathcal{A}^*$ be the space defining the intersection of $\mathcal{A}$ and the solution set of (14.5.32) and $\boldsymbol{\psi}(\boldsymbol{\alpha})$ be the Jacobian matrix $[\partial\boldsymbol{\psi}_i/\partial\alpha_j]$. Then, if we define $V(\boldsymbol{\alpha})$ by

$$V(\boldsymbol{\alpha}) = \begin{bmatrix} I(\boldsymbol{\alpha}) \\ \boldsymbol{\psi}(\boldsymbol{\alpha}) \end{bmatrix} \tag{14.5.33}$$

we may state the following theorem [Rothenberg (1971)].

THEOREM

> Suppose $\boldsymbol{\alpha}^0 \epsilon \mathcal{R}^K$ is a regular point of both $\boldsymbol{\psi}(\boldsymbol{\alpha})$ and $V(\boldsymbol{\alpha})$. Then $\boldsymbol{\alpha}^0$ is locally identifiable if and only if $V(\boldsymbol{\alpha}^0)$ has full column rank K.

The meaning of "regular" in this context is that there exists an open neighborhood of $\boldsymbol{\alpha}^0$ where the matrix (or matrices) in question has (have) constant rank. Global identification results are more difficult to obtain and the reader is referred to Rothenberg for the appropriate theorems.

An important special case of the above result arises when there exist reduced form parameters. That is, if the probability density of $\mathbf{y}$ depends on $\boldsymbol{\alpha}$ only through an r-dimensional reduced form parameter vector $\boldsymbol{\pi}$. That is, there exist r known continuously differentiable functions $\pi_i = h_i(\boldsymbol{\alpha})$, $i = 1, \ldots, r$, and a function $f^*(\mathbf{y}|\boldsymbol{\pi})$ such that $f(\mathbf{y}|\boldsymbol{\alpha}) = f^*(\mathbf{y}|\mathbf{h}(\boldsymbol{\alpha})) = f^*(\mathbf{y}|\boldsymbol{\pi})$ for all $\mathbf{y}$ and $\boldsymbol{\alpha}$. Also, let $\mathcal{A}^{**}$ be the image of $\mathcal{A}^*$ under the mapping $\mathbf{h}$. Then every $\boldsymbol{\pi}$ in $\mathcal{A}^{**}$ is assumed to be identified. Define the Jacobian matrices

$$H(\boldsymbol{\alpha}) = [\partial h_i/\partial \alpha_j], \qquad \boldsymbol{\psi}(\boldsymbol{\alpha}) = [\partial \psi_i/\partial \alpha_j]$$

and the $((r + J) \times K)$ partitioned matrix

$$W(\boldsymbol{\alpha}) = \begin{bmatrix} H(\boldsymbol{\alpha}) \\ \boldsymbol{\psi}(\boldsymbol{\alpha}) \end{bmatrix} \tag{14.5.34}$$

If the functions h_i and ψ_i are linear, then $\boldsymbol{\alpha}^0$ is globally identified if and only if the constant matrix W has rank K. Otherwise, if $\boldsymbol{\alpha}^0$ is a regular point of $W(\boldsymbol{\alpha})$, then $\boldsymbol{\alpha}^0$ is locally identified if and only if $W(\boldsymbol{\alpha}^0)$ has rank K. Again global results are more difficult to obtain and the reader is referred to Rothenberg's paper. Rothenberg also specializes the results to the usual simultaneous equations models and derives conditions equivalent to those stated earlier in this chapter.

14.6 SUMMARY

In this chapter, we have specified the simultaneous equations model and stated the usual assumptions associated with it. We showed that a single equation from a simultaneous equations system cannot be estimated consistently using LS. The reason is that the presence of an endogenous variable on the right-hand side of the equation ensures that there will be contemporaneous, nonvanishing correlation between the error term and the set of explanatory variables, even as the sample size grows toward infinity. The reduced form equations, however, can be consistently estimated by LS because current endogenous variables do not appear in the RHS of those equations.

The notion of the identification problem was presented and necessary and sufficient conditions for identification stated, both for a specific equation and the whole system of equations. The complexities that arise when a system is nonlinear, either in the variables or in the parameters, were also briefly discussed. The reader should be reminded that the identification problem is logically prior to any problems of estimation. If a structural parameter is not identified, then no estimation technique exists that will allow its consistent estimation. It should also be noted that the identification problem forces one to recognize and deal with the limits of sample information alone. The theoretical underpinning of the statistical model must be rich enough to satisfy the conditions for identification before progress in learning about the structure can be made. This interdependence between economic theory and statistical inference is one of the fascinating aspects of simultaneous equations models.

For those interested in the historical development of the identification literature, the following references may be of interest. The rank and order conditions, first stated as conditions on a submatrix of the reduced form coefficients, stem from Koopmans (1949), Koopmans and Reiersol (1950), and Wald (1950). Fisher (1959, 1963) generalizes these results and extended them to nonlinear systems [Fisher (1961, 1965)]. Fisher (1966) summarizes the identification literature. Wegge (1965) and Rothenberg (1971) examine the identification of whole systems, the former using the Jacobian matrix and the latter using the information matrix. Following these works, Bowden (1973) shows the equivalence of the identification problem to a nonlinear programming problem and Richmond (1974) provides conditions for the identification of parametric functions. Kelly (1971, 1975) provides results on the identification of ratios of parameters and the use of cross-equation constraints. Gabrielsen (1978) and Deistler and Seifert (1978) independently investigate the relationship between identification and consistent estimation, and obtained conditions under which identifiability and consistency are equivalent almost everywhere. Hausman and Taylor (1983) establish from a recursive system that an equation is identified if jointly determined endogenous variables become predetermined in the equation under consideration. Sargan (1983) discusses cases where an econometric model linear in the variables is identified, but where the estimators are not asymptotically normally distributed. See also Hausman (1983) for a good summary of identification.

Special problems of identification occur where autocorrelation or measurement error is present. If equation errors are autocorrelated, then the equation error and lagged endogenous variables cannot be considered predetermined. See Hatanaka (1975), Deistler (1976, 1978), and Deistler and Schrader (1979) or Chapter 16 for discussions of identifiability and autocorrelated errors. The effects of measurement error on identification can be found in Hsiao (1976, 1977), Geraci (1976), Aigner, Hsiao, Kapteyn, and Wansbeek (1981), and Hsiao (1982).

One can approach identification and estimation from a Bayesian perspective. As stated above, identification deals with the amount of nonsample information required to combine with sample data to permit consistent estimation of structural parameters. In the context of the Bayesian approach the identification problem may be viewed as whether the posterior distribution of the relevant parameters has a unique mode, so that the set of parameters in question may be uniquely estimated. See Zellner (1971), Kadane (1974), and Drèze (1974) for a discussion of the Bayesian approach.

14.7 EXERCISES

Exercise 14.1

Find the reduced form equations from the following structural equations.

$$y_{t1}^2\gamma_{11} + y_{t2}^2\gamma_{21} + x_{t1}\beta_{11} + x_{t2}\beta_{21} + e_{t1} = 0$$
$$y_{t1}^2\gamma_{12} + y_{t2}^2\gamma_{22} + x_{t1}\beta_{12} + x_{t3}\beta_{32} + e_{t2} = 0$$

Exercise 14.2

Let $\mathbf{a}_i$ be the ith column of A. Define $\text{vec}(A) = (\mathbf{a}_1' \, \mathbf{a}_2' \, . \, . \, . \, \mathbf{a}_n')'$, where A has n columns.

1. Show that $\operatorname{vec}(ABC) = (C' \otimes A)\operatorname{vec}(B)$, where A is $(m \times n)$, B is $(n \times p)$, and C is $(p \times q)$.
2. Show that

$$(I_p \otimes A)\operatorname{vec}(B) = (B' \otimes I_m)\operatorname{vec}(A)$$

Exercise 14.3

For the system $Y\Gamma + XB + \mathbf{E} = 0$ with reduced form equation $Y = X\Pi + V$, show that

$$\operatorname{vec}(V) = -((\Gamma^{-1})' \otimes I_T)\operatorname{vec}(\mathbf{E})$$

Exercise 14.4

Consider the model

$$\mathbf{y}_1\gamma_{11} + \mathbf{y}_2\gamma_{21} + \mathbf{x}_1\beta_{11} + \mathbf{x}_2\beta_{21} + \mathbf{x}_3\beta_{31} + \mathbf{e}_1 = \mathbf{0}$$
$$\mathbf{y}_1\gamma_{12} + \mathbf{y}_2\gamma_{22} + \mathbf{x}_1\beta_{12} + \mathbf{x}_2\beta_{22} + \mathbf{x}_3\beta_{32} + \mathbf{e}_2 = \mathbf{0}$$

Suppose that the prior restrictions on parameters are

$$\gamma_{11} = -1, \quad \gamma_{22} = -1, \quad \beta_{31} = 0, \quad \text{and} \quad \beta_{21} = \beta_{12}$$

Examine the order and rank conditions of the whole system.

Exercise 14.5

For the two-equation system in Exercise 14.1, suppose that the a priori restrictions on parameters are

$$\gamma_{11} = -1, \quad \beta_{21} = 0, \quad \beta_{32} = 0, \quad \text{and} \quad \gamma_{22} = -1.$$

Examine the order and rank conditions for each equation and the system as a whole.

Exercise 14.6

Consider the following three-equation system:

$$\mathbf{y}_1\gamma_{11} + \mathbf{y}_2\gamma_{21} + \mathbf{y}_3\gamma_{31} + \mathbf{x}_1\beta_{11} + \mathbf{x}_2\beta_{21} + \mathbf{x}_3\beta_{31} + \mathbf{e}_1 = \mathbf{0}$$
$$\mathbf{y}_1\gamma_{12} + \mathbf{y}_2\gamma_{22} + \mathbf{y}_3\gamma_{32} + \mathbf{x}_1\beta_{12} + \mathbf{x}_2\beta_{22} + \mathbf{x}_3\beta_{32} + \mathbf{e}_2 = \mathbf{0}$$
$$\mathbf{y}_1\gamma_{13} + \mathbf{y}_2\gamma_{23} + \mathbf{y}_3\gamma_{33} + \mathbf{x}_1\beta_{13} + \mathbf{x}_2\beta_{23} + \mathbf{x}_3\beta_{33} + \mathbf{e}_3 = \mathbf{0}$$

Suppose that the prior restrictions on coefficients are

$$\beta_{11} = 0, \quad \beta_{22} = 0, \quad \beta_{33} = 0, \quad \beta_{31} = 0$$

and the covariance restrictions are

$$\sigma_{12} = 0 \quad \text{and} \quad \sigma_{13} = 0.$$

Examine the identification for each equation.

Exercise 14.7

Examine the identification of each equation in the following model nonlinear in variables and linear in parameters:

$$y_{t1}\gamma_{11} + y_{t2}\gamma_{21} + e_{t1} = 0$$

$$y_{t1}^2\gamma_{32} + y_{t2}^2\gamma_{42} + y_{t1}y_{t2}\gamma_{52} + x_{t1}\beta_{12} + x_{t2}\beta_{22} + e_{t2} = 0$$

14.8 REFERENCES

Aigner, D. J., C. Hsiao, A. Kapteyn and T. Wansbeek (1981) "Latent Variable Models in Econometrics," unpublished manuscript.

Bowden, R. (1973) "The Theory of Parametric Identification," *Econometrica,* 41, 1069–1074.

Brown, B. (1983) "The Identification Problem in Systems Nonlinear in the Variables," *Econometrica,* 51, 175–196.

Deistler, M. (1976) "The Identifiability of Linear Econometric Models with Autocorrelated Errors," *International Economic Review,* 17, 26–45.

Deistler, M. (1978) "The Structural Identifiability of Linear Models with Autocorrelated Errors in the Case of Affine Cross-Equation Restrictions," *Journal of Econometrics,* 8, 23–31.

Deistler, M. and H. G. Seifert (1978) "Identifiability and Consistent Estimability in Econometric Models," *Econometrica,* 46, 969–980.

Deistler, M. and J. Schrader (1979) "Linear Models with Autocorrelated Errors: Structural Identifiability in the Absence of Minimality Assumptions," *Econometrica,* 47, 495–504.

Drèze, J. H. (1974) "Bayesian Theory of Identification in Simultaneous Equation Models," in *Studies in Bayesian Econometrics and Statistics,* S. E. Fienberg and A. Zellner, eds., North-Holland, Amsterdam.

Fisher, F. M. (1959) "Generalization of the Rank and Order Conditions for Identifiability," *Econometrica,* 27, 431–447.

Fisher, F. M. (1961) "Identifiability Criteria in Nonlinear Systems," *Econometrica,* 29, 574–590.

Fisher, F. M. (1963) "Uncorrelated Disturbances and Identifiability Criteria," *International Economic Review,* 4, 134–152.

Fisher, F. M. (1965) "Identifiability Criteria in Nonlinear Systems: A Further Note," *Econometrica,* 33, 197–205.

Fisher, F. M. (1966) *The Identification Problem in Econometrics,* McGraw Hill, New York.

Gabrielsen, A. (1978) "Consistency and Identifiability," *Journal of Econometrics,* 8, 261–263.
Geraci, V. J. (1976) "Identification of Simultaneous Equation Models with Measurement Error," *Journal of Econometrics,* 4, 263–284.
Girshick, M. A. and T. Haavelmo (1953) "Statistical Analysis of the Demand for Food: Examples of Simultaneous Estimation of Structural Equations," in W. C. Hood and T. C. Koopmans, eds., *Studies in Econometric Method,* Yale University Press, pp. 92–111.
Haavelmo, T. (1943) "The Statistical Implications of a System of Simultaneous Equations," *Econometrica,* 11, 1–12.
Hatanaka, M. (1975) "On the Global Identification of the Dynamic Simultaneous Equations Model with Stationary Disturbances," *International Economic Review,* 16, 545–554.
Hausman, J. A. and W. E. Taylor (1983) "Identification in Linear Simultaneous Equations Models with Covariance Restrictions: An Instrumental Variables Interpretation," *Econometrica,* 51, 1527–1549.
Hausman, J. A. (1983) "Specification and Estimation of Simultaneous Equation Models," Chapter 7 of *Handbook of Econometrics,* North-Holland, Amsterdam, 392–448.
Hsiao, C. (1976) "Identification and Estimation of Simultaneous Equation Models with Measurement Error," *International Economic Review,* 17, 319–339.
Hsiao, C. (1977) "Identification for a Linear Dynamic Simultaneous Error-Shock Model," *International Economic Review,* 18, 181–194.
Hsiao, C. (1982) "Identification," unpublished manuscript, Institute for Policy Analysis, University of Toronto.
Judge, G., R. Hill, W. Griffiths, H. Lütkepohl and T. Lee (1982) *Introduction to the Theory and Practice of Econometrics,* Wiley, New York.
Kadane, J. B. (1974) "The Role of Identification in Bayesian Theory," in S. E. Fienberg and A. Zellner, eds., *Studies in Bayesian Econometrics and Statistics,* North-Holland, Amsterdam.
Kelejian, H. H. (1971) "Two-Stage Least Squares and Econometric Systems Linear in Parameters but Nonlinear in Endogenous Variables," *Journal of the American Statistical Association,* 66, 373–374.
Kelly, J. S. (1971) "The Identification of Ratios of Parameters in Unidentified Equations," *Econometrica,* 39, 1049–1051.
Kelly, J. S. (1975) "Linear Cross-Equation Constraints and the Identification Problem," *Econometrica,* 43, 125–140.
Koopmans, T. C. (1949) "Identification Problems in Economic Model Construction," *Econometrica,* 17, 125–144.
Koopmans, T. C. (1953) "Identification Problems in Economic Model Construction," in W. C. Hood and T. C. Koopmans, eds., *Studies in Econometric Method,* Yale University Press, pp. 27–48.
Koopmans, T. C. and O. Reiersol (1950) "The Identification of Structural Characteristics," *Annals of Mathematical Statistics,* 21, 165–181.
Marschak, J. (1950), "Statistical Inference in Economics," in T. C. Koop-

mans, ed., *Statistical Inference in Dynamic Economic Models,* Wiley, New York, pp. 1–50.

Marschak, J. (1953), "Economic Measurements for Policy and Prediction," W. C. Hood and T. C. Koopmans, eds., *Studies in Econometric Method,* Yale University Press, pp. 1–26.

Richmond, J. (1974) "Identifiability in Linear Models," *Econometrica,* 42, 731–736.

Richmond, J. (1976) "Aggregation and Identification," *International Economic Review,* 17, 47–56.

Rothenberg, T. J. (1971) "Identification in Parametric Models," *Econometrica,* 39, 577–592.

Schmidt, P. (1976) *Econometrics,* Marcel Dekker, New York.

Wald, A. (1950) "Note on the Identification of Economic Relations," in *Statistical Inference in Dynamic Economic Models,* Cowles Commission Monograph 10, Wiley, New York.

Wegge, L. L. (1965) "Identification Criteria for a System of Equations as a Whole," *Australian Journal of Statistics,* 7, 67–77.

Zellner, A. (1971) *An Introduction to Bayesian Inference in Econometrics,* Wiley, New York.

Chapter 15

Estimation and Inference in a System of Simultaneous Equations

15.1 INTRODUCTION

As noted in the previous chapter, economic data are often viewed as being passively generated by a system of equations that are dynamic, simultaneous and stochastic. In this chapter we consider the problems of estimation and inference in the context of a structural equation system, assuming sufficient a priori information exists to identify the system. We first review traditional estimation procedures for both single equations within the system and the system as a whole. We then present general classes of estimators that contain the traditional estimators as special cases. While the large sample properties of the traditional estimators are well known, it is only fairly recently that the small sample properties have begun to be studied analytically. Some of this literature is reviewed in Section 15.4. Procedures for testing hypothesis about structural parameters are presented in Section 15.5, as well as tests for the orthogonality between the disturbances and explanatory variables in a regression equation. Following these discussions of basic material, sections are presented on efficient estimation of reduced form parameters, methods for nonlinear systems, Bayesian methods, and disequilibrium models. The structure of the chapter is summarized in Table 15.1.

15.2 TRADITIONAL METHODS OF ESTIMATING LINEAR STATISTICAL MODELS

This section deals with the problem of estimating the parameters of the model

$$Y\Gamma + XB + \mathbf{E} = 0 \qquad (15.2.1)$$

with notation defined in Chapter 14. For the ith equation,

$$Y\mathbf{\Gamma}_i + X\mathbf{B}_i + \mathbf{e}_i = \mathbf{0} \qquad (15.2.2)$$

TABLE 15.1 ***ESTIMATION AND INFERENCE IN A SYSTEM OF SIMULTANEOUS EQUATIONS***

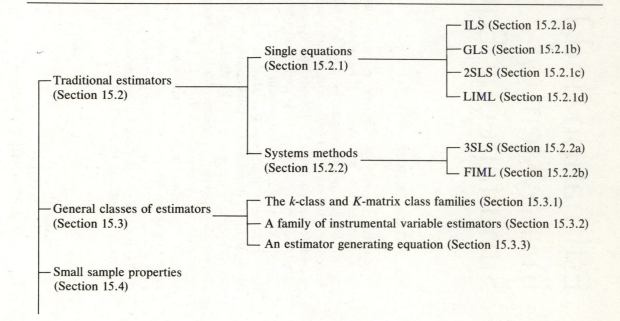

- Traditional estimators (Section 15.2)
  - Single equations (Section 15.2.1)
    - ILS (Section 15.2.1a)
    - GLS (Section 15.2.1b)
    - 2SLS (Section 15.2.1c)
    - LIML (Section 15.2.1d)
  - Systems methods (Section 15.2.2)
    - 3SLS (Section 15.2.2a)
    - FIML (Section 15.2.2b)
- General classes of estimators (Section 15.3)
  - The k-class and K-matrix class families (Section 15.3.1)
  - A family of instrumental variable estimators (Section 15.3.2)
  - An estimator generating equation (Section 15.3.3)
- Small sample properties (Section 15.4)

- Inference (Section 15.5)
  - Tests of Parameter Significance (Section 15.5.1)
  - Tests of Overidentification (Section 15.5.2)
  - Misspecification tests (Section 15.5.3)
- Efficient estimation of reduced form parameters (Section 15.6)
- Methods for nonlinear systems (Section 15.7)
  - Single equation methods (Section 15.7.1)
  - Systems methods (Section 15.7.2)
- Bayesian methods (Section 15.8)
  - Single equation Bayesian analysis (Section 15.8.1)
  - Full system Bayesian analysis (Section 15.8.2)
  - A minimum expected loss approach (Section 15.8.3)
- Disequilibrium models (Section 15.9)

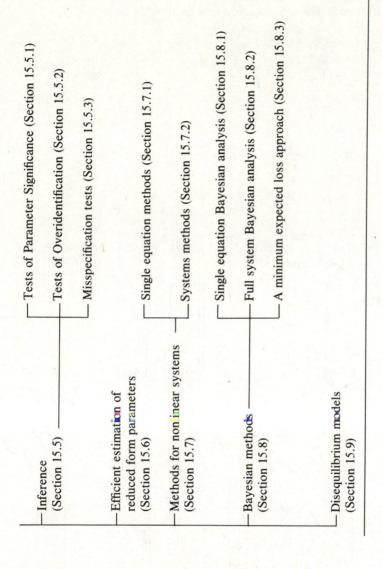

it is assumed that there are m_i^* endogenous variables and k_i^* predetermined variables in the equation with zero coefficients. The remaining $m_i - 1 = M - m_i^* - 1$ unknown elements of $\boldsymbol{\Gamma}_i(\gamma_{ii} = -1)$ and $k_i = K - k_i^*$ unknown elements of $\mathbf{B}_i$ are to be estimated. The ith equation can be written as

$$\begin{aligned}\mathbf{y}_i &= Y_i\boldsymbol{\gamma}_i + X_i\boldsymbol{\beta}_i + \mathbf{e}_i \\ &= (Y_i \quad X_i)\begin{pmatrix}\boldsymbol{\gamma}_i \\ \boldsymbol{\beta}_i\end{pmatrix} + \mathbf{e}_i \\ &= Z_i\boldsymbol{\delta}_i + \mathbf{e}_i, \qquad i = 1, 2, \ldots, M \end{aligned} \tag{15.2.3}$$

where

$$\boldsymbol{\Gamma}_i = \begin{pmatrix}-1 \\ \boldsymbol{\gamma}_i \\ \mathbf{0}\end{pmatrix}, \qquad \mathbf{B}_i = \begin{pmatrix}\boldsymbol{\beta}_i \\ \mathbf{0}\end{pmatrix}, \qquad \text{and} \qquad \boldsymbol{\delta}_i = \begin{pmatrix}\boldsymbol{\gamma}_i \\ \boldsymbol{\beta}_i\end{pmatrix}$$

If all M equations of (15.2.3) are considered jointly, the statistical model can be written as the set of equations:

$$\begin{bmatrix}\mathbf{y}_1 \\ \mathbf{y}_2 \\ \vdots \\ \mathbf{y}_M\end{bmatrix} = \begin{bmatrix}Z_1 & & & \\ & Z_2 & & \\ & & \ddots & \\ & & & Z_M\end{bmatrix}\begin{bmatrix}\boldsymbol{\delta}_1 \\ \boldsymbol{\delta}_2 \\ \vdots \\ \boldsymbol{\delta}_M\end{bmatrix} + \begin{bmatrix}\mathbf{e}_1 \\ \mathbf{e}_2 \\ \vdots \\ \mathbf{e}_M\end{bmatrix} \tag{15.2.4}$$

or compactly

$$\mathbf{y} = Z\boldsymbol{\delta} + \mathbf{e} \tag{15.2.5}$$

where

$$\mathbf{y} = \begin{bmatrix}\mathbf{y}_1 \\ \mathbf{y}_2 \\ \vdots \\ \mathbf{y}_M\end{bmatrix}, \quad Z = \begin{bmatrix}Z_1 & & & \\ & Z_2 & & \\ & & \ddots & \\ & & & Z_M\end{bmatrix}, \quad \boldsymbol{\delta} = \begin{bmatrix}\boldsymbol{\delta}_1 \\ \boldsymbol{\delta}_2 \\ \vdots \\ \boldsymbol{\delta}_M\end{bmatrix}, \quad \text{and} \quad \mathbf{e} = \begin{bmatrix}\mathbf{e}_1 \\ \mathbf{e}_2 \\ \vdots \\ \mathbf{e}_M\end{bmatrix}$$

Below we consider estimation of the equations (15.2.3) individually (single equation or limited information methods) or jointly, as in (15.2.5) (system or full information methods). Since these estimation procedures are well known, our presentation will be brief. For a more detailed discussion, see Judge et al. (1982, Chapter 13).

15.2.1 Single Equation or Limited Information Methods

15.2.1a Indirect Least Squares

The name of indirect least squares stems from the fact that the estimator is derived from the consistent estimator

$$\hat{\Pi} = (X'X)^{-1}X'Y \tag{15.2.6}$$

via the relation $\Pi\boldsymbol{\Gamma}_i = -\mathbf{B}_i$. In particular, we derive the estimator $\hat{\boldsymbol{\delta}}_i$ from

$$(X'X)^{-1}X'Y\begin{pmatrix} -1 \\ \hat{\boldsymbol{\gamma}}_i \\ \mathbf{0} \end{pmatrix} = \begin{pmatrix} -\hat{\boldsymbol{\beta}}_i \\ \mathbf{0} \end{pmatrix}$$

or

$$X'\mathbf{y}_i = X'Y_i\hat{\boldsymbol{\gamma}}_i + X'X_i\hat{\boldsymbol{\beta}}_i = X'Z_i\hat{\boldsymbol{\delta}}_i \tag{15.2.7}$$

Solving (15.2.7) for $\hat{\boldsymbol{\delta}}_i$, providing $X'Z_i$ is square and nonsingular, yields the indirect least squares (ILS) estimator of $\boldsymbol{\delta}_i$.

$$\hat{\boldsymbol{\delta}}_{i(\text{ILS})} = (X'Z_i)^{-1}X'\mathbf{y}_i \tag{15.2.8}$$

The matrix $X'Z_i$ is square if $K = m_i - 1 + k_i$, since X is $(T \times K)$ and Z_i is $[T \times (m_i - 1 + k_i)]$. The ILS estimator exists and is unique if the ith structural equation is just identified. If the equation is overidentified, then $K > m_i - 1 + k_i$ and $X'Z_i$ is not square. In this case (15.2.7) provides more equations than unknowns and thus the ILS estimator is not unique. The solution to any $m_i - 1 + k_i$ relations from (15.2.7) provides a consistent estimator of $\boldsymbol{\delta}_i$, though it is not efficient since some information has been discarded.

When the ith equation is just identified, $\sqrt{T}(\hat{\boldsymbol{\delta}}_{i(\text{ILS})} - \boldsymbol{\delta}_i)$ is asymptotically normally distributed with mean vector zero and covariance matrix

$$\begin{aligned}\boldsymbol{\Sigma}_{\hat{\boldsymbol{\delta}}_{i(\text{ILS})}} &= \sigma_{ii}\ \text{plim}\left(\frac{Z_i'X}{T}\right)^{-1}\text{plim}\left(\frac{X'X}{T}\right)\text{plim}\left(\frac{X'Z_i}{T}\right)^{-1} \\ &= \sigma_{ii}\,\boldsymbol{\Sigma}_{z_ix}^{-1}\,\boldsymbol{\Sigma}_{xx}\,\boldsymbol{\Sigma}_{xz_i}^{-1}\end{aligned} \tag{15.2.9}$$

where

$$\boldsymbol{\Sigma}_{xz_i} = \text{plim}\left(\frac{X'Z_i}{T}\right) = \boldsymbol{\Sigma}_{z_ix}'$$

and

$$\Sigma_{xx} = \text{plim}(X'X/T)$$

In finite samples the covariance matrix (15.2.9) can be estimated by

$$\hat{\Sigma}_{\hat{\boldsymbol{\delta}}_i} = T\hat{\sigma}_{ii}(Z_i'X)^{-1}(X'X)(X'Z_i)^{-1}$$

with

$$\hat{\sigma}_{ii} = (\mathbf{y}_i - Z_i\hat{\boldsymbol{\delta}}_i)'(\mathbf{y}_i - Z_i\hat{\boldsymbol{\delta}}_i)/\tau_i$$

Both $\tau_i = T$ and $\tau_i = T - m_i + 1 - k_i$ make $\hat{\sigma}_{ii}$ a consistent estimator of σ_{ii}. If Z_i contains only nonstochastic exogenous variables, the choice $\tau_i = T - m_i + 1 - k_i$ provides an unbiased estimator of the residual variance.

15.2.1b A Generalized Least Squares Estimator

In order to motivate a generalized least squares estimation technique for $\boldsymbol{\delta}_i$, consider premultiplication of Equation 15.2.3 by X' to obtain

$$X'\mathbf{y}_i = X'Z_i\boldsymbol{\delta}_i + X'\mathbf{e}_i \tag{15.2.10}$$

If $X'Z_i$ is square and nonsingular, the ILS estimator can be viewed as an ordinary least squares estimator of (15.2.10):

$$\begin{aligned}\hat{\boldsymbol{\delta}}_{i(\text{ILS})} &= (Z_i'XX'Z_i)^{-1}Z_i'XX'\mathbf{y}_i \\ &= (X'Z_i)^{-1}X'\mathbf{y}_i\end{aligned} \tag{15.2.11}$$

In order to estimate $\boldsymbol{\delta}_i$ from (15.2.10) in an "efficient" way, the covariance of $X'\mathbf{e}_i$ must be considered. The covariance matrix of $X'\mathbf{e}_i$ can be taken to be $\sigma_{ii}X'X$, at least in large samples under some reasonably strong assumptions [see Dhrymes (1974, pp. 183–184)], making the application of GLS appropriate. Applying generalized least squares to (15.2.10) yields

$$\begin{aligned}\hat{\hat{\boldsymbol{\delta}}}_i &= [(X'Z_i)'(\sigma_{ii}X'X)^{-1}(X'Z_i)]^{-1}(X'Z_i)'(\sigma_{ii}X'X)^{-1}X'\mathbf{y}_i \\ &= [Z_i'X(X'X)^{-1}X'Z_i]^{-1}Z_i'X(X'X)^{-1}X'\mathbf{y}_i\end{aligned} \tag{15.2.12}$$

provided that the matrix $[Z_i'X(X'X)^{-1}X'Z_i]$ has an inverse. Since Z_i is $[T \times (m_i - 1 + k_i)]$ and X is $(T \times K)$, for the matrix $[Z_i'X(X'X)^{-1}X'Z_i]$ to be a nonsingular matrix of order $m_i - 1 + k_i$, the condition $m_i - 1 + k_i \leq K$, or $m_i - 1 \leq k_i^*$ must hold. This is the order condition for identification developed in Chapter 14. In the case of just identification, $m_i - 1 + k_i = K$ and $Z_i'X$ is a square matrix, and the estimator (15.2.12) can be simplified to the indirect least squares estimator (15.2.11). Asymptotically, assuming the rank condition for identification of the ith equation holds as well as some other fairly general conditions [see Dhrymes (1974, Section 4.5)],

$$\sqrt{T}(\tilde{\boldsymbol{\delta}}_i - \boldsymbol{\delta}_i) \xrightarrow{d} N(\mathbf{0}, \sigma_{ii}(\Sigma_{z_i x}\Sigma_{xx}^{-1}\Sigma_{xz_i})^{-1}) \tag{15.2.13}$$

For the just identified case, the limiting covariance matrix (15.2.13) is the same as (15.2.9) because $\Sigma_{z_i x}$ will be a square matrix. In finite samples, the unknown covariance matrix of $\tilde{\boldsymbol{\delta}}_i$ can be estimated by

$$\tilde{\Sigma}_{\tilde{\boldsymbol{\delta}}_i} = \tilde{\sigma}_{ii}[Z_i'X(X'X)^{-1}X'Z_i]^{-1}$$

with

$$\tilde{\sigma}_{ii} = (\mathbf{y}_i - Z_i\tilde{\boldsymbol{\delta}}_i)'(\mathbf{y}_i - Z_i\tilde{\boldsymbol{\delta}}_i)/\tau_i$$

where both $\tau_i = T$ and $\tau_i = T - m_i + 1 - k_i$ make $\tilde{\sigma}_{ii}$ a consistent estimator of σ_{ii}. As noted above, the choice of $\tau_i = T - m_i + 1 - k_i$ provides an unbiased estimator of the residual variance if Z_i contains only nonstochastic exogenous variables.

15.2.1c The Two-Stage Least Squares Estimator

The generalized least squares estimator $\tilde{\boldsymbol{\delta}}_i$ may be interpreted as a two-stage least squares (2SLS) estimator. If we let

$$\begin{aligned} \hat{Z}_i &= [\hat{Y}_i \quad X_i] \\ &= \left[X\hat{\Pi}_i \quad X\begin{pmatrix} I_{k_i} \\ 0 \end{pmatrix}\right] \\ &= [X(X'X)^{-1}X'Y_i \quad X(X'X)^{-1}X'X_i] \\ &= X(X'X)^{-1}X'Z_i \end{aligned} \tag{15.2.14}$$

then the generalized least squares estimator (15.2.12) can be written as

$$\begin{aligned} \tilde{\boldsymbol{\delta}}_i &= [Z_i'X(X'X)^{-1}X'Z_i]^{-1}Z_i'X(X'X)^{-1}X'\mathbf{y}_i \\ &= [Z_i'X(X'X)^{-1}X'X(X'X)^{-1}X'Z_i]^{-1}Z_i'X(X'X)^{-1}X'\mathbf{y}_i \\ &= (\hat{Z}_i'\hat{Z}_i)^{-1}\hat{Z}_i'\mathbf{y}_i \end{aligned}$$

This estimator is also obtained if the least squares rule is applied to the statistical model

$$\mathbf{y}_i = (\hat{Y}_i \quad X_i)\boldsymbol{\delta}_i + \mathbf{e}_i^*$$

where $\mathbf{e}_i^* = \mathbf{e}_i + \hat{V}_i\boldsymbol{\gamma}_i$ and $\hat{V}_i = Y_i - \hat{Y}_i$. In this context, the 2SLS estimator $\tilde{\boldsymbol{\delta}}_i$ may be obtained in two stages. In the first stage, Y_i is regressed on X to obtain

$\hat{\Pi}_i = (X'X)^{-1}X'Y_i$ and $\hat{Y}_i = X\hat{\Pi}_i$. In the second stage, $\mathbf{y}_i$ is regressed on $\hat{Y}_i$ and X_i to obtain $\tilde{\boldsymbol{\delta}}_i$. The sampling properties of $\tilde{\boldsymbol{\delta}}_i$ are given by (15.2.13).

15.2.1d The Limited Information Maximum Likelihood Estimator

The limited information maximum likelihood (LIML) estimation method is concerned with maximizing the likelihood function that is constructed from the stochastic elements involved in a single structural equation

$$\mathbf{y}_i = Z_i\boldsymbol{\delta}_i + \mathbf{e}_i$$

under the assumption that the errors are normally distributed. The likelihood function is

$$\ell(\boldsymbol{\delta}_*, \Sigma_* | \mathbf{y}_*) = (2\pi)^{-m_iT/2}|\Sigma_* \otimes I_T|^{-1/2}|\Gamma_*|^T \cdot \exp[-\tfrac{1}{2}(\mathbf{y}_* - Z_*\boldsymbol{\delta}_*)'(\Sigma_*^{-1} \otimes I_T)(\mathbf{y}_* - Z_*\boldsymbol{\delta}_*)]$$

where $\mathbf{y}_* = \text{vec}(\mathbf{y}_i \quad Y_i)$ is a $(Tm_i \times 1)$ subvector of $\mathbf{y}$, Σ_* is an $(m_i \times m_i)$ submatrix of Σ relating to structural equation errors of $\mathbf{y}_*$, Z_* is a matrix of Z involving $Z_1, Z_2, \ldots, Z_{m_i}$, and $\boldsymbol{\delta}_*$ is a subvector of $\boldsymbol{\delta}$ involving $\boldsymbol{\delta}_1, \boldsymbol{\delta}_2, \ldots, \boldsymbol{\delta}_{m_i}$. When the above likelihood function is maximized subject to the identification restriction of the ith equation, the resultant estimator is known as the limited information maximum likelihood (LIML) estimator. For a complete development of this estimator see Schmidt (1976, Section 4.8). If the ith equation is identified, then the LIML estimator is consistent and has the same asymptotic distribution as the 2SLS estimator.

Pagan (1979) shows that the LIML estimates can be computed by using the seemingly unrelated regression technique, if we write the structural equation to be estimated as

$$\mathbf{y}_i = Z_i\boldsymbol{\delta}_i + \mathbf{e}_i$$

together with the reduced form equation for Y_i in a vector form

$$\mathbf{y}_R = (I_{m_i-1} \otimes X)\boldsymbol{\pi}_R + \mathbf{v}_R$$

where $Z_i = (Y_i \quad X_i)$, $\mathbf{y}_R = \text{vec}(Y_i)$, $\boldsymbol{\pi}_R = \text{vec}(\Pi_i)$, and $\mathbf{v}_R = \text{vec}(V_i)$. This results because the restrictions imposed on the reduced form of $\mathbf{y}_i$ and $\mathbf{y}_R$ are exactly the LIML restrictions. The seemingly unrelated regression is

$$\begin{bmatrix} \mathbf{y}_i \\ \mathbf{y}_R \end{bmatrix} = \begin{bmatrix} Z & 0 \\ 0 & I_{m_i-1} \otimes X \end{bmatrix} \begin{bmatrix} \boldsymbol{\delta} \\ \boldsymbol{\pi}_R \end{bmatrix} + \begin{bmatrix} \mathbf{e}_i \\ \mathbf{v}_R \end{bmatrix}$$

If the covariance matrix between $\mathbf{e}_i$ and $\mathbf{v}_R$ is

$$\begin{bmatrix} \sigma_i^2 & \boldsymbol{\phi}' \\ \boldsymbol{\phi} & \Omega^* \end{bmatrix}$$

the estimator is

$$\begin{bmatrix} \hat{\boldsymbol{\delta}}_{i(\text{LIML})} \\ \hat{\boldsymbol{\pi}}_{R(\text{LIML})} \end{bmatrix} = \begin{bmatrix} Z_i'(a \otimes I)Z_i & Z_i'(\mathbf{b}' \otimes X) \\ (\mathbf{b} \otimes X')Z_i & C \otimes X'X \end{bmatrix}^{-1} \begin{bmatrix} Z_i'(a \otimes I) & Z_i'(\mathbf{b}' \otimes X) \\ \mathbf{b} \otimes X' & C \otimes X' \end{bmatrix} \begin{bmatrix} \mathbf{y}_i \\ \mathbf{y}_R \end{bmatrix}$$

where

$$\begin{bmatrix} \sigma_i^2 & \boldsymbol{\phi}' \\ \boldsymbol{\phi} & \Omega^* \end{bmatrix}^{-1} = \begin{bmatrix} a & \mathbf{b}' \\ \mathbf{b} & C \end{bmatrix}$$

By partitioned inversion, the result for the LIML estimator of $\boldsymbol{\delta}_i$ is

$$\hat{\boldsymbol{\delta}}_{i(\text{LIML})} = \sigma_i^2 QZ_i'M\mathbf{y}_i + aQZ_i'\bar{M}\mathbf{y}_i + QZ_i'(\mathbf{b}' \otimes \bar{M})\mathbf{y}_R$$

where $Q^{-1} = \sigma_i^{-2}Z_i'MZ_i + aZ_i'\bar{M}Z_i$, $M = X(X'X)^{-1}X'$ and $\bar{M} = I - M$. Let $\hat{Z}_i = (\hat{Y}_i \quad X_i)$ and $\hat{W}_i = Z_i - \hat{Z}_i$, then Q^{-1} can be simplified to $Q^{-1} = \sigma_i^{-2}\hat{Z}_i'\hat{Z}_i + a\hat{W}_i'\hat{W}_i$, and the following relation results

$$\begin{aligned} \hat{\boldsymbol{\delta}}_{i(\text{LIML})} = \hat{\boldsymbol{\delta}}_{i(2\text{SLS})} &- (\hat{Z}_i'\hat{Z}_i)^{-1}F(\hat{Z}_i'\hat{Z}_i)^{-1}\hat{Z}_i'\mathbf{y}_i + aQ\hat{Z}_i'M\mathbf{y}_i \\ &+ Q\hat{Z}_i'(\mathbf{b}' \otimes \bar{M})\mathbf{y}_R \end{aligned} \qquad (15.2.15)$$

where $F = \hat{W}_i'(k_iI + \hat{W}_i(\hat{Z}_i'\hat{Z}_i)^{-1}\hat{W}_i')^{-1}\hat{W}_i$, $k_i = \sigma_i^{-2}a$, and $\hat{\boldsymbol{\delta}}_{i(2\text{SLS})} = (\hat{Z}_i'\hat{Z}_i)^{-1}\hat{Z}_i'\mathbf{y}_i$. Equation (15.2.15) establishes a relation between LIML and 2SLS.

15.2.2 Systems or Full Information Methods

15.2.2a The Three-Stage Least Squares Estimator

Under conditions normally fulfilled in practice the efficiency of the single equation estimators discussed above can be improved upon if all structural equations are estimated jointly. The M structural equations in the form of (15.2.10) can be written as

$$\begin{bmatrix} X'\mathbf{y}_1 \\ X'\mathbf{y}_2 \\ \vdots \\ X'\mathbf{y}_M \end{bmatrix} = \begin{bmatrix} X'Z_1 & & & \\ & X'Z_2 & & \\ & & \ddots & \\ & & & X'Z_M \end{bmatrix} \begin{bmatrix} \boldsymbol{\delta}_1 \\ \boldsymbol{\delta}_2 \\ \vdots \\ \boldsymbol{\delta}_M \end{bmatrix} + \begin{bmatrix} X'\mathbf{e}_1 \\ X'\mathbf{e}_2 \\ \vdots \\ X'\mathbf{e}_M \end{bmatrix} \qquad (15.2.16)$$

or compactly as

$$(I \otimes X')\mathbf{y} = (I \otimes X')Z\boldsymbol{\delta} + (I \otimes X')\mathbf{e} \qquad (15.2.17)$$

where

$$Z = \begin{bmatrix} Z_1 & & & \\ & Z_2 & & \\ & & \ddots & \\ & & & Z_M \end{bmatrix} \text{ is a } \left[TM \times \sum_{i=1}^{M} (m_i - 1 + k_i)\right] \text{ matrix}$$

$$\mathbf{y} = \begin{bmatrix} \mathbf{y}_1 \\ \mathbf{y}_2 \\ \vdots \\ \mathbf{y}_M \end{bmatrix} \text{ is a } [TM \times 1] \text{ vector, } \boldsymbol{\delta} = \begin{bmatrix} \boldsymbol{\delta}_1 \\ \boldsymbol{\delta}_2 \\ \vdots \\ \boldsymbol{\delta}_M \end{bmatrix} \text{ is a } \left[\sum_{i=1}^{M} (m_i - 1 + k_i) \times 1\right] \text{ vector}$$

and

$$\mathbf{e} = \begin{bmatrix} \mathbf{e}_1 \\ \mathbf{e}_2 \\ \vdots \\ \mathbf{e}_M \end{bmatrix} \text{ is a } [TM \times 1] \text{ vector}$$

The covariance matrix of $(I \otimes X')\mathbf{e}$ can be taken to be, in large samples and under conditions given in Dhrymes (1974, pp. 183–184), $\Sigma \otimes E(X'X)$, where Σ is an unknown $(M \times M)$ matrix. Assuming that $(X'X/T)$ converges to a nonstochastic limit, $X'X/T$ will be a consistent estimator for $T^{-1}E[X'X]$. Thus for large samples, we may use $\Sigma \otimes X'X$ in place of $\Sigma \otimes E[X'X]$ in estimation. The GLS (SUR) estimator of $\boldsymbol{\delta}$ is

$$\begin{aligned} \tilde{\boldsymbol{\delta}}^* &= \{Z'(I \otimes X')'[\Sigma^{-1} \otimes (X'X)^{-1}](I \otimes X')Z\}^{-1} \\ &\quad \times Z'(I \otimes X')'[\Sigma^{-1} \otimes (X'X)^{-1}](I \otimes X')\mathbf{y} \\ &= \{Z'[\Sigma^{-1} \otimes X(X'X)^{-1}X']Z\}^{-1}Z'[\Sigma^{-1} \otimes X(X'X)^{-1}X']\mathbf{y} \end{aligned}$$

The unknown matrix Σ can be consistently estimated by $\hat{\Sigma}$ with elements

$$\hat{\sigma}_{ij} = (\mathbf{y}_i - Z_i\tilde{\boldsymbol{\delta}}_i)'(\mathbf{y}_j - Z_j\tilde{\boldsymbol{\delta}}_j)/\tau_{ij} \tag{15.2.18}$$

where $\tilde{\boldsymbol{\delta}}_i$ is the 2SLS estimator and τ_{ij} may be calculated as $\tau_{ij} = T$ or $\tau_{ij} = [(T - m_i + 1 - k_i)(T - m_j + 1 - k_j)]^{1/2}$. A feasible 3SLS estimator

$$\hat{\boldsymbol{\delta}}^* = \{Z'[\hat{\Sigma}^{-1} \otimes X(X'X)^{-1}X']Z\}^{-1}Z'[\hat{\Sigma}^{-1} \otimes X(X'X)^{-1}X']\mathbf{y} \tag{15.2.19}$$

may be calculated in three stages. In the first stage, each endogenous variable $\mathbf{y}_i$

is regressed on all predetermined variables X to obtain estimates of the reduced form parameters, $\hat{\boldsymbol{\pi}}_i = (X'X)^{-1}X'\mathbf{y}_i$. These in turn are used to obtain the predicted value of $\mathbf{y}_i$ as $\hat{\mathbf{y}}_i = X\hat{\boldsymbol{\pi}}_i = X(X'X)^{-1}X'\mathbf{y}_i$. In the second stage the estimated covariance matrix $\hat{\Sigma}$ is formed from the 2SLS residuals based on (15.2.18). In the third stage, $\hat{\Sigma}$ is used in (15.2.19) to obtain the 3SLS estimator $\tilde{\boldsymbol{\delta}}^*$. Asymptotically, under conditions outlined in Dhrymes (1974, pp. 212–216)

$$\sqrt{T}(\tilde{\boldsymbol{\delta}}^* - \boldsymbol{\delta}) \xrightarrow{d} N(\mathbf{0}, \text{plim}\{[T^{-1}Z'(\Sigma^{-1} \otimes X(X'X)^{-1}X')Z]^{-1}\},$$

The covariance matrix of $\tilde{\boldsymbol{\delta}}^*$ can be consistently estimated in small samples by $\{Z'[\hat{\Sigma}^{-1} \otimes X(X'X)^{-1}X']Z\}^{-1}$.

15.2.2b The Full Information Maximum Likelihood Method

The structural parameters $\boldsymbol{\delta} = (\boldsymbol{\delta}_1' \; \boldsymbol{\delta}_2' \; . \; . \; . \; \boldsymbol{\delta}_M')'$ can also be estimated by maximizing the likelihood function, assuming that the structural errors are normally distributed. Given the model

$$\mathbf{y} = Z\boldsymbol{\delta} + \mathbf{e} \tag{15.2.20}$$

the joint probability density function for $\mathbf{e}$ is

$$g(\mathbf{e}) = (2\pi)^{-MT/2}|\Sigma \otimes I_T|^{-1/2} \exp[-\tfrac{1}{2}\mathbf{e}'(\Sigma \otimes I_T)^{-1}\mathbf{e}] \tag{15.2.21}$$

and the joint pdf for $\mathbf{y}$ is

$$f(\mathbf{y}) = (2\pi)^{-MT/2}|\Sigma \otimes I_T|^{-1/2}|\Gamma|^T \exp[-\tfrac{1}{2}(\mathbf{y} - Z\boldsymbol{\delta})'(\Sigma^{-1} \otimes I_T)(\mathbf{y} - Z\boldsymbol{\delta})] \tag{15.2.22}$$

Whe.. viewed as a function of the parameters $\boldsymbol{\delta}$ and Σ, given observations $\mathbf{y}$ and Z, the expression (15.2.22) is the likelihood function. The log likelihood function is

$$\ln \ell(\boldsymbol{\delta},\Sigma|\mathbf{y},Z) = -\frac{MT}{2}\ln(2\pi) + \frac{T}{2}\ln|\Sigma|^{-1} + T\ln|\Gamma| - \tfrac{1}{2}(\mathbf{y} - Z\boldsymbol{\delta})'(\Sigma^{-1} \otimes I_T)(\mathbf{y} - Z\boldsymbol{\delta}) \tag{15.2.23}$$

Full information maximum likelihood (FIML) estimation involves maximization of (15.2.23) subject to any restrictions on the parameters Γ, B, and Σ. For a complete treatment of the FIML method see Schmidt (1976, pp. 216–236). For a treatment of FIML estimation under the assumption that the disturbances are distributed as a multivariate t with known degrees of freedom, see Prucha and Kelejian (1984).

15.3 GENERAL CLASSES OF ESTIMATORS

In this section we will discuss briefly the relative merits of the estimators of the parameters of the structural equations. To do so, we identify the estimators with their characteristics within a certain family so that related estimators can be compared. The special characteristics that we will consider in this section are the values of k in the k-class estimators, the instrumental variables used, and numerical solution algorithms used in approximating the full information maximum likelihood estimator.

15.3.1 The *k*-Class and *K*-Matrix-Class Families

Theil (1958, 1961) proposes a class of estimators called k-class estimators, where member of the class is characterized by a value of the scalar k. The general expression for the k-class estimators denoted by $\hat{\boldsymbol{\delta}}_{i(k)}$ is

$$\hat{\boldsymbol{\delta}}_{i(k)} = \begin{bmatrix} Y_i'Y_i - k\hat{V}_i'\hat{V}_i & Y_i'X_i \\ X_i'Y_i & X_i'X_i \end{bmatrix}^{-1} \begin{bmatrix} Y_i' - k\hat{V}_i' \\ X_i' \end{bmatrix} \mathbf{y}_i \qquad (15.3.1)$$

It can be shown that ordinary and two-stage least squares are members of the k-class with k chosen equal to be 0 and 1, respectively. The k-class estimator is consistent if plim $k = 1$ and it has the same asymptotic covariance matrix as 2SLS if plim $\sqrt{T}(k - 1) = 0$. See Schmidt (1976, pp. 167–169) for a proof. Since OLS corresponds to the choice $k = 0$, it is not consistent as noted in the previous chapter.

Another well known member of the k-class estimators is the limited information maximum likelihood estimator, the value of k being equal to the smallest root l of the characteristic equation

$$|W_i - lW| = 0 \qquad (15.3.2)$$

where

$$W_i = Y_i'M_iY_i, \qquad M_i = I - X_i(X_i'X_i)^{-1}X_i'$$
$$W = Y_i'MY_i, \qquad M = I - X(X'X)^{-1}X'$$

For the proof, see, for example, Goldberger (1964, pp. 338–344) or Schmidt (1976, pp. 169–200). To examine the consistency of the LIML estimator, we make use of the result of Anderson and Rubin (1950) that the asymptotic distribution of $T(l - 1)$ is $\chi^2_{(k_i^* - m_i + 1)}$. The asymptotic expectation of $\sqrt{T}(l - 1)$ is $(k_i^* - m_i + 1)/\sqrt{T}$ and the asymptotic variance of $\sqrt{T}(l - 1)$ is $2(k_i^* - m_i + 1)/T$. Since both the mean and variance go to zero as T approaches infinity, the asymptotic distribution of $\sqrt{T}(l - 1)$ is degenerate at 0. Therefore, we have plim $\sqrt{T}(l - 1) = 0$, which implies that the LIML estimator is consistent and has the same asymptotic covariance matrix as the 2SLS estimator.

Generalizing the k-class estimator, Nagar (1962) introduced the double k-class estimators. The double k-class estimator is given by

$$\boldsymbol{\delta}_{i(k_1,k_2)} = \begin{bmatrix} Y_i'Y_i - k_1\hat{V}_i'\hat{V}_i & Y_i'X_i \\ X_i'Y_i & X_i'X_i \end{bmatrix}^{-1} \begin{bmatrix} Y_i' - k_2\hat{V}_i' \\ X_i' \end{bmatrix} \mathbf{y}_i \tag{15.3.3}$$

The generalization makes the k-class estimator a special case ($k_1 = k_2 = k$). If $k_1 = k_2 = 1$ it is the 2SLS estimator. Another special case is Theil's (1961) h-class of estimators, when $k_1 = 1 - h^2$ and $k_2 = 1 - h$. The double k-class estimator is consistent and has the same asymptotic covariance matrix as that of the 2SLS estimator if plim $\sqrt{T}(k_1 - 1) =$ plim $\sqrt{T}(k_2 - 1) = 0$. Nagar (1959, 1962) works out some approximate small sample properties of the k-class and double k-class estimators under the assumptions that k_1 and k_2 are nonstochastic, the disturbances are normal and serially independent and all predetermined variables are nonstochastic and exogenous. For more discussion of the small sample properties, see Section 15.4.

Generalizations of the double-k-class estimator to full information simultaneous system estimation are attempted by Roy and Srivastava (1966), Srivastava (1971), Savin (1973), and Scharf (1976). Realizing that the k-class normal equations are obtained from the 2SLS normal equations if the matrix $X(X'X)^{-1}X'$ is replaced by $I - k_iM$ with $M = I - X(X'X)^{-1}X'$, Scharf (1976) replaces the matrices $X(X'X)^{-1}X'$ occurring in each submatrix of the 3SLS normal equations by $I - k_{ij}M$ to define the K-matrix-class estimators. When all k_{ij} are equal to k, the K-matrix-class can be easily expressed as

$$\hat{\boldsymbol{\delta}}^*_{(k)} = \{Z'[\Sigma^{-1} \otimes (I - kM)]Z\}^{-1}Z'[\Sigma^{-1} \otimes (I - kM)]\mathbf{y} \tag{15.3.4}$$

If each k_{ij} has the property that plim $\sqrt{T}(k_{ij} - 1) = 0$ for all $i,j = 1, 2, \ldots, M$, then the K matrix class and 3SLS estimators have the same asymptotic distribution. Scharf (1976) has proved that the FIML estimator is an estimator of the K-matrix-class with $(M \times M)$ matrix K given by

$$K = (k_{ij}) = (w^{ij}/s^{ij})$$

where w^{ij} and s^{ij} are the (i,j)th element of

$$W^{-1} = \{\Gamma'Y'[I - X(X'X)^{-1}X']Y\Gamma/T\}^{-1}$$

and

$$S^{-1} = [(Y\Gamma + XB)'(Y\Gamma + XB)/T]^{-1}$$

respectively. In practice any consistent estimators of Γ and B may be used to compute the estimator.

15.3.2 A Family of Instrumental Variable Estimators

For a system of simultaneous structural equations written as $\mathbf{y} = Z\boldsymbol{\delta} + \mathbf{e}$, the instrumental variable estimator is defined as

$$\hat{\boldsymbol{\delta}}_{(IV)} = (W'Z)^{-1}W'\mathbf{y} \tag{15.3.5}$$

where W is a matrix of instruments that has the same dimension and rank as Z, the elements of W are uncorrelated with $\mathbf{e}$ so that

$$\text{plim}(W'\mathbf{e}/T) = \mathbf{0} \tag{15.3.6}$$

and are correlated with Z so that

$$\text{plim}(W'Z/T) = \Sigma_{wz} \tag{15.3.7}$$

is nonsingular. Under these assumptions and using procedures discussed in Chapter 5, the estimator $\hat{\boldsymbol{\delta}}_{(IV)}$ is consistent because

$$\text{plim}\ \hat{\boldsymbol{\delta}}_{(IV)} = [\text{plim}(W'Z/T)]^{-1}[\text{plim}(W'Z\boldsymbol{\delta}/T) + \text{plim}(W'\mathbf{e}/T)] = \boldsymbol{\delta}$$

If $\mathbf{e}$ is normal with mean $\mathbf{0}$ and covariance $\Sigma \otimes I$, then $W'\mathbf{e}/\sqrt{T}$ converges in distribution to $N[\mathbf{0}, \text{plim}\ W'(\Sigma \otimes I)W/T]$. Thus $\sqrt{T}(\hat{\boldsymbol{\delta}}_{(IV)} - \boldsymbol{\delta})$ is asymptotically normal with mean zero and covariance

$$\text{plim}(W'Z/T)^{-1}\ \text{plim}[W'(\Sigma \otimes I)W/T]\ \text{plim}(Z'W/T)^{-1} \tag{15.3.8}$$

Given the definition of the instrumental variable estimator and its asymptotic properties, we can now give the well-known estimators discussed in previous sections an instrumental variable interpretation. Based on the amount of information employed in forming the instrumental variables, we will be able to compare alternative estimators in terms of their asymptotic efficiency.

We will start with the OLS estimator of the structural parameter vector, $\boldsymbol{\delta}$,

$$\hat{\boldsymbol{\delta}}_{(OLS)} = (Z'Z)^{-1}Z'\mathbf{y}$$

In this case, the instrumental variable matrix used is Z itself. Since $\text{plim}\ Z'\mathbf{e}/T \neq \mathbf{0}$, the condition (15.3.6) is violated and the OLS estimator is thus inconsistent. The system 2SLS estimator can be written as

$$\hat{\boldsymbol{\delta}}_{(2SLS)} = \{Z'[I \otimes X(X'X)^{-1}X']Z\}^{-1}Z'[I \otimes X(X'X)^{-1}X']\mathbf{y}$$

In this case, the instrumental variable matrix W' is

$$W' = Z'[I \otimes X(X'X)^{-1}X']$$

which is asymptotically uncorrelated with $\mathbf{e}$ because plim$(W'\mathbf{e}/T) = \mathbf{0}$. Also, plim$(W'Z/T)$ has a limit that may be assumed nonsingular. Thus the 2SLS estimator is consistent. The asymptotic covariance matrix of $\sqrt{T}(\tilde{\boldsymbol{\delta}}_{(2SLS)} - \boldsymbol{\delta})$ is

$$\text{plim}\{[T^{-1}Z'(I \otimes M)Z]^{-1}[T^{-1}Z'(\Sigma \otimes M)Z][T^{-1}Z'(I \otimes M)Z]^{-1}\}$$

where $M = X(X'X)^{-1}X'$. For the 3SLS estimator,

$$\tilde{\boldsymbol{\delta}}^*_{(3SLS)} = [Z'(\hat{\Sigma}^{-1} \otimes M)Z]^{-1}Z'(\hat{\Sigma}^{-1} \otimes M)\mathbf{y}$$

where the matrix of instrumental variables

$$W' = Z'(\hat{\Sigma}^{-1} \otimes M)$$

is also asymptotically uncorrelated with $\mathbf{e}$ and plim$(W'Z/T)$ has a limit that is assumed nonsingular. Thus, the 3SLS estimator is consistent and the asymptotic covariance matrix of $\sqrt{T}(\tilde{\boldsymbol{\delta}}^*_{(3SLS)} - \boldsymbol{\delta})$ is

$$\text{plim}[T^{-1}Z'(\Sigma^{-1} \otimes M)Z]^{-1}$$

It can be shown that the difference between the covariance matrix of the 2SLS estimator and the 3SLS estimator is a positive semidefinite symmetric matrix. The efficiency of 3SLS over 2SLS is seen from the amount of information contained in the instrumental variables $Z'(\hat{\Sigma}^{-1} \otimes M)$ as compared to $Z'(I \otimes M)$ used in 2SLS. The 2SLS estimator ignores the information in Σ^{-1}.

Hausman (1975) has given an interesting instrumental variable interpretation of FIML. Hausman shows that by maximizing the log likelihood function $L(\Gamma,B,\Sigma)$, the FIML estimator $\tilde{\boldsymbol{\delta}}_{(FI)}$ of the unknown elements of $\boldsymbol{\delta}$ is

$$\tilde{\boldsymbol{\delta}}_{(FI)} = (\bar{W}'Z)^{-1}\bar{W}'\mathbf{y}$$

where the instruments are

$$\bar{W}' = \hat{Z}'(S \otimes I_T)$$

with

$$\hat{Z} = \text{diag}(\hat{Z}_1, \hat{Z}_2, \ldots, \hat{Z}_M)$$
$$\hat{Z}_i = [X(\hat{B}\hat{\Gamma}^{-1})_i \quad X_i] = (X\hat{\boldsymbol{\pi}}_i \quad X_i)$$
$$S = T^{-1}(Y\hat{\Gamma} + X\hat{B})'(Y\hat{\Gamma} + X\hat{B})$$

and the a priori restrictions of zero and normalized coefficients have been imposed. The estimator $\tilde{\boldsymbol{\delta}}_{(FI)}$ is the instrumental variable estimator that fulfills the assumptions of orthogonality, plim$(\bar{W}'\mathbf{e}/T) = \mathbf{0}$ and the existence and nonsingularity of the second order moment matrices. Note that both $\hat{Z}$ and S

depend on $\hat{\Gamma}$ and $\hat{B}$, which are elements of $\tilde{\boldsymbol{\delta}}$. Therefore, $\tilde{\boldsymbol{\delta}}^*_{(\mathrm{FI})}$ could be obtained by an iterative process

$$\tilde{\boldsymbol{\delta}}^*_{(\mathrm{FI})}(k+1) = (W'_{(k)}Z)^{-1}W'_{(k)}\mathbf{y}$$

where k and $k+1$ denote iteration numbers. The limit of the iterative process, if it converges, $\tilde{\delta}^*_{(\mathrm{FI})}$, is the FIML estimator with estimated covariance matrix $[\hat{Z}^{*\prime}(S^* \otimes I_T)^{-1}\hat{Z}^*]^{-1}$, since asymptotically $\sqrt{T}(\tilde{\boldsymbol{\delta}}^*_{(\mathrm{FI})} - \boldsymbol{\delta}) \sim N(\mathbf{0},V^{-1})$, where $V = \lim[-E(T^{-1}\,\partial^2 L/\partial\boldsymbol{\delta}\,\partial\boldsymbol{\delta}')]$, and $\hat{Z}^*$ and S^* are computed using $\tilde{\delta}^*_{(\mathrm{FI})}$.

By an examination of the difference in instruments between $Z'(\hat{\Sigma}^{-1} \otimes M)$ and $\hat{Z}'(S \otimes I)$, we can state that the FIML estimator uses all a priori restrictions in constructing the instruments, while 3SLS uses an unrestricted estimator in constructing the instruments. In other words, in FIML, zero restrictions have been imposed to construct $\hat{Z}_i$, while the 3SLS does not impose the known parameter constraints. In short, the difference between FIML and 3SLS lies in the latter not making complete use of the identifying restrictions in constructing the instruments and different estimators of the covariance matrix Σ. The two methods are equivalent when each structural equation is just identified since the instruments are identical. The 3SLS estimator and the FIML estimator converge to the same limiting distribution since both are consistent and asymptotically normal and have covariance matrices that converge asymptotically to the inverse of the information matrix.

Since iterative procedures are used in computing the FIML estimator, the convergence properties are not clear. For a test of the method and certain proposed alternatives, see Hausman (1974). Alternative ways of constructing instruments for FIML are also available in Lyttkens (1970), Dhrymes (1971), and Brundy and Jorgenson (1971). These alternative estimators are shown by Hausman (1975) to be particular cases of the FIML iteration discussed above.

15.3.3 An Estimator Generating Equation

A grouping system to clarify the structure of large groups of estimators and their asymptotic equivalency has been proposed by Hendry (1976). The formula for the FIML estimator for a linear simultaneous system is demonstrated by Hendry to be an estimator generating equation in that all presently known estimators are readily derivable from that formula if they are considered as numerical approximations to its solution.

In deriving the generating equation, Hendry (1976) starts from the log likelihood function

$$L(\Gamma,B,\Sigma|W) = \text{const.} + T\ln\|\Gamma\| - (T/2)\ln|\Sigma| - (T/2)\,\mathrm{tr}[\Sigma^{-1}A'(W'W/T)A]$$

for the model

$$Y\Gamma + XB + \mathbf{E} = 0$$

or

$$WA + \mathbf{E} = 0$$

where $W = (Y \quad X)$, $A = (\Gamma' \quad B')'$, and $\mathbf{E} = (\mathbf{e}_1 \ \mathbf{e}_2 \ . \ . \ . \ \mathbf{e}_M)$. Taking the derivatives of L with respect to unrestricted elements of Γ, B, and Σ^{-1} and setting them to zero, we obtain, respectively,

$$[T(\Gamma')^{-1} - Y'WA\Sigma^{-1}]^u = 0$$

$$(-X'WA\Sigma^{-1})^u = 0$$

and

$$T\Sigma - A'W'WA = 0$$

where the superscript u denotes choosing only the elements corresponding to the unrestricted elements of Γ and B. The last condition yields

$$\Sigma = A'(W'W/T)A$$

and the first two conditions can be combined and simplified to

$$(\Gamma^{-1} \quad 0)^u = (\Sigma^{-1}A'W'Y/T \quad \Sigma^{-1}A'W'X/T)^u$$

which can be further reduced to

$$[\Sigma^{-1}A'(W'X/T)Q]^u = 0$$

where

$$Y = X\Pi + V$$

$$\Pi = -B\Gamma^{-1}$$

$$Q = (\Pi \quad I)$$

$$W = (Y \quad X) = XQ + (V \quad 0)$$

are used. In solving for Γ, B, and Σ, alternative solution algorithms are available for either implementing or approximating FIML. The following algorithm approximating FIML is well defined:

Step 1 Use any consistent estimator $\Gamma_{(1)}$ and $B_{(1)}$ of Γ and B to obtain $\Pi_{(1)}$ with $\Pi_{(1)} = -B_{(1)}\Gamma_{(1)}^{-1}$.

Step 2 Compute $Q_{(1)} = (\Pi_{(1)} \quad I)$.

Step 3 Compute $\Sigma_{(2)} = A'_{(2)}(W'W/T)A_{(2)}$.

Step 4 Solve $A_{(3)}$ from $[\Sigma_{(2)}^{-1}A'_{(3)}(W'X/T)Q_{(1)}]^u = 0$.

In the above steps, the subscripts in the parentheses denote that different estimators may be used in each expression, where the number shows the order in which the estimators are often obtained. The equation $[\Sigma^{-1}A'(W'X/T)Q]^u = 0$ is linear in A and constitutes a generating equation for estimators in that variations in the choice of Q and Σ generate almost all known estimators for A.

The matrix $[\Sigma^{-1}A'(W'X/T)Q]^u$ is the result of the first derivatives of the concentrated likelihood function $L(A|\Sigma)$. Thus the second derivatives of $L(A|\Sigma)$ with respect to the elements of A will give the information matrix. To determine these derivatives, it will be easier to consider $\mathbf{d} = \text{vec}(A) = (\mathbf{a}_1' \; \mathbf{a}_2' \; . \; . \; . \; \mathbf{a}_M')'$, retain the unrestricted coefficients and pack together to obtain $\boldsymbol{\delta}$, then take the derivative with respect to $\boldsymbol{\delta}$. With the vectorization, the matrix in question can be written

$$(\Sigma^{-1} \otimes Q'X'W)^u \boldsymbol{\delta}$$

where again we remind the reader that u denotes choosing only the elements corresponding to the unrestricted coefficients $\boldsymbol{\delta}$. The derivative of $(\Sigma^{-1} \otimes Q'X'W)^u \boldsymbol{\delta}$ with respect to $\boldsymbol{\delta}$ is

$$(\Sigma^{-1} \otimes Q'X'W)^u \qquad \text{or} \qquad (\Sigma^{-1} \otimes Q'X'XQ)^u$$

by dropping the asymptotically negligible terms. Thus, the covariance matrix of the FIML estimator of $\boldsymbol{\delta}$ is

$$[(\Sigma^{-1} \otimes Q'X'XQ)^u]^{-1}$$

which is often used in numerical iteration procedures such as gradient methods.

To show that $[\Sigma^{-1}A'(W'X/T)Q]^u = 0$ is a generating function for estimators, we consider evaluating $\Sigma_{(2)}$ with consistent 2SLS or instrumental variable estimates for $A_{(2)}$. Denote this estimator by $\hat{\Sigma}$. Replace $Q_{(1)}$ by $\hat{Q} = (\hat{\Pi} \quad I)$, where $\hat{\Pi} = (X'X)^{-1}X'Y$. Then, $W'XQ = W'X(X'X)^{-1}W = W'MW$. Normalizing the diagonal of Γ and moving the corresponding constants of $\Sigma^{-1}A'W'XQ = 0$ to the right-hand side, we have

$$(\Sigma^{-1} \otimes W'MW)^u \boldsymbol{\delta} = (\Sigma^{-1} \otimes W'M)^u \mathbf{y}$$

where $\mathbf{y} = \text{vec}(Y)$ has been formed by collecting the elements of W corresponding to the normalization constants of -1. The last expression is the set of normal equations for 3SLS. If it is iterated numerically revising only $\Sigma_{(2)}$, the convergence point will in general differ from FIML for all finite T, but the asymptotic distribution will be unaffected. The asymptotic property in general is seen from the limit of the asymptotic covariance:

$$\text{plim} \frac{\partial}{\partial \boldsymbol{\delta}'} \text{vec} \left[\Sigma^{-1}A' \left(\frac{W'X}{T}\right) Q\right]^u = \text{plim} \frac{\partial}{\partial \boldsymbol{\delta}'} \text{vec} \left[\Sigma^{-1} \left(\frac{V'X}{T}\right) Q\right]^u = 0$$

because $\text{plim}(V'X/T) = 0$.

For the generation and discussion of other estimators, the reader is referred to Hendry (1976), Hendry and Harrison (1974), Maasoumi and Phillips (1982), Hendry (1982), Anderson (1984), and Prucha and Kelejian (1984).

15.4 SMALL SAMPLE PROPERTIES OF ESTIMATORS

In Section 15.3, where general classes of estimators were discussed, the comparisons of alternative estimators were primarily based on the similarities in the asymptotic properties. In other words, the estimators were compared when the sample size was assumed large. For example, the distribution of the FIML estimator and 3SLS estimator are known to converge to the same limiting distribution. However, in small samples their behavior may be very different. In this section, we will concentrate on the small sample properties of simultaneous equations estimators.

During the 1950s and 1960s, studies of small sample properties of estimators were often performed by Monte Carlo experiments. For a classified bibliography of such Monte Carlo experiments over the period 1948–1972, see Sowey (1973). The sampling experiments are often performed by setting up a structural model with specified values of structural coefficients and specified distributions of equation errors. The values of the predetermined variables are also specified, and the values of the jointly dependent variables obtained through the reduced form equations in conjunction with the reduced form disturbances that may be generated by a random number generator of a digital computer. Many samples of different sizes are generated and used to estimate the structural parameters with different estimators. The resultant distributions of the sample estimates are summarized and compared. Although past Monte Carlo studies have provided insights into the comparative merits of statistical procedures, there are limitations on the generalization that may be made from these experiments. The results may be specific to the set of parameter values assumed in the simulation and may be subject to sampling variations. Monte Carlo experiments neither permit a systematic analysis of the relationship between parameter values and the corresponding distributions, nor allow a way to reveal that moments of the exact distribution may exist. However, they may give very strong indication of such nonexistence. Recent efforts to cope with these issues are discussed in Hendry and Harrison (1974), Hendry and Mizon (1980), and Dempster, Schatzoff, and Wermuth (1977).

Recent studies of small sample properties have concentrated on analytical work. Although there are pioneering works by Nagar (1959), Basmann (1960, 1961), and Bergstrom (1962), most of the results appear in the literature after 1970. In the past 10 to 15 years, although we have seen many achievements, results are available only for certain special cases because of the analytical complexities involved in carrying through the necessary derivations. Recent contributions by Basmann (1974), Phillips (1980a), Mariano (1982), Anderson (1982, 1984), Greenberg and Webster (1983), Phillips (1983) and Taylor (1983) summarize many of these results. Most of the results are about the 2SLS estimators, k-class estimators, LIML estimators, instrumental variable (IV) estimators, and maximum likelihood estimators. Results are different for the cases of two and three or more included endogenous variables. Some methods used in comparing the behavior of the estimates are:

1. Exact small-sample densities of distributions.
2. Moments or other characteristics of the exact distributions.
3. Approximate densities of distributions, possibly asymptotic expansions.
4. Moments or other characteristics of the approximate distributions.
5. Tables of the distributions for a range of parameter values.
6. Tables of moments or other characteristics of distributions for a range of parameter values.

In the following, we try to summarize the highlights of the analytical finite sample results for estimators in simultaneous equation models.

The simplest form of a structural equation in a complete model is the one that contains two endogenous variables and has the form

$$\mathbf{y}_2 = \gamma \mathbf{y}_1 + \beta \mathbf{x}_1 + \mathbf{e}$$

where $\mathbf{y}_1$, $\mathbf{y}_2$ are $(T \times 1)$ vectors of observations on the two endogenous variables, $\mathbf{x}_1$ is a $(T \times 1)$ vector of one's, and $\mathbf{e}$ is a $(T \times 1)$ vector of errors. Richardson (1968) and Sawa (1969) have independently derived the exact sampling distribution of the 2SLS estimator for the above model. While Richardson (1968) derives the distribution directly from the 2SLS procedure, Sawa (1969) derives the distribution for the 2SLS estimator from the distribution of the OLS estimator. Richardson and Wu (1971), show that the distribution function of the OLS estimator of γ in the above model has the same form as the 2SLS distribution.

Using the above model, Sawa (1969) first derives the distribution of the OLS estimator for γ and shows that the moments of order less than $T - 1$ exist and those of high order do not. Based on the fact that the 2SLS estimator is essentially the instrumental variables method using all exogenous variables as instrumental variables, the 2SLS estimator of γ may be obtained by applying the OLS method directly to the equation

$$W'\mathbf{y}_2 = \gamma W'\mathbf{y}_1 + \beta W'\mathbf{x}_1 + W'\mathbf{e}$$

where $W = X(X'X)^{-1}X'Z_2$, $Z_2 = (\mathbf{y}_1 \;\; \mathbf{x}_1)$, and X is the $(T \times K)$ matrix of observations on all predetermined (assuming only exogenous and no lagged endogenous) variables. Therefore, the distribution of the 2SLS estimator of γ is essentially the same as that of the OLS estimator, except for the degrees of freedom. Thus, the moments of the 2SLS estimator of order less than k_i^* exist and those of higher order do not. The results can be easily extended to the case where the equation of interest includes two endogenous variables and k_i exogenous variables, hence the moments of the 2SLS estimator of order less than k_i^*

exist and those of higher order do not. An interesting special case arises when the number of excluded exogenous variables is $k_i^* = K - k_i = 1$, which corresponds to the case that the equation with two included endogenous variables is just identified. In this case, the moments do not exist for the 2SLS estimator.

Sawa's (1969) results for the density functions for the OLS and 2SLS are complicated in mathematical structure and it is difficult to deduce any definite conclusions concerning small sample properties. Therefore, Sawa evaluates the density functions numerically for $\gamma = 0.6$, $\sigma_{11} = \sigma_{22} = 1$, and for several values of T, K, and τ^2 (which is T times the square of the reduced form coefficients for $\mathbf{y}_1$). His graphs show that:

1. 2SLS has a smaller bias than OLS.
2. Both OLS and 2SLS are biased in the same direction.
3. The distributions are extremely sensitive to the value of $\rho = \sigma_{12}/\sigma_{11}$.
4. When $\rho = 0$, both OLS and 2SLS become more concentrated as T increases, but the mode of the OLS estimator remains at approximately 0.5, while that of the 2SLS is about 0.6.
5. For a fixed T, the 2SLS distribution is affected by K, and the bias increases with K.

Both Richardson (1968) and Sawa (1969) have independently confirmed Basmann's (1961) conjecture that the moments of the 2SLS estimator of an equation in a simultaneous system of linear stochastic equations exist if the order is less than $k_i^* - m_i + 1$, where m_i and k_i^* are respectively the numbers of endogenous variables included and predetermined variables excluded from the equation being estimated. Also in the case of two included endogenous variables, Mariano and Sawa (1972) derive the exact probability density function of the LIML estimator and show that for arbitrary values of the parameters in the model, the LIML estimator does not possess moments of any order. Mariano (1972) further proves for the general case with an arbitrary number of included endogenous variables, even moments of the 2SLS estimator exist if and only if the order is less than $k_i^* - m_i + 1$, and that even moments of the OLS estimator exist if and only if the order is less than $T - k_i - m_i + 1$.

The exact distributions derived for the 2SLS and LIML estimators are too complicated to provide any basis for a comparison of the two estimators. Hoping that approximations to the distribution functions of these two estimators will provide more tractable expressions for comparison, Mariano (1973a) approximates the distribution function of the 2SLS estimators up to terms whose order of magnitude is $1/\sqrt{T}$, where T is the sample size. Anderson and Sawa (1973) also give an asymptotic expansion of the distribution of the k-class estimates in terms of an Edgeworth or Gram-Charlier series. The density of the approximate distribution is a normal density multiplied by a polynomial. The first correction term to the normal distribution involves a cubic divided by the square root of the sample size, and other correction terms involve a polynomial of higher degree divided by higher powers of the square root of the sample size. The approach of Anderson and Sawa (1973) permits expression of the distribution of the 2SLS and OLS estimates in terms of the doubly noncentral F distribution. Anderson and Sawa (1973) also give an asymptotic expansion of the cumulative density function of the 2SLS estimate in terms of the noncentrality parameter for a fixed number of excluded exogenous variables. Their expansion agrees with that given by Sargan and Mikhail (1971). Mariano (1973b) also approximates the distribution of the k-class estimators extending the method he used for the 2SLS (Mariano, 1973a). Anderson (1974) makes an asymptotic expansion of the distribution of the LIML estimate for the two included endogenous variables case.

Anderson and Sawa (1979) complete their study of the distribution function of 2SLS by giving extensive numerical tables of the exact cumulative density function of the 2SLS estimator and examining the accuracy of the approximate distributions based on the asymptotic expansion in the noncentrality parameter. The distribution of the estimator depends on the values taken by the noncentrality parameter and a standardization of the structural coefficients as well as the number of the excluded endogenous variables. Anderson, Kunitomo, and Sawa (1982) present corresponding tables for the LIML estimator. The distribution of this estimator depends on the same factors that affect the distribution of the 2SLS estimator plus the number of degrees of freedom in the estimator of the covariance matrix of the reduced form. They also show that the LIML estimator approaches normality much faster than the 2SLS estimator and LIML is strongly preferred to 2SLS. Holly and Phillips (1979) point out that approximations based on the Edgeworth expansion are sometimes unsatisfactory in the tail area and propose the use of the saddle point approximation. Their numerical computations suggest that the new approximation performs very well relative to Edgeworth approximations, particularly when the degree of overidentification in the equation is large.

Kinal (1980) summarizes the conditions for the existence of moments of k-class estimators for the special case of two included endogenous variables as follows: The rth-order moment of k-class estimators, of the coefficient of an endogenous variable of an equation in a simultaneous system of linear stochastic equations, exists for nonstochastic k if and only if $r < N$, where

$$N = \begin{cases} T - k_i - m_i + 2 & \text{for } 0 \leq k < 1 \\ k_i^* - m_i + 2 & \text{for } k = 1 \end{cases}$$

and where T is the number of observations, m_i is the number of endogenous variables included in the equation, and k_i and k_i^* are, respectively, the number of predetermined variables included in and excluded from the equation. He proves the above conditions for all m_i and k_i^*.

Phillips (1980b) derives the exact probability density function of instrumental variable estimators of the coefficient vector of endogenous variables in a structural equation containing $n + 1$ endogenous variables and any degrees of overidentification. The numerical computations for n equal to 1 and 2 and both parameters equal to 0.6 show that the distribution appears to concentrate more quickly as T becomes large when $n = 1$ than when $n = 2$. The density of the instrumental variable estimator displays more bias as the number of additional instruments used for the n right-hand side endogenous variables increases. The density appears to be sensitive to the degree of correlation in the matrix of products of reduced form coefficients. When the two endogenous coefficients γ_1 and γ_2 are different, the distribution of the IV estimator for γ_1 becomes less well centered about the true value of γ_1. The bias becomes positive and the dispersion increases rapidly as the difference between γ_2 and γ_1 increases.

Finite sample properties of instrumental variable estimators of structural coefficients are also studied by Mariano (1977). The class he considered consisted of instrumental variable estimators generated by stochastic instruments. Some known estimators in this class are OLS, 2SLS, and IV estimators studied by Sargan and Mikhail (1971), which are, equivalently, modified 2SLS where the first stage regressors are exogenous variables including those contained in the equation being estimated. These estimators have finite moments up to order $h - (m_i - 1)$, where h denotes the degrees of freedom of the Wishart matrix involved and m_i is the number of included exogenous variables. The exact pdf's of these estimators can also be obtained from the procedure of Sargan (1976). Another class of instrumental variable estimators uses nonstochastic instruments. This type of estimators is characterized in terms of multinormal random vectors in exactly the same way as the 2SLS estimator for a just identified equation and as a consequence, these estimators will have no finite moments at all.

In closing this section, we summarize the existence and nonexistence of moments of the small sample distributions of various estimators. Consider an identified equation in a linear simultaneous system satisfying classical assumptions. The moments of coefficient estimates for various estimators in this structural equation exist up to orders given in the following:

1. For 2SLS and 3SLS, the finite moments exist up to $k_i^* - m_i + 1$, the number of overidentifying restrictions.
2. For modified 2SLS, the finite moments exist up to $r - k_i + m_i + 1$, where r is the number of linearly independent first stage regressors.
3. For the k-class estimators with k nonstochastic and $0 \leq k < 1$, the finite moments exist up to $T - k_i - m_i + 1$, or T minus the number of parameters in the equation to be estimated.
4. For the k-class estimator with nonstochastic k exceeding 1, no moments exist.
5. For LIML and FIML, no finite moments exist.
6. For instrumental variable estimators with nonstochastic instruments, no finite moments exist.

15.5 INFERENCE

Several kinds of tests have been proposed for the estimated coefficients of equations in a system of simultaneous linear equations. In this section, we will present selected test procedures for parameter significance, overidentification and the orthogonality assumption.

15.5.1 Tests of Parameter Significance

As we discussed in Section 15.4, for small sample sizes the probability distributions of estimators in a system of simultaneous equations are unknown except for a few highly special cases. Consequently, tests of parameter significance are usually based on the asymptotic distributions of the estimators.

Let the general linear hypothesis be H_0: $R\boldsymbol{\delta} = \mathbf{r}$, where R is $(J \times n)$, $\mathbf{r}$ is $(J \times 1)$, and $n = \Sigma_i(m_i + k_i)$. To demonstrate how a test of these constraints can be derived, we use the 3SLS estimator $\tilde{\boldsymbol{\delta}}^*$. A test statistic for the 2SLS estimator can be obtained analogously. Since $T^{1/2}(\tilde{\boldsymbol{\delta}}^* - \boldsymbol{\delta})$ is asymptotically distributed $N(\mathbf{0},\Sigma_{\tilde{\delta}^*})$, where $\Sigma_{\tilde{\delta}^*} = \text{plim}\{T^{-1}Z'[\hat{\Sigma}^{-1} \otimes X(X'X)^{-1}X']Z\}^{-1}$,

$$T^{1/2}R(\tilde{\boldsymbol{\delta}}^* - \boldsymbol{\delta}) \xrightarrow{d} N(\mathbf{0},R\Sigma_{\tilde{\delta}^*}R') \tag{15.5.1}$$

and

$$T(\tilde{\boldsymbol{\delta}}^* - \boldsymbol{\delta})'R'(R\Sigma_{\tilde{\delta}^*}R')^{-1}R(\tilde{\boldsymbol{\delta}}^* - \boldsymbol{\delta}) \xrightarrow{d} \chi^2_{(J)} \tag{15.5.2}$$

In finite samples the test statistic can be computed as

$$(\tilde{\boldsymbol{\delta}}^* - \boldsymbol{\delta})'R'(R\{Z'[\hat{\Sigma}^{-1} \otimes X(X'X)^{-1}X']Z\}^{-1}R')^{-1}R(\tilde{\boldsymbol{\delta}}^* - \boldsymbol{\delta}) \tag{15.5.3}$$

Similarly, for 2SLS estimation, we have

$$(\tilde{\boldsymbol{\delta}} - \boldsymbol{\delta})'R'(R\Sigma_{\tilde{\delta}}R')^{-1}R(\tilde{\boldsymbol{\delta}} - \boldsymbol{\delta}) \xrightarrow{d} \chi^2_{(J)} \tag{15.5.4}$$

where $\tilde{\boldsymbol{\delta}}$ is the 2SLS estimator. Therefore tests involving groups of coefficients estimated by 2SLS or 3SLS methods can be carried out by using the chi-square distribution.

For testing a single parameter δ_{ij}, the ith parameter of the jth equation, the matrix R is a unit vector and the test statistic for 3SLS reduces to

$$(\tilde{\delta}^*_{ij} - \delta_{ij})^2/\text{var}(\tilde{\delta}^*_{ij}) \xrightarrow{d} \chi^2_{(1)} \tag{15.5.5}$$

or

$$(\tilde{\delta}^*_{ij} - \delta_{ij})/\sqrt{\text{var}(\tilde{\delta}^*_{ij})} \xrightarrow{d} N(0,1) \tag{15.5.6}$$

Thus asymptotic tests on individual parameters can be carried out in finite samples using (15.5.6) with the estimated standard error of $\tilde{\delta}^*_{ij}$ and critical values from the standard normal or "t" distribution, since they are the same asymptotically.

15.5.2 Tests of Overidentification

Consistent estimation of the parameters of a system of linear simultaneous equations requires identifying restrictions on the parameters. Therefore, the identifying restrictions are of particular interest and tests are available for the overidentifying restrictions.

A well-known overidentification test is Anderson and Rubin's (1949) likelihood ratio test. The essential idea of the test is the following: If all the a priori restrictions on parameters are correct, then the ratio of the likelihood function for the restricted and unrestricted models should be close to one. If the ratio deviates from one too much in a statistical sense, then the hypotheses, here the overidentifying restrictions, are concluded not to agree with the sample data. Since $\hat{l}$ is the minimum value of the ratio of two residual variances $\boldsymbol{\gamma}_i' W_i \boldsymbol{\gamma}_i / \boldsymbol{\gamma}_i' W \boldsymbol{\gamma}_i$, the likelihood ratio test statistic turns out to be the smallest root $\hat{l}$ of

$$|W_i - lW| = 0 \tag{15.5.7}$$

where $W_i = Y_i'M_iY_i$, $M_i = I - X_i(X_i'X_i)^{-1}X_i'$, $W = Y_i'MY_i$, and $M = I - X(X'X)^{-1}X'$. Anderson and Rubin (1949) show that the asymptotic distribution of $T(\hat{l} - 1)$ is $\chi^2_{(k_i^* - m_i + 1)}$, the degrees of freedom being the number of overidentifying restrictions. Consequently, the asymptotic test procedure is to reject the hypothesis that the overidentifying restrictions are valid if the value of $T(\hat{l} - 1)$ is large. The test does not work for just identified equations, because in that case $k_i^* - m_i + 1 = 0$, so that there are no degrees of freedom and $\hat{l}$ always turns out to be exactly 1 and consequently $T(\hat{l} - 1) = 0$. For details on this test in the context of LIML estimation, see Koopmans and Hood (1953).

Basmann (1960) also proposes two alternative tests of the hypothesis of overidentification based on the F distribution, one for LIML estimation and one for 2SLS estimation. For LIML estimation, Basmann (1960) shows that the test statistic $(\hat{l} - 1)(T - K)/(k_i^* - m_i + 1)$ is asymptotically distributed as $F_{(k_i^* - m_i + 1, T-K)}$. For 2SLS estimation, $\tilde{l}$ is used in place of $\hat{l}$, where $\tilde{l}$ is the minimum value of the ratio $\boldsymbol{\gamma}_i' W_i \boldsymbol{\gamma}_i / \boldsymbol{\gamma}_i' W \boldsymbol{\gamma}_i$ when the 2SLS estimator is used for $\boldsymbol{\gamma}_i$.

Byron (1974) proposes tests of overidentification based on the use of only the unrestricted reduced form parameter estimates. Overidentifying structural restrictions are expressed as nonlinear reduced form restrictions, and the Wald principle is then applied to test overidentification. The idea is as follows: If the maintained hypothesis is correct, then the relationship between the reduced form parameters implied by the structure will tend to be reproduced by any consistent estimates of the reduced form parameters because the reduced form population parameters will satisfy the restrictions exactly.

Let $\mathbf{h}(\boldsymbol{\pi}) = \mathbf{0}$ be the J-dimensional set of J restrictions, nonlinear in the elements of $\boldsymbol{\pi}$, transformed from the overidentifying structural restrictions, where $\boldsymbol{\pi} = \text{vec}(\Pi)$. For an example of such a transformation, see Hwang (1980b). If $\mathbf{h}(\hat{\boldsymbol{\pi}})$ is near enough to zero, where $\hat{\boldsymbol{\pi}}$ is an unrestricted parameter estimator, the null hypothesis is accepted.

Byron's (1974) test is based on the first-order Taylor expansion of the components of $\mathbf{h}(\hat{\boldsymbol{\pi}})$ about the true parameter $\boldsymbol{\pi}$,

$$\mathbf{h}(\hat{\boldsymbol{\pi}}) \simeq \mathbf{h}(\boldsymbol{\pi}) + H'(\hat{\boldsymbol{\pi}} - \boldsymbol{\pi}) \tag{15.5.8}$$

where $H = \partial \mathbf{h}(\boldsymbol{\pi})'/\partial \boldsymbol{\pi}$. If the null hypothesis is true, $\mathbf{h}(\boldsymbol{\pi}) = \mathbf{0}$ and

$$\mathbf{h}(\hat{\boldsymbol{\pi}}) \simeq H'(\hat{\boldsymbol{\pi}} - \boldsymbol{\pi}) \tag{15.5.9}$$

Since $\sqrt{T}(\hat{\boldsymbol{\pi}} - \boldsymbol{\pi})$ is asymptotically $N(\mathbf{0},\boldsymbol{\Psi})$, where $\boldsymbol{\Psi} = \lim[-(ET^{-1}\partial^2 \ln L/\partial\boldsymbol{\pi}\partial\boldsymbol{\pi}')^{-1}]$, $\sqrt{T}\mathbf{h}(\hat{\boldsymbol{\pi}})$ is asymptotically $N(\mathbf{0},H'\boldsymbol{\Psi}H)$. Therefore, under the null hypothesis $\mathbf{h}(\boldsymbol{\pi}) = \mathbf{0}$, the quadratic form

$$q = T\mathbf{h}(\hat{\boldsymbol{\pi}})'(H'\boldsymbol{\Psi}H)^{-1}\mathbf{h}(\hat{\boldsymbol{\pi}}) \tag{15.5.10}$$

which is the Wald test statistic, is asymptotically $\chi^2_{(J)}$, where J is the number of restrictions that overidentify the structural equation. Byron shows that under the null hypothesis, the Wald test is asymptotically equivalent to a likelihood ratio test.

Wegge (1978) treats an overidentified model as an exact identified model that is subject to overidentifying restrictions. Consider the just identified ith structural equation

$$\mathbf{y}_i = Y_i\boldsymbol{\gamma}_i + X_i\boldsymbol{\beta}_i + X_i^*\boldsymbol{\beta}_i^* + \mathbf{e}_i \tag{15.5.11}$$

in which $\boldsymbol{\beta}_i^* = \mathbf{0}$ overidentifies the equation. Let $M_i = I - X_i(X_i'X_i)^{-1}X_i'$, $M = I - X(X'X)^{-1}X'$, $W^* = M_i - M$, and $M^* = W^* - W^*Y_i(Y_i'W^*Y_i)^{-1}X_i^*W^*\mathbf{y}$. The 2SLS estimator of $\boldsymbol{\beta}_i^*$ is given by

$$\hat{\boldsymbol{\beta}}_i^* = (X_i^{*\prime}M^*X_i^*)^{-1}X_i^{*\prime}M^*\mathbf{y} \tag{15.5.12}$$

Since

$$\sqrt{T}(\hat{\boldsymbol{\beta}}_i^* - \boldsymbol{\beta}_i^*) \xrightarrow{d} N(\mathbf{0}, \sigma_{ii} \operatorname{plim}(X_i^{*\prime}M^*X_i^*/T)^{-1}) \tag{15.5.13}$$

the quadratic form

$$(\hat{\boldsymbol{\beta}}_i^* - \boldsymbol{\beta}_i^*)'(X_i^{*\prime}M^*X_i^*)(\hat{\boldsymbol{\beta}}_i^* - \boldsymbol{\beta}_i^*)/\hat{\sigma}_{ii} \xrightarrow{d} \chi^2_{(k_i^*)}$$

where $\hat{\sigma}_{ii}$ is the 2SLS estimate of σ_{ii}. Under the null hypothesis $\boldsymbol{\beta}_i^* = \mathbf{0}$, so that the test statistic becomes $\hat{\boldsymbol{\beta}}_i^{*\prime}(X_i^{*\prime}M^*X_i^*)\hat{\boldsymbol{\beta}}_i^*/\hat{\sigma}_{ii}$. For a comparison of alternative test procedures, see Hwang (1980b).

15.5.3 Misspecification Tests

In specification of a system of simultaneous linear equations, the predetermined variables X are assumed to be uncorrelated with the structural equation errors [i.e., $E(X'e) = \mathbf{0}$ or in large samples, $\operatorname{plim}(X'\mathbf{e}/T) = \mathbf{0}$]. However, if in fact a specified predetermined variable $\mathbf{x}_i$ is not orthogonal to $\mathbf{e}$, it is possible that the variable under consideration is not a predetermined variable but should be correctly specified as an endogenous variable. The violation of the orthogonality assumption is possible under a variety of circumstances. Examples are omission of the relevant explanatory variables, errors in variables, inappropriate aggregation over time, simultaneity, and incorrect functional form. Therefore, rejection of the null hypothesis that $\text{plim}(X'\mathbf{e}/T) = \mathbf{0}$ will not in general allow us to identify a specific alternative hypothesis.

When the orthogonality assumption is not appropriate, the use of ordinary least squares (OLS) leads to biased and inconsistent parameter estimates, and the usual t and F tests for these parameters are no longer appropriate. In this case, consistent parameter estimates can be obtained by the use of an instrumental variables (IV) estimator. However, the use of an IV estimator involves a certain loss of efficiency. Based on the trade-off between consistency and efficiency, Durbin (1954) proposes a test for this specification error of the orthogonality assumption in the form appropriate for choosing between OLS and IV estimation. Wu (1973) addresses the same problem and proposes four tests: two finite sample tests and two alternative asymptotic tests for the hypothesis that the stochastic regressors and disturbances are independent. Providing a basis for choosing among the four tests, Wu (1974) determines analytically the set of parameters that enter the power functions of these tests and then compares the power functions of these tests using sampling experiments. Perhaps because the test statistics appear computationally cumbersome, they are rarely used in empirical studies. However, a fair amount of theoretical work has appeared in the literature. For a list of references, see Nakamura and Nakamura (1981).

In a recent article, Hausman (1978) proposes a general form of specification test. The test is based on the existence of two alternative estimators: one that is consistent and asymptotically efficient under the null hypothesis and one that is not asymptotically efficient under the null hypothesis but is consistent under both null and alternative hypotheses. By comparing the estimates from both estimators and noting that their difference is uncorrelated with the efficient estimator when the null hypothesis is true, a test is derived based on the asymptotic distribution of the difference in the two estimators. For a single equation model, the efficient estimator under the null hypothesis is, of course, the least squares estimator. The comparison estimator will be an instrumental variable estimator based on the instrument that is correlated with the explanatory variables but independent of the equation error. In a test of system specification within a simultaneous equations context, the efficient estimator would be provided by 3SLS and the alternative estimator would be 2SLS, since the latter is consistent under both hypotheses as long as any misspecification occurs in another equation, while the former transmits misspecification throughout the entire system, affecting the estimates of all coefficients. Hausman (1978) shows that $\sqrt{T}\,\hat{\mathbf{q}} = \sqrt{T}(\hat{\boldsymbol{\delta}}^* - \hat{\boldsymbol{\delta}})$ and $\sqrt{T}(\hat{\boldsymbol{\delta}}^* - \boldsymbol{\delta})$ have zero covariance, where $\hat{\boldsymbol{\delta}}^*$ and $\hat{\boldsymbol{\delta}}$ are 3SLS and 2SLS estimators, respectively. Given the above result, a general misspecification test can be specified by considering the statistic

$$m = T\hat{\mathbf{q}}'\hat{V}(\hat{\mathbf{q}})^{-1}\hat{\mathbf{q}} \tag{15.5.14}$$

where $\hat{V}(\hat{\mathbf{q}})$ is a consistent estimate of the variance of $\hat{\mathbf{q}}$. This statistic is shown to be distributed asymptotically as central $\chi^2_{(n)}$ under the null hypothesis, where n is the number of unknown parameters in $\boldsymbol{\delta}$ when no misspecification is present. In practice, Hausman suggests that an equivalent alternative procedure is to consider the regression for

$$\mathbf{y} = \hat{Z}\boldsymbol{\delta} + \tilde{Z}\boldsymbol{\alpha} + \boldsymbol{\epsilon} \tag{15.5.15}$$

where $\hat{Z} = (I_M \otimes X(X'X)^{-1}X')Z$, $\tilde{Z} = (\hat{\Sigma}^{-1} \otimes X(X'X)^{-1}X')Z$, and to test whether $\boldsymbol{\alpha} = \mathbf{0}$.

Since the misspecification represented by the alternative hypothesis is not specific, one only knows that misspecification is present somewhere in the system. If one is confident that one or more equations are correctly specified, then the specification of other equations could be checked by using them to form a 3SLS-type estimator. By using this sequential method, the misspecification might be isolated, but the test is complicated.

Building on the same idea as Hausman's Spencer and Berk (1981) explicitly propose a misspecification test for a single equation without specifying the entire system in order to obtain asymptotically efficient estimators such as 3SLS. The single equation test relies on the fact that the 2SLS estimator is efficient in the class of instrumental variable estimators having instruments that are linear functions of the exogenous variables. If an alternative estimator is chosen from the same class that is not efficient but is consistent under the alternative hypothesis, then Hausman's (1978) test is applicable. Spencer and Berk (1981) show that $\sqrt{T}\,\hat{\mathbf{q}} = \sqrt{T}(\hat{\boldsymbol{\delta}}_i - \hat{\boldsymbol{\delta}}_{i(\mathrm{IV})})$ and $\sqrt{T}(\hat{\boldsymbol{\delta}}_i - \boldsymbol{\delta}_i)$ have zero covariance matrix and consider the test statistic

$$m = T\hat{\mathbf{q}}'\hat{V}(\hat{\mathbf{q}})^{-1}\hat{\mathbf{q}} \tag{15.5.16}$$

which is distributed asymptotically as $\chi^2_{(n)}$, where n is the number of unknown parameters in $\boldsymbol{\delta}_i$. An alternative equivalent test that may be easier to apply using existing computer programs is the test of the hypothesis that $\boldsymbol{\alpha} = \mathbf{0}$ in the regression:

$$\mathbf{y}_i = \hat{Z}_i\boldsymbol{\delta}_i + \tilde{Z}_i\boldsymbol{\alpha} + \boldsymbol{\epsilon} \tag{15.5.17}$$

where $\hat{Z}_i = X(X'X)^{-1}X'Z_i$, $\tilde{Z}_i = X_*(X_*'X_*)^{-1}X_*'Z_i$, and X_* is a submatrix of X excluding the first column and the column corresponding to the variable under the test of orthogonality with $\mathbf{e}_i$. The first column of X is deleted in forming $\tilde{Z}_i$ in order to avoid multicollinearity. For the details, see Spencer and Berk (1981).

The interrelationship among Durbin's, Wu's, and Hausman's statistics is discussed in Nakamura and Nakamura (1981). They show that Hausman's (1978) IV test is identical to one of Wu's (1973) four tests, but the former is computationally more convenient than the latter. The IV statistic presented by Hausman is also identical to Durbin's (1954) test statistic since they are given in forms appropriate for choosing between ordinary least squares and IV estimation. Both Hausman's IV test statistic and Durbin's (1954) test statistic are also identical to Wu's (1973) two other test statistics depending on the estimator used for the nuisance parameter of the variance of the equation error. None of these tests, however, are true Lagrange multiplier or Wald tests, since they are not based on maximum likelihood estimates.

15.6 EFFICIENT ESTIMATION OF REDUCED FORM PARAMETERS

The estimation of reduced form equations was discussed earlier for the purpose of using the results to consistently estimate structural parameters. For certain applications of estimated econometric models, such as forecasting, interest centers on the reduced form of the model rather than on the structural form. In such cases it appears desirable to estimate the reduced form by the most efficient means available.

In Chapter 14, we have shown that the direct application of the OLS to the reduced form equations results in consistent estimates of the reduced form parameters. The method is computationally simple, but the estimates are not efficient since the method does not take account of overidentifying restrictions. In other words, each endogenous variable is regressed on all predetermined variables disregarding the fact that restrictions may relate some reduced form coefficients. Therefore, in the following discussion, we will explore alternative methods of estimating the reduced form parameters.

A well-known method is to derive the estimator for the reduced form coefficients from the known consistent estimators of structural parameters. The result is known as the derived reduced form. This method incorporates all overidentifying restrictions on all structural coefficients, but the computations require use of consistent estimators of the structural coefficients. In addition, the covariance matrix of the reduced form estimators must also be derived from the already very complicated covariance matrix of the consistent estimates of the structural estimates. Moreover, the covariances of reduced form estimates and of forecasts are available only to order $1/T$, where T is the sample size. Besides, accumulation of rounding errors in computing the derived covariance matrix for a large model may become a significant problem. See Schmidt (1976, pp. 236–247) for a summary of the properties of derived reduced form parameter estimates.

Alternatively, direct estimation of reduced forms can be improved by incorporating a priori restrictions on the reduced form coefficients. The procedure is feasible if the a priori restrictions on reduced form coefficients are known in advance. However, such a priori restrictions on reduced forms implied by the restrictions on structural parameters are often hard to derive. This is particularly true when the model is large. Besides, if the restrictions are not correct, the resulting estimators are biased.

Kakwani and Court (1972) propose the use of overidentifying information on the coefficients of one structural equation at a time. Recall that a structural equation $\mathbf{y}_i = Y_i\boldsymbol{\gamma}_i + X_i\boldsymbol{\beta}_i + \mathbf{e}_i$ can be written as

$$\begin{aligned}\mathbf{y}_i &= (X\Pi_i \quad X_i)\boldsymbol{\delta}_i + \mathbf{v}_i \\ &= \bar{Z}_i\boldsymbol{\delta}_i + \mathbf{v}_i\end{aligned}$$

where $\mathbf{v}_i = \mathbf{e}_i + V_i\boldsymbol{\gamma}_i$ and $\bar{Z}_i = (X\Pi_i \quad X_i)$. Let $H = \left(\Pi_i \quad \begin{pmatrix} I \\ 0 \end{pmatrix}\right)$, then $\bar{Z}_i =$ XH and the ith structural equation can be written as

$$\mathbf{y}_i = XH\boldsymbol{\delta}_i + \mathbf{v}_i$$

Comparing the coefficients with its own reduced form equation, we have

$$\boldsymbol{\pi}_i = H\boldsymbol{\delta}_i \tag{15.6.1}$$

Kakwani and Court (1972) define the partially restricted reduced form estimator $\tilde{\boldsymbol{\pi}}_i$ as

$$\tilde{\boldsymbol{\pi}}_i = \hat{H}\hat{\boldsymbol{\delta}}_i \tag{15.6.2}$$

where

$$\hat{H} = (X'X)^{-1}X'Z_i \tag{15.6.3}$$

is the least squares estimator of H and

$$\begin{aligned}\hat{\boldsymbol{\delta}}_i &= (Z_i'MZ_i)^{-1}Z_i'M\mathbf{y}_i \\ &= (\hat{H}'X'X\hat{H})^{-1}\hat{H}'X'\mathbf{y}_i\end{aligned} \tag{15.6.4}$$

is the 2SLS estimator of $\boldsymbol{\delta}_i$, where $M = X(X'X)^{-1}X'$. An estimate of the entire reduced form coefficient matrix Π can be built by estimating $\boldsymbol{\pi}_i$, $i = 1, 2, \ldots, M$, column by column.

In practice, the forecast value of $\mathbf{y}_i$, or $\hat{\mathbf{y}}_i = X\tilde{\boldsymbol{\pi}}_i$, can be calculated in two stages. In the first stage Z_i is regressed on X to obtain the calculated values $\hat{Z}_i = X(X'X)^{-1}X'Z_i$. In the second stage $\mathbf{y}_i$ is regressed on $\hat{Z}_i$ to obtain the calculated values of $\mathbf{y}_i$,

$$\begin{aligned}\hat{\mathbf{y}}_i &= \hat{Z}_i(\hat{Z}_i'\hat{Z}_i)^{-1}\hat{Z}_i'\mathbf{y}_i \\ &= X(X'X)^{-1}X'Z_i[Z_i'X(X'X)^{-1}X'Z_i]^{-1}Z_i'X(X'X)^{-1}X'\mathbf{y}_i \\ &= X\hat{H}\hat{\boldsymbol{\delta}}_i\end{aligned} \tag{15.6.5}$$

Kakwani and Court (1972) showed that the partially restricted reduced form estimates can be regarded as a first approximation to the derived reduced form coefficients. An iterative procedure is thus proposed. The initially estimated $\hat{\Pi}$

(built from the $\hat{\boldsymbol{\pi}}_i$)implies a new $\hat{H} = \left(\hat{\Pi}\begin{pmatrix} I \\ 0 \end{pmatrix}\right)$, which may be used to obtain a new $\hat{\boldsymbol{\pi}}_i = H\hat{\boldsymbol{\delta}}_i$. The process is repeated until it has converged.

An alternative iterative procedure is to incorporate the new $\hat{\boldsymbol{\delta}}_i = (\hat{H}'X'X\hat{H})^{-1}\hat{H}'X'\mathbf{y}_i$ in addition to the new $\hat{H}$ in updating $\hat{\boldsymbol{\pi}}_i = \hat{H}\hat{\boldsymbol{\delta}}_i$. Note that this iteration method changes the estimates of the structural parameters. An empirical study by Nagar (1959) shows unsatisfactory results in certain cases.

Under the assumptions that X is nonstochastic and has full column rank, and that $\mathbf{e}_i$ is normally distributed with $E[\mathbf{e}_i] = \mathbf{0}$ and $E[\mathbf{e}_i\mathbf{e}_i'] = \sigma_{ii}I$, the estimator $\hat{\boldsymbol{\pi}}_i$ described above is biased to order $1/T$. For the moment matrix of $\hat{\boldsymbol{\pi}}_i$, see Kakwani and Court (1972). Other work on the partially restricted reduced form can be found in Knight (1977), Nagar and Sahay (1978), Sant (1978), Swamy and Mehta (1980, 1981), and McCarthy (1981).

Court (1973) proposes a method of estimating the parameters of some (or all) of the reduced form equations jointly, by 3SLS, with the parameters of some (or all) of the structural equations. Specifically, let several of the structural equations $\mathbf{y}_i = Z_i\boldsymbol{\delta}_i + \mathbf{e}_i$ be stated as

$$\mathbf{y}_s = Z_s\boldsymbol{\delta}_s + \mathbf{e}_s$$

where the subscript s refers to the fact that not all M equations may be present. Similarly, several of the reduced form equations $\mathbf{y}_j = X\boldsymbol{\pi}_j + \mathbf{v}_j$ can be jointly written as

$$\mathbf{y}_R = (I_R \otimes X)\boldsymbol{\pi}_R + \mathbf{v}_R$$

where again the subscript R implies that not all of the reduced form equations may be present. If these two equations are written jointly as

$$\begin{bmatrix} \mathbf{y}_s \\ \mathbf{y}_R \end{bmatrix} = \begin{bmatrix} Z_s & 0 \\ 0 & I_R \otimes X \end{bmatrix} \begin{bmatrix} \boldsymbol{\delta}_s \\ \boldsymbol{\pi}_R \end{bmatrix} + \begin{bmatrix} \mathbf{e}_s \\ \mathbf{v}_R \end{bmatrix} \tag{15.6.6}$$

and then estimated by 3SLS, Court shows that the resulting estimates of the structural parameters are unaffected by the presence of the reduced form equations, but the estimators of the reduced form parameters are more efficient than the estimators of the reduced form parameters by least squares. He also shows that if $\mathbf{y}_s$ and $\mathbf{y}_R$ are complete and contain all the endogenous variables in the system, the resulting estimators of the structural parameters are simply the 3SLS estimates and the estimators of the reduced form parameters are the derived reduced form estimators from the 3SLS estimators of the structural parameters. One convenience of this approach is a formula for the covariance matrix of the derived reduced form parameter estimators that appears easier to compute than that of Goldberger, Nagar, and Odeh (1961).

Maasoumi (1978) proposes to combine the corresponding restricted 3SLS and the unrestricted least squares estimators for the reduced form coefficients to obtain a modified Stein-like estimator. The proposed estimator is

$$\hat{\Pi}_{\text{MS}} = \lambda\hat{\Pi}_{\text{3SLS}} + (1 - \lambda)\hat{\Pi}_{\text{OLS}} \tag{15.6.7}$$

where $\hat{\Pi}_{\text{3SLS}} = -\hat{B}\hat{\Gamma}^{-1}$ with $\hat{B}$ and $\hat{\Gamma}$ obtained from 3SLS, $\hat{\Pi}_{\text{OLS}} = (X'X)^{-1}X'Y$, and the value of λ is

$$\lambda = \begin{cases} 1 & \text{if } \phi^* \leq c_p \\ \left(\dfrac{\phi_2}{\phi^*}\right)^{1/2} \quad \text{or} \quad \left(\dfrac{\phi_2}{\phi^*}\right) & \text{if } \phi^* > c_p \end{cases} \tag{15.6.8}$$

depending on (1) the chosen critical value c_p of the test of the validity of the parameter constraints (and specification) on reduced form parameters, and (2) the value of the test statistic

$$\phi^* = \text{tr}[W^{-1}(\hat{\Pi}_{\text{OLS}} - \hat{\Pi}_{\text{3SLS}})'(Z'Z)(\hat{\Pi}_{\text{OLS}} - \hat{\Pi}_{\text{3SLS}})] \tag{15.6.9}$$

which is asymptotically $\chi^2_{(N)}$, with N equal to the total number of overidentifying restrictions in the system, and (3) the value of ϕ_2, which is less than c_p and may be chosen so as to minimize a desired quadratic loss measure.

The similarity of $\hat{\Pi}_{\text{MS}}$ to the Stein-like estimators is seen from the following:

$$\begin{aligned} \hat{\Pi}_{\text{MS}} &= \hat{\Pi}_{\text{3SLS}} + (1 - \lambda)(\hat{\Pi}_{\text{OLS}} - \hat{\Pi}_{\text{3SLS}}) \\ &= \hat{\Pi}_{\text{3SLS}} + I_{(c_p,\infty)}(\phi^*)(1 - \phi_2/\phi^*)(\hat{\Pi}_{\text{OLS}} - \hat{\Pi}_{\text{3SLS}}) \end{aligned} \tag{15.6.10}$$

in which $I_{(c_p,\infty)}(\phi^*) = 1$ if the argument ϕ^* falls within (c_p,∞) and zero otherwise. The combined OLS–3SLS estimator for Π can be seen to be the same as that derived from 3SLS when the model is correctly specified, but is closer to the direct OLS estimates of Π when the specification is less reliable.

Maasoumi (1978) shows that whereas the restricted (derived) 3SLS and 2SLS reduced form estimates possess no finite moments, the modified Stein-like reduced form estimator $\hat{\Pi}_{\text{MS}}$ has finite moments of up to order $(T - M - K)$. For a discussion of the existence of moments, see Section 15.4. He argues that the difference between $\hat{\Pi}_{\text{MS}}$ and $\hat{\Pi}_{\text{3SLS}}$ is asymptotically negligible and Monte Carlo experiments support the above observations [Maasoumi (1977)].

15.7 METHODS FOR NONLINEAR SYSTEMS

In many empirical studies structural equations cannot be properly represented by a system of equations linear in both parameters and variables. This section deals with the estimation of a system of equations that are nonlinear in the parameters and/or the variables. We assume in line with Section 14.5.3 that the equations to be estimated are identified.

15.7.1 Single Equation Methods

Amemiya (1974a) considers a general class of nonlinear regression equations

$$y_{ti} = f_{ti}(\mathbf{z}_{ti}, \boldsymbol{\delta}_i) + e_{ti} \tag{15.7.1}$$

where y_{ti} is a scalar random variable, e_{ti} is a scalar random variable with zero mean and constant variance σ_{ii}, $\mathbf{z}_{ti}$ is a $[(m_i + k_i) \times 1]$ vector of m_i endogenous variables and k_i exogenous variables, $\boldsymbol{\delta}_i$ is a $(g \times 1)$ vector of unknown parameters, and f_{ti} is a nonlinear function in both $\mathbf{z}_{ti}$ and $\boldsymbol{\delta}_i$ having continuous first and second derivatives with respect to $\boldsymbol{\delta}_i$.

The nonlinear two stage least squares estimator (NL2SLS) of $\boldsymbol{\delta}_i$ is defined by Amemiya (1974a) as the value of $\boldsymbol{\delta}_i$ that minimizes

$$\mathbf{e}_i' D(D'D)^{-1}D'\mathbf{e}_i = (\mathbf{y}_i - \mathbf{f}_i)'D(D'D)^{-1}D'(\mathbf{y}_i - \mathbf{f}_i) \tag{15.7.2}$$

where $\mathbf{e}_i$, $\mathbf{y}_i$, and $\mathbf{f}_i$ are $(T \times 1)$ vectors of elements e_{ti}, y_{ti}, and $f_{ti}(\mathbf{z}_{ti}, \boldsymbol{\delta}_i)$, respectively, and D is a $(T \times K)$ matrix of certain constants with rank K. The matrix D may consist of low-order polynomials of all exogenous variables of the system, as in Kelejian's (1971) model that is nonlinear in only the variables, or just all the exogenous variables of the system, as in the usual linear model or that of Zellner, Huang, and Chau (1965), which is nonlinear only in the parameters. Under the assumption that the elements of $\mathbf{e}_i$ are independent, plus others concerning the limiting behavior of the derivatives of $\mathbf{f}_i$ and the matrix D, Amemiya shows that the NL2SLS estimator $\hat{\boldsymbol{\delta}}_i$ converges in probability to the true value of $\boldsymbol{\delta}_i$, $\boldsymbol{\delta}_i^*$, and $\sqrt{T}(\hat{\boldsymbol{\delta}}_i - \boldsymbol{\delta}_i^*)$ converges in distribution to

$$N\left\{\mathbf{0}, \sigma_{ii}\left[\text{plim}\,\frac{1}{T}\left(\frac{\partial \mathbf{f}_i'}{\partial \boldsymbol{\delta}_i}\bigg|_{\boldsymbol{\delta}_i^*}\right) D(D'D)^{-1}D'\left(\frac{\partial \mathbf{f}_i}{\partial \boldsymbol{\delta}_i'}\bigg|_{\boldsymbol{\delta}_i^*}\right)\right]^{-1}\right\} \tag{15.7.3}$$

For the proof, see Amemiya (1974). Minimization of the criterion function (15.7.2) can be accomplished using the Gauss–Newton iterative procedure with iterations

$$\hat{\boldsymbol{\delta}}_i(n) = \hat{\boldsymbol{\delta}}_i(n-1) + \left(\frac{\partial \mathbf{f}_i'}{\partial \boldsymbol{\delta}_i} D(D'D)^{-1}D' \frac{\partial \mathbf{f}_i}{\partial \boldsymbol{\delta}_i'}\right)^{-1} \frac{\partial \mathbf{f}_i'}{\partial \boldsymbol{\delta}_i} D(D'D)^{-1}(\mathbf{y}_i - \mathbf{f}_i) \tag{15.7.4}$$

where $\mathbf{f}_i$ and $\partial \mathbf{f}_i'/\partial \boldsymbol{\delta}_i$ in the right-hand side are evaluated at $\hat{\boldsymbol{\delta}}_i(n-1)$, the estimate obtained in the $(n-1)$th iteration (see Appendix B).

The consequences of several different choices of the matrix D are examined by Amemiya (1975), who considers the special case where both simultaneity and nonlinearity appear only in the ith equation. That is,

$$\mathbf{y}_i = \mathbf{f}_i(Y_i, \boldsymbol{\delta}_i) + \mathbf{e}_i \tag{15.7.5}$$

and all other equations are linear in parameters

$$Y_i = X\Pi_i + V_i \tag{15.7.6}$$

where Y_i and V_i are $[T \times (m_i - 1)]$ matrices of random variables and Π_i is a $[k_i \times (m_i - 1)]$ matrix of unknown parameters [Amemiya (1975)]. It is additionally assumed that the rows of $(\mathbf{e}_i \quad V_i)$ are multivariate normal with mean zero and covariance matrix

$$\Sigma = \begin{bmatrix} \Sigma_{11} & \Sigma_{12} \\ \Sigma_{21} & \Sigma_{22} \end{bmatrix}$$

where subscripts refer to $\mathbf{e}_i$ and V_i. Then, using $D = X$ in (15.7.2), Amemiya called the resulting estimator the standard nonlinear two-stage least squares estimator (SNL2S), denoted as $\hat{\boldsymbol{\delta}}_{i2S}$. Choosing $D = E(\partial\mathbf{f}_i/\partial\boldsymbol{\delta}_i')$ the estimator is called the best nonlinear two-stage least squares estimator (BNL2S), denoted as $\hat{\boldsymbol{\delta}}_{iB}$.

The asymptotic covariance matrix of $\hat{\boldsymbol{\delta}}_{i2S}$ is given by

$$V_{2S} = \Sigma_{11} \text{ plim } TH^{-1} \tag{15.7.7}$$

where

$$H = \frac{\partial\mathbf{f}_i'}{\partial\boldsymbol{\delta}_i} X(X'X)^{-1}X' \frac{\partial\mathbf{f}_i}{\partial\boldsymbol{\delta}_i'} \tag{15.7.8}$$

The asymptotic covariance matrix of $\hat{\boldsymbol{\delta}}_{iB}$ is given by

$$V_B = \Sigma_{11} \text{ plim } T\left[E\left(\frac{\partial\mathbf{f}_i'}{\partial\boldsymbol{\delta}_i}\right) E\left(\frac{\partial\mathbf{f}_i}{\partial\boldsymbol{\delta}_i'}\right)\right]^{-1} \tag{15.7.9}$$

Amemiya shows that $V_B \leq V_{2S}$. However, SNL2S may be practically more useful than BNL2S because $E(\partial\mathbf{f}_i'/\partial\boldsymbol{\delta}_i)$ does not always exist or may be difficult to find. Moreover, SNL2S is consistent with the spirit of limited information estimation whereas BNL2S is not. In the linear case, both SNL2S and BNL2S reduce to the usual 2SLS estimator.

To obtain the nonlinear limited-information maximum likelihood estimator (NLLI), we write the log likelihood function as

$$L^{**} = -(T/2)\ln|\Sigma| - (1/2)\operatorname{tr}\Sigma^{-1}S$$

where

$$S = \begin{bmatrix} \mathbf{e}_i'\mathbf{e}_i & \mathbf{e}_i'V_i \\ V_i'\mathbf{e}_i & V_i'V_i \end{bmatrix}$$

Solving $\partial L^{**}/\partial\Sigma = 0$ for Σ, we get

$$\Sigma = S/T$$

Inserting $\Sigma = S/T$ into L^{**}, we obtain the concentrated likelihood function

$$L^* = -(T/2)(\ln \mathbf{e}_i'\mathbf{e}_i + \ln|V_i'AV_i|)$$

where

$$A = I - \mathbf{e}_i(\mathbf{e}_i'\mathbf{e}_i)^{-1}\mathbf{e}_i'$$

Solving $\partial L^*/\partial\Pi_i = 0$ for Π_i, we obtain

$$\Pi_i = (X'AX)^{-1}X'AY_i$$

Inserting $\Pi_i = (X'AX)^{-1}X'AY_i$ into L^*, we obtain the further concentrated likelihood function

$$L = -(T/2)[\ln \mathbf{e}_i'\mathbf{e}_i + \ln|Y_i'AY_i - Y_i'AX(X'AX)^{-1}X'AY_i|]$$

The NLLI of $\boldsymbol{\delta}_i$, denoted by $\hat{\boldsymbol{\delta}}_{iLI}$ is the value of $\boldsymbol{\delta}_i$ that maximizes L. The asymptotic covariance matrix of $\hat{\boldsymbol{\delta}}_{iLI}$ is

$$V_{LI} = \text{plim } T[\Sigma_{11}^{*-1}G - (\Sigma_{11}^{*-1} - \Sigma_{11}^{-1})H]^{-1}$$

where

$$\Sigma_{11}^* = \Sigma_{11} - \Sigma_{12}\Sigma_{22}^{-1}\Sigma_{21}$$

and

$$G = \frac{\partial \mathbf{f}_i'}{\partial \boldsymbol{\delta}_i}[I - V_i(V_i'V_i)^{-1}V_i']\frac{\partial \mathbf{f}_i}{\partial \boldsymbol{\delta}_i'}$$

It can be shown that $V_{LI} \leq V_B$, that is, $V_B - V_{LI}$ is positive semidefinite.

The maximization of L may be carried out using an iterative technique. Because of the particular form of the likelihood function L^*, the maximum likelihood estimator of $\boldsymbol{\delta}_i$ given Π_i is the value of $\boldsymbol{\delta}_i$ that minimizes

$$\phi(\boldsymbol{\delta}_i,\Pi_i) = (\mathbf{y}_i - \mathbf{f}_i)'[I - V_i(V_i'V_i)^{-1}V_i'](\mathbf{y}_i - \mathbf{f}_i)$$

Consequently, the following iterative procedure can be followed: Estimate Π_i initially by $\hat{\Pi}_i = (X'X)^{-1}X'Y_i$. Insert that value into $\phi(\boldsymbol{\delta}_i,\Pi_i)$ and find the value of $\boldsymbol{\delta}_i$ that minimizes $\phi(\boldsymbol{\delta}_i,\hat{\Pi}_i)$. Use that value of $\boldsymbol{\delta}_i$ to obtain the value for $\mathbf{e}_i$, then A and then $\hat{\Pi}_i = (X'AX)^{-1}X'AY_i$, the second round estimator of Π_i. Repeat the procedure until convergence. The second round estimator described above is called by Amemiya (1975) the modified nonlinear two-stage least squares estimator (MNL2S) denoted by $\hat{\boldsymbol{\delta}}_{iM}$. It is equivalent to the value $\hat{\boldsymbol{\delta}}_{iM}$ that minimizes

$$\phi(\boldsymbol{\delta}_i, \hat{\Pi}_i) = (\mathbf{y}_i - \mathbf{f}_i)'[I - MY_i(Y_i'MY_i)^{-1}Y_i'M](\mathbf{y}_i - \mathbf{f}_i)$$

where $M = I - X(X'X)^{-1}X'$. It can be shown that in the linear case, MNL2S is identical to the 2SLS estimator. The asymptotic covariance matrix of $\hat{\boldsymbol{\delta}}_{iM}$ is

$$V_{\mathrm{M}} = \operatorname{plim} TG^{-1}[\Sigma_{11}^{*}G + (\Sigma_{11} - \Sigma_{11}^{*})H]G^{-1}$$

It can also be shown that $V_{\mathrm{LI}} \leq V_{\mathrm{M}} \leq V_{\mathrm{B}} \leq V_{2\mathrm{S}}$ in the nonlinear case in general. In the linear case, they have the same asymptotic variance, and the estimators NLLI, MNL2S, and BNL2S are identical for every sample. Thus, NLLI and MNL2S are recommended by Amemiya (1975) in the limited information context. For a computational simplification of NLLI, see Raduchel (1978).

15.7.2 Systems Methods

For a system method, all of the M structural equations are considered simultaneously in estimation. A system of M nonlinear structural equations can be written as

$$f_{ti}(\mathbf{y}_t', \mathbf{x}_t', \boldsymbol{\delta}_i) = e_{ti}, \qquad i = 1, 2, \ldots, M$$
$$t = 1, 2, \ldots, T \qquad (15.7.10)$$

where $\mathbf{y}_t$ is an M-dimensional vector of endogenous variables, $\mathbf{x}_t$ is a vector of exogenous variables, and $\boldsymbol{\delta}_i$ is a vector of unknown parameters. We assume that the Jacobian of the system is nonvanishing in a domain containing the observations $\mathbf{y}_t$, or

$$\det|J_t| = \det\left(\frac{\partial f_{ti}}{\partial y_{tj}}\right) \neq 0$$

so that it is possible to find the reduced form of the system. A likelihood function based on a multivariate normal distribution for e_{ti} with zero mean and the nonsingular covariance matrix $\Sigma = [\sigma_{ij}]$ is

$$L^{**}(\boldsymbol{\delta},\Sigma|\mathbf{y}_t,\mathbf{x}_t) = (2\pi)^{-TM/2}(\det \Sigma)^{-T/2} \prod_{t=1}^{T} |\det J_t| \exp\left(-\frac{1}{2}\sum_{tij} f_{ti}\sigma^{ij}f_{tj}\right)$$

where σ^{ij} is the (i,j)th element of Σ^{-1} and Σ_{tij} denotes a triple summation. The logarithmic likelihood function may be written

$$L^* = -\left(\frac{T}{2}\right) \ln|\Sigma| + \sum_{t=1}^{T} \ln \left\|\frac{\partial \mathbf{f}_t}{\partial \mathbf{y}_t'}\right\| - \frac{1}{2}\sum_{t=1}^{T} \mathbf{f}_t'\Sigma^{-1}\mathbf{f}_t$$

where $\mathbf{f}_t = (f_{t1}\ f_{t2}\ .\ .\ .\ f_{tM})'$, and a constant is dropped. Equating the partial derivatives of L^* with respect to Σ to zero, we obtain

$$\Sigma = T^{-1} \sum_{t=1}^{T} \mathbf{f}_t\mathbf{f}_t' \tag{15.7.11}$$

Inserting (15.7.11) into L^*, we obtain the concentrated likelihood function

$$L = \sum_{t=1}^{T} \ln \left\|\frac{\partial \mathbf{f}_t}{\partial \mathbf{y}_t'}\right\| - \left(\frac{T}{2}\right) \ln \left|T^{-1} \sum_{t=1}^{T} \mathbf{f}_t\mathbf{f}_t'\right| \tag{15.7.12}$$

The maximum likelihood estimator of $\boldsymbol{\delta}_i$ is defined as a root of the equation $\partial L/\partial \boldsymbol{\delta} = \mathbf{0}$ provided that it exists, where $\boldsymbol{\delta}' = (\boldsymbol{\delta}_1'\ \boldsymbol{\delta}_2'\ .\ .\ .\ \boldsymbol{\delta}_M')$. Amemiya (1977) has proved that at least one root exists and that asymptotically one of the roots, denoted by $\hat{\boldsymbol{\delta}}_{SM}$, is consistent. The consistency proof depends on the assumption of normality. The maximum likelihood estimator $\hat{\boldsymbol{\delta}}$ is such that $\sqrt{T}(\hat{\boldsymbol{\delta}} - \boldsymbol{\delta}^*)$ converges in distribution to

$$N\left[\mathbf{0}, -\text{plim}\ T^{-1}\left(\left.\frac{\partial^2 L}{\partial \boldsymbol{\delta}\, \partial \boldsymbol{\delta}'}\right|_{\boldsymbol{\delta}^*}\right)^{-1}\right]$$

where $\boldsymbol{\delta}^*$ is the true parameter vector.

Computation of the maximum likelihood estimator can be done iteratively. The gradient class of iteration methods may be represented as

$$\hat{\boldsymbol{\delta}}(2) = \hat{\boldsymbol{\delta}}(1) - A\left(\left.\frac{\partial L}{\partial \boldsymbol{\delta}}\right|_{\hat{\boldsymbol{\delta}}(1)}\right)$$

where $\hat{\boldsymbol{\delta}}(1)$ is an initial estimator and A is some positive definite matrix that may be stochastic. Amemiya (1977) proposes iterations

$$\hat{\boldsymbol{\delta}}(2) = \hat{\boldsymbol{\delta}}(1) - [\hat{G}'(\hat{\Sigma}^{-1} \otimes I)G]^{-1}\hat{G}'(\hat{\Sigma}^{-1} \otimes I)\mathbf{f} \tag{15.7.13}$$

where

$$G = \text{diag}(G_1, G_2, \ldots, G_M)$$

$$\hat{G} = \text{diag}(\hat{G}_1, \hat{G}_2, \ldots, \hat{G}_M)$$

$$G_i = \text{the matrix whose } i\text{th row is } \partial f_{ti}/\partial \boldsymbol{\delta}_i'$$

$$\hat{G}_i = G_i' - T^{-1}\sum \frac{\partial f_{ti}}{\partial \mathbf{e}\, \partial \mathbf{e}'} F'$$

$$F = \text{the } (T \times M) \text{ matrix whose } (i,j)\text{th element is } f_{ti}$$

$$\mathbf{e} = (\mathbf{e}_1' \ \mathbf{e}_2' \ . \ . \ . \ \mathbf{e}_M')'$$

$$\mathbf{f} = (\mathbf{f}_1' \ \mathbf{f}_2' \ . \ . \ . \ \mathbf{f}_M')' = \text{vec}(F)$$

and

$$\hat{\Sigma} = T^{-1}F'F$$

Amemiya has shown that the asymptotic distribution of the second round estimator in the above iteration depends on the asymptotic distribution of the initial estimator and is not asymptotically efficient. Although (15.7.13) may not be a good method of iteration, it serves to demonstrate a certain similarity between the maximum likelihood estimator and the nonlinear three stage least squares estimator (NL3S) that is discussed below.

Extending the result of NL2S described in Section 15.7.1, Jorgenson and Laffont (1974) defined the NL3S as the value of $\boldsymbol{\delta}$ that minimizes

$$\mathbf{f}(\boldsymbol{\delta})'[\hat{\Sigma}^{-1} \otimes X(X'X)^{-1}X']\mathbf{f}(\boldsymbol{\delta})$$

where $\hat{\Sigma}$ is some consistent estimator of Σ, and X is a matrix of exogenous variables that may not coincide with the exogenous variables that appear originally as the arguments of $\mathbf{f}$. The asymptotic variance-covariance matrix is given by

$$\left[\text{plim } T^{-1} \left(\frac{\partial \mathbf{f}'}{\partial \boldsymbol{\delta}}\bigg|_{\boldsymbol{\delta}^*}\right) [\Sigma^{-1} \otimes X(X'X)^{-1}X'] \left(\frac{\partial \mathbf{f}}{\partial \boldsymbol{\delta}'}\bigg|_{\boldsymbol{\delta}^*}\right)\right]^{-1}$$

Amemiya (1977) further extends the definition of NL3S to be the value of $\boldsymbol{\delta}$ that minimizes $\mathbf{f}'A\mathbf{f}$, where A could take any of the following three forms:

$$A_1 = \hat{\Lambda}^{-1/2}S_1(S_1'S_1)^{-1}S_1'\hat{\Lambda}^{-1/2}$$

$$A_2 = S_2(S_2'\hat{\Lambda}S_2)^{-1}S_2'$$

and

$$A_3 = \hat{\Lambda}^{-1}S_3(S_3'\hat{\Lambda}^{-1}S_3)^{-1}S_3'\hat{\Lambda}^{-1}$$

where S_1, S_2, and S_3 are matrices of at least asymptotically nonstochastic variables and $\hat{\Lambda} = \hat{\Sigma} \otimes I$. The general asymptotic-covariance matrix is

$$\left[\text{plim } T^{-1} \left(\frac{\partial \mathbf{f}'}{\partial \boldsymbol{\delta}}\bigg|_{\boldsymbol{\delta}^*}\right) A \left(\frac{\partial \mathbf{f}}{\partial \boldsymbol{\delta}'}\bigg|_{\boldsymbol{\delta}^*}\right)\right]^{-1} \qquad (15.7.14)$$

If we choose S_1, S_2, and S_3 to be $S_1 = S_2 = S_3 = (I \otimes X)$, all three formulations A_1, A_2, and A_3 are equal and the estimators reduce to Jorgenson-Laffont's NL3S. For all A_1, A_2, and A_3, the lower bound of the covariance matrix (15.7.14) is equal to

$$\left[\lim T^{-1}E\left(\frac{\partial \mathbf{f}'}{\partial \boldsymbol{\delta}}\bigg|_{\delta^*}\right)(\Sigma^{-1} \otimes I)E\left(\frac{\partial \mathbf{f}}{\partial \boldsymbol{\delta}'}\bigg|_{\delta^*}\right)\right]^{-1}$$

which can be attained when

$$S_1 = \Lambda^{-1/2}E(\partial \mathbf{f}/\partial \boldsymbol{\delta}')$$

$$S_2 = \Lambda^{-1}E(\partial \mathbf{f}/\partial \boldsymbol{\delta}')$$

and

$$S_3 = E(\partial \mathbf{f}/\partial \boldsymbol{\delta}')$$

where $\boldsymbol{\delta}$ that appears in $E(\partial \mathbf{f}/\partial \boldsymbol{\delta}')$ is assumed estimated consistently. Thus, the estimator whose covariance attains the lower bound is called the best nonlinear three-stage least squares estimator or BNL3S. As mentioned in Section 15.7.1, $E(\partial \mathbf{f}/\partial \boldsymbol{\delta}')$ is difficult to obtain in explicit form, and thus BNL3S is often not a practical estimator. Besides, BNL3S is asymptotically less efficient than the maximum likelihood estimator. For a proof, see Amemiya (1977). However, NL3S is more robust against nonnormality because it is consistent, provided the error term has mean zero and certain higher order finite moments, whereas the consistency of the maximum likelihood estimator in the nonlinear model depends crucially on the normality assumption.

The similarity of NL3S and the maximum likelihood estimator is seen from the Gauss–Newton iteration to obtain the BNL3S:

$$\hat{\boldsymbol{\delta}}(2) = \hat{\boldsymbol{\delta}}(1) - [\bar{G}'(\hat{\Sigma}^{-1} \otimes I)\bar{G}]^{-1}\bar{G}'(\hat{\Sigma}^{-1} \otimes I)\mathbf{f}$$

where $\bar{G}' = \text{diag}(\bar{G}_1', \bar{G}_2', \ldots, \bar{G}_M')$, and $\bar{G}_i' = E[G_i']$. The resulting NL3S is asymptotically less efficient than the BNL3S but is much more practical.

The NL3S has been extended to the estimation of the parameters of a system of simultaneous, nonlinear, implicit equations in the recent literature. Within this context, it is not assumed that it is possible to write one endogenous variable in each structural equation explicitly in terms of the remaining variables of the system and nonlinear parametric restrictions across equations are permitted. Interested readers should refer to Gallant (1977), Gallant and Jorgenson (1979), and Gallant and Holly (1980).

For the case of nonlinearity in the parameters, a nonlinear 3SLS and a nonlinear full information instrumental variables estimator are proposed by Hausman (1975). A system of M simultaneous equations with nonlinearity only in the parameters can be written as

$$Y\Gamma(\boldsymbol{\alpha}) + XB(\boldsymbol{\alpha}) = \mathbf{E}$$

or

$$\mathbf{y}_i = Y_i\boldsymbol{\gamma}_i(\boldsymbol{\alpha}) + X_i\boldsymbol{\beta}_i(\boldsymbol{\alpha}) + \mathbf{e}_i,\ i = 1, 2, \ldots, M$$

where $\Gamma(\boldsymbol{\alpha})$ and $B(\boldsymbol{\alpha})$ denote matrices, and $\boldsymbol{\gamma}_i(\boldsymbol{\alpha})$ and $\boldsymbol{\beta}_i'(\boldsymbol{\alpha})$ denote vectors with each element a function of a $(g \times 1)$ parameter vector $\boldsymbol{\alpha}$. The system can be written compactly as

$$\mathbf{y} = Z\boldsymbol{\delta}(\boldsymbol{\alpha}) + \mathbf{e}$$

where $\boldsymbol{\delta}(\boldsymbol{\alpha}) = (\boldsymbol{\delta}_1'(\boldsymbol{\alpha})\ \boldsymbol{\delta}_2'(\boldsymbol{\alpha}) \ldots \boldsymbol{\delta}_M'(\boldsymbol{\alpha}))'$ and $\boldsymbol{\delta}_i(\boldsymbol{\alpha}) = (\boldsymbol{\gamma}_i(\boldsymbol{\alpha})\ \boldsymbol{\beta}_i(\boldsymbol{\alpha}))'$. An example of such a system is a linear simultaneous equations model with autoregressive errors. Other examples are partial adjustment or distributed lag models containing a desired stock that is a function of structural parameters. The log likelihood function of the elements of $(\boldsymbol{\alpha},\Sigma)$ is

$$\begin{aligned} L(\boldsymbol{\alpha},\Sigma) = {} & \text{const.} + (T/2)\ln\det(\Sigma^{-1}) + T\ln\det\Gamma(\boldsymbol{\alpha}) \\ & - (T/2)\,\mathrm{tr}\{T^{-1}\Sigma^{-1}[Y\Gamma(\boldsymbol{\alpha}) + XB(\boldsymbol{\alpha})]'[Y\Gamma(\boldsymbol{\alpha}) + XB(\boldsymbol{\alpha})]\} \end{aligned}$$

Solving the first-order conditions for $\boldsymbol{\alpha}$ and Σ yields the following nonlinear iterative equation:

$$\hat{\boldsymbol{\alpha}}_{(k+1)} - \hat{\boldsymbol{\alpha}}_{(k)} = \left[\bar{\bar{W}}_{(k)}'Z\left(\frac{\partial\boldsymbol{\delta}(\boldsymbol{\alpha})}{\partial\boldsymbol{\alpha}}\bigg|_{\hat{\boldsymbol{\alpha}}_{(k)}}\right)\right]^{-1}\bar{\bar{W}}_{(k)}'(\mathbf{y}\text{-}Z\boldsymbol{\delta}(\hat{\boldsymbol{\alpha}}_{(k)}))$$

where the instruments are

$$\bar{\bar{W}}_{(k)}' = \left[\hat{Z}\left(\frac{\partial\boldsymbol{\delta}(\boldsymbol{\alpha})}{\partial\boldsymbol{\alpha}}\bigg|_{\hat{\boldsymbol{\alpha}}_{(k)}}\right)\right]'(S \otimes I_T)^{-1}$$

and $Z(\partial\boldsymbol{\delta}(\boldsymbol{\alpha})/\partial\boldsymbol{\alpha}|_{\hat{\boldsymbol{\alpha}}_{(k)}})$ is a $(TM \times g)$ matrix of derivatives evaluated at the kth estimate of $\boldsymbol{\alpha}$. The elements of $\bar{\bar{W}}_{(k)}'$ are

$$\begin{aligned} \hat{Z} &= \mathrm{diag}(\hat{Z}_1, \hat{Z}_2, \ldots, \hat{Z}_M) \\ \hat{Z}_i &= [X(\hat{B}(\boldsymbol{\alpha})\hat{\Gamma}(\boldsymbol{\alpha})^{-1})_i\quad X_i] \end{aligned}$$

and

$$S = T^{-1}[Y\hat{\Gamma}(\boldsymbol{\alpha}) + X\hat{B}(\boldsymbol{\alpha})]'[Y\hat{\Gamma}(\boldsymbol{\alpha}) + X\hat{B}(\boldsymbol{\alpha})]$$

Calculation of the FIML estimator follows:

Step 1 Choose an arbitrary vector $\boldsymbol{\alpha}_0$ for $\boldsymbol{\alpha}$.

Step 2 Form $\boldsymbol{\delta}(\boldsymbol{\alpha})$, $\hat{Z}$, and S.

Step 3 Calculate $Z(\partial\boldsymbol{\delta}(\boldsymbol{\alpha})/\partial\boldsymbol{\alpha})$ and $\hat{Z}(\partial\boldsymbol{\delta}(\boldsymbol{\alpha})/\partial\boldsymbol{\alpha})$ evaluated at $\boldsymbol{\alpha}_0$.

Step 4 Form the instruments $\bar{\bar{W}}_{(k)}$ and calculate the new $\hat{\boldsymbol{\alpha}}_{(1)}$.

Repeat steps 2 through 4 until $\hat{\boldsymbol{\alpha}}_{(k)}$ converges. The result is the NLFIML estimator $\hat{\boldsymbol{\alpha}}_{\text{NLM}}$. A consistent estimate of the covariance matrix of $\hat{\boldsymbol{\alpha}}_{\text{NLM}}$ is $[(\hat{Z}\partial\boldsymbol{\delta}(\boldsymbol{\alpha})/\partial\boldsymbol{\alpha})'(S \otimes I_T)^{-1}(\hat{Z}\partial\boldsymbol{\delta}(\boldsymbol{\alpha})/\partial\boldsymbol{\alpha})]^{-1}$.

By analogy, a nonlinear 3SLS or NL3SLS estimator $\tilde{\boldsymbol{\alpha}}$ may be defined as

$$\tilde{\boldsymbol{\alpha}}_{(k+1)} - \tilde{\boldsymbol{\alpha}}_{(k)} = \left[\tilde{W}'_{(k)}Z\left(\frac{\partial\boldsymbol{\delta}(\boldsymbol{\alpha})}{\partial\boldsymbol{\alpha}}\bigg|_{\tilde{\boldsymbol{\alpha}}_{(k)}}\right)\right]^{-1}\tilde{W}'_{(k)}(\mathbf{y}\text{-}Z\boldsymbol{\delta}(\tilde{\boldsymbol{\alpha}}_{(k)}))$$

with instruments

$$\tilde{W}'_{(k)} = \left[\hat{Z}\left(\frac{\partial\boldsymbol{\delta}(\boldsymbol{\alpha})}{\partial\boldsymbol{\alpha}}\bigg|_{\tilde{\boldsymbol{\alpha}}_{(k)}}\right)\right]'(\tilde{S}^{-1} \otimes X(X'X)^{-1}X')$$

where $\tilde{S}$ is a consistent estimate of Σ. The NL3SLS and FIML are asymptotically equivalent. A consistent estimator of the asymptotic covariance matrix of $\tilde{\boldsymbol{\alpha}}$ is

$$\{[\hat{Z}(\partial\boldsymbol{\delta}(\boldsymbol{\alpha})/\partial\boldsymbol{\alpha}|_{\tilde{\boldsymbol{\alpha}}})]'(\tilde{S}^{-1} \otimes X(X'X)^{-1}X')[\hat{Z}(\partial\boldsymbol{\delta}(\boldsymbol{\alpha})/\partial\boldsymbol{\alpha}|_{\tilde{\boldsymbol{\alpha}}})]\}^{-1}$$

For a variation of instrumental variable construction and interpretation see Hausman (1975). For the discussion of inconsistency of FIML in the non-linear case when equation errors are not normal, see Hausman (1983).

15.8 BAYESIAN METHODS

In the sampling theory approach, the a priori restrictions are imposed in exact form, through equalities or inequalities with known coefficients, and certain parameters are left completely unrestricted. However, the a priori information provided by economic theory is often not of such an exact nature and might be better reflected in probabilistic statements. The Bayesian approach allows the flexibility of stochastic restrictions reflecting the imprecise nature of the prior information. In estimation, we assume that the parameters of the equations to be estimated are identified in the sense that the posterior pdf of the parameters is unique. In the following section we will discuss the single equation, limited information, and full system Bayesian analysis. For a discussion of Bayesian inference the reader should review Chapter 4.

15.8.1 Single Equation Bayesian Analysis

Using the notation defined in Section 15.2, consider the ith structural equation of an M-equation model

$$
\begin{aligned}
\mathbf{y}_i &= Y_i\boldsymbol{\gamma}_i + Y_i^*\boldsymbol{\gamma}_i^* + X_i\boldsymbol{\beta}_i + X_i^*\boldsymbol{\beta}_i^* + \mathbf{e}_i \\
&= Y_i\boldsymbol{\gamma}_i + X_i\boldsymbol{\beta}_i + \mathbf{e}_i
\end{aligned} \tag{15.8.1}
$$

where $\boldsymbol{\gamma}_i^* = \mathbf{0}$ and $\boldsymbol{\beta}_i^* = \mathbf{0}$ are identifying restrictions. The reduced form equations for Y_i are

$$
Y_i = X\Pi_i + V_i \tag{15.8.2}
$$

and for $\mathbf{y}_i$ it is

$$
\begin{aligned}
\mathbf{y}_i &= (X\Pi_i + V_i)\boldsymbol{\gamma}_i + X_i\boldsymbol{\beta}_i + \mathbf{e}_i \\
&= X\Pi_i\boldsymbol{\gamma}_i + X_i\boldsymbol{\beta}_i + \mathbf{e}_i + V_i\boldsymbol{\gamma}_i \\
&= (X\Pi_i \quad X_i)\boldsymbol{\delta}_i + \mathbf{v}_i
\end{aligned} \tag{15.8.3}
$$

where $\mathbf{v}_i = \mathbf{e}_i + V_i\boldsymbol{\gamma}_i$. Thus for given Π_i, say $\Pi_i = \hat{\Pi}_i = (X'X)^{-1}X'Y_i$, (15.8.3) is in the form of a multiple regression model. The Bayesian approach of Chapter 4 is directly applicable.

A result following the approach taken by Drèze (1968) and Zellner (1971) is summarized in the following. Under the assumption that the rows of $(\mathbf{v}_i \quad V_i)$ are independent and $N(\mathbf{0},\Omega_i)$, the covariance matrix of $(\mathbf{e}_i \quad \mathbf{v}_i)$ or Ω_*, can be formed and the likelihood function of $\boldsymbol{\gamma}_i$, $\boldsymbol{\beta}_i$, Π_i, and Ω_*, given $\mathbf{y}_i$ and Y_i, can be constructed as

$$
\ell(\boldsymbol{\gamma}_i,\boldsymbol{\beta}_i,\Pi_i,\Omega_*|\mathbf{y}_i,Y_i) \propto |\Omega_*|^{-T/2} \exp[-\tfrac{1}{2}\operatorname{tr}(W - X\Pi_*)'(W - X\Pi_*)\Omega_*^{-1}] \tag{15.8.4}
$$

where

$$
W = (\mathbf{y}_i - Y_i\boldsymbol{\gamma}_i \quad Y_i), \qquad \Pi_* = \left[\begin{pmatrix} \boldsymbol{\beta}_i \\ \boldsymbol{\beta}_i^* \end{pmatrix} \quad \Pi_i\right]
$$

with $\boldsymbol{\beta}_i^* = \mathbf{0}$ to be incorporated in the prior pdf. The prior pdf employed is

$$
p(\boldsymbol{\gamma}_i,\boldsymbol{\beta}_i,\Pi_i,\Omega_*|\boldsymbol{\beta}_i^* = \mathbf{0}) \propto p_i|\Omega_*|^{-m_i/2} \tag{15.8.5}
$$

where $p_i \equiv p_i(\boldsymbol{\gamma}_i,\boldsymbol{\beta}_i|\boldsymbol{\beta}_i^* = \mathbf{0})$ is the prior pdf for $\boldsymbol{\gamma}_i$ and $\boldsymbol{\beta}_i$. Combining the likelihood and prior pdf we obtain the posterior pdf

$$
\begin{aligned}
&p(\boldsymbol{\gamma}_i,\boldsymbol{\beta}_i,\Pi_i,\Omega_*|\text{data and prior assumptions}) \\
&\qquad \propto p_i|\Omega_*|^{-(T+m_i)/2} \exp[-\tfrac{1}{2}\operatorname{tr}(W - X\Pi_*)'(W - X\Pi_*)\Omega_*^{-1}]
\end{aligned} \tag{15.8.6}
$$

By integrating the pdf for $\boldsymbol{\gamma}_i$, $\boldsymbol{\beta}_i$, Π_i, and Ω_* with respect to the elements of Ω_*, the resulting marginal posterior pdf for $\boldsymbol{\gamma}_i$, $\boldsymbol{\beta}_i$, and Π_i has the form of a generalized Student t pdf. If Π_i is further integrated out, the resulting marginal posterior pdf for $\boldsymbol{\delta}_i$ has the form

$$p(\boldsymbol{\delta}_i|\text{data and prior assumptions}) \propto p_i a_{ii}^{-K/2}[1 + (\boldsymbol{\delta}_i - \hat{\boldsymbol{\delta}}_i)'H(\boldsymbol{\delta}_i - \hat{\boldsymbol{\delta}}_i)]^{-(K-m_i)} \quad (15.8.7)$$

where p_i is the prior pdf of $\boldsymbol{\gamma}_i$ and $\boldsymbol{\beta}_i$, $a_{ii} = (\hat{\mathbf{v}}_i - \hat{V}_i\boldsymbol{\gamma}_i)'(\hat{\mathbf{v}}_i - \hat{V}_i\boldsymbol{\gamma}_i)$, $(\hat{\mathbf{v}}_i \quad \hat{V}_i) = (\mathbf{y}_i \quad Y_i) - X(\hat{\boldsymbol{\pi}}_i \quad \hat{\Pi}_i)$, $H = \hat{Z}_i'\hat{Z}_i/a_{ii}$, $\hat{Z}_i = (\hat{Y}_i \quad X_i)$, and $\hat{\boldsymbol{\delta}}_i$ is identical to the 2SLS estimator. If the prior pdf of $\boldsymbol{\gamma}_i$ and $\boldsymbol{\beta}_i$ is diffuse, then p_i is a constant and the marginal posterior pdf for $\boldsymbol{\delta}_i$ would be in the form of a multivariate t centered at the quantity $\boldsymbol{\delta}_i$ were it not for the fact that a_{ii} depends on $\boldsymbol{\gamma}_i$. The posterior mean of $\boldsymbol{\delta}_i$ is

$$E(\boldsymbol{\delta}_i|\mathbf{y}_i, Y_i) = \begin{bmatrix} \hat{\Pi}_i'X'X\hat{\Pi}_i & \hat{\Pi}_i'X'X_i \\ X_i'X\hat{\Pi}_i & X_i'X_i \end{bmatrix}^{-1} \begin{bmatrix} \hat{\Pi}_i'X'X\hat{\Pi}_i \\ X_i'X_i\hat{\boldsymbol{\pi}}_i \end{bmatrix} + \text{remainder} \quad (15.8.8)$$

If $\hat{\Pi}_i$ is given, the conditional posterior pdf for $\boldsymbol{\gamma}_i$ and $\boldsymbol{\beta}_i$ is in the multivariate Student t form with mean vector given by

$$\hat{\boldsymbol{\delta}}_i = \begin{bmatrix} \hat{\Pi}_i'X'X\hat{\Pi}_i & \hat{\Pi}_i'X'X_i \\ X_i'X\hat{\Pi}_i & X_i'X_i \end{bmatrix}^{-1} \begin{bmatrix} \hat{\Pi}_i'X'\mathbf{y}_i \\ X_i'\mathbf{y}_i \end{bmatrix} \quad (15.8.9)$$

which is just the 2SLS estimate. Furthermore, given $\boldsymbol{\gamma}_i$, the conditional posterior pdf for $\boldsymbol{\beta}_i$ is in the multivariate Student t form, which when integrated over $\boldsymbol{\beta}_i$ yields the marginal posterior pdf of $\boldsymbol{\gamma}_i$:

$$p(\boldsymbol{\gamma}_i|\text{data and assumptions}) \propto a_{ii}^{-(K-k_i)/2}[1 + (\boldsymbol{\gamma}_i - \hat{\boldsymbol{\gamma}}_i)'H_i(\boldsymbol{\gamma}_i - \hat{\boldsymbol{\gamma}}_i)]^{-(v+m_i)} \quad (15.8.10)$$

where $v = T - 2m_i - k_i$ and $H_i = [Y_i'Y_i - Y_i'(X_i'X_i)^{-1}X_i'Y_i]/a_{ii}$. If $\boldsymbol{\gamma}_i$ has just a small number of elements, numerical integration techniques can be employed to evaluate the remaining posterior pdf.

15.8.2 Full System Bayesian Analysis

In the previous section, we dealt with the posterior pdf for the parameters of a single equation, using just the identifying prior information for those parameters. In this section, we will deal with a joint posterior pdf for the parameters of all structural equations incorporating the prior identifying information for all parameters of an M-equation system.

If we write the model in the notation of Section 15.2 as

$$Y\Gamma + XB + \mathbf{E} = 0$$

then, under the assumption that the rows of **E** are normally and independently distributed, each with zero mean vector and $(M \times M)$ covariance matrix Σ, the likelihood function is

$$\ell(\Gamma,B,\Sigma|\text{data}) \propto |\Gamma|^T \exp[-\tfrac{1}{2}\,\text{tr}(Y\Gamma + XB)'(Y\Gamma + XB)\Sigma^{-1}] \quad (15.8.11)$$

If the prior pdf for the parameters is

$$p(\Gamma,B,\Sigma) \propto p_1(\Gamma,B)|\Sigma|^{-(M+1)/2} \quad (15.8.12)$$

then the posterior pdf is

$$p(\Gamma,B,\Sigma|\text{data and prior assumptions})$$
$$\propto p_1(\Gamma,B)|\Sigma|^{-(T+M+1)/2}|\Gamma|^T \exp[-\tfrac{1}{2}\,\text{tr}(Y\Gamma + XB)'(Y\Gamma + XB)\Sigma^{-1}] \quad (15.8.13)$$

Zellner (1971) finds that the marginal posterior pdf for Γ and B, after integrating (15.8.13) with respect to the elements of Σ, is

$$p(\Gamma,B|\text{data, prior assumptions}) \propto \frac{p_1(\Gamma,B)|\Gamma'\hat{\Omega}\Gamma|^{T/2}}{|T\Gamma'\hat{\Omega}\Gamma + (B - \hat{B})'X'X(B - \hat{B})|^{T/2}} \quad (15.8.14)$$

where $\hat{B} = -(X'X)^{-1}X'Y\Gamma = -\hat{\Pi}\Gamma$ and $T\hat{\Omega} + (Y - X\hat{\Pi})'(Y - X\hat{\Pi}) = \hat{V}'\hat{V}$. From the form of the above expression (15.8.14), one can conclude that if the conditional prior pdf for B, given Γ, $p_2(B|\Gamma) \propto$ constant, the conditional posterior pdf for the elements of B, given Γ, is in the generalized Student t form with mean $\hat{B} = -(X'X)^{-1}X'Y\Gamma$.

Since the pdf for Γ and B, $p_1(\Gamma,B)$, incorporates the prior identifying information that certain elements of (Γ,B) are equal to zero, the posterior pdf can be simplified to

$$p(\boldsymbol{\delta},\Omega|\text{data and prior assumptions})$$
$$\propto |\Omega|^{-(T+M+1)/2} \exp\left(-\frac{T}{2}\,\text{tr}\,\hat{\Omega}\Omega^{-1}\right) \exp[-\tfrac{1}{2}(\boldsymbol{\delta} - \hat{\boldsymbol{\delta}})'Q(\boldsymbol{\delta} - \hat{\boldsymbol{\delta}})] \quad (15.8.15)$$

where $\boldsymbol{\delta}$ is a vector of all nonzero structural coefficients excluding M normalizing coefficients of -1 as defined earlier. The above expression (15.8.15) shows that Ω and $\boldsymbol{\delta}$ are independently distributed, with elements of Ω having an inverted Wishart pdf and those of $\boldsymbol{\delta}$ having a multivariate normal pdf, with mean vector

$$\hat{\boldsymbol{\delta}} = [\hat{Z}'(\hat{\Sigma}^{-1} \otimes I_T)\hat{Z}]^{-1}\hat{Z}'(\hat{\Sigma}^{-1} \otimes I_T)\hat{\mathbf{y}} \quad (15.8.16)$$

and covariance matrix

$$Q^{-1} = [\hat{Z}'(\hat{\Sigma}^{-1} \otimes I_T)\hat{Z}]^{-1} \quad (15.8.17)$$

where $\hat{\mathbf{y}} = X\hat{\boldsymbol{\pi}}$, $\hat{Z} = \text{diag}(\hat{Z}_1, \hat{Z}_2, \ldots, \hat{Z}_M)$, $\hat{Z}_i = (\hat{Y}_i \quad X_i)$, and $\hat{Y}_i = X\hat{\Pi}_i$. The above results are analogous to the large sample covariance matrix estimator. For details, see Zellner (1971).

In Sections 15.8.1 and 15.8.2 we have presented the highlights of the basic Bayesian analysis for a system of simultaneous equations utilizing a diffuse prior pdf for the structural parameters Γ, B, and Σ. For a detailed analysis of special models and the use of some informative prior pdf's, Monte Carlo experiments, and so on, the reader is referred to Chetty (1968), Harkema (1971), Zellner (1971), Morales (1971), Richard (1973), Rothenberg (1974), Kaufman (1974), Zellner and Vandaele (1975), Drèze (1976), van Dijk and Kloek (1977), and Kloek and van Dijk (1978). In the following section, we will discuss the further use of a posterior distribution in formulating an estimator.

15.8.3 A Minimum Expected Loss Approach

It is well known that many widely used estimators such as 2SLS, LIML, 3SLS, FIML, and so on, can fail to possess finite moments as discussed in Sawa (1972, 1973), Bergstrom (1962), Hatanaka (1973), and others. See also Section 15.4. As a consequence those estimators can have infinite risk relative to quadratic and other loss functions. Further, means of posterior distributions based on diffuse or natural conjugate prior distributions, often fail to exist. In these cases, the usual Bayesian point estimate using the posterior mean is not available.

This section deals with parameter estimators that minimize the posterior expectation of generalized quadratic loss functions for structural coefficients of linear structural models. Parameter estimators that minimize posterior expected loss, called MELO estimators, have at least a finite second moment and thus finite risk relative to quadratic and other loss functions. We first consider a single structural equation and then go on to consider joint estimation of parameters of a set of structural equations.

As we discussed in Section 15.6, the ith structural equation can be written as

$$\begin{aligned}\mathbf{y}_i &= X\Pi_i\boldsymbol{\gamma}_i + X_i\boldsymbol{\beta}_i + \mathbf{v}_i \\ &= (X\Pi_i \quad X_i)\boldsymbol{\delta}_i + \mathbf{v}_i \\ &= \bar{Z}_i\boldsymbol{\delta}_i + \mathbf{v}_i \end{aligned} \tag{15.8.18}$$

where $\mathbf{v}_i = \mathbf{e}_i + V_i\boldsymbol{\gamma}_i$ and $\bar{Z}_i = (X\Pi_i \quad X_i)$. By comparing the coefficient of (15.8.18) and that of $\mathbf{y}_i = X\boldsymbol{\pi}_i + \mathbf{v}_i$, we obtain

$$X\boldsymbol{\pi}_i = \bar{Z}_i\boldsymbol{\delta}_i \tag{15.8.19}$$

If $\hat{\boldsymbol{\delta}}_i$ is an estimate of $\boldsymbol{\delta}_i$, let $\boldsymbol{\epsilon} = X\pi_i - \bar{Z}_i\hat{\boldsymbol{\delta}}_i$ and we define the loss function as

$$\begin{aligned}L = \boldsymbol{\epsilon}'\boldsymbol{\epsilon} &= (X\boldsymbol{\pi}_i - \bar{Z}_i\hat{\boldsymbol{\delta}}_i)'(X\boldsymbol{\pi}_i - \bar{Z}_i\hat{\boldsymbol{\delta}}_i) \\ &= (\boldsymbol{\delta}_i - \hat{\boldsymbol{\delta}}_i)'\bar{Z}_i'\bar{Z}_i(\boldsymbol{\delta}_i - \hat{\boldsymbol{\delta}}_i)\end{aligned} \tag{15.8.20}$$

where $X\boldsymbol{\pi}_i = \bar{Z}_i\boldsymbol{\delta}_i$ is used. Thus, the loss function (15.8.20) is quadratic in $\boldsymbol{\delta}_i - \hat{\boldsymbol{\delta}}_i$ with a positive definite symmetric matrix $\bar{Z}_i'\bar{Z}_i$ as the weight matrix.

Given a posterior pdf for $(\boldsymbol{\pi}_i \quad \Pi_i)$ that possesses finite first and second moments, the value of $\boldsymbol{\delta}_i$, $\boldsymbol{\delta}_i^*$, that minimizes the posterior expected loss

$$E(L) = E(X\boldsymbol{\pi}_i - \bar{Z}_i\boldsymbol{\delta}_i)'(X\boldsymbol{\pi}_i - \bar{Z}_i\boldsymbol{\delta}_i) \tag{15.8.21}$$

is the MELO estimator:

$$\begin{aligned}\hat{\boldsymbol{\delta}}_i^* &= (E\bar{Z}_i'\bar{Z}_i)^{-1}E\bar{Z}_i'X\boldsymbol{\pi}_i \\ &= \begin{bmatrix} E\Pi_i'X'X\Pi_i & E\Pi_i'X'X_i \\ EX_i'X\Pi_i & X_i'X_i \end{bmatrix}^{-1}\begin{bmatrix} E\Pi_i'X'X\boldsymbol{\pi}_i \\ EX_i'X\boldsymbol{\pi}_i \end{bmatrix}\end{aligned} \tag{15.8.22}$$

The above result is quite general in that any posterior pdf may be employed in evaluating the posterior expectation. In a specific case where a diffuse prior pdf for Π and Ω is used, or

$$p(\Pi,\Omega) \propto |\Omega|^{-(M+1)/2} \tag{15.8.23}$$

the marginal posterior pdf for Π is in the following matrix Student t form (see Zellner, 1971, p. 229):

$$p(\Pi|\,Y, \text{prior information}) \propto |S + (\Pi - \hat{\Pi})'X'X(\Pi - \hat{\Pi})|^{-T/2}$$

where $\hat{\Pi} = (X'X)^{-1}X'Y$, which is the posterior mean of Π, and $S = (Y - X\hat{\Pi})'(Y - X\hat{\Pi}) = \hat{V}'\hat{V}$. Using this specific posterior distribution to evaluate the posterior expectation in (15.8.22), we obtain, after simplifying,

$$\hat{\boldsymbol{\delta}}_i^* = \begin{bmatrix} \hat{\Pi}_i'X'X\hat{\Pi}_i + k\bar{S}_{22} & \hat{\Pi}_i'X'X_i \\ X_i'X\hat{\Pi}_i & X_i'X_i \end{bmatrix}^{-1}\begin{bmatrix} \hat{\Pi}_i'X'X\hat{\boldsymbol{\pi}}_i + k\bar{\mathbf{s}}_{12} \\ X_i'X\hat{\boldsymbol{\pi}}_i \end{bmatrix} \tag{15.8.24}$$

where

$$\bar{S} = \frac{(Y - X\hat{\Pi})'(Y - X\hat{\Pi})}{(v - 2)} = \begin{bmatrix} \bar{s}_{11} & \bar{\mathbf{s}}_{12}' \\ \bar{\mathbf{s}}_{12} & \bar{S}_{22} \end{bmatrix}$$

and $v = T - K - (M - 1) > 2$ are employed.

From (15.8.24), it can be seen that the estimator $\hat{\boldsymbol{\delta}}_i^*$ for $\boldsymbol{\delta}_i$ is in the form of a k-class estimator. The value of k is $k^* = 1 - K/(v - 2)$, with $v = T - K - (M - 1) > 2$. Since k^* is less than one, and the order condition for identification and other conditions specified by Hatanaka (1973, pp. 12–14) are met in this case, the first two finite sample moments of k-class estimators exist. Therefore, $\hat{\boldsymbol{\delta}}_i^*$ has finite first and second moments and bounded risk relative to quadratic loss functions. Further, as T approaches infinity, k^* approaches 1, and thus $\hat{\boldsymbol{\delta}}_i^*$ is consistent and asymptotically equivalent to other consistent and asymptotically normal k-class estimators.

To derive MELO estimators of all the structural coefficients of the system, we write each structural equation in the form of (15.8.19) and express them jointly as

$$\begin{bmatrix} X\boldsymbol{\pi}_1 \\ X\boldsymbol{\pi}_2 \\ \vdots \\ X\boldsymbol{\pi}_M \end{bmatrix} = \begin{bmatrix} \bar{Z}_1 & & & \\ & \bar{Z}_2 & & \\ & & \ddots & \\ & & & \bar{Z}_M \end{bmatrix} \begin{bmatrix} \boldsymbol{\delta}_1 \\ \boldsymbol{\delta}_2 \\ \vdots \\ \boldsymbol{\delta}_M \end{bmatrix}$$

or

$$\bar{\mathbf{w}} = \bar{Z}\boldsymbol{\delta} \tag{15.8.25}$$

Thus, the loss function can be formulated as

$$\begin{aligned} L &= (\bar{\mathbf{w}} - \bar{Z}\hat{\boldsymbol{\delta}})'Q(\bar{\mathbf{w}} - \bar{Z}\hat{\boldsymbol{\delta}}) \\ &= (\boldsymbol{\delta} - \hat{\boldsymbol{\delta}})'\bar{Z}'Q\bar{Z}(\boldsymbol{\delta} - \hat{\boldsymbol{\delta}}) \end{aligned} \tag{15.8.26}$$

where Q is a positive definite symmetric matrix that may have elements that are parameters with unknown values.

Given a posterior pdf for the reduced form coefficients and elements of Q, the posterior expectation $E(L)$ can be minimized to find the general MELO estimator of $\boldsymbol{\delta}$ to be

$$\hat{\boldsymbol{\delta}}_i^* = (E\bar{Z}'Q\bar{Z})^{-1}E\bar{Z}'Q\bar{\mathbf{w}} \tag{15.8.27}$$

A particular MELO estimator can be obtained by using $Q = \Omega^{-1} \otimes I_T$, and a posterior pdf resulting from incorporating a diffuse prior pdf for Π and Ω (see Zellner, 1971, p. 227). The estimator $\hat{\boldsymbol{\delta}}^*$ given Ω is derived by Zellner (1978) as

$$\hat{\boldsymbol{\delta}}^* = \left\{\begin{bmatrix} \hat{Y}_i'\hat{Y}_j + k\Omega_{ij}\omega^{ij} & Y_i'X_j \\ X_i'Y_j & X_i'X_j \end{bmatrix}\right\}^{-1}\left\{\left[\sum_{j=1}^{M}\begin{pmatrix} \hat{Y}_i\mathbf{y}_j + k\boldsymbol{\omega}_{ij}\omega^{ij} \\ X_i'\mathbf{y}_j \end{pmatrix}\right]\right\} \tag{15.8.28}$$

where the entry in the first pair of curly braces is a typical submatrix, $i, j = 1, 2, \ldots, M$, and in the second pair, a typical subvector, $\hat{Y}_i = X\hat{\Pi}_i$, ω^{ij} is the (i,j)th element of Ω^{-1}, Ω_{ij} is a submatrix of Ω that is equal to the sampling covariance between corresponding rows of $V_i = Y_i - X\Pi_i$ and $V_j = Y_j - X\Pi_j$, and $\boldsymbol{\omega}_{ij}$ is a vector of sampling covariances between elements of $\mathbf{v}_i = \mathbf{y}_i - X\boldsymbol{\pi}_i$ and corresponding rows of $V_i = Y_i - X\Pi_i$. For the properties of MELO estimators, the reader is referred to Zellner (1978), Zellner and Park (1979), and Park (1982).

15.9 A SPECIAL SYSTEM— DISEQUILIBRIUM MODELS

In view of the recent developments in disequilibrium microeconomics, the estimation of supply and demand schedules for disequilibrium markets has become a problem of practical importance. Fair and Jaffee (1972) discuss several interesting models of markets in disequilibrium and propose four possible methods of estimation. The limitations of the methods are discussed and some modifications are proposed by Fair and Kelejian (1974). Amemiya (1974b) derives 2SLS and ML estimators for a disequilibrium model. Maddala and Nelson (1974) present appropriate maximum likelihood methods for alternative models using a formulation similar to that for models with limited dependent variables. Hartley and Mallela (1977) examine the maximum likelihood estimator and derive the asymptotic properties for disequilibrium models. Gourieroux, Laffont, and Monfort (1980) consider the econometric problems raised by multi-market disequilibrium models and propose LIML and FIML estimators. Ito (1980) also develops disequilibrium models that consider the spill-over effects of the unsatisfied demand or supply in other markets. A small number of empirical applications and disequilibrium theories have appeared in the literature. For a literature review, see Gourieroux, Laffont, and Monfort (1980).

In the following, we will deal with a basic model discussed by Fair and Kelejian (1974) and Amemiya (1974b). The basic disequilibrium model consists of the following equations:

$$d_t = \mathbf{x}_t'\boldsymbol{\alpha} + u_t \tag{15.9.1}$$

$$s_t = \mathbf{z}_t'\boldsymbol{\beta} + v_t \tag{15.9.2}$$

$$q_t = \min(d_t, s_t) \tag{15.9.3}$$

$$\Delta p_t = \gamma(d_t - s_t) \tag{15.9.4}$$

where $\boldsymbol{\alpha}$ and $\boldsymbol{\beta}$ are vectors of unknown parameters, γ is an unknown positive scalar parameter, d_t is demand, s_t is supply, $\mathbf{x}_t$ and $\mathbf{z}_t$ are vectors of predetermined variables including the lagged price p_{t-1}, q_t is the observed quantity, $\Delta p_t = p_t - p_{t-1}$, and u_t and v_t are serially and contemporaneously independent with distributions $N(0,\sigma_u^2)$ and $N(0,\sigma_v^2)$, respectively. The problem is to estimate $\boldsymbol{\alpha}$, $\boldsymbol{\beta}$, γ, σ_u^2, and σ_v^2 with the observations on $\mathbf{x}_t$, $\mathbf{z}_t$, q_t, and p_t for $t = 1, 2, \ldots, T$. Note that in the absence of an equilibrium condition the observed quantity traded in the market may not satisfy both the demand and supply schedule. Therefore, d_t and s_t are not completely observed. The model is assumed identified by different sets of variables in $\mathbf{x}_t$ and $\mathbf{z}_t$.

The above model can be reformulated by considering the period of rising prices $\Delta p_t > 0$ and the period of falling prices $\Delta p_t < 0$. In periods with rising prices, there will be excess demand and thus the observed quantity will equal the supply. Consequently, the supply function (15.9.2) can be estimated using the observed quantity as the dependent variable. In this case, equation (15.9.4) can be used to write the demand function (15.9.1) as

$$q_t = \mathbf{x}_t'\boldsymbol{\alpha} - \frac{1}{\gamma}\Delta p_t + u_t, \qquad \Delta p_t > 0 \tag{15.9.5}$$

Similarly, in the periods with falling prices, there will be excess supply and thus the observed quantity will equal the demand. Consequently, the demand function (15.9.1) can be estimated using the observed quantity as the dependent variable. In this case, equation (15.9.4) can be used to write (15.9.2) as

$$q_t = \mathbf{z}_t'\boldsymbol{\beta} + \frac{1}{\gamma}\Delta p_t + v_t, \qquad \Delta p_t < 0 \tag{15.9.6}$$

In summary, the model becomes

$$q_t = \mathbf{x}_t'\boldsymbol{\alpha} - \frac{1}{\gamma} g_t + u_t \tag{15.9.7a}$$

where

$$g_t = \begin{cases} \Delta p_t & \text{if } \Delta p_t > 0 \\ 0 & \text{otherwise} \end{cases} \tag{15.9.7b}$$

and

$$q_t = \mathbf{z}_t'\boldsymbol{\beta} - \frac{1}{\gamma} h_t + v_t \tag{15.9.8a}$$

where

$$h_t = \begin{cases} -\Delta p_t & \text{if } \Delta p_t < 0 \\ 0 & \text{otherwise} \end{cases} \tag{15.9.8b}$$

With the model (15.9.7) and (15.9.8), the parameters can be consistently estimated by first regressing g_t and h_t on all the exogenous variables, $\mathbf{x}_t$ and $\mathbf{z}_t$ in order to obtain their calculated values $\hat{g}_t$ and $\hat{h}_t$, and then in the second stage, regressing q_t on $\mathbf{x}_t$ and $\hat{g}_t$ for (15.9.7) and regressing q_t on $\mathbf{z}_t$ and $\hat{h}_t$ for (15.9.8). The 2SLS estimator is consistent but not asymptotically efficient in this model because no restriction is imposed to force the same γ to appear in both equations and furthermore, g_t and h_t are not, strictly speaking, linear functions of exogenous variables.

Amemiya (1974b) proposes the following iterative method of obtaining the maximum likelihood estimator. Since in period A when $d_t > s_t$, the conditional density of Δp_t given q_t is $N(\gamma(q_t - \mathbf{z}_t'\boldsymbol{\beta}), \gamma^2\sigma_v^2)$, and in period B when $s_t > d_t$, the conditional density of Δp_t given q_t is $N(\gamma(q_t - \mathbf{x}_t'\boldsymbol{\alpha}), \gamma^2\sigma_u^2)$, the log likelihood function is

$$\ln \ell = \text{const.} - T \ln \gamma - T \ln \sigma_u - T \ln \sigma_v$$
$$- \frac{1}{2\sigma_u^2} \sum_A (q_t - \mathbf{x}_t'\boldsymbol{\alpha})^2 - \frac{1}{2\gamma^2\sigma_v^2} \sum_A [\Delta p_t - (q_t - \mathbf{z}_t'\boldsymbol{\beta})]^2$$
$$- \frac{1}{2\sigma_v^2} \sum_B (q_t - \mathbf{z}_t'\boldsymbol{\beta})^2 - \frac{1}{2\gamma^2\sigma_u^2} \sum_B [\Delta p_t + (q_t - \mathbf{x}_t'\boldsymbol{\alpha})]^2 \tag{15.9.9}$$

Taking the derivatives with respect to zero yields a set of conditions that are to be solved jointly for the parameters. Amemiya (1974b) shows that the equations for $\boldsymbol{\alpha}$ and $\boldsymbol{\beta}$ are the same as the LS estimator of $\boldsymbol{\alpha}$ and $\boldsymbol{\beta}$ given γ applied to (15.9.7a) and (15.9.8a), respectively. The equations for σ_u^2 and σ_v^2 are the residual sums of squares of equations (15.9.7a) and (15.9.8a), given γ, divided by T as for the usual ML estimators, and the equation for γ is

$$T\gamma + \frac{1}{\sigma_v^2} \sum_A \left(q_t - \frac{1}{\gamma} p_t - \mathbf{z}_t'\boldsymbol{\beta}\right) \Delta p_t - \frac{1}{\sigma_u^2} \sum_B \left(q_t + \frac{1}{\gamma} p_t - \mathbf{x}_t'\boldsymbol{\alpha}\right) \Delta p_t = 0 \tag{15.9.10}$$

which is a quadratic function in γ. Thus, the parameter estimates can be solved for by using the following iterative procedure:

Step 1 Use the 2SLS estimates of $\boldsymbol{\alpha}$, $\boldsymbol{\beta}$, σ_u^2, and σ_v^2 as the initial estimates.

Step 2 Substitute the estimates $\hat{\boldsymbol{\alpha}}$, $\hat{\boldsymbol{\beta}}$, $\hat{\sigma}_u^2$, and $\hat{\sigma}_v^2$ into (15.9.10) and solve for the positive root of γ, $\hat{\gamma}$.

Step 3 Use $\hat{\gamma}$ in (15.9.7a) and (15.9.8a) to obtain least squares estimates of $\boldsymbol{\alpha}$, $\boldsymbol{\beta}$, σ_u^2, and σ_v^2.

The iteration repeats steps 2 and 3 until the solutions converge.

For the cases when (a) u_t and v_t are serially correlated, (b) u_t and v_t are contemporaneously correlated but serially uncorrelated, and (c) p_t is contained in $\mathbf{x}_t$ and $\mathbf{z}_t$, Amemiya (1974b) also shows that the maximum likelihood estimates can be obtained by a standard iterative technique such as the Newton-Raphson method (see Appendix B).

In this section, we have presented the most basic model of a market in disequilibrium. For estimation and inference of advanced models and applications, the reader is referred to Maddala and Nelson (1974), Barro and Grossman (1971), Grossman (1971), Laffont and Garcia (1977), Quandt and Rosen (1978), Quandt (1978), Bowden (1978a,b), and Hwang (1980a).

15.10 SUMMARY

In this chapter, we have discussed alternative methods of estimation and inference for the parameters of structural and reduced form equations. The traditional methods of estimation including ILS, 2SLS, 3SLS, LIML, and FIML estimators are presented. The methods for nonlinear models are heavily based on Amemiya's work and the Bayesian methods are basically Zellner's results. A recent advancement in the MELO approach, which makes use of the posterior pdf in evaluating the expectation of a loss function, is included as a part of Bayesian results. Reduced form parameter estimation methods that incorporate overidentifying restrictions are also discussed. In comparing the relative merits of estimators, some characteristics of estimators within a certain family are identified. The special characteristics that we considered are the value of k in the k-class family, the construction of instrumental variables, and the numerical solution algorithm used in approximating the full information maximum likelihood estimator. The comparisons of sampling properties are mainly of an asymptotic nature. On the small sample properties of estimators, a literature review is given and the highlights of the research regarding the derivation of exact densities and/or distributions, the existence of moments, and their approximations, are discussed. With respect to statistical inference, we have discussed three types of hypothesis tests, namely tests of parameter significance, overidentification, and the orthogonality assumption. Finally, a special model of a single market disequilibrium is discussed with its special econometric problems. There are many other interesting topics related to simultaneous equations in recent advancements of econometrics, that are not included in this volume. Some of the neglected topics are two-stage least absolute deviation estimators, an indirect least squares estimator using the Moore-Penrose inverse for overidentified equations, the extension of 3SLS for a singular covariance matrix, tests of serial correlation, heteroscedasticity and normality for simultaneous equation errors, problems in simultaneous forecasts, undersized and incomplete samples and the use of auxiliary regression, and treatments of vector autoregressive errors, systems of simultaneous differential equations in the time domain or in the frequency domain. Models with truncated normal errors, binary exogenous variables and the use of switching regime, binary endogenous variables are discussed in Chapter 18, as are multiple logit and generalized probit models. Some of the other topics are also discussed in later chapters. Other topics related to simultaneous equations, such as multiple time series and the rational expectations hypothesis, are discussed in Chapter 16.

15.11 EXERCISES

Exercise 15.1

Let $\hat{\mathbf{y}} = \hat{Z}\boldsymbol{\delta} + \hat{\mathbf{e}}$, where $\hat{Z} = PZ$, $\hat{\mathbf{e}} = P\mathbf{e}$, $\hat{\mathbf{y}} = P\mathbf{y}$, and $P = (I_M \otimes X(X'X)^{-1}X')$. Show that $\hat{\boldsymbol{\delta}} = (\hat{Z}'\hat{Z})^{-1}\hat{Z}'\hat{\mathbf{y}}$ is the 2SLS estimator.

Exercise 15.2

Let $\mathbf{y} = Z\boldsymbol{\delta} + \mathbf{e}$, $\tilde{Z} = P_*Z$, and $P_* = (\Sigma^{-1} \otimes X(X'X)^{-1}X')$. Show that $\tilde{\boldsymbol{\delta}}^* = (\tilde{Z}'Z)^{-1}\tilde{Z}'\mathbf{y}$ is the 3SLS estimator.

Exercise 15.3

Show that when an equation is just identified, its 2SLS estimator is identical to the indirect least squares estimator.

Exercise 15.4

Show that if all structural equations are just identified, the 3SLS and 2SLS estimators have the same asymptotic covariance matrix.

Exercise 15.5

Let $Z_i = (Y_i \quad X_i)$, $\hat{Z}_i = (\hat{Y}_i \quad X_i)$, $\hat{Y}_i = X(X'X)^{-1}X'Y_i$, $\mathbf{y} = Z\boldsymbol{\delta} + \mathbf{e}$, $Z = \text{diag}(Z_1, Z_2, \ldots, Z_M)$, and $\hat{Z} = \text{diag}(\hat{Z}_1, \hat{Z}_2, \ldots, \hat{Z}_M)$. Show that $\hat{Z} = (I_M \otimes X(X'X)^{-1}X')Z$ and $\hat{\mathbf{y}} = (I_M \otimes X(X'X)^{-1}X')\mathbf{y}$.

Exercise 15.6

Let $\hat{\mathbf{y}} = \hat{Z}\boldsymbol{\delta} + \hat{\mathbf{e}}$, with estimated covariance $(\hat{\Sigma}^{-1} \otimes I_T)$, where $\hat{Z} = \text{diag}(\hat{Z}_1, \hat{Z}_2, \ldots, \hat{Z}_M)$, $\hat{Z}_i = (\hat{Y}_i \quad X_i)$, $\hat{Y}_i = X\hat{\Pi}_i$, $\hat{\Pi}_i = (X'X)^{-1}X'Y_i$, $\hat{\mathbf{y}} = X\hat{\boldsymbol{\pi}}$. Show that $\boldsymbol{\delta}^* = (\hat{Z}'(\hat{\Sigma}^{-1} \otimes I_T)\hat{Z})^{-1}\hat{Z}'(\hat{\Sigma}^{-1} \otimes I_T)\hat{\mathbf{y}}$ is the 3SLS estimator of $\boldsymbol{\delta}$ in $\mathbf{y} = Z\boldsymbol{\delta} + \mathbf{e}$.

Exercise 15.7

Show that minimizing $l = \ln(\boldsymbol{\gamma}_i' W_i \boldsymbol{\gamma}_i / \boldsymbol{\gamma}_i' W \boldsymbol{\gamma}_i)$ is equivalent to finding the smallest (characteristic) root of $|W_i - lW| = 0$, where $W_i = Y_i'[I - X_i(X_i'X_i)^{-1}X_i']Y_i$, and $W = Y_i'[I - X(X'X)^{-1}X']Y_i$.

Exercise 15.8

Since the reduced form equation of $\mathbf{y}_i$ can be expressed as $\mathbf{y}_i = Y_i\boldsymbol{\gamma}_i + X_i\boldsymbol{\beta}_i + \mathbf{e}_i = (X\Pi_i \quad X_i)\boldsymbol{\delta} + \mathbf{v}_i$, where $\mathbf{v}_i = \mathbf{e}_i + V_i\boldsymbol{\gamma}_i$, $Y_i = X\Pi_i + V_i$, and $\boldsymbol{\delta} = (\boldsymbol{\gamma}_i'\boldsymbol{\beta}_i')'$, show that the structural parameter $\boldsymbol{\delta}$ can be expressed as a function of reduced form coefficients $\boldsymbol{\pi}_i$ and Π_i as follows:

$$\boldsymbol{\delta}_i = \begin{bmatrix} \Pi_i'X'X\boldsymbol{\pi}_i & \Pi_i'X'X_i \\ X_i'X\boldsymbol{\pi}_i & X_i'X_i \end{bmatrix}^{-1} \begin{bmatrix} \Pi_i'X'X\pi_i \\ X_i'X\boldsymbol{\pi}_i \end{bmatrix}$$

Exercise 15.9

Let $W_i = (Y_i - k\hat{V}_i \quad X_i)$, where $\hat{V}_i = Y_i - \hat{Y}_i$, and $\hat{Y}_i = X(X'X)^{-1}X'Y_i$. Show that $\hat{\boldsymbol{\delta}}_i = (W_i'Z_i)^{-1}W_i'\mathbf{y}_i$ is the k-class estimator for $\boldsymbol{\delta}_i$ in $\mathbf{y}_i = Z_i\boldsymbol{\delta}_i + \mathbf{e}_i$.

Exercise 5.10

In Hausman's instrumental variable interpretation of FIML and 3SLS, show that when all the structural equations are just identified, the instruments are identical.

Exercise 15.11

In Hendry's derivation of the estimator generation equation, show that $(\Gamma^{-1} \quad 0) = \Sigma^{-1}A'W'W/T$ holds given that $T(\Gamma')^{-1} - Y'WA\Sigma^{-1} = 0$ and $-X'WA\Sigma^{-1} = 0$.

Exercise 15.12

Consider the model $Y\Gamma + XB + \mathbf{E} = 0$. Let

$$A = \begin{pmatrix} \Gamma \\ B \end{pmatrix} = \begin{bmatrix} -1 & 0.2 & 0 \\ -10 & -1 & 2 \\ 2.5 & 0 & -1 \\ -60 & 40 & -10 \\ 0 & -4 & 80 \\ 0 & -6 & 0 \\ 0 & 1.5 & 0 \\ 0 & 0 & 5 \end{bmatrix}$$

and

$$\Sigma = \begin{bmatrix} 227.55 & 8.91 & -56.89 \\ 8.91 & 0.66 & -1.88 \\ -56.89 & -1.88 & 15.76 \end{bmatrix}$$

or equivalently

$$\Omega = \begin{bmatrix} 4 & 1.26 & -1.52 \\ 1.26 & 1 & -0.69 \\ -1.52 & -0.69 & 9 \end{bmatrix}.$$

Consistent with the covariance structure Σ, the reduced form equation errors $\mathbf{v}_1$, $\mathbf{v}_2$, $\mathbf{v}_3$, and $\mathbf{v}_4$ are simulated and a sample is listed in Table 15.2 together with the fixed values of $\mathbf{x}_1$, $\mathbf{x}_2$, $\mathbf{x}_3$, $\mathbf{x}_4$, and $\mathbf{x}_5$.

1. Find the reduced form equations with the particular assumed structural coefficients.
2. Calculate the systematic part of Y, using the fixed value of X.
3. Generate a sample of data Y by adding the systematic part of Y and the reduced form equation errors listed in Table 15.2.
4. Generate your own samples of data Y by adding to the systematic part of Y different sets of equation errors that are consistent with your own assumed values of Σ and Ω. (*Hint:* See p. 810 in Judge et al. (1982) for the method of generating multivariate normal random variables.)

Exercise 15.13

Using the data generated from Exercise 15.12, calculate the following estimators for each equation: (a) OLS, (b) 2SLS, (c) 3SLS, (d) LIML, and (e) FIML.

TABLE 15.2 ***FIXED VALUES OF X AND A SAMPLE OF V***

x_1	x_2	x_3	x_4	x_5	v_1	v_2	v_3
1	3.06	1.34	8.48	28	0.83	0.27	−3.66
1	3.19	1.44	9.16	35	1.17	1.55	−3.37
1	3.30	1.54	9.90	37	2.10	0.28	−3.93
1	3.40	1.71	11.02	36	−2.07	0.84	−3.46
1	3.48	1.89	11.64	29	−3.26	−1.73	−3.04
1	3.60	1.99	12.73	47	−1.98	−2.06	0.81
1	3.68	2.22	13.88	50	2.06	1.06	−4.56
1	3.72	2.43	14.50	35	2.49	−0.94	1.43
1	3.92	2.43	15.47	33	−1.26	−0.30	−1.71
1	4.15	2.31	16.61	40	−0.69	0.67	−0.67
1	4.35	2.39	17.40	38	−2.50	−0.21	1.96
1	4.37	2.63	18.83	37	2.98	1.19	2.58
1	4.59	2.69	20.62	56	−0.10	0.20	−4.41
1	5.23	3.35	23.76	88	−0.60	−0.41	4.40
1	6.04	5.81	26.52	62	−0.78	−0.80	−0.97
1	6.36	6.38	27.45	51	−1.23	−0.45	0.78
1	7.04	6.14	30.28	29	−2.28	−1.05	−1.69
1	7.81	6.14	25.40	22	−2.78	−0.23	−1.54
1	8.09	6.19	28.84	38	−0.66	0.57	5.81
1	9.24	6.69	34.36	41	−1.04	0.79	4.17

Exercise 15.14

Consider the following disequilibrium model:

$$d_t = \alpha_0 + \alpha_1 p_{t-1} + \alpha_2 y_t + u_t$$

$$s_t = \beta_0 + \beta_1 p_{t-1} + \beta_2 w_t + v_t$$

$$q_t = \min(d_t, s_t)$$

$$p_t = p_{t-1} + \gamma(d_t - s_t)$$

where u_t and v_t are equation errors, α's, β's, and γ are parameters to be estimated, and

d_t is the quantity demanded in time t,

s_t is the quantity supplied in time t,

p_t is the price in time t,

y_t is income in time t, and

w_t is wage rate in time t.

Now let $\alpha_0 = 60,\quad \alpha_1 = -1.8,\quad \alpha_2 = 0.05,\quad \gamma = 0.04,$

$\beta_0 = 10,\quad \beta_1 = 2.5,\quad \beta_2 = -3.$

TABLE 15.3 FIXED VALUES OF y_t, w_t, AND A SAMPLE OF u_t AND v_t

t	y_t	w_t	u_t	v_t
1	574.21	1.69	0.41	0.46
2	653.85	1.88	−0.09	4.78
3	733.81	1.94	0.39	2.76
4	818.29	1.96	−0.52	−2.83
5	899.29	2.15	1.37	3.12
6	972.78	2.16	−0.80	0.28
7	1057.56	2.29	0.63	−0.02
8	1132.86	2.31	1.83	2.81
9	1215.80	2.59	−0.85	2.41
10	1292.58	2.67	−0.85	0.09
11	1373.82	2.76	−1.29	−1.37
12	1459.22	2.73	−0.46	0.23
13	1538.38	2.94	−0.79	−0.45
14	1617.47	3.06	−0.63	2.64
15	1692.97	3.19	−0.62	3.83
16	1777.61	3.17	−1.53	1.23
17	1858.21	3.30	0.61	−0.81
18	1939.75	3.44	0.92	−1.04
19	2010.60	3.46	−0.26	3.33
20	2090.36	3.62	−0.93	1.92

Assume that u_t and v_t are serially and contemporaneously independent with distributions $N(0,\sigma_u^2)$ and $N(0,\sigma_v^2)$, respectively. Let $\sigma_u^2 = 1$ and $\sigma_v^2 = 4$. Consistent with the error structure, simulated equation errors are given in Table 15.3 together with the fixed values of y_t and w_t and the initial price $p_0 = 43.21$.

1. Using the given information, generate the data for p_t, d_t, s_t, and q_t.
2. Using your own equation errors u_t and v_t that are consistent with your own assumptions, generate the data for p_t, d_t, s_t, and q_t.

Exercise 15.15

Pretending that d_t and s_t are not observed and using the data q_t and p_t generated in Exercise 15.14 together with the fixed values of y_t and w_t, estimate the parameters α's, β's, and γ by the (a) 2SLS procedure and (b) iterative maximum likelihood procedure.

Exercise 15.16

Using the following data on q_t and p_t (Table 15.4) together with y_t and w_t of Table 15.3, estimate the parameters of the disequilibrium model of Exercise 15.14 by (a) 2SLS and (b) iterative maximum likelihood procedure.

TABLE 15.4
OBSERVED VALUES OF p_t AND q_t

t	p_t	q_t
1	39.11	11.33
2	36.03	21.98
3	33.43	32.53
4	31.67	40.65
5	30.30	47.50
6	29.26	52.07
7	28.42	58.54
8	28.13	65.12
9	27.92	69.51
10	28.03	71.64
11	28.44	68.32
12	28.78	73.68
13	29.34	70.85
14	29.95	74.64
15	30.62	74.55
16	31.37	74.81
17	32.07	80.28
18	32.87	78.52
19	33.66	81.36
20	34.50	82.78

15.12 REFERENCES

Amemiya, T. (1974a) "The Nonlinear Two-Stage Least-Squares Estimator," *Journal of Econometrics,* 2, 105–110.

Amemiya, T. (1974b) "A Note on a Fair and Jaffee Model," *Econometrica,* 42, 759–762.

Amemiya, T. (1975) "The Nonlinear Limited-Information Maximum Likelihood Estimator and the Modified Nonlinear Two-Stage Least Squares Estimator," *Journal of Econometrics,* 3, 375–386.

Amemiya, T. (1977) "The Maximum Likelihood Estimator and the Nonlinear Three-Stage Least Squares Estimator in the General Nonlinear Simultaneous Equation Model," *Econometrica,* 45, 955–968.

Anderson, T. W. (1974) "An Asymptotic Expansion of the Distribution of the Limited Information Maximum Likelihood Estimate of a Coefficient in a Simultaneous Equation System," *Journal of the American Statistical Association,* 69, 565–573.

Anderson, T. W. (1982) "Some Recent Developments on the Distributions of Single Equation Estimators," in *Advances in Econometrics,* W. Hildenbrand, ed., Cambridge University Press, Cambridge.

Anderson, T. W. (1984) "The 1982 Wald Memorial Lectures: Estimating Linear Statistical Relationships," *Annals of Statistics,* 12, 1–145.

Anderson, T. W., N. Kunitomo, and T. Sawa (1982) "Evaluation of the Distribution Function of the Limited Information Maximum Likelihood Estimator," *Econometrica,* 50, 1009–1028.

Anderson, T. W. and H. Rubin (1949) "Estimation of the Parameters of a Single Equation in a Complete System of Stochastic Equations," *Annals of Mathematical Statistics,* 20, 46–63.

Anderson, T. W. and H. Rubin (1950) "The Asymptotic Properties of Estimators of Estimates of the Parameters of A Single Equation in A Complete System of Stochastic Equations," *Annals of Mathematical Statistics,* 21, 570–582.

Anderson, T. W. and T. Sawa (1973) "Distributions of Estimates of Coefficients of a Single Equation in a Simultaneous System and Their Asymptotic Expansions," *Econometrica,* 41, 683–714.

Anderson, T. W. and T. Sawa (1979) "Evaluation of the Distribution Function of the Two-Stage Least Squares Estimate," *Econometrica,* 47, 163–182.

Barro, R. J. and H. T. Grossman (1971) "A General Disequilibrium Model of Income and Employment," *American Economic Review,* 61, 82–93.

Basmann, R. L. (1960) "On Finite Sample Distributions of Generalized Classical Linear Identifiability Test Statistics," *Journal of the American Statistical Association,* 55, 650–659.

Basmann, R. L. (1961) "A Note on the Exact Finite Sample Frequency Functions of Generalized Classical Linear Estimators in Two Leading Overidentified Cases," *Journal of the American Statistical Association,* 56, 619–636.

Basmann, R. L. (1974) "Exact Finite Sample Distribution for Some Econometric Estimators and Test Statistics: A Survey and Appraisal," Chapter 4 in *Frontiers of Quantitative Econometrics,* Volume 2, Intriligator and Kendrick, eds., North-Holland, Amsterdam.

Benassy, J. P. (1975) "Neo-Keynesian Disequilibrium in a Monetary Economy," *Review of Economic Studies,* 42, 503–524.

Bergstrom, A. R. (1962) "The Exact Sampling Distributions of Least Squares and Maximum Likelihood Estimators of the Marginal Propensity to Consume," *Econometrica,* 30, 480–490.

Bowden, R. J. (1978a) "Specification, Estimation and Inference for Models of Markets in Disequilibrium," *International Economic Review,* 19, 711–726.

Bowden, R. J. (1978b) *The Econometrics of Disequilibrium,* North-Holland, Amsterdam.

Brundy, J. and D. W. Jorgenson (1971) "Efficient Estimation of Simultaneous Equation Systems by Instrumental Variables," *Review of Economics and Statistics,* 53, 207–224.

Byron, R. P. (1974) "Testing Structural Specification Using the Unrestricted Reduced Form," *Econometrica,* 42, 869–884.

Chetty, V. K. (1968) "Bayesian Analysis of Haavelmo's Models," *Econometrica,* 36, 582–602.

Court, R. H. (1973) "Efficient Estimation of the Reduced Form From Incomplete Econometric Models," *Review of Economic Studies,* 40, 411–417.

Dempster, A. P., M. Schatzoff, and M. Wermuth (1977) "A Simulation Study of Alternatives to Ordinary Least Squares," *Journal of the American Statistical Association,* 72, 77–106.

Dhrymes, P. J. (1971) "A Simplified Structural Estimator for Large-Scale Econometric Models," *The Australian Journal of Statistics,* 13, 168–175.

Dhrymes, P. J. (1974) *Econometrics,* Springer-Verlag, New York.

Drèze, J. H. (1976) "Bayesian Limited Information Analysis of the Simultaneous Equation Model," *Econometrica,* 46, 1045–1075.

Durbin, J. (1954) "Errors in Variables," *Review of the International Statistical Institute,* 22, 23–32.

Fair, R. C. and D. M. Jaffee (1972) "Methods of Estimation for Markets in Disequilibrium," *Econometrica,* 40, 497–514.

Fair, R. C. and H. H. Kelejian (1974) "Methods of Estimation for Markets in Disequilibrium: A Further Study," *Econometrica,* 42, 177–190.

Gallant, A. R. (1977) "Three-Stage Least Squares Estimates for a System of Simultaneous Nonlinear Implicit Equations," *Journal of Econometrics,* 5, 71–88.

Gallant, A. R. and A. Holly (1980) "Statistical Inference in an Implicit, Nonlinear, Simultaneous Equation Model in the Context of Maximum Likelihood Estimation," *Econometrica,* 48, 697–720.

Gallant, A. R. and D. W. Jorgenson (1979) "Statistical Inference for a System of Simultaneous, Nonlinear, Implicit Equations in the Context of Instrumental Variable Estimation," *Journal of Econometrics,* 11, 275–302.

Gourieroux, C., J. J. Laffont, and A. Monfort (1980) "Disequilibrium Econometrics in Simultaneous Equations Systems," *Econometrica,* 48, 75–96.

Goldfeld, S. M. and R. E. Quandt (1975) "Estimation in a Disequilibrium Model and the Value of Information," *Journal of Econometrics,* 3, 325–348.

Greenberg, E. and C. E. Webster (1983) *Advanced Econometrics: A Bridge to the Literature,* Wiley, New York.

Grossman, H. I. (1971) "Money, Interest and Prices in Market Disequilibrium," *Journal of Political Economy,* 79, 943–961.

Grossman, H. I. (1974) "The Nature of Quantities in Market Disequilibrium," *American Economic Review,* 64, 509–514.

Harkema, R. (1971) *Simultaneous Equations, A Bayesian Approach,* University Press, Rotterdam.

Hartley, M. J. and P. Mallela (1977) "The Asymptotic Properties of a Maximum Likelihood Estimator for a Model of Markets in Disequilibrium," *Econometrica,* 45, 1205–1220.

Hatanaka, M. (1973) "On the Existence and the Approximation Formulae for the Moments of the *k*-Class Estimators," *The Economic Studies Quarterly,* 24, 1–15.

Hausman, J. A. (1974) "Full Information Instrumental Variable Estimation of Simultaneous Equation Models," *Annals of Economic and Social Measurement,* 3, 641–652.

Hausman, J. A. (1975) "An Instrumental Variable Approach to Full-Information Estimators for Linear and Certain Nonlinear Econometric Models," *Econometrica,* 43, 727–738.

Hausman, J. A. (1978) "Specification Tests in Econometrics," *Econometrica,* 46, 1251–1271.

Hendry, D. F. (1976) "The Structure of Simultaneous Equations Estimators," *Journal of Econometrics,* 4, 51–88.

Hendry, D. F. (1982) "A Reply to Professors Maasoumi and Phillips," *Journal of Econometrics,* 19, 203–213.

Hendry, D. F. and R. W. Harrison (1974) "Monte Carlo Methodology and the Small Sample Behavior of Ordinary and Two Stage Least Squares," *Journal of Econometrics,* 2, 151–174.

Hendry, D. F. and C. Mizon (1980) "An Empirical Application and Monte Carlo Analysis of Tests of Dynamic Specification," *Review of Economic Studies,* 47, 21–45.

Holly, A. and P. C. B. Phillips (1979) "A Saddlepoint Approximation to the Distribution of the *k*-Class Estimator of a Coefficient in a Simultaneous System," *Econometrica,* 47, 1527–1547.

Hwang, H. S. (1980a) "A Test of Disequilibrium Model," *Journal of Econometrics,* 12, 319–333.

Hwang, H. S. (1980b) "A Comparison of Tests of Overidentifying Restrictions," *Econometrica,* 48, 1821–1826.

Ito, T. (1980) "Methods of Estimation for Multi-Market Disequilibrium Models," *Econometrica,* 48, 97–126.

Jorgenson, D. W. and J. Laffont (1974) "Efficient Estimation of Nonlinear Simultaneous Equations with Additive Disturbances," *Annals of Economic and Social Measurement,* 3, 615–640.

Judge, G. G., R. C. Hill, W. E. Griffiths, H. Lütkepohl, and T. C. Lee (1982) *Introduction to the Theory and Practice of Econometrics,* Wiley, New York.

Kakwani, N. C. and R. H. Court (1972) "Reduced-form Coefficient Estimation and Forecasting from a Simultaneous Equation Model," *Australian Journal of Statistics,* 14, 143–160.

Kaufman, G. M. (1974) "Posterior Inference for Structural Parameters Using Cross-Section and Time Series Data," Section 9.2 of *Studies in Bayesian Econometrics and Statistics,* 383–404, S. E. Fienbeg and A. Zellner, eds.

Kelejian, H. H. (1971) "Two-Stage Least Squares and Econometric Systems Linear in Parameters but Nonlinear in Endogenous Variables," *Journal of the American Statistical Association,* 66, 373–374

Kinal, T. W. (1980) "The Existence of Moments of *k*-Class Estimators," *Econometrica,* 48, 241–249.

Kloek, T. and H. K. van Dijk (1978) "Bayesian Estimates of Equation System Parameters: An Application of Integration by Monte Carlo," *Econometrica,* 46, 1–19.

Knight, J. L. (1977) "On the Existence of Moments of the Partially Restricted Reduced Form Estimators from a Simultaneous-Equation Model," *Journal of Econometrics,* 5, 315–322.

Koopmans, T. C. and W. C. Hood (1953) "The Estimation of Simultaneous Linear Economic Relationships," Chapter VI in Hood and Koopmans eds. *Studies in Econometric Method,* Yale University Press, 112–199.

Laffont, J. J. and R. Garcia (1977) "Disequilibrium Econometrics for Business Loans," *Econometrica,* 45, 1187–1204.

Lyttkens, E. (1970) "Symmetric and Asymmetric Estimation Methods," in E. Mosback and H. Wold, eds., *Independent Systems,* North-Holland, Amsterdam.

Maasoumi, E. (1977) "A Study of Improved Methods of Estimating Reduced Form Coefficients Based Upon 3SLS," unpublished Ph.D. Thesis, London School of Economics.

Maasoumi, E. (1978) "A Modified Stein-like Estimator for the Reduced Form Coefficients of Simultaneous Equations," *Econometrica,* 46, 695–704.

Maasoumi, E. and P. C. B. Phillips (1982) "On the Behavior of Inconsistent Instrumental Variable Estimations," *Journal of Econometrics,* 19, 183–201.

Maddala, G. S. (1976) "Weak Priors and Sharp Posteriors in Simultaneous Equation Models," *Econometrica,* 44, 345–352.

Maddala, G. S. and F. D. Nelson (1974) "Maximum Likelihood Methods for the Estimation of Models of Markets in Disequilibrium," *Econometrica,* 42, 1013–1030.

Mariano, R. S. (1972) "The Existence of Moments of the Ordinary Least Squares and Two-Stage Least Squares Estimators," *Econometrica,* 40, 643–652.

Mariano, R. S. (1973a) "Approximations to the Distribution Functions of the OLS and 2SLS Estimators in the Case of Two Included Endogenous Variables," *Econometrica,* 41, 67–77.

Mariano, R. S. (1973b) "Approximations to the Distribution Functions of Theil's *k*-Class Estimators," *Econometrica,* 41, 715–721.

Mariano, R. S. (1977) "Finite Sample Properties of Instrumental Variable Estimators of Structural Coefficients," *Econometrica,* 45, 487–496.

Mariano, R. S. (1982) "Analytical Small-Sample Distribution Theory in Econometrics: The Simultaneous-Equations Case," *International Economic Review,* 23, 503–534.

Mariano, R. S. and T. Sawa (1972) "The Exact Finite-Sample Distribution of the Limited Information Maximum Likelihood Estimator in the Case of Two Included Exogenous Variables," *Journal of the American Statistical Association,* 67, 159–163.

McCarthy, M. (1981) "A Note on the Moments of Partially Restricted Reduced Forms," *Journal of Econometrics,* 17, 383–388.

Morales, J. A. (1971) *Bayesian Full Information Structural Analysis,* Springer-Verlag, Berlin.

Nagar, A. L. (1959) "The Bias and Moment Matrix of the General *k*-Class Estimators of the Parameters in Simultaneous Equations," *Econometrica,* 27, 575–595.

Nagar, A. L. (1962) "Double *k*-Class Estimators of Parameters in Simultaneous Equations and Their Small Sample Properties," *International Economic Review,* 3, 168–188.

Nagar, A. L. and S. Sahay (1978) "The Bias and Mean Squared Error of Forecasts From Partially Restricted Reduced Forms," *Journal of Econometrics,* 7, 227–244.

Nakamura, A. and M. Nakamura (1981) "On the Relationships Among Several Specification Error Tests Presented by Durbin, Wu, and Hausman," *Econometrica,* 49, 1583–1588.

Pagan, A. (1979) "Some Consequences of Viewing LIML as an Iterated Aitken Estimator," *Economics Letters,* 3, 369–372.

Park, S. B. (1982) "Some Sampling Properties of Minimum Expected Loss (MELO) Estimators of Structural Coefficients," *Journal of Econometrics,* 18, 295–311.

Phillips, P. C. B. (1980a) "Finite Sample Theory and the Distributions of Alternative Estimators of the Marginal Propensity to Consume," *Review of Economic Studies,* 47, 183–224.

Phillips, P. C. B. (1980b) "The Exact Distribution of Instrumental Variable Estimators in an Equation Containing $n + 1$ Endogenous Variables," *Econometrica,* 48, 861–878.

Phillips, P. C. B. (1983) "Exact Small Sample Theory in The Simultaneous Equation Model," Chapter 8 of *Handbook of Econometrics,* Vol. I Edited by Z. Griliches and M. D. Intriligator, North-Holland, Amsterdam, 451–516.

Prucha, I. R. and H. H. Kelejian (1984) "The Structure of Simultaneous Equation Estimators: A Generalization Towards Nonnormal Disturbances," *Econometrica* 52, 721–736.

Quandt, R. E. (1978) "Tests of Equilibrium vs. Disequilibrium Hypotheses," *International Economic Review,* 19, 435–452.

Quandt, R. E. and H. S. Rosen (1978) "Estimation of a Disequilibrium Aggregate Labor Market," *Review of Economics and Statistics,* 60, 371–379.

Raduchel, W. J. (1978) "A Note on Non-Linear Limited-Information Maximum-Likelihood," *Journal of Econometrics,* 7, 119–122.

Richard, J. F. (1973) *Posterior and Predictive Densities for Simultaneous Equation Models,* Springer-Verlag, Berlin.

Richardson, D. H. (1968) "The Exact Distribution of a Structural Coefficient Estimator," *Journal of the American Statistical Association,* 63, 1214–1226.

Richardson, D. H. and D. M. Wu (1971) "A Note on the Comparison of Ordinary and Two-Stage Least Squares," *Econometrica,* 39, 973–982.

Rothenberg, T. J. (1974) "Bayesian Analysis of Simultaneous Equations Models," Section 9.3 of *Studies in Bayesian Econometrics and Statistics,* 405–424, Fienberg, S. E. and A. Zellner, eds.

Roy, A. R. and V. K. Srivastava (1966) "Generalized Double *K*-Class Estimators," *Journal of the Indian Statistical Association,* 4, 38–46.

Sant, D. (1978) "Partially Restricted Reduced Forms: Asymptotic Relative Efficiency," *International Economic Review,* 19, 739–748.

Sargan, J. D. (1976) "Econometric Estimators and the Edgeworth Approximation," *Econometrica,* 44, 421–448.

Sargan, J. D. and Mikhail (1971) "A General Approximation to the Distribution of Instrumental Variable Estimates," *Econometrica,* 39, 131–169.

Sawa, T. (1969) "The Exact Sampling Distribution of Ordinary Least Squares

and Two Stage Least Squares Estimators," *Journal of the American Statistical Association,* 64, 923–937.
Sawa, T. (1972) "Finite-Sample Properties of the *k*-Class Estimators," *Econometrica,* 40, 653–680.
Sawa, T. (1973) "Almost Unbiased Estimator in Simultaneous Equations Systems," *International Economic Review,* 14, 97–106.
Savin, N. E. (1973) "Systems *k*-Class Estimators," *Econometrica,* 41, 1125–1136.
Scharf, W. (1976) "*K*-Matrix Class Estimators and the Full Information Maximum-Likelihood Estimator as a Special Case," *Journal of Econometrics,* 4, 41–50.
Schmidt, P. (1976) *Econometrics,* Marcel Dekker, New York.
Sowey, E. R. (1973) "A Classified Bibliography of Monte Carlo Studies in Econometrics," *Journal of Econometrics,* 1, 377–395.
Spencer, D. E. and K. N. Berk (1981) "A Limited Information Specification Test," *Econometrica,* 49, 1079–1085.
Srivastava, V. K. (1971) "Three Stage Least-Squares Generalized Double *K*-Class Estimators: A Mathematical Relationship," *International Economic Review,* 12, 312–316.
Swamy, P. and J. Mehta (1980) "On the Existence of Moments of Partially Restricted Reduced Form Coefficients," *Journal of Econometrics,* 14, 183–194.
Swamy, P. and J. Mehta (1981) "On the Existence of Moments of Partially Restricted Reduced Form Estimators: A Comment," *Journal of Econometrics,* 17, 389–392.
Taylor, W. E. (1983) "On the Relevance of Finite Sample Distribution Theory," *Econometric Reviews,* 2, 1–139.
Theil, H. (1958) *Economic Forecasts and Policy,* North-Holland, Amsterdam (second edition, 1961).
Van Dijk, H. K. and T. Kloek (1977) "Predictive Moments of Simultaneous Econometric Models, A Bayesian Approach," in *New Developments in the Applications of Bayesian Methods,* A. Aykac and C. Brumat, eds., North-Holland, Amsterdam.
Wegge, L. L. (1978) "Constrained Indirect Least Squares Estimators," *Econometrica,* 46, 435–499.
Wu, D. (1973) "Alternative Tests of Independence Between Stochastic Regressors and Disturbances," *Econometrica,* 41, 733–750.
Wu, D. (1974) "Alternative Tests of Independence Between Stochastic Regressors and Disturbances: Finite Sample Results," *Econometrica,* 42, 529–546.
Zellner, A. (1971) *An Introduction to Bayesian Inference in Econometrics,* Wiley, New York.
Zellner, A. (1978) "Estimation of Functions of Population Means and Regression Coefficients Including Structural Coefficients: A Minimum Expected Loss (MELO) Approach," *Journal of Econometrics,* 8, 127–158.
Zellner, A., D. S. Huang and L. C. Chau (1965) "Further Analysis of the Short Run Consumption Function with Emphasis on the Role of Liquid Assets," *Econometrica,* 33, 571–581

Zellner, A. and S. B. Park (1979) "Minimum Expected Loss (MELO) Estimators for Functions of Parameters and Structural Coefficients of Econometric Models," *Journal of the American Statistical Association,* 74, 185–193.

Zellner, A. and W. Vandaele (1975) "Bayes-Stein Estimators for *K*-Means, Regression and Simultaneous Equation Models," in *Studies in Bayesian Econometrics and Statistics,* S. E. Feinberg and A. Zellner, eds., North Holland, Amsterdam.

Chapter 16

Multiple Time Series and Systems of Dynamic Simultaneous Equations

In Part Three of this book we discussed simple examples of single equation dynamic econometric models. We now consider more general dynamic models with several endogenous variables. These models can also be regarded as generalizations of the simultaneous equations models discussed in Chapters 14 and 15. However, in the present context, economic theory will usually not provide a complete specification of the dynamic structure of the relationship between the variables of interest and sample information has to be used at the specification stage. The resulting problems will be discussed as follows:

In Section 16.1 vector stochastic processes will be developed as a framework for discussing dynamic simultaneous equations systems considered in Section 16.2. The consequences of aggregating dynamic models are discussed in Section 16.3 and some other problems rendering the interpretation of such models difficult are listed in Section 16.4. Estimation is considered in Section 16.5 and procedures for specifying the dynamic structure based on sample information are presented in Section 16.6. Conclusions are set forth in Section 16.7. To provide an overview the content of this chapter is summarized in Table 16.1. It will be advantageous for the reader to be familiar with the material on univariate time series analysis in Chapter 7 and with the infinite distributed lag models discussed in Chapter 10. Also a preliminary reading of Chapter 26 in Judge et al. (1982) could be helpful.

TABLE 16.1 *MULTIPLE TIME SERIES AND SYSTEMS OF DYNAMIC SIMULTANEOUS EQUATIONS*

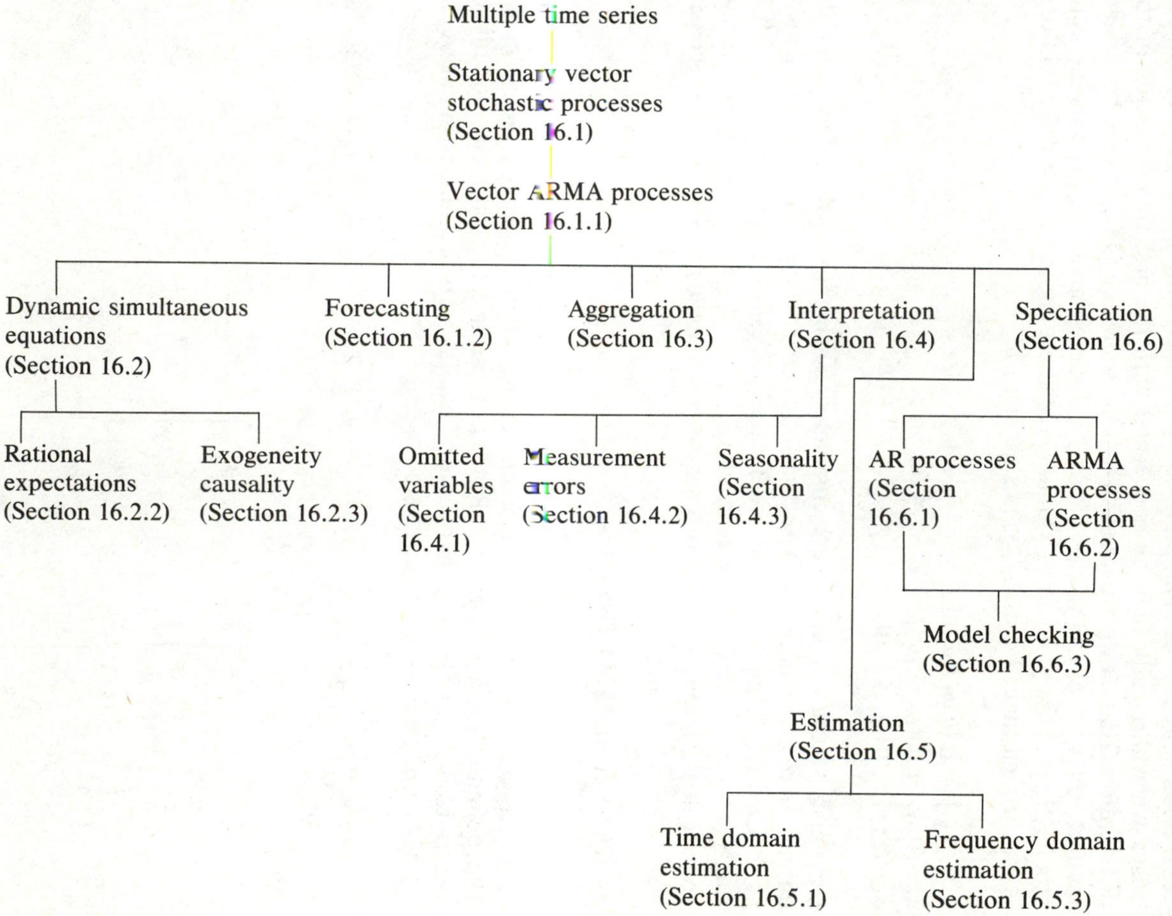

16.1 STATIONARY VECTOR STOCHASTIC PROCESSES

Instead of having data only on a single variable as in Chapter 7, we now assume the availability of observations on a set of variables, say $\mathbf{y}_t = (y_{1t}, \ldots, y_{kt})'$. In order to model the data generation process, we associate a random vector $\mathbf{y}_t$ with each integer $t = 0, \pm 1, \pm 2, \ldots$ similar to the univariate case. The resulting sequence is called a k-dimensional (discrete) vector stochastic process. Such a process is characterized by its distribution and for practical purposes we will usually only be concerned with the first two moments of this distribution. That is, we are interested in the sequence $E[\mathbf{y}_t]$ and the covariance matrices $E[(\mathbf{y}_t - E[\mathbf{y}_t])(\mathbf{y}_{t+h} - E[\mathbf{y}_{t+h}])']$. Like a univariate process, a vector stochastic process $\mathbf{y}_t$ is called *stationary* if these moments are finite and constant through time. Formally, $\mathbf{y}_t$ is stationary if:

1. $E[\mathbf{y}_t] = \boldsymbol{\mu} < \infty$ for all t.
2. $E[(\mathbf{y}_t - \boldsymbol{\mu})(\mathbf{y}_t - \boldsymbol{\mu})'] = \Sigma_{\mathbf{y}} < \infty$ for all t.
3. $E[(\mathbf{y}_t - \boldsymbol{\mu})(\mathbf{y}_{t+h} - \boldsymbol{\mu})'] = \Gamma_{\mathbf{y}}(h)$ for all t and h. (16.1.1)

Obviously, these conditions are completely analogous to those given for the univariate case in Chapter 7. Also, we define *strict stationarity* in the same way as in Chapter 7, and a vector stochastic process is called Gaussian if it is stationary and all finite subsequences $\mathbf{y}_t, \ldots, \mathbf{y}_{t+h}$ have a joint multivariate normal distribution. We now discuss some examples of stationary stochastic processes.

16.1.1 Vector ARMA Processes

Vector autoregressive-moving average (ARMA) processes have proved to be useful tools to describe dynamic relationships between economic variables. The definition of a univariate ARMA process in Chapter 7 can directly be generalized to the multivariate case. That is, $\mathbf{y}_t$ is a k-dimensional vector ARMA(p,q) process if it is generated as

$$\mathbf{y}_t = \Theta_1 \mathbf{y}_{t-1} + \cdots + \Theta_p \mathbf{y}_{t-p} + \mathbf{v}_t + A_1 \mathbf{v}_{t-1} + \cdots + A_q \mathbf{v}_{t-q} \quad (16.1.2)$$

where

$$\Theta_n = \begin{bmatrix} \theta_{11,n} & \cdots & \theta_{1k,n} \\ \vdots & \ddots & \vdots \\ \theta_{k1,n} & \cdots & \theta_{kk,n} \end{bmatrix}, \qquad n = 1, \ldots, p$$

$$A_n = \begin{bmatrix} \alpha_{11,n} & \cdots & \alpha_{1k,n} \\ \vdots & \ddots & \vdots \\ \alpha_{k1,n} & \cdots & \alpha_{kk,n} \end{bmatrix}, \qquad n = 1, \ldots, q$$

and $\mathbf{v}_t$ is k-dimensional *vector* (or *multivariate*) *white noise* defined by $E[\mathbf{v}_t] = \mathbf{0}$, $E[\mathbf{v}_t\mathbf{v}_t'] = \Sigma_v$ (positive definite) and $\mathbf{v}_t$ and $\mathbf{v}_s$ are independent for $s \neq t$.

The process $\mathbf{y}_t$ is called a vector AR(p) process if $q = 0$; that is,

$$\mathbf{y}_t = \Theta_1\mathbf{y}_{t-1} + \ldots + \Theta_p\mathbf{y}_{t-p} + \mathbf{v}_t \tag{16.1.3}$$

and $\mathbf{y}_t$ is called a vector MA(q) process if $p = 0$; that is,

$$\mathbf{y}_t = \mathbf{v}_t + A_1\mathbf{v}_{t-1} + \ldots + A_q\mathbf{v}_{t-q} \tag{16.1.4}$$

In shorthand notation (16.1.2) can be written as

$$\Theta_p(L)\mathbf{y}_t = A_q(L)\mathbf{v}_t \tag{16.1.5}$$

where

$$\Theta_p(L) = I - \Theta_1 L - \ldots - \Theta_p L^p$$

and

$$A_q(L) = I + A_1 L + \ldots + A_q L^q$$

and L is the lag operator defined such that $L^n\mathbf{y}_t = \mathbf{y}_{t-n}$ (see Chapter 7). The vector ARMA process (16.1.5) is stationary if

$$\begin{aligned}\det[\Theta_p(z)] &= |\Theta_p(z)| \\ &= |I - \Theta_1 z - \ldots - \Theta_p z^p| \neq 0 \quad \text{for} \quad |z| \leq 1\end{aligned} \tag{16.1.6}$$

and a stationary vector ARMA process has a (possibly infinite order) MA representation

$$\mathbf{y}_t = \mathbf{v}_t + M_1\mathbf{v}_{t-1} + \ldots = M(L)\mathbf{v}_t \tag{16.1.7}$$

where $M(L) = \Theta_p(L)^{-1}A_q(L)$ and the coefficient matrices M_i can be evaluated using the following recursions:

$$\begin{aligned}M_0 &= I \\ M_1 &= A_1 - \Theta_1 \\ M_2 &= A_2 - \Theta_2 - \Theta_1 M_1 \\ &\vdots \\ M_i &= A_i - \sum_{j=1}^{\min(i,p)} \Theta_j M_{i-j}, \qquad i \leq q \\ M_i &= - \sum_{j=1}^{\min(i,p)} \Theta_j M_{i-j}, \qquad i > q\end{aligned} \tag{16.1.8}$$

The autocovariance matrices of the process $\mathbf{y}_t$ can be shown to be

$$\Gamma_{\mathbf{y}}(h) = E[\mathbf{y}_t\mathbf{y}'_{t+h}] = \sum_{j=0}^{\infty} M_j\Sigma_{\mathbf{v}}M'_{j+h}, \qquad h \geq 0 \tag{16.1.9}$$

and $\Gamma_{\mathbf{y}}(h) = \Gamma'_{\mathbf{y}}(-h)$ for $h < 0$. In fact, by a multivariate version of Wold's Decomposition Theorem [e.g., Hannan (1970)] any nondeterministic stationary vector stochastic process has an infinite MA representation.

The MA part of (16.1.2) or, for simplicity, the process $\mathbf{y}_t$ is called *invertible* if

$$|A_q(z)| = |I + A_1z + \ldots + A_qz^q| \neq 0 \quad \text{for} \quad |z| \leq 1 \tag{16.1.10}$$

If this condition is satisfied $\mathbf{y}_t$ has an AR representation

$$\mathbf{y}_t - \Phi_1\mathbf{y}_{t-1} - \Phi_2\mathbf{y}_{t-2} - \ldots = \Phi(L)\mathbf{y}_t = \mathbf{v}_t \tag{16.1.11}$$

where $\Phi(L) = A_q(L)^{-1}\Theta_p(L)$. The coefficient matrices Φ_i can be determined by a recursion similar to (16.1.8).

Note that an ARMA representation of a stationary vector stochastic process is not unique. For example, if $\mathbf{y}_t$ has the representation (16.1.5) and $\Theta_p(L)$ satisfies (16.1.6), then we may left-multiply (16.1.5) by $\Theta_p^*(L) = |\Theta_p(L)|\Theta_p^{-1}(L)$, the adjoint of $\Theta_p(L)$. This results in

$$|\Theta_p(L)|\mathbf{y}_t = \Theta_p^*(L)A_q(L)\mathbf{v}_t \tag{16.1.12}$$

Since both $|\Theta_p(L)|$ and $\Theta_p^*(L)$ are finite-order operators, (16.1.12) is another finite order ARMA representation of $\mathbf{y}_t$; that is, (16.1.12) represents the same autocovariance structure as (16.1.5). Interestingly, $|\Theta_p(L)|$ is a (1×1) operator and thus, the same AR operator is applied to each component of $\mathbf{y}_t$ in (16.1.12). This result has received considerable attention in the literature and has been used in practical multiple time series analyses [e.g., Zellner and Palm (1974), Wallis (1977), Chan and Wallis (1978)].

The problem of nonuniqueness of the ARMA representation of a stochastic process—that is, the problem that two different vector ARMA models may represent processes with identical covariance structure—corresponds of course to the identification problem discussed in Chapter 14 in the context of simultaneous equations models. In the multiple time series context this problem was raised by Quenouille (1957) in his pioneering book on the subject. Subsequently, conditions for the uniqueness of ARMA representations have been developed [e.g., Hannan (1969, 1970, 1976, 1979), Deistler and Hannan (1981)]. The following conditions are due to Hannan [see Priestley (1981, Section 10.5) and Granger and Newbold (1977, Section 7.3)].

Suppose the model is of the general form (16.1.5) and (16.1.6) and (16.1.10) are satisfied. Assume further that $\Theta_p(L)$ and $A_q(L)$ have no common left divisors; that is,

$$\Theta_p(L) = \Psi(L)\bar{\Theta}(L) \quad \text{and} \quad A_q(L) = \Psi(L)\bar{A}(L) \text{ implies that } |\Psi(L)| \text{ is constant} \tag{16.1.13}$$

Then any of the following conditions guarantees uniqueness of the ARMA representation.

1. $\Theta_p(L)$ is upper triangular and deg $\theta_{ii}(L) \geq$ deg $\theta_{ij}(L)$, $i = 1, \ldots, k$ and $j = 1, \ldots, k$, where deg $\theta(L)$ denotes the degree of the operator $\theta(L)$.
2. The AR operator $\Theta_p(L)$ is a scalar [(1×1) matrix] and the pth coefficient $\Theta_p \neq 0$.
3. Out of the class of all equivalent ARMA models choose q to be minimal and then choose p to be minimal. Then if the matrix $[\Theta_p \quad A_q]$ has full rank, uniqueness of the representation is guaranteed.

Besides those mentioned above, there are various other representations of vector ARMA processes that are useful occasionally. For instance, left-multiplying (16.1.2) by a nonsingular $(k \times k)$ matrix Φ does not alter the correlation structure of $\mathbf{y}_t$ and hence results in an equivalent representation. Also, if we define s such that $SS' = \Sigma_{\mathbf{v}}$ and $\mathbf{u}_t = S^{-1}\mathbf{v}_t$, then $E[\mathbf{u}_t\mathbf{u}_t'] = I_k$ and

$$\mathbf{y}_t = \Theta_1\mathbf{y}_{t-1} + \ldots + \Theta_p\mathbf{y}_{t-p} + S\mathbf{u}_t + A_1S\mathbf{u}_{t-1} + \ldots + A_qS\mathbf{u}_{t-q} \tag{16.1.14}$$

is equivalent to (16.1.2) and (16.1.5).

Another equivalent representation results if we define a triangular matrix P with unit diagonal such that $P\Sigma_{\mathbf{v}}P'$ is a diagonal matrix. In this case

$$P\mathbf{y}_t = P\Theta_1\mathbf{y}_{t-1} + \ldots + P\Theta_p\mathbf{y}_{t-p} + \mathbf{w}_t + PA_1P^{-1}\mathbf{w}_{t-1} + \ldots + PA_qP^{-1}\mathbf{w}_{t-q} \tag{16.1.15}$$

is an ARMA representation where the white noise process $\mathbf{w}_t = P\mathbf{v}_t$ has a diagonal variance-covariance matrix $\Sigma_{\mathbf{w}}$.

16.1.2 Forecasting Vector ARMA Processes

To forecast vector ARMA processes, the formulas developed in Chapter 7 for the univariate case can be generalized. Assuming again that $\mathbf{y}_t$ is as in (16.1.2) with (16.1.6) and (16.1.10) fulfilled, we denote the h-step forecast at time T by $\mathbf{y}_T(h)$. The objective is to find $\mathbf{y}_T(h)$ such that $\hat{\Sigma}(h) - \Sigma(h)$ is positive semidefinite where

$$\Sigma(h) = E\{[\mathbf{y}_{T+h} - \mathbf{y}_T(h)][\mathbf{y}_{T+h} - \mathbf{y}_T(h)]'\} \tag{16.1.16}$$

and $\hat{\Sigma}(h)$ is the MSE matrix of any other linear h-step ahead predictor at time T. Similar to the univariate case it can be shown that

$$\mathbf{y}_T(1) = \Theta_1\mathbf{y}_T + \ldots + \Theta_p\mathbf{y}_{T-p+1} + A_1\mathbf{v}_T + A_2\mathbf{v}_{T-1} + \ldots + A_q\mathbf{v}_{T-q+1}$$

$$\mathbf{y}_T(2) = \Theta_1\mathbf{y}_T(1) + \Theta_2\mathbf{y}_T + \ldots + \Theta_p\mathbf{y}_{T-p+2} + A_2\mathbf{v}_T + A_3\mathbf{v}_{T-1} + \ldots + A_q\mathbf{v}_{T-q+2} \tag{16.1.17}$$

and so on.

If the infinite AR representation (16.1.11) is given, the optimal h-step forecast is

$$\mathbf{y}_T(h) = \Phi_1\mathbf{y}_T(h-1) + \ldots + \Phi_{h-1}\mathbf{y}_T(1) + \Phi_h\mathbf{y}_T + \ldots \tag{16.1.18}$$

Alternatively, if the infinite MA representation (16.1.7) is given,

$$\mathbf{y}_T(h) = M_h\mathbf{v}_T + M_{h+1}\mathbf{v}_{T-1} + \ldots \tag{16.1.19}$$

The corresponding mean square forecasting error matrix is

$$\begin{aligned}\Sigma(h) &= \Sigma_{\mathbf{v}} + M_1\Sigma_{\mathbf{v}}M_1' + \ldots + M_{h-1}\Sigma_{\mathbf{v}}M_{h-1}' \\ &= \Sigma(h-1) + M_{h-1}\Sigma_{\mathbf{v}}M_{h-1}'\end{aligned} \tag{16.1.20}$$

and can be computed recursively.

This shows that, once the data generation process is known, optimal forecasting is a routine affair. Of course, the true process will in practice not be known and thus has to be derived from the available data. In that case the same arguments apply as in the univariate case. In particular, the forecasting variance (16.1.20) will only be an approximation to the actual variance. The *asymptotic* forecasting variance if the parameters of the process are estimated is considered by Yamamoto (1980, 1981), Reinsel (1980), and Baillie (1979, 1981).

16.2 DYNAMIC SIMULTANEOUS EQUATIONS MODELS

16.2.1 Structural Form, Reduced Form, and Final Form

Dynamic econometric models can often be interpreted as parts of vector ARMA processes. If $\mathbf{y}_t' = (\mathbf{z}_t', \mathbf{x}_t')$ and $\mathbf{z}_t$ and $\mathbf{x}_t$ are g endogenous and l exogenous variables of a system, respectively, an ARMA model for $\mathbf{y}_t$ has the form

$$\Theta_p(L)\mathbf{y}_t = \begin{bmatrix}\Theta_{11}(L) & \Theta_{12}(L) \\ 0 & \Theta_{22}(L)\end{bmatrix}\begin{bmatrix}\mathbf{z}_t \\ \mathbf{x}_t\end{bmatrix} = \begin{bmatrix}A_{11}(L) & 0 \\ 0 & A_{22}(L)\end{bmatrix}\begin{bmatrix}\mathbf{v}_{1t} \\ \mathbf{v}_{2t}\end{bmatrix} \tag{16.2.1}$$

or

$$\Theta_{11}(L)\mathbf{z}_t + \Theta_{12}(L)\mathbf{x}_t = A_{11}(L)\mathbf{v}_{1t} \tag{16.2.2}$$

$$\Theta_{22}(L)\mathbf{x}_t = A_{22}(L)\mathbf{v}_{2t} \tag{16.2.3}$$

where $\mathbf{v}_{1t}$ and $\mathbf{v}_{2t}$ are assumed to be independent white noise processes. Equation 16.2.2 obviously looks very much like the systems of simultaneous equations discussed in Chapters 14 and 15, the difference being that the lagged endogenous and exogenous variables are expressed by means of matrix polynomials in the lag operator and the error terms $\mathbf{e}_t = A_{11}(L)\mathbf{v}_{1t}$ are serially correlated. Models of the form (16.2.2) are sometimes called ARMAX models. There has been some discussion of exogeneity of variables and the above is but one possible use of the term. We will return to this topic in Section 16.2.3.

Written without the lag operator (16.2.2) is

$$\Theta_{11,0}\mathbf{z}_t + \ldots + \Theta_{11,p}\mathbf{z}_{t-p} + \Theta_{12,0}\mathbf{x}_t + \ldots + \Theta_{12,r}\mathbf{x}_{t-r} = \mathbf{e}_t \quad (16.2.4)$$

where it has been used that $\Theta_{11}(L)$ and $\Theta_{12}(L)$ do not necessarily have the same order. In this case these operators are assumed to have the orders p and r, respectively. Equation 16.2.4 is a *structural form* of a system of simultaneous equations. The corresponding *reduced form* is

$$\mathbf{z}_t = -\Theta_{11,0}^{-1}(\Theta_{11,1}\mathbf{z}_{t-1} + \ldots + \Theta_{11,p}\mathbf{z}_{t-p}) - \Theta_{11,0}^{-1}\Theta_{12}(L)\mathbf{x}_t + \Theta_{11,0}^{-1}\mathbf{e}_t \quad (16.2.5)$$

and the *final form* is

$$\mathbf{z}_t = -\Theta_{11}^{-1}(L)\Theta_{12}(L)\mathbf{x}_t + \Theta_{11}^{-1}(L)\mathbf{e}_t \quad (16.2.6)$$

[e.g., Zellner and Palm (1974), Prothero and Wallis (1976), Wallis (1977), Harvey (1981, Chapter 9)]. In this form the infinite matrix polynomial

$$\Xi(L) = \sum_{i=0}^{\infty} \Xi_i L^i = -\Theta_{11}^{-1}(L)\Theta_{12}(L)$$

contains the *dynamic multipliers,* describing the response of $\mathbf{z}_t$ to unit shocks in the exogenous variables $\mathbf{x}_t$. $\Xi(1) = \sum_{i=0}^{\infty} \Xi_i$ represents the total response of $\mathbf{z}_t$ to unit changes in $\mathbf{x}_t$ and is therefore called the matrix of *total multipliers,* whereas $\sum_{i=0}^{n} \Xi_i$ is the matrix of the nth *interim multipliers*. The matrix Ξ_0 represents the immediate effects of a unit increase in the components of $\mathbf{x}_t$ and is called the matrix of *impact multipliers*.

Note that the precise form of the lag polynomials $\Theta_{11}(L)$, $\Theta_{12}(L)$, and $A_{11}(L)$ is usually not known from economic theory and the data have to be used to determine these operators. In this case the dynamic multipliers have to be interpreted carefully since, as we have seen in Section 16.1.1, the ARMA representation of a stochastic process is in general not unique. If identifying restrictions are not available from economic theory the dynamic multipliers are to some extent arbitrary (see Section 16.2.3). Before we make some more remarks about the identification of systems of dynamic simultaneous equations we will now consider an example.

16.2.1a An Example

Zellner and Palm (1974) postulate the following dynamic model for quarterly U.S. data:

$$C_t = \beta + \gamma(L)Y_t + e_{1t} \tag{16.2.7a}$$

$$S_t = \nu + \eta(L)(C_t + I_t) + e_{2t} \tag{16.2.7b}$$

$$Y_t = C_t + I_t - S_t \tag{16.2.7c}$$

where C_t denotes personal consumption expenditures, Y_t is personal disposable income, S_t stands for gross business saving and I_t denotes gross investment. The variables C_t, Y_t, and S_t are endogenous, I_t is exogenous and e_{1t} and e_{2t} are disturbance terms that may be temporally correlated. The operators $\gamma(L) = \gamma_0 + \gamma_1 L + \ldots + \gamma_p L^p$ and $\eta(L) = \eta_0 + \eta_1 L + \ldots + \eta_r L^r$ have finite but unknown order. The quantities β and ν denote constants. For expository purposes in the ARMA processes in Section 16.1 and in the system (16.2.2), deterministic terms like *intercept* or *polynomial trends* have been neglected. However, if only (16.2.2) is considered and an analysis is done conditionally on the exogenous variables, some components of $\mathbf{x}_t$ may be assumed nonstochastic and thus may contain deterministic terms unless otherwise noted.

Eliminating the identity of (16.2.7) we get the two-equation system

$$C_t = \beta + \gamma(L)Y_t + e_{1t} \tag{16.2.8a}$$

$$Y_t = -\nu + \delta(L)(C_t + I_t) - e_{2t} \tag{16.2.8b}$$

where $\delta(L) = [1 - \eta(L)] = \delta_0 + \delta_1 L + \ldots + \delta_r L^r$. In vector and matrix notation we get

$$\begin{bmatrix} 1 & -\gamma_0 \\ -\delta_0 & 1 \end{bmatrix} \begin{bmatrix} C_t \\ Y_t \end{bmatrix} = \begin{bmatrix} \beta \\ -\nu \end{bmatrix} + \begin{bmatrix} \gamma_1 Y_{t-1} + \ldots + \gamma_p Y_{t-p} \\ \delta_1 C_{t-1} + \ldots + \delta_r C_{t-r} \end{bmatrix} + \begin{bmatrix} 0 \\ \delta(L) \end{bmatrix} I_t + \begin{bmatrix} e_{1t} \\ -e_{2t} \end{bmatrix} \tag{16.2.9}$$

and, assuming invertibility of the left-hand side matrix, the reduced form is

$$\begin{bmatrix} C_t \\ Y_t \end{bmatrix} = \begin{bmatrix} 1 & -\gamma_0 \\ -\delta_0 & 1 \end{bmatrix}^{-1} \left(\begin{bmatrix} \beta \\ -\nu \end{bmatrix} + \begin{bmatrix} \gamma_1 Y_{t-1} + \ldots + \gamma_p Y_{t-p} \\ \delta_1 C_{t-1} + \ldots + \delta_r C_{t-r} \end{bmatrix} + \begin{bmatrix} 0 \\ \delta(L) \end{bmatrix} I_t + \begin{bmatrix} e_{1t} \\ -e_{2t} \end{bmatrix} \right) \tag{16.2.10}$$

The final form is obtained from

$$\begin{bmatrix} 1 & -\gamma(L) \\ -\delta(L) & 1 \end{bmatrix} \begin{bmatrix} C_t \\ Y_t \end{bmatrix} = \begin{bmatrix} \beta \\ -\nu \end{bmatrix} + \begin{bmatrix} 0 \\ \delta(L) \end{bmatrix} I_t + \begin{bmatrix} e_{1t} \\ -e_{2t} \end{bmatrix}$$

by multiplying by the inverse of the left-hand side matrix:

$$\begin{bmatrix} C_t \\ Y_t \end{bmatrix} = \frac{1}{1-\delta(1)\gamma(1)} \begin{bmatrix} 1 & \gamma(1) \\ \delta(1) & 1 \end{bmatrix} \begin{bmatrix} \beta \\ -\nu \end{bmatrix} + \begin{bmatrix} \dfrac{\gamma(L)\delta(L)}{1-\gamma(L)\delta(L)} \\ \dfrac{\delta(L)}{1-\gamma(L)\delta(L)} \end{bmatrix} I_t + \mathbf{u}_t \tag{16.2.11}$$

where

$$\mathbf{u}_t = \frac{1}{1-\gamma(L)\delta(L)} \begin{bmatrix} 1 & \gamma(L) \\ \delta(L) & 1 \end{bmatrix} \begin{bmatrix} e_{1t} \\ -e_{2t} \end{bmatrix}$$

16.2.1b Identification of ARMAX Models

As we have seen in Section 16.1.1, without any a priori constraints the ARMA representation of a stochastic process will not be unique. Identifying restrictions for the system (16.2.1) have been mentioned in Section 16.1.1. However, in the context of dynamic simultaneous equations systems it is desirable to identify (16.2.2) without reference to (16.2.3). Identification conditions for this case are for example given by Hatanaka (1975). He assumes that the lag lengths of the endogenous and exogenous variables are unknown and the error process $\mathbf{e}_t$ is stationary but does not have to be specified. Furthermore, it is assumed that the exogenous variables $\mathbf{x}_t$ do not contain deterministic terms such as intercepts, seasonal dummy variables, or polynomial trend terms. With these assumptions conditions similar to the classical rank and order conditions (see Chapter 14) can be formulated. However, instead of placing zero restrictions on individual parameters, a variable is now said to be excluded from an equation if neither current nor lagged values of the variable appear in the equation. Thus, elements of $\Theta_{11}(L)$ and $\Theta_{12}(L)$ in (16.2.2) are restricted to zero. For example, in the first equation

$$[\boldsymbol{\theta}'_{11,1}(L) \quad \boldsymbol{\theta}'_{11,2}(L)] \begin{bmatrix} \mathbf{z}_{1t} \\ \mathbf{z}_{2t} \end{bmatrix} + [\boldsymbol{\theta}'_{12,1}(L) \quad \boldsymbol{\theta}'_{12,2}(L)] \begin{bmatrix} \mathbf{x}_{1t} \\ \mathbf{x}_{2t} \end{bmatrix} = e_{1t} \tag{16.2.12}$$

where $\boldsymbol{\theta}_{11,1}(L)$ and $\mathbf{z}_{1t}$ are $(g_1 \times 1)$, $\boldsymbol{\theta}_{11,2}(L)$ and $\mathbf{z}_{2t}$ are $(g_2 \times 1)$, $\boldsymbol{\theta}_{12,1}(L)$ and $\mathbf{x}_{1t}$ are $(l_1 \times 1)$, and $\boldsymbol{\theta}_{12,2}(L)$ and $\mathbf{x}_{2t}$ are $(l_2 \times 1)$, the variables $\mathbf{z}_{2t}$ and $\mathbf{x}_{2t}$ are said to be excluded if $\boldsymbol{\theta}_{11,2}(L)$ and $\boldsymbol{\theta}_{12,2}(L)$ are zero. Partitioning the $[(g_1 + g_2) \times (g_1 + g_2)]$ matrix $\Theta_{11}(L)$ and the $[(g_1 + g_2) \times (l_1 + l_2)]$ matrix $\Theta_{12}(L)$ comformably, we get

$$[\Theta_{11}(L) \quad \Theta_{12}(L)] = \begin{bmatrix} \boldsymbol{\theta}'_{11,1}(L) & \mathbf{0}' & \boldsymbol{\theta}'_{12,1}(L) & \mathbf{0}' \\ \Theta_{11,1}(L) & \Theta_{11,2}(L) & \Theta_{12,1}(L) & \Theta_{12,2}(L) \end{bmatrix} \tag{16.2.13}$$

In this case a generalization of the *rank condition* states that the first equation of the model is identified if and only if the matrix $[\Theta_{11,2}(L) \quad \Theta_{12,2}(L)]$ has rank $g_1 + g_2 - 1$ and the rank is defined to be the order of the largest submatrix for which the determinant does not vanish *identically* for all L. The *order condition* states that for the first equation to be identified the number of excluded exogenous variables, l_2, has to be greater than or equal to $g_1 - 1$, the number of included endogenous variables minus one.

Note that without any normalization (16.2.12) is still not unique if the rank condition is satisfied, since multiplication by any polynomial $\eta(L)$ will result in an equivalent structure. However, uniqueness can be insured by requiring that no further cancellation is possible and that the zero order coefficient of the first endogenous variable is 1.

Occasionally exclusion restrictions of the type discussed by Hatanaka will not suffice to decide the identifiability of an equation. An example is Equation 16.2.8b of the example model. Other conditions have been discussed by Deistler (1976, 1978), Deistler and Schrader (1979), and others. For the case of white noise errors $\mathbf{e}_t$ see also Chapter 14.

16.2.2 Rational Expectations

An extension of the model (16.2.2) is obtained when expectations of economic agents formed in previous periods are assumed to have an impact on the system; for example,

$$\Theta_{11}(L)\mathbf{z}_t + \Phi\,\mathbf{z}_t^* + \Theta_{12}(L)\mathbf{x}_t = A_{11}(L)\mathbf{v}_{1t} \tag{16.2.14}$$

where $\mathbf{z}_t^*$ are expectations of $\mathbf{z}_t$ formed in period $t-1$ and Φ is a $(g \times g)$ matrix [e.g., Wallis (1980), Shiller (1978)]. By following Muth (1961) the expectations are called *rational* if they are formed using all information available at time $t - 1$. In other words,

$$\mathbf{z}_t^* = E[\mathbf{z}_t|\mathbf{z}_s, \mathbf{x}_s, s < t] = E[\mathbf{z}_t|\mathbf{y}_s, s < t] \tag{16.2.15}$$

Taking conditional expectations of (16.2.14) gives

$$\begin{aligned}\Theta_{11,0}\mathbf{z}_t^* &+ \Theta_{11,1}\mathbf{z}_{t-1} + \dots + \Theta_{11,p}\mathbf{z}_{t-p} + \Phi\mathbf{z}_t^* \\ &+ \Theta_{12,0}E[\mathbf{x}_t|\mathbf{y}_s, s < t] + \Theta_{12,1}\mathbf{x}_{t-1} + \dots + \Theta_{12,r}\mathbf{x}_{t-r} \\ &= A_{11,1}\mathbf{v}_{1,t-1} + \dots + A_{11,q}\mathbf{v}_{1,t-q}\end{aligned}$$

or, provided $\Psi = (\Theta_{11,0} + \Phi)$ is invertible,

$$\begin{aligned}\mathbf{z}_t^* = &-\Psi^{-1}[\Theta_{11}(L) - \Theta_{11,0}]\mathbf{z}_t - \Psi^{-1}\Theta_{12,0}E[\mathbf{x}_t|\mathbf{y}_s, s < t] \\ &-\Psi^{-1}[\Theta_{12}(L) - \Theta_{12,0}]\mathbf{x}_t + \Psi^{-1}[A_{11}(L) - A_{11,0}]\mathbf{v}_{1t}\end{aligned} \tag{16.2.16}$$

Using (16.2.3)

$$E[\mathbf{x}_t|\mathbf{y}_s, s < t] = -\Theta_{22,0}^{-1}\{[\Theta_{22}(L) - \Theta_{22,0}]\mathbf{x}_t + [A_{22}(L) - A_{22,0}]\mathbf{v}_{2t}\} \tag{16.2.17}$$

where $\Theta_{22,0}$ and $A_{22,0}$ are the zero-order coefficient matrices of $\Theta_{22}(L)$ and $A_{22}(L)$, respectively. Substituting (16.2.17) in (16.2.16) and using the resulting expression for $\mathbf{z}_t^*$ in (16.2.14) results in a model of the general form (16.2.2), (16.2.3). Thus, the rational expectations model (16.2.14) implies, under our assumptions, that the data are generated by a vector ARMA process. Note however that the rational expectations hypothesis implies restrictions on the parameters that can be tested. Hoffman and Schmidt (1981) consider the likelihood ratio and the Wald test for this purpose and Hoffman and Schlagenhauf (1983) discuss applications. Theoretically (16.2.14) could be extended to include expectations several periods ahead or expectations formed in earlier periods [see Shiller (1978), Wallis (1980)].

As a simple example of a model involving expectations consider the following two-equation model:

$$\text{Supply:}\quad z_{1t} = \alpha_1 z_{2t}^* + e_{1t} \tag{16.2.18a}$$

$$\text{Demand:}\quad z_{1t} = \beta_1 z_{2t} + \beta_2 x_t + e_{2t} \tag{16.2.18b}$$

where z_{1t} represents quantity, z_{2t} is the market price in the tth period, z_{2t}^* is the unobservable market price expected to prevail during the tth period on the basis of information available through the $(t-1)$st period, x_t is income, and e_{1t} and e_{2t} are stochastic disturbance terms. All variables are measured as deviations from equilibrium values.

Equation 16.2.18a can be rewritten as

$$z_{2t} = \left(\frac{\alpha_1}{\beta_1}\right) z_{2t}^* - \left(\frac{\beta_2}{\beta_1}\right) x_t + \frac{e_{1t} - e_{2t}}{\beta_1} \tag{16.2.19}$$

Using

$$z_{2t}^* = E[z_{2t}|\Omega_{t-1}]$$

where Ω_{t-1} contains the information up to period $t-1$, and taking conditional expectations of (16.2.19), we have

$$z_{2t}^* = \left(\frac{\alpha_1}{\beta_1}\right) z_{2t}^* - \left(\frac{\beta_2}{\beta_1}\right) E[x_t|\Omega_{t-1}] + \frac{E[e_{1t} - e_{2t}|\Omega_{t-1}]}{\beta_1} \tag{16.2.20}$$

Assuming that the disturbances e_{1t} and e_{2t} are nonautocorrelated and independent of Ω_{t-1}, and have zero means, we obtain the rational expectation

$$z_{2t}^* = -\frac{\beta_2}{\beta_1 - \alpha_1} E[x_t|\Omega_{t-1}] \tag{16.2.21}$$

where the conditional expected value is the optimal 1-step ahead predictor of the exogenous variable. If we assume that Ω_{t-1} contains only z_{1s}, z_{2s}, and x_s,

$s < t$, and x_t is an ARMA process,

$$\psi(L)x_t = \eta(L)w_t \tag{16.2.22}$$

where w_t is white noise, the optimal 1-step forecast is

$$E[x_t|\Omega_{t-1}] = \delta(L)x_{t-1} \tag{16.2.23}$$

where

$$\delta(L) = \frac{1}{L}[1 - \eta^{-1}(L)\psi(L)] = \delta_1 + \delta_2 L + \delta_3 L^2 + \ldots$$

Therefore, when (16.2.23) is substituted into (16.2.21),

$$z_{2t}^* = -\frac{\beta_2}{\beta_1 - \alpha_1}\delta(L)x_{t-1}$$

Further substitution of the above equation into (16.2.18a) and (16.2.19) results in

$$z_{1t} = \frac{\alpha_1\beta_2}{(\alpha_1 - \beta_1)}\delta(L)x_{t-1} + e_{1t}$$

and

$$z_{2t} = \frac{\alpha_1\beta_2}{(\alpha_1 - \beta_1)\beta_1}\delta(L)x_{t-1} - \frac{\beta_2}{\beta_1}x_t + \frac{e_{1t} - e_{2t}}{\beta_1}$$

In each of these equations the endogenous variable is a distributed lag function of the observable exogenous variable x.

Lucas (1976) noted that a rational economic agent will take into account changes in policy rules. This situation can be accommodated in the present framework if the conditional expected value of x_t in (16.2.21) is not simply replaced by the optimal forecast (16.2.23), but is modified so as to take account of the policy change. For instance, a change in the tax rule could have an impact on the income of the agents operating in the considered market and could be taken into account when expectations are being built.

In (16.2.14) the expectations enter the model in an ad hoc way. However, it is possible to base the underlying theory on optimizing behavior of the involved agents. For instance, a firm could be assumed to maximize its discounted expected future profits [e.g., Hansen and Sargent (1980)]. Such an assumption would introduce expectations in the model. The implied constraints on the vector ARMA structure would become rather more complicated in this case.

Work with the rational expectations hypothesis has been done on topics such as inflation, interest, and employment. An excellent collection of papers in this area is provided by Lucas and Sargent (1981), where also a very good introduction to the topic and many further references are given.

16.2.3 Exogeneity and Causality

There has been some discussion about a meaningful definition of a variable being exogenous [e.g., Sims (1977), Geweke (1978a, 1982), Engle, Hendry, and Richard (1983), to give only a few references]. The definition of exogeneity implicit in the foregoing is closely related to the concept of causality in Granger's (1969) sense and we will now introduce this concept. Before we give details some general remarks may be useful.

Given the nonexperimental nature of most economic data it is difficult and often impossible to determine cause and effect relationships from the available data. Therefore, economic theory usually has to provide a model that postulates the direction of causality. Since many controversial economic theories exist, it would be preferable to examine such models including the causal directions with statistical tools. Therefore, a concept of "causality" has been developed that can be tested with statistical tools. Since this concept is not based on an acceptable definition of cause and effect in a strict philosophical sense, "causality" is, strictly speaking, not the appropriate word in this context. Nonetheless, we will follow the tradition of the recent literature on the subject and use the term here.

Broadly speaking, a set of variables $\mathbf{z}_t$ is said to be caused by $\mathbf{x}_t$ in Granger's sense if the information in past and present $\mathbf{x}_t$ helps to improve the forecasts of $\mathbf{z}_t$. To formalize, suppose Ω_t contains all the information in the universe up to time t and define $\Sigma(\mathbf{z}_{t+1}|\Omega_t)$ to be the 1-step expected quadratic forecasting error matrix if all the information in Ω_t is used to predict $\mathbf{z}_{t+1}$. A vector of variables $\mathbf{x}_t$ is said to *cause* $\mathbf{z}_t$ if for some t

$$\Sigma(\mathbf{z}_{t+1}|\Omega_t) \neq \Sigma(\mathbf{z}_{t+1}|\Omega_t \backslash \{\mathbf{x}_s|s \leq t\}) \qquad (16.2.24)$$

where $\Omega_t \backslash \{\mathbf{x}_s|s \leq t\}$ denotes the set of elements of Ω_t that are not in $\{\mathbf{x}_s|s \leq t\}$, and $\mathbf{x}_t$ *causes* $\mathbf{z}_t$ *instantaneously* if

$$\Sigma(\mathbf{z}_{t+1}|\Omega_t \cup \{\mathbf{x}_{t+1}\}) \neq \Sigma(\mathbf{z}_{t+1}|\Omega_t) \qquad (16.2.25)$$

If (16.2.24) is not true, $\mathbf{z}_t$ is *not caused* by $\mathbf{x}_t$ and if (16.2.25) does not hold, then $\mathbf{z}_t$ is *not caused instantaneously* by $\mathbf{x}_t$. If $\mathbf{x}_t$ causes $\mathbf{z}_t$ and $\mathbf{z}_t$ causes $\mathbf{x}_t$, then $\mathbf{y}_t' = (\mathbf{z}_t', \mathbf{x}_t')$ is a *feedback* system.

Assuming $\mathbf{y}_t' = (\mathbf{z}_t', \mathbf{x}_t')$ is generated by the ARMA process (16.2.1) with invertible operators $A_{11}(L)$ and $A_{22}(L)$, the process has an AR representation

$$\begin{aligned} \mathbf{z}_t &= \Phi_{11,1}\mathbf{z}_{t-1} + \Phi_{12,1}\mathbf{x}_{t-1} + \Phi_{11,2}\mathbf{z}_{t-2} + \Phi_{12,2}\mathbf{x}_{t-2} + \cdots + \mathbf{v}_{1t} \\ \mathbf{x}_t &= \Phi_{22,1}\mathbf{x}_{t-1} + \Phi_{22,2}\mathbf{x}_{t-2} + \cdots + \mathbf{v}_{2t} \end{aligned} \qquad (16.2.26)$$

where $\mathbf{v}_{1t}$ and $\mathbf{v}_{2t}$ are independent white noise processes. Here transformations similar to those in Section 16.1.1 have been used. Using (16.1.18) the optimal 1-step ahead forecasts of $\mathbf{z}_t$ and $\mathbf{x}_t$ are

$$\mathbf{z}_t(1) = \Phi_{11,1}\mathbf{z}_t + \Phi_{12,1}\mathbf{x}_t + \Phi_{11,2}\mathbf{z}_{t-1} + \Phi_{12,2}\mathbf{x}_{t-1} + \ldots \tag{16.2.27}$$

and

$$\mathbf{x}_t(1) = \Phi_{22,1}\mathbf{x}_t + \Phi_{22,2}\mathbf{x}_{t-1} + \ldots \tag{16.2.28}$$

Thus, $\mathbf{z}_t$ does not cause $\mathbf{x}_t$ if we assume that

$$\Omega_t = \{\mathbf{z}_s | s \leq t\} \cup \{\mathbf{x}_s | s \leq t\} \tag{16.2.29}$$

That is, we assume $\mathbf{z}_t$ and $\mathbf{x}_t$ contain all relevant information in the universe. In other words, the exogenous variables are not Granger-caused by the endogenous variables.

More generally, it can be shown that for a Gaussian process $(\mathbf{z}_t', \mathbf{x}_t')$ with conformably partitioned AR representation,

$$\begin{bmatrix} \mathbf{z}_t \\ \mathbf{x}_t \end{bmatrix} = \begin{bmatrix} \Phi_{11,1} & \Phi_{12,1} \\ \Phi_{21,1} & \Phi_{22,1} \end{bmatrix} \begin{bmatrix} \mathbf{z}_{t-1} \\ \mathbf{x}_{t-1} \end{bmatrix} + \begin{bmatrix} \Phi_{11,2} & \Phi_{12,2} \\ \Phi_{21,2} & \Phi_{22,2} \end{bmatrix} \begin{bmatrix} \mathbf{z}_{t-2} \\ \mathbf{x}_{t-2} \end{bmatrix} + \ldots + \begin{bmatrix} \mathbf{v}_{1t} \\ \mathbf{v}_{2t} \end{bmatrix} \tag{16.2.30}$$

$\mathbf{z}_t$ does not cause $\mathbf{x}_t$ if and only if $\Phi_{21,i} = 0, i = 1, 2, \ldots$, if the information set Ω_t is as in (16.2.29). It follows immediately for an invertible Gaussian MA process

$$\begin{bmatrix} \mathbf{z}_t \\ \mathbf{x}_t \end{bmatrix} = \begin{bmatrix} \mathbf{v}_{1t} \\ \mathbf{v}_{2t} \end{bmatrix} + \begin{bmatrix} M_{11,1} & M_{12,1} \\ M_{21,1} & M_{22,1} \end{bmatrix} \begin{bmatrix} \mathbf{v}_{1,t-1} \\ \mathbf{v}_{2,t-1} \end{bmatrix} + \ldots \tag{16.2.31}$$

that $\mathbf{z}_t$ does not Granger-cause $\mathbf{x}_t$ if and only if $M_{21,i} = 0, i = 1, 2, \ldots$, [e.g., Pierce and Haugh (1977)]. Furthermore, if $\mathbf{v}_{1t}$ and $\mathbf{v}_{2t}$ are independent in (16.2.30) and (16.2.31), there is no instantaneous causality. The restrictions on the MA and AR coefficients matrices can be tested with standard techniques and this is the main virtue of the concept of Granger-causality. The money-income relationship is a popular example where such tests have been applied [e.g., Sims (1972), Barth and Bennett (1974), Williams, Goodhart, and Gowland (1976), Ciccolo (1978), Feige and Pearce (1979), Hsiao (1979a,b, 1981, 1982)].

It must be clear, however, that to make Granger's concept operational some quite restrictive assumptions have been made. First, the information set Ω_t has been reduced to the information in the past and present of $\mathbf{z}_t$ and $\mathbf{x}_t$ that will usually be short of some information in the universe and expanding the information set may change the causal structure [e.g., Lütkepohl (1982a), Webster (1982a)]. Second, "optimal forecasts" have been replaced by "optimal linear forecasts.'' This is appropriate if $(\mathbf{z}_t', \mathbf{x}_t')$ is assumed Gaussian but may clearly be restrictive for non-Gaussian processes. Third, one could question the mean square forecasting error as a measure for forecasting accuracy. As mentioned earlier, in addition to these more technical problems, the fundamental objection has been raised against the concept of Granger-causality that reference is made only to the concept of ''predictability'' and not to the concept of ''cause and effect'' in an acceptable philosophical sense. To demonstrate the involved problems more clearly a simple example may be helpful.

Consider the two-dimensional Gaussian AR(1) process

$$\begin{bmatrix} z_t \\ x_t \end{bmatrix} = \begin{bmatrix} \theta_{11} & 0 \\ 0 & \theta_{22} \end{bmatrix} \begin{bmatrix} z_{t-1} \\ x_{t-1} \end{bmatrix} + \begin{bmatrix} v_{1t} \\ v_{2t} \end{bmatrix}, \qquad \Sigma_{\mathbf{v}} = \begin{bmatrix} \sigma_1^2 & \sigma_{12} \\ \sigma_{12} & \sigma_2^2 \end{bmatrix} \tag{16.2.32}$$

By the foregoing discussion we know that x_t does not cause z_t and z_t does not cause x_t in Granger's sense. However, the process can be written equivalently as

$$\begin{aligned} z_t &= \theta_{11} z_{t-1} + \lambda x_t - \lambda \theta_{22} x_{t-1} + u_{1t} \\ x_t &= \theta_{22} x_{t-1} + u_{2t} \end{aligned} \tag{16.2.33}$$

where λ is a constant $u_{1t} = v_{1t} - \lambda v_{2t}$, and $u_{2t} = v_{2t}$ [see (16.1.15)]. Clearly, if this is the appropriate characterization of the relationship between z_t and x_t, then variations in x_t have an effect on z_t although, as we have seen above, z_t is not Granger-caused by x_t. This example also shows the possible arbitrariness of multipliers if economic theory is not capable of providing a unique model form.

Further discussions of Granger-causality include Zellner (1979), Caines and Chan (1975, 1976), Pierce (1977), Price (1979), Skoog (1977), Tjøstheim (1981), Caines and Sethi (1979), Newbold (1982), Florens and Mouchart (1982a,b), Chamberlain (1982) and Schwert (1979). Geweke, Meese, and Dent (1983) discuss and compare various tests for causality.

Engle, Hendry, and Richard (1983) emphasize that the concepts of Granger noncausality and exogeneity serve different purposes. They characterize a variable as *weakly exogenous* if inference for a set of parameters can be made conditionally on that variable without loss of information. Thus, this notion of exogeneity is not explicitly based on a variable's importance for prediction. If a variable is weakly exogenous and is not Granger-caused by any of the endogenous variables, then it is called *strongly exogenous* by Engle, Hendry, and Richard.

16.3 AGGREGATION OF VECTOR ARMA PROCESSES

Most economic data are aggregates. Examples are not only macro economic variables like the GNP, but also micro economic data like the monthly sales figure of a department store that is the sum of all individual items sold during a month. Furthermore, the yearly sales figure is the sum of all monthly sales figures. These examples contain two types of aggregation: contemporaneous aggregation and temporal aggregation. Very often both types of aggregation arise simultaneously and it seems desirable to analyze the consequences jointly. Nevertheless, we will first consider contemporaneous aggregation and then show how the results can be extended to variables subject to both types of aggregation. This section is mainly based on Lütkepohl (1984a, 1984b) where also further references are given. We will only consider aggregation of discrete time processes and refer the reader to Sims (1971) and Geweke (1978b) for results on temporal aggregation of continuous time processes.

16.3.1 The Structure of Aggregated ARMA Processes

16.3.1a Contemporaneous Aggregation

Contemporaneous aggregation of a vector ARMA process comes down to considering a linear transformation of the process. For example, if $\mathbf{y}_t = (y_{1t}, \ldots, y_{kt})'$, $z_{1t} = y_{1t} + \ldots + y_{lt}$, and $z_{2t} = y_{l+1,t} + \ldots + y_{kt}$, then

$$\mathbf{z}_t = \begin{bmatrix} z_{1t} \\ z_{2t} \end{bmatrix} = \begin{bmatrix} \underbrace{\begin{matrix} 1 & 1 & \ldots & 1 \\ 0 & 0 & \ldots & 0 \end{matrix}}_{l\text{-times}} & \underbrace{\begin{matrix} 0 & 0 & \ldots & 0 \\ 1 & 1 & \ldots & 1 \end{matrix}}_{(k-l)\text{-times}} \end{bmatrix} \mathbf{y}_t \tag{16.3.1}$$

Therefore, in order to study the consequences of contemporaneous aggregation, we may consider linear transformations of vector ARMA processes.

Suppose $\mathbf{y}_t$ is a k-dimensional ARMA(p,q) process as in (16.1.2) and (16.1.5) and F is an $(l \times k)$ matrix of rank l. Then it can be shown that $\mathbf{z}_t = F\mathbf{y}_t$ has an ARMA(p^*,q^*) representation with

$$p^* \leq kp \tag{16.3.2}$$

and

$$q^* \leq (k-1)p + q \tag{16.3.3}$$

This result follows from the representation (16.1.12) and the fact that a linear transformation of a moving average process is a moving average process of at most the same order. As shown in Section 16.1.1, $\mathbf{z}_t$ has various different finite order ARMA representations. The above result means that the orders of one of these representations are bounded by the quantities in (16.3.2) and (16.3.3). For tighter bounds see Lütkepohl (1984a). The process $\mathbf{z}_t = F\mathbf{y}_t$ is stationary if $\mathbf{y}_t$ is stationary.

16.3.1b Temporal and Contemporaneous Aggregation

To show how the foregoing results can be used to study the consequences of both contemporaneous and temporal aggregation over m periods we define a *macro process*

$$\boldsymbol{\Theta}_0\mathscr{y}_t + \boldsymbol{\Theta}_1\mathscr{y}_{t-1} + \ldots + \boldsymbol{\Theta}_P\mathscr{y}_{\tau-P} = \mathbf{A}_0\mathscr{v}_\tau + \mathbf{A}_1\mathscr{v}_{\tau-1} + \ldots + \mathbf{A}_Q\mathscr{v}_{\tau-Q} \qquad \tau = 0, \pm 1, \pm 2, \ldots \tag{16.3.4}$$

where

$$\mathscr{y}_\tau = \underset{(mk \times 1)}{\begin{bmatrix} \mathbf{y}_{(\tau-1)m+1} \\ \mathbf{y}_{(\tau-1)m+2} \\ \vdots \\ \mathbf{y}_{(\tau-1)m+m} \end{bmatrix}}, \qquad \mathscr{v}_\tau = \underset{(mk \times 1)}{\begin{bmatrix} \mathbf{v}_{(\tau-1)m+1} \\ \mathbf{v}_{(\tau-1)m+2} \\ \vdots \\ \mathbf{v}_{(\tau-1)m+m} \end{bmatrix}} \tag{16.3.5}$$

and $\boldsymbol{\Theta}_i$ and $\mathbf{A}_i$ consist of rows $imk + 1$ through $imk + mk$ of the following matrices:

$$\underset{(Pmk \times mk)}{\begin{bmatrix} I_k & 0 & 0 & \ldots & 0 \\ -\Theta_1 & I_k & 0 & \ldots & 0 \\ -\Theta_2 & -\Theta_1 & I_k & \ldots & 0 \\ \vdots & \vdots & \vdots & \ddots & \vdots \\ -\Theta_p & -\Theta_{p-1} & -\Theta_{p-2} & & I_k \\ 0 & -\Theta_p & -\Theta_{p-1} & \ddots & \vdots \\ 0 & 0 & -\Theta_p & \ddots & -\Theta_{p-2} \\ & & \ddots & \ddots & -\Theta_{p-1} \\ \vdots & \vdots & & \ddots & -\Theta_p \\ & & & \ddots & 0 \\ & & & & \vdots \\ 0 & 0 & 0 & \ldots & 0 \end{bmatrix}} \quad \text{and} \quad \underset{(Qmk \times mk)}{\begin{bmatrix} I_k & 0 & 0 & \ldots & 0 \\ A_1 & I_k & 0 & \ldots & 0 \\ A_2 & A_1 & I_k & \ldots & 0 \\ \vdots & \vdots & \vdots & \ddots & \vdots \\ & & & & I_k \\ A_q & A_{q-1} & A_{q-2} & \ddots & \vdots \\ 0 & A_q & A_{q-1} & \ddots & A_{q-2} \\ 0 & 0 & A_q & \ddots & A_{q-1} \\ \vdots & \vdots & & \ddots & A_q \\ & & & \ddots & 0 \\ & & & & \vdots \\ 0 & 0 & 0 & \ldots & 0 \end{bmatrix}} \tag{16.3.6}$$

respectively. Here

$$P = \min\{n \in \mathfrak{N} | nm \geq p\} \tag{16.3.7}$$

and

$$Q = \min\{n \in \mathfrak{N} | nm \geq q\} \tag{16.3.8}$$

where $\mathfrak{N}$ denotes the nonnegative integers.

As an example consider the vector ARMA(2,1) process

$$\mathbf{y}_t = \Theta_1 \mathbf{y}_{t-1} + \Theta_2 \mathbf{y}_{t-2} + \mathbf{v}_t + A_1 \mathbf{v}_{t-1} \tag{16.3.9}$$

For $m = 3$, $\mathfrak{y}_\tau$ is an ARMA(1,1) process of dimension $3k$,

$$\mathbf{\Theta}_0 \mathfrak{y}_\tau + \mathbf{\Theta}_1 \mathfrak{y}_{\tau-1} = \mathbf{A}_0 \mathfrak{v}_\tau + \mathbf{A}_1 \mathfrak{v}_{\tau-1} \tag{16.3.10}$$

where

$$\mathfrak{y}_\tau = \begin{bmatrix} \mathbf{y}_{(\tau-1)3+1} \\ \mathbf{y}_{(\tau-1)3+2} \\ \mathbf{y}_{3\tau} \end{bmatrix}, \qquad \mathfrak{v}_\tau = \begin{bmatrix} \mathbf{v}_{(\tau-1)3+1} \\ \mathbf{v}_{(\tau-1)3+2} \\ \mathbf{v}_{3\tau} \end{bmatrix}$$

$$\mathbf{\Theta}_0 = \begin{bmatrix} I_k & 0 & 0 \\ \Theta_1 & I_k & 0 \\ \Theta_2 & \Theta_1 & I_k \end{bmatrix}, \qquad \mathbf{\Theta}_1 = \begin{bmatrix} 0 & \Theta_2 & \Theta_1 \\ 0 & 0 & \Theta_2 \\ 0 & 0 & 0 \end{bmatrix}$$

$$\mathbf{A}_0 = \begin{bmatrix} I_k & 0 & 0 \\ A_1 & I_k & 0 \\ 0 & A_1 & I_k \end{bmatrix}, \qquad \mathbf{A}_1 = \begin{bmatrix} 0 & 0 & A_1 \\ 0 & 0 & 0 \\ 0 & 0 & 0 \end{bmatrix}$$

The macro process $\mathfrak{y}_\tau$ can be used to investigate temporal aggregates of $\mathbf{y}_t$. For example, if $\mathbf{y}_t$ is a vector of flow variables and m consecutive vectors are added starting with $t = 1$, we get a process

$$\underset{(k \times mk)}{\mathfrak{z}_\tau = [I_k \quad I_k \quad . \; . \; . \quad I_k]} \mathfrak{y}_\tau = F \mathfrak{y}_\tau \tag{16.3.11}$$

where the definition of F is obvious. That is, the resulting process $\mathfrak{z}_\tau$ is a linear transformation of $\mathfrak{y}_\tau$. Similarly, if $\mathbf{y}_t$ consists of stock variables and observations are only available every mth period, we get a process

$$\underset{(k \times mk)}{\mathfrak{z}_\tau = [0 \quad I_k]} \mathfrak{y}_\tau = F \mathfrak{y}_\tau \tag{16.3.12}$$

and if $\mathfrak{z}_\tau$ is an average of m consecutive $\mathbf{y}_t$ we have

$$\mathfrak{z}_\tau = \frac{1}{m} \underset{(k \times mk)}{[I_k \quad I_k \quad . \quad . \quad . \quad I_k]} \mathfrak{y}_\tau \tag{16.3.13}$$

Of course, this framework permits us to treat stock and flow variables simultaneously in one system. More generally, to jointly investigate temporal and contemporaneous aggregation problems we can consider the process $\mathfrak{z}_\tau = F\mathfrak{y}_\tau$, where F is a suitable $(l \times mk)$ matrix.

Given this framework, the results of Section 16.3.1a can be used to investigate the properties of the aggregated process $\mathfrak{z}_\tau$. If $\mathbf{y}_t$ is an ARMA(p,q) process, $\mathfrak{y}_\tau$ is the corresponding macro process for a given m, and $F \neq 0$ is an $(l \times mk)$ matrix, $\mathfrak{z}_\tau = F\mathfrak{y}_\tau$ can be shown to have an ARMA(p^*,q^*) representation with

$$p^* \leq kp \tag{16.3.14}$$

and

$$q^* \leq kp + Q \tag{16.3.15}$$

where Q is as defined in (16.3.8). If $m \geq p \geq q$,

$$q^* \leq kp \tag{16.3.16}$$

Furthermore, stationary $\mathbf{y}_t$ implies that $\mathfrak{z}_\tau$ is stationary. Note, however, that the aggregate $\mathfrak{z}_\tau$ being stationary does not necessarily imply that the underlying process $\mathbf{y}_t$ is stationary.

Another result of practical importance is that, under general conditions, a stationary ARMA process tends to become vector white noise if m, the period of temporal aggregation, approaches infinity. This result implies that highly temporally aggregated data may not contain much information about the disaggregates. Tiao and Wei (1976) show that even the causal structure may be spoiled by temporal aggregation. For instance, if a variable is Granger-caused by some other variable in the basic underlying system, there may be no causal relationship between the two variables in the temporally aggregated system. Also a one-way causal system may become a feedback structure when temporally aggregated.

16.3.2 Forecasting Aggregated Vector ARMA Processes

Using an aggregated model also has implications for the forecasts obtained for the involved variables. Assuming that the model has vector ARMA form we will again begin with the consequences of contemporaneous aggregation. In the remainder of this section we assume that $\mathbf{y}_t$ is a k-dimensional *stationary*

ARMA process with invertible MA part. As before, $F \neq 0$ is an $(l \times k)$ matrix of rank l and $\mathbf{z}_t = F\mathbf{y}_t$.

Suppose the objective is to forecast $\mathbf{z}_{t+h}$ at time t. There are some obvious ways to obtain a forecast. First, the optimal h-step forecast $\mathbf{y}_t(h)$ of $\mathbf{y}_{t+h}$ can be evaluated (see Section 16.1.2) and

$$\tilde{\mathbf{z}}_t(h) = F\mathbf{y}_t(h) \tag{16.3.17}$$

is then used as a forecast for $\mathbf{z}_{t+h}$. This forecast can be shown to be optimal given the information set $\{\mathbf{y}_s | s \leq t\}$. However, often it is difficult in practice to derive the process $\mathbf{y}_t$ from the data and univariate ARMA models may be constructed for the individual components of $\mathbf{y}_t$. These ARMA processes can be used to forecast the individual components of $\mathbf{y}_t$ giving a predictor that we denote by $\hat{\mathbf{y}}_t(h)$. This forecast in turn can be used to form

$$\hat{\mathbf{z}}_t(h) = F\hat{\mathbf{y}}_t(h) \tag{16.3.18}$$

As a third alternative, if only aggregated data and the aggregated process $\mathbf{z}_t$ are available, an optimal linear predictor $\mathbf{z}_t(h)$ based on $\{\mathbf{z}_s | s \leq t\}$ can be evaluated.

To compare the performance of the three forecasts $\tilde{\mathbf{z}}_t(h)$, $\hat{\mathbf{z}}_t(h)$, and $\mathbf{z}_t(h)$, we denote the corresponding mean square error matrices by

$$\tilde{\Sigma}(h) = E[\tilde{\mathbf{z}}_t(h) - \mathbf{z}_{t+h}][\tilde{\mathbf{z}}_t(h) - \mathbf{z}_{t+h}]' \tag{16.3.19}$$

$$\hat{\Sigma}(h) = E[\hat{\mathbf{z}}_t(h) - \mathbf{z}_{t+h}][\hat{\mathbf{z}}_t(h) - \mathbf{z}_{t+h}]' \tag{16.3.20}$$

and

$$\Sigma(h) = E[\mathbf{z}_t(h) - \mathbf{z}_{t+h}][\mathbf{z}_t(h) - \mathbf{z}_{t+h}]' \tag{16.3.21}$$

As mentioned above, $\tilde{\mathbf{z}}_t(h)$ is the best linear forecast. In particular, $\Sigma(h) - \tilde{\Sigma}(h)$ and $\hat{\Sigma}(h) - \tilde{\Sigma}(h)$ are positive semidefinite for $h = 1, 2, \ldots$. However, it is not possible in general to give a ranking of $\mathbf{z}_t(h)$ and $\hat{\mathbf{z}}_t(h)$. In other words, it may be better to forecast the aggregated process directly rather than forecasting the individual series and aggregate the individual forecasts. Of course, if the individual components of $\mathbf{y}_t$ are independent, forecasting them individually results in $\hat{\mathbf{y}}_t(h) = \mathbf{y}_t(h)$ so that in this case $\hat{\mathbf{z}}_t(h)$ is in general preferable to $\mathbf{z}_t(h)$. Lütkepohl (1984a) gives conditions for equality of $\tilde{\mathbf{z}}_t(h)$, $\hat{\mathbf{z}}_t(h)$, and $\mathbf{z}_t(h)$ and further discussions of the above results include Kohn (1982), Tiao and Guttman (1980), and Wei and Abraham (1981).

Using again the macro process $\mathcal{Y}_\tau$ corresponding to $\mathbf{y}_t$ and a prespecified positive integer m, it is easy to extend the above results to the case where both temporal and contemporaneous aggregation are present. Theoretically, forecasting the basic disaggregate process and then aggregating the forecasts turns out to be best.

Note that the above results also have interesting implications for comparing forecasts from econometric models and single series ARMA models. Theoretically, if the econometric model involving the variables $\mathbf{y}_t$ is specified correctly, the generation process of an individual variable, say y_{1t}, can be obtained by considering a linear transformation, $y_{1t} = [1 \quad 0 \quad . \ . \ . \quad 0]\mathbf{y}_t$. Thus, by the above results, single series forecasts cannot be better than forecasts from correctly specified econometric models. Webster (1982b) provides a more detailed discussion of this issue. In practice, however, it has been observed in various studies that single series forecasts may outperform econometric forecasts. For a survey of some of the literature on this topic, see Granger and Newbold (1977, Chapter 8).

16.4 INTERPRETATION OF MULTIPLE TIME SERIES MODELS

One objective of building multiple time series models is to better understand the interrelationships within the considered set of variables $\mathbf{y}_t$. For this purpose Sargent and Sims (1977) and Sims (1980) suggest tracing the system's response to so-called typical shocks. For simplicity we assume that $\mathbf{y}_t$ is a zero-mean stationary vector ARMA process with MA representation

$$\mathbf{y}_t = \mathbf{v}_t + M_1\mathbf{v}_{t-1} + M_2\mathbf{v}_{t-2} + \ . \ . \ . = M(L)\mathbf{v}_t \qquad (16.4.1)$$

Suppose that the system has been in equilibrium up to time $t = 0$; that is, $\mathbf{y}_t = \mathbf{0}$ for $t < 0$. Then a typical shock is a unit increase in one of the variables at $t = 0$, for instance $\mathbf{y}_0 = (1, 0, \ . \ . \ . \ , 0)'$. Equivalently, this can be expressed by requiring $\mathbf{v}_t = \mathbf{0}$, $t < 0$, and $\mathbf{v}_0 = (1, 0, \ . \ . \ . \ , 0)'$. Tracing out the system's response to such a shock over time gives the first column of M_1, M_2, and so on. Similarly, if $\mathbf{y}_0 = (0, 1, 0, \ . \ . \ . \ , 0)'$, we get the second columns of the MA coefficient matrices, and so on. Thus, the MA coefficient matrices represent the system's response to a unit shock in each of the variables. In other words, the MA coefficients are "*dynamic multipliers*" of the system. Note that the definition of exogeneity in Section 16.2 ensures that an exogenous variable does not react to a shock in any of the endogenous variables. This is easily seen by considering the MA representation of (16.2.1).

Note that MA representations other than (16.4.1) exist and thus the multipliers are not unique (see Sections 16.1.1 and 16.2). To ensure uniqueness economic theory has to supply a priori restrictions on the model structure. In addition, there are other obstacles that render the interpretation of the multipliers difficult. In particular, we need to assume that all "important" variables are included in the system, there are no measurement errors and prior transformations such as seasonal adjustment are such that the actual structure is not distorted. These problems are discussed in the following sections.

16.4.1 Omitted Variables

Assume that $\mathbf{y}_t$ consists of two subvectors $\mathbf{y}_{1t}$ and $\mathbf{y}_{2t}$ of dimension k_1 and k_2, respectively, and $\mathbf{v}_t$ is partitioned accordingly, so that

$$\mathbf{y}_t = \begin{bmatrix} \mathbf{y}_{1t} \\ \mathbf{y}_{2t} \end{bmatrix} = \sum_{i=0}^{\infty} \begin{bmatrix} M_{11,i} & M_{12,i} \\ M_{21,i} & M_{22,i} \end{bmatrix} \begin{bmatrix} \mathbf{v}_{1,t-i} \\ \mathbf{v}_{2,t-i} \end{bmatrix} \tag{16.4.2}$$

where $M_{11,0} = I_{k_1}$, $M_{22,0} = I_{k_2}$, $M_{12,0} = 0$, $M_{21,0} = 0$. If only $\mathbf{y}_{1t}$ is considered, the response of this subsystem to typical shocks is represented by the $M_{11,i}$, $i = 1, 2, \ldots$ and Lütkepohl (1982a) calls the corresponding process

$$\mathbf{z}_t = \sum_{i=0}^{\infty} M_{11,i}\mathbf{v}_{1,t-i} \tag{16.4.3}$$

a k_1-dimensional *partial process* of $\mathbf{y}_t$.

In contrast, the k_1-dimensional *subprocess* of the first k_1 components of $\mathbf{y}_t$ is

$$\mathbf{y}_{1t} = \sum_{i=0}^{\infty} [M_{11,i} \quad M_{12,i}]\mathbf{v}_{t-i} \tag{16.4.4}$$

This process is stationary and has an MA representation

$$\mathbf{y}_{1t} = \sum_{i=0}^{\infty} \Phi_i \mathbf{u}_{t-i}, \qquad \Phi_0 = I_{k_1} \tag{16.4.5}$$

where $\mathbf{u}_t$ is k_1-dimensional white noise. The subprocess is useful for forecasting purposes as the coefficient matrices Φ_i can be used to compute optimal forecasts given only information on past and present $\mathbf{y}_{1t}$ (see Section 16.1.2). However, the subprocess is in general not useful for structural analyses since it differs from the partial process (16.4.3) unless $M_{12,i} = 0$, $i = 1, 2, \ldots$. If a data-based modeling procedure is applied to determine the generation process for $\mathbf{y}_{1t}$ (see Section 16.6), the objective can only be to find a model for the subprocess from which the partial process can usually not be recovered.

Given the substantial number of interrelated economic variables and, on the other hand, given the available tools for multiple time series model building, it seems rather unlikely that multiple time series models are suitable for structural analyses unless the dimensionality of the system of interest can be limited on the basis of nonsample information that may, for example, be available from economic theory. It has indeed been found in practice that structural analyses based on low-dimensional time series models can be quite misleading [see Sims (1981) and Lütkepohl (1982a,b)]. Even the causal structure of the $\mathbf{y}_1$-variables may change.

16.4.2 Measurement Errors

Measurement errors represent another obstacle to structural analyses of multiple time series models. Let us assume that the observed variables are

$$\mathbf{y}_t^* = \mathbf{y}_t + \mathbf{z}_t \tag{16.4.6}$$

where the $\mathbf{z}_t$ are the measurement errors also assumed to be generated by a vector stationary stochastic process with MA representation,

$$\mathbf{z}_t = \mathbf{w}_t + \Phi_1\mathbf{w}_{t-1} + \ldots = \Phi(L)\mathbf{w}_t \tag{16.4.7}$$

This stochastic process may be singular—that is, some components of $\mathbf{z}_t$, and thus $\mathbf{w}_t$, may be identically zero since some of the components of $\mathbf{y}_t$ may be measured without error. Substituting for $\mathbf{y}_t$ and $\mathbf{z}_t$ in (16.4.6), we get

$$\mathbf{y}_t^* = M(L)\mathbf{v}_t + \Phi(L)\mathbf{w}_t \tag{16.4.8}$$

which is again a stationary stochastic process that has an infinite MA representation

$$\mathbf{y}_t^* = \mathbf{u}_t + \Psi_1\mathbf{u}_{t-1} + \ldots = \Psi(L)\mathbf{u}_t \tag{16.4.9}$$

where $\mathbf{u}_t$ is vector white noise. In general $\Psi(L) \neq M(L)$ so that this process does not allow conclusions concerning the structure of $\mathbf{y}_t$, which is often the process of interest. Newbold (1978) has shown that a one-way causal system may turn into a feedback system due to measurement error.

Occasionally a researcher or a user of the model for the considered variables may really be interested in $\mathbf{y}^*$ rather than in the $\mathbf{y}$ variables. For instance, close to an election a politician may want to have a small *measured* unemployment rate whatever the true unemployment rate may be. In that case the goal may be to control the system contaminated by measurement error.

16.4.3 Seasonality

Under suitable assumptions seasonality can be treated in the same framework as measurement errors. If the seasonal part $\mathbf{s}_t$ of $\mathbf{y}_t$ is assumed to be added to the nonseasonal part $\mathbf{n}_t$ so that

$$\mathbf{y}_t = \mathbf{n}_t + \mathbf{s}_t \tag{16.4.10}$$

we obviously have the same situation as in the previous section. Again, without further information it is not possible to deduce the MA structure of $\mathbf{n}_t$ or $\mathbf{s}_t$ from the MA representation of $\mathbf{y}_t$.

Since interest often seems to focus on $\mathbf{n}_t$, seasonally adjusted data have been used in many analyses of multiple time series. Commonly the seasonal adjustment procedure is applied to the univariate time series separately. Hence, a rather special structure of $\mathbf{y}_t$ is implicitly assumed. For instance, adjusting the data by a linear filter, say

$$\begin{aligned} y_{it}^a &= \delta_{-s}^{(i)} y_{i,t+s} + \ldots + \delta_{-1}^{(i)} y_{i,t+1} + \delta_0^{(i)} y_{it} + \delta_1^{(i)} y_{i,t-1} + \ldots + \delta_s^{(i)} y_{i,t-s} \\ &= \delta^{(i)}(L) y_{it} \end{aligned} \tag{16.4.11}$$

(see Section 7.7.2) implies that

$$\mathbf{n}_t = \mathbf{y}_t^a = \Delta(L)\mathbf{y}_t \tag{16.4.12}$$

is assumed, where

$$\Delta(L) = \begin{bmatrix} \delta^{(1)}(L) & & 0 \\ & \ddots & \\ 0 & & \delta^{(k)}(L) \end{bmatrix}$$

and $\mathbf{y}_t^a = (y_{1t}^a, \ldots, y_{kt}^a)'$. To be appropriate this adjustment clearly requires a very special structure of $\mathbf{y}_t$.

The impact of seasonal adjustment in a multiple time series context has been studied by Sims (1974) and Wallis (1974, 1978). In practice the MA structure of the seasonally adjusted data may have little to do with the MA structure of $\mathbf{n}_t$ so that seasonal adjustment can be another source for misinterpreting a multiple time series model.

In addition to omitted variables, measurement errors, and seasonality, we have seen in Section 16.3 that aggregation can lead to erroneous interpretations of multiple time series models. In the light of all these problems one might well argue that such models are useless for structural analyses at least if the model specification is based primarily on sample information. (See also the comments at the beginning of Section 16.6 below.) Even if one does not share this extreme viewpoint, it is useful to be aware of these potential problems when conclusions for the structure of an economic system are drawn from multiple time series models.

16.5 ESTIMATION OF VECTOR ARMA PROCESSES

To estimate the parameters of a vector ARMA process, maximum likelihood (ML) procedures are recommended as they result in consistent, asymptotically efficient, and normally distributed estimators under very general conditions. The small sample properties of these procedures are in general unknown. Below we will briefly consider estimation in the time and in the frequency domain. Generally optimization of the likelihood function results in a complicated nonlinear optimization problem. However, we will consider some special cases where estimation is computationally straightforward.

The following discussion of general time and frequency domain estimation is based on Anderson (1980) where details and some more references can be found. A substantial list of references on the subject is also given in Kashyap and Nasburg (1974).

16.5.1 Time Domain Maximum Likelihood Estimation

Consider the stationary, invertible k-dimensional process

$$\mathbf{y}_t - \Theta_1 \mathbf{y}_{t-1} - \ldots - \Theta_p \mathbf{y}_{t-p} = \mathbf{v}_t + A_1 \mathbf{v}_{t-1} + \ldots + A_q \mathbf{v}_{t-q} \tag{16.5.1}$$

or, compactly,

$$\Theta_p(L)\mathbf{y}_t = A_q(L)\mathbf{v}_t \tag{16.5.2}$$

where $\mathbf{v}_t$ is Gaussian white noise with variance-covariance matrix $\Sigma_\mathbf{v}$ and we assume that a set of identifying restrictions is fulfilled (see Section 16.1.1). The negative log likelihood function, given a sample of size T, is

$$\begin{aligned}-\ln \ell &= \frac{Tk}{2}\ln 2\pi + \frac{T}{2}\ln|\Sigma_\mathbf{v}| + \frac{1}{2}\sum_{t=1}^{T} \mathbf{v}_t' \Sigma_\mathbf{v}^{-1} \mathbf{v}_t \\ &= \frac{Tk}{2}\ln 2\pi + \frac{T}{2}\ln|\Sigma_\mathbf{v}| \\ &\quad + \frac{1}{2}\sum_{t=1}^{T} \{[\mathbf{y}_t - \Theta_1\mathbf{y}_{t-1} - \ldots - \Theta_p\mathbf{y}_{t-p} - A_1\mathbf{v}_{t-1} - \ldots - A_q\mathbf{v}_{t-q}]'\Sigma_\mathbf{v}^{-1} \\ &\quad \cdot [\mathbf{y}_t - \Theta_1\mathbf{y}_{t-1} - \ldots - \Theta_p\mathbf{y}_{t-p} - A_1\mathbf{v}_{t-1} - \ldots - A_q\mathbf{v}_{t-q}]\}\end{aligned} \tag{16.5.3}$$

We will assume that the $\mathbf{y}_t$ and $\mathbf{v}_t$ with $t \leq 0$ are zero since this will not affect the asymptotic properties of the resulting estimators. Instead of setting the presample values at zero, we could treat the first p observations as fixed presample values and $\mathbf{v}_{p+1-q} = \ldots = \mathbf{v}_p = \mathbf{0}$. If the sample mean of the time series is nonzero, we assume that it has been subtracted from the data previously.

Since the $\mathbf{v}_t$ in (16.5.3) are unobserved, they have to be expressed in terms of the observed $\mathbf{y}_t$, and we use the relation

$$\mathbf{v}_t = A_q(L)^{-1}\Theta_p(L)\mathbf{y}_t \tag{16.5.4}$$

[see (16.1.11)]. Thus, the parameters will enter nonlinearly in (16.5.3) and a nonlinear, iterative optimization routine like the *Newton–Raphson method* is required for the minimization of $-\ln \ell$ (see Appendix B). Assuming that $\boldsymbol{\theta}$ is a vector containing all the parameters except the elements of $\Sigma_\mathbf{v}$, the nth iteration of the Newton–Raphson algorithm has the form:

$$\boldsymbol{\theta}_{n+1} = \boldsymbol{\theta}_n - \left(\frac{\partial^2 \ln \ell}{\partial\boldsymbol{\theta}\,\partial\boldsymbol{\theta}'}\bigg|_{\boldsymbol{\theta}=\boldsymbol{\theta}_n}\right)^{-1}\left(\frac{\partial \ln \ell}{\partial\boldsymbol{\theta}}\bigg|_{\boldsymbol{\theta}=\boldsymbol{\theta}_n}\right) \tag{16.5.5}$$

where the index n denotes the parameter vector obtained in the $(n - 1)$th iteration. The derivatives on the right-hand side of (16.5.5) are given in Anderson's article and the choice of starting values $\boldsymbol{\theta}_1$ for the iteration is discussed in Section 16.5.3. As noted in Chapter 6, if $\boldsymbol{\theta}_1$ is a consistent estimator of $\boldsymbol{\theta}$, the method will provide an efficient estimator in one iteration under general conditions.

Replacing the matrix of second derivatives in (16.5.5) by the information matrix

$$I(\boldsymbol{\theta}_n) = -E\left(\frac{\partial^2 \ln \ell}{\partial \boldsymbol{\theta}\, \partial \boldsymbol{\theta}'}\bigg|_{\boldsymbol{\theta}=\boldsymbol{\theta}_n}\right) \tag{16.5.6}$$

results in the *method of scoring* (see Appendix B). The elements of $I(\boldsymbol{\theta})$ are also given by Anderson (1980). The inverse information matrix $I(\hat{\boldsymbol{\theta}})^{-1}$, where $\hat{\boldsymbol{\theta}}$ is the ML estimate, can be used as an estimate of the asymptotic covariance matrix of $\hat{\boldsymbol{\theta}}$. Other nonlinear optimization algorithms that could be used to minimize (16.5.3) are given in Appendix B.

The asymptotic normality of $\hat{\boldsymbol{\theta}}$ holds under more general conditions than those stated above. In particular, the $\mathbf{v}_t$ need not be normally distributed. In that case the procedure is a pseudo-ML procedure. Also, there may be constraints on the parameters. Such constraints are sometimes provided by economic theory as we have seen earlier. Furthermore, the system may contain nonstochastic exogenous variables; that is, $\mathbf{y}_t$ may be generated by an ARMAX process. For a discussion of these and other generalizations, see, for example, Dunsmuir and Hannan (1976), Deistler, Dunsmuir and Hannan (1978), Hannan (1979), Hannan, Dunsmuir, and Deistler (1980), and Hillmer and Tiao (1979).

16.5.2 Special Cases

There are various special processes for which the estimation problem is computationally easier than may be suggested by the above discussion, and we will consider some of these cases in more detail since they are of practical importance.

16.5.2a Vector Autoregressive Processes

If $\mathbf{y}_t$ is a stationary k-dimensional AR(p) process—that is,

$$\mathbf{y}_t = \Theta_1 \mathbf{y}_{t-1} + \ldots + \Theta_p \mathbf{y}_{t-p} + \mathbf{v}_t \tag{16.5.7}$$

where $\mathbf{v}_t$ is again Gaussian white noise—consistent and asymptotically efficient estimates can be obtained by estimating each of the k equations separately by linear least squares (LS). In this case the model has the form of a seemingly unrelated regression model with equal regressors in each equation so that LS estimation is efficient (see Chapter 12).

If there are zero constraints on the parameter matrices, there may be different regressors in different equations. In that case (16.5.7) can be premultiplied by an upper triangular matrix P with unit diagonal defined such that $P\Sigma_{\mathbf{v}}P'$ is a diagonal matrix. Thus,

$$\mathbf{y}_t = B_0\mathbf{y}_t + B_1\mathbf{y}_{t-1} + \ldots + B_p\mathbf{y}_{t-p} + \mathbf{w}_t \tag{16.5.8}$$

where $B_0 = I - P$, $B_j = P\Theta_j$, $j = 1, \ldots, p$, and $\mathbf{w}_t = P\mathbf{v}_t$ [see (16.1.15)]. The virtue of (16.5.8) lies in the residual term $\mathbf{w}_t$ having diagonal variance-covariance matrix so that LS estimation of each separate equation is efficient even if some coefficients of the transformed model are constrained to zero.

If a model is given in the form of a system of structural equations like

$$\Theta_{11}(L)\mathbf{z}_t + \Theta_{12}(L)\mathbf{x}_t = \mathbf{e}_t \tag{16.5.9}$$

[see (16.2.2)], then a transformation of the above type is not necessarily desirable if interest centers on the structural form parameters contained in $\Theta_{11}(L)$ and $\Theta_{12}(L)$. However, if the $\mathbf{e}_t$ are not autocorrelated, then the system (16.5.9) has the form of the models considered in Chapter 15 with predetermined variables $\mathbf{z}_{t-1}, \mathbf{z}_{t-2}, \ldots$ and $\mathbf{x}_t, \mathbf{x}_{t-1}, \ldots$. Such a system can be estimated using the techniques presented in Chapter 15. Estimation techniques especially designed for rational expectations models (see Section 16.2.2) are considered by Wallis (1980), Chow (1980), Hansen and Sargent (1980), Pagan (1984), Wickens (1982), Cumby, Huizinga, and Obstfeld (1983), and others.

16.5.2b AP Processes

Another subclass of ARMA processes that can be estimated efficiently by LS is the class of autoregressive-discounted-polynomial (AP) processes. These processes are discussed in this context by Lütkepohl (1982c) and are generalizations of the discounted polynomial lag models (see Chapter 10). The idea is to impose some kind of smoothness constraint on the AR operator, since fitting finite order AR processes has the disadvantage of picking up distortions that do not reflect the actual underlying structure but are merely due to the randomness in the sample.

The general form of an AP process is

$$\sum_{n=0}^{\infty} \Phi_n \mathbf{y}_{t-n} = \mathbf{v}_t \tag{16.5.10}$$

where

$$\Phi_n = \lambda^n P(n) \tag{16.5.11}$$

$0 < |\lambda| < 1$ and the $P(n)$ are $(k \times k)$ matrices of polynomials in n,

$$P(n) = [p_{ij}(n)] = \left[\sum_{l=0}^{v_{ij}} p_{ij,l}n^l\right]$$

It can be shown that

$$\sum_{n=0}^{\infty} \lambda^n P(n) L^n = \frac{Q_v(L)}{(1 - \lambda L)^{v+1}} \tag{16.5.12}$$

where $v = \max\{v_{ij} | i, j = 1, \ldots, k\}$, L is the lag operator, and $Q_v(L)$ is a $(k \times k)$ matrix of polynomials in the lag operator of degree v. Thus, the above AP process has a vector ARMA$(v, v + 1)$ representation. For any fixed λ between 0 and 1 these processes can approximate any finite order stationary ARMA process to any desired degree of accuracy in a relevant sense. For the details see Lütkepohl (1982c).

We may assume that the variance-covariance matrix $\Sigma_{\mathbf{v}}$ of $\mathbf{v}_t$ in (16.5.10) is a diagonal matrix if $P(0)$ is allowed to be upper triangular with unit diagonal. In this case the ith equation of (16.5.10) can be written as

$$y_{i,t} - s_{i0,t} = \sum_{l=i+1}^{k} p_{il,0}(s_{l0,t} - y_{l,t}) + \sum_{l=1}^{k} \sum_{j=1}^{v_{il}} p_{il,j} s_{lj,t} - r_{i,t} + v_{i,t} \tag{16.5.13}$$

where

$$s_{lj,t} = -\sum_{n=1}^{t-1} \lambda^n n^j y_{l,t-n}$$

$$r_{i,t} = \sum_{j=0}^{v_i} \eta_{i,j} \lambda^t t^j$$

and

$$v_i = \max\{v_{il} | l = 1, 2, \ldots, k\}$$

The $\eta_{i,j}$ are independent of t and thus, for a fixed λ, (16.5.13) is a linear regression equation with parameters $p_{il,j}$ and $\eta_{i,j}$, which can be estimated by LS. The $\eta_{i,j}$ contain the presample values $\mathbf{y}_t$, $t \leq 0$, and cannot be estimated consistently since the $r_{i,t}$ approach zero rapidly as t goes to infinity. Replacing these terms by zero—that is, assuming $\mathbf{y}_t = \mathbf{0}$ for $t \leq 0$—does not affect the asymptotic properties of the estimators of the $p_{il,j}$, in which we are primarily interested. If $\mathbf{y}_t$ is Gaussian, the LS estimators of the $p_{il,j}$ are consistent, asymptotically efficient, and normally distributed. The AR coefficients can be obtained via (16.5.11) and it is easy to see that the coefficients of the Φ_n are linearly related to the $p_{il,j}$ if λ is fixed so that the asymptotic distribution of the AR coefficients is also normal.

16.5.3 Spectral Estimation

A univariate stationary stochastic process y_t with autocorrelation function $\gamma_y(h)$ has spectral density

$$f_y(\omega) = \frac{1}{2\pi} \sum_{h=-\infty}^{\infty} \gamma_y(h) e^{-i\omega h}, \qquad -\pi \leq \omega \leq \pi \tag{16.5.14}$$

(see Section 7.6). Analogously the spectral density for a stationary vector stochastic process $\mathbf{y}_t$ with autocorrelation matrices

$$\Gamma_{\mathbf{y}}(h) = E[(\mathbf{y}_t - E[\mathbf{y}_t])(\mathbf{y}_{t+h} - E[\mathbf{y}_{t+h}])'] \tag{16.5.15}$$

is defined as

$$f_{\mathbf{y}}(\omega) = \frac{1}{2\pi} \sum_{h=-\infty}^{\infty} \Gamma_{\mathbf{y}}(h) e^{-i\omega h}, \qquad -\pi \leq \omega \leq \pi \tag{16.5.16}$$

It can be shown that

$$\Gamma_{\mathbf{y}}(h) = \int_{-\pi}^{\pi} e^{i\omega h} f_{\mathbf{y}}(\omega)\, d\omega \tag{16.5.17}$$

Thus, a zero-mean Gaussian process can be characterized either by its autocovariance matrices or by its spectral density.

For the ARMA process $\mathbf{y}_t$ in (16.5.2) the spectral density can be shown to be

$$f_{\mathbf{y}}(\omega) = \frac{1}{2\pi} \Theta_p(e^{i\omega})^{-1} A_q(e^{i\omega}) \Sigma_{\mathbf{v}} A_q(e^{-i\omega})' \Theta_p(e^{-i\omega})'^{-1} \tag{16.5.18}$$

Rather than maximizing the likelihood, Dunsmuir and Hannan (1976) show that

$$H = -\frac{T}{2} \ln|\Sigma_{\mathbf{v}}| - \frac{1}{2} \sum_{t=1}^{T} \operatorname{trace} f_{\mathbf{y}}^{-1}(\omega_t) P(\omega_t) \tag{16.5.19}$$

can be maximized. Here $\omega_t = 2\pi t/T$, $t = 1, \ldots, T$, and $P(\omega)$ is the periodogram given by

$$P(\omega) = \frac{1}{2\pi} \sum_{h=-(T-1)}^{T-1} C_{\mathbf{y}}(h) e^{-i\omega h} \tag{16.5.20}$$

where

$$C_{\mathbf{y}}(h) = \frac{1}{T} \sum_{t=1}^{T-h} \mathbf{y}_t \mathbf{y}_{t+h}' \quad \text{for} \quad h \geq 0 \tag{16.5.21}$$

and $C_{\mathbf{y}}(h) = C_{\mathbf{y}}(-h)'$ for $h < 0$. Maximization of (16.5.19) can have computational advantages due to the special structure of the matrix of second derivatives although it is of course also a nonlinear optimization problem as can be seen from (16.5.18). Again the Newton-Raphson algorithm or the method of scoring can be used for the numerical optimization.

Initial estimates for the AR coefficients $\Theta_j, j = 1, \ldots, p$, can be obtained via the *multivariate Yule-Walker equations* that are derived by taking expectations of

$$\begin{aligned}\mathbf{y}_t\mathbf{y}_{t-h}' &= \Theta_1\mathbf{y}_{t-1}\mathbf{y}_{t-h}' + \ldots + \Theta_p\mathbf{y}_{t-p}\mathbf{y}_{t-h}' \\ &\quad + \mathbf{v}_t\mathbf{y}_{t-h}' + A_1\mathbf{v}_{t-1}\mathbf{y}_{t-h}' + \ldots + A_q\mathbf{v}_{t-q}\mathbf{y}_{t-h}' \end{aligned} \tag{16.5.22}$$

For $h > q$ this gives

$$\Gamma_{\mathbf{y}}(-h) = \sum_{j=1}^{p} \Theta_j\Gamma_{\mathbf{y}}(j-h) \tag{16.5.23}$$

Replacing the $\Gamma_{\mathbf{y}}(m)$ by $C_{\mathbf{y}}(m)$ and solving (16.5.23) for $h = q+1, \ldots, q+p$ gives the desired initial estimates $\tilde{\Theta}_j$ for the $\Theta_j, j = 1, \ldots, p$. These values can be used to compute residuals

$$\tilde{\mathbf{e}}_t = \mathbf{y}_t - \tilde{\Theta}_1\mathbf{y}_{t-1} - \ldots - \tilde{\Theta}_p\mathbf{y}_{t-p} \tag{16.5.24}$$

which in turn can be used to estimate the spectral density of the error process

$$\mathbf{e}_t = \mathbf{v}_t + A_1\mathbf{v}_{t-1} + \ldots + A_q\mathbf{v}_{t-q} \tag{16.5.25}$$

by

$$\tilde{f}_{\mathbf{e}}(\omega) = \frac{1}{2\pi}\sum_{h=-q}^{q} C_{\tilde{\mathbf{e}}}(h)e^{-i\omega h} \tag{16.5.26}$$

where the $C_{\tilde{\mathbf{e}}}(h)$ are defined analogous to (16.5.21). The actual spectral density of $\mathbf{e}_t$ is

$$f_{\mathbf{e}}(\omega) = \frac{1}{2\pi} A_q(e^{i\omega})\Sigma_{\mathbf{v}}A_q(e^{-i\omega})' \tag{16.5.27}$$

and the estimate $\tilde{f}_{\mathbf{e}}(\omega)$ is such that it can be factored accordingly in order to obtain initial estimates of the $A_j, j = 1, \ldots, q$, and $\Sigma_{\mathbf{v}}$.

16.5.4 Some Problems

The small sample behavior of the different methods are in general unknown and therefore we cannot give well-founded advice as to which method to use for a particular data set. Also, little seems to be known about the best treatment of the initial conditions terms. Furthermore, in general we do not know the asymptotic distribution of the parameter estimates for nonstationary and noninvertible ARMA processes. In fact, the full likelihood function cannot even be maximized if the AR operator has a unit root [see Deistler, Dunsmuir, and Hannan (1978)]. Also, it would be useful to know the consequences of estimating a misspecified model. Clearly these problems are sufficiently important to deserve further investigation.

16.6 DATA-BASED SPECIFICATION OF VECTOR ARMA PROCESSES

So far we have assumed that the model is completely specified and merely involves some unknown parameters that can be estimated from the data. Although there are economic theories that result in dynamic econometric specifications, Sims (1980) has persuasively argued that economic theory is not likely to provide a completely and uniquely specified model. The following are his main objections to identifying restrictions in macroeconometric models:

(1) Restrictions are often not based on economic theory but rather on the "econometrician's version of psychological and sociological theory." Economic theory often tells us only "that any variable which appears on the right-hand side of one of these equations belongs in principle on the right-hand side of all of them." [Sims (1980, p. 3).]
(2) In dynamic models with lagged endogenous variables and temporally correlated error terms where the exact lag lengths are not known a priori, the conditions for exact or overidentification require to distinguish between lagged dependent and strictly exogenous variables. However, sometimes variables are "treated as exogenous only because seriously explaining them would require an extensive modeling effort in areas away from the main interests of the model-builders." [Sims (1980, pp. 5,6).]
(3) Including expectations variables in an econometric model may create identification problems since the expected future values must have "a rich enough pattern of variation to identify the parameters of the structure. This will ordinarily require restrictions on the form of serial correlation in the exogenous variables." [Sims (1980, p. 7).]

If economic theory is not able to provide a fully specified model, it will be necessary to use sample information for model specification, and we will now discuss some methods proposed for this purpose. We will begin with pure AR models and then discuss the specification of vector ARMA processes.

16.6.1 AR Processes

We assume that a given set of data $\mathbf{y}_1, \ldots, \mathbf{y}_T$ is generated by a k-dimensional, stationary Gaussian AR(p) process—that is,

$$\mathbf{y}_t = \Theta_1\mathbf{y}_{t-1} + \ldots + \Theta_p\mathbf{y}_{t-p} + \mathbf{v}_t \qquad (16.6.1)$$

and the sample mean is assumed to be zero or previously subtracted from the data. Of course, in practice many economic time series have trends and cannot be regarded as being generated by a stationary AR process. Therefore, a trend or seasonal component is often removed prior to fitting an AR model [e.g., Sims (1980, 1981), Hsiao (1979a, 1981, 1982)]. Although in practice differencing is a valuable device to remove nonstationarities of univariate time series, it is pointed out by Lütkepohl (1982d) and others that care has to be exercised in differencing the data prior to fitting an AR model. Differencing univariate series may lead to overdifferenced multiple time series for which an appropriate AR model does not exist. For illustrative purposes we will nevertheless assume in the following that a stationary AR model is adequate for the data under consideration and we will ignore the problem of prior detrending or seasonal adjustment.

In Chapter 7 a number of criteria and procedures are discussed for estimating the order of a univariate AR process. These procedures can be generalized to the multivariate case and we will briefly do so in the following discussion.

16.6.1a Estimating the Order of an Unconstrained Vector AR Process

Sequential testing procedures are a traditional tool for determining the order of an AR process. Likelihood ratio tests can be used in such procedures. The likelihood ratio statistic for testing an AR(m) against an AR(l), $l < m$, is

$$\Lambda = T(\ln|\hat{\Sigma}_l| - \ln|\hat{\Sigma}_m|) \tag{16.6.2}$$

[e.g., Hannan (1970)]. Here

$$\hat{\Sigma}_j = \frac{1}{T}[\hat{\mathbf{v}}_1, \ldots, \hat{\mathbf{v}}_T]\begin{bmatrix} \hat{\mathbf{v}}_1' \\ \vdots \\ \hat{\mathbf{v}}_T' \end{bmatrix} \tag{16.6.3}$$

where $\hat{\mathbf{v}}_t$ is the tth vector of residuals obtained by LS (ML) estimation of an AR(j). The statistic Λ is asymptotically χ^2 distributed with $k^2(m - l)$ degrees of freedom. Alternatively a Lagrange multiplier test could be applied [Hosking (1981a)].

Other procedures are based on minimizing an objective function. An upper bound m for the AR order is specified and the objective function is evaluated for all AR orders $j = 0, 1, \ldots, m$. Then the estimate $\hat{p}$ is chosen such that the objective function assumes its minimum for an AR($\hat{p}$). For instance, Akaike's (1969, 1971) FPE criterion is designed to minimize the asymptotic 1-step ahead prediction error. In the present context the objective function is

$$\text{FPE}(j) = \left(\frac{T + j}{T - j}\right)^k |\hat{\Sigma}_j| \tag{16.6.4}$$

and the estimator $\hat{p}$ is chosen such that

$$\text{FPE}(\hat{p}) = \min\{\text{FPE}(j)|j = 0, 1, \ldots, m\} \tag{16.6.5}$$

Another example is Akaike's (1973, 1974) AIC criterion, which is based on the Kullback-Leibler mean information for discriminating between different densities and can be regarded as a generalization of the ML principle. Its general form is

$$-2 \ln(\text{maximum likelihood}) + 2(\text{number of parameters})$$

so that

$$\text{AIC}(j) = \ln|\hat{\Sigma}_j| + \frac{2k^2 j}{T} \tag{16.6.6}$$

is the criterion to be minimized in the present situation.

A Bayesian treatment led Schwarz (1978) to develop a criterion that reduces to

$$\text{SC}(j) = \ln|\hat{\Sigma}_j| + \frac{k^2 j \ln T}{T} \tag{16.6.7}$$

for our purposes and Parzen (1974, 1977) suggests to minimize

$$\text{CAT}(j) = \text{trace}\left[\frac{k}{T}\sum_{s=1}^{j}\left(\frac{T}{T-sk}\hat{\Sigma}_s\right)^{-1} - \left(\frac{T}{T-jk}\hat{\Sigma}_j\right)^{-1}\right] \tag{16.6.8}$$

in order to minimize an approximate mean square difference between the estimated and the true autoregressive transfer function.

Quinn (1980) discusses the problem of finding a consistent estimate of the true AR order p. He shows that for $m \geq p$, minimization of

$$\Phi(j) = \ln|\hat{\Sigma}_j| + \frac{2jc_T \ln \ln T}{T} \tag{16.6.9}$$

leads to a consistent estimator $\hat{p}$ if and only if $\lim_{T\to\infty} \sup c_T > 1$. Quinn suggests using $c_T = k^2$ so that we get a criterion

$$\text{HQ}(j) = \ln|\hat{\Sigma}_j| + \frac{2jk^2 \ln \ln T}{T} \tag{16.6.10}$$

From Quinn's result it easily follows that SC also provides a consistent estimator of p. On the other hand it can be shown that FPE and AIC asymptotically overestimate the true order with positive probability. For more details on the above criteria see the references given.

A comparison of the above criteria and further references can be found in Lütkepohl (1982e). For example, it is easy to show that

$$\ln \text{FPE}(j) = \text{AIC}(j) + O\left(\frac{1}{T^2}\right) \tag{16.6.11}$$

Furthermore, if $T \geq 8$, $\hat{p}(\text{AIC}) \geq \hat{p}(\text{SC})$ and, for all T, $\hat{p}(\text{HQ}) \geq \hat{p}(\text{SC})$. Overall Lütkepohl's results clearly favor the SC criterion for small and moderate samples. In his Monte Carlo studies SC chooses the correct order most often and the resulting estimated AR processes provide the best forecasts. Some of the above criteria have been extended for estimating the order of a vector ARMA process [e.g., Hannan (1981)].

Determining p and estimating the resulting AR process without any zero constraints will often lead to a wastefully parameterized model in practice and methods have been proposed to reduce the number of parameters in an AR model. We will sketch one of them in the following.

16.6.1b Constrained Vector AR Models

Different ways to limit the number of parameters in a pure AR model have been suggested [e.g., Sargent and Sims (1977), Reinsel (1983), Hsiao (1979a), Penm and Terrell (1982)]. As one example we will briefly introduce Hsiao's (1979a) proposal and we will assume data on only two variables, y_1 and y_2. Thus, the objective is to specify a two-dimensional AR model

$$\Theta(L)\mathbf{y}_t = \begin{bmatrix} \theta_{11}(L) & \theta_{12}(L) \\ \theta_{21}(L) & \theta_{22}(L) \end{bmatrix} \begin{bmatrix} y_{1t} \\ y_{2t} \end{bmatrix} = \begin{bmatrix} v_{1t} \\ v_{2t} \end{bmatrix} = \mathbf{v}_t \qquad (16.6.12)$$

where

$$\theta_{ij}(L) = \theta_{ij,0} - \theta_{ij,1}L - \ldots - \theta_{ij,p_{ij}}L^{p_{ij}}, \qquad i, j = 1, 2 \quad (16.6.13)$$

$$\theta_{ij,0} = \begin{cases} 1 & \text{if } i = j \\ 0 & \text{if } i \neq j \end{cases} \qquad (16.6.14)$$

and $\mathbf{v}_t$ is Gaussian white noise with covariance matrix $\Sigma_{\mathbf{v}}$. We assume that $\mathbf{y}_t$ is stationary. Defining $p = \max\{p_{ij}|i, j = 1, 2\}$, $\mathbf{y}_t$ is of course a bivariate AR(p) process. However, some of the p_{ij} may be less than p, which implies that the corresponding $\theta_{ij,p_{ij}+1}, \ldots, \theta_{ij,p} = 0$.

Allowing the $\theta_{ij}(L)$, $i, j = 1, 2$, to have different degrees can lead to a substantial reduction of the number of parameters in the final AR model. However, instead of only p we now have to determine all four degrees p_{ij}. The criteria presented in the previous section can be employed for that purpose. Hsiao suggests choosing $\hat{p}_{ij}$ such that FPE is minimized—that is,

$$\text{FPE}(\hat{p}_{11}, \hat{p}_{12}, \hat{p}_{21}, \hat{p}_{22}) = \min\{\text{FPE}(i,j,l,n)|0 \leq i,j,l,n \leq m\} \quad (16.6.15)$$

where m is a prespecified number that is known to be at least as great as p. In specifying the orders the two equations in (16.6.12) are treated separately. Let us focus on the first equation

$$\theta_{11}(L)y_{1t} + \theta_{12}(L)y_{2t} = v_{1t} \qquad (16.6.16)$$

For this case the FPE criterion is defined as

$$\mathrm{FPE}(l,n) = \frac{T + l + n}{T - l - n}\,\tilde{\sigma}^2(l,n) \tag{16.6.17}$$

where

$$\tilde{\sigma}^2(l,n) = \frac{1}{T}\sum_{t=1}^{T} \hat{v}_{1t}^2 \tag{16.6.18}$$

and the $\hat{v}_{1t}$ are the LS residuals when (16.6.16) is fitted with $p_{11} = l$ and $p_{12} = n$.

To find the minimum of (16.6.17) over all l,n between 0 and m requires that $(m + 1)^2$ regressions be run or, if k variables are involved, $(m + 1)^k$ regressions have to be fitted to specify only one of the equations. Clearly this may require a quite substantial amount of computing time and Hsiao suggests the following abbreviated procedure for a bivariate process.

Step 1 Determine $\tilde{p}_{11}$ such that

$$\mathrm{FPE}(\tilde{p}_{11},-) = \min\{\mathrm{FPE}(l,-)|l = 0, 1, \ldots, m\} \tag{16.6.19}$$

where the dash indicates that the second variable, y_{2t}, is not included. In other words, the optimal univariate AR model for y_{1t} is determined.

Step 2 Choose $\hat{p}_{12}$ such that

$$\mathrm{FPE}(\tilde{p}_{11},\hat{p}_{12}) = \min\{\mathrm{FPE}(\tilde{p}_{11},n)|n = 0, 1, \ldots, m\} \tag{16.6.20}$$

Step 3 Select $\hat{p}_{11}$ so that

$$\mathrm{FPE}(\hat{p}_{11},\hat{p}_{12}) = \min\{\mathrm{FPE}(l,\hat{p}_{12})|l = 0, 1, \ldots, \tilde{p}_{11}\} \tag{16.6.21}$$

This procedure will not necessarily lead to the minimum FPE over all combinations (l,n), $l,n = 0, 1, \ldots, m$. Therefore, Hsiao suggests overfitting and underfitting of the final model and checking the significance of extra parameters or deleted parameters by likelihood ratio tests. For the second equation the procedure is analogous, and, of course, other criteria could be used in place of FPE. Currently it is not clear which criterion is preferable in small samples.

A similar procedure could be applied to fit an AP model to a given set of data. From (16.5.13) the first estimation equation for a bivariate model is known to be

$$y_{1t} - s_{10,t} = p_{12,0}(s_{20,t} - y_{2t}) + \sum_{j=1}^{v_{11}} p_{11,j}s_{1j,t} + \sum_{j=1}^{v_{12}} p_{12,j}s_{2j,t} - r_{1t} + v_{1t} \tag{16.6.22}$$

where all symbols are as defined in (16.5.13). To specify this equation of the AP model, v_{11} and v_{12} have to be determined. Obviously, as in the above AR model, varying these degrees comes down to varying the number of regressors in the regression equation (16.6.22) if λ is fixed (see Section 16.5.2b). Similarly we can proceed for the second equation. For details and applications see Lütkepohl (1982b,c).

While the above procedures are relatively easy to carry out, they may result in nonparsimonious specifications which in turn may have adverse effects on their forecasting performance. Therefore, choosing a model from the larger ARMA class is often desirable.

16.6.2 Modeling ARMA Processes

Different procedures have been proposed for vector ARMA model building and it is beyond the scope of this chapter to offer a detailed account of each. We will only give brief sketches of some of the methods in the following.

16.6.2a Granger-Newbold Procedure

For simplicity we assume again that $\mathbf{y}_t = (y_{1t}, y_{2t})'$ is a bivariate stationary Gaussian ARMA process. It may be assumed that y_{1t} and y_{2t} are appropriately differenced to induce stationarity of the individual series although this may occasionally be a source of problems in the following procedure.

Being a stationary ARMA process, $\mathbf{y}_t$ has a representation of the form

$$y_{1t} = \frac{v_1(L)}{\beta_1(L)} y_{2t} + \frac{\psi_1(L)}{\omega_1(L)} v_{1t} \tag{16.6.23}$$

$$y_{2t} = \frac{v_2(L)}{\beta_2(L)} y_{1t} + \frac{\psi_2(L)}{\omega_2(L)} v_{2t} \tag{16.6.24}$$

where $\mathbf{v}_t = (v_{1t}, v_{2t})'$ is a bivariate white noise process and the operators $v_j(L)$, $\beta_j(L)$, $\psi_j(L)$, and $\omega_j(L)$, $j = 1, 2$, are of finite order. To determine the orders of these operators Granger and Newbold (1977) suggest to build univariate ARMA models for y_{1t} and y_{2t} first, say

$$\theta_j(L) y_{jt} = \alpha_j(L) w_{jt}, \qquad j = 1, 2 \tag{16.6.25}$$

where the w_{jt} are white noise and $\theta_j(L)$ and $\alpha_j(L)$, $j = 1, 2$, are finite order operators. The models (16.6.25) can be specified using the Box-Jenkins approach presented in Chapter 7.

Although the w_{it} are *univariate* white noise processes, $\mathbf{w}_t = (w_{1t}, w_{2t})'$ will in general not be a *bivariate* white noise process. Therefore, a bivariate model, say

$$w_{1t} = \frac{\zeta_1(L)}{\phi_1(L)} w_{2t} + \frac{\mu_1(L)}{\delta_1(L)} v_{1t} \tag{16.6.26}$$

$$w_{2t} = \frac{\zeta_2(L)}{\phi_2(L)} w_{1t} + \frac{\mu_2(L)}{\delta_2(L)} v_{2t} \tag{16.6.27}$$

is built in the next step. Using the fact that the w_{jt} are univariate white noise processes makes it possible to infer the orders of the $\zeta_j(L)$, $\phi_j(L)$, $j = 1, 2$, from the cross-correlations between w_{1t} and w_{2s}, $t,s = 0, \pm 1, \pm 2, \ldots$. Finally, the orders of the $\mu_j(L)$ and $\delta_j(L)$ are inferred from the residual correlations of the resulting models and the model (16.6.26)–(16.6.27) is amalgamated with (16.6.25) to obtain a tentative bivariate specification for $\mathbf{y}_t$. After having been estimated by some efficient method the adequacy of this model has to be checked and, if necessary, modifications have to be made. Since model checking is an important step in all modeling procedures, we will mention some possible checks in Section 16.6.3.

Granger and Newbold admit that their approach, although theoretically feasible, will be of little use in practice if more than three variables are involved. A similar model building strategy is proposed and applied by Haugh and Box (1977) and Jenkins (1979) and a slightly different procedure is discussed by Wallis (1977) and Chan and Wallis (1978). These latter authors also "prewhiten" the single series first; that is, they build univariate ARMA models first, and make use of the representation (16.1.12) of a vector ARMA model. Also Zellner and Palm (1974) start from univariate models and then gradually complicate the multivariate model structure. They explicitly make use of information from economic theory. Furthermore, common factor analysis can be used to specify multivariate ARMA models (see Chapter 10).

16.6.2b Tiao and Box's Approach

Viewing the problems involved in starting a multivariate analysis from univariate models for the individual time series, Tiao and Box (1981) propose using multivariate quantities at the initial stage of the model building procedure. In particular, they suggest using the autocorrelation and partial autoregression matrices to determine a tentative model. Partial autoregression matrices are obtained from multivariate Yule-Walker equations in a similar way as partial autocorrelations for univariate time series. In other words Tiao and Box advocate a direct generalization of the univariate Box-Jenkins procedure described in Chapter 7.

In practice the autocorrelations and partial autoregressions are estimated from the available data and it may be difficult to infer a tentative model by visual inspection of the estimates. For details and examples see Tiao and Box (1981) and Tiao and Tsay (1983). Other authors who have used the autocorrelation matrices for multiple time series model building include Jenkins and Alavi (1981). As these methods involve subjective elements, they require some experience for their successful application.

16.6.3 Model Checking

After a tentative model has been specified by any of the above procedures, checks of its adequacy have to be carried out. As in a univariate analysis the significance of the individual parameters should be tested and insignificant parameters should be deleted in accordance with the principle of parsimony.

Also overfitting and testing the significance of the extra parameters is a useful check. Suitable tests for this purpose have been proposed and discussed by Quenouille (1957) and Hosking (1981a) among others.

Furthermore, a residual analysis can be based on a multivariate version of the portmanteau test [Chitturi (1974), Hosking (1980, 1981b), Li and McLeod (1981)]. A special case of this test is discussed in Section 10.4. For the present case the appropriate statistic is

$$Q = T \sum_{l=1}^{K} \operatorname{tr}(C_l' C_0^{-1} C_l C_0^{-1}) \tag{16.6.28}$$

where T is the sample size, K is small relative to T, and C_l is the lth covariance matrix of the residuals,

$$C_l = \frac{1}{T} \sum_{t=l+1}^{T} \hat{\mathbf{v}}_t \hat{\mathbf{v}}_{t-l}' \tag{16.6.29}$$

and the $\hat{\mathbf{v}}_t$ are the estimation residuals. Under the null hypothesis that the model is a k-dimensional ARMA(p,q) process, the statistic Q is asymptotically distributed as χ^2 with $k^2(K - p - q)$ degrees of freedom. A modification of Q with possibly superior small sample behavior is noted by Hosking (1980). For further details and references on model checking see Newbold (1981).

16.6.4 A Comment on Data-based Modeling

None of the above procedures is suitable for building multiple time series models comparable in size to large scale econometric models. Currently we cannot recommend a particular procedure for universal use. If the objective is forecasting, then it seems logical to judge a model and thus the corresponding modeling procedure by its forecasting performance, and it would be desirable to compare different models for a set of economic data on this basis. It seems fair to say that multivariate time series model building for economic data is still in its infancy and there is much opportunity for further research in this area.

16.7 SUMMARY

In this chapter a framework is presented for simultaneously analyzing the dynamic structure of a set of time series. Vector ARMA models are introduced as a general type of generation process of a multiple time series and their relationship to dynamic simultaneous equations models is discussed.

Since economic data are often aggregates, the temporal and contemporaneous aggregation of vector ARMA processes is considered. The main consequences are a possible loss in forecasting precision and a distortion of the generation process of the disaggregate data. In general it will not be possible to recover the disaggregate process from the aggregated process. Therefore, aggregation is one possible source of misinterpretations of time series models. Other sources are omitted variables, measurement errors, and seasonal adjustment of the individual time series. Dynamic multipliers are possible tools for interpreting time series models and these will be affected if important variables are omitted or the data are contaminated by measurement errors. Seasonal adjustment procedures are commonly applied to individual univariate time series, and subjecting the adjusted series to a multiple time series analysis does not necessarily result in an adequate model for the nonseasonal part of the time series. In summary, multiple time series models must be interpreted carefully and further research is necessary to fully understand the message in the dynamic multipliers regarding the structure of the interrelationships within a set of time series variables.

Once a model is specified its parameters can be estimated from the given data. Maximum likelihood methods have been developed for that purpose. In general these involve solving a highly nonlinear optimization problem and only in special cases linear estimation methods may be used. Despite some progress over the last few years the estimation of ARMA and ARMAX systems is still an area of much potential for active research. For instance, the small sample behavior of the different methods is in general unknown so that it is not clear whether using time domain or spectral estimation is preferable and how the involved initial conditions are best treated. Also, the effects of estimating a misspecified model need further consideration. Furthermore, in general the asymptotic distribution seems to be unknown for nonstationary and noninvertible ARMA processes.

Since economic theory is often not very explicit about the lags in econometric relationships, the specification of multiple time series models usually has to rely at least to some extent on the sample information. We have briefly discussed some specification methods. Unfortunately multiple time series model building based on economic data is still in its infancy so that an evaluation of the different proposed methods is difficult at this point. In particular, the forecasting performance of models constructed with different model building strategies needs to be compared. None of the methods presented in this chapter is suitable for a simultaneous analysis of as many variables as are found in large scale econometric models. Perhaps knowledge from economic theory can help at the modeling stage of a high-dimensional multiple time series analysis.

Multiple time series analysis is far too big a field to be covered completely in a chapter of this size and many interesting problems remain untouched. For instance, we have only discussed a very special kind of nonstationarity. Recalling the definition of stationarity it is clear that nonstationarity may have other sources than unit roots in the AR operator of an ARMA process. A time-dependent correlation structure could also be caused by time-dependent parameters of the process. Kalman filters (see Appendix C) have been used to cope with this problem and a detailed treatment in the present context is beyond the scope of this chapter [see, e.g., Hannan (1970)].

Furthermore, we have limited the discussion to linear models. Since even they are difficult to cope with, it may seem unreasonable to ask for anything but linear multiple time series models at this point. However, nonlinear models have proved their value in univariate analyses and eventually (perhaps in the remote future) they may also become a useful tool in multivariate analyses. In summary, it does not require much expertise in the business of forecasting to predict that the analysis of multiple economic time series will remain an active field of research over the years to come.

16.8 EXERCISES

The following problems are based on the bivariate AR(1) process

$$\mathbf{y}_t = \begin{bmatrix} z_t \\ x_t \end{bmatrix} = \begin{bmatrix} \alpha & \beta \\ \gamma & \delta \end{bmatrix} \begin{bmatrix} z_{t-1} \\ x_{t-1} \end{bmatrix} + \mathbf{v}_t \tag{16.8.1}$$

where $\alpha = \delta = 0.5$, $\beta = 0.8$, $\gamma = 0$, and $\mathbf{v}_t$ is bivariate Gaussian white noise with variance-covariance matrix

$$\Sigma_{\mathbf{v}} = \begin{bmatrix} 1 & 1 \\ 1 & 2 \end{bmatrix}$$

One hundred samples of size 100 should be generated using a random number generator. A procedure to generate bivariate normal random variables is described in Judge et al. (1982, p. 810).

16.8.1 Individual Exercises

Exercise 16.1
Use five samples of Monte Carlo data to estimate the parameters α, β, γ, and δ by applying least squares to each of the two equations in (16.8.1) separately.

Exercise 16.2
Using the five samples of Exercise 16.1, reestimate the parameters by the seemingly unrelated regression method.

Exercise 16.3
Transform the model (16.8.1) so that the disturbance terms of the two equations are independent and estimate the parameters of the transformed model by LS using the five samples of data from Exercise 16.1.

Exercise 16.4
Perform tests to investigate the causal structure of the system $\mathbf{y}_t$ using the five sets of Monte Carlo data from Exercise 16.1.

Exercise 16.5
Assume that in (16.8.1) $\Sigma_{\mathbf{v}}$ is diagonal and $\gamma = 0$. Determine the reduced form and the final form of the model.

Exercise 16.6

Determine the moving average representation of the model (16.8.1) and derive an ARMA representation of the univariate subprocesses z_t and x_t.

Exercise 16.7

Using the five samples from Exercise 16.1, compute the sample autocorrelations. Try to determine an adequate model for $\mathbf{y}_t$ based on these quantities.

Exercise 16.8

Use the AIC and the SC criteria of Section 16.6.1 and a maximum order of six and estimate the order of an AR model for $\mathbf{y}_t$ for the five different samples of Exercise 16.1. Interpret your results.

Exercise 16.9

Using the five samples of Monte Carlo data from Exercise 16.1, apply Hsiao's method as described in Section 16.6.1b to specify an AR model for $\mathbf{y}_t$. Assume the maximum lag to be four.

16.8.2 Class Exercises

Exercise 16.10

Repeat Exercises 16.1 and 16.2 with 100 bivariate samples of size 100. Compute the means, variances, and mean square errors (MSE's) of the resulting estimators, construct frequency distributions, and interpret.

Exercise 16.11

Repeat Exercise 16.3 with all 100 samples. Compute the means, variances, and MSE's of the resulting estimators and construct frequency distributions.

Exercise 16.12

Make use of all 100 samples generated from the model (16.8.1) and repeat Exercise 16.8. Construct frequency distributions for the AR orders estimated by AIC and SC and interpret.

Exercise 16.13

Repeat Exercise 16.9 with all 100 samples of size 100. Construct frequency distributions for the estimated orders and interpret.

16.9 REFERENCES

Akaike, H. (1969) "Fitting Autoregressive Models for Prediction," *Annals of the Institute of Statistical Mathematics*, 21, 243–247.

Akaike, H. (1971) "Autoregressive Model Fitting for Control," *Annals of the Institute of Statistical Mathematics*, 23, 163–180.

Akaike, H. (1973) "Information Theory and an Extension of the Maximum Likelihood Principle," in B. N. Petrov and F. Csáki (eds.), *2nd International Symposium on Information Theory*, Adadémiai Kiadó, Budapest, 267–281.

Akaike, H. (1974) "A New Look at the Statistical Model Identification," *IEEE Transactions on Automatic Control,* AC-19, 716–723.

Anderson, T. W. (1980) "Maximum Likelihood Estimation for Vector Autoregressive Moving Average Models," in D. R. Brillinger and G. C. Tiao, eds., *Directions in Time Series,* Institute of Mathematical Statistics, 49–59.

Baillie, R. T. (1979) "Asymptotic Prediction Mean Squared Error for Vector Autoregressive Models," *Biometrika,* 66, 675–678.

Baillie, R. T. (1981) "Prediction from the Dynamic Simultaneous Equation Model with Vector Autoregressive Errors," *Econometrica,* 49, 1331–1337.

Barth, J. R. and J. T. Bennett (1974) "The Role of Money in the Canadian Economy: An Empirical Test," *Canadian Journal of Economics,* 7, 306–311.

Caines, P. E. and C. W. Chan (1975) "Feedback Between Stationary Stochastic Processes," *IEEE Transactions on Automatic Control,* AC-20, 498–508.

Caines, P. E. and C. W. Chan (1976) "Estimation, Identification and Feedback," in R. K. Mehra and D. G. Lainiotis, eds., *System Identification: Advances and Case Studies,* Academic, New York.

Caines, P. E. and S. P. Sethi (1979) "Recursiveness, Causality and Feedback," *IEEE Transactions on Automatic Control,* AC-24, 113–115.

Chamberlain, G. (1982) "The General Equivalence of Granger and Sims Causality," *Econometrica,* 50, 569–581.

Chan, W. Y. T. and K. F. Wallis (1978) "Multiple Time Series Modeling: Another Look at the Mink-Muskrat Interaction," *Applied Statistics,* 27, 168–175.

Chitturi, R. V. (1974) "Distribution of Residual Autocorrelations in Multiple Autoregressive Schemes," *Journal of the American Statistical Association,* 69, 928–934.

Chow, G. C. (1980) "Estimation of Rational Expectations Models," *Journal of Economic Dynamics and Control,* 2, 47–59.

Ciccolo, J. H., Jr. (1978) "Money, Equity Values, and Income: Tests for Exogeneity," *Journal of Money, Credit, and Banking,* 10, 46–64.

Cumby, R. E., J. Huizinga, and M. Obstfeld (1983) "Two-Step Two-Stage Least Squares Estimation in Models with Rational Expectations," *Journal of Econometrics,* 21, 333–355.

Deistler, M. (1976) "The Identifiability of Linear Econometric Models with Autocorrelated Errors," *International Economic Review,* 17, 26–45.

Deistler, M. (1978) "The Structural Identifiability of Linear Models with Autocorrelated Errors in the Case of Cross-Equation Restrictions," *Journal of Econometrics,* 8, 23–31.

Deistler, M., W. T. M. Dunsmuir, and E. J. Hannan (1978) "Vector Linear Time Series Models: Corrections and Extensions," *Advances in Applied Probability,* 10, 360–372.

Deistler, M. and E. J. Hannan (1981) "Some Properties of the Parameterization of ARMA Systems with Unknown Order," *Journal of Multivariate Analysis,* 11, 474–484.

Deistler, M. and J. Schrader (1979) "Linear Models with Autocorrelated Errors: Structural Identifiability in the Absence of Minimality Assumptions," *Econometrica,* 47, 495–504.

Dunsmuir, W. T. M. and E. J. Hannan (1976) "Vector Linear Time Series Models," *Advances in Applied Probability,* 8, 339–364.

Engle, R. F., D. F. Hendry, and J.-F. Richard (1983) "Exogeneity," *Econometrica,* 51, 277–304.

Feige, E. L. and D. K. Pearce (1979) "The Casual Causal Relationship Between Money and Income: Some Caveats for Time Series Analysis," *The Review of Economics and Statistics,* 61, 521–533.

Florens, J. P. and M. Mouchart (1982a) "A Note on Noncausality," *Econometrica,* 50, 583–591.

Florens, J. P. and M. Mouchart (1982b) "A Linear Theory for Noncausality," paper presented at the European Meeting of the Econometric Society, Dublin, Ireland.

Geweke, J. (1978a) "Testing the Exogeneity Specification in the Complete Dynamic Simultaneous Equations Model," *Journal of Econometrics,* 7, 163–185.

Geweke, J. (1978b) "Temporal Aggregation in the Multiple Regression Model," *Econometrica,* 46, 643–661.

Geweke, J. (1982) "Causality, Exogeneity and Inference," in W. Hildenbrand, ed., *Advances in Econometrics,* Cambridge University Press, New York, 209–235.

Geweke, J., R. Meese, and W. Dent (1983) "Comparing Alternative Tests of Causality in Temporal Systems: Analytic Results and Experimental Evidence," *Journal of Econometrics,* 21, 161–194.

Granger, C. W. J. (1969) "Investigating Causal Relations by Econometric Models and Cross-Spectral Methods," *Econometrica,* 37, 424–438.

Granger, C. W. J. and P. Newbold (1977) *Forecasting Economic Time Series,* Academic, New York.

Hannan, E. J. (1969) "The Identification of Vector Mixed Autoregressive Moving Average Systems," *Biometrika,* 56, 223–225.

Hannan, E. J. (1970) *Multiple Time Series,* Wiley, New York.

Hannan, E. J. (1976) "The Identification and Parameterization of ARMAX and State Space Forms," *Econometrica,* 44, 713–723.

Hannan, E. J. (1979) "The Statistical Theory of Linear Systems," in P. R. Krishnaiah, ed., *Developments in Statistics,* Academic, New York.

Hannan, E. J. (1981) "Estimating the Dimension of a Linear System," *Journal of Multivariate Analysis,* 11, 459–473.

Hannan, E. J., W. T. M. Dunsmuir, and M. Deistler (1980) "Estimation of Vector ARMAX Models," *Journal of Multivariate Analysis,* 10, 275–295.

Hansen, L. P. and T. J. Sargent (1980) "Formulating and Estimating Dynamic Linear Rational Expectations Models," *Journal of Economic Dynamics and Control,* 2, 7–46.

Harvey, A. C. (1981) *The Econometric Analysis of Time Series,* Allan, Oxford.

Hatanaka, M. (1975) "On the Global Identification of the Dynamic Simultaneous Equation Model with Stationary Disturbances," *International Economic Review,* 16, 545–554.

Haugh, L. D. and G. E. P. Box (1977) "Identification of Dynamic Regression (Distributed Lag) Models Connecting Two Time Series," *Journal of the American Statistical Association,* 72, 121–130.

Hillmer, S. C. and G. C. Tiao (1979) "Likelihood Function of Stationary Multiple Autoregressive Moving Average Models," *Journal of the American Statistical Association,* 74, 652–660.

Hoffman, D. L. and D. E. Schlagenhauf (1983) "Rationality, Specification Tests, and Macroeconomic Models," *Journal of Econometrics,* 21, 367–386.

Hoffman, D. L. and P. Schmidt (1981) "Testing the Restrictions Implied by the Rational Expectations Hypothesis," *Journal of Econometrics,* 15, 265–287.

Hosking, J. R. M. (1980) "The Multivariate Portmanteau Statistic," *Journal of the American Statistical Association,* 75, 602–608.

Hosking, J. R. M. (1981a) "Lagrange Multiplier Tests of Multivariate Time Series Models," *Journal of the Royal Statistical Society B,* 43, 219–230.

Hosking, J. R. M. (1981b) "Equivalent Forms of the Multivariate Portmanteau Statistic," *Journal of the Royal Statistical Society B,* 43, 261–262.

Hsiao, C. (1979a) "Autoregressive Modeling of Canadian Money and Income Data," *Journal of the American Statistical Association,* 74, 553–560.

Hsiao, C. (1979b) "Causality Tests in Econometrics," *Journal of Economic Dynamics and Control,* 1, 321–346.

Hsiao, C. (1981) "Autoregressive Modeling and Money-Income Causality Detection," *Journal of Monetary Economics,* 7, 85–106.

Hsiao, C. (1982) "Time Series Modeling and Causal Ordering of Canadian Money, Income and Interest Rates," in O. D. Anderson, ed., *Time Series Analysis: Theory and Practice 1,* North-Holland, Amsterdam, 671–699.

Jenkins, G. M. (1979) "Practical Experiences with Modeling and Forecasting Time Series," in O. D. Anderson, ed., *Forecasting,* North-Holland, Amsterdam, 43–166.

Jenkins, G. M. and A. S. Alavi (1981) "Some Aspects of Modeling and Forecasting Multivariate Time Series," *Journal of Time Series Analysis,* 2, 1–47.

Judge, G. G., R. C. Hill, W. E. Griffiths, H. Lütkepohl, and T. C. Lee (1982) *Introduction to the Theory and Practice of Econometrics,* Wiley, New York.

Kashyap, R. L. and R. E. Nasburg (1974) "Parameter Estimation in Multivariate Stochastic Difference Equations," *IEEE Transactions on Automatic Control,* AC-19, 784–797.

Kohn, R. (1982) "When is an Aggregate of a Time Series Efficiently Forecast by Its Past?," *Journal of Econometrics,* 18, 337–349.

Li, W. K. and A. I. McLeod (1981) "Distribution of the Residual Autocorrelations in Multivariate ARMA Time Series Models," *Journal of the Royal Statistical Society B,* 43, 231–239.

Lucas, R. E. Jr. (1976) "Econometric Policy Evaluation: A Critique," in K. Brunner and A. H. Meltzer, *The Phillips Curve and Labor Markets,* Carnegie-Rochester Conference Series on Public Policy, 1, North-Holland, Amsterdam, 19–46.

Lucas, R. E. Jr. and T. J. Sargent, eds., (1981) *Rational Expectations and Econometric Practice,* Vol. 1 and 2, The University of Minnesota Press, Minneapolis.

Lütkepohl, H. (1982a) "Non-Causality Due to Omitted Variables," *Journal of Econometrics,* 19, 367–378.

Lütkepohl, H. (1982b) "The Impact of Omitted Variables on the Structure of Multiple Time Series: Quenouille's Data Revisited," in O. D. Anderson, ed., *Time Series Analysis: Theory and Practice 2,* North-Holland, Amsterdam, 143–159.

Lütkepohl, H. (1982c) "Discounted Polynomials for Multiple Time Series Model Building," *Biometrika,* 69, 107–115.

Lütkepohl, H. (1982d) "Differencing Multiple Time Series: Another Look at Canadian Money and Income Data," *Journal of Time Series Analysis,* 3, 235–243.

Lütkepohl, H. (1982e) "Comparison of Criteria for Estimating the Order of a Vector Autoregressive Process," Working Paper #8207, Fachbereich Wirtschaftswissenschaften, Universität Osnabrück.

Lütkepohl, H. (1984a) "Linear Transformations of Vector ARMA Processes," *Journal of Econometrics,* 25, forthcoming.

Lütkepohl, H. (1984b) "Linear Aggregation of Vector Autoregressive Moving Average Processes," *Economics Letters,* 14, 345–350.

Muth, J. F. (1961) "Rational Expectations and the Theory of Price Movements," *Econometrica,* 29, 315–335.

Newbold, P. (1978) "Feedback Induced by Measurement Errors," *International Economic Review,* 19, 787–791.

Newbold, P. (1981) "Model Checking in Time Series Analysis," paper presented at the Conference on Applied Time Series Analysis of Economic Data, Arlington, VA.

Newbold, P. (1982) "Causality Testing in Economics," in O. D. Anderson, ed., *Time Series Analysis: Theory and Practice 1,* North-Holland, Amsterdam, 701–716.

Pagan, A. (1984) "Econometric Issues in the Analysis of Regressions with Generated Regressors," *International Economic Review,* 25, forthcoming.

Parzen, E. (1974) "Some Recent Advances in Time Series Modeling," *IEEE Transactions on Automatic Control,* AC-19, 723–730.

Parzen, E. (1977) "Multiple Time Series: Determining the Order of Approximating Autoregressive Schemes," in P. R. Krishnaiah, ed., *Multivariate Analysis-IV,* North-Holland, Amsterdam, 283–295.

Penm, J. H. W. and R. D. Terrell (1982) "On the Recursive Fitting of Subset Autoregressions," *Journal of Time Series Analysis,* 3, 43–59.

Pierce, D. A. (1977) "Relationships—and the Lack Thereof—Between Economic Time Series, with Special Reference to Money, Reserves and Interest Rates," *Journal of the American Statistical Association,* 72, 11–22.

Pierce, D. A. and L. D. Haugh (1977) "Causality in Temporal Systems: Characterizations and a Survey," *Journal of Econometrics,* 5, 265–293.

Price, J. M. (1979) "The Characterization of Instantaneous Causality: A Correction," *Journal of Econometrics,* 10, 253–256.

Priestley, M. B. (1981) *Spectral Analysis and Time Series,* Vol. I and II, Academic, London.

Prothero, D. L. and K. F. Wallis (1976) "Modeling Macroeconomic Time Series," *Journal of the Royal Statistical Society A,* 139, 468–500.

Quenouille, M. H. (1957) *The Analysis of Multiple Time-Series,* Griffin, London.

Quinn, B. G. (1980) "Order Determination for a Multivariate Autoregression," *Journal of the Royal Statistical Society B,* 42, 182–185.

Reinsel, G. (1980) "Asymptotic Properties of Prediction Errors for the Multivariate Autoregressive Model Using Estimated Parameters," *Journal of the Royal Statistical Society B,* 42, 328–333.

Reinsel, G. (1983) "Some Results on Multivariate Autoregressive Index Models," *Biometrika,* 70, 145–156.

Sargent, T. J. and C. A. Sims (1977) "Business Cycle Modeling Without Pretending to Have Too Much A Priori Economic Theory," in *New Methods in Business Cycle Research: Proceedings from a Conference,* Federal Reserve Bank of Minneapolis, Minnesota, 45–109.

Schwarz, G. (1978) "Estimating the Dimension of a Model," *The Annals of Statistics,* 6, 461–464.

Schwert, G. W. (1979) "Tests of Causality: The Message in the Innovations," in K. Brunner and A. H. Meltzer, eds., *Three Aspects of Policy and Policymaking: Knowledge, Data and Institutions,* Carnegie-Rochester Conference Series on Public Policy, 10, 55–96.

Shiller, R. J. (1978) "Rational Expectations and the Dynamic Structure of Macroeconomic Models: A Critical Review," *Journal of Monetary Economics,* 4, 1–44.

Sims, C. A. (1971) "Discrete Approximation to Continuous Time Distributed Lags in Econometrics," *Econometrica,* 39, 545–563.

Sims, C. A. (1972) "Money, Income and Causality," *American Economic Review,* 62, 540–555.

Sims, C. A. (1974) "Seasonality in Regression," *Journal of the American Statistical Association,* 69, 618–626.

Sims, C. A. (1977) "Exogeneity and Causal Ordering in Macroeconomic Models," in *New Methods in Business Cycle Research: Proceedings from a Conference,* Federal Reserve Bank of Minneapolis, Minnesota, 23–43.

Sims, C. A. (1980) "Macroeconomics and Reality," *Econometrica,* 48, 1–48.

Sims, C. A. (1981) "An Autoregressive Index Model for the U.S. 1948–1975," in J. Kmenta and J. B. Ramsey, eds., *Large-Scale Macroeconometric Models,* North-Holland, Amsterdam, 283–327.

Skoog, G. R. (1977) "Causality Characterizations: Bivariate, Trivariate and Multivariate Propositions," Graduate School of Business, University of Chicago.

Tiao, G. C. and G. E. P. Box (1981) "Modeling Multiple Time Series With Applications," *Journal of the American Statistical Association,* 76, 802–816.

Tiao, G. C. and I. Guttman (1980) "Forecasting Contemporal Aggregates of Multiple Time Series," *Journal of Econometrics,* 12, 219–230.

Tiao, G. C. and R. S. Tsay (1983) "Multiple Time Series Modeling and Extended Sample Cross-Correlations," *Journal of Business and Economic Statistics,* 1, 43–56.

Tiao, G. C. and W. S. Wei (1976) "Effects of Temporal Aggregation on the Dynamic Relationship of Two Time Series Variables," *Biometrika,* 63, 513–523.

Tjøstheim, D. (1981) "Granger-Causality in Multiple Time Series," *Journal of Econometrics,* 17, 157–176.

Wallis, K. F. (1974) "Seasonal Adjustment and Relations Between Variables," *Journal of the American Statistical Association,* 69, 18–31.

Wallis, K. F. (1977) "Multiple Time Series Analysis and the Final Form of Econometric Models," *Econometrica,* 45, 1481–1497.

Wallis, K. F. (1978) "Seasonal Adjustment and Multiple Time Series Analysis," in A. Zellner, ed., *Seasonal Analysis of Economic Time Series,* U.S. Department of Commerce, Bureau of the Census, 347–357.

Wallis, K. F. (1980) "Econometric Implications of the Rational Expectations Hypothesis," *Econometrica,* 48, 49–73.

Webster, C. E. (1982a) "Structural Economic Models and Univariate Tests of Causality," Working Paper #32, Department of Economics, Washington University, St. Louis, Missouri.

Webster, C. E. (1982b) "The Relative Forecasting Properties of ARIMA and Econometric Models," Working Paper #34, Department of Economics, Washington University, St. Louis, Missouri.

Wei, W. W. S. and B. Abraham (1981) "Forecasting Contemporal Time Series Aggregates," *Communications in Statistics Part A—Theory and Methods,* 10, 1335–1344.

Wickens, M. R. (1982) "The Efficient Estimation of Econometric Models with Rational Expectations," *Review of Economic Studies,* 49, 55–68.

Williams, D., C. A. Goodhart, and D. H. Gowland (1976) "Money, Income and Causality: The U.K. Experience," *American Economic Review,* 66, 417–423.

Yamamoto, T. (1980) "On the Treatment of Autocorrelated Errors in the Multiperiod Prediction of Dynamic Simultaneous Equation Models," *International Economic Review,* 21, 735–748.

Yamamoto, T. (1981) "Prediction of Multivariate Autoregressive-Moving Average Models," *Biometrika,* 68, 485–492.

Zellner, A. (1979) "Causality and Econometrics," in K. Brunner and A. H. Meltzer, eds., *Three Aspects of Policy and Policymaking: Knowledge, Data and Institutions,* Carnegie-Rochester Conference Series on Public Policy, 10, 9–54.

Zellner, A. and F. Palm (1974) "Time Series Analysis and Simultaneous Equation Econometric Models," *Journal of Econometrics,* 2, 17–54.

PART SIX

FURTHER MODEL EXTENSIONS

Chapter 17

Unobservable Variables

17.1 UNOBSERVABLE VARIABLES IN ECONOMETRIC MODELS

In this chapter we continue to relax the restrictive assumptions underlying the classical statistical model analyzed in Chapter 2. Just as we earlier recognized that economic relations are seldom deterministic or exact, we now acknowledge that few if any economic variables are measured or observed without error. In addition, many economic variables of great interest are sometimes unobserved or unobservable. To cope with this situation, in this chapter we deal with the statistical implications of the use of unobservable variables in econometric models. For an introductory discussion of some of the material covered in this chapter, see Judge, et al. (1982).

The problem of unobservable and erroneously observed variables takes on greater importance as researchers explore new areas of empirical research. The models constructed for many areas of scientific inquiry include theoretical or abstract variables, for which the measures are known to be imperfect or the scales of measurement do not exist at all. Examples of such variables are utility, ability, achievement, ambition, political attitudes, and other human capital concepts. No one has yet observed or measured ability, but it is often used in explaining an individual's earning or status attainment. In a model by Chamberlain and Griliches (1974), observable measures of an individual's success, such as income and occupational standing, depend on schooling and an alleged unobservable ability variable. In another model, Rosen (1973) states that the permanent change in the earnings of individuals during any time period is the sum of an unobserved initial human capital level and the previously accumulated permanent change in earnings.

Unobservable variables may also be the result of measurement error in the observed magnitudes. One example is Friedman's (1957) permanent income hypothesis. In his consumption function model, permanent consumption c_p is proportional to permanent income y_p, that is, $c_p = \beta y_p$. The actual observable measured income of any individual or economy consists of the sum of permanent and transitory components y_T, that is, $y = y_T$. Also, actual measured consumption is viewed as consisting of a basic permanent component plus a random transitory component, which means, $c = c_p + c_T$. Another example is Cagan's adaptive expectations model (1956), in which the quantity supplied may depend on the unobservable expected price, and the expectations are revised in proportion to the error associated with the previous level of expectations. Also, in Nerlove's (1956) partial adjustment model, current values of the independent variables determine the unobservable desired values of the dependent variable, but only some fixed fraction of the desired adjustment is accomplished in one period. Thus the errors in variables problem is not only inseparable from the problem of unobservable variables, but is also related to distributed lag models, such as those discussed in Chapters 9 and 10.

In some cases in empirical analysis, the variables we measure are not really what we want to measure. For example, observed test scores may be used as a proxy for years of education and consequently the proxy variables may be subject to large random measurement errors.

Even for the observable variables, the data may be subject to a variety of errors. Errors may be introduced by the wording of the survey questionnaires. Words such as weak or strong may imply different things to different respondents. Griliches (1974) notes that these errors arise because (1) in economics the data producers and data analyzers are separate, (2) there is fuzziness about what it is we would like to observe, and (3) the phenomena we are trying to measure are complex.

In the following sections, the inadequacy of the least squares rule, when applied to a statistical model containing errors in variables, is evaluated and the dilemma of using proxy variables versus ignoring the unobservable variables is discussed. The classical model in which both the dependent and independent variables are subject to error is demonstrated to be unidentified due to insufficient information. For identification, additional information is required. For a single equation model, information regarding error variances may be used to identify the equation and these error variances can often be estimated by the use of repeated observations. When additional outcome indicators are available or if unobservable variables can be specified as a function of observable explanatory variables (causes), multiple equation models result. In multiple equations, alternative procedures of estimation are available and factor analysis and path analysis are of special interest. Finally, we also discuss simultaneous equation models that involve errors in the exogenous variables and models that are dynamic in nature. An overview of this chapter is given in Table 17.1.

17.2 LEAST SQUARES CONSEQUENCES OF ERRORS IN VARIABLES

The problem of using least squares on a model that contains errors in variables is that the equation error is no longer independent of the explanatory variables that are measured with errors. To see the problem, consider the following model:

$$\mathbf{y} = Z\boldsymbol{\gamma} + X^*\boldsymbol{\beta} + \mathbf{v} \tag{17.2.1}$$

where $\mathbf{y}$ is a $(T \times 1)$ vector of observations on a dependent variable, $\mathbf{v}$ is a $(T \times 1)$ vector of equation errors, Z is a $(T \times g)$ matrix of observations on variables subject to no errors, X^* is a $(T \times h)$ matrix of unobservable true variables, and $\boldsymbol{\gamma}$ is a $(g \times 1)$, and $\boldsymbol{\beta}$ is an $(h \times 1)$ vector of parameters. Suppose that X^* is observed as X with a $(T \times h)$ matrix of errors U; that is,

$$X = X^* + U \tag{17.2.2}$$

TABLE 17.1 ***UNOBSERVABLE VARIABLES***

- Unobservable variables in econometric models (Section 17.1)
  - Inadequacy of OLS (Section 17.2)
  - Dilemma of (Section 17.3)
    - Using proxy variables
    - Deleting unobservable variables
  - The problem of identification (Section 17.4)
  - Single equation models
    - Additional error information (Section 17.5.1)
    - Repeated observations (Section 17.5.2)
  - Multiple equations (Section 17.6)
    - Multiple indicators (Section 17.6.1)
    - Multiple causes (Section 17.6.2)
    - Multiple causes multiple indicators model (Section 17.6.3)
    - Causal models and path analysis (Section 17.6.4)
    - Instrumental variables (Section 17.6.5)
  - Simultaneous equation models (Section 17.7)
  - Dynamic models (Section 17.8)

We assume that $E(U) = O$, $E(\mathbf{v}) = \mathbf{0}$, and $E(\mathbf{u}_i\mathbf{v}') = 0$ where $\mathbf{u}$ is the i-th column of U. Using the observations X of (17.2.2) in (17.2.1), we obtain a regression model

$$\begin{aligned} \mathbf{y} &= Z\boldsymbol{\gamma} + X\boldsymbol{\beta} + \mathbf{e} \\ &= W\boldsymbol{\delta} + \mathbf{e} \end{aligned} \tag{17.2.3}$$

where $W = (Z \quad X)$, $\boldsymbol{\delta} = (\boldsymbol{\gamma}' \quad \boldsymbol{\beta}')'$, and

$$\mathbf{e} = \mathbf{v} - U\boldsymbol{\beta} \tag{17.2.4}$$

If least squares method is used, the least squares estimator of $\boldsymbol{\delta}$ in (17.2.3)

$$\hat{\boldsymbol{\delta}} = (W'W)^{-1}W'\mathbf{y} \tag{17.2.5}$$

is biased because $\mathbf{e}$ and W, which contains X, are not independent. Making use of procedures and assumptions outlined in Chapter 5, we obtain, for large samples

$$\begin{aligned} \text{plim}(X'\mathbf{e}/T) &= \text{plim}[U'(\mathbf{v} - U\boldsymbol{\beta})/T] \\ &= -\,\text{plim}[(U'U/T)\boldsymbol{\beta}] \\ &= -\Sigma_{uu}\boldsymbol{\beta} \end{aligned} \tag{17.2.6a}$$

where $\text{plim}(U'U/T) = \Sigma_{uu}$ is assumed to exist. Thus the least squares estimator $\hat{\boldsymbol{\delta}}$ is also inconsistent and the inconsistency is

$$\text{plim}(\hat{\boldsymbol{\delta}} - \boldsymbol{\delta}) = \text{plim}(W'W)^{-1}TT^{-1}W'(\mathbf{v} - U\boldsymbol{\beta}) \tag{17.2.6b}$$

If we assume that the following limits exist:

$$\text{plim}(W'W/T) = \text{plim}\begin{bmatrix} Z'Z/T & Z'X/T \\ X'Z/T & X'X/T \end{bmatrix} = \begin{bmatrix} \Sigma_{zz} & \Sigma_{zx} \\ \Sigma_{xz} & \Sigma_{xx} \end{bmatrix} \tag{17.2.7}$$

$$\begin{aligned} \text{plim}[W'(\mathbf{v} - U\boldsymbol{\beta})/T] &= \text{plim}\begin{bmatrix} Z'(\mathbf{v} - U\boldsymbol{\beta})/T \\ X'(\mathbf{v} - U\boldsymbol{\beta})/T \end{bmatrix} \\ &= \begin{bmatrix} 0 \\ -\Sigma_{uu}\boldsymbol{\beta} \end{bmatrix} \end{aligned} \tag{17.2.8}$$

then the inconsistency may be expressed as

$$\text{plim}\begin{bmatrix} \hat{\boldsymbol{\gamma}} - \boldsymbol{\gamma} \\ \hat{\boldsymbol{\beta}} - \boldsymbol{\beta} \end{bmatrix} = \begin{bmatrix} \Sigma_{zz}^{-1}\Sigma_{zx}(\Sigma_{xx} - \Sigma_{xz}\Sigma_{zz}^{-1}\Sigma_{zx})^{-1}\Sigma_{uu}\boldsymbol{\beta} \\ -(\Sigma_{xx} - \Sigma_{xz}\Sigma_{zz}^{-1}\Sigma_{zx})^{-1}\Sigma_{uu}\boldsymbol{\beta} \end{bmatrix} \tag{17.2.9}$$

where the partitioned inverse of $\text{plim}(W'W/T)$ is used. The direction of bias is not easy in general to determine. However, for a special case, when X is a single variable $\mathbf{x}$, then Σ_{uu} is σ_u^2 and $(\Sigma_{xx} - \Sigma_{xz}\Sigma_{zz}^{-1}\Sigma_{zx})$ becomes $\sigma_x^2(1 - R_{xz}^2)$, where R_{xz} is the multiple correlation coefficient between $\mathbf{x}$ and Z. Since σ_u^2 and $\sigma_x^2(1 - R_{xz}^2)$ are positive scalars, the sampling bias of the parameter estimate of β will be biased downward. The bias of $\hat{\boldsymbol{\gamma}}$ depends on $\Sigma_{zz}^{-1}\Sigma_{zx}$, which is the probability limit of the least squares estimator of the parameters in the "auxiliary" regression of $\mathbf{x}$ on Z. Thus, if a variable is subject to measurement error, it will not only affect its own parameter estimate, but will also affect the parameter estimates of other variables that are measured without error.

In another special case when Z does not exist and X is a single variable $\mathbf{x}$, then (17.2.9) becomes

$$\text{plim}(\hat{\beta} - \beta) = -\frac{\beta\sigma_u^2}{\sigma_x^2} = -\frac{\beta\sigma_u^2}{\sigma_{x^*}^2 + \sigma_u^2} \tag{17.2.10}$$

Thus for a single independent variable model, $\hat{\beta}$ will always underestimate β by $\beta\sigma_u^2/\sigma_x^2$, which can be small only if σ_x^2 or $\sigma_{x^*}^2$ is larger relative to σ_u^2. In other words, the inconsistency can only be small if the variation of the true variable is large relative to that of the measurement error.

In regard to hypothesis testing, the impact of errors in variables on the F-test statistic is demonstrated by Dhrymes (1978). He shows that

$$\text{plim}\frac{R^2}{1 - R^2} > \text{plim}\frac{R_*^2}{1 - R_*^2} \tag{17.2.11}$$

where R denotes the multiple correlation coefficient for the regression model with the true variables and R_* denotes the multiple correlation coefficient for the regression model containing errors in the variables. Since the F statistic is proportional to $R^2/(1 - R^2)$, or

$$F_{(K-1,T-K)} = \frac{R^2}{1 - R^2}\frac{T - K}{K - 1} \tag{17.2.12}$$

where K is the total number of parameters in the equation, the F statistic is unambiguously understated when the variables subject to errors are used in the regression. Consequently, we would expect to reject models more often than we should. Dhrymes (1978) also examines the t ratio of the least squares estimator of the parameters for the errors in variables model and finds that no unambiguous statements can be made.

17.3 THE DILEMMA OF PROXY VARIABLES

We mentioned in Section 17.2 that in research we often encounter a variable that is unobservable. For example, in studying the effect of education ($\mathbf{x}^*$), and other explanatory variables (Z), on income ($\mathbf{y}$), that is,

$$\mathbf{y} = Z\gamma + \mathbf{x}^*\beta + \mathbf{v} \tag{17.3.1}$$

where Z is a $(T \times g)$ matrix, $\mathbf{y}$, $\mathbf{x}^*$, and $\mathbf{v}$ are $(T \times 1)$ vectors, γ is a $(g \times 1)$ vector of unknown parameters, and β is a scalar unknown parameter, one possibility is to measure the years of education ($\mathbf{x}^*$). However, the data available are the years of schooling ($\mathbf{x}$). Since there is a discrepancy between years of schooling and years of education.

$$\mathbf{x} = \mathbf{x}^* + \mathbf{u} \tag{17.3.2}$$

we are confronted with the choice of either using the years of schooling as a proxy variable in place of the unobservable variable, years of education; that is,

$$\mathbf{y} = Z\boldsymbol{\gamma} + \mathbf{x}\beta + \mathbf{e} \tag{17.3.3}$$

or simply omitting the unobservable variable ($\mathbf{x}^*$) and using instead the resulting misspecified equation

$$\mathbf{y} = Z\boldsymbol{\gamma} + \mathbf{e} \tag{17.3.4}$$

Since both (17.3.3) and (17.3.4) are misspecified equations of (17.3.1) together with (17.3.2), the estimators of $\boldsymbol{\gamma}$ are both biased and inconsistent [Theil (1957)]. The question then is, "Which course of action will produce estimators with less bias or inconsistency?"

McCallum (1972) and Wickens (1972) independently show, assuming that $\mathbf{u}$ is independent of $\mathbf{e}$, $\mathbf{x}^*$, and Z, that the bias of the estimator

$$\hat{\boldsymbol{\gamma}}_s = (Z'Z)^{-1}Z'\mathbf{y} \tag{17.3.5}$$

is always greater than the bias of the estimator $\hat{\boldsymbol{\gamma}}_E$ obtained from

$$\begin{bmatrix} \hat{\boldsymbol{\gamma}}_E \\ \hat{\beta} \end{bmatrix} = \begin{bmatrix} Z'Z & Z'\mathbf{x} \\ \mathbf{x}'Z & \mathbf{x}'\mathbf{x} \end{bmatrix}^{-1} \begin{bmatrix} Z'\mathbf{y} \\ \mathbf{x}'\mathbf{y} \end{bmatrix} \tag{17.3.6}$$

The inconsistency of $\hat{\boldsymbol{\gamma}}_s$ is

$$\text{plim}(\hat{\boldsymbol{\gamma}}_s - \boldsymbol{\gamma}) = \beta \Sigma_{zz}^{-1} \Sigma_{zx^*} \tag{17.3.7}$$

provided that $\Sigma_{zz} = \text{plim}(Z'Z/T)$ and $\Sigma_{zx^*} = \text{plim}(Z'\mathbf{x}^*/T)$ exist and the former is nonsingular. On the other hand, the inconsistency of $\hat{\boldsymbol{\gamma}}_E$ is

$$\text{plim}(\hat{\boldsymbol{\gamma}}_E - \boldsymbol{\gamma}) = \frac{\beta \Sigma_{zz}^{-1} \Sigma_{zx^*} \sigma_{uu}}{\delta} \tag{17.3.8}$$

where $\sigma_{uu} = \text{plim}\, \mathbf{u}'\mathbf{u}/T$, $\delta = \sigma_{uu} + \sigma_{x^*x^*}[1 - (\Sigma_{zx^*}' \Sigma_{zz}^{-1} \Sigma_{zx^*}/\sigma_{x^*x^*})]$, and $\sigma_{x^*x^*} = \text{plim}\, \mathbf{x}^{*\prime}\mathbf{x}^*/T$. It can be shown that $|\sigma_{\mathbf{x}^*\mathbf{x}^*}/\delta| < 1$. Consequently the inconsistency of $\hat{\boldsymbol{\gamma}}_E$ is always smaller than that of $\hat{\boldsymbol{\gamma}}_s$.

Thus, if our major concern is inconsistency, it is better to use even a poor proxy than to omit the unobservable variable. However, the above conclusion is not without reservation. First, the relationship between the proxy variable ($\mathbf{x}$) and the unobservable variable ($\mathbf{x}^*$) is not necessarily in the form of errors in variables (17.3.2). If the proxy variable is a linear function of the unobservable variable with intercept and slope parameter(s) [Aigner (1974a)], and also influenced by other variables [Maddala (1977, p. 160)], or the proxy variable is in the form of the dummy variable [Maddala (1977, p. 161)], the situation will be different. Second, the bias comparisons of McCallum (1972) and Wickens (1972) are based on asymptotic properties. They do not provide sufficient evidence for a choice among estimators in small samples. If we have large samples, the bias of the estimator for the model that includes the proxy variable can be eliminated asymptotically if we can find an appropriate instrument and use the instrumental variable method. However, the estimator is inefficient.

Other criteria may be used to compare the estimators. If we use the variance criterion in choosing the estimator, the variance of $\hat{\gamma}_E$ may be larger than the variance of $\hat{\gamma}_s$. Aigner (1974a) compares both estimators in terms of the mean square error (MSE), and as discussed in Chapter 3 this measure is the sum of the variance and the squared bias. He finds that in terms of the MSE criterion $\hat{\gamma}_E$ does not dominate $\hat{\gamma}_s$. Without loss of generality, he used a simple case of one other explanatory variable to establish the condition $\text{MSE}(\hat{\gamma}_E) \geq \text{MSE}(\hat{\gamma}_s)$ if and only if

$$\frac{(1 - (1 - \lambda T)\rho^2_{zx^*})}{(1 - (1 - \lambda)\rho^2_{zx^*})^2}\,\frac{\lambda}{T} \geq \rho^2_{zx^*} \tag{17.3.9}$$

where $\lambda = \sigma_{uu}/(\sigma_{x^*x^*} + \sigma_{uu})$ and $\rho^2_{zx^*}$ denotes the squared simple (population) correlation coefficient between z and x^*.

The condition (17.3.9) depends on the values of T and the unknown parameters $\rho^2_{zx^*}$, and λ. If, for example, $\rho^2_{zx^*} = 0.3$, $T = 10$, and $\lambda = 0.9$, the condition holds and $\text{MSE}(\hat{\gamma}_E) > \text{MSE}(\hat{\gamma}_s)$. In this case, omitting the unobservable variable x^* from the regression is the optimal choice. However, the map of the "contours of dominance" based on the above condition (17.3.9) shows that the area in favor of $\hat{\gamma}_s$ in terms of MSE is relatively small. When λ is small (relative to the above numerical example) and $\rho^2_{zx^*}$ and T are large, then the use of a proxy variable in a multiple regression of $\mathbf{y}$ on $\mathbf{z}$ and $\mathbf{x}$ will be favorable in terms of MSE.

In summary, with the assumptions of McCallum (1972) and Wickens (1972), it is true that the use of the proxy variable leads to a smaller inconsistency. Aigner's (1974a) findings also broadly support the use of a proxy. However, in cases when the proxy is not simply in the form of errors in variables, other techniques may be preferable. This is particularly true when the proxy is a function of its own unobservable variable and other additional variables that may be subject to errors. In the following sections, we discuss other techniques of estimating equations with unobservable variables that do not make use of proxy variables.

17.4 THE PROBLEM OF IDENTIFICATION

Consider the following classical model of errors in variables:

$$\mathbf{y} = \mathbf{x}^*\beta + \mathbf{v} \tag{17.4.1}$$

and

$$\mathbf{x} = \mathbf{x}^* + \mathbf{u} \tag{17.4.2}$$

where $\mathbf{y}$ and $\mathbf{x}$ are $(T \times 1)$ vectors of observations $\mathbf{x}^*$ is a $(T \times 1)$ vector of unobservable true values, and $\mathbf{u}$ and $\mathbf{v}$ are $(T \times 1)$ vectors of errors. We assume that $\mathbf{u}$ and $\mathbf{v}$ are normally and independently distributed, with $E[\mathbf{u}] = \mathbf{0}$, $E[\mathbf{v}] = \mathbf{0}$, $E[\mathbf{uu}'] = \sigma_u^2 I$, $E[\mathbf{vv}'] = \sigma_v^2 I$, and $E[\mathbf{uv}'] = 0$. In (17.4.1), the parameter β cannot be estimated consistently because there is insufficient information to identify the parameter.

The problem of insufficient information is detected when the maximum likelihood method is applied. The joint pdf for $\mathbf{u}$ and $\mathbf{v}$ is

$$f(\mathbf{u},\mathbf{v}) = (2\pi\sigma_u^2)^{-T/2} \exp\{-(\mathbf{x} - \mathbf{x}^*)'(\mathbf{x} - \mathbf{x}^*)/2\sigma_u^2\} \times (2\pi\sigma_v^2)^{-T/2} \exp\{-(\mathbf{y} - \mathbf{x}^*\beta)'(\mathbf{y} - \mathbf{x}^*\beta)/2\sigma_v^2\} \quad (17.4.3)$$

The log likelihood function is

$$\ln \ell(\beta,\sigma_u^2,\sigma_v^2,\mathbf{x}^*|\mathbf{y},\mathbf{x}) = \text{const.} - \frac{T}{2}(\ln \sigma_u^2 + \ln \sigma_v^2) - (\mathbf{x} - \mathbf{x}^*)'(\mathbf{x} - \mathbf{x}^*)/2\sigma_u^2 - (\mathbf{y} - \mathbf{x}^*\beta)'(\mathbf{y} - \mathbf{x}^*\beta)/2\sigma_v^2 \quad (17.4.4)$$

Taking the partial derivatives of $\ln(\ell)$ or (17.4.4) with respect to β, σ_u^2, σ_v^2, and $\mathbf{x}^*$, setting the derivation equal to zero and simplifying gives

$$\tilde{\mathbf{x}}^{*\prime}(\mathbf{y} - \tilde{\mathbf{x}}^*\tilde{\beta}) = 0 \quad (17.4.5)$$

$$(\mathbf{x} - \tilde{\mathbf{x}}^*)'(\mathbf{x} - \tilde{\mathbf{x}}^*) = T\tilde{\sigma}_u^2 \quad (17.4.6)$$

$$(\mathbf{y} - \tilde{\mathbf{x}}^*\tilde{\beta})'(\mathbf{y} - \tilde{\mathbf{x}}^*\tilde{\beta}) = T\tilde{\sigma}_v^2 \quad (17.4.7)$$

and

$$(\mathbf{x} - \tilde{\mathbf{x}}^*)\tilde{\sigma}_v^2 + \tilde{\beta}(\mathbf{y} - \tilde{\mathbf{x}}^*\tilde{\beta})\tilde{\sigma}_u^2 = \mathbf{0} \quad (17.4.8)$$

provided that σ_u^2 and σ_v^2 are not zero. Solving equations (17.4.5) through (17.4.8) jointly, we obtain an undesirable relation

$$\tilde{\sigma}_v^2 = \tilde{\beta}^2\tilde{\sigma}_u^2 \quad (17.4.9)$$

It is undesirable because in large samples, the result in (17.4.9) implies $\beta^2 = \sigma_v^2/\sigma_u^2$, which is unreasonable and not true. The ratio σ_v^2/σ_u^2 as an estimator of β^2 was first deduced by Lindley (1947) and is considered an unacceptable solution by some researchers, for example, Kendall and Stuart (1961, p. 384) and Johnston (1963, p. 152). The failure of the maximum likelihood method to yield a unique estimate is, in this case, the result of insufficient information. In other words, the model is not identified.

To see the lack of information, we note that elements of **x** and **y** are normally distributed with zero mean vector and covariance matrix

$$\begin{bmatrix} \sigma_x^2 & \sigma_{xy} \\ \sigma_{xy} & \sigma_y^2 \end{bmatrix} = \begin{bmatrix} \sigma_{x^*}^2 + \sigma_u^2 & \beta\sigma_{x^*}^2 \\ \beta\sigma_{x^*}^2 & \beta^2\sigma_{x^*}^2 + \sigma_v^2 \end{bmatrix} \tag{17.4.10}$$

Consistent estimates of σ_x^2, σ_y^2, and σ_{xy} are available from the maximum likelihood estimators of the moments:

$$m_{xx} = \Sigma x_t^2/T \tag{17.4.11}$$

$$m_{yy} = \Sigma y_t^2/T \tag{17.4.12}$$

and

$$m_{xy} = \Sigma x_t y_t/T \tag{17.4.13}$$

respectively. The model implies three equations relating the structural parameters β, σ_u^2, σ_v^2, and $\sigma_{x^*}^2$, to population moments of the observable variables, or, in practice, to their sample counterparts:

$$\tilde{\sigma}_{x^*}^2 + \tilde{\sigma}_u^2 = m_{xx} \tag{17.4.14}$$

$$\tilde{\beta}^2\tilde{\sigma}_{x^*}^2 + \tilde{\sigma}_v^2 = m_{yy} \tag{17.4.15}$$

$$\tilde{\beta}\tilde{\sigma}_{x^*}^2 = m_{xy} \tag{17.4.16}$$

These three equations are not sufficient to determine the four parameters, and the model is underidentified.

The basic concept of identification is the same as that of a system of simultaneous equations. In the latter, the problem of identification is to derive Γ and B from $\Pi\Gamma = -B$, while the former is to derive the parameters β, σ_u^2, σ_s^2, and $\sigma_{x^*}^2$ from (17.4.10). Just as in a system of simultaneous equations, for identification, more information regarding the parameter restrictions is required. In the following sections, we discuss the types of parameter restrictions that will help identify the parameters. Parameter restrictions therefore become an important part of the model specification.

17.5 SINGLE EQUATION MODELS

Within the context of the previous section, in this section we consider the identification of the equation

$$\mathbf{y} = \beta\mathbf{x} + \mathbf{e} \tag{17.5.1}$$

where $\mathbf{x} = \mathbf{x}^* + \mathbf{u}$, $\mathbf{y} = \mathbf{y}^* + \mathbf{v}$, $\mathbf{e} = \mathbf{v} - \beta\mathbf{u}$, and $\mathbf{x}^*$ and $\mathbf{y}^*$ are unobservable. To mitigate the impact of underidentification, we make use of additional a priori information regarding the parameters β, σ_u^2, σ_v^2, and $\sigma_{x^*}^2$, or extraneous information in the form of repeated observations of **x** and **y**.

17.5.1 Use of Information on the Errors in Variables

Recall that for the model (17.5.1), the parameters β, σ_u^2, σ_v^2, and $\sigma_{x^*}^2$ are to be derived from the equations (17.4.14) through (17.4.16) plus additional information. The additional information may involve one or more of the following relations:

1. $\sigma_u^2 = c_1$
2. $\sigma_v^2 = c_2$
3. $\sigma_u^2 = \lambda\sigma_v^2$
4. $\sigma_{x^*}^2 = \gamma\sigma_u^2$

where c_1, c_2, λ, and γ are known constants. If any of the above information is used together with Equations (17.4.14)–(17.4.16), then there are four equations and four unknowns and we have a complete system. However, the system is not linear but is instead a third-order system. Therefore, there could be as many as six different solutions since (17.4.15) is third order and (17.4.16) is second order. By imposing nonnegativity conditions on σ_u^2, σ_v^2, and $\sigma_{x^*}^2$, some infeasible solutions can be ruled out.

If either σ_u^2 is known to be c_1, or σ_v^2 is known to be c_2, then estimates of the parameters can be obtained from (17.4.14) through (17.4.16), but the estimates may be infeasible (negative variance) or feasible but inefficient. The maximum likelihood estimator in this case is demonstrated by Birch (1964) and its sampling properties are discussed by Fuller (1978). For the case when both σ_u^2 and σ_v^2 are known at the same time, the results are developed in Birch (1964) and a summary of the results is available in Judge et al. (1980).

The case when the ratio $\sigma_u^2/\sigma_v^2 = \lambda$ is known is well documented in the literature. In this case the system of nonlinear equations reduces to

$$\beta^2 m_{xy} + \beta(m_{xx} - m_{yy}) - m_{xy} = 0 \tag{17.5.2}$$

The estimator $\tilde{\beta}$ is one of the roots of (17.5.2) with algebraic sign that is consistent with the sign of m_{xy}, since $\tilde{\beta}$ measures the slope of the relation between the true values y^* and x^*. The other parameter estimators are $\tilde{\sigma}_{x^*}^2 = m_{xy}/\tilde{\beta}$, $\tilde{\sigma}_u^2 = m_{xx} - m_{xy}/\tilde{\beta}$, and $\tilde{\sigma}_v^2 = \tilde{\sigma}_u^2/\lambda$. For the asymptotic properties, see Fuller (1978).

In another case, the ratio $\sigma_{x^*}^2/\sigma_x^2$ or the ratio σ_u^2/σ_x^2 may be known, where $\sigma_x^2 = \sigma_{x^*}^2 + \sigma_u^2$. If the ratio $\sigma_{x^*}^2/\sigma_x^2$, which is often called the measure of reliability, is known, the biased least squares estimator $b = m_{xy}/m_{xx}$ may be transformed to yield an estimator

$$\hat{\beta} = b\sigma_x^2/\sigma_{x^*}^2 \tag{17.5.3}$$

which is unbiased; that is,

$$\begin{aligned} E[\hat{\beta}] &= E[b\sigma_x^2/\sigma_{x^*}^2] = (\beta - \beta\sigma_u^2/\sigma_x^2)\sigma_x^2/\sigma_{x^*}^2 \\ &= \beta(\sigma_x^2 - \sigma_u^2)/\sigma_{x^*}^2 = \beta \end{aligned} \tag{17.5.4}$$

The variance of $\hat{\beta}$, and the test statistic that may be used for inference purposes are developed by Fuller (1978).

17.5.2 Repeated Observations

When there are repeated observations on the observable counterparts of the same true unobservable variables, this additional information provides a basis for obtaining estimates of the unknown parameters. For a generalization of the statistical model, let us consider the case where n repeated observations are available for $\mathbf{y}$ alone. The model is

$$\mathbf{y}_j = \beta\mathbf{x}^* + \mathbf{v}_j, \qquad j = 1, 2, \ldots, n \tag{17.5.5}$$

where $\mathbf{y}_j$ is a $(T \times 1)$ vector of observations y_{tj}, $\mathbf{v}_j$ is a $(T \times 1)$ vector of unobservable errors v_{tj}, and $\mathbf{x}^*$ is a $(T \times 1)$ vector of true values x_t^*. We assume that $E[\mathbf{v}_j] = \mathbf{0}$, $E[\mathbf{v}_j\mathbf{v}_j'] = \sigma_v^2 I$, and $\mathbf{x}^*$ and $\mathbf{v}_j$ are independent. Although, in this case, it is impossible to obtain an estimator of β, estimators of $\beta\mathbf{x}^*$ and σ_v^2 are possible because of the repeated observations. The vector $\boldsymbol{\alpha} = \beta\mathbf{x}^*$ can be estimated by least squares as

$$\hat{\boldsymbol{\alpha}} = \sum_j \mathbf{y}_j/n \tag{17.5.6}$$

and σ_v^2 can be estimated as

$$\hat{\sigma}_v^2 = \sum_{j=1}^{n} (\mathbf{y}_j - \hat{\boldsymbol{\alpha}})'(\mathbf{y}_j - \hat{\boldsymbol{\alpha}})/(Tn - n) \tag{17.5.7}$$

provided that $Tn > n$. Both of the estimators $\hat{\boldsymbol{\alpha}}$ and $\hat{\sigma}_v^2$ are unbiased.

A generalization of (17.5.5) is the addition of explanatory Z_j variables, which leads to the specification

$$\mathbf{y}_j = Z_j\boldsymbol{\gamma} + \beta\mathbf{x}^* + \mathbf{v}_j, \qquad j = 1, 2, \ldots, n \tag{17.5.8}$$

where Z_j is a $(T \times g)$ matrix of observable explanatory variables and $\boldsymbol{\gamma}$ is a $(g \times 1)$ vector of parameters. Under the assumption that Z_j is independent of $\mathbf{v}_j$ and all variables have zero expectations, the model (17.5.8) can be formulated as

$$\mathbf{y} = Z\boldsymbol{\delta} + \mathbf{v} \tag{17.5.9}$$

where

$$\mathbf{y} = (\mathbf{y}_1' \quad \mathbf{y}_2' \; . \; . \; . \; \mathbf{y}_n')',$$
$$\mathbf{v} = (\mathbf{v}_1' \quad \mathbf{v}_2' \; . \; . \; . \; \mathbf{v}_n')',$$
$$\boldsymbol{\delta} = (\boldsymbol{\alpha}' \; \boldsymbol{\gamma}')',$$

and

$$Z = \begin{bmatrix} I_T & Z_1 \\ I_T & Z_2 \\ \vdots & \vdots \\ I_T & Z_n \end{bmatrix}$$

The least squares estimator

$$\hat{\boldsymbol{\delta}} = (Z'Z)^{-1}Z'\mathbf{y} \tag{17.5.10}$$

is unbiased. Thus, the parameter σ_v^2 can be estimated by

$$\hat{\sigma}_v^2 = (\mathbf{y} - Z\hat{\boldsymbol{\delta}})'(\mathbf{y} - Z\hat{\boldsymbol{\delta}})/(Tn - T - g) \tag{17.5.11}$$

In summary, $\boldsymbol{\gamma}$ and $\boldsymbol{\alpha}$ can be estimated, but β and $\mathbf{x}^*$ cannot be separated from $\beta\mathbf{x}^*$. A classical example of the model is the specification of an unobservable management variable in a Cobb-Douglas production function (Mundlak, 1961). To separate β from $\mathbf{x}^*$, we need additional information. For example, Mundlak (1961) assumes constant returns to scale, which implies the restriction that the elements in $\boldsymbol{\gamma}$ and β add to one.

Now suppose that $\mathbf{x}^*$ has a measurable counterpart $\mathbf{x}$ but with error $\mathbf{u}$; that is,

$$\mathbf{x} = \mathbf{x}^* + \mathbf{u} \tag{17.5.12}$$

where $E[\mathbf{u}] = \mathbf{0}$, $E[\mathbf{uu}'] = \sigma_u^2 I$, $E[\mathbf{uv}'] = 0$, and $\mathbf{u}$ is independent of Z. The information in (17.5.12) provides the relation

$$\sigma_x^2 = \sigma_{x^*}^2 + \sigma_u^2 \tag{17.5.13}$$

which can be incorporated with the following relation obtained from (17.5.8),

$$\sigma_y^2 = \beta^2\sigma_{x^*}^2 + \sigma^2 \tag{17.5.14}$$

and the relation obtained from (17.5.8) and (17.5.12),

$$\sigma_{xy} = \beta\sigma_{x^*}^2 \tag{17.5.15}$$

to obtain estimates of the parameters. Since the population variances σ_x^2, σ_y^2, and covariance σ_{xy} can be estimated by sample counterparts m_{xx}, m_{yy}, and m_{xy}, respectively, and σ_v^2 can be estimated from (17.5.11), the three unknowns $\sigma_{x^*}^2$, σ_u^2, and β can be estimated from the three relations (17.5.13) through (17.5.15).

Further, if repeated observations are also available on $\mathbf{x}$ so that

$$\mathbf{x}_j = \mathbf{x}^* + \mathbf{u}_j, \qquad j = 1, 2, \ldots, n \tag{17.5.16}$$

where $\mathbf{x}_j$, $\mathbf{x}^*$, and $\mathbf{u}_j$ are all $(T \times 1)$ vectors, then clearly there is overidentification, since σ_u^2 and $\sigma_{x^*}^2$ can be estimated from (17.5.16) and both (17.5.14) and (17.5.15) determine β.

For an overidentified situation, the maximum likelihood estimator provides a solution. Examples are Villegas (1961), Barnett (1970), and Dolby and Freeman (1975). For a treatment of repeated observations within the context of analysis of variance, see Tukey (1951) and Madansky (1959), and for a summary, see Judge et al. (1980).

17.6 MULTIPLE EQUATIONS

The repeated observation model of Section 17.5, $\mathbf{y}_j = \beta\mathbf{x}^* + \mathbf{v}_j, j = 1, 2, \ldots, n$, becomes a multiple equation model when the observations are not exactly repeated but obtained under different conditions β_j. In this case a relevant statistical model is

$$\mathbf{y}_j = \beta_j\mathbf{x}^* + \mathbf{v}_j, \qquad j = 1, 2, \ldots, n \tag{17.6.1}$$

where $\mathbf{y}_j, j = 1, 2, \ldots, n$, are known as observable indicators of the unobservable variable $\mathbf{x}^*$.

17.6.1 Multiple Indicators

For the multiple equation model (17.6.1), the errors $\mathbf{v}_j$ do not necessarily come from the same distribution. In this case, the underlying stochastic assumptions are that each $\mathbf{v}_j$ and $\mathbf{x}^*$ are independent and

$$E[\mathbf{v}_j\mathbf{v}_j'] = \sigma_{v_j}^2 I = \sigma_{v_j v_j} I \tag{17.6.2}$$

Thus, observations generated under different conditions increase the number of parameters in β_j and $\sigma_{v_i v_j}$ as compared to the traditional model of repeated observations.

In the two indicator model, the equations are

$$\mathbf{y}_1 = \beta_1\mathbf{x}^* + \mathbf{v}_1 \tag{17.6.3}$$

and

$$\mathbf{y}_2 = \beta_2\mathbf{x}^* + \mathbf{v}_2 \tag{17.6.4}$$

If we set $\beta_2 = 1$ (normalization) and read $\mathbf{y}_1$ as $\mathbf{y}$, $\mathbf{y}_2$ as $\mathbf{x}$, $\mathbf{v}_1$ as $\mathbf{v}$, and $\mathbf{v}_2$ as $\mathbf{u}$, then we have the classical errors in variables model discussed in the form of (17.4.1) and (17.4.2). This model is underidentified as we noted in Section 17.4.

Suppose that we have three indicators, and the three equations are

$$\begin{aligned} \mathbf{y}_1 &= \beta_1 \mathbf{x}^* + \mathbf{v}_1 \\ \mathbf{y}_2 &= \beta_2 \mathbf{x}^* + \mathbf{v}_2 \\ \mathbf{y}_3 &= \beta_3 \mathbf{x}^* + \mathbf{v}_3 \end{aligned} \tag{17.6.5}$$

Instead of normalizing $\beta_1 = 1$, we may for convenience normalize the variance of $\mathbf{x}^*$ to be one—that is, $\sigma_{x^*}^2 = 1$. In this way, the equations relating population moments of the observables σ_{ij} to the six structural parameters β_1, β_2, β_3, σ_{v1}^2, σ_{v2}^2, and σ_{v3}^2 can be written in a triangular form as

$$\begin{bmatrix} \sigma_{11} & & \\ \sigma_{21} & \sigma_{22} & \\ \sigma_{31} & \sigma_{32} & \sigma_{33} \end{bmatrix} = \begin{bmatrix} \beta_1^2 + \sigma_{v1}^2 & & \\ \beta_1\beta_2 & \beta_2^2 + \sigma_{v2}^2 & \\ \beta_1\beta_3 & \beta_2\beta_3 & \beta_3^2 + \sigma_{v3}^2 \end{bmatrix} \tag{17.6.6}$$

where the upper triangle elements are omitted for simplicity. There are six relations and six unknowns. The model is just identified. If a fourth indicator is available, it would add two additional parameters β_4 and σ_{v4}^2 but there will be four additional relations relating population moments of the observables to parameters. The model is then overidentified.

In general, the multiple indicator model can be written as

$$\mathbf{y} = \boldsymbol{\beta} x^* + \mathbf{v} \tag{17.6.7}$$

$$E(x^*\mathbf{v}) = \mathbf{0} \tag{17.6.8}$$

$$E(\mathbf{v}\mathbf{v}') = \Omega \text{ diagonal} \tag{17.6.9}$$

where $\mathbf{y}$ is an $(M \times 1)$ vector of observable indicators, $\boldsymbol{\beta}$ is an $(M \times 1)$ vector of parameters, x^* is an unobservable scalar, $\mathbf{v}$ is an $(M \times 1)$ error vector, and Ω is the $(M \times M)$ diagonal matrix of error variances. The implied population second moment matrix of the observable $\mathbf{y}$ variables is

$$\Sigma = E[\mathbf{y}\mathbf{y}'] = \boldsymbol{\beta}\boldsymbol{\beta}' + \Omega \tag{17.6.10}$$

There are $M(M + 1)/2$ distinct elements in $\Sigma = \boldsymbol{\beta}\boldsymbol{\beta}' + \Omega$, that when equated with sample second moments, provide $M(M + 1)/2$ estimating equations. There are only $2M$ parameters in $\boldsymbol{\beta}$ and Ω. Thus if $M > 3$, there will be more equations than unknown parameters and overidentification results. There will be many estimators that are consistent but may not be fully efficient. Efficient estimators of $\boldsymbol{\beta}$ and Ω may be obtained by the ML method.

Under the normality assumption, the log likelihood function with constants dropped may be written as

$$L = \tfrac{1}{2}T[\ln |\Sigma| + \text{tr}\,(\Sigma^{-1}S)] \tag{17.6.11}$$

where

$$S = T^{-1} \sum_{t=1}^{T} \mathbf{y}(t)\mathbf{y}'(t) \tag{17.6.12}$$

is the $(M \times M)$ sample second moment matrix of $\mathbf{y}$, and $\Sigma = \boldsymbol{\beta}\boldsymbol{\beta}' + \Omega$ was defined in (17.6.10). Taking the derivative of L with respect to $\boldsymbol{\beta}$ and setting it to zero, we obtain

$$(S\Omega^{-1} - \lambda I)\boldsymbol{\beta} = \mathbf{0} \tag{17.6.13}$$

where

$$\lambda = 1 + \frac{\boldsymbol{\beta}'\Omega^{-1}S\Omega^{-1}\boldsymbol{\beta}}{1 + \boldsymbol{\beta}'\Omega^{-1}\boldsymbol{\beta}} \tag{17.6.14}$$

Thus $\boldsymbol{\beta}$ is a characteristic vector of $S\Omega^{-1}$ corresponding to the root λ but must be normalized by $\boldsymbol{\beta}'\Omega^{-1}\boldsymbol{\beta} = \lambda - 1$ due to the relationship between (17.6.13) and (17.6.14). It can be shown that L is an increasing function of λ. Therefore, we should choose λ as large as possible. In summary, the maximum likelihood estimator of $\boldsymbol{\beta}$ is the characteristic vector corresponding to the largest root λ of $S\Omega^{-1}$ and is normalized by $\boldsymbol{\beta}'\Omega^{-1}\boldsymbol{\beta} = \lambda - 1$.

The estimators for the diagonal elements of Ω^{-1} may be obtained by differentiating L with respect to $\sigma_{v_i}^2$ $(i = 1, 2, \ldots, M)$, setting them to zero, and solving for $\sigma_{v_i}^2$. The result expressed in diagonal matrices is

$$\text{diag}\,\Omega = \text{diag}\,(S - \boldsymbol{\beta}\boldsymbol{\beta}') \tag{17.6.15}$$

For a detailed derivation, see Goldberger (1974). Although Goldberger does not derive the variance for the ML estimator, the ML estimator is consistent and efficient.

The multiple indicators model can be viewed as a special case of the factor analysis model that has long been used in psychometrics. For details of factor analysis, see Lawley and Maxwell (1971) and Harman (1976).

17.6.2 Multiple Causes

An extension of the above basic multiple indicators model is the addition of multiple causes. The model is

$$\mathbf{y} = \boldsymbol{\beta}x^* + \mathbf{v} \tag{17.6.16}$$

with

$$x^* = \boldsymbol{\alpha}'\mathbf{x} \tag{17.6.17}$$

where $\mathbf{y}$ is the $(M \times 1)$ vector of observable random variables, $\mathbf{x}$ is the $(K \times 1)$ vector of observable exogenous causes, $\mathbf{v}$ is the $(M \times 1)$ vector of errors, $\boldsymbol{\alpha}$ and $\boldsymbol{\beta}$ are respectively $(K \times 1)$ and $(M \times 1)$ parameter vectors, x^* is the unobservable scalar, the variance of which can be standardized

$$\sigma_{x^*}^2 = E[x^*x^*] = \boldsymbol{\alpha}'E[\mathbf{x}\mathbf{x}']\boldsymbol{\alpha} = 1 \tag{17.6.18}$$

Substituting (17.6.17) into (17.6.16) results in the reduced form

$$\mathbf{y} = \boldsymbol{\beta}\boldsymbol{\alpha}'\mathbf{x} + \mathbf{v} = \Pi'\mathbf{x} + \mathbf{v} \tag{17.6.19}$$

where

$$\Pi = \boldsymbol{\alpha}\boldsymbol{\beta}' \tag{17.6.20}$$

In Equation 17.6.19, the KM elements of Π are expressed in terms of $K + M$ parameters, one of which may be normalized. Thus, there are $KM - K - M + 1$ overidentifying restrictions on Π. A natural way of estimating an overidentified equation would be to use the maximum likelihood method.

Under the assumption that $\mathbf{v}$ is a normal vector with mean zero and $E[\mathbf{v}\mathbf{v}'] = \Omega$ and independent of $\mathbf{x}$, that is, $E[\mathbf{v}\mathbf{x}'] = 0$, the likelihood function for a sample of T joint observations on $\mathbf{y}$ and $\mathbf{x}$, $\mathbf{y}(1) \ldots \mathbf{y}(T)$, $\mathbf{x}(1) \ldots \mathbf{x}(T)$, is given by

$$\ell = (2\pi)^{-T/2}|\Omega|^{-T/2} \exp[-\tfrac{1}{2}T \operatorname{tr}(\Omega^{-1}W)] \tag{17.6.21}$$

where

$$W = (Y - X\Pi)'(Y - X\Pi) \tag{17.6.22}$$

is the sample covariance matrix of reduced form errors $\mathbf{v}$, and

$$Y = T^{-1/2}(\mathbf{y}(1) \ldots \mathbf{y}(T))' \tag{17.6.23}$$

$$X = T^{-1/2}(\mathbf{x}(1) \ldots \mathbf{x}(T))' \tag{17.6.24}$$

It can be shown (Goldberger, 1974) that the solution value for $\boldsymbol{\beta}$ is the characteristic vector of QS^{-1} corresponding to the root λ; that is,

$$(QS^{-1} - \lambda I)\boldsymbol{\beta} = \mathbf{0} \tag{17.6.25}$$

where

$$Q = Y'X(X'X)^{-1}X'Y \tag{17.6.26}$$

$$S = (Y - XP)'(Y - XP) \tag{17.6.27}$$

$$P = (X'X)^{-1}X'Y \tag{17.6.28}$$

Further, it can be shown that $\boldsymbol{\beta}$ is the first principal component of QS^{-1} since $\lambda = \boldsymbol{\beta}'S^{-1}\boldsymbol{\beta}$ corresponds to the largest characteristic root of QS^{-1}. The solution value for $\boldsymbol{\alpha}$ is shown by Goldberger (1974) to be

$$\boldsymbol{\alpha} = \lambda^{-1}PS^{-1}\boldsymbol{\beta} \tag{17.6.29}$$

For a special case of only two indicators, Zellner (1970) and Goldberger (1972a) develop generalized least squares and maximum likelihood algorithms under alternative assumptions about the errors of the two indicators. Zellner (1970) considers the following model that involves ancillary variables:

$$\mathbf{y} = \mathbf{x}_1\alpha + \mathbf{x}^*\beta + \mathbf{v} \tag{17.6.30}$$

$$\mathbf{x} = \mathbf{x}^* + \mathbf{u} \tag{17.6.31}$$

$$\mathbf{x}^* = \mathbf{x}_1\pi_1 + \mathbf{z}_2\pi_2 + \ldots + \mathbf{z}_K\pi_K \tag{17.6.32}$$

where $\mathbf{x}_1$ is a $(T \times 1)$ column vector of ones and the π's are additional unknown parameters. An example of this model can be found in Crockett (1960). In Crockett's model $\mathbf{y}$ is a vector of observed consumption levels, $\mathbf{x}^*$ is permanent income, and the $\mathbf{z}$'s are such variables as house value, educational attainment, age, and so forth.

In the above formulation the number of parameters in the model is no longer dependent on the sample size, and the T unknown incidental parameters $\mathbf{x}^*$ are now replaced by the K-dimensional unknown coefficient vector $\boldsymbol{\pi}$. The model was first considered by Zellner (1970) as a system of simultaneous equations. Indeed, substitution of (17.6.32) into (17.6.30) and (17.6.31) results in the two equation model

$$\mathbf{y} = \mathbf{x}_1(\alpha + \beta\pi_1) + \mathbf{z}_2\beta\pi_2 + \ldots + \mathbf{z}_K\beta\pi_K + \mathbf{v} \tag{17.6.33}$$

$$\mathbf{x} = \mathbf{x}_1\pi_1 + \mathbf{z}_2\pi_2 + \ldots + \mathbf{z}_K\pi_K + \mathbf{u} \tag{17.6.34}$$

or, more compactly,

$$\mathbf{y} = Z\boldsymbol{\pi}_x\beta + \mathbf{v} \tag{17.6.35}$$

$$\mathbf{x} = Z\boldsymbol{\pi}_x + \mathbf{u} \tag{17.6.36}$$

where, for simplicity, all the variables are measured as deviations from their means so that the intercepts α and π_1 may be eliminated, $Z = (\mathbf{z}_2\ \mathbf{z}_3 \ldots \mathbf{z}_K)$ is a

$[T \times (K - 1)]$ matrix,

$$\boldsymbol{\pi}_x = \begin{bmatrix} \pi_2 \\ \pi_3 \\ \cdot \\ \cdot \\ \cdot \\ \pi_K \end{bmatrix}$$

is a $[(K - 1) \times 1]$ vector of parameters, and β is a scalar.

To estimate β in (17.6.35) we must know $Z\boldsymbol{\pi}_x$. Although Z is known, $\boldsymbol{\pi}_x$ is unknown. However, $\boldsymbol{\pi}_x$ can be estimated from (17.6.36). Thus a two-stage least squares procedure is suggested. In the first stage $\mathbf{x}$ is regressed on Z to obtain

$$\hat{\boldsymbol{\pi}}_x = (Z'Z)^{-1}Z'\mathbf{x} \tag{17.6.37}$$

In the second stage $\mathbf{y}$ is regressed on $\hat{\mathbf{x}}(=Z\hat{\boldsymbol{\pi}}_x)$ to obtain one of the two stage least squares estimators denoted by $\tilde{\beta}_{(\infty)}$ as

$$\tilde{\beta}_{(\infty)} = (\mathbf{x}'Z(Z'Z)^{-1}Z'\mathbf{x})^{-1}\mathbf{x}'Z(Z'Z)^{-1}Z'\mathbf{y} \tag{17.6.38}$$

The use of infinity in $\tilde{\beta}_{(\infty)}$ is related to the variance ratio $\lambda = \sigma_v^2/\sigma_u^2$ and will become apparent in what follows. On the other hand, if we define

$$\boldsymbol{\pi}_y = \boldsymbol{\pi}_x\beta \tag{17.6.39}$$

we can rearrange (17.6.35) and (17.6.36) as

$$\mathbf{y} = Z\boldsymbol{\pi}_y + \mathbf{v} \tag{17.6.40}$$

$$\mathbf{x} = Z\boldsymbol{\pi}_y/\beta + \mathbf{u} \tag{17.6.41}$$

In this case, the two-stage least squares procedure is reversed. In the first stage $\mathbf{y}$ is regressed on Z to obtain

$$\hat{\boldsymbol{\pi}}_y = (Z'Z)^{-1}Z'\mathbf{y} \tag{17.6.42}$$

and in the second stage, $\mathbf{x}$ is regressed on $\hat{\mathbf{y}}(=Z\hat{\boldsymbol{\pi}}_y)$ to obtain

$$\widehat{\left(\frac{1}{\beta}\right)} = (\mathbf{y}'Z(Z'Z)^{-1}Z'\mathbf{y})^{-1}\mathbf{y}'Z(Z'Z)^{-1}Z'\mathbf{x} \tag{17.6.43}$$

We take the reciprocal of (17.6.43) as the basis for the estimator

$$\tilde{\beta}_{(0)} = (\mathbf{y}'Z(Z'Z)^{-1}Z'\mathbf{x})^{-1}\mathbf{y}'Z(Z'Z)^{-1}Z'\mathbf{y} \tag{17.6.44}$$

Thus there are two 2SLS estimators, $\tilde{\beta}_{(\infty)}$ and $\tilde{\beta}_{(0)}$. The former may be interpreted as a regression of $\mathbf{y}$ on $\mathbf{x}$ using $\hat{\mathbf{x}}$ as an instrumental variable, and the latter may be interpreted as a regression of $\mathbf{y}$ on $\mathbf{x}$ using $\hat{\mathbf{y}}$ as an instrumental variable. Both 2SLS estimators are consistent but are not efficient, because in the process of estimating $\boldsymbol{\pi}_x$, information contained in $\mathbf{y}$ is not used, and in estimating $\boldsymbol{\pi}_y$, information contained in $\mathbf{x}$ is not used.

To improve the efficiency of the estimator for β, Zellner (1970) minimizes the following weighted sum of squares

$$S = \frac{1}{\sigma_u^2}(\mathbf{x} - Z\boldsymbol{\pi}_x)'(\mathbf{x} - Z\boldsymbol{\pi}_x) + \frac{1}{\sigma_v^2}(\mathbf{y} - Z\boldsymbol{\pi}_x\beta)'(\mathbf{y} - Z\boldsymbol{\pi}_x\beta) \tag{17.6.45}$$

In the above weighted sum of squares, information contained in both $\mathbf{x}$ and $\mathbf{y}$ is utilized, and the resulting estimator should be more efficient. Minimization of (17.6.45) yields the following generalized least squares estimator (see Zellner, 1970) for $\boldsymbol{\pi}_x$

$$\tilde{\boldsymbol{\pi}}_x = [\hat{\boldsymbol{\pi}}_x + (\beta^2/\lambda)(\hat{\boldsymbol{\pi}}_y/\beta)]/(1 + \beta^2/\lambda) \tag{17.6.46}$$

and the estimator for β

$$\tilde{\beta}_{(\lambda)} = \frac{\hat{\mathbf{y}}'\hat{\mathbf{y}} - \lambda\hat{\mathbf{x}}'\hat{\mathbf{x}} + \sqrt{(\lambda\hat{\mathbf{x}}'\hat{\mathbf{x}} - \hat{\mathbf{y}}'\hat{\mathbf{y}})^2 + 4\lambda(\hat{\mathbf{x}}'\hat{\mathbf{y}})^2}}{2\hat{\mathbf{x}}'\hat{\mathbf{y}}} \tag{17.6.47}$$

where $\lambda = \sigma_v^2/\sigma_u^2$ may be estimated as

$$\hat{\lambda} = \frac{s_{yy}}{s_{xx}} \tag{17.6.48}$$

with

$$s_{yy} = T^{-1}(\mathbf{y} - Z\hat{\boldsymbol{\pi}}_y)'(\mathbf{y} - Z\hat{\boldsymbol{\pi}}_y) \tag{17.6.49}$$

$$s_{xx} = T^{-1}(\mathbf{x} - Z\hat{\boldsymbol{\pi}}_x)'(\mathbf{x} - Z\hat{\boldsymbol{\pi}}_x) \tag{17.6.50}$$

Zellner (1970) noted that

$$|\tilde{\beta}_{(\infty)}| \le |\tilde{\beta}_{(\lambda)}| \le |\tilde{\beta}_{(0)}| \tag{17.6.51}$$

Noting that the weighted sum of squares (17.6.45) is only a part of a log likelihood function, Goldberger (1972a) suggests that $\boldsymbol{\pi}_x$, $\boldsymbol{\pi}_y$, σ_u^2, and σ_v^2 be estimated jointly from the likelihood function. The parameter β may be estimated from (17.6.39) after $\boldsymbol{\pi}_x$ and $\boldsymbol{\pi}_y$ are estimated. To show the symmetry Goldberger writes the model in the reduced form as

$$\mathbf{y} = Z\boldsymbol{\pi}_y + \mathbf{v} \tag{17.6.52}$$

$$\mathbf{x} = Z\boldsymbol{\pi}_x + \mathbf{u} \tag{17.6.53}$$

where $(\mathbf{u}' \ \mathbf{v}')'$ is normally distributed with mean zero and variance Ω

$$E\left[\begin{pmatrix}\mathbf{u}\\ \mathbf{v}\end{pmatrix}\begin{pmatrix}\mathbf{u}\\ \mathbf{v}\end{pmatrix}'\right] = \Omega = \begin{pmatrix}\sigma_u^2 I_T & 0\\ 0 & \sigma_v^2 I_T\end{pmatrix} \tag{17.6.54}$$

The joint *pdf* for $\mathbf{u}$ and $\mathbf{v}$ is

$$f(\mathbf{u},\mathbf{v}) = (2\pi)^{-T}|\Omega|^{-1/2} \cdot \exp\left[-\frac{1}{2\sigma_v^2}(\mathbf{y} - Z\boldsymbol{\pi}_y)'(\mathbf{y} - Z\boldsymbol{\pi}_y) - \frac{1}{2\sigma_u^2}(\mathbf{x} - Z\boldsymbol{\pi}_x)'(\mathbf{x} - Z\boldsymbol{\pi}_x)\right] \tag{17.6.55}$$

which, when viewed as a function of the parameters $\boldsymbol{\pi}_x$, $\boldsymbol{\pi}_y$, σ_u^2, and σ_v^2, given $\mathbf{y}$ and $\mathbf{x}$, is the likelihood function. The log likelihood is

$$\ln \ell(\boldsymbol{\pi}_x, \boldsymbol{\pi}_y, \sigma_u^2, \sigma_v^2|\mathbf{y}, \mathbf{x}) = -T\ln(2\pi) - \tfrac{1}{2}\ln|\Omega| - \frac{1}{2\sigma_v^2}(\mathbf{y} - Z\boldsymbol{\pi}_y)'(\mathbf{y} - Z\boldsymbol{\pi}_y) - \frac{1}{2\sigma_u^2}(\mathbf{x} - Z\boldsymbol{\pi}_x)'(\mathbf{x} - Z\boldsymbol{\pi}_x) \tag{17.6.56}$$

Note that the last two terms of (17.6.56) contain the weighted sum of squares (17.6.45). If Ω is known, then maximizing (17.6.56) is equivalent to minimizing (17.6.45). If Ω is unknown, (17.6.56) or $\ell(\cdot)$ is maximized by taking the derivatives of $\ln \ell(\cdot)$ with respect to σ_u^2 and σ_v^2, setting them to zero, and solving for σ_u^2 and σ_v^2 to obtain the ML estimators $\tilde{\sigma}_u^2$ and $\tilde{\sigma}_v^2$. Then $\tilde{\sigma}_u^2$ and $\tilde{\sigma}_v^2$ are inserted back into (17.6.55) to obtain the concentrated likelihood function, which in turn is maximized with respect to $\boldsymbol{\pi}_x$ and $\boldsymbol{\pi}_y$. Since the first step produces

$$\tilde{\sigma}_v^2 = T^{-1}(\mathbf{y} - Z\tilde{\boldsymbol{\pi}}_y)'(\mathbf{y} - Z\tilde{\boldsymbol{\pi}}_y) \tag{17.6.57}$$

$$\tilde{\sigma}_u^2 = T^{-1}(\mathbf{x} - Z\tilde{\boldsymbol{\pi}}_x)'(\mathbf{x} - Z\tilde{\boldsymbol{\pi}}_x) \tag{17.6.58}$$

Goldberger suggests an iterative procedure to obtain $\tilde{\sigma}_u^2$, $\tilde{\sigma}_v^2$, $\tilde{\boldsymbol{\pi}}_x$, and $\tilde{\boldsymbol{\pi}}_y$. The generalized least squares estimators $\hat{\boldsymbol{\pi}}_x$ and $\hat{\boldsymbol{\pi}}_y$, as proposed by Zellner, are used as initial estimates in order to compute (17.6.57) and (17.6.58), or, equivalently, (17.6.49) and (17.6.50), then (17.6.48) and hence the new generalized least squares estimator (17.6.47). Then, (17.6.56) is maximized, given $\tilde{\sigma}_u^2$ and $\tilde{\sigma}_v^2$, to obtain $\tilde{\boldsymbol{\pi}}_x$ and $\tilde{\boldsymbol{\pi}}_y$. The procedure is repeated until the estimates converge.

It should be noted at this point that for this particular model, Pagan (1984) has shown that the maximum likelihood estimator and the 2SLS estimator of β happen to have the same asymptotic distribution. It turns out that, in this case, the 2SLS estimator is asymptotically efficient and no asymptotic efficiency gains are available by switching from the 2SLS estimator to a full maximum likelihood estimator. In other situations, however, the maximum likelihood method is a preferred alternative.

With the likelihood function $\ell(\cdot)$ we can incorporate, following the Bayesian procedures used in Chapter 4, the following prior *pdf*

$$p(\beta, \boldsymbol{\pi}_x, \lambda, \sigma_v^2) \propto p_1(\lambda)p_2(\beta)/\sigma_v^2 \tag{17.6.59}$$

where $0 < \sigma_v^2 < \infty$, $0 < \lambda < \infty$, $-\infty < \pi_i < \infty$, $i = 1, 2, \ldots, K$, and $p_1(\lambda)$ and $p_2(\beta)$ are of unspecified form. In (17.6.59) we have assumed that β, λ, $\ln \sigma_v^2$, and the elements of $\boldsymbol{\pi}_x$ are independently distributed and the *pdf*'s for $\ln \sigma_v^2$ and the elements of $\boldsymbol{\pi}_x$ are uniform. The multiplication of (17.6.59) and (17.6.56) results in the posterior *pdf* for the parameters β, $\boldsymbol{\pi}_x$, λ, and σ_v^2. Numerical integration techniques required to compute the joint and marginal posterior *pdf*'s were discussed in Chapter 4.

A generalization of the basic multiple causes model (17.6.16) is to include some exogenous variables $\mathbf{x}_1$ that directly affect the indicators:

$$\mathbf{y} = \boldsymbol{\beta}x^* + \Pi_1'\mathbf{x}_1 + \mathbf{v} \tag{17.6.60}$$

$$x^* = \boldsymbol{\alpha}'\mathbf{x}_2 \tag{17.6.61}$$

with assumptions $E[\mathbf{v}] = \mathbf{0}$, $E[\mathbf{vv}'] = \Omega$, where $\mathbf{x}_1$ is $(K_1 \times 1)$, $\mathbf{x}_2$ is $(K_2 \times 1)$, $\mathbf{x} = (\mathbf{x}_1' \quad \mathbf{x}_2')'$, Π_1 is $(K_1 \times M)$, $\boldsymbol{\alpha}$ is $(K_2 \times 1)$. In this case, the reduced form becomes

$$\begin{aligned}\mathbf{y} &= \Pi_1'\mathbf{x}_1 + \boldsymbol{\beta}(\boldsymbol{\alpha}'\mathbf{x}_2) + \mathbf{v}\\ &= \Pi_1'\mathbf{x}_1 + \Pi_2'\mathbf{x}_2 + \mathbf{v}\\ &= \Pi'\mathbf{x} + \mathbf{v}\end{aligned} \tag{17.6.62}$$

where $\Pi_2' = \boldsymbol{\beta\alpha}'$, $\Pi = (\Pi_1' \quad \Pi_2')'$. The previous procedure of solving (17.6.19) and (17.6.20) for $\boldsymbol{\alpha}$ and $\boldsymbol{\beta}$ is still applicable.

17.6.3 A Model with Multiple Indicators and Multiple Causes

When a stochastic error is added to the equation of multiple causes, the following model can be specified:

$$\mathbf{y} = \boldsymbol{\beta}x^* + \mathbf{u} \tag{17.6.63}$$

$$x^* = \boldsymbol{\alpha}'\mathbf{x} + \varepsilon \tag{17.6.64}$$

where $E[\mathbf{xu}'] = 0$, $E[\mathbf{x}\varepsilon] = \mathbf{0}$, $E[\varepsilon\mathbf{u}'] = \mathbf{0}'$, and $E[\mathbf{uu}'] = \Omega$ is a diagonal covariance matrix so that elements of $\mathbf{v}$ are mutually independent. Here again, $\mathbf{y}$ is an $(M \times 1)$ vector of observable effects, $\mathbf{x}$ is a $(K \times 1)$ vector of observable causes, $\mathbf{u}$ is an $(M \times 1)$ vector of errors, and x^* is the unobservable scalar.

The reduced form equation is

$$\begin{aligned} \mathbf{y} &= \boldsymbol{\beta}(\boldsymbol{\alpha}'\mathbf{x} + \varepsilon) + \mathbf{u} \\ &= \boldsymbol{\beta}\boldsymbol{\alpha}'\mathbf{x} + \boldsymbol{\beta}\varepsilon + \mathbf{u} \\ &= \Pi'\mathbf{x} + \mathbf{v} \end{aligned} \tag{17.6.65}$$

where $\Pi = \boldsymbol{\alpha}\boldsymbol{\beta}'$ and $\mathbf{v} = \boldsymbol{\beta}\varepsilon + \mathbf{u}$. Following the maximum likelihood procedure and adopting the normalization $\sigma_\varepsilon^2 = E[\varepsilon^2] = 1$, Goldberger (1974) shows that the following condition results:

$$(R\Omega^{-1} - \lambda I)\boldsymbol{\beta} = \mathbf{0} \tag{17.6.66}$$

where

$$\begin{aligned} R &= \frac{f}{1+f}S + Q \\ \lambda &= \frac{f}{1+f} + \frac{fg}{(1+f)^2} + \frac{h}{f} \\ f &= \boldsymbol{\beta}'\Omega^{-1}\boldsymbol{\beta}, \qquad g = \boldsymbol{\beta}'\Omega^{-1}S\Omega^{-1}\boldsymbol{\beta}, \qquad h = \boldsymbol{\beta}'\Omega^{-1}Q\Omega^{-1}\boldsymbol{\beta} \\ S &= (Y - XP)'(Y - XP) \\ P &= (X'X)^{-1}X'Y \\ Q &= P'X'XP \end{aligned}$$

Thus, conditional on Ω and f, the maximum likelihood estimator of $\boldsymbol{\beta}$ is a characteristic vector corresponding to the largest root λ of $R\Omega^{-1}$.

17.6.4 Causal Models and Path Analysis

The problem of unobservable variables can be approached by the path analysis method, which originated with Sewall Wright and dates back to the 1920s. However, it was not until 1966 when Dudley Duncan published an exposition of path analysis for sociologists that path analysis was brought to the attention of social scientists.

Path analysis starts by displaying a structural model as a flow diagram with one-way arrows flowing from causal variables to their direct effects, and with curved two-headed arrows connecting exogenous variables, whose causal linkage is not investigated. The structural coefficients, also called path coefficients, are placed on the one-headed arrows. For example, the following path diagram shows the causal relationships among variables x_t, y_t, z_t, u_t, v_t, and e_t. In Figure 17.1, the simple causal chain is that z_t and the error e directly affect x_t^*, which in turn together with v_t affects y_t, but x_t^* is not directly observed and its observed counterpart x_t is contaminated with error u_t. Thus, the causal model that con-

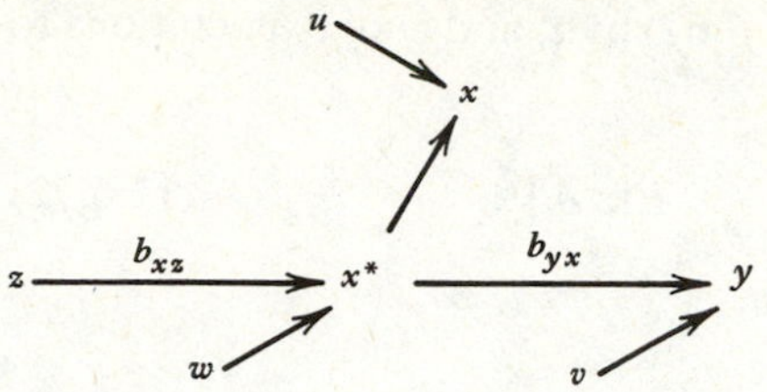

Figure 17.1 A path diagram.

tains measurement errors can be written in equation form as follows:

$$y_t = b_{yx}x_t^* + v_t \tag{17.6.67}$$

$$x_t = x_t^* + u_t \tag{17.6.68}$$

$$x_t^* = b_{xz}z_t + w_t \tag{17.6.69}$$

We assume that u_t is uncorrelated with x_t^* and also with y_t and z_t, $E[x_t^*u_t] = E[z_tu_t] = E[y_tu_t] = 0$, and $E[z_tw_t] = E[x_t^*v_t] = E[x_tv_t] = E[z_tv_t] = 0$. As a consequence, $E[u_tv_t] = E[u_tw_t] = E[v_tw_t] = 0$. The above model is a special case of the model in Section 17.6.3.

When the structural coefficients b_{yx} and b_{xz} are adjusted by population standard deviations, they are called by Wright path coefficients and are denoted by p_{yx} and p_{xz}, respectively, that is, $p_{yx} = b_{yx}\sigma_x/\sigma_y$ and $p_{xz} = b_{xz}\sigma_z/\sigma_x$. If the data are standardized, then $\sigma_x = \sigma_y = \sigma_z = 1$, $b_{yx} = p_{yx}$ and $b_{xz} = p_{xz}$. Here we assume that all variables are standardized so that

$$E[x_t^2] = E[y_t^2] = E[z_t^2] = E[u_t^2] = E[v_t^2] = E[w_t^2] = 1$$

$$E[x_t^*y_t] = E[x_ty_t] = \rho_{xy}$$

and

$$E[x_t^*z_t] = E[x_tz_t] = \rho_{xz}$$

where ρ_{xy} and ρ_{xz} denote population correlation between x_t and y_t, and x_t and z_t, respectively.

If we multiply equation (17.6.69) by z_t, and take expectations, we obtain

$$E[z_tx_t^*] = b_{xz}E[z_t^2] + E[z_tw_t] \tag{17.6.70}$$

or

$$\rho_{xz} = b_{xz} \tag{17.6.71}$$

Thus, the sample simple correlation r_{xz} provides an unbiased estimator of b_{xz}.

To estimate b_{yx}, we multiply equation (17.6.67) by z_t and take expectations to obtain

$$E[z_t y_t] = b_{yx} E[z_t x_t^*] + E[z_t v_t] \tag{17.6.72}$$

or

$$\rho_{zy} = b_{yx} \rho_{zx} \tag{17.6.73}$$

Therefore, $b_{yx} = \rho_{zy}/\rho_{zx}$ can be estimated by the ratio of the sample correlations r_{zy}/r_{zx}. Note that b_{yx} cannot be consistently estimated by r_{yx} because from Equation 17.6.67

$$E[x_t y_t] = b_{yx} E[x_t x_t^*] + E[x_t v_t] \tag{17.6.74}$$

or

$$\rho_{xy} = b_{yx}(1 - \sigma_u^2) \tag{17.6.75}$$

Therefore, the greater the variance in the errors σ_u^2, the greater the bias in using r_{xy} as an estimator of b_{yx}. Note also that the use of r_{zy}/r_{zx} as an estimator of b_{yx} is actually the same as the instrumental variable method, where the instrument variable is z_t. Other possible instrumental variables are discussed in the following section.

For other structural equation models and methods, see Hauser and Goldberger (1971), Goldberger (1972a,b), Goldberger and Duncan (1973), Duncan (1975), and Bagozzi (1980).

17.6.5 Instrumental Variables

Consider the basic errors in variables model

$$\mathbf{y} = \beta \mathbf{x}^* + \mathbf{v} \tag{17.6.76}$$

$$\mathbf{x} = \mathbf{x}^* + \mathbf{u} \tag{17.6.77}$$

where $\mathbf{y}$ and $\mathbf{x}$ are $(T \times 1)$ vectors of observations subject to error vectors $\mathbf{v}$ and $\mathbf{u}$, respectively, $\mathbf{x}^*$ is a $(T \times 1)$ vector of true but unobservable values, and β is the parameter to be estimated. We assume that all variables are in deviation form and $\mathbf{u}$, $\mathbf{v}$, and $\mathbf{x}^*$ are independent. The model, as discussed in Section 17.6.3, is underidentified. Additional information is required to identify the parameters.

Suppose that a third $(T \times 1)$ vector $\mathbf{z}$ is known to be correlated with $\mathbf{x}^*$ (or equivalently $\mathbf{x}$) but is independent of $\mathbf{u}$ and $\mathbf{v}$. In this event $\mathbf{z}$ can be used as an instrument to estimate β. Specifically, this is equivalent to specifying a third equation:

$$\mathbf{x}^* = \alpha\mathbf{z} + \mathbf{w} \qquad (17.6.78)$$

where **w** is independent of **z**, **u**, and **v**,

$$\text{plim}(\mathbf{z}'\mathbf{x}/T) = \text{plim}(\mathbf{z}'\mathbf{x}^*/T) = \sigma_{zx} \qquad (17.6.79)$$

exists and is nonzero, and

$$\text{plim}(\mathbf{z}'\mathbf{u}/T) = \text{plim}(\mathbf{z}'\mathbf{v}/T) = 0 \qquad (17.6.80)$$

In estimating β, we combine the first two equations (17.6.76) and (17.6.77) to obtain

$$\mathbf{y} = \beta\mathbf{x} + \mathbf{e} \qquad (17.6.81)$$

where $\mathbf{e} = \mathbf{v} - \beta\mathbf{u}$. The instrumental variable estimator

$$\beta_{\text{IV}} = (\mathbf{z}'\mathbf{x})^{-1}\mathbf{z}'\mathbf{y} \qquad (17.6.82)$$

is consistent since

$$\begin{aligned} \text{plim } \beta_{\text{IV}} &= \text{plim}(\mathbf{z}'\mathbf{x}/T)^{-1}(\mathbf{z}'\mathbf{x}\beta + \mathbf{z}'\mathbf{e})/T \\ &= \beta + \text{plim}(\mathbf{z}'\mathbf{x}/T)^{-1}[-\beta \text{ plim}(\mathbf{z}'\mathbf{u}/T) + \text{plim}(\mathbf{z}'\mathbf{v}/T)] \\ &= \beta \end{aligned} \qquad (17.6.83)$$

Thus, estimation of the parameters of a model that contains an unobservable variable is possible by an instrumental variable method, if one can justify the existence of the third variable **z** that relates to $\mathbf{x}^*$ in the additional third equation (17.6.78).

If the third equation (17.6.78) is specified, the parameter in the additional equation (17.6.78) can be estimated by the least squares rule with the following equation that combines (17.6.77) and (17.6.78):

$$\mathbf{x} = \alpha\mathbf{z} + (\mathbf{w} + \mathbf{u}) \qquad (17.6.84)$$

Since $(\mathbf{w} + \mathbf{u})$ is independent of **z**, the least squares estimator of α

$$\hat{\alpha} = (\mathbf{z}'\mathbf{z})^{-1}\mathbf{z}'\mathbf{x} \qquad (17.6.85)$$

is consistent.

A difficulty in using the instrumental variable method is the choice of an appropriate instrument that is correlated with the explanatory variable and uncorrelated with the error term. A variable that is likely to satisfy these two conditions is the discrete grouping variable. In other words, we classify the observations according to whether they fall into certain discrete groups and treat this classification as a discrete-valued variable. Several grouping instruments are available. If a two group classification is appropriate, then a binary variable

$$z_t = \begin{cases} 1 & \text{for one group} \\ 0 & \text{otherwise} \end{cases}$$

may be used as an instrument. This is equivalent to Wald's (1940) two group method. He suggests that if observations are divided into two groups, then the means of two groups can be connected to obtain an estimator of a slope parameter. He shows that the estimator is consistent if the grouping is independent of the errors, and significantly identifies the difference of the two means. An example is Friedman's grouping for cross-sectional data for his permanent-transitory income model of consumption. Friedman (1957) suggests connecting means of these variables across cities or occupations to estimate the slope of the consumption. This is equivalent to assuming that the distribution of the unobservable permanent income variable has a particular city or occupation component structure and using city or occupation dummies as instrumental variables.

If a three group classification is appropriate, then the following instrumental variable may be used:

$$z_t = \begin{cases} 1 & \text{for the top group} \\ 0 & \text{for the middle group} \\ -1 & \text{for the bottom group} \end{cases}$$

The three group method is discussed extensively by Nair and Shrivastava (1942), Nair and Banerjee (1942), Bartlett (1949), Theil and van Ijzeren (1956), Gibson and Jowett (1957), and Madansky (1959).

Another way of constructing an instrumental variable is to rank the observations x_j according to their ascending order and use the rank j as the instrument z. The method was suggested by Durbin (1954).

An efficient estimator can be obtained by using the 2SLS procedure. In the first stage, regress $\mathbf{x}$ on all possible instrumental variables $\mathbf{z}_1, \mathbf{z}_2, \ldots, \mathbf{z}_k$ to obtain linear combination constants $c_1, c_2, \ldots, c_k$ so that an instrumental variable $\hat{\mathbf{x}} = \Sigma_i c_i \mathbf{z}_i$ can be constructed. In the second stage, regress $\mathbf{y}$ on $\hat{\mathbf{x}}$ to obtain the instrumental variable estimator.

One problem is that we may not be able to identify all possible instrumental variables. Even if we can identify many instrumental variables, the first-stage regression in creating a combined instrument may run short of observations. In summary, the problem of finding an efficient estimator is equivalent to how well the researcher can specify the third equation $\mathbf{x}^* = Z\boldsymbol{\alpha} + \mathbf{w}$ that contains k extraneous variables in the $(T \times k)$ matrix Z.

17.7 SIMULTANEOUS EQUATIONS MODELS

Although the models considered in Section 17.6 contain multiple equations, they are recursive in nature and no simultaneity is involved among variables. In this section, we consider errors in the exogenous variables of a system of simultaneous equations. We assume that the errors in the endogenous variables can be absorbed into the structural equation errors. Errors in endogenous variables should not affect the identifiability of the structural coefficients if the covariance matrix of the structural equation errors is unrestricted.

Recalling the standard simultaneous equation model described in Chapters 14 and 15, we write the model with errors in exogenous variables as

$$Y\Gamma + X^*B + \mathbf{E} = 0 \tag{17.7.1}$$

where X^* is not observable but

$$X = X^* + U \tag{17.7.2}$$

is observable. We assume that X^* is independent of $\mathbf{E}$ and U,

$$\text{plim}(X^{*\prime}\mathbf{E}/T) = 0 \tag{17.7.3}$$

$$\text{plim}(X^{*\prime}U/T) = 0 \tag{17.7.4}$$

and for simplicity

$$\text{plim}(U'U/T) = \Theta \tag{17.7.5}$$

is diagonal. We also assume that the model would be overidentified if X^* were observable. If we allow some exogenous variables to be measured accurately, then the corresponding diagonal elements of Θ will be zero.

Denote the population covariance matrix of the observed X by Φ, then, under the usual assumptions

$$\begin{aligned}\Phi = \text{plim}(X'X/T) &= \text{plim}(X^* + U)'(X^* + U)/T \\ &= \text{plim}(X^{*\prime}X^*/T) + \Theta \end{aligned} \tag{17.7.6}$$

Noting that the reduced form equation is

$$\begin{aligned} Y &= -X^*B\Gamma^{-1} - \mathbf{E}\Gamma^{-1} \\ &= X^*\Pi^* + V \end{aligned} \tag{17.7.7}$$

where $\Pi^* = -B\Gamma^{-1}$ and $V = -\mathbf{E}\Gamma^{-1}$, we let Π be the coefficient matrix in the population linear regression of Y on X,

$$\begin{aligned}\Pi &= \text{plim}(X'X/T)^{-1}\,\text{plim}(X'Y/T)\\ &= \Phi^{-1}\,\text{plim}(X^* + U)'(X^*\Pi^* + V)/T\\ &= \Phi^{-1}\,\text{plim}(X^{*\prime}X^*/T)\Pi^*\\ &= \Phi^{-1}(\Phi - \Theta)\Pi^* \end{aligned} \tag{17.7.8}$$

Premultiplying (17.7.8) by Φ results in

$$\Phi\Pi = (\Phi - \Theta)\Pi^* \tag{17.7.9}$$

Solving for Π^* yields

$$\Pi^* = (\Phi - \Theta)^{-1}\Phi\Pi \tag{17.7.10}$$

which provides the relation connecting the observable moments and coefficients Φ and Π, to the parameters, Π^* and Θ. This relation, in conjunction with prior restrictions of zeros in Θ and the overidentifying restrictions on Π^*, may be sufficient to identify Π^*, which in turn, identifies the structural parameters. In general, overidentifying restrictions on the reduced-form coefficients can be used to identify measurement error variances if the error variances are properly located. However, operational rules for assessing the identifiability of parameters in a simultaneous equation model with unobservable variables, remain to be worked out.

For the subject of identification involving errors in exogenous variables, see Anderson and Hurwicz (1949), Wiley (1973), Geraci (1973), and Aigner, Hsiao, Kapteyn, and Wansbeck (1983). For estimation, see Chernoff and Rubin (1953), Sargan (1958), Jöreskog (1973), and Geraci (1983). In the presence of errors in variables, Geraci finds conditions under which simultaneous equations can be analyzed and estimated on a recursive equation by equation basis. Examples of models involving errors in exogenous variables are given by Goldberger (1972b, 1974), Duncan et al. (1968), Hauser (1972), and Duncan and Featherman (1972).

17.8 DYNAMIC MODELS

In order to consider a dynamic specification, we write the basic model in the nonvector form

$$y_t = x_t^*\beta + v_t \tag{17.8.1}$$

$$x_t = x_t^* + u_t \tag{17.8.2}$$

Without additional information, the above model is underidentified. Now suppose that x_t^* is serially correlated and we know that

$$E[x_t^* x_{t-1}^*] = E[x_t x_{t-1}] = \sigma_{xx}(1) \neq 0 \tag{17.8.3}$$

where the number in the parentheses indicates the order of lags in the variable of the second subscript. With the extraneous information of $E[x_t^* x_{t-1}^*] \neq 0$, β is identified by the following relation:

$$\begin{aligned}\sigma_{yx}(1) &= E[y_t x_{t-1}] \\ &= E[(x_t\beta + v_t - u_t\beta)x_{t-1}] \\ &= \beta E[x_t x_{t-1}] \\ &= \beta\sigma_{xx}(1) \qquad (17.8.4)\end{aligned}$$

Therefore,

$$\beta = \sigma_{yx}(1)/\sigma_{xx}(1) \qquad (17.8.5)$$

which can be estimated by the ratio of the sample moments $m_{yx}(1)$ and $m_{xx}(1)$ of $\sigma_{yx}(1)$ and $\sigma_{xx}(1)$, respectively, where

$$m_{yx}(1) = \Sigma y_t x_{t-1}/T \qquad (17.8.6)$$

$$m_{xx}(1) = \Sigma x_t x_{t-1}/T \qquad (17.8.7)$$

All variables are in deviation form. The estimator

$$\hat{\beta} = \Sigma y_t x_{t-1}/\Sigma x_t x_{t-1} \qquad (17.8.8)$$

is the instrumental variable estimator, the instrument being x_{t-1}. This is equivalent to specifying a dynamic equation

$$x_t^* = \alpha x_{t-1} + w_t \qquad (17.8.9)$$

as the third equation, where α can be estimated by

$$\hat{\alpha} = \Sigma x_t x_{t-1}/\Sigma x_{t-1}^2 \qquad (17.8.10)$$

In another situation, if it is known that

$$x_t^* = y_{t-1}^* \qquad (17.8.11)$$

in addition to the first two equations (17.8.1) and (17.8.2), then the covariance between lagged variables

$$\text{Cov}(y_t, y_{t-1}) = \sigma_{yy}(1) = \beta\sigma_{y^*y} = \beta\sigma_y^2 \qquad (17.8.12)$$

provides an estimation equation for β. Thus, an estimator for β is based on

$$\beta = \sigma_{yy}(1)/\sigma_y^2 \qquad (17.8.13)$$

Similarly, consider a simultaneous equation model

$$Y\Gamma + X^*B + \mathbf{E} = 0 \tag{17.8.14}$$

where

$$X = X^* + U \tag{17.8.15}$$

If the dynamic information

$$\text{plim}(X^{*\prime}_{-1}X^*/T) = \text{plim}(X'_{-1}X/T) = \Sigma_{x-1,x} \tag{17.8.16}$$

is known to be nonsingular, where X^*_{-1} and X_{-1} denote the matrices with lagged values of elements in X^* and X, respectively, then the following equation

$$\begin{aligned}\text{plim}(X'_{-1}Y/T) &= \Sigma_{x-1,y} \\ &= \text{plim}(X'_{-1}X/T)\Pi^* \\ &= \Sigma_{x-1\,x}\Pi^* \end{aligned} \tag{17.8.17}$$

can be used to identify Π as

$$\Pi^* = \Sigma^{-1}_{x-1,x}\Sigma_{x-1,y} \tag{17.8.18}$$

Therefore, the reduced form coefficients Π^* can be estimated by the sample covariances of Y and X_{-1}, and X and X_{-1}. This is equivalent to using X_{-1} as an instrumental variable in regressing Y on X, or

$$Y = X\Pi^* + W \tag{17.8.19}$$

where $W = V - U\Pi^*$, and

$$\hat{\Pi}^* = (X'_{-1}X)^{-1}X'_{-1}Y \tag{17.8.20}$$

To estimate the parameters in Γ, B, and Σ, the conventional order and rank conditions specified in Chapter 14 are necessary and sufficient. Details for identification are given by Hsiao (1978).

17.9 SUMMARY

In this chapter, we have considered statistical models that involve unobservable variables and variables that contain errors of measurement. We have shown that the least squares estimators of the parameters in these models that contain unobservable variables or observable variables measured with errors will be biased and inconsistent because the classical assumption about the independency of the stochastic term and the regressors is violated. We also noted that either omitting an unobservable variable or making use of a proxy variable in a regression equation results in a misspecification of the true model. Within the framework of least squares, McCallum (1972) and Wickens (1972) independently have shown that the use of the proxy variable leads to smaller inconsistency. Thus if one's major concern is inconsistency, it is better to use even a poor proxy than to omit the unobservable variable. On the other hand, Aigner (1974a) shows that based on the mean square error (MSE) criterion, the use of a poor proxy may result in a larger MSE than the omission of the unobservable variable. In any event, consistent parameter estimators can be obtained with other procedures such as the instrumental variable method.

Estimation of the parameters in models that contain measurement errors and unobservable variables is not as straightforward as in classical models. The maximum likelihood procedure for the simple regression with both dependent and independent variables subject to errors fails due to insufficient information in the model and thus raises the question of model identification. The classical errors in variables model is unidentified because there are many unknown parameters in the model to be solved from a smaller number of estimation equations. From the discussions involving both functional and structural relationships, we conclude that additional information is required to estimate the parameters. This outcome results because there are alternative structures with different parameter values that will produce the same expected moment matrix of observable variables. *If we can place sufficient restrictions on the parameters, the covariance matrix of the unobservable variables, and the covariance matrix of the disturbances, then it may be possible to find only one structure that is consistent with the observed information and the restrictions.*

Additional information may come in different forms. We may know the variances of the error terms associated with dependent or independent variables or both, or we may know the covariance matrix of the error terms up to a scalar factor. Sometimes we may know the ratio of error variance to total variance, for example, the reliability of test scores to represent ability. When additional information is available, the new information may be used to identify the particular structure. Excessive information may result in overidentification in the sense that there will be more equations than the number of unknown parameters to be solved, and thus alternative estimates will be available. However, as sample size increases, they all converge to the true parameter value.

Another source of information about the variances and covariances of the error terms is from repeated observations. Within the sets of repeated observations, one will be able to estimate the covariance matrix of the error terms. The parameters then can be estimated from this additional information on error variances.

Another type of additional information is related to unobservable variables in the form of indicators or causes. In either case, an additional equation is specified to explain the unobservable variable with exogenous causes or to show the relationship between the observable counterpart and the unobservable variables. An example of an additional observable indicator of the true but unobservable variable is another type of test score as an indicator of human ability. For an identifiable model, the maximum likelihood estimation procedure reduces to the problem of finding the largest characteristic root and the associated normalized characteristic vector. If we know the relationship between the true but unknown variable and a set of observable variables, we can add this new equation to the model to achieve identification. Addition of the equation that explains the unobservable variable circumvents the complication of the problem associated with incidental parameters—namely, the number of unknowns increases as the sample size increases. For a special case of only two indicators, Zellner (1970) and Goldberger (1972a) develop generalized least squares and maximum likelihood procedures under alternative assumptions about the errors of the two indicators.

The generalized least squares (GLS) approach utilizes information contained in both dependent and independent variables and results in a "better" estimate than those of the 2SLS. The formula for the GLS estimator is quite similar to the classical case when the ratio of error variances is known. The only difference is that the moments of the original variables are replaced by the moments of the calculated variables. The GLS estimator may be viewed as an initial estimate of the maximum likelihood estimate, since the variances of the error terms are given by the mean square of the first-stage least squares residuals, and are not estimated jointly with other parameters in the likelihood function.

An iterative procedure can be used to update the estimates of the error variances and other parameter estimates. If one further incorporates prior knowledge about the distribution of the unknown parameters, Bayesian estimation can be used. When a diffuse or vague prior pdf for the parameters is used, the mode of the posterior pdf is close to the previously mentioned GLS estimate given the ratio of error variances. Both the variance ratio and the regression parameter can be analyzed from the joint posterior pdf and their marginal pdf by numerical analysis.

In the multiple equation cases, the maximum likelihood procedure is available and the estimates can be obtained by solving a characteristic root problem. The procedure used is similar to that employed in factor analysis, which is often used in psychology. Path analysis, which is often used in sociology, is also quite capable of solving unobservable variable problems. An instrumental variable interpretation of an estimate of a path coefficient leads to discussions of alternative instrumental variables that are related to the grouping methods.

The problem of unobservable variables may be extended to a system of simultaneous equations, in which the exogenous variables may be unobservable. Goldberger (1972b) has shown that the overidentification conditions can be used to offset the underidentification introduced by errors in variables in a contemporaneous simultaneous equations model. In the case of a dynamic model, Hsiao (1978) shows that under certain conditions, conventional order and rank conditions are necessary to identify the model that has measurement errors. Spectral estimation procedures to deal with the model that contains lagged endogenous variables and measurement errors are investigated by Hsiao

(1978). Because of computational complexities, its applicability is somewhat limited.

The pace of theoretical developments in the error in variables and unobservable variables models is rapid. Jöreskog (1970) discusses the estimation of the general model in which means, variances, and covariances are structured in terms of another set of parameters that are to be estimated. Browne (1974) discusses generalized least squares estimators in the analysis of covariance structures. Robinson (1974) examines the identification and estimation of elaborate models containing arbitrarily many observables and unobservables and also presents a large-sample theory for the estimates.

Chamberlain and Griliches (1975) develop and estimate a somewhat more general structural model whose reduced form disturbances are connected by a common unobservable variable having a within- and between-group variance component structure. Robinson and Ferrara (1977) further discuss the estimation of a model for an unobservable variable with endogeneous causes. Maravall and Aigner (1977) present the basic identification theorem for a single-equation dynamic model containing a latent endogeneous variable and latent exogenous variables with an autocorrelated shock, but with no a priori parameter restrictions. Geweke (1977) examines a factor analysis model from the aspect of frequency domain using the spectral technique. Geraci (1977) examines the estimation of a normal, contemporaneous, simultaneous equation model in which some of the exogenous variables are measured with error. Fuller (1971) studies properties of some estimators for the errors in variables model. Wolter and Fuller (1978) propose an iterative estimation procedure for nonlinear errors in variables models. The list goes on and on.

On the other hand, since the path-breaking articles by Zellner (1970) and Goldberger (1972a), unobservable variables models of various types have also been the subject of empirical study. Aigner (1974b), using the 1967 Survey of Economic Opportunity file, presents an explicit treatment of the errors in variables problem arising in the estimation of a labor-supply function. Griliches and Mason (1972), Chamberlain and Griliches (1974, 1975) and Chamberlain (1977) have considered the empirical problem of the bias in income-schooling regressions caused by the omission of unobservable initial "ability" variables. Bielby, Hauser, and Featherman (1977) consider models of the achievement process, in which the covariation among the indicators is generated by unobserved true scores. Kadane, McGuire, Sanday, and Staelin (1977) study the effect of environmental factors on changes in IQ.

The methodology of errors in variables also extends to the estimation of distributed lag models. For the explicit connection of distributed lags to the errors in variables, see Klein (1958), Muth (1960), Nerlove (1967), and Grether and Nerlove (1970). Detailed discussions of the distributed lag models were presented in Part Three.

The existing literature on theoretical and empirical analysis of errors in variables or unobservable variables provides good references on how to handle similar problems. The choice of estimation procedures depends on the kind of extraneous information that is available. Without extraneous information, the classical errors in variables model is unidentified. For an identifiable model, the maximum likelihood procedure provides consistent and efficient estimators of parameters. For the maximum likelihood procedures we have discussed, we need extraneous information regarding the variances of the error terms, in one form or another, or additional information regarding indicators of the true unobservable variables, or information regarding the causes that explain the variations of the unobservable variables.

Since the error term at the end of the equation that contains unobservable variables is partly due to these explanatory variables, the error term cannot be independent of the explanatory variables. As a consequence, no linear unbiased estimator can be obtained. The best we can do is to find the most efficient estimator among the consistent estimators. In this context the maximum likelihood estimator is consistent and asymptotically efficient. Although these properties are only asymptotic, this is about all that we can hope for. *The small-sample properties of these estimators are unfortunately unknown.*

17.10 EXERCISES

Some data for exercises in this section are generated from the following basic model:

$$\begin{aligned} y_t^* &= \alpha + \beta x_t^* + \gamma z_t \\ x_t &= x_t^* + u_t \\ y_t &= y_t^* + v_t \end{aligned} \tag{17.10.1}$$

where $\alpha = 8.0$, $\beta = 0.6$, and $\gamma = 0.03$; y_t^* and x_t^*, the unobservable variables, and z_t, the observable variable, measured without errors, are given in Table 17.2. With the assumptions that $u_t \sim N(0,1)$ and $v_t \sim N(0,9)$, for all t, a sample of x_t and y_t of size 20 has been generated and is listed in Table 17.2.

Data in Table 17.3 are generated from the model

$$\begin{aligned} y_t^* &= \alpha + \beta x_t^* \\ x_t &= x_t^* + u_t \\ y_t &= y_t^* + v_t \end{aligned} \tag{17.10.2}$$

with $\alpha = 10$, $\beta = 0.9$, $u_t \sim N(0,1)$, and $v_t \sim N(0,9)$, and y_t^* and x_t^* as listed in Table 17.2.

Exercise 17.1

Using 20 observations of x, y, and z in Table 17.2, compute the least squares estimates of α, β, and γ in $y_t = \alpha + \beta x_t + \gamma z_t + v_t$, where the true variable x_t^* is replaced by the observable proxy variable x_t. Compare the results to their theoretical counterparts.

TABLE 17.2 ***TRUE UNOBSERVABLE VARIABLES y*, x*, OBSERVABLE VARIABLE MEASURED WITHOUT ERRORS z, AND OBSERVABLE VARIABLES MEASURED WITH ERRORS y, x***

y*	x*	z	y	x
20.30	18.86	32.87	12.40	16.12
19.21	17.09	31.81	21.61	17.08
18.62	16.25	28.89	20.58	17.71
17.14	13.95	25.69	18.14	15.16
16.85	13.50	25.13	15.88	13.91
17.34	14.20	27.27	13.47	15.61
18.10	15.44	27.80	22.45	15.46
19.17	17.22	27.94	21.50	18.88
19.48	17.67	29.29	20.59	18.97
18.68	16.37	28.59	17.79	16.64
19.39	17.56	28.40	19.67	19.33
19.97	18.49	29.10	22.49	18.77
21.45	20.84	31.49	16.63	19.62
23.16	23.53	34.82	22.00	21.27
23.67	24.29	36.41	23.85	24.25
24.02	24.85	37.13	28.19	24.01
23.66	24.20	37.99	19.93	23.71
23.42	23.51	43.88	24.45	24.34
22.76	22.12	49.70	19.44	21.78
23.32	22.88	53.13	21.37	22.09

Exercise 17.2
Using the observations in Table 17.2, compute the least squares estimates α and γ in $y_t = \alpha + \gamma z_t + e_t$, where the true unobservable variable x_t^* is omitted. Compare the results to their theoretical counterparts.

Exercise 17.3
Assuming that we know that $\sigma_u^2 = 1$ and using the observations in Table 17.2, estimate the parameters α and β of the model (17.10.1).

Exercise 17.4
Repeat 17.3 but assume that $\sigma_v^2 = 9$ is known.

Exercise 17.5
Repeat 17.3 but assume that $\sigma_v^2/\sigma_u^2 = 9$ is known.

Exercise 17.6
Repeat 17.3 but assume that both $\sigma_u^2 = 1$ and $\sigma_v^2 = 9$ are known.

TABLE 17.3 *SAMPLES OF OBSERVABLE VARIABLES MEASURED WITH ERRORS*

y_1	x_1	y_2	x_2	y_3	x_3	y_4	x_4
19.07	16.12	17.61	15.63	19.14	15.14	17.67	15.65
27.78	17.08	27.73	17.06	27.67	17.04	30.61	18.02
26.59	17.71	20.35	17.63	23.11	16.55	25.87	16.47
23.55	15.16	18.79	14.57	29.03	13.98	21.27	13.39
21.18	13.91	26.66	14.74	23.14	12.57	19.62	13.39
18.91	15.61	21.40	14.44	26.89	14.27	23.37	14.10
28.24	15.46	22.37	14.50	25.50	15.55	19.63	15.59
27.83	18.88	28.77	18.19	23.70	17.50	30.64	18.81
27.02	18.97	22.84	18.58	27.66	17.19	23.48	17.79
23.84	16.64	25.47	15.18	24.10	15.73	19.73	16.27
26.08	19.33	27.68	16.86	23.28	18.39	27.88	18.92
29.16	18.77	30.83	18.32	26.50	17.88	25.17	17.44
23.94	19.62	25.63	20.18	21.31	20.74	26.00	21.31
30.02	21.27	31.48	24.76	32.94	24.25	31.40	22.73
32.05	24.25	34.78	24.16	34.51	26.07	31.24	23.98
36.53	24.01	28.50	24.33	29.46	25.66	30.43	24.98
28.05	23.71	37.12	23.74	28.19	24.76	37.27	22.79
32.19	24.34	31.14	22.99	36.09	22.64	32.05	24.29
26.59	21.78	24.56	23.10	31.53	21.43	26.50	21.75
28.64	22.09	23.88	21.50	31.12	23.92	32.37	24.33

Exercise 17.7

Using 20 observations from Table 17.3 and x_{t-1} as an instrument, estimate the parameters α and β in the model (17.10.2).

Exercise 17.8

Repeat 17.7 but use Wald's two-group method.

Exercise 17.9

Repeat 17.7 but use the three-group method.

Exercise 17.10

Repeat 17.7 but use the ranks as an instrument.

Exercise 17.11

Treat the four samples in Table 17.3 as repeated observations of the same unobservable variable listed in Table 17.4. Using the method of repeated observations described in Section 17.5.2, estimate the parameters of the model (17.10.2).

A second indicator y_{2t} is assumed observable, where $y_{2t} = \alpha_2 + \beta_2 x_t^* + v_{2t}$ and $v_{2t} \sim N(0,\sigma_{\theta 2}^2)$. Four samples of indicator values that are generated with $\alpha_2 = -0.2$, $\beta_2 = 7$, and $v_{2t} \sim N(0,4)$ are given by Table 17.5.

TABLE 17.4 ***TRUE UNOBSERVABLE VARIABLES, y* AND x****

y*	x*
26.97	18.86
25.38	17.09
24.62	16.25
22.55	13.95
22.15	13.50
22.78	14.20
23.90	15.44
25.50	17.22
25.90	17.67
24.73	16.37
25.80	17.56
26.64	18.49
28.76	20.84
31.18	23.53
31.86	24.29
32.36	24.85
31.78	24.20
31.16	23.51
29.91	22.12
30.59	22.88

TABLE 17.5 ***A SECOND INDICATOR***

y_{21}	y_{22}	y_{23}	y_{24}
187.57	186.60	179.62	182.64
178.69	176.65	178.61	174.57
175.88	169.71	175.55	171.39
156.61	157.43	158.26	159.08
154.73	152.38	154.03	153.69
157.27	158.93	162.59	160.24
166.83	170.91	167.00	167.08
180.08	178.71	179.33	179.96
182.00	181.21	180.43	179.64
171.20	172.28	173.37	172.45
179.27	180.33	179.40	178.46
187.09	188.20	187.32	186.43
199.11	200.23	203.36	202.48
219.01	219.98	214.96	221.93
223.16	226.99	224.81	222.63
227.58	226.23	226.87	229.52
220.26	224.31	218.36	222.40
217.63	214.93	218.24	217.54
211.41	210.05	208.70	207.35
210.93	217.75	216.58	213.41

Exercise 17.12

Using any of the four samples of $\mathbf{y}_1$ in Table 17.3 and any of the four samples of $\mathbf{y}_2$ in Table 17.5, estimate the parameters in the following model:

$$\mathbf{y}_1 = \alpha_1 \mathbf{j} + \beta_1 \mathbf{x}^* + \mathbf{v}_1$$
$$\mathbf{y}_2 = \alpha_2 \mathbf{j} + \beta_2 \mathbf{x}^* + \mathbf{v}_2$$
$$\mathbf{x} = \mathbf{x}^* + \mathbf{u} \tag{17.10.3}$$

where $\mathbf{j} = (1 \quad 1 \quad . \; . \; . \quad 1)'$.

Exercise 17.13

Repeat Exercise 17.12 but use the factor analysis approach described in Section 17.6.2.

Suppose that two causes of x_t^* can be identified as z_1 and z_2 in the form $x_t^* = \pi_0 + \pi_1 z_{1t} + \pi_2 z_{2t}$. In generating data for the purpose of exercises, the values for z_1 are given and values for z_2 are generated with $\pi_0 = 7$, $\pi_1 = -2$, $\pi_2 = 3$, so that the values of x_t^* are those listed in Table 17.2. The values of the two causes are listed in Table 17.6.

TABLE 17.6
ADDITIONAL CAUSES

$\mathbf{z}_1$	$\mathbf{z}_2$
305.80	207.82
305.29	206.89
308.45	208.72
313.88	211.57
323.93	218.12
323.05	217.77
321.61	217.22
312.66	211.85
309.80	210.09
308.40	208.72
305.47	207.17
301.18	204.62
289.14	197.37
261.86	180.08
248.15	171.20
244.20	168.75
254.03	175.09
258.29	177.70
243.83	167.59
241.94	166.59

Exercise 17.14

Using 20 observations of any of the four samples of y_t and x_t in Table 17.3 and the two causes z_1 and z_2 in Table 17.6, estimate the parameters of the model

$$y_t = \alpha + \beta x_t^* + v_t$$

$$x_t = x_t^* + u_t$$

$$x_t^* = \pi_0 + \pi_1 z_{1t} + \pi_2 z_{2t} \tag{17.10.4}$$

with the two-stage least squares estimator.

Exercise 17.15

Repeat 17.14 but use the generalized least squares procedure described in Section 17.6.3.

Exercise 17.16

Repeat 17.14 but use the maximum likelihood procedure described in Section 17.6.3.

17.11 REFERENCES

Aigner, D. J. (1973) "Regression with a Binary Independent Variable Subject to Errors of Observation," *Journal of Econometrics,* 1, 49–60.

Aigner, D. J. (1974a) "MSE Dominance of Least Squares with Errors of Observation," *Journal of Econometrics,* 2, 365–372.

Aigner, D. J. (1974b) "An Appropriate Econometric Framework for Estimating a Labor-Supply Function from the SEO File," *International Economic Review,* 15, 59–68.

Aigner, D. J. and A. S. Goldberger, eds. (1977) *Latent Variables in Socioeconomic Models,* North-Holland, Amsterdam.

Aigner, D. J., C. Hsiao, A. Kapteyn, and T. Wansbeek (1984) "Latent Variable Models in Econometrics," Chapter 23 in *Handbook of Econometrics,* Vol. II, Z. Griliches and M. D. Intriligator, eds., North-Holland, Amsterdam.

Allen, R. G. D. (1939) "Assumptions of Linear Regression," *Economica,* 6, 199–204.

Anderson, T. W. and L. Hurwicz (1949) "Errors and Shocks in Economic Relationships," *Econometrica, Suppl.* 17, 23–25.

Bagozzi, R. P. (1980) *Causal Models in Marketing,* Wiley, New York.

Barnett, V. D. (1967) "A Note on Linear Functional Relationships When Both Residual Variances Are Known," *Biometrika,* 54, 670–672.

Barnett, V. D. (1970) "Fitting Straight Lines: The Linear Functional Relationship with Replicated Observations," *Applied Statistics,* 54, 670–672.

Bartlett, M. S. (1949) "Fitting of Straight Lines When Both Variables Are Subject to Error," *Biometrics,* 5, 207–212.

Bielby, W. T., R. M. Hauser, and D. L. Featherman (1977) "Response Errors of Non-Black Males in Models of the Stratification Process," in D. J. Aigner and A. S. Goldberger, eds., *Latent Variables in Socio-economic Models,* North-Holland, Amsterdam, pp. 227–251.

Birch, M. W. (1964) "A Note on the Maximum Likelihood Estimation of a Linear Structural Relationship," *Journal of the American Statistical Association,* 59, 1175–1178.

Blalock, H. M. Jr., ed. (1971) *Causal Models in the Social Sciences,* Aldine-Atheron, Chicago.

Blalock, H. M. Jr. (1971) "Four-Variable Causal Models and Partial Correlations," *American Journal of Sociology,* 77, 1962–1963.

Blalock, H. M. Jr. (1969) "Multiple Indicators and the Causal Approach to Measurement Error," *American Journal of Sociology,* 75, 264–272.

Bowles, S. (1972) "Schooling and Inequality from Generation to Generation," *Journal of Political Economy,* 80, 219–251.

Browne, M. W. (1974) "Generalized Least-Squares Estimators in the Analysis of Covariance Structures," *South African Statistical Journal,* 8, 1–24; reprinted in D. J. Aigner and A. S. Goldberger, eds., (1977), *Latent Variables in Socio-economic Models,* North-Holland, Amsterdam, pp. 205–226.

Cagan, P. (1956) "The Monetary Dynamics of Hyper-inflation," in M. Friedman, ed., *Studies in the Quantity Theory of Money,* University of Chicago Press, Chicago, Ill.

Carlson F. D., F. Sobel, and G. S. Watson (1966) "Linear Relationship Between Variables Affected by Errors," *Biometrics,* 22, 252–267.

Chamberlain, G. (1973) "Unobservables in Econometric Models," unpublished Ph.D. dissertation. Harvard University, Cambridge, Mass.

Chamberlain, G. (1977) "Education, Income, and Ability Revisited," *Journal of Econometrics,* 5, 241–257.

Chamberlain, G. and Z. Griliches (1974) "Returns to Schooling of Brothers and Ability as an Unobservable Variance Component," Harvard Institute of Economic Research, Discussion Paper No. 340, Cambridge, Mass.

Chamberlain, G. and Z. Griliches (1975) "Unobservables with a Variance-Components Structure: Ability, Schooling, and the Economic Success of Brothers," *International Economic Review,* 16, 422–449.

Chernoff, H. and H. Rubin (1953) "Asymptotic Properties of Limited-Information Estimates under Generalized Conditions," in W. C. Hood and T. C. Koopmans, eds., *Studies in Econometric Method,* Wiley, New York.

Clutton-Brock, M. (1967) "Likelihood Distributions for Estimating Functions When Both Variables Are Subject to Error," *Technometrics,* 9, 261–269.

Cochran, W. G. (1968) "Errors of Measurement in Statistics," *Technometrics,* 10, 637–666.

Crockett, J. (1960) "Technical Note," in I. Friend and R. Jones, *Proceedings of the Conference on Consumption and Saving,* University of Pennsylvania, Philadelphia, pp. 213–222.

DeGracie, J. S. and W. A. Fuller (1972) "Estimation of the Slope and Analysis of Covariance When the Concomitant Variable Is Measured with Error," *Journal of the American Statistical Association,* 67, 930–937.

Dhrymes, P. J. (1978) *Introductory Econometrics,* Springer-Verlag, New York.

Dolby, C. R. and S. Lipton (1972) "Maximum Likelihood Estimation of the General Nonlinear Functional Relationship with Replicated Observations and Correlated Errors," *Biometrika,* 59, 121–129.

Dolby, G. R. and T. G. Freeman (1975) "Functional Relationships Having Many Independent Variables and Errors with Multivariate Normal Distribution," *Journal of Multivariate Analysis,* 5, 466–478.

Duncan, O. D. (1966) "Path Analysis: Sociological Examples," *American Journal of Sociology,* 72, 1–16.

Duncan, O. D. (1975) *Introduction to Structural Equation Models,* Academic, New York.

Duncan, O. D. and D. L. Featherman (1972) "Psychological and Cultural Factors in The Process of Occupational Achievement," *Social Science Research,* 1, 121–145.

Duncan, O. D., A. O. Haller, and A. Portes (1968) "Peer Influences on Aspirations: A Reinterpretation," *American Journal of Sociology,* 74, 119–137.

Durbin, J. (1954) "Errors in Variables," *Review of the International Statistics Institute,* 1, 23–32.

El-Sayyad, G. M. (1968) "The Bayesian Estimation of a Linear Functional Relationship," *Journal of the Royal Statistical Society, Series B,* 30, 190–202.

Feldstein, M. S. (1974) "Errors in Variables: A Consistent Estimator with Smaller MSE in Finite Samples," *Journal of the American Statistical Association,* 69, 990–996.

Florens, J. P., M. Mouchart, and J. P. Richard (1974) "Bayesian Inference in Errors-in-Variables Models," *Journal of Multivariate Analysis,* 4, 419–452.

Friedman, M. (1957) *A Theory of the Consumption Function,* Princeton University Press, Princeton, N.J.

Fuller, W. A. (1971) "Properties of Some Estimators for the Errors-in-Variables Model," paper presented at the Econometric Society meeting, New Orleans, December.

Fuller, W. A. (1978) "Measurement Error Models," mimeograph, Iowa State University, Ames.

Fuller, W. A. and M. A. Hidiroglou (1978) "Regression Estimation After Correcting for Attenuation," *Journal of the American Statistical Association,* 73, 99–104.

Geary, R. C. (1942) "Inherent Relations Between Random Variables," *Proceedings of the Royal Irish Academy,* A47, 63–76.

Geary, R. C. (1949) "Determination of Linear Relations Between Systematic Parts of Variables with Errors of Observations the Variance of Which Are Unknown," *Econometrica,* 17, 30–58.

Geraci, V. J. (1973) "Simultaneous Equation Models with Measurement Error," unpublished Ph.D. dissertation, University of Wisconsin, Madison, Wisconsin.

Geraci, V. J. (1976) "Identification of Simultaneous Equation Models with Measurement Error," *Journal of Econometrics,* 4, 262–283.

Geraci, V. J. (1977) "Estimation of Simultaneous Equation Models with Measurement Error," *Econometrica,* 45, 1243–1253.

Geraci, V. J. (1983) "Errors in Variables and Individual Structural Equations," *International Economic Review,* 24, 217–236.

Geweke, J. (1977) "The Dynamic Factor Analysis of Economic Time-Series Models," in D. J. Aigner, and A. S. Goldberger, eds., *Latent Variables in Socio-economic Models,* North-Holland, Amsterdam, pp. 366–383.

Gibson, W. M. and G. H. Jowett (1957) "Three-Group Regression Analysis, Part I, Simple Regression Analysis," *Applied Statistics,* 6, 114.

Goldberger, A. S. (1964) *Econometric Theory,* Wiley, New York.

Goldberger, A. S. (1972a) "Maximum-Likelihood Estimation of Regressions Containing Unobservable Independent Variables," *International Economic Review,* 13, 1–15.

Goldberger, A. S. (1972b) "Structural Equation Methods in the Social Sciences," *Econometrica,* 40, 979–1002.

Goldberger, A. S. (1974) "Unobservable Variables in Econometrics," in P. Zarembka, ed., *Frontiers of Econometrics,* Academic, New York, pp. 193–213.

Goldberger, A. S. and O. D. Duncan, eds. (1973) *Structural Equation Models in the Social Sciences,* Seminar Press, New York.

Goodman, L. A. (1974) "The Analysis of Systems of Qualitative Variables When Some of the Variables are Unobservable, Part I—A Modified Latent Structure Approach," *American Journal of Sociology,* 79, 1179–1259.

Grether, D. M. and M. Nerlove (1970) "Some Properties of 'Optimal' Seasonal Adjustment," *Econometrica,* 38, 682–703.

Griliches, Z. (1970) "Notes on the Role of Education in Production Functions and Growth Accounting," in W. L. Hansen, ed., *Education, Income and Human Capital,* National Bureau of Economic Research, New York.

Griliches, Z. (1974) "Errors in Variables and Other Unobservables," *Econometrica,* 42, 971–998.

Griliches, Z. (1977) "Estimating the Returns to Schooling: Some Econometric Problems," *Econometrica,* 45, 1–22.

Griliches, Z. and W. M. Mason (1972) "Education and Ability," *Journal of Political Economy,* 80, 74–103.

Griliches, Z. and V. Ringstad (1970) "Errors-in-the-Variables Bias in Nonlinear Contexts," *Econometrica,* 38, 368–370.

Halperin, M. J. (1961) "Fitting of Straight Lines and Prediction when Both Variables Are Subject to Error," *Journal of the American Statistical Association,* 56, 657–669.

Hanushek, E. A. and J. E. Jackson (1977) *Statistical Methods for Social Scientists,* Academic, New York, Chapter 10.

Harman, H. H. (1976) *Modern Factor Analysis,* 3rd ed., revised. University of Chicago Press, Chicago, Ill.

Hauser, R. M. (1972) "Disaggregating A Social-Psychological Model of Educational Attainment," *Social Science Research,* 1, 159–188.

Hauser, R. M. and A. S. Goldberger (1971) "The Treatment of Unobservable Variables in Path Analysis," in H. L. Costner, ed., *Sociological Methodology,* Jossey-Bass, San Francisco.

Holbrook, R. and F. Stafford (1971) "The Propensity to Consume Separate Types of Income: A Generalized Permanent Income Hypothesis," *Econometrica,* 39, 1–22.

Hooper, J. W. and H. Theil (1958) "The Extension of Wald's Method of Fitting Straight Lines to Multiple Regression," *Review of the International Statistical Institute,* 26, 37–47.

Hsiao, C. (1976) "Identification and Estimation of Simultaneous Equation Models with Measurement Error," *International Economic Review,* 17, 319–339.

Hsiao, C. (1978) "Measurement Error in A Dynamic Simultaneous Equations Model Without Stationary Disturbances," Technical Report No. 263, Institute For Mathematical Studies in The Social Sciences, Stanford University, Stanford, California.

Johnston, J. (1963) *Econometric Methods,* McGraw-Hill, New York.

Jöreskog, K. G. (1970) "A General Method for Analysis of Covariance Structures," *Biometrika,* 57, 239–251.

Jöreskog, K. G. (1973) "A General Method for Estimating a Linear Structure Equation System," in A. S. Goldberger and O. D. Duncan, eds., *Structural Equation Models in the Social Sciences,* Seminar Press, New York. pp. 85–112.

Jöreskog, K. G. and A. S. Goldberger (1972) "Factor Analysis by Generalized Least Squares," *Psychometrika,* 37, 243–260.

Jöreskog, K. G. and D. Sorbom (1977) "Statistical Models and Methods for Analysis of Longitudinal Data," in D. J. Aigner and A. S. Goldberger, eds., *Latent Variables in Socio-economic Models,* North-Holland, Amsterdam, pp. 285–325.

Judge, G. G., W. E. Griffiths, R. C. Hill, and T. C. Lee (1980) *The Theory and Practice of Econometrics,* Wiley, New York.

Judge, G. G., R. C. Hill, W. E. Griffiths, H. Lütkepohl, and T. C. Lee (1982) *Introduction to the Theory and Practice of Econometrics,* Wiley, New York.

Kadane, J. B., T. W. McGuire, P. R. Sanday, and R. Staelin (1977) "Estimation of Environmental Effects on the Pattern of IQ Scores over Time," in D. J. Aigner and A. S. Goldberger, eds., *Latent Variables in Socio-economic Models,* North-Holland, Amsterdam, pp. 327–348.

Kendall, M. G. (1951) "Regression, Structure, and Functional Relationships, Part I," *Biometrika,* 38, 11–25.

Kendall, M. G. (1952) "Regression, Structure, and Functional Relationships, Part II," *Biometrika,* 39, 96–108.

Kendall, M. G. (1957) *A Course in Multivariate Analysis,* Charles Griffin, London.

Kendall, M. G. and A. Stuart (1961) *The Advanced Theory of Statistics,* Vol. 2, Hafner, New York, Chapter 29.

Kiefer, J. and J. Wolfowitz (1956) "Consistency of the Maximum Likelihood Estimator in the Presence of Infinitely Many Incidental Parameters," *Annals of Mathematical Statistics,* 27, 887–906.

Klein, L. R. (1958) "The Estimation of Distributed Lags," *Econometrica,* 26, 553–565.

Konijn, H. S. (1962) "Identification and Estimation in a Simultaneous Equation Model with Errors in Variables," *Econometrica,* 30, 79–87.

Lawley, D. N. and A. E. Maxwell (1963) *Factor Analysis as a Statistical Method,* Butterworth, London.

Lawley, D. N. and A. E. Maxwell (1971) *Factor Analysis as a Statistical Method,* Second Edition, American Elsevier, New York.

Levi, M. D. (1973) "Errors in the Variables Bias in the Presence of Correctly Measured Variables," *Econometrica,* 41, 985–986.

Levi, M. D. (1977) "Measurement Errors and Bounded OLS Estimates," *Journal of Econometrics,* 6, 165–171.

Lindley, D. V. (1947) "Regression Lines and the Linear Functional Relationship," *Supplement to the Journal of the Royal Statistical Society,* 218–244.

Liviatan, N. (1961) "Errors in Variables and Engel Curve Analysis," *Econometrica,* 29, 336–362.

McCallum, B. T. (1972) "Relative Asymptotic Bias from Errors of Omission and Measurement," *Econometrica,* 40, 757–758.

Madansky, A. (1959) "The Fitting of Straight Lines When Both Variables Are Subject to Error," *Journal of the American Statistical Association,* 54, 173–205.

Madansky, A. (1964) "Instrumental Variables in Factor Analysis," *Psychometrika,* 29, 105–113.

Madansky, A. (1976) "Errors-in-Variables Models," *Foundations of Econometrics,* North-Holland, Amsterdam, Chapter 4.

Maddala, G. S. (1971) "The Use of Variance Component Models in Pooling Cross-Section and Time Series Data," *Econometrica,* 39, 341–358.

Maddala, G. S. (1977) *Econometrics,* McGraw-Hill, New York.

Malinvaud, E. (1970) *Statistical Methods of Econometrics,* 2nd ed., North-Holland, Amsterdam.

Maravall, A. and D. J. Aigner (1977) "Identification of the Dynamic Shock-Error Model, The Case of Dynamic Regression," in D. J. Aigner and A. S. Goldberger, eds., *Latent Variables in Socio-economic Models,* North-Holland, Amsterdam, pp. 349–363.

Marschak, J. and W. H. Andrews (1944) "Random Simultaneous Equations and the Theory of Production," *Econometrica,* 12, 143–206.

Morgenstern, O. (1950) *On the Accuracy of Economic Observations,* Princeton University Press, Princeton, N.J.

Mouchart, M. (1977) "A Regression Model with an Explanatory Variable Which Is Both Binary and Subject to Errors," in D. J. Aigner and A. S. Goldberger, eds., *Latent Variables in Socio-economic Models,* North-Holland, Amsterdam, pp. 49–66.

Mundlak, Y. (1961) "Empirical Production Function Free of Management Bias," *Journal of Farm Economics,* 43, 44–56.

Muth, J. (1960) "Optimal Properties of Exponentially Weighted Forecasts with Permanent and Transitory Components," *Journal of the American Statistical Association,* 55, 299–306.

Nair, K. R. and K. S. Banerjee (1942) "A Note on Fitting of Straight Lines if Both Variables Are Subject to Error," *Sankhyā,* 6, 331.

Nair, K. R. and Shrivastava, M. P. (1942) "On a Simple Method of Curve Fitting," *Sankhya,* 6, 121.

Nerlove, M. (1956) "Estimates of The Elasticities of Supply and Selected Agricultural Commodities," *Journal of Farm Economics,* 38, 496–506.

Nerlove, M. (1958a) "The Implications of Friedman's Permanent Income Hypothesis for Demand Analysis," *Agricultural Economics Research,* 10, 1–14.

Nerlove, M. (1958b) *Distributed Lags and Demand Analysis,* U.S. Department of Agriculture Handbook, No. 14.

Nerlove, M. (1967) "Distributed Lags and Unobserved Components in Economic Time Series," in W. Fellner et al., eds., *Ten Economic Studies in the Tradition of Irving Fisher,* Wiley, New York.

Neyman, J. and E. L. Scott (1951) "On Certain Methods of Estimating the Linear Structural Relationship," *Annals of Mathematical Statistics,* 22, 352–361.

O'Neill, M., L. G. Sinclair, and F. J. Smith (1969), "Polynomial Curve Fitting When Abscissas and Ordinates Are Both Subject to Error," *Computer Journal,* 12, 52–56.

Pagan, A. (1984) "Econometric Issues in The Analysis of Regressions With Generated Regressors," *International Economic Review,* forthcoming.

Rao, P. (1973) "Some Notes on the Errors-in-Variables Model," *The American Statistician,* 27, 217–218.

Reiersol, O. (1941) "Confluence Analysis by Means of Lag Moments and Other Methods of Confluence Analysis," *Econometrica,* 9, 1–24.

Reiersol, O. (1945) "Confluence Analysis by Means of Instrumental Sets of Variables," *Arkiv for Matematik, Astronomi och Fysik,* Almquist and Wicksells Boktryckeri—AB, Uppsala, 1–119.

Reiersol, O. (1950) "Identifiability of Linear Relation Between Variables Which Are Subject to Error," *Econometrica,* 18, 375–389.

Richardson, D. H. and De-min Wu (1970) "Least Squares and Grouping Method Estimators in the Errors in Variables Models," *Journal of the American Statistical Association,* 65, 724–748.

Robinson, P. M. (1974) "Identification, Estimation, and Large-Sample Theory for Regressions Containing Unobservable Variables," *International Economic Review,* 15, 680–692.

Robinson, P. M. and M. C. Ferrara (1977) "The Estimation of a Model for an Unobservable Variable with Endogenous Causes," in D. J. Aigner and A. S. Goldberger, eds. *Latent Variables in Socio-economic Models,* North-Holland, Amsterdam, pp. 131–142.

Rosen, S. (1973) "Income Generating Functions and Capital Accumulation," Harvard Institute of Economic Research Discussion Paper No. 36, Harvard University, Cambridge, Mass.

Sargan, J. D. (1958) "The Estimation of Economic Relationships Using Instrumental Variables," *Econometrica,* 26, 393–415.

Siegal, P. M. and R. W. Hodge (1968) "A Causal Approach to the Study of Measurement Error," in H. M. Blalock, Jr., and A. B. Blalock, eds., *Methodology in Social Research,* McGraw-Hill, New York, Chapter 2, pp. 28–59.

Theil, H. (1950) "A Rank-Invariant Method of Linear and Polynomial Regression Analysis," *Proceedings of the Royal Netherland Academy of Sciences,* 53, 386–392.

Theil, H. (1957) "Specification Errors and the Estimation of Economic Relationships," *Review of the International Statistical Institute,* 25, 41–51.

Theil, H. (1971) *Principles of Econometrics,* North-Holland, Amsterdam.

Theil, H. and J. van Ijzeren (1956) "On the Efficiency of Wald's Method of Fitting Straight Lines," *Review of the International Statistical Institute,* 24, 17–26.

Tintner, G. (1952) *Econometrics,* Wiley, New York, Chapter 6.

Tukey, J. W. (1951) "Components in Regression," *Biometrics,* 7, 33–70.

Villegas, C. (1961) "Maximum Likelihood Estimation of a Linear Functional Relationship," *Annals of Mathematical Statistics,* 32, 1040–1062.

Wald, A. (1940) "The Fitting of Straight Lines if Both Variables Are Subject to Errors," *Annals of Mathematical Statistics,* 11, 284–300.

Warren, R. D., J. K. White, and W. A. Fuller (1974) "An Errors-in-Variables Analysis of Managerial Role Performance," *Journal of the American Statistical Association,* 69, 886–893.

Welch, F. (1975) "Human Capital Theory: Education, Discrimination, and Life Cycles," *American Economic Review,* 65, 63–73.

Wickens, M. R. (1972) "A Note on the Use of Proxy Variables," *Econometrica,* 40, 759–761.

Wiley, D. E. (1973) "The Identification Problem for Structural Equation Models with Unmeasured Variables," in A. S. Goldberger and O. D. Duncan, eds., *Structural Equation Models in the Social Sciences,* Seminar Press, New York, pp. 69–84.

Wolter, K. M. and W. A. Fuller (1975) "Estimating a Nonlinear Error-in-Variables Model with Singular Error Covariance Matrix," 1975 Proceedings of the Business and Economic Statistics Section, American Statistical Association.

Wolter, K. M. and W. A. Fuller (1978) "Estimation of Nonlinear Errors-in-Variables Models," mimeograph, Iowa State University, Ames, Iowa.

Wright, S. (1960) "Path Coefficients and Path Regressions Alternative or Complementary Concepts?", *Biometrics,* 16, 189–202.

Zellner, A. (1970) "Estimation of Regression Relationships Containing Unobservable Independent Variables," *International Economic Review,* 11, 441–454.

Zellner, A. (1971) *An Introduction to Bayesian Inference in Econometrics*, Wiley, New York, Chapter 5.
Zellner, A. and M. Geisel (1970) "Analysis of Distributed Lag Models with Application to Consumption Function Estimation," *Econometrica*, 38, 865–888.

CHAPTER 18

Qualitative and Limited Dependent Variable Models

18.1 INTRODUCTION

Social scientists are concerned in general with the problem of explaining and predicting individual behavior. Within this context economists examine individual choice behavior in a wide variety of settings. Often the choices can be considered to be selections from a continuum of alternatives, as illustrated by the conventional theory of the household and firm that deals with, among other things, "how much" to consume or produce of a certain primary, intermediate, or final commodity. Economic theory provides models of individual behavior in these circumstances, and standard procedures allow statistical inferences about "average" population behavior given a random sample of data from a population of individuals. Increasingly, however, as microdata become more widely available, researchers are faced with situations in which the choice alternatives are limited in number—that is, the alternatives are discrete or "quantal." Examples of situations where such choices arise include efforts at modeling occupation choice, the labor force participation decision, voting behavior, and housing choice.

Statistical analysis of general population choice behavior is complicated by the fact that such behavior must be described in probabilistic terms. That is, models describing choices from a limited number of alternatives attempt to relate the conditional probability of a particular choice being made to various explanatory factors that include the attributes of the alternatives as well as the characteristics of the decision makers. Several well-known problems arise when usual regression procedures are applied to such models and a substantial body of literature exists suggesting alternative methods for dealing with these problems. Our purpose is (1) to point out the difficulties in applying the usual techniques to such models, (2) summarize proposed solutions that are applicable under alternative circumstances, and (3) note some advantages and disadvantages of the various methods proposed in (2). These and related issues are discussed in Sections 18.2 (for binary choice models) and 18.3 (for multinomial choice models).

In addition to examining models describing "quantal" choice, a related set of models will be considered that deal with choices not involving a finite number of alternatives but are limited in some other way. Examples include situations when a model's dependent variable can take only a certain range of values (the "truncated" variables problem) or where some range of responses is unobservable (the case of "censored" samples). Pioneering work on such models has been done by Tobin (1958), Amemiya (1973), and Heckman (1974, 1976, 1979). Recently a number of new procedures have been proposed that improve and extend these results. One important extension carries qualitative and limited endogenous variables into the simultaneous equations context. Single equation limited dependent variable models are presented in Section 18.4 and extensions to simultaneous equations in Section 18.5. A visual overview of the chapter is presented in Table 18.1. For extensions of these topics and a complete survey of the literature see Amemiya (1981, 1984) and Maddala (1983).

18.2 BINARY CHOICE MODELS

In this section we consider modeling the choice behavior of individuals when two alternatives are available and one must be chosen. The binary decision by the ith individual can be conveniently represented by a random variable y_i that takes the value one if one choice is made and the value zero if the other is made. Let P_i represent the probability that y_i takes the value one. While it may be of interest to estimate the probabilities P_i, economists are typically interested in the more general problem of studying how various explanatory variables affect P_i.

There are several ways to motivate such economic models. The first is based on the maximization of expected utility by an individual decision maker. Assume that the utility derived from a choice is based on the attributes of the choice, which are specific to the individual decision maker, the individual's socio-economic characteristics and a random disturbance. Let U_{i1} and U_{i0} denote the utilities of the two choices, $\mathbf{z}_{i1}'$ and $\mathbf{z}_{i0}'$ vectors of characteristics of the alternatives as perceived by individual i and $\mathbf{w}_i'$ a vector of socio-economic characteristics of the ith individual. Then, assuming linearity,

$$U_{i0} = \bar{U}_{i0} + e_{i0} = \alpha_0 + \mathbf{z}_{i0}'\boldsymbol{\delta} + \mathbf{w}_i'\boldsymbol{\gamma}_0 + e_{i0}$$

$$U_{i1} = \bar{U}_{i1} + e_{i1} = \alpha_1 + \mathbf{z}_{i1}'\boldsymbol{\delta} + \mathbf{w}_i'\boldsymbol{\gamma}_1 + e_{i1}$$

Thus $y_i = 1$ if $U_{i1} > U_{i0}$ and $y_i = 0$ if $U_{i0} > U_{i1}$. Consequently,

$$\begin{aligned}\Pr(y_i = 1) = \Pr(U_{i1} > U_{i0}) &= \Pr[(e_{i0} - e_{i1}) < (\alpha_1 - \alpha_0) + (\mathbf{z}_{i1} - \mathbf{z}_{i0})'\boldsymbol{\delta} \\ &\qquad + \mathbf{w}_i'(\boldsymbol{\gamma}_1 - \boldsymbol{\gamma}_0)] \\ &= F(\mathbf{x}_i'\boldsymbol{\beta}),\end{aligned}$$

where $\mathbf{x}_i' = (1, (\mathbf{z}_{i1} - \mathbf{z}_{i0})', \mathbf{w}_i')$, $\boldsymbol{\beta}' = ((\alpha_1 - \alpha_0), \boldsymbol{\delta}', (\boldsymbol{\gamma}_1 - \boldsymbol{\gamma}_0)')$, and F is the cumulative distribution function (CDF) of $(e_{i0} - e_{i1})$. Note that if an individual

TABLE 18.1 ***QUALITATIVE AND LIMITED DEPENDENT VARIABLE MODELS***

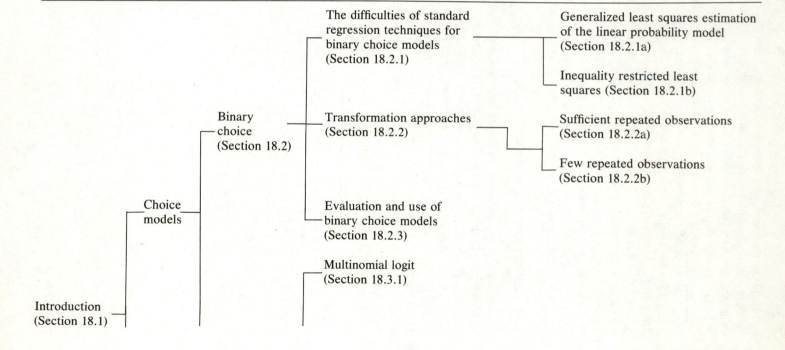

- Introduction (Section 18.1)
- Choice models
  - Binary choice (Section 18.2)
    - The difficulties of standard regression techniques for binary choice models (Section 18.2.1)
      - Generalized least squares estimation of the linear probability model (Section 18.2.1a)
      - Inequality restricted least squares (Section 18.2.1b)
    - Transformation approaches (Section 18.2.2)
      - Sufficient repeated observations (Section 18.2.2a)
      - Few repeated observations (Section 18.2.2b)
    - Evaluation and use of binary choice models (Section 18.2.3)
  - Multinomial logit (Section 18.3.1)

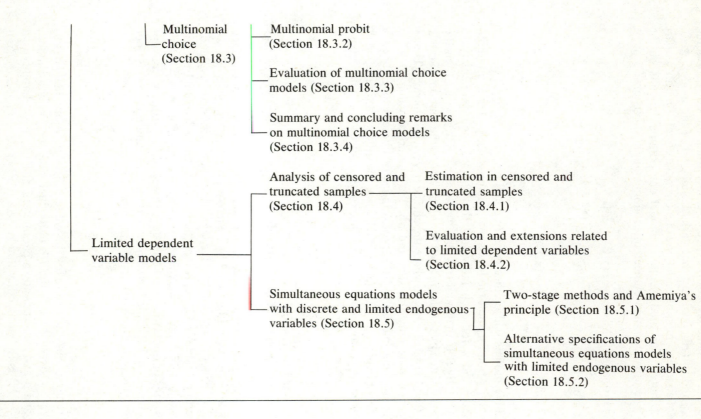

- Multinomial choice (Section 18.3)
  - Multinomial probit (Section 18.3.2)
  - Evaluation of multinomial choice models (Section 18.3.3)
  - Summary and concluding remarks on multinomial choice models (Section 18.3.4)
- Limited dependent variable models
  - Analysis of censored and truncated samples (Section 18.4)
    - Estimation in censored and truncated samples (Section 18.4.1)
    - Evaluation and extensions related to limited dependent variables (Section 18.4.2)
  - Simultaneous equations models with discrete and limited endogenous variables (Section 18.5)
    - Two-stage methods and Amemiya's principle (Section 18.5.1)
    - Alternative specifications of simultaneous equations models with limited endogenous variables (Section 18.5.2)

characteristic has the same effect on expected utility, then the corresponding elements of γ_0 and γ_1 are equal and that variable falls out of the model. Also, the presence of an intercept implies that the choices have effects on utility apart from their attributes. The kind of choice model one obtains depends on the choice of F. The most common choices in economic applications are:

The Linear Probability Model: $F(\mathbf{x}_i'\boldsymbol{\beta}) = \mathbf{x}_i'\boldsymbol{\beta}$

The Probit Model: $F(\mathbf{x}_i'\boldsymbol{\beta}) = \int_{-\infty}^{\mathbf{x}_i'\boldsymbol{\beta}} \frac{1}{\sqrt{2\pi}} e^{-t^2/2}\, dt$

The Logit Model: $F(\mathbf{x}_i'\boldsymbol{\beta}) = \frac{1}{1 + e^{-\mathbf{x}_i'\boldsymbol{\beta}}}$

These alternative models will be discussed in detail below.

A second motivation for such models is that it is possible to define an unobservable random index for each individual that defines their propensity to choose an alternative. If that unobservable index is $y_i^* = \mathbf{x}_i'\boldsymbol{\beta} + e_i$, then the binary choice is defined by assuming a pdf for e_i and letting the random variable $y_i = 1$ if $y_i^* > 0$ and $y_i = 0$ if $y_i^* \leq 0$, where the choice of zero is arbitrary. This is equivalent to assuming only the sign and not the numerical value of y_i^* is observed. Finally, one may model the probabilities of choices directly as a function of a set of explanatory variables and bypass the utility maximization or threshold arguments noted above. We now turn to an analysis of the models so generated.

18.2.1 The Difficulties of Standard Regression Techniques for Binary Choice Models

The difficulties of using standard regression procedures when a quantal choice model is adopted are easily illustrated by a simple example. Suppose that we are interested in the factors that determine whether or not an individual attends college in a certain year. We can represent the choice of any individual by using a dummy variable, which takes the value one or zero depending upon whether the individual does or does not attend college, respectively. Furthermore, suppose that this decision is modeled to depend upon income and nothing else but random effects. Then this model can be represented as

$$y_i = \alpha + \beta x_i + e_i, \qquad i = 1, \ldots, T \tag{18.2.1}$$

where y_i is a random variable that takes the value 1 if the ith individual goes to college and zero otherwise, x_i is the ith individual's income, e_i is a random disturbance, and α and β are unknown parameters. If P_i is the probability that $y_i = 1$ and $(1 - P_i)$ is the probability that $y_i = 0$, then $E[y_i] = P_i = \alpha + \beta x_i$ if $E[e_i] = 0$, and (18.2.1) is called the *linear probability model.*

This specification has several readily apparent problems. First, if we want to make the usual assumption that the random variable e_i has mean zero—that is, $E(e_i) = 0$ for all i—we must face the fact that while y_i can take but two values, zero and one, the systematic portion of the right-hand side can take any value. This means that e_i can take only two values given x_i—namely, $-(\alpha + \beta x_i)$ and $1 - (\alpha + \beta x_i)$. Furthermore, if $E(e_i)$ is to be zero, they must take these values with probabilities $1 - (\alpha + \beta x_i)$ and $(\alpha + \beta x_i)$, respectively. Since $\alpha + \beta x_i$ can take on values greater than one or less than zero, the probabilities above can be greater than one or less than zero. Second, given the results above, the usual assumption that $E(e_i^2) = \sigma^2$ is no longer tenable. The Bernoulli character of y_i implies a variance for e_i of $(\alpha + \beta x_i)(1 - \alpha - \beta x_i)$. Since the variance of e_i depends on i, the e_i are heteroscedastic and, apart from the first problem mentioned, the use of ordinary least squares will result in inefficient estimates and imprecise predictions (see Chapter 11, Section 11.1). Third, even if $E(y_i|x_i)$ is confined to the unit interval, predictions outside the unit interval can be produced for values of x outside the sample range even if the coefficient estimates are derived by minimizing the sum of squared residuals subject to the condition that within-sample predictions lie in the unit interval (which leads to a quadratic programming problem). Fourth, the fitted relationship will be very sensitive to the values taken by the explanatory variable(s) especially where they are "bunched." Fifth, the usual tests of significance for the estimated coefficients do not apply, estimated standard errors are not consistent, and the summary measure R^2 is no longer meaningful. Sixth, in this model, a change in the explanatory variable has the same effect on P_i whether the initial value is near zero or near one. In many economic applications the effect of a change in an independent variable would be expected to be greater when P_i is initially near 0.5. Finally, since the y_i's are not normally distributed, no method of estimation that is linear in the y_i's is in general efficient. That is, any estimator that is linear in the y_i's, such as least squares (LS) or generalized least squares (GLS), can be improved upon.

18.2.1a Generalized Least Squares Estimation of the Linear Probability Model

An approach that corrects only for the heteroscedasticity noted above has been suggested by Goldberger (1964, p. 248) and Zellner and Lee (1965, p. 387). Generalizing the model in (18.2.1), we allow for the possibility of $n_i \geq 1$ observations on each of $i = 1, \ldots, T$ "settings" of a $(K \times 1)$ vector of independent variables $\mathbf{x}_i$. Let y_i be the number of occurrences of the event E in n_i repetitions of the setting $\mathbf{x}_i$. The linear probability model considers the ith sample proportion $p_i = y_i/n_i$ and relates it to determining variables, at least over a region, by a relationship that is linear in the parameters, say $\mathbf{x}_i'\boldsymbol{\beta}$, where $\boldsymbol{\beta}$ is a $(K \times 1)$ vector of unknown parameters. The full set of T observations then can be written

$$\mathbf{p} = X\boldsymbol{\beta} + \mathbf{e} \tag{18.2.2}$$

where $\mathbf{p}$ is a $(T \times 1)$ random vector of sample proportions, X is a $(T \times K)$ nonstochastic observation matrix of rank K and $\mathbf{e}$ is a $(T \times 1)$ vector of random disturbances. The GLS estimator of $\boldsymbol{\beta}$ is

$$\hat{\boldsymbol{\beta}} = (X'\boldsymbol{\Phi}^{-1}X)^{-1}X'\boldsymbol{\Phi}^{-1}\mathbf{p} \tag{18.2.3}$$

where $\boldsymbol{\Phi}$ is the diagonal covariance matrix of $\mathbf{e}$. The true proportions P_i are related to the sample proportions p_i by

$$p_i = P_i + e_i, \qquad i = 1, \ldots, T \tag{18.2.4}$$

Consequently the random variable e_i has mean zero and variance $P_i(1 - P_i)/n_i$, which is the ith diagonal value of $\boldsymbol{\Phi}$. If the P_i are not known, a feasible GLS estimator is

$$\hat{\hat{\boldsymbol{\beta}}} = (X'\hat{\boldsymbol{\Phi}}^{-1}X)^{-1}X'\hat{\boldsymbol{\Phi}}^{-1}\mathbf{p} \tag{18.2.5}$$

where $\hat{\boldsymbol{\Phi}}$ is a consistent estimator of the covariance matrix of $\mathbf{e}$ in the sense that plim $\hat{\boldsymbol{\Phi}}_{ij} = \boldsymbol{\Phi}_{ij}$ for all i,j. The diagonal elements of $\hat{\boldsymbol{\Phi}}$ are $\hat{p}_i(1 - \hat{p}_i)/n_i$ with $\hat{p}_i$ the ith element of $\hat{\mathbf{p}} = X\mathbf{b}$, where $\mathbf{b} = (X'X)^{-1}X'\mathbf{p}$, the unweighted least squares estimator of $\boldsymbol{\beta}$. Note that the covariance matrix of $\mathbf{b}$ is $\boldsymbol{\Sigma}_{\mathbf{b}} = (X'X)^{-1}X'\boldsymbol{\Phi}X(X'X)^{-1}$. The "conventional" least squares covariance formula $\hat{\sigma}^2(X'X)^{-1}$, where $\hat{\sigma}^2 = (\mathbf{p} - X\mathbf{b})'(\mathbf{p} - X\mathbf{b})/(T - K)$, is a biased and inconsistent estimator of $\boldsymbol{\Sigma}_{\mathbf{b}}$. This result is true despite the fact that $\mathbf{b}$ is unbiased and consistent if $\lim_{T\to\infty}(X'\boldsymbol{\Phi}X/T)$ is finite.

Statistical inference procedures for this model may be used on the usual asymptotic normal distribution of $\hat{\hat{\boldsymbol{\beta}}}$ if conditions defined in Chapter 5 hold. Despite the ease and simplicity of this approach, several disturbing facts remain. First, there is no guarantee that the elements of $\hat{\mathbf{p}} = X\mathbf{b}$ will fall in the unit interval unless they are constrained to do so. This means that one is usually faced with "fixing up" any values $\hat{p}_i$ that are negative or greater than one. Methods suggested range from setting $\hat{p}_i = 0.5$ or $\hat{p}_i = 0.98$ when $\hat{p}_i(1 - \hat{p}_i) \leq 0$ to replacing it by $|\hat{p}_i(1 - \hat{p}_i)|$. Monte Carlo results of Smith and Cicchetti (1975) support the conclusion that none of these procedures is especially appealing. Second, apart from the above problem, there is still no guarantee that the predicted proportion of successes based on $\hat{\hat{\boldsymbol{\beta}}}$ for any $\mathbf{x}_i$ will fall in the unit interval. Since there is no way of knowing whether a particular observation will result in the event in question occurring or not, we are interested in the conditional probability of the event's occurring, given some $\mathbf{x}_i$, and the way in which it varies as $\mathbf{x}_i$ is changed. This means that we are faced with the problem of restricting this quantity to the unit interval. Because usual unconstrained regression procedures applied to the linear probability model are unsatisfactory in this regard, we turn to a method that deals more directly with this problem.

18.2.1b Inequality-Restricted Least Squares

To ensure that the predicted proportion of success will fall within the unit interval, the inequality-restricted least squares method described in Chapter 3 may be used. The method is satisfactory in restricting the predicted proportion inside the unit interval for the given sample of X, but it may not be satisfactory when prediction is required for any $\mathbf{x}_i$. However, if the range of the yet unobserved $\mathbf{x}_i$ is known a priori, this additional knowledge may be incorporated to guarantee a meaningful forecast.

The inequality-restricted least squares estimator minimizes the quadratic form

$$(\mathbf{p} - X\boldsymbol{\beta})'\Phi^{-1}(\mathbf{p} - X\boldsymbol{\beta}) \tag{18.2.6}$$

subject to the linear inequality restrictions that the predicted proportions $\tilde{\mathbf{p}} = X\tilde{\boldsymbol{\beta}}$ fall within the unit interval; that is,

$$X\boldsymbol{\beta} \leq \boldsymbol{\eta}_T \tag{18.2.7}$$

and

$$X\boldsymbol{\beta} \geq \mathbf{0} \tag{18.2.8}$$

where $\boldsymbol{\eta}_T$ is a $(T \times 1)$ vector of one's. If a priori knowledge is available on future values of the explanatory variables, say an $(N \times K)$ matrix X_*, additional restrictions may be imposed:

$$X_*\boldsymbol{\beta} \leq \boldsymbol{\eta}_N \tag{18.2.9}$$

and

$$X_*\boldsymbol{\beta} \geq \mathbf{0} \tag{18.2.10}$$

where $\boldsymbol{\eta}_N$ is an $(N \times 1)$ vector of one's. In practice, only those $\mathbf{x}_i$'s that will produce extreme values for P_i need to be considered since, if the extreme values of the predicted P_i are within the range between 0 and 1, then the predicted value of P_i for all other values of $\mathbf{x}_i$ is also within the specified interval. Economic data often show an increasing or decreasing trend. The extreme values of P_i often correspond to the smallest and the largest values of $\mathbf{x}_i$. Thus, by selecting possible binding restrictions, the number of restrictions can be reduced to a manageable size. Combining the restrictions (18.2.7) through (18.2.10), we can write

$$\begin{bmatrix} \tilde{X} \\ -\tilde{X} \end{bmatrix} \boldsymbol{\beta} \leq \begin{bmatrix} \boldsymbol{\eta} \\ \mathbf{0} \end{bmatrix} \tag{18.2.11}$$

where

$$\tilde{X} = \begin{bmatrix} X \\ X_* \end{bmatrix} \tag{18.2.12}$$

and $\boldsymbol{\eta}$ is a $[(T + N) \times 1]$ vector of one's. The Lagrangian function is

$$L = (\mathbf{p} - X\boldsymbol{\beta})'\boldsymbol{\Phi}^{-1}(\mathbf{p} - X\boldsymbol{\beta}) + 2\boldsymbol{\lambda}_1'(\boldsymbol{\eta} - \tilde{X}\boldsymbol{\beta}) + 2\boldsymbol{\lambda}_2'\tilde{X}\boldsymbol{\beta} \tag{18.2.13}$$

where $\boldsymbol{\lambda}_1$ and $\boldsymbol{\lambda}_2$ are both $[(T + N) \times 1]$ vectors of Langrange multipliers. Applying the Kuhn–Tucker conditions, we obtain

$$-X'\boldsymbol{\Phi}^{-1}(\mathbf{p} - X\boldsymbol{\beta}) - \tilde{X}'\boldsymbol{\lambda}_1 + \tilde{X}'\boldsymbol{\lambda}_2 = \mathbf{0}$$

$$\boldsymbol{\eta} - \tilde{X}\boldsymbol{\beta} \geq \mathbf{0}$$

$$\boldsymbol{\lambda}_1'(\boldsymbol{\eta} - \tilde{X}\boldsymbol{\beta}) = 0$$

$$\tilde{X}\boldsymbol{\beta} \geq \mathbf{0}$$

and

$$\boldsymbol{\lambda}_2'\tilde{X}\boldsymbol{\beta} = 0$$

Let $\mathbf{e}_1 = \boldsymbol{\eta} - \tilde{X}\boldsymbol{\beta}$ and $\mathbf{e}_2 = \tilde{X}\boldsymbol{\beta}$. The above conditions can be summarized as follows:

$$X'\boldsymbol{\Phi}^{-1}\mathbf{p} = \tilde{X}'\boldsymbol{\lambda}_2 - \tilde{X}'\boldsymbol{\lambda}_1 + X'\boldsymbol{\Phi}^{-1}X\boldsymbol{\beta} \tag{18.2.14}$$

$$\boldsymbol{\eta} = \tilde{X}\boldsymbol{\beta} + \mathbf{e}_1 \tag{18.2.15}$$

$$\mathbf{0} = -\tilde{X}\boldsymbol{\beta} + \mathbf{e}_2 \tag{18.2.16}$$

with the bilinear conditions

$$\boldsymbol{\lambda}_1'\mathbf{e}_1 = 0, \qquad \boldsymbol{\lambda}_2'\mathbf{e}_2 = 0 \tag{18.2.17}$$

and the nonnegativity conditions

$$\boldsymbol{\lambda}_1 \geq \mathbf{0} \qquad \boldsymbol{\lambda}_2 \geq \mathbf{0} \qquad \mathbf{e}_1 \geq \mathbf{0} \qquad \mathbf{e}_2 \geq \mathbf{0} \tag{18.2.18}$$

The system of equations (18.2.14) through (18.2.16) is linear and can be solved by a simplex algorithm with a modification that incorporates side conditions (18.2.17) and the nonnegativity conditions (18.2.18). For such a modification, see Wolfe (1959). For similar applications, see Lee, Judge, and Zellner (1968) and Lee and Judge (1972).

It is interesting to note that the inequality-restricted least squares estimator includes the feasible, unrestricted least squares estimator (18.2.3). In other words, if the estimator $\hat{\boldsymbol{\beta}}$ will forecast $\mathbf{p}$ within the unit interval, then $\boldsymbol{\lambda}_1 = \boldsymbol{\lambda}_2 = \mathbf{0}$ and the inequality-restricted least squares estimator from (18.2.14) is also the unconstrained estimator:

$$\begin{aligned}\tilde{\boldsymbol{\beta}} &= (X'\boldsymbol{\Phi}^{-1}X)^{-1}X'\boldsymbol{\Phi}^{-1}\mathbf{p} + (X'\boldsymbol{\Phi}^{-1}X)^{-1}X'(\tilde{X}'\boldsymbol{\lambda}_1 - \tilde{X}'\boldsymbol{\lambda}_2) \\ &= (X'\boldsymbol{\Phi}^{-1}X)^{-1}X'\boldsymbol{\Phi}^{-1}\mathbf{p} = \hat{\boldsymbol{\beta}} \end{aligned} \tag{18.2.19}$$

The inequality-restricted least squares estimator will yield a satisfactory forecast if appropriate restrictions are incorporated. The method is also applicable to the multiple attributes problem, which involves a system of linear probability functions. In this case Zellner's seemingly unrelated regression formulation may be applied before adding the inequality restrictions. For an example, see Lee, Judge, and Zellner (1977, Appendix B).

One limitation of the inequality-restricted estimator is that it depends on the availability of the future values of X. Another problem is that the sampling properties of the inequality-restricted estimator when Φ is estimated have not been analytically developed. Sampling experiments based on Monte Carlo experiments are available for some specific, restricted least squares estimators (e.g., Lee, Judge, and Zellner, 1977). The results show that variances of restricted estimates are smaller than those of unrestricted estimates. Thus a conservative way of testing the significance of parameters is to use the variances of the unrestricted estimates as upper bounds. When Φ is known, the inequality sampling results of Section 3.3 are applicable.

18.2.2 Transformation Approaches

If we assume that the larger the value of the index $I_i = \mathbf{x}_i'\boldsymbol{\beta}$, the greater the probability that the event E in question will occur, we can think of a monotonic relationship between the value of I_i and the probability of E occurring. Under these assumptions the "true" probability function would have the characteristic shape of a cumulative distribution function (CDF). Theoretical arguments for the use of particular CDFs have appeared recently and will be examined in Section 18.3, but in most economic applications choices seem to have only casual justification. The two most widely used CDFs are the normal and the logistic, with the associated analyses called probit and logit, respectively. One argument for adopting the normal CDF is as follows: Each individual makes a choice, between E and not-E, by comparing I_i to some critical value of the random index I^*, which reflects individual tastes. If there are many independent factors determining the critical level for each individual, the central limit theorem may be used to justify assuming that I^* is a normally distributed random variable. If an individual chooses E only if $I_i \geq I^*$, the conditional probability of event E occurring, given I_i, is

$$\Pr(E|I_i) = \Pr(I^* \leq I_i) = F(\mathbf{x}_i'\boldsymbol{\beta}) \tag{18.2.20}$$

where $F(\cdot)$ is the normal CDF evaluated at the value of the argument. The logistic CDF

$$F(\mathbf{x}_i'\boldsymbol{\beta}) = \frac{1}{1 + \exp(-\mathbf{x}_i'\boldsymbol{\beta})}, \qquad -\infty < \mathbf{x}_i'\boldsymbol{\beta} < \infty \tag{18.2.21}$$

is used because of its close approximation to the normal CDF [see Cox (1970, p. 28) and Amemiya (1981, p. 1487)] and its numerical simplicity. Alternative estimation procedures exist for these models, the alternatives depending on the number of repeated observations (n_i) and hence how precise p_i is as an estimator for P_i. These two cases will now be treated.

18.2.2a Transformation Procedures When Sufficient Repeated Observations Are Available

For the *probit* transformation the probability of the event E occurring given the value of the index $I_i = \mathbf{x}_i'\boldsymbol{\beta}$ is

$$\Pr(E|I_i) = P_i = F(I_i) = \frac{1}{\sqrt{2\pi}} \int_{-\infty}^{I_i} e^{-t^2/2}\, dt \tag{18.2.22}$$

Then, if F^{-1} is the inverse of the normal CDF, using (18.2.4),

$$F^{-1}(p_i) = F^{-1}(P_i + e_i) \tag{18.2.23}$$

Expanding $F^{-1}(P_i + e_i)$ by a Taylor's series about P_i, we obtain

$$F^{-1}(p_i) = F^{-1}(P_i) + e_i \frac{dF^{-1}(P_i)}{dP_i} + R_i \tag{18.2.24}$$

Since R_i is a remainder that goes to zero in probability as $n_i \to \infty$, we get

$$F^{-1}(p_i) \doteq F^{-1}(P_i) + \frac{e_i}{f[F^{-1}(P_i)]}$$

using

$$\frac{dF^{-1}(P_i)}{dP_i} = \frac{1}{f[F^{-1}(P_i)]}$$

where $f(\cdot)$ is the value of the standard normal density evaluated at its argument.

Alternatively,

$$v_i = I_i + u_i = \mathbf{x}_i'\boldsymbol{\beta} + u_i \tag{18.2.25}$$

where $v_i = F^{-1}(p_i)$ is called the "observed" probit, $I_i = F^{-1}(P_i)$ is the "true" probit, and the random disturbance u_i has $E(u_i) = 0$ and

$$\mathrm{var}(u_i) = \frac{P_i(1 - P_i)}{n_i(f[F^{-1}(P_i)])^2} \tag{18.2.26}$$

If (18.2.25) is written as

$$\mathbf{v} = X\boldsymbol{\beta} + \mathbf{u} \tag{18.2.27}$$

the appropriate estimator for $\boldsymbol{\beta}$ is

$$\tilde{\boldsymbol{\beta}} = (X'\boldsymbol{\Phi}^{-1}X)^{-1}X'\boldsymbol{\Phi}^{-1}\mathbf{v}$$

where $\boldsymbol{\Phi}$ is a diagonal matrix whose ith diagonal element is (18.2.26). Since $\boldsymbol{\Phi}$ is unknown, a feasible GLS estimator, also called the minimum chi-square estimator [Amemiya (1981, p. 1498)], is

$$\tilde{\tilde{\boldsymbol{\beta}}} = (X'\hat{\boldsymbol{\Phi}}^{-1}X)^{-1}X'\hat{\boldsymbol{\Phi}}^{-1}\mathbf{v} \tag{18.2.28}$$

where $\hat{\boldsymbol{\Phi}}$ is based on an estimator of P_i. Alternative estimators are sample proportions, the least squares predictor $\hat{\mathbf{P}} = X(X'X)^{-1}X'\mathbf{p}$, the predictor from the linear probability model, or the predictor based on least squares estimation of $\boldsymbol{\beta}$ in (18.2.27) and obtained from $\tilde{P}_i = F(\hat{v}_i)$, where $\hat{v}_i = \mathbf{x}_i'(X'X)^{-1}X'\mathbf{v}$. The advantage of this latter approach is, of course, that not only are the $\tilde{P}_i$ confined to the zero one interval, but they are also based on the information provided by the structure (18.2.27).

Since the remainder R_i in (18.2.24) vanishes in probability, the usual results of estimated generalized least squares hold. Namely, under some general conditions the EGLS estimators of (18.2.28) are consistent and have an asymptotic normal distribution. Therefore, the usual tests of hypotheses can be based on the consistent estimator $(X'\hat{\boldsymbol{\Phi}}^{-1}X)^{-1}$.

For the *logit* transformation,

$$\Pr(E|I_i) = P_i = \frac{1}{1 + \exp(-I_i)} \tag{18.2.29}$$

This formulation has the property that the odds ratio is a loglinear function of $\mathbf{x}'\boldsymbol{\beta}$, and is given by

$$\ln\left[\frac{p_i}{1 - p_i}\right] \doteq \mathbf{x}_i'\boldsymbol{\beta} + \frac{e_i}{P_i(1 - P_i)} \tag{18.2.30}$$

The generalized least squares estimator for $\boldsymbol{\beta}$ in this formulation is

$$\hat{\boldsymbol{\beta}} = (X'\boldsymbol{\Phi}^{-1}X)^{-1}X'\boldsymbol{\Phi}^{-1}\mathbf{v} \tag{18.2.31}$$

where the diagonal elements of $\mathbf{\Phi}$ are

$$\operatorname{var}\left[\frac{e_i}{P_i(1 - P_i)}\right] = \frac{1}{n_i P_i(1 - P_i)} \tag{18.2.32}$$

and $\mathbf{v}$ is the vector of observed logits,

$$\ln\left[\frac{p_i}{1 - p_i}\right]$$

The feasible logit estimator $\hat{\hat{\boldsymbol{\beta}}}$ is obtained by replacing $\mathbf{\Phi}$ with a consistent estimator. One consistent estimator for P_i is the sample proportion. Others can be obtained from the linear probability model or least squares applied to (18.2.30).

Other CDFs have been suggested by Zellner and Lee (1965, p. 386) and Nerlove and Press (1973, p. 15), but probit and logit are the most popular in economic applications. An extensive list of applications is given by McFadden (1976, pp. 382–390), Hensher and Johnson (1981), and Amemiya (1981).

18.2.2b Transformation Procedures When Few Repeated Observations are Available

When the number of repeated observations on the choice experiment n_i is small and P_i cannot be reliably estimated using the sample proportion, then maximum likelihood estimation of the logit and probit models can be carried out. If P_i is the probability that the event E occurs on the ith trial of the experiment, then the random variable y_i, which is one if the event occurs but zero otherwise, has probability function

$$y_i = \begin{cases} 1 & \text{with probability } P_i \\ 0 & \text{with probability } 1 - P_i \end{cases} \tag{18.2.33}$$

Consequently, if T observations are available, then the likelihood function is

$$\ell = \prod_{i=1}^{T} P_i^{y_i}(1 - P_i)^{1-y_i} \tag{18.2.34}$$

The logit or probit model arises when P_i is specified as the logistic or normal CDF evaluated at $\mathbf{x}_i'\boldsymbol{\beta}$. If $F(\mathbf{x}_i'\boldsymbol{\beta})$ denotes either of the CDF's evaluated at $\mathbf{x}_i'\boldsymbol{\beta}$, then the likelihood function for both models is

$$\ell = \prod_{i=1}^{T} [F(\mathbf{x}_i'\boldsymbol{\beta})]^{y_i}[1 - F(\mathbf{x}_i'\boldsymbol{\beta})]^{1-y_i} \tag{18.2.35}$$

and the log-likelihood function is

$$\ln \ell = \sum_{i=1}^{T} \{y_i \ln[F(\mathbf{x}_i'\boldsymbol{\beta})] + (1 - y_i) \ln[1 - F(\mathbf{x}_i'\boldsymbol{\beta})]\} \tag{18.2.36}$$

Whether $F(\cdot)$ is chosen to be the standard normal or logistic CDF, the first-order conditions for a maximum will be nonlinear, so maximum likelihood estimates must be obtained numerically. From Chapter 6 and Appendix B, we know that the Newton-Raphson iterative procedure for maximizing a nonlinear objective function leads to the recursive relation

$$\tilde{\boldsymbol{\beta}}_{n+1} = \tilde{\boldsymbol{\beta}}_n - \left[\frac{\partial^2 \ln \ell}{\partial \boldsymbol{\beta}\, \partial \boldsymbol{\beta}'}\bigg|_{\boldsymbol{\beta}=\tilde{\boldsymbol{\beta}}_n}\right]^{-1}\left[\frac{\partial \ln \ell}{\partial \boldsymbol{\beta}}\bigg|_{\boldsymbol{\beta}=\tilde{\boldsymbol{\beta}}_n}\right] \tag{18.2.37}$$

where $\tilde{\boldsymbol{\beta}}_n$ is the nth round estimate, and the matrix of second partials and the gradient vector are evaluated at the nth round estimate. This is convenient since, under the usual regularity conditions, the maximum likelihood estimator, say $\tilde{\boldsymbol{\beta}}$, is consistent and

$$\sqrt{T}(\tilde{\boldsymbol{\beta}} - \boldsymbol{\beta}) \xrightarrow{d} N\left(\mathbf{0}, \lim\left[-T^{-1}E\frac{\partial^2 \ln \ell}{\partial \boldsymbol{\beta}\, \partial \boldsymbol{\beta}'}\right]^{-1}\right)$$

For finite samples, the asymptotic distribution of $\tilde{\boldsymbol{\beta}}$ can be approximated by

$$N\left(\boldsymbol{\beta}, -\left[\frac{\partial^2 \ln \ell}{\partial \boldsymbol{\beta}\, \partial \boldsymbol{\beta}'}\bigg|_{\boldsymbol{\beta}=\tilde{\boldsymbol{\beta}}}\right]^{-1}\right)$$

The Method of Scoring could also be used with iterations defined by

$$\tilde{\boldsymbol{\beta}}_{n+1} = \tilde{\boldsymbol{\beta}}_n - \left[E\frac{\partial^2 \ln \ell}{\partial \boldsymbol{\beta}\, \partial \boldsymbol{\beta}'}\bigg|_{\boldsymbol{\beta}=\tilde{\boldsymbol{\beta}}_n}\right]^{-1}\left[\frac{\partial \ln \ell}{\partial \boldsymbol{\beta}}\bigg|_{\boldsymbol{\beta}=\tilde{\boldsymbol{\beta}}_n}\right]$$

where

$$E\left[\frac{\partial^2 \ln \ell}{\partial \boldsymbol{\beta}\, \partial \boldsymbol{\beta}'}\right] = -\sum_{i=1}^{T} \frac{[f(\mathbf{x}_i'\boldsymbol{\beta})]^2}{F(\mathbf{x}_i'\boldsymbol{\beta})[1 - F(\mathbf{x}_i'\boldsymbol{\beta})]}\mathbf{x}_i\mathbf{x}_i'$$

and we use as the asymptotic covariance matrix $-(E\partial^2 \ln \ell/\partial\boldsymbol{\beta}\, \partial\boldsymbol{\beta}')^{-1}$. The reader should confirm that this is the asymptotic covariance matrix of the feasible GLS estimator presented in Section 18.2.2.

Thus, in order to carry out optimization the first and second derivatives of the log-likelihood function are required. While derivatives could be approximated numerically, there is no reason to do so for the probit and logit models since they are quite tractable analytically.

For the probit model, where F and f are the standard normal CDF and pdf,

$$\frac{\partial \ln \ell}{\partial \boldsymbol{\beta}} = \sum_{i=1}^{T}\left[y_i\frac{f(\mathbf{x}_i'\boldsymbol{\beta})}{F(\mathbf{x}_i'\boldsymbol{\beta})} - (1 - y_i)\frac{f(\mathbf{x}_i'\boldsymbol{\beta})}{1 - F(\mathbf{x}_i'\boldsymbol{\beta})}\right]\mathbf{x}_i \tag{18.2.38}$$

and

$$\frac{\partial^2 \ln \ell}{\partial \boldsymbol{\beta}\, \partial \boldsymbol{\beta}'} = -\sum_{i=1}^{T} f(\mathbf{x}_i'\boldsymbol{\beta}) \left[y_i \frac{f(\mathbf{x}_i'\boldsymbol{\beta}) + (\mathbf{x}_i'\boldsymbol{\beta})F(\mathbf{x}_i'\boldsymbol{\beta})}{[F(\mathbf{x}_i'\boldsymbol{\beta})]^2} + (1 - y_i)\frac{f(\mathbf{x}_i'\boldsymbol{\beta}) - (\mathbf{x}_i'\boldsymbol{\beta})[1 - F(\mathbf{x}_i'\boldsymbol{\beta})]}{[1 - F(\mathbf{x}_i'\boldsymbol{\beta})]^2} \right] \mathbf{x}_i\mathbf{x}_i' \tag{18.2.39}$$

For the logit model, where F and f are the logistic CDF and pdf,

$$\begin{aligned}\frac{\partial \ln \ell}{\partial \boldsymbol{\beta}} &= \sum_{i=1}^{T} y_i \frac{1}{1 + \exp(\mathbf{x}_i'\boldsymbol{\beta})}\mathbf{x}_i - \sum_{i=1}^{T} (1 - y_i)\frac{1}{1 + \exp(-\mathbf{x}_i'\boldsymbol{\beta})}\mathbf{x}_i \\ &= \sum_{i=1}^{T} [y_i F(-\mathbf{x}_i'\boldsymbol{\beta}) - (1 - y_i)F(\mathbf{x}_i'\boldsymbol{\beta})]\mathbf{x}_i \end{aligned} \tag{18.2.40}$$

and

$$\begin{aligned}\frac{\partial^2 \ln \ell}{\partial \boldsymbol{\beta}\, \partial \boldsymbol{\beta}'} &= -\sum_{i=1}^{T} \frac{\exp(-\mathbf{x}_i'\boldsymbol{\beta})}{[1 + \exp(-\mathbf{x}_i'\boldsymbol{\beta})]^2}\mathbf{x}_i\mathbf{x}_i' \\ &= -\sum_{i=1}^{T} f(\mathbf{x}_i'\boldsymbol{\beta})\mathbf{x}_i\mathbf{x}_i' \end{aligned} \tag{18.2.41}$$

Using these derivatives and the recursive relation (18.2.37), maximum likelihood estimators can be obtained given some initial estimates $\tilde{\boldsymbol{\beta}}_1$. For probit and logit models the choice of the initial estimates does not matter since it can be shown [see Dhrymes (1978, pp. 344–347)], that, for both of these models, the matrix of second partials $\partial^2 \ln \ell/\partial \boldsymbol{\beta}\, \partial \boldsymbol{\beta}'$ is negative definite for *all* values of $\boldsymbol{\beta}$. Consequently, the Newton-Raphson procedure will converge, ultimately, to the unique maximum likelihood estimators regardless of the initial estimates. Computationally, of course, the choice does matter since the better the initial estimates the fewer iterations must be carried out to attain the maximum of the likelihood function. While several alternatives for initial estimates exist, one can simply use the least squares estimators of $\boldsymbol{\beta}$ obtained by regressing y_i on the explanatory variables.

18.2.3 Evaluation and Use of Binary Choice Models

When evaluating binary choice models, care must be taken with regard to several points. First, estimated coefficients do not indicate the increase in the probability of the event occurring given a one unit increase in the corresponding independent variable. Rather, the coefficients reflect the effect of a change in an independent variable upon $F^{-1}(P_i)$ for the probit model and upon $\ln[P_i/(1 - P_i)]$ for the logit model. In both cases the amount of the increase in the probability depends upon the original probability and thus upon the initial values of all the independent variables and their coefficients. This is true since $P_i = F(\mathbf{x}_i'\boldsymbol{\beta})$ and $\partial P_i/\partial x_{ij} = f(\mathbf{x}_i'\boldsymbol{\beta}) \cdot \beta_j$, where $f(\cdot)$ is the pdf associated with $F(\cdot)$. Thus, while the sign of the coefficient does indicate the *direction* of the change, the magnitude depends upon $f(\mathbf{x}_i'\boldsymbol{\beta})$, which, of course, reflects the *steepness* of the CDF at $\mathbf{x}_i'\boldsymbol{\beta}$. Naturally, the steeper the CDF the greater the impact of a change in the value of an explanatory variable will be.

Second, usual individual or joint hypothesis tests about coefficients and confidence intervals can be constructed from the estimate of the asymptotic covariance matrix using either the Wald or LR statistics, and relying on the asymptotic normality of the EGLS or ML estimator being used.

A test of the hypothesis H_0: $\beta_2 = \beta_3 = \ldots = \beta_K = 0$ can be easily carried out using the likelihood ratio procedure. If n is the number of successes ($y_i = 1$) observed in the T observations, then for both the logit and probit models the maximum value of the log-likelihood function under the null hypothesis H_0 is

$$\ln \ell(\hat{\omega}) = n \ln \left(\frac{n}{T}\right) + (T - n) \ln \left(\frac{T - n}{T}\right)$$

Consequently, if the hypothesis is true, then asymptotically

$$-2[\ln \ell(\hat{\omega}) - \ln \ell(\hat{\Omega})] \tag{18.2.42}$$

has a $\chi^2_{(K-1)}$ distribution, where $\ln \ell(\hat{\Omega})$ is the value of the log-likelihood function evaluated at $\tilde{\boldsymbol{\beta}}$. Acceptance of this hypothesis would, of course, imply that none of the explanatory variables has any effect on the probability of E occurring. In that case the probability that $y_i = 1$ is estimated by $\hat{P}_i = n/T$, which is simply the sample proportion.

Investigators are also frequently interested in a scalar measure of model performance, such as R^2 is for the linear model. Amemiya (1981, pp. 1502–1507) suggests several measures that can be used. Two popular ones are the value of the chi-square statistic in (18.2.42) and the pseudo-R^2, defined as

$$\rho^2 = 1 - \frac{\ln \ell(\hat{\Omega})}{\ln \ell(\hat{\omega})}$$

This measure is 1 when the model is a perfect predictor, in the sense that $\hat{P}_i = F(\mathbf{x}_i'\tilde{\boldsymbol{\beta}}) = 1$ when $y_i = 1$ and $\hat{P}_i = 0$ when $y_i = 0$, and is 0 when $\ln \ell(\hat{\Omega}) = \ln \ell(\hat{\omega})$. Between these limits the value of ρ^2 has no obvious intuitive meaning. However, Hauser (1978) shows that ρ^2 can be given meaning in an information theoretic context. Specifically, ρ^2 measures the percent of the "uncertainty" in the data explained by the empirical results. This concept is discussed more fully in Section 18.3.3.

Logit and probit models might be used as alternatives to discriminant analysis for classifying individuals into one population or another. Specifically if $\hat{P}_i \geq 0.5$ a set of characteristics $\mathbf{x}_i$ may be asserted to "predict" that $y_i = 1$. See Press and Wilson (1978) for a discussion of the relation between discrimination based on logistic models and a discriminant function. However, from a summary point of view, it is frequently worthwhile to report the in-sample predictive success of the model. In particular, the number of "correct" predictions, where a prediction is correct when $\hat{P}_i \geq .5$ and $y_i = 1$ or $\hat{P}_i < .5$ and $y_i = 0$. An interesting feature of the logit model is that the predicted share of occurrences of the event E—that is, the number of times $\hat{P}_i \geq .5$ over T—is equal to the actual share n/T.

In this same context one might wish to ask when the use of logit, for example, would be preferable to usual discriminant analysis. Amemiya and Powell (1980) investigate this issue and note that if the $\mathbf{x}_i$ are multivariate normal, then the discriminant analysis estimator is the ML estimator and is asymptotically efficient. On the other hand, the discriminant analysis estimator is not consistent when the $\mathbf{x}_i$ are not normal, but logit is. On the basis of a comparison of large sample properties, however, they conclude that the discriminant estimator does quite well in prediction and reasonably well in estimation even with nonnormal populations.

Finally, while this chapter reflects the sampling theory approach to binary choice models, the Bayesian approach is also feasible. Zellner and Rossi (1982) consider the binary choice model with diffuse and informative priors. They present hypothesis testing and model selection procedures and compare alternative numerical integration techniques that are available.

18.3 MULTINOMIAL CHOICE MODELS

A typical quantal choice model considers subjects who face $J \geq 2$ alternatives and must choose one of these. In this sense these models are generalizations of those presented in Section 18.2. Let y_{ij} be a binary variable that takes the value one if the jth alternative, $j = 1, \ldots, J$, is chosen and zero otherwise. Let $P_{ij} = \Pr[y_{ij} = 1]$. Then

$$\sum_{j=1}^{J} y_{ij} = \sum_{j=1}^{J} P_{ij} = 1$$

and given a sample of T individuals the likelihood function is

$$\ell = \prod_{i=1}^{T} P_{i1}^{y_{i1}} P_{i2}^{y_{i2}} \ldots P_{iJ}^{y_{iJ}} \tag{18.3.1}$$

Each observation is assumed to be drawn from independent, but not identical, multinomial distributions; hence the name, multinomial choice models. Note that the numbers of alternatives that face different individuals might vary, so that J could be indexed by i, but we will not pursue that generalization. This model is made into a behavioral one by relating the selection probabilities to attributes of the alternatives in the choice set and the attributes of the individuals making the choices.

As in Section 18.2, such models can be motivated by assuming that individuals maximize utility, and that the utility that the ith individual derives from the choice of the jth alternative can be represented as

$$U_{ij} = \bar{U}_{ij} + e_{ij} = \mathbf{x}_{ij}'\boldsymbol{\beta} + e_{ij} \tag{18.3.2}$$

where $\mathbf{x}_{ij}$ is a vector of variables representing the attributes of the jth choice to the ith individual, $\boldsymbol{\beta}$ is a vector of unknown parameters, and e_{ij} is a random disturbance. The presence of the random disturbance e_{ij} can be rationalized as reflecting intrinsically random choice behavior, and measurement and/or specification error. In particular it may reflect unobserved attributes of the alternatives.

Having specified a utility function, each individual is assumed to make selections that maximize their utility. The probability that the first alternative is chosen is

$$\begin{aligned} P_{i1} &= \Pr[U_{i1} > U_{i2} \quad \text{and} \quad U_{i1} > U_{i3} \ldots \quad \text{and} \quad U_{i1} > U_{iJ}] \\ &= \Pr[e_{i2} < \bar{U}_{i1} - \bar{U}_{i2} + e_{i1} \quad \text{and} \quad e_{i3} < \bar{U}_{i1} - \bar{U}_{i3} + e_{i1} \\ &\quad \ldots \quad \text{and} \quad e_{iJ} < \bar{U}_{i1} - \bar{U}_{iJ} + e_{i1}] \end{aligned} \tag{18.3.3}$$

Similar expressions hold for all other P_{ij}'s and the P_{ij}'s become well-defined probabilities once a joint density function is chosen for the e_{ij}. It is convenient to look at (18.3.3) in differenced form as

$$P_{i1} = \Pr[e_{i2} - e_{i1} < \bar{U}_{i1} - \bar{U}_{i2} \quad \ldots \quad \text{and} \quad e_{iJ} - e_{i1} < \bar{U}_{i1} - \bar{U}_{iJ}] \tag{18.3.4}$$

This transformation reduces by one the number of integrals that must be evaluated in order to determine the P_{ij}'s. It also explains why distributions that are closed under subtraction, or produce convenient distributions under subtraction, are popular candidates for the joint density of the e_{ij}.

In the two sections that follow, the logit and probit formulations, respectively, will be presented. The logit model has been extensively considered by McFadden (1974, 1976), who discusses the discrete choice theory implied by the logit specification and develops appropriate estimation and inference procedures. The logit model rests upon a very strong behavioral assumption, the independence of irrelevant alternatives. The implications of this assumption will be investigated in Section 18.3.1. The probit model has been considered by Albright, Lerman, and Manski (1977) and Hausman and Wise (1978), and represents an attempt to avoid the strong assumption upon which logit analysis depends.

18.3.1 Multinomial Logit

The multinomial logit model follows from the assumption that the e_{ij} in (18.3.2) are independently and identically distributed with Weibull [Johnson and Kotz (1970)] density functions. Corresponding cumulative distribution functions are of the form

$$\Pr(e_{ij} \leq \varepsilon) = \exp[-\exp(-\varepsilon)]$$

McFadden (1974) has shown that a necessary and sufficient condition for the random utility model (18.3.2) with independent and identically distributed errors to yield the logit model is that the errors have Weibull distributions. The difference between any two random variables with this distribution has a logistic distribution function, giving the multinomial logit model. The probabilities arising from this model can be expressed as

$$P_{ij} = \frac{\exp(\mathbf{x}'_{ij}\boldsymbol{\beta})}{\sum_{j=1}^{J} \exp(\mathbf{x}'_{ij}\boldsymbol{\beta})} \tag{18.3.5}$$

which is a general form of the logistic distribution function. Recall that $\boldsymbol{\beta}$ is an unknown $(K \times 1)$ vector of taste parameters common to all members of the population and $\mathbf{x}_{ij}$ is a $(K \times 1)$ vector of observations on variables that are functions of the characteristics of the alternatives and the individual decision-makers. We now note some consequences of this specification.

First, consider the effect on the odds of choosing alternative 1 rather than alternative 2 where the number of alternatives facing the individual are increased from J to J^*. The odds of alternative 1 being chosen rather than 2 where J alternatives are available is

$$\frac{P_{i1}}{P_{i2}} = \frac{\exp(\mathbf{x}'_{i1}\boldsymbol{\beta}) \Big/ \sum_{j=1}^{J} \exp(\mathbf{x}'_{ij}\boldsymbol{\beta})}{\exp(\mathbf{x}'_{i2}\boldsymbol{\beta}) \Big/ \sum_{j=1}^{J} \exp(\mathbf{x}'_{ij}\boldsymbol{\beta})} = \frac{\exp(\mathbf{x}'_{i1}\boldsymbol{\beta})}{\exp(\mathbf{x}'_{i2}\boldsymbol{\beta})}$$

The odds when J^* alternatives are available is *still*

$$\frac{P_{i1}}{P_{i2}} = \frac{\exp(\mathbf{x}'_{i1}\boldsymbol{\beta})}{\exp(\mathbf{x}'_{i2}\boldsymbol{\beta})}$$

since the denominators of (18.3.5) divide out. Thus, for this model the odds of a particular choice are *unaffected* by the presence of additional alternatives. This property is called the *independence of irrelevant alternatives* and can represent a serious weakness in the logit model. Suppose, for example, members of a population, when offered a choice between a pony and a bicycle, choose the pony in two-thirds of the cases. If an additional alternative is made available, say an additional bicycle just like the first except of a different color, then one would still expect two-thirds of the population to choose the pony and the remaining one-third to split their choices among the bicycles according to their color preference. In the logit model, however, the proportion choosing the pony must fall to one-half if the odds relative to either bicycle is to remain two-to-one in favor of the pony. This illustrates the point that when two or more of the J alternatives are close substitutes, the conditional logit model may not produce reasonable results. As Albright, Lerman, and Manski (1977) note, this feature is a consequence of assuming the errors e_{ij} are independent. On the other hand, there are many circumstances where the alternatives are distinct enough for this feature of the logit model not to be a negative factor.

Second, in this formulation none of the K variables represented in $\mathbf{x}_{ij}$ can be constant across all alteratives since then the associated parameter would not be identified. For example, consider again the odds of choosing alternative one rather than alternative two,

$$\frac{P_{i1}}{P_{i2}} = \frac{\exp(\mathbf{x}_{i1}'\boldsymbol{\beta})}{\exp(\mathbf{x}_{i2}'\boldsymbol{\beta})} = \exp(\mathbf{x}_{i1}' - \mathbf{x}_{i2}')\boldsymbol{\beta}$$

If any corresponding elements of $\mathbf{x}_{i1}$ and $\mathbf{x}_{i2}$ are equal, the associated variable has no influence on the odds. If this is the case for all alternatives, then the variable in question does not contribute to the explanation of why one alternative is chosen over another and its parameter cannot be estimated. Intuitively, if the parameter vector $\boldsymbol{\beta}$ is to remain constant across all alternatives, only factors that change from alternative to alternative can help explain why one is chosen rather than another. Consequently, variables like age, sex, income, or race that are constant across alternatives provide no information about the choice process given this model. Variables that *would* provide information about the choices made include the cost of a particular alternative to each individual (for instance the cost of transportation by car, bus, train or taxi to a particular destination) or the return to an individual from each available alternative. These factors vary across alternatives for each individual.

Unfortunately, economists rarely have data that varies over both the individual in the sample and over each alternative faced by an individual. Such data are both costly to collect and difficult to characterize. The data economists usually have access to varies across individuals but not across alternatives, so that for any individual $\mathbf{x}_{i1} = \mathbf{x}_{i2} = \ldots = \mathbf{x}_{iJ} = \mathbf{x}_i$. Given this circumstance, the model must be modified in some way before it can be used to characterize choice behavior. One possible modification is to allow the explanatory variables to have differential impacts upon the odds of choosing one alternative rather than another. That is, the coefficient vector must be made alternative-specific. That is, let the selection probabilities be given by

Model w/o variables that vary across alternatives

$$P_{ij} = \frac{\exp(\mathbf{x}_{ij}'\boldsymbol{\beta}_j)}{\sum_{j=1}^{J} \exp(\mathbf{x}_{ij}'\boldsymbol{\beta}_j)} \tag{18.3.6}$$

where now the parameter vector is indexed by j, indicating that explanatory variables may have differential impacts depending upon the alternative.

Now the odds of the kth alternative relative to the first are

$$\frac{P_{ik}}{P_{i1}} = \frac{\exp(\mathbf{x}_{ik}'\boldsymbol{\beta}_k)}{\exp(\mathbf{x}_{i1}'\boldsymbol{\beta}_1)} = \exp(\mathbf{x}_{ik}'\boldsymbol{\beta}_k - \mathbf{x}_{i1}'\boldsymbol{\beta}_1), \qquad k = 2, \ldots, J \tag{18.3.7}$$

If the vectors $\mathbf{x}_{ik}$ and $\mathbf{x}_{i1}$ contain variables that are constant across alternatives, then $\mathbf{x}_{ik} = \mathbf{x}_{i1} = \mathbf{x}_i$, for all $k = 2, \ldots, J$, and (18.3.7) becomes

$$\frac{P_{ik}}{P_{i1}} = \exp[\mathbf{x}_i'(\boldsymbol{\beta}_k - \boldsymbol{\beta}_1)] \tag{18.3.8}$$

Some sort of normalization rule is clearly needed, and a convenient one is to assume $\boldsymbol{\beta}_1 = \mathbf{0}$. This condition, together with the $(J - 1)$ equations in (18.3.8), uniquely determines the selection probabilities and guarantees they sum to 1 for each i. The resulting selection probabilities are

$$P_{i1} = \frac{1}{1 + \sum_{j=2}^{J} \exp(\mathbf{x}_i'\boldsymbol{\beta}_j)}$$

$$P_{ij} = \frac{\exp(\mathbf{x}_i'\boldsymbol{\beta}_j)}{1 + \sum_{j=2}^{J} \exp(\mathbf{x}_i'\boldsymbol{\beta}_j)}, \qquad j = 2, \ldots, J \tag{18.3.9}$$

Estimation of the parameters of the multiple logit model with the selection probabilities given by (18.3.5) or (18.3.9) can be carried out by using maximum likelihood procedures. The appropriate likelihood function is obtained by substituting the relevant expression for P_{ij} into (18.3.1). See McFadden (1974) for details concerning estimation when probabilities are given by (18.3.5) and Schmidt and Strauss (1975) for the case represented in (18.3.9). In both cases the likelihood function is concave in the unknown parameters and any convergent numerical optimization algorithm discussed in Appendix B can be used. The expressions for first and second derivatives are given in the cited references.

18.3.2 Multinomial Probit

The multinomial probit model overcomes some of the weaknesses of the logit formulation by permitting the disturbances e_{ij} in (18.3.2) to be correlated and by allowing tastes to vary across individuals in the population. The correlation of the e_{ij}'s arises as a consequence of their embodiment of unobserved attributes and individual effects. For two similar choices, j and k, it is reasonable to expect e_{ij} and e_{ik} to be similar also, and thus not independent. It follows that the multinomial probit model does not exhibit the characteristic of independence of irrelevant alternatives.

Variation in taste parameters is achieved by rewriting (18.3.2) as

$$U_{ij} = \mathbf{x}'_{ij}\boldsymbol{\beta}_i + e_{ij} \tag{18.3.10}$$

where $\boldsymbol{\beta}_i = \bar{\boldsymbol{\beta}} + \mathbf{v}_i$ is a vector of taste parameters specific to the ith individual, $\bar{\boldsymbol{\beta}}$ is the mean taste parameter, and $\mathbf{v}_i$ is a vector of random elements that represent the ith person's deviation from that mean. Since $\mathbf{v}_i$ is unobservable, the resulting random utility model is

$$U_{ij} = \mathbf{x}'_{ij}\bar{\boldsymbol{\beta}} + (\mathbf{x}'_{ij}\mathbf{v}_i + e_{ij}) \tag{18.3.11}$$

In this model the disturbances $\mathbf{x}'_{ij}\mathbf{v}_i + e_{ij}$ are not independent because of the relation between the e_{ij}'s and also because for two choices j and k the errors will have the common random element $\mathbf{v}_i$.

The random utility model is made complete by assuming that the random parameters $\boldsymbol{\beta}_i$ and the random errors e_{ij} are multivariate normal and independent of one another. This assumption poses some practical problems since (18.3.4) now represents $(J - 1)$ integrals of the pdf of a multivariate normal random vector. Several versions of the multinomial probit model, and the computational problems, are discussed by Albright, Lerman, and Manski (1977), Hausman and Wise (1978), and Daganzo (1979).

18.3.3 Evaluation of Multinomial Choice Models

With respect to evaluation of results from multinomial choice models, one topic of interest is measuring the effects of changes of the independent variables upon the selection probabilities. This is a straightforward generalization of the results in Section 18.2.3. The difficulties in using the relevant partial derivatives are considered by Crawford and Pollak (1982). They obtain bounding values for the partials and their standard errors. They also carefully define two notions of "order" in qualitative response models, and give necessary and sufficient conditions for the presence of each.

Procedures currently used to validate quantal choice models also involve attempts to measure the "goodness" of the predictions of the model. This is not straightforward, since the statistical model predicts conditional probabilities that must be compared to actual choices. Current measures of model goodness include:

1. First preference recovery is the percent of individuals that actually choose the alternative which the model indicates has the highest probability. This measure can then be compared to the percent that would choose the alternative by chance, $1/J$, or the share of the sample or population that chooses the alternative.

2. A comparison of the actual share in the sample for each alternative with the predicted share $\Sigma_{i=1}^{T}\hat{P}_{ij}/T$, or the root mean square percent error, allows an evaluation of different model specifications.
3. The log likelihood chi-square test, where the null model, with all coefficients equal to zero, implies that all alternatives are equally likely.
4. A pseudo-R^2, the likelihood ratio index

$$\rho^2 = 1 - \frac{L(\hat{\boldsymbol{\beta}})}{L(\hat{\boldsymbol{\beta}}^H)}$$

where $L(\hat{\boldsymbol{\beta}})$ is the log likelihood of the unconstrained model and $L(\hat{\boldsymbol{\beta}}^H)$ is the log likelihood of the model defined by the null hypothesis. This measure is zero when $L(\hat{\boldsymbol{\beta}}) = L(\hat{\boldsymbol{\beta}}^H)$ and when the model is a perfect predictor $\rho^2 = 1$.

These measures have some obvious weaknesses. The evaluation of criteria (1) and (2) must take into account both the number of alternatives available and the population share of each alternative, for what is a "good" value of these measures depends on these factors. The chi-square test (3) can statistically reject null hypotheses and allows comparisons of one model versus another if the models are nested. But this test does not provide an indication of how accurate the predictions are. The pseudo-R^2 is a convenient measure, but it does not have an intuitive interpretation between its limits.

Given these difficulties, it is useful to consider an approach to evaluating quantal choice models that is consistent and has intuitive meaning. Such an approach can be based upon information theory [see Theil (1967, 1970, 1971); Hauser (1978)]. A brief statement of some information theoretic concepts follows with their applications to quantal choice models.

Suppose that a message is received saying that some event y has occurred. The informational content of the message depends upon the probability P of the event. If P had been close to one, little information would have been received, since y was practically certain to occur. On the other hand, if P had been small, and in spite of this y did occur, then the informational content of the message would have been large. It is natural, then, to relate the informational content of a message concerning y to y's probability P by some decreasing function. A choice with many convenient properties is [see Theil (1967)]

$$I(P) = \ln \frac{1}{P}$$

which decreases from infinity (infinite surprise when $P = 0$) to zero (no information when $P = 1$ and y was certain to occur).

Prior to receiving any message about y, the informational content of a message is known to be either $I(P)$ or $I(1 - P)$, depending upon whether the message states that y occurred or that it did not. The expected informational content of the message, or entropy, then is

$$H = PI(P) + (1 - P)I(1 - P)$$

H-entropy

$$= P \ln \left[\frac{1}{P}\right] + (1 - P) \ln \left[\frac{1}{1 - P}\right]$$

This measure can be extended to several events, say $y_1, \ldots, y_J$, with probabilities $P_1, \ldots, P_J$, which sum to one, meaning that it is known with certainty that one of the events will occur. The expected information in this case is

$0 < H < \ln J$

$$H = \sum_{i=1}^{J} P_i I(P_i) = \sum_{i=1}^{J} P_i \ln \left[\frac{1}{P_i}\right]$$

measures total uncertainty

(18.3.12)

This measure is nonnegative and varies between zero, corresponding to the case when one of the prior probabilities $P_i = 1$, and $\ln J$, which is the case when all prior probabilities are equal to $1/J$. Thus the maximum expected informational content increases as the number of alternatives increases, since there are more possible outcomes and more uncertainty. In fact, uncertainty and expected information are complementary notions. The larger the uncertainty prior to the reception of the message, the larger the amount of information, on the average, that it contains. Thus the entropy H is a measure of uncertainty associated with the distribution of events $y_1, \ldots, y_J$, whose probabilities are $P_1, \ldots, P_J$.

Given these concepts, the informational content of a message that does not indicate whether the event y occurred or not, but causes a change in the probability of occurrence of y from P to Q, can be defined. As we have defined it, information is additive [Theil (1967, p. 4)], and a natural way to define the informational content of a message is the difference

$$I(P) - I(Q) = \ln \left[\frac{Q}{P}\right]$$

measure of info content in Δ in prob of occurrence

(18.3.13)

This measure is zero when $P = Q$, which implies that the message did not change the odds in favor of y and thus provided no information. Its value is $\ln(1/P)$ when $Q = 1$, which is the case when the message indicates that y has occurred. The value is negative when $Q < P$, which corresponds to the case when the message indicates y is less likely and then y does occur, implying that the message provided negative or bad information. In the general case, when J mutually exclusive events are considered, the information on each event is $\ln(Q_i/P_i)$ and the probability of y_i is Q_i so that the expected information is

$$I(\mathbf{P}) - I(\mathbf{Q}) = \sum_{i=1}^{J} Q_i \ln \left[\frac{Q_i}{P_i}\right]$$

(18.3.14)

where $\mathbf{P}' = (P_1, \ldots, P_J)$ and $\mathbf{Q}' = (Q_1, \ldots, Q_J)$. Note that this measure may be infinitely large if some Q_i is positive when the corresponding P_i was zero and is zero if $P_i = Q_i$ for all i. Such a message would imply that y_i, previously considered to have zero chance, now has a positive probability and represents an infinite informational increase. Also, as should be expected, if the message states that one outcome, y_i, has probability one, then the expected information is $\ln(1/P_i)$, as in the simple case.

With these definitions and ideas the problem of evaluating quantal choice models can be considered. Let $\mathbf{y}' = (y_1, \ldots, y_J)$ be the set of alternatives to the ith individual, who is observed to have characteristics $\mathbf{x}_i$. A multinomial choice model estimates the probabilities $P_{ij} = \Pr(y_j|\mathbf{x}_i)$; we wish to compare these estimates with the actual choices made, represented by δ_{ij}, which is unity if individual i chooses alternative j and zero otherwise. If we let $\Pr(y_j|\mathbf{x}_i) = Q_{ij}$, the probability of alternative j's being chosen by the ith individual given the "message" $\mathbf{x}_i$, and $\Pr(y_j) = P_j$, the prior probability of the jth alternative being chosen, then the informational content of the model (18.3.14) becomes

$$I(y_j;\mathbf{x}_i) = \ln \frac{\Pr(y_j|\mathbf{x}_i)}{\Pr(y_j)}$$

The expected information (18.3.14) generalizes to the expected information provided by the model over all observation vectors $\mathbf{x}_i$ as

$$\begin{aligned} EI(\mathbf{y};X) &= \sum_{\mathbf{x}_i} \Pr(\mathbf{x}_i) \sum_j \Pr(y_j|\mathbf{x}_i) \ln \frac{\Pr(y_j|\mathbf{x}_i)}{\Pr(y_j)} \\ &= \sum_{\mathbf{x}_i} \sum_j \Pr(y_j,\mathbf{x}_i) \ln \frac{\Pr(y_j|\mathbf{x}_i)}{\Pr(y_j)} \end{aligned} \tag{18.3.15}$$

where X is the set of sample observations, and $\Pr(y_j,\mathbf{x}_i)$ is the joint probability of an observation $\mathbf{x}_i$ and an event y_j. The uncertainty after the observations $\mathbf{x}_i$ are available is

$$H(\mathbf{y}|X) = \sum_{\mathbf{x}_i} \Pr(\mathbf{x}_i) \sum_j \Pr(y_j|\mathbf{x}_i) \ln \frac{1}{\Pr(y_j|\mathbf{x}_i)}$$

which is a straightforward generalization of (18.3.12).

To apply these concepts to a specific problem, $\Pr(\mathbf{x}_i)$ and $\Pr(y_j)$ must be given. If a sample of T individuals is available, Hauser (1978) suggests that $\Pr(\mathbf{x}_i)$ be specified as

$$\Pr(\mathbf{x}_i) = \frac{\text{number of times } \mathbf{x}_i \text{ occurs}}{T}$$

which in most cases will be $1/T$, since observations will not in general be repeated. The distribution $\Pr(y_j)$ could be any prior distribution, but two particularly useful specifications are $\Pr(y_j) = 1/J$, the equally likely case, or to set

$\Pr(y_j)$ equal to the known population or sample share of each of the alternatives. Then, within the information theoretic framework, the following procedures may be used to evaluate a model of qualitative choice:

1. Theil (1971, p. 645), suggests comparing the sample shares of each alternative with their predicted shares $\Sigma_i \hat{P}_{ij}$. If $q_1, \ldots, q_J$ are the observed shares and $p_1, \ldots, p_J$ the predicted shares, then (18.3.14) is an inverse measure of the accuracy of these predictions; zero when $p_i = q_i$ for all alternatives and positive otherwise. The expected information is called the information inaccuracy of the forecast and may be regarded as a measure of lack of fit.

2. A measure of the "empirical information" provided by the model can be computed by evaluating

$$I(\mathbf{y};X) = \frac{1}{T}\sum_i \sum_j \delta_{ij} \ln \frac{\hat{P}_{ij}}{\Pr(y_j)}$$

where $\Pr(y_j)$ is the selected prior distribution of the alternatives and $\hat{P}_{ij}$ is a predicted choice probability from the model. The empirical information can be compared to the total uncertainty in the system (18.3.12), which has maximum value $\ln J$ under the assumption of equally likely alternatives. Hauser (1978) has shown that this ratio is a generalization of the pseudo-R^2 measure in that if the null hypothesis or prior distribution does not depend on i, then the two are numerically equal. Thus the pseudo-R^2 may be interpreted as the percent of uncertainty explained by the empirical results.

3. Alternatively, we could compare the empirical information to the expected information from the model (18.3.15). Hauser (1978) states that a test for the adequacy of the probabilistic model could be carried out by testing the closeness of the empirical information to the expected information. He argues that $I(\mathbf{y};X)$ is asymptotically normally distributed with mean $EI(\mathbf{y};X)$ and variance

$$V(\mathbf{y};X) = \frac{1}{T}\sum_{i=1}^{T}\left\{\sum_{j=1}^{J} \Pr(y_j|\mathbf{x}_i)\left[\ln \frac{\Pr(y_j|\mathbf{x}_i)}{\Pr(y_j)}\right]^2 - \left[\sum_{j=1}^{J} \Pr(y_j|\mathbf{x}_i) \ln \frac{\Pr(y_j|\mathbf{x}_i)}{\Pr(y_j)}\right]^2\right\}$$

If $I(\mathbf{y};X)$ is not statistically close to $EI(\mathbf{y};X)$, the probabilistic model may be rejected as unable to explain the empirical observations.

These measures, along with the chi-square test, provide useful, consistent, and interpretable ways of evaluating the probabilistic model for quantal choice. Also, regression diagnostic techniques have recently been extended to logistic models by Pregibon (1981) and graphical diagnostic procedures are suggested by Landwehr et al. (1984). As usual, none of these validation procedures should be used as a vehicle for model specification. Although pretest estimates have not been examined for these models, it is clear that the resulting estimators may not have the expected distributions under such procedures.

18.3.4 Summary and Concluding Remarks on Multinomial Choice Models

As formulated above, the multinomial probit model is less restrictive than the multinomial logit model, but the generality is gained at considerable computational expense. The multinomial logit model assumes that the parameters of the random utility function are constant across individuals in the population and that the random utilities are independent, even for alternatives that are similar. The multinomial probit relaxes both of these assumptions. By adopting a random utility function of the form (18.3.10) taste parameters are assumed to vary normally across the population of decisionmakers and utilities can be correlated. Hausman and Wise (1978) assume the random parameters β_{ij} are uncorrelated across i and that the e_{ij} are uncorrelated across i and j. Thus U_{ij} and U_{ik} are correlated because the same $\boldsymbol{\beta}$'s appear for all the alternatives. The computational procedure they adopt is feasible for a model with up to five alternatives. They compare their general model, and a special case that assumes the variances of the random coefficients to be zero (called independent probit) to multinomial logit. They conclude that in their example the results of logit and independent probit are similar, and their general model fits best and produces significantly different estimates and forecasts concerning a new alternative. Albright, Lerman and Manski's (1977) model is more general and they consider alternative procedures for evaluating the integral of the normal pdf. Their procedure can handle models with up to ten alternatives. They applied their model to the Hausman and Wise data and concluded that the logit and probit results did not differ by much. Furthermore, they could not obtain accurate estimates of the covariance matrix of $\boldsymbol{\beta}_i$, the increase in the value of the log likelihood using probit rather than logit did not seem substantial relative to the decrease in degrees of freedom, and the probit model required much more computer time per iteration than did the logit model. Thus while they demonstrated the feasibility of the multinomial probit model, they could not justify its additional cost, at least for the data set they used.

In addition to literature on the choice between multinomial logit and probit, additional work has appeared on a variety of related topics. McFadden (1977, 1981) introduces a nonindependent logit model that eliminates some of the weakness of the multinomial logit model described above. Misspecification in the context of choice models has been considered by several authors. Lee (1982) considers the effect of omitting a relevant variable from a multinomial logit model. Ruud (1983) considers the effects of applying maximum likelihood techniques to a multinomial choice model when the distribution has been misspecified. Parks (1980) extends the procedure of Amemiya and Nold (1975) to allow for an additional disturbance to reflect misspecification of the random utility function in the context of a sample with repeated observations. Fomby and Pearce (1982) present standard errors for the selection probabilities, partial derivatives and the expected response in the multinomial logit model. Zellner (1983) presents a Bayesian analysis of a simple multinomial logit model.

18.4 ANALYSIS OF CENSORED AND TRUNCATED SAMPLES

In the two previous sections of this chapter we have considered discrete choice models. They explain the behavior of variables that represent the choice of one of a finite number of alternatives by a decisionmaker, and consequently are of the multinomial form. A more general way to view these models is as regression models in which a dependent variable can only be observed in a limited range or in a limited way. In the binary probit model, for example, we only observe whether or not a certain threshold is crossed by an unobservable index variable. In this section we consider other models in this framework. In particular we explore the case of a dependent variable that is continuous, but not completely observable. For example, the dependent variable, and, perhaps, some independent variables as well, is observed and recorded only if the dependent variable is positive. The dependent variable is thus continuous, but observed only on a limited range.

A unifying framework for the current literature on models with limited dependent variables is to consider them as models with missing data, as is done by Heckman (1976, 1979) and Hartley (1976). Samples with missing observations arise in different ways, and the biases that result and the statistical procedures required to deal with them depend upon why the observations are missing. Such situations involving either censored or truncated samples are discussed by Kendall and Stuart (1973, p. 541).

A *censored sample* is one in which some observations on the dependent variable corresponding to known sets of independent variables are not observable. For example, suppose shots are fired under controlled conditions at a vertical circular target of fixed radius R. The distance of the shot from the center, the random variable in question, will be unobservable if the shot misses the target entirely. The observable range of the random variable will be limited to the range $[0,R]$ and no observations can be recorded for some experimental trials. A familiar example in economics is Tobin's (1958) model in which a consumer durable is purchased if a consumer's desire is high enough, where a measure of that desire is provided by the dollar amount spent by the purchaser. On the other hand, no measure is obtained if no purchase is made so that the sample is censored at zero, and those observations are incomplete in that no value is available for the dependent variables.

A *truncated sample* results when knowledge of the independent variables is available only when the dependent variable is also observed. Thus, in the shooting range example, the experimental setting is recorded only if the trial results in the target's being hit, resulting in some trials in which neither dependent nor independent variables are observed. One must simply assume, then, that the values of the random variable occurring come from a *distribution* that is truncated at R. Kendall and Stuart (1973, p. 541) note that censoring is a property of the sample while truncation is a property of the distribution. In the consumer durable example, a truncated sample would occur if customer characteristics were recorded only if a purchase were made. As should be expected, dealing with truncation problems is more difficult than censoring problems, since less information is available. In this section both the censored and truncated sample problems will be considered, as well as the more general selectivity problem framework of Heckman (1976).

18.4.1 Estimation in Censored and Truncated Samples

Let us consider a model in which the dependent variable is observed *only* if it is nonnegative and otherwise takes the value zero, although the choice of zero is arbitrary. Then this model can be written

$$y_t = \begin{cases} \mathbf{x}_t'\boldsymbol{\beta} + e_t & \text{if } y_t > 0 \\ 0 & \text{otherwise} \end{cases} \tag{18.4.1}$$

Furthermore, assume that, of T observations, the last s y_t's are zero, but y_t, $t = 1, \ldots, T - s$ is observable. Thus the sample is *censored* and is often called the *Tobit* model. In this case the regression function can be written

$$E(y_t|\mathbf{x}_t, y_t > 0) = \mathbf{x}_t'\boldsymbol{\beta} + E(e_t|y_t > 0), \qquad t = 1, \ldots, T - s$$

If the conditional expectation of the error term is zero, there is no problem, since then a least squares regression on the $T - s$ available observations will provide an unbiased estimate of $\boldsymbol{\beta}$. This, unfortunately, is not the case. If the e_t are independent and normally distributed random variables, with mean zero and variance σ^2, then

$$E(e_t|y_t > 0) = E(e_t|e_t > -\mathbf{x}_t'\boldsymbol{\beta}) = \sigma\lambda_t \tag{18.4.2}$$

where

$$\lambda_t = \frac{f(\psi_t)}{1 - F(\psi_t)}, \; \psi_t = -\mathbf{x}_t'\boldsymbol{\beta}/\sigma \tag{18.4.3}$$

and $f(\cdot)$ and $F(\cdot)$ are, respectively, the density and CDF of a standard normal random variable evaluated at the argument. Thus, the regression function can be written

$$E(y_t|\mathbf{x}_t, y_t > 0) = \mathbf{x}_t'\boldsymbol{\beta} + \sigma\lambda_t, \qquad t = 1, \ldots, T - s \tag{18.4.4}$$

The difficulty with least squares is that it omits the second term on the right-hand side of (18.4.4). The least squares estimator of $\boldsymbol{\beta}$ is biased and inconsistent, using either the entire sample or the subsample of complete observations. Greene (1981a) and Goldberger (1981) consider in more detail the properties of the OLS estimators in Tobit models when the explanatory variables are multivariate normal.

Two-step and maximum likelihood estimation procedures are available for the censored sample problem. A simple two-step procedure can be carried out as follows: Let y_t^* be a random variable that is 1 when y_t is observed and zero otherwise. Then the likelihood function for the sample is

$$\begin{aligned}\ell &= \prod_{t=1}^{T} [\Pr(e_t \leq -\mathbf{x}_t'\boldsymbol{\beta})]^{1-y_t^*} [\Pr(e_t > -\mathbf{x}_t'\boldsymbol{\beta})]^{y_t^*} \\ &= \prod_{t=1}^{T} \Pr\left[\frac{e_t}{\sigma} \leq \frac{-\mathbf{x}_t'\boldsymbol{\beta}}{\sigma}\right]^{1-y_t^*} \Pr\left[\frac{e_t}{\sigma} > \frac{-\mathbf{x}_t'\boldsymbol{\beta}}{\sigma}\right]^{y_t^*} \\ &= \prod_{t=1}^{T} F\left[\frac{\mathbf{x}_t'\boldsymbol{\beta}}{\sigma}\right]^{y_t^*} \left\{1 - F\left[\frac{\mathbf{x}_t'\boldsymbol{\beta}}{\sigma}\right]\right\}^{1-y_t^*} \qquad (18.4.5)\end{aligned}$$

since $F(-t) = 1 - F(t)$ for the normal distribution. This is the likelihood function for probit estimation of the model

$$E[y_t^*] = \mathbf{x}_t'\boldsymbol{\beta}/\sigma$$

Thus the first step of the two-step procedure is to estimate a probit model where the dependent variable is 1 or zero depending on whether y_t is observed or not. This provides a consistent estimator of $\boldsymbol{\beta}/\sigma$, which can be used to provide a consistent estimator of ψ_t and λ_t. The consistent estimator of λ_t is then inserted into (18.4.4) and the second step of the two-step procedure is the application of least squares to the resulting equation. The estimator of $\boldsymbol{\beta}$ produced by this process is consistent and asymptotically normally distributed. See Heckman (1976, 1979) and Greene (1981b) for the proofs, expressions for the asymptotic covariance matrix and other generalizations.

Amemiya (1973) considers maximum likelihood estimation of the parameters of (18.4.1) under the assumption that the errors e_t are independent and $N(0,\sigma^2)$. Since the likelihood function is highly nonlinear, we will, following Amemiya, seek a consistent estimator with which to begin an iterative search process. The availability of a consistent initial estimator will also allow use of the linearized maximum likelihood estimator, which is known to have the same asymptotic distribution as the maximum likelihood estimator if the initial estimator is consistent.

Let S be a s-element subset of the T integers $1, 2, \ldots, T$ such that $y_t = 0$ for t in S. Let $\bar{S}$ be the set of $T - s$ elements such that $y_t > 0$ for t in $\bar{S}$. The likelihood function is defined as

$$\ell = \Pi_S G(-\mathbf{x}_t'\boldsymbol{\beta},\sigma^2)\Pi_{\bar{S}}\, g(y_t - \mathbf{x}_t'\boldsymbol{\beta},\sigma^2)$$

where $G(\cdot)$ and $g(\cdot)$ are the CDF and pdf of a $N(0,\sigma^2)$ random variable, respectively. The likelihood function can be simplified since

$G(-\mathbf{x}_t'\boldsymbol{\beta},\sigma^2) = 1 - G(\mathbf{x}_t'\boldsymbol{\beta},\sigma^2) = 1 - G_t$

$$\ell = \Pi_S[1 - G_t]\Pi_{\bar{S}} \frac{1}{\sqrt{2\pi}\sigma} \exp\left(-\frac{1}{2\sigma^2}(y_t - \mathbf{x}_t'\boldsymbol{\beta})^2\right)$$

This likelihood function is a mixture of normal CDF's (discrete probabilities) and density functions. The log-likelihood function, apart from constants, is

$$\ln \ell = \sum_S \ln(1 - G_t) - \frac{T - s}{2} \ln \sigma^2 - \frac{1}{2\sigma^2} \sum_{\bar{S}} (y_t - \mathbf{x}_t'\boldsymbol{\beta})^2$$

The normal equations are highly nonlinear and thus a root must be obtained numerically. Furthermore, because of the nature of the likelihood function usual theorems about the asymptotic normality and consistency of the maximum likelihood estimator do not hold. Amemiya (1973) shows that a root $\hat{\boldsymbol{\theta}}$ of the normal equations $\partial(\ln \ell)/\partial\boldsymbol{\theta} = \mathbf{0}$, where $\boldsymbol{\theta} = (\boldsymbol{\beta}',\sigma^2)'$, is consistent and

$$\sqrt{T}(\hat{\boldsymbol{\theta}} - \boldsymbol{\theta}) \xrightarrow{d} N\left(\mathbf{0}, \left[-\frac{\partial^2 Q(\boldsymbol{\theta})}{\partial\boldsymbol{\theta}\,\partial\boldsymbol{\theta}'}\right]^{-1}\right)$$

where

$$\frac{\partial^2 Q(\boldsymbol{\theta})}{\partial\boldsymbol{\theta}\,\partial\boldsymbol{\theta}'} = -\lim \frac{1}{T} \begin{bmatrix} \sum_1^T a_t\mathbf{x}_t\mathbf{x}_t' & \sum_1^T b_t\mathbf{x}_t \\ \sum_1^T b_t\mathbf{x}_t' & \sum_1^T c_t \end{bmatrix} \tag{18.4.6}$$

and

$$a_t = -\frac{1}{\sigma^2}\left(z_tf_t - \frac{f_t^2}{1 - F_t} - F_t\right)$$

$$b_t = \frac{1}{2\sigma^2}\left(z_t^2f_t + f_t - \frac{z_tf_t^2}{1 - F_t}\right)$$

$$c_t = -\frac{1}{4\sigma^4}\left(z_t^3f_t + z_tf_t - \frac{z_t^2f_t^2}{1 - F_t} - 2F_t\right)$$

where $z_t = \mathbf{x}_t'\boldsymbol{\beta}/\sigma$, $F(\mathbf{x}_t'\boldsymbol{\beta}/\sigma) = F_t$, and $f(\mathbf{x}_t'\boldsymbol{\beta}/\sigma) = f_t$. This means that the sampling density of $\boldsymbol{\theta}$ may be approximated by

$$N\left(\boldsymbol{\theta}, \left[-T\left(\frac{\partial^2 Q(\boldsymbol{\theta})}{\partial\boldsymbol{\theta}\,\partial\boldsymbol{\theta}'}\right)\bigg|_{\boldsymbol{\theta}=\hat{\boldsymbol{\theta}}}\right]^{-1}\right)$$

where the limit sign in (18.4.6) is removed.

Since the normal equations are nonlinear, their solution may be obtained by an iterative process. The method of Newton gives the second round estimate

$$\hat{\boldsymbol{\theta}}_2 = \hat{\boldsymbol{\theta}}_1 - \left(\left.\frac{\partial^2 \ln \ell(\boldsymbol{\theta})}{\partial\boldsymbol{\theta}\,\partial\boldsymbol{\theta}'}\right|_{\boldsymbol{\theta}=\hat{\boldsymbol{\theta}}_1}\right)^{-1}\left(\left.\frac{\partial \ln \ell(\boldsymbol{\theta})}{\partial\boldsymbol{\theta}}\right|_{\boldsymbol{\theta}=\hat{\boldsymbol{\theta}}_1}\right) \tag{18.4.7}$$

Expressions for the necessary partial derivatives are given in Amemiya (1973). In order for the second round estimator to be consistent, a consistent initial estimator must be used. Amemiya shows that the instrumental variables estimator,

$$\hat{\boldsymbol{\theta}}_1 = \begin{bmatrix} \hat{\boldsymbol{\beta}}_1 \\ \hat{\sigma}_1^2 \end{bmatrix} = \left[\sum_{\bar{s}} \begin{bmatrix} \hat{y}_t\mathbf{x}_t \\ 1 \end{bmatrix} (y_t\mathbf{x}_t', 1)\right]^{-1} \sum_{\bar{s}} \begin{bmatrix} \hat{y}_t\mathbf{x}_t \\ 1 \end{bmatrix} y_t^2$$

where $\hat{y}_t$ is the least squares predictor of y_t based on the set of $T - s$ complete observations, is consistent and asymptotically normal, and, therefore, a suitable first round estimator for use in the two-step estimator (18.4.7).

The above analysis was carried out for the censored sample case, where a total of T observations are available, $T - s$ of which correspond to positive values for the dependent variable. For the truncated sample case, only $T - s$ observations are available on $\mathbf{x}_t$ and the logarithmic likelihood function is given by

$$-\sum_{t=1}^{T-s} \ln F_t - \frac{T-s}{2} \ln \sigma^2 - \frac{1}{2\sigma^2} \sum_{t=1}^{T-s} (y_t - \boldsymbol{\beta}'\mathbf{x}_t)^2$$

The initial estimator $\hat{\boldsymbol{\theta}}_1$ proposed above is still consistent and asymptotically normal, since it only depends on observations for which the dependent variable is positive. Furthermore, Amemiya states that the second-round estimator is asymptotically efficient so that one must only obtain the information matrix for the likelihood function given above in order to apply the method to the truncated data case.

18.4.2 Evaluation and Extensions Related to Limited Dependent Variable Models

As with the probit and logit models, the estimated coefficients in a Tobit model must be interpreted with some care. McDonald and Moffitt (1980) explore the interpretation and use of the estimated Tobit coefficients. They show that

$$\frac{\partial E y_t}{\partial x_{tj}} = F(z_t)\frac{\partial E y_t^*}{\partial x_{tj}} + E y_t^* \frac{\partial F(z_t)}{\partial x_{tj}} \tag{18.4.8}$$

where $z_t = \mathbf{x}_t'\boldsymbol{\beta}/\sigma$, Ey_t^* is the expected value of the dependent variable y_t given that $y_t > 0$, and $F(\cdot)$ is the cumulative normal distribution function. Furthermore,

$$\frac{\partial Ey_t^*}{\partial x_{tj}} = \beta_j \left(1 - \frac{z_t f(z_t)}{F(z_t)} - \frac{(f(z_t))^2}{(F(z_t))^2}\right)$$

where $f(\cdot)$ is the value of the standard normal density, and

$$Ey_t^* = \mathbf{x}_t'\boldsymbol{\beta} + \sigma f(z_t)/F(z_t)$$

$$Ey_t = F(z_t) \cdot Ey_t^*$$

Thus, the total change in Ey_t in (18.4.8) is disaggregated into two parts: first the change in y for those above the limit, weighted by the probability of being above the limit and second, the change in probability of being above the limit, weighted by the expected value of y_t given that it is above the limit. These values, of course, depend upon the parameter estimates for $\boldsymbol{\beta}$ and σ^2 as well as the values of the explanatory variables $\mathbf{x}_t$. For the purposes of reporting the results, one might choose $\mathbf{x}_t$ to be the mean values of the explanatory variables. Also note that the coefficient β_j is *not* $\partial y_t^*/\partial x_{tj}$. See the McDonald and Moffitt paper for some examples of the use of this decomposition.

In the past several years a substantial amount of work has appeared on alternative estimation procedures for models with qualitative and limited dependent variables as well as the effects of and tests for specification errors in such models. First, Olsen (1978) and Pratt (1981) have shown the concavity of the log likelihood function for the Tobit model, so that if an iteration procedure converges, it converges to a consistent and asymptotically normal estimate. Fair (1977) has suggested a more efficient iteration procedure than the usual method of Newton. Greene (1981a, 1983) suggests "corrected" OLS estimates that are close to the ML estimates under the assumption that the explanatory variables are multivariate normal. Powell (1981) offers a least absolute deviation estimator that is consistent and does not depend on the distribution of the errors. Paarsch (1984) evaluates Powell's estimator, Heckman's two-step estimator, the ML estimator and OLS under various distributional, censoring and sample size assumptions. Nelson (1984) studies the efficiency of Heckman's two-step estimator relative to the ML estimator. These investigations show that ML can be substantially more efficient than the two-step estimator.

The sensitivity of ML estimation to errors in the specification of the error distribution in Tobit models has begun to be documented. Goldberger (1980), Chung and Goldberger (1984) and Arabmazer and Schmidt (1982) show and discuss the inconsistency of the MLE when the errors are not normal. Bera, Jarque, and Lee (1982) define a Lagrange multiplier test that can be used to test for normality in probit as well as truncated and censored sample models. Nelson (1981) offers a Hausman-like test for misspecification in the Tobit model. Hurd (1979) and Arabmazer and Schmidt (1981) study the effect of heteroscedasticity in the estimation of truncated and censored models, respectively. Heteroscedasticity makes the usual ML estimator inconsistent in both cases.

Based on numerical experiments, the degree of inconsistency is substantially greater in the truncated model case. The effect of autocorrelation has been studied by Robinson (1982). He shows, under certain conditions on the dependence of the errors that the Tobit estimator is strongly consistent and asymptotically normal, but not efficient. Finally, Stapleton and Young (1981) consider measurement error on the nonzero observations of the dependent variable, and show that the usual Tobit MLE is inconsistent in this case.

18.5 SIMULTANEOUS EQUATIONS MODELS WITH DISCRETE AND LIMITED ENDOGENOUS VARIABLES

In this section we briefly consider estimation of simultaneous equations systems where some of the endogenous variables are discrete or limited in some way. Such models have been considered by Amemiya (1974, 1978b, 1979), Heckman (1978), Lee (1978, 1979), Nelson and Olson (1978), Duncan (1980), Brownstone (1980), and Sickles and Schmidt (1978) among others. A class of models will be presented for which computationally feasible two-stage estimation techniques exist. Alternative estimators that were derived using Amemiya's principle (1978b, 1979) and that are more efficient than the two-stage estimators will be given. Other variants of such models will also be discussed briefly.

18.5.1 Two-Stage Methods and Amemiya's Principle

Following Lee (1981), consider the simultaneous equations model

$$Y\Gamma + XB + E = 0 \tag{18.5.1}$$

where the systems notation is defined in Chapter 14. In contrast to Chapter 14, however, where all endogenous variables were assumed to be completely observable, continuous variables, here we are going to permit some of the endogenous variables to be limited or even unobservable. Specifically, assume that $0 \leq M_1 \leq M_2 \leq M_3 \leq M$ and the following:

1. The first M_1 variables in Y, $\mathbf{y}_1, \ldots, \mathbf{y}_{M_1}$, are observable, continuous variables.
2. The next $M_2 - M_1$ variables, $\mathbf{y}_{M_1+1}, \ldots, \mathbf{y}_{M_2}$, are limited in the sense that they can be observed only if they are positive. (Tobit structure)
3. The next $M_3 - M_2$ variables, $\mathbf{y}_{M_2+1}, \ldots, \mathbf{y}_{M_3}$, are unobservable latent variables. However, corresponding to each is an observable binary indicator variable that takes the value unity or zero depending on whether the unobservable variable is positive or nonpositive. (Probit structure)
4. The final $M - M_3$ variables are censored by a subset of the variables $\mathbf{y}_{M_2+1}, \ldots, \mathbf{y}_{M_3}$. That is, the variables $\mathbf{y}_{M_3+1}, \ldots, \mathbf{y}_M$ each are associated with

a specific latent variable and are observable themselves only when its associated latent variable is positive. (Censored structure)

For the model (18.5.1), in the presence of these limited endogenous variables, maximum likelihood methods are conceptually possible but complicated in practice. As an alternative we consider consistent two-stage techniques. Each of these relies on consistent estimation of the reduced form in the first stage. For (18.5.1), under usual completeness assumptions, the reduced form is

$$Y = X\Pi + V \tag{18.5.2}$$

where $\Pi = -B\Gamma^{-1}$ and $V = -\mathbf{E}\Gamma^{-1}$. The reduced form equations for specific endogenous variables can be written as

$$\mathbf{y}_i = X\boldsymbol{\pi}_i + \mathbf{v}_i \tag{18.5.3}$$

The parameters $\boldsymbol{\pi}_i$ can be estimated consistently using probit, tobit, and so on, depending upon the specific form of $\mathbf{y}_i$.

In the second stage the structural parameters are estimated. Let the ith structural equation be

$$\mathbf{y}_i = Y_i\boldsymbol{\gamma}_i + X_i\boldsymbol{\beta}_i + \mathbf{e}_i \tag{18.5.4}$$

and partition the reduced form (18.5.2) as

$$[\mathbf{y}_i \quad Y_i \quad Y_i^*] = X[\boldsymbol{\pi}_i \quad \Pi_i \quad \Pi_i^*] + [\mathbf{v}_i \quad V_i \quad V_i^*] \tag{18.5.5}$$

where the partitions correspond to the LHS endogenous variable ($\mathbf{y}_i$), the RHS endogenous variables (Y_i), and the excluded endogenous variables (Y_i^*) in the ith equation. Note that $Y_i = X\Pi_i + V_i$. Substituting for Y_i in (18.5.4), we obtain

$$\begin{aligned} \mathbf{y}_i &= (X\Pi_i + V_i)\boldsymbol{\gamma}_i + X_i\boldsymbol{\beta}_i + \mathbf{e}_i \\ &= X\Pi_i\boldsymbol{\gamma}_i + X_i\boldsymbol{\beta}_i + V_i\boldsymbol{\gamma}_i + \mathbf{e}_i \\ &= X\Pi_i\boldsymbol{\gamma}_i + X_i\boldsymbol{\beta}_i + \mathbf{v}_i \end{aligned} \tag{18.5.6}$$

where the relation $\mathbf{v}_i = V_i\boldsymbol{\gamma}_i + \mathbf{e}_i$ was used, since $V\boldsymbol{\Gamma}_i = -\mathbf{E}\Gamma^{-1}\boldsymbol{\Gamma}_i = -\mathbf{e}_i$ and $V\boldsymbol{\Gamma}_i = -\mathbf{v}_i + V_i\boldsymbol{\gamma}_i$. If $X\hat{\Pi}_i\boldsymbol{\gamma}_i$ is added to and subtracted from (18.5.6), we obtain

$$\begin{aligned} \mathbf{y}_i &= X\hat{\Pi}_i\boldsymbol{\gamma}_i + X_i\boldsymbol{\beta}_i + X(\Pi_i - \hat{\Pi}_i)\boldsymbol{\gamma}_i + \mathbf{v}_i \\ &= X\hat{\Pi}_i\boldsymbol{\gamma}_i + X_i\boldsymbol{\beta}_i + \boldsymbol{\omega}_i \end{aligned} \tag{18.5.7}$$

The second stage of estimation consists of estimating (18.5.7) by probit, tobit, and so on, depending on the nature of $\mathbf{y}_i$.

Instead of estimating (18.5.7), Amemiya suggests that structural parameters be solved for in terms of reduced form parameters by regression methods. Specifically, let $X_i = XJ_i$, where J_i is an appropriately constructed matrix of ones and zeroes. Then (18.5.6) can be written

$$\begin{aligned}\mathbf{y}_i &= X\Pi_i\boldsymbol{\gamma}_i + XJ_i\boldsymbol{\beta}_i + \mathbf{v}_i \\ &= X(\Pi_i\boldsymbol{\gamma}_i + J_i\boldsymbol{\beta}_i) + \mathbf{v}_i \qquad (18.5.8)\end{aligned}$$

Comparing (18.5.8) to (18.5.3) it is clear that

$$\boldsymbol{\pi}_i = \Pi_i\boldsymbol{\gamma}_i + J_i\boldsymbol{\beta}_i$$

Amemiya suggests estimating $\boldsymbol{\gamma}_i$ and $\boldsymbol{\beta}_i$ by OLS or GLS from

$$\begin{aligned}\hat{\boldsymbol{\pi}}_i &= \hat{\Pi}_i\boldsymbol{\gamma}_i + J_i\boldsymbol{\beta}_i + (\hat{\boldsymbol{\pi}}_i - \boldsymbol{\pi}_i) - (\hat{\Pi}_i - \Pi_i)\boldsymbol{\gamma}_i \\ &= \hat{\Pi}_i\boldsymbol{\gamma}_i + J_i\boldsymbol{\beta}_i + \mathbf{u}_i \qquad (18.5.9)\end{aligned}$$

Under general conditions these estimation methods give parameter estimates that are consistent and asymptotically normal. Extending the work of Amemiya (1978b, 1979), Lee (1981) shows that the GLS estimates from (18.5.9) are asymptotically more efficient than the corresponding two-stage estimator when (i) the LHS variable is latent, but with an observable indicator variable, giving rise to a probit structure, (ii) the LHS variable is an observable continuous variable, (iii) the LHS variable is censored, and (iv) when the LHS variable is limited, giving rise to the Tobit structure. In each of these cases Lee provides the asymptotic covariance matrices of the two-stage estimators and those from Amemiya's principle.

18.5.2 Alternative Specifications of Simultaneous Equations Models with Limited Endogenous Variables

In order to make some interpretive comments consider the following two equation model:

$$\mathbf{y}_1 = \mathbf{y}_2^*\gamma_1 + X_1\boldsymbol{\beta}_1 + \mathbf{e}_1 \qquad (18.5.10a)$$

$$\mathbf{y}_2^* = \mathbf{y}_1\gamma_2 + X_2\boldsymbol{\beta}_2 + \mathbf{e}_2 \qquad (18.5.10b)$$

where $\mathbf{y}_1$ is an observable continuous endogenous variable and $\mathbf{y}_2^*$ is an unobservable latent variable. Corresponding to $\mathbf{y}_2^*$ we may observe a binary indicator variable (probit) or positive values of $\mathbf{y}_2^*$ (tobit). Whatever is observed, a key feature of this system is that $\mathbf{y}_1$ and $\mathbf{y}_2^*$ have unique reduced form equations.

Note that in this specification the relevant endogenous variables are $\mathbf{y}_1$ and the *unobservable* $\mathbf{y}_2^*$.

On the other hand suppose the relevant structural equation system is

$$\mathbf{y}_1 = \mathbf{y}_2\gamma_1 + X_1\boldsymbol{\beta}_1 + \mathbf{e}_1 \tag{18.5.11a}$$

$$\mathbf{y}_2^* = \mathbf{y}_1\gamma_2 + X_2\boldsymbol{\beta}_2 + \mathbf{e}_2 \tag{18.5.11b}$$

In this case it is the observed, limited variable that appears on the RHS of (18.5.11a), not the continuous, but unobservable, latent variable $\mathbf{y}_2^*$ as in (18.5.10). Thus the difference between these two models is whether $\mathbf{y}_2$ or $\mathbf{y}_2^*$ should appear on the RHS of Equation 18.5.11a. The answer should certainly depend on the economic interpretation in any particular application. There is a considerable difference in the estimation procedure for the two models. The reason for the difference is that the system (18.5.11) does not have a single set of reduced form equations and certain conditions must be imposed on the parameters in order for the model to be internally consistent. See Schmidt (1981) for a discussion of the restrictions that are imposed on the parameters of (18.5.11) and for the restrictions that arise in other forms of the model. Sickles and Schmidt (1978) discuss the estimation of (18.5.11). Also see Heckman (1978) for a model in which both the latent variable and its observable counterpart appear in the equation. This permits an endogenous structural shift to occur. Lee (1981) notes that Amemiya's principle can be applied to obtain more efficient parameter estimates than the two stage procedure suggested by Heckman. A generalization of Heckman's model is provided by Lee (1978, 1979). His model is a switching simultaneous equations model that uses sample separation information. All structural parameters are allowed to vary depending on the value of the latent variable. Lee (1981) provides two estimators that are more efficient than those based on Amemiya's principle in this case. See Lee, et al. (1980) for derivation of the asymptotic covariance matrices of two-stage probit and tobit estimators.

18.6 SUMMARY

In this chapter we have considered models where the dependent variable is not a continuously observable variable. These models fall into two primary categories: those where the dependent variable is qualitative, and takes values (usually) reflecting choices made by an economic unit, and those where the dependent variable is continuous, but not completely observable for one reason or another. As the literature survey in this chapter should indicate, there is substantial research activity in this area. Much has been discussed here, but certainly not all of it. The reader is referred to the excellent surveys by Amemiya (1981, 1984), Maddala (1983), Manski and McFadden (1981), and Hensher and Johnson (1981).

For an investigator modeling situations in which decision makers choose from a finite set of alternatives, the choice of statistical procedure depends upon the number of repeated observations for each experimental setting and the number of alternatives faced by each decision maker. If decision makers face only two alternatives and enough responses per experimental setting are available to adequately estimate selection probabilities using relative frequencies, then straightforward, generalized least squares versions of the linear probability model, logit, or probit may be used. If a binary choice is to be made and only one or just a few observations for each experimental setting are available, maximum likelihood approaches to the estimation of probit and logit functions are suggested. Procedures are simply special cases of those for multiple-choice situations. There is little theoretical justification for choosing one formulation over the other in most circumstances involving binary choices. The logit model provides a good approximation to the probit model and has computational advantages but both are widely used.

If decision makers face more than two options, whether there are few or many observations for each experimental setting, the choice between generalized logit and probit models becomes more important. The logit model is again computationally more simple, but it is based on assumptions that may be violated if some of the alternatives from which a choice is to be made are close substitutes. The differences between the two models may be summarized by saying that although the probit model is computationally more difficult, it is more flexible and does not suffer from the possible weakness of the logit model just described.

The other type of limited dependent variable model discussed in this chapter is designed for situations when the available sample is incomplete. Incomplete samples may arise in two ways. First, observations on the dependent variable may be unavailable for some sets of known values of independent variables. Such samples are said to be censored. A well-known model dealing with this problem is Tobin's (1958) analysis of consumer durable purchases.

Procedures for dealing with censored samples are provided by Heckman (1976, 1979) and Amemiya (1973). Both provide parameter estimates with good asymptotic properties, but the former is numerically simpler. A second situation in which incomplete samples arise is when neither the dependent nor independent variables are observable for some trials of an experiment so that some observations are not recorded. An example would be a case when only purchasers buying a product are interviewed about their attitude toward it and the nonbuying customers were excluded or not observed. Such samples are said to be truncated. The relatively simple approach suggested by Heckman for censored samples is no longer easy to apply because certain prior information is required that is not likely to be known. The maximum likelihood method proposed for censored samples by Amemiya is still a viable method.

All of these models may be generalized to simultaneous equations where endogenous variables may be discrete or limited. For these models full maximum likelihood estimation appears very burdensome, but computationally feasible two-step estimation procedures exist.

18.7 EXERCISES

18.7.1 General Exercises

Exercise 18.1
Verify the Taylor's series expansion (18.2.24) for the probit model.

Exercise 18.2
Verify (18.2.38)–(18.2.41).

Exercise 18.3
Given the likelihood function (18.3.1) for the multinomial choice model and choice probabilities (18.3.9), derive the explicit expression for the Newton-Raphson iterations.

18.7.2 Individual Monte Carlo Exercises

Exercise 18.4
Using the X_1 matrix defined in Section 2.5.1, let the design matrix for a probit model be $X = (X_1' \, X_1' \, X_1' \, X_1')'$, so that X is (80×3) and let the parameter vector be $\boldsymbol{\beta}' = (0, .6, -.6)$. Then the probability that $y_i = 1$ is

$$P_i = \int_{-\infty}^{\mathbf{x}_i'\boldsymbol{\beta}} \frac{1}{\sqrt{2\pi}} e^{-t^2/2}\, dt$$

Construct five samples of size 80. The values of y_i should be assigned according to the values P_i. One way to do this is to draw a uniform random number u in the [0,1] interval and assign the value $y_i = 1$ if u is in $[0,P_i]$, and let $y_i = 0$ otherwise.

For each of the five samples of size 80 constructed from the probit model, construct maximum likelihood estimates of the probit and logit models.

Exercise 18.5
For each of the five samples, compute and compare the values of the partial derivatives of P_i with respect to each of the explanatory variables, evaluated at the mean.

Exercise 18.6
Construct a 95% confidence interval for β_2 using each of the five samples.

Exercise 18.7
Repeat Exercises 18.4, 18.5, and 18.6, but generate the observations from the logit specification. That is, let

$$P_i = \frac{1}{1 + \exp(-\mathbf{x}_i'\boldsymbol{\beta})}.$$

In order to illustrate the use of limited dependent variable models, consider

$$y_t = \beta_1 + \beta_2 x_{t2} + e_t, \qquad t = 1, \ldots, 80$$

and let $\beta_1 = -15$, $\beta_2 = 1$, and $x_{t2} = t$. Using five sets of random numbers from a $N(0,2)$ population, generate five samples of values on the dependent variable.

Exercise 18.8
Set all the nonpositive values of y to zero in the five samples generated above. Obtain LS estimates of the parameters and compare them to the ML estimates using the censored sample model, Heckman's two-step estimates, and to Amemiya's two-step estimates.

Exercise 18.9
Repeat Exercise 18.8 except discard the complete observation for nonpositive values of y. Compare the LS estimates to the ML estimates and Amemiya's two-step estimates.

18.7.3 Group Monte Carlo Exercises

Exercise 18.10
Consider 30 samples from the probit model as constructed in Exercise 18.4 as repeated observations. Construct EGLS estimates based on the linear probability, probit, and logit models.

Exercise 18.11
Construct 100 samples as in Exercise 18.8 and compare the empirical densities of the alternative estimators of the unknown parameters.

18.8 REFERENCES

Albright, R. L., S. R. Lerman, and C. F. Manski (1977) "Report on the Development of an Estimation Program for the Multinomial Probit Model," prepared for the Federal Highway Administration.

Amemiya, T. (1973) "Regression Analysis When The Dependent Variable Is Truncated Normal," *Econometrica,* 42, 999–1012.

Amemiya, T. (1974) "Multivariate Regression and Simultaneous Equation Models When the Dependent Variables are Truncated Normal," *Econometrica,* 42, 999–1012.

Amemiya, T. (1978a) "On a Two-Step Estimation of a Multivariate Logit Model," *Journal of Econometrics,* 8, 13–22.

Amemiya, T. (1978b) "The Estimation of a Simultaneous Equation Generalized Probit Model," *Econometrica,* 46, 1193–1205.

Amemiya, T. (1979) "The Estimation of a Simultaneous Equation Tobit Model," *International Economic Review,* 20, 169–181.

Amemiya, T. (1981) "Qualitative Response Models: A Survey," *Journal of Economic Literature,* 19, 1483–1536.

Amemiya, T., ed. (1984) "Censored or Truncated Regression Models," *Journal of Econometrics,* 24, 1–222.

Amemiya, T. and F. Nold (1975) "A Modified Logit Model," *Review of Economics and Statistics,* 57, 255–257.

Amemiya, T. and J. Powell (1980) "A Comparison of the Logit Model and Normal Discriminant Analysis When Independent Variables Are Binary," Technical Report No. 320, Institute for Mathematical Studies in the Social Sciences, Encina Hall, Stanford University, Stanford, California.

Arabmazer, A. and P. Schmidt (1981) "Further Evidence on the Robustness of the Tobit Estimator to Heteroscedasticity," *Journal of Econometrics,* 17, 253–258.

Arabmazer, A. and P. Schmidt (1982) "An Investigation of the Robustness of the Tobit Estimator to Nonnormality," *Econometrica,* 50, 1055–1063.

Bera, A., C. Jarque, and L. Lee (1982) "Testing for the Normality Assumption in Limited Dependent Variable Models," mimeo.

Brownstone, D. (1980) "A Joint Discrete/Continuous Choice Model for Consumer Durables," Unpublished Ph.D. Dissertation, Department of Economics, University of California, Berkeley.

Chung, C. and A. Goldberger (1984) "Proportional Projections in Limited Dependent Variable Models," *Econometrica,* 52, 531–534.

Cox, D. (1970) *Analysis of Binary Data,* Methuen, London.

Crawford, D. and R. Pollak (1982) "Order and Inference in Qualitative Response Models," Discussion Paper #82-4, Bureau of Economic Research Rutgers University, New Brunswick, N.J.

Daganzo, C. (1979) *Multinomial Probit,* Academic, New York.

Dhrymes, P. J. (1978) *Introductory Econometrics,* Springer-Verlag, New York.

Duncan, G. (1980) "Formulation and Statistical Analysis of the Mixed, Continuous/Discrete Dependent Variable Model in Classical Production Theory," *Econometrica,* 48, 839–852.

Fair, R. (1977) "A Note on the Computation of the Tobit Estimator," *Econometrica,* 45, 1723–1727.

Fomby, T. and J. Pearce (1982) "Additional Standard Errors of the Multinomial Logit Model," mimeo, Department of Economics, Southern Methodist University, Dallas, TX.

Goldberger, A. S. (1964) *Econometric Theory,* Wiley, New York.

Goldberger, A. (1980) "Abnormal Selection Bias," SSRI Discussion Paper 8006, University of Wisconsin, Madison, WI.

Goldberger, A. (1981) "Linear Regression After Selection," *Journal of Econometrics,* 15, 357–366.

Greene, W. (1981a) "On the Asymptotic Bias of the Ordinary Least Squares Estimator of the Tobit Model," *Econometrica,* 49, 505–513.

Greene, W. (1981b) "Sample Selection Bias as a Specification Error: Comment," *Econometrica,* 49, 795–798.

Greene, W. (1983) "Estimation of Limited Dependent Variable Models by

Ordinary Least Squares and the Method of Moments,'' *Journal of Econometrics,* 21, 195–212.

Hartley, M. J. (1976) ''The Tobit and Probit Models: Maximum Likelihood Estimation by Ordinary Least Squares,'' Discussion Paper Number 374, Department of Economics, State University of New York at Buffalo.

Hauser, J. (1978) ''Testing the Accuracy, Usefulness and Significance of Probabilistic Choice Models: An Information Theoretic Approach,'' *Operations Research,* 26, 406–421.

Hausman, J. A. and D. A. Wise (1978) ''A Conditional Probit Model for Qualitative Choice: Discrete Decisions Recognizing Interdependence and Heterogeneous Preferences,'' *Econometrica,* 46, 403–426.

Heckman, J. (1974) ''Shadow Prices, Market Wages, and Labor Supply,'' *Econometrica,* 42, 679–694.

Heckman, J. (1976) ''The Common Structure of Statistical Models of Truncation, Sample Selection, and Limited Dependent Variables and a Simple Estimator for Such Models,'' *Annals of Economic and Social Measurement,* 5, 475–492.

Heckman, J. (1978) ''Dummy Endogenous Variables in a Simultaneous Equation System,'' *Econometrica,* 46, 931–951.

Heckman, J. (1979) ''Sample Bias as a Specification Error,'' *Econometrica,* 47, 153–162.

Hensher, D. and L. Johnson (1981) *Applied Discrete-Choice Modelling,* Halsted, New York.

Hurd, M. (1979) ''Estimation in Truncated Samples When There is Heteroscedasticity,'' *Journal of Econometrics,* 11, 247–258.

Johnson, N. L. and S. Kotz (1970) *Continuous Univariate Distributions,* Vol. 1, Wiley, New York.

Kendall, M. G. and A. Stuart (1973) *The Advanced Theory of Statistics,* Vol. 2, Hafner, New York.

Landwehr, J. M., D. Pregibon and A. C. Shoemaker (1984) ''Graphical Methods for Assessing Logistic Regression Models,'' *Journal of the American Statistical Association,* 79, 61–83.

Lee, L. (1978) ''Unionism and Wage Rates: A Simultaneous Equation Model with Qualitative and Limited Dependent Variables,'' *International Economic Review,* 19, 415–433.

Lee, L. (1979) ''Identification and Estimation in Binary Choice Models with Limited (Censored) Dependent Variables,'' *Econometrica,* 47, 977–996.

Lee, L. (1981) ''Simultaneous Equations Models With Discrete and Censored Dependent Variables,'' in C. Manski and D. McFadden, eds., *Structural Analysis of Discrete Data with Econometric Applications,* MIT Press, Cambridge, Mass., 346–364.

Lee, L. (1982) ''Specification Error in Multinomial Logit Models: Analysis of Omitted Variable Bias,'' *Journal of Econometrics,* 20, 197–210.

Lee, L. (1983) ''Generalized Econometric Models with Selectivity,'' *Econometrica,* 51, 507–512.

Lee, L., G. Maddala, and R. Trost (1980) ''Asymptotic Covariance Matrices of

Two-Stage Probit and Two-Stage Tobit Models of Simultaneous Equations Models with Selectivity,'' *Econometrica,* 48, 491–503.

Lee, L. and R. Trost (1978) ''Estimation of Some Limited Dependent Variable Models with Applications to Housing Demand,'' *Journal of Econometrics,* 8, 357–382.

Lee, T. C. and G. G. Judge (1972) ''Estimation of Transition Probabilities in a Non-Stationary Finite Markov Chain,'' *Metroeconomica,* 24, 180–201.

Lee, T. C., G. G. Judge, and A. Zellner (1968) ''Maximum Likelihood and Bayesian Estimation of Transition Probabilities, *Journal of the American Statistical Association,* 63, 1162–1179.

Lee, T. C., G. G. Judge, and A. Zellner (1977) *Estimating the Parameters of the Markov Probability Model from Aggregate Time Series Data,* 2nd ed., North-Holland, Amsterdam.

Maddala, G. S. (1983) *Limited Dependent and Qualitative Variables in Econometrics,* Cambridge University Press, London.

Manski, C. F. and D. McFadden, eds. (1981) *Structural Analysis of Discrete Data with Econometric Applications,* MIT Press, Cambridge, Mass.

McDonald, J. and R. Moffitt (1980) ''The Uses of Tobit Analysis,'' *Review of Economics and Statistics,* 62, 318–321.

McFadden, D. (1974) ''Conditional Logit Analysis of Qualitative Choice Behavior,'' in P. Zarembka, ed., *Frontiers in Econometrics,* Academic, New York, 105–142.

McFadden, D. (1976) ''Quantal Choice Analysis: A Survey,'' *Annals of Economic and Social Measurement,* 5, 363–390.

McFadden, D. (1977) ''Quantitative Methods for Analyzing Travel Behavior of Individuals: Some Recent Developments,'' Cowles Foundation Discussion Paper No. 474.

McFadden, D. (1981) ''Econometric Models of Probabilistic Choice,'' in *Structural Analysis of Discrete Data with Econometric Applications,* C. Manski and D. McFadden, eds., MIT Press, Cambridge, Mass., 198–272.

McFadden, D. (1984) ''Econometric Analysis of Qualitative Response Models,'' in *Handbook of Econometrics,* Z. Griliches and M. Intriligator, eds., North-Holland Publishing, Amsterdam.

Nelson, F. (1977) ''Censored Regression Models with Unobserved, Stochastic Censoring Thresholds,'' *Journal of Econometrics,* 6, 309–328.

Nelson, F. (1981) ''A Test for Misspecification in the Censored Normal Model,'' *Econometrica,* 49, 1317–1329.

Nelson, F. (1984) ''Efficiency of the Two-Step Estimator for Models with Endogenous Sample Selection,'' *Journal of Econometrics,* 24, 181–196.

Nelson, F. and L. Olson (1978) ''Specification and Estimation of A Simultaneous Equation Model with Limited Dependent Variables,'' *International Economic Review,* 19, 695–710.

Olsen, R. (1978) ''A Note on the Uniqueness of the Maximum Likelihood Estimator for the Tobit Model,'' *Econometrica,* 46, 1211–1215.

Olsen, R. (1980) ''A Least Squares Correction for Selectivity Bias,'' *Econometrica,* 48, 1815–1820.

Olsen, R. (1982) "Distributional Tests for Selectivity Bias and a More Robust Likelihood Estimator," *International Economic Review,* 23, 223–240.

Paarsch, H. J. (1984) "A Monte Carlo Comparison of Estimators for Censored Regression Models," *Journal of Econometrics,* 24, 197–214.

Parks, R. (1980) "On the Estimation of Multinomial Logit Models From Relative Frequency Data," *Journal of Econometrics,* 13, 293–303.

Powell, J. (1981) "Least Absolute Deviations Estimation for Censored and Truncated Regression Models," Technical Report No. 356, The Economics Series, Institute for Mathematical Studies in the Social Sciences, Stanford University, Stanford, California.

Pratt, J. (1981) "Concavity of the Log Likelihood," *Journal of the American Statistical Association,* 76, 103–106.

Pregibon, D. (1981) "Logistic Regression-Diagnostics," *Annals of Statistics,* 9, 705--724.

Press, S. and S. Wilson (1978) "Choosing Between Logistic Regression and Discriminant Analysis," *Journal of the American Statistical Association,* 23, 699–705.

Robinson, P. (1982) "On the Asymptotic Properties of Estimators of Models Containing Limited Dependent Variables," *Econometrica,* 50, 27–41.

Ruud, P. (1983) "Sufficient Conditions for the Consistency of Maximum Likelihood Estimation Despite Misspecification of Distribution in Multinomial Discrete Choice Models," *Econometrica,* 51, 225–228.

Schmidt, P. (1980) "Constraints on the Parameters in Simultaneous Tobit and Probit Models," in *Structural Analysis of Discrete Data with Econometric Applications,* C. Manski and D. McFadden, eds., MIT Press, Cambridge, Mass.

Schmidt, P. and R. Strauss (1975) "The Prediction of Occupation Using Multiple Logit Models," *International Economic Review,* 16, 471–486.

Sickles, R. and P. Schmidt (1978) "Simultaneous Equations Models with Truncated Dependent Variables: A Simultaneous Tobit Model," *Journal of Economics and Business,* 31, 11–21.

Smith, V. and C. Cicchetti (1975) "Regression Analysis with Dichotomous Dependent Variables," paper presented at the Third World Congress of the Econometric Society, Toronto, Canada.

Stapleton, D. and D. Young (1981) "Censored Normal Regression with Measurement Error in the Dependent Variable," Discussion Paper No. 81-30, Department of Economics, University of British Columbia.

Theil, H. (1967) *Economics and Information Theory,* Rand McNally, Chicago, and North-Holland, Amsterdam.

Theil, H. (1970) "On the Estimation of Relationships Involving Qualitative Variables," *American Journal of Sociology,* 76, 103–154.

Theil, H. (1971) *Principles of Econometrics,* Wiley, New York.

Tobin, J. (1958) "Estimation of Relationships for Limited Dependent Variables," *Econometrica,* 26, 24–36.

Wales, T. and A. Woodland (1980) "Sample Selectivity and Estimation of Labor Supply Functions," *International Economic Review,* 21, 437–468.

Wolfe, P. (1959) "The Simple Simplex Method of Quadratic Programming," *Econometrica,* 27, 382–398.

Zellner, A. (1983) "Bayesian Analysis of a Simple Multinomial Logit Model," *Economics Letters,* 11, 133–136.

Zellner, A. and P. Rossi (1982) "Bayesian Analysis of Dichotomous Quantal Response Models," H. G. B. Alexander Research Foundation Paper, Graduate School of Business, University of Chicago.

Zellner, A. and T. H. Lee (1965) "Joint Estimation of Relationships Involving Discrete Random Variables," *Econometrica,* 33, 382–394.

Chapter 19

Varying and Random Coefficient Models

19.1 INTRODUCTION

Throughout this book we discuss problems that economists and other nonexperimental scientists face as a result of their use of data that has not been generated by controlled experiments. In this chapter we consider another aspect of this problem—namely, the assumption of fixed or constant parameters. Those who work with classical linear models usually assume that the economic structure generating the sample observations remains constant. That is, there exists not only a single parameter vector relating the dependent and independent variables, but also a constant set of error process parameters and a single functional form. Unfortunately, the microparameter systems along with their aggregate counterparts for economic processes and institutions are not constant, and given that our data are generated by uncontrolled and often unobservable experiments, it is frequently argued that the traditional assumption of fixed coefficients is a poor one.

For example, when using cross-sectional data on micro-units, such as firms or households, it is unlikely that the response to a change in an explanatory variable will be the same for all micro-units. Similarly, when using time series data, it is often difficult to explicitly model a changing economic environment and, in these circumstances, the response coefficients are likely to change over time. These considerations have led to the development of a number of stochastic or variable parameter models.

Varying parameter models can be classified into three types. First, the parameters can vary across subsets of observations within the sample but be nonstochastic. Examples of such models are discussed in Sections 19.2 and 19.3 and include a general systematically varying parameter model, seasonality models, and a variety of "switching regression" models where the sample observations are generated by two (or more) distinct regimes.

A second class of models is where the parameters are stochastic, and can be thought of as being generated by a stationary stochastic process. We have seen examples of such models in Chapter 13 where the Swamy and Hsiao random coefficient models were used to combine time series and cross-sectional data. In Sections 19.4 and 19.5 two more models of this type are presented, the Hildreth–Houck random coefficient model and its generalization, the return to normality model.

TABLE 19.1 *VARYING AND RANDOM COEFFICIENT MODELS*

Varying but nonstochastic parameters	A general systematically varying parameter model (Section 19.2)
	Switching regression models (Section 19.3)
Random parameters from a stationary process	Hildreth–Houck model (Section 19.4)
	Return to normality model (Section 19.5)
Random parameters from a nonstationary process	Cooley–Prescott model (Section 19.6)

Finally, the third class of models consists of those where the stochastic parameters are generated by a process that is not stationary. The Cooley–Prescott model is of this type and is presented in Section 19.6. A visual overview of the chapter is provided in Table 19.1.

19.2 A MODEL OF SYSTEMATICALLY VARYING PARAMETERS

Consider the general linear model

$$y_{it} = \mathbf{x}_{it}'\boldsymbol{\beta}_{it} + e_{it}, \qquad i = 1, \ldots, N; t = 1, \ldots, T \tag{19.2.1}$$

where y_{it} is the ith cross-sectional observation on the dependent variable in the tth time period; $\mathbf{x}_{it}$ is a $(K \times 1)$ nonstochastic vector of observations on explanatory variables, $\boldsymbol{\beta}_{it}$ is a $(K \times 1)$ coefficient vector, possibly unique to the ith cross section and tth time period, and the e_{it} are normally and independently distributed random disturbances with zero means and variances σ^2. This formulation of the linear regression model allows the response coefficient for the explanatory variables to differ for each cross-sectional unit and each time period. The difficulty with this model is that there are $KNT + 1$ parameters to be estimated with only NT observations. Additional information must be introduced that places some structure on how the coefficients vary across observations if reasonable estimation procedures are to be developed.

Following Belsley (1973a), let the nonsample information be

$$\boldsymbol{\beta}_{it} = Z_{it}\boldsymbol{\gamma} \tag{19.2.2}$$

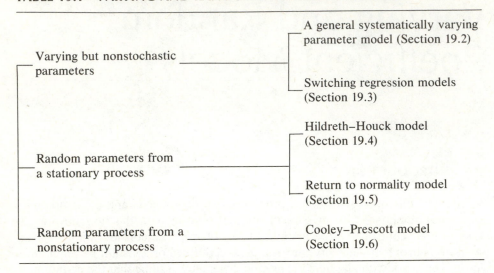

where Z_{it} is a $(K \times M)$ matrix of variables that "explain" the variation in the $\boldsymbol{\beta}_{it}$ across observations and $\boldsymbol{\gamma}$ is an $(M \times 1)$ vector of associated coefficients.

It is unlikely that each element of $\boldsymbol{\beta}_{it}$ will be the same linear function of a set of explanatory variables. Equation 19.2.2 is sufficiently general to cover such circumstances if, in Z_{it}, zeros are included in the appropriate places. In general, the matrix of explanatory variables Z_{it} may contain (1) functions of variables already included in $\mathbf{x}_{it}$, implying that (19.2.1) is not linear in the original explanatory variables; (2) functions of other variables that do not appear in $\mathbf{x}_{it}$; or (3) qualitative variables that may be stochastic or nonstochastic, implying the existence of separate regression regimes. With these alternative specifications for Z_{it} the model in (19.2.1) and (19.2.2) includes a number of special models that have appeared in the literature. The following sections identify some of these models and discuss the consequences of their adoption.

Estimation of the model (19.2.1)–(19.2.2) is carried out straightforwardly. Equation 19.2.2 is combined with (19.2.1) to produce

$$y_{it} = \mathbf{x}_{it}'Z_{it}\boldsymbol{\gamma} + e_{it} = \mathbf{w}_{it}'\boldsymbol{\gamma} + e_{it} \tag{19.2.3}$$

where $\mathbf{w}_{it}' = \mathbf{x}_{it}'Z_{it}$ is a $(1 \times M)$ vector of observations on interaction variables. Under the assumptions we have made about e_{it}, the best linear unbiased estimator of $\boldsymbol{\gamma}$, and thus $\boldsymbol{\beta}_{it}$, is the least squares estimator. Thus, when Z_{it} is known and nonstochastic, no real difficulties are encountered. On the other hand, if Z_{it} is not known with certainty, we face exactly those difficulties that exist when there is uncertainty about the correct set of regressors (Chapter 21). Belsley (1973b) presents a traditional test procedure for comparing alternative Z_{it} matrices. Unfortunately, the consequences of preliminary test procedures here are exactly those discussed in Chapter 3—namely, that the pretest estimator of $\boldsymbol{\gamma}$ is inferior to the least squares estimator under a variety of loss functions and over large portions of the parameter space. Black (1982) discussed the interpretation of the parameters.

It is possible to make (19.2.2) stochastic of course by adding a $(K \times 1)$ random disturbance vector, say $\mathbf{v}_{it}$. The resulting model is $y_{it} = \mathbf{w}_{it}'\boldsymbol{\gamma} + u_{it}$, where $u_{it} = \mathbf{x}_{it}'\mathbf{v}_{it} + e_{it}$ is heteroscedastic. This is a special case of the model presented by Hsiao (1975) and is discussed in Chapter 13. When $T = 1$, so that only cross-sectional observations are available, the procedures discussed in Section 19.4 for the Hildreth–Houck model can be applied to construct EGLS estimates. Singh et al. (1976) consider the special case when $N = 1$, so only time series observations are available. In their model Z_{it} contains functions of calendar time and the $\mathbf{v}_t$ is normal with mean zero and diagonal covariance matrix. The justification for using calendar time to "explain" the variation in $\boldsymbol{\beta}_t$ is the same as that used when time-trend variables are included in regression models. These variables act as surrogates for all the unknown time-related dynamic forces within the economy. The usefulness of this model then depends upon the acceptability of that substitution. The estimation problem is exactly the same as above. Singh et al. (1976) develop both a modified Hildreth–Houck estimator and the maximum likelihood estimator for this reformulated statistical model.

19.3 SWITCHING REGRESSIONS

The models in Section 19.2 allow response coefficients to be different for each observation. Often this completely general formulation can be usefully modified to allow the regression coefficients to be constant within subsets or partitions of the observations, but to be different across partitions. These models may be thought of as situations where the Z_{it} matrix in (19.2.2) contains qualitative variables that "sort out" observations into different partitions. Examples include models with dummy variables, seasonality models, and the piecewise regression models such as those developed by Hinkley (1971); McGee and Carlton (1970); Gallant and Fuller (1973); Poirier (1973, 1976); Quandt (1958); and Goldfeld and Quandt (1973a, 1973b). Analysis of these models re-emphasizes the close relationship between the "varying parameter" and "pooling" models.

19.3.1 Seasonality Models

Many important economic variables such as output, consumption, and employment, which are reported on a weekly, monthly, or quarterly basis, exhibit seasonal patterns. Some of these series, have been deseasonalized by using a moving-average process. Unfortunately, seasonally adjusted data contain little or no information about seasonal variation in the parameters and, as Wallis (1974) and Sims (1974) note, the use of seasonally adjusted data in dynamic statistical models such as distributed lag models, can have serious statistical consequences. This important aspect of using deseasonalized data is discussed in Chapter 10. Also see Havenner and Swamy (1981) for a random coefficient approach to seasonal adjustment. In this section we consider economic variables that contain seasonal patterns or components and consider how to identify and estimate seasonal variation in the parameters in the intertemporal relationships. Those interested in procedures for deseasonalizing data are referred to a recent volume by Zellner (1979).

If the seasonal data pattern is exogenously determined and the process is a stable one, then the Zellner seemingly unrelated regression specification outlined in Chapter 12 provides a convenient framework for estimating and statistically evaluating the significance of the seasonal variation in the intercept and/or variable treatment parameters. For example, with data exhibiting quarterly seasonality, if the seasonal effect is reflected in the parameters of both the intercept and treatment variables, the quarterly set of equations

$$\mathbf{y}_1 = X_1\boldsymbol{\beta}_1 + \mathbf{e}_1 \tag{19.3.1a}$$

$$\mathbf{y}_2 = X_2\boldsymbol{\beta}_2 + \mathbf{e}_2 \tag{19.3.1b}$$

$$\mathbf{y}_3 = X_3\boldsymbol{\beta}_3 + \mathbf{e}_3 \tag{19.3.1c}$$

$$\mathbf{y}_4 = X_4\boldsymbol{\beta}_4 + \mathbf{e}_4 \tag{19.3.1d}$$

may be rewritten in single equation form as

$$\begin{bmatrix} \mathbf{y}_1 \\ \mathbf{y}_2 \\ \mathbf{y}_3 \\ \mathbf{y}_4 \end{bmatrix} = \begin{bmatrix} X_1 & & & \\ & X_2 & & \\ & & X_3 & \\ & & & X_4 \end{bmatrix} \begin{bmatrix} \boldsymbol{\beta}_1 \\ \boldsymbol{\beta}_2 \\ \boldsymbol{\beta}_3 \\ \boldsymbol{\beta}_4 \end{bmatrix} + \begin{bmatrix} \mathbf{e}_1 \\ \mathbf{e}_2 \\ \mathbf{e}_3 \\ \mathbf{e}_4 \end{bmatrix} \tag{19.3.2}$$

or more compactly as

$$\mathbf{y} = Z\boldsymbol{\gamma} + \boldsymbol{\omega} \tag{19.3.3}$$

If $\boldsymbol{\omega} \sim N(\mathbf{0},\sigma^2 I)$, the least squares rule would be applied to estimate the parameters of the quarterly equations, and the general hypothesis

$$R\boldsymbol{\gamma} = \begin{bmatrix} I_1 & -I_2 & 0 & 0 \\ 0 & I_2 & -I_3 & 0 \\ 0 & 0 & I_3 & -I_4 \end{bmatrix} \begin{bmatrix} \boldsymbol{\beta}_1 \\ \boldsymbol{\beta}_2 \\ \boldsymbol{\beta}_3 \\ \boldsymbol{\beta}_4 \end{bmatrix} = \begin{bmatrix} \mathbf{0} \\ \mathbf{0} \\ \mathbf{0} \end{bmatrix} \tag{19.3.4}$$

could be used to test the statistical significance of the seasonal effects on all or some combination of the parameters. In (19.3.3), if the quarterly equations are error related and $\boldsymbol{\omega} \sim N(\mathbf{0},\boldsymbol{\Phi})$, where $\boldsymbol{\Phi}$ is some positive definite, symmetric matrix, the coefficient vector $\boldsymbol{\gamma}$ may be efficiently estimated by using the Aitken generalized least squares rule, where the covariance $\boldsymbol{\Phi}$ is estimated. See Chapter 12. In this case the standard Zellner type of aggregation tests could be applied to the quarterly parameters.

If the parameters of the treatment variables do not have a seasonal pattern and the seasonal effect is only exhibited in the intercept parameter for each of the quarterly equations, (19.3.3) may be reformulated as

$$\begin{bmatrix} \mathbf{y}_1 \\ \mathbf{y}_2 \\ \mathbf{y}_3 \\ \mathbf{y}_4 \end{bmatrix} = \begin{bmatrix} \mathbf{x}_{11} & X_{12} & & & \\ & X_{22} & \mathbf{x}_{21} & & \\ & X_{32} & & \mathbf{x}_{31} & \\ & X_{42} & & & \mathbf{x}_{41} \end{bmatrix} \begin{bmatrix} \beta_{11} \\ \boldsymbol{\beta}_2 \\ \beta_{21} \\ \beta_{31} \\ \beta_{41} \end{bmatrix} + \begin{bmatrix} \mathbf{e}_1 \\ \mathbf{e}_2 \\ \mathbf{e}_3 \\ \mathbf{e}_4 \end{bmatrix} \tag{19.3.5}$$

where $\boldsymbol{\beta}_2$ is a $(K-1)$-dimensional parameter vector and β_{11}, β_{21}, β_{31}, and β_{41} are parameters for the quarterly equations corresponding to the intercept variables $\mathbf{x}_{11}$, $\mathbf{x}_{21}$, $\mathbf{x}_{31}$, and $\mathbf{x}_{41}$. Seasonal intercept parameter variability could be tested by using an appropriate variation of the general linear hypothesis given in (19.3.4).

Alternatively, as Kmenta (1971, pp. 422–443) and Johnston (1984, pp. 234–239) suggest, the variable seasonal parameter problem could be equivalently formulated by using zero-one dummy variables to indicate the parameter variability alternatives. However, the seemingly unrelated format of (19.3.3) appears more straightforward in terms of estimation and inference. When the dummy variable format is used, additional calculations are required to obtain estimates of the original coefficients and their standard errors.

When the seasonal variation is determined by identifiable economic and noneconomic factors, the models in Section 19.2 can be applied directly.

19.3.2 Piecewise Regression Models: Known Join Point

Models that use dummy variables imply the presence of identifiable parameter "regimes" that hold for partitions of the entire sample. Although dummy variable models are easily extended to situations where both time series and cross-sectional data are available, we will, for expository purposes and without loss of generality, consider only time series models. This corresponds to setting $N = 1$ in (19.2.1). Only two partitions will be considered because extension to a greater number of partitions follows directly. If the observations for which the different parameter regimes hold are readily identifiable, then the total of T observations may be split into two groups of T_1 and T_2 observations, where $T_1 + T_2 = T$. These groupings do not necessarily have to contain observations that are sequential in time; thus this formulation is a generalization of the model in Section 19.3.1. Let us write the two regimes as

$$y_t = \begin{cases} \mathbf{x}_t'\boldsymbol{\beta}_1 + e_{1t} & \text{if } t \in \{T_1\} \\ \mathbf{x}_t'\boldsymbol{\beta}_2 + e_{2t} & \text{if } t \in \{T_2\} \end{cases} \tag{19.3.6}$$

or in convenient matrix notation

$$\begin{bmatrix} \mathbf{y}_1 \\ \mathbf{y}_2 \end{bmatrix} = \begin{bmatrix} X_1 & 0 \\ 0 & X_2 \end{bmatrix} \begin{bmatrix} \boldsymbol{\beta}_1 \\ \boldsymbol{\beta}_2 \end{bmatrix} + \begin{bmatrix} \mathbf{e}_1 \\ \mathbf{e}_2 \end{bmatrix} \tag{19.3.7}$$

If some of the coefficients are not expected to change, restrictions may be imposed across the sample partitions that guarantee the equality of the corresponding elements of $\boldsymbol{\beta}_1$ and $\boldsymbol{\beta}_2$.

The model formulated in (19.3.7) separates the linear regression model into as many pieces as there are regimes, and these pieces are not necessarily joined. If the observations in T_1 and T_2 are sequential in time and if the regressions for the two regimes are assumed to join at the point $t_0 \in [1,T]$, the statistical model (19.3.7) would be estimated subject to the condition that

$$E[y_{t_0}] = \mathbf{x}_{t_0}'\boldsymbol{\beta}_1 = \mathbf{x}_{t_0}'\boldsymbol{\beta}_2 \tag{19.3.8}$$

or

$$\mathbf{x}_{t_0}'(\boldsymbol{\beta}_1 - \boldsymbol{\beta}_2) = 0 \tag{19.3.9}$$

The imposition of these parameter restrictions implies that the two regression functions will join at the point t_0.

Poirier (1973, 1976) has considered a piecewise regression function called a cubic spline function, whose pieces join more smoothly than in the model considered above. Cubic splines have been used extensively by physical scientists as approximating functions. In reality cubic splines are cubic polynomials in a single independent variable, which are joined together smoothly at known points. The smoothness restrictions are such that at the point where the cubic polynomials meet, their first and second derivatives are also equal; thus the transition from one regime to another does not occur abruptly. In particular, let the regression function be

$$y_t = g_1(t)I_{[1,t_0]}(t) + g_2(t)I_{[t_0,T]}(t) + e_t \tag{19.3.10}$$

where $I(\cdot)$ are indicator functions that take the value one if the argument is in the stated interval and zero otherwise. The $g_i(t)$, $i = 1,2$, are cubic polynomials of the form

$$g_i(t) = a_i t^3 + b_i t^2 + c_i t + d_i$$

In the cubic spline literature the point t_0, where the two cubic functions meet, is referred to as the "knot" point. The functions $g_i(t)$ obey the following smoothness (derivative) restrictions:

$$g_1(t_0) = g_2(t_0),\ g_1'(t_0) = g_2'(t_0),\ g_1''(t_0) = g_2''(t_0) \tag{19.3.11}$$

This information, which can be written in terms of linear equality restrictions on the coefficients of the cubic polynomials, has been shown by Buse and Lim (1977) to be equivalent to the formulation originally presented by Poirier (1973). This means, of course, that the restricted least squares estimator may be used to estimate the unknown coefficients.

One difficulty with the use of cubic splines is that although these functions are very flexible approximating functions, the form of the implied structural change is very restrictive. Although the fitted curve may approximate the available data well, the straightforward application of this technique offers little chance for investigating the nature of the structural change.

19.3.3 Piecewise Regression Models: Unknown Join Point

The models above have presumed that the point(s) of structural change were known. If this is not the case, then the unknown point(s) where the regimes switch, become unknowns and thus are parameters to be estimated. This problem has been surveyed by Goldfeld and Quandt (1973b). Given the model in (19.3.6), they assume $e_{1t} \sim N(0,\sigma_1^2)$ and $e_{2t} \sim N(0,\sigma_2^2)$ and in general that $(\boldsymbol{\beta}_1,\sigma_1^2) \neq (\boldsymbol{\beta}_2,\sigma_2^2)$. The choice between the two regimes is then assumed either deterministic, where some observed variable is compared to some unknown threshold, or stochastic and dependent upon unknown probabilities.

19.3.3a Deterministic Switching on the Basis of Time

First, consider the deterministic case where the switch occurs on the basis of a time index. Specifically, assume that the first regime in (19.3.6) holds if $t \leq t_0$ and the second if $t > t_0$. The likelihood function, conditional on t_0, is

$$\ell(\beta_1, \beta_2, \sigma_1^2, \sigma_2^2 | t_0) = (2\pi)^{-T/2}\sigma_1^{-t_0}\sigma_2^{-(T-t_0)}$$
$$\times \exp\left\{-\frac{1}{2\sigma_1^2}\sum_{t=1}^{t_0}(y_t - \mathbf{x}_t'\boldsymbol{\beta}_1)^2 - \frac{1}{2\sigma_2^2}\sum_{t=t_0+1}^{T}(y_t - \mathbf{x}_t'\boldsymbol{\beta}_2)^2\right\} \tag{19.3.12}$$

The estimate of t_0 chosen is the value that maximizes the likelihood function. A likelihood ratio test for the hypothesis of no switching can then be carried out by comparing the value of the likelihood function (19.3.12) to that for a single regression over the entire sample. Again this search process has pretest estimator sampling consequences.

A detection procedure similar in spirit has been suggested by Brown, Durbin, and Evans (1975). They investigate the constancy of regression relations over time by considering functions of recursive residuals generated by moving regressions. Comparison of the standardized sum and standardized sum of squares of these residuals to approximate confidence bounds provide evidence of regression stability or instability and approximately where any structural change may have taken place.

An alternative test for shifts in slope parameters where the shift point is unknown has been suggested by Farley and Hinich (1970) and Farley, Hinich, and McGuire (1975). They approximate a discrete shift in the slope at an unknown point by a continuous linear shift using the model

$$y_t = \mathbf{x}_t'\boldsymbol{\beta}_t + e_t$$

where

$$\boldsymbol{\beta}_t = \boldsymbol{\beta} + t\boldsymbol{\delta}$$

This means the full model can be written as

$$y_t = \mathbf{x}_t'\boldsymbol{\beta} + t\mathbf{x}_t'\boldsymbol{\delta} + e_t \tag{19.3.13}$$

The test for constant slopes is then the usual likelihood ratio test of the hypothesis that $\boldsymbol{\delta} = \mathbf{0}$. Farley et al. (1975) provide Monte Carlo evidence that their test is robust with respect to gradual parameter shifts in one or more parameters. They also note, however, that unless the sample is large or the shift great, tests for model instability are not very powerful. Furthermore, the properties of any estimators produced after this preliminary test are not discussed and thus are presumably unknown.

The Bayesian approach can offer useful insights into the switching regression problem. See, for example, Chin Choy and Broemeling (1980), Ferreira (1975), Smith and Cook (1980), Tsurumi (1982), Booth and Smith (1982), Holbert (1982), Hsu (1982), and Ohtani (1982).

19.3.3b Deterministic Switching on the Basis of Other Variables

The procedures suggested above can be directly applied to cases where a single variable determines the switching process. If there is no autocorrelation present in the disturbance term nor any distributed lag variables, we simply reorder the observations according to increasing magnitudes of the variable that controls the switching process.

Goldfeld and Quandt (1973b) offer a more general formulation. They assume that there exist variables with observations $z_{1t}, \ldots, z_{mt}$, $t = 1, \ldots, T$ such that nature selects regimes according to whether $\mathbf{z}_t'\boldsymbol{\gamma} \le 0$, or $\mathbf{z}_t'\boldsymbol{\gamma} > 0$, where $\boldsymbol{\gamma}$ is an unknown coefficient vector. By letting $D_t = 0$ if $\mathbf{z}_t'\boldsymbol{\gamma} \le 0$ and $D_t = 1$ otherwise, the two regimes in (19.3.6) can be combined as

$$y_t = \mathbf{x}_t'[(1 - D_t)\boldsymbol{\beta}_1 + D_t\boldsymbol{\beta}_2] + (1 - D_t)e_{1t} + D_t e_{2t} \tag{19.3.14}$$

where $\boldsymbol{\beta}_1$, $\boldsymbol{\beta}_2$, σ_1^2, σ_2^2 and the D_t's must be estimated. To make the problem tractable, the D_t's may be approximated by a continuous function. One possible approximation is to use the probit function

$$D_t = \int_{-\infty}^{\mathbf{z}_t'\boldsymbol{\gamma}} \frac{1}{\sqrt{2\pi\sigma^2}} \exp\left(-\frac{u^2}{2\sigma^2}\right) du$$

with log likelihood function

$$\begin{aligned} L = &-\frac{T}{2}\ln 2\pi - \frac{1}{2}\sum_{1}^{T} \ln[\sigma_1^2(1 - D_t)^2 + \sigma_2^2 D_t^2] \\ &- \frac{1}{2}\sum_{1}^{T} \frac{\{y_t - \mathbf{x}_t'[\boldsymbol{\beta}_1(1 - D_t) + \boldsymbol{\beta}_2 D_t]\}^2}{\sigma_1^2(1 - D_t)^2 + \sigma_2^2 D_t^2} \end{aligned} \tag{19.3.15}$$

Upon replacing D_t by its approximating function, the log likelihood can be maximized with respect to $\boldsymbol{\beta}_1$, $\boldsymbol{\beta}_2$, $\boldsymbol{\gamma}$, σ_1^2 and σ_2^2. If the sample discrimination is not perfect so that $\hat{D}_t$ is not exactly one or zero, then Goldfeld and Quandt (1973b) suggest that one solution is to create two subsamples on the basis of whether $\mathbf{z}_t'\hat{\boldsymbol{\gamma}}$ is ≤ 0 or $\mathbf{z}_t'\hat{\boldsymbol{\gamma}} > 0$. Separate regressions are then estimated for each sample. A likelihood ratio test for the null hypothesis of no separate regimes can be carried out. Again the sampling properties of the outcome generated by using this rule are unknown.

19.3.3c Stochastic Choice of Regimes

A nondeterministic alternative is to assume that nature chooses between the first and second regimes on the basis of unknown probabilities λ and $1 - \lambda$. The density of y_t is

$$g(y_t|\mathbf{x}_t) = \lambda f_1(y_t|\mathbf{x}_t) + (1 - \lambda)f_2(y_t|\mathbf{x}_t)$$
$$= \frac{\lambda}{\sqrt{2\pi}\sigma_1} \exp\left(-\frac{1}{2}\frac{(y_t - \mathbf{x}_t'\boldsymbol{\beta}_1)^2}{\sigma_1^2}\right) + \frac{1 - \lambda}{\sqrt{2\pi}\sigma_2} \exp\left(-\frac{1}{2}\frac{(y_t - \mathbf{x}_t'\boldsymbol{\beta}_2)^2}{\sigma_2^2}\right) \tag{19.3.16}$$

The log likelihood function $L = \Sigma_{t=1}^{T} \ln g(y_t|\mathbf{x}_t)$ may then be maximized with respect to the $\boldsymbol{\beta}$'s, σ^2's, and λ. The reader might want to note the relationship between this formulation and the nonnested hypothesis testing problem of Section 21.8. An immediate extension of this alternative would be to make λ a function of exogenous variables.

Another modification of the stochastic alternatives is to allow the probability λ of choosing the first regime in the time period t_0 to depend upon the state of the system in the previous trial. Specifically, Goldfeld and Quandt (1973a) introduce a Markov model in which transition probabilities are explicitly introduced. The transition probabilities may be considered fixed or nonstationary and functions of exogenous variables. In each case the likelihood function is formed and maximized with respect to all relevant variables. The reader is referred to Goldfeld and Quandt (1973a) for further details. Also see Tishler and Zang (1978) who develop approximations to the likelihood function which are computationally simple and Swamy and Mehta (1975) for a Bayesian and other generalizations. Lee and Porter (1984) suggest a model for which some imperfect sample separation information is available.

19.4 THE HILDRETH-HOUCK RANDOM COEFFICIENT MODEL

Consider the linear model (19.2.2) where $t = 1$, and is thus suppressed, the parameters are assumed stochastic, so $\boldsymbol{\beta}_i = Z_i\boldsymbol{\gamma} + \mathbf{v}_i$, and that $Z_i = I_K$ and $\boldsymbol{\gamma} = \bar{\boldsymbol{\beta}}$. The resulting model is

$$y_i = \mathbf{x}_i'\boldsymbol{\beta}_i \tag{19.4.1}$$

where

$$\boldsymbol{\beta}_i = \bar{\boldsymbol{\beta}} + \mathbf{v}_i \tag{19.4.2}$$

This is the random coefficient model of Hildreth and Houck (1968). The vector

$\boldsymbol{\beta}_i' = (\beta_{1i}, \beta_{2i}, \ldots, \beta_{Ki})$ contains the actual (random) response coefficients for the ith individual, $\bar{\boldsymbol{\beta}}' = (\bar{\beta}_1, \ldots, \bar{\beta}_K)$ is a vector of nonstochastic mean response coefficients and $\mathbf{v}_i' = (v_{1i}, v_{2i}, \ldots, v_{Ki})$ is a vector of random disturbances. We assume $E[\mathbf{v}_i] = \mathbf{0}$, $E[\mathbf{v}_i\mathbf{v}_i'] = A$ and $E[\mathbf{v}_i\mathbf{v}_j'] = 0$ if $i \neq j$. Note that a separate equation disturbance in (19.4.1) could not be distinguished from v_{1i} if the first variable is an intercept, and thus it is ignored.

This type of model is often reasonable when we have cross-sectional data on a number of micro-units. In such a case we are likely to be interested in estimating the mean coefficients, $\bar{\boldsymbol{\beta}}$, the actual coefficients, $\boldsymbol{\beta}_i$, and the covariance matrix A.

To consider estimation, combine (19.4.1) and (19.4.2) and rewrite as

$$y_i = \mathbf{x}_i'\bar{\boldsymbol{\beta}} + e_i \tag{19.4.3}$$

where $\mathbf{x}_i' = (1, x_{2i}, \ldots, x_{Ki})$, $e_i = \mathbf{x}_i'\mathbf{v}_i$, $E[e_i] = 0$, and $\sigma_i^2 = E[e_i^2] = \mathbf{x}_i'A\mathbf{x}_i$. Then, if A is known, the generalized least squares estimator for $\bar{\boldsymbol{\beta}}$

$$\hat{\bar{\boldsymbol{\beta}}} = \left(\sum_{i=1}^{N} \sigma_i^{-2}\mathbf{x}_i\mathbf{x}_i'\right)^{-1} \sum_{i=1}^{N} \sigma_i^{-2}\mathbf{x}_i y_i \tag{19.4.4}$$

is best linear unbiased and has covariance matrix $(\Sigma_{i=1}^{N}\sigma_i^{-2}\mathbf{x}_i\mathbf{x}_i')^{-1}$.

For estimating, or more correctly "predicting," the individual coefficient vector $\boldsymbol{\beta}_i$, the predictor

$$\hat{\boldsymbol{\beta}}_i = \hat{\bar{\boldsymbol{\beta}}} + A\mathbf{x}_i(\mathbf{x}_i'A\mathbf{x}_i)^{-1}(y_i - \mathbf{x}_i'\hat{\bar{\boldsymbol{\beta}}}) \tag{19.4.5}$$

is best linear unbiased [Griffiths (1972), Swamy and Mehta (1975), Lee and Griffiths (1979)]. It is unbiased in the sense that $E[\hat{\boldsymbol{\beta}}_i - \boldsymbol{\beta}_i] = \mathbf{0}$, and best in the sense that the covariance matrix of the prediction error of any other linear unbiased predictor exceeds the covariance matrix of $(\hat{\boldsymbol{\beta}}_i - \boldsymbol{\beta}_i)$ by a nonnegative definite matrix.

Since A will be unknown, for $\hat{\bar{\boldsymbol{\beta}}}$ and $\hat{\boldsymbol{\beta}}_i$ to be operational, we need to find an estimator for A. For this purpose it is convenient to let $P = K(K + 1)/2$ and write the variance of e_i as

$$\sigma_i^2 = \mathbf{x}_i'A\mathbf{x}_i = \mathbf{z}_i'\boldsymbol{\alpha} \tag{19.4.6}$$

where $\boldsymbol{\alpha}$ is a $(P \times 1)$ vector containing the distinct elements of A and $\mathbf{z}_i' = (1, z_{2i}, \ldots, z_{Pi})$ is found by calculating the Kronecker product $\mathbf{x}_i' \otimes \mathbf{x}_i'$ and combining the identical elements. For example, if $K = 3$ and

$$A = \begin{bmatrix} \alpha_{11} & \alpha_{12} & \alpha_{13} \\ \alpha_{21} & \alpha_{22} & \alpha_{23} \\ \alpha_{31} & \alpha_{32} & \alpha_{33} \end{bmatrix} \tag{19.4.7}$$

then $\boldsymbol{\alpha}' = (\alpha_{11}, \alpha_{12}, \alpha_{13}, \alpha_{22}, \alpha_{23}, \alpha_{33})$ and $\mathbf{z}_i' = (1, 2x_{2i}, 2x_{3i}, x_{2i}^2, 2x_{2i}x_{3i}, x_{3i}^2)$.

From Equation 19.4.6 it is clear that the Hildreth-Houck random coefficient model belongs to the class of heteroscedastic error models, where the variance of y_i is a linear function of a set of exogeneous variables. This class of models was discussed in Section 11.2.4. The discussion included (1) a number of alternative estimators for $\boldsymbol{\alpha}$ and their properties, and (2) information on Monte Carlo studies of the finite sample properties of estimated, generalized least squares estimators for $\bar{\boldsymbol{\beta}}$, which were based on various estimators for $\boldsymbol{\alpha}$. The interested reader should consult that section.

However, in this case there is an additional consideration. Because the elements of $\boldsymbol{\alpha}$ are now regarded as elements of a covariance matrix, the estimators should satisfy certain restrictions. In particular, they should be such that A is nonnegative definite. For the estimators outlined in Section 11.2.4, there is no guarantee this will be true. For example, if $X = (\mathbf{x}_1, \mathbf{x}_2, \ldots, \mathbf{x}_N)'$ and $Z = (\mathbf{z}_1, \mathbf{z}_2, \ldots, \mathbf{z}_N)'$, it can be shown that

$$E[\dot{\hat{\mathbf{e}}}] = F\boldsymbol{\alpha} \tag{19.4.8}$$

where $\dot{\hat{\mathbf{e}}}$ contains the squares of the least squares residuals, and $F = \dot{M}Z$ with $\dot{M}$ containing the squares of the elements of $M = I - X(X'X)^{-1}X'$. The estimator $\hat{\boldsymbol{\alpha}} = (F'F)^{-1}F'\dot{\hat{\mathbf{e}}}$ is unbiased, but because it is a least squares estimator, its elements will not be constrained.

For the case where A is diagonal, Hildreth and Houck (1968) suggest changing negative estimates to zero or using the quadratic programming estimator obtained by minimizing $(\dot{\hat{\mathbf{e}}} - F\boldsymbol{\alpha})'(\dot{\hat{\mathbf{e}}} - F\boldsymbol{\alpha})$ subject to $\boldsymbol{\alpha} \geq \mathbf{0}$. Unfortunately, when A is not diagonal, the constraints become nonlinear so that there is not an obvious, more general form for the quadratic programming estimator. For example, when $K = 3$, the constraints can be written as

$$\alpha_{11} \geq 0, \quad \begin{vmatrix} \alpha_{11} & \alpha_{12} \\ \alpha_{12} & \alpha_{22} \end{vmatrix} \geq 0, \quad \begin{vmatrix} \alpha_{11} & \alpha_{12} & \alpha_{13} \\ \alpha_{12} & \alpha_{22} & \alpha_{23} \\ \alpha_{13} & \alpha_{23} & \alpha_{33} \end{vmatrix} \geq 0 \tag{19.4.9}$$

One solution is to make ad hoc adjustments to the variances and covariances in an estimated A such that it is nonnegative definite. Because it leaves one in doubt about the properties of the resulting estimator, this is not a completely satisfactory procedure. See Schwaille (1982) for a reparameterization that can be used to produce a positive semidefinite estimated A without the constraints in Equation 19.4.9. At this point it is worth noting that the above discussion is relevant for Section 13.6, where the topic was estimation of variances in the Hsiao random coefficient model.

Four other estimators for A have been suggested by Swamy and Mehta (1975). One is the maximum likelihood estimator under the assumption of normality, and two are based on prior information about A. For the fourth they suggest beginning with an "initial guess" for A and based on this, calculating $\hat{\boldsymbol{\beta}}_i$ and $\hat{\bar{\boldsymbol{\beta}}}$ from Equations 19.4.5 and 19.4.4, respectively. Following this calculation, an estimator for A can be derived from the sum of cross products $\Sigma_{i=1}^{N}(\hat{\boldsymbol{\beta}}_i - \hat{\bar{\boldsymbol{\beta}}})(\hat{\boldsymbol{\beta}}_i - \hat{\bar{\boldsymbol{\beta}}})'$. Also see Srivastava et al. (1981), who consider using a mixed estimation procedure to estimate the coefficient variances.

In addition to estimation, the applied worker is likely to be interested in testing for randomness in the coefficients. The type of randomness discussed in this section leads to a heteroscedastic error model, and so, for testing purposes, the tests discussed in Section 11.3 are relevant. In particular, the Breusch–Pagan (1979) test (Section 11.3.1) is likely to be a satisfactory one.

Additional references that relate to the Hildreth–Houck model include Raj, et al. (1980), who obtain a finite sample approximation to the moment matrix of the limiting distribution when the errors are normal and assuming disturbances are small. For Bayesian treatments of the Hildreth–Houck model and a generalization, see Griffiths, et al. (1979) and Liu (1981).

19.5 THE RETURN TO NORMALITY MODEL

The return to normality model is specifically suited to use with time series data where the assumption that the coefficients in the regression model are constant over time is not a reasonable one. The parameters in this model are dynamic and this represents a generalization of the random coefficient model previously discussed in Section 19.4. Models with dynamic parameters can be further classified into those where the parameters follow a stationary stochastic process about a fixed but unknown mean, which is the topic of this section, and those where the parameters follow a stochastic process that is nonstationary. The nonstationary type parameter process is illustrated in Section 19.6 with the discussion of the Cooley–Prescott (1976) model.

19.5.1 The Model

Following Harvey and Phillips (1982), write the regression model as

$$y_t = \mathbf{x}_t'\boldsymbol{\beta}_t, \qquad t = 1, \ldots, T \tag{19.5.1a}$$

$$\boldsymbol{\beta}_t - \bar{\boldsymbol{\beta}} = \Phi(\boldsymbol{\beta}_{t-1} - \bar{\boldsymbol{\beta}}) + \mathbf{e}_t \tag{19.5.1b}$$

where y_t is an observation on the dependent variable, $\mathbf{x}_t$ is a $(K \times 1)$ vector of nonstochastic observations and $\boldsymbol{\beta}_t$ is a vector of stochastic parameters with $\bar{\boldsymbol{\beta}}$ being a nonstochastic $(K \times 1)$ vector. The parameter matrix Φ is $(K \times K)$ with characteristic roots less than one in absolute value. Note that if $\Phi = 0$ the model reduces to the Hildreth–Houck random coefficient model, and thus represents a dynamic generalization. The $(K \times 1)$ vector of random disturbances $\mathbf{e}_t \sim N(\mathbf{0},\sigma^2 Q)$ and $E(\mathbf{e}_t\mathbf{e}_s') = 0$, $t \neq s$. Note that (19.5.1a) is written without an error term. It is assumed that the first element of $\mathbf{x}_t$ is unity so that the variance of the first parameter is indistinguishable from the equation error variance, and thus it is ignored.

Rewriting (19.5.1a), we obtain

$$y_t = \mathbf{x}_t'\bar{\boldsymbol{\beta}} + v_t \tag{19.5.2a}$$

where

$$v_t = \mathbf{x}_t'(\boldsymbol{\beta}_t - \bar{\boldsymbol{\beta}}) \tag{19.5.2b}$$

Equation 19.5.2a represents a linear regression model with fixed coefficients, but serially correlated and heteroscedastic disturbances, v_t; where $E(v_t) = 0$, $E(v_t v_s) = \sigma^2 \mathbf{x}_t' \Gamma_\tau \mathbf{x}_s$, $\tau = t - s$ and $\sigma^2\Gamma_\tau$ is the autocovariance matrix of $(\boldsymbol{\beta}_t - \bar{\boldsymbol{\beta}})$ at lag τ. Estimation could be carried out by maximum likelihood, conditional on Φ and Q, by using the usual GLS estimator. This would involve inversion of the $(T \times T)$ covariance matrix. Luckily, the Kalman filter (see Appendix C) can be used here to computational advantage.

19.5.2 State Space Form of the Model and Generalized Least Squares

The model (19.5.1) can be put in state space form with transition equation

$$\boldsymbol{\alpha}_t = \begin{bmatrix} \bar{\boldsymbol{\beta}}_t \\ \boldsymbol{\delta}_t \end{bmatrix} = \begin{bmatrix} I_K & 0 \\ 0 & \Phi \end{bmatrix} \begin{bmatrix} \bar{\boldsymbol{\beta}}_{t-1} \\ \boldsymbol{\delta}_{t-1} \end{bmatrix} + \begin{bmatrix} 0 \\ I_K \end{bmatrix} \mathbf{e}_t \tag{19.5.3}$$

where $\bar{\boldsymbol{\beta}}_t = \bar{\boldsymbol{\beta}}$ for all t and $\boldsymbol{\delta}_t = \boldsymbol{\beta}_t - \bar{\boldsymbol{\beta}}$. The associated measurement equation is

$$y_t = (\mathbf{x}_t' \ \mathbf{x}_t') \begin{bmatrix} \bar{\boldsymbol{\beta}}_t \\ \boldsymbol{\delta}_t \end{bmatrix} \tag{19.5.4}$$

Consequently, all that is needed to carry out the Kalman filter iterations, and obtain the GLS estimator of $\bar{\boldsymbol{\beta}}$ conditional on Φ and Q, is some starting values. Harvey and Phillips (1982, p. 311) suggest using the first K observations to obtain initial estimates of $\boldsymbol{\alpha}_t$ and its covariance matrix. Finally, full maximum likelihood estimation would involve maximizing the concentrated log likelihood function with respect to the unknown elements of Φ and Q. A numerical optimization procedure would require initial estimates of these unknown parameters. Harvey and Phillips (1982, pp. 314–315), under the assumption that Φ and Q are diagonal, with elements $\phi_1, \ldots, \phi_K$ and $1, q_2, \ldots, q_K$, respectively, note that

$$E(v_t^2) = \sigma^2 \sum_{j=1}^{K} \frac{x_{tj}^2 q_j}{(1 - \phi_j^2)}$$

where $q_1 = 1$ and $x_{t1} = 1$, and

$$E(v_t v_{t-1}) = \sigma^2 \sum_{j=1}^{K} \frac{x_{tj} x_{t-1,j} q_j \phi_j}{(1 - \phi_j^2)}$$

This suggests that starting estimates of diag(Φ) and diag(Q) could be obtained by computing the least squares residuals $\hat{e}_1, \ldots, \hat{e}_T$ and regressing $\hat{e}_t^2$ on $x_{t1}^2, x_{t2}^2, \ldots, x_{tK}^2$ and $\hat{e}_t\hat{e}_{t-1}$ on $x_{t1}x_{t-1,1}, \ldots, x_{tK}x_{t-1,K}$. Given the consistency of these initial estimates, an estimated GLS estimator of $\bar{\boldsymbol{\beta}}$ is then computed by a single pass of the Kalman filter. In Monte Carlo experiments, Harvey and Phillips found a clear mean square error gain by using ML over OLS or the two-step EGLS estimator, and the EGLS estimator provided substantial improvement over OLS.

19.5.3 Generalizations

The return to normality model can be generalized. Instead of (19.5.1b) the process generating the parameters could be $A(L)(\boldsymbol{\beta}_t - \bar{\boldsymbol{\beta}}) = \mathbf{e}_t$, where $A(L)$ is a rational function of finite polynomials, implying that $\boldsymbol{\beta}_t - \bar{\boldsymbol{\beta}}$ follows a multivariate ARMA process. Burnett and Guthrie (1970) and Rosenberg (1972, 1973) consider such a model as do Cooley and Prescott (1973, 1976) whose model is presented in Section 19.6. Pagan (1980) discusses sufficient conditions for asymptotic identification of such models, assuming $\boldsymbol{\beta}_t - \bar{\boldsymbol{\beta}}$ is stationary, and also establishes sufficient conditions for the consistency and asymptotic normality of ML estimators without assuming stationarity, but assuming asymptotic identifiability. He also notes conditions under which the conventional Aitken GLS form of the likelihood function is equivalent to the state space form, which are both widely used. Swamy and Tinsley (1980) investigate a similar general model that also allows the errors e_t to follow an ARMA process. Liu and Hanssens (1981) consider estimation of (19.5.1) from a Bayesian perspective using noninformative priors.

19.6 THE COOLEY–PRESCOTT MODEL

To this point we have reviewed models where parameter shifts have been given considerable structure. In this section variable parameter models are presented that place a less restrictive structure on the parameter variation. In particular, we consider the random walk model of Cooley and Prescott (1973, 1976). In this model the parameters vary from one time period to another on the basis of a nonstationary probabilistic scheme. Similar models are discussed by Sarris (1973), Cooper (1973), Sant (1977), Belsley (1973a), and Rausser and Mundlak (1978).

Cooley and Prescott consider a time series regression model

$$y_t = \mathbf{x}_t'\boldsymbol{\beta}_t, \qquad t = 1, \ldots, T \tag{19.6.1}$$

where $\mathbf{x}_t$ is a vector of observations on K explanatory variables, and $\boldsymbol{\beta}_t$ is a conformable parameter vector subject to stochastic variation. The parameter variation is of two types, permanent and transitory, the former allowing some persistent "drift" in the parameter values. These sources of variation are modeled as

$$\boldsymbol{\beta}_t = \boldsymbol{\beta}_t^p + \mathbf{u}_t$$
$$\boldsymbol{\beta}_t^p = \boldsymbol{\beta}_{t-1}^p + \mathbf{v}_t \tag{19.6.2}$$

where $\boldsymbol{\beta}_t^p$ is the permanent component of the parameter vector. The terms $\mathbf{u}_t$ and $\mathbf{v}_t$ are independent, normal random vectors with mean vectors zero and covariance matrices $E(\mathbf{u}_t\mathbf{u}_t') = (1 - \gamma)\sigma^2\Sigma_u$ and $E(\mathbf{v}_t\mathbf{v}_t') = \gamma\sigma^2\Sigma_v$. The matrices Σ_u and Σ_v are assumed to be known up to a scale factor and normalized so that the element corresponding to the intercept is unity. That is, the first regressor is the constant term and the transitory component of the corresponding parameter's variation plays the role of the additive disturbance in the regression equation. Note that the parameterization adopted is such that γ reflects the relative magnitudes of the permanent and transitory changes. If γ is close to 1, then the permanent changes are large relative to transitory ones.

Straightforward maximum likelihood estimation of σ^2, γ, and the permanent components of the $\boldsymbol{\beta}_t$ is not possible, since the process generating the parameters is not stationary. However, by considering the value of the parameter process at a particular point as the parameter vector of interest, a well-defined likelihood function can be constructed.

Cooley and Prescott focus on the value of the parameter process one period past the sample, which is convenient for forecasting. Then, by repeated substitutions,

$$\boldsymbol{\beta}_{T+1}^p = \boldsymbol{\beta}_T^p + \mathbf{v}_{T+1} = \boldsymbol{\beta}_t^p + \sum_{j=t+1}^{T+1} \mathbf{v}_j \tag{19.6.3}$$

and so

$$\boldsymbol{\beta}_t = \boldsymbol{\beta}_{T+1}^p - \sum_{j=t+1}^{T+1} \mathbf{v}_j + \mathbf{u}_t \tag{19.6.4}$$

Substituting (19.6.4) into (19.6.1), we obtain

$$y_t = \mathbf{x}_t'\boldsymbol{\beta}_{T+1}^p + e_t, \qquad t = 1, \ldots, T \tag{19.6.5}$$

where

$$e_t = \mathbf{x}_t'\mathbf{u}_t - \mathbf{x}_t' \sum_{j=t+1}^{T+1} \mathbf{v}_j$$

The random vector $\mathbf{e} = (e_1, \ldots, e_T)'$ is normally distributed with mean vector zero and covariance matrix

$$E(\mathbf{ee}') = \sigma^2[(1 - \gamma)R + \gamma Q] = \sigma^2\Omega(\gamma) \tag{19.6.6}$$

where R is a diagonal matrix with elements $r_{ii} = \mathbf{x}_i'\Sigma_u\mathbf{x}_i$ and Q is a matrix with elements

$$q_{ij} = \min(T - i + 1, T - j + 1)\mathbf{x}_i'\Sigma_v\mathbf{x}_j$$

If γ is known, generalized least squares can be directly applied to obtain estimates of $\boldsymbol{\beta}_{T+1}^p$. If the full model is written

$$\mathbf{y} = X\boldsymbol{\beta}_{T+1}^p + \mathbf{e}$$

the log likelihood of the observations is

$$L = -\frac{T}{2}\ln 2\pi - \frac{T}{2}\ln \sigma^2 - \frac{1}{2}\ln|\Omega(\gamma)| - \frac{1}{2\sigma^2}(\mathbf{y} - X\boldsymbol{\beta}_{T+1}^p)'\Omega(\gamma)^{-1}(\mathbf{y} - X\boldsymbol{\beta}_{T+1}^p) \tag{19.6.7}$$

Maximizing (19.6.7) with respect to $\boldsymbol{\beta}_{T+1}^p$ and σ^2, we obtain the conditional estimators

$$\hat{\boldsymbol{\beta}}_{T+1}^p(\gamma) = [X'\Omega(\gamma)^{-1}X]^{-1}X'\Omega(\gamma)^{-1}\mathbf{y}$$

and

$$\hat{\sigma}^2(\gamma) = \frac{1}{T}[\mathbf{y} - X\hat{\boldsymbol{\beta}}_{T+1}^p]'\Omega(\gamma)^{-1}[\mathbf{y} - X\hat{\boldsymbol{\beta}}_{T+1}^p] \tag{19.6.8}$$

Substituting these estimators back into (19.6.7) yields the concentrated log likelihood function

$$\begin{aligned} L &= -\frac{T}{2}\ln 2\pi - \frac{T}{2}\ln \hat{\sigma}^2(\gamma) - \frac{1}{2}\ln|\Omega(\gamma)| - \frac{T}{2} \\ &= -\frac{T}{2}(\ln 2\pi + 1) - \frac{T}{2}\ln \hat{\sigma}^2(\gamma) - \frac{1}{2}\ln|\Omega(\gamma)| \end{aligned} \tag{19.6.9}$$

Maximization of (19.6.7) may now be carried out by maximizing (19.6.9) with respect to $\gamma \in [0,1]$. The value of γ that maximizes (19.6.9), say $\hat{\gamma}$, can be inserted into (19.6.8) to obtain estimates of $\boldsymbol{\beta}_{T+1}^p$ and σ^2. Cooley and Prescott show that $\hat{\gamma}$ is consistent for γ and that $\boldsymbol{\beta}_{T+1}^p(\hat{\gamma})$ is asymptotically efficient and asymptotically yields optimal predictions. Note, however, that the nature of the problem precludes any notion of consistent estimation of $\boldsymbol{\beta}_{T+1}^p$.

Hypotheses about γ can be tested using the variance of the asymptotic distribution of $\hat{\gamma}$,

$$\operatorname{var}\sqrt{T}(\hat{\gamma} - \gamma) = 2\Big/\left[\frac{1}{T}\sum_i \frac{(d_i - 1)^2}{d_i(\gamma)^2} - \left(\frac{1}{T}\sum_i \frac{(d_i - 1)^2}{d_i(\gamma)}\right)\right]^2$$

where $d_i(\gamma) = (1 - \gamma) + \gamma d_i$ and d_i are the characteristic roots of Q^*, with $q_{ij}^* = q_{ij}/\sqrt{r_{ii}r_{jj}}$. The matrix Q^* arises from a transformation of the model suggested by Cooley and Prescott (1976, pp. 172–173), which reduces the computational burden of estimation. The reader is referred to the Cooley–Prescott paper for that discussion.

Although estimation and interpretation of the Cooley–Prescott model is relatively straightforward, its application is not without difficulties. The specification of Σ_u and Σ_v must come from theoretical considerations. In particular, their specification presumes the ability to specify the relative variability of the parameters.

19.7 SUMMARY

In this chapter, we have reviewed a variety of statistical models that have been developed for situations where the coefficients of the general linear model are assumed to vary across observations. Justification for the use of varying parameter models usually follows one of two lines. First in importance is the situation when the coefficients of an otherwise properly specified relationship are different for some subsets of the available sample; that is, the sample data cannot be pooled. Estimation with a model that does not take this into account would produce results that do not accurately represent the existing economic structure and do not serve as a good basis for forecasting. The exact consequences of ignoring the parameter variation would, of course, depend on the nature and degree of the misspecification. The other justification for the use of a model with varying parameters is that econometric models are necessarily abstractions from and simplifications of reality. Adoption of the classical linear model may then imply misspecifications that cause the coefficients of the model to apparently vary across the sample even though the true underlying structure is not changing. Some examples of this are the following:

1. If important explanatory variables are excluded from the model and if they are related to included variables, the effects of the included variables on the dependent variable can be expected to vary across the sample. As a minimum, omitted variables can be expected to produce variations in the intercept. In other words, the effects of omitted variables are (incorrectly) attributed to variables that do appear in the model.
2. Economists often use proxy variables that only partially reflect the economic effects they represent. If the relationship between the proxy and its true counterpart is not constant across observations, the coefficient of the proxy variable will not be constant.
3. When aggregate data are used, the potential for coefficient variation is present. Coefficients in the aggregate equation will remain constant as long as the relationship between microunits remains constant.
4. Coefficients of a linear model can vary across the sample if the true relationship is nonlinear and observations fall outside the narrow range where the linear approximation is acceptable.

The use of random or varying parameter models under these circumstances leaves one a bit uneasy. Models with random but not systematically varying parameters force recognition of another source of estimation and forecasting inaccuracy and thus to some extent prevent overstatement of the quality of statistical results. *Modeling a changing economic structure by allowing response parameters to vary over observations may be a realistic approach, but the chances for misspecification are many.* Although it may be possible to forecast the conditional mean of the dependent variable more accurately by letting model parameters vary systematically with trend variables, this does little to reveal the nature of the actual structure change. As always, we return to the fact that inferences about economic processes based on statistical models are conditioned by the theoretical and institutional knowledge of the economic structure on which the sampling model is based.

In Section 19.2 a general model of nonstochastic (although it is easily made stochastic) parameter variation is presented in which the parameters vary as a function of some explanatory variables. It is suitable for use with time series, cross-sectional, or combined data, where subsets of the observations are thought to be generated by a different parametric structure. The primary difficulty in using this model is, of course, that one must specify the structure causing the parameter variation. Errors in specification will lead to familiar and unfortunate consequences. Section 19.3 contains two special cases of the general model. Namely, seasonality models, where a different parametric structure is appropriate for different seasons, and switching or piecewise regression models, in which there are two, or a few, subsets of observations for which different structures exist.

Models with a *stochastic* parametric structure are presented in Sections 19.4 and 19.5. The Hildreth–Houck model has random coefficients that are drawn from a population with fixed mean and covariance. When using cross-sectional data, we could argue that the Hildreth–Houck random coefficient model should always be used, since its assumptions are more general than those of a constant coefficient model. However, this is not the only issue. If the number of observations is such that the covariance matrix of the disturbance vector cannot be accurately estimated, we may be better off assuming the coefficients are constant. Also, if all models are regarded as an approximation to some underlying process, the random coefficient approximation may not be better than a constant coefficient approximation. Thus we recommend using the Hildreth–Houck random coefficient model when it has advantages in terms of both realism of assumptions and estimation efficiency. Where some doubt exists it might be worthwhile using statistical tests for heteroscedastic errors.

The return to normality model in Section 19.5 is like the Hildreth–Houck model in that parameters are assumed to be generated by a stationary stochastic process. However, it is more general in that the coefficients reflect a dynamic stochastic structure. The Cooley–Prescott model in Section 19.6 also presents a dynamic, stochastic parameter structure, but in this case the process is nonstationary. Both the return to normality model and the Cooley–Prescott model are more likely to be used with time series data.

19.8 EXERCISES

The data in Table 19.2 were generated from a linear statistical model with a systematically varying parameter. In particular, the five samples of y's shown are generated using the statistical model $\mathbf{y} = X\boldsymbol{\beta} + \mathbf{e} = 10\mathbf{x}_1 + \beta_2\mathbf{x}_2 + 0.6\mathbf{x}_3 + \mathbf{e}$, where $\mathbf{x}_1$, $\mathbf{x}_2$, and $\mathbf{x}_3$ are given in Section 2.5.1, $\mathbf{e} \sim N(\mathbf{0}, I)$, and the coefficient β_2 varies with the trend variable t, $t = 1, \ldots, 20$, as

$$\beta_2 = \gamma_1 t^2 + \gamma_2 t + \gamma_3 = -t^2 + 22t - 21$$

19.8.1 Individual Exercises (Section 19.2)

Exercise 19.1
Obtain the least squares estimates of the model $\mathbf{y} = X\boldsymbol{\beta} + \mathbf{e}$ for the five samples ignoring the presence of the varying parameter. Examine the residuals for each of the samples.

Exercise 19.2
Obtain estimates of the coefficients in the correctly specified model for the five samples.

TABLE 19.2 *DATA FOR EXERCISES 19.1–19.3*

$\mathbf{y}_1$	$\mathbf{y}_2$	$\mathbf{y}_3$	$\mathbf{y}_4$	$\mathbf{y}_5$
9.37	8.97	11.83	10.76	9.15
43.23	42.64	44.10	43.72	44.34
34.37	35.54	35.48	35.16	35.33
97.37	98.07	100.07	98.45	99.28
52.70	51.95	54.38	53.63	54.45
184.13	185.05	184.38	184.98	184.56
155.54	156.26	155.26	156.81	153.13
224.40	222.01	223.04	221.99	223.45
234.41	234.83	235.05	233.53	234.68
78.83	79.70	79.36	78.94	80.72
79.43	81.06	78.71	78.19	77.68
182.42	180.68	182.45	180.63	179.25
177.68	176.89	176.73	175.18	176.47
72.12	72.97	73.91	71.79	72.59
206.93	210.39	205.76	205.56	207.82
141.22	140.43	140.15	138.52	139.43
160.18	160.38	160.17	160.64	161.47
127.26	129.67	131.35	129.15	129.41
73.60	72.35	73.03	72.87	73.08
22.49	23.50	22.08	23.72	24.64

Exercise 19.3
Test for the presence of a systematically varying parameter in the correctly specified model by testing the hypothesis that $\gamma_1 = \gamma_2 = 0$.

19.8.2 Individual Exercises (Section 19.6)

The data in Table 19.3 were generated from a linear model with time-varying parameters. In particular, the five samples of y's shown were generated using the statistical model

$$\mathbf{y} = \beta_1\mathbf{x}_1 + \beta_2\mathbf{x}_2 + \beta_3\mathbf{x}_3 + \mathbf{e}$$

where $\mathbf{x}_1$, $\mathbf{x}_2$, and $\mathbf{x}_3$ are given in Section 2.5.1, $\mathbf{e} \sim N(\mathbf{0},I)$ and the coefficients β_1, β_2, β_3 vary following the Cooley–Prescott formulation (Section 19.6) with $\gamma = 0.8$, $\Sigma_u = \Sigma_v = I$, and the initial values being $\boldsymbol{\beta}_0' = (10, 0.4, 0.6)$.

Exercises 19.4
For the five samples in Table 19.3 compute the usual least squares coefficient estimates. Obtain the predicted conditional mean of the dependent variable for observation $(T + 1)$, where $\mathbf{x}_{T+1}' = (1, 1.5, 2)$.

TABLE 19.3 *DATA FOR EXERCISES 19.4–19.6*

$\mathbf{y}_1$	$\mathbf{y}_2$	$\mathbf{y}_3$	$\mathbf{y}_4$	$\mathbf{y}_5$
11.11	9.99	12.20	10.21	9.59
8.68	8.63	12.59	12.40	9.97
4.67	5.90	12.29	12.15	9.21
5.55	8.49	12.33	13.51	8.80
3.12	6.43	10.34	15.24	14.97
14.18	6.47	8.22	17.27	11.98
16.63	1.55	10.58	23.87	16.77
16.77	−1.64	2.00	21.95	18.25
16.28	−2.08	4.29	26.04	20.51
11.94	7.81	9.25	15.89	16.65
13.13	6.81	10.57	14.03	21.84
20.54	4.51	7.66	17.86	17.30
15.47	3.11	4.86	18.97	20.66
13.28	3.58	8.65	14.99	25.17
26.98	5.43	5.06	23.46	15.20
21.47	7.19	4.61	19.55	23.75
27.46	5.96	−1.39	21.41	9.82
29.79	5.57	0.07	17.49	17.91
27.09	10.61	5.89	17.16	12.36
14.48	11.92	5.55	14.15	14.47

Exercise 19.5

For the five samples in Table 19.3 use the estimation procedure suggested by Cooley and Prescott and described in Section 19.4.1 to estimate $\boldsymbol{\beta}_{T+1}$, the set of parameters generated by the indicated process for the $(T + 1)$ time period. Refer to the Cooley–Prescott paper for a transformation that eases the computational burden. Use the estimated coefficients to predict Ey_{T+1} using $\mathbf{x}_{T+1}$ in Exercise 19.4. Compare these forecasts to the least squares forecasts.

Exercise 19.6

For each of the five samples given in Table 19.3 test the hypothesis that $\gamma = 0$ using the variance of the asymptotic distribution of γ given in Section 19.4.1.

19.8.3 Class or Group Exercises (Section 19.6)

Exercise 19.7

Repeat the methodology described to generate the data for Exercise 19.4 to generate 100 samples of data. For each sample compute forecasts of $E[y_{T+1}]$ using the least squares and Cooley–Prescott estimates of $\boldsymbol{\beta}_{T+1}$. Compare the empirical mean square errors of prediction for the 100 samples for each of the estimators.

19.9 REFERENCES

Belsley, D. (1973a) "On the Determination of Systematic Parameter Variation in the Linear Regression Model," *Annals of Economic and Social Measurement,* 2, 487–494.

Belsley, D. (1973b) "A Test for Systematic Variation in Regression Coefficients," *Annals of Economic and Social Measurement,* 2, 494–499.

Booth, N. and A. Smith (1982) "A Bayesian Approach to Retrospective Identification of Change Points," *Journal of Econometrics,* 19, 7–22.

Breusch, T. and A. Pagan (1979) "A Simple Test for Heteroscedasticity and Random Coefficient Variation," *Econometrica,* 47, 1287–1294.

Brown, R., J. Durbin, and J. Evans (1975) "Techniques for Testing the Constancy of Regression Relationships over Time," *Journal of the Royal Statistical Society,* Series B, 149–163.

Burnett, T. D. and D. Guthrie (1970) "Estimation of Stationary Stochastic Regression Parameters," *Journal of the American Statistical Association,* 65, 1547–1553.

Buse, A. and L. Lim (1977) "Cubic Splines as a Special Case of Restricted Least Squares," *Journal of the American Statistical Association,* 72, 64–68.

Chin Choy, J. and L. Broemeling (1980) "Some Bayesian Inferences for a Changing Linear Model," *Technometrics,* 22, 71–78.

Cooley, T. and E. Prescott (1973) "Varying Parameter Regression, A Theory and Some Applications," *Annals of Economic and Social Measurement,* 2, 463–474.

Cooley, T. and E. Prescott (1976) "Estimation in the Presence of Stochastic Parameter Variation," *Econometrica,* 44, 167–184.

Cooper, J. (1973) "Time-Varying Regression Coefficients: A Mixed Estimation Approach and Operational Limitations of the General Markov Structure," *Annals of Economic and Social Measurement,* 2, 525–530.

Farley, J. and M. Hinich (1970) "Testing for a Shifting Slope Coefficient in a Linear Model," *Journal of the American Statistical Association,* 65, 1320–1329.

Farley, J., M. Hinich, and T. McGuire (1975) "Some Comparisons of Tests for a Shift in the Slopes of a Multivariate Linear Time Series Model," *Journal of Econometrics,* 3, 297–318.

Ferreira, P. (1975) "A Bayesian Analysis of a Switching Regression Model: Known Number of Regimes," *Journal of the American Statistical Association,* 70, 370–374.

Gallant, A. and W. Fuller (1973) "Fitting Segmented Polynomial Regression Models Whose Join Points Have to be Estimated," *Journal of the American Statistical Association,* 68, 144–147.

Goldfeld, S. and R. Quandt (1973a) "A Markov Model for Switching Regressions," *Journal of Econometrics,* 1, 3–16.

Goldfeld, S. and R. Quandt (1973b) "The Estimation of Structural Shifts by Switching Regressions," *Annals of Economic and Social Measurement,* 2, 475–485.

Griffiths, W. E. (1972) "Estimation of Actual Response Coefficients in the Hildreth–Houck Random Coefficients Model," *Journal of the American Statistical Association,* 67, 633–635.

Griffiths, W. E., R. Drynan, and S. Prakash (1979) "Bayesian Estimation of a Random Coefficient Model," *Journal of Econometrics,* 10, 201–220.

Harvey, A. and G. Phillips (1982) "Estimation of Regression Models with Time Varying Parameters," in *Games, Economic Dynamics and Time Series Analysis,* M. Deistler, E. Fürst, and G. Schwödiauer, eds., Physica-Verlag, Wien-Würzburg, 306–321.

Hildreth, C. and J. P. Houck (1968) "Some Estimators for a Linear Model with Random Coefficients," *Journal of the American Statistical Association,* 63, 584–595.

Hinkley, D. (1971) "Inference in Two-Phase Regression," *Journal of the American Statistical Association,* 66, 736–743.

Holbert, D. (1982) "A Bayesian Analysis of a Switching Linear Model," *Journal of Econometrics,* 19, 77–87.

Hsiao, C. (1975) "Some Estimation Methods for a Random Coefficient Model," *Econometrica,* 43, 305–325.

Hsu, D. (1982) "Robust Inferences for Structural Shift in Regression Models," *Journal of Econometrics,* 19, 89–107.

Johnston, J. (1984) *Econometric Methods,* 3rd ed., McGraw-Hill, New York.

Kmenta, J. (1971) *Elements of Econometrics,* Macmillan, New York.

Lee, L. F. and W. E. Griffiths (1979) "The Prior Likelihood and Best Linear

Unbiased Prediction in Stochastic Coefficient Linear Models,'' University of New England Working Papers in Econometrics and Applied Statistics No. 1, Armidale, Australia.

Lee, L. F. and R. H. Porter (1984) ''Switching Regression Models with Imperfect Sample Separation Information—With an Application on Cartel Stability,'' *Econometrica,* 52, 427–448.

Liu, L. (1981) ''Estimation of Random Coefficient Regression Models,'' *Journal of Statistical Computation and Simulation,* 13, 27–39.

Liu, L. and D. Hanssens (1981) ''A Bayesian Approach to Time Varying Cross-Sectional Regression Models,'' *Journal of Econometrics,* 15, 341–356.

McGee, V. E. and W. T. Carlton (1970) ''Piecewise Regression,'' *Journal of the American Statistical Association,* 65, 1109–1124.

Ohtani, K. (1982) ''Bayesian Estimation of the Switching Regression Model with Autocorrelated Errors,'' *Journal of Econometrics,* 18, 251–261.

Pagan, A. (1980) ''Some Identification and Estimation Results for Regression Models with Stochastically Varying Coefficients,'' *Journal of Econometrics,* 13, 341–363.

Poirier, D. (1973) ''Piecewise Regressions Using Cubic Splines,'' *Journal of the American Statistical Association,* 68, 515–524.

Poirier, D. (1976) *The Economics of Structural Change,* North-Holland, Amsterdam.

Quandt, R. (1958) ''The Estimation of the Parameters of a Linear Regression System Obeying Two Separate Regimes,'' *Journal of the American Statistical Association,* 53, 873–880.

Raj, B., V. Srivastava, and S. Upadhyaya (1980) ''The Efficiency of Estimating a Random Coefficient Model,'' *Journal of Econometrics,* 12, 285–299.

Rausser, G. and Y. Mundlak (1978) ''Structural Change, Parameter Variation, and Agricultural Forecasting,'' unpublished mimeo, Harvard University.

Rosenberg, B. (1972) ''The Estimation of Stationary Stochastic Regression Parameters Reexamined,'' *Journal of the American Statistical Association,* 67, 650–654.

Rosenberg, B. (1973) ''The Analysis of a Cross Section of Time Series by Stochastically Convergent Parameter Regression,'' *Annals of Economic and Social Measurement,* 2, 399–428.

Sant, D. (1977) ''Generalized Least Squares Applied to Time-Varying Parameter Models,'' *Annals of Economic and Social Measurement,* 6, 301–314.

Sarris, A. (1973) ''A Bayesian Approach to Estimation of Time-Varying Regression Coefficients,'' *Annals of Economic and Social Measurement,* 2, 501–523.

Schwaille, D. (1982) ''Unconstrained Maximum Likelihood Estimation of Contemporaneous Covariances,'' *Economics Letters,* 9, 359–364.

Sims, C. A. (1974) ''Seasonality in Regression,'' *Journal of the American Statistical Association,* 69, 618–626.

Singh, B., A.L. Nagar, N. K., Choudhry, and B. Raj (1976) ''On the Estimation of Structural Change: A Generalization of the Random Coefficients Regression Model,'' *International Economic Review,* 17, 340–361.

Smith, F. and D. Cook (1980) "Straight Lines with a Change Point: A Bayesian Analysis of Some Renal Transplant Data," *Applied Statistics,* 29, 180–189.
Srivastava, V., G. Mishva, and A. Chaturvedi (1981) "Estimation of Linear Regression Model with Random Coefficients Ensuring Almost Non-Negativity of Variance Estimators," *Biometric Journal,* 23, 3–8.
Swamy, P. and P. Tinsley (1980) "Linear Prediction and Estimation Methods for Regression Models with Stationary Stochastic Coefficients," *Journal of Econometrics,* 12, 103–142.
Swamy, P. A. V. B. and J. S. Mehta (1975) "Bayesian and Non-Bayesian Analysis of Switching Regressions and of Random Coefficient Regression Models," *Journal of the American Statistical Association,* 70, 593–602.
Tishler, A. and I. Zang (1979) "A Switching Regression Method Using Inequality Conditions," *Journal of Econometrics,* 11, 259–274.
Tsurumi, H. (1982) "A Bayesian and Maximum Likelihood Analysis of a Gradual Switching Regression in a Simultaneous Equation Framework," *Journal of Econometrics,* 19, 165–182.
Wallis, K. F. (1974) "Seasonal Adjustment and Relations Between Variables," *Journal of the American Statistical Association,* 69, 18–31.
Zellner, A., ed. (1979) *Seasonal Analysis of Economic Time Series*, U.S. Government Printing Office, Washington, D.C.

Chapter 20

Nonnormal Disturbances

Throughout this book it is frequently assumed that the random variables of interest are normally distributed. In this chapter we (1) make more explicit the results that depend on normality (Section 20.1), (2) make reference to alternative tests of the normality assumption (Section 20.2), (3) examine estimation of some specific nonnormal cases (Sections 20.3 to 20.5), and (4) discuss the question of an additive or a multiplicative disturbance (Section 20.6).

In Section 20.3 the estimation of frontier production functions is considered while in Section 20.4 some robust estimation procedures, particularly relevant when the disturbances have an infinite variance, are discussed. The "Box–Cox transformation," which can be used to induce normality and which is also used to give a more flexible functional form and homoscedastic disturbances, is discussed in Section 20.5. Table 20.1 illustrates the different directions taken in the chapter.

20.1 THE CONSEQUENCES OF NONNORMAL DISTURBANCES

In this section we summarize the consequences of nonnormal disturbances in the general linear model. Two separate cases will be considered, one where the variance of the disturbance is finite and the other where it is infinite.

20.1.1 Finite Variance

Consider the general linear model

$$\mathbf{y} = X\boldsymbol{\beta} + \mathbf{e} \qquad (20.1.1)$$

where (1) the usual definitions hold, (2) X is nonstochastic of rank K, (3) $\lim_{T\to\infty} T^{-1}X'X$ is a finite nonsingular matrix, and (4) the random vector $\mathbf{e}$ is such that $E[\mathbf{e}] = \mathbf{0}$ and $E[\mathbf{ee}'] = \sigma^2 I$, σ^2 finite. If, in addition, $\mathbf{e}$ is normally distributed

1. The least squares estimator $\mathbf{b} = (X'X)^{-1}X'\mathbf{y}$ is unbiased, minimum variance from within the class of *all* unbiased estimators, asymptotically efficient and consistent.
2. The variance estimator $\hat{\sigma}^2 = (\mathbf{y} - X\mathbf{b})'(\mathbf{y} - X\mathbf{b})/(T - K)$ is unbiased, minimum variance from within the class of all unbiased estimators, asymptotically efficient, and consistent.

TABLE 20.1 *NONNORMAL DISTURBANCES*

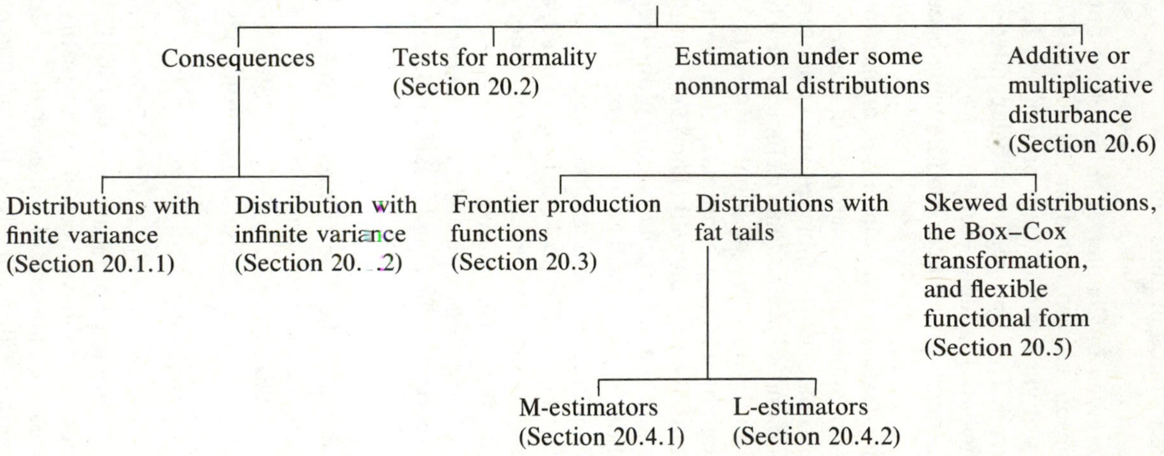

3. The respective distributions for **b** and $(T - K)\hat{\sigma}^2/\sigma^2$ are normal and $\chi^2_{(T-K)}$ and, furthermore, they are independent.
4. The F test on a set of linear restrictions $R\boldsymbol{\beta} = \mathbf{r}$, and t tests on the individual coefficients, are justified in finite samples.

These results are given in Chapter 2; an excellent outline of the necessary assumptions and proofs can be found in Schmidt (1976a). In Chapter 3 the sampling properties of various restricted, preliminary test, and Stein-rule estimators were discussed. These properties also depended on the assumption that **e** is a normally distributed random vector.

When **e** is not normally distributed, the following occur.

1. The least squares estimator **b** is unbiased minimum variance from within the class of *linear* unbiased estimators, and consistent.
2. The variance estimator $\hat{\sigma}^2$ is unbiased and consistent.
3. The estimators **b** and $\hat{\sigma}^2$ are no longer efficient or asymptotically efficient. If the form of the probability distribution of **e** is known, the likelihood function for **y** can be used to obtain maximum likelihood estimators for $\boldsymbol{\beta}$ and σ^2. In general, the maximum likelihood estimator for $\boldsymbol{\beta}$ will be *nonlinear* and, under appropriate regularity conditions (see Chapter 5), the ML estimators for both $\boldsymbol{\beta}$ and σ^2 will be asymptotically efficient. If the form of the probability distribution of **e** is unknown, one of the nonlinear robust estimators outlined in Section 20.4 can be employed, and, depending on the unknown underlying distribution, such an estimator may be more asymptotically efficient than least squares.
4. The respective distributions of **b** and $(T - K)\hat{\sigma}^2/\sigma^2$ are no longer normal and χ^2 and, consequently, the F and t tests on $\boldsymbol{\beta}$ are not necessarily valid in finite samples. However, they do have an asymptotic justification. Also, appropriate asymptotic tests such as the Wald test can be constructed. See Chapter 5 for details. These tests may, however, have reduced power under certain departures from normality.
5. The various restricted, preliminary test, and Stein-rule estimators given in Chapter 3 no longer possess the sampling properties that were outlined in that chapter.

Two of the above results—namely, that (i) **b** is best linear unbiased, and (ii) the conventional tests are asymptotically justified in the sense that they have asymptotically correct size—have been used to justify the use of the least squares estimator under conditions of nonnormality. Most econometric textbooks [e.g., Malinvaud (1970, p. 100)] use this argument, either explicitly, or implicitly. However, Koenker (1982) argues that neither of the points is very compelling. He notes that the class of linear estimators is computationally appealing, but it may be drastically restrictive. Also, the power of the asymptotic tests can be extremely sensitive to the hypothesized error distribution. The least squares estimator does not satisfy a robustness requirement that the distribution of an estimator or test statistic be altered only slightly when the distribution of the error term is altered only slightly [see Koenker (1982) for details]. These facts, coupled with the fact that arguments justifying the existence of normally distributed errors are often weak, have led Koenker and others to advocate use of robust estimation techniques (Section 20.4). Such techniques will be particularly desirable if the error distribution has infinite variance, and we now discuss some aspects of this situation.

20.1.2 Infinite Variance

There is a large body of literature [e.g., Mandlebrot (1963a and b, 1966, 1967, 1969) and Fama (1963, 1965, 1970)] which suggests that many economic data series, particularly prices in financial and commodity markets, are well represented by a class of distributions with infinite variance. An example is the Pareto distribution, with density $f(e) = c(e - e_0)^{-\alpha-1}$, where c, e_0, and α are constants and where the variance does not exist for $\alpha < 2$. Thus it is natural to ask whether, in the context of the general linear model, one should assume that the disturbance comes from a distribution with finite variance. It is frequently argued that the disturbance is made up of the sum of a large number of separate influences and, from a central limit theorem, that the distribution of this sum will approach normality. However, as Koenker (1982) notes, the necessary Lindeberg condition may not be met, and, as Bartels (1977) points out, there are other limit theorems which are just as likely to be relevant when considering the sum of a number of components in a regression disturbance; some of these theorems lead to nonnormal stable distributions characterized by infinite variance. Thus, it is worthwhile considering the consequences of an infinite error variance for our usual least squares estimation techniques.

An infinite variance distribution has "fat tails," which implies that large values or "outliers" will be relatively frequent. Because the least squares technique minimizes *squared* deviations, it places a relatively heavy weight on outliers, and their presence can lead to estimates that are extremely sensitive. Thus, in repeated samples, least squares estimates will vary more than in the finite variance case. Also, we will be unable to reliably estimate the variance of the disturbance or the least squares estimates. If the variance does not exist, it is obviously impossible to obtain a meaningful variance estimator and the least squares estimator will not possess its usual minimum variance property. This in turn implies that the conventional F and t tests on the coefficients could be very misleading.

Malinvaud (1970, p. 308) points out that, in practice, one can always assume that the distribution of the disturbances is bounded and this will lead to a finite variance. However, he also points out that this will not overcome the problem. The relatively large number of outliers will still lead to variance estimates that are unstable in repeated samples and, in general, the estimates will behave as if the variance were infinite.

The possibility of nonnormal disturbances in general, and infinite variance disturbances in particular, has led to the development of alternative estimation techniques which, relative to least squares, place less weight on outliers. As mentioned above, these techniques come under the general heading of robust estimation and are discussed in Section 20.4.

Before closing this section, it should be mentioned that in the estimation of economic relationships, the issue of a finite versus infinite disturbance variance is far from settled. Blattberg and Gonedes (1974) give evidence which suggests that the data which Fama (1965) originally fitted to a Pareto distribution could equally well be fitted to a t distribution with finite variance. This, of course, does not necessarily carry over to a regression disturbance. However, Jeffreys (1961) found that a t distribution with low degrees of freedom was a reasonable model for noise. Thus, the t distribution may be a reasonable way of modeling tails that are fatter than those of the normal distribution. If the disturbance vector has a multivariate t distribution in which the individual disturbances are uncorrelated, then the least squares estimator is also the maximum likelihood estimator [Zellner (1976) and Kelejian and Prucha (1983)]. Prucha and Kelejian (1984) consider a general linear simultaneous equation system with a multivariate student t disturbance vector.

20.2 TESTS FOR NORMALITY

Because of the possible consequences of nonnormal disturbances, it is worthwhile testing to see if the disturbances could have come from a normal distribution. Most available tests for normality consider whether or not a set of observations could be *independent* drawings from a normal distribution. In the general linear model $\mathbf{y} = X\boldsymbol{\beta} + \mathbf{e}$, where $E[\mathbf{e}] = \mathbf{0}$ and $E[\mathbf{ee}'] = \sigma^2 I$, the disturbances, although independent, are unobservable. We can estimate the disturbances with the least squares residual vector $\hat{\mathbf{e}} = (I - X(X'X)^{-1}X')\mathbf{y}$, but $E[\hat{\mathbf{e}}\hat{\mathbf{e}}'] = \sigma^2(I - X(X'X)^{-1}X')$, and so the elements of $\hat{\mathbf{e}}$ are correlated. Despite this fact, under appropriate conditions [White and MacDonald (1980)], many of the tests remain asymptotically valid when $\mathbf{e}$ is replaced by $\hat{\mathbf{e}}$. Alternatively, the problem can be overcome by transforming $\hat{\mathbf{e}}$ to a new $(T - K)$ vector of uncorrelated residuals such as the BLUS residual vector $\tilde{\mathbf{e}}$ or a vector of recursive residuals $\mathbf{e}^*$. See Chapter 5. Then, $\mathbf{e}$ can be replaced by either $\tilde{\mathbf{e}}$ or $\mathbf{e}^*$.

The literature on testing for normality is vast. See, for example, Pearson, D'Agostino, and Bowman (1977), Gastwirth and Owens (1977), Locke and Spurrier (1977), Spiegelhalter (1977), Saniga and Miles (1979), Mardia (1980), White and MacDonald (1980), Franck (1981), Bera and Jarque (1981), Bera and John (1983), and Kiefer and Salmon (1983). These papers contain details of alternative tests, further references to the literature, and Monte Carlo evidence on the relative performance of the tests. We have chosen to report just one test, the Shapiro–Wilk statistic, that has performed reasonably well in a wide variety of circumstances [Shapiro, Wilk and Chen (1968), Huang and Bolch (1974)]. Using, for example, the BLUS residual vector, this statistic is given by

$$W = \frac{(\sum_{i=1}^{h} a_{in}[\tilde{e}_{(n-i+1)} - \tilde{e}_{(i)}])^2}{\sum_{i=1}^{n}(\tilde{e}_i - \bar{\tilde{e}})^2} \tag{20.2.1}$$

where

1. $n = T - K$.
2. $\tilde{e}_{(1)} \le \tilde{e}_{(2)} \le \ldots \le \tilde{e}_{(n)}$ are the ordered BLUS residuals.

3. $\bar{\tilde{e}} = \Sigma_{i=1}^{n} \tilde{e}_i / n$.
4. $h = n/2$ or $(n - 1)/2$ according to whether n is even or odd.
5. The coefficients a_{in} are tabulated by Shapiro and Wilk (1965).

The null hypothesis is that the disturbances are normally distributed and the critical region is given by low values of W. Significance points are provided by Shapiro and Wilk (1965).

It is interesting to note that although the test assumes that the observations are independent, both Huang and Bolch (1974) and Ramsey (1974) report on Monte Carlo studies where the least squares vector $\hat{\mathbf{e}}$ led to a more powerful test than that obtained using the BLUS residual vector $\tilde{\mathbf{e}}$.

20.3 FRONTIER PRODUCTION FUNCTIONS

An excellent example of statistical models in which errors are nonnormal, and where the maximum likelihood technique provides a more efficient nonlinear estimator, is provided by the study of frontier production function models. Such models have been studied and applied by Aigner, Lovell, and Schmidt (1977); Schmidt (1976b); Lee and Tyler (1978); Waldman (1982); Greene (1982); Lee (1983); and Aigner, Amemiya, and Poirier (1976) among others. See also the special journal issue edited by Aigner and Schmidt (1980). The basis for the model is that a production function defines the *maximum* amount of output available from any input bundle given fixed technology. As a result, any observed levels of production must lie *inside* the production frontier. Thus a simple model of maximum production is

$$y_t = \beta_1 + \sum_{i=2}^{K} \beta_i X_{it} + e_t, \qquad t = 1, \ldots, T \tag{20.3.1}$$

where y is the log of maximum output, given the X_i's, the logs of the various inputs. Since observed production must lie inside this frontier, every disturbance must be negative, that is, $e_t \leq 0$.

If we assume that the e_t are independently and identically distributed random variables with mean $\mu < 0$ and finite variance σ^2, then the model may be estimated by least squares (LS). For $i \neq 1$ the estimates of the β_i's will be best linear unbiased. The estimator for β_1 will be biased but it will be unbiased for $\beta_1 + \mu$. Furthermore, while the LS estimates will not be normal in small samples, they will be asymptotically normal, so the usual tests for the β_i will be asymptotically valid. However, this method does not allow us to obtain a reliable estimate for β_1, nor can the frontier itself be estimated.

If one is willing to assume a distribution for e_t, the parameters of the model can be estimated by maximum likelihood (ML). Schmidt (1976b) notes that one may conveniently assume either that the e_t's have a half-normal distribution

$$f(e_t) = \frac{2}{\sqrt{2\pi}\sigma} \exp\left(-\frac{e_t^2}{2\sigma^2}\right), \qquad e_t \leq 0 \tag{20.3.2}$$

or that $u_t = -e_t$ has an exponential distribution

$$f(u) = \frac{1}{\sigma} \exp\left(-\frac{u}{\sigma}\right), \qquad u \geq 0 \tag{20.3.3}$$

He also notes that, unfortunately, one of the maximum likelihood regularity conditions is violated. Thus, although ML estimation is possible, the properties of the resulting estimators are uncertain.

It has been argued recently, however, that strictly negative errors may not be appropriate. Aigner, Lovell, and Schmidt (1977) suggest that the error be considered made up of two components, one normal and one having a one-sided distribution. They suggest that one component, which is nonpositive, occurs because each firm's output must lie on or below a stochastic frontier. Such a deviation results from inefficiency factors from within the firm. It is also assumed that the frontier itself can vary across firms or over time, and is thus stochastic. The component that allows for this variation has mean zero and is the result of factors beyond the control of the firm like climate, topography, luck, or errors of measurement in y. Thus we have $e_t = v_t + u_t$, $t = 1, \ldots, T$, where (1) the error component v_t represents the symmetric disturbance, assumed to be i.i.d. $N(0,\sigma_v^2)$, and (2) the component u_t is independent of v_t and satisfies $u_t \leq 0$. In particular, it is assumed that u_t has the above-mentioned half-normal distribution or that $-u_t$ has the exponential distribution. Given these assumptions, Aigner et al. present the likelihood function for the half-normal case and its first and second derivatives. Maximum likelihood estimates, having all their usual properties, may be obtained using one of the optimization techniques, such as the Davidon–Fletcher–Powell algorithm, outlined in Appendix B.

Aigner et al. apply their model to two examples and find that the symmetric component v_t dominates the error term and that the resulting estimates differ little from least squares. However, Lee and Tyler (1978) and Kopp and Smith (1978) present examples where this is not the case.

20.4 SOME ROBUST ESTIMATORS

In Section 20.1.2 we discussed the effects of nonnormality of the disturbances when the nonnormal distribution has infinite variance or is characterized by a relatively large proportion of outliers. The possible existence of this, or some other type of nonnormal distribution of the disturbances, has led to a search for estimators that are more "robust" than least squares (LS) in the sense that they are reasonably efficient irrespective of the form of the underlying distribution. When the disturbances are independent identically distributed normal random variables, the LS estimator is known to be efficient, and so the relevant question is: Are there estimators that are not much worse than LS when the disturbances are normal but are considerably better for nonnormal distributions?

With this in mind a large number of estimators has been suggested and a considerable body of literature has developed. See, for example, the surveys of

Huber (1972, 1973, 1977), Bickel (1976), Koenker (1982), and Dielman and Pfaffenberger (1982), the books by Mosteller and Tukey (1977), Bierens (1981) and Huber (1981), the special journal issue edited by Hogg (1977), and the papers by Koenker and Bassett (1978, 1982a), McKean and Hettmansperger (1978), and Joiner and Hall (1983). In this section we concentrate on two classes of robust estimators—namely, M-estimators (Section 20.4.1) and L-estimators (Section 20.4.2). A third classification where estimators are based on a ranking of the residuals in linear models is known as R-estimators. For details and additional references in this area, we refer the reader to Koenker (1982), Jaeckel (1972), McKean and Hettmansperger (1978), and Sievers (1978). Other work that is not described or referred to here but is worthy of mention is that of Kadiyala (1972), Hogg and Randles (1975), Chambers and Heathcote (1975, 1978), Krasker (1980), and Moberg et al. (1980). Gilstein and Leamer (1983) suggest an approach where the *set* of maximum likelihood estimators for a given set of error distributions is identified. Maximum likelihood estimation of density functions that include the normal as a special case has been investigated by Zeckhauser and Thompson (1970) and Goldfeld and Quandt (1981).

Finally, it is important to note that when James and Stein (1961) considered the problem of the simultaneous estimation of location parameters under quadratic loss that we discussed in Chapter 3, they also showed the assumption of normality was unnecessary and suggested an estimator of the form $\delta(\tilde{\boldsymbol{\beta}}) = \{1 - b/(a + \tilde{\boldsymbol{\beta}}'\tilde{\boldsymbol{\beta}})\}\tilde{\boldsymbol{\beta}}$, which is better than the maximum likelihood estimator $\tilde{\boldsymbol{\beta}}$ if a and b are suitably chosen. Since the values a and b were not explicitly determined it was left to Shinozaki (1984) to demonstrate explicit estimators which dominate the best invariant estimator when the coordinates of the best invariant estimator are independently, identically, and symmetrically distributed. Ullah, Srivastava, and Chandra (1983) consider a class of shrinkage estimators and study their sampling properties when the disturbances are small and possess moments of the fourth order. Alternatively, Stein (1981) proposed a coordinate-wise limited translation estimator to improve on the conventional Stein type estimator in the case of possibly heavy-tailed prior distributions. Dey and Berger (1983) analyzed this estimator for a number of heavy-tailed distributions, noted its risk performance and proposed an operational adaptive version. Judge, Yancey, and Miyazaki (1984) analyzed the sampling performance of this family of Stein-like estimators under multivariate t and independent t error distributions with 1, 3, and 5 degrees of freedom and found the risk performance of a variety of Stein estimators over the range of the parameter space, to be superior to some of the conventional robust estimators to be discussed in this section.

20.4.1 M-Estimators

We are concerned with estimating the $(K \times 1)$ parameter vector $\boldsymbol{\beta}$ in the linear model

$$y_t = \mathbf{x}_t'\boldsymbol{\beta} + e_t, \qquad t = 1, 2, \ldots, T \tag{20.4.1}$$

where the e_t are independent, identically distributed, random variables with distribution function $F(y_t - \mathbf{x}_t'\boldsymbol{\beta})$. It is assumed that the e_t are symmetrically distributed around zero, but that they do not necessarily possess a finite mean and variance.

For least squares estimation we find that $\boldsymbol{\beta}$ which minimizes $\Sigma(y_t - \mathbf{x}_t'\boldsymbol{\beta})^2$, or, equivalently, that $\boldsymbol{\beta}$ which satisfies the equations

$$\sum_{t=1}^{T} \mathbf{x}_t(y_t - \mathbf{x}_t'\boldsymbol{\beta}) = \mathbf{0} \tag{20.4.2}$$

Similarly, for maximum likelihood estimation where e_t has density function $f(y_t - \mathbf{x}_t'\boldsymbol{\beta})$, we find that $\boldsymbol{\beta}$ which minimizes $-\Sigma \ln f(y_t - \mathbf{x}_t'\boldsymbol{\beta})$, or, equivalently, we find that $\boldsymbol{\beta}$ which is a solution to

$$\sum_{t=1}^{T} \mathbf{x}_t \frac{f'(y_t - \mathbf{x}_t'\boldsymbol{\beta})}{f(y_t - \mathbf{x}_t'\boldsymbol{\beta})} = \mathbf{0} \tag{20.4.3}$$

where $f'(z) = df(z)/dz$. Of course, if the e_t are normally distributed, (20.4.2) and (20.4.3) are identical.

If the density function f is unknown, and, therefore, f'/f is unknown, the equations in (20.4.3) cannot be solved. However, we can obtain a "maximum likelihood like" estimator by replacing f'/f with another function, say ψ, and then solving. Such an estimator is known as an "M-estimator"; it is considered desirable to choose a function ψ that leads to an estimator for $\boldsymbol{\beta}$ which is robust under alternative specifications of f. The estimation problem can be set up in terms of finding that $\boldsymbol{\beta}$ which minimizes the function

$$\sum_{t=1}^{T} \rho(y_t - \mathbf{x}_t'\boldsymbol{\beta}) \tag{20.4.4}$$

or, alternatively, that $\boldsymbol{\beta}$ which satisfies the equations

$$\sum_{t=1}^{T} \mathbf{x}_t\psi(y_t - \mathbf{x}_t'\boldsymbol{\beta}) = \mathbf{0} \tag{20.4.5}$$

where, if $\rho(z)$ is a strictly convex function, $\rho'(z) = \psi(z)$. In the least squares case, $\rho(y_t - \mathbf{x}_t'\boldsymbol{\beta}) = \frac{1}{2}(y_t - \mathbf{x}_t'\boldsymbol{\beta})^2$ and $\psi(y_t - \mathbf{x}_t'\boldsymbol{\beta}) = y_t - \mathbf{x}_t'\boldsymbol{\beta}$. However, for robust estimation we typically choose ρ and ψ so that outliers are weighted less heavily than they are in the least squares situation. One set of functions that has been popularized by Huber and that possesses some desirable minimax properties in the presence of a "contaminated" normal distribution [see Huber (1981) for details] is

$$\rho(y_t - \mathbf{x}_t'\boldsymbol{\beta}) = \begin{cases} \frac{1}{2}(y_t - \mathbf{x}_t'\boldsymbol{\beta})^2 & \text{if } |y_t - \mathbf{x}_t'\boldsymbol{\beta}| \leq k \\ k|y_t - \mathbf{x}_t\boldsymbol{\beta}| - \frac{1}{2}k^2 & \text{if } |y_t - \mathbf{x}_t'\boldsymbol{\beta}| > k \end{cases} \tag{20.4.6}$$

and

$$\psi(y_t - \mathbf{x}_t'\boldsymbol{\beta}) = \max\{-k, \min(k, y_t - \mathbf{x}_t'\boldsymbol{\beta})\}$$
$$= \begin{cases} -k & \text{if } y_t - \mathbf{x}_t'\boldsymbol{\beta} < -k \\ y_t - \mathbf{x}_t'\boldsymbol{\beta} & \text{if } |y_t - \mathbf{x}_t'\boldsymbol{\beta}| \leq k \\ k & \text{if } y_t - \mathbf{x}_t'\boldsymbol{\beta} > k \end{cases} \tag{20.4.7}$$

where k is a preassigned multiple of a robust measure of dispersion of the e_t. From (20.4.6) we see that this scheme treats "small" residuals in the traditional way, by minimizing their sum of squares. However, so that outliers do not have an undue influence on the estimation procedure, the sum of the *absolute values* of "large" residuals is minimized. In terms of the normal equations in (20.4.5), the scheme implies that small residuals are treated in the usual manner, but residuals greater than k in absolute value are replaced by $\pm k$. See Equation 20.4.7.

Let us introduce the measure of dispersion (or the scale factor) more explicitly. If $k = c\sigma$, where σ is a measure of dispersion and c is a constant usually taken as about 1.5, then (20.4.7) can be written as

$$\psi\left(\frac{y_t - \mathbf{x}_t'\boldsymbol{\beta}}{\sigma}\right) = \begin{cases} -c & \text{if } y_t - \mathbf{x}_t'\boldsymbol{\beta} < -c\sigma \\ (\mathbf{y}_t - \mathbf{x}_t'\boldsymbol{\beta})/\sigma & \text{if } |y_t - \mathbf{x}_t'\boldsymbol{\beta}| \leq c\sigma \\ c & \text{if } y_t - \mathbf{x}_t'\boldsymbol{\beta} > c\sigma \end{cases} \tag{20.4.8}$$

The scale factor is introduced in the general case in a similar manner. In particular, to ensure an M-estimator for $\boldsymbol{\beta}$ is scale invariant we replace (20.4.5) with

$$\sum_{t=1}^{T} \mathbf{x}_t \psi\left(\frac{y_t - \mathbf{x}_t'\boldsymbol{\beta}}{\sigma}\right) = \mathbf{0} \tag{20.4.9}$$

Of course, σ is unknown, but it can be replaced by an estimate, preferably one that is robust. One way of obtaining a robust scale estimate is to find the residuals from the l_1-estimator for $\boldsymbol{\beta}$ (see Section 20.4.2), and to take the median of the absolute values of these residuals. Another robust scale estimate is the interquartile range of the l_1-residuals.

A more appealing approach, however, is to set up "pseudo maximum likelihood equations" for both $\boldsymbol{\beta}$ and σ. Those suggested by Huber (1981, p. 179) are (20.4.9) and

$$\frac{1}{T}\sum_{t=1}^{T} \chi\left(\frac{y_t - \mathbf{x}_t'\boldsymbol{\beta}}{\sigma}\right) = a \tag{20.4.10}$$

where $\chi(z) = z\psi(z) - \rho(z)$,

$$a = \frac{T - K}{T} E_\Phi(\chi) \tag{20.4.11}$$

E_Φ is the expectation with respect to Φ, and Φ is the distribution function for a standard normal random variable. The choice of a in (20.4.11) is mainly for convenience. It leads to the classical estimates for the least squares choice $\rho(z) = \frac{1}{2}z^2$, and it ensures the scale estimate will be consistent if the errors are normally distributed.

Let us examine the nature of (20.4.9) and (20.4.10) for the special case where ψ is defined by (20.4.8). Also, we will investigate how to solve the equations for this particular case. Working in this direction we define what are often termed the "Winsorized residuals"

$$e_t^* = \begin{cases} -c\sigma & \text{if } y_t - \mathbf{x}_t'\boldsymbol{\beta} < -c\sigma \\ e_t = y_t - \mathbf{x}_t'\boldsymbol{\beta} & \text{if } |y_t - \mathbf{x}_t'\boldsymbol{\beta}| \leq c\sigma \\ c\sigma & \text{if } y_t - \mathbf{x}_t'\boldsymbol{\beta} > c\sigma \end{cases} \tag{20.4.12}$$

That is, the residuals with absolute values greater than $c\sigma$ are replaced by $\pm c\sigma$. Then, for ψ defined in (20.4.8), Equation 20.4.9 can be written as

$$\sum_{t=1}^{T} \frac{\mathbf{x}_t e_t^*}{\sigma} = \mathbf{0} \tag{20.4.13}$$

To rewrite (20.4.10) we first note that, in this case, $\chi(z) = \frac{1}{2}\psi(z)^2$, and so (20.4.10) becomes

$$\frac{1}{2T}\sum_{t=1}^{T} \frac{e_t^{*2}}{\sigma^2} = a \tag{20.4.14}$$

Furthermore, $a = [(T - K)/T]E_\Phi \frac{1}{2}\psi^2 = [(T - K)/2T]\gamma$, where $\gamma = E_\Phi \psi^2 = 2[c^2\Phi(-c) + \int_0^c z^2\, d\Phi(z)]$. Rewriting (20.4.13) and (20.4.14) yields

$$X'\mathbf{e}^* = \mathbf{0} \tag{20.4.15}$$

and

$$\sigma^2 = \frac{\mathbf{e}^{*\prime}\mathbf{e}^*}{(T - K)\gamma} \tag{20.4.16}$$

where $\mathbf{e}^*$ and X (and for future reference $\mathbf{y}$) have obvious vector and matrix definitions. In the classical least squares case $\gamma = 1$ and $\mathbf{e}^* = \mathbf{y} - X\boldsymbol{\beta}$, and thus the least squares solutions are obtained immediately from (20.4.15) and (20.4.16). In our case, however, $\mathbf{e}^*$ depends on both $\boldsymbol{\beta}$ and σ through the Winsorizing of residuals, and an iterative procedure is needed to solve (20.4.15) and (20.4.16).

One algorithm is as follows. We begin with some initial estimates $\hat{\boldsymbol{\beta}}^{(0)}$ and $\hat{\sigma}^{(0)}$, which could be least squares estimates, or, preferably, those obtained from l_1-estimation. See Andrews (1974), Hinich and Talwar (1975), and Harvey (1977) for some discussion on initial estimates. Using $\hat{\boldsymbol{\beta}}^{(0)}$ and $\hat{\sigma}^{(0)}$, some Winsorized residuals $\mathbf{e}^{*(0)}$ are calculated from (20.4.12). A second scale estimate

$\hat{\sigma}^{2(1)} = \mathbf{e}^{*(0)\prime}\mathbf{e}^{*(0)}/(T - K)\gamma$ can then be calculated. To obtain a second estimate of $\boldsymbol{\beta}$ we define $\mathbf{y}^{(1)} = X\hat{\boldsymbol{\beta}}^{(0)} + \mathbf{e}^{*(0)}$ and take $\hat{\boldsymbol{\beta}}^{(1)}$ as the solution obtained when $\mathbf{e}^*$ in $X'\mathbf{e}^* = \mathbf{0}$ is replaced by $\mathbf{y}^{(1)} - X\boldsymbol{\beta}^{(1)}$. That is, we solve

$$X'(\mathbf{y}^{(1)} - X\hat{\boldsymbol{\beta}}^{(1)}) = \mathbf{0} \tag{20.4.17}$$

The solution to (20.4.17) is identical to

$$\hat{\boldsymbol{\beta}}^{(1)} = \hat{\boldsymbol{\beta}}^{(0)} + (X'X)^{-1}X'\mathbf{e}^{*(0)} \tag{20.4.18}$$

The estimates $\hat{\boldsymbol{\beta}}^{(1)}$ and $\hat{\sigma}^{(1)}$ can be used to obtain a new set of Winsorized residuals $\mathbf{e}^{*(1)}$, and the process continues until convergence. For details of convergence properties, see Huber (1981, Ch. 7) and references therein.

Another possible algorithm is an iterative weighted least squares scheme. Specifically, at the mth iteration we minimize $\Sigma_{t=1}^{T} w_t^{(m)}(y_t - \mathbf{x}_t'\boldsymbol{\beta}^{(m)})^2$, where

$$w_t^{(m)} = \begin{cases} 1 & \text{if } |y_t - \mathbf{x}_t'\hat{\boldsymbol{\beta}}^{(m-1)}| \leq c\hat{\sigma}^{(m-1)} \\ \dfrac{c\hat{\sigma}^{(m-1)}}{|y_t - \mathbf{x}_t'\hat{\boldsymbol{\beta}}^{(m-1)}|} & \text{if } |y_t - \mathbf{x}_t'\hat{\boldsymbol{\beta}}^{(m-1)}| > c\hat{\sigma}^{(m-1)} \end{cases} \tag{20.4.19}$$

The resulting estimator is $\hat{\boldsymbol{\beta}}^{(m)} = (X'W^{(m)}X)^{-1}X'W^{(m)}\mathbf{y}$, where $W^{(m)} =$ diagonal$(w_1^{(m)}, w_2^{(m)}, \ldots, w_T^{(m)})$.

The asymptotic properties of M-estimators have been investigated by, among others, Huber (1973, 1981) and Yohai and Maronna (1979). If, in addition to some mild conditions on ψ and F, we assume that (i) $E_F\psi(e_t) = 0$, (ii) $E_F\psi(e_t)^2 < \infty$, and (iii) $\lim T^{-1}X'X = Q$ is positive definite, then it is possible to show that the corresponding M-estimator, say $\hat{\boldsymbol{\beta}}$, is consistent, and that

$$\sqrt{T}(\hat{\boldsymbol{\beta}} - \boldsymbol{\beta}) \xrightarrow{d} N[\mathbf{0}, \sigma^2(\psi,F)Q^{-1}] \tag{20.4.20}$$

where $\sigma^2(\psi,F) = E_F\psi(e_t)^2/[E_F\psi'(e_t)]^2$. For the special case where ψ is defined by (20.4.8), Huber (1971) recommends estimating the asymptotic covariance of $\hat{\boldsymbol{\beta}}$ with

$$\hat{\Sigma}_{\hat{\boldsymbol{\beta}}} = \frac{g^2\mathbf{e}^{*\prime}\mathbf{e}^*}{T - K}(X'X)^{-1} \tag{20.4.21}$$

where $g = [1 + (K/T)(1 - \mu)/\mu]/\mu$ and μ is the proportion of "non-Winsorized" residuals. From these results we can construct approximate confidence intervals for the elements in $\boldsymbol{\beta}$, as well as test hypotheses about $\boldsymbol{\beta}$.

We conclude this section with two more points. First, a number of other ψ functions have been suggested in the literature. For some examples see Anscombe (1967), Hill and Holland (1977), and Serfling (1980, Chapter 7). Second, observations that could be regarded as outliers with respect to a true underlying regression model will not necessarily show up as outliers in the residuals of a fitted regression. Such will be the case if these observations are "high leverage" points—they exert a strong influence on the position of the fitted regression. Also, highly influential observations become particularly important if we regard our linear model as an approximation to a nonlinear one, and we are concerned with the robustness of this approximation. For work in this area see Belsley, Kuh and Welsch (1980), Krasker and Welsch (1982), and Huber (1983).

20.4.2 L-Estimators

When estimating the simple location model

$$y_t = \beta + e_t \tag{20.4.22}$$

where the y_t are independent identically distributed random variables with symmetric distribution function F and median β, the title L-estimators is used for estimators which are linear combinations of the order statistics $y_{(1)}, y_{(2)}, \ldots, y_{(T)}$. In this section we discuss Koenker and Bassett's (1978) generalized versions of these estimators for the linear model.

We begin by briefly considering quantiles for the simple location model in (20.4.22). If F is continuous, then its θth quantile $(0 < \theta < 1)$, denoted by ξ_θ, is that value of y for which $P(y < \xi_\theta) = F(\xi_\theta) = \theta$. If θT is not an integer, the θth *sample quantile* is $y_{(n)}$, where $n = [\theta T] + 1$, and the quantity $[\theta T]$ denotes the greatest integer not exceeding θT. If θT is an integer, then the θth sample quantile is not unique, and is taken as any value between $y_{(\theta T)}$ and $y_{(\theta T+1)}$. For example, in (20.4.22), $\xi_{0.5} = \beta$ is the median and, if $T = 25$ (say), $y_{(13)}$ is the sample median. For $T = 24$ the sample median is any value between $y_{(12)}$ and $y_{(13)}$, but usually some rule, such as median $= (y_{(12)} + y_{(13)})/2$, is used to obtain a unique value. Thus, the sample quantiles, and any linear function of them, are L-estimators of location. In addition to the median, examples of L-estimators that have been suggested are the Gastwirth (1966)

$$\hat{\beta}_G = 0.3\hat{\xi}_{1/3} + 0.4\hat{\xi}_{0.5} + 0.3\hat{\xi}_{2/3} \tag{20.4.23}$$

where $\hat{\xi}_\theta$ is the θth sample quantile; and the trimmed mean that is the sample mean of all observations lying between two quantiles, say $\hat{\xi}_\alpha$ and $\hat{\xi}_{1-\alpha}$.

When we consider the more general linear model, our usual concept of order statistics is no longer adequate because what constitutes an appropriate ordering depends on the vector $\boldsymbol{\beta}$. One possible approach is to obtain the residuals from a preliminary fit (such as least squares or least absolute values) and to estimate the quantiles of the error distribution on the basis of these residuals. A more appealing approach, however, is that suggested by Koenker and Bassett (1978). They begin by noting that, in the location model, the θth sample quantile can be equivalently defined as any solution to the following minimization problem:

$$\min_{\beta} \left[\sum_{\{t|y_t \geq \beta\}} \theta|y_t - \beta| + \sum_{\{t|y_t < \beta\}} (1 - \theta)|y_t - \beta| \right] \tag{20.4.24}$$

This definition extends readily to the more general case. Specifically, if we have the linear model

$$y_t = \mathbf{x}_t'\boldsymbol{\beta} + e_t \tag{20.4.25}$$

where the e_t are independent and identically distributed with distribution function F, which is symmetric around zero, and the other notation is identical to that used previously, then the θth *regression quantile* $(0 < \theta < 1)$ is defined as any solution to the minimization problem,

$$\min_{\boldsymbol{\beta}} \left[\sum_{\{t|y_t \geq \mathbf{x}_t'\boldsymbol{\beta}\}} \theta|y_t - \mathbf{x}_t'\boldsymbol{\beta}| + \sum_{\{t|y_t < \mathbf{x}_t'\boldsymbol{\beta}\}} (1-\theta)|y_t - \mathbf{x}_t'\boldsymbol{\beta}| \right] \tag{20.4.26}$$

When $k = 1$ and $x_{t1} \equiv 1$, (20.4.26) reduces to (20.4.24). Also, for $\theta = \frac{1}{2}$, (20.4.26) is equivalent to minimizing $\Sigma_t|y_t - \mathbf{x}_t'\boldsymbol{\beta}|$, and the resulting estimator is often known as the least absolute value or l_1-estimator. We shall discuss this estimator in more detail in Section 20.4.2a. The minimization problem in (20.4.26) is a linear programming problem whose computational aspects are discussed in Appendices in Koenker and Bassett (1978) and Bassett and Koenker (1982).

A number of properties of the estimators $\hat{\boldsymbol{\beta}}^*(\theta)$ that are solutions to (20.4.26) are outlined in Koenker and Bassett (1978), and properties of the empirical quantile functions are studied further in Bassett and Koenker (1982, 1983) and Koenker and Bassett (1982a). We will report just the asymptotic distribution results for $\hat{\boldsymbol{\beta}}^*(\theta)$. It is convenient to define $\boldsymbol{\beta}^*(\theta) = (\beta_1^*(\theta), \beta_2, \beta_3, \ldots, \beta_K)'$, where $\beta_1^*(\theta) = \beta_1 + \xi_\theta$ and $\xi_\theta = F^{-1}(\theta)$ is the θth quantile of the error distribution. We assume that $x_{t1} \equiv 1$ and so $\boldsymbol{\beta}^*(\theta)$ is identical to $\boldsymbol{\beta}$ except for an adjustment to the intercept, with the adjustment equal to the θth quantile. Note that, in the case of the median, we have $\xi_{0.5} = 0$ and $\boldsymbol{\beta}^*(0.5) = \boldsymbol{\beta}$. Let $\hat{\boldsymbol{\delta}}' = (\hat{\boldsymbol{\beta}}^{*\prime}(\theta_1), \hat{\boldsymbol{\beta}}^{*\prime}(\theta_2), \ldots, \hat{\boldsymbol{\beta}}^{*\prime}(\theta_M))$ with $0 < \theta_1 < \theta_2 < \ldots < \theta_M < 1$ denote a sequence of unique regression quantile estimates, and, correspondingly let $\boldsymbol{\delta}' = (\boldsymbol{\beta}^{*\prime}(\theta_1), \boldsymbol{\beta}^{*\prime}(\theta_2), \ldots, \boldsymbol{\beta}^{*\prime}(\theta_M))$. Then, it can be shown that

$$\sqrt{T}\,(\hat{\boldsymbol{\delta}} - \boldsymbol{\delta}) \xrightarrow{d} N(\mathbf{0}, \Omega \otimes Q^{-1}) \tag{20.4.27}$$

where:

(i) Ω has typical element

$$\omega_{ij} = \frac{\min(\theta_i, \theta_j) - \theta_i\theta_j}{f(\xi_{\theta_i})f(\xi_{\theta_j})} \tag{20.4.28}$$

(ii) F has density function f that is assumed to be continuous and positive at ξ_{θ_i}, $i = 1, 2, \ldots, M$; and
(iii) $\lim T^{-1}X'X = Q$ is a positive definite matrix.

Necessary and sufficient conditions for the uniqueness of $\hat{\boldsymbol{\delta}}$ are given by Koenker and Bassett (1978). Uniqueness can always be achieved by selecting an appropriate design or by using an arbitrary rule to select from any set of multiple solutions. Note that, apart from the intercept term, $\hat{\boldsymbol{\beta}}^*(\theta_1)$, $\hat{\boldsymbol{\beta}}^*(\theta_2)$, . . . , $\hat{\boldsymbol{\beta}}^*(\theta_M)$ can all be regarded as alternative estimators for the same coefficient vector $\boldsymbol{\beta}$. In the following subsections we use some special cases to indicate how approximate inference procedures can be based on the result in (20.4.27).

20.4.2a l_1-Estimation

As mentioned above, when $\theta = \frac{1}{2}$ the minimization problem in (20.4.26) is equivalent to finding that $\boldsymbol{\beta}$ which minimizes $\Sigma|y_t - \mathbf{x}_t'\boldsymbol{\beta}|$. This estimator, $\hat{\boldsymbol{\beta}}^*(0.5)$, is sometimes referred to as the l_1-estimator since it is a special case of the l_P-estimator that minimizes $\Sigma_t|y_t - \mathbf{x}_t'\boldsymbol{\beta}|^P$. It has also been called the least absolute value (LAV) estimator, the least absolute residual (LAR) estimator, the least absolute error (LAE) estimator, and the minimum absolute deviation (MAD) estimator. See Dielman and Pfaffenberger (1982) for a review of computational algorithms, small sample (Monte Carlo) properties, and asymptotic properties. Examples of computational algorithms are the linear programming algorithms suggested by Spyropoulos et al. (1973), Abdelmalek (1974), and Bassett and Koenker (1982), and the iterative weighted least squares algorithm suggested by Schlossmacher (1973) and Fair (1974).

With respect to the statistical properties of $\hat{\boldsymbol{\beta}}^*(0.5)$, we first note [see Blattberg and Sargent (1971)] that, if the disturbances follow a two-tailed exponential distribution with density function

$$f(e_t) = (2\lambda)^{-1} \exp\left\{-\frac{|e_t|}{\lambda}\right\} \tag{20.4.29}$$

then maximization of the likelihood function is equivalent to minimization of $\Sigma_{t=1}^{T}|e_t|$ and so $\hat{\boldsymbol{\beta}}^*(0.5)$ will be the maximum likelihood estimator. Relative to the normal distribution this density is more peaked and has fatter tails, but unlike many other distributions with fat tails, it does have a finite variance. The maximum likelihood estimator thus has the usual desirable asymptotic properties. Also, the superiority of $\hat{\boldsymbol{\beta}}^*(0.5)$ over LS in finite samples, when the errors follow the density in (20.4.29), was confirmed in a Monte Carlo study by Smith and Hall (1972).

For the more general case where e_t comes from any distribution, some results on unbiasedness have been provided by Sielken and Hartley (1973) and Taylor (1974). The estimator will be unbiased if it is a unique solution to the minimization problem; alternatively, if multiple solutions exist, unbiasedness can be obtained by using Sielken and Hartley's algorithm.

The limiting distribution of $\hat{\boldsymbol{\beta}}^*(0.5)$ is given by considering the appropriate subvector of $\hat{\boldsymbol{\delta}}$ in (20.4.27). In particular, ω_{ij} becomes $[2f(0)]^{-2}$ and we have

$$\sqrt{T}\,[\hat{\boldsymbol{\beta}}^*(0.5) - \boldsymbol{\beta}] \xrightarrow{d} N(\mathbf{0},[2f(0)]^{-2}Q^{-1}) \tag{20.4.30}$$

where $f(0)$ is the value of the density at the median [Bassett and Koenker (1978)]. The term $[2f(0)]^{-2}$ is the asymptotic variance of the sample median from samples with distribution function F. Thus, the l_1-estimator will be more efficient than the least squares estimator for all error distributions where the median is superior to the mean as an estimator of location. This class of error distributions includes the Cauchy, the two-tailed exponential, and a number of other distributions where "outliers" are prevalent.

It is straightforward to use (20.4.30) to formulate a Wald statistic for testing hypotheses about $\boldsymbol{\beta}$, providing that we can find a consistent estimator for $f(0)$. One such estimator is [Cox and Hinkley (1974, p. 470)]

$$\hat{f}(0) = \frac{r - s}{T(\hat{e}_{(r)} - \hat{e}_{(s)})} \tag{20.4.31}$$

where $r = [T/2] + v$, $s = [T/2] - v$, $[\cdot]$ indicates the integer portion of the argument, v is an integer and $\hat{e}_{(1)}, \hat{e}_{(2)}, \ldots, \hat{e}_{(T)}$ are the ordered l_1-residuals. The best choice of v is not clear; however, since (20.4.31) is essentially a smoothing procedure, it will depend upon the smoothness of the empirical function and the number of observations. Also, this estimator may not be satisfactory when (K/T) is large. For further information on this and other estimators, and access to the literature, see Sheather and Maritz (1983).

In addition to the Wald test, Koenker and Bassett (1982b) suggest tests that are analogous to the likelihood ratio (LR) and Lagrange multiplier tests, and which are also based on l_1-estimation methods. For testing a set of linear restrictions on $\boldsymbol{\beta}$, their LR statistic is

$$\lambda_{\text{LR}} = 2[2f(0)]^{-1}(S_R - S_U) \tag{20.4.32}$$

where S_U and S_R are the sums of the absolute values of the residuals in the unrestricted and restricted models, respectively. For the hypothesis $\boldsymbol{\beta}_2 = \mathbf{0}$ in the partitioning $y_t = \mathbf{x}_{t1}'\boldsymbol{\beta}_1 + \mathbf{x}_{t2}'\boldsymbol{\beta}_2 + e_t$ the LM statistic is

$$\lambda_{\text{LM}} = \mathbf{g}'D\mathbf{g} \tag{20.4.33}$$

where $\mathbf{g} = \Sigma_t \mathbf{x}_{t2} \operatorname{sign}(y_t - \mathbf{x}_{t1}'\tilde{\boldsymbol{\beta}}_1)$, $\tilde{\boldsymbol{\beta}}_1$ is the restricted l_1-estimator for $\boldsymbol{\beta}_1$, and D is the second diagonal block of $(X'X)^{-1}$ corresponding to the above partitioning of $\mathbf{x}_t'\boldsymbol{\beta}$. Under the null hypothesis both statistics have limiting $\chi^2_{(J)}$-distributions, where J is the number of restrictions. The LM test has the advantage that it does not require estimation of $f(0)$. Koenker and Bassett (1982b) compare the asymptotic efficiency of the tests with that of the more conventional ones based on least squares residuals, and suggest some finite sample correction factors. As expected, the tests based on l_1-estimation are more powerful for heavytailed distributions.

Before turning to more general functions of regression quantiles, we note that Amemiya (1982) and Powell (1983) have extended l_1-methods to simultaneous equation models.

20.4.2b Linear Functions of Regression Quantiles

The l_1-estimator is, of course, one example of a linear function of regression quantiles where all the weight is placed on $\theta = 0.5$. It is also possible to construct estimators that are more general functions of the regression quantiles and that are analogous to some of the L-estimators suggested for the simple location model (c.f. Equation 20.4.23). Consider the estimator

$$\hat{\boldsymbol{\beta}}(\boldsymbol{\pi}) = \sum_{i=1}^{M} \pi(\theta_i)\hat{\boldsymbol{\beta}}^*(\theta_i) \tag{20.4.34}$$

where $\boldsymbol{\pi} = (\pi(\theta_1), \pi(\theta_2), \ldots, \pi(\theta_M))'$ is a symmetric weighting scheme, and the assumptions and notation used throughout this section still hold. Because both $\pi(\theta_i)$ and the distribution of e_t are symmetric, we can treat $\hat{\boldsymbol{\beta}}(\boldsymbol{\pi})$ as an estimator for $\boldsymbol{\beta}$ rather than a particular $\boldsymbol{\beta}^*(\theta)$, and we have the result [Koenker and Bassett (1978)]

$$\sqrt{T}\,(\hat{\boldsymbol{\beta}}(\boldsymbol{\pi}) - \boldsymbol{\beta}) \xrightarrow{d} N(\mathbf{0},\boldsymbol{\pi}'\Omega\boldsymbol{\pi}Q^{-1}) \tag{20.4.35}$$

Examples of weighting schemes are the Gastwirth scheme mentioned above, where $\boldsymbol{\pi}' = (\pi(\frac{1}{3}), \pi(\frac{1}{2}), \pi(\frac{2}{3})) = (0.3, 0.4, 0.3)$, or the trimean suggested by Tukey, where $\boldsymbol{\pi}' = (\pi(\frac{1}{4}), \pi(\frac{1}{2}), \pi(\frac{3}{4})) = (0.25, 0.5, 0.25)$. The result in (20.4.35) can be used to formulate approximate tests for testing hypotheses about $\boldsymbol{\beta}$, providing we substitute $X'X/T$ for Q, and use a consistent estimator for the elements of Ω. For this latter estimator we need an estimator for $f(\xi_{\theta_i})$—see Equation 20.4.28. Along the lines of (20.4.31) such an estimator is given by

$$\hat{f}(\xi_\theta) = \frac{r - s}{T(\hat{e}_{(r)} - \hat{e}_{(s)})} \tag{20.4.36}$$

where $r = [T\theta] + v$, $s = [T\theta] - v$, and $\hat{e}_{(1)}, \hat{e}_{(2)}, \ldots, \hat{e}_{(T)}$ are the ordered l_1-residuals. For another possible method of estimating the density function ordinates $f(\xi_\theta)$, see Koenker and Bassett (1982a).

20.4.2c Trimmed Least Squares

An obvious analogue to the trimmed mean of the simple location model is the trimmed least squares estimator suggested by Koenker and Bassett (1978) and studied further by Ruppert and Carroll (1980). To obtain this estimator we first calculate $\hat{\boldsymbol{\beta}}^*(\alpha)$ and $\hat{\boldsymbol{\beta}}^*(1 - \alpha)$, where α is the desired trimming proportion $(0 < \alpha < 0.5)$. Then, observations where $y_t - \mathbf{x}_t'\hat{\boldsymbol{\beta}}^*(\alpha) \le 0$ or $y_t - \mathbf{x}_t'\hat{\boldsymbol{\beta}}^*(1 - \alpha) \ge 0$ are discarded, and least squares is applied to the remaining observations. Denoting this estimator by $\tilde{\boldsymbol{\beta}}_\alpha$, under appropriate conditions it can be shown that [Ruppert and Carroll (1980)]

$$\sqrt{T}\,(\tilde{\boldsymbol{\beta}}_\alpha - \boldsymbol{\beta}) \xrightarrow{d} N(\mathbf{0},\sigma^2(\alpha,F)Q^{-1}) \tag{20.4.37}$$

where $\sigma^2(\alpha,F)$ denotes the asymptotic variance of the corresponding α-trimmed mean from a population with distribution F. A consistent estimator for $\sigma^2(\alpha,F)$ is given by [Ruppert and Carroll (1980)]

$$\hat{\sigma}^2(\alpha,F) = \frac{1}{(1-2\alpha)^2}\left(\frac{S}{T-K} + \alpha(c_1^2 + c_2^2) - \alpha^2(c_1 + c_2)^2\right) \quad (20.4.38)$$

where S is the sum of squares of residuals from the trimmed sample,

$$c_1 = \bar{\mathbf{x}}'(\hat{\boldsymbol{\beta}}^*(\alpha) - \tilde{\boldsymbol{\beta}}_\alpha), \quad c_2 = \bar{\mathbf{x}}'(\hat{\boldsymbol{\beta}}^*(1-\alpha) - \tilde{\boldsymbol{\beta}}_\alpha) \quad (20.4.39)$$

and $\bar{\mathbf{x}}$ is a K-vector containing the means of the observations on the explanatory variables. Ruppert and Carroll find that $\tilde{\boldsymbol{\beta}}_\alpha$ is preferable to trimmed estimators where the trimming is based on a preliminary estimate such as the least squares or l_1-estimator. Also, the trimmed least squares estimator has been shown [Jurečková (1983)] to be asymptotically equivalent to Huber's M-estimator; it has the added virtue of scale invariance. The l_1-estimator can be viewed as the limiting case of the trimmed least squares estimator where $\alpha = \frac{1}{2}$.

20.4.2d Heteroscedastic Errors

We conclude this section by mentioning some work investigating the consequences of relaxing the assumption that the e_t are identically distributed. As we have seen, when the errors are identically distributed, the intercept term in $\boldsymbol{\beta}^*(\theta)$ depends on θ, but the slope coefficients do not. When heteroscedasticity exists, however, the slope coefficients for the θth quantile are also likely to depend on θ. This scenario has been investigated by Koenker and Bassett (1982a) who suggest testing for heteroscedasticity on the basis of whether or not the estimated slope coefficients for different quantiles are significantly different.

20.5 THE BOX–COX TRANSFORMATION

For some statistical models the dependent variable may not be normally distributed, but there may exist a transformation such that the transformed observations are normally distributed. For example, consider the nonlinear model

$$y_t = \exp\{\mathbf{x}_t'\boldsymbol{\beta}\} \cdot \exp\{e_t\}, \qquad t = 1, 2, \ldots, T \quad (20.5.1)$$

where y_t is the tth observation on a dependent variable, $\mathbf{x}_t$ is a $(K \times 1)$ vector containing the tth observation on some explanatory variables, $\boldsymbol{\beta}$ is a $(K \times 1)$ vector of parameters to be estimated, and the e_t are i.i.d. $N(0,\sigma^2)$. In this model the y_t are log normally distributed and heteroscedastic with variances

$$V(y_t) = [\exp(\mathbf{x}_t'\boldsymbol{\beta})]^2 \cdot \exp(\sigma^2) \cdot [\exp(\sigma^2) - 1], \qquad t = 1, 2, \ldots, T$$

However, taking logs of Equation 20.5.1 yields

$$\ln y_t = \mathbf{x}_t'\boldsymbol{\beta} + e_t \tag{20.5.2}$$

where $\ln y_t$ is normally distributed, homoscedastic, and a linear function of $\boldsymbol{\beta}$, and so application of least squares to (20.5.2) gives a minimum variance unbiased estimator for $\boldsymbol{\beta}$.

This is a special case of a class of transformations considered by Box and Cox (1964). For this class they assume there exists a value λ such that

$$\frac{y_t^\lambda - 1}{\lambda} = \mathbf{x}_t'\boldsymbol{\beta} + e_t \tag{20.5.3}$$

where the e_t are i.i.d. $N(0,\sigma^2)$. Thus they assume that there exists a transformation of the dependent variable, of the form given in (20.5.3), such that the transformed dependent variable:

1. Is normally distributed.
2. Is homoscedastic.
3. Has an expectation that is linear in $\boldsymbol{\beta}$.

It can be shown that $\lim_{\lambda\to 0}[(y_t^\lambda - 1)/\lambda] = \ln y_t$, and so Equation 20.5.2 is regarded as a special case of (20.5.3), where $\lambda = 0$. Also, apart from a difference in the intercept, $\lambda = 1$ yields the familiar linear model $y_t = \mathbf{x}_t'\boldsymbol{\beta} + e_t$. If λ were known, the application of least squares to (20.5.3) would yield a minimum variance unbiased estimator for $\boldsymbol{\beta}$. However, it is usually assumed that λ is unknown and, along with $\boldsymbol{\beta}$, it needs to be estimated.

Before discussing maximum likelihood estimation of the parameters, some comments on model specification and "functional form analysis" are in order. Despite the fact that this transformation may be useful for inducing normality on observations from skewed distributions, and despite the fact that this section appears in a chapter entitled "Nonnormal Disturbances," the main use of the Box–Cox transformation in empirical econometrics has been as a device for generalizing functional form. Because the functional forms $E[y_t] = \mathbf{x}_t'\boldsymbol{\beta}$ and $E[\ln y_t] = \mathbf{x}_t'\boldsymbol{\beta}$ are both special cases of Equation (20.5.3), estimation of this equation can be regarded as one way of letting the data determine the most appropriate functional form. In economics this is frequently one source of uncertainty so that the approach has a great deal of appeal.

Also, it can be readily extended to include more general cases. If $y_t^{(\lambda)}$ is used to denote $(y_t^\lambda - 1)/\lambda$ for $\lambda \neq 0$ and $\ln y_t$ for $\lambda = 0$, and the explanatory variables, as well as the dependent variable, are transformed, we have

$$y_t^{(\lambda)} = \beta_1 + \beta_2 x_{2t}^{(\lambda)} + \dots + \beta_K x_{Kt}^{(\lambda)} + e_t \tag{20.5.4}$$

This includes as special cases the models

$$y_t = \beta_1 + \beta_2 x_{2t} + \dots + \beta_K x_{Kt} + e_t \tag{20.5.5}$$

and

$$\ln y_t = \beta_1 + \beta_2 \ln x_{2t} + \ . \ . \ . + \beta_K \ln x_{Kt} + e_t \tag{20.5.6}$$

Further flexibility, and additional computations, are introduced if we use a different transformation parameter for each variable. In this case the function can be written as

$$y_t^{(\lambda_1)} = \beta_1 + \beta_2 x_{2t}^{(\lambda_2)} + \ . \ . \ . + \beta_K x_{Kt}^{(\lambda_K)} + e_t \tag{20.5.7}$$

A problem with the above approaches is that they assume that the transformation *simultaneously* yields the appropriate functional form *and* disturbances that are approximately normally distributed and homoscedastic. Such an assumption may be unreasonable. Zarembka (1974) has shown that when the e_t are heteroscedastic, the estimated λ will be biased in the direction required for the transformed dependent variable to be more nearly homoscedastic. To overcome this problem maximum likelihood estimation of a model that allows for both a flexible functional form and heteroscedasticity has been considered by Egy and Lahiri (1979). See also Gaudry and Dagenais (1979) and Seaks and Layson (1983).

Alternative computational methods for obtaining maximum likelihood estimates for the models in (20.5.3), (20.5.4), and (20.5.7) have been reviewed by Spitzer (1982a, 1982b). Considering, for example, the model in (20.5.3), we can write the log of the likelihood function as

$$L = \text{const} - \frac{T}{2} \ln \sigma^2 - \frac{(\mathbf{y}^{(\lambda)} - X\boldsymbol{\beta})'(\mathbf{y}^{(\lambda)} - X\boldsymbol{\beta})}{2\sigma^2} + (\lambda - 1) \sum_{t=1}^{T} \ln y_t \tag{20.5.8}$$

where $\mathbf{y}^{(\lambda)} = (y_1^{(\lambda)}, y_2^{(\lambda)}, \ . \ . \ . \ , y_T^{(\lambda)})'$ and $X' = (\mathbf{x}_1, \mathbf{x}_2, \ . \ . \ . \ , \mathbf{x}_T)$. This function can be maximized directly using one of the algorithms outlined in Appendix B, we can obtain the concentrated likelihood function that depends only on λ and carry out a search procedure over λ, or we can employ one of the other methods suggested by Spitzer (1982a, 1982b). Substituting the conditional ML estimators $\hat{\boldsymbol{\beta}}(\lambda) = (X'X)^{-1}X'\mathbf{y}^{(\lambda)}$ and $\hat{\sigma}^2(\lambda) = [\mathbf{y}^{(\lambda)} - X\hat{\boldsymbol{\beta}}(\lambda)]' \ [\mathbf{y}^{(\lambda)} - X\hat{\boldsymbol{\beta}}(\lambda)]/T$ into (20.5.8) gives, apart from a constant, the concentrated likelihood function

$$L(\lambda) = -\frac{T}{2} \ln \hat{\sigma}^2(\lambda) + (\lambda - 1) \sum_{t=1}^{T} \ln y_t \tag{20.5.9}$$

Thus ML estimates can be found by (1) choosing a reasonable range of values for λ, (2) using least squares to find $\hat{\boldsymbol{\beta}}(\lambda)$ and $\hat{\sigma}^2(\lambda)$ for each value of λ, and (3) choosing that set of estimates for which (20.5.9) is a minimum. This is a convenient procedure because it can be carried out using most least squares computer packages. Also, we can make the procedure even more amenable to analysis by a least squares computer package by dividing each y_t by the geometric mean of the y_t's. This transformation has the effect of eliminating the second term in (20.5.9) so that maximizing the likelihood becomes equivalent to minimizing the transformed residual sum of squares. See Spitzer (1982a) for details of the transformation and the relationship between the transformed and untransformed parameters.

A potential danger from using a standard least squares computer package is that the standard errors provided by the program will be taken as a proper reflection of the reliability of the parameter estimates. These standard errors will, however, be *conditional on* λ, and will underestimate the more relevant unconditional ones. Details of the transformation necessary to obtain unconditional standard errors are given by Spitzer (1982a). Because of the model implications of $\lambda = 0$ and $\lambda = 1$, a confidence interval for λ is frequently of interest. In the usual way, such a confidence interval can be constructed using the asymptotic normality of the maximum likelihood estimator $\tilde{\lambda}$, and its standard error.

Empirical applications of the Box–Cox transformation include the work of Zarembka (1968, 1974); White (1972); Spitzer (1976): Kau and Lee (1976); and Chang (1977); and two extensions are its use in simultaneous equations models [Spitzer (1977)] and the introduction of first-order autoregressive errors [Savin and White (1978)]. Spitzer (1978) has provided some Monte Carlo evidence on the small-sample properties of the ML estimates, and Hill, Johnson, and Kau (1977) suggest, in terms of response variation characteristics, that the Box–Cox transformation model is similar to a class of systematically varying parameter models. Because it makes the model restrictions more explicit, they prefer this latter class of models. Further properties of estimators based on the Box–Cox transformation have been investigated by Bickel and Doksum (1981) [see also Box and Cox (1982)], Carroll (1982) and Doksum and Wong (1983).

20.6 A MULTIPLICATIVE OR AN ADDITIVE DISTURBANCE?

Hazell and Scandizzo (1975, 1977) and Turnovsky (1976), among others, have pointed out some of the different implications of multiplicative and additive disturbances in stochastic economic relationships. This question concerning the type of disturbance is somewhat related to heteroscedasticity, functional form, and the Box–Cox transformation, and so this is a convenient place to discuss certain aspects of it.

We assume that the applied worker is faced with choosing between the two alternatives

$$y_t = f(\mathbf{x}_t, \boldsymbol{\beta}) + e_t \tag{20.6.1}$$

and

$$y_t = f(\mathbf{x}_t, \boldsymbol{\beta}) v_t \tag{20.6.2}$$

where y_t, $\mathbf{x}_t$, and $\boldsymbol{\beta}$ have the usual definitions, f is not necessarily linear, the e_t in Equation 20.6.1 are assumed to be i.i.d. $(0,\sigma_e^2)$, and the v_t in Equation 20.6.2 are assumed to be i.i.d. (μ,σ_v^2). The error in (20.6.1) is given the title additive disturbance while in (20.6.2) it is known as a multiplicative disturbance. The distinction is important, for example, when dealing with stochastic supply functions, where it has implications for the welfare effects of price stabilization policies [Hazell and Scandizzo (1975), Turnovsky (1976)].

From a statistical standpoint the real difference between Equations (20.6.1) and (20.6.2) seems to be whether or not y_t is heteroscedastic with a variance that depends on $\mathbf{x}_t$. To illustrate this, we define a disturbance $e_t^* = v_t - \mu$ and rewrite (20.6.2) as

$$\begin{aligned} y_t &= f(\mathbf{x}_t,\boldsymbol{\beta})\mu + f(\mathbf{x}_t,\boldsymbol{\beta})e_t^* \\ &= f(\mathbf{x}_t,\boldsymbol{\beta})\mu + u_t \end{aligned} \tag{20.6.3}$$

where $u_t = f(\mathbf{x}_t,\boldsymbol{\beta})e_t^*$ is a new "additive" disturbance with $E[u_t] = 0$ and $E[u_t^2] = f^2(\mathbf{x}_t,\boldsymbol{\beta})\sigma_v^2$. Thus it is possible to transform a model with a multiplicative homoscedastic disturbance into one with an additive heteroscedastic disturbance.

If the choice between an additive and a multiplicative disturbance is viewed as a choice between (20.6.1) and (20.6.3), then a reasonable way to proceed is to model the heteroscedasticity along one of the lines suggested in Chapter 11 and to test for the presence of a homoscedastic disturbance. If f is nonlinear, one of the estimation techniques outlined in Appendix B rather than generalized least squares, would have to be used. This type of an approach does not recognize that the precise form of the heteroscedasticity in (20.6.3) depends on $\boldsymbol{\beta}$. Thus, if, a priori, the variance formulation $E[u_t^2] = f^2(\mathbf{x}_t,\boldsymbol{\beta})\sigma_v^2$ was considered appropriate, it would be desirable to estimate (20.6.3) via nonlinear least squares or maximum likelihood such that this assumption is incorporated. However, the assumption may be too restrictive. Even in the economic theoretic papers, the critical issue seems to be whether or not $E[u_t^2]$ is a function of $\mathbf{x}_t$, not whether or not it depends on $\boldsymbol{\beta}$.

A similar argument can be made with respect to models such as

$$y_t = f(\mathbf{x}_t,\boldsymbol{\beta})v_t + e_t \tag{20.6.4}$$

which possess both additive and multiplicative components [Goldfeld and Quandt (1970, 1972); Kelejian (1972)]. In this case the variance of y_t consists of a constant component and a heteroscedastic component, but it still could be modeled along the lines in Chapter 11.

Frequently, the decision concerning whether or not y_t should be treated as heteroscedastic (or whether there is a multiplicative disturbance) is not separated from the decision about an appropriate functional form. For example, considering a two-explanatory-variable case, a choice is often made between the models $y_t = \beta_1 x_{2t}^{\beta_2} x_{3t}^{\beta_3} \cdot \exp\{e_t\}$ and $y_t = \beta_1 + \beta_2 x_{2t} + \beta_3 x_{3t} + e_t$, where the e_t

are assumed to be i.i.d. $N(0,\sigma^2)$. This is a choice between a constant elasticity model with heteroscedastic y_t and a constant slope model with homoscedastic y_t. If the decisions about modeling heteroscedasticity and functional form were separated, which seems more appropriate, two other alternatives would have to be considered, namely a constant elasticity model with homoscedastic y_t, such as $y_t = \beta_1 x_{2t}^{\beta_2} x_{3t}^{\beta_3} + e_t$, and a constant slope model with heteroscedastic y_t such as $y_t = (\beta_1 + \beta_2 x_{2t} + \beta_3 x_{3t}) \cdot \exp\{e_t\}$. Another obvious example of where the two decisions are not separated is when the Box–Cox transformation, discussed in Section 20.5, is employed. As it was pointed out in that section, the model assumes that the transformation simultaneously yields the appropriate functional form and homoscedastic errors.

Thus we argue that the choice between a multiplicative and an additive disturbance is really a choice between assuming that y_t is heteroscedastic or homoscedastic, and this choice can be made using the framework described in Chapter 11. However, the multiplicative–additive distinction does have an advantage. It helps to separate explicitly the decisions concerning how to model heteroscedasticity and how to model functional form.

Under the assumption that the functional form is known, Leech (1975) demonstrates how the Box–Cox transformation can be used to try and discriminate between the additive specification in (20.6.1) when e_t is normally distributed and the multiplicative specification in (20.6.2) when v_t is lognormally distributed. Given the above discussion this is essentially a test designed to discriminate between the assumptions:

1. y_t is normally distributed and homoscedastic.
2. y_t is lognormally distributed and heteroscedastic.

We conclude this section with a description of the test.

Specifically, the two models are

$$y_t = f(\mathbf{x}_t, \boldsymbol{\beta}) + e_t \tag{20.6.5}$$

and

$$y_t = f(\mathbf{x}_t, \boldsymbol{\beta}) \cdot \exp\{\eta_t\} \tag{20.6.6}$$

where the e_t are i.i.d. $N(0,\sigma_e^2)$ and the η_t are i.i.d. $N(0,\sigma_\eta^2)$. A more general model, which includes these two as special cases, is

$$y_t^{(\lambda)} = [f(\mathbf{x}_t, \boldsymbol{\beta})]^{(\lambda)} + \delta_t \tag{20.6.7}$$

where the δ_t are assumed to be i.i.d. $N(0,\sigma^2)$,

$$\begin{aligned} y_t^{(\lambda)} &= \frac{y_t^\lambda - 1}{\lambda} \qquad \text{if } \lambda \neq 0 \\ &= \ln y_t \qquad \text{if } \lambda = 0 \end{aligned}$$

and $[f(\mathbf{x}_t,\boldsymbol{\beta})]^{(\lambda)}$ is defined in a similar way. When $\lambda = 0$, (20.6.7) reduces to (20.6.6) and when $\lambda = 1$, it reduces to (20.6.5). Note the difference between the transformation in (20.6.7) and that used in Section 20.5. In this case the complete function on the right-hand side, rather than each variable separately, is subject to the power transformation.

Using the likelihood ratio statistic to test the hypothesis $\lambda = 0$, we compute

$$u = T(\ln S(\hat{\boldsymbol{\beta}},0) - \ln S(\tilde{\boldsymbol{\beta}},\tilde{\lambda})) + 2\tilde{\lambda}\sum_{t=1}^{T}\ln y_t \tag{20.6.8}$$

where

1. $\hat{\boldsymbol{\beta}}$ is the maximum likelihood estimate from the model in (20.6.6).
2. $\tilde{\boldsymbol{\beta}}$ and $\tilde{\lambda}$ are maximum likelihood estimates obtained by maximizing the log likelihood function

$$L = \text{const} - \frac{T}{2}\ln\sigma^2 + (\lambda - 1)\sum_{t=1}^{T}\ln y_t - \frac{S(\boldsymbol{\beta},\lambda)}{2\sigma^2}$$

3. $$S(\boldsymbol{\beta},\lambda) = \sum_{t=1}^{T}\{y_t^{(\lambda)} - [f(\mathbf{x}_t,\boldsymbol{\beta})]^{(\lambda)}\}^2$$

Under the null hypothesis that $\lambda = 0$, u is asymptotically distributed as $\chi^2_{(1)}$.

To test the hypothesis that $\lambda = 1$, the statistic becomes

$$u = T[\ln S(\hat{\boldsymbol{\beta}},1) - \ln S(\tilde{\boldsymbol{\beta}},\tilde{\lambda})] + 2(\tilde{\lambda} - 1)\sum_{t=1}^{T}\ln y_t \tag{20.6.9}$$

where, in this case, $\hat{\boldsymbol{\beta}}$ is the maximum likelihood estimate of $\boldsymbol{\beta}$ from (20.6.5).

For applications of this test see Leech (1975), Mizon (1977), and Griffiths and Anderson (1978). Other general transformations that include the features of this section as well as those of Section 20.5 are those studied by Blaylock (1980), Godfrey and Wickens (1981) and Bera and McAleer (1983).

20.7 RECOMMENDATIONS

In the estimation of economic relationships the applied worker is likely to be interested in whether the normality assumption is a reasonable one and, if it is not, how one should proceed. It is not possible to give blanket recommendations that are suitable for all circumstances but, in general, the following strategies seem reasonable.

1. If one has a priori information about the likely form of a nonnormal distribution, then, because of its known desirable properties, maximum likelihood estimation should be used.

2. If the error distribution is not likely to be one where outliers occur, use least squares; otherwise use one of the robust estimation techniques. In particular, the trimmed least squares estimator or the l_1-estimator seem to be attractive alternatives.
3. When observations on the dependent variable come from a skewed distribution the Box–Cox transformation may be useful. However, because it also makes assumptions about the functional form and the homoscedasticity of the transformed observations, it should be used cautiously.
4. When a researcher is choosing an appropriate functional form, this decision should not be made independently of the decision concerning how to model the stochastic term.

20.8 EXERCISES

For the problems below we recommend generating 100 samples of Monte Carlo data from the model

$$y_t = \beta_1 + \beta_2 x_{t2} + \beta_3 x_{t3} + e_t, \tag{20.8.1}$$

where $\beta_1 = 10$, $\beta_2 = \beta_3 = 1$, the e_t are independent identically distributed drawings from a Cauchy distribution (t distribution with one degree of freedom), and $t = 1, 2, \ldots, 20$. Choose any convenient design for x_{t2} and x_{t3}.

20.8.1 Individual Exercises

Exercise 20.1

Choose five samples and, for each of the samples, find values for the following estimators:

1. The least squares estimator.
2. The "Huber-estimator" obtained by solving (20.4.14) and (20.4.15).
3. The l_1-estimator.
4. The trimmed least squares estimator with $\alpha = 0.1$.

Compare the estimates with each other and the true parameter values.

Exercise 20.2

For the same five samples, use what in each case would be the conventional covariance matrix estimator to estimate the covariance matrices of the four estimators in Exercise 20.1. Comment.

Exercise 20.3

Using the same four estimators and the same five samples, calculate "t statistics" that would be used to test (a) H_0: $\beta_2 = 0$ against H_1: $\beta_2 \neq 0$, and (b) H_0: $\beta_3 = 1$ against H_1: $\beta_3 \neq 1$. Comment on the outcomes of these tests.

20.8.2 Group or Class Exercises

Exercise 20.4

Using all 100 samples calculate the mean and mean square error matrices for each of the estimators in Exercise 20.1. Comment on the relative efficiency.

Exercise 20.5

Use all 100 samples to calculate the averages of the estimated covariance matrices found in Exercise 20.2. Are these averages good estimates of the mean square error matrices found in Exercise 20.4?

Exercise 20.6

Consider the tests in Exercise 20.3. Use all 100 samples to calculate the proportion of Type I (Part b) and Type II (Part a) errors. Also, construct empirical distributions of the t statistics. From these results comment on the validity of the tests and their relative power.

20.9 REFERENCES

Abdelmalek, N. N. (1974) "On the Discrete Linear L_1 Approximation and L_1 Solutions of Overdetermined Linear Equations," *Journal of Approximation Theory,* 11, 38–53.

Aigner, D. J., T. Amemiya, and D. J. Poirier (1978) "On the Estimation of Production Frontiers: Maximum Likelihood Estimation of the Parameters of a Discontinuous Density Function," *International Economic Review,* 17, 377–396.

Aigner, D. J., A. K. Lovell, and P. Schmidt (1977) "Formulation and Estimation of Stochastic Frontier Production Function Models," *Journal of Econometrics,* 6, 21–38.

Aigner, D. J. and P. Schmidt, eds. (1980) "Specification and Estimation of Frontier Production, Profit and Cost Functions," *Journal of Econometrics,* 13, 1–138.

Amemiya, T. (1982) "Two-Stage Least Absolute Deviations Estimators," *Econometrica,* 50, 689–712.

Anscombe, F. J. (1967) "Topics in the Investigation of Linear Relations Fitted by the Method of Least Squares," *Journal of the Royal Statistical Society, Series B,* 29, 1–52.

Bartels, R. (1977) "On the Use of Limit Theorem Arguments in Economic Statistics," *American Statistician,* 31, 85–87.

Bassett, G. and R. Koenker (1978) "Asymptotic Theory of Least Absolute Error Regression," *Journal of the American Statistical Association,* 73, 618–622.

Bassett, G. and R. Koenker (1982) "An Empirical Quantile Function for Linear Models with iid Errors," *Journal of the American Statistical Association,* 77, 407–415.

Bassett, G. and R. Koenker (1983) "Strong Consistency of Regression Quantiles," *Journal of Econometrics,* forthcoming.

Belsley, D. A., E. Kuh, and R. E. Welsch (1980) *Regression Diagnostics: Identifying Influential Data and Sources of Collinearity,* Wiley, New York.

Bera, A. K. and C. M. Jarque (1981) "An Efficient Large-Sample Test for Normality of Observations and Regression Residuals," Australian National University working papers in Econometrics No. 40, Canberra.

Bera, A. K. and S. John (1983) "Tests for Multivariate Normality with Pearson Alternatives," *Communications in Statistics,* A12, forthcoming.

Bera, A. K. and M. McAleer (1983) "Some Exact Tests for Model Specification", *The Review of Economics and Statistics,* 65, 351–354.

Bickel, P. J. (1976) "Another Look at Robustness," *Scandinavian Journal of Statistics,* 3, 145–168.

Bickel, P. J. and Doksum, K. A. (1981) "An Analysis of Transformations Revisited," *Journal of American Statistical Association,* 76, 296–311.

Bierens, H. J. (1981) *Robust Methods and Asymptotic Theory in Nonlinear Econometrics,* Springer Verlag, Berlin.

Blattberg, R. C. and N. J. Gonedes (1974) "A Comparison of the Stable and Student Distributions as Statistical Models for Stock Prices," *Journal of Business,* 47, 244–280.

Blattberg, R. C. and T. Sargent (1971) "Regression with Non-Gaussian Stable Disturbances: Some Sampling Results," *Econometrica,* 39, 501–510.

Blaylock, J. R. (1980) "The Application of Transformations to Non-Linear Models," *Economics Letters,* 5, 161–164.

Box, G. E. P. and D. R. Cox (1964) "An Analysis of Transformations," *Journal of the Royal Statistical Society, Series B,* 26, 211–243.

Box, G. E. P. and D. R. Cox (1982) "An Analysis of Transformations Revisited, Rebutted," *Journal of the American Statistical Association,* 77, 209–210.

Carroll, R. J. (1982) "Prediction and Power Transformations When the Choice of Power is Restricted to a Finite Set," *Journal of the American Statistical Association,* 77, 908–915.

Chambers, R. L. and C. R. Heathcote (1975) "A Linear Model with Errors Lacking a Variance I," *Australian Journal of Statistics,* 17, 173–185.

Chambers, R. L. and C. R. Heathcote (1978) "A Linear Model with Errors Lacking a Variance II," *Australian Journal of Statistics,* 20, 161–175.

Chang, H. S. (1977) "Functional Form and the Demand for Meat in the United States," *Review of Economics and Statistics,* 59, 355–359.

Cox, D. R. and D. V. Hinkley (1974) *Theoretical Statistics,* Chapman and Hall, London.

Dey, D. K. and J. O. Berger (1983) "On the Truncation of Shrinkage Estimators in Simultaneous Estimation of Normal Means", *Journal of the American Statistical Association,* 78, 865–869.

Dielman, T. and R. Pfaffenberger (1982) "LAV (Least Absolute Value) Estimation in Linear Regression: A Review," *TIMS Studies in the Management Sciences,* 19, 31–52.

Doksum, K. A. and C.-W. Wong (1983) "Statistical Tests Based on Transformed Data", *Journal of the American Statistical Association,* 78, 411–417.

Egy, D. and K. Lahiri (1979) "On Maximum Likelihood Estimation of Functional Form and Heteroscedasticity," *Economics Letters,* 2, 155–159.

Fair, R. C. (1974) "On the Robust Estimation of Econometric Models," *Annals of Economic and Social Measurement,* 3, 667–678.

Fama, E. F. (1963) "Mandlebrot and the Stable Paretian Hypothesis," *Journal of Business,* 36, 420–429.

Fama, E. F. (1965) "The Behavior of Stock Market Prices," *Journal of Business,* 38, 34–105.

Fama, E. F. (1970) "Efficient Capital Markets: A Review of Theory and Empirical Work," *Journal of Finance,* 25, 383–417.

Franck, W. E. (1981) "The Most Powerful Invariant Test of Normal Versus Cauchy with Applications to Stable Alternatives," *Journal of the American Statistical Association,* 76, 1002–1005.

Gastwirth, J. L. (1966) "On Robust Procedures," *Journal of the American Statistical Association,* 61, 929–948.

Gastwirth, J. L. and M. E. B. Owens (1977) "On Classical Tests of Normality," *Biometrika,* 64, 135–139.

Gaudry, M. J. I. and M. G. Dagenais (1979) "Heteroscedasticity and the Use of Box–Cox Transformations," *Economics Letters,* 2, 225–229.

Gilstein, C. Z. and E. E. Leamer (1983) "Robust Sets of Regression Estimates," *Econometrica,* 51, 321–334.

Godfrey, L. G. and M. R. Wickens (1981) "Testing Linear and Log-linear Regressions for Functional Form", *Review of Economic Studies,* 48, 487–496.

Goldfeld, S. M. and R. E. Quandt (1970) "The Estimation of Cobb–Douglas Type Functions with Multiplicative and Additive Errors," *International Economic Review,* 11, 251–257.

Goldfeld, S. M. and R. E. Quandt (1972) *Nonlinear Methods of Econometrics,* North-Holland, Amsterdam.

Goldfeld, S. M. and R. E. Quandt (1981) "Econometric Modeling with Nonnormal Disturbances," *Journal of Econometrics,* 17, 141–155.

Greene, W. H. (1982) "Maximum Likelihood Estimation of Stochastic Frontier Production Models", *Journal of Econometrics,* 18, 285–290.

Griffiths, W. E. and J. R. Anderson (1978) "Specification of Agricultural Supply Functions—Empirical Evidence on Wheat in Southern N.S.W.," *Australian Journal of Agricultural Economics,* 22, 115–128.

Harvey, A. C. (1977) "A Comparison of Preliminary Estimators for Robust Regression," *Journal of the American Statistical Association,* 72, 910–913.

Hazell, P. B. R. and P. L. Scandizzo (1975) "Market Intervention Policies When Production is Risky," *American Journal of Agricultural Economics,* 57, 641–649.

Hazell, P. B. R. and P. L. Scandizzo (1977) "Farmers' Expectations, Risk Aversion, and Market Equilibrium Under Risk," *American Journal of Agricultural Economics,* 59, 204–209.

Hill, R. C., S. R. Johnson, and J. B. Kau (1977) "An Alternative Perspective on Functional Form Analysis,'' paper presented at the Econometric Society Meetings, New York.

Hill, R. W. and P. W. Holland (1977) ''Two Robust Alternatives to Least-Squares Regression,'' *Journal of the American Statistical Association,* 72, 828–833.

Hinich, M. J. and P. P. Talwar (1975) ''A Simple Method for Robust Regression,'' *Journal of the American Statistical Association,* 70, 113–119.

Hogg, R. V. ed. (1977) ''Special Issue on Robustness,'' *Communications in Statistics,* A6, 789–894.

Hogg, R. V. and R. H. Randles (1975) ''Adaptive Distribution—Free Regression Methods and Their Applications,'' *Technometrics,* 17, 399–407.

Huang, C. J. and B. W. Bolch (1974) ''On the Testing of Regression Disturbances for Normality,'' *Journal of the American Statistical Association,* 69, 330–335.

Huber, P. J. (1972) ''Robust Statistics: A Review,'' *The Annals of Mathematical Statistics,* 43, 1041–1067.

Huber, P. J. (1973) ''Robust Regression: Asymptotics, Conjectures, and Monte Carlo,'' *The Annals of Statistics,* 1, 799–821.

Huber, P. J. (1977) *Robust Statistical Procedures,* SIAM, Philadelphia.

Huber, P. J. (1981) *Robust Statistics,* Wiley, New York.

Huber, P. J. (1983) ''Minimax Aspects of Bounded-Influence Regression,'' *Journal of the American Statistical Association,* 78, 66–80.

Jaeckel, L. A. (1972) ''Estimating Regression Coefficients by Minimizing the Dispersion of the Residuals,'' *Annals of Mathematical Statistics,* 42, 1328–1338.

Jeffreys, H. (1961) *Theory of Probability,* Oxford: Clarendon.

Joiner, B. L. and D. L. Hall (1983) ''The Ubiquitous Role of f'/f in Efficient Estimation of Location,'' *The American Statistician,* 37, 128–133.

Judge, G. G., T. A. Yancey and S. Miyazaki (1984) ''Sampling Performance of Stein Type Estimators under Weakened Error Assumptions'', Economics Working Paper, University of Illinois.

Jurečková, J. (1983) ''M-, L- and R- Estimators'' in P. R. Krishnaiah and P. K. Sen, editors, *Handbook of Statistics Vol. 4,* Amsterdam: North-Holland.

Kadiyala, K. R. (1972) ''Regression with Non-Guassian Stable Disturbances: Some Sampling Results,'' *Econometrica,* 40, 719–722.

Kau, J. B. and C. F. Lee (1976) ''The Functional Form in Estimating the Density Gradient: An Empirical Investigation,'' *Journal of the American Statistical Association,* 71, 326–327.

Kelejian, H. H. (1972) ''The Estimation of Cobb–Douglas Type Functions with Multiplicative and Additive Errors: A Further Analysis,'' *International Economic Review,* 13, 179–182.

Kelejian, H. H. and I. R. Prucha (1983) ''Independent or Uncorrelated Disturbances in Regression'', Economics Working Paper, University of Maryland.

Kiefer, N. M. and M. Salmon (1983) ''Testing Normality in Econometric Models,'' *Economics Letters,* 11, 123–128.

Koenker, R. W. (1982) ''Robust Methods in Econometrics,'' *Econometric Reviews,* 1, 213–290.

Koenker, R. W. and G. W. Bassett (1978) "Regression Quantiles," *Econometrica,* 46, 33–50.

Koenker, R. W. and G. W. Bassett (1982a) "Robust Tests for Heteroscedasticity Based on Regression Quantiles," *Econometrica,* 50, 43–62.

Koenker, R. W. and G. W. Bassett (1982b) "Tests of Linear Hypotheses and l_1-Estimation," *Econometrica,* 50, 1577–1583.

Kopp, R. and V. K. Smith (1978) "The Characteristics of Frontier Production Function Estimates for Steam Generating Electric Plants: An Econometric Analysis", *Southern Economic Journal,* 47, 1049–1059.

Krasker, W. S. (1980) "Estimation of Linear Regression Models with Disparate Data Points," *Econometrica,* 48, 1333–1346.

Krasker, W. S. and R. E. Welsch (1982) "Efficient Bounded-Influence Regression Estimation," *Journal of the American Statistical Association,* 77, 595–605.

Lee, L.-F. (1983) "On Maximum Likelihood Estimation of Stochastic Frontier Production Models", *Journal of Econometrics,* 23, 269–274.

Lee, L. F. and W. G. Tyler (1978) "A Stochastic Frontier Production Function and Average Efficiency: An Empirical Analysis," *Journal of Econometrics,* 7, 385–390.

Leech, D. (1975) "Testing the Error Specification in Nonlinear Regression," *Econometrica,* 43, 719–726.

Locke, C. and J. S. Spurrier (1977) "The Use of U-Statistics for Testing Normality Against Alternatives with Both Tails Heavy or Both Tails Light," *Biometrika,* 64, 638–640.

McKean, J. W. and T. P. Hettmansperger (1978) "A Robust Analysis of the General Linear Model Based on One Step *R*-Estimates," *Biometrika,* 65, 571–579.

Maddala, G. S. (1977) *Econometrics,* McGraw-Hill, New York.

Malinvaud, E. (1970) *Statistical Methods in Econometrics,* 2nd ed., North-Holland, Amsterdam.

Mandlebrot, B. B. (1963a) "The Variation of Certain Speculative Prices," *Journal of Business,* 36, 394–419.

Mandlebrot, B. B. (1963b) "New Methods in Statistical Economics," *Journal of Political Economy,* 71, 421–440.

Mandlebrot, B. B. (1966) "Forecasts of Future Prices, Unbiased Markets, and 'Martingale' Models," *Journal of Business,* 39, 242–255.

Mandlebrot, B. B. (1967) "The Variation of Some Other Speculative Prices," *Journal of Business,* 40, 393–413.

Mandlebrot, B. B. (1969) "Long Run Linearity, Locally Gaussian Process, H-Spectra and Infinite Variances," *International Economic Review,* 10, 82–111.

Mardia, K. V. (1980) "Tests of Univariate and Multivariate Normality," *Handbook of Statistics,* Vol. 1, P. R. Krishnaiah, ed., North Holland, Amsterdam, pp. 279–320.

Mizon, G. E. (1977) "Inferential Procedures in Nonlinear Models: An Application in a U.K. Industrial Cross Section Study of Factor Substitution and Returns to Scale," *Econometrica,* 45, 1221–1242.

Moberg, T. E., J. S. Ramber, and R. H. Randles (1980) "An Adaptive Multiple Regression Procedure Based on M-Estimators," *Technometrics,* 22, 213–224.

Mosteller, F. and J. W. Tukey (1977) *Data Analysis and Regression,* Addison-Wesley, Reading, Mass.

Pearson, E. S., R. B. D'Agostino, and K. O. Bowman (1977) "Tests for Departure from Normality: Comparison of Powers," *Biometrika,* 64, 231–246.

Powell, J. L. (1983) "The Asymptotic Normality of Two-Stage Least Absolute Deviations Estimators", *Econometrica,* 51, 1569–1576.

Prucha, I. R. and H. K. Kelejian (1984) "The Structure of Simultaneous Equation Estimators: A Generalization Toward Nonnormal Disturbances" *Econometrica,* 52, 721–736.

Ramsey, J. B. (1974) "Classical Model Selection Through Specification Error Tests," in P. Zarembka, ed., *Frontiers in Econometrics,* Academic, New York.

Ruppert, D. and J. Carroll (1980) "Trimmed Least Squares Estimation in the Linear Model," *Journal of the American Statistical Association,* 75, 828–838.

Saniga, E. M. and J. A. Miles (1979) "Power of Some Standard Goodness-of-Fit Tests of Normality Against Asymmetric Stable Alternatives," *Journal of the American Statistical Association,* 74, 861–865.

Savin, N. E. and K. J. White (1978) "Estimation and Testing for Functional Form and Autocorrelation: A Simultaneous Approach," *Journal of Econometrics,* 8, 1–12.

Schlossmacher, E. J. (1973) "An Iterative Technique for Absolute Deviations Curve Fitting," *Journal of the American Statistical Association,* 68, 857–859.

Schmidt, P. (1976a) *Econometrics,* Dekker, New York.

Schmidt, P. (1976b) "On the Statistical Estimation of Parametric Frontier Production Functions," *Review of Economics and Statistics,* 58, 238–239.

Seaks, T. G., and S. K. Layson (1983) "Box–Cox Estimation with Standard Econometric Problems", *The Review of Economics and Statistics,* 65, 160–164.

Serfling, R. J. (1980) *Approximation Theorems of Mathematical Statistics,* Wiley, New York.

Shapiro, S. S. and M. B. Wilk (1965) "An Analysis of Variance Test for Normality (Complete Samples)," *Biometrika,* 52, 591–611.

Shapiro, S. S., M. B. Wilk, and H. J. Chen (1968) "A Comparative Study of Various Tests of Normality," *Journal of the American Statistical Association,* 63, 1343–1372.

Sheather, S. and J. S. Maritz (1983) "An Estimate of the Asymptotic Standard Error of the Sample Median," *Australian Journal of Statistics,* 25, 109–122.

Shinozaki, N. (1984) "Simultaneous Estimation of the Location Parameters under Quadratic Loss", *The Annals of Statistics,* 12, 322–335.

Sielken, R. L. and H. O. Hartley (1973) "Two Linear Programming Algorithms for Unbiased Estimation of Linear Models," *Journal of the American Statistical Association,* 68, 639–641.

Sievers, G. L. (1978) "Weighted Rank Statistics for Linear Regression," *Journal of the American Statistical Association,* 73, 628–631.

Smith, V. K. and T. W. Hall (1972) "A Comparison of Maximum Likelihood Versus BLUE Estimators," *The Review of Economics and Statistics,* 54, 186–190.

Spiegelhalter, D. J. (1977) "A Test for Normality Against Symmetric Alternatives," *Biometrika,* 64, 415–418.

Spitzer, J. J. (1976) "The Demand for Money, the Liquidity Trap, and Functional Forms," *International Economic Review,* 17, 220–227.

Spitzer, J. J. (1977) "A Simultaneous Equations System of Money Demand and Supply Using Generalized Functional Forms," *Journal of Econometrics,* 5, 117–128.

Spitzer, J. J. (1982a) "A Primer on Box–Cox Estimation," *Review of Economics and Statistics,* 64, 307–313.

Spitzer, J. J. (1982b) "A Fast and Efficient Algorithm for the Estimation of Parameters in Models with the Box-and-Cox Transformation", *Journal of the American Statistical Association,* 77, 760–766.

Spitzer, J. J. (1978) "A Monte Carlo Investigation of the Box–Cox Transformation in Small Samples," *Journal of the American Statistical Association,* 73, 488–495.

Stein, C. M. (1981) "Estimation of the Mean of a Multivariate Normal Distribution", *The Annals of Statistics,* 9, 1135–1151.

Taylor, L. D. (1974) "Estimation by Minimizing the Sum of Absolute Errors," in P. Zarembka, ed., *Frontiers in Econometrics,* Academic, New York.

Turnovsky, S. J. (1976) "The Distribution of Welfare Gains from Price Stabilization: The Case of Multiplicative Disturbances," *International Economic Review,* 17, 133–148.

Ullah, A., V. K. Srivastava and R. Chandra (1983) "Properties of Shrinkage Estimators in Linear Regression when Disturbances are not Normal", *Journal of Econometrics,* 21, 389–402.

Waldman, D. M. (1982) "A Stationary Point for the Stochastic Frontier Likelihood", *Journal of Econometrics,* 18, 275–280.

White, H. and G. M. MacDonald (1980) "Some Large-Sample Tests for Nonnormality in the Linear Regression Model," *Journal of the American Statistical Association,* 75, 16–28.

White, K. J. (1972) "Estimation of the Liquidity Trap with a Generalized Functional Form," *Econometrica,* 40, 193–199.

Yohai, V. J. and Maronna, R. A. (1979) "Asymptotic Behavior of M-Estimators for the Linear Model," *Annals of Statistics,* 7, 258–268.

Zarembka, P. (1968) "Functional Form in the Demand for Money," *Journal of the American Statistical Association,* 63, 502–511.

Zarembka, P. (1974) "Transformation of Variables in Econometrics," in P. Zarembka, ed., *Frontiers in Econometrics,* Academic, New York.

Zeckhauser, R. and M. Thompson (1970) "Linear Regression with Nonnormal Error Terms," *Review of Economics and Statistics,* 52, 280–286.

Zellner, A. (1976) "Bayesian and Non-Bayesian Analysis of the Regression Model with Multivariate Student-t Error Terms," *Journal of the American Statistical Association,* 71, 400–405.

Chapter 21

On Selecting the Set of Regressors

1.1 INTRODUCTION

Much of the literature concerned with estimation and inference from a sample of economic data deals with a situation when the statistical model is correctly specified. Consequently, as discussed in Chapter 2 and in much of econometric practice, it is customary to assume that the parameterized linear statistical model used for purposes of inference is consistent with the sampling process from which the sample observations were generated. In this happy event, statistical theory provides techniques for obtaining point and interval estimators of the population parameters and for hypothesis testing. In practice, however, the possibilities for model misspecification are numerous and false statistical models are most likely the rule rather than the exception.

In many of the previous chapters various types of uncertainty relative to the specification of the statistical model were recognized and procedures were suggested for identifying the misspecification and/or mitigating its statistical impact. Among the various possible sources of false statistical models, the omission of relevant explanatory variables or the inclusion of extraneous explanatory variables, are the most likely and pervasive. Consequently, in this chapter, within the context of nonexperimental model building and the linear statistical model framework introduced in Chapter 2, we consider the statistical consequences of and the possibilities for dealing with uncertainty concerning the appropriate column dimension of the design matrix X. Variable selection procedures are considered within a broad context that encompasses both discrimination among the nested alternatives and the testing of separate models. Although we are concerned with both nested and nonnested models, the main focus is on the nested variety.

Nonexperimental model building or the selection of the statistical model that is consistent with the sampling process whereby the data are generated, is an old and important problem in econometrics. Over the years various criteria, search processes, empirical rules, and testing mechanisms have been proposed as aids in the choice process. Many of these procedures are discussed in recent literature survey articles by Gaver and Geisel (1974), Hocking (1976), Thompson (1978), Amemiya (1980), MacKinnon (1983), Sawyer (1980), McAleer (1984), a specification search book by Leamer (1978), and special issues of the *Journal of Econometrics* by Maddala (1981) and White (1982, 1983). Most model search procedures recognize the importance of economic theory in narrowing the range of admissible design matrix specifications. Some suggested search procedures have little or no theoretical basis and have, it would appear, solved the problem by making reference to magic, mysticism, or possibly revelation. Others have suggested various criteria or rules of thumb for adding to or deleting explanatory variables from the design matrix. In any event, whatever the choice procedure employed, seldom in a sampling theory context have we known the sampling properties of the estimators thereby generated and in a decision context the risk associated with a particular rule (action).

Our objective in this chapter as in others is to sort out the statistical implications of using some of the various model selection rules and to provide some guides for choice. Toward this objective the organization of the chapter is as follows:

First, we consider within a nested model context the statistical consequences of *incorrectly* specifying the dimension of the design matrix. Next we specify a range of variable selection criteria and discuss their interrelationships, statistical pitfalls, and possible uses. Information criteria are then discussed, and the Jeffrey–Bayes posterior odds ratio and Stein-rule alternatives are considered. Nonnested models and the choice of functional form of the variables appearing in the design matrix are then discussed and procedures for handling these problems are evaluated. Finally, in the final sections, model identification procedures are compared within a decision context, a basis for coping with the variable choice problem is suggested and a set of exercises is given that permits a range of model choice rules to be applied to a particular set of data.

The problem of a near-degenerate, singular design matrix that may result from non-experimental data falls within the regressor choice domain, but because of its importance in econometric research, this problem is discussed as a separate topic in Chapter 22.

As an aid to the reader, an overview of some of the alternative search procedures to be discussed is given in Table 21.1.

21.2 NESTED STATISTICAL MODELS

Assume there exists a general model represented by the density $f_1(\cdot|\boldsymbol{\beta})$, which is the true sampling model underlying the observed values of the random vector $\mathbf{y}$. Further assume there are $(J - 1)$ alternative statistical models $f_2(\cdot|\boldsymbol{\beta}_1)$, $f_3(\cdot|\boldsymbol{\beta}_2)$, . . . , $f_J(\cdot|\boldsymbol{\beta}_{J-1})$ that are also candidates for explaining the random vector $\mathbf{y}$. Let us further assume that all of the J alternative models can be derived by imposing appropriate restrictions on the parameter vector $\boldsymbol{\beta}$, the parameter vector for the general (true) model; that is, the J statistical models make up a nested set of alternatives for describing the sampling process underlying $\mathbf{y}$. Although these assumptions are restrictive they are general enough to contain some important model selection problems both in a sampling theory and Bayesian context.

TABLE 21.1 *AN OVERVIEW OF SOME MODEL SELECTION PROCEDURES*

Nested Statistical Models						Nonnested Statistical Models
Classical hypothesis testing framework (Section 21.2.2)		Residual error sum of squares rules (Section 21.2.3)	Information criteria (Section 21.2.5)	Bayes criteria (Section 21.2.5e)	Stein rules (Section 21.2.6)	Variants of likelihood ratio test (Section 21.3)
F test statistic	Mean square error norm test statistic	Coefficient of multiple determination	Information criteria AIC and BIC	Jeffrey–Bayes posterior odds ratio	Positive Stein rule, zero null hypothesis	Cox
Pretest rules	Pretest rules	Adjusted coefficient of multiple determination	Bayes criterion			Atkinson
		Amemiya's criterion, PC	Chow posterior probability criterion			Quandt
		Mallows criterion C_p				Pesaran and Deaton
						Davidson and MacKinnon
						Fisher and McAleer

21.2.1 Statistical Consequences of an Incorrect Design Matrix

The problem considered in this section is posed by Efron and Morris (1975, p. 318) as follows:

> ". . . The statistician wants to estimate the parameters of a linear model that are known to lie in a high dimensional parameter space H_1; but he suspects that they may lie close to a specified lower dimensional parameter space $H_0 \subset H_1$. Then, estimates unbiased for every parameter vector in H_1 may have large variance, while estimates restricted to H_0 have smaller variance but possibly large bias. . . ."

To see the underlying basis for this conclusion for expository purposes let us consider the regressor choice problem within the context of a general two-decision setting and make use of the parameterized linear statistical model

$$\mathbf{y} = X\boldsymbol{\beta} + \mathbf{e} = X_1\boldsymbol{\beta}_1 + X_2\boldsymbol{\beta}_2 + \mathbf{e} \tag{21.2.1}$$

where $\mathbf{y}$ is a T-dimensional vector of observations; $X = [X_1, X_2]$ is a $(T \times K)$ matrix of constants of rank K; X_1 and X_2 are known matrices of dimension $(T \times K_1)$ and $(T \times K_2)$, respectively, with $K_1 + K_2 = K$; $\boldsymbol{\beta}$ is a K-dimensional vector of unknown parameters that is partitioned conformably into components $\boldsymbol{\beta}_1$ and $\boldsymbol{\beta}_2$; and $\mathbf{e}$ is a $(T \times 1)$ normal random vector with mean vector zero and covariance matrix $\sigma^2 I_T$ with the scalar σ^2 unknown. If we let X_1 contain the included variables and X_2 contain the excluded or omitted variables, where $K_1 \leq K$, the statistical model (21.2.1) can be made to represent all of the possible subsets (combinations) of X by varying the column dimensions and content of X_1 and X_2. The least squares (maximum likelihood) estimator of $\boldsymbol{\beta}$ and an estimator of σ^2 are

$$\mathbf{b} = \begin{bmatrix} \mathbf{b}_1 \\ \mathbf{b}_2 \end{bmatrix} = (X'X)^{-1}X'\mathbf{y} = \begin{bmatrix} X_1'X_1 & X_1'X_2 \\ X_2'X_1 & X_2'X_2 \end{bmatrix}^{-1} \begin{bmatrix} X_1'\mathbf{y} \\ X_2'\mathbf{y} \end{bmatrix} \tag{21.2.2}$$

and

$$\hat{\sigma}^2 = \frac{(\mathbf{y} - X\mathbf{b})'(\mathbf{y} - X\mathbf{b})}{T - K} = \frac{\mathbf{y}'[I_T - X(X'X)^{-1}X']\mathbf{y}}{T - K} \tag{21.2.3}$$

If the statistical model (21.2.1) is correct; that is, if the column dimension of the design matrix X is K, then $\mathbf{b}$ and $\hat{\sigma}^2$ are minimum variance *unbiased* estimators. The maximum likelihood estimator $\mathbf{b}$ is a normally distributed random vector with mean vector $\boldsymbol{\beta}$ and covariance $E[(\mathbf{b} - \boldsymbol{\beta})(\mathbf{b} - \boldsymbol{\beta})'] = \sigma^2(X'X)^{-1}$. In regard to the unbiased estimator $\hat{\sigma}^2$, the random variable $(T - K)\hat{\sigma}^2/\sigma^2$ is distributed as a central χ^2 random variable with $(T - K)$ degrees of freedom.

Consider only the X_1 subset of X and assume that the X_2 set of variables appears in the equation with a zero coefficient vector. Thus if we assume the X_2

variables are extraneous and are omitted from the statistical model, then we may represent this information by the set of restrictions

$$R\boldsymbol{\beta} = \mathbf{r} = [0, I_{K_2}]\begin{bmatrix}\boldsymbol{\beta}_1 \\ \boldsymbol{\beta}_2\end{bmatrix} = \mathbf{0}_{K_2} \tag{21.2.4}$$

where R is a $(K_2 \times K)$ known matrix of rank K_2 and $\mathbf{0}_{K_2}$ is a K_2 dimensional zero vector. Under this scenario, the general restricted least squares estimator is

$$\mathbf{b}^* = \mathbf{b} - (X'X)^{-1}R'[R(X'X)^{-1}R']^{-1}(R\mathbf{b} - \mathbf{r}) \tag{21.2.5a}$$

If the elements of $\boldsymbol{\beta}_2$ are restricted to zero, the restricted least squares estimator for this special case becomes

$$\mathbf{b}^* = \begin{bmatrix}\mathbf{b}_1^* \\ \mathbf{0}_{K_2}\end{bmatrix} = \begin{bmatrix}(X_1'X_1)^{-1}X_1'\mathbf{y} \\ \mathbf{0}_{K_2}\end{bmatrix} \tag{21.2.5b}$$

We recognize the fact that some or possibly all of the elements of $\boldsymbol{\beta}_2$ may not be zero by letting $R\boldsymbol{\beta} - \mathbf{r} = \boldsymbol{\delta}$, a vector of parameter specification errors of dimension K_2. If the restrictions are correct, which for our special case implies $\boldsymbol{\beta}_2 = \mathbf{0}$, then $\boldsymbol{\delta}$ is a null vector. Within this context the mean of the restricted estimator $\mathbf{b}^*$ is

$$\begin{aligned} E[\mathbf{b}^*] &= E[\mathbf{b} - (X'X)^{-1}R'[R(X'X)^{-1}R']^{-1}(R\mathbf{b} - \mathbf{0})] \\ &= \boldsymbol{\beta} - (X'X)^{-1}R'[R(X'X)^{-1}R']^{-1}\boldsymbol{\delta} = \begin{bmatrix}\boldsymbol{\beta}_1 + (X_1'X_1)^{-1}X_1'X_2\boldsymbol{\beta}_2 \\ \boldsymbol{\beta}_2 - \boldsymbol{\delta}\end{bmatrix} \end{aligned} \tag{21.2.6}$$

If $\boldsymbol{\beta}_2 = \mathbf{0}$ and thus $\boldsymbol{\delta} = \mathbf{0}$, then $\mathbf{b}_1^*$ is an unbiased estimator of $\boldsymbol{\beta}_1$. Otherwise, unless the regressor sets X_1 and X_2 are orthogonal, the estimator (21.2.5) is a biased estimator of $\boldsymbol{\beta}_1$ with the bias being proportional to the magnitudes of the $\boldsymbol{\beta}_2$ vector. The covariance matrix of $\mathbf{b}^*$ is

$$\begin{aligned} &E\{[\mathbf{b}^* - E(\mathbf{b}^*)][\mathbf{b}^* - E(\mathbf{b}^*)]'\} \\ &\quad = \sigma^2\{(X'X)^{-1} - (X'X)^{-1}R'[R(X'X)^{-1}R']^{-1}R(X'X)^{-1}\} \end{aligned} \tag{21.2.7a}$$

or

$$E\left[\begin{bmatrix}\mathbf{b}_1^* - E(\mathbf{b}_1^*) \\ \mathbf{b}_2^* - E(\mathbf{b}_2^*)\end{bmatrix}\begin{bmatrix}\mathbf{b}_1^* - E(\mathbf{b}_1^*) \\ \mathbf{b}_2^* - E(\mathbf{b}_2^*)\end{bmatrix}'\right] = \begin{bmatrix}\sigma^2(X_1'X_1)^{-1} & 0 \\ 0 & 0_{K_2}\end{bmatrix} \tag{21.2.7b}$$

The second expression on the right-hand side of (21.2.7a) is a positive semidefinite matrix. Also, the difference between the covariance matrices of the restricted and unrestricted estimators is

$$E\{(\mathbf{b} - \boldsymbol{\beta})(\mathbf{b} - \boldsymbol{\beta})' - [\mathbf{b}^* - E(\mathbf{b}^*)][\mathbf{b}^* - E(\mathbf{b}^*)]'\} = \Delta \qquad (21.2.8)$$

where Δ is a positive semidefinite matrix. This implies, among other things, that the covariance matrix (21.2.7a) or (21.2.7b), for the estimator involving restriction (21.2.4), has diagonal elements (sampling variabilities or measures of precision) that are equal to or less than the corresponding unrestricted elements of the least squares estimator $\mathbf{b}$ for the statistical model (21.2.1).

An estimator of σ^2 that uses the restricted least squares estimator $\mathbf{b}^*$ is

$$\overset{*}{\sigma}{}^2 = \frac{(\mathbf{y} - X\mathbf{b}^*)'(\mathbf{y} - X\mathbf{b}^*)}{T - K_1} = \frac{\mathbf{y}'(I_T - X_1(X_1'X_1)^{-1}X_1')\mathbf{y}}{T - K_1} \qquad (21.2.9)$$

and has mean

$$E[\overset{*}{\sigma}{}^2] = \sigma^2 + \frac{\boldsymbol{\beta}_2'X_2'(I - X_1(X_1'X_1)^{-1}X_1')X_2\boldsymbol{\beta}_2}{T - K_1} \qquad (21.2.10)$$

Therefore, unless $\boldsymbol{\beta}_2 = \mathbf{0}$ and the subset model is correct, $\overset{*}{\sigma}{}^2$ yields a biased estimator of σ^2. Also, when $\boldsymbol{\beta}_2 \neq \mathbf{0}$, the ratio $(T - K_1)\overset{*}{\sigma}{}^2/\sigma^2$ is distributed as a noncentral $\chi^2_{(T-K_1)}$ random variable.

These results bring out clearly the following statistical consequences of using a subset X_1 of the possible design matrix X:

1. The estimator $\mathbf{b}_1^*$ is biased unless $\boldsymbol{\beta}_2 = \mathbf{0}$ or X_1 and X_2 are orthogonal.
2. Whether or not $\boldsymbol{\beta}_2 = \mathbf{0}$, the unrestricted least squares estimate of $\mathbf{b}_1$, when both X_1 and X_2 *are included,* has lower precision than the estimate $\mathbf{b}_1^*$ from the subset model, that is, the sampling variability of $\mathbf{b}_1^*$ is equal to or less than the sampling variability of $\mathbf{b}_1$ from the unrestricted model.
3. Unless $\boldsymbol{\beta}_2 = \mathbf{0}$, the subset (restricted) model estimator $\overset{*}{\sigma}{}^2$ has a positive bias.
4. If $\boldsymbol{\beta}_2 \neq \mathbf{0}$, then either $\mathbf{b}_1^*$ is biased or $\overset{*}{\sigma}{}^2$ is biased or both are biased.

These results are summarized in Table 21.2 as a two-state, two-action structure presented on page 860.

21.2.2 Mean Squared Error Norms

The above conclusions cast the incentive for correct model choice in terms of bias and/or variance. The mean square error measure, which in the case of biased estimators is a composite of the two, provides a basis for reflecting a trade-off between bias and precision [Section 3.1.3 and Judge and Bock (1978, pp. 28, 29)].

Within the context of Section 21.2.1 if $\boldsymbol{\beta}_2 \neq \mathbf{0}$ and thus $\boldsymbol{\delta} \neq \mathbf{0}$, then $\mathbf{b}^*$ is a biased estimator with mean square error (MSE),

TABLE 21.2 *MODEL ALTERNATIVES AND STATISTICAL IMPLICATIONS*

Investigators Actions	States of World: True Model $\mathbf{y} = X_1\boldsymbol{\beta}_1 + X_2\boldsymbol{\beta}_2 + \mathbf{e}$	States of World: True Model $\mathbf{y} = X_1\boldsymbol{\beta}_1 + X_2\boldsymbol{\beta}_2 + \mathbf{e}$, $\boldsymbol{\beta}_2 = \mathbf{0}$
Assume statistical model $\mathbf{y} = X_1\boldsymbol{\beta}_1 + X_2\boldsymbol{\beta}_2 + \mathbf{e}$	**b** is minimum variance unbiased	**b** is unbiased but not minimum variance
Assume statistical model $\mathbf{y} = X_1\boldsymbol{\beta}_1 + X_2\boldsymbol{\beta}_2 + \mathbf{e}$; $\boldsymbol{\beta}_2 = \mathbf{0}$	**b*** is biased, but its sampling variability is less than that of the unbiased estimator **b**. $\overset{*}{\sigma}{}^2$ is biased upward	**b*** is minimum variance unbiased

$$\begin{aligned}\text{MSE}_{\mathbf{b}^*} &= E[(\mathbf{b}^* - \boldsymbol{\beta})(\mathbf{b}^* - \boldsymbol{\beta})'] \\ &= \sigma^2(X'X)^{-1} - \sigma^2(X'X)^{-1}R'[R(X'X)^{-1}R']^{-1}R(X'X)^{-1} \\ &\quad + (X'X)^{-1}R'[R(X'X)^{-1}R']^{-1}\boldsymbol{\delta}\boldsymbol{\delta}'[R(X'X)^{-1}R']^{-1}R(X'X)^{-1} \qquad (21.2.11)\end{aligned}$$

which is the sum of the covariance matrix (21.2.7a) and the bias matrix. Of course, if the specification error $\boldsymbol{\delta} = \mathbf{0}$, the restricted estimator is unbiased and (21.2.11) is equal to (21.2.7b).

In particular, the mean square error matrix for the restricted estimator $\mathbf{b}_1^*$ is, from (21.2.6) and (21.2.7),

$$\text{MSE}_{\mathbf{b}_1^*} = \sigma^2(X_1'X_1)^{-1} + (X_1'X_1)^{-1}X_1'X_2\boldsymbol{\beta}_2\boldsymbol{\beta}_2'X_2'X_1(X_1'X_1)^{-1} \qquad (21.2.12)$$

Correspondingly, by making use of the partitioned inverse rule [Appendix A, Section A.5] in regard to the covariance (MSE) matrix of **b**, the mean square error of $\mathbf{b}_1$ is

$$\begin{aligned}\text{MSE}_{\mathbf{b}_1} &= \sigma^2\{(X_1'X_1)^{-1} + (X_1'X_1)^{-1}X_1'X_2[X_2'X_2 \\ &\quad - X_2'X_1(X_1'X_1)^{-1}X_1'X_2]^{-1}X_2'X_1(X_1'X_1)^{-1}\} \qquad (21.2.13)\end{aligned}$$

The difference in the mean square error matrices for $\mathbf{b}_1^*$ and $\mathbf{b}_1$ is

$$\begin{aligned}\text{MSE}_{\mathbf{b}_1} - \text{MSE}_{\mathbf{b}_1^*} &= \Delta_1 \\ &= (X_1'X_1)^{-1}X_1'X_2\{\sigma^2[X_2'X_2 - X_2'X_1(X_1'X_1)^{-1}X_1'X_2]^{-1} - \boldsymbol{\beta}_2\boldsymbol{\beta}_2'\} \\ &\quad X_2'X_1(X_1'X_1)^{-1} \\ &= (X_1'X_1)^{-1}X_1'X_2\{\boldsymbol{\Sigma}_{\mathbf{b}_2} - \boldsymbol{\delta}\boldsymbol{\delta}'\}X_2'X_1(X_1'X_1)^{-1} \qquad (21.2.14)\end{aligned}$$

The expression inside { } is the covariance matrix for $\mathbf{b}_2$ and the bias matrix for

$\mathbf{b}_2^*$. The Δ_1 matrix in (21.2.14) will be positive semidefinite if $\Sigma_{\mathbf{b}_2} - \boldsymbol{\beta}_2\boldsymbol{\beta}_2'$ is positive semidefinite.

If in terms of gauging the performance of the estimators **b** and **b*** we use the squared error loss measure, where interest centers on the diagonal elements of the mean square or risk matrix, that is, the sum of the variance plus the bias squared for each element of $\boldsymbol{\beta}$, the risk outcome is

$$E[(\mathbf{b} - \boldsymbol{\beta})'(\mathbf{b} - \boldsymbol{\beta})] = \sigma^2 \operatorname{tr}(X'X)^{-1} \tag{21.2.15}$$

for the least squares–maximum likelihood estimator and

$$\begin{aligned} E[(\mathbf{b}^* - \boldsymbol{\beta})'(\mathbf{b}^* - \boldsymbol{\beta})] = {} & \sigma^2 \operatorname{tr}(X'X)^{-1} \\ & - \sigma^2 \operatorname{tr}(X'X)^{-1}R'[R(X'X)^{-1}R']^{-1}R(X'X)^{-1} \\ & + \operatorname{tr}\{(X'X)^{-1}R'[R(X'X)^{-1}R']^{-1}\boldsymbol{\delta}\boldsymbol{\delta}' \\ & \times [R(X'X)^{-1}R']^{-1}R(X'X)^{-1}\} \end{aligned} \tag{21.2.16}$$

for the restricted or subset estimator. Judge and Bock [(1978), pp. 29–33] present the conditions under squared error loss for which the risk of the restricted subset estimator **b*** is less than the risk of the maximum likelihood estimator **b**. As one special case, consider the conditional mean forecasting problem concerned with estimating $X\boldsymbol{\beta}$, the mean values of **y** at the sample points X. The risk of the maximum likelihood estimator $X\mathbf{b}$ under squared error loss is

$$\begin{aligned} E[(\mathbf{b} - \boldsymbol{\beta})'X'X(\mathbf{b} - \boldsymbol{\beta})] &= \sigma^2 \operatorname{tr} X(X'X)^{-1}X' = \sigma^2 \operatorname{tr} X'X(X'X)^{-1} = \sigma^2 \operatorname{tr} I_K \\ &= \sigma^2 K \end{aligned} \tag{21.2.17}$$

which is an increasing function of the number of variables K. Within the context of Section 3.2.1, for the restricted estimator $X\mathbf{b}^*$ the risk is

$$\begin{aligned} E[(\mathbf{b}^* - \boldsymbol{\beta})'X'X(\mathbf{b}^* - \boldsymbol{\beta})] &= \operatorname{tr}\{\sigma^2 I_K - \sigma^2(X'X)^{-1}R'[R(X'X)^{-1}R']^{-1}R \\ &\quad + (X'X)^{-1}R'[R(X'X)^{-1}R']^{-1}\boldsymbol{\delta}\boldsymbol{\delta}'[R(X'X)^{-1}R']^{-1}R\} \\ &= \sigma^2 K - \sigma^2 K_2 + \boldsymbol{\delta}'[R(X'X)^{-1}R']^{-1}\boldsymbol{\delta} = \sigma^2(K - K_2) + \boldsymbol{\delta}'[R(X'X)^{-1}R']^{-1}\boldsymbol{\delta} \\ &= \sigma^2 K_1 + \boldsymbol{\delta}'[R(X'X)^{-1}R']^{-1}\boldsymbol{\delta} = \sigma^2 K_1 + \boldsymbol{\beta}_2'[X_2'X_2 - X_2'X_1(X_1'X_1)^{-1}X_1'X_2]\boldsymbol{\beta}_2 \end{aligned} \tag{21.2.18}$$

where $\sigma^2 K_1$ is the risk penalty for the included variables (complexity) and the second term is the risk penalty for misspecification (incorrect variable selection). Consequently,

$$E[(\mathbf{b} - \boldsymbol{\beta})'X'X(\mathbf{b} - \boldsymbol{\beta})] - E[(\mathbf{b}^* - \boldsymbol{\beta})'X'X(\mathbf{b}^* - \boldsymbol{\beta})] \geq 0 \tag{21.2.19}$$

if

$$\frac{\boldsymbol{\delta}'[R(X'X)^{-1}R']^{-1}\boldsymbol{\delta}}{2\sigma^2} \le \frac{K_2}{2} \tag{21.2.20}$$

and one would select the subset model X_1 over the complete model involving X_1, X_2 if the expected loss (21.2.18) is less than the expected loss (21.2.17). However in (21.2.18) the specification error $\boldsymbol{\delta}$ depends on $\boldsymbol{\beta}_2$, which is unknown. Therefore, for variable selection purposes the rule is not operational. The search for an operational rule is the subject of the next few sections.

21.2.3 Some Alternative Variable Selection Rules

In this section we specify, discuss, and compare a range of sampling theory and Bayesian decision rules that have been proposed for coping with the nested model selection problem. In general most of these rules rely on discrimination criteria such as maximizing some modified R^2 and each one measures how well the models fit the data after some adjustment for parsimony.

21.2.3a The R^2 and $\bar{R}^2$ Criteria

If one reviews the econometric literature, there appears to have been a strong urge by many to make available some single statistic or index to gauge the "goodness" of an econometric model. One natural competitor for this honor is the coefficient of multiple determination R^2, which is a measure of the proportion of the total variance accounted for by the linear influence of the explanatory variables. For the complete statistical model (21.1.1) the total sum of squares of $\mathbf{y}$ about its mean may be partitioned as follows:

total sum		regression		error sum
of squares	=	sum of squares	+	of squares
(SST)		(SSR)		(SSE)

$$(\mathbf{y} - \bar{\mathbf{y}})'(\mathbf{y} - \bar{\mathbf{y}}) = (\hat{\mathbf{y}} - \bar{\mathbf{y}})'(\hat{\mathbf{y}} - \bar{\mathbf{y}}) + \hat{\mathbf{e}}'\hat{\mathbf{e}}$$

where $\bar{\mathbf{y}}$ is a vector with elements $\bar{y} = \Sigma_t y_t/T$, and $\hat{\mathbf{y}} = X\mathbf{b}$. Given this decomposition of the sample variation of $\mathbf{y}$ about its mean, the coefficient of determination may be defined as

$$R^2 = 1 - \frac{\text{SSE}}{\text{SST}} = 1 - \frac{(\mathbf{y} - X\mathbf{b})'(\mathbf{y} - X\mathbf{b})}{(\mathbf{y} - \bar{\mathbf{y}})'(\mathbf{y} - \bar{\mathbf{y}})}. \tag{21.2.21}$$

As a basis for model choice, the R^2 measure has an obvious fault; it can be increased by increasing the number of explanatory variables, that is, by increasing the column dimension of the design matrix. To take this characteristic of the measure into account, Theil (1971, p. 178) proposed a corrected coefficient of multiple determination $\bar{R}^2$, which uses unbiased estimators of the respective variances. For the subset model involving the design matrix X_1, the corrected or adjusted R^2 may be defined as

$$\bar{R}_1^2 = 1 - \frac{(\mathbf{y} - X_1\mathbf{b}_1^*)'(\mathbf{y} - X_1\mathbf{b}_1^*)/(T - K_1)}{(\mathbf{y} - \bar{\mathbf{y}})'(\mathbf{y} - \bar{\mathbf{y}})/(T - 1)} = 1 - \left(\frac{T - 1}{T - K_1}\right)(1 - R_1^2), \tag{21.2.22}$$

where T is the sample size, K_1 is the number of variables included, and $K_1 < K$. Given the measure, Theil's recommendation is to seek that subset of explanatory variables that maximizes the corrected or adjusted R^2. Such a rule, he states, will lead us to the right model "on the average." However, the expectation property alone is no guarantee of high power. Also, as Pesaran (1974) notes, the $\bar{R}^2$ criterion need not be the most powerful of the criteria involving the quadratic form of the residuals that have as their property: The expected value is minimized by the true model. Perhaps the most uncomfortable aspect of both the R^2 and adjusted R^2 measures is that they do not include a consideration of the losses associated with choosing an incorrect model; that is, they do not consider within a decision context the purpose for which the model is to be used. With the goal of eliminating this deficiency, we now turn to two criteria that are based on the mean square error measure.

21.2.3b The C_p—Conditional Mean Square Error Prediction Criterion

As one solution to the variable selection problem for statistical model (21.2.1), consider a criterion based on conditional mean square prediction error. For the subset model $\mathbf{y} = X_1\boldsymbol{\beta}_1 + \boldsymbol{\epsilon}$, where $\boldsymbol{\epsilon} = X_2\boldsymbol{\beta} + \mathbf{e}$, this criterion, in line with (21.2.18), may be defined as

$$\begin{aligned}
\rho(X\mathbf{b}^*, X\boldsymbol{\beta}) &= E[(X\mathbf{b}^* - X\boldsymbol{\beta})'(X\mathbf{b}^* - X\boldsymbol{\beta})] \\
&= E\left[\begin{pmatrix} X_1\mathbf{b}_1^* - X_1\boldsymbol{\beta}_1 \\ X_2\mathbf{0} - X_2\boldsymbol{\beta}_2 \end{pmatrix}'\begin{pmatrix} X_1\mathbf{b}_1^* - X_1\boldsymbol{\beta}_1 \\ X_2\mathbf{0} - X_2\boldsymbol{\beta}_2 \end{pmatrix}\right] \\
&= E\left[\begin{pmatrix} \mathbf{b}_1^* - \boldsymbol{\beta}_1 \\ \mathbf{0} - \boldsymbol{\beta}_2 \end{pmatrix}' X'X \begin{pmatrix} \mathbf{b}_1^* - \boldsymbol{\beta}_1 \\ \mathbf{0} - \boldsymbol{\beta}_2 \end{pmatrix}\right] \\
&= \sigma^2 K_1 + \boldsymbol{\beta}_2' X_2'[I - X_1(X_1'X_1)^{-1}X_1']X_2\boldsymbol{\beta}_2 \\
&= \sigma^2 K_1 + (\text{bias})^2,
\end{aligned} \tag{21.2.23}$$

where the last term on the right-hand side is the sum of squares of the bias and follows from the fact that $\mathbf{b}_1^* = \boldsymbol{\beta}_1 + (X_1'X_1)^{-1}X_1'X_2\boldsymbol{\beta}_2 + (X_1'X_1)^{-1}X_1'\mathbf{e}$, since $\mathbf{y} = X_1\boldsymbol{\beta}_1 + X_2\boldsymbol{\beta}_2 + \mathbf{e}$. Since (21.2.23) contains unknown parameters, one way to proceed is to use an estimate for the unknown parameters and, based on the estimate, choose the model with the smallest estimated risk.

In terms of standardized risk under squared error loss, (21.2.23) can be rewritten as

$$\frac{\rho(X_1\mathbf{b}_1^*,X\boldsymbol{\beta})}{\sigma^2} = \frac{\sigma^2K_1 + (\text{bias})^2}{\sigma^2}$$

$$= K_1 + \frac{(\text{bias})^2}{\sigma^2} \qquad (21.2.24)$$

Noting that

$$E[(\mathbf{y} - X_1\mathbf{b}_1^*)'(\mathbf{y} - X_1\mathbf{b}_1^*)] = E[(T - K_1)\overset{*}{\sigma}{}_1^2]$$

$$= \boldsymbol{\beta}_2'X_2'[I - X_1(X_1'X_1)^{-1}X_1']X_2\boldsymbol{\beta}_2 + \sigma^2(T - K_1)$$

$$= (\text{bias})^2 + \sigma^2(T - K_1) \qquad (21.2.25)$$

we can express the squared bias as

$$(\text{bias})^2 = E[(T - K_1)\overset{*}{\sigma}{}_1^2] - (T - K_1)\sigma^2 \qquad (21.2.26)$$

Substituting (21.2.26) in (21.2.24) yields

$$\frac{\rho(X_1\mathbf{b}_1^*,X\boldsymbol{\beta})}{\sigma^2} = \frac{E[(T - K_1)\overset{*}{\sigma}{}_1^2]}{\sigma^2} + (2K_1 - T) \qquad (21.2.27)$$

If the unknown parameters in (21.2.27) are replaced by unbiased sample values, we can write the unbiased estimator of (21.2.24) as

$$\hat{\rho}(X_1\mathbf{b}_1^*,X_1\boldsymbol{\beta}) = C_p = \frac{(T - K_1)\overset{*}{\sigma}{}_1^2}{\hat{\sigma}^2} + (2K_1 - T)$$

$$= \frac{(T - K_1)(1 - \bar{R}_1^2)}{1 - \bar{R}^2} + (2K_1 - T) \qquad (21.2.28)$$

where $\hat{\sigma}^2 = (\mathbf{y} - X\mathbf{b})'(\mathbf{y} - X\mathbf{b})/(T - K)$. When the subset model has small bias, then $\overset{*}{\sigma}{}_1^2$ is approximately equal to $\hat{\sigma}^2$, and C_p is approximately equal to K_1. Therefore, in the (C_p,K_1) space, C_p values with small bias will tend to cluster about a 45° line, where $C_p = K_1$. In using the C_p criterion, a procedure sometimes recommended is to obtain a C_p value for all of the possible 2^K subsets of models and choose the model in which C_p is approximately equal to K_1. No rule such as minimizing C_p is advised in applied work but the implication is that variable sets with C_p less than K_1 are thought to have smaller prediction error.

If alternatively in (21.2.23) a consistent estimator of $\boldsymbol{\beta}_2$ is chosen, we are led to a consistent estimator of the risk and to selection rules such as those proposed by Allen (1971) and discussed by Leamer (1983).

21.2.3c An Unconditional Mean Square Error Criterion

In order to include a consideration of the losses associated with choosing an incorrect model, Amemiya (1980) developed a criterion based on the mean square prediction error. Amemiya considers the problem of predicting y_0 by $\hat{y}_0 = \mathbf{x}_{01}'(X_1'X_1)^{-1}X_1'\mathbf{y}$, where $\mathbf{x}_{01}$ is a *vector* of values of X_i for the prediction period. Using the loss function $(y_0 - \hat{y}_0)^2$, the mean square prediction error given $\mathbf{x}_{01}$ is for this special case,

$$E[(y_0 - \hat{y}_0)^2] = \sigma^2[1 + \mathbf{x}_{01}'(X_1'X_1)^{-1}\mathbf{x}_{01}] + [\mathbf{x}_0'\boldsymbol{\beta} - \mathbf{x}_{01}'(X_1'X_1)^{-1}X_1'X_1\boldsymbol{\beta}]^2 \tag{21.2.29}$$

and involves the unknown parameters $\boldsymbol{\beta}$ and σ^2. Amemiya then regards $\mathbf{x}_0$ as a random vector that satisfies the condition $E[\mathbf{x}_0\mathbf{x}_0'] = (1/T)X'X$. Under this assumption we obtain, by substitution in (21.2.29),

$$E[(y_0 - \hat{y}_0)^2] = \sigma^2\left(1 + \frac{K_1}{T}\right) + \left(\frac{1}{T}\right)\boldsymbol{\beta}_2'X_2'[I - X_1(X_1'X_1)^{-1}X_1']X_2\boldsymbol{\beta}_2 \tag{21.2.30}$$

and Amemiya calls this the unconditional mean square prediction error. Unfortunately, (21.2.30) still contains unknown parameters. In typical econometric form, σ^2 is replaced by its unbiased estimator, and $\boldsymbol{\beta}_2$ is made equal to a null (zero) vector. Since $\boldsymbol{\beta}_2$ is assumed zero, the corresponding unbiased estimator of σ^2 is

$$\overset{*}{\sigma}{}_1^2 = \frac{\mathbf{y}'[I - X_1(X_1'X_1)^{-1}X_1']\mathbf{y}}{T - K_1} = \frac{\mathbf{y}'M_1\mathbf{y}}{T - K_1}$$

This sequence of assumptions yields what Amemiya calls the prediction criterion (PC)

$$\text{PC} = \overset{*}{\sigma}{}_1^2\left(1 + \frac{K_1}{T}\right) \tag{21.2.31}$$

which when minimized and expressed in terms of R^2 is

$$\text{PC} = \left(\frac{T + K_1}{T - K_1}\right)(1 - R_1^2)\left(\frac{\text{SST}}{T}\right) \tag{21.2.32}$$

If we compare this with (21.2.22), it is evident that the PC has a higher penalty for adding variables than Theil's adjusted R^2.

If we do not assume that $\boldsymbol{\beta}_2 = \mathbf{0}$ in (21.2.30) but instead estimate the bias component from the relation

$$E[\mathbf{y}'M_1\mathbf{y}] = \boldsymbol{\beta}_2'X_2'M_1X_2\boldsymbol{\beta}_2 + (T - K_1)\sigma^2 \tag{21.2.33}$$

or, in other words, if we estimate the last right-hand term in (21.2.30) by $(\mathbf{y}'M_1\mathbf{y}/T) - [(T - K_1)\sigma^2/T]$ and insert this in (21.2.30), we get, following Amemiya,

$$\text{MC} = \frac{2K_1\sigma^2 + \mathbf{y}'M_1\mathbf{y}}{T} \tag{21.2.34}$$

Since σ^2 is unknown, if we estimate this by $\hat{\sigma}^2 = (\mathbf{y}'M\mathbf{y})/(T - K)$, which assumes that none of the K variables are irrelevant, we get the Mallows (1973) criterion

$$\text{MC} = \left(\frac{1}{T}\right)\left[2K_1\left(\frac{\mathbf{y}'M\mathbf{y}}{T - K}\right) + \mathbf{y}'M_1\mathbf{y}\right] = \left(\frac{1}{T}\right)[2K_1\hat{\sigma}^2 + (T - K_1)\overset{*}{\sigma}{}_1^2] \tag{21.2.35}$$

As Amemiya notes, a monotonic transformation of (21.2.35) yields the well-known, Mallows, conditional mean squared error of prediction criterion given in (21.2.28).

21.2.3d An *F* Test Statistic Interpretation

Since all the criteria discussed in this section are functions of the error sum of squares, it is interesting and informative to interpret them through the well-known, F test statistic. In Chapter 3 and in (21.2.14) and (21.2.20), when using the parameterized linear statistical model $\mathbf{y} = X_1\boldsymbol{\beta}_1 + X_2\boldsymbol{\beta}_2 + \mathbf{e}$ and the general linear hypothesis or variable omission design system $R\boldsymbol{\beta} = \mathbf{0}$, where $R = [0, I_{K_2}]$, we found the following:

1. Under the general mean square error criterion $E[(\tilde{\boldsymbol{\beta}} - \boldsymbol{\beta})(\tilde{\boldsymbol{\beta}} - \boldsymbol{\beta})']$, in order for the subset of regressors to be preferred over the complete set of regressors, it is necessary that

$$\frac{(R\boldsymbol{\beta})'[R(X'X)^{-1}R']^{-1}(R\boldsymbol{\beta})}{\sigma^2} \le 1 \tag{21.2.36}$$

2. Under the squared error loss criterion $E[(\tilde{\boldsymbol{\beta}} - \boldsymbol{\beta})'(\tilde{\boldsymbol{\beta}} - \boldsymbol{\beta})]$, in order for the subset of regressors to have lower risk than the complete set of regressors, it is necessary that

$$\frac{(R\boldsymbol{\beta})'[R(X'X)^{-1}R']^{-1}(R\boldsymbol{\beta})}{\sigma^2} \le K_2 = K - K_1 \tag{21.2.37}$$

If we replace the unknown parameters in (21.2.36) and (21.2.37) by their unbiased estimators from the complete model, then (21.2.36) and (21.2.37) become, when divided by K_2,

$$\frac{(R\mathbf{b})'[R(X'X)^{-1}R']^{-1}(R\mathbf{b})}{K_2\hat{\sigma}^2} \leq \frac{1}{K_2} \qquad (21.2.38)$$

and

$$\frac{(R\mathbf{b})'[R(X'X)^{-1}R']^{-1}(R\mathbf{b})}{K_2\hat{\sigma}^2} \leq 1 \qquad (21.2.39)$$

where the left-hand ratios of (21.2.38) and (21.2.39) are F random variables with K_2 and $(T - K)$ degrees of freedom. According to these criteria, the variables in the set K_2 would be deleted if, depending on the criterion, the F test statistic was less than or equal to $1/K_2$ or the weaker requirement, less than or equal to 1. The commonly suggested rule of thumb of deleting variables whose t statistics are less than 1 in absolute value has a basis in (21.2.39), which requires the t statistics associated with the K_2 regressors to be less than 1 in magnitude.

By noting that

$$F_{(K_2,T-K)} = \frac{(R\mathbf{b})'[R(X'X)^{-1}R']^{-1}(R\mathbf{b})}{K_2\hat{\sigma}^2} = \frac{(T-K)}{K_2}\frac{\mathbf{y}'M_1\mathbf{y} - \mathbf{y}'M\mathbf{y}}{\mathbf{y}'M\mathbf{y}}$$
$$= \left(\frac{\mathbf{y}'M_1\mathbf{y}}{\mathbf{y}'M\mathbf{y}} - 1\right)\left(\frac{T-K}{K_2}\right) \qquad (21.2.40)$$

we may establish the relationship between the Theil adjusted $\bar{R}^2$, the Amemiya PC, and the Mallows C_p criteria. Following Amemiya (1980), in order to make bilateral comparison between models containing K and $K - K_2 = K_1$ variables in terms of the F random variable, we have

1. For the adjusted $\bar{R}^2$ criterion

$$F = \frac{T-K}{K_2}\frac{\bar{R}^2_{K_1}}{\bar{R}^2_K} - \frac{T-K}{K_2} < 1 \qquad (21.2.41)$$

when the subset (K_1) model is selected.

2. For the Mallows C_p criterion (21.2.28), if we rewrite (21.2.19) as

$$K_2F_{(K_2,T-K)} = \left(\frac{\mathbf{y}'M_1\mathbf{y}}{\hat{\sigma}^2}\right) - (T-K) \qquad (21.2.42)$$

Then

$$\frac{(T-K_1)\overset{*}{\sigma}{}_1^2}{\hat{\sigma}^2} = K_2F_{(K_2,T-K)} + (T-K) \qquad (21.2.43)$$

If (21.2.43) is substituted into (21.2.28), C_p may be expressed in terms of the $F_{(K_2,T-K)}$ random variable as

$$C_p = [K_2 F_{(K_2,T-K)} + (T - K)] - T + 2K_1$$
$$= K_2 F_{(K_2,T-K)} + (T - K_1 - K_2) - T + 2K_1 \qquad (21.2.44)$$

This may be rewritten as

$$C_p - K_1 = K_2[F_{(K_2,T-K)} - 1] \qquad (21.2.45)$$

Therefore, $C_p \leq K_1$ implies that $F_{(K_2,T-K)} \leq 1$, and the hypothesis that $\boldsymbol{\beta}_{K_2} = \mathbf{0}$ is accepted when $F_{(K_2,T-K)} < 1$. Note that the critical value of $F_{(K_2,T-K)}$ is smaller than that implied by the traditional $\alpha = 0.05$ significance level.

3. For the prediction criterion (PC)

$$F = \frac{(T - K_1)(T + K)}{K_2(T + K_1)} \frac{\text{PC}_{K_1}}{\text{PC}_K} - \frac{T - K}{K_2} \qquad (21.2.46)$$

Therefore, $\text{PC}_{K_1}/\text{PC}_K > 1$ if $F > 2K/(T + K_1)$. If K_1/T is "small," the critical value for F approaches 2.00.

Alternatively, the ad hoc procedure of using an $F_{(K_2,T-K)} \leq 2$ as the criterion means that C_p must satisfy the condition $C_p \leq K$.

21.2.3e The S_p Criterion—How Many Variables

The problem of the optimal number of regressors to minimize the mean squared prediction error is also considered by Breiman and Freedman (1983). As the number of regressors grows large, their S_p criterion provides an asymptotically optimal choice as to the number of regressors. Within the context of Section 2.2.3c they consider how to choose the dimension of K_1 so as to minimize v, the unconditional mean squared prediction error. First playing the role of an omniscient statistician where K_1 is much smaller than T, they show that approximately $v \doteq \sigma^2 + \sigma^2_{K_2} + \sigma^2 K_1/T$, where σ^2 measures the impact of e_0 on the error, $\sigma^2_{K_2}$ measures the impact of omitted variables, and $\sigma^2 K_1/T$ measures the impact of the random error on the K_1 coefficient estimates and increases as K_1 increases. Since $\sigma^2_{K_2}$ decreases as K_1 increases and $\sigma^2 K_1/T$ increases with K_1, there is an optimal K_1.

When the parameters of the equation are unknown the S_p criterion involves the smallest $K_1 \leq T/2$ that minimizes $\hat{\sigma}^2_{K_1}\,(1 + K_1/(T - 1 - K_1))$. These results are closely related to that for the prediction criterion (Section 21.2.3c) which is asymptotically equivalent to the Akaike (1973) information criterion that is discussed in Section 21.2.5a.

21.2.3f A Comment

Other selection criteria are, of course, possible, and an exhaustive list of these rules is included in Hocking's (1976) review article. All are functions of the equation error sum of squares and thus are related. Since all the procedures lead in reality to a pretest estimator in one form or another, they all lead to inadmissible estimators whose exact sampling properties are not known. Consequently, inference relative to the estimators that result from any of these search processes should be viewed with caution by the applied researcher.

In closing this section perhaps we should mention two papers where the model selection problem is in a way regarded as part of the estimation procedure—that is, the properties of the estimators are derived. Geweke and Meese (1981) consider the problem of estimation when the correct specification of the statistical model is unknown but it is known to be one of an infinite sequence of nested alternatives. Procedures for model selection are set forth that provide choices that lead to the correct model with unit probability *asymptotically*. Shibata (1981) considers the optimal selection of regression variables in a model involving infinitely many parameters or where the number of variables increases with sample size. His criterion is the same as that used by Breiman and Freedman (1983) and his method is asymptotically equivalent to the Mallows and Akaike methods.

21.2.4 Model Selection Tests

In assessing the validity of the statistical model, one type of diagnosis often employed is to use a hypothesis test that compares the null model with a generalized alternative. Rejection of a hypothesis based on the test statistic(s) suggests incompatibility of the data and the model and is taken as evidence of variable misspecification. Within this testing framework the Wald, likelihood ratio and Lagrange multiplier tests are traditionally used. These tests, which were discussed in Chapter 5, have the nice property of being asymptotically locally most powerful unbiased. They are designed to test a set of parametric restrictions and are in contrast to the Hausman (1978) specification test, which is, as Holly (1982) notes, designed to test the implications of an hypothesis in terms of inconsistency.

In most cases hypothesis and specification testing are done with an eye toward estimation. This means that the final estimation stage proceeds conditionally on the hypothesis (statistical model) that has been selected. This process, which makes the model and thus the estimation procedure dependent on the test based on the data at hand, leads to what we referred to in Chapter 3 as pretest estimators. This testing mechanism leads to estimators that are inadmissible under a squared error loss measure. Little is known of the sampling properties of many of these pretest estimators and even less is known of the sampling properties of higher order sequential test procedures—that is, repeated tests that typically use the same set of data. Therefore, it would appear that traditional hypothesis testing procedures with their corresponding optimum significance level problem, do not offer a viable way to handle the best subset problem.

Hocking (1976) summarized under the descriptive heading "computational techniques" many of the forward selection and backward elimination of variables procedures that are based on some form of pre-testing. In general these procedures lead to different or contradictory results and are long on method and heuristic arguments, but strangely silent as to the sampling properties of the estimators thereby generated.

As an aside, since it is known we generally work with false models and since the power of statistical tests increases with sample size, a statistical test can be relied on in virtually every application to reject the restricted model (hypothesis) for a *large-enough sample*.

21.2.5 Information Criteria for Model Selection

The information measure or criterion seeks to incorporate in model selection the divergent considerations of accuracy of estimation and the "best" approximation to reality. Thus use of this criterion involves a statistic that incorporates a measure of the precision of the estimate and a measure of the rule of parsimony in the parameterization of a statistical model. In this section we discuss variants of the Akaike (1973) information criterion, which is based on the Kullback–Leibler or entropy criterion [Kullback (1959), Akaike (1981)]. In this context, the adequacy of an approximation to the true distribution of a random variable is measured by the distance between the "model of reality" and the true distribution. The basis for this criterion is discussed in detail in Akaike (1973, 1974, 1981) and in Sawa (1978) and to date has probably been discussed more extensively in connection with model identification in the time series literature. However, the work of Sawa (1978) and the expository efforts of Amemiya (1980) have helped to introduce this criterion in the econometric literature.

21.2.5a The Akaike Information Criterion (AIC)

As a basis for discussing the AIC, let $\ell(\boldsymbol{\beta}|\mathbf{y})$ be the likelihood function and consider the statistical model (21.2.1), where the design matrix X is partitioned into components X_1 and X_2 with corresponding partitioning of the $\boldsymbol{\beta}$ vector. Under the hypothesis $R\boldsymbol{\beta} = (0_{(K_2 \times K_1)}, I_{K_2})\boldsymbol{\beta} = \mathbf{0}$; that is, the last $K - K_1 = K_2$ elements of $\boldsymbol{\beta}$ are assumed to be zero, the Akaike information criterion (AIC) is

$$\text{AIC} = -\frac{2}{T} \ln \ell(\mathbf{b}_1^*|\mathbf{y}) + \frac{2K_1}{T} \tag{21.2.47}$$

and under this criterion, (21.2.47) is to be minimized among all of the possible linear hypotheses $R\boldsymbol{\beta} = \mathbf{0}$. For the statistical model (21.2.1), this criterion reduces to

$$\mathrm{AIC}_{(R\boldsymbol{\beta}=\mathbf{0})} = \ln \frac{\mathbf{y}'M_1\mathbf{y}}{T} + \frac{2K_1}{T} \tag{21.2.48}$$

where K_1 and thus $M_1 = I - X_1(X_1'X_1)^{-1}X_1'$ is chosen so as to numerically minimize (21.2.48). Therefore, as K_1 increases, $\mathbf{y}'M_1\mathbf{y}$ decreases and the value of the likelihood function increases; thus the trade-off between parsimony and precision is clear, and the penalty for increasing the number of parameters is explicit.

If, as Amemiya shows, one proceeds as if the parameter σ^2 were known in the likelihood function, then AIC becomes

$$\mathrm{AIC}_{(R\boldsymbol{\beta}=\mathbf{0},\sigma^2 \text{ known})} = \left(\frac{\mathbf{y}'M_1\mathbf{y}}{T}\right) + \frac{\sigma^2(2K_1)}{T} \tag{21.2.49}$$

Since in reality σ^2 is not known and if σ^2 is replaced by an estimate, the question becomes which estimate to use. If $\hat{\sigma}^2 = \mathbf{y}'(I - X(X'X)^{-1}X')\mathbf{y}/(T - K)$, then as Amemiya notes, (21.2.49) is the same as the Mallows C_p criterion defined in (21.2.35). Alternatively, if $\hat{\sigma}^2 = \mathbf{y}'M_1\mathbf{y}/(T - K)$, then (21.2.49) is equal to the Amemiya PC defined in (21.2.31). In these cases, of course, AIC suffers all the defects of C_p and PC.

Chow (1981) has noted that since in general $\sigma_1^2 > \sigma^2$ an adjustment should be made in Akaike's formula. If this is done the Chow rule turns out to favor the small model more than Akaike's rule.

Leamer (1983) questions whether the estimation problem inherent in the information criterion implies a model selection problem. He observes that the fundamental reason why the information criterion does not imply anything especially different from maximum methods is that it uses the scoring rule underlying maximum likelihood estimation.

21.2.5b Sawa's Criterion (BIC)

Sawa (1978), on the other hand, departs from the idea of a true model and develops the information criterion within the context of what he calls pseudo-true parameter values; that is, he measures the distance between the pseudo-true parameters and the postulated parametric model, by the Kullback–Leibler information criterion, where $f(\mathbf{y}|\boldsymbol{\theta}_0)$ is the density function of the pseudo-true model and $\mathbf{y}$ is $N(X\boldsymbol{\beta}_0,\sigma_0^2I)$. If we assume with an incorrect model that our objective is to estimate the pseudo-true parameter values, Sawa's criterion, which he calls BIC, is

$$\mathrm{BIC} = \ln \mathbf{y}'M_1\mathbf{y} + 2\left[(K_1 + 2)\frac{\hat{w}^2}{\overset{*}{\sigma}{}^2} - \left(\frac{\hat{w}^2}{\overset{*}{\sigma}{}^2}\right)^2\right] \tag{21.2.50}$$

where $\hat{w}^2$ is an independent estimate of the true variance. If we assume $w^2 = \sigma^2$

and thus the pseudo-true model closely approximates the *true* model, then (21.2.50) becomes the AIC. However, if $\overset{*}{\sigma}^2$ is used to estimate w^2 in BIC (21.2.50), then $\hat{w}^2/\overset{*}{\sigma}^2 \leq 1$ and relative to AIC, a model with fewer explanatory variables and larger $\mathbf{y}'M_1\mathbf{y}$ is preferred to a competing model with a larger number of variables and smaller squared errors. In a two-model choice problem, the rule that emerges is to compute BIC for each model and choose that model with a minimum outcome where $\hat{w}^2$ is replaced by $\hat{\sigma}^2$ from the higher-dimension model.

As Sawa (1978) shows, these criteria can be related to a decision rule based on the conventional F statistic, and when this happens for "normal" values of K_1, the implied α significance level varies for AIC from 30% to 16% as the degrees of freedom increase and for BIC, from 10% to 16%. This stands in contrast to the conventional pretest level of 5% or 1%, which is relatively parsimonious toward the inclusion of additional variables, a procedure that has severe risk consequences when the hypotheses are wrong.

21.2.5c The Reformulated AIC

Since these methods are based on heuristic arguments and the only justification is through performance in applications, there have been other attempts to tinker with the criterion. Akaike (1978), using a Bayesian framework, proposed a second criterion, which we call AIC_1, that is a function of familiar quadratic forms and is given by

$$\text{AIC}_1 = (T - K_1) \ln \left(\frac{\mathbf{y}'M_1\mathbf{y}}{T - K_1}\right) + K_1 \ln \left(\frac{\mathbf{y}'X_1(X_1'X_1)^{-1}X_1'\mathbf{y}}{K_1}\right) \tag{21.2.51}$$

Akaike notes that this criterion is more parsimonious in selecting regressors than the original AIC.

Alternatively, Akaike (1978) introduces a definition of the likelihood determined by the data, where the definition is based on the proposition that the log likelihood is the basic quantity to use to measure the goodness of fit of a model. The likelihood of a model is so defined that its logarithm will be an unbiased estimator of the expected log likelihood of the model with respect to a future observation, where the expectation is taken with respect to the distribution of the present and future observations.

This formulation leads to

$$\begin{aligned}\text{AIC}_2 &= \exp\{\ln \text{(maximum likelihood)} - K_1\} \\ &= \exp\{-(\tfrac{1}{2})\text{AIC}\}\end{aligned} \tag{21.2.52}$$

where AIC, for comparison purposes, may be written as $(-2 \ln \text{(maximum likelihood)} + 2K_1)$. Akaike (1978) suggests that (21.2.52) is asymptotically a reasonable definition of the likelihood of a model specified by the parameters determined by the method of maximum likelihood. The practical utility of this approach is demonstrated by numerical examples in Akaike's article.

21.2.5d The Posterior Probability Criterion

Finally, within this context, Schwarz (1978) treats the problem of selecting a model from a number of models of different dimensions by finding its Bayes solution and then evaluating the leading term of its asymptotic expansion. Since the terms are valid within a large-sample context, they do not depend on a particular prior distribution. In contrast to the Akaike criterion, which in effect suggests maximizing the likelihood functions (minimizing the error sums of squares) for each alternative model, taking its logarithm, and then subtracting the number of parameters in the corresponding model and choosing the model that has the largest numerical value, the criterion proposed by Schwarz (SC) is choose the model for which

$$\text{SC} = \ln(\text{maximum likelihood}) - (\tfrac{1}{2})K_1 \ln T \tag{21.2.53}$$

is largest. Thus the Schwarz criterion differs from the Akaike criterion in that the dimension of the model is multiplied by $(\frac{1}{2})\ln T$. For the number of observations usually found with economic data, the Schwarz criterion favors a lower-dimensional model than the Akaike criterion. As T grows, the difference between the two criteria grows. Schwarz notes that under his formulation of the problem, Akaike's criterion cannot be asymptotically optimal. Using a posterior probability criterion Akaike (1978) attempted to derive the choice rule (21.2.52) to approximate the Schwarz rule. Chow (1981) rightly points out there is no need to justify the information criterion in terms of the posterior probability criterion since they are designed to answer different questions. Within this context let us turn to the Bayesian approach to statistical model choice.

21.2.5e Jeffreys-Bayes Posterior Odds Ratio

Zellner (1971), Gaver and Geisel (1974), and others building on the work of Jeffreys, Thornber and Geisel, have developed a framework for using the posterior odds ratio as a basis for discriminating among hypotheses or models. If within the context of the linear statistical model (21.2.1) we are interested in the hypothesis $H_0: \boldsymbol{\beta}_2 = \mathbf{0}$ versus the alternative hypothesis $H_A: \boldsymbol{\beta}_2 \neq \mathbf{0}$, we can, following Zellner (1971) and Chapter 4, and assuming σ is known, write the posterior odds ratio as

$$K_{0A} = \frac{\pi_0}{\pi_A} \frac{\int P(\boldsymbol{\beta}_1)\ell(\boldsymbol{\beta}_1|\mathbf{y}, \sigma)\, d\boldsymbol{\beta}_1}{\int P(\boldsymbol{\beta}_1, \boldsymbol{\beta}_2)\ell(\boldsymbol{\beta}_1, \boldsymbol{\beta}_2|\mathbf{y}, \sigma)\, d\boldsymbol{\beta}_1\, d\boldsymbol{\beta}_2} \tag{21.2.54}$$

where π_0/π_A is the prior odds ratio, $P(\boldsymbol{\beta}_1)$ and $P(\boldsymbol{\beta}_1, \boldsymbol{\beta}_2)$ are prior distributions under H_0 and H_A, and the $\ell(\cdot)$ are likelihood functions under the two hypotheses. Under "reasonable" assumptions about the prior distributions, Zellner (1978) approximates the posterior odds ratio as

$$K_{0A} \doteq \frac{\pi_0}{\pi_A} \frac{P(\mathbf{b}_1)}{P(\mathbf{b})} \left(\frac{|X_1'X_1|}{|X'X|}\right)^{-1/2} \exp\left[\frac{(T-K_1)\overset{*}{\sigma}{}^2 - (T-K)\hat{\sigma}^2}{2\sigma^2}\right]\left(\frac{1}{2\pi\sigma^2}\right)^{K_2/2} \tag{21.2.55}$$

Thus, among other things, the posterior odds ratio depends on the prior odds ratio, the compatibility of the prior distributions and maximum likelihood estimates for $\boldsymbol{\beta}_1$ and $\boldsymbol{\beta}$, a ratio of the determinants of the two design matrices, and a ratio of the likelihoods and therefore a goodness of fit consideration. Acting to minimize expected loss in a symmetric loss structure, we choose H_0 if $K_{0A} > 1$ and H_A if $K_{0A} < 1$, or in other words, we choose the hypothesis with the higher posterior probability. Note again that the posterior odds are equal to the prior odds times the ratio of the average likelihoods weighted by the prior probability density functions. In large samples the posterior odds are the conventional likelihood ratio multiplied by the prior odds. It is interesting to note that for the classical normal linear statistical model (21.2.1) and the corresponding hypotheses, if the priors are chosen to be natural conjugate–multivariate normal and inverted gamma, the posterior odds reflects the relative sizes of the error quadratic form for each hypothesis. If the priors are diffuse and the prior odds equal, the quadratic form comparisons dominate the posterior odds.

In order to compare the posterior odds ratio to the Akaike criterion, Zellner (1978) rewrites (21.2.55) as

$$\begin{aligned} -2 \ln K_{0A} &= -2 \ln \left(\frac{\pi_0}{\pi_A}\right) \frac{P(\mathbf{b}_1)}{P(\mathbf{b})} + \frac{(T - K_1)\overset{*}{\sigma}{}^2 - (T - K)\hat{\sigma}^2}{\sigma^2} \\ &\quad - K_2 \left[\ln \left(\frac{|X_1'X_1|}{|X'X|} \right)^{1/K_2} - \ln 2\pi\sigma^2 \right] \end{aligned} \tag{21.2.56}$$

and this criterion reduces to the rule, choose H_0 if $-2 \ln K_{0A} < 0$ and choose H_A if $-2 \ln K_{0A} > 0$.

Alternatively for comparison purposes, Zellner (1978) writes the Alkaike information criterion as

$$\begin{aligned} \text{AIC} &= -2[\ln \ell(\mathbf{b}_1|\mathbf{y}) - \ln \ell(\mathbf{b}|\mathbf{y})] + 2[K_1 - K] \\ &= -2 \left[\frac{-(T - K_1)\overset{*}{\sigma}{}^2 + (T - K)\hat{\sigma}^2}{2\sigma^2} \right] - 2K_2 \\ &= \left(\frac{(T - K_1)\overset{*}{\sigma}{}^2 - (T - K)\hat{\sigma}^2}{\sigma^2} \right) - 2K_2 \end{aligned} \tag{21.2.57}$$

While somewhat similar, the two criteria obviously differ as to how prior information and prior odds are used, and are equal under only some very strong conditions.

As a further basis for seeing how the various criteria are interrelated, let us note that for AIC (21.2.57), if $\hat{\sigma}^2$ replaces the unknown σ^2, the result is the Mallows C_p criterion. Also if $\overset{*}{\sigma}{}^2$ replaces the unknown σ^2 in (21.2.57), we have the Amemiya prediction criterion (PC). Therefore, a link between these criteria and the Jeffrey–Bayes posterior odds ratio is provided. It should also be clear that Bayesians evaluate inference procedures in terms of posterior expected losses while sampling theorists are concerned with sampling properties or risk functions. This distinction is highlighted relative to the model choice problem by Kiefer and Richard (1982).

21.2.6 Stein Rules for Model Choice

Continue to consider the problem of the investigator who suspects that the data generation process may be described by a high-dimensional parameter space K but who has good reason to believe some of the variables are not necessary, since they have little or no effect on the outcome of $\mathbf{y}$. Therefore, the conjecture is that the data process can be adequately modeled by a lower-dimensional parameter space K_1. We know from Chapter 3 and the preceding sections of this chapter that including extraneous variables in the design matrix or excluding important explanatory variables from the design matrix conditions the precision and bias with which the parameter vector $\boldsymbol{\beta}$ is estimated. The maximum likelihood (least squares) rule for the complete model involving K parameters and the restricted maximum likelihood (least squares) procedure, which excludes some of the extraneous and other variables and thus reduces the dimension of the parameter space to K_1, are end points on the bias–variance continuum. In this section we leave the traditional estimator and pretest estimation worlds and consider the bias–variance choice within a Stein-rule context, where the data are used to determine the compromise between bias and variance and the *appropriate dimension or transformation* of the parameter vector.

21.2.6a The Conditional Mean Forecasting Problem Restated

In motivating the consideration of the Stein rules for this problem, consider the conditional mean forecasting problem of estimating $E[\mathbf{y}_1] = \tilde{X}\boldsymbol{\beta}$, where $\mathbf{y}_1 = \tilde{X}\boldsymbol{\beta} + \mathbf{e}_1$, is a $(\tau \times 1)$ vector and $\tilde{X}$ is the subsequent $(\tau \times K)$ design matrix. The maximum likelihood estimator $\tilde{X}\mathbf{b}$ has mean $\tilde{X}\boldsymbol{\beta}$ and covariance matrix $E[\tilde{X}(\mathbf{b} - \boldsymbol{\beta})(\mathbf{b} - \boldsymbol{\beta})'\tilde{X}'] = \sigma^2\tilde{X}(X'X)^{-1}\tilde{X}'$, and under quadratic loss the risk is $E[(\tilde{X}\mathbf{b} - X\boldsymbol{\beta})'(\tilde{X}\mathbf{b} - X\boldsymbol{\beta})] = \sigma^2 \operatorname{tr} \tilde{X}(X'X)^{-1}\tilde{X}'$. If one is willing to leave the class of unbiased estimators and consider biased estimators, it is instructive to follow King (1972, 1974) and consider all estimators of the form $c\mathbf{b}$, where c is any constant, and to ask what c minimizes the squared error loss function [Judge and Bock (1978, p. 22)]. For the estimator $c\tilde{X}\mathbf{b}$ the risk function for the conditional mean forecasting problem is

$$\begin{aligned}\rho(\tilde{X}\boldsymbol{\beta}, c\tilde{X}\mathbf{b}) &= E[(c\tilde{X}\mathbf{b} - \tilde{X}\boldsymbol{\beta})'(c\tilde{X}\mathbf{b} - \tilde{X}\boldsymbol{\beta})] \\ &= E[(c\tilde{X}(\boldsymbol{\beta} + (X'X)^{-1}X'\mathbf{e}) - \tilde{X}\boldsymbol{\beta})'(c\tilde{X}(\boldsymbol{\beta} + (X'X)^{-1}X'\mathbf{e}) - \tilde{X}\boldsymbol{\beta})]\end{aligned} \tag{21.2.58a}$$

which after a little algebra becomes

$$\rho(\tilde{X}\boldsymbol{\beta}, c\tilde{X}\mathbf{b}) = (c - 1)^2\boldsymbol{\beta}'\tilde{X}'\tilde{X}\boldsymbol{\beta} + c^2\sigma^2 \operatorname{tr} [\tilde{X}(X'X)^{-1}\tilde{X}'] \tag{21.2.58b}$$

The optimality condition for the minimum of (22.2.58) is

$$\frac{d\rho(\tilde{X}\boldsymbol{\beta}, c\tilde{X}\mathbf{b})}{dc} = 2(c - 1)\boldsymbol{\beta}'\tilde{X}'\tilde{X}\boldsymbol{\beta} + 2c\sigma^2 \operatorname{tr}[\tilde{X}(X'X)^{-1}\tilde{X}'] = 0 \tag{21.2.59}$$

Unfortunately, the minimum choice c, which is

$$c = \frac{\boldsymbol{\beta}'\tilde{X}'\tilde{X}\boldsymbol{\beta}}{\boldsymbol{\beta}'\tilde{X}'\tilde{X}\boldsymbol{\beta} + \sigma^2 \operatorname{tr}[\tilde{X}(X'X)^{-1}\tilde{X}']} \tag{21.2.60}$$

depends upon the unknown parameter vector $\boldsymbol{\beta}$ and the scalar σ^2. If after making the proper substitutions, we replace the unknown $\boldsymbol{\beta}$ and σ^2 in (21.2.60) with their unbiased estimators, then

$$\begin{aligned} c &= \frac{\mathbf{b}'\tilde{X}'\tilde{X}\mathbf{b} - \hat{\sigma}^2 \operatorname{tr}(\tilde{X}(X'X)^{-1}\tilde{X}')}{\mathbf{b}'\tilde{X}'\tilde{X}\mathbf{b}} \\ &= 1 - \left(\frac{\hat{\sigma}^2 \operatorname{tr} \tilde{X}(X'X)^{-1}\tilde{X}'}{\mathbf{b}'\tilde{X}'\tilde{X}\mathbf{b}}\right) \end{aligned} \tag{21.2.61}$$

This result looks suspiciously like the general form of the Stein-rule adjustment for the maximum likelihood estimator that was discussed in Chapter 3 and suggests that perhaps some member of the Stein-rule family might be of use in the estimation-model selection problem. Use of the Stein-rule estimator in this context is particularly appealing, since we know the sampling properties of this estimator and know little about the sampling properties of the criteria or decision rules discussed in the previous sections of this chapter or for that matter the estimator suggested in (21.2.61).

21.2.6b Stein-Rule Formulation

To investigate the problem in a Stein-rule context, assume that the set of explanatory variables that is consistent with a general design matrix and a high-dimensional parameter space can be partitioned into the following disjoint sets: (1) the set of explanatory variables X_1, which are important in determining the outcome of $\mathbf{y}$; and (2) the set of variables X_2, which have no impact on the outcome of $\mathbf{y}$, and thus are extraneous variables in terms of describing the process by which $\mathbf{y}$ is generated. Usually, the investigator for a particular applied problem does not know with certainty which particular variables fall in each class or set. The problem of model choice then narrows to finding, out of the total set of variables $X = \{X_1, X_2\}$ of dimension $K_1 + K_2 = K$, the variables that are in the set X_1, and how to exclude the extraneous variables X_2 from the model so that the precision with which the parameters of X_1 variables are estimated can be increased.

In considering this problem within a Stein-rule context, first consider the conditional mean forecast problem under a squared error loss measure. The risk function may be stated as

$$E[(X\tilde{\boldsymbol{\beta}} - X\boldsymbol{\beta})'(X\tilde{\boldsymbol{\beta}} - X\boldsymbol{\beta})] = E[(\tilde{\boldsymbol{\beta}} - \boldsymbol{\beta})'X'X(\tilde{\boldsymbol{\beta}} - \boldsymbol{\beta})] \tag{21.2.62}$$

which by the transformations given in Chapter 2 may be written as

$$E[(X\tilde{\boldsymbol{\beta}} - X\boldsymbol{\beta})'(X\tilde{\boldsymbol{\beta}} - X\boldsymbol{\beta})] = E[(\tilde{\boldsymbol{\theta}} - \boldsymbol{\theta})'(\tilde{\boldsymbol{\theta}} - \boldsymbol{\theta})] \tag{21.2.63}$$

where $\mathbf{y} = XS^{-1/2}S^{1/2}\boldsymbol{\beta} + \mathbf{e} = Z\boldsymbol{\theta} + \mathbf{e}$, with $\tilde{\boldsymbol{\theta}} = S^{1/2}\tilde{\boldsymbol{\beta}}$, $S^{1/2}S^{1/2} = X'X$, and $Z'Z = I_K$. Under this specification, the maximum likelihood estimator $\hat{\boldsymbol{\theta}} = (Z'Z)^{-1}Z'\mathbf{y} = Z'\mathbf{y}$ has mean $\boldsymbol{\theta}$ and covariance $\sigma^2 I_K$.

From Chapter 3 and from Judge and Bock (1978, pp. 167–206) the generalized James and Stein estimator for the complete model, with corresponding hypotheses $\boldsymbol{\theta} = \boldsymbol{\theta}_0$ for all parameters, may be written as

$$\boldsymbol{\theta}^* = \left[1 - \frac{c^*}{u}\right](\hat{\boldsymbol{\theta}} - \boldsymbol{\theta}_0) + \boldsymbol{\theta}_0 = \left[1 - \frac{c(T-K)\hat{\sigma}^2}{(\hat{\boldsymbol{\theta}} - \boldsymbol{\theta}_0)'(\hat{\boldsymbol{\theta}} - \boldsymbol{\theta}_0)}\right](\hat{\boldsymbol{\theta}} - \boldsymbol{\theta}_0) + \boldsymbol{\theta}_0 \tag{21.2.64}$$

where $c^* = (T-K)(K-2)/K(T-K+2)$ and $u = (\hat{\boldsymbol{\theta}} - \boldsymbol{\theta}_0)'(\hat{\boldsymbol{\theta}} - \boldsymbol{\theta}_0)/K\hat{\sigma}^2$ is the likelihood ratio statistic that, assuming the hypotheses are correct, is distributed as a central F random variable with K and $(T - K)$ degrees of freedom. Furthermore, from the results of James and Stein (1961) and Judge and Bock (1978), we know that under the squared error loss measure of performance, the James and Stein estimator is uniformly superior to the maximum likelihood estimator $\hat{\boldsymbol{\theta}} = Z'\mathbf{y}$. If the null hypothesis is $\boldsymbol{\theta}_0 = \mathbf{0}$, the James and Stein estimator simplifies to

$$\boldsymbol{\theta}^*_{(\boldsymbol{\theta}_0=\mathbf{0})} = \left(1 - \frac{c^*}{u}\right)\hat{\boldsymbol{\theta}} \tag{21.2.65}$$

One important thing to note in (21.2.65) is that except for the case when $u = c^*$, although the parameters are transformed, the dimension of the parameter space is maintained at K. In the case $u = (T-K)(K-2)/K(T-K+2) = c^*$, all elements of the K-dimensional parameter vector are set equal to $\boldsymbol{\theta}_0 = \mathbf{0}$.

These results are interesting, since we now have an estimator (21.2.64) and (21.2.65) that is a function of the maximum likelihood estimator but has risk equal to or less than the maximum likelihood estimator over the whole parameter space. If we use a Stein-rule that shrinks to a null vector when the extraneous variables are included, under loss (21.2.63), the risk function is

$$\frac{\rho(\boldsymbol{\theta}^*_{(\boldsymbol{\theta}_0=\mathbf{0})}, \boldsymbol{\theta})}{\sigma^2} = K - (K-2)^2 \frac{(T-K)}{T-K+2} E\left[\frac{1}{\chi^2_{(K,\lambda)}}\right] \tag{21.2.66}$$

where the noncentrality parameter $\lambda = \boldsymbol{\theta}'\boldsymbol{\theta}/2\sigma^2$. When $\boldsymbol{\theta} = \mathbf{0}$ the risk is

$K - (K - 2)(T - K)/(T - K + 2)$ and increases to K the maximum likelihood risk, as $\lambda \to \infty$. Under the correct model the risk of the Stein-rule estimator is

$$\frac{\rho(\boldsymbol{\theta}^*_{1(\boldsymbol{\theta}_{10}=\mathbf{0})}, \boldsymbol{\theta}_1)}{\sigma^2} = K_1 - (K_1 - 2)^2 \frac{(T - K_1)}{T - K_1 + 2} E\left[\frac{1}{\chi^2_{(K_1,\lambda)}}\right] \qquad (21.2.67)$$

A variant of the Stein-rule that does exclude variables for a range of values of u, or in other words, values of the F statistic, is the Baranchik (1964) positive-part, Stein-rule estimator. For the formulation resulting in (21.2.65) involving a zero null hypothesis for the complete parameter vector, the positive rule estimator is

$$\boldsymbol{\theta}^{*+} = I_{[c^*,\infty)}(u)\left[1 - \frac{c^*}{u}\right]\hat{\boldsymbol{\theta}} \qquad (21.2.68)$$

By this rule, unless u or F falls in the range c^* to ∞, where

$$c_0 = (K - 2)(T - K)/(K(T - K + 2))$$

and $c_0 \leq c^* \leq 2c_0$, the parameter vector $\boldsymbol{\theta}$ should be estimated by $\boldsymbol{\theta}_0 = \mathbf{0}$. The positive Stein estimator produces an estimator that, under squared error loss, dominates the corresponding maximum likelihood and James and Stein estimators. In addition, for comparable levels of the test, the positive Stein-rule dominates the conventional pre-test estimator.

The implied statistical level of significance for the F random variable, when using the positive Stein-rule is given in Table 21.3 for various K and $T - K$. As is evident from Table 21.3, the above criterion and the corresponding rules require critical values of the F statistic that result in higher significance levels α than those recommended by many of the informal criteria discussed in the previous sections. This means, on the average, that a larger subset of variables would be retained with the Stein-rule criterion than, for example, the information, Amemiya, and Mallows-type criteria.

TABLE 21.3 ***IMPLIED α LEVELS OF THE TEST CORRESPONDING TO THE POSITIVE STEIN-RULE ESTIMATOR FOR c^* AND $2c^*$ WHERE*** **$c^* = K^{-1}(T - K)(K - 2)(T - K + 2)^{-1}$**

		Possible Number of Extraneous Variables			
		$K_2 = 5$	$K_2 = 10$	$K_2 = 20$	$K_2 = 30$
$T - K = K_2$	c^*	0.81	0.73	0.67	0.64
	$2c^*$	0.57	0.33	0.14	0.07

Source: S. L. Sclove, C. Morris, and R. Radhakrishnan (1972), *Annals of Mathematical Statistics*, 43, p. 1486.

In practical applications the investigator would estimate the parameters of the orthogonal model by least squares procedures, compute the F statistic under a zero ($K > 2$) vector null hypothesis, exclude the K variables when the test statistic $u_K \leq k[(T - K)(K - 2)/K(T - K + 2)]$, where $1 \leq k \leq 2$, or otherwise use the James and Stein estimator (21.2.65). Even if one thinks that the K set of variables is empty and there is no uncertainty about the dimensions of the parameter space, one would still gain from the squared error loss point of view from using the James and Stein estimator (21.2.65) or its positive rule counterpart for the complete model.

This suggested criterion makes use of the data to determine (1) the dimensions or transformations of the parameter space and therefore (2) the compromise between variance and bias. Since the Stein positive rule estimator is neither Bayesian nor admissible under squared error loss, it can be beaten, but we suspect the superior rule or criterion does not yet exist.

There is for the positive rule estimator no optimum value of c^*, and for the estimator to satisfy the minimax condition, c^* must take on values $0 \leq c^* \leq 2(K - 2)(T - K)/K(T - K + 2)$. However, Efron and Morris (1973) have shown that the range of $c^* = k(T - K)(K - 2)/K(T - K + 2)$, when $1 \leq k \leq 2$, dominates any choice of k in the range $0 \leq k \leq 1$.

It is possible, of course, within a sampling context, that one or more of the critical variables in the set X_1 would be omitted. However, the high α levels suggested for the F statistic would act to help avoid placing a critical variable in the X_2 category. If, however, the initial model is misspecified and some X_1 variables are omitted, then the estimator of the variance is biased and as noted by Mittlehammer (1984) the F random variable in (21.2.64) has a double noncentral F distribution. As Mittlehammer shows, under this scenario, the Stein estimator no longer dominates, under squared error loss, the restricted maximum likelihood estimator that has unbounded risk. Alternatively when the model is over specified the estimator of the variance is biased by a factor $(T - K_1)(T - K_1 - K_2)^{-1}$ and the previous relative risk outcomes hold.

Another alternative is to follow Efron and Morris (1972) and modify the James-Stein estimator by requiring that no coordinate of the X_1 set be changed by more than a preassigned quantity. This leads to improvement in the James-Stein risk when the empirical distribution of β_i is long tailed. Building on this work Stein (1981), using order statistics, has modified the Efron and Morris limited translation estimator to obtain an even larger improvement over the James-Stein risks. Since these estimators are defined on a coordinate-wise basis they may be especially useful in handling model choice problems of the type noted at the beginning of Section 21.2.6.

21.2.6c A General Stein-Rule

In many situations in econometric practice, it is more reasonable to base the choice of the model on a more general loss function and work with the following risk $E[(\mathbf{b} - \boldsymbol{\beta})'(\mathbf{b} - \boldsymbol{\beta})]$. In this case, one may choose a generalized variant of the Stein-rule [Judge and Bock (1978, pp. 229–257)] such as

$$\mathbf{b}_1^* = \left[1 - \left(\frac{a(T-K)\hat{\sigma}^2}{\mathbf{b}'X'X\mathbf{b}}\right)\right]\mathbf{b} \tag{21.2.69}$$

or the generalized counterpart

$$\begin{aligned}\mathbf{b}_2^* &= \left[1 - \frac{a(T-K)\hat{\sigma}^2}{(\mathbf{b}-\boldsymbol{\beta}_0)'X'X(\mathbf{b}-\boldsymbol{\beta}_0)}\right](\mathbf{b}-\boldsymbol{\beta}_0) + \boldsymbol{\beta}_0 \\ &= \left[1 - \frac{a(T-K)\hat{\sigma}^2}{(\mathbf{r}-R\mathbf{b})'[R(X'X)^{-1}R']^{-1}(\mathbf{r}-R\mathbf{b})}\right](\mathbf{b}-\mathbf{b}^*) + \mathbf{b}^*\end{aligned} \tag{21.2.70}$$

where $\mathbf{b}^* = \mathbf{b} - (X'X)^{-1}R'[R(X'X)^{-1}R']^{-1}(R\mathbf{b} - \mathbf{r})$ is the restricted least squares estimator, and R is a $(J \times K)$ restriction matrix with $J \leq K$. For expository purposes, let us rewrite (21.2.69) as

$$\mathbf{b}_1^* = \left[1 - \frac{a(T-K)J^{-1}}{u_1}\right](\mathbf{b}-\mathbf{b}^*) + \mathbf{b}^* \tag{21.2.71}$$

where $u_1 = (\mathbf{r} - R\mathbf{b})'[R(X'X)^{-1}R']^{-1}(\mathbf{r} - R\mathbf{b})/J\hat{\sigma}^2$, a test statistic that is distributed as an $F_{(J,T-K)}$ random variable. As Judge and Bock (1978) demonstrate, this version of the James–Stein rule is, under squared error loss, $E[(\mathbf{b} - \boldsymbol{\beta})'(\mathbf{b} - \boldsymbol{\beta})/\sigma^2]$, uniformly superior to the least squares estimator $\mathbf{b}$, if

$$0 \leq a \leq \frac{2\{\text{tr}\,[R(X'X)^{-1}R']^{-1}R(X'X)^{-2}R'\; d_L^{-1} - 2\}}{(T-K+2)}$$

and $\text{tr}\,[R(X'X)^{-1}R']^{-1}R(X'X)^{-2}R' > 2\,d_L$, where d_L is the largest characteristic root of the matrix $[R(X'X)^{-1}R']^{-1}R(X'X)^{-2}R'$ and $J \geq 3$. Judge and Bock (1978, p. 246) also show that the positive-part Stein-rule estimator

$$\mathbf{b}_3^* = I_{(a^*,\infty)}(u_1)\left[1 - \frac{a^*}{u_1}\right](\mathbf{b}-\mathbf{b}^*) + \mathbf{b}^* \tag{21.2.72}$$

where $a^* = a(T-K)J^{-1}$, dominates the James and Stein estimator (21.2.70) if $0 \leq a^* \leq 2(T-K)\{\text{tr}\,[R(X'X)^{-1}R']\,d_L^{-1} - 2\}/J(T-K+2)$ and $\text{tr}\,R(X'X)^{-1}R' \geq 2\,d_L$ or

$$\frac{\text{tr}\,R(X'X)^{-1}R'}{d_L} \geq 2 \tag{21.2.73}$$

As in the orthonormal case in the $\boldsymbol{\theta}$ (prediction) space, where $\text{tr}\,[R(X'X)^{-1}R']/d_L \geq 2$ implies that $K_2 \geq 2$, we are provided with a basis for choosing a model in the K-dimensional space. The rule is: (1) if $u_1 \leq a^*$, use $\mathbf{b}^*$; (2) if $u_1 > a^*$, use the K-dimensional space where the estimator (21.2.71) becomes operational (i.e., the James and Stein estimator) and transform all the elements in the K-dimensional vector. The case when $\{\text{tr}\,[R(X'X)^{-1}R']d_L^{-1}\} < 2$ will be discussed in Chapter 22. If we assume that the characteristic root condition (21.2.73) is fulfilled, the critical value of the $F_{(J,T-K)}$ test statistic is

$$F_{(J,T-K)} \leq a^* = \frac{2(T-K)\{\text{tr}\,[R(X'X)^{-1}R']\,d_L^{-1} - 2\}}{J(T-K+2)} \leq 1 \quad (21.2.74)$$

As in the orthonormal case for the positive Stein-rule estimator, there is no optimal value of a^* and the risk functions for

$$0 < a^* < 2\left[a_0 = \frac{(T-K)\{\text{tr}[R(X'X)^{-1}R']\,d_L^{-1} - 2\}}{J(T-K+2)}\right]$$

cross somewhere in the parameter space. A choice of $a^* = a_0$ provides one basis for choosing between the K- and J-dimensional restricted model or its K-dimensional transformed counterpart. The Stein positive rule always ensures when $0 \leq a^* \leq 2a_0$ that, on the average, a model chosen in this way will, under squared error loss, have risk equal to or less than that of the K-dimensional unrestricted model or its conventional pretest counterpart. Consequently, we are provided with a rule that yields a risk function that is superior to that of the unrestricted maximum likelihood estimator and its conventional pretest counterpart; and happily, the sampling properties for the rule are known. Since the Mallows et al. rules for model selection result in the choice of a critical F value as the decision variable, the above results imply that for comparable critical values or levels of the test, the Stein positive rule will dominate its implied pretest counterparts. This result demonstrates the questionable normative content of the family of informal and not so informal rules. We should, in closing, note that, as discussed by Judge and Bock (1978, pp. 275–291), these results also hold for the stochastic regressor case.

21.3 NONNESTED STATISTICAL MODELS

In many cases in applied econometrics, there is a need for statistical procedures for testing nonnested, or *separate,* parametric families of hypotheses. Economic examples of nonnested hypotheses include additive or multiplicative errors in a Cobb–Douglas production function and a lognormal versus a Pareto distribution for personal incomes. In these situations, one model cannot be obtained from the other by imposing appropriate restrictions or as a limiting suitable approximation. The variants of the various F norm test statistics, which were discussed in the previous sections for nested hypotheses, cannot in general be used for hypotheses of the *nonnested* type. These tests of *separate* models are specification tests that use information about a specific alternative and test whether the null can predict the performance of the alternative. Although there are differences among researchers as to the appropriate way to test separate families of hypotheses [see, e.g., Atkinson (1970) and Quandt (1974)], the initial results on this subject are based on the work of Cox (1961, 1962). Pesaran (1974) extended the work of Cox to include the regression model and considered the autocorrelated disturbance case, and Pesaran and Deaton (1978) have extended the Pesaran results so that one does not have to assume linearity of the models and competing *systems* of nonlinear equations can be handled. Atkinson (1970) proposes a procedure that nests the nonnested models into a general model. Dastoor (1983) notes an inequality between the Cox and Atkinson statistics and along with Fisher and McAleer (1981) modifies the Cox test for linear regressions. For model specification testing Davidson and MacKinnon (1981) have proposed procedures that are linearized versions of the Cox test and closely related to the nonnested hypothesis tests of Pesaran and Deaton (1978). Pesaran (1982) has compared the local power of several of the tests noted above. A bibliography of papers concerning separate families of hypotheses is given by Pereira (1977b). A special issue of the *Journal of Econometrics* edited by White (1983) contains a set of articles concerned with interpretation, extension, and application of the Cox approach to nonnested hypothesis testing.

In one interesting paper in White's special issue Gourieroux, Monfort and Trognon (1983) present a testing approach that is applicable to both nested and nonnested models. Their procedure rests on the notion of a Sawa-type pseudo-true value and the statistic proposed is similar to the Wald statistics used in the case of nested models.

In the nonnested hypothesis case, we have the following scenario: a data system and a set of alternative hypotheses that are, by assumption, nonnested and thus unranked as to generality. Each of the models (hypotheses) H_i is considered equally likely. Tests of each pair of hypotheses are made, and in each case, a check is made to see if the performance of H_i against the data is consistent with the truth of H_j. One outcome, of course, is that both hypotheses may be rejected.

21.3.1 The Nonnested Framework and a Traditional Test

Suppose for expository purposes that we have two hypotheses H_1 and H_2 about the random vector $\mathbf{y}$. Under H_1 the random vector $\mathbf{y}$ is assumed to be generated by a density function $f_1(\mathbf{y}|X, \boldsymbol{\beta}_1, \sigma_1^2)$, where $(\boldsymbol{\beta}_1, \sigma_1^2)\epsilon\Omega_1$, and under H_2 the random vector $\mathbf{y}$ is assumed to be reflected by the density function $f_2(\mathbf{y}|Z, \boldsymbol{\beta}_2, \sigma_2^2)$, where $(\boldsymbol{\beta}_2, \sigma_2^2)\epsilon\Omega_2$. The union of Ω_1 and Ω_2 is assumed not equal to Ω_1 or Ω_2, and, under this framework, we do not consider approximating one hypothesis by another. Within the linear hypothesis framework for the linear statistical model, the above two nonnested hypotheses become

$$H_1 : \mathbf{y} = X\boldsymbol{\beta}_1 + \mathbf{e}_1 \qquad (21.3.1)$$

where $\mathbf{e}_1 \sim N(\mathbf{0},\sigma_1^2 I_T)$, and

$$H_2 : \mathbf{y} = Z\boldsymbol{\beta}_2 + \mathbf{e}_2 \tag{21.3.2}$$

where $\mathbf{e}_2 \sim N(\mathbf{0},\sigma_2^2 I_T)$, and $\boldsymbol{\beta}_1$ and $\boldsymbol{\beta}_2$ are K_1- and K_2-dimensional parameter vectors. Thus attention is focused on specification tests for separate models and following Pesaran (1982) we assume that transformations on Z result in $Z = [Z_1 \quad XA]$, where Z_1 cannot be obtained from X by the imposition of linear parametric restrictions, and Z_1 is a $(T \times J)$ matrix, where J is the number of nonoverlapping variables. In this context the general model that includes both hypotheses is

$$\begin{aligned}\mathbf{y} &= X\boldsymbol{\beta}_1 + [Z_1 \quad XA]\begin{bmatrix}\boldsymbol{\beta}_{21}\\ \boldsymbol{\beta}_{22}\end{bmatrix} + \mathbf{e}\\ &= X[\boldsymbol{\beta}_1 + A\boldsymbol{\beta}_{22}] + Z_1\boldsymbol{\beta}_{21} + \mathbf{e}\end{aligned} \tag{21.3.3}$$

A test of H_1 against H_2 might then be performed by using the conventional likelihood ratio or the Lagrange multiplier test for testing the hypothesis $\boldsymbol{\beta}_{21} = \mathbf{0}$. Asymptotically the appropriate test statistic, under hypothesis H_1, will be distributed as a central $\chi^2_{(J)}$ random variable.

21.3.2 The Cox Test

In specifying a test for nonnested hypotheses, Cox (1961, 1962) developed a variant of the Neyman-Pearson likelihood ratio test, which compares the value of this statistic to its expected value when the null hypothesis is true, and considers the asymptotic distribution of a function of the generalized log likelihood ratio. A useful derivation of the Cox test for the regression case is given by Pesaran (1974) and McAleer (1984) provides a useful interpretation. For the statistical hypotheses under consideration we have the expression

$$\begin{aligned}c_{12} &= \left(\frac{T}{2}\right) \ln \left\{\frac{\hat{\sigma}_2^2}{\hat{\sigma}_1^2 + \frac{1}{T}\hat{\boldsymbol{\beta}}_1' X'[I - Z(Z'Z)^{-1}Z']X\hat{\boldsymbol{\beta}}_1}\right\}\\ &= \left(\frac{T}{2}\right) \ln \frac{\hat{\sigma}_2^2}{\hat{\sigma}_{21}^2}\end{aligned} \tag{21.3.4}$$

where $\hat{\sigma}_{21}^2$ can be interpreted as the residual variance of H_2 predicted by H_1. In the expression $\hat{}$ denotes maximum likelihood estimators and σ_{21}^2 denotes the probability limit of $\hat{\sigma}_2^2$ under hypothesis H_1.

As Cox has shown, if H_1 holds, c_{12} will be asymptotically normally distributed with mean zero and variance $V(c_{12})$. At this point, it should be noted that the small-sample distribution of the test statistic c_{12} depends on unknown parameters and thus cannot be derived. However, if $[I - Z(Z'Z)^{-1}Z']X = M_2X = 0$, then the models are nested, and for this case an exact test exists.

Given the asymptotic variance $V(c_{12})$, if H_1 holds, $c_{12}/[V(c_{12})]^{1/2}$ is asymptotically distributed as a standard normal random variable. If the unknown parameters are replaced by consistent estimators, then, as Pesaran (1974) shows, $\hat{V}(c_{12}) = (\hat{\sigma}_1^2/\hat{\sigma}_{21}^4)\hat{\boldsymbol{\beta}}_1 X'M_2M_1M_2X\hat{\boldsymbol{\beta}}_1$ can be used to estimate $V(c_{12})$, where M_2 is as defined above and $M_1 = I - X(X'X)^{-1}X'$. Then the test statistic

$$\frac{c_{12}}{[\hat{V}(c_{12})]^{1/2}} = \frac{T}{2}\ln\frac{\hat{\sigma}_2^2}{\hat{\sigma}_{21}^2}\Big/\left[\frac{\hat{\sigma}_1^2}{\hat{\sigma}_{21}^4}\,\hat{\boldsymbol{\beta}}_1'X'M_2M_1M_2X\hat{\boldsymbol{\beta}}_1\right]^{1/2} \tag{21.3.5}$$

can be approximated if H_1 is true, by using a standard normal variable.

Two tests are performed, where each model has a turn at being the true model. A "significant" value for the test statistic suggests rejecting H_1. The outcome of the tests may indicate the data are (1) consistent with H_1, (2) consistent with H_2, or (3) consistent with neither H_1 nor H_2, or (4) consistent with both. It should be noted that in the nonnested case one may not believe either H_1 or H_2 is true. If H_2 involves q separate models, then a joint separate test among these alternatives would involve $q(q + 1)$ paired test statistics. Alternatively H_1 can be simultaneously tested against all q models in H_2 using a $\chi^2_{(q)}$ test or $F_{(q,n-k_1-q)}$.

21.3.3 The *J* Test

Next we consider a linearized version of the Cox test statistic that has been suggested by Davidson and MacKinnon (1981) and is very much related to Ramsey's tests (1974). As one of the alternative tests proposed, Davidson and MacKinnon consider embedding the alternatives in a general model that uses a mixing parameter λ in the combined statistical model

$$\mathbf{y} = (1 - \lambda)X\boldsymbol{\beta}_1 + \lambda Z\boldsymbol{\beta}_2 + \mathbf{e} \tag{21.3.6}$$

Under the hypothesis H_2, Davidson and MacKinnon replace the unknown $Z\boldsymbol{\beta}_2$ with its estimate $Z\hat{\boldsymbol{\beta}}_2 = (I - M_2)\mathbf{y}$. Therefore, (21.3.6) may be rewritten as

$$\begin{aligned}\mathbf{y} &= X\boldsymbol{\beta}_1(1 - \lambda) + \lambda(Z\hat{\boldsymbol{\beta}}_2) + \mathbf{e}\\ &= X\boldsymbol{\beta}_1(1 - \lambda) + \lambda\hat{\mathbf{y}}_2 + \mathbf{e}\end{aligned} \tag{21.3.7}$$

Set up in this form, if hypothesis H_1 is true, then $\lambda = 0$. Since $\hat{\mathbf{y}}$ is asymptotically independent of $\mathbf{e}$, they suggest testing whether $\lambda = 0$ in (21.3.7) by using a likelihood ratio test or the conventional t test, which they call a J test. Therefore, if H_1 is true, as Pesaran (1982) notes, this results in the test statistic

$$J_1 = \hat{\boldsymbol{\beta}}_2'Z'M_1\mathbf{y}/\hat{\sigma}(\hat{\boldsymbol{\beta}}_2'Z'M_1Z\hat{\boldsymbol{\beta}}_2)^{1/2} \tag{21.3.8}$$

where $\hat{\sigma}$ is an estimate of the standard error of regression in (21.3.7). This test statistic is asymptotically distributed as a standard normal random variable and is asymptotically equivalent to the *JA* test proposed by Fisher and McAleer (1981). By using different estimates of $\boldsymbol{\beta}_2$, a number of alternative tests may be generated. For example, if $Z\hat{\hat{\boldsymbol{\beta}}}_2 = (I - M_2)(I - M_1)\mathbf{y}$, then we have the *JA* test noted above.

21.3.4 Some Comments

As noted in the introduction to this section there is a rich literature on separate families of hypotheses that make use of the modified likelihood ratio principle and permit a probabilistic statement to be made regarding model selection. We have only looked at a few of the alternative tests from a very rich and growing set. Many of these tests have the correct size asymptotically, besides being consistent for the testing of H_1 against H_2. This result means that the choice between the tests will depend on the behavior of their power functions. Pesaran (1982) sheds some light on the local power of the Cox and *J* tests, but much work remains in this area. At this point little is known about the small sample properties of the various tests although some preliminary Monte Carlo work has been done in this area. Since we are destined to work with false structural models, it is important to learn about the properties of the tests when neither the null or the alternative are correctly specified. McAleer, Fisher, and Volker (1982) have shown that when the alternative model is misspecified, the test of the null may not be consistent in the sense of rejecting a false null with probability one in large samples; that is, many tests are not, in general, robust in the presence of the other misspecifications. McAleer (1982) discusses other results in this area.

In regard to many of the tests, there is a problem of symmetry relative to the reference hypothesis; that is, the conclusions are not invariant as to the choice of the reference hypothesis. Also, as in other hypothesis tests or pretests, the nagging questions remain: (1) what is the optimal level of the test, and (2) what are the sampling properties of the pretest estimator we have created? To make the test of great use in applied work, these questions must be answered.

Finally, we note that Aneuryn–Evans and Deaton (1980) have proposed a separate family of hypothesis tests based on Cox (1961, 1962) that permits us to test for both functional form and model specification in a very general way. The competing hypotheses for the linear statistical model result when one model might explain the level of a variable up to an additive error and the other would be concerned with its logarithm. Since the main focus of their work is on a test for functional form, we will discuss this procedure in the next section.

21.4 CHOOSING THE FUNCTIONAL FORM

Economic theory has much to offer the researcher in describing how economic data are generated, how economic variables are classified, which economic variables should be considered, and the direction of possible relationships between the variables. Unfortunately, economic theory, which treats most variables symmetrically, is of little help when one reaches the stage in quantitative analysis of specifying the appropriate functional form. Intuitively, it would seem that the data underlying many economic processes and institutions are generated by economic relations that may be nonlinear both in the variables and in the parameters. The problem of estimation and inference in statistical models that are nonlinear in the parameters and the variables was discussed in Chapter 6.

In this section we consider the problem of choosing the algebraic form for statistical models that are nonlinear in the variables and consider the choice problem relating to whether the variables should be represented as linear in their natural units or linear in their transformed values.

In the econometric literature much of the focus is on specifying a wide range of functional forms and then indicating how the statistical model can be transformed to a specification that is linear in the variables to facilitate estimation and inference. The implication of traditional discussions is that, in many cases, variable transformations exist that permit us ultimately to specify models that are nonlinear in the variables as linear in both the variables and the parameters. For example, if we let ε represent the random equation error and consider a single treatment variable $\mathbf{x}_2$, some simple variants of functional forms that have found much use in econometric practice because of the ease of obtaining a linear counterpart are

$$y_t = \beta_1 + x_{2t}\beta_2 + x_{2t}^2\beta_3 + \varepsilon_t = \beta_1 + x_{2t}\beta_2 + x_{3t}\beta_3 + \varepsilon_t \qquad (21.4.1)$$

$$y = \beta_1 x_{2t}^{\beta_2} e^{\varepsilon_t} \qquad \text{or} \qquad \ln y_t = \ln \beta_1 + \beta_2 \ln x_{2t} + \varepsilon_t \qquad (21.4.2)$$

and

$$y_t = \beta_1 e^{x_{2t}\beta_2} e^{\varepsilon_t} \qquad \text{or} \qquad \ln y_t = \ln \beta_1 + x_{2t}\beta_2 + \varepsilon_t \qquad (21.4.3)$$

These specifications suggest that many alternative functional forms exist for reflecting the relationship between the treatment variables and the outcome variable $\mathbf{y}$. Given this array of algebraic alternatives, the central econometric problem is how best to use a sample of data so that we can discriminate between the alternative possible functional forms. It is conventional to bundle this choice problem within a hypothesis-testing framework. For example, power series representations, such as the parabolic specification given in (21.4.1), can be represented in a nested model context, since the linear formulation $\mathbf{y} = \mathbf{x}_1\beta_1 + \mathbf{x}_2\beta_2 + \boldsymbol{\epsilon}$ is a subset of the more general quadratic model. Consequently, the statistical consequences of the choice of a functional form can be evaluated in an omitted variable context—that is, the contrast between the least squares result under the restriction $\beta_3 = 0$ and the unrestricted model (21.4.1). Unfortunately, a test of the hypothesis that the model is linear in terms of $\mathbf{x}_2$ versus the alternative that it may be represented by some polynomial in $\mathbf{x}_2$ leads to a pretest estimator and thus has all the negative statistical consequences discussed in Chapter 3 and in the previous sections of this chapter. So the question is, not whether we can represent our variables in terms of a polynomial or exponential function, but rather how we can use the data to learn something about the correct functional form. Here again, the positive Stein rule may be a useful alternative to conventional hypothesis testing and ad hoc rules.

In the area of consumer and production theories a variety of functional forms, such as the translog, the generalized Leontief, and the generalized Cobb–Douglas, have recently been introduced. Many of these are of the flexible type, in the sense that a priori they do not constrain the relevant elasticities of substitution. These functions provide a local approximation to an arbitrary, twice differentiable cost or direct or indirect utility or production function. Building on this work Appelbaum (1979) uses the Box–Cox (1964) transformation function to demonstrate new generalized forms that can be polynomials, quadratic in logarithms, or various mixed combinations of both. Gallant (1981) goes outside of the Taylor series approximation traditionally used with flexible functional forms and proposes a Fourier flexible form in an attempt to find an indirect utility function whose derived expenditure system will adequately approximate those resulting from a broad class of utility functions. Guilkey, Knox and Sickles (1983) consider the translog, the generalized Leontief and the generalized Cobb-Douglas and analyze the ability of estimating models derived from these functional forms to track a known technology over a range of observations. They conclude the translog form provides a dependable approximation to reality, provided reality is not too complex. They were not able to turn up a flexible functional form more reliable than the translog. Although these generalizations enrich the family of specification alternatives, the question of how to choose among the functional forms remains.

One alternative in specifying and selecting a functional form is to use the Box and Cox (1964) transformation, which includes linearity as a special case. For a single treatment variable specification, we can, following Section 20.5 of Chapter 20 write the Box and Cox transformation as

$$\frac{y_t^{\lambda} - 1}{\lambda} = \beta_1 + \frac{\beta_2(x_{2t}^{\lambda} - 1)}{\lambda} + \varepsilon_t \tag{21.4.4}$$

When $\lambda = 0$, (21.4.4) reduces to

$$\ln y_t = \beta_1 + \beta_2 \ln x_{2t} + \varepsilon_t \tag{21.4.5}$$

and when $\lambda = 1$, (21.4.4) reduces to

$$y_t = (\beta_1 - \beta_2 + 1) + x_{2t}\beta_2 + \varepsilon_t = \beta_0 + x_{2t}\beta_2 + \varepsilon_t \tag{21.4.6}$$

a linear formulation. Since a family of functions is defined by (21.4.4), a conventional likelihood ratio hypothesis test of linearity would involve the null hypothesis H_0: $\lambda = 1$ versus the alternative H_A: $\lambda \neq 1$. The usual negative statistical consequences of this functional form search (pretest) procedure apply directly.

Finally, Aneuryn–Evans and Deaton (1980) consider two competing statistical models, one of which explains the level of a variable up to an additive error and the other explains its logarithm up to an additive error. The variables that appear in the design matrix may be linear or nonlinear. In their paper, they develop a test based on the Cox (1961, 1962) procedure for testing separate families of hypotheses; that is, they develop two test statistics that are, if correct, asymptotically distributed as $N(0,1)$ random variables. Their work is therefore related to the nonnested models hypothesis procedures discussed in Section 21.3. They conclude that the large-sample properties of the test are closely approximated in small samples. Their results also imply that if the investigator knows that one or the other model is correct, that is, in (21.4.4), either $\lambda = 0$ or $\lambda = 1$, then the likelihood ratio criterion proposed by Sargan (1964) is a useful basis for discriminating between the two models. However, in case neither model is true, the Cox test has the possibility of rejecting both models, which is the correct decision. Building on the work of Andrews (1971), and Aneuryn–Evans and Deaton (1980), Godfrey and Wickens (1981) develop a basis for testing the adequacy of the linear and log-linear forms against the more general Box–Cox regression model. Their approach, which treats the linear and log-linear forms as special cases of the general model, leads to a Lagrange multiplier test that is easy to compute and that can as one outcome reject both models. An informative discussion of testing linear and log-linear models may be found in McAleer (1984).

21.5 SUMMARY

Someone once said that econometrics is a curious set of recipes. Nowhere in the subject areas of econometrics is this proposition more true than it is for the problem of statistical model selection. Nonexperimental model building is a difficult task, and our desire to try to obtain so much information from a limited set of observations is perhaps doomed from the start to some degree to failure. But the appropriate parameterization of a linear statistical model is a hard and important problem, and despite the productive efforts of many, it remains just that. One indication of this state of affairs comes from the concluding remarks sections of competent and knowledgeable literature review articles concerned with model identification. In each case the authors make clear that their intention has been to present the current state of the art, perhaps offer a suggestion or two here and there, and to give no definite solutions. This, of course, is in itself an important result, because it is very important to know the limits of our knowledge so that we do not feel comfortable in our state of ignorance and do not continue to fool ourselves and perhaps others.

Although there is a certain intuitive appeal and logic to many of the ad hoc, informal model selection rules that have been suggested, we should not forget (1) *their heuristic base,* (2) *the fact that their sampling properties are virtually unknown,* and (3) *that their practical utility is mainly demonstrated by numerical examples*. Consequently, there is in the background the nagging question of applicability of the results to a broader set of data. The classical theory of estimation as it relates to the process of statistical model building, usually results in various types of two- or more stage pretest estimation-type procedures. As discussed in Chapter 3, these pretest-type search procedures lead to rules that are inadmissible under a squared error loss measure, that is, the measure usually used to justify the procedure in the first place. The Bayesian approach to statistical inference with a decision oriented focus has done much to provide conceptual clarification for the process of learning from economic data. However, the posterior odds depend on the prior probabilities of the models and the parameters, and many practitioners have difficulty in choosing the appropriate priors.

In much of this chapter we have been concerned with researchers who believe they can identify in *general* the ingredients of the economic processes and institutions by which their data are generated. However, they suspect the real world may be much simpler, and indeed, there are several admissible alternative nested and nonnested models that do not contradict their knowledge of economic behavior. Therefore, questions arise as to the appropriate dimension of the parameterized statistical model. From the standpoint of inference, we need to know, out of the possible set of variables, how to choose the "appropriate ones" so that we can successfully walk the parameter performance tightrope, which has bias on one end and precision (variance) on the other or resolve some of the debates currently raging in economic theory.

For the most part the criteria or choice rules we have discussed, relating to model selection with quadratic loss, have involved, in one form or another, the residual error sum of squares corresponding to each model specification. Therefore, it has been possible to relate them to one another by way of one or more traditional test statistics and to discuss the implied level of statistical significance. Most of the criteria involve unknown parameters, and therefore operational counterparts for these criteria vary, depending on the estimates used to substitute for the unknown parameters. Furthermore, with each criterion there is uncertainty, in a decision theory context, as to the corresponding loss or risk function, and even if we could identify the appropriate risk function, we are unsure as to the part of the parameter space that is applicable. None of these procedures can assure that the model that most accurately estimates the parameters of interest will be selected. Furthermore, in using these discrimination procedures one model will always be chosen even if it cannot predict the consequences of separate alternatives.

When we leave the nested model case, the problem becomes more difficult and the results perhaps a bit more shaky. To be sure, it is important to have statistical procedures for checking separate families of hypotheses, and toward this end, the tests suggested by Cox (1961, 1962) are suggestive. The work, for example, of Atkinson (1970), Quandt (1974), Pesaran (1974), Pesaran and Deaton (1978), Davidson and MacKinnon (1981), Pesaran (1982), and Mizon and Richard (1983) adds to the knowledge in this area. However, until we know more of the small-sample properties and power of the tests proposed, the robustness of the tests under unusual error structures and specification errors, and something about the risk functions for the estimators thereby generated, we should use these tests, for model identification purposes, with caution.

Perhaps within both the nested and nonnested worlds, a requirement for introducing any new criterion or test should be that its sampling properties should be demonstrated under alternative loss structures. This requirement would profoundly curtail or reduce the current and prospective criterion sets.

21.6 EXERCISES

In order to demonstrate the reach of some of the model selection procedures discussed in this chapter, consider the following statistical model and design matrix:

$$\mathbf{y} = X\boldsymbol{\beta} + \mathbf{e} = 10\mathbf{x}_1 + 0.4\mathbf{x}_2 + 0.6\mathbf{x}_3 + 0.0\mathbf{x}_4 + 0.0\mathbf{x}_5 + 0.0\mathbf{x}_6 + \mathbf{e} \quad (21.6.1)$$

where $\mathbf{e}$ is a normal random vector with mean vector zero and variance $\sigma^2 = .0625$. Assume the (20×6) design matrix is

$$X = \begin{array}{c} \begin{matrix} \mathbf{x}_1 & \mathbf{x}_2 & \mathbf{x}_3 & \mathbf{x}_4 & \mathbf{x}_5 & \mathbf{x}_6 \end{matrix} \\ \begin{bmatrix} 1 & 0.693 & 0.693 & 0.610 & 1.327 & -2.947 \\ 1 & 1.733 & 0.693 & -1.714 & 2.413 & 0.788 \\ 1 & 0.693 & 1.386 & 0.082 & 3.728 & -0.813 \\ 1 & 1.733 & 1.386 & -0.776 & -0.757 & 1.968 \\ 1 & 0.693 & 1.792 & 1.182 & -0.819 & 3.106 \\ 1 & 2.340 & 0.693 & 3.681 & 2.013 & -3.176 \\ 1 & 1.733 & 1.792 & -1.307 & 0.464 & -2.407 \\ 1 & 2.340 & 1.386 & 0.440 & -2.493 & 0.136 \\ 1 & 2.340 & 1.792 & 1.395 & -1.637 & 3.427 \\ 1 & 0.693 & 0.693 & 0.281 & 0.504 & 0.687 \\ 1 & 0.693 & 1.386 & -1.929 & -0.344 & -2.609 \\ 1 & 1.733 & 0.693 & 1.985 & -0.212 & -0.741 \\ 1 & 1.733 & 1.386 & -2.500 & -0.875 & 0.264 \\ 1 & 0.693 & 1.792 & 0.335 & 2.137 & 0.631 \\ 1 & 2.340 & 0.693 & 0.464 & 1.550 & -1.169 \\ 1 & 1.733 & 1.792 & 4.110 & -1.664 & 1.585 \\ 1 & 2.340 & 1.386 & -2.254 & -0.285 & -0.131 \\ 1 & 2.340 & 1.792 & -1.906 & 1.162 & 0.903 \\ 1 & 1.733 & 1.386 & 0.125 & 0.399 & -1.838 \\ 1 & 0.693 & 0.693 & -2.935 & -2.600 & -2.634 \end{bmatrix} \end{array} \quad (21.6.2)$$

Using the statistical model described by (21.6.1) and (21.6.2) and the sampling process described in Chapter 2, use Monte Carlo procedures to generate 100 $\mathbf{y}$ samples of size 20.

21.6.1 Individual Exercises

Choose five samples of data and for *each* sample do the following:

Exercise 21.1
Select a final model using the $\bar{R}^2$ criterion.

Exercise 21.2
Select a final model using the C_p criterion.

Exercise 21.3
Select a final model using the PC criterion.

Exercise 21.4
Select a final model using the AIC criterion.

Exercise 21.5
Select a final model using the BIC criterion.

Exercise 21.6
Select a final model by the general Stein positive rule when the coefficients of $\mathbf{x}_4$, $\mathbf{x}_5$, and $\mathbf{x}_6$ are hypothesized to be zero, that is $R\boldsymbol{\beta} = [0,I_3]\boldsymbol{\beta} = \mathbf{0}$.

Exercise 21.7
Using the conventional and J tests for nonnested models, discriminate between the two models that involve $\mathbf{x}_1$, $\mathbf{x}_2$, and $\mathbf{x}_3$, and $\mathbf{x}_4$, $\mathbf{x}_5$, and $\mathbf{x}_6$.

Exercise 21.8
Compare and contrast your model choice results for both the nested and nonnested cases.

21.6.2 Joint or Class Exercises

Using the 100 samples of data previously generated involving the design matrix (21.6.2), an error variance of .0625 and the risk function $(\tilde{\boldsymbol{\beta}} - \boldsymbol{\beta})'X'X(\tilde{\boldsymbol{\beta}} - \boldsymbol{\beta})$, where $\tilde{\boldsymbol{\beta}}$ is the relevant estimator, develop empirical risk functions associated with the following variable selection criteria over the specification error parameter space $\boldsymbol{\beta}'\boldsymbol{\beta}$ and discuss:

Exercise 21.9
The C_p criterion.

Exercise 21.10
The PC criterion.

Exercise 21.11
The AIC criterion.

Exercise 21.12
The positive Stein-rule criterion under the hypothesis

$$R\boldsymbol{\beta} = [0, I_3]\boldsymbol{\beta} = \mathbf{0}.$$

Exercise 21.13
The traditional pretest estimator under the hypothesis $R\boldsymbol{\beta} = \mathbf{0}$.

21.7 REFERENCES

Akaike, H. (1973) "Information Theory and the Extension of the Maximum Likelihood Principle," in B. N. Petrov and F. Csaki, eds., *2nd International Symposium on Information Theory,* Akailseoniai-Kiudo, Budapest, pp. 267–281.

Akaike, H. (1974) "A New Look at the Statistical Identification Model," *IEEE: Trans. Auto. Control,* 19, 716–723.

Akaike, H. (1978) "On the Likelihood of a Time Series Model," Paper presented at the Institute of Statisticians 1978 Conference on Time Series Analysis, Cambridge University, Cambridge, England, July 1978.

Akaike, H. (1981) "Likelihood of a Model and Information Criteria," *Journal of Econometrics,* 16, 3–14.

Allen, D. M. (1971) "Mean Square Error of Predictions as a Criterion for Selecting Variables," *Technometrics,* 13, 469–475.

Amemiya, T. (1980) "Selection of Regressors," *International Economic Review,* 21, 331–354.

Andrews, D. F. (1971) "A Note on the Selection of Data Transformations," *Biometrika,* 58, 249–254.

Aneuryn-Evans, G. and A. Deaton (1980) "Testing Linear Versus Logarithmic Regression Models," *Review of Economic Studies,* 47, 275–291.

Appelbaum, E. (1979) "On the Choice of Functional Forms," *International Economic Review,* 20, 449–458.

Atkinson, A. C. (1970) "A Method for Discriminating Between Models," *Journal of the Royal Statistical Society, Series B,* 32, 323–345.

Baranchik, A. (1964) "Multiple Regression and Estimation of the Mean of the Multivariate Normal Mean," Technical Report No. 51, Department of Statistics, Stanford University.

Box, G. E. P. and D. R. Cox (1964) "An Analysis of Transformations," *Journal of the Royal Statistical Society, Series B,* 26, 211–243.

Breiman, L. and D. Freedman (1983) "How Many Variables Should be Entered in a Regression Equation?" *Journal of American Statistical Association,* 78, 131–136.

Brook, R. J. (1976) "On the Use of a Regret Function to Set Significance Points in Prior Tests of Estimation," *Journal of the American Statistical Association,* 71, 126–131.

Chow, G. C. (1981) "A Comparison of the Information and Posterior Probability Criteria for Model Selection," *Journal of Econometrics,* 16, 21–33.

Cox, D. R. (1961) "Test of Separate Families of Hypotheses," *Proceedings of the Fourth Berkeley Symposium on Mathematical Statistics and Probability,* Vol. 1, University of California Press, Berkeley.

Cox, D. R. (1962) "Further Results on Tests of Separate Families of Hypothesis," *Journal of the Royal Statistical Society, Series B,* 24, 406–424.

Dastoor, N. K. (1983) "Some Aspects of Testing Nonnested Hypotheses," *Journal of Econometrics,* 21, 213–228.

Davidson, R. and J. G. MacKinnon (1981) "Several Tests for Model Specification in the Presence of Alternative Hypotheses," *Econometrica,* 49, 781–793.

Edwards, J. B. (1969) "The Relationship Between the F Test and R^2," *American Statistician,* 23, 28.

Efron, B. and C. Morris (1975) "Data Analysis Using Stein's Estimator and Its Generalizations," *Journal of the American Statistical Association,* 70, 311–319.

Efron, B. and C. Morris (1972) "Limiting the Risk of Bayes and Empirical Bayes Estimators—Part II: The Empirical Bayes Case" *Journal of the American Statistical Association,* 67, 130–139.

Efron, B. and C. Morris (1973) "Stein's Estimation Rule and Its Competitors—An Empirical Bayes Approach," *Journal of the American Statistical Association,* 68, 117–130.

Efroymson, M. A. (1966) "Stepwise Regression—A Backward and Forward Look," *Paper presented at the Eastern Regional Meetings of the Institute of Mathematical Statistics.*

Fisher, G. R. and M. McAleer (1981) "Alternative Procedures and Associated Tests of Significance for Nonnested Hypotheses," *Journal of Econometrics,* 16, 103–119.

Gallant, R. (1981) "On the Bias in Flexible Functional Forms and an Essentially Unbiased Form: The Fourier Flexible Form," *Journal of Econometrics,* 15, 211–246.

Gaver, K. M. and M. S. Geisel (1974) "Discriminating Among Alternative Models: Bayesian and Non-Bayesian Methods," in Paul Zarembka, ed., *Frontiers of Econometrics,* Academic, New York, 49–80.

Geweke, J. and R. Meese (1981) "Estimating Regression Models of Finite but Unknown Order," *International Economic Review,* 22, 55–70.

Godfrey, L. G. and M. R. Wickens (1981) "Testing Linear and Log-Linear Regressions for Functional Form," *Review of Economic Studies,* 48, 487–496.

Gourieroux, C., A. Monfort, and A. Trognon (1983) "Testing Nested or Nonnested Hypotheses," *Journal of Econometrics,* 21, 83–115.

Guilkey, D. K., C. A. Knox and R. C. Sickles (1983) "A Comparison of the Performance of Three Flexible Functional Forms," *International Economic Review,* 24, 591–616.

Hausman, J. A. (1978) "Specification Tests in Econometrics," *Econometrica,* 46, 1251–1271.

Hocking, R. R. (1976) "The Analysis and Selection of Variables in Linear Regression," *Biometrics,* 32, 1–49.

Holly, A. (1982) "A Remark on Hausman's Specification Test," *Econometrica,* 50, 749–759.

James, W. and C. Stein (1961) "Estimation with Quadratic Loss," *Proceedings of the Fourth Berkeley Symposium Mathematical Statistics and Probability,"* Vol. 1, University of California Press, Berkeley, 361–379.

Judge, G. G. and M. E. Bock (1978) *Statistical Implications of Pre-Test and Stein-Rule Estimators in Econometrics,* North-Holland, Amsterdam.

Kiefer, N. M. and J. F. Richard (1982) "A Bayesian Approach to Model Choice and Evaluating Estimating Strategies," unpublished paper, Cornell University.

King, N. (1972) "An Alternative for the Linear Regression Equation When the Predictor Variable Is Uncontrolled and the Sample Is Small," *Journal of American Statistical Association,* 67, 217–219.

King, N. (1974) "An Alternative for Multiple Regression When the Prediction Variables Are Uncontrolled and the Sample Size Is Not Too Small," unpublished manuscript, Minneapolis, Minnesota.

Kullback, S. (1959) *Information Theory and Statistics,* Wiley, New York.

Leamer, E. E. (1978) *Specification Searches,* Wiley, New York.

Leamer, E. E. (1979) "Information Criteria for the Choice of Regression Models, A Comment," *Econometrica,* 47, 507–510.

Leamer, E. E. (1983) "Model Choice and Specification Analysis," in *Handbook of Econometrics,* Z. Griliches and M. Intriligator, eds., North-Holland, Amsterdam, Vol. 1.

Lindley, D. V. (1968) "The Choice of Variables in Multiple Regression," (with discussion), *Journal of the Royal Statistical Society, Series B,* 30, 31–66.

MacKinnon, J. (1983) "Model Specification Tests Against Nonnested Alternatives," *Econometric Reviews,* Vol. 2.

Maddala, G. S. (1981) "Model Selection," *Journal of Econometrics,* 16, 1–170.

Mallows, C. L. (1973) "Some Comments on C_p," *Technometrics,* 15, 661–676.

McAleer, M. and G. R. Fisher (1981) "Separate Misspecified Regressions," *Biometrika,*

McAleer, M. (1984) "Specification Tests for Separate Models: A Survey," forthcoming in M. L. King and D. E. A. Giles (eds.), *Specification Analysis in the Linear Model: Essays in Honour of Donald Cochrane.*

McAleer, M., G. Fisher, and P. Volker (1982) "Separate Misspecified Regressions and the U.S. Long-run Demand for Money Function," *The Review of Economics and Statistics,* LXIV, 572–583.

Mittlehammer, R. C. (1984) "Restricted Least Squares, Pretest, OLS and Stein Rule Estimator Comparison," *Journal of Econometrics,* forthcoming.

Mizon, G. E. and J-F. Richard (1983) "The Encompassing Principle and Its Application to Testing Nonnested Hypothesis," CORE Discussion Paper—8330, Universite Catholique de Louvain.

Periera, B. de B. (1977a) "A Note on the Consistency and the Finite Sample Comparisons of Some Tests of Separate Families of Hypotheses," *Biometrika,* 66, 122–131.

Pereira, B. de B. (1977b) "Discriminating Among Separate Models: A Bibliography," *International Statistical Review,* 45, 163–172.

Pesaran, M. H. (1974) "On the General Problem of Model Selection," *Review of Economic Studies,* 41, 153–171.

Pesaran, M. H., and A. S. Deaton (1978) "Testing Nonnested Nonlinear Regression Models," *Econometrica,* 46, 677–694.

Pesaran, M. H. (1982) "Comparison of Local Power of Alternative Tests of Nonnested Regression Models," *Econometrica,* 50, 1287–1306.

Quandt, R. E. (1974) "A Comparison of Methods for Testing Nonnested Hypotheses," *Review of Economics and Statistics,* 56, 92–99.

Ramsey, J. B. (1974) "Classical Model Selection Through Specification Error Tests," in Paul Zarembka, ed., *Frontiers in Econometrics,* Academic, New York, 13–47.

Sargan, J. D. (1964) "Wages and Prices in the United Kingdom," in P. E. Hart, ed., *Econometric Analysis for National Economic Planning,* Butterworths, London.

Sawa, T. (1978) "Information Criteria for Discriminating Among Alternative Regression Models," *Econometrica,* 46, 1273–1291.

Sawyer, K. (1980) "The Theory of Econometric Model Selection," unpublished Ph.D. Thesis, Department of Statistics, The Australian National University.

Schwarz, G. (1978) "Estimating the Dimension of a Model," *Annals of Statistics,* 6, 461–464.

Sclove, S. L. (1968) "Improved Estimator for Coefficients in Linear Regression," *Journal of the American Statistical Association,* 63, 596–606.

Sclove, S. L., C. Morris, and R. Radhakrishnan (1972) "Non-Optimality of Preliminary-Test Estimators for the Mean of a Multivariate Normal Distribution," *Annals of Mathematical Statistics,* 43, 1481–1490.

Shibata, R. (1981) "An Optimal Selection of Regression Variables," *Biometrika,* 68, 45–54.

Stein, C. (1966) "An Approach to Recovery of Interblock Information in Incomplete Block Designs," in F. N. David, ed., *Research Papers in Statistics.* Festschrift for J. Neyman, Wiley, New York, 351–366.

Stein, C. M. (1981) "Estimation of the Mean of a Multivariate Normal Distribution" *The Annals of Statistics,* 9, 1135–1151.

Theil, H. (1971) *Principles of Econometrics,* Wiley, New York.

Thompson, M. L. (1978) "Selection of Variables in Multiple Regression," *International Statistical Review,* 46, 1–19 and 129–146.

Wallace, T. D. and V. G. Ashar (1972) "Sequential Methods in Model Construction," *Review of Economics and Statistics,* 54, 172–178.

White, H. (1982) "Model Specification," Special issue of the *Journal of Econometrics,* 20, 1–157.

White, H. (1983) "Nonnested Models," Special Issue of the *Journal of Econometrics,* 21, 1–160.

Zellner, A. (1971) *An Introduction to Bayesian Inference in Econometrics,* Wiley, New York.

Zellner, A. (1978) "Jeffreys–Bayes Posterior Odds Ratio and the Akaike Information Criterion for Discriminating Between Models," *Economic Letters,* 1, 337–342.

Chapter 22

Multicollinearity

22.1 INTRODUCTION

Economists, to a large extent, can be described as nonexperimental scientists. Experimental scientists can carefully design controlled experiments to try to ensure that sufficient sample information is present to estimate relevant parameters of the model in question with desired sampling precision. Estimation and inference under these circumstances can be a relatively straightforward procedure. In contrast, in the nonexperimental sciences, much of the data used are passively generated. Consequently, data often are generated by an experimental design proposed by society and collected by agencies for administrative rather than for research purposes. As a result, we are presented in most cases with an implicit experimental design and a data collection process that are not of our choosing. The number of observations are sometimes limited, variables do not vary over a very wide range, and thus the samples often do not provide enough information to support investigation of the parameter space in question and give us precise responses to all the questions for which we would like answers. In the extreme, not enough information may be present to obtain, for example, unique least squares estimates of all relevant parameters in the model. This lack of sufficient information and the corresponding loss of precision of statistical results based on such data leads to what is commonly called the multicollinearity problem.

The inadequacy of the experimental designs most frequently encountered is reflected by the existence of general interrelationships among the set of explanatory variables in the design matrix. Examples are countless, but one simple illustration comes from the consumption function, which is an attempt to explain household consumption as a function of, among other things, household income and wealth. In a cross-sectional sample we are likely to observe that wealth and income of surveyed households obey a strong positive relationship. Households with small incomes are likely to have a small amount of wealth and those with high incomes are likely to have a large amount of wealth. Thus, in the sample, because we are faced with a poor experimental design, the two variables may be collinear. For a particular sample the consequences of this collinearity, or multicollinearity in the case of several variables, follow:

1. It becomes very difficult to precisely identify the separate effects of the variables involved. In fact, since the regression coefficients are interpreted as reflecting the effects of changes in their corresponding variables, all other things held constant, our ability to interpret the coefficients declines the more persistent and severe the collinearity. The lack of precision is manifested by the existence of potentially large sampling variances for estimators of the unknown parameters and high correlations between affected estimators.

2. Given the above, unknown parameters may not appear significantly different from zero, and consequently variables may be dropped from the analysis, not because they have no effect but simply because the sample is inadequate to isolate the effect precisely. This result obtains despite possibly high R^2 or "F values," indicating "significant" explanatory power of the model.

3. Estimators may be very sensitive to the addition or deletion of a few observations or the deletion of an apparently insignificant variable.

4. Despite the difficulties in isolating the effects of individual variables from such a sample, accurate forecasts may still be possible even outside the sample. This is only true, however, if the pattern of interrelationships among the explanatory variables is the same in the forecast period as in the sample period.

Once detected, the best and obvious solution to the problem is to obtain and incorporate more information. This additional information may be reflected in the form of new data, a priori restrictions based on theoretical relations, prior statistical information in the form of previous statistical estimates of some of the coefficients and/or subjective information. Unfortunately, the possibilities for "solving" the problems caused by multicollinearity by these procedures are all too limited.

For the researcher unable to obtain more information, procedures have been developed that offer hope of culling more information from the sample and producing correspondingly more precise parameter estimates. These procedures include, for example, principal components regression, ridge regression, and various variable selection procedures (Chapter 21). Unfortunately, if one considers the sampling properties of the resulting estimators, these procedures are in general unsatisfactory. Nontraditional estimators, which have been recently developed, offer point estimates of parameters superior to those provided by traditional procedures under a variety of loss functions. Although these estimators do not provide solutions to all statistical problems, as their sampling distributions are as yet unknown, they do in many cases provide important risk gains. The magnitude of those gains may not be substantial, however, when data are collinear.

In this chapter the dimensions of the multicollinearity problem are discussed, and procedures that may be used for its identification and mitigation are summarized and evaluated. A visual outline of the chapter is given in Table 22.1. The statistical consequences of multicollinearity are specified in Section 22.2. Methods that have been proposed for detecting the presence and nature of multicollinearity are reviewed in Section 22.3 and possible methods for mitigating the effects of collinearity are discussed in Sections 22.4 to 22.6. In Section 22.7 we consider multicollinearity in the context of the stochastic regressor model. All other sections assume that the design matrix is nonstochastic and

TABLE 22.1 *MULTICOLLINEARITY*

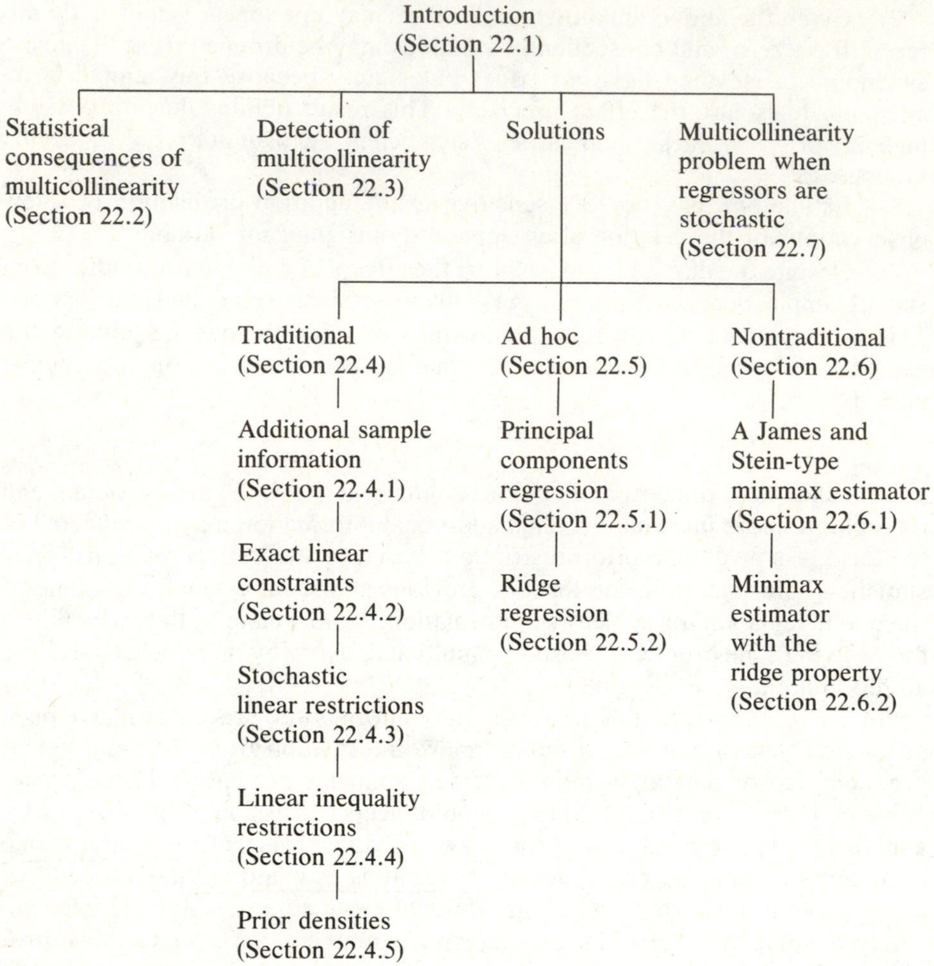

the results are thus conditional. Finally, a summary and concluding comments are provided in Section 22.8.

22.2 STATISTICAL CONSEQUENCES OF MULTICOLLINEARITY

In order to fully explore the consequences of multicollinearity, consider the general linear model introduced in Chapter 2:

$$\mathbf{y} = X\boldsymbol{\beta} + \mathbf{e} \tag{22.2.1}$$

where $\mathbf{y}$ is a $(T \times 1)$ vector of observations, X is a nonstochastic $(T \times K)$ matrix of observations on explanatory variables, $\boldsymbol{\beta}$ is a $(K \times 1)$ vector of unknown regression coefficients, and $\mathbf{e}$ a $(T \times 1)$ vector of normally distributed random disturbances with zero mean and common variance σ^2. Extreme multicollinearity exists when there is at least one linear dependency among the columns of X, and this means that the X matrix is less than full column rank. Although this state of affairs is uncommon in practice, it could arise for several reasons. First, a physical constraint upon the explanatory variables might exist. This can occur in physical sciences when, for example, for a chemical reaction to occur certain ingredients must appear in fixed proportions. In economics a corresponding case is the oftmentioned "dummy variable trap" where, for instance, male and female dummy variables and a vector of unit values for the intercept are included in a cross-sectional regression model. Second, one may possess an implicit design so poor that an exact linear dependency exists in the sample although none exists in the population. The probability that this will occur is, of course, low. Third, the model may have more explanatory variables than observations. This can occur in large-scale econometric models in the first stage of two-stage least squares. The fact that many economic variables move together over time has plagued econometricians over the decades. Much of the early work of Tinbergen and Frisch was concerned with how to cope with the near singularity of the design matrix of many econometric models based on passively generated or nonexperimental data.

The extreme situation described above provides a useful starting point for our discussion of multicollinearity. In the case where the rank of X is less than K, at least one relation of the form

$$c_1\mathbf{x}_1 + c_2\mathbf{x}_2 + \ldots + c_K\mathbf{x}_K = \mathbf{0} \tag{22.2.2}$$

holds, where the c_i are constants not all equal to zero and $\mathbf{x}_i$ is the ith column of X. Thus the observation matrix $[\mathbf{y} : X]$ obeys a second linear relation beside (22.2.1), the one we are interested in. The presence of linear relations like (22.2.2) implies that certain real linear parametric functions, such as

$$\mathbf{w}'\boldsymbol{\beta} = w_1\beta_1 + w_2\beta_2 + \ldots + w_K\beta_K$$

do not possess unbiased linear estimators. In fact, $\mathbf{w}'\boldsymbol{\beta}$ possesses an unbiased linear estimator if and only if $\mathbf{w}'$ can be expressed as a linear combination of the rows of X. If this is true, then the minimum variance, linear unbiased estimator of $\mathbf{w}'\boldsymbol{\beta}$ exists, is unique, and is given by $\mathbf{w}'\mathbf{b}^*$, where $\mathbf{b}^*$ is *any* solution to the normal equations $X'X\mathbf{b}^* = X'\mathbf{y}$ [Theil (1971, pp. 147–152)].

An equivalent and useful condition for $\mathbf{w}'\boldsymbol{\beta}$ to be *estimable* is that the vector $\mathbf{w}$ can be expressed as a linear combination of the rows, or columns, of $X'X$. See Rao (1973, p. 223) for a proof. Silvey (1969) uses this result to prove that the linear parametric function $\mathbf{w}'\boldsymbol{\beta}$ is estimable if and only if $\mathbf{w}$ is a linear combination of the characteristic vectors of $X'X$ corresponding to nonzero characteristic roots of this matrix.

Following Silvey, consider a reparameterized version of (22.2.1) by writing

$$\mathbf{y} = X\boldsymbol{\beta} + \mathbf{e} = (XT)(T^{-1}\boldsymbol{\beta}) + \mathbf{e} \tag{22.2.3}$$

where T is a square nonsingular matrix chosen so that the columns of XT are orthogonal. One choice of T is P, an orthogonal matrix whose columns are orthonormal characteristic vectors of $X'X$. Since $PP' = I$, we can write

$$\mathbf{y} = X\boldsymbol{\beta} + \mathbf{e} = (XP)(P'\boldsymbol{\beta}) + \mathbf{e} = Z\boldsymbol{\theta} + \mathbf{e} \tag{22.2.4}$$

where $Z = XP$ and $\boldsymbol{\theta} = P'\boldsymbol{\beta}$. The columns of Z are orthogonal as

$$Z'Z = (XP)'XP = P'X'XP = \Lambda \tag{22.2.5}$$

where Λ is a diagonal matrix whose elements are $\lambda_1, \ldots, \lambda_K$, the characteristic roots of $X'X$. If X has rank $K - J$, then $X'X$ has J characteristic roots that are zero, and J columns of XP are zero; say the last J. It follows that the last J components of $\boldsymbol{\theta}$ are simply eliminated from the model. Therefore, θ_{K-J+1}, $\theta_{K-J+2}, \ldots, \theta_K$ cannot be estimated from the available observations X. On the other hand, $\theta_1, \ldots, \theta_{K-J}$, or any linear combination of these can be estimated. Therefore, we can estimate $\mathbf{w}'\boldsymbol{\beta}$ if and only if $\mathbf{w}'\boldsymbol{\beta}$ transforms into a linear combination of $\theta_1, \ldots, \theta_{K-J}$. Since

$$\mathbf{w}'\boldsymbol{\beta} = \mathbf{w}'PP'\boldsymbol{\beta} = (P'\mathbf{w})'\boldsymbol{\theta}$$

we can estimate $\mathbf{w}'\boldsymbol{\beta}$ if and only if the last J components of $P'\mathbf{w}$ are zero. This result is of practical importance, since there are numerous computer programs that can be used to obtain P and Λ.

This analysis not only allows us to determine which functions $\mathbf{w}'\boldsymbol{\beta}$ are estimable, but also which of these functions can be estimated relatively precisely and which only imprecisely. If $\mathbf{p}$ is a normalized characteristic vector of $X'X$ corresponding to a nonzero characteristic root λ, then $\mathbf{p}'\boldsymbol{\beta}$ is estimable, and its minimum variance linear unbiased estimator is $\mathbf{p}'\mathbf{b}^*$, where $\mathbf{b}^*$ is any solution of the normal equations $X'X\mathbf{b}^* = X'\mathbf{y}$. The variance of $\mathbf{p}'\mathbf{b}^*$ is given by σ^2/λ, since

$$\mathbf{p}'X'\mathbf{y} = \mathbf{p}'X'X\mathbf{b}^* = \lambda\mathbf{p}'\mathbf{b}^* \tag{22.2.6}$$

using $\mathbf{p}'X'X = \lambda\mathbf{p}'$, so that from (22.2.6),

$$\lambda^2 \operatorname{var}(\mathbf{p}'\mathbf{b}^*) = \mathbf{p}'X'\operatorname{var}(\mathbf{y})X\mathbf{p} = \sigma^2\mathbf{p}'X'X\mathbf{p} = \lambda\sigma^2$$

Similarly, it can be shown that if $\mathbf{p}_1$ and $\mathbf{p}_2$ are characteristic vectors of $X'X$ corresponding to nonzero roots, then $\operatorname{cov}(\mathbf{p}_1'\mathbf{b}^*, \mathbf{p}_2'\mathbf{b}^*) = 0$. If the function $\mathbf{w}'\boldsymbol{\beta}$ is estimable, implying that

$$\mathbf{w} = k_1\mathbf{p}_1 + \ldots + k_{K-J}\mathbf{p}_{K-J} \tag{22.2.7}$$

where the k_i are constants and the $\mathbf{p}_i$ are characteristic vectors corresponding to the nonzero roots $\lambda_1, \ldots, \lambda_{K-J}$, the variance of the estimator $\mathbf{w}'\mathbf{b}^*$ is

$$\text{var}(\mathbf{w}'\mathbf{b}^*) = \sigma^2 \left(\frac{k_1^2}{\lambda_1} + \frac{k_2^2}{\lambda_2} + \cdots + \frac{k_{K-J}^2}{\lambda_{K-J}}\right) \tag{22.2.8}$$

This expression summarizes what we know about the precision with which we may estimate an estimable function. Consequently, the precision depends on the error variance σ^2, the magnitudes of the constants k_i and the magnitudes of the nonzero characteristic roots λ_i. As noted by Silvey (1969, p. 542),

> . . . Relatively precise estimation is possible in the directions of (characteristic) vectors of $X'X$ corresponding to large (characteristic) roots; relatively imprecise estimation in those directions corresponding to small (characteristic) roots . . .

That is, the linear combination of $\mathbf{w}'\boldsymbol{\beta}$, if estimable, will be relatively less precisely estimated if $\mathbf{w}$, as written in (22.2.7), has large weights k_i attached to characteristic vectors that correspond to the small characteristic roots; the smaller those roots, the larger the estimator's variance will be. This approach may, of course, be extended to the case where there are no exact linear combinations among the columns of X. Therefore, all functions of the form $\mathbf{w}'\boldsymbol{\beta} = (k_1\mathbf{p}_1 + \cdots + k_K\mathbf{p}_K)'\boldsymbol{\beta}$ are estimable and the minimum variance unbiased estimator is $\mathbf{w}'\mathbf{b}$, where $\mathbf{b} = (X'X)^{-1}X'\mathbf{y}$ is the least squares estimator, and the corresponding variance is

$$\begin{aligned}\text{var}(\mathbf{w}'\mathbf{b}) &= \mathbf{w}'\text{var}(\mathbf{b})\mathbf{w} = \sigma^2\mathbf{w}'(X'X)^{-1}\mathbf{w} = \sigma^2\mathbf{w}'\left[\sum_{i=1}^{K} \lambda_i^{-1}\mathbf{p}_i\mathbf{p}_i'\right]\mathbf{w} \\ &= \sigma^2 \sum_{i=1}^{K} \frac{k_i^2}{\lambda_i}\end{aligned} \tag{22.2.9}$$

The only question here is about the variance of the estimator, and the same conclusions that were made about (22.2.8) hold. Expression (22.2.9) is also useful in explaining why multicollinearity does not necessarily produce a model that is a poor predictor. The predictor for the conditional mean of the dependent variable, corresponding to the set of independent variables in the tth row of X, is $\mathbf{x}_t'\mathbf{b}$, where $\mathbf{x}_t'$ is the tth row of X. The variance of the predictor, by the next to last expression in (12.2.9), is

$$\sigma^2\mathbf{x}_t'\left[\sum_{i=1}^{K} \lambda_i^{-1}\mathbf{p}_i\mathbf{p}_i'\right]\mathbf{x}_t \tag{22.2.10}$$

If, for instance, λ_k is small, the $\mathbf{x}_t'\mathbf{p}_k$ will be small and the effect of the small λ_k will be canceled out. Thus predictors will not necessarily be imprecise because of multicollinearity, as long as the values of the independent variables for which a prediction is desired obey the same near exact restrictions as the X matrix.

22.3 DETECTION OF MULTICOLLINEARITY

Determination of the severity and form of near exact linear dependencies is an obvious initial step before any remedial measures for poor sample design are undertaken. While views on the usefulness of such exercises vary (see for example Leamer (1983)) some progress has been made recently in this direction. For a survey of methods historically used, but which cannot be advocated, see Farrar and Glauber (1967), Kumar (1975), Willan and Watts (1978), Marquardt and Snee (1975), Friedmann (1982), and Belsley, Kuh, and Welsch (1980).

The results of Section 22.2 show that an analysis of the characteristic roots and vectors of $X'X$ can reveal the presence and perhaps the nature of multicollinearity in a sample with poor design. The spectral decomposition of $X'X$ is

$$X'X = \sum_{i=1}^{K} \lambda_i \mathbf{p}_i \mathbf{p}_i'$$

which both identifies the presence of multicollinearity, by one or more characteristic root(s) λ_i, being small, and the nature of the near-linear dependencies, since, λ_i being small implies that $X\mathbf{p}_i \cong \mathbf{0}$. Belsley, Kuh, and Welsch (1980) advocate a similar analysis called the singular value decomposition.

The advantages of the spectral and singular value decompositions are that not only can they isolate which explanatory variables are interrelated, but they also deal with the issues of what constitutes a "small" characteristic root, or singular value, and whether collinearity is "harmful" from the point of view of a particular application.

The question of what is a small characteristic root can be addressed from a numerical analysis point of view where interest is on the properties of a matrix A in linear systems like $A\mathbf{x} = \mathbf{c}$. One such system is, of course, the normal equations, $X'X\mathbf{b} = X'\mathbf{y}$. Belsley et al. (1980, pp. 100–104) show that the condition number of X, $\kappa(X) = (\lambda_1/\lambda_K)^{1/2}$ is a measure of the sensitivity (elasticity) of $\mathbf{b}$ to changes in $X'\mathbf{y}$ or $X'X$. They present numerical experiments from which they conclude that, when the independent variables are scaled to unit length but not centered, weak dependencies are associated with condition indices around 5 or 10, whereas moderate to strong relations are associated with condition indices 30 to 100. While these are simple rules of thumb, they represent the best decision criteria currently available.

Given the identification of the existence and form of near exact linear dependencies, the question arises as to the nature and extent of the effect on parameter estimates. This can be shown by using (22.2.9) to express the variance of a single coefficient in $\mathbf{b}$ as

$$\operatorname{var}(b_k) = \sigma^2 \sum_{j=1}^{K} \frac{p_{kj}^2}{\lambda_j}$$

Consequently, the proportion of $\operatorname{var}(b_k)$ associated with any single characteristic root is

$$\phi_{kj} = \frac{p_{kj}^2/\lambda_j}{\sum_{j=1}^{K} p_{kj}^2/\lambda_j}$$

It is useful to array these values as in Table 22.2.

The columns in Table 22.2 sum to one. The presence of *two or more* large values of ϕ_{kj} in a *row* of Table 22.2 indicates that multicollinearity, and in particular the linear dependence associated with the corresponding characteristic root, is adversely affecting the precision of estimation of the associated coefficients. Belsley et al. (1980) suggest that values of ϕ_{kj} greater than .50 are large for this purpose. Several comments are in order here. First, note that a small characteristic root does not necessarily imply that using a least squares estimator results in the same imprecision for each of the parameters. The kth coefficient is unaffected by a small root λ_j as long as p_{kj} is small. Practically, this means that the kth variable is not involved in the collinearity relationship. See Vinod and Ullah (1981, Chapter 1) for a geometric interpretation and Belsley et al. (1980, pp. 107–108). Second, there has been substantial confusion and disagreement about the appropriateness of standardization of the variables in regression models. See, for example, Marquardt and Snee (1975), Smith and Campbell (1980), Belsley et al. (1980, pp. 177–185), and Belsley (1982a). From the point of view of diagnosing the presence and nature of multicollinearity, one may *scale* the data so that the variables have a specified length, perhaps unity, but it is not advisable to *center* the data by subtracting variables' sample means. The reason for this, which is fully discussed in Belsley (1982a), is that centering obscures any linear dependence that involves the constant term. An example illustrating this possibility can be found in Judge et al. (1982, Chapter 23).

Finally, we note a weakness of this method of detecting and assessing multicollinearity, and one that is also shared by the spectral decomposition approach. Using the procedures noted above we can detect the presence of multi-

TABLE 22.2 *VARIANCE-DECOMPOSITION PROPORTIONS*

Characteristic Root	$\text{var}(b_1)$	$\text{var}(b_2)$	$\cdots$	$\text{var}(b_K)$
λ_1	ϕ_{11}	ϕ_{21}		ϕ_{K1}
λ_2	ϕ_{12}	ϕ_{22}		ϕ_{K2}
$\vdots$	$\vdots$	$\vdots$	$\cdots$	$\vdots$
λ_K	ϕ_{1K}	ϕ_{2K}		ϕ_{KK}

ple linear dependencies. When multiple dependencies exist, our analyses indicate the set of variables involved in the linear dependencies, as well as which coefficients' variances are adversely affected by the multicollinearity. What we cannot do is determine the exact and separate nature of the linear dependencies among the explanatory variables. To make this notion more precise assume that two characteristic roots, λ_K and λ_{K-1}, are near zero. Thus we have $X\mathbf{p}_K \cong \mathbf{0}$ and $X\mathbf{p}_{K-1} \cong \mathbf{0}$. The "true" linear dependencies between the columns of X are in the space spanned by $\mathbf{p}_K$ and $\mathbf{p}_{K-1}$, but that is all we know without further analysis. See Belsley et al. (1980, pp. 154–155) for more on this difficulty.

Belsley (1982b) takes a slightly different approach to diagnosing the collinearity problem that may prove useful. He defines X to possess a weak-data problem relative to the estimation of β_k (which must be assumed *a priori* to be nonzero) if the variance of the corresponding LS estimator, denoted $\sigma^2_{b_k}$, is "too large." This definition suggests a test of the magnitudes of the signal-to-noise (s/n) parameter $\tau = \beta_k/\sigma_{b_k}$. This approach differs from others in that it takes into account the error variance σ^2. Several comments are in order at the outset. Note that such an approach must presume $\beta_k \neq 0$, for if it were possible to entertain the hypothesis $\beta_k = 0$, then the rejection of a high τ could reflect either $\beta_k = 0$ or a low s/n ratio and it would be impossible to distinguish between these causes. Second, τ bears a resemblance to the usual t-statistic, $t = b_k/s_{b_k}$. In general, t has a noncentral t distribution with noncentrality parameter τ. Under the hypothesis $\beta_k = 0$, t is centrally distributed for all σ_{b_k}. Under the test Belsley proposes, a test that $|\tau|$ exceeds some threshold, the t statistic is noncentrally distributed with $\tau \neq 0$. An immediate consequence of this is that usual critical values may not be large enough for tests concerning τ. For generalization of this procedure, see Belsley's paper.

22.4 TRADITIONAL SOLUTIONS TO THE MULTICOLLINEARITY PROBLEM

In the discussion so far we have noted some of the consequences associated with the presence of multicollinearity and the difficulties with procedures for detecting it. The conventional prescription for multicollinearity, once it has been detected and deemed harmful, is to obtain, in one form or another, more information. This bit of wisdom follows from the understanding of multicollinearity as being caused by a poor sample design that provides insufficient information, when traditional estimators are used, to obtain the desired sampling precision and to isolate the individual effects of all the independent variables in the model. It is, of course, good advice to follow but not always easy to carry out. Sometimes the cure leads to undesirable consequences. In this section we will review the common procedures for introducing empirical and subjective information. We note for each case how the introduction of additional information helps solve the multicollinearity problem and how it affects the sampling properties of the estimator thereby generated.

22.4.1 Additional Sample Information

Given that poor sample design is a basic problem, the most obvious solution is to obtain additional sample data. Silvey (1969) has considered the problem of what values of the independent variables are optimal in some sense if one new observation is to be taken. Suppose, in the model $\mathbf{y} = X\boldsymbol{\beta} + \mathbf{e}$, that there is one exact linear dependency. Then there is one vector $\mathbf{p}$ such that $X'X\mathbf{p} = \mathbf{0}$, which means that $\mathbf{p}'\boldsymbol{\beta}$ is not estimable, nor is any linear function $\mathbf{w}'\boldsymbol{\beta}$ for which $\mathbf{w}$ has a nonzero component in the direction of $\mathbf{p}$. Since $X'X\mathbf{p} = \mathbf{0}$ if and only if $X\mathbf{p} = \mathbf{0}$, the multicollinearity problem exists if every row of X is orthogonal to $\mathbf{p}$. Thus, to get rid of multicollinearity, we must choose a new observation that is not orthogonal to $\mathbf{p}$. An obvious choice is to choose an observation in the direction of $\mathbf{p}$ itself, say $\mathbf{x}_{T+1} = l\mathbf{p}$, where l is a scalar.

A similar analysis holds true if $X'X$ has no zero roots, but some that are small. Suppose that $X'X$ has one small root λ corresponding to the characteristic vector $\mathbf{p}$, which defines the direction in which estimation is imprecise. Then we take an additional observation y_{T+1} at values $\mathbf{x}_{T+1} = l\mathbf{p}$. The model for the complete set of observations is

$$\begin{bmatrix} \mathbf{y} \\ y_{T+1} \end{bmatrix} = \begin{bmatrix} X \\ \mathbf{x}'_{T+1} \end{bmatrix} \boldsymbol{\beta} + \begin{bmatrix} \mathbf{e} \\ e_{T+1} \end{bmatrix}$$

or

$$\mathbf{y}_* = X_*\boldsymbol{\beta} + \mathbf{e}_*$$

Then

$$X'_*X_* = X'X + \mathbf{x}_{T+1}\mathbf{x}'_{T+1} = X'X + l^2\mathbf{p}\mathbf{p}'$$

and

$$X'_*X_*\mathbf{p} = X'X\mathbf{p} + l^2\mathbf{p}\mathbf{p}'\mathbf{p} = \lambda\mathbf{p} + l^2\mathbf{p} = (\lambda + l^2)\mathbf{p}$$

so that $\mathbf{p}$ is a characteristic vector of X'_*X_* corresponding to the root $l^2 + \lambda$. Thus, by choosing a new observation in the direction of $\mathbf{p}$, the precision of estimation can be improved in the direction that was previously the most imprecise. This, of course, generalizes to the case when there are J small roots.

Silvey proceeds to investigate two more interesting questions. First, how is the precision of estimation affected by taking another observation at $\mathbf{x}_{T+1}$ not necessarily in the direction of the characteristic vectors of $X'X$? To answer this question let $\mathbf{b}_T$ and $\mathbf{b}_{T+1}$ be the least squares estimators of $\boldsymbol{\beta}$ based on T and the $T + 1$ observations, respectively. Then

$$\text{var}(\mathbf{w}'\mathbf{b}_T) - \text{var}(\mathbf{w}'\mathbf{b}_{T+1}) = \frac{\sigma^2\mathbf{a}'\Lambda^{-1}\mathbf{z}\mathbf{z}'\Lambda^{-1}\mathbf{a}}{1 + \mathbf{z}'\Lambda^{-1}\mathbf{z}}$$

where $\mathbf{a} = P'\mathbf{w}$, $\mathbf{z} = P'\mathbf{x}_{T+1}$, and Λ = diagonal $(\lambda_1, \ldots, \lambda_K)$. This expression provides the improvement of precision of the estimator of any linear combination $\mathbf{w}'\boldsymbol{\beta}$ from adding a new observation $\mathbf{x}_{T+1}$. Second, and perhaps the most interesting, how should $\mathbf{x}_{T+1}$ be chosen to improve as much as possible the estimation of a specific linear function $\mathbf{w}'\boldsymbol{\beta}$? This may arise either when one is interested in a certain linear combination of parameters or when one is interested in making a prediction for a particular set of the explanatory values $\mathbf{w}$. Silvey proves that, given the usual linear model and the condition $\mathbf{x}'_{T+1}\mathbf{x}_{T+1} = d^2$ satisfied by a new set of observations $\mathbf{x}_{T+1}$ on the explanatory variables, the optimum direction of $\mathbf{x}_{T+1}$ for improving the precision of estimation of $\mathbf{w}'\boldsymbol{\beta}$ is that of the vector $\mathbf{v}$, where $\mathbf{v} = (I + d^{-2}X'X)^{-1}\mathbf{w}$. In other words, the new observation should be proportional to $\mathbf{v}$. It is assumed that the error associated with the new observation is uncorrelated with errors in the original model and has the same variance as each of them. No condition is imposed on the rank of X. The constraint $\mathbf{x}'_{T+1}\mathbf{x}_{T+1} = d^2$ is placed on the values of the explanatory variables because the greater the length of $\mathbf{x}_{T+1}$, the greater the improvement in the precision of estimation of $\mathbf{w}'\boldsymbol{\beta}$. Note that this result holds even when there is an exact linear relation among the columns of X. Thus even if $\mathbf{w}'\boldsymbol{\beta}$ cannot be initially estimated, the optimal direction for a new observation is still provided by Silvey's result.

22.4.2 Exact Linear Constraints

The effects of imposing exact linear constraints upon the parameters of a linear regression model have been discussed in Chapter 3, Section 3.2.1. The restrictions imposed presumably describe some physical constraint on the variables involved and are the product of a theory relating the variables. Alternatively, we may simply observe relations like $X\mathbf{p} \cong \mathbf{0}$ and use those sample specific results to place restrictions on the parameter space. This procedure will be discussed in Section 22.5.1 on principal components regression.

One effect of using exact parameter restrictions is to reduce the sampling variability of the estimators, a desirable end given multicollinear data. The imposition of binding constraints, even if incorrect, may reduce the mean square error of the estimator although incorrect restrictions produce biased parameter estimators.

Exact linear restrictions may be employed in case of both extreme and near-extreme multicollinearity. Exact restrictions "work" by reducing the dimensionality of the parameter space, one dimension for each independent linear constraint. Thus, by adding K-rank(X) restrictions in the extreme multicollinearity situation, all parametric functions $\mathbf{w}'\boldsymbol{\beta}$ become estimable. One still incurs bias, however, if the restrictions are incorrect.

When multicollinearity is present researchers often try a great number of model specifications until they obtain one that "works." The variable selection procedures described in Chapter 21 represent ways of evaluating exact exclusion restrictions. As noted in Chapter 21, these sequential procedures produce estimators whose sampling properties are largely unknown. This is, of course, a price researchers pay for coming to a problem with an incompletely specified theory. Although it is acceptable for Holmes to say, "Never theorize before the facts, Watson," such advice is unacceptable to econometricians.

22.4.3 Stochastic Linear Restrictions

Stochastic linear restrictions arise from prior statistical information, usually in the form of previous estimates of parameters that are also included in a current model, or, as discussed in Chapter 3, subjective considerations on the part of the investigator. For the purposes of this section these linear stochastic restrictions act just like additional observations, if the statistical information is unbiased, and thus they may serve to aid in both situations of extreme and near-extreme multicollinearity. The consequences of using biased statistical information and pretesting are discussed in Chapter 3.

Marquardt (1970) noted that the ridge regression estimator, which will be fully discussed in Section 22.5.2, is equivalent to a least squares estimator where the actual data are supplemented by a fictitious set of data points taken according to an orthogonal experiment with each response being set to zero. It naturally follows then, as noted by Bacon and Hausman (1974), Fomby and Johnson (1977), and Lin and Kmenta (1982) that a ridge estimator is numerically equal to the estimator obtained by constraining the linear model with certain stochastic linear restrictions. However, the resulting estimator has a covariance matrix different from the ridge estimator, which is discussed in Section 22.5.2. More specifically in line with Section 3.2.2 of Chapter 3, assume that prior information of the form

$$\mathbf{r} = \boldsymbol{\beta} + \mathbf{v}$$

is available, where $\mathbf{r}$ is a vector of prior estimates of $\boldsymbol{\beta}$, and $\mathbf{v}$ is a random disturbance with $E\mathbf{v} = \mathbf{0}$, and $E\mathbf{v}\mathbf{v}' = (\sigma^2/k)I_K$. Combining the stochastic information with the sample information (22.2.1), we find that the stochastic restricted least squares estimator is

$$\mathbf{b}^*(k) = (X'X + kI)^{-1}(X'\mathbf{y} + k\mathbf{r})$$

The ridge estimator of Section 22.5 results when $\mathbf{r} = \mathbf{0}$. This may be viewed as taking the conservative position that an explanatory variable is assumed to have no effect on the dependent variable in the absence of contrary information. The appropriateness of this rationalization is questionable when *all* coefficients are shrunk toward zero. The parameter k reflects the confidence with which this stochastic prior information is held. As $k \to 0$, the prior information becomes less important relative to the sample information and as $k \to \infty$ the restrictions become more strongly held. Thus one approach to selecting k would be to either test the compatibility of the stochastic prior information implied by a specific k using Theil's (1963) compatibility statistic, or transform the stochastic restrictions into nonstochastic ones via the transformation in

Judge, Yancey, and Bock (1973) and apply the MSE tests of Toro-Vizcarrondo and Wallace (1968) or Wallace (1972) as suggested by Fomby and Johnson (1977). Either of these procedures, of course, produces pretest estimators whose properties are not in general favorable. Furthermore, if the pretest estimator based on exact restrictions is adopted, it is known that there is a superior estimator, namely, the modified positive part estimator proposed by Sclove, Morris, and Radhakrishnan (1972). See Chapter 3, Section 3.4.4, for a discussion of this estimator.

22.4.4 Linear Inequality Restrictions

Linear inequality restrictions are discussed in Chapter 3, Section 2.3. Their use can improve the precision of estimation when near-extreme multicollinearity is present, but cannot, in the extreme multicollinearity situation, make it possible to estimate a function that cannot be estimated because inexact restrictions may not affect the dimensionality of the parameter space. Presumably, however, inequality constraints upon parameters involved in an estimable function improve the precision of estimation of those parametric functions. The consequences of incorrect inequality constraints and pretesting are discussed in Chapter 3, Section 3.2.3.

22.4.5 Prior Densities

If one is operating within a Bayesian framework, the incorporation of prior information to mitigate multicollinearity, extreme or near extreme, is achieved as usual by the use of a prior density function (see Chapter 4, Section 4.3) upon the parameter vector $\boldsymbol{\beta}$. For the Bayesian, no special problems are caused by a singular or near-singular $X'X$ matrix. For details see Zellner (1971, pp. 75–81). However, as Leamer (1978) points out, the difficulty Bayesians have when data are multicollinear is that the posterior distribution becomes very sensitive to changes in the prior distribution. This means that use and analysis of the reported empirical results is difficult, since a given sample might suggest widely different posteriors to individual researchers. Thus how the sample evidence fits with the prior information and the sensitivity of the posterior distribution to changes in the prior, respectively, define and measure the multicollinearity problem. This is exactly the same set of problems faced by sampling theorists. For more on the Bayesian approach, see Leamer (1983).

One particular prior density that is discussed widely in the context of multicollinearity is the "null" prior noted in Section 22.4.3. Specifically, Lindley and Smith (1972) and Goldstein and Smith (1974) discuss the Bayesian analogue of ridge regression. In particular, Lindley and Smith note that the ridge estimator is numerically equal to the Bayesian estimator with an exchangeable prior distribution, which implies that all parameters have identical prior means and variances. They are correctly adamant about the sensibility of the resulting estimates depending upon the appropriateness of exchangeability within the regression equation. Specifically, they assume

$$\mathbf{y} \sim N(X\boldsymbol{\beta}, \sigma^2 I_T)$$

and assume exchangeable priors

$$\beta_j \sim N(\xi, \sigma_\beta^2)$$

The posterior mean under quadratic loss when $\xi = 0$ is then

$$\mathbf{b}^*(k) = [I_K + k(X'X)^{-1}]^{-1}\mathbf{b}$$

which is the usual ridge estimator, where $k = \sigma^2/\sigma_\beta^2$. Given that k represents a ratio of variances, they go on to suggest an iterative Bayes approach to the choice of k.

22.5 AD HOC SOLUTIONS TO THE MULTICOLLINEARITY PROBLEM

In the previous section we noted that conventional procedures for combining sample and nonsample information can be used in an attempt to reduce the ill effects of multicollinearity. This of course presumes that nonsample information is available, either from some underlying theory, previous statistical work, or subjective considerations. In this section we consider two estimators that can mitigate the effects of collinearity, but which are *ad hoc* in the sense that the information they introduce is specific to the sample in hand. Furthermore, in their conventional forms, these estimators have unbounded risk, and thus may or may not actually provide risk gains over LS.

22.5.1 Principal Components Regression

As noted above, when faced with ill-conditioned data, investigators frequently choose to reduce information demands on the sample by considering only subspaces of the K-dimensional parameter space. These subspaces may be suggested by economic theory, previous statistical results, or ad hoc dimensionality reduction procedures. Whatever the rationale, reducing the dimensionality of the estimation problem implies an obvious trade-off. Unless the true parameter vector lies in the subspace chosen for examination, the resulting estimators will be biased. The trade-off then involves balancing reduced sampling variances for the estimators against bias.

These considerations are of particular importance in the case of principal components regression, which has received considerable attention in recent years as a method for dealing with ill-conditioned data. See, for example, Farebrother (1972); Fomby and Hill (1978b); Fomby, Hill, and Johnson (1978);

Greenberg (1975); Hill, Fomby, and Johnson (1977); Johnson, Reimer, and Rothrock (1973); Lott (1973); McCallum (1970); and Massey (1975). Principal components regression is a method of inspecting the sample data or design matrix for directions of variability and using this information to reduce the dimensionality of the estimation problem. The reduction in dimensionality is achieved by imposing exact linear constraints that are sample specific but have certain maximum variance properties [see Greenberg (1975) and Fomby, Hill, and Johnson (1978)] that make their use attractive.

Let the model under consideration be

$$\mathbf{y} = X\boldsymbol{\beta} + \mathbf{e} \tag{22.5.1}$$

where $\mathbf{y}$ is $(T \times 1)$, X is $(T \times K)$ and nonstochastic, $\boldsymbol{\beta}$ is $(K \times 1)$, and $\mathbf{e}$ is $(T \times 1)$ and distributed as $N(\mathbf{0},\sigma^2 I)$. Consider the transformation

$$\mathbf{y} = XPP'\boldsymbol{\beta} + \mathbf{e} = XP\boldsymbol{\theta} + \mathbf{e} = Z\boldsymbol{\theta} + \mathbf{e} \tag{22.5.2}$$

where $P = (\mathbf{p}_1, \ldots, \mathbf{p}_K)$ is a $(K \times K)$ matrix whose columns $(\mathbf{p}_i)$ are orthogonal characteristic vectors of $X'X$ ordered to correspond to the relative magnitudes of the characteristic roots of the positive definite matrix $X'X$ and $Z = (\mathbf{z}_1, \ldots, \mathbf{z}_K)$ is the $(T \times K)$ matrix of principal components. Accordingly, $\mathbf{z}_i = X\mathbf{p}_i$ is called the ith principal component, where $\mathbf{z}_i'\mathbf{z}_i = \lambda_i$ and λ_i is the ith largest characteristic root of $X'X$.

The principal components estimator of $\boldsymbol{\beta}$ is obtained by deleting one or more of the variables $\mathbf{z}_i$, applying ordinary least squares to the resulting model and making a transformation back to the original parameter space. Assume for the moment that Z has been partitioned into two parts Z_1, the $\mathbf{z}_i$ to be retained, and Z_2, the $\mathbf{z}_i$ to be deleted. This partitioning imposes an identical partitioning on P. Thus (22.5.2) becomes

$$\mathbf{y} = XP_1\boldsymbol{\theta}_1 + XP_2\boldsymbol{\theta}_2 + \mathbf{e} = Z_1\boldsymbol{\theta}_1 + Z_2\boldsymbol{\theta}_2 + \mathbf{e} \tag{22.5.3}$$

where $X\{P_1 : P_2\} = \{Z_1 : Z_2\}$. Properties of $\hat{\boldsymbol{\theta}}_1 = (Z_1'Z_1)^{-1}Z_1'\mathbf{y}$, the LS estimator of $\boldsymbol{\theta}_1$ with Z_2 omitted from Equation 22.5.3, are easily obtained. Specifically, $\hat{\boldsymbol{\theta}}_1$ is unbiased, due to the orthogonality of Z_1 and Z_2, and has covariance matrix $\sigma^2(Z_1'Z_1)^{-1}$. The principal components estimator is obtained by an inverse linear transformation. Since $\boldsymbol{\beta} = P\boldsymbol{\theta} = P_1\boldsymbol{\theta}_1 + P_2\boldsymbol{\theta}_2$, omitting the components in Z_2 means that $\boldsymbol{\theta}_2$ has implicitly been set equal to zero. Hence $P_2\boldsymbol{\theta}_2 = \mathbf{0}$ and the principal components estimator of $\boldsymbol{\beta}$ is

$$\hat{\boldsymbol{\beta}}^* = P_1\hat{\boldsymbol{\theta}}_1 = P\hat{\boldsymbol{\theta}}^*$$

where $\hat{\boldsymbol{\theta}}^* = (\hat{\boldsymbol{\theta}}_1', \mathbf{0}')'$ with $\mathbf{0}$ a null vector of conformable dimension. The properties of $\hat{\boldsymbol{\beta}}^*$ follow straightforwardly from its equivalence to the restricted least squares estimator obtained by estimating (22.5.1) subject to $P_2'\boldsymbol{\beta} = \mathbf{0}$. Thus the principal components estimator, like all restricted least squares estimators, is known to have smaller sampling variance than the least squares estimator **b**, but is biased unless the restrictions $P_2'\boldsymbol{\beta} = \mathbf{0}$ are true.

Identifying the restricted least squares estimator equivalent of the principal components estimator has several advantages. First, one is reminded that data reduction techniques impose restrictions on and sometimes reduce the dimension of the parameter space. Second, explicit recognition of the restrictions permits evaluation of their theoretical implications. However, as argued in Section 22.3, it is very difficult to interpret the restrictions when more than one near exact dependency is present.

22.5.1a Component Selection Procedures

A major question that remains is, "How does one select components to delete and what are the consequences of each choice?" Two approaches have received attention in the literature. First, we can include in Z_2 those components associated with "small" characteristic roots. This, of course, amounts to assuming that the "nearly exact" linear dependencies among the columns of X discussed in Section 22.2 are, in fact, exact. Although such an assumption is invalid, it is usually justified on the basis of preserving as much of the variability in the sample data as possible while reducing the dimensionality of the estimation problem. It is also appealing because these linear restrictions provide a greater reduction in the sampling variances of the estimators than any other set of linear restrictions with an equal number of restrictions [Fomby, Hill, and Johnson (1978)]. However, the adoption of such arbitrary restrictions is not a good strategy in general.

A second approach to deleting components is based upon tests of hypotheses of the sample specific restrictions $P_2'\boldsymbol{\beta} = \mathbf{0}$ using classical or MSE tests. Hill, Fomby, and Johnson (1977) give a summary listing of such tests and their interpretations. Such an approach is equivalent to testing whether or not these linear dependencies "almost" hold for the population variables. They cannot hold exactly, of course, since the characteristic roots based on the sample would be exactly zero. If components are deleted on the basis of these tests of significance, the resulting pretest estimators are known to be inferior to least squares estimators over a wide range of the parameter space and are inadmissible, as noted in Chapter 3. In fact, the use of testing procedures for selecting a principal components estimator where the components are not interpretable only delays problems by one analytical step, since the range under which the preliminary test estimator is superior to the least squares estimator, depends upon unknown population parameters.

As noted above, principal components regression does not provide estimators with better sampling properties than the least squares estimators over the entire parameter space. Its failure reflects the failure of all such ad hoc data search procedures. If interest centers on obtaining good point estimates, however, it is clear that the linear hypotheses suggested by principal components estimators may be combined with sample information by using the James- and Stein-type minimax estimators or their positive rule counterparts discussed by

Judge and Bock (1978, Chapter 10, Section 3). Under certain conditions these estimators are known to dominate the maximum likelihood estimator under squared error loss. More will be said about this possibility in Section 22.6.

22.5.1b The Benchmark Function of Principal Components Regression

The primary usefulness of principal components analysis lies in its function as an exploratory tool. It can serve to identify multicollinearities in the data and suggest useful data transformations. That is, it can detect exact linear dependencies that exist so that any physical constraints on the population variables may be identified; and it can provide a variance reduction benchmark. The latter function deserves more comment. Following Fomby and Hill (1978b), let λ_i, $i = 1, 2, \ldots, K$, be the characteristic roots of $X'X$, where $\lambda_1 \geq \lambda_2 \geq \ldots \geq \lambda_K$. The trace of the covariance matrix of the principal components estimator with J components deleted is $\sigma^2 \Sigma_{i=1}^{K-J}(1/\lambda_i)$. The trace of the covariance matrix of the LS estimator is $\sigma^2 \Sigma_{i=1}^{K}(1/\lambda_i)$. Therefore, the maximum percentage reduction in the trace of the covariance matrix obtainable from using a least squares estimator with J independent linear restrictions is

$$V_J = \frac{\sum_{i=K-J+1}^{K} (1/\lambda_i)}{\sum_{i=1}^{K} (1/\lambda_i)} \times 100\%, \qquad J = 1, 2, \ldots, K$$

For an application illustrating this case, see Fomby and Hill (1978b).

22.5.2 Ridge Regression

Since the publication of the original papers on ridge regression by Hoerl and Kennard (1970a, 1970b), there have been a large number of papers written on the subject. Because of the difficulty of obtaining analytical results for this type of estimator, Monte Carlo experiments have been carried out to investigate the properties of the resulting estimators. Hoerl and Kennard (1979) offer a survey article with an annotated bibliography. Vinod (1978), Vinod and Ullah (1981), Draper and Van Nostrand (1979) and Judge and Bock (1983) also survey the ridge regression literature.

Ridge regression was originally suggested as a procedure for investigating the sensitivity of least squares estimates based on data exhibiting near-extreme multicollinearity, where small perturbations in the data may produce large changes in the magnitudes of the estimated coefficients. Also discussed, however, is the hope that the ridge regression estimator is an "improved estimator," in the sense that it may have smaller risk than the conventional least squares estimator.

In this section we discuss the ridge estimators and their properties. The literature devoted to the selection of a member from the ridge family for use is reviewed and recent results on the minimax properties of ridge regression presented. These studies suggest that the conditions on ridge regression that guarantee its mean square error improvement over least squares may not be fulfilled when the data are extremely, or even moderately, ill-conditioned. In fact, there may be a basic conflict between estimators that are minimax and those that exhibit stability in the face of ill-conditioned data. These aspects of the problem will also be investigated.

22.5.2a The Ridge Family of Estimators

Consider again the linear regression model $\mathbf{y} = X\boldsymbol{\beta} + \mathbf{e}$. In discussions of ridge regression it is typically assumed that X has been standardized so that $X'X$ is the matrix of simple correlations among the independent variables. This is *not* necessary for any results related to ridge regression and is *not* assumed here. See Vinod and Ullah (1981, p. 179) for more discussion of the standardization issue.

The generalized ridge regression estimator introduced by Hoerl and Kennard (1970a,b) is

$$\mathbf{b}^*(D) = [X'X + PDP']^{-1}X'\mathbf{y} \tag{22.5.4}$$

where P is the matrix whose columns are the orthonormal characteristic vectors of $X'X$ and D is a diagonal matrix of constants $d_i \geq 0$. If the constants d_i are all equal and take the value $d_i = k$, the generalized ridge estimator reduces to the ordinary ridge estimator

$$\mathbf{b}^*(k) = (X'X + kI)^{-1}X'\mathbf{y} \tag{22.5.5}$$

Note that the LS estimator is a member of this family with $k = 0$ and the principal components estimator of Section 22.5.1 can be viewed as (22.5.4) with $d_1 = \ldots = d_{K-J} = 0$ and $d_{K-J+1} = \ldots = d_K = \infty$.

One property of the least squares estimator $\mathbf{b}$ that is frequently noted in the ridge regression literature is

$$E(\mathbf{b}'\mathbf{b}) = \boldsymbol{\beta}'\boldsymbol{\beta} + \sigma^2 \operatorname{tr}(X'X)^{-1} > \boldsymbol{\beta}'\boldsymbol{\beta} + \frac{\sigma^2}{\lambda_K}$$

where λ_K is the minimum characteristic root of $X'X$. Thus, where the data are ill-conditioned, and λ_K is small, this implies that the expected squared length of the least squares coefficient vector is greater than the squared length of the true coefficient vector, and the smaller λ_K, the greater the difference. Brook and Moore (1980) give a valid evaluation of the usual statement that the least squares estimator is longer than the true parameter vector. Hoerl (1962, 1964) suggested that to control the coefficient inflation and general instability associated with the use of the least squares estimator, one could use the ordinary ridge estimator $\mathbf{b}^*(k)$. The properties of $\mathbf{b}^*(k)$ include:

1. $\mathbf{b}^*(k)$ minimizes the sum of squared residuals on the sphere centered at the origin whose radius is the length of $\mathbf{b}^*(k)$. That is, for a given sum of squared residuals, it is the coefficient vector with minimum length.
2. The sum of squared residuals is an increasing function of k.
3. $\mathbf{b}^*(k)'\mathbf{b}^*(k) < \mathbf{b}'\mathbf{b}$, and $\mathbf{b}^*(k)'\mathbf{b}^*(k) \to 0$ as $k \to \infty$.
4. The ratio of the largest characteristic root of the design matrix $(X'X + kI)$ to the smallest root is $(\lambda_1 + k)/(\lambda_K + k)$, where $\lambda_1 \geq \lambda_2 \geq \ldots \geq \lambda_K$ are the ordered roots of $X'X$, and is a decreasing function of k. The square root of this ratio is called the condition number of X. See Belsley et al. (1980, pp. 100–104). The condition number is often taken as a measure of data ill-conditioning and is related to the stability of the coefficient estimates.
5. The ridge estimator

$$\mathbf{b}^*(k) = [I_K + k(X'X)^{-1}]^{-1}\mathbf{b} = W\mathbf{b}$$

is a linear transformation of the least squares estimator.
6. The mean square error of $\mathbf{b}^*(k)$ is

$$\begin{aligned} E[(\mathbf{b}^*(k) - \boldsymbol{\beta})'(\mathbf{b}^*(k) - \boldsymbol{\beta})] &= E[(\mathbf{b} - \boldsymbol{\beta})'W'W(\mathbf{b} - \boldsymbol{\beta})] \\ &\quad + (W\boldsymbol{\beta} - \boldsymbol{\beta})'(W\boldsymbol{\beta} - \boldsymbol{\beta}) \\ &= \sigma^2 \sum_{i=1}^{K} \frac{\lambda_i}{(\lambda_i + k)^2} + k^2\boldsymbol{\beta}'(X'X + kI)^{-2}\boldsymbol{\beta} \end{aligned} \tag{22.5.6}$$

where the first term on the RHS of (22.5.6) is the sum of the variances of the estimators and the second term is the total squared bias introduced by using $\mathbf{b}^*(k)$ rather than $\mathbf{b}$. The total variance is a monotonically decreasing function of k and the squared bias a monotonically increasing function of k.
7. $\lim_{\boldsymbol{\beta}'\boldsymbol{\beta}\to\infty} \text{MSE}[\mathbf{b}^*(k)] = \infty$, thus for fixed k, the estimator $\mathbf{b}^*(k)$ is not minimax, and in fact has unbounded risk.
8. There always exists a $k > 0$, such that $\mathbf{b}^*(k)$ has a smaller MSE than $\mathbf{b}$ [Hoerl and Kennard (1970a)].

Hoerl and Kennard (1970a) show that under squared error loss, a sufficient condition for property 8 is that $k < \sigma^2/\theta^2_{\max}$, where $\theta^2_{\max}$ is the largest element of the vector $\boldsymbol{\theta} = P'\boldsymbol{\beta}$ (P is a matrix of orthonormal characteristic vectors of $X'X$). Theobald (1974) has generalized this result to weighted squared error loss and has shown that a sufficient condition is $k < 2\sigma^2/\boldsymbol{\beta}'\boldsymbol{\beta}$. Property 8 is, of course, the property of the ridge family that has provided *hope* for some that ridge regression can improve upon the least squares estimator.

However $\mathbf{b}^*(k)$ *improves upon* $\mathbf{b}$ *only for a limited range of the parameter space, and the region of improvement depends upon the unknown parameters* $\boldsymbol{\beta}$ *and* σ^2. Consequently, as a practical matter property 8 is useless. The hope has been, however, that one could use the data to help select a k value that will produce an estimator superior to least squares. We will call such an estimator an *adaptive ridge estimator. These estimators, where the parameter k is a function of the sample data and thus stochastic, do not have the same properties as the ridge estimator based on fixed k. In particular, the MSE gain is no longer guaranteed.*

For the generalized ridge estimator $\mathbf{b}^*(D)$ a similar result holds. The optimal value of $d_i = \sigma^2/\theta_i^2$ under squared error loss. This optimal value is of little practical value as it requires knowledge of the true parameter values. Adaptive generalized ridge estimators are subject to the same caveats expressed above about the adaptive ordinary ridge estimator.

22.5.2b Adaptive Ordinary Ridge Estimators

In this section various proposals for selecting values of k for use in $\mathbf{b}^*(k)$ are briefly reviewed and evaluated.

The Ridge Trace The ridge trace is a two-dimensional plot of values of ridge coefficient estimates $b_i^*(k)$ and the residual sum of squares for a number of values of k. One curve or trace is made for each coefficient. Hoerl and Kennard (1970b) suggest selecting a value of k on the basis of criteria like stability of the estimated coefficients as k increases, reasonable signs, coefficient magnitudes, sum of squared residuals and the maximum variance inflation factor, that is, the maximum diagonal element of $(X'X)^{-1}$, that Marquardt and Snee (1975) claim to be the best single measure of data conditioning. While Marquardt and Snee say that in practice the value of k is not hard to select using the ridge trace, others, noted below, have expressed greater concern.

Brown and Beattie (1975, p. 27) specify the following decision rule that attempts to formalize use of the ridge trace: "Select a value of k at that point where the last ridge estimate attains its maximum absolute magnitude after having attained its "ultimate" sign, where "ultimate" sign is defined as being the sign at, say $k = 0.9$."

Vinod (1976) offers a rescaled horizontal axis, the m-scale, which compresses the $[0,\infty]$ range of k to the interval $[0,K]$ for m, where m is defined by $m = K - \Sigma_i\lambda_i/(\lambda_i + k)$, and the regressors are assumed standardized. He also attempts to quantify the concept of coefficient stability using an index of stability of relative magnitudes (ISRM), which is zero for orthogonal data. Vinod suggests selecting a value of m for which ISRM is smallest, which also defines a nonstochastic value of k, since ISRM depends only on X. Also see Vinod and Ullah (1981, pp. 180–183) and Friedmann (1982) for interpretations of ISRM.

Others such as Conniffe and Stone (1973) have criticized the use of the ridge trace. To make a long academic dialogue short, however, we can summarize the usefulness of the ridge trace, scaled or unscaled, by simply saying that it is an art form. There may be those who can learn from the data using the ridge trace, but determination of k by visual inspection leads to estimates whose properties cannot be determined. In particular, we have no guarantee of the superiority of these estimators to the least squares estimator in terms of MSE.

The rules that have been proposed to quantify concepts associated with the ridge trace are also analytically void. The ISRM criterion, although nonstochastic, does not guarantee that k falls in the region where the corresponding ridge estimator would have lower MSE than the LS estimator. Any nonstochastic k produces an estimator that is admissible; but although inadmissibility is bad, admissibility by itself is not necessarily a valuable property. Thus the use of the ridge trace as a way of obtaining improved estimators may be rejected. It can illustrate the sensitivity of coefficients to small data perturbations, but that is all.

The Hoerl–Kennard–Baldwin Estimator Hoerl, Kennard, and Baldwin (1975) suggest adopting a k value of

$$k_{\text{HKB}} = \frac{K\hat{\sigma}^2}{\mathbf{b}'\mathbf{b}}$$

where k_{HKB} is the sample analogue of $K\sigma^2/\boldsymbol{\beta}'\boldsymbol{\beta}$, which is the harmonic mean of the optimal generalized ridge element $d_i = \sigma^2/\theta_i^2$. Hoerl and Kennard (1976) consider iterative estimation of the biasing parameter. Hoerl, Kennard, and Baldwin (1975) and Lawless and Wang (1976) produced Monte Carlo results that show the ridge estimator using k_{HKB} superior to least squares.

The Lawless–Wang Estimator Lawless and Wang (1976) suggest use of the ridge estimator

$$\theta_i^{\text{LW}} = \frac{\lambda_i}{\lambda_i + k_{\text{LW}}} \hat{\theta}_i$$

where

$$k_{\text{LW}} = \frac{K\hat{\sigma}^2}{\sum_{i=1}^{K} \lambda_i \hat{\theta}_i^2}$$

They carry out Monte Carlo experiments that support the conclusion that θ_i^{LW} performs substantially better than the HKB or LS rules against squared error loss or squared error of prediction loss.

The McDonald–Galarneau Estimator Recall that the expected squared length of the LS estimator is greater than that of the true coefficient vector. McDonald and Galarneau (1975) note that

$$E[\mathbf{b}'\mathbf{b} - \sigma^2 \operatorname{tr}(X'X)^{-1}] = \boldsymbol{\beta}'\boldsymbol{\beta}$$

and suggest that k be chosen such that

$$\mathbf{b}^*(k)'\mathbf{b}^*(k) = \mathbf{b}'\mathbf{b} - \hat{\sigma}^2 \operatorname{tr}(X'X)^{-1}$$

which means that the adaptative ridge estimator has the same expected squared length as the true parameter vector. They carry out a Monte Carlo experiment and conclude that none of the ridge-type estimators they consider is better than LS in all cases.

RIDGM Dempster, Schatzoff, and Wermuth (1977) in a large simulation study, suggest an estimator RIDGM, which is motivated by the Bayesian interpretation and is similar to the McDonald–Galarneau estimator. Specifically, RIDGM selects $k = \sigma^2/\sigma_\theta^2$, where σ_θ^2 is the prior variance of the θ_i in the canonical form of the model, such that $\Sigma\hat{\theta}_i^2/(\sigma_\theta^2 + \sigma^2/\lambda_i)$ is equal to its prior expectation K. Efron and Morris (1977) note the empirical Bayes nature of RIDGM.

The properties of the rules listed above have been studied primarily through the use of Monte Carlo experiments. In addition to those experiments already mentioned, see Lin and Kmenta (1982), Gibbons (1981), and Wichern and Churchill (1978). The difficulty with such work is that usually no one rule is shown to be superior under all conditions and the scope of the results is limited to the experimental designs and parameter values considered.

There has been some analytical work, however, investigating the risk properties of ridge estimators that result from alternative choices for empirically determining k. See, for example, Thisted and Morris (1980), Thisted (1977, 1978a, 1978b), and Casella (1977). In these works, conditions are derived under which a ridge estimator (for example, using the Hoerl–Kennard–Baldwin rule or the Lawless–Wang rule) has smaller risk under squared error or squared error of prediction loss than the LS estimator. The conditions are similar to those required for minimaxity of the Stein-like rules discussed in the next section, and thus will not be presented here in detail. Suffice it to say there are necessary design related conditions (in particular related to the characteristic roots of $X'X$ and the number of regressors K) that must be satisfied if the ridge rules are to be minimax, and that these conditions are less likely to be satisfied when multicollinearity is present.

22.5.2c Adaptive Generalized Ridge Estimators

There are a variety of rules for empirically determining values of the constants d_i in the generalized ridge estimator $\mathbf{b}^*(D)$. One choice that has been widely considered is an operational version of the optimal choice, in a mean squared error sense, of $d_i = \sigma^2/\theta_i^2$. Hoerl and Kennard (1970a) and Goldstein and Smith (1974) suggest an iterative procedure for estimating d_i. Alternative convergence criteria and constraints are suggested by Hocking, Speed, and Lynn (1976) and Hemmerle (1975). Hemmerle (1975) and Teekens and de Boer (1977) have shown that iteration is not necessary as the limiting value can be determined analytically. Teekens and de Boer also determine the region of parameter space, assuming σ^2 is known, where the corresponding ridge estimator has smaller MSE than the LS estimator.

Following Allen (1974), Hemmerle and Brantle (1978) suggest choosing an adaptive generalized estimator that minimizes the unbiased estimators of expected squared error loss and expected squared error of prediction loss. Although the sampling properties of the resulting estimator are unknown, they carry out Monte Carlo experiments, which suggest that this estimator is more conservative in departing from least squares than other adaptive procedures. They also report results when the estimated expected loss functions are minimized subject to general inequality restrictions. The reader is referred to their paper for the results of those numerical experiments. For a more detailed survey of these and other adaptive generalized ridge rules, see Vinod and Ullah (1981, Chapter 8). Our conclusions about these adaptive generalized ridge rules are that they do not guarantee risk improvement over LS for all parameter values and thus their use is based on unspecified nonsample information.

As noted above, however, there is an increasing amount of research on determining analytic expressions for the risk of shrinkage estimators, like the adaptive ordinary and generalized ridge estimators, whose shrinkage is determined by stochastic factors. For adaptive generalized ridge rules, examples are Vinod (1978), Vinod, Ullah, and Kadiyala (1981), Ullah and Vinod (1979), Casella (1977), and Strawderman (1978). We will consider Strawderman's results in more detail.

Hoerl and Kennard (1970a) and others have studied generalized ridge rules of the form $[X'X + kB]^{-1}X'\mathbf{y}$, where B is a symmetric, positive definite matrix. This rule can be re-expressed as $[(X'X)(I + k(X'X)^{-1}B)]^{-1}X'\mathbf{y}$ or $[I + kC]^{-1}\mathbf{b}$, where $C = (X'X)^{-1}B$. Strawderman (1978) considers rules of this form and explicitly allows the factor k to be a function of the data—that is, $k(\mathbf{y})$. He then writes the ridge rule as

$$\boldsymbol{\delta}(\mathbf{b},s) = [I + k(\mathbf{y})C]^{-1}\mathbf{b}$$

His goal is to produce estimators within this class that are minimax and exhibit some of the stability properties of traditional ridge rules.

Strawderman's procedure is to consider the problem in reduced form—namely, that of estimating the mean vector of a multivariate normal random vector. By doing so, the techniques of proof developed by those who have considered the problem of obtaining minimax estimators for the multivariate normal mean become applicable. Strawderman's results relating to ridge rules can be summarized as follows: Let $\mathbf{y} = X\boldsymbol{\beta} + \mathbf{e}$, where all the usual assumptions of the classical, normal linear regression model hold. If loss is measured by

$$L(\boldsymbol{\beta},\boldsymbol{\delta}) = \frac{1}{\sigma^2}(\boldsymbol{\beta} - \boldsymbol{\delta})'Q(\boldsymbol{\beta} - \boldsymbol{\delta})$$

where Q is an arbitrary, positive definite symmetric matrix, and if $K \geq 3$, the following adaptive generalized ridge estimator is minimax:

$$\boldsymbol{\delta}(\mathbf{b},s) = \left[I + \frac{asQ^{-1}X'X}{\mathbf{b}'X'X\mathbf{b} + gs + h}\right]^{-1}\mathbf{b} \tag{22.5.7}$$

where

$$s = (\mathbf{y} - X\mathbf{b})'(\mathbf{y} - X\mathbf{b}), \qquad 0 \le a \le \frac{2(K-2)}{(T-K+2)} \frac{1}{\lambda_{\max}[Q^{-1}X'X]}$$

$h \ge 0$ and $g \ge 2K/(T - K + 2)$. Also, $\lambda_{\max}[\cdot]$ is the largest characteristic root of the matrix argument. This corresponds to the general form with $k(\mathbf{y}) = as/(\mathbf{b}'X'X\mathbf{b} + gs + h)$ and $C = Q^{-1}X'X$.

It is interesting that the usual ridge rule

$$[I + k(X'X)^{-1}]^{-1}\mathbf{b}$$

is minimax when the matrix of the loss function is $Q = (X'X)^2$ rather than the more usual cases $Q = I$ (squared error of estimation loss) or $Q = X'X$ (squared error of prediction loss). The consequences of this fact are quite important if we relate it back to the multicollinearity problem. Recall that the motivation for ridge regression, or in fact any sort of biased estimation procedure, is to gain improved information about the unknown parameters of the linear regression model by using an estimator that has smaller risk, over the range of the parameter space, than the conventional least squares estimator. This consideration is especially important, of course, when a lack of precision due to poor implicit sample design is a problem. The class of shrink estimators, those that improve on least squares by shrinking the least square estimators toward some specified point in the parameter space, includes both the ridge estimators and the general Stein-like minimax estimators to be considered in Section 22.6. One important question that remains is: "How does the choice of Q affect the shrink estimators?" Furthermore, given the previously mentioned instability of least squares estimates based on multicollinear data, is it possible to obtain shrink estimators that are more stable than least squares estimates?

To investigate the questions raised above, consider the model in its canonical form

$$\mathbf{y} = X\boldsymbol{\beta} + \mathbf{e} = XPP'\boldsymbol{\beta} + \mathbf{e} = Z\boldsymbol{\theta} + \mathbf{e}$$

where P is the orthogonal matrix of characteristic vectors of $X'X$ ordered so that $P'X'XP = \Lambda = \text{diag}(\lambda_1, \lambda_2, \ldots, \lambda_K)$ with $\lambda_1 \ge \lambda_2 \ge \ldots \ge \lambda_K$. The relevant risk function becomes

$$\begin{aligned} \rho(\boldsymbol{\beta}^*,\boldsymbol{\beta}) &= E(\boldsymbol{\beta}^* - \boldsymbol{\beta})'Q(\boldsymbol{\beta}^* - \boldsymbol{\beta})/\sigma^2 \\ &= E(\boldsymbol{\theta}^* - \boldsymbol{\theta})'P'QP(\boldsymbol{\theta}^* - \boldsymbol{\theta})/\sigma^2 \end{aligned}$$

The Strawderman estimator in (22.5.7) is

$$\boldsymbol{\delta}(\mathbf{b},s) = P\boldsymbol{\delta}(\hat{\boldsymbol{\theta}},s) = P\left[I + \frac{asP'Q^{-1}P\Lambda}{\hat{\boldsymbol{\theta}}'\Lambda\hat{\boldsymbol{\theta}} + gs + h}\right]^{-1}\hat{\boldsymbol{\theta}}$$

where $\hat{\boldsymbol{\theta}} = (Z'Z)^{-1}Z'\mathbf{y} = \Lambda^{-1}Z'\mathbf{y}$ and for minimaxity $g \geq 2K/(T-K+2)$, $h \geq 0$ and

$$0 \leq a \leq \frac{2(K-2)}{(T-K+2)} \frac{1}{\lambda_{\max}[Q^{-1}P\Lambda P']}$$

How the choice of Q and multicollinearity affect the properties of the ridge estimator can be seen by examining the following cases:

1. Let $Q = I$. Then

$$\begin{aligned}\rho(\boldsymbol{\beta}^*,\boldsymbol{\beta}) &= E[(\boldsymbol{\theta}^* - \boldsymbol{\theta})'P'P(\boldsymbol{\theta}^* - \boldsymbol{\theta})]/\sigma^2 \\ &= E[(\boldsymbol{\theta}^* - \boldsymbol{\theta})'(\boldsymbol{\theta}^* - \boldsymbol{\theta})]/\sigma^2\end{aligned}$$

and the loss function penalizes errors in all components equally, regardless of how well they may be estimated, given the sample design. The Strawderman estimator becomes

$$\boldsymbol{\delta}(\mathbf{b},s) = P\left[I + \frac{as\Lambda}{\hat{\boldsymbol{\theta}}'\Lambda\hat{\boldsymbol{\theta}} + gs + h}\right]^{-1}\hat{\boldsymbol{\theta}}$$

If we recall that $\mathrm{cov}(\hat{\boldsymbol{\theta}}) = \sigma^2\Lambda^{-1}$, it is clear that this estimator shrinks the components $\hat{\theta}_i$ with the smallest variances the most. If (22.5.7) is rewritten as

$$\boldsymbol{\delta}(\mathbf{b},s) = \left[X'X + \frac{asX'XQ^{-1}X'X}{\mathbf{b}'X'X\mathbf{b} + gs + h}\right]^{-1} X'\mathbf{y} \tag{22.5.8}$$

we can examine the influences of this type of shrinkage on the stability of the estimator by comparing the condition number of the design matrix of the least squares estimator $X'X$ and the design matrix in (22.5.8). If $Q = I$, the design matrix is $[X'X + k(\mathbf{y})(X'X)^2]$. The condition of this matrix is $[\lambda_1 + \lambda_1^2 k(\mathbf{y})]/[\lambda_K + \lambda_K^2 k(\mathbf{y})]$. This ratio is greater than the condition number λ_1/λ_K of $X'X$, which implies that this ridge estimator is less stable than the least squares estimator. This is not a desirable result if we are concerned with the effects of collinearity upon the stability of the estimator.

Another consideration is how much the resulting minimax rule will be different from the conventional estimator. For minimaxity,

$$0 \leq a \leq \frac{2(K-2)}{(T-K+2)} \frac{1}{\lambda_{\max}[Q^{-1}X'X]}$$

Factors that affect the width of the interval containing the constant a are important, since that determines the amount of shrinkage allowable for the estimator to remain minimax. Furthermore, it is of interest to examine the effects of multicollinearity upon the bound of the interval that contains a. Since $Q = I$ and $\lambda_{max}[X'X] = \lambda_1$, the range of a becomes the interval

$$\left[0, \frac{2(K-2)}{(T-K+2)}\ \frac{1}{\lambda_1}\right]$$

The upper bound of the interval is a function of T, K, and λ_1. As T increases, the interval narrows, which reflects the fact that the usual estimator is consistent and a departure from it makes less sense as the sample size becomes large. As K increases, the interval lengthens so that the more regressors there are, other things remaining the same, the more shrinkage is allowable. Finally, as λ_1 is larger, that is, the more of the total variation in the data that is oriented in a single direction, indicating more severe multicollinearity, the narrower the range of a and the less shrinkage is allowable for a minimax estimator. Consequently, when multicollinearity is severe, the less difference there can be between this minimax ridge estimator and **b**.

2. Let $Q = X'X$. Then the loss function is $\rho(\boldsymbol{\beta}^*,\boldsymbol{\beta}) = E(\boldsymbol{\theta}^* - \boldsymbol{\theta})'\Lambda(\boldsymbol{\theta}^* - \boldsymbol{\theta})/\sigma^2$ and errors in those components with the smallest variances (largest λ_i's) are penalized more than those components with the largest variances (smallest λ_i's). The Strawderman estimator becomes

$$\delta(\mathbf{b},s) = P\left[I + \frac{asI}{\hat{\boldsymbol{\theta}}'\Lambda\hat{\boldsymbol{\theta}} + gs + h}\right]^{-1}\hat{\boldsymbol{\theta}}$$

All components $\hat{\theta}_i$ are shrunk by the same fraction. The design matrix becomes $[X'X + k(\mathbf{y})X'X]$, which has condition number $[\lambda_1 + k(\mathbf{y})\lambda_1]/[\lambda_K + k(\mathbf{y})\lambda_K]$, which equals λ_1/λ_K, the condition number of $X'X$. Thus this type of shrinkage has no effect on the stability of the resulting etimates under the criterion.

For this loss function the upper bound on the shrinkage constant a becomes $2(K-2)/(T-K+2)$. Therefore, only the number of regressors and number of observations affect the maximum minimax amount of shrinkage and not the multicollinearity in the data. Since this loss function is appropriate for situations in which prediction is the primary concern of the analysis, this is not a surprising result.

3. Let $Q = (X'X)^2$. The risk function is $\rho(\boldsymbol{\beta}^*,\boldsymbol{\beta}) = E(\boldsymbol{\theta}^* - \boldsymbol{\theta})'\Lambda^2(\boldsymbol{\theta}^* - \boldsymbol{\theta})/\sigma^2$ and losses on components with small variances are magnified more than in the case where $Q = X'X$. The Strawderman estimator becomes

$$\delta(\mathbf{b},s) = P\left[I + \frac{as\Lambda^{-1}}{\hat{\boldsymbol{\theta}}'\Lambda\hat{\boldsymbol{\theta}} + gs + h}\right]^{-1}\hat{\boldsymbol{\theta}}$$

and now components with large variances are shrunk more than components with small variances. Casella (1977) terms this the "ridge property," which serves to distinguish this class of estimators from other shrinkage estimators.

The design matrix is $[X'X + k(\mathbf{y})I]$, which has condition number $[\lambda_1 + k(\mathbf{y})]/[\lambda_K + k(\mathbf{y})]$, which is less than λ_1/λ_K, the condition number of $X'X$. Thus this choice of Q ensures the improved stability of the estimators as measured on this criterion.

The upper bound on the shrinkage constant a is now

$$\frac{2(K-2)}{(T-K+2)} \frac{1}{\lambda_{\max}[(X'X)^{-1}]} = \frac{2(K-2)}{T-K+2} \lambda_K$$

where λ_K is the smallest root of $X'X$. The smaller λ_K—that is, the more severe the multicollinearity—the smaller the amount of minimax shrinkage allowed. Therefore, although this estimator is minimax and improves the condition number of the design matrix, the more severe the collinearity the less different this estimator will be from the conventional estimator. This reaffirms the comment of Efron and Morris (1973, p. 93) that there is "tension" between minimaxity and the stability of estimated coefficients.

22.6 NONTRADITIONAL SOLUTIONS TO THE MULTICOLLINEARITY PROBLEM: STEIN-LIKE ESTIMATORS

The work of Stein and its extensions have been discussed in Chapter 3 as a superior method of incorporating prior information when its validity is uncertain. In this section we consider a general class of minimax estimators discussed by Judge and Bock (1978) as a way of obtaining more precise information about unknown population parameters when implicit design is poor. In the usual regression case where σ^2 is unknown, Judge and Bock (1978, p. 234) propose a class of rules

$$\boldsymbol{\delta}(\mathbf{b},s) = \left[I_K - h\left(\frac{\mathbf{b}'B\mathbf{b}}{s}\right) C\right] \mathbf{b} \tag{22.6.1}$$

where B and C are square matrices and h is a differentiable function. This rule is minimax for $\boldsymbol{\beta}$ against

$$L(\boldsymbol{\delta},\boldsymbol{\beta}) = \frac{1}{\sigma^2}(\boldsymbol{\delta} - \boldsymbol{\beta})'Q(\boldsymbol{\delta} - \boldsymbol{\beta})$$

under certain conditions on B, C, Q, $h(\cdot)$ and if $K \geq 3$. We consider some special cases of this rule and their implications for the multicollinearity problem.

22.6.1 A James- and Stein-type Minimax Estimator

In the general estimator (22.6.1) let $Q = C = I$, $B = X'X$, and $h(u) = a/u$. The resulting estimator is

$$\boldsymbol{\delta}(\mathbf{b},s) = \left[1 - \frac{as}{\mathbf{b}'X'X\mathbf{b}}\right]\mathbf{b} \tag{22.6.2}$$

which in matrix form is

$$\boldsymbol{\delta}_1(\mathbf{b},s) = [I - k(\mathbf{y})I]\mathbf{b}$$

where $k(\mathbf{y}) = as/(\mathbf{b}'X'X\mathbf{b})$. This estimator is minimax if

$$0 \leq a \leq \frac{2}{(T-K+2)}\left[\operatorname{tr}(X'X)^{-1}\ \frac{1}{\lambda_{\max}[(X'X)^{-1}]} - 2\right]$$

Since $\operatorname{tr}(X'X)^{-1} = \operatorname{tr}\Lambda^{-1}$ and $\lambda_{\max}[(X'X)^{-1}] = 1/\lambda_K$, this condition becomes

$$0 \leq a \leq \frac{2}{(T-K+2)}[\lambda_K \operatorname{tr}\Lambda^{-1} - 2]$$

Note that the width of this interval, determining the amount of shrinking that is allowed for minimaxity, is positively related to K and negatively related to T. The remaining factor $[\lambda_K \operatorname{tr}\Lambda^{-1} - 2]$ must be positive and is positively related to the width of the interval. Since this factor depends upon the characteristic roots of the design matrix, and therefore on whatever patterns of multicollinearity are present, it is important to have an idea of what characteristic root spectra lead to the satisfaction of this condition. Our first intuition that increasingly severe multicollinearity implies λ_K increasingly small and therefore limited range of improvement of the Stein-rule estimator over least squares is not completely accurate. Recall that each small characteristic root corresponds to a nearly exact linear relationship among the columns of the X matrix. The condition

$$[\lambda_K \operatorname{tr}\Lambda^{-1} - 2] > 0$$

will fail in general when there is one, but not more than one, small characteristic root. If there are two or more small characteristic roots, implying two or more near-exact linear dependencies among the columns of X, then the condition may be satisfied.

Fomby and Hill (1978a), Trenkler (1984) and Oman (1982) have investigated this condition for several patterned $X'X$ matrices that could be thought to represent general multicollinearity conditions. For example, let $X'X = (z_{ij})$, where $z_{ij} = 1$ if $i = j$ and z otherwise. The characteristic roots of $X'X$ are $1 + (K - 1)z$ and $(K - 1)$ values to $1 - z$. The condition $[\lambda_K \text{ tr } \Lambda^{-1} - 2] > 0$ is satisfied for all $K \geq 3$ regardless of the value of $z \in [0,1]$. Thus the results indicate, perhaps contrary to intuition, that the more small characteristic roots λ_i there are, the more likely it is that the necessary condition will be fulfilled, but the narrower the interval of minimax shrinkage. This can be verified in the above example by noting that $\lambda_K \text{ tr } \Lambda^{-1}$ is a decreasing function of z. Hill and Ziemer (1983, 1984) report Monte Carlo results that indicate that the extent of risk gains over LS can degenerate rapidly with only moderate degrees of collinearity depending on the form of the collinearity.

Finally, we must ask whether this estimator provides more stable estimates than the least squares estimators. Since a matrix and its inverse have the same condition number, for the estimator (22.6.2), the condition number of the design matrix is $[\lambda_1 - k(\mathbf{y})\lambda_1]/[\lambda_K k(\mathbf{y})\lambda_K] = \lambda_1/\lambda_K$. Thus the use of this estimator has no effect on the stability of the estimates using the condition number criterion.

As an alternative to the Stein-like rule (22.6.2) that shrinks the OLS estimates toward the origin, one might consider the Stein-like rule that shrinks toward the restricted least squares estimator $\mathbf{b}^*$. That rule is given by

$$\boldsymbol{\delta}_2^*(\mathbf{b},s) = \left[1 - \frac{as}{(\mathbf{r} - R\mathbf{b})'(RS^{-1}R')^{-1}(\mathbf{r} - R\mathbf{b})}\right](\mathbf{b} - \mathbf{b}^*) + \mathbf{b}^*$$

where $S = X'X$, $\mathbf{b}^* = \mathbf{b} - S^{-1}R'(RS^{-1}R')^{-1}(R\mathbf{b} - \mathbf{r})$, R is a known $(J \times K)$ matrix of rank J and $\mathbf{r}$ is a known $(J \times 1)$ vector. This estimator has risk that is less than or equal to that of $\mathbf{b}$ if $J \geq 3$ and the constant a is in the interval

$$0 \leq a \leq \frac{2}{(T - K + 2)}\left[\frac{\text{tr}(RS^{-1}R')^{-1}RS^{-1}QS^{-1}R'}{\zeta} - 2\right]$$

where ζ is the largest characteristic root of $(RS^{-1}R')^{-1}RS^{-1}QS^{-1}R'$ [Mittelhammer (1984)]. Given uncertain nonsample information, use of the mimimax rule $\boldsymbol{\delta}_2^*(\mathbf{b},s)$ to combine the sample and nonsample information in order to gain more precise parameter estimates in the presence of multicollinearity would seem useful. Hill and Ziemer (1984) have evaluated the risk function of this estimator under varying degrees of collinearity using principal components restrictions, and have found that the extent of risk improvement over LS increases with the dimension of the design matrix K and the number of restrictions J, but again the risk gains can dissipate rapidly as collinearity increases in certain cases. Thus while the Stein-like rules seem to offer substantial risk gains in near orthogonal designs, little improvement over LS may be forthcoming in nonorthogonal designs. Stein (1981) has proposed a coordinate-wise limited translation Stein-estimator that may correct some of the deficiencies noted above.

22.6.2 Minimax Estimators with the Ridge Property

Members of the class (22.6.1) that do shrink with the ridge property are illustrated in the following cases:

1. Let $Q = I$, $C = (X'X)^{-1}$, $B = X'X$, and $h(u) = a/u$. The resulting estimator is

$$\delta(\mathbf{b},s) = \left[I - \frac{as(X'X)^{-1}}{\mathbf{b}'X'X\mathbf{b}}\right]\mathbf{b} \tag{22.6.3}$$

or expressed in the canonical form

$$\delta(\mathbf{b},s) = P\left[I - \frac{as\Lambda^{-1}}{\hat{\boldsymbol{\theta}}'\Lambda\hat{\boldsymbol{\theta}}}\right]\hat{\boldsymbol{\theta}}$$

As is clear from examining (22.6.3), this estimator shrinks most those components, $\hat{\theta}_i$, which have the largest variance σ^2/λ_i. The condition for minimaxity is

$$0 \le a \le 2\,\frac{\lambda_K[\lambda_K^2 \operatorname{tr}\Lambda^{-2} - 2]}{T - K + 2} \tag{22.6.4}$$

Note that the necessary condition for minimaxity is now

$$\operatorname{tr}\Lambda^{-2} > \frac{2}{\lambda_K^2} \tag{22.6.5}$$

The same general remarks about the satisfaction of (22.6.5) hold as discussed in Section 22.6.1. In particular, for the equicorrelation example considered there, (22.6.5) is satisfied for $K \ge 3$ regardless of the value of z. Again the interval in (22.6.4) decreases in width as z gets larger. As for the stability of the estimator in (22.6.3) the condition number of the design matrix is that of

$$[(X'X)^{-1} - k(\mathbf{y})(X'X)^{-2}] = \frac{1/\lambda_K - k(\mathbf{y})(1/\lambda_K)^2}{1/\lambda_1 - k(\mathbf{y})(1/\lambda_1)^2} = \frac{\lambda_1}{\lambda_K}\,\frac{1 - k(\mathbf{y})/\lambda_K}{1 - k(\mathbf{y})/\lambda_1}$$

which is a decreasing function of $k(\mathbf{y})$. Therefore, the use of (22.6.3) improves the stability of the estimates and is minimax with respect to squared error loss. However, these positive qualities are diminished by the fact that the interval (22.6.4) may get narrower as collinearity gets worse so that when multicollinearity is most severe, the estimator (22.6.3) may not be much different from **b**, implying little actual gain.

2. Let $Q = X'X$, $C = (X'X)^{-1}$, $B = X'X$, and $h(u) = a/u$. The resulting estimator is identical to (22.6.3) except that the condition for minimaxity is

$$0 \leq a \leq \frac{2\lambda_K[\lambda_K \operatorname{tr} \Lambda^{-1} - 2]}{T - K + 2}$$

Again, the smaller λ_K, the less difference there will be between this estimator and the least squares estimator despite the fact that it is minimax and is more stable on the condition number criterion.

3. To obtain an estimator with more desirable properties, but which is slightly different in form from the estimators presented above, let $Q = (X'X)^2$, $C = (X'X)^{-1}$, $B = I$, and $h(u) = a/u$. This estimator has the form

$$\delta_3(\mathbf{b},s) = \left[I - \frac{as(X'X)^{-1}}{\mathbf{b}'\mathbf{b}}\right]\mathbf{b} = P\left[I - \frac{as\Lambda^{-1}}{\hat{\boldsymbol{\theta}}'\hat{\boldsymbol{\theta}}}\right]\hat{\boldsymbol{\theta}}$$

and the condition for minimaxity is

$$0 \leq a \leq \frac{2(K - 2)}{(T - K + 2)}$$

These estimators offer properties that are desirable when data are multicollinear. What remains to investigate is the extent of risk gains among the various rules and the circumstances when one is preferred to another.

22.7 THE MULTICOLLINEARITY PROBLEM WHEN REGRESSORS ARE STOCHASTIC

Consider the linear regression model with stochastic regressors

$$\mathbf{y} = X\boldsymbol{\beta} + \mathbf{e}$$

where $\mathbf{y}$ is a $(T \times 1)$ vector of observations on the dependent variable, X is a $(T \times K)$ stochastic matrix; that is, the tth row $\mathbf{x}_t'$ is a $(1 \times K)$ random vector, $\boldsymbol{\beta}$ is a $(K \times 1)$ vector of unknown parameters, and $\mathbf{e}$ is a $(T \times 1)$ stochastic error vector that is distributed independently of X so that $E(\mathbf{e}|X) = \mathbf{0}$ and $E(\mathbf{ee}'|X) = \sigma^2 I$. The properties of this model are discussed in Chapter 5.

Since we are presuming that our data are generated by independent drawings from the distribution of X and $\mathbf{e}$, it is clear that as experimenters we no longer have a carefully controlled experimental design to work with. Thus it is possible to draw a sample of T observations on the independent variables that have poor sample design. We may analyze this sample in one of two ways. First, we could analyze the sample design as if X were nonstochastic with all results conditional on the values of the sample actually drawn. Multicollinearity can then be properly analyzed as a feature of the sample, not the population, and all the comments of previous sections apply. This is usually the position taken.

On the other hand, we may wish to know if the independent variables obey some significant auxiliary relations among themselves. Such relations could lead to exact or stochastic restrictions on the parameter vector if they could be identified. If we are willing to assume that the $\mathbf{x}_t$ are normally and independently distributed, the tests of Farrar and Glauber (1967) are available and confidence statements can be made. Kumar (1975) notes that the test statistic derived by Farrar and Glauber depends on independent sample observations from a joint normal population, which is not likely to be the case. Wichers (1975) proposes a modification of the Farrar and Glauber tests designed to identify the nature of the linear dependencies. Alternatively, we may test hypotheses about the characteristic roots, which are now themselves stochastic. We are interested in whether or not J roots are indistinguishable, and presumably small. Dhrymes (1974, p. 61) suggests testing the hypothesis that $\lambda_{K-J+1} = \ldots = \lambda_K$, using a chi-square test statistic developed by Lawley (1956). Note that we are not testing for the singularity or nonsingularity of X, for if exact linear constraints were obeyed in the population, the sample would obey those constraints with probability one and $X'X$ would be singular. Thus we are testing only whether or not there is little independent variation within a set of explanatory variables. Such information is important for two related reasons. If we are aware of auxiliary relations among the regressors, their identification and use could provide improved estimates of the unknown parameters. Second if these auxiliary relations exist, and are strong, the interpretation of the regression coefficients of the variables involved becomes difficult, as the variables exhibit little independent variation.

Given the assumptions of the stochastic regressor model, the search for improved estimators becomes difficult. We might replace the necessary conditions in Sections 22.5 and 22.6 by their analogues, as suggested by Trivedi (1978). Unfortunately, even if the risk improvement carries over when $E(X'X)$ is known, it is unlikely to hold when the sample counterpart is used to estimate it. Although little has been done in this area, Judge and Bock (1978, p. 268) carry out some sampling experiments, in a different context, which indicate that the Stein-like estimators may do well when the covariance matrix is estimated rather than known. This, however, remains an area where research must be done.

The results of Baranchik (1973) represent solid analytical work and provide hope that improved estimates for the stochastic regressor model may be found. He considers the situation where $\mathbf{y}$ and X are jointly normal. Under this model and if the loss function is the mean square error of prediction, Baranchik presents an estimator that dominates the usual maximum likelihood estimator. King (1972, 1974) has also investigated this problem. His results, as well as Baranchik's, are summarized in Judge and Bock (1978, Chapter 12).

22.8 SUMMARY

In this chapter the problem of multicollinearity has been considered and its statistical consequences noted. The presence of multicollinearity implies poor implicit sample design, and means that not all parameters in the model can be estimated precisely. Which linear combinations of parameters will be estimated relatively imprecisely using least squares with a given sample can be determined by examining the characteristic roots and vectors of the $X'X$ matrix. If the linear combinations of parameters on which interest centers are not affected by the multicollinearity, then one can proceed using classical methods. If, however, the parameters of interest cannot be estimated precisely with the given sample using classical methods, then other alternatives should be considered.

One possibility for improving the precision of parameter estimation is to introduce nonsample information that can be combined with the existing sample information. The statistical consequences of this approach may be summarized as follows: Over the region of the parameter space where the nonsample information is "close" to being correct, the estimator that combines sample and other information has a lower risk than the conventional estimator. If the information is uncertain, however, there is a potential cost—namely, that the estimator that combines both types of information may not be better than the conventional estimator. Because of this fact, investigators have adopted the practice of performing statistical tests of the compatibility of the sample and prior information and making a decision whether or not to pool based upon the outcome of that test. The resulting pretest estimator protects against large losses due to the incorporation of erroneous information. It is superior to the conventional estimator over only a portion of the parameter space. Furthermore, the sampling distributions of these pretest estimators are not presently known and thus the basis for inference is limited.

If the statistical consequences of pretesting are ignored, then it is possible to make empirical results "look good" by locating a specification of the model that fits the data well in the sense that the "t values" are high. Such exercises do not generally represent positive contributions to knowledge. Like other statistical theories with the sampling theory approach to estimation and inference, a particular empirical result cannot be judged either good or bad. What people typically mean when they say that the results "look good" is that they agree with prior notions. This, however, does not necessarily imply correctness.

Another suggested route to improving the precision of estimators is to inspect the (nonstochastic) design matrix X to determine what information it contains and then incorporate that information into the estimation process. Examples of these ad hoc techniques include principal components regression, ridge regression, and various variable selection procedures. These procedures as usually presented have little or no conceptual basis and lead to estimators that are inferior to the conventional estimator over a large range of the parameter space. Consequently, their use is not recommended. Recently, Strawderman (1978) has produced a ridge-like estimator, which under certain conditions is superior to the maximum likelihood estimator over the entire parameter space. To achieve improvement in risk and estimator stability, an unusually weighted loss function must be adopted. It is possible, however, to obtain risk improvement over least squares under a wide range of loss functions. Sampling distributions are not available for these estimators, and thus neither hypothesis tests nor confidence interval statements can be made.

Finally, Stein-like estimators provide an alternative route to improved precision of estimation. These estimators can be thought of as superior ways of combining sample and uncertain nonsample information. They have the property that regardless of the correctness of the nonsample information, if certain conditions are met, they dominate the conventional estimator under a wide range of loss functions. Once more, however, these results are useful only where point estimates are sought because the sampling distributions of these estimators are not yet known. Furthermore, the extent of the risk gain can diminish substantially when certain forms of multicollinearity are present because of the limited shrinkage permitted by the minimaxity condition on the shrinkage constant. A generalized coordinate-wise Stein (1981) estimator may remedy this deficiency.

Given the alternatives noted above, what solid guidance may be given to the investigators who feel that their samples may not be rich enough in information to precisely estimate specific linear parametric functions?

First, in general, investigators who have only vaguely defined objectives when carrying out empirical work are more likely to be troubled by poor sample design problems than investigators who have more limited or narrowly defined objectives. Multicollinear data do not imply that one should despair immediately, since in some cases linear combinations of parameters may permit estimation with acceptable sampling precision. What should be done is to assess whether or not key parametric functions can be estimated relatively precisely. If the data will not allow this, then other sources of information must be sought.

Second, adoption of estimation procedures that have low risk relative to least squares over only a narrow range of the parameter space should be avoided in general. This includes a vast array of ad hoc data search procedures and pretest estimators outlined in this chapter and Chapter 21.

Third, if the sample does not contain sufficient information for precise parameter estimation, then those who wish to test hypotheses or make confidence interval statements are in a difficult position. Most of the procedures available to improve the precision and/or stability of parameter estimates, such as the Stein-rule family of estimators, have unknown sampling distributions. Finally, for those who are only interested in point estimates, Stein-like alternatives are superior to least squares. The degree of improvement in estimator precision and stability, however, depends on the loss function adopted, the number of regressors, the nature of the multicollinearity, and the type and quality of both the available sample and prior information.

Finally, what are some suggestions for research in this area? First and foremost is the course to continue efforts to develop estimators, perhaps in the Stein-family, that provide risk improvements over LS and that are robust to data ill-conditioning. Part of this work, of course, is careful investigation of potential risk gains provided by current estimators under varying conditions of collinearity. A second avenue of research that has yet to receive much attention is the effect of near exact linear dependencies on the finite sampling precision of estimators in nonlinear models like Tobit, Probit, and so on. These questions become increasingly important given the growing use of nonlinear models in applied work.

22.9 EXERCISES

In order to demonstrate the effect of multicollinearity and to help the reader understand the alternative proposals that have been suggested for "curing" the problem, consider the linear statistical model $\mathbf{y} = 10.0\mathbf{x}_1 + 0.4\mathbf{x}_2 + 0.6\mathbf{x}_3 + \mathbf{x}_4 + 2\mathbf{x}_5 + \mathbf{e}$, where $\mathbf{x}_1$, $\mathbf{x}_2$, and $\mathbf{x}_3$ are given in Section 2.7 of Chapter 2. The variables $\mathbf{x}_4$ and $\mathbf{x}_5$ are presented in Table 22.3. They were constructed as $\mathbf{x}_4 = \mathbf{x}_2 + \mathbf{x}_3 + \mathbf{w}_1$ and $\mathbf{x}_5 = \mathbf{x}_2 + \mathbf{w}_2$, where $\mathbf{w}_1$ is a random vector from a uniform distribution over the unit interval and $\mathbf{w}_2$ is a random vector from a uniform distribution over the interval $[0,\frac{1}{2}]$. Let $\mathbf{e}$, as in the problem set in Chapter 2, be a vector of normally and independently distributed random variables with mean zero and constant variance 1.0. Using this statistical model, five samples of data were generated and are presented in Table 22.4.

22.9.1 Individual Exercises (Section 22.3)

Exercise 22.1
For the model outlined above, and using the data in Table 22.4, compute the least squares estimates of the coefficients, their means, and their sample variances. Compare the sample variances with their theoretical counterparts.

Exercise 22.2
For the given design matrix compute and evaluate each of the multicollinearity "detection" methods outlined in Section 22.3.

TABLE 22.3 ***ADDITIONAL DESIGN VARIABLES***

$\mathbf{x}_4$	$\mathbf{x}_5$	$\mathbf{x}_4$	$\mathbf{x}_5$
0.88839	2.05464	1.10589	2.17026
2.13713	3.12292	1.74341	3.40309
1.16983	2.51224	1.99744	3.87633
1.95618	4.06982	0.85438	3.35228
0.79418	3.44152	2.49910	3.72893
2.56843	3.99406	2.13015	3.53070
2.05807	3.98592	2.82119	4.49139
2.52166	3.76541	2.49415	4.90527
2.69760	4.54431	1.89954	3.56241
0.70151	1.62394	0.85161	1.51745

TABLE 22.4 *SAMPLES GENERATED USING MULTICOLLINEAR DATA*

y_1	y_2	y_3	y_4	y_5
16.64	15.81	15.48	16.97	15.97
17.77	18.76	19.38	18.35	18.94
16.98	17.31	16.70	18.92	15.38
22.40	20.02	20.73	22.41	22.44
19.19	16.51	17.79	18.58	19.33
22.03	21.88	19.72	20.70	21.75
22.22	22.87	20.96	23.66	23.03
20.85	22.01	20.77	21.14	22.29
22.68	22.49	23.05	21.50	23.33
16.24	14.29	14.52	14.87	14.71
17.85	17.17	16.63	17.15	17.77
18.95	21.98	19.97	20.37	19.99
21.12	20.76	22.29	21.72	19.98
19.85	19.45	19.24	18.29	20.27
21.34	23.66	22.17	20.85	21.08
22.74	20.99	21.37	19.15	19.58
24.36	24.18	21.34	24.10	24.14
24.70	25.19	23.71	24.81	23.27
18.92	20.59	20.81	21.00	20.17
15.31	13.12	16.08	15.58	13.16

22.9.2 Joint or Class Exercises (Section 22.3)

Exercise 22.3

Generate 100 samples of size 20 for the statistical model outlined above. Compute the least squares estimates, their sample means, variances, and squared error loss, $\Sigma_{i=1}^{100}(\mathbf{b}_i - \boldsymbol{\beta}_i)'(\mathbf{b}_i - \boldsymbol{\beta}_i)/100$. Construct empirical frequency distributions of the least squares estimates of the coefficients and the unbiased estimate of the error variance. Compare these distributions to the true distributions.

22.9.3 Individual Exercises (Section 22.4)

Exercise 22.4

Assume that exact prior information of the form $\beta_2 + \beta_3 = \beta_4$ is available. Compute the restricted least squares estimates for the five samples of data from Exercise 22.1 and compare these outcomes with the corresponding least squares results. See Section 3.1.

Exercise 22.5

Assume stochastic prior information of the form $R\boldsymbol{\beta} + \mathbf{v} = \beta_2 + \beta_3 - \beta_4 + v = 0$, where v is assumed to be a normal random variable with mean zero and variance $\frac{1}{64}$. Using this information in conjunction with the sample data, estimate the parameter vector $\boldsymbol{\beta}$ and compare it with the least squares and restricted least squares results. See Section 3.2.

Exercise 22.6

Use the inequality restricted estimator and the inequality restriction $R\boldsymbol{\beta} = \beta_2 + \beta_3 - \beta_4 \geq 0$ to estimate the unknown $\boldsymbol{\beta}$ parameters for the five samples. Compare these results with those of the least squares, restricted least squares, and stochastically restricted least squares estimators. See Section 3.2.

Exercise 22.7

Apply principal components regression (Section 22.5.1), deleting in turn one, two, and three principal components, to obtain parameter estimates for the five samples. Compute the sample means of the principal components estimates and their sample variance.

22.9.4 Joint or Class Exercises (Section 22.4)

Exercise 22.8

Compute the restricted least squares estimator for the 100 samples constructed as outlined above, using the exact prior information $\beta_2 + \beta_3 = \beta_4$. Compute the sample means and variances of the resulting estimates and compare them to their theoretical counterparts. Compute the squared error loss of the estimates and compare it to that for the least squares estimator.

Exercise 22.9

Compute the stochastically restricted estimator based on the prior information $R\boldsymbol{\beta} + \mathbf{v} = \beta_2 + \beta_3 - \beta_4 + v = 0$, where v is a normal random variable with mean zero and variance $\frac{1}{64}$, for 100 samples. Compute the sample means and variances of the estimates and compare with their theoretical counterparts. Compute the squared error loss of these estimates and compare them with the least squares estimates.

Exercise 22.10

Use the inequality restricted estimator and the prior information that $R\boldsymbol{\beta} = \beta_2 + \beta_3 - \beta_4 \geq 0$ to estimate the model parameters for 100 samples. Compute the sample means, variances, and squared error loss of these estimates and compare them to the least squares results.

Exercise 22.11

Apply principal components regression, deleting in turn one, two, and three components, to 100 samples. Compute the sample means and variances of these estimates and compare them with the least squares results.

22.9.5 Individual Exercises (Section 22.5)

Exercise 22.12
Adopt one of the rules outlined in Section 22.5.2b for selecting the biasing parameter k used in ridge regression and compute the ridge estimates for five samples. Compute the sample means and variances of the estimated coefficients and compare them with the least squares results.

Exercise 22.13
Use Strawderman's adaptive generalized ridge estimator (Section 22.5.2c) to estimate the model's coefficients for five samples. Compute the means and variances of these estimates and compare them to the least squares results.

22.9.6 Joint or Class Exercises (Section 22.5)

Exercise 22.14
Use the sample data from Exercise 22.3 and Strawderman's adaptive generalized ridge estimator to estimate the model's coefficients for 100 samples. Compute the sample means, variances, and squared error loss for these estimates and compare them to the least squares results.

22.9.7 Individual Exercises (Section 22.6)

Exercise 22.15
Use the James- and Stein-type minimax estimator (22.6.2) to estimate the model's parameters for five samples. Compute the sample means and variances of these estimates and compare them to the least squares results.

22.9.8 Joint or Class Exercises (Section 22.6)

Exercise 22.16
Use the sample data from Exercise 22.3 and the James- and Stein-type minimax estimator (22.6.2) to estimate the model's parameters for 100 samples. Compute the sample means, variances, and squared error loss of these estimates and compare them to the least squares results.

22.9.9 Joint or Class Exercises (Section 22.8)

Exercise 22.17
Contrast the results for the various estimators and diagnostic checks and discuss the best way to deal with this model and the corresponding data.

22.10 REFERENCES

Allen, D. M. (1974) "The Relationship Between Variable Selection and Data Augmentation and a Method for Prediction," *Technometrics,* 16, 125–127.

Bacon, R. W. and J. A. Hausman (1974) ''The Relationship Between Ridge Regression and the Minimum Mean Squared Error Estimator of Chipman,'' *Oxford Bulletin of Economics and Statistics,* 36, 115–124.

Baranchik, A. J. (1973) ''Inadmissibility of Maximum Likelihood Estimators in Some Multiple Regression Problems with Three or More Independent Variables,'' *Annals of Statistics,* 1, 312–321.

Belsley, D., E. Kuh, and R. E. Welsh (1980) *Regression Diagnostics,* Wiley, New York.

Belsley, D. (1982a) ''Centering, the Constant and Diagnosing Collinearity,'' Technical Report #33, Boston College.

Belsley, D. (1982b) ''Assessing the Presence of Harmful Collinearity and other Forms of Weak Data through a Test for Signal to Noise,'' *Journal of Econometrics,* 20, 211–253.

Brooks, R. J. and T. Moore (1980) ''On the Expected Length of the Least Squares Coefficient Vector,'' *Journal of Econometrics,* 12, 245–246.

Brown, W. G. and B. R. Beattie (1975) ''Improving Estimates of Economic Parameters by Use of Ridge Regression with Production Function Applications,'' *American Journal of Agricultural Economics,* 57, 21–32.

Casella, G. (1977) Minimax Ridge Estimation, unpublished Ph.D. dissertation, Purdue University, Lafayette, Ind.

Conniffe, D. and J. Stone (1973) ''A Critical View of Ridge Regression,'' *The Statistician,* 22, 181–187.

Dempster, A. P., M. Schatzoff, and M. Wermuth (1977) ''A Simulation Study of Alternatives to Ordinary Least Squares,'' *Journal of the American Statistical Association,* 72, 77–104.

Dhrymes, P. J. (1974) *Econometrics: Statistical Foundations and Applications,* Springer-Verlag, New York.

Draper, N. and R. Van Nostrand (1979) ''Ridge Regression and James and Stein Estimation: Review and Comments,'' *Technometrics,* 21, 451–466.

Efron, B. and C. Morris (1977) ''Comment,'' *Journal of the American Statistical Association,* 72, 91–94.

Farebrother (1972) ''Principal Component Estimators and Minimum Mean Square Error Criteria in Regression Analysis,'' *Review of Economics and Statistics,* 54, 332–336.

Farrar, D. E. and R. R. Glauber (1967) ''Multicollinearity in Regression Analysis: The Problem Revisited,'' *Review of Economics and Statistics,* 49, 92–107.

Fomby, T. B. and S. R. Johnson (1977) ''MSE Evaluation of Ridge Estimators Based on Stochastic Prior Information,'' *Communications in Statistics, A,* 6, 1245–1258.

Fomby, T. B. and R. C. Hill (1978a) ''Multicollinearity and the Minimax Conditions for the Bock Stein-Like Estimator,'' *Econometrica,* 47, 211–212.

Fomby, T. B. and R. C. Hill (1978b) ''Multicollinearity and the Value of a Priori Information,'' *Communications in Statistics, A,* 8, 477–486.

Fomby, T. B., R. C. Hill, and S. R. Johnson (1978) ''An Optimality Property of Principal Components Regression,'' *Journal of the American Statistical Association,* 73, 191–193.

Fourgeaud, C., C. Gourieroux, and J. Pradel (1984) "Some Theoretical Results for Generalized Ridge Regression Estimator," *Journal of Econometrics,* forthcoming.

Friedmann, R. (1982) "Multicollinearity and Ridge Regression," *Allgemeines Statistisches Archiv,* 66, 120–128.

Gibbons, D. (1981) "A Simulation Study of Some Ridge Estimators," *Journal of the American Statistical Association,* 76, 131–139.

Goldstein, M. and A. F. M. Smith (1974) "Ridge Type Estimators for Regression Analysis," *Journal of the Royal Statistical Society B,* 36, 284–291.

Greenberg, E. (1975) "Minimum Variance Properties of Principal Components Regression," *Journal of the American Statistical Association,* 70, 194–197.

Hemmerle, W. J. (1975) "An Explicit Solution for Generalized Ridge Regression," *Technometrics,* 17, 309–314.

Hemmerle, W. J. and T. F. Brantle (1978) "Explicit and Constrained Generalized Ridge Regression," *Technometrics,* 20, 109–120.

Hill, R. C., and R. Ziemer (1983a) "Small Sample Performance of the Stein-Rule in Nonorthogonal Designs," *Economics Letters,* 10, 285–292.

Hill, R. C., and R. Ziemer (1984) "The Risk of Stein-Like Estimators in the Presence of Multicollinearity," *Journal of Econometrics,* forthcoming.

Hill, R. C., T. B. Fomby, and S. R. Johnson (1977) "Component Selection Norms for Principal Components Regression," *Communications in Statistics, A,* 6, 309–333.

Hocking, R. R., F. M. Speed, and M. J. Lynn (1976) "A Class of Biased Estimators in Linear Regression," *Technometrics,* 18, 425–437.

Hoerl, A. E. (1962) "Application of Ridge Analysis to Regression Problems," *Chemical Engineering Progress,* 58, 54–59.

Hoerl, A. E. (1964) "Ridge Analysis," Chemical Engineering Progress Symposium, Series 60, 67–77.

Hoerl, A. E. and R. W. Kennard (1970a) "Ridge Regression: Biased Estimation of Nonorthogonal Problems," *Technometrics,* 12, 55–67.

Hoerl, A. E. and R. W. Kennard (1970b) "Ridge Regression: Application to Nonorthogonal Problems," *Technometrics,* 12, 69–82.

Hoerl, A. E. and R. W. Kennard (1976) "Ridge Regression: Iterative Estimation of the Biasing Parameter," *Communications in Statistics, A,* 5, 77–88.

Hoerl, A. E. and R. W. Kennard (1979) "Ridge Regression-1979," unpublished mimeo.

Hoerl, A. E., R. W. Kennard, and K. F. Baldwin (1975) "Ridge Regression: Some Simulations," *Communications in Statistics, A,* 4, 105–123.

Johnson, S. R., S. C. Reimer, and T. P. Rothrock (1973) "Principal Components and the Problem of Multicollinearity," *Metroeconomica,* 25, 306–317.

Judge, G. G. and M. Bock (1983) "Biased Estimation," in *Handbook in Econometrics, Vol. I,* Z. Griliches and M. Intriligator, eds., North Holland, Amsterdam, 599–660.

Judge, G. G., R. Hill, W. Griffiths, H. Lütkepohl, and T. Lee (1982) *Introduction to the Theory and Practice of Econometrics,* Wiley, New York.

Judge, G. G. and M. E. Bock (1978) *The Statistical Implications of Pre-Test and Stein-Rule Estimators in Econometrics,* North-Holland, Amsterdam.

Judge, G. G., T. A. Yancey, and M. E. Bock (1973) "Properties of Estimators After Preliminary Tests of Significance When Stochastic Restrictions Are Used in Regression," *Journal of Econometrics,* 1, 29–48.

King, N. (1972) "An Alternative for the Linear Regression Equation When the Predictor Variable Is Uncontrolled and the Sample Size Is Small," *Journal of the American Statistical Association,* 67, 217–219.

King, N. (1974) "An Alternative for Multiple Regression When the Prediction Variable Are Uncontrolled and the Sample Size Is Not So Small," unpublished manuscript.

Kumar, T. K. (1975) "Multicollinearity in Regression Analysis," *Review of Economics and Statistics,* 57, 365–366.

Lawless, J. F. and P. Wang (1976) "A Simulation Study of Ridge and Other Regression Estimators," *Communications in Statistics, A,* 5, 307–323.

Lawley, D. N. (1965) "Tests of Significance for the Latent Roots of Covariance and Correlation Matrices," *Biometrika,* 43, 128–136.

Leamer, E. (1983) "Model Choice and Specification Analysis," in *Handbook of Econometrics, Vol. I,* Z. Griliches and M. Intriligator, eds., North Holland, Amsterdam, 285–331.

Leamer, E. (1978) *Specification Searches: Ad Hoc Inference with Nonexperimental Data,* Wiley, New York.

Lin, K. and J. Kmenta (1982) "Ridge Regression Under Alternative Loss Criteria," *Review of Economics and Statistics,* 64, 488–494.

Lindley, D. V. and A. F. M. Smith (1972) "Bayes Estimates for the Linear Model," *Journal of the Royal Statistical Society, B,* 34, 1–41.

Lott, W. F. (1973) "The Optimal Set of Principal Component Restrictions on a Least Squares Regression," *Communications in Statistics, A,* 2, 449–464.

Marquardt, D. W. (1970) "Generalized Inverses, Ridge Regression, Biased Linear Estimation, and Nonlinear Estimation," *Technometrics,* 12, 591–612.

Marquardt, D. W. and R. D. Snee (1975) "Ridge Regression in Practice," *American Statistician,* 29, 3–20.

Mason, R. L., R. F. Gunst, and J. T. Webster (1975) "Regression Analysis and Problems of Multicollinearity," *Communications in Statistics,* 4, 277–292.

Massey, W. F. (1965) "Principal Components Regression Exploratory Statistic Research," *Journal of the American Statistical Association,* 60, 234–256.

McCallum, B. T. (1979) "Artificial Orthogonalization in Regression Analysis," *Review of Economics and Statistics,* 52, 110–113.

McDonald, G. C. and D. I. Galarneau (1975) "A Monte Carlo Evaluation of Some Ridge-Type Estimators," *Journal of the American Statistical Association,* 70, 407–416.

Mittelhammer, R. (1984) "Risk Comparisons of Restricted Least Squares, Pretest, OLS and Stein Estimators Under Model Misspecification," *Journal of Econometrics,* forthcoming.

Obenchain, R. L. (1975) "Ridge Regression Following a Preliminary Test of a Shrunken Hypothesis," *Technometrics,* 17, 431–441.

O'Hagen, J. and B. McCabe (1975) "Tests for the Severity of Multicollinearity in Regression Analysis: A Comment," *Review of Economics and Statistics,* 57, 368–370.

Oman, S. (1982) "Contracting Towards Subspaces When Estimating the Mean of a Multivariate Normal Distribution," *Journal of Multivariate Analysis,* 12, 270–290.

Rao, C. R. (1973) *Linear Statistical Inference and Its Applications,* 2nd ed., Wiley, New York.

Schmidt, P. (1976) *Econometrics,* Dekker, New York.

Sclove, S. L., C. Morris, and R. Radhakrishnan (1972) "Nonoptimality of Preliminary Test Estimators for the Multinormal Mean, *Annals of Mathematical Statistics,* 42, 1481–1490.

Silvey, S. D. (1969) "Multicollinearity and Imprecise Estimation," *Journal of the Royal Statistical Society, Series B,* 35, 67–75.

Smith, G. (1974) "Multicollinearity and Forecasting," Cowles Foundation Discussion Paper No. 33.

Smith, G. and F. Campbell (1980) "A Critique of Some Ridge Regression Methods," *Journal of the American Statistical Association,* 75, 74–103.

Srivastava, V. and D. Giles (1982) "A Pre-Test General Ridge Regression Estimator: Exact Finite Sample Properties," Working paper No. 3/82, Department of Econometrics and Operations Research, Monash, University.

Stein, C. (1973) "Estimation of the Mean of a Multivariate Normal Distribution," Technical Report No. 48, Department of Statistics, Stanford University, Stanford, Calif.

Stein, C. (1981) "Estimation of the Mean of a Multivariate Normal Distribution," *Annals of Statistics,* 9, 1135–1151.

Stone, R. (1947) "On the Interpendence of Blocks of Transactions," Supplement to the *Journal of the Royal Statistical Society,* 9, 1–45.

Strawderman, W. E. (1978) "Minimax Adaptive Generalized Ridge Regression Estimators," *Journal of the American Statistical Association,* 73, 623–627.

Teekens, R. and P. M. C. de Boer (1977) "The Exact MSE-Efficiency of the General Ridge Estimator Relative to OLS," presented at the summer 1977 meeting of the Econometric Society.

Theil, H. (1963) "On the Use of Incomplete Prior Information in Regression Analysis," *Journal of the American Statistical Association,* 58, 401–414.

Theil, H. (1971) *Principles of Econometrics,* Wiley, New York.

Theobold, C. M. (1974) "Generalizations of Mean Square Error Applied to Ridge Regression," *Journal of the Royal Statistical Society, Series B,* 36, 103–106.

Thisted, R. (1977) Ridge Regression, Minimax Estimation, and Empirical Bayes Methods, unpublished Ph.D. dissertation, Stanford University, Stanford, Calif.

Thisted, R. (1978a) "Multicollinearity, Information and Ridge Regression," Technical Report No. 66, Department of Statistics, University of Chicago.

Thisted, R. (1978b) "On Generalized Ridge Regressions," Technical Report No. 57, Department of Statistics, University of Chicago.

Thisted, R. and C. Morris (1980) "Theoretical Results for Adaptive Ordinary Ridge Regression Estimators," Technical Report No. 94, Department of Statistics, University of Chicago.

Toro-Vizcarrondo, C. and T. D. Wallace (1968) "A Test of the Mean Square

Error Criterion for Restrictions in Linear Regression,'' *Journal of the American Statistical Association,* 63, 558–572.

Trenkler, G. (1984) ''Some Further Remarks on Multicollinearity and the Minimax Conditions of the Bock Stein-Like Estimator,'' *Econometrica,* forthcoming.

Trivedi, P. K. (1978) ''Estimation of a Distributed Lag Model Under Quadratic Loss,'' *Econometrica,* 46, 1181–1192.

Vinod, H. (1978) ''A Ridge Estimator Whose MSE Dominates OLS,'' *International Economic Review,* 19, 727–737.

Vinod, H., A. Ullah, and K. Kadiyala, (1979) ''Evaluation of the Mean Squared Error of Certain Generalized Ridge Estimators Using Confluent Hypergeometric Functions,'' Bell Laboratories Economic Discussion Paper 137, Murry Hill, N.J.

Vinod, H. D. (1976) ''Application of New Ridge Regression Methods to a Study of Bell System Scale Economies,'' *Journal of the American Statistical Association,* 71, 835–841.

Vinod, H. D. (1978) ''A Survey of Ridge Regression and Related Techniques for Improvements over Ordinary Least Squares,'' *Review of Economics and Statistics,* 60, 121–131.

Vinod, H. D. and A. Ullah (1981) *Recent Advances in Regression Methods,* Marcel Dekker, New York.

Wichern, D. and G. Churchill (1978) ''A Comparison of Ridge Estimators,'' *Technometrics,* 20, 301–311.

Wichers, C. (1975) ''The Detection of Multicollinearity: A Comment,'' *Review of Economics and Statistics,* 57, 366–368.

Willan, A. R. and D. G. Watts (1978) ''Meaningful Multicollinearity Measures,'' *Technometrics,* 20, 407–411.

Zellner, A. (1971) *An Introduction to Bayesian Inference in Econometrics,* Wiley, New York.

Appendix A

Some Matrix and Distribution Theorems

For reference purposes some of the matrix and distribution theorems used in derivations in this book and elsewhere are summarized in this Appendix. For a more complete treatment see linear algebra or linear statistical model books such as *Introduction to Matrices with Applications to Statistics* and *The Theory and Application of the Linear Model,* both by F. Graybill and *Linear Statistical Inference* by C. R. Rao.

A.1 MATRIX AND VECTOR DIFFERENTIATION

A.1.1

Let $c(B,\mathbf{x})$ be a differentiable, real-valued function of the $(T \times K)$ matrix B and the $(T \times 1)$ column vector $\mathbf{x}$ and $\mathbf{b}(\mathbf{x})$ a differentiable function of $\mathbf{x}$ with values in the K-dimensional Euclidean space. Then

1. $\partial c/\partial \mathbf{x}$ is a T-dimensional column vector with ith element $\partial c/\partial x_i$.
2. $\partial c/\partial B$ is a $(T \times K)$ matrix with ijth element $\partial c/\partial b_{ij}$.
3. $\partial \mathbf{b}/\partial \mathbf{x}'$ is a $(K \times T)$ matrix with ijth element $\partial b_i/\partial x_j$.

A.1.2

Let $\mathbf{a}$ and $\mathbf{x}$ be $(T \times 1)$ vectors; $\mathbf{y}$, a $(K \times 1)$ vector; A, a $(T \times T)$ matrix; and B, a $(T \times K)$ matrix. Then the above notation implies that

$$\frac{\partial \mathbf{a}'\mathbf{x}}{\partial \mathbf{x}} = \mathbf{a}, \quad \frac{\partial \mathbf{x}'A\mathbf{x}}{\partial \mathbf{x}} = (A + A')\mathbf{x}, \quad \frac{\partial^2(\mathbf{x}'A\mathbf{x})}{\partial \mathbf{x}\partial \mathbf{x}'} = A + A', \quad \frac{\partial(\mathbf{x}'B\mathbf{y})}{\partial B} = \mathbf{x}\mathbf{y}'.$$

Also

$$\frac{\partial \operatorname{tr} A}{\partial A} = I; \qquad \frac{\partial |A|}{\partial A} = \begin{cases} |A|(A')^{-1} & \text{provided that } A \text{ is nonsingular} \\ 0 & \text{if } A \text{ is singular} \end{cases}$$

and

$$\frac{\partial \log |A|}{\partial A} = (A')^{-1} \qquad \text{provided that } |A| > 0.$$

A.1.3

The kth-order Taylor expansion of $c(\mathbf{x})$ around a vector $\mathbf{x}^*$ is

$$c(\mathbf{x}) = c(\mathbf{x}^*) + \Sigma_i \left[\frac{\partial c}{\partial x_i}\bigg|_{\mathbf{x}^*} \right] (x_i - x_i^*) + \ldots$$

$$+ \frac{1}{(k-1)!} \Sigma_i \ldots \Sigma_j \left[\frac{\partial^{k-1} c}{\partial x_i \ldots \partial x_j}\bigg|_{\mathbf{x}^*} \right] (x_i - x_i^*) \ldots (x_j - x_j^*)$$

$$+ \frac{1}{k!} \Sigma_i \ldots \Sigma_j \Sigma_l \left[\frac{\partial^k c}{\partial x_i \ldots \partial x_j \, \partial x_l}\bigg|_{\bar{\mathbf{x}}} \right]$$

$$\cdot (x_i - x_i^*) \ldots (x_j - x_j^*)(x_l - x_l^*)$$

where $\bar{\mathbf{x}}$ is on the line segment between $\mathbf{x}$ and $\mathbf{x}^*$ and $c(\cdot)$ is assumed to be at least k times continuously differentiable.

A.2 MATRIX ALGEBRA RELEVANT TO NORMAL DISTRIBUTION THEORY

A.2.1

The characteristic roots of a $(T \times T)$ matrix A are the T roots of the polynomial in the scalar λ given by $|A - \lambda I| = 0$.

A.2.2

The two K-dimensional vectors $\mathbf{y}$ and $\mathbf{z}$ are said to be orthogonal if $\mathbf{y}'\mathbf{z} = 0$. If in addition $\mathbf{y}'\mathbf{y} = 1$ and $\mathbf{z}'\mathbf{z} = 1$, they are said to be orthonormal. For a $(T \times T)$ orthogonal matrix $C, C'C = CC' = I$, and, if C is orthogonal, then C' is orthogonal.

A.2.3

If C is orthogonal, then the determinant $|C|$ is either 1 or -1.

A.2.4

If A is a $(T \times T)$ symmetric matrix, then there exists a $(T \times T)$ matrix P that is orthogonal and $P'AP = D$, a diagonal matrix with diagonal elements that are the characteristic roots of A. The rank of A is equal to the number of nonzero roots.

A.2.5

A symmetric matrix A is called positive definite if $\mathbf{y}'A\mathbf{y} > 0$ for all $\mathbf{y} \neq \mathbf{0}$. A symmetric matrix A is positive definite if and only if all its characteristic roots are positive.

A.2.6

If A is a $(T \times T)$ positive definite matrix, then $|A| > 0$, the rank of A is equal to T, and A is nonsingular.

A.2.7

If A is a $(T \times T)$ positive definite matrix and B is a $(T \times K)$ matrix with rank K, then $B'AB$ is positive definite.

A.2.8

If A is a $(T \times T)$ positive definite matrix, then there exists a positive definite matrix $A^{-1/2}$ such that $A^{-1/2}AA^{-1/2} = I$ and $A^{-1/2}A^{-1/2} = A^{-1}$. Also we may write $A^{1/2} = (A^{-1/2})^{-1}$ and $A^{1/2}A^{1/2} = A$. In particular, if Q is an orthogonal matrix such that

$$A = Q \begin{bmatrix} \lambda_1 & & 0 \\ & \ddots & \\ 0 & & \lambda_T \end{bmatrix} Q'$$

where the λ_i are the characteristic roots of A, then

$$A^{1/2} = Q \begin{bmatrix} \lambda_1^{1/2} & & 0 \\ & \ddots & \\ 0 & & \lambda_T^{1/2} \end{bmatrix} Q'$$

A.2.9

If λ is a characteristic root of the $(T \times T)$ matrix A and $\mathbf{x}$ is a characteristic vector of A corresponding to the root λ, then λ^k is a characteristic root of A^k and $\mathbf{x}$ is a characteristic vector of A^k corresponding to the root λ^k (k is any positive integer).

A.2.10

If A is a $(T \times T)$ nonsingular matrix and λ is a characteristic root of A, then $1/\lambda$ is a characteristic root of A^{-1}, and the characteristic vectors of A and A^{-1} are the same.

A.2.11

Let A be a $(T \times T)$ symmetric idempotent matrix (i.e., $A = A'$ and $AA = A$) of rank J, then A has J characteristic roots equal to 1 and $(T - J)$ roots equal to zero. The rank of A is equal to tr A, and there is an orthogonal matrix C such that

$$C'AC = \begin{bmatrix} I_J & 0_{(J\times(T-J))} \\ 0 & 0_{(T-J)\times(T-J)} \end{bmatrix}$$

The identity matrix is the only nonsingular idempotent matrix, and a symmetric idempotent matrix is positive semidefinite.

A.2.12

If A and B are $(T \times T)$ symmetric matrices and B is positive definite, there exists a nonsingular matrix Q such that $Q'AQ = \Lambda$ and $Q'BQ = I$, where Λ is a diagonal matrix.

A.2.13

If A and B are two symmetric matrices, a necessary and sufficient condition for an orthogonal matrix C to exist such that $C'AC = \Lambda$ and $C'BC = M$, where Λ and M are diagonal, is that A and B commute, that is, $AB = BA$.

A.3 NORMAL DISTRIBUTION

A.3.1

If y is a normal random variable with mean δ and variance σ^2, that is, $N(\delta,\sigma^2)$, then $z = ay$ is a normal random variable with mean $a\delta$ and variance $a^2\sigma^2$, for $a \neq 0$. If $\mathbf{y}$ is a $(T \times 1)$ normally distributed random vector with mean vector $\boldsymbol{\delta}$ and covariance $\sigma^2 I_T$ and A is a $(K \times T)$ matrix of rank $K < T$, then $\mathbf{z} = A\mathbf{y}$, is a normal random vector with mean $A\boldsymbol{\delta}$ and covariance $\sigma^2 AA'$.

A.3.2

If y is $N(\delta,\sigma^2)$, then the random variable $(y - \delta)/\sigma$ is a standard normal random variable, that is, $N(0,1)$.

A.3.3

If $y_1, y_2, \ldots, y_T$ are independent normal random variables, then $\Sigma_t y_t$ is normally distributed.

A.3.4

If y is $N(\delta,\sigma^2)$ and $(y_1, y_2, \ldots, y_T)$ is a random sample of y, then $\Sigma_t y_t/T$ is $N(\delta,\sigma^2/T)$.

A.3.5

If y is any random variable with mean δ and variance σ^2, then, when T is large, $\Sigma_t y_t/T$ has approximately the distribution $N(\delta,\sigma^2/T)$.

A.4 CHI-SQUARE, *t*, AND *F* DISTRIBUTIONS

A.4.1

If y is a standard normal random variable $N(0,1)$, then y^2 is distributed as a chi-square random variable with 1 degree of freedom, that is, $\chi^2_{(1)}$.

A.4.2

If y is $N(0,1)$ and $y_1, y_2, \ldots, y_T$ is a random sample of independent and identically distributed, standard normal random variables, then the quadratic form $\Sigma_t y_t^2$ is distributed as a chi-square random variable with T degrees of freedom, that is, $\chi^2_{(T)}$.

A.4.3

If y is $N(\delta,\sigma^2)$ and $y_1, y_2, \ldots, y_T$ is a random sample of T independent normally distributed random variables, then $\Sigma_t(y_t - \delta)^2/\sigma^2$ is distributed as a $\chi^2_{(T)}$ random variable.

A.4.4

If $\mathbf{y}$ is a $(T \times 1)$ normal random vector $N(\mathbf{0},I_T)$, then the quadratic form $\mathbf{y}'\mathbf{y}$ is distributed as a $\chi^2_{(T)}$ random variable.

A.4.5

If $\mathbf{y}$ is a $(T \times 1)$ random vector distributed as $N(\mathbf{0},I_T)$ and A is a $(T \times T)$ symmetric idempotent matrix of rank J, then $\mathbf{y}'A\mathbf{y}$ is distributed as a $\chi^2_{(J)}$ random variable.

A.4.6

If $\mathbf{y}$ is a $(T \times 1)$ random vector that is distributed as $N(\boldsymbol{\delta},\sigma^2 I_T)$, A is a $(T \times T)$ symmetric idempotent matrix, B is a $(K \times T)$ matrix, and $AB' = 0$, then $B\mathbf{y}$ is distributed independently of the quadratic form $\mathbf{y}'A\mathbf{y}$.

A.4.7

If $\mathbf{y}$ is a $(T \times 1)$ random vector that is distributed as $N(\mathbf{0},\sigma^2 I_T)$, A and B are symmetric idempotent $(T \times T)$ matrices of rank J and K, and $AB = 0$, then $\mathbf{y}'A\mathbf{y}$ is distributed independently of the quadratic form $\mathbf{y}'B\mathbf{y}$.

A.4.8

If $\mathbf{y}$ is a $(T \times 1)$ random vector distributed as $N(\mathbf{0},\sigma^2 I_T)$ and A and B are as defined above, then u, the ratio of $\mathbf{y}'A\mathbf{y}/\sigma^2$ and $\mathbf{y}'B\mathbf{y}/\sigma^2$ each divided by its rank, that is,

$$u = \frac{\mathbf{y}'A\mathbf{y}}{J\sigma^2} \bigg/ \frac{\mathbf{y}'B\mathbf{y}}{K\sigma^2}$$

is distributed as an $F_{(J,K)}$ random variable.

A.4.9

If u is $F_{(T,K)}$, then $z = 1/u$ is distributed as an $F_{(K,T)}$ random variable.

A.4.10

If the $(T \times 1)$ vector $\mathbf{y}$ is distributed as $N(\boldsymbol{\delta},A)$, then $\mathbf{y}'A^{-1}\mathbf{y}$ is distributed as a noncentral $\chi^2_{(T,\lambda)}$ with noncentrality parameter $\lambda = \boldsymbol{\delta}'A^{-1}\boldsymbol{\delta}/2$.

A.4.11

If the random vectors $\mathbf{y}$ and $\mathbf{z}$ are distributed $N(\boldsymbol{\delta},\sigma^2 I_T)$ and $N(\mathbf{0},\sigma^2 I_T)$, respectively, and A and B are symmetric idempotent matrices of rank K and J, respectively, where $BA = 0$, then the ratio $[(\mathbf{y}'A\mathbf{y}/\sigma^2)/(\mathbf{z}'B\mathbf{z}/\sigma^2)](J/K) = u$ is distributed as a noncentral $F_{(K,J,\lambda)}$ random variable with $\lambda = \boldsymbol{\delta}'A\boldsymbol{\delta}/2\sigma^2$.

A.4.12

If the $(K \times 1)$ random vector $\mathbf{b}$ is distributed as $N(\boldsymbol{\beta},\sigma^2 C)$, the random element b_i is distributed as $N(\beta_i,\sigma^2 c_{ii})$, where c_{ii} is the ith diagonal element of C. The random variable $(b_i - \beta_i)/\sigma\sqrt{c_{ii}}$ is distributed as $N(0,1)$. Also suppose the quadratic form $\mathbf{y}'A\mathbf{y}/\sigma^2$ for the $(T \times 1)$ random vector $\mathbf{y}$, where A is a symmetric idempotent matrix of rank q, is distributed as $\chi^2_{(q)}$. Let $\mathbf{y}'A\mathbf{y}/q = \hat{\sigma}^2$, then

$[(b_i - \beta_i)/\sigma\sqrt{c_{ii}}]/\sqrt{(\mathbf{y}'A\mathbf{y}/\sigma^2)/q} = (b_i - \beta_i)/\hat{\sigma}\sqrt{c_{ii}} = v$ is distributed as a t random variable with q degrees of freedom.

A.4.13

If the $(K \times 1)$ random vector $\mathbf{b}$ is distributed as $N(\boldsymbol{\beta},\sigma^2(X'X)^{-1})$, where X is $(T \times K)$ and $K < T$, then $(\mathbf{b} - \boldsymbol{\beta})$ is distributed as $N(\mathbf{0},\sigma^2(X'X)^{-1})$ and the quadratic expression $(\mathbf{b} - \boldsymbol{\beta})'(X'X)(\mathbf{b} - \boldsymbol{\beta})/\sigma^2$ is distributed as $\chi^2_{(K)}$.

A.4.14

If the $(K \times 1)$ vector $\mathbf{b}$ is distributed as $N(\boldsymbol{\beta},\sigma^2(X'X)^{-1})$, where X is $(T \times K)$ and $K < T$, then

1. $R\mathbf{b}$ is distributed as $N(R\boldsymbol{\beta},\sigma^2R(X'X)^{-1}R')$, where R is $(J \times K)$ and of rank $J \leq K$.
2. $(R\mathbf{b} - R\boldsymbol{\beta})$ is distributed as $N(\mathbf{0},\sigma^2R(X'X)^{-1}R')$.
3. The quadratic expression $(R\mathbf{b} - R\boldsymbol{\beta})'[R(X'X)^{-1}R']^{-1}(R\mathbf{b} - R\boldsymbol{\beta})/\sigma^2$ is distributed as $\chi^2_{(J)}$.

A.4.15

If the $(n \times 1)$ random vector $\mathbf{y}$ is $N(\mathbf{0},\sigma^2I_n)$ the expected value of the quadratic form $\mathbf{y}'A\mathbf{y}/\sigma^2$ is equal to tr A. Therefore, if A is an $(n \times n)$ symmetric idempotent matrix of rank r, then $E(\mathbf{y}'A\mathbf{y})/\sigma^2 = r$.

A.4.16

The reciprocal of the central χ^2 random variable with r degrees of freedom has expected value $E[(\chi^2_{(r)})^{-1}] = 1/(r - 2)$, for $r \geq 3$.

A.4.17

The central χ^2 random variable with r degrees of freedom has variance $2r$.

A.4.18

The square of the reciprocal of a central χ^2 random variable with r degrees of freedom has expected value $E[(\chi^2_{(r)})^{-2}] = 1/[(r - 2)(r - 4)]$, for $r \geq 5$.

A.4.19

Any non-central χ^2 random variable with r degrees of freedom and non-centrality parameter λ, may be represented as a central χ^2 random variable with $(r + 2j)$ degrees of freedom (conditional on j), where j is a Poisson random variable with parameter λ.

A.4.20

Let $\chi^2_{(k,\lambda)}$ have a noncentral chi-square distribution with noncentrality parameter λ. If k is an even integer greater than two, then

$$E[(\chi^2_{(k,\lambda)})^{-1}] = \frac{1}{2}\left(\frac{k}{2} - 2\right)!\left(\frac{-2}{\lambda}\right)^{k/2-1}\left[e^{-\lambda/2} - \sum_{l=0}^{k/2-2}\frac{(-\lambda/2)^l}{l!}\right]$$

If k is an odd integer greater than two, then

$$E[(\chi^2_{(k,\lambda)})^{-1}] = \frac{1}{2}\left(\frac{\Gamma[(k-2)/2]}{\Gamma(\frac{1}{2})}\right)\left(-\frac{2}{\lambda}\right)^{((k-1)/2)-1}\left[2\left(\frac{\lambda}{2}\right)^{-1/2}\mathcal{D}\left(\left(\frac{\lambda}{2}\right)^{-1/2}\right)\right.$$
$$\left. - \underset{[5,\infty)}{I(k)}\sum_{n=0}^{((k-1)/2)-2}\left(-\frac{\lambda}{2}\right)^n\frac{\Gamma(n+1+\frac{1}{2})}{\Gamma(\frac{1}{2})}\right]$$

where $\mathcal{D}(y) = e^{-y^2}\int_0^y e^{t^2}\,dt$ is Dawson's integral. For large y, $\mathcal{D}(y)$ is approximately $\frac{1}{2}y^{-1}$. For $k = 4$, $E[(\chi^2_{(4,\lambda)})^{-1}] = \lambda^{-1}[1 - e^{-(\lambda/2)}]$. For $k = 6$, $E[(\chi^2_{(6,\lambda)})^{-1}] = 2\lambda^{-2}(e^{-\lambda/2} - 1 + \lambda/2)$. If $k = 3$,

$$E[(\chi^2_{(3,\lambda)})^{-1}] = \left(\frac{\lambda}{2}\right)^{1/2}\mathcal{D}\left(\left(\frac{\lambda}{2}\right)^{1/2}\right)$$

For "A Simple Form for the Inverse Moments of Non-Central χ^2 and F Random Variables and for Certain Confluent Hypergeometric Functions," see Bock, Judge and Yancey (1984), *Journal of Econometrics*.

A.5 KRONECKER PRODUCT AND PARTITIONED AND GENERALIZED INVERSES

A.5.1

If A is an $(M \times N)$ matrix with elements a_{ij} and B is a matrix of dimension $(K \times L)$, then the Kronecker product of A and B is an $(MK \times NL)$ matrix given by

$$A \otimes B = \begin{bmatrix} a_{11}B & a_{12}B & \cdots & a_{1N}B \\ a_{21}B & a_{22}B & \cdots & a_{2N}B \\ \vdots & \vdots & \vdots & \vdots \\ a_{M1}B & a_{M2}B & \cdots & a_{MN}B \end{bmatrix}$$

The following results hold

1. $(A \otimes B)(C \otimes D) = AC \otimes BD$.
2. $(A \otimes B)^{-1} = A^{-1} \otimes B^{-1}$.

3. $(A \otimes B)' = A' \otimes B'$.
4. $A \otimes (B + C) = A \otimes B + A \otimes C$.

A.5.2

Consider the following partitioned matrix

$$A = \begin{bmatrix} A_{11} & A_{12} \\ A_{21} & A_{22} \end{bmatrix}$$

where A_{11} and A_{22} are square matrices. The partitioned inverse of A

$$A^{-1} = \begin{bmatrix} A_{11} & A_{12} \\ A_{21} & A_{22} \end{bmatrix}^{-1}$$

$$= \begin{bmatrix} (A_{11} - A_{12}A_{22}^{-1}A_{21})^{-1} & -(A_{11} - A_{12}A_{22}^{-1}A_{21})^{-1}A_{12}A_{22}^{-1} \\ -A_{22}^{-1}A_{21}(A_{11} - A_{12}A_{22}^{-1}A_{21})^{-1} & A_{22}^{-1} + A_{22}^{-1}A_{21}(A_{11} - A_{12}A_{22}^{-1}A_{21})^{-1}A_{12}A_{22}^{-1} \end{bmatrix}$$

provided A_{22} and $(A_{11} - A_{12}A_{22}^{-1}A_{21})$ are nonsingular.

A.5.3

Let A, B, C, D be $(M \times M)$, $(M \times N)$, $(N \times M)$, and $(N \times N)$ matrices, respectively, and A and D are nonsingular. Then $[A + BDC]^{-1} = A^{-1} - A^{-1}B\,(CA^{-1}B + D^{-1})^{-1}\,CA^{-1}$, if the matrix $A + BDC$ is nonsingular.

A.5.4

For any matrix A, there exists a unique matrix A^+ that satisfies the following four conditions:

1. $AA^+A = A$
2. $A^+AA^+ = A^+$
3. $(A^+A)' = A^+A$
4. $(AA^+)' = AA^+$

The matrix A^+ is called the (Penrose–Moore) generalized inverse of A.

A.5.5

If we define a matrix G, called g-inverse, of A as the one that satisfies (1) of A.5.4, that is, $AGA = A$, then the g-inverse may not be unique unless (2), (3), and (4) of A.5.4 are also satisfied. Thus A^+ is a special case of G.

A.5.6

If G is a g-inverse of $X'X$, as defined in A.5.5, then the following statements hold:

1. G' is also a g-inverse of $X'X$;
2. $XGX'X = X$; that is, GX' is a g-inverse of X;
3. XGX' is invariant to G; that is, if F is also a g-inverse of $X'X$, then $XGX' = XFX'$;
4. XGX' is symmetric, whether or not G is symmetric.

A.5.7

If A is a $(T \times T)$ matrix with rank $G \leq T$, and K is the $(T \times G)$ orthonormal matrix such that $K'AK = I_G$, then $A^+ = KK'$.

A.5.8

If $A = BC$, where A, B, C are, respectively, $(M \times N)$, $(M \times G)$, and $(G \times N)$, and all three matrices are of rank G, then $A^+ = C'(CC')^{-1}(B'B)^{-1}B'$.

A.5.9

The generalized inverse as defined in A.5.4 has the following properties:

1. If A is $(M \times N)$, then A^+ is $(N \times M)$.
2. $\text{Rank}(A^+) = \text{Rank}(A)$
3. If A is symmetric, then A^+ is also symmetric.
4. $(A^+)' = (A')^+$
5. $(A^+)^+ = A$
6. $(cA)^+ = (1/c)A^+$, where c is a scalar constant.
7. $(AB)^+ \neq B^+A^+$ in general.
8. If A is $(M \times G)$, B is $(G \times N)$ and both matrices are of rank G, then $(AB)^+ = B^+A^+$.
9. If A is a square nonsingular matrix, then $A^+ = A^{-1}$.

A.6 THE LAG OPERATOR

A.6.1

Define $Ly_t = y_{t-1}$, then:

1. $L(ay_t + z_t) = aLy_t + Lz_t = ay_{t-1} + z_{t-1}$.
2. $L^k y_t = L^{k-1}Ly_t = L^{k-1}y_{t-1} = \ldots = y_{t-k}$.
3. $L^kL^q = L^{k+q}$.
4. $L^0 y_t = y_t$.

5. $La = a$.
6. $L^{-1}L = LL^{-1} = 1$.

A.6.2

Define $\theta_q(L)$ as a polynomial of degree q in the lag operator—that is, $\theta_q(L) = 1 + \theta_1 L + \theta_2 L^2 + \ldots + \theta_q L^q$ and similarly for $\phi_p(L)$ and $B_r(L)$. Then:

1. $\theta_q(L) + \phi_p(L) = B_r(L)$, where $r \leq \max(q,p)$.
2. $\theta_q(L) \cdot \phi_p(L) = B_r(L)$, where $r = q + p$.
3. $\theta_q^{-1}(L) = B_\infty(L)$ and, for convergence, the roots of $\theta_q(z) = 0$ must be greater than one in absolute value.

A.7 VECTORIZATION OF MATRICES

A.7.1

Define $\text{vec}(A) = (\mathbf{a}_1' \, \mathbf{a}_2' \ldots \mathbf{a}_n')'$ to be an $(mn \times 1)$ column vector, where A has n columns $\mathbf{a}_1, \mathbf{a}_2, \ldots, \mathbf{a}_n$, each with m elements; that is, A is $(m \times n)$.

A.7.2

If A and B are $(m \times n)$ matrices. Then $\text{vec}(A + B) = \text{vec}(A) + \text{vec}(B)$.

A.7.3

Let A be $(m \times n)$, B be $(n \times p)$, and C be $(p \times q)$.

1. $\text{vec}(ABC) = (C' \otimes A)\,\text{vec}(B)$.
2. $\text{vec}(AB) = (I_p \otimes A)\,\text{vec}(B)$
   $= (B' \otimes I_m)\,\text{vec}(A)$.
3. $\text{vec}(ABC) = (I_q \otimes AB)\,\text{vec}(C)$
   $= (C'B' \otimes I_n)\,\text{vec}(A)$.

A.7.4

If A and B are $(m \times n)$ and $(n \times m)$, respectively, then $\text{vec}(B')'\,\text{vec}(A) = \text{tr}(AB) = \text{vec}(A')'\,\text{vec}(B)$.

A.7.5

If A is $(m \times n)$, B is $(n \times p)$, and C is $(p \times m)$, then

$$\begin{aligned}\text{tr}(ABC) &= \text{vec}(A')'(C' \otimes I_n)\,\text{vec}(B)\\ &= \text{vec}(A')'(I_m \otimes B)\,\text{vec}(C)\end{aligned}$$

$$= \text{vec}(B')'(A \otimes I_p)\,\text{vec}(C)$$
$$= \text{vec}(B')'(I_n \otimes C)\,\text{vec}(A)$$
$$= \text{vec}(C')'(B' \otimes I_m)\,\text{vec}(A)$$
$$= \text{vec}(C')'(I_p \otimes A)\,\text{vec}(B).$$

A.8 DETERMINANTS

A.8.1

If D is a nonsingular diagonal matrix of order K and $\boldsymbol{\beta}$ is a $(K \times 1)$ column vector, then $\det(D + \boldsymbol{\beta}\boldsymbol{\beta}') = \det D(1 + \boldsymbol{\beta}'D^{-1}\boldsymbol{\beta})$.

A.8.2

If A, D are nonsingular matrices of orders m, n and B, C are $(m \times n)$ and $(n \times m)$ matrices, respectively, then $\det A \det(D + CA^{-1}B) = \det D \det(A + BD^{-1}C)$.

A.8.3

If $\mathbf{u}$ and $\mathbf{v}$ are $(m \times 1)$ column vectors, then $\det(I_m + \mathbf{u}\mathbf{v}') = 1 + \mathbf{u}'\mathbf{v}$.

Appendix B

Numerical Optimization Methods

B.1 INTRODUCTION

Estimating the parameters of a statistical model usually requires optimizing some kind of objective function. For instance, least squares estimates are obtained by minimizing a sum of squares, and maximum likelihood estimation is done by maximizing the likelihood function. In many situations it is not possible to give a closed form expression for the estimates as a function of the sample values. This occurs, for example, when the statistical model is nonlinear in the parameters, as in Chapter 6, or, more generally, when the likelihood function or sum of squares cannot be transformed so that the normal equations are linear.

In the following discussion we will assume that an objective function $H(\boldsymbol{\theta})$ is given that is to be *minimized* with respect to the $(K \times 1)$ parameter vector $\boldsymbol{\theta}$. This vector may of course contain variance-covariance parameters. The objective function is assumed to be sufficiently often differentiable so that all required derivatives exist. Note that *maximization* problems can be solved in this framework by simply minimizing the negative of the original objective function. In Section B.2 we will present some unconstrained optimization algorithms and in Section B.3 constrained minimization is discussed. Throughout we will give references for further details on the considered topics. For general reading and many more references the reader is referred to Bard (1974), Himmelblau (1972a), Künzi and Oettli (1969), Lootsma (1972a), Murray (1972a), Fletcher (1969), Fiacco and McCormick (1968), Powell (1982a), and Quandt (1983).

Computer software is available for the methods outlined in the following discussion. Some programs are listed in Bard (1974, Appendix G), and FORTRAN programs can be found in Himmelblau (1972a, Appendix B). For a discussion of FORTRAN subroutines and ALGOL 60 procedures, see Fletcher (1972b). Also, many computer packages contain easily used algorithms. For a general discussion of the available computer software see Powell (1982a, Part 6). In many programs slight modifications of the methods described here are used.

B.2 UNCONSTRAINED OPTIMIZATION

Most of the minimization methods discussed in the following are *iterative* and follow the general scheme depicted in Figure B.1. In this approach we try to

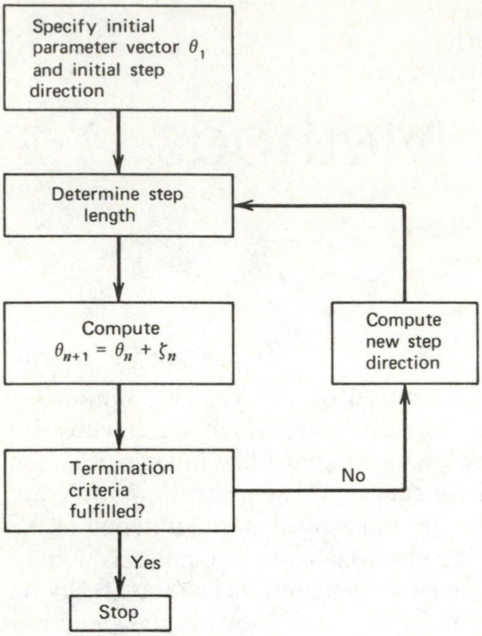

Figure B.1 Flow diagram for iterative optimization methods.

find a sequence $\boldsymbol{\theta}_1, \boldsymbol{\theta}_2, \ldots, \boldsymbol{\theta}_N$ of vectors in the parameter space such that $\boldsymbol{\theta}_N$ minimizes $H(\boldsymbol{\theta})$ approximately. Starting with some *initial vector* $\boldsymbol{\theta}_1$, each of the following elements in the sequence is based on the preceding one in that we add a vector $\boldsymbol{\zeta}_n$, called a *step*, to $\boldsymbol{\theta}_n$ in order to determine $\boldsymbol{\theta}_{n+1}$. Thus

$$\boldsymbol{\theta}_{n+1} = \boldsymbol{\theta}_n + \boldsymbol{\zeta}_n \tag{B.2.1}$$

Although this might not be the shortest way to the minimum of $H(\boldsymbol{\theta})$, we usually require $H(\boldsymbol{\theta}_n) > H(\boldsymbol{\theta}_{n+1})$. A step that meets this condition is called *acceptable*.

Ideally, the procedure should terminate when no further reduction of the objective function can be obtained. For practical purposes the iteration stops, for example, if for a prespecified small $\varepsilon > 0$:

1. $(\boldsymbol{\theta}_{n+\ell} - \boldsymbol{\theta}_n)'(\boldsymbol{\theta}_{n+\ell} - \boldsymbol{\theta}_n) < \varepsilon$.
2. $H(\boldsymbol{\theta}_n) - H(\boldsymbol{\theta}_{n+\ell}) < \varepsilon$ for a positive integer ℓ.
3. $\left[\left.\dfrac{\partial H}{\partial \boldsymbol{\theta}}\right|_{\boldsymbol{\theta}_n}\right]'\left[\left.\dfrac{\partial H}{\partial \boldsymbol{\theta}}\right|_{\boldsymbol{\theta}_n}\right] < \varepsilon$.
4. A prespecified upper bound for the number of iterations is attained.
5. A prespecified upper limit for the computation time is reached.

Usually, we do not wish to rely on a single one of these criteria, since (1) does not guarantee a termination if, for example, the minimum is not unique and (2) and (3) may never occur if no minimum exists or the algorithm used does not approach the existing minimum for some reason. Conditions (4) and (5) are useful to stop a search in a region of the parameter space far away from a minimum. Different starting values may be tried to locate the minimum in a reasonable number of iterations. Let us now turn to a discussion of some of the possibilities in choosing a step.

B.2.1 Gradient Methods

Given a point $\boldsymbol{\theta}_n$ in the parameter space, we seek a direction $\boldsymbol{\delta}$ in which to go downhill—that is, a direction in which the objective function declines. However, we have to be careful not to step too far in this direction, since this may carry us beyond the trough and uphill again. On the other hand, too short a step will be inefficient. In other words, we have to choose an appropriate *step length* t and a *step direction* $\boldsymbol{\delta}$ such that

$$H(\boldsymbol{\theta}_n + t\boldsymbol{\delta}) < H(\boldsymbol{\theta}_n) \qquad \text{(B.2.2)}$$

If $\boldsymbol{\delta}$ is a downhill direction, a small step in that direction will always decrease the objective function. Thus we are looking for $\boldsymbol{\delta}$ such that $H(\boldsymbol{\theta}_n + t\boldsymbol{\delta})$ is a decreasing function of t for t sufficiently close to zero. Consequently, for our $\boldsymbol{\delta}$,

$$\left.\frac{d[H(\boldsymbol{\theta}_n + t\boldsymbol{\delta})]}{dt}\right|_{t=0} = \left[\left.\frac{\partial H}{\partial \boldsymbol{\theta}}\right|_{\boldsymbol{\theta}_n}\right]' \left[\left.\frac{d(\boldsymbol{\theta}_n + t\boldsymbol{\delta})}{dt}\right|_{t=0}\right] = \left[\left.\frac{\partial H}{\partial \boldsymbol{\theta}}\right|_{\boldsymbol{\theta}_n}\right]' \boldsymbol{\delta} \qquad \text{(B.2.3)}$$

has to be less than zero. Abbreviating the *gradient* of the objective function

$$\left.\frac{\partial H}{\partial \boldsymbol{\theta}}\right|_{\boldsymbol{\theta}_n}$$

by $\boldsymbol{\gamma}_n$, it is clear that we can choose

$$\boldsymbol{\delta} = -P_n \boldsymbol{\gamma}_n \qquad \text{(B.2.4)}$$

where P_n is any positive definite matrix, that is, $\boldsymbol{\gamma}' P_n \boldsymbol{\gamma} > 0$ for all vectors $\boldsymbol{\gamma} \neq \mathbf{0}$ and, therefore, $\boldsymbol{\gamma}_n' \boldsymbol{\delta} = -\boldsymbol{\gamma}_n' P_n \boldsymbol{\gamma}_n < 0$ if $\boldsymbol{\gamma}_n \neq \mathbf{0}$. For $\boldsymbol{\gamma}_n = \mathbf{0}$, we can hope that we have reached the trough. As the general form of an iteration we get from (B.2.1)

$$\boldsymbol{\theta}_{n+1} = \boldsymbol{\theta}_n - t_n P_n \boldsymbol{\gamma}_n \qquad \text{(B.2.5)}$$

where t_n is the step length in the nth iteration.

Clearly, there are many downhill directions in these mountains, at least as many as there are positive definite matrices. Since our limited horizon in most cases does not allow an a priori optimal choice, many different ways to the trough are proposed in the literature. In some algorithms the step length is determined simultaneously with the direction, whereas other methods specify the direction only and allow various possibilities for the step length selection. These can range from using the first trial of t that fulfills (B.2.2) to an optimization of the step length in the given direction. For a description of some possible procedures, see Flanagan, Vitale, and Mendelsohn (1969). Determination of the optimal step length in each iteration is likely to decrease the number of steps to the trough but increases the computational cost for each iteration. Bard (1970) and Flanagan, Vitale, and Mendelsohn (1969) found that for their test problems it did not pay to use the most expensive procedures for the step length selection and according to Dennis (1973, p. 161) efforts to improve the gradient methods focus on modifications of the direction rather than the step length.

Usually, the gradient methods are differentiated by the step direction, or since almost all use the basic formula (B.2.5), by the *direction matrix* P_n. In the following section we will discuss possible choices, some of which are summarized in Table B.1.

TABLE B.1 ***SOME GRADIENT METHODS***

Method	Direction Matrix in the nth Iteration P_n	Section
Steepest descent	I_K	B.2.2
Newton–Raphson	$\left[\left.\frac{\partial^2 H}{\partial \boldsymbol{\theta}\, \partial \boldsymbol{\theta}'}\right\|_{\boldsymbol{\theta}_n}\right]^{-1}$	B.2.3
Rank one correction	$P_{n-1} + \frac{\boldsymbol{\eta}_{n-1}\boldsymbol{\eta}_{n-1}'}{\boldsymbol{\eta}_{n-1}'(\boldsymbol{\gamma}_n - \boldsymbol{\gamma}_{n-1})}$	B.2.4
Davidon–Fletcher–Powell	$P_{n-1} + \frac{\boldsymbol{\zeta}_{n-1}\boldsymbol{\zeta}_{n-1}'}{\boldsymbol{\zeta}_{n-1}'(\boldsymbol{\gamma}_n - \boldsymbol{\gamma}_{n-1})} - \frac{P_{n-1}(\boldsymbol{\gamma}_n - \boldsymbol{\gamma}_{n-1})(\boldsymbol{\gamma}_n - \boldsymbol{\gamma}_{n-1})'P_{n-1}}{(\boldsymbol{\gamma}_n - \boldsymbol{\gamma}_{n-1})'P_{n-1}(\boldsymbol{\gamma}_n - \boldsymbol{\gamma}_{n-1})}$	B.2.4
Gauss	$[Z(\boldsymbol{\theta}_n)'Z(\boldsymbol{\theta}_n)]^{-1}$	B.2.5
Method of scoring	$-\left[E\left.\frac{\partial^2 \ln \ell}{\partial \boldsymbol{\theta}\, \partial \boldsymbol{\theta}'}\right\|_{\boldsymbol{\theta}_n}\right]^{-1}$	B.2.5
Brown–Dennis	$\left[Z(\boldsymbol{\theta}_n)'Z(\boldsymbol{\theta}_n) - \sum_{t,t'=1}^{T} [y_t - f_t(\boldsymbol{\theta}_n)]F_{t',n}\right]^{-1}$	B.2.6
Marquardt	$[Z(\boldsymbol{\theta}_n)'Z(\boldsymbol{\theta}_n) + \lambda_n I_K]^{-1}$	B.2.7
Quadratic hill climbing	$\left[\left.\frac{\partial^2 H}{\partial \boldsymbol{\theta}\, \partial \boldsymbol{\theta}'}\right\|_{\boldsymbol{\theta}_n} + \lambda_n I_K\right]^{-1}$	B.2.7

B.2.2 Method of Steepest Descent

It can be shown that the initially steepest descent is obtained if we choose

$$P_n = I_K \tag{B.2.6}$$

in all iterations, where K is the dimension of the parameter space as before. Although this method is very simple, its use cannot be recommended in most cases, since it may converge very slowly if the minimum is in a long and narrow valley, that is, if the objective function is ill-conditioned. It is clear that using the same direction matrix P_n in each iteration does not allow a flexible adjustment to different shapes of the objective function surface. However, the steepest descent method can be valuable if it is combined with other algorithms as discussed in Section B.2.7.

B.2.3 Newton–Raphson Method

The Newton–Raphson or simply Newton algorithm uses the inverse of the Hessian matrix to specify the step direction in each iteration; that is,

$$P_n = \left[\frac{\partial^2 H}{\partial \boldsymbol{\theta}\, \partial \boldsymbol{\theta}'}\bigg|_{\boldsymbol{\theta}_n} \right]^{-1} \tag{B.2.7}$$

In the sequel the Hessian of $H(\boldsymbol{\theta})$ in $\boldsymbol{\theta}_n$ will be denoted by $\mathcal{H}_n$. To see why this direction matrix is chosen, we approximate $H(\boldsymbol{\theta})$ at $\boldsymbol{\theta}_n$ by its Taylor series expansion up to the quadratic terms:

$$H(\boldsymbol{\theta}) \simeq H(\boldsymbol{\theta}_n) + \boldsymbol{\gamma}_n'(\boldsymbol{\theta} - \boldsymbol{\theta}_n) + \tfrac{1}{2}(\boldsymbol{\theta} - \boldsymbol{\theta}_n)'\mathcal{H}_n(\boldsymbol{\theta} - \boldsymbol{\theta}_n) \tag{B.2.8}$$

First-order conditions for a minimum of the right-hand side are

$$\boldsymbol{\gamma}_n + \mathcal{H}_n(\boldsymbol{\theta} - \boldsymbol{\theta}_n) = \mathbf{0} \tag{B.2.9}$$

or

$$\boldsymbol{\theta} = \boldsymbol{\theta}_n - \mathcal{H}_n^{-1}\boldsymbol{\gamma}_n \tag{B.2.10}$$

Hence, if $H(\boldsymbol{\theta})$ is quadratic, that is, we have an exact equality in (B.2.8), we reach the minimum in one step of length one. In general, however, the Hessian may not be positive definite outside a small neighborhood of the minimum, and thus iterations of the form (B.2.10) may carry us to a maximum or saddle point. Consequently, a step (B.2.10) may not be acceptable. Other disadvantages are that first and second partial derivatives have to be determined analytically, which places a heavy burden on the user of this algorithm. Whereas the analytic determination of the ingredients of the gradient is acceptable in most cases, analytic computation of higher-order partial derivatives is considered to be at least a possible error source. The gradient methods described in the following subsections can be viewed as efforts to overcome the disadvantage that analytic determination of second-order partial derivatives is necessary, without giving up the advantage of fast local convergence.

To illustrate the Newton algorithm we use an example that is discussed in more detail in Judge et al. (1982, Chapter 24). We consider the nonlinear statistical model

$$y_t = \theta_1^* + \theta_2^* x_{t2} + \theta_2^{*2} x_{t3} + e_t, \qquad t = 1, \ldots, 20 \tag{B.2.11}$$

$$\mathbf{y} = \mathbf{f}(\boldsymbol{\theta}^*) + \mathbf{e} \tag{B.2.12}$$

where $\mathbf{y} = (y_1, y_2, \ldots, y_{20})'$, $\boldsymbol{\theta}^* = (\theta_1^*, \theta_2^*)'$ is the true parameter vector, $\mathbf{e} = (e_1, e_2, \ldots, e_{20})'$ and

$$\mathbf{f}(\boldsymbol{\theta}) = \begin{bmatrix} \theta_1 + \theta_2 x_{12} + \theta_2^2 x_{13} \\ \theta_1 + \theta_2 x_{22} + \theta_2^2 x_{23} \\ \vdots \\ \theta_1 + \theta_2 x_{20,2} + \theta_2^2 x_{20,3} \end{bmatrix}$$

TABLE B.2 ***DATA FOR EXAMPLE MODEL***

t	y_t	x_{t1}	x_{t2}	x_{t3}
1	4.284	1.000	0.286	0.645
2	4.149	1.000	0.973	0.585
3	3.877	1.000	0.384	0.310
4	0.533	1.000	0.276	0.058
5	2.211	1.000	0.973	0.455
6	2.389	1.000	0.543	0.779
7	2.145	1.000	0.957	0.259
8	3.231	1.000	0.948	0.202
9	1.998	1.000	0.543	0.028
10	1.379	1.000	0.797	0.099
11	2.106	1.000	0.936	0.142
12	1.428	1.000	0.889	0.296
13	1.011	1.000	0.006	0.175
14	2.179	1.000	0.828	0.180
15	2.858	1.000	0.399	0.842
16	1.388	1.000	0.617	0.039
17	1.651	1.000	0.939	0.103
18	1.593	1.000	0.784	0.620
19	1.046	1.000	0.072	0.158
20	2.152	1.000	0.889	0.704

The data used for this example are given in Table B.2. The x_{t2} and x_{t3} are pseudo-random numbers from a uniform distribution on the unit interval, and the y_t are computed by adding a normal pseudo-random number to $\theta_1^* + \theta_2^* x_{t2} + \theta_2^{*2} x_{t3}$, where the true parameters θ_1^* and θ_2^* were chosen to be $\theta_1^* = \theta_2^* = 1$. That is, we have actually added the random error to $1 + x_{t2} + x_{t3}$.

To determine the least squares estimate of $\boldsymbol{\theta}^*$ we have to minimize

$$H(\boldsymbol{\theta}) = [\mathbf{y} - \mathbf{f}(\boldsymbol{\theta})]'[\mathbf{y} - \mathbf{f}(\boldsymbol{\theta})] \tag{B.2.13}$$

Loci in the parameter space with constant $H(\boldsymbol{\theta})$ are depicted in Figure B.2. Using the iterations

$$\boldsymbol{\theta}_{n+1} = \boldsymbol{\theta}_n - \mathcal{H}_n^{-1} \boldsymbol{\gamma}_n$$

and three different starting values, we obtained the results given in Table B.3. The algorithm terminates at two different points in the parameter space. This outcome is not surprising since $H(\boldsymbol{\theta})$ has two different local minima (see Figure B.2). The example shows that an optimization algorithm does not necessarily converge to the global minimum. We will return to this problem later on.

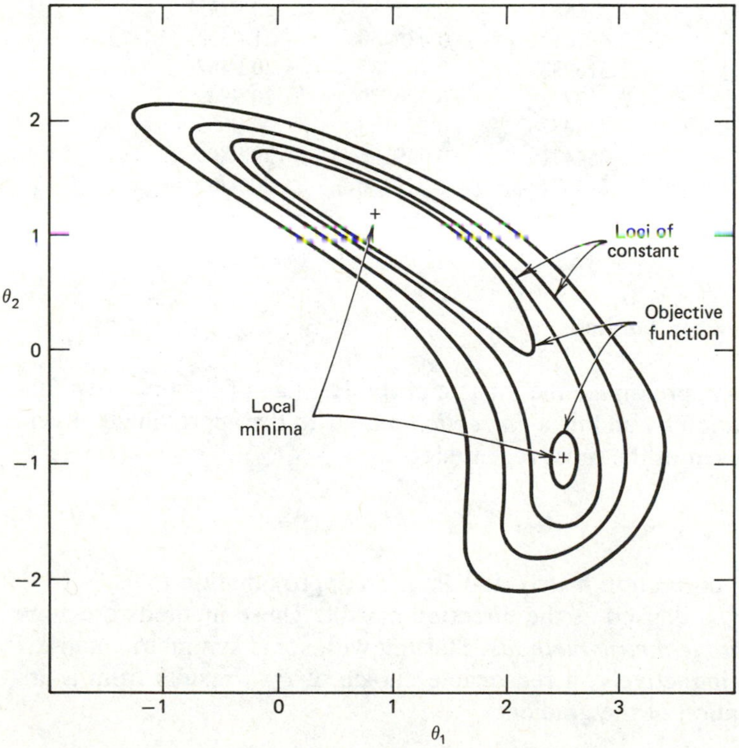

Figure B.2 Loci of constant objective function $H(\boldsymbol{\theta})$.

TABLE B.3 *ITERATIONS OF THE NEWTON ALGORITHM*

n	$\theta_{n,1}$	$\theta_{n,2}$	$H(\boldsymbol{\theta}_n)$
1	3.000000	2.000000	264.3918
2	−0.084033	1.811210	20.6328
3	0.625029	1.423940	16.5105
4	0.817259	1.272776	16.0961
5	0.862590	1.237516	16.0818
6	0.864782	1.235753	16.0817
7	0.864787	1.235748	16.0817
8	0.864787	1.235748	16.0817
1	0.000000	2.000000	29.2758
2	0.334936	1.600435	17.7382
3	0.735040	1.336953	16.1955
4	0.849677	1.247743	16.0832
5	0.864541	1.235946	16.0817
6	0.864787	1.235749	16.0817
7	0.864787	1.235748	16.0817
8	0.864787	1.235748	16.0817
1	1.500000	0.500000	20.2951
2	2.256853	0.007135	20.7735
3	2.467047	−0.436460	21.0312
4	2.316982	−0.202435	20.9467
5	2.359743	−0.320579	20.9809
6	2.354457	−0.319153	20.9805
7	2.354471	−0.319186	20.9805
8	2.354471	−0.319186	20.9805

B.2.4 Quasi-Newton Methods

Some algorithms approximate the inverse of the Hessian of the objective function in each iteration by adding a *correction matrix* to the approximate inverse of the Hessian used in the most recent step,

$$P_{n+1} = P_n + M_n \tag{B.2.14}$$

where M_n is the correction matrix and P_n is an approximation to $\mathcal{H}_n^{-1}$. In the $(n + 1)$st step P_{n+1} is used as the direction matrix. These methods are sometimes called *variable metric methods*. Starting with some symmetric matrix P_1 and proceeding inductively, a reasonable choice of P_{n+1} results from a first-order approximation of the gradient

$$\boldsymbol{\gamma}_n \simeq \boldsymbol{\gamma}_{n+1} + \mathcal{H}_{n+1}(\boldsymbol{\theta}_n - \boldsymbol{\theta}_{n+1}) \tag{B.2.15}$$

which leads to

$$\mathcal{H}_{n+1}^{-1}(\boldsymbol{\gamma}_{n+1} - \boldsymbol{\gamma}_n) \simeq (\boldsymbol{\theta}_{n+1} - \boldsymbol{\theta}_n) \tag{B.2.16}$$

if the Hessian $\mathcal{H}_{n+1}$ is nonsingular. Replacing $\mathcal{H}_{n+1}^{-1}$ in this equation by $P_{n+1} = P_n + M_n$, we get

$$M_n(\boldsymbol{\gamma}_{n+1} - \boldsymbol{\gamma}_n) = \boldsymbol{\eta}_n \tag{B.2.17}$$

where $\boldsymbol{\eta}_n = (\boldsymbol{\theta}_{n+1} - \boldsymbol{\theta}_n) - P_n(\boldsymbol{\gamma}_{n+1} - \boldsymbol{\gamma}_n)$. Of course, M_n is required to be symmetric in order to obtain the symmetry of P_{n+1}. But even with this restriction the $K(K + 1)/2$ possibly different elements of M_n are not uniquely determined by the K equations (B.2.17) if $K > 1$. Thus different correction matrices fulfilling (B.2.17) are suggested in the literature; for example, one alternative is

$$M_n = \frac{\boldsymbol{\eta}_n\boldsymbol{\eta}_n'}{\boldsymbol{\eta}_n'(\boldsymbol{\gamma}_{n+1} - \boldsymbol{\gamma}_n)} \tag{B.2.18}$$

This is the only symmetric matrix of rank one which meets the requirements of (B.2.17) [Broyden (1965, 1967)]. The resulting algorithm is therefore called the *rank one correction* (ROC) method. This choice does not necessarily lead to an acceptable step, since $P_n + M_n$ may not be positive definite.

Another famous member of this family of algorithms is the *Davidon–Fletcher–Powell* (DFP) method [Davidon (1959), Fletcher and Powell (1963)] for which

$$M_n = \frac{\boldsymbol{\zeta}_n\boldsymbol{\zeta}_n'}{\boldsymbol{\zeta}_n'(\boldsymbol{\gamma}_{n+1} - \boldsymbol{\gamma}_n)} - \frac{P_n(\boldsymbol{\gamma}_{n+1} - \boldsymbol{\gamma}_n)(\boldsymbol{\gamma}_{n+1} - \boldsymbol{\gamma}_n)'P_n}{(\boldsymbol{\gamma}_{n+1} - \boldsymbol{\gamma}_n)'P_n(\boldsymbol{\gamma}_{n+1} - \boldsymbol{\gamma}_n)} \tag{B.2.19}$$

As shown by Fletcher and Powell (1963), if the step length t_n for each step $\boldsymbol{\zeta}_n = -t_nP_n\boldsymbol{\gamma}_n$ is selected so as to minimize $H(\boldsymbol{\theta}_n + \boldsymbol{\zeta}_n)$ for the given $\boldsymbol{\theta}_n$, P_n, and $\boldsymbol{\gamma}_n$, then $P_{n+1} = P_n + M_n$ will always be positive definite. Therefore, choosing P_n as the step direction in the nth iteration guarantees an acceptable step. The identity matrix I_K can be used as P_1. In practice, however, the necessary computations may not be precise enough to obtain a positive definite P_n in each iteration [Bard (1968)]. Nevertheless, the DFP method is very popular and has proved very efficient in many applications.

Clearly, the choice of the step size is crucial in this algorithm, and many procedures have been developed to efficiently minimize the objective function in the direction $-P_n\boldsymbol{\gamma}_n$ in the nth iteration. Some methods are discussed in Himmelblau (1972a, Section 2.6) and Dixon (1972).

Many other possible formulae have been suggested for the correction matrix M_n. Some are presented in Himmelblau (1972a, Table 3.5–1), and Huang (1970) has given a classification of many of them. See also Huang and Levy (1970), Dennis and Moré (1977), and Brodlie (1977).

Sometimes the inverse Hessian of the objective function is used to construct approximate confidence intervals for the parameter estimates. If a quasi-Newton algorithm is started with $P_1 = I_K$ and converges after only a few iterations, the direction matrix obtained in the last step may not be a good approximation to the inverse of the Hessian of the objective function. In that case this matrix should not be used to compute asymptotic confidence intervals for the parameter estimates. It is suggested to restart the algorithm and do some more iterations.

Instead of its inverse, the Hessian can also be approximated directly. In that case the inverse of the approximating matrix is used as the direction matrix. Dual formulae for many of the above-mentioned algorithms exist.

B.2.5 Gauss Method

The Gauss method, sometimes called the *Gauss-Newton method,* is based on another possibility to approximate the Hessian if the objective function is of a special form. Suppose, for instance, that we have a statistical model of the type

$$\mathbf{y} = \mathbf{f}(X,\boldsymbol{\theta}^*) + \mathbf{e} = \mathbf{f}(\boldsymbol{\theta}^*) + \mathbf{e} \tag{B.2.20}$$

where $\mathbf{y} = (y_1, \ldots, y_T)'$, $\mathbf{f}(\boldsymbol{\theta}) = [f_1(\boldsymbol{\theta}), \ldots, f_T(\boldsymbol{\theta})]'$, and $\mathbf{e} = (e_1, \ldots, e_T)'$, as discussed in Chapter 6, and the objective function is the sum of squared errors,

$$H(\boldsymbol{\theta}) = [\mathbf{y} - \mathbf{f}(\boldsymbol{\theta})]'[\mathbf{y} - \mathbf{f}(\boldsymbol{\theta})] = \mathbf{e}(\boldsymbol{\theta})'\mathbf{e}(\boldsymbol{\theta}) \tag{B.2.21}$$

Then the Hessian of $H(\boldsymbol{\theta})$ is

$$\mathscr{H}(\boldsymbol{\theta}) = 2Z(\boldsymbol{\theta})'Z(\boldsymbol{\theta}) - 2\sum_{t,t'=1}^{T} [y_t - f_t(\boldsymbol{\theta})]\left[\left.\frac{\partial^2 f_{t'}(\boldsymbol{\theta})}{\partial\boldsymbol{\theta}\,\partial\boldsymbol{\theta}'}\right|_{\boldsymbol{\theta}}\right] \tag{B.2.22}$$

where $Z(\boldsymbol{\theta}) = [\partial\mathbf{f}/\partial\boldsymbol{\theta}'|_{\boldsymbol{\theta}}]$. Since the mean of $e_t = y_t - f_t(\boldsymbol{\theta}^*)$ is assumed to be zero the second term on the right-hand side is deleted and the first term is taken as an approximation of $H(\boldsymbol{\theta})$. Consequently,

$$P_n = [2Z(\boldsymbol{\theta}_n)'Z(\boldsymbol{\theta}_n)]^{-1} \tag{B.2.23}$$

and, since $\boldsymbol{\gamma}_n = -2Z(\boldsymbol{\theta}_n)'[\mathbf{y} - \mathbf{f}(\boldsymbol{\theta}_n)]$, we get with step length 1,

$$\begin{aligned}\boldsymbol{\theta}_{n+1} &= \boldsymbol{\theta}_n + [Z(\boldsymbol{\theta}_n)'Z(\boldsymbol{\theta}_n)]^{-1}Z(\boldsymbol{\theta}_n)'[\mathbf{y} - \mathbf{f}(\boldsymbol{\theta}_n)] \\ &= [Z(\boldsymbol{\theta}_n)'Z(\boldsymbol{\theta}_n)]^{-1}Z(\boldsymbol{\theta}_n)'[\mathbf{y} - \mathbf{f}(\boldsymbol{\theta}_n) + Z(\boldsymbol{\theta}_n)\boldsymbol{\theta}_n]\end{aligned} \tag{B.2.24a}$$

which is the least squares estimator for the model

$$\bar{\mathbf{y}}(\boldsymbol{\theta}_n) = Z(\boldsymbol{\theta}_n)\boldsymbol{\theta} + \mathbf{e} \tag{B.2.25}$$

where

$$\bar{\mathbf{y}}(\boldsymbol{\theta}_n) = \mathbf{y} - \mathbf{f}(\boldsymbol{\theta}_n) + Z(\boldsymbol{\theta}_n)\boldsymbol{\theta}_n \tag{B.2.26}$$

This shows that the Gauss algorithm can be viewed as a sequence of linear regressions. In each step we compute the LS estimator for a linear approximation of the nonlinear model. It is sometimes useful to write (B.2.24a) as

$$\boldsymbol{\theta}_{n+1} = \boldsymbol{\theta}_n - \left(\left[\left.\frac{\partial \mathbf{e}}{\partial \boldsymbol{\theta}'}\right|_{\boldsymbol{\theta}_n}\right]'\left[\left.\frac{\partial \mathbf{e}}{\partial \boldsymbol{\theta}'}\right|_{\boldsymbol{\theta}_n}\right]\right)^{-1}\left[\left.\frac{\partial \mathbf{e}}{\partial \boldsymbol{\theta}'}\right|_{\boldsymbol{\theta}_n}\right]' \mathbf{e}(\boldsymbol{\theta}_n) \tag{B.2.24b}$$

where

$$\left.\frac{\partial \mathbf{e}}{\partial \boldsymbol{\theta}'}\right|_{\boldsymbol{\theta}} = -Z(\boldsymbol{\theta})$$

has been used.

Another interesting feature of the Gauss algorithm is its relationship to the *method of scoring* [e.g., Maddala (1977)], which can be used for maximum likelihood estimation. For this algorithm the direction matrix is given by

$$P_n = -\left[E\left.\frac{\partial^2 \ln \ell}{\partial \boldsymbol{\theta}\, \partial \boldsymbol{\theta}'}\right|_{\boldsymbol{\theta}_n}\right]^{-1} \tag{B.2.27}$$

where ℓ is the likelihood function. Thus, using the negative log likelihood function as the objective function, the Hessian is approximated by its expected value. Assuming independently, identically, normally distributed errors and deleting the variance σ^2 in the usual way from the minimization procedure, $[Z(\boldsymbol{\theta}_n)'Z(\boldsymbol{\theta}_n)]^{-1}$ can be used as direction matrix instead of (B.2.27). For a generalization of this method see Berndt, Hall, Hall, and Hausman (1974).

The Gauss method is also applicable for objective functions different from (B.2.21). [See Bard (1974, Sections 5-9 to 5-11)]. The simplicity of this algorithm and its good local convergence properties [Dennis (1973)] make it an attractive method where applicable. However, in general, P_n is singular and thus not positive definite if $\boldsymbol{\theta}_n$ is not close to $\boldsymbol{\theta}_{\min}$, which minimizes $H(\boldsymbol{\theta})$ and, if the linear approximation of the nonlinear model is poor or the residuals are large, convergence can be slow. For the example model (B.2.11) iterations of the Gauss algorithm are given in Table B.4.

B.2.6 Combining Gauss and Quasi-Newton Methods

Since the performance of the Gauss method depends on the size of the residuals in a particular model or more precisely on

$$\sum_{t,t'=1}^{T} [y_t - f_t(\boldsymbol{\theta})] \left[\left.\frac{\partial^2 f_{t'}}{\partial \boldsymbol{\theta}\, \partial \boldsymbol{\theta}'}\right|_{\boldsymbol{\theta}}\right] \tag{B.2.28}$$

TABLE B.4 *ITERATIONS OF THE GAUSS ALGORITHM*

n	$\theta_{n,1}$	$\theta_{n,2}$	$H(\boldsymbol{\theta}_n)$
1	3.000000	2.000000	264.3918
2	0.723481	1.404965	16.6635
3	0.837007	1.259230	16.0880
4	0.861002	1.238408	16.0818
5	0.864359	1.236040	16.0817
6	0.864740	1.235780	16.0817
7	0.864782	1.235752	16.0817
8	0.864787	1.235749	16.0817
9	0.864787	1.235749	16.0817
1	3.000000	−1.000000	25.5156
2	2.498561	−0.989894	20.4856
3	2.498566	−0.985678	20.4824
4	2.498571	−0.983903	20.4823
5	2.498574	−0.983154	20.4823
6	2.498575	−0.982837	20.4823
7	2.498576	−0.982703	20.4823
8	2.498576	−0.982646	20.4823
9	2.498576	−0.982623	20.4823
10	2.498576	−0.982612	20.4823
11	2.498576	−0.982607	20.4823
12	2.498576	−0.982605	20.4823
13	2.498576	−0.982605	20.4823
1	1.500000	0.500000	20.2951
2	1.067414	1.213585	16.6646
3	0.868351	1.233424	16.0818
4	0.865161	1.235496	16.0817
5	0.864828	1.235721	16.0817
6	0.864792	1.235746	16.0817
7	0.864788	1.235748	16.0817
8	0.864787	1.235748	16.0817
9	0.864787	1.235748	16.0817

Brown and Dennis (1971) suggest the possibility of combining the Gauss algorithm with a quasi-Newton method. Instead of the inverse Hessian of the objective function, we approximate the Hessian of $f_t(\boldsymbol{\theta})$ iteratively; that is, we choose

$$F_{t,n+1} = F_{t,n} + M_{t,n} \tag{B.2.29}$$

where $F_{t,n}$ is an approximation to

$$\left.\frac{\partial^2 f_t}{\partial \boldsymbol{\theta}\, \partial \boldsymbol{\theta}'}\right|_{\boldsymbol{\theta}_n} \tag{B.2.30}$$

From

$$\left.\frac{\partial f_t}{\partial \boldsymbol{\theta}}\right|_{\boldsymbol{\theta}_n} \simeq \left.\frac{\partial f_t}{\partial \boldsymbol{\theta}}\right|_{\boldsymbol{\theta}_{n+1}} + \left[\left.\frac{\partial^2 f_t}{\partial \boldsymbol{\theta}\, \partial \boldsymbol{\theta}'}\right|_{\boldsymbol{\theta}_{n+1}}\right](\boldsymbol{\theta}_n - \boldsymbol{\theta}_{n+1}) \tag{B.2.31}$$

it follows that $M_{t,n}$ should satisfy

$$M_{t,n}(\boldsymbol{\theta}_{n+1} - \boldsymbol{\theta}_n) = \boldsymbol{\mu}_{t,n} \tag{B.2.32}$$

with

$$\boldsymbol{\mu}_{t,n} = \left.\frac{\partial f_t}{\partial \boldsymbol{\theta}}\right|_{\boldsymbol{\theta}_{n+1}} - \left.\frac{\partial f_t}{\partial \boldsymbol{\theta}}\right|_{\boldsymbol{\theta}_n} - F_{t,n}(\boldsymbol{\theta}_{n+1} - \boldsymbol{\theta}_n) \tag{B.2.33}$$

[compare (B.2.15) to (B.2.17)]. For instance, a correction matrix of rank one such as

$$M_{t,n} = \frac{\boldsymbol{\mu}_{t,n}(\boldsymbol{\theta}_{n+1} - \boldsymbol{\theta}_n)'}{(\boldsymbol{\theta}_{n+1} - \boldsymbol{\theta}_n)'(\boldsymbol{\theta}_{n+1} - \boldsymbol{\theta}_n)} \tag{B.2.34}$$

could be used.

The direction matrix for this algorithm is

$$P_n = \{Z(\boldsymbol{\theta}_n)'Z(\boldsymbol{\theta}_n) - \sum_{t,t'=1}^{T} [y_t - f_t(\boldsymbol{\theta}_n)]F_{t',n}\}^{-1} \tag{B.2.35}$$

As one alternative the unit matrix could be substituted for $F_{t,1}$ for all t. For another possible choice see Dennis (1973, p. 173). Brown and Dennis (1971) found a good performance of this algorithm in a comparison with other methods. However, the computer storage requirements for this procedure are relatively high.

B.2.7 Modifications

B.2.7a Marquardt's Method

The Marquardt algorithm [Marquardt (1963)], sometimes referred to as the *Marquardt–Levenberg method,* can be used to modify procedures that do not guarantee a positive definite direction matrix P_n. This algorithm utilizes the fact that

$$P_n + \lambda_n \bar{P}_n \tag{B.2.36}$$

is always positive definite if $\bar{P}_n$ is positive definite and the scalar λ_n is sufficiently large. A possible choice for $\bar{P}_n$ is the identity matrix. Typically, this method is used in combination with the Gauss algorithm and $Z(\boldsymbol{\theta}_n)'Z(\boldsymbol{\theta}_n)$ is modified rather than its inverse. Thus the new direction matrix is given by

$$P_n = [Z(\boldsymbol{\theta}_n)'Z(\boldsymbol{\theta}_n) + \lambda_n \bar{P}_n]^{-1} \tag{B.2.37}$$

where I_K can be used as $\bar{P}_n$. For a λ_n close to zero, this method is equivalent to the Gauss algorithm. On the other hand, for increasing λ_n, the steepest descent method is approached. Since the Gauss algorithm performs very well in a neighborhood of the minimum, we start with a small λ_1 and decrease $\lambda_n > 0$ in each iteration unless this results in an unacceptable step. Note that the step length is determined simultaneously with the step direction. For the typical step (B.2.5) t_n always takes the value one.

Similarly, we could modify the Hessian of the objective function and use

$$P_n = [\mathcal{H}_n + \lambda_n I_K]^{-1} \tag{B.2.38}$$

as the direction matrix. This algorithm is usually referred to as the *quadratic hill-climbing method,* since it was introduced in a maximization context [Goldfeld, Quandt, and Trotter (1966)]. The performance of these algorithms is not invariant under transformations of the parameter space and thus an improvement may be obtained by using a matrix $\bar{P}_n$ that is different from I_K [Marquardt (1963), Goldfeld and Quandt (1972, Chapter 1)]. Marquardt's method appears to perform very well in practice even if the initial parameter vector $\boldsymbol{\theta}_1$ is not close to the minimum of the objective function.

B.2.7b Some Other Modifications

Some other possibilities to enforce acceptable steps are based upon the eigenvalue decomposition of the direction matrix

$$P_n = U_n'\Lambda_n U_n \tag{B.2.39}$$

where U_n is an orthogonal matrix and Λ_n a diagonal matrix with diagonal elements consisting of the characteristic roots $\lambda_j, j = 1, 2, \ldots, K$, of P_n. If P_n is not positive definite, then some λ_j are negative or zero and can be replaced by

$$\lambda_j^* = \max[|\lambda_j|, \mu] \tag{B.2.40}$$

[Greenstadt (1967)], or

$$\bar{\lambda}_j = \begin{cases} \max[|\lambda_j|, \mu] & \text{if } |\lambda_j|^{-1} > \varepsilon \\ \eta & \text{if } |\lambda_j|^{-1} \leq \varepsilon \end{cases} \tag{B.2.41}$$

[Bard (1974), p. 93]. Here 0^{-1} is defined to be infinity and ε, μ, and η are suitable positive constants. In these proposals a positive lower bound for the absolute value of the characteristic roots is given, since in practical computations a very small number is treated as zero.

Another possibility is to replace a nonpositive definite matrix P_n by the identity matrix and perform a step in the direction of steepest descent. This modification is sometimes used in conjunction with quasi-Newton methods and can be interpreted as a restarting of the algorithm.

B.2.8 Conjugate Gradient Algorithm

This algorithm was suggested by Fletcher and Reeves (1964) and is based on an idea that is different from the other gradient methods. Suppose the objective function $H(\boldsymbol{\theta})$ is quadratic and thus the Hessian $\mathcal{H}$ is constant. Two directions $\boldsymbol{\delta}$ and $\bar{\boldsymbol{\delta}}$ in the K-dimensional $\boldsymbol{\theta}$-space are called *conjugate* if $\boldsymbol{\delta}'\mathcal{H}\bar{\boldsymbol{\delta}} = 0$. For a given $\boldsymbol{\delta} \neq \mathbf{0}$ there are $K - 1$ conjugate directions in the parameter space. Starting at an initial vector $\boldsymbol{\theta}_1$ with a step in the steepest descent direction and then performing steps in all conjugate directions will lead to the global minimum, provided that $H(\boldsymbol{\theta})$ is minimized in the given direction at each stage, that is, the optimal step length has to be chosen in each iteration. It turns out that the conjugate directions can be computed inductively by the formula

$$\boldsymbol{\delta}_{n+1} = -\boldsymbol{\gamma}_n + \frac{\boldsymbol{\gamma}_n'\boldsymbol{\gamma}_n}{\boldsymbol{\gamma}_{n-1}'\boldsymbol{\gamma}_{n-1}}\boldsymbol{\delta}_n \tag{B.2.42}$$

using $\boldsymbol{\delta}_1 = -\boldsymbol{\gamma}_1$, the direction of steepest descent. As before, $\boldsymbol{\gamma}_n$ denotes the gradient at $\boldsymbol{\theta}_n$. In the conjugate gradient algorithm a step is thus chosen to be of the form

$$\boldsymbol{\zeta}_n = t_n\boldsymbol{\delta}_n \tag{B.2.43}$$

where t_n is selected so as to minimize $H(\boldsymbol{\theta}_n + t_n\boldsymbol{\delta}_n)$. This guarantees a nonincreasing objective function in each step, but it does not guarantee an arrival at the minimum in K steps if $H(\boldsymbol{\theta})$ is not quadratic. Therefore, the algorithm has to be restarted periodically in the direction of the negative gradient.

An obvious advantage of this method is the simple nature of the steps. In fact, it is only necessary to store the gradient and the step direction vector at each iteration stage whereas the storage of the gradient and the direction matrix is required for other gradient algorithms. Note that the DFP method can also be interpreted as a conjugate gradient procedure. For a further discussion see Polak (1971) and Fletcher (1972a).

B.2.9 Jacobi's Method and the Gauss-Seidel Algorithm

From (B.2.5) it follows that the above-mentioned algorithms consist of iterations of the general form

$$\boldsymbol{\theta}_{n+1} = \mathbf{F}(\boldsymbol{\theta}_n) \tag{B.2.44}$$

where $\mathbf{F}(\boldsymbol{\theta}) = [F_1(\boldsymbol{\theta}), \ldots, F_K(\boldsymbol{\theta})]'$ and the optimum is reached when $\boldsymbol{\theta}_{n+1} = \boldsymbol{\theta}_n$. In other words, the algorithms determine a *fixed point* of the function $\mathbf{F}(\cdot)$. If the original problem is formulated in this way, the iteration (B.2.44) can be used directly. This procedure is called *Jacobi method*. It does not converge in general.

The *Gauss-Seidel algorithm* follows similar ideas. It is applicable if the original problem is set up so that, in the optimum,

$$\theta_i = G_i(\theta_1, \ldots, \theta_{i-1}, \theta_{i+1}, \ldots, \theta_K), \qquad i = 1, 2, \ldots, K \qquad \text{(B.2.45)}$$

In this case iterations similar to (B.2.44) can be carried out. For further details and references see Quandt (1983).

B.2.10 Derivative Free Methods

One disadvantage of the gradient methods is that they require analytic computation of at least first partial derivatives to find the step direction. Actually, it is possible to let the computer remove this burden from the user, since approximately

$$\left.\frac{\partial H}{\partial \theta_i}\right|_{\boldsymbol{\theta}} \simeq [H(\theta_1, \ldots, \theta_{i-1}, \theta_i + \Delta\theta_i, \theta_{i+1}, \ldots, \theta_K) - H(\theta_1, \ldots, \theta_{i-1}, \theta_i - \Delta\theta_i, \theta_{i+1}, \ldots, \theta_K)]/2\Delta\theta_i \qquad \text{(B.2.46)}$$

if $\Delta\theta_i$ is sufficiently small. Also, a similar one-sided approximation could be used. But it is clear that this convenience will not only increase the computational cost but also the inaccuracy of the calculations. Of course, it is possible to compute other necessary derivatives in a similar way. Details are given in Bard (1974, Section 5-18) and Quandt (1983).

B.2.10a Direct Search Methods

Another possible way of avoiding partial derivatives is to apply a *direct search method*. These procedures are useful if the first partial derivatives of the objective function do not exist or are difficult to compute. For an example see Goldfeld and Quandt (1972, Chapter 5). Starting from some initial $(K \times 1)$ parameter vector $\boldsymbol{\theta}_1$, a search is performed in K directions $\boldsymbol{\delta}_1, \boldsymbol{\delta}_2, \ldots, \boldsymbol{\delta}_K$, which are at least linearly independent but often orthogonal. A typical iteration is

$$\boldsymbol{\theta}_{n+1} = \boldsymbol{\theta}_n + t_n \boldsymbol{\delta}_j \qquad \text{(B.2.47)}$$

The step length t_n is chosen such that $H(\boldsymbol{\theta}_{n+1}) \leq H(\boldsymbol{\theta}_n)$. The methods differ in how they select step length and direction and how and when they apply a new set of direction vectors. An algorithm suggested by Powell (1964) has proved quite successful in some applications. As in the conjugate gradient method, a search is performed along conjugate directions. For details see Powell's article or Himmelblau (1972a, Chapter 4), where other derivative free methods are also described. A short review and comparison of some procedures is given by Fletcher (1965). Other references include Rosenbrock (1960), Hooke and Jeeves (1961), Powell (1965), and Swann (1972).

B.2.10b Simplex Algorithm

A search method based on yet another idea is the so-called *simplex algorithm* suggested by Spendley, Hext, and Himsworth (1962), not to be confused with the simplex method for the solution of linear programming problems. A simplex is spanned by $K + 1$ vectors $\boldsymbol{\theta}_1, \boldsymbol{\theta}_2, \ldots, \boldsymbol{\theta}_{K+1}$ in the K-dimensional space. These vectors are the vertices of the simplex. For example, in the plane the two-dimensional simplexes are triangles and in three-space tetrahedrons are simplexes of maximum dimension. Suppose that m is such that

$$H(\boldsymbol{\theta}_m) = \max_{j=1,2,\ldots,K+1} H(\boldsymbol{\theta}_j)$$

Then $\boldsymbol{\theta}_m$ is replaced by $\bar{\boldsymbol{\theta}}$, say, a point on the ray from $\boldsymbol{\theta}_m$ through the centroid of the remaining points. The procedure is repeated, always replacing the vertex that leads to a maximum value of the objective function as illustrated in Figure B.3. Usually, modifications of this basic step will be necessary in order to guarantee satisfactory progress in locating the minimum of $H(\boldsymbol{\theta})$. A detailed

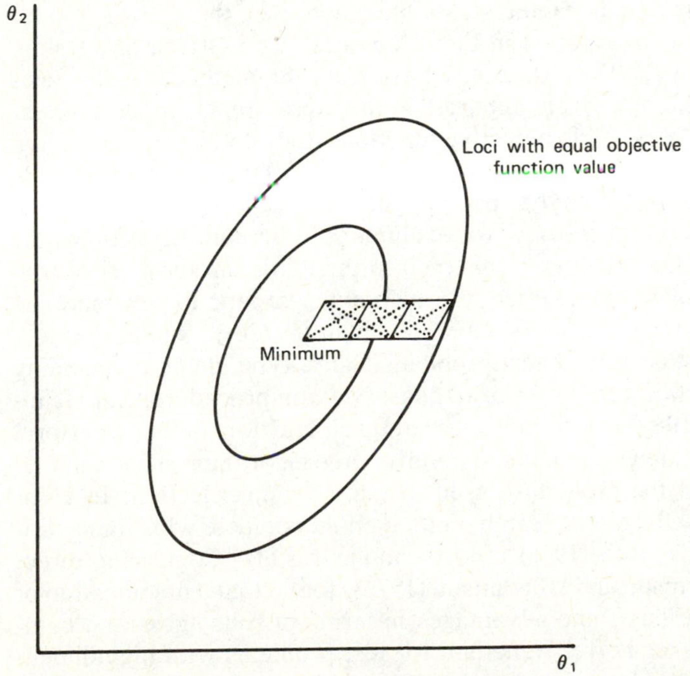

Figure B.3 Iterations of the simplex algorithm.

description of the algorithm is given by Nelder and Mead (1965); for some modifications see Parkinson and Hutchinson (1972a, 1972b). The method seems to be robust and has been successfully applied for problems with a high-dimensional parameter space. Computer programs for the simplex method and also for Powell's algorithm are given in Himmelblau (1972a, Appendix B).

B.2.10c Grid Search

If the statistical model is nonlinear in only one parameter, and if the feasible range of this parameter is small as, for example, in the discounted polynomial lag model (Chapter 10), then sometimes a simple grid search over the range of this parameter is used. The optimal values of the linear parameters are computed conditionally on the given values of the nonlinear parameter at each grid point by applying linear estimation techniques.

A grid search is also recommended to find reasonable starting values for gradient or direct search methods. If the feasible region in the parameter space is large, a search over randomly selected points can be carried out to keep the cost of this procedure in acceptable limits. Some possible strategies for a random search are discussed in Schrack and Borowski (1972).

B.2.11 Concluding Remarks and Critique

Since for applied researchers the actual performance of an algorithm for their particular problems is of major interest, we have not given theoretical convergence results. These can be found in the references [e.g., Ortega and Rheinboldt (1970) and Dennis (1977)]. Rather, we compare the methods on the basis of some performance comparisons reported in the literature. It should be clear that the wide variety of possible objective functions does not permit an evaluation that is correct for any given problem and also the differences in the evaluation criteria used in different studies hamper generally valid statements. Criteria such as (1) robustness measured, for example, by the number of times the algorithm under consideration has converged to the minimum for a set of trial problems, (2) precision in the solution, (3) the number of function evaluations, and (4) execution time, are often used [Himmelblau (1972b)].

Bard (1970) found that for his test problems Gauss-type methods including the Marquardt algorithm were superior to quasi-Newton procedures, and Himmelblau's (1972b) results seem to indicate that quasi-Newton methods perform better than the conjugate gradient and derivative-free algorithms. This ranking, however, depends on the procedure used for step length selection. In Himmelblau's study, Powell's direct search method could compete with some variable metric algorithms. Box (1966) reports similar results. Comparing direct search methods, Parkinson and Hutchinson (1972a) found that a modification of the simplex algorithm has some advantages in terms of robustness and computer storage space over Powell's method for test problems with high-dimensional parameter spaces. Although the conjugate gradient method appears to be less efficient than quasi-Newton procedures in most comparisons, Sargent and

Sebastian (1972) mention its good performance for some functions involving many parameters. As we have seen, this algorithm needs less storage space than most other gradient methods.

Summarizing, there seems to be evidence that the Gauss-type methods are preferable if applicable, but a general ranking of other algorithms appears to be difficult and possibly for the applied worker not too useful. A combination of Gauss and quasi-Newton methods might be the first choice if the residuals are expected to be relatively large. However, this procedure is more costly in terms of computer storage space than other algorithms. An application of the Newton–Raphson algorithm or a modification thereof is often hampered by the inconvenience of providing analytic second partial derivatives. To find the optimal algorithm in the first trial requires some experience and even then it will be difficult or impossible. Bard (1974, pp. 116–117) remarks "that the state of the art of nonlinear optimization is such that one cannot as yet write a computer program that will produce the correct answer to every parameter estimation problem in a single computer run." This, however, should not discourage the applied researcher from using the described procedures, since even for a few trials the cost will usually be in acceptable limits if the number of parameters is relatively small. Moreover, the application of the methods is very easy if the available computer packages are used. For a discussion of computer related problems see Murray (1972b).

Generally, all possible simplifications of the minimization procedure should be utilized. A reparameterization of ill-conditioned objective functions, for instance, can sometimes simplify the minimization problem. An example is given in Draper and Smith (1981, Chapter 10). Unfortunately, the difficulty of finding a good reparameterization is one limitation of this method. If the model under consideration is linear in some parameters, a nonlinear procedure can sometimes be combined profitably with the methods to solve a linear estimation problem. At each stage of the iteration procedure the optimal values of the linear parameters are computed conditional on the given values for the nonlinear parameters.

Finally, we remind the reader that the described algorithms usually converge only to local minima. To find the global minimum, it can be helpful to apply different methods and starting values (see Section B.2.3). The reader is referred to Quandt (1983) and Dixon and Szegö (1975) for a discussion of more sophisticated, global optimization techniques.

B.3 CONSTRAINED OPTIMIZATION

In Section B.2 we have assumed that a priori any point in the parameter space qualifies as a solution of the optimization problem. In practice, nonsample information about the parameters is often available in the form of equality and/or inequality constraints. Knowledge of this kind can help to find good starting values for an optimization algorithm and also reduces the region in which we have to search for the minimum of the objective function. Moreover, it can aid in picking the correct optimizing vector if the optimization problem has no unique solution.

On the other hand, the algorithms described in Section B.2 are designed for unconstrained problems and therefore either the algorithms have to be modified or the objective function has to be changed in such a way that the solution of an unconstrained optimization fulfills the constraints. In the following we will first discuss equality constraints and then consider inequality constraints.

B.3.1 Equality Constraints

Suppose that the true parameters are known to fulfill equality constraints given in the form

$$\mathbf{q}(\boldsymbol{\theta}) = \mathbf{0} \tag{B.3.1}$$

where $\mathbf{q}(\boldsymbol{\theta})$ is a differentiable function with values in the J-dimensional Euclidean space. The differentiability assumption will be met in almost all practical situations and covers, for instance, the case of linear constraints $R\boldsymbol{\theta} = \mathbf{r}$, where R is a $(J \times K)$ matrix and $\mathbf{r}$ a $(J \times 1)$ vector. In this case $\mathbf{q}(\boldsymbol{\theta}) = R\boldsymbol{\theta} - \mathbf{r}$. In the following section we will discuss some possible modifications of the objective function $H(\boldsymbol{\theta})$.

B.3.1a Reparameterization

Sometimes equality restrictions can be introduced by reducing the dimension of the parameter space. For instance, if $\boldsymbol{\theta} = (\theta_1,\theta_2)'$ and a constraint is $\theta_2 = \theta_1^2$, then we can define

$$\mathbf{g}(\theta_1) = \begin{bmatrix} \theta_1 \\ \theta_2 \end{bmatrix}$$

and minimize $H_R(\theta_1) = H(\mathbf{g}(\theta_1))$ with respect to θ_1 only. Generally, if the restrictions can be expressed in the form

$$\boldsymbol{\theta} = \mathbf{g}(\boldsymbol{\alpha}) \tag{B.3.2}$$

where $\boldsymbol{\alpha}$ is a $(J \times 1)$ vector, the constrained optimum of $H(\boldsymbol{\theta})$ can be found by an unconstrained minimization of $H_R(\boldsymbol{\alpha}) = H(\mathbf{g}(\boldsymbol{\alpha}))$.

B.3.1b Lagrange Multipliers

If a reparameterization of the above-described form is not possible, a vector $\boldsymbol{\lambda} = (\lambda_1, \lambda_2, \ldots, \lambda_J)'$ of Lagrange multipliers can be introduced and the constraints are incorporated in the minimization procedure by defining

$$\hat{H}_R(\boldsymbol{\theta},\boldsymbol{\lambda}) = H(\boldsymbol{\theta}) + \boldsymbol{\lambda}'\mathbf{q}(\boldsymbol{\theta}) \tag{B.3.3}$$

It can be shown that a constrained minimum of $H(\boldsymbol{\theta})$ is obtained at a stationary point of $\hat{H}_R(\boldsymbol{\theta},\boldsymbol{\lambda})$. Thus we have to find a solution to $(\partial \hat{H}_R/\partial \boldsymbol{\nu}|_{\boldsymbol{\nu}}) = \mathbf{0}$, where $\boldsymbol{\nu}' = (\boldsymbol{\theta}',\boldsymbol{\lambda}')$. This can be done by minimizing

$$H_R(\boldsymbol{\nu}) = \left[\frac{\partial \hat{H}_R}{\partial \boldsymbol{\nu}}\bigg|_{\boldsymbol{\nu}}\right]'\left[\frac{\partial \hat{H}_R}{\partial \boldsymbol{\nu}}\bigg|_{\boldsymbol{\nu}}\right]$$

But notice that this method increases the number of parameters in the objective function and thereby may increase the minimization difficulties, whereas a reduction of the parameter space as described above is likely to reduce the computational burden. Furthermore, $(\partial \hat{H}_R/\partial \boldsymbol{\nu}|_{\boldsymbol{\nu}}) = \mathbf{0}$ is only a necessary condition for a constrained minimum of $H(\boldsymbol{\theta})$.

B.3.1c Penalty Functions

Since using Lagrange multipliers has the above-mentioned disadvantages, other methods, for instance adding a *penalty function,* $A(\boldsymbol{\theta})$ say, to $H(\boldsymbol{\theta})$ are proposed. The penalty function $A(\boldsymbol{\theta})$ has to be chosen such that it is zero or almost zero for feasible $\boldsymbol{\theta}$ and very large outside the feasible region, for example,

$$A(\boldsymbol{\theta}) = d\mathbf{q}(\boldsymbol{\theta})'\mathbf{q}(\boldsymbol{\theta}) \tag{B.3.4}$$

where d is a sufficiently large constant to guarantee a minimum in the feasible region. The modified objective function is

$$H_R(\boldsymbol{\theta}) = H(\boldsymbol{\theta}) + A(\boldsymbol{\theta}) \tag{B.3.5}$$

For more details and other possible penalty functions, see Fletcher (1977) and Lootsma (1972b).

If the constraints are simple enough to permit an easy computation of second partial derivatives of $A(\boldsymbol{\theta})$, Gauss-type methods can still be applied to minimize the modified objective function if $H(\boldsymbol{\theta})$ has the form discussed in Section B.2.5. The direction matrix for the nth iteration becomes

$$\bar{P}_n = \left[P_n^{-1} + \frac{\partial^2 A}{\partial \boldsymbol{\theta}\, \partial \boldsymbol{\theta}'}\bigg|_{\boldsymbol{\theta}_n}\right]^{-1} \tag{B.3.6}$$

where P_n is the direction matrix used in the Gauss or modified Gauss algorithm.

B.3.1d Augmented Lagrangian Method

The augmented Lagrangian method combines (B.3.3) and (B.3.5) giving an objective function

$$H_R(\boldsymbol{\theta},\boldsymbol{\lambda}) = H(\boldsymbol{\theta}) + \boldsymbol{\lambda}'\mathbf{q}(\boldsymbol{\theta}) + d\mathbf{q}(\boldsymbol{\theta})'\mathbf{q}(\boldsymbol{\theta}) \tag{B.3.7}$$

Using this specification the λ's can be given fixed nonzero values in a first round and $H_R(\boldsymbol{\theta},\boldsymbol{\lambda})$ is minimized with respect to $\boldsymbol{\theta}$ without constraints. The resulting $\boldsymbol{\theta}$ vector can be used in (B.3.3) to determine a new $\boldsymbol{\lambda}$ that is used as a fixed vector in (B.3.7) in the next round. This procedure is repeated until convergence. For details see Fletcher (1975) and Powell (1978). Powell (1982b) recommends the method in conjunction with the conjugate gradient algorithm when the number of parameters is large and the number of restrictions is small.

B.3.2 Inequality Constraints

Suppose now that constraints for the parameters are given in the form of inequalities

$$\mathbf{q}(\boldsymbol{\theta}) \geq \mathbf{0} \tag{B.3.8}$$

where $\mathbf{q}(\boldsymbol{\theta})$ is a differentiable function with values in the J-dimensional Euclidean space. Let us first look at possible modifications of the objective functions that transform the optimization problem into an unconstrained one.

B.3.2a Modifications of the Objective Function

A *barrier function* $B(\boldsymbol{\theta})$, which is almost zero for all $\boldsymbol{\theta}$ satisfying the constraints and very large at the boundary of the feasible region, can have the form

$$B_n(\boldsymbol{\theta}) = c_n \sum_{j=1}^{J} [1/q_j(\boldsymbol{\theta})] \tag{B.3.9}$$

[Carroll (1961)] or

$$B_n(\boldsymbol{\theta}) = -c_n \sum_{j=1}^{J} \ln[q_j(\boldsymbol{\theta})] \tag{B.3.10}$$

[Lootsma (1967)], where the c_n are small positive constants with $c_1, c_2, c_3, \ldots$, approaching zero. In order to find the minimum of the original objective function in the feasible region

$$H_n(\boldsymbol{\theta}) = H(\boldsymbol{\theta}) + B_n(\boldsymbol{\theta}) \tag{B.3.11}$$

has to be minimized starting with a feasible initial vector $\boldsymbol{\theta}_1$, for consecutive n until $\min H_{n-1}(\boldsymbol{\theta}) = \min H_n(\boldsymbol{\theta})$ approximately. A method of this type is called an *interior point method*. The general form of the barrier function is

$$B(\boldsymbol{\theta}) = c \sum_{j=1}^{J} \rho[q_j(\boldsymbol{\theta})] \tag{B.3.12}$$

where $\rho[\cdot]$ is a continuously differentiable function defined on the positive real numbers, with $\rho[q_j(\boldsymbol{\theta})] \rightarrow \infty$ if $q_j(\boldsymbol{\theta}) \rightarrow 0$. This formulation restricts the parameters to the interior of the feasible region, and problems can arise if the minimum is obtained on or near the boundary. In this case an *exterior point method* may be appropriate. A penalty function of the general form

$$A(\boldsymbol{\theta}) = d \sum_{j=1}^{J} \eta[q_j(\boldsymbol{\theta})] \tag{B.3.13}$$

is added to the original objective function. In (B.3.13), $\eta[\cdot]$ is a continuously differentiable function defined on the real number line and satisfying

$$\eta[q_j(\boldsymbol{\theta})] \begin{cases} = 0 & \text{for } q_j(\boldsymbol{\theta}) \geq 0 \\ > 0 & \text{for } q_j(\boldsymbol{\theta}) < 0 \end{cases} \tag{B.3.14}$$

A possible choice is

$$\eta[q_j(\boldsymbol{\theta})] = \{\min[0, q_j(\boldsymbol{\theta})]\}^2 \tag{B.3.15}$$

If we add $A(\boldsymbol{\theta})$ to $H(\boldsymbol{\theta})$, the penalty for leaving the feasible region grows with d. Thus an increasing series of d-values may have to be tried in order to obtain a feasible minimum of the objective function. Note that the Hessian of the new objective function does not exist at the boundary of the feasible region. For more details about the use of barrier and penalty functions, as well as other methods and references, see Lootsma (1972b), Davies and Swann (1969), Powell (1969), Fiacco and McCormick (1968), Fletcher (1977), and Murray (1969). The Gauss method can be modified to allow for a penalty or barrier function term in the objective function as in (B.3.6).

Sometimes inequality constraints can be eliminated by a parameter transformation. For instance, if θ_i is restricted to be greater than zero it can be replaced by $e^{\bar{\theta}_i}$. Since we are dealing with nonlinear models anyway, such a transformation may not increase the computational burden. Other possible transformations are listed in Box (1966) and Powell (1972).

B.3.2b Modifications of the Optimization Algorithm

In this subsection we discuss methods of how to modify the optimization procedure rather than the objective function. The *gradient projection method* proposed by Rosen (1960, 1961) can be applied combined with any gradient method. An unconstrained minimization is carried out as long as all steps remain inside the feasible region. If the nth iteration, say, leads to a $\boldsymbol{\theta}_{n+1}$ outside the feasible region, the step length t_n is reduced such that $\boldsymbol{\theta}_{n+1}$ is on the boundary and consequently fulfills some of the inequality constraints, called *active constraints,* with an equality sign. If the next unconstrained iteration results in a $\boldsymbol{\theta}_{n+1}$ outside the feasible region, we treat the active constraints for $\boldsymbol{\theta}_n$ as equality constraints and perform the next step along the boundary, and so forth. If we have strict inequalities, the gradient projection may not be applicable, since for the boundary values $H(\boldsymbol{\theta})$ may simply not be defined. For example, this occurs if the restriction is $\theta_i > 0$ and this parameter appears as the argument of a logarithm in the objective function. In this case the application of the gradient projection method requires a modification of the constraint of the form $\theta_i - \varepsilon \geq 0$, where ε is a small positive number.

The same applies for the so-called *projection method*. Any iterative algorithm is used for an unconstrained minimization, but each infeasible $\boldsymbol{\theta}_n$ is projected on $\bar{\boldsymbol{\theta}}_n$, a vector on the boundary of the feasible region, and the next step is started from $\bar{\boldsymbol{\theta}}_n$. This method is very easy if the constraints are of a simple type, for instance, $\theta_{ni} \geq 0$. Then if θ_{ni}, the ith coordinate of $\boldsymbol{\theta}_n$, is less than zero and thus $\boldsymbol{\theta}_n$ is infeasible, θ_{ni} is simply replaced by zero, and all other coordinates are left unchanged. Unfortunately, this method does not guarantee a constrained minimum if the procedure terminates at the boundary of the feasible region [Jennrich and Sampson (1968)]. But its simplicity makes it worth trying especially if the minimum of the restricted objective function is expected to be in the interior of the feasible region.

B.3.3 Joint Equality and Inequality Constraints

Sometimes both equality and inequality constraints for the parameter vector $\boldsymbol{\theta}$ are present. In this case the methods discussed in Sections B.3.1 and B.3.2 can be combined. Suppose the restrictions are given as

$$\mathbf{q}_1(\boldsymbol{\theta}) = \mathbf{0} \qquad \text{and} \qquad \mathbf{q}_2(\boldsymbol{\theta}) \geq \mathbf{0} \tag{B.3.16}$$

where $\mathbf{q}_1(\cdot)$ is $(J_1 \times 1)$ and $\mathbf{q}_2(\cdot)$ is $(J_2 \times 1)$. Combining (B.3.4) and (B.3.15) we get a new objective function,

$$H_R(\boldsymbol{\theta}) = H(\boldsymbol{\theta}) + d\{\mathbf{q}_1(\boldsymbol{\theta})'\mathbf{q}_1(\boldsymbol{\theta}) + \sum_{j=1}^{J_2} (\min[0, q_{2j}(\boldsymbol{\theta})])^2\} \tag{B.3.17}$$

where $q_{2j}(\boldsymbol{\theta})$ is the jth coordinate of $\mathbf{q}_2(\boldsymbol{\theta})$.

B.3.4 Some Comments

Having presented a range of different possibilities for constrained and unconstrained optimization, the question arises as to which method to use with each inequality-constrained problem, and how this method should be combined with an optimization algorithm. This, of course, depends on the model under consideration. Generally, problems can arise when quasi-Newton methods and penalty or barrier functions are applied, since these methods iteratively approximate the Hessian of the objective function, which is increasingly ill-conditioned if the sequence of weighting parameters c_n for an interior point barrier function approaches zero; and does not even exist at the boundary of the feasible region if the exterior point penalty function is used. Moreover, the performance of the quasi-Newton methods depends on the unidimensional search. Therefore, relatively sophisticated, unidimensional search procedures, which are in many cases not adequate in the presence of penalty or barrier functions, are usually applied in ready-for-use computer programs. It is possible that a long trial step is carried out beyond the barrier at the boundary of the feasible region. This can cause trouble especially if the original objective function is not defined outside the feasible region. Also, the use of the simple projection method together with a quasi-Newton method cannot be recommended, since frequent interruptions of the unconstrained iteration process hinder a successful approximation of the Hessian.

Consequently, Gauss-type algorithms should be used in the presence of inequality constraints, if possible. In a first-round minimization the projection method can be applied to guarantee a feasible estimate. If the minimization procedure terminates at the boundary of the feasible region, other methods should be tried. If the structure of the objective function prohibits the use of Gauss-type methods, then a quasi-Newton method with a special unidimensional search procedure [Lasdon, Fox, and Ratner (1973)] or an algorithm designed particularly for the minimization of objective functions with penalty or barrier function terms could be applied [Lasdon (1972)].

In general it is desirable to utilize any possible simplifications that may for instance result from a reparameterization of the objective function. Also, if the objective functions or restrictions have a particular form, simplifications may be possible. For a discussion of linear constraints see Powell (1982b) and the references given in that article. Of course, at the extreme end, where the normal equations and restrictions are linear, the above methods are not required (see Chapters 2 and 3).

B.4 REFERENCES

Bard, Y. (1968) "On a Numerical Instability of Davidon-Like Methods," *Mathematics of Computation,* 22, 665–666.

Bard, Y. (1970) "Comparison of Gradient Methods for the Solution of Nonlinear Parameter Estimation Problems," *SIAM Journal of Numerical Analysis,* 7, 157–186.

Bard, Y. (1974) *Nonlinear Parameter Estimation,* Academic, New York.

Berndt, E. R., B. H. Hall, R. E. Hall, and J. A. Hausman (1974) "Estimation and Inference in Nonlinear Structural Models," *Annals of Economic and Social Measurement,* 3, 653–665.

Box, M. J. (1966) "A Comparison of Several Current Optimization Methods, and the Use of Transformations in Constrained Problems," *The Computer Journal,* 9, 67–77.

Brodlie, K. W. (1977) "Unconstrained Minimization," in D. Jacobs, ed., *The State of the Art in Numerical Analysis,* Academic, London, 229–268.

Brown, G. G. (1974) "Nonlinear Statistical Estimation with Numerical Maximum Likelihood," Working Paper No. 222, University of California, Los Angeles.

Brown, K. M. and J. E. Dennis, Jr. (1971) "A New Algorithm for Nonlinear

Least-Squares Curve Fitting," in J. R. Rice, ed., *Mathematical Software*, Academic, New York, 391–396.

Broyden, C. G. (1965) "A Class of Methods for Solving Nonlinear Simultaneous Equations," *Mathematics of Computation*, 19, 577–593.

Broyden, C. G. (1967) "Quasi-Newton Methods and Their Application to Function Minimization," *Mathematics of Computation*, 21, 368–381.

Carroll, C. W. (1961) "The Created Response Surface Technique for Optimizing Nonlinear, Restrained Systems," *Operations Research*, 9, 169–184.

Davidon, W. C. (1959) "Variable Metric Method for Minimization," A.E.C. Research and Development Report, ANL-5990 (revised).

Davies, D. and W. H. Swann (1969) "Review of Constrained Optimization," in R. Fletcher, ed., *Optimization*, Academic, London, 187–202.

Dennis, J. E. Jr. (1973) "Some Computational Techniques for the Nonlinear Least Squares Problem," in G. D. Bryne and C. A. Hall, eds., *Numerical Solutions of Systems of Nonlinear Algebraic Equations*, Academic, New York, 157–183.

Dennis, J. E., Jr. (1977) "Non-linear Least Squares and Equations," in D. Jacobs, ed., *The State of the Art in Numerical Analysis*, Academic, London, 269–312.

Dennis, J. E. and J. J. Moré (1977) "Quasi-Newton Methods, Motivation and Theory," *SIAM Review*, 9, 46–89.

Dixon, L. C. W. (1972) "The Choice of Step Length, a Crucial Factor in the Performance of Variable Metric Algorithms," in F. R. Lootsma, ed., *Numerical Methods for Non-linear Optimization*, Academic, London, 149–170.

Dixon, L. C. W. and G. P. Szegö (1975) *Towards Global Optimization*, North-Holland, Amsterdam.

Draper, N. R. and H. Smith (1981) *Applied Regression Analysis*, 2nd ed., Wiley, New York.

Fiacco, A. V. and G. P. McCormick (1968) *Nonlinear Programming: Sequential Unconstrained Minimization Techniques*, Wiley, New York.

Flanagan, P. D., P. A. Vitale, and J. Mendelsohn (1969) "A Numerical Investigation of Several One-Dimensional Search Procedures in Nonlinear Regression Problems," *Technometrics*, 11, 265–284.

Fletcher, R. (1965) "Function Minimization Without Evaluating Derivatives—A Review," *The Computer Journal*, 8, 33–41.

Fletcher, R., ed. (1969) *Optimization*, Academic, London.

Fletcher, R. (1972a) "Conjugate Direction Methods," in W. Murray, ed., *Numerical Methods for Unconstrained Optimization*, Academic, London, 73–86.

Fletcher, R. (1972b) "A Survey of Algorithms for Unconstrained Optimization," in W. Murray, ed., *Numerical Methods for Unconstrained Optimization*, Academic, London, 123–129.

Fletcher, R. (1975) "An Ideal Penalty Function for Constrained Optimization," in O. L. Mangasarian, R. R. Meyer, and S. M. Robinson, eds., *Nonlinear Programming 2*, Academic, New York, 121–163.

Fletcher, R. (1977) "Methods for Solving Non-Linearly Constrained Optimization Problems,'' in D. Jacobs, ed., *The State of the Art in Numerical Analysis,* Academic, London, 365–407.

Fletcher, R. and M. J. D. Powell (1963) ''A Rapidly Convergent Descent Method for Minimization,'' *The Computer Journal,* 6, 163–168.

Fletcher, R. and C. M. Reeves (1964) ''Function Minimization by Conjugate Gradients,'' *The Computer Journal,* 7, 149–154.

Goldfeld, S. M. and R. E. Quandt (1972) *Nonlinear Methods in Econometrics,* North-Holland, Amsterdam.

Goldfeld, S. M., R. E. Quandt, and H. F. Trotter (1966) ''Maximization by Quadratic Hill-Climbing,'' *Econometrica,* 34, 541–551.

Greenstadt, J. (1967) ''On the Relative Efficiencies of Gradient Methods,'' *Mathematics of Computation,* 21, 360–367.

Himmelblau, D. M. (1972a) *Applied Nonlinear Programming,* McGraw-Hill, New York.

Himmelblau, D. M. (1972b) ''A Uniform Evaluation of Unconstrained Optimization Techniques,'' in F. R. Lootsma, ed., *Numerical Methods for Nonlinear Optimization,* Academic, London, 69–97.

Hooke, R. and T. A. Jeeves (1961) ''Direct Search Solution of Numerical and Statistical Problems,'' *Journal of the Association for Computing Machinery,* 8, 212–229.

Huang, H. Y. (1970) ''A Unified Approach to Quadratically Convergent Algorithms for Function Minimization,'' *Journal of Optimization Theory and Applications,* 5, 405–423.

Huang, H. Y. and A. V. Levy (1970) ''Numerical Experiments on Quadratically Convergent Algorithms for Function Minimization,'' *Journal of Optimization Theory and Applications,* 6, 269–282.

Jennrich, R. I. and P. F. Sampson (1968) ''Application of Stepwise Regression to Non-Linear Estimation,'' *Technometrics,* 10, 63–72.

Judge, G. G., R. C. Hill, W. E. Griffiths, H. Lütkepohl, and T. C. Lee (1982) *Introduction to the Theory and Practice of Econometrics,* Wiley, New York.

Künzi, H. P. and W. Oettli (1969) *Nichtlineare Optimierung: Neuere Verfahren Bibliographie,* Lecture Notes in Operations Research and Mathematical Systems, 16, Springer, Berlin.

Lasdon, L. S. (1972) ''An Efficient Algorithm for Minimizing Barrier and Penalty Functions,'' *Mathematical Programming,* 2, 65–106.

Lasdon, L. S., R. L. Fox, and M. W. Ratner (1973) ''An Efficient One-Dimensional Search Procedure for Barrier Functions,'' *Mathematical Programming,* 4, 279–296.

Lootsma, F. R. (1967) ''Logarithmic Programming: A Method of Solving Nonlinear-Programming Problems,'' *Philips Research Reports,* 22, 329–344.

Lootsma, F. R., ed. (1972a) *Numerical Methods for Non-linear Optimization,* Academic, London.

Lootsma, F. R. (1972b) ''A Survey of Methods for Solving Constrained Minimization Problems via Unconstrained Minimization,'' in F. R. Lootsma, ed., *Numerical Methods for Non-linear Optimization,* Academic, London, 313–347.

Maddala, G. S. (1977) *Econometrics,* McGraw-Hill, New York.

Marquardt, D. W. (1963) "An Algorithm for Least Squares Estimation of Nonlinear Parameters," *Journal of the Society for Industrial and Applied Mathematics,* 11, 431–441.

Murray, W. (1969) "An Algorithm for Unconstrained Minimization," in R. Fletcher, ed., *Optimization,* Academic, London, 247–258.

Murray, W., ed. (1972a) *Numerical Methods for Unconstrained Optimization,* Academic, London.

Murray, W. (1972b) "Failure, the Causes and Cures," in W. Murray, ed., *Numerical Methods for Unconstrained Optimization,* Academic, London, 107–122.

Nelder, J. A. and R. Mead (1965) "A Simplex Method for Function Minimization," *The Computer Journal,* 7, 308–313.

Ortega, J. M. and W. C. Rheinboldt (1970) *Iterative Solution of Nonlinear Equations in Several Variables,* Academic, New York.

Parkinson, J. M. and D. Hutchinson (1972a) "A Consideration of Non-gradient Algorithms for the Unconstrained Optimization of Functions of High Dimensionality," in F. R. Lootsma, ed., *Numerical Methods for Non-linear Optimization,* Academic, London, 99–113.

Parkinson, J. M. and D. Hutchinson (1972b) "An Investigation into the Efficiency of Variants on the Simplex Method," in F. R. Lootsma, ed., *Numerical Methods for Non-linear Optimization,* Academic, London, 115–135.

Polak, E. (1971) *Computational Methods in Optimization,* Academic, New York.

Powell, M. J. D. (1964) "An Efficient Method for Finding the Minimum of a Function of Several Variables Without Calculating Derivatives," *The Computer Journal,* 7, 155–162.

Powell, M. J. D. (1965) "A Method for Minimizing a Sum of Squares of Nonlinear Functions Without Calculating Derivatives," *The Computer Journal,* 7, 303–307.

Powell, M. J. D. (1969) "A Method for Nonlinear Constraints in Minimization Problems," in R. Fletcher, ed., *Optimization,* Academic, London, 283–298.

Powell, M. J. D. (1972) "Problems Related to Unconstrained Optimization," in W. Murray, ed., *Numerical Methods for Unconstrained Optimization,* Academic, London, 29–55.

Powell, M. J. D. (1978) "Algorithms for Nonlinear Constraints that Use Lagrangian Functions," *Mathematical Programming,* 14, 224–248.

Powell, M. J. D., ed. (1982a) *Nonlinear Optimization 1981,* Academic, London.

Powell, M. J. D. (1982b) "Algorithms for Constrained and Unconstrained Optimization Calculations," in M. Hazewinkel and A. H. G. Rinnooy Kan, eds., *Current Developments in the Interface: Economics, Econometrics, Mathematics,* Reidel, Dordrecht, 293–312.

Quandt, R. E. (1983) "Computational Problems and Methods," in Z. Griliches and M. Intriligator, eds., *Handbook of Econometrics,* Vol. I, North-Holland, Amsterdam.

Rosen, J. B. (1960) "The Gradient Projection Method for Nonlinear Programming: I. Linear Constraints," *SIAM Journal,* 8, 181–217.

Rosen, J. B. (1961) "The Gradient Projection Method for Nonlinear Programming: II. Nonlinear Constraints," *SIAM Journal,* 9, 514–532.

Rosenbrock, H. H. (1960) "An Automatic Method for Finding the Greatest or Least Value of a Function," *The Computer Journal,* 3, 175–184.

Sargent, R. W. H. and D. J. Sebastian (1972) "Numerical Experience with Algorithms for Unconstrained Minimization," in F. R. Lootsma, ed., *Numerical Methods for Non-linear Optimization,* Academic, London, 45–68.

Schrack, G. and N. Borowski (1972) "An Experimental Comparison of Three Random Searches," in F. R. Lootsma, ed., *Numerical Methods for Non-linear Optimization,* Academic, London, 137–147.

Spendley, W., G. R. Hext, and F. R. Himsworth (1962) "Sequential Application of Simplex Designs in Optimization and Evolutionary Operation," *Technometrics,* 4, 441–461.

Swann, W. H. (1972) "Direct Search Methods," in W. Murray, ed., *Numerical Methods for Unconstrained Optimization,* Academic, London, 13–28.

Appendix C

The Kalman Filter

C.1 INTRODUCTION

Kalman Filters are used in different parts of this book. They provide a rather general framework in which to handle a range of different problems. In the following discussion we will summarize the basic formulas. More details can be found, for example, in Kalman (1960), Kalman and Bucy (1961), Hannan (1970), Harvey (1981, 1982), Priestley (1981), Anderson and Moore (1979), and Meinhold and Singpurwalla (1983).

Suppose interest centers on a $(K \times 1)$ vector $\boldsymbol{\gamma}_t$ of *state variables* that are generated by the process

$$\boldsymbol{\gamma}_t = \Phi_t \boldsymbol{\gamma}_{t-1} + \mathbf{c}_t + \boldsymbol{\Psi}_t \mathbf{v}_t, \qquad t = 1, 2, \ldots, T \tag{C.1.1}$$

where $\mathbf{c}_t$ is a nonstochastic $(K \times 1)$ vector, Φ_t and $\boldsymbol{\Psi}_t$ are fixed $(K \times K)$ and $(K \times M)$ matrices, respectively, and $\mathbf{v}_t$ is an M-dimensional white noise vector; that is, $E\mathbf{v}_t = \mathbf{0}$ and

$$E[\mathbf{v}_t \mathbf{v}_s'] = \begin{cases} \Sigma_{\mathbf{v}_t} & \text{if } s = t \\ 0 & \text{if } s \neq t \end{cases}$$

and we assume that the $\mathbf{v}_t$ are uncorrelated with the initial state vector $\boldsymbol{\gamma}_0$. Note that the above definition of vector white noise differs from the definition given in Chapter 16 in that the covariance matrix may depend on t. Equation C.1.1 is called the *transition equation*.

Suppose that $\boldsymbol{\gamma}_t$ cannot be observed directly. Instead the $(N \times 1)$ vector

$$\mathbf{y}_t = Z_t \boldsymbol{\gamma}_t + S_t \mathbf{w}_t, \qquad t = 1, 2, \ldots, T \tag{C.1.2}$$

is observed, where Z_t and S_t are $(N \times K)$ and $(N \times m)$ matrices, respectively, and $\mathbf{w}_t$ is m-dimensional white noise defined analogously to $\mathbf{v}_t$ with covariance matrix $\Sigma_{\mathbf{w}_t}$. We assume that $E[\mathbf{v}_t \mathbf{w}_s'] = 0$ and $E[\mathbf{w}_t \boldsymbol{\gamma}_0'] = 0$ for all s and t. Equation C.1.2 is called the *measurement equation*. Together the transition equation and the measurement equation represent a *state space model*.

This set-up is rather general and includes for example the ARMA models introduced in Chapter 7. For instance, an ARMA(2,1) model

$$y_t = \theta_1 y_{t-1} + \theta_2 y_{t-2} + v_t + \alpha v_{t-1} \tag{C.1.3}$$

can be written as

$$\begin{bmatrix} y_t \\ \theta_2 y_{t-1} + \alpha v_t \end{bmatrix} = \begin{bmatrix} \theta_1 & 1 \\ \theta_2 & 0 \end{bmatrix} \begin{bmatrix} y_{t-1} \\ \theta_2 y_{t-2} + \alpha v_{t-1} \end{bmatrix} + \begin{bmatrix} 1 \\ \alpha \end{bmatrix} v_t \tag{C.1.4}$$

$$y_t = [1 \quad 0] \begin{bmatrix} y_t \\ \theta_2 y_{t-1} + \alpha v_t \end{bmatrix} \tag{C.1.5}$$

which has precisely the form (C.1.1)–(C.1.2) if we define

$$\boldsymbol{\gamma}_t = \begin{bmatrix} y_t \\ \theta_2 y_{t-1} + \alpha v_t \end{bmatrix}, \qquad \Phi_t = \begin{bmatrix} \theta_1 & 1 \\ \theta_2 & 0 \end{bmatrix}, \qquad \mathbf{c}_t = \mathbf{0}, \qquad \boldsymbol{\Psi}_t = \begin{bmatrix} 1 \\ \alpha \end{bmatrix}$$

$$Z_t = [1 \quad 0], \qquad S_t = 0$$

More generally, an ARMA (p,q) process

$$y_t = \theta_1 y_{t-1} + \ldots + \theta_p y_{t-p} + v_t + \alpha_1 v_{t-1} + \ldots + \alpha_q v_{t-q} \tag{C.1.6}$$

has a representation

$$\boldsymbol{\gamma}_t = \underset{(K \times K)}{\begin{bmatrix} \theta_1 & 1 & 0 & \ldots & 0 \\ \theta_2 & 0 & 1 & \ldots & 0 \\ \vdots & \vdots & \vdots & \ddots & \vdots \\ \theta_{K-1} & 0 & 0 & \ldots & 1 \\ \theta_K & 0 & 0 & \ldots & 0 \end{bmatrix}} \boldsymbol{\gamma}_{t-1} + \underset{(K \times 1)}{\begin{bmatrix} 1 \\ \alpha_1 \\ \vdots \\ \alpha_{K-1} \end{bmatrix}} v_t \tag{C.1.7a}$$

$$y_t = \underset{(1 \times K)}{[1 \quad \mathbf{0}']} \boldsymbol{\gamma}_t \tag{C.1.7b}$$

where K is the maximum of p and $q + 1$, $\theta_i = 0$ for $i > p$, and $\alpha_i = 0$ for $i > q$.

The *Kalman Filter* is a tool to estimate the state vector in an optimal way and to update the estimate when new observations become available. Denoting by $\hat{\boldsymbol{\gamma}}_t$ the optimal (minimum mean square error) linear estimator of $\boldsymbol{\gamma}_t$ based on the information available at time t and denoting the corresponding mean square error (MSE) matrix by Ω_t, we get the *prediction equations*

$$\hat{\boldsymbol{\gamma}}_{t|t-1} = \Phi_t \hat{\boldsymbol{\gamma}}_{t-1} + \mathbf{c}_t \tag{C.1.8a}$$

and

$$\Omega_{t|t-1} = \Phi_t \Omega_{t-1} \Phi_t' + \boldsymbol{\Psi}_t \Sigma_{\mathbf{v}_t} \boldsymbol{\Psi}_t', \qquad t = 1, \ldots, T \tag{C.1.8b}$$

where $\hat{\boldsymbol{\gamma}}_{t|t-1}$ is the optimal linear prediction of $\hat{\boldsymbol{\gamma}}_t$ given $\hat{\boldsymbol{\gamma}}_{t-1}$ and $\Omega_{t|t-1}$ is the optimal linear estimator of Ω_t given Ω_{t-1}. When $\mathbf{y}_t$ becomes available the *updating equations*

$$\hat{\gamma}_t = \hat{\gamma}_{t|t-1} + \Omega_{t|t-1}Z_t'F_t^{-1}(\mathbf{y}_t - Z_t\hat{\gamma}_{t|t-1}) \tag{C.1.9a}$$

$$\Omega_t = \Omega_{t|t-1} - \Omega_{t|t-1}Z_t'F_t^{-1}Z_t\Omega_{t|t-1}, \qquad t = 1, \ldots, T \tag{C.1.9b}$$

can be used to update the predictions $\hat{\gamma}_{t|t-1}$ and $\Omega_{t|t-1}$. In (C.1.9)

$$F_t = Z_t\Omega_{t|t-1}Z_t' + S_t\Sigma_{\mathbf{w}_t}S_t' \tag{C.1.10}$$

is the covariance matrix of the prediction error

$$\mathbf{e}_t = \mathbf{y}_t - Z_t\hat{\gamma}_{t|t-1} \tag{C.1.11}$$

The recursions in (C.1.8) and (C.1.9) are called Kalman Filters and can be solved if $\mathbf{y}_1, \ldots, \mathbf{y}_T, \gamma_0, \Omega_0, \Phi_t, \mathbf{c}_t, \Psi_t, Z_t$, and S_t are given.

When working backwards, the Kalman Filter can also be used for smoothing. Since the estimator $\hat{\gamma}_T$ uses all the sample information, the recursion is started at the end of the sample period using the *smoothing equations*

$$\hat{\gamma}_{t|T} = \hat{\gamma}_t + P_t(\hat{\gamma}_{t+1|T} - \Phi_{t+1}\hat{\gamma}_t) \tag{C.1.12a}$$

and

$$\Omega_{t|T} = \Omega_t + P_t(\Omega_{t+1|T} - \Omega_{t+1|t})P_t' \tag{C.1.12b}$$

where

$$P_t = \Omega_t\Phi_{t+1}'\Omega_{t+1|t}^{-1}, \qquad t = T-1, \ldots, 1 \tag{C.1.13}$$

Smoothing is sometimes called *signal extraction* and the above recursions provide an optimal solution to this problem.

C.2 AN APPLICATION

Given a normally distributed sample of $(K \times 1)$ vectors $\mathbf{y}_1, \mathbf{y}_2, \ldots, \mathbf{y}_T$, the logarithm of the likelihood function is

$$\ln \ell = -\frac{KT}{2}\ln 2\pi - \frac{1}{2}\ln|\Sigma_{\mathbf{y}}| - \frac{1}{2}(\mathbf{y} - \boldsymbol{\mu})'\Sigma_{\mathbf{y}}^{-1}(\mathbf{y} - \boldsymbol{\mu}) \tag{C.2.1}$$

where $\mathbf{y}' = (\mathbf{y}_1', \mathbf{y}_2', \ldots, \mathbf{y}_T')$ and $\boldsymbol{\mu}$ and $\Sigma_{\mathbf{y}}$ are the mean and covariance matrix of $\mathbf{y}$. Usually $\boldsymbol{\mu}$ and $\Sigma_{\mathbf{y}}$ depend on unknown parameters that are to be estimated. Since $\Sigma_{\mathbf{y}}$ is a $(KT \times KT)$ matrix, its inversion may be rather expensive if the sample size and/or the dimension of $\mathbf{y}_t$ is large. Therefore, if the model for $\mathbf{y}_t$ can be written in state space form, from a computational point of view, the following equivalent form of (C.2.1) may be easier to handle:

$$\ln \ell = -\frac{KT}{2}\ln 2\pi - \frac{1}{2}\sum_{t=1}^{T}\ln|F_t| - \frac{1}{2}\sum_{t=1}^{T}\mathbf{e}_t'F_t^{-1}\mathbf{e}_t \qquad \text{(C.2.2)}$$

where F_t and $\mathbf{e}_t$ are as defined in (C.1.10) and (C.1.11), respectively. This form of the log likelihood function follows by noting that the joint density of the sample can be written as

$$\begin{aligned} f(\mathbf{y}_1, \ldots, \mathbf{y}_T) &= f(\mathbf{y}_T|\mathbf{y}_{T-1}, \ldots, \mathbf{y}_1)\cdot f(\mathbf{y}_{T-1}, \ldots, \mathbf{y}_1) = \ldots \\ &= f(\mathbf{y}_T|\mathbf{y}_{T-1}, \ldots, \mathbf{y}_1)\cdot f(\mathbf{y}_{T-1}|\mathbf{y}_{T-2}, \ldots, \mathbf{y}_1)\ldots f(\mathbf{y}_1) \end{aligned}$$

and the conditional mean $E(\mathbf{y}_t|\mathbf{y}_{t-1}, \ldots, \mathbf{y}_1)$ is the optimal predictor of $\mathbf{y}_t$ given the information up to time $t-1$. For a detailed derivation of (C.2.2) see Harvey (1981, Chapter 1). Thus, if the model for $\mathbf{y}_t$ can be written in state space form, the Kalman Filter can be used in developing useful maximum likelihood estimation algorithms [see Harvey and Phillips (1979)].

Kalman Filters have also been applied to treat missing observations [e.g., Jones (1980)], aggregation problems [e.g., Harvey and McKenzie (1981)], unobserved components [e.g., Engle (1978) and Burmeister and Wall (1982)], data revisions [e.g., Howrey (1978), Conrad and Corrado (1979), Harvey et al. (1981)], and varying parameter models [e.g., Harvey and Phillips (1981), Liu and Hanssens (1981)]. For more details and references on these topics see Harvey (1982) and Watson (1983).

C.3 REFERENCES

Anderson, B. D. O. and J. B. Moore (1979) *Optimal Filtering,* Prentice-Hall, Englewood Cliffs.

Burmeister, E. and K. D. Wall (1982) "Kalman Filtering Estimation of Unobserved Rational Expectations with an Application to the German Hyperinflation," *Journal of Econometrics,* 20, 255–284.

Conrad, W. and C. Corrado (1979) "Application of the Kalman Filter to Revisions in Monthly Retail Sales Estimates," *Journal of Economic Dynamics and Control,* 1, 177–198.

Engle, R. F. (1978) "Estimating Structural Models of Seasonality," in A. Zellner, ed., *Seasonal Analysis of Economic Time Series,* Bureau of the Census, Washington, DC, 281–308.

Hannan, E. J. (1970) *Multiple Time Series,* Wiley, New York.

Harvey, A. C. (1981) *Time Series Models,* Philip Allan, Oxford.

Harvey, A. C. (1982) "The Kalman Filter and Its Applications in Econometrics and Time Series Analysis," *Methods of Operations Research,* 44, 3–18.

Harvey, A. C. and C. R. McKenzie (1981) "Estimation of Systems of Equations when there is Contemporaneous Aggregation of the Dependent Variables," LSE discussion paper.

Harvey, A. C., C. R. McKenzie, D. P. C. Blake, and M. J. Desai (1981) "Modeling the Structure of Irregular Data Revisions," Paper presented at the Conference on Applied Time Series Analysis of Economic Data, Arlington, VA.

Harvey, A. C. and G. D. A. Phillips (1979) "Maximum Likelihood Estimation of Regression Models with Autoregressive-Moving Average Disturbances," *Biometrika,* 66, 49–58.

Harvey, A. C. and G. D. A. Phillips (1981) "The Estimation of Regression Models with Time-Varying Parameters," in M. Deistler, E. Fürst, and G. Schwödiauer, eds., *Games, Economic Dynamics, and Time Series Analysis,* Physica-Verlag, Wien, 306–321.

Howrey, E. P. (1978) "The Use of Preliminary Data in Econometric Forecasting," *Review of Economics and Statistics,* 60, 193–201.

Jones, R. H. (1980) "Maximum Likelihood Fitting of ARMA Models to Time Series with Missing Observations," *Technometrics,* 22, 389–395.

Kalman, R. E. (1960) "A New Approach to Linear Filtering and Prediction Problems," Transactions of ASME, Series D, *Journal of Basic Engineering,* 82, 35–45.

Kalman, R. E. and R. Bucy (1961) "New Results in Linear Filtering and Prediction Theory," Transactions of ASME, Series D, *Journal of Basic Engineering,* 83, 95–108.

Liu, L.-M. and D. M. Hanssens (1981) "A Bayesian Approach to Time-Varying Cross-Sectional Regression Models," *Journal of Econometrics,* 15, 341–356.

Meinhold, R. J. and N. D. Singpurwalla (1983) "Understanding the Kalman Filter," *The American Statistician,* 37, 123–127.

Priestley, M. B. (1981) *Spectral Analysis and Time Series, Vol. II,* Academic, London.

Watson, P. K. (1983) "Kalman Filtering as an Alternative to Ordinary Least Squares—Some Theoretical Considerations and Empirical Results" *Empirical Economics,* 8, 71–85.

Author Index

Numbers in *italics* indicate pages where full references appear.

Subject Index

Applied Probability and Statistics (Continued)

JUDGE, HILL, GRIFFITHS, LÜTKEPOHL and LEE • Introduction to the Theory and Practice of Econometrics
JUDGE, GRIFFITHS, HILL, LÜTKEPOHL and LEE • The Theory and Practice of Econometrics, *Second Edition*
KALBFLEISCH and PRENTICE • The Statistical Analysis of Failure Time Data
KISH • Survey Sampling
KUH, NEESE, and HOLLINGER • Structural Sensitivity in Econometric Models
KEENEY and RAIFFA • Decisions with Multiple Objectives
LAWLESS • Statistical Models and Methods for Lifetime Data
LEAMER • Specification Searches: Ad Hoc Inference with Nonexperimental Data
LEBART, MORINEAU, and WARWICK • Multivariate Descriptive Statistical Analysis: Correspondence Analysis and Related Techniques for Large Matrices
LINHART and ZUCCHINI • Model Selection
LITTLE and RUBIN • Statistical Analysis with Missing Data
McNEIL • Interactive Data Analysis
MAINDONALD • Statistical Computation
MANN, SCHAFER and SINGPURWALLA • Methods for Statistical Analysis of Reliability and Life Data
MARTZ and WALLER • Bayesian Reliability Analysis
MIKÉ and STANLEY • Statistics in Medical Research: Methods and Issues with Applications in Cancer Research
MILLER • Beyond ANOVA, Basics of Applied Statistics
MILLER • Survival Analysis
MILLER, EFRON, BROWN, and MOSES • Biostatistics Casebook
MONTGOMERY and PECK • Introduction to Linear Regression Analysis
NELSON • Applied Life Data Analysis
OSBORNE • Finite Algorithms in Optimization and Data Analysis
OTNES and ENOCHSON • Applied Time Series Analysis: Volume I, Basic Techniques
OTNES and ENOCHSON • Digital Time Series Analysis
PANKRATZ • Forecasting with Univariate Box-Jenkins Models: Concepts and Cases
PIELOU • Interpretation of Ecological Data: A Primer on Classification and Ordination
PLATEK, RAO, SARNDAL and SINGH • Small Area Statistics: An International Symposium
POLLOCK • The Algebra of Econometrics
PRENTER • Splines and Variational Methods
RAO and MITRA • Generalized Inverse of Matrices and Its Applications
RÉNYI • A Diary on Information Theory
RIPLEY • Spatial Statistics
RIPLEY • Stochastic Simulation
RUBIN • Multiple Imputation for Nonresponse in Surveys
RUBINSTEIN • Monte Carlo Optimization, Simulation, and Sensitivity of Queueing Networks
SCHUSS • Theory and Applications of Stochastic Differential Equations
SEAL • Survival Probabilities: The Goal of Risk Theory
SEARLE • Linear Models
SEARLE • Matrix Algebra Useful for Statistics
SPRINGER • The Algebra of Random Variables
STEUER • Multiple Criteria Optimization
STOYAN • Comparison Methods for Queues and Other Stochastic Models
TIJMS • Stochastic Modeling and Analysis: A Computational Approach
TITTERINGTON, SMITH, and MAKOV • Statistical Analysis of Finite Mixture Distributions
UPTON • The Analysis of Cross-Tabulated Data
UPTON and FINGLETON • Spatial Data Analysis by Example, Volume I: Point Pattern and Quantitative Data

(*continued from front*)